The SAT Prep Black Book

"The Most Effective SAT Strategies Ever Published"

Second Edition

By Mike Barrett and Patrick Barrett

Do not let your fire go out, spark by irreplaceable spark. In the hopeless swamps of the not quite, the not yet, and the not at all, do not let the hero in your soul perish and leave only frustration for the life you deserved, but never have been able to reach. The world you desire can be won, it exists, it is real, it is possible, it is yours.
Ayn Rand

Dedication

When the first edition of *The SAT Prep Black Book* was released, I had no idea how warmly it would be received. Readers from around the world have shared their experiences with the book—and bits of their personal stories, too. I am grateful to be a small part of their lives.

Some readers asked for more question explanations, which is why this edition has full walkthroughs for every question in the first four SAT Practice Tests released by the College Board (you can find those Practice Tests themselves on the College Board's web site for free, or you can purchase them in the 2016 or 2018 editions of the College Board's Blue Book). In addition, the walkthroughs are now presented in a way that makes them easier to skim if you want, and also reflects the ideal mental processes for exploiting the repetitive nature of the SAT more directly. Again, I'm grateful to the readers who offered the guidance that led to those adaptations. I thank you all for your patience as I researched the new version of the test and assembled this edition of the book.

To the students of all ages and backgrounds who have shared their hopes, frustrations, personal stories, and feedback: I wish you the best of luck as you navigate the challenges and opportunities before you. Some of you have told me that my Black Books have helped you think differently about situations apart from standardized testing, which makes me happier than I can express. That's the real goal.

To the parents, guardians, teachers, and counselors who have given my books to the test-takers in their lives, or used them to help others: Thank you for trusting me to be part of such important work. It's a responsibility I don't take lightly, and I strive not to let you down.

I'm also grateful to the many people in my life whose enthusiasm, support, and guidance helped make this book possible—above all, my brother and co-author, Patrick.

Finally, I would like to thank the people at Amazon for allowing me and everyone else to share our work with the world through the most sophisticated and open publishing platform ever built. We're only beginning to glimpse the changes that such a platform can bring.

This book is dedicated to all of you.

Check Us Out Online

All you need to prepare for the SAT is this Black Book, and SAT Practice Tests #1-4 (which are available for free on the College Board's website, as well as in the College Board publication *The Official SAT Study Guide*, also called the Blue Book).

But if you'd like more from me—including sample videos and updates related to test preparation, admissions, and the college experience—please connect with me on the following channels:

SATprepVideos.com

This is where you can sign up for my e-mail newsletter and check out sample videos of question walkthroughs to see how I think through real SAT practice questions in real time.

YouTube.com/TestingIsEasy

This is my YouTube channel, where you can find sample videos from my online video courses, as well as videos about other aspects of test prep and admissions.

Facebook.com/TestingIsEasy

This is my Facebook page, the primary place where I keep in touch with my students, and also a place to share updates, interesting articles, commentary, and the occasional gif of a goat riding a dirt bike through a mall. This feed is also posted on Instagram.com/TestingIsEasy and Twitter.com/TestingIsEasy, if you prefer to follow it there.

TestingIsEasy.com

This is my main website and blog where you can find videos and articles about many different aspects of test preparation and college admissions.

And look for more soon—including a podcast where I answer your questions . . .

Table of Contents

PLEASE Read This First!!!

Victorious warriors win first and then go to war, while defeated warriors go to war first and then seek to win.
Sun Tzu

Yeah, so . . . this book is over 600 pages long.

You may be wondering if I expect you to read all of it, or if reading *any* of it is really going to help you at all. At least, that's what I'd be wondering if I were you. Most SAT-prep books are pretty long and pretty useless.

So let me explain a few things that will hopefully help set your mind at ease.

First, you should know that I've been tutoring people for standardized tests since I was in high school (which was in the 90's, if you've ever heard of those). But instead of focusing on memorizing concepts from the classroom like math formulas and grammar rules, which is what most test-prep sources teach, my approach to standardized testing has always been based on understanding how a test is designed, and then thinking strategically about how to exploit the weaknesses of that design. (Different tests have different weaknesses, but any multiple-choice test that's designed to be given to huge numbers of people and provide reliable data must follow some kind of design rules, and those rules always introduce weaknesses that we can beat.)

I also think about testing from the standpoint of performance. In addition to my years of tutoring, I draw on my training as a fencing coach and my experience as a mentor to explain all aspects of test-taking with an eye towards helping you figure out how to *implement* what I'm teaching you—everything from stuff like dealing with testing anxiety and time management all the way down to explaining why an individual answer choice is right or wrong, and what lessons you can draw from a mistake that will help you on future questions.

My personal tutoring clients pay me hundreds of dollars per hour and only come to me through word of mouth. In other words, I only have tutoring clients because previous clients recommend me to their friends and family.

So, in short: my approach to the SAT is likely to be actually helpful to you, instead of just wasting your time with mindless repetition of stuff you've already heard, which probably didn't help anyway.

And here's more good news . . .

You Probably Don't Need to Read This Whole Crazy Long Book to Raise Your Score Significantly.

This Black Book has lots of pages, and it's structured so that certain kinds of ideas are repeated and demonstrated in different ways throughout the text. For example, my walkthroughs of real SAT questions show the specific application of generalized ideas that appear in the training sections of this book. Some people only skim the generalized training, and then dive right into the walkthroughs. Some people only focus on the training parts of the book and don't read many walkthroughs. And even if you're really into the walkthroughs, you'll probably decide on your own that they're so repetitive you don't need to read all of them. (I didn't set out to make the walkthroughs repetitive on my own; it's just that they're based on real SAT questions, and the SAT is a very repetitive test, so there's not much I can do to keep the walkthroughs from touching on the same concepts over and over again).

So you may be wondering why I bothered to write such a long book—if most readers don't need to read the whole thing, then why does the whole thing exist?

The reason is that different readers will benefit from different aspects of the book . . . and I know from years of experience that a sizable number of readers actually *want* to understand every single aspect of the SAT, and will welcome the chance to digest this Black Book in its entirety.

Choosing Which Parts of this Black Book to Read, and in What Order

This book consists of a few different types of material, which can be loosely grouped as follows:

- General articles on topics like managing your time (in preparation and on test day), when and how to guess, and so on.
- Training sections on the three main types of SAT questions (Reading, Writing and Language, and Math)
- Detailed walkthroughs of every SAT question from the first four official SAT Practice Tests released by the College Board in the current format of the test, showing you how the training from the rest of this Black Book can actually be implemented on test day against real SAT questions.

You can choose your own path through the ideas in this book, based on your needs and your learning style. Here are two examples of ways that readers in my test audience have reported going through it:

- If you're new to the SAT in general, then you'd probably be better off reading this Black Book basically in order, starting with the general training articles, moving on to training articles for individual parts of the SAT, and finishing with the walkthroughs, so you can see the ideas in action.
- If you're satisfied that you completely understand how to handle some parts of the test and you're just looking for help on other parts, then you can consider getting right to work on your problem areas—but I'd advise you to come back to

the other parts of the book later on, because they might help you get even better at the areas you currently consider to be your strongest. And when you decide that you really want to maximize your overall SAT score and give yourself the best possible chances in your college admissions campaign, then you'll want to be sure to check out these particular articles on overall prepping and test strategy:

- The Importance of Details: Avoiding "Careless Errors" (Page 16)
- Only Work with Questions from the College Board! (page 18)
- Setting (the Right) Goals (page 26)
- How to Train for the SAT—Mastering the Ideas in this Black Book (page 27)
- Where to Find "Missing Points" (page 28)
- Guessing on the SAT (page 33)
- Time Management on Test Day (page 36)

My only somewhat firm recommendation on how to digest this Black Book is that you make sure you look through the training for a section of the SAT before you read the walkthroughs, because that will make it easier for you to make sure you get the maximum benefit from the walkthroughs. My question walkthroughs are much more thorough than the ones provided by the College Board itself, and they draw on concepts that aren't obvious but that are spelled out in the training sections.

At the same time, if you feel like you fully understand how a particular kind of question should be attacked, then there's no reason to go through every single walkthrough for that question type in this Black Book. As I mentioned, the SAT is incredibly repetitive (that's part of what makes it standardized, in fact), which means the walkthroughs can start to feel repetitive once you really understand the test.

Keep an open mind!

If you want me to be on your team for the SAT, then you have to give us both a fighting chance. That means reading this book with an open mind, looking carefully at the many example solutions to get an idea of how the principles apply to real College Board questions, going to www.SATprepVideos.com to watch the free video demonstrations, and—above all—sticking with it when you run into difficulties. I've done my part to help you beat the test by laying bare exactly how the SAT works and exactly where it's vulnerable. Now it's up to you to read the battle plan and mount your attack.

Even though there are a variety of effective ways you could choose to tackle this material, as I explained above, *you won't get the full benefit of this book if you don't pay attention to what you read!*

Stick with it!

I can guarantee you that you will encounter real test questions that *seem* to violate the rules and patterns I talk about in this book. This is a normal part of the process—everyone, including myself, occasionally runs into a question that seems to break the rules.

When this happens, it's always because the test-taker has made a mistake.

So it's crucial that we remember that SAT questions must always follow a set of predictable rules, no matter how much any particular question might seem to break those rules. It will be tempting to think, "Oh, I guess this one math question requires me to know calculus, even though Mike said that would never happen," or "Well, I guess this passage question requires me to think about symbolism, even though that's supposed to be impossible on the SAT." As soon as you go down that road—as soon as you stop playing by the rules of the test and start treating the SAT like something it's not—your score will suffer.

So don't do that :)

Using Real SAT Practice Tests

The SAT Prep Black Book that you're reading right now will teach you all the rules, patterns, and design principles of real SAT questions, and will show you hundreds of solutions for real SAT questions, but you'll only be able to practice these ideas if you have real SAT Practice Tests from the College Board.

I want to make sure I mention this up-front because some readers think it's okay to work with practice questions from test prep companies like Kaplan, Barron's, et cetera. See "Only Work with Questions from the College Board!" on page 18 for an in-depth examination of all the reasons why those fake questions should be avoided.

Don't Believe Me? Don't Worry.

As you read this book, you may encounter advice that surprises you, or that contradicts "conventional wisdom" in test preparation (if there is such a thing).

Don't worry. This book contains walkthroughs for all the questions in SAT Practice Tests #1 – 4 from the College Board. That means you'll be able read along as I give detailed, practical, non-obvious explanations for every real SAT question in those four tests, using the ideas in this Black Book. You'll see for yourself that the advice in this book can be successfully and consistently applied to real SAT practice questions.

Remember that the true test of SAT prep advice from *any* source, myself included, is whether that advice can be used successfully against real SAT practice questions from the College Board.

Using this Black Book to Prepare for the PSAT

On a question-by-question basis, the SAT and the PSATs are the same: any question, passage, or figure that appears on either test could conceivably appear on the other. This makes it pretty easy for you to prepare for the PSAT and the SAT at the same time, because anything you learn about a question type on one test applies completely to the other test (except when it comes to the SAT Essay, since there's no handwritten essay task on the PSAT).

In short, the only differences between the SAT and PSAT are the following:

- The PSAT has slightly fewer questions than the SAT, and is 15 minutes shorter as well. Consider the following:

Section name	No. of PSAT Q's	PSAT time limit	No. of SAT Q's	SAT time limit
Reading	47	60	52	65
Writing and Language	44	35	44	35
Math (No-calc)	17	25	20	25
Math (Calc)	31	45	38	55

- The PSAT offers slightly more time per question than the SAT does (except for Writing and Language questions):

Section name	Approximate seconds per question	
	PSAT	SAT
Reading	76.6	75.0
Writing and Language	47.7	47.7
Math (No-calc)	88.2	75.0
Math (Calc)	87.1	86.8

- The PSAT doesn't offer the option to write an essay, but the SAT does.

So, as a practical matter, the best way to prepare for the PSAT is simply to prepare for the SAT as you normally would—the PSAT might even seem a little easier in comparison, since it has fewer questions overall and allows you a little extra time on some questions.

A Note on Repetition

There's a good chance that you will feel like parts of this book are repetitive. You're right—they are. This is because the SAT is very, very repetitive test, which means that my discussions of how different questions and sections work will often involve repeating myself to some extent.

I've found that the best way for students to understand this test, and how it differs from classroom tests, is to reinforce all the basic information about the test until it becomes second nature. If you finish this Black Book and you're so familiar with the SAT that basic information about the test feels obvious and boring because you've heard it several times in a variety of situations, then that means you're probably in a good position to do really well on the test. Spending the extra time to read through this book will probably save you dozens and dozens of hours of practice and re-testing—and it will get you a better score besides. So I think it's worth it to hear me mention key aspects of the test's design more than once.

About My Writing Style . . .

You may have already noticed that I use an informal, conversational writing style in this Black Book. I do this because my students tend to find that style much easier to read and digest than a formal "textbook" style.

This means I might do a few things your English teacher wouldn't love, such as starting sentences with conjunctions like "and" or "but." Most teachers will tell you not to do that in formal writing, even though famous and respected authors like John Locke, W. E. B. DuBois, and Jane Austen did it all the time.

You'll also find that many of my sentences would be unacceptable if they appeared on the Writing and Language section of the SAT. Don't worry about that, though; as we'll discuss in the training for that section, you'll find that most writers don't follow all the rules of that section in real life. (In fact, most or all of the passages on the SAT Reading section—and many of the prompts and answer choices written by the College Board itself—violate rules that the SAT expects you to follow on the Writing and Language section.)

So I don't think of my Black Books as examples of formal writing (see? I just started a sentence with a conjunction again . . . and now I'm putting an ellipsis inside parentheses . . . and I'm not sure how to punctuate the end of this sentence, so I might just go all out and resort to multiple exclamation points and a smiley face!!!!! ☺). I prefer to write in a way that feels less like a textbook and more like a conversation, while still making sure my meaning is clear. In my experience, students find this approach much more engaging and ultimately much more effective—which is the whole point.

Part 1: The Secrets of SAT Success

In this part of the Black Book, we'll cover the most important concepts that underlie effective SAT preparation. Unfortunately, these are things that most untrained test-takers never realize, which causes them to spend more time than necessary on their SAT preparation . . . and come away with very little to show for all that effort.

The rest of this Black Book will build on these critical concepts; you'll see them at work in all of my training and walkthroughs.

In this part of the Black Book, you'll learn the following:

- why the SAT isn't designed like a regular high school test
- how the College Board manages to create difficult questions based on relatively simple concepts
- why some people do better in school than they do on the SAT, or vice-versa
- why there can only be one valid answer for each SAT question
- some fundamental errors that keep most untrained test-takers from ever approaching the SAT correctly
- how everyday experiences in high school can set you up with the wrong expectations on test day
- how to react when it seems like a question has more than one good answer
- important differences between classroom discussions and the analysis you'll need to use on the SAT
- why it's so important to see each SAT question as a system of ideas
- why any detail can potentially reveal the best way to answer a question, no matter how insignificant it seems
- and more . . .

The "Big Secrets" of the SAT: Simplicity, Repetition, Weirdness, and Details

There are no secrets that time does not reveal.
Jean Racine

Before we get into all the strategies and advice for specific areas of the test, I want to start out by sharing something very important with you: the "secret" of the SAT.

Here it is: the SAT frustrates so many test-takers because it asks about basic things in very strange (but repetitive) ways.

The simple reason so many people struggle with the test is that they're looking at it in completely the wrong way.

Let's examine why this is.

Imagine you're the College Board. Colleges use your test scores to help figure out which applicants to admit, and they only trust your test because it consistently provides them with reliable measurements. So how do you go about making a test that can be given to millions of students a year and still compare them all in a meaningful way, despite the wide variations in their backgrounds and abilities?

You can't just make a super-difficult test, because that won't really provide useful information to the colleges who rely on you. For example, you can't just focus the math test on advanced ideas from calculus and statistics, because many of the test-takers have never taken those subjects—and, even if they had, the results from your test wouldn't really tell the colleges anything that wasn't already reflected in students' transcripts. And you can't make a test that relies on arbitrary interpretation of literature, because then the test results won't correlate to anything meaningful on a large scale, and colleges won't be able to rely on the data from your test.

So, if you're the College Board, you need to design the SAT so it avoids advanced concepts and arbitrary interpretation. Otherwise, your test will be useless for colleges, because colleges want to use a test that measures something meaningful about every applicant in the same way every time.

In other words, you have to test *basic* ideas in an *objective* way, rather than testing *advanced* ideas in a *subjective* way.

But then you have another problem: if you give a traditional objective test of basic ideas to millions of college-bound, motivated students, a lot of them are going to do really well on it—and then your results will be useless for a different reason, because there will be so many high scores that colleges won't be able to use the results in their admissions decisions.

So how do you solve this problem?

The College Board solves this problem by combining basic ideas in weird (but repetitive and predictable) ways. The result is that doing well on the SAT involves the ability to look at a new test question and then figure out how it follows the rules that all SAT questions of that type must follow. And that's what this book will teach you to do.

This is why there are so many people who do so well in advanced classes in high school but have a relatively hard time with the SAT: the SAT tests simpler stuff in a stranger way. It basically requires a totally different skill-set from high school or college. (You may be wondering why some students do well on both the SAT and school. These people are just good at both skill-sets. It's a bit like being good at both football and wrestling: there's enough of an overlap that some people are naturally good at both, but enough of a difference that many people struggle with one or the other. Or both.)

Now that you know the SAT's big secret, the rest of this Black Book—and the SAT itself—will probably make a lot more sense to you. This book is basically a road map to all the weird things the SAT does. It will teach you how to navigate the SAT's bizarre design, and how to exploit the many weaknesses inherent in that design.

Certainty and the SAT

I've spent more hours than I can count helping my students raise their SAT scores, and all of that time has made me realize that there's a serious problem blocking most SAT-takers from realizing their full potential.

It's not a problem that has to do with strategy, memorization, timing, focus, or anything like that. This problem is at the root of the very nature of the SAT itself. And if you don't come to terms with it, your score can only be mediocre at best.

The problem is that the SAT only gives you one correct answer choice for each question, and this correct answer choice is totally, definitively, incontrovertibly the correct answer—there are no arguments to be made against it (once we know the test's rules).

But a lot of untrained test-takers never realize this. In this book, I talk a lot about all the specific ways that the SAT is different from tests you take in high school. But I really want to pound this one difference into your head, because it will affect every single thing you do as you prepare for the test.

So I'm saying it again—read closely:

Multiple-choice SAT questions always have ONE, and only ONE, correct answer. Furthermore, the issue of which answer choice is the correct one is absolutely beyond disagreement. As surely as 2 and 2 make 4, and not 5 or 3, every single multiple-choice SAT question has exactly one correct answer choice. And you can find it with total certainty once you know how to identify it, which is what you'll learn to do in this Black Book.

A Real-Life Example

Why is this such a big deal, you ask?

Imagine this common high school situation, which you've probably been through yourself. Your history teacher is going over the answers to a multiple-choice test with your class. It's a test he wrote himself, and he wrote it just for your class. And as he's going through the test, he tells you that the answer to number 9 is choice (D). Half the class groans—they all marked (B). One of the students who marked (B) raises her hand and makes a convincing argument that she should get credit for marking (B). She explains that if you read the question a certain way, (B) and (D) are equally good answers. The teacher, who wants to be open-minded and fair, reconsiders the question, and decides that it's poorly written. In light of the student's argument, he can understand why (B) might have looked like the right answer. And, because he's fair, he announces that he'll give equal credit for both (B) and (D).

That sort of thing happens every day in high schools all across the country. It's the natural result of a system in which teachers have to write their own classes' exams, and don't have enough time to proof-read them or even test them out on sample classes in advance. Inevitably, some poorly written questions get past the teacher. The teacher corrects the problem later by giving credit as necessary, or throwing questions out, or whatever.

What message does this send to students? Unfortunately, students come to believe that the answers to *all* tests are open to discussion and debate, that *all* questions are written by stressed-out teachers who work with specific students in mind, that *all* questions are potentially flawed and open to interpretation.

Then, when these students take the SAT, things get crazy. They can never settle on anything, because they've been taught that the proper approach to a multiple-choice test is to look for any way at all to bend every answer until it's correct. They mark wrong answers left and right—usually they manage to eliminate one or two choices, and then the rest all seem equally correct, so they take a stab at each question and move on to the next, never really being certain of anything.

Most of these untrained test-takers are wrong way more often than they think.

And the worst part is that they never even realize what's holding them back.

Two Key Realizations

If you're going to do well on the SAT, you have to realize two things.

First, you have to know that the SAT is a totally objective test, and that every single question has only one right answer, as we've discussed. The SAT is written by teams of people; before a question appears on the SAT, it's been reviewed and tested by experts. No matter how much it might seem otherwise, every multiple-choice question on the SAT has only one right answer that follows the rules of the test.

Once you come to accept that, the second thing you have to realize is that you—specifically YOU, the person reading this—can find the answer to every SAT question if you learn what to look for. You can. And with the right training and practice, you will.

So let's wrap this whole thing up nice and simple:

1. The only way to do really well on the SAT is to mark the correct answer to most or all of the questions on the test.
2. The only reliable way to mark the correct answer consistently is to be able to identify it consistently.
3. Before you can identify the correct answer consistently, you have to know and believe that there will always be one correct answer for every question—if you're open to the possibility that more than one answer could be acceptable, you won't be strict about eliminating answers by using the rules and patterns of the test.
4. Most untrained test-takers never realize this, and as a result they never maximize their performance. Instead, they treat the SAT like a regular high school test, which is a huge mistake for the reasons we just discussed.

Now that we've established this important concept, we have to talk about something that comes up often in testing situations . . .

What to Do When it Looks Like There Might be Two Right Answers to a Question

Even though you know there can only be one valid answer to a real SAT question, there will be times when you think more than one choice might be correct. It happens to everybody. It happens to me, and it will happen to you. When it does happen, you must immediately recognize that you've done something wrong—you misread a key word, you left off a minus sign, something like that.

There are two ways to fix this situation. One way is to cut your losses and go on to the next question, planning to return to the difficult question later on, when your head has cleared. This is what I usually do, and we cover it in more detail in "Time Management on Test Day," which starts on page 36 of this Black Book.

The second way is to keep working on the difficult question. Try and figure out what might be causing the confusion while the question is still fresh in your mind, and resolve the issue right then and there. I'm not such a big fan of this approach because I tend to find that things are clearer to me when I return to a question after skipping it. But some people find that moving on without answering a question just means they have to familiarize themselves with it all over again when they come back, and they prefer to stay focused on a particular question until they either find the right answer or decide to guess on it.

To see which type of person you are, just do what comes naturally, and experiment a little bit with both approaches in your practice sessions—then check your results and see which approach yields more total correct answers per section.

The Importance of Details: Avoiding "Careless Errors"

You will make all kinds of mistakes; but as long as you are generous and true, and also fierce, you cannot hurt the world or even seriously distress her.

Winston Churchill

As you go through the test-taking strategies in this Black Book, one thing will become very clear to you: at every turn, the SAT is obsessed with details in a way that high school and college courses typically are not.

The right answer to an SAT Reading question might rely on the subtle difference between the words "unique" and "rare." A 5-word answer choice in a Writing and Language question might be wrong because of a single comma. A Math question involving algebra and fractions might have the reciprocal and the opposite of the right answer as two of the wrong answers. And so on.

This means that doing extremely well on the SAT isn't just a matter of knowing the proper strategies (though that's a big part of it, of course!). It's also a matter of being almost fanatically obsessed with the tiniest details. In fact, I would say that in most cases the biggest difference between someone who scores a 600 on a section of the SAT and someone who scores an 800 is not that the 800-scorer is any smarter or any more knowledgeable, but that she's much more diligent about paying attention to details.

This strong orientation to detail is exactly the opposite of what most teachers in most high schools reward in their classes. Generally speaking, teachers are more interested in things like participation, an ability to defend your position, and a willingness to think of the big picture, especially in humanities classes. On the SAT, those things rarely come in handy. What matters on the SAT is your ability to execute relatively simple strategies over and over again on a variety of questions without missing small details that would normally go overlooked in a classroom discussion.

For this reason, the attitude that most test-takers typically have towards so-called "careless errors"—which is that they don't really matter as long as you basically understand what the question is about—is very destructive when you take the SAT.

In fact, I'd even say that most test-takers could improve their scores by at least 50 to 100 points per section—usually more—if they would just eliminate these kinds of errors completely. But most people don't take these small mistakes seriously, and they don't know a reliable way to separate right answers from wrong answers anyway. So they usually end up making the same kinds of small errors, often without realizing it, no matter how much they practice.

Why are Careless Errors so Easy to Make on the SAT?

As always, when we try to figure out why the SAT is the way it is, we have to remember why the test exists in the first place: colleges and universities find the data from the test to be useful when they're evaluating applicants. This is only possible because the test questions are written according to specific rules and patterns that don't change, and because the test uses the multiple-choice format, which limits student responses and allows the grading to be objective, in the sense that a test-taker either marks the correct answer to a question, or she doesn't.

Here's the kicker: the multiple-choice format itself, and the SAT's rules and patterns specifically, would be useless for the purpose of making fine, meaningful distinctions among millions of test-takers unless the questions were written in a very detail-oriented way.

In other words, the College Board has to be obsessed with details because otherwise its data would be useless.

So the questions on the SAT are extremely nit-picky.

How Can We Pay Attention to Details and Avoid Careless Mistakes?

When we get into the walkthroughs of real SAT questions later in this book, you'll notice that I always talk about each question as a system of ideas. Instead of just explaining how the right answer satisfies the prompt, I also talk about the patterns we can see in the wrong answers, and about how the wrong answers relate to the right answer. I do this for a variety of reasons, but one of the biggest reasons is that being aware of the interplay of the parts of a question is one of the best ways to verify that an answer choice is right. If the choice you like makes sense within the larger context of the test's design, then you can have more confidence in your decisions and a greater degree of certainty that you haven't made a mistake.

On the other hand, most of the time when people do make a mistake on the test, it's because they haven't considered the question in its entirety. Instead, they catch a couple of phrases or concepts, make an unwarranted assumption or a faulty calculation, see an answer choice that reflects their mistake, and then move on to the next question without reconsidering their decisions.

So please do us both a favor and take a lesson from the way I think carefully about parts of each question that most people might consider irrelevant. I do that for a reason.

Part 2: When to Use College Board Materials . . . And When Not To

In this part of the Black Book, I'll explain why it's so important to work with real SAT questions from the College Board . . . but also important to ignore the College Board's own "explanations" of those real SAT questions (you'll see why I put the word "explanations" in quotation marks like that, too). Finally, if you've already run out of official questions from the College Board, I'll give you some ideas of other sources you can use in a pinch.

Among other things, you'll learn the following:

- why it's so important to practice with questions that follow the same rules as the questions you'll see on test day
- what really holds most people back from scoring as high as they should (it isn't subject-matter knowledge!)
- where we can find real test questions from the College Board
- some common differences between questions from the College Board and questions from other companies
- where to find real College Board questions, including free resources
- why it makes no sense to practice with "harder" questions than you'll see on test day
- why the College Board's "explanations" are often unhelpful for most test-takers who need them
- the elements of a good explanation for an official SAT question
- the most important part of using real SAT questions in your training
- why your analysis of an SAT question should always be directed at diagnosing similar situations on test day
- how the College Board's "explanations" of math often ignore the techniques that high-scorers actually use
- how the College Board's "explanations" of Verbal questions use circular reasoning to avoid revealing too much
- how to use the walkthroughs in this Black Book
- why you should read the entire walkthrough when you use this Black Book to help you with an SAT question
- why my walkthroughs are more thorough than you'll need to be on test day, and what to do on test day instead
- why you probably won't run out of practice material if you use the College Board's materials wisely
- which other practice materials to use—and which to avoid—if you do feel like you need more practice questions
- and more . . .

Only Work with Questions from the College Board!

> *One must learn by doing the thing.*
> Sophocles

Three of the most important themes in this book, which are reflected on almost every level of my SAT advice, are the following:

- SAT questions are written according to specific rules and patterns, and . . .
- . . . beating the SAT is a matter of learning to exploit the inherent weaknesses of those rules and patterns systematically, because . . .
- . . . most of the problems that most people have on the SAT are the result of poor test-taking skills, not of deficiencies in subject-matter knowledge.

I'll expand on these ideas in the rest of this Black Book, but for right now I want to impress something upon you that is extremely, extremely important: it's absolutely critical that you practice with real SAT questions written by the actual College Board itself, and not with any other kind of practice test or practice questions.

Only the real questions written by the actual College Board are guaranteed to behave like the questions you'll see on test day. Questions written by other companies (Kaplan, Barron's, or anybody else) are simply not guaranteed to behave like the real thing. In some cases, the differences are obvious, and, frankly, shocking. Some companies write fake practice SAT Writing and Language questions in which the passive voice is the difference between a right answer and a wrong answer. Some fake SAT Math questions rely on math formulas the real SAT doesn't test; many fake SAT Reading questions require literary analysis. And so on.

Fake practice questions that break the rules of the real test will encourage you to develop bad test-taking habits, and will keep you from being able to develop good habits. For our purposes, then, fake SAT questions written by any company except the College Board are basically useless. If you want to learn how to beat the SAT, you should work with real SAT questions. (You can find them in the College Board's "Blue Book," *The Official SAT Study Guide* (any edition from 2016 or later). You can also get all the SAT Practice Tests from that book for free on the College Board's website.)

At the time of this writing, there are 8 official SAT Practice Tests available from the College Board, but you could really prepare effectively even if you only had access to 2 or 3 tests, so 8 is plenty. See "How to Train for the SAT—Mastering the Ideas in this Black Book" on page 27 for ideas on the best ways to use the official tests along with this Black Book. (And see "But What if I Run Out of Practice Materials?!" on page 22 if you're nervous about using up all the official tests.)

What About "Harder" Questions?

One of the most common objections to the idea of using real SAT questions is that some companies (most notably Barron's) are known for writing practice questions that are "harder" than real test questions—the argument is that working with more difficult questions will make the real test seem like a breeze in comparison.

Unfortunately, this approach is too clever for its own good! It overlooks the nature of difficulty on the SAT. If the "harder" practice questions from a third-party company were hard *in the same way that "hard" SAT questions are hard,* then using them might be a good idea. But those fake questions are harder in a way that makes them totally unlike real questions, so they're a waste of time.

When a third-party company writes fake questions to be hard, it does so by incorporating skills that a high-school student would need to use in advanced classes: complicated math concepts, subtle literary analysis, and so on. But these skills have no place on the SAT, because the SAT limits itself to very basic ideas, and tries to fool you by asking you about basic things in weird ways.

So if you want to raise your SAT score, the skill you need to develop is the ability to look at real SAT questions, figure out whatever basic thing they actually want you to do, and then do it. That's what this Black Book teaches you. In fact, the more familiar you become with the SAT, the more you'll see that "hard" official SAT questions aren't really any different from "easy" ones when you get right down to it. This is why it's pointless to use fake questions, even if they're supposed to be more challenging.

Whenever students ask if they should use "harder" questions to get ready for the SAT, I always answer with this analogy: it's true that performing on the flying trapeze is harder than making an omelet, but getting better at the trapeze won't make your omelets any better, because the two things have nothing in common. Just because something is harder doesn't mean it's helpful.

I really can't stress this enough: If you're serious about raising your score, then you need to practice with real SAT questions written by the College Board, because real test questions are what you'll see on test day. (I sometimes have students who ignore this part of my SAT advice, and the results are never good. Seriously. Trust me on this. Use questions from the College Board :))

Why it's so Important for Me to "Re-Explain" Questions from the College Board

Whatever is worth doing at all is worth doing well.

Philip Stanhope

You may have realized by now that the College Board already provides "explanations" for every official practice question in their released practice tests, and that this Black Book also contains explanations for the same official practice questions. You may also be asking yourself why I'd bother writing out a ton of in-depth explanations for questions that already have "explanations" by the College Board.

On top of that, you may have noticed that I just put the word "explanations" in quotation marks every time I referred to "explanations" written by the College Board. And you may be wondering what's up with all of that.

Actually, it relates to a very important question that underlies our entire method of preparation: what's the purpose of practicing with official test questions from the College Board, and how do the official practice questions you work on relate to the questions that you'll see on test day?

The questions that you see on test day won't be word-for-word repetitions of the questions in the official SAT Practice Tests from the College Board, but the questions on test-day will follow the same design principles as the official practice questions. They'll observe the same rules and patterns, and they'll try to trick you in the same ways, even if that's not immediately obvious to an untrained test-taker.

That means you'll miss out on the true value of practicing with real SAT questions from the College Board *unless you analyze them effectively afterwards.* You'll never see a specific practice question on a real SAT again, but you *will* see lots of other questions that follow the same underlying principles as the questions you practice with. So your analysis of your practice sessions needs to get into those underlying principles, or your preparation won't be nearly as effective as it could be.

For these reasons, a good explanation of an official SAT practice question should point out 5 things:

1. Specifically why the right answer is right—what attributes does it have that you can expect to find in other right answers that you'll see on test day?

2. Specifically why the wrong answers are wrong, and which of their attributes you'll see again in the wrong answers on test day.

3. The fastest and easiest way that you could have arrived at the right answer to the question.

4. The attributes of the question that will appear in other questions on test day, so you can exploit them when you see them in the future.

5. The tricks that the College Board tried to play on untrained test-takers when it constructed the question, and how we can avoid similar tricks on test day.

In general, the College Board's own "explanations" don't address these issues. Instead, they typically provide some kind of limited or circular statement about Reading or Writing and Language questions, and a relatively formulaic approach for Math questions. The College Board occasionally provides more detailed explanations for some questions, but, for the most part, the College Board's explanations do almost nothing to help you learn the deeper lessons from a practice question and then apply them to future questions (which makes sense, really, because if the College Board fully explained how SAT questions actually work, it would be working against its own interests . . .).

This is why it's necessary for me to provide separate explanations for the College Board's practice questions. My explanations address the elements above so that you can learn what you should actually do on test day.

You can see what I'm talking about if you randomly flip through the Blue Book to almost any question "explanation." But I'll provide a few randomly selected examples of what I'm talking about below, to make sure we're on the same page.

College Board Explanations on the Reading Section

The College Board's explanations for its Reading questions are often circular, essentially boiling down to a statement like "Choice (A) is right because it's the right answer, while the other choices are wrong because they're not right." Instead of trying to help you understand what the College Board considers to be correct, or why the SAT is constructed the way it is, this type of "explanation" generally adds nothing to your understanding.

One example of this kind of non-explanation can be found in the College Board's "explanation" for question 5 on the Reading section of SAT Practice Test #3. The prompt for that question asks us about a line of text from the passage, and the correct answer says that the line "provides a humorous insight into" the main character from the passage. The "explanation" for the question quotes some lines from the passage and then tells us that those lines "suggest" the main character "has a sense of humor"—in other words, the "explanation" tells us that the answer choice mentioning humor is correct because the quoted line suggests something humorous. But the "explanation" doesn't tell us *why* the College Board thinks the quoted line is humorous, nor does it tell us how we might be able to identify other "humorous" portions of text in the future. The explanation concludes by telling us that the three wrong answers are wrong because the quote in the prompt doesn't fit with any of the wrong answers—in other words, the "explanation" just tells us that the wrong answers are wrong, without explaining *why* the College Board thinks those answers are wrong, or what we might be able to learn about those answers that we could expect to find in the wrong answers to future SAT questions.

On the other hand, the walkthrough for that question later in this Black Book actually explains what "humor" means on the SAT, why it's appropriate for the right answer to refer to humor, and how you'll be able to apply the College Board's unwritten definition of "humor" to other questions on test day. Of course, our walkthrough also explains what's wrong with the other choices from a test-taking standpoint. (Take a look at the walkthrough on page 124 of this Black Book to see what I mean).

College Board Explanations on the Math Section

When the College Board "explains" an SAT Math question, it generally avoids the kind of non-formulaic approaches that high-scoring test-takers would actually use on the question; in fact, the College Board rarely explains alternative approaches for its Math questions. And while the College Board's "explanations" sometimes address the idea that errors in reading or calculation might lead to a wrong answer, they don't address what most of those errors actually involve, nor tell you how to look out for them in the future.

For an example, consider the College Board's "explanation" to question 10 on section 3 of SAT Practice Test #4. The College Board simply walks the reader through the algebraic solution to the question, and then says that the wrong answers "may be the result of calculation errors," or of "using the distribution property improperly." There's no mention of other ways to approach the question, and no mention of the features of the prompt and the answer choices that a trained test-taker would notice when deciding which approach to use. There's also no description of the specific miscalculations that could lead a test-taker to one of the wrong answers. Beyond that, the solution that does appear is quite brief, with almost no elaboration of its steps. This sort of "explanation" usually only makes sense to a test-taker who already knows how to answer the question . . . but that kind of test-taker doesn't need an explanation for the question. Meanwhile, a test-taker who found the question difficult would be unlikely to benefit much from reading the College Board's explanation.

In contrast, my walkthrough for that question (which appears on page 300 in this Black Book) provides two solutions for this question, and each solution is accompanied by a much more detailed explanation of its steps, so a student who didn't already know how to answer a question like this one could actually learn how to apply similar solutions on test day. (Most SAT Math walkthroughs in this Black Book provide two or more solutions, to help you learn that there are multiple ways to approach most SAT Math questions) .

College Board Explanations on the Writing and Language Section

The College Board's "explanations" for the Writing and Language Test are often circular in a way that's similar to what we just saw on the Reading Test: they tell us that the right answer is right and the wrong answers are wrong, without explaining *why*.

As one example, consider the "explanation" of question 4 on the Writing and Language section of SAT Practice Test #2. The correct answer says that the text in the prompt provides "specific examples," and then the "explanation" says, "without these specific examples, readers have only a vague sense" of what's being discussed—but since "not vague" is basically the definition of "specific," this "explanation" is really just repeating what the correct answer said, without adding any further insight. The College Board never tells us *why* it thinks the text in the prompt is specific, nor what the SAT will consider to be too "vague" on future questions, which means the "explanation" really doesn't help a reader understand what to look out for in the future.

Similarly, the rest of the explanation tells us that the wrong answers "are incorrect because each represents a misinterpretation" of what the prompt asked for—in other words, we're basically told each one is wrong because it represents something wrong. The "explanation" never says *why* the other interpretations are wrong, so if you picked one of the "misinterpretation[s]," all this "explanation" tells you is that you got the question wrong, which is something you already knew just from reading the answer key.

In fact, the actual unwritten rules that govern this type of question don't have much of anything to do with the specific ideas brought up by the College Board in their explanation, and have more to do with the way the answer choices describe the phrase or sentence in the question. Those rules aren't discussed in the College Board's explanation for the correct answer to this question, just as the specific reasons the wrong answers are wrong aren't actually discussed. (For an explanation of those unwritten rules, see "Including or excluding a phrase or sentence" starting on page 433 of this Black Book. For more on this specific question, see its walkthrough on page 484 in this Black Book.)

Three Important Notes on the Question Walkthroughs in this Book

Before we move on, let's talk about three important ideas related to the walkthroughs in this book.

Look at the Sample Walkthroughs!

I've included a sample diagram and explanation for each type of walkthrough at the beginning of each walkthrough section. These diagrams explain how the walkthroughs are organized, and show you how the walkthrough reflects the ideal thought process as you attack each question according to the training in this Black Book. While the walkthroughs are designed so that each one can stand on its own, you'll get more out of each walkthrough if you take a few seconds to look at the sample layouts first.

- The sample diagram for my SAT Reading walkthroughs is on page 78.
- The sample diagram for my SAT Math walkthroughs is on page 230.
- The sample diagram for my SAT Writing and Language walkthroughs is on page 462.

Read the Entire Walkthrough!

If you're going to look up a walkthrough in this book for a particular question from an SAT Practice Test, be sure to read the whole thing, including any introductory text explaining the key concepts involved in the question, and any notes at the end of the walkthrough! If you just read part of the walkthrough, you may not realize many of the key details of the question that will actually be useful to you on test day.

My Walkthroughs are More Thorough Than You'll Need to be on Test Day!

My walkthroughs often go into a lot of detail, but that doesn't mean that applying these techniques on test day should take you a long time! Remember that the point of my walkthrough is to show you everything of importance that's going on in the question, so you can understand how the SAT really works—but even though the description of a particular question might go on for pages, we could often have chosen the correct answer in 10 seconds or less on test day, and pretty much always in 30 seconds or less, if all we were trying to do was to answer the question and not thoroughly dissect it as part of our training.

Remember that on test day, you don't have to explain to someone every single aspect of what's going on in each question the way we do in this book; you just have to find the correct answer in the way that's quickest and most comfortable for you. In the Math walkthroughs, for example, we might look at 2 or 3 different ways to answer one question—but you won't need to find multiple solutions to these questions on test day. We're just looking at a lot of different ways to show you that multiple approaches can be successful, so you can find which one works best for you.

My purpose in this Black Book is to communicate the ideal thought process when encountering a new SAT question, so I often need to go into great detail. But your purpose on test day is to find the correct answer with total certainty as quickly and easily as possible, so you should focus on that goal. In time, you'll find that a lot of the thoughts I spell out on the page in a walkthrough become second-nature for you, so that you don't even consciously register them for more than a split second as you work through a question.

"But What if I Run Out of Practice Materials?!"

If you're totally on board with the idea that the real SAT Practice Tests available from the College Board are all you need for your preparation, and you have no interest in other practice materials, then you can probably skip this section. But if you're curious about the pros and cons of other practice material options, read on.

At the time of this writing, there are eight real SAT Practice Tests available from the College Board. They can be purchased in one of the editions of the Blue Book that corresponds to the current format of the SAT, or downloaded for free from the College Board's website.

The tests available from the College Board should be more than enough practice for anyone preparing for the SAT according to the methods in this Black Book—in fact, three or four tests is plenty for most people, if they review their practice work properly as we discuss in "How to Train for the SAT—Mastering the Ideas in this Black Book" on page 27. But I sometimes hear from students who want more real tests to practice with—sometimes because they had already used all the available tests from the College Board before reading my book, and sometimes because they just wanted the security of knowing more practice materials were available for them.

This is a bit tricky. As we've already discussed, you should only work with real SAT Practice Tests written by the College Board, because only practice materials from the College Board are guaranteed to follow all the subtle, important standards used to make the SAT. Working with practice materials created by other companies means you won't get a chance to practice all the SAT-specific techniques that work on real questions—and you'll also pick up habits that work on the fake question but WON'T work on test day.

So my first bit of advice for you if you've already gone through all the SAT Practice Tests from the College Board is to go back through those same practice tests again. Take a second look (and maybe a third and fourth look) at all of those questions—especially the ones you missed on your first attempt—and really re-analyze each one, thinking about what makes the right answer right, what makes the wrong answers wrong, what you need to know to choose the correct answer, how you could find that information quickly, and so on.

After that, if you *insist* on using other practice materials—which, again, really shouldn't be necessary for just about anybody, and, again, isn't really something I recommend—then here's a list of your various practice material options, and the pros and cons of each one, listed roughly in order from most acceptable to least acceptable.

Previous Generation SAT Practice Tests

You should probably be able to find old copies of previous editions of the College Board's "Blue Book." These previous editions contain a number of official practice tests from previous generations of the SAT.

- **Pros:** The passage-based reading questions on these tests are highly similar to passage-based reading questions on the current version of the SAT. The math is also pretty similar. You can use the passage-based reading questions and a lot of the math questions from these old tests as reasonably decent real SAT practice questions written by the College Board, although they're still not always perfectly identical to the questions you'll see on the current version of the SAT.

- **Cons:** The structure and format of these old tests (number of sections, number of questions per section, etc.) is different from the current structure and format of the SAT, so the timing of each section won't be the same as it will be on test day. These old tests also include some obviously different question types, like Sentence Completion or even Analogies questions, depending on the age of the test. Ignore any old, obviously different question types that don't appear on the current version of the SAT. Further, the Writing section on the 2004-2016 version of the test isn't very useful practice for the current version of the Writing and Language Test.

ACT Practice Tests

The SAT and ACT are definitely not identical tests, but they're pretty similar in a lot of ways.

- **Pros:** The ACT Reading section is pretty similar to the SAT Reading section, the ACT Math section is pretty similar to the SAT Math section, and the ACT English test is pretty similar to the SAT Writing and Language section. If you practice with those materials, you *will* be using questions written by a creator of a nationally standardized test—just not the College Board.

- **Cons:** The ACT is a different test from the SAT, made by a different organization. The standards on the two tests overlap somewhat, but they aren't exactly the same. You may pick up some habits that work well against ACT questions but that aren't as effective against SAT questions. Some questions on the ACT Science section are actually more similar to questions that could appear on the SAT than a lot of people realize (though it's true that the SAT incorporates those kinds of questions on each of the sections on the test, rather than confining them all to one section like the ACT does). But it's still not a good idea to use practice questions from the ACT Science section to prepare for anything other than the ACT Science section.

SAT Subject Practice Tests

The SAT Literature Subject Test and SAT Math Level 1 and Level 2 Subject Tests are generally similar to the SAT Reading Test and SAT Math Tests, respectively.

- **Pros:** These tests have similar standards to the standards used to create the SAT, and they were created by the same organization: the College Board.
- **Cons:** SAT subject tests rely a bit more on subject matter knowledge than the SAT does, so practicing with subject tests may give you the false impression that you need to brush up on a lot of subject-matter knowledge to prepare for the SAT itself.

AP Practice Tests

The AP English Tests and AP Math Tests are somewhat similar to the SAT Reading Test and SAT Math Tests, respectively.

- **Pros:** These tests have roughly similar standards to the standards used to create the SAT, because they were also created by the College Board, but AP tests are even less directly comparable to the SAT than Subject Tests are.
- **Cons:** AP tests have the same basic problem as the SAT Subject Practice Tests, only more so—they rely even more heavily on subject matter knowledge.

Third-Party Practice Tests

These are potentially the worst practice questions you could use, because the companies that write them don't necessarily understand the way the real SAT is designed, and they have no incentive to develop questions that consistently adhere to rules and standards.

- **Pros:** None to speak of.
- **Cons:** These tests may seem to imitate the real SAT on the surface, especially to untrained test-takers, which can make it even harder for them to realize the important differences that can exist between these tests and the real SAT. I would strongly advise you to stay far away from practice materials written by third-party companies. In theory, I suppose it's conceivable that a third-party company could create practice questions that followed the same rules as the actual SAT, but I've never seen it done. There are plenty of other types of question sources earlier in this list, and I'd be willing to trust any of them before I used practice questions from a third-party company.

A Gray Area—Khan Academy Practice Materials

The College Board has partnered with Khan Academy to provide, among other things, additional free practice materials to prepare for the SAT. Students often ask me what I think about those practice tests.

This is sort of a gray area. On the one hand, Khan Academy does have an official relationship with the College Board. On the other hand, at the time of this writing, the practice materials from Khan Academy that are separate from the free official SAT Practice Tests aren't actually described as official SAT practice materials by the College Board or by Khan Academy. In other words, the Khan Academy website (at the time of this writing) features two kinds of practice SAT material, and only one of those is described as coming from the College Board:

1. the same real SAT Practice Tests that are on the College Board's website, which are described as "real" SAT practice tests
2. other "practice" material that is obviously targeted at the SAT, but is never called "real," and is never specifically described as coming from the College Board

The Khan Academy practice questions in that second category seem to be a bit more like questions you might see in a classroom, rather than questions that could appear on the SAT on test day: the reading and writing questions seem to require a little interpretation here and there, the math seems a little more formulaic than SAT math, and so on. These additional questions are certainly much closer to the real SAT than other third-party practice materials, but my gut tells me that if all of these practice materials on the Khan Academy website were written by the College Board AND subjected to the same rigorous process used by the College Board to create real SAT questions that can appear on a real SAT on test day, then the College Board and Khan Academy would just come out and say so. But they don't say that—at least, not at the time that I'm writing this.

So I'm not going to tell you that working with Khan Academy practice materials will hurt your score, or that people who work with Khan Academy practice materials can't get a good score. I'm just saying there are actual full-length SAT Practice Tests on the College Board's website that are definitely real, official SAT practice materials from the College Board itself, and that amount of material should be plenty for anybody. So there's no real reason to risk picking up bad habits with practice materials that might not be made according to the same process as the real thing, whether they come from Khan Academy or from anybody else.

Conclusion

So now you've read my take on all the most common alternatives to real SAT practice materials. But I want to make it absolutely clear, one more, time, that *I don't actually recommend using any of them if you can possibly avoid it.* There are real, official, full-length SAT tests available *for free* from the College Board's website (and they're also available in the College Board's Blue Book). Those practice tests should be more than enough for almost anyone.

If you've already done those practice tests, you can still review them, using some of the drills and exercises that I described in "How to Train for the SAT—Mastering the Ideas in this Black Book" on page 27. The key to doing your absolute best on the SAT isn't to churn out as many hours of mindless practice as you can; it's to review your practice until you understand every mistake you've ever made from the College Board's perspective, so you can avoid those issues in the future.

Part 3: Goals and Training

Now we'll talk about the right way to set goals during your SAT training, and then we'll arm you with a bunch of ideas for scheduling your time, and creative exercises that are far more effective than just taking practice tests over and over again.

In this part of the Black Book, you'll learn the following:

- the key skillsets you need to pull off a perfect SAT score (or any other score you want)
- what you actually need to do in order to get better at the SAT
- how to set goals that will make progress both easier to achieve and easier to track
- the approach I recommend for mastering the ideas in this Black Book
- how to focus on the critical step that usually comes before you stop making mistakes
- what to fix in your approach before you start worrying about time management on test day
- the best order of attack for most people to use against the different sections of the SAT
- why you shouldn't attack your weak areas first, especially if you need to hit a specific target score
- why mindlessly taking a lot of practice tests doesn't help most people as much as they expect
- a variety of unusual drills and exercises that will help you understand how the SAT really works
- how to arrange your preparation schedule (that is, if you even need a schedule in the first place)
- why you probably shouldn't put your faith in diagnostic tests, even if they come from the College Board
- and more . . .

Setting (the Right) Goals

The secret of all victory lies in the organization of the non-obvious.
Marcus Aurelius

At some point, most of my tutoring clients ask me what I think is the highest possible score they can hope for on the SAT. Sometimes they frame it in terms of their previous scores—"If I already have a 1260, can I possibly bring that up to a 1600?"

The answer to this question is simple on the surface, but there are actually many other issues surrounding this question that you want to make sure you consider.

But let's start with the simple stuff first.

If you can read American English pretty well, and if you know the basic principles of arithmetic, geometry, algebra, and trig, then there's no reason why you can't *eventually* make a 1600, or any other score you want, because every question on the SAT relies on your ability to read and understand American English and/or to use relatively basic math principles.

Please read that last sentence carefully . . . especially the word "eventually!" I'm absolutely not saying that a person whose highest score so far is an 1100 can just snap her fingers and make a 1600 overnight. What I'm saying is that the SAT is a test of basic skills, and if we have those basic skills then there's no reason, in theory, why we shouldn't be able to answer every question correctly.

Of course, raising an SAT score significantly is going to take some effort, in just about every case. Approaching the SAT in the right way isn't necessarily *difficult*, but it is definitely *different* from the way you would approach tests in high school or college. If you want to raise your score a lot, then you'll really have to try to think like the test—which, again, is not an extremely difficult thing to do, but will take some conscious effort on your part.

(By the way, if you don't read American English very well, check out "Advice for Non-Native Speakers of American English" on page 572 of this Black Book. And if you don't know the basic concepts of arithmetic, geometry, algebra, and trig, then review the SAT Math Toolbox, which starts on page 168.)

Getting Better at the SAT

We should think of the SAT as a test that asks us to do basically the same things over and over again.

And over again.

And over again, again. And then again.

For this reason, once you have a handle on the concepts spelled out in this book, getting better at the SAT isn't a matter of *learning* anything further—it's a matter of *improving your accuracy* in the application of principles you already know.

So once you know the basics, it's a bit like improving your free-throws in basketball, or practicing for a piano recital, or even getting better at a video game. It's more an exercise in improving your technical execution, and less an exercise in broadening your intellect.

(Of course, this metaphor doesn't hold up completely. There are some parts of the SAT—most notably the Math sections—in which you'll have to think a bit creatively. But the way we attack the test should always rely on the basic concepts and strategies described in this Black Book. The simple fact remains that the difference between a 600 and an 800 on a given section nearly always comes down to strategy, execution, and accuracy, and not to knowledge or intelligence.)

How to Set Goals

The most popular way to set an SAT goal is usually to target a particular score. That can work fine, of course, but it's not the way I like to do it.

Instead, I recommend that you target particular levels of accuracy in particular skillsets, and then let the scores rise on their own as a consequence of your improved abilities.

In other words, rather than say, "I want to try to get a 600 in Reading on my next practice test," say something like, "I want to go an entire section without missing a single question in which I know the meanings of all the words." Then try to achieve that standard of execution (which, by the way, would lead to a score much higher than 600 for most test-takers). Or, in the Math sections, set a goal like "I want to go an entire practice test without making a 'careless' mental error," or "I want to make sure I understand at least one wrong answer choice with each question that I answer," and so on.

If you set these kinds of task-based goals, rather than score-based goals, your improvement will generally be more meaningful and lasting, and it will come more quickly and easily.

How to Train for the SAT—Mastering the Ideas in this Black Book

After questions about the structure of the test itself, the most common question I get has to do with the right way to "study" for the SAT. People want to know the best order for tackling the different parts of the test, what kind of schedule they should follow, whether they should take a practice SAT on the day before the real test—all kinds of stuff.

The short answer to all of these questions is that there really is no single best way to tackle the material in this Black Book, because no two students will have the same exact needs when it comes to prepping. Different people will have different strengths and weaknesses, different schedules, different target scores, different starting points, different attention spans, and so on. So I'm not going to tell you exactly how to manage your preparation schedule. Instead, I'm going to give you guidelines and important considerations for you to weigh on your own, and then it'll be up to you to piece those things together in a way that works well for you.

So we'll handle it in this order:

- the recommended skill progression
- guidelines for the order in which you tackle different parts of the test
- ideas for drills and exercises
- general notes on scheduling

Let's get started.

The Recommended Skill Progression

Most people measure their progress by the scores they make on practice tests, but I don't advise that, at least not in the beginning. I'd rather see you measure your progress in terms of your overall understanding of the SAT. This is a subjective measurement, to be sure, but it's actually a lot more reliable than practice test results when you're just starting out.

So your first goal is to get a general grasp of the mechanics of each part of the test. You do this by reading the relevant portion of this Black Book, following along with some or all of the sample solutions, and checking out the free videos at www.SATprepVideos.com until you feel like you can understand the reasoning behind most or all of the test.

After you have a grasp of the foundation of the test, your next goal is to understand the mistakes you make when you look at questions on your own (whether we're talking about practice tests, practice sections, or just individual questions—more on that below). In other words, at this stage your main goal isn't really to keep from making mistakes; it's simply to *understand* your mistakes *after you make them*. You want to figure out what the mistake was, of course, but you also want to figure out why it happened, and what you should have noticed in the question that would have kept you from making the mistake in the first place, or would have allowed you to catch it and correct it after it was made. This is why I spend so much time in this Black Book talking about each question as a system of concepts and relationships, and explaining the ways that right answers differ from wrong answers, and the relationships that typically exist among them. Those are the things you want to get in the habit of noticing when you look at an SAT question, because if those things seem to be in order then you've probably understood the question correctly.

Once you have a solid grasp of the reasons you're making mistakes and the things you could do to avoid them, your next goal is to actually eliminate those mistakes, either by avoiding them in the first place or by noticing them after they happen and then correcting them. This is where it really helps to be aware of the test's rules and patterns, particularly when it comes to answer choices. At this stage, your goal is to make sure that you never miss a question as a result of a mistake on your part—you want to get to a point where the only reason you ever miss a question is that it might involve a word, grammar principle, or math concept that you were unfamiliar with, and that you can't work around. In other words, your goal is to eliminate so-called "careless mistakes."

When you have essentially eliminated careless mistakes, you'll probably be at a point where your scores on practice tests are more than satisfactory. If not, you need to think carefully about what's causing you to miss the remaining questions, and how to fix those issues. (But be careful here—too many people jump to the incorrect conclusion that they missed an SAT Math question, for example, because they didn't know the right formula, when they may have simply misread the prompt, a figure, or an answer choice.)

You may also have to think about timing issues at this stage in your progression, though most people who get to a point where they've eliminated "careless errors" find that timing is no longer a concern. If timing is still an issue, review "Time Management on Test Day" on page 36 of this Black Book, and remember that your goal on the test isn't to do a lot of work very quickly—it's to streamline and reduce the amount of work that goes into answering each question in the first place.

The Order of Attack

I pretty much always recommend that students start with the Reading section, because it's typically the part of the test where it's easiest to start noticing how the SAT uses rules and patterns to make questions predictable and objective even when they might seem not to be. It's also a good introduction to the extreme importance of reading carefully and paying attention to details.

There are really only two reasons I might recommend not starting with the Reading section. One would be if you already consistently answered all questions on that section correctly. The other reason would be if you really wanted to work on Math or Writing questions AND you just didn't have enough time before your test date to start with Reading questions. In all other situations, though, I'd start with Reading, even if that isn't the part of the test that bothers you most. It's the foundation for the rest of the SAT.

When you feel like you understand the Reading questions, you can move on to the Math sections. As I mention many times in this book, the Math sections combine relatively basic concepts and present them in strange ways, so we have to learn how to look at a Math question and figure out which basic concepts are involved, and then use those concepts to answer the question. After you've learned how the College Board uses consistent rules to make Reading questions formulaic and objective, it's easier to see the rules at work in the Math questions, and combine that idea with the subject matter knowledge required by the Math sections, which is usually at least a little familiar for most test-takers, since most test-takers have had classes in algebra, geometry, and basic trigonometry.

Once you feel like the Reading and Math sections make sense, you can turn your attention to the Writing and Language questions. Many of these questions involve the restatement and demonstration that we see in the Reading section, while other questions include some subject-matter knowledge (which is related to the grammar and style conventions that the College Board rewards). Many test-takers haven't really studied American English grammar in school, so I provide the key grammar, style, and punctuation ideas you'll need in the Grammar/Style/Punctuation Toolbox starting on page 435.

I would advise most test-takers to focus on the SAT Essay last—of course, this assumes that you plan to take the SAT Essay, and that your target schools will even care about it. Many schools ignore the SAT Essay completely. If your target schools don't care about it, then there's probably no point in taking it. You can quickly find out if your target schools consider the SAT Essay score by looking at their websites, or by contacting their admissions departments and asking directly.

Where to Find "Missing Points"

Most test-takers have some idea of a target score that will make them competitive for their target schools, or for certain scholarship programs, and those target scores are usually somewhere in the range of 1200 to 1600, depending on the student's goals and situation (of course, there are some people whose target scores might be different).

Most people try to hit their target scores by improving in the areas where they're weakest, and that's certainly understandable. But I would recommend that you also consider working to improve the areas where you're *strongest* first, for 3 reasons:

1. People usually feel more comfortable working on their strong areas, so there's less stress.
2. The mistakes you're making in your strong areas are more likely to be things related to "careless errors," or things you can correct with minimal effort.
3. The closer you are to the top of the scoring scale, the bigger the impact of each additional question that you answer correctly. In other words, if you're scoring around a 710 in SAT Math, then answering one or two more questions correctly might increase your math score by 30 points or more. But if you're scoring around a 520—closer to the middle of the scoring scale—then answering another one or two questions correctly might only raise your score 10 points. This is the result of the norming process that the College Board uses to "curve" the test scores. (The "curve" differs slightly from test to test, so the numbers aren't always exactly the same, but the general trend is consistent.)

So if you find yourself short of your goal score, it might be a good idea to focus first on making your strong areas even stronger, rather than struggling to bring your weak areas up.

But what if you need to meet a target score within a single section?

Some test-takers don't just need to reach a certain overall score; sometimes schools or programs are looking for scores on individual sections to meet particular cutoffs. But you can still use the strategy of improving on your strong areas even in these situations, because every section has different question types, and most students are naturally more inclined to some questions types than to others. I would recommend focusing on your preferred question types until you're basically perfect at answering them before going on to question types that you don't like as much.

Drills and Exercises

Most people get ready for the SAT or PSAT the same way they'd get ready for a school test: they try to memorize stuff, and then they do a lot of practice questions. After you've read the sections of this Black Book that deal with the way SAT questions work, you'll understand why this approach won't really help most people. The SAT isn't a test of advanced knowledge, so memorizing obscure definitions and math formulas won't do much. And it doesn't repeat test items exactly, so taking tons of practice tests with the idea that you'll see the exact same questions on test day is also a bad idea.

(This, by the way, is why you probably know so many people who work so hard on the SAT or PSAT and have so little to show for it. They're getting ready for the test as though it were a final exam in a geometry class, and that's not what it is.)

Of course, that raises an important question: if you're not supposed to get ready for the SAT by memorizing stuff and doing a million practice questions, then what are you supposed to do instead?

You're supposed to try to *understand* the test instead. When you understand how the SAT works—really, truly understand it—you'll find that it's a relatively basic test, and that you really don't need to spend a hundred hours getting ready for it. (If you're going for a perfect 1600, then you will probably need to spend a bit more time than the average person—but we'll talk about that later).

You come to understand the SAT by thinking about how the test is designed and why it's designed that way, so that you can eventually see it the same way the College Board sees it. And you get to that point by thinking about the things that we talk about in this book, and by making a conscious and intentional effort to apply them to a sufficient sample of real test questions.

This process may incidentally involve a little memorization—you'll want to remember what kinds of patterns to look for, for example. And it will also involve a certain amount of practice as you learn to apply these ideas against real SAT questions. But our ultimate goal is to see the SAT as a coherent, predictable system of rules and patterns we understand, instead of having to say, "I've done 8 practice tests, but my score just isn't improving."

Ultimately, you want to realize that the SAT tests the same underlying principles according to the same rules and patterns on every test, but that each individual SAT question will appear unique to people who don't know how the test works. And you want to be able to identify the ways that an individual question follows those rules and patterns, so that you can "decode" each question and mark the answer that the College Board will reward.

Now let's talk about some different options for getting to that point. Here are four of my favorite exercises. I've given them ridiculous names to help them stick in your head, and to emphasize that they're different from just mindlessly taking practice tests.

1. The Semi-Structured Stare-and-Ponder

The Semi-Structured Stare-And-Ponder is a great way to begin to appreciate how the SAT is actually designed. You start out by learning the general idea of how a certain question type works by reading the relevant portions of this Black Book and looking at a good number of the sample solutions in here. Then you find a question of the same general type (Reading, Math, whatever) in a real SAT practice test from the College Board.

And then you stare at the question.

And you ponder it.

You try to figure out how that question is doing the kinds of things that I talk about in this Black Book. You think carefully about the wording, the answer choices, all that stuff. Ultimately, your goal is to understand the College Board's motivation for writing the question in that way—why the right answer is right, why the wrong answers are wrong, and why the College Board thinks the wrong answers would be appealing to different types of test-takers who might make different types of mistakes.

When you feel you've stared at a particular question and pondered it long enough, you move on to another one, and stare at it (and ponder it, too). You look for the same types of design elements and relationships, with the same ultimate goal of seeing the question through the College Board's eyes, and being able to explain every aspect of the question's design.

Then you move on to the next question. Or you eat a sandwich, or go for a walk or something—when staring and pondering in a semi-structured way gets boring, you stop. You come back to it later, when you're interested to see how much more of the SAT you can figure out. Ideally, the process is relaxed, with no real consideration of time. You're just letting the ideas rattle around in your head, and letting your brain get used to looking for them in real SAT questions. You don't get frustrated if you can't see how something works. You're just getting used to a new way of looking at test questions in a low-pressure setting.

Of course, when you actually take the test, you won't want to approach it in this way. That goes without saying. But that shouldn't stop you from pondering all the different aspects of the test in this kind of relaxed way as a part of your preparation, because the more you do this kind of thing, the more quickly you'll be able to analyze and diagnose real test questions in the future. Let things percolate a bit and you may be surprised what you start to notice in the future.

2. Practice-and-a-Postie

The word "postie" here is short for the phrase "post mortem," which in this case refers to the idea of analyzing a test or a practice session after the fact. I included the word "postie" in the name of this exercise because I really, really want to emphasize that if you don't make a serious analysis of your practice work after you finish it, then you're really wasting the time you spend practicing.

So basically you start out by doing practice parts of a test, or even an entire practice test. You can do these practice sections with or without time limits, as you see fit (of course, the actual SAT will have a time limit, so you'll probably want to practice with a time limit at some point, but it might not be beneficial in the beginning).

I wouldn't recommend that you use practice sections or full practice tests until you've made some progress in understanding the rules and patterns of the individual SAT questions—otherwise, you'll just end up wasting lots of time and getting frustrated when you miss a lot of questions and don't understand why.

I also wouldn't recommend that you do practice tests or sections without doing a full post-mortem on them, in which you go through all the questions and try to understand the following things:

- why the College Board wrote each question the way it did
- what you could have done to answer the question correctly as quickly and directly as possible
- what lessons you can learn from that question that might be applicable to future questions

This post-mortem step is absolutely critical if you want to make a serious improvement on the SAT, but it's something that most people completely ignore, or do only halfway.

Since the whole point of your practice sessions is to prepare you to do well on test day, the most important thing you can learn from any question is how to recognize its rules and patterns at work *in future questions.* In other words, as weird as it may sound, the actual answer to a particular practice question doesn't really matter that much; what matters is whether the question can teach us how to answer *future questions on test day.* So it's much better to miss a practice question and learn something from it than to get lucky on a practice question and not learn anything.

And if you don't really sit and think about the questions you've missed, you're going to keep missing similar questions in the future—maybe not questions that seem similar on the surface (there may not even be any that seem similar on the surface), but you'll definitely miss questions with similar fundamentals, and there will probably be a lot of them.

So please make sure you give some serious thought to the questions you answer in practice sessions after you finish them. Otherwise, the time you spend doing them is basically wasted. (By the way, if you do a good job on your post-mortems you should find that you dramatically reduce the amount of practice that you need to reach your goal, so you save yourself a ton of time in the long run.)

3. The Shortcut Search

In this exercise, which can be part of a post-mortem or just an exercise on its own, you look at some real SAT questions for which you already know the answers. It's best to do this with questions you've already practiced with, as opposed to just looking at the answer key for questions you haven't tried to answer yet, so you can save questions you haven't seen for a practice session.

Our goal with this exercise is not to figure out the right answer to a question, but to figure out the fastest and easiest way to arrive at that answer with certainty, using the various SAT-specific rules and patterns that you can learn in this Black Book.

4. WWMIR?

This abbreviation stands for "What Would Make It Right?" In this drill, you go through each answer choice in a question and ask yourself what would have to change about the question for that choice to be the correct one. If a Math question asks for the value of one cell on a table, and one wrong answer is the value of another cell, then the answer to "WWMIR" is something like "if the College Board had asked for the value in the other cell." The answer to "WWMIR" for a Writing and Language question might be something like "if this noun had been singular instead of plural, or if the word 'it' had been 'they.'" Forcing yourself to try to re-imagine the questions in ways that would make the wrong answers right will help reinforce your understanding of how right and wrong answers work for particular parts of the SAT.

Things to Think about for Scheduling

As I mentioned above, years of working with a wide variety of students have left me convinced that there is no single best schedule for every test-taker. In fact, I think it would be closer to the truth to say that no two test-takers would probably have the exact same optimal preparation schedule. So now that we've talked about general ideas to use in your preparation, let's talk about the things you'll need to think about when you schedule that preparation.

Do You Like to Get an Early Start, or are You an Adrenaline Junkie?

Imagine that you're in a history class, and the teacher announces a massive research assignment that will be due in 2 months. There are two general reactions to a situation like this: some people rush home and start working on it right away, and some people already know that they'll pull a couple of all-nighters right before it's due and knock it out like that. I find that the same general tendencies exist when it comes to test prep. If you'd get started on a 2-month project when the due date is still 2 months away, then you should probably start as early as possible on your test preparation. If you're more of a last-minute person, then you're probably more of a last-minute prepper, too. I've seen both approaches work out very well tons of times, as long as the test-taker was comfortable with the particular approach and had been successful with similar timelines on other projects.

How Long Can You Stand to Stare at the Same Page?

Some people have longer attention spans than others, and some are just naturally more interested in the SAT than others. If you really can't coax more than 10 to 30 minutes of sustained attention to the test out of yourself, then you'll probably want to do shorter and more frequent bouts of preparation. On the other hand, if you're the kind of person who can easily spend 2 hours thinking about the SAT without wanting to scream, then it may make more sense for you to do an hour or two each weekend and largely ignore the test during the week.

What Kind of Score Increase do You Need?

This one is probably obvious: the bigger the score increase you need, the earlier you'll want to start prepping.

How Much Free Time do You Have?

Again, fairly obvious: the less free time you have in your schedule, the earlier you need to start prepping in order to accommodate a particular amount of prep time. (But one potential wrinkle in this part of the discussion is the fact that the actual amount of prep time you need may be significantly more or significantly less than you'd expect at the outset.)

How Many Questions/Sections/Tests do You Need to Do?

It may come as a surprise, but there is no magic number of practice questions that will guarantee you hit your target score. Based on my fairly wide experience, I would say that over 99% of people do need to do some kind of actual practice work with the ideas in this Black Book—it's very rare that a person is able to implement the strategies on test day with full effectiveness after merely reading about them. So you'll want to do some number of practice questions or sections. The operative question is "how many?"

And the issue is one of quality, not quantity. Most people will assume (very incorrectly) that if they simply do a certain number of questions they're guaranteed to improve. But that really isn't the case, because of the unique way in which the SAT is designed. It's much more important to try to *understand* a representative sample of questions than it is to crank out a million repetitions simply for its own sake. If you can look at a single real SAT practice test and really, thoroughly understand what the College Board is doing in that test, and why, and how you can use the strategies in this book to beat that test, then you're ready.

Do You Even Need a Schedule?

Finally, I'd like to close by pointing out that a specific test-prep schedule might not even be ideal for you in the first place. In my experience, students are often very bad at predicting how long it will take them to master a particular skill on the SAT, because the SAT is so different from traditional tests. You may pick up the Reading very quickly and take longer to build good SAT Math skills, or the other way around, and there may not be any correlation between those lengths of time and your academic strengths. Or you might rapidly build up good test-taking instincts for all the question types, and then have a difficult time eliminating your "careless mistakes" and spend weeks perfecting that. You may be full of enthusiasm and excitement one week, and then suddenly find yourself with no time at all the next week. And so on. An overly rigid schedule may prevent you from adapting to these kinds of situations, or to others.

My general "scheduling" advice, then, is simple. If I were you, I would try to start prepping as early as you can, even if that just means flipping absent-mindedly through this Black Book in the very beginning. The earlier you start, the more gradual the prep can be, and the more likely it is to stick. At the same time, I'd recommend prepping in ways that you find mentally engaging, and taking breaks when it gets boring and counter-productive. After every practice section or full-length practice test, I would *strongly* recommend a serious post-mortem.

And that's basically it. Modify it and make it your own as you see fit.

Be Careful with Diagnostics, Even from the College Board!

A lot of test-takers try to assess their weaknesses with some kind of diagnostic test, whether from the College Board itself, or from a tutor or test prep company. In fact, even the score report you get from the College Board after taking the SAT or PSAT provides a breakdown of your supposed strengths and weaknesses based on which questions you missed.

In my opinion, you want to be very careful when you consider this kind of feedback, because it overlooks the fact that there are many, many ways to miss any given SAT question, and they might not have anything to do with someone's idea of the question's "type."

For instance, you might miss a Reading question because you don't know some of the words in the question, or you might miss it because you misread the question, or because you were in a hurry and didn't have time to consider it carefully enough. You might miss a Math question for any of the same reasons, or because you made a simple mistake in the arithmetic component of an algebra question, or because you keyed something into the calculator incorrectly. But diagnostic reports on multiple-choice tests can't measure your *reasons* for missing things—they can only try to classify each question into types, and then assume that people who miss a question are bad at answering questions of that type, without considering all the other reasons a question might have been missed.

So I rarely pay any attention to such diagnostic reports, and I don't encourage my students to worry about them in most cases. The only limited exception I would make would be in an extreme case. For example, if you miss every single question on a diagnostic that involves a chart, graph, or other figure, and you don't miss any other questions on the entire test, then there's a good chance that you do need to work on your approach to questions involving figures.

But outside of those kinds of rare situations, I'd recommend that you pay more attention to your own feelings about where your weak areas are, as long as you're trying to diagnose those weaknesses honestly. For instance, it's tempting to look at an SAT Math question you missed that involves circles, and assume that you missed it because you're not good with circles. But, if you pay close attention to how you tried to answer the question, then you may realize that you actually missed it because you ignored two of the answer choices, or you didn't notice a word in the prompt. Either way, the experience of looking back over a question you missed and trying to figure out why the correct answer is correct, and how you might have arrived at that correct answer if you had looked at the question differently, is far more helpful than accepting a diagnostic report at face value.

Part 4: Guessing and Time-Management on Test Day

This part of the Black Book will explore the key factors that should impact your decisions about how to invest every second on test day. We'll start with a detailed discussion of the right way to think about guessing on test day (which is very important!), and then we'll build on that and have a broader discussion about using your time in the most effective way possible.

In this part of the Black Book, you'll learn the following:

- why just marking your best guess for every question isn't a good strategy
- why you should never forget your training, even when a question seems impossible
- why you shouldn't worry about being stumped a few times on test day
- how the SAT is designed to punish most people's guessing instincts
- the right way to think about guessing, so it can help your score instead of getting in the way
- key, section-specific considerations to keep in mind when you get stuck on different kinds of SAT questions
- the two types of guessing on the SAT, and why the one you probably haven't heard of might be better for you
- the important implications of viewing time as an investment on test day
- how quickly a trained test-taker can generally answer a real SAT question
- why and how you should approach each section of the SAT in multiple passes
- different ways to handle questions related to a single passage
- easily overlooked test-taking mistakes that can cost you points and undo your hard work
- how to diagnose any remaining issues with time management
- why skipping questions sooner may be key to raising your score
- why you should never worry about the average amount of time you spend on each question
- and more . . .

Guessing on the SAT

If things go wrong, don't go with them.

Roger Babson

It's important for us to talk about the correct approach to guessing on the SAT, because most untrained test-takers go about it in ways that don't help their scores as much as possible.

Let's start with the most basic fact: the SAT has no wrong-answer penalty. In other words, the test doesn't take any points away from you if you answer a question incorrectly, instead of just leaving it blank.[1]

With that in mind, you should always mark an answer to every question on a section before time runs out, even if you're just randomly choosing an answer. It can't hurt you, and there's a chance it could help.

Most untrained test-takers realize this on their own . . .

. . . and that's about where they stop thinking about SAT guessing altogether, unfortunately.

As a result, most people develop the habit of just putting down their "best guess" right away on any question they can't answer. For most untrained test-takers, this eventually bleeds into a general approach of marking down their first hunch on any question they see.

Even though this approach is very popular, it can still be a huge mistake, lowering your score for the following reasons:

- It ignores the fact that every official SAT question has a correct answer that's inarguable and totally predictable once you know how the test actually works.

- It ignores the SAT's habit of intentionally misleading people who only understand a small part of a question.

Let's explore those reasons in more detail, because it's very important to understand them if you're going to maximize your score.

Don't Forget that Every Real SAT Question has Exactly One Correct Answer.

Remember that every right answer on the SAT must be bulletproof, and that there's always exactly one correct answer, and that the correct answer is undeniably right, according to the rules of the test—no matter how strange it might seem to an untrained test-taker.

If you forget this fundamental idea, you may end up being tempted to abandon your training when you face a challenging question that you can't quite figure out right away. You might let yourself decide that this one question is the exception, and that two or three of the answers are all equally valid in this one case. Then you might start to doubt or abandon the strategies you've learned as you go through the rest of the test, causing you to end up with a much worse score than you could have achieved if you'd stuck to the rules.

So if you find yourself guessing on something, you have to remember that it's NOT because there's something wrong with the question that makes it impossible to answer with certainty, and it's NOT because the strategies you learn in this Black Book don't work. If you find yourself wanting to guess on a question, it's because there's something about this question that you just aren't seeing. It might be a word you don't really know, or it might be a math concept that you've forgotten, or a complicated sentence you don't quite understand. It might even just be that you're getting flustered and forgetting something important about how the question should work.

That's fine—it happens at least a few times to every single person who takes the SAT. And the way the test is designed, you can be totally stumped a few times and still get a great score, or even a perfect score. There's no need to beat yourself up about being unable to figure out a question. Just make sure you don't lose faith in your training simply because you're unable to execute that training sometimes.

So, for a trained test-taker, guessing should NEVER be the first instinct on a standardized test. You need to maintain a disciplined approach to every real SAT question you encounter, because that's the only way to make sure you attack each question using the principles in this Black Book—which, in turn, is the most effective way to maximize your score.

At this point, I know it might still be difficult to adjust to the fact that every real SAT question must follow certain rules you can learn, because it's so tempting to say that a difficult question "just doesn't follow the rules." But once you do adjust to the right way of thinking about the test, you'll have the comfort of knowing you can't really be surprised on test day—you can only be momentarily confused from looking at something the wrong way. We'll see more proof of this as we proceed with your training, and in the walkthroughs later in this book.

Of course, if you've been trying to figure out a tough SAT question and you've got no idea what to do, then you should eventually guess, rather than leave the question blank. But guessing is a last-ditch option, and it shouldn't change your mindset or mess up your overall game plan for the rest of the test. On top of that, there are specific ideas you should keep in mind if you have to guess on the SAT—and they're not things that most untrained test-takers ever think about.

That leads us into the other big problem with the normal approach to SAT guessing.

---

[1] At the time of this writing, the SAT Subject Tests *do* penalize you for missing a question instead of leaving it blank, so make sure you keep that in mind when you take your Subject Tests!

Don't Forget that the SAT is Designed to Lead You to Wrong Answers if You Don't Understand a Question.

As we'll see in more detail later on in this Black Book, the SAT is intentionally designed so that wrong answer choices often seem like the right answer to people who don't know how to approach a particular question. In other words, the very thing that keeps you from understanding a question in the first place is also the thing that's likely to attract you to a wrong answer if you decide to guess.

When untrained test-takers come to a question they're not sure about, they usually just put down the first choice that looks appealing to them, and move on to the next question—and this often means that they fall for a trap somewhere in the question, as we'll see in my walkthroughs of official SAT questions later on.

Instead of immediately guessing when a question can't be answered right away, a trained test-taker knows that she has to keep the design of the test in mind, and try to work around the issue that prevented her from immediately identifying the correct answer in the first place. This gives her a much better chance of correctly understanding how the question follows the rules and patterns of the SAT, which gives her a much better chance of answering the question correctly than she would have if she made a guess based on a poor understanding of the question.

Here are some guidelines of the kinds of things that tend to get overlooked when you can't figure out which choice is correct. I've broken them up by section. (Of course, we'll go into much more detail with instructions and examples of these ideas later in this book.)

Reading

- Are you reading the wrong part of the passage?
- Have you misunderstood, misread, or overlooked a word or phrase in the prompt, answer choice, or passage?
- Have you made an everyday assumption that isn't actually supported by the text?

Writing and Language

- Did you misread or overlook part of the underlined portion of the text?
- Did you misread or overlook part of an answer choice?
- Is it possible that the question involves a grammar or punctuation rule you haven't considered?
- Is it possible that a sentence before or after the underlined part of the passage might contain a parallel phrase that indicates which answer choice is correct?

Math

- Did you misread the prompt, answer choices, or diagram?
- Did you make any calculation mistakes? (Remember that it's still possible to make a mistake when you use a calculator—you might mis-key, for example.)
- Could the question involve a math concept you haven't considered? (Remember that the question might involve concepts that are directly related to the concepts in the question and the answer choices—but the question can't require you to know calculus, for example.)

Very often, a trained test-taker will remember to refer to elements of her training like the ones I've sketched out above, and then actually be able to identify the mistake she made when she first saw the question. From there, it's often possible to identify the correct answer to the question, rather than try to make a misguided guess.

Of course, it can sometimes happen that a trained test-taker will be unable to figure out the correct answer to a question with total certainty, no matter how hard she tries. In those circumstances, she should still mark an answer before time runs out, for obvious reasons … but the best way to pick which choice you'll commit to may not be what you'd expect. This is a good time to talk about the different ways to guess on the SAT.

The Recommended Approach to Guessing on the SAT

These are the two main approaches to SAT guessing:

- Hunch guessing
- Constant guessing

Let's explore them in more detail.

Hunch Guessing: The Most Common Approach

Hunch guessing is exactly what it sounds like: choosing an answer based entirely on your subjective assessment of which choice feels right to you, based on what you think you understand about the question. This approach tends to result in wrong answers for a lot of untrained test-takers, largely because it keeps them from working to understand how a difficult question follows the rules and patterns of the SAT, and because the College Board likes to include wrong answer choices that seem tempting to test-takers who don't fully understand the question.

But hunch guessing can be a useful strategy for some trained test-takers! There are two general types of test-takers who can benefit from hunch guessing:

- Test-takers who lack the confidence to know for sure that they're right, even though they're well trained.
- Very high-performing trained test-takers who have developed reliable instincts about how the SAT works. These test-takers usually only feel the need to guess once or twice per section, and can often intuitively identify the correct answer to a tough question even if they feel like they've overlooked a key piece of the question that would make them certain

In a moment, we'll talk about how you can find out whether you should employ hunch guessing or not.

Constant Guessing: The More Reliable Approach?

One way to avoid being influenced by the question and answer choices—and possibly picking the wrong answer as a result—is the technique of "constant" guessing. In this kind of guessing, once we've gone through our passes and answered every question we can handle with confidence, we then go back before time runs out and mark the same answer choice to every single skipped question. For example, we might mark all (A)s, or all (C)s. It doesn't matter which choice we pick; the goal is just to remove any kind of conscious interference from the process of guessing, and hope that random chance will cause us to get about 1/4 of our guesses right (since multiple choice questions on the SAT have four answer choices).

A lot of test-takers dislike constant guessing at first because it often involves marking down answers that seem like they must be wrong. But that's part of the process, and actually part of the rationale: when we use this approach, we're deliberately acknowledging that we don't understand the questions we're guessing on, and we're deliberately opening ourselves up to the possibility that answers might be correct even if we don't understand why.

Guessing Wrap-Up

With hunch guessing, the hope is that a test-taker will somehow figure out the answer without understanding a question, and the result is often that the test-taker misses all the questions he guesses on; with constant guessing, the hope is that random chance will allow us to mark correct answers for a predictable fraction of the questions we can't figure out.

As we've discussed, different guessing approaches will work better for different test-takers. The following key factors will influence the best approach for you on test day:

- Your level of training and awareness of how the SAT works as a test.
- Your level of confidence in the choices that you mark as correct answers.
- Whether your general intuitions about a particular question tend to be reliable.

Most untrained test-takers use the hunch-guessing approach on nearly every question, never even realizing that it's possible to know for sure which choice will be correct if we understand the rules and patterns of the SAT. This heavy reliance on hunch-guessing will nearly always result in a low-to-average score on any standardized test.

For most (but not all) trained test-takers, constant-guessing will result in at least as many correct answers as hunch-guessing will.

The only real way to know which approach is most likely to boost your score on test day is to experiment with each approach during your training, and see which one works best for you—that is, which one causes you to choose the correct answer more often when you guess.

A Critically Important Note on SAT Guessing

As we've discussed in other parts of this book, third-party questions from well-known test prep companies often break the actual rules and patterns of the real SAT, which can sometimes make it easier to hunch-guess your way to a correct answer on those fake questions. This is why it's EXTREMELY IMPORTANT that you test out your guessing with real SAT questions written by the College Board, and NOT with third-party questions written by other companies!

Time Management on Test Day

I recommend you read this section carefully, even if you feel like you don't need help with time management right now. My experience with students has shown me that everyone can improve their time management to some degree—no matter how good they think they already are when it comes to that aspect of testing performance—and improving your time management on test day is one of the fastest and easiest ways to raise your score.

We'll start by discussing the key underlying concept to keep in mind as you make decisions on test day. Then we'll go over the general process I recommend on test day in order to decide which question you should be answering at any given time. Finally, we'll discuss some other aspects of time management that might still be an issue after you've tried to implement everything else.

Remember that Time is an Investment.

We always want to spend our time in the ways that are most likely to increase our score in the most efficient way. For example, we don't want to spend 90 seconds on a question that seems difficult to us if we could have spent those 90 seconds correctly answering 2 or 3 questions that seem easier to us. If we have time to go back and try the harder question later, instead of just guessing on it, that's great—but we should take care of the ones we can answer more quickly first.

All of this leads to the following conclusions:

- We want to invest time in questions that we'll be able to answer correctly.

- We want to avoid working on questions that we'll end up having to guess on anyway.

- If we're not sure about an answer, we should use the guessing strategy that works best for us (for more on the issue of guessing on the SAT, see "Guessing on the SAT" on page 33 of this Black Book).

Now that we've discussed some key ideas underlying time management, let's talk about some ways we can apply them practically.

Answer Questions in the Order You Choose, not in the Order They're Presented.

Most untrained test-takers answer questions in the order that the College Board chooses to present them, instead of prioritizing the questions they find easier. This is almost always a bad idea—sticking to the College Board's order can't possibly *help* your score, and the only way it could fail to *hurt* your score is if you're so good at the SAT that you know you'll finish every question quickly and correctly . . . in which case you wouldn't need to be reading this Black Book in the first place.

So instead of just accepting the order that the College Board chooses for its questions, we should decide on our own whether to answer each question as we first encounter it, or skip it for the moment. To help us make that decision, we should keep in mind the fundamentals of time management:

- Every question within a section has the same potential impact on your score.

- Working on a question and then having to guess on it is usually a waste of time.

- Getting a question wrong is also a waste of time.

When we first come to a question, we shouldn't assume that we have to try to answer it right away. We're the ones who decide what we'll work on next, not the College Board. Instead of just diving right in and trying to find a solution, we should read the question and decide quickly if we think we'll be able to find the correct answer with total confidence in a fairly short time. My general rule of thumb is that I give myself 10 seconds to see if I can figure out how to arrive at an answer in 30 seconds or less. In other words, I spend 10 seconds reading through the question and trying to figure out how I could solve it in under 30 seconds. If 10 seconds have gone by and I still have no idea how to attack the question, then I skip it for the moment. I can always come back to it later if I want to, and I'll definitely mark some kind of guess for the question if I can't figure out the answer before time expires, but it's silly to invest more time in the question now, when I could be working on other questions that would be quicker and easier for me. I always keep in mind that every question in the section has the same impact on my score, so I should ideally be working on the easiest unanswered question at any given moment.

Remember that SAT Questions are Designed so Trained Test-Takers can Answer them Quickly—Usually in Under 30 Seconds.

As we've discussed in general, and as you'll see in more detail when we get into the section-specific training and walkthroughs, the SAT is actually a relatively simple and repetitive test once you understand its design. The SAT isn't interested in making us work out complicated solutions to advanced questions, because those kinds of skills are already measured in classroom settings or even on AP tests; instead, it's interested in seeing how quickly we can diagnose a question, identify the key information on the page, and apply the most efficient solution to arrive at the right answer. Questions are generally designed so that test-takers who know the unwritten rules of the test can answer them quickly. So if we know how the test works and we're still having a hard time answering a question, then we've probably misread or misunderstood some key element of the prompt, answer choices, or other information on the page; in these situations, continuing to spend a lot of time on the troublesome question is unlikely to yield results in the way that, say, spending more time on a complicated physics question in school is often the only way to arrive at the correct answer.

In general, I find that trained test-takers can expect to work through a question in less than 30 seconds if all goes well—in fact, people often find they can work through certain types of question, such as relatively easy Math questions or Writing and Language questions, in 10 seconds or less. Of course, this doesn't mean that you're guaranteed to get a question wrong if you need more time, or that you should feel bad if you routinely take longer than 30 seconds to answer certain questions. I'm just mentioning this idea to help you understand how the test is designed and what the rhythm of working through the questions efficiently can feel like.

All of this leads to the next idea, which is VERY important, and which most test-takers don't seem to realize:

Approach Each Section in Multiple Passes—Probably More than Two.

I've mentioned the idea of skipping questions if we don't think we'd be able to answer them with certainty, but there's a bit more to this idea than we've discussed so far.

A trained test-taker should approach a section of the SAT with the expectation of doing at least three or four passes through the section. This allows us to be fairly certain that we're not wasting time on questions that are more challenging for us when we could be scoring points on easier questions that we haven't seen yet.

Here's the basic idea—of course, you should feel free to modify this as you see fit, but this is roughly how I divide up the passes when I take a standardized test:

First Pass: Low-Hanging Fruit and Information-Gathering

I have two primary goals in mind the first time I go through a section of the SAT:

- I want to mark down correct answers for all the questions I feel I can work through pretty quickly and easily.
- I want to get an idea of what the harder questions look like.

I start the first pass by reading the first question on the section. If I can figure out a quick, easy way to attack the question and find the answer, then I do that—making EXTREMELY sure, as always, that I don't take the question for granted and fall for some kind of trick that causes me to mark the wrong answer. If I've looked at the first question for 10 seconds or so and I still don't feel like I have an idea of how to find the answer, then I skip it. I can always come back to it in a later pass if I want, or eventually guess on it.

After I handle the first question, either by finding the answer quickly and easily or by deciding to skip it for the moment, I go on to the second question, and repeat the process: if I look at the question for 10 seconds, and I think I can answer with total certainty by working on the question for another 30 seconds or less, then I do; if not, I skip it and save it for later.

I repeat this process until I've gone through every question on the section.

After the first pass, I've marked correct answers to all the questions that seemed pretty easy to me . . . and I've also put my eyes on *every single question on the section*, even if it was only to glance at the question and decide quickly that it was something that probably required more time than I wanted to spend on my first pass.

I'm going to use my knowledge of the various questions on the section when I do my next pass.

Second Pass: Questions that Require a Little More Thought

Keeping in mind what I saw during my first pass, I go back to the beginning of the section and find the first question that I skipped during my first pass. I read it a bit more carefully and think about it a bit more deliberately than I might have done on my first pass, when I was just trying to answer the questions that seemed obvious to me.

Just like on the first pass, I skip or answer each question, and I don't let myself get too bogged down on any one question; it's just that, now, I'm more willing to invest a few extra seconds trying to figure out how to approach a question than I was before. (Again, I'm NOT willing to spend several minutes on a single question, because I know that the College Board never sets up a question in a way that would require a trained test-taker to work on the question for several minutes. I'm willing to spend more time analyzing the wording of a question, the relationships among the choices, and the other things we consider as trained test-takers, but I still know that when I figure out how to execute a solution, that solution will usually take less than 30 seconds per question.)

Unlike my first pass, though, I have some idea of what the other questions on the test look like when I go through my second pass, and I use that information to help me decide which questions I should skip again for a later pass, and which of the remaining questions seem easier to me. I let that knowledge guide me.

I always keep in mind that my goal at any given moment is to invest my time in the activities that are most likely to result in getting me the most points in the least time, which generally means answering the remaining questions that seem quickest and easiest to me, and making sure I don't make any careless errors.

When I've reached the end of my second pass, the only questions left unanswered are the ones that seem the most challenging, because I've now looked through the whole section twice and still decided not to attack them yet. Now it's time for the third pass.

Third Pass: Remain Upbeat and Remember Your Training

Most untrained test-takers would be very discouraged at the thought of focusing on the questions that seemed hardest initially, but we know two things that untrained test-takers don't know:

- The College Board generally makes questions seem challenging by using test-design principles that make the test seem harder than it is, not by writing questions that actually require advanced knowledge.

- On most days we can miss or leave blank a handful of questions and still get an elite score if everything else is answered correctly. This means we never need to get flustered about a few questions that seem extra hard to us, as long as we're careful to answer all the other questions correctly.

So on the third pass through the test, we need to keep in mind that our goal is basically to identify the unanswered questions that we're most likely to be able to answer correctly with a little extra attention and reflection in the time we have left. In general, these will be the questions that contain words and concepts we feel like we're familiar with, as opposed to questions that include phrases we may not recognize—but it's important to keep in mind that you'll sometimes find you can work out the meaning of an unknown phrase if you stay calm and analyze the parts of the question that make sense to you. (For an example of how this can work, consider question 23 from Section 4 of SAT Practice Test #4, which involves the phrase "standard deviation." Even if a test-taker is uncomfortable with that term, he might be able to work out roughly what it means and then answer the question correctly if he notices that the values in one set of numbers vary significantly more from their average than the values in the other set do. See my walkthrough of that question on page 417, including my note on a way to attack the question if you don't know the term "standard deviation.")

By the time you start this third pass, you're likely to have used up half of your allotted time on the section, or maybe even three-quarters of it, or more. You may only have enough time to expect to answer 5 or fewer additional questions, so it's especially important to tackle the remaining questions in the order that you want. If you feel like the last question on the test is likely to be the easiest remaining question to figure out, then start there. Start this pass on the question that seems like the one that's most likely to result in a correct answer in the shortest possible time, and then go on to the question that seems the next most likely to result in a right answer in the shortest possible time, and so on.

At some point, you may be ready for a fourth pass, either because you've answered all the questions on the section, or you've decided that there are some questions on the section you just won't be able to answer with certainty before time runs out. This is when we might consider shifting our focus a little bit.

Review and Clean-Up Pass

I usually recommend you start your review pass through the section when you've answered all the questions that you think you can answer with certainty, or when there are about 10 minutes left, whichever comes first.

On this last pass, the goal is to go back through all the questions you've answered and make sure that you haven't made any mistakes in the answers that you've marked. Be especially careful to check for all the little kinds of mistakes that the College Board likes to trick us into—stuff like looking at the wrong part of a Reading passage, overlooking the subject of a verb on the Writing and Language section, solving for the wrong variable on a Math question, and so on.

I often like to check my work by seeing if I can figure out the kinds of mistakes the College Board was trying to anticipate with the wrong answers that it set out. If I can do that for a particular question, I can usually be pretty sure I've answered it correctly.

Of course, you should also have been very careful to avoid mistakes during the other passes, when you previously answered the questions, so this last pass usually shouldn't turn up too many mistakes. But we should always be on the lookout for them, because we always need to remember that one of the College Board's main goals is to trick untrained test-takers into answering questions incorrectly even when they think they understand a question. Never forget that rigorous attention to detail is the main thing that separates top-scoring test-takers from everybody else—not advanced knowledge!

After we've reviewed the questions we felt certain about, we may still have some questions on the section that are unanswered. In our last pass before time expires, we'll consider how to guess on those remaining questions.

Guessing Pass

If you find yourself still working on a section with only a few minutes left before time expires, then you'll want to make sure that you mark down an answer for every question on the section, even if you have to guess blindly on some of them, because you'll at least be giving yourself the chance to get lucky on the questions you guess at. (Of course, if you've implemented the ideas in this Black Book and been diligent in your training, you probably won't find yourself guessing blindly at the end of a section—my point is just that you should always make sure to manage your time so that you've marked an answer for every question before time runs out, since there's no penalty for marking an incorrect answer on the SAT.)

There are two main ways to approach guessing on the SAT, and I cover them in "Guessing on the SAT" on page 33 of this Black Book. For now, the important thing to keep in mind is that, as trained test-takers, we need to make sure that we distinguish between questions whose answers we're certain about, and questions when we know we're guessing, so that we don't develop the mindset that the right answer to every question is subjective and up for discussion. That way we can optimize our results from any guessing we need to do.

Make it your Own and Remember What Counts.

As I mentioned earlier, you should feel free to modify this idea of approaching the test in passes, and make it your own. The key thing to keep in mind is that you should always be investing your time in the activities that are most likely to improve your score in the least time, instead of mindlessly tackling whatever the College Board decides to throw at you next.

What about Passages on the Reading Section and the Writing and Language Section?

Both the Reading Test and the Writing and Language Test feature questions grouped around separate passages, which can complicate the idea of approaching the test in passes for some test-takers: they wonder whether they should decide to skip individual questions, or to skip all the questions for an entire passage if they find the passage difficult in general.

As it turns out, some test-takers will do better when they skip an entire passage altogether, and some will do better when they skip individual questions. The only real way to know for sure what works for you is to experiment with how you structure your passes during your practice sessions.

Personally, I generally prefer to save individual questions for later passes, because my approach to the Reading and Writing and Language sections involves treating each question as its own issue, rather than lumping them together with other questions about the same passage. As you'll see when we get into the training for those kinds of questions, I generally approach each one by reading the prompt, finding the relevant part of the passage, and then using my knowledge of the SAT's design to identify the correct answer based on the relevant text. Because I understand how the test works, I know that we never need to keep an entire passage in mind when we answer an individual question about that passage. Once you learn the proper way to approach the test, you'll understand why this is so, and you'll probably prefer to decide whether to skip a question without considering which passage it refers to. Still, some test-takers just prefer to work on all the questions for a passage anyway, even when they understand that it isn't technically necessary. If that's what works best for you, then that's what you should do.

You may also wonder whether to do multiple "mini-passes" within the questions for a given passage, or to just go through all the questions for all the passages before coming back to the beginning of the whole section. The answer is basically the same—either approach can work fine. Just try each one out in practice and go with whichever works better for you.

A Few More Things to Keep in Mind

Below, I'd like to address a few other important considerations when you approach the test in this way.

Don't Mis-bubble the Answer Sheet!

As you're skipping questions and working in passes like this, it's important to make sure that the answers you do fill in are marked in the proper place on your answer sheet. For example, if you skip question 17 to work on question 18, make sure that you mark the answer for 18 next to the 18 on your answer sheet—not next to the 17. This idea of working in passes will save you a lot of time and frustration if you do it right, but if you end up having to erase a bunch of answers and re-enter them, you'll undo a lot of the benefits. So pay attention, and make sure you're always marking each answer next to the right number.

Don't Lose Track of Time.

As we've discussed, the idea of approaching the test in passes is an essential part of optimal test-taking, because it allows us to make sure we invest our time in ways that are mostly likely to get us more points. But we still have to make sure we move through each pass with an appropriate sense of urgency. Sometimes, finishing a pass can make us feel like we're done with the section overall, because we find ourselves considering how to answer the last few questions of the section much earlier than untrained test-takers will see them. But it's important to remember that we're not expecting to answer every question when we complete a pass! We're just looking for the easiest remaining questions on each pass, even though it might feel like we're completing the section multiple times. So we can't take breaks, even though it might be tempting to pause sometimes. When I finish one pass, I go right back to the questions that are still unanswered and start the next pass, and I repeat this process until time is called—even after I've finished answering the questions, I keep re-checking my work, because I know how important it is to make sure I avoid mistakes.

Mistakes will Undo Your Hard Work. Don't Make Them.

You've probably noticed by now that I constantly remind you of the importance of avoiding small mistakes. This is because every wrong answer costs you in two ways:

- You lose the time you invested in the question, which you could have invested in a question you would have answered correctly.
- You lose the opportunity to mark a correct answer for the question you got wrong.

So when you're going through your passes, you want to make sure to remain thorough and diligent on the questions that you answer, because it doesn't help you to work on a question and get it wrong.

Similarly, you should take your final review and guessing passes seriously, because correcting a question that you'd previously marked wrong is just as valuable as marking a correct answer on a blank question.

Other Time-Management Issues

Up until now, we've been discussing general time-management strategies that apply to all trained test-takers. But you may still feel that you have other concerns when it comes to timing, and we'll address some of those now.

Actually, a lot of test-takers worry about having enough time on the SAT, because they're used to having timing issues on regular high school tests, and they don't realize how different the SAT is from non-standardized tests. Then test day comes around, and untrained test-takers see questions that look strange to them, and they start to panic . . . none of which helps with their time-management issues.

But my first piece of advice for a student in this position is to put the issue of time-management aside until after you learn about everything else in this Black Book. You might very well find that you no longer have any issues with time-management after you adopt my approach to the SAT.

In most situations, test-takers who worry about time are using the wrong approach to the test in the first place. So they don't need to get quicker at the old approach—instead, they need to start using a method that's more efficient and, therefore, inherently faster. You'll learn a much more efficient approach in this Black Book; it takes less time and produces better results than the traditional approach that most untrained test-takers will use.

So, again, the first thing I'd recommend you do is ignore your timing issues at the beginning of your preparation, and see if they go away on their own as you come to understand how the test really works. They often do.

If they don't go away, though, there's still plenty of stuff we can work on. Read on.

Reading Speed

Some test-takers are naturally slower at reading than others, but most people find they read fast enough for the SAT if they're approaching questions in the most efficient way. As a general rule of thumb, if you don't have problems with the speed of your reading in your classes in school, then you probably read fast enough to do very well on the SAT if you're using the right strategies.

For what it's worth, most of us can make some kind of improvement on our reading speed just by making a conscious effort to read faster. I know that might sound simplistic, but it's true. If you constantly remind yourself to read faster, you'll find yourself reading faster. It's a bit like walking—most of us could walk noticeably faster if we just made a deliberate effort to do so.

If you have a serious issue with reading speed that can be diagnosed by a professional, then it might be a good idea to try to petition the College Board for extra time when you take the test.

Nerves

A lot of people get nervous at the thought of taking the SAT, and some people freeze up when they're nervous. If this kind of thing is affecting your time management, there are two different ways to attack it. First, you can work on consciously channeling your nervousness into productive energy. Let it make you read more carefully, or drive you to consider a new angle on a question that's troubling you. Second, you can recognize that the root of your nervousness is probably a feeling of frustration or even powerlessness when it comes to the SAT—and the best way to beat that feeling is by learning how the test works so you can see that it's actually not scary at all. It's just weird, and detail-oriented.

You May Need to Work on Deciding to Skip Questions Faster.

If you're using the multiple-pass approach that I described in "Time Management on Test Day" on page 36 of this Black Book, but still having difficulties with time, then you may need to make a conscious effort to get better at recognizing when to skip a question during a pass. As I said in that discussion, my general recommendation is that students should move on to the next question if ten seconds have gone by and they still can't figure out how to attack the question they're looking at. You may want to play around with trying to make that decision even faster.

(To be clear, I don't try to *answer* the question in ten seconds. I'm just saying that I try to figure out what my approach is going to be within the first ten seconds of reading a question. For example, it might take me ten seconds to read a question, look at the answer choices, and think, "I could find the answer by graphing each answer choice and comparing it to the text in the prompt." I haven't actually found the answer yet, but I know how to approach the question, and would probably do so right then, rather than saving the question for a later pass. This is an important distinction.)

If I can't see how I'm going to approach a question within the first ten seconds of reading it, I immediately forget about that question for the time being, and go on to the next one. I recommend you do the same thing. Remember that our goal is to invest our time in the easiest questions available.

Everyone runs into questions that just don't "click." This is a completely normal part of taking a standardized test, and you need to train yourself to act accordingly. So it's important to learn to skip questions as soon as you realize you can't work productively on them. There's no shame in it—in fact, working on questions in passes like this is a major part of smart, disciplined test-taking.

Don't Think about the Average Time per Question.

A lot of untrained test-takers try to maintain a constant pace throughout a given section, which ends up causing unnecessary worry and costing them points. These test-takers usually find the average amount of time allotted for each question by dividing the number of minutes allotted for a section by the number of questions in the section. Then they mistakenly adopt this average-time-per-question as a guideline for how long they should spend on every single question, no matter what. As they go through the test, if they find a question they can answer quickly, they slow down a little so that the question still takes up the average amount of time per question on that section; if they find a question that seems harder for them, they panic and rush because they still want to try to get it done in the average amount of time per question on that section.

This approach might make sense if most of the questions on a given section were very similar to one another in terms of subject matter, difficulty, and complexity . . . but they aren't. Some questions will naturally take you 10 or 15 seconds to figure out with total certainty (especially as you get better at implementing the strategies in this Black Book, which you'll see in the question walkthroughs later on). In these situations, it would be silly to spend extra time staring at a question once you've checked your solution and made sure you're right. On the other hand, sometimes you'll misunderstand a question, or keep making a small mistake that causes you not to arrive at any of the answer choices, or you'll have some other issue on a question that might cause you to skip it twice and then finally be forced to guess on it, and you'll end up spending a total of two minutes or more on one question. For these kinds of questions, it makes no sense to try to cram all of that thinking into an arbitrary time limit.

So the smart way to approach the SAT is to realize that some questions take much less time than average, and some questions might take you more than a minute or two. You should try to handle every question as quickly as you can without sacrificing accuracy—whether that means solving it on your current pass, saving it for later, or deciding to skip it altogether. If you keep this attitude, you'll find that the questions you answer quickly will help you have enough time to devote extra energy to the occasional question that stumps you in the later passes.

Analyze and Adjust Your Performance.

If you're still having timing issues, you may need to do some analysis on the specific questions that are slowing you down. When you practice with real test questions, make a mark next to questions that take you a lot of time. Go back to them after your practice session is over, and try to identify the elements they have in common that made them take so long. Every test-taker has different triggers that might cause him to spend more time than necessary on some questions, and your goal is to figure out what causes it to happen to you. You might think about issues like the following, just as examples:

- Do you have trouble reading the prompt carefully if it involves more than two or three lines of text?
- Do you re-check work three or four times on each question, even after you're sure you haven't made a mistake?
- Do you panic when passages involve figures?

Try to pinpoint the kinds of things that generally slow you down. Then do some untimed review of relevant practice questions from the College Board, along with the walkthroughs from this Black Book, and really analyze and break down the aspect of solving that question that takes you the most time. Then, keep in mind what you've learned when you do your next timed practice, and try to modify the behavior that was costing you extra time before.

Breaking down your performance like this, and thinking about how you react to different elements of official practice questions from the College Board, can give you some insights into where you should focus as you try to increase your speed. For example, if you find that certain calculations take a lot of time for you to do by hand, consider using your calculator a little more; if you find that you're frequently re-reading long blocks of text, focus on trying to absorb all the necessary information in one or two tries. You'll find that identifying the causes of your issues as precisely as you possibly can will make it a lot easier to figure out the likely solutions to your problems.

On the Reading and Writing Sections, Remember that We Never Need to Memorize Every Detail in a Passage.

Some test-takers have a difficult time accepting the fact that the rules and patterns of the SAT prevent the College Board from writing questions that would require test-takers to remember and understand an entire passage at once. This causes them to spend much more time and energy than necessary on trying to keep an entire passage in their head, instead of identifying the small portions of any individual passage that are actually relevant to a particular question. As we'll see later on in the training for questions on both the Reading section and the Writing and Language section, and as I'll demonstrate in the walkthroughs for those question types, we never need to understand an entire passage at once to answer a question—in fact, we generally don't need to read any passage all the way through if we don't want to.

On Math Sections, Remember that the College Board Rewards Us for Finding Informal Solutions.

Sometimes, a test-taker will waste time unnecessarily writing out extra steps to a solution as though she were going to submit the work to a teacher, forgetting that the College Board will only grade her on the bubbles she fills in on the answer sheet. In fact, as we'll see in the walkthroughs in this Black Book, the fastest solutions to many questions don't involve formulas, or even written solutions at all.

If you find yourself writing out a lot of steps for most questions, then give yourself permission to be more efficient, and focus on finding answers without doing so much writing. As we'll discuss in more detail later on, these solutions might involve analyzing the answer choices as part of the question, using a calculator, noticing a shortcut that's possible because of a diagram, and so on.

Consider Petitioning the College Board for Accommodations.

If you've been working on implementing the ideas in this Black Book, and particularly in this section, but you're still feeling totally overwhelmed by the time limits on the SAT, then you may want to consider contacting the College Board for special timing accommodations. The requirements of the conditions for getting these accommodations can change at any time (as can the nature of the accommodations themselves), so I won't discuss them here. If you're interested in more information on these accommodations, you can look them up on the College Board's website, or ask a teacher or guidance counselor for advice.

Part 5: "Science" on the SAT

In the following articles, we'll briefly discuss the minor role that scientific knowledge will actually play on test day, and uncover what you'll need to know when the College Board tries to confuse you with questions that might seem to be based on science.

Among other things, you'll learn the following:

- why the College Board has increased its apparent focus on science in the current version of the test

- why you shouldn't worry when questions mention experiments or scientific jargon

- the importance of understanding graphs, tables, and other figures, and the key rules for reading them

- how to tell when you need to combine information from a passage with information from a figure

- a common pattern for wrong answers on questions related to figures

- why it's so important to be familiar with a wide variety of figures BEFORE test day

- how to read a wide range of figures that you might encounter on test day

- and more . . .

Facebook.com/TestingIsEasy   Youtube.com/TestingIsEasy

How Science Appears on the SAT

The College Board wants you to think that you'll need some kind of scientific knowledge to perform well on the SAT. This might be for any number of reasons, including (but not limited to) the following:

- The SAT's number one competitor—the ACT—has a Science section, and the College Board doesn't want the SAT to seem to fall short of the ACT in this regard.

- The College Board likes to make it seem like the SAT requires more advanced skills than it actually does.

- The College Board wants the SAT to be seen as a test of college-readiness, and most people will study some kind of science in college, so it would probably look good if the SAT seemed to test scientific understanding.

But you don't actually need to understand the scientific method, experiments, hypotheses, independent and dependent variables, or anything along those lines to answer SAT questions. (You *will* need to understand a couple of basic ideas related to surveys and sampling to answer a small percentage of SAT Math questions, but we'll cover that in "The Basics of Surveys and Sampling" on page 206 of this Black Book).

You will occasionally see a Reading or Writing and Language passage that mentions an experiment or a hypothesis or something along those lines, but you won't actually need to understand what those words mean in order to answer those questions—instead, you'll just need to be able to tell which answer choice is restated or demonstrated by ideas from the passage, and which ones contradict the passage or aren't supported by the passage in some way—more on that in the training for those sections.

To be clear, I'm not saying that it isn't important in general to understand science or the scientific method. I actually think that understanding the scientific method is really, really important, and that it's very unfortunate that most schools don't really teach it to their students anymore. But you don't need to know about any of that to answer questions on the SAT, so don't get nervous if you see questions on scientific topics on test day—just stick to your training for the section where the question appears and you'll be fine, with no outside knowledge of science required (again, except for that small survey and sampling issue that appears on the SAT Math section, which we'll cover on page 206).

Reading Graphs, Charts, Tables, and Other Figures

The importance of careful reading on the SAT extends beyond passages, prompts, and answer choices. We also need to be able to read graphs, charts, tables, and a variety of other figures that can appear on every section of the test, because the College Board includes figures throughout the test in an effort to make the SAT seem more in keeping with recent trends in education.

By now, it should be no surprise that every figure on the SAT obeys certain rules and conventions—whether it's a scatterplot, a table, a map, or some other kind of figure—because we know that the SAT is highly standardized.

You may already be comfortable with reading data from a variety of different kinds of figures in school or in your hobbies (for example, histograms are often encountered in photography, while line graphs and bar graphs come up in fantasy sports, and so on). If that's the case, then you'll probably find that you can understand the figures on the SAT relatively easily, and you just need to understand the test's extra rules and conventions in order to be ready to read figures on test day.

But many test-takers will find that at least some of the charts, graphs, and diagrams on the SAT are surprisingly tricky to read at first. The College Board likes to present us with some pretty non-standard figures, and you can almost be sure that you'll encounter at least one kind of figure that you haven't seen before on test day.

But there's no need to worry! Even the stranger figures on the SAT will always follow rules we'll discuss. So, as trained test-takers, we realize we can always answer data-related questions correctly if we keep the SAT's rules in mind and read carefully.

In this section, we'll start out by discussing the rules we need to follow when reading figures on the SAT. Then, we'll review some types of figures that you might see on test day, in case you're not feeling confident with graphical representations of data in general.

Reading Figures Rule 1: No Judgment Calls or Outside Knowledge

Whenever the SAT asks us to answer a question based on data in a figure, the data in the figure will always clearly and directly support one correct answer choice, with no interpretation on our part. We'll never run into a situation in which two different aspects of the data contradict each other and the only way to find the answer is to make a subjective decision that one aspect of the data is more important than the other one, or anything like that. The wording in the question, the wording in the figure, and the wording in the passage (if relevant) will always point to one clear, correct answer that follows the rules of the relevant section of the SAT (whether it's a Reading, Writing and Language, or Math question). On top of that, you'll never need any outside knowledge about a topic in the data; for example, if a question asks about a table showing the growth rates of populations of bacteria, you won't be required to know anything about the bacteria on your own in order to answer the question (although you may have to find some information in a relevant passage or label, or somewhere else on the page, as we'll discuss below, and as you'll see in the question walkthroughs later in this Black Book).

For an example from a real SAT practice question, look at question 20 from the Reading section of SAT Practice Test #2 from the College Board. That question asks for the period of time during which "the greatest difference between per-pound profits from fair trade coffee and those from regular coffee occurred." As we can see in the walkthrough for that question on page 109 of this Black Book, we don't need to make any kind of judgment call whatsoever in answering this question—the graph clearly shows that the greatest difference appeared during one particular period. Also, we don't need any outside knowledge—all the information required to answer the question is present in the graph, and we don't need to have prior knowledge of coffee, profits, or anything else from the question to find the right answer. (For a detailed discussion of that question, see the walkthrough on page 109.)

Reading Figures Rule 2: ALL Text and Labels are Important.

This might sound like an obvious piece of advice, but you'd be surprised how often untrained test-takers mistakenly think a question can't be answered because they don't realize they overlooked a label on a table, or because they misread the title of a graph, or something else along those lines.

Generally, you'll find that key phrases in the prompt or answer choices are nearly identical to phrases that appear in figures as labels, titles, headings, and other text elements. For this reason, it's very important that you notice all the text in a figure! Make a deliberate point of looking for text above, below, and to both sides of all figures, as well as within the figures themselves. We'll see examples of how important this can be throughout the walkthroughs in this Black Book.

Remember that figures on the SAT often don't look like figures we encounter in the classroom! Don't make the mistake of thinking that reading the labels of the x- and y-axes on a graph will always give you all the information you need to answer the question, even though that's often the case in science and math classes. There may be multiple labels on any axis, or there may be a label along the top or right side of a figure, or there may be sub-titles, or keys, or notes about scale, or other elements in the figure. If you don't notice a particular text element in a particular figure, you may not be able to answer a question about that figure with certainty.

Reading Figures Rule 3: Be Sure to Use the Right Data.

Figures on the SAT often display a variety of different pieces of information, which means that a big part of answering a question about a figure is identifying the data you need, and ignoring the data that's not relevant. *Make sure you're looking in the right place when you answer a data-related question.*

Here are some examples of common mistakes that can lead untrained test-takers to consider the wrong data when they try to answer a question:

- A bar graph may use multiple shades of gray in a cluster of bars, leading an untrained test-taker to misread the key and pay attention to the wrong bar.
- An untrained test-taker may not realize her eyes have skipped to a different line of data when she tries to read a value off a table.
- An untrained test-taker may look at one figure in the passage without realizing the question is asking about another figure.

So when you refer back to a figure, make sure that the data you consider is actually the data that the question is asking about.

Again, I know this might sound obvious if you're not familiar with the SAT, but we have to remember that one of the College Board's most effective tactics, on any section, is to give untrained test-takers the opportunity to make small, simple mistakes without noticing them. As trained test-takers, we always have to look out for those potential small mistakes. One of the easiest ways to fall for a wrong answer is to look at the wrong data in a figure, because the College Board often writes the wrong answers to data-based questions so they accurately reflect parts of a figure that aren't relevant to the prompt. Remember the importance of careful reading at all times!

For an example from a real SAT practice question, look at question 28 from the Reading section of SAT Practice Test #1. That question asks for the correct percentages of the purines in yeast DNA. Wrong answer choice (B) is the result we get if we accidentally find the data for the pyrimidines in yeast DNA, not the purines. (For a detailed discussion of that question, see its walkthrough on page 90 in this book. Also, don't worry if you don't know what purines or pyrimidines are—the passage for that question provides all the information you need to know to answer the question, which is typical for technical terms on the SAT.)

Reading Figures Rule 4: Sometimes You'll Need Info from the Passage, Too.

There will be times when we encounter a question about a figure, and we won't immediately see how the question and the figure are related, even though we've read the question and the figure correctly. In these situations, the passage itself often provides a necessary piece of information to link the prompt, the figure, and the correct answer.

We can often tell that a portion of a passage might be relevant to a data question if we notice that the concepts in the answer choices aren't present in the labels and text that we see in the figure.

For example, question 21 on the Reading section of SAT Practice Test #2 asks which idea in the passage is directly supported by the data in the graph. The graph in question compares profits on fair trade coffee to profits on regular coffee from 2000 to 2008. But when we read the answer choices, we can see that none of them mentions anything about coffee or profits. An untrained test-taker might feel as though he's being asked to make a judgment call—or even form an opinion—about an idea that appears in the passage.

But trained test-takers know there must be direct support in the passage and/or figure for any correct answer choice. When we carefully read the passage, we see that paragraph 6 (lines 57-66) discusses fair trade coffee, then says "common ground like this suggests that . . . ethical economics is still possible." So the passage tells us that fair trade coffee is an example of ethical economics, and question 21 asks us which idea from the passage is supported by a graph displaying data related to fair trade coffee profits. Since the graph gives us information about fair trade coffee profits, and the passage tells us that fair trade coffee indicates that "ethical economics is still possible" (line 66), we know the correct answer must be (C), "Ethical economics is still possible." (See my walkthrough of this question on page 110 for more details if you'd like.)

Notice that—even though we had to rely on some information in the passage—there was a clear logical connection between the passage, the graph, and the correct answer choice, and that all the information we needed to arrive at the one correct answer was right there on the page in front of us. Even on this figure question, which is one of the more challenging figure questions the College Board has released, we were able to find the correct answer with certainty just by reading carefully.

Reading Figures Rule 5: Wrong Answers Frequently Mention Ideas that aren't on the Page at All.

The College Board often likes to create wrong answers for data questions that mention ideas that appear neither in the figure, nor in the passage itself. As an example, consider question 20 from the Reading section of SAT Practice Test #3. It asks about two figures, which provide information about the occupations of people who use public transportation, and the purposes of trips on public transportation. Choices (C) and (D) are both incorrect, and they both refer to ideas that aren't in the figures or in the passage. (C) makes a distinction between people's habits during the week and on the weekends . . . but neither figure mentions days of the week at all, let alone anything about what people do during the week as opposed to on the weekends. The passage itself is also silent on that issue. Similarly, choice (D) mentions the idea of people waiting to be able to afford a car, but, again, neither figure mentions anything about people saving up to buy cars, and the passage doesn't say anything about that idea either. So (C) and (D) are wrong because they mention ideas that don't appear in the figures at all. (For more on this question, see its walkthrough on page 131 of this Black Book.)

The College Board probably includes answer choices like this because they encourage untrained test-takers to try to interpret the given data subjectively, rather than focus on the information that's actually on the page. This gives an untrained test-taker one more way to make a mistake on a question. Many people will find it easier to rule out answer choices that contradict the figures than to rule out choices that don't even mention information from the figures, because there's nothing in the figure that says an irrelevant choice is wrong—we just have to know it's wrong because irrelevant choices are always wrong on the SAT. In fact, an untrained test-taker who sees an irrelevant choice might think she missed something in the passage, or that she misread a figure, or even that the choice might be correct because it just seems to make sense, as (C) or (D) on question 20 might seem to make subjective sense to some people.

So it's important for us to remember that sometimes the College Board will include answer choices for a data question that contain ideas that just don't appear anywhere on the page—not in the figure, and not in the passage itself. When you see these kinds of choices, don't get flustered and start thinking that you must have misread something. Instead, just carefully re-read the figure and any relevant part of the passage; if you can see that the answer choice doesn't restate or demonstrate information from the figure or passage, then you can be confident the answer choice is wrong.

Reading Figures Rule 6: Get Comfortable with Figures on the SAT BEFORE Test Day.

Getting comfortable with reading figures on the SAT is like getting comfortable with any other part of the SAT: it's a little different from what you're used to in a classroom setting, but, once you learn how the test works and you get in some practice, you'll find that the stuff you need to do on the SAT is usually less complicated and more straightforward and predictable than stuff you have to do in school.

Remember that figures will appear in the Reading, Writing and Language, and Math sections on the SAT, so you'll encounter a variety of SAT questions with figures as you prepare for the test. If you have trouble with any SAT questions that involve figures, review those questions carefully to understand why you got them wrong and what you could do to answer a similar question correctly in the future (and, of course, review the relevant walkthroughs in this Black Book).

Common Types of Figures

Now we'll discuss the different ways to read data from some of the most common types of figures you'll see on test day.

Tables

A table consists of rows and columns. A row is a horizontal grouping of individual boxes or "cells," and a column is a vertical grouping of cells. Each row or column has its own label. The label for a row is usually in the left-most cell in that row. The label for a column is usually in the highest cell in that column. The example table below shows the height and vertical leap of four students.

Students' Heights And Vertical Leaps (m)

Student Name	Susan	James	Derek	Lauren
Height (m)	1.67	1.78	1.61	1.72
Vertical Leap (m)	0.40	0.45	0.65	0.51

In the example above, the row labeled "Vertical Leap" tells us the vertical leap of each student in the table. The column labeled "Lauren" gives us the data for the student named Lauren.

The cell shared by a particular row and column—that is, the cell located at the intersection of that row and column—contains the numerical data that reflects the combination of the data in the labels for the row and column. In the example above, the row labeled "Vertical Leap" intersects with the column labeled "Lauren" at the cell that contains the number "0.51." This tells us that the "Vertical Leap" for "Lauren" is "0.51." In other words, the student named Lauren has a vertical leap of 0.51 meters.

Sub-groupings

Tables are often used to show a breakdown of data into certain groups or classes, especially through "sub-groupings." Sometimes we'll see multiple layers of labels on either the horizontal or vertical axis of the table, or on both axes. This indicates sub-groupings of data. The example table below shows us which types of lunches were served on which days in a school cafeteria over a 10-week period.

Type Of Lunch Served In Cafeteria Over 10-Week Period

Day Of Week	Hot Lunches			Cold Lunches		
	Pasta	Pizza	Tacos	Sandwich	Salad	Smoothie
Monday	2	3	0	1	4	0
Tuesday	1	2	2	3	0	2
Wednesday	1	3	1	2	2	1
Thursday	0	0	4	2	1	3
Friday	2	1	1	4	2	0
Total	6	9	8	12	9	6

In the example table above, we can see the title of the table, "Type Of Lunch Served In Cafeteria Over 10-Week Period," at the top. Below the title, we can see that the lunches are divided into two sub-groupings: "Hot Lunches" and "Cold Lunches." Under the "Hot Lunches" sub-grouping, we can see "Pasta," "Pizza," and "Tacos," while under the "Cold Lunches" sub-grouping, we can see "Sandwich," "Salad," and "Smoothie."

(For an example of these kinds of sub-groupings in an SAT question, see passage 5 in the Reading section of SAT Practice Test #3 from the College Board. Beneath the label "Percent of colonies affected by pathogen" in the table, there are two sub-groupings: "Colonies with colony collapse disorder (%)" and "Colonies without colony collapse disorder (%).")

Double lines

Sometimes the College Board uses double lines in a table to make the layout of the information more clear. For example, in the table in question 21 on section 4 of SAT Practice Test #1, the horizontal double line helps separate the top row, which explains what the numbers in the table represent, from the other rows in the table. The same table could also have appeared without the double line and we would still be able to tell what the table was showing us, but the College Board just likes to use double lines in tables sometimes. I only mention them here because some test-takers might think the double lines have a special meaning, but they really don't—so you don't need to give them much thought.

Bar Graphs

A bar graph is just a different graphical demonstration of the same kind of information that can appear in a table. The bar graphs below show the information from the table above entitled "Students' Heights And Vertical Leaps (m)."

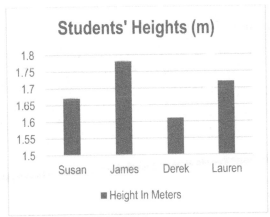
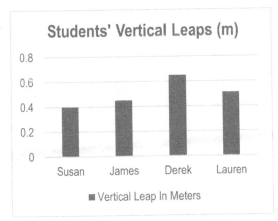

In both bar graphs, the vertical axis on the left shows the range of numerical values, and the horizontal axis along the bottom shows the different students whose data appears in the graph. For example, in the bar graph titled "Students' Vertical Leaps (m)," we can find Lauren's vertical leap by finding the bar labeled "Lauren," then seeing how far up Lauren's value travels against the numerical values on the left side of the graph. When we do that, we can see that Lauren's vertical leap is right around 0.5 m.

Multiple bars in a cluster

Sometimes a bar graph will use clusters of bars to show more than one type of data. The different bars in a cluster will often be color-coded according to a key or legend. The example below uses clusters of bars to combine the data from the two previous graphs:

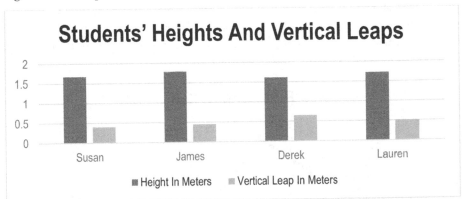

In the bar graph above, the key at the bottom tell us that the gray bar represents the student's height in meters, while the black bar represents the student's vertical leap in meters.

A bar graph can be oriented either horizontally or vertically. It doesn't really change anything important about the data itself, or the way we should read it, except that the x- and y-axes are switched. The graph below shows the same information as the previous graph labeled "Students' Heights And Vertical Leaps," but the graph is oriented horizontally instead of vertically:

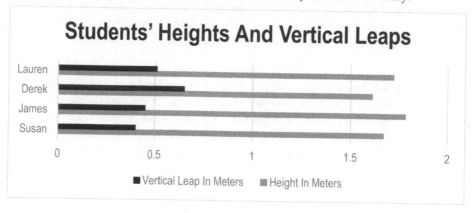

Histograms

A histogram is a special type of bar graph used to show the distribution of frequency for a particular type of data.

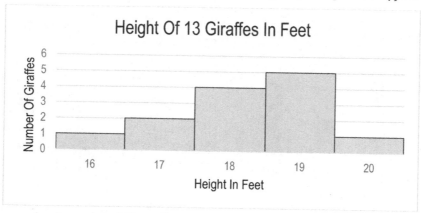

The histogram above shows us that, in a group of 13 giraffes,

- 1 is 16 feet tall
- 2 are 17 feet tall
- 4 are 18 feet tall
- 5 are 19 feet tall
- 1 is 20 feet tall.

For an example from a real SAT practice question, look at question 12 from Section 4 of SAT Practice Test #1. That question includes a histogram entitled "Number of Seeds in Each of 12 Apples," and asks us to find the average number of seeds per apple. For a detailed discussion of that question, see its walkthrough on page 320 in this book.

Line Graphs

Line graphs are often used to show the change in a data set over time. Typically, the horizontal axis shows different points in time—days, months, years, etc.—and the vertical axis shows the range of numerical values. The data is plotted as coordinate points on the graph, and the points are connected to form a line that shows how the data changes between the increments on the horizontal axis. The example line graph below shows the population of Kansas City from 1960 to 2010:

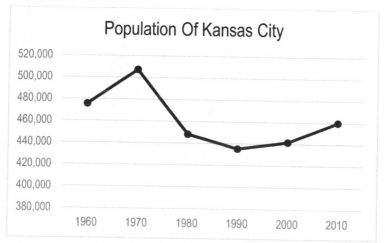

Multiple lines

Some line graphs track the changes in more than one variable. In situations with multiple lines, the lines will often involve different patterns of dots and dashes, explained in a key, so that it's easier to see which line represents which data. The line graph below shows the population of Kansas City, Boise, and Detroit from 1960 to 2010:

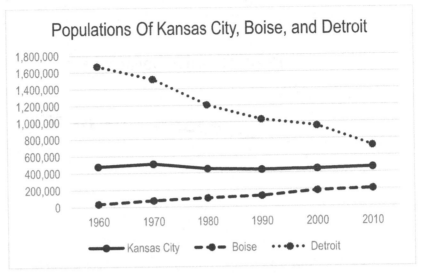

Scatterplots

A scatterplot is used to demonstrate the general relationship between two variables as that relationship is revealed in a population. A scatterplot is similar in some ways to what we see when we plot the points for a line graph, except that we don't connect the points in the scatterplot, and it's acceptable to have multiple points with the same x- and/or y-values. The example scatterplot below shows the relationship between height and age in a population of people. Each point represents the height and age of one person.

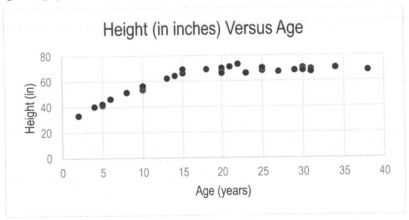

Line of best fit

A "line of best fit" or "trend line" is a line that can be drawn through a scatterplot to represent the overall trend of the data in the scatterplot. There's a mathematical formula for determining a line of best fit for a given dataset, but we'll never need that formula for the SAT. Instead, we just need to be able to do things like identify a proper line of best fit in a set of answer choices, or imagine what a line of best fit might look like if a question requires that.

If we add a line of best fit to the scatterplot above, we get this:

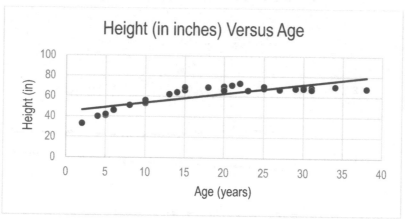

We must remember that the line of best fit *does not* represent actual data—*it only represents a trend in data.* The line of best fit might coincidentally cross an actual data point in the scatterplot, but the line itself still doesn't represent actual data. For more on the line of best fit, please see the section on statistics on page 202 in the Math Toolbox of this Black Book.

Associations within data

Sometimes, the College Board will ask you about the associations within a dataset. These associations basically have three different types, for SAT purposes:

- positive association
- negative association
- lack of association

For more on these types of associations, please see the section on statistics on page 202 in the Math Toolbox of this Black Book.

Maps

A map can be used to indicate a geographic breakdown of data (to show, for example, how many car accidents happen in different counties within a state, or how many people over a particular age live in each country in a region, and so on). It's very important to make sure you read all the relevant labels on a map, because they usually don't have the level of clarity and organization that's made possible by the axes in tables and graphs. (See question 31 on section 2 of SAT Practice Test #4 for an example of a real SAT question with a map, and see my walkthrough for that question on page 536 of this Black Book for further discussion of it.)

Pie Charts and Percentages

A pie chart is used to demonstrate portions of a whole. Remember that pie charts don't always indicate absolute numbers—they may only indicate relative percentages and relationships among quantities. The following example pie chart shows the percentages of students who favor different desserts:

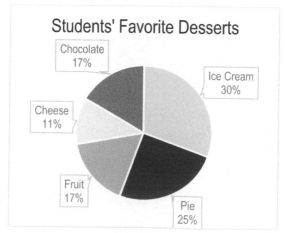

Comparing percentages across multiple pie charts

When multiple pie charts discuss similar data, it's important to remember that we can't compare "wedges" across different pie charts unless the labeling specifically indicates that such a comparison is valid because the given percentages are percentages of the same number. For example, the largest portion of one chart doesn't necessarily contain the same people (or elements of the population) as the largest portion in a different chart. Further, a large portion of one chart may not actually represent a larger absolute number than a small portion of another chart.

For example, consider the pie charts for questions 19 and 20 in the Reading section of SAT Practice Test #3. Neither the passage nor the pie charts themselves tell us how many people are represented by the percentages in either pie chart. We have no way of knowing whether the 6.4% of public transportation passengers who are unemployed in Figure 1 represent more people or fewer people than the 10.6% of people who use public transportation for school according to Figure 2. For all we know, Figure 1 represents a survey of 3,000 people, while Figure 2 represents a survey of 500,000 people—or vice versa. We aren't given any information about the number of people in either survey, so we can't make absolute comparisons between the two pie charts.

Conclusion

We've discussed the rules for reading figures on the SAT, and we've also discussed the more common types of figures that appear on the test. Remember that you may also see other figures that we haven't specifically discussed! The SAT likes to use unusual figures sometimes, so we can't know *exactly* what we'll see on test day. But any figures that do appear will follow the rules discussed in this section, and will have enough in common with the figures we've talked about that we'll always be able to read them carefully and figure out the answers to any relevant questions if we understand the above examples.

For more in-depth explanations of real figures in real SAT practice questions, see the walkthroughs in this Black Book of questions involving figures.

Part 6: Key Techniques for the Whole SAT

Before we discuss more specific training for the different kinds of SAT questions, we'll briefly discuss two concepts that you'll be able to use many times throughout the test.

In this part of the Black Book, you'll learn the following:

- how most people look at a set of answer choices, and why it holds them back
- a habit that will help you catch your mistakes (and answer questions more effectively in the first place)
- how a question's answer choices can often reveal SAT-specific shortcuts that untrained test-takers don't notice
- what the vertical scan is, why it's so useful on the SAT, and how to execute it
- and more . . .

Always Consider Every Answer Choice!

When untrained test-takers think they've found the right answer to a question, they typically mark it immediately and then move on to the next question—even if the choice they've selected is the very first one in the set, and they haven't looked at the others at all. This is a very common way to go through the test, but it's a terrible habit to get into!

As we know by now, the College Board deliberately creates wrong answers so they'll appeal to people who've made a mistake in addressing the question—whether through misreading, miscalculating, or even just being nervous.

So as trained test-takers, we always want to make sure that we're giving ourselves every opportunity to assess what's really going on in a question . . . and to catch any mistakes we might make so we can correct them and get the high scores we deserve.

Catching Your Mistakes

One of the best ways to catch your mistakes on the SAT is to check *every* answer choice whenever you answer a question.

When you read through the whole set of answer choices, you're giving yourself access to more information about the question, which is always helpful for a trained test-taker who understands how SAT questions are constructed. You might end up realizing that more than one of the choices seems like a valid answer at first, in which case you know that you need to revisit the question and keep your training in mind so you can figure out which choice really is correct. Or you might realize that some of the other choices fit hidden patterns that suggest the choice you like really is correct, in which case you can have even more confidence that you've answered the question correctly. These are advantages that other test-takers won't have.

Finding the Easiest Approach to Any Question

And as we'll see throughout this Black Book, trained test-takers can almost always use the relationships among a set of answer choices to help them diagnose what's going on in a question before they even start thinking about which answer is likely to be correct:

- On the Reading section, being aware of the options in the answer choices can help you zero in on the parts of the passage that might be relevant to a question, allowing you to focus your energies effectively.

- On the Writing and Language section, noticing the similarities and differences among the answer choices can help you realize which grammatical concepts are actually being tested by a question, while untrained test-takers might incorrectly focus on ideas that aren't relevant to finding the right answer at all.

- On the Math sections, being aware of the relationships among a set of answer choices can help you identify solutions that might take less than 10 seconds and not even require a calculation, while untrained test-takers waste unnecessary time on a formal solution that will involve more steps and a greater potential for errors and frustration.

Every SAT Question is a System of Ideas

You'll see throughout this Black Book that we try to understand each question as a whole system of ideas—and that system includes all of the answer choices! When you read each answer choice, you're in a better position to see what's going on in the whole question: what kinds of mistakes the College Board hopes you'll make, what you need to focus on to find the correct answer in the most efficient way, and so on.

So remember to check every answer choice, even if you're sure you've found the right answer after the first choice or two! You'll understand questions better in the first place, which will allow you to attack them more quickly and more successfully; when you do make a mistake, you'll have a much better chance of catching it and correcting it.

On the next page, we'll explore one specialized way of considering every answer choice: the vertical scan.

The Vertical Scan: A Key Tactic for Trained Test-Takers

Before we start discussing the details of the different kinds of questions you'll encounter on test day in a few pages, I want to discuss a special technique that will often come in handy on the SAT (and, indeed, on most standardized multiple-choice tests). I call this technique the "vertical scan," and it can help you notice the similarities, differences, and other relationships within a set of answer choices more easily, and keep them clear in your head with less effort.

An Important Note Before We Get Started!

The vertical scan is just one way to get a quick, accurate impression of the similarities and differences among a set of answer choices. It doesn't have to be the only way you read the answer choices for a question, and you don't have to use it on every question! You'll probably run into a few situations in which the vertical scan gives you enough information to be able to answer a question with total certainty, but there will also be lots of times when you decide to scan the answer choices vertically *and* read them horizontally as well. I'm not suggesting that you never read horizontally on test day! I'm just giving you another tool for evaluating answer choices that a lot of untrained test-takers never think of.

How to Execute the Vertical Scan

Performing the vertical scan is relatively easy: we just mentally divide a set of answers choices into a few "columns" based on the similarities and differences that initially leap out at us, and then we proceed to read *down* each column, instead of reading or skimming *across* each choice as a separate row, which is what most untrained test-takers do when they read a set of answer choices.

An Example from the Writing and Language Section

See the diagram below for a general demonstration of the difference between the way an untrained test-taker looks at a set of answer choices, and the way we analyze those answer choices with a vertical scan. These choices are taken from question 26 on section 2 of SAT Practice Test #1:

Normal Horizontal Reading and the Vertical Scan
(dashed arrows indicate reading direction)

Untrained / horizontal-only reading approach	Trained / vertical scanning approach
A) equipment, such as	A) equipment, such as
B) equipment, such as:	B) equipment, such as:
C) equipment such as:	C) equipment such as:
D) equipment, such as,	D) equipment, such as,

On the left side, we can see the answer choices more or less as they appear in the test booklet. Most untrained test-takers will just read them in sequence from left to right, and try to remember each item separately afterward. Their inner monologue while reading might be something like this: "Okay, the choices are equipment-comma-such-as, equipment-comma-such-as-colon, equipment-such-as-colon, and equipment-comma-such-as-comma."

On the right side, we can see the same answer choices visualized as four rough "columns." When we scan down the columns, it's easier to note several things:

- In the first "column," we can see quickly that every choice uses the word "equipment" (that is, no choice uses a word like the possessive noun "equipment's," nor the verb "equip," as the first word in the choice).

- The second "column" shows us that three of the four choices have a comma after "equipment," while one choice has no punctuation after that word.

- The third "column" shows us that every choice has the phrase "such as."

- The fourth "columns" shows us the following:

  - Two choices include a colon after "such as."

  - One choice includes a comma in that position.

  - One choice ends with no punctuation at all after "such as."

Our inner monologue while we do a vertical scan on this question might sound something like this: "It looks like every choice starts with 'equipment,' and then most choices have a comma after that but one doesn't, and then every choice has 'such as,' and then one choice ends with no punctuation, two choices end with a colon, and one ends with a comma."

When we use the vertical scan to look at the choices in this way, it becomes easier to realize which options the question is actually presenting to us. For example, in this question, we can see that if we figure out which punctuation (if any) should go after "such as," then we can eliminate two or three answers. (For a complete discussion of that question, take a look at the corresponding walkthrough in the SAT Writing and Language section of this Black Book, on page 475.)

An Example from the Math Section

Let's look at an example from the SAT Math section as well. The following choices are taken from question 24 on section 4 of SAT Practice Test #1:

Normal Horizontal Reading and the Vertical Scan
(dashed arrows indicate reading direction)

Untrained / horizontal-only reading approach

A) $x^2 + (y - 4)^2 = \frac{25}{9}$

B) $x^2 + (y + 4)^2 = \frac{25}{9}$

C) $x^2 + (y - 4)^2 = \frac{5}{3}$

D) $x^2 + (y + 4)^2 = \frac{3}{5}$

Trained / vertical scanning approach

A) $x^2 + (y - 4)^2 = \frac{25}{9}$

B) $x^2 + (y + 4)^2 = \frac{25}{9}$

C) $x^2 + (y - 4)^2 = \frac{5}{3}$

D) $x^2 + (y + 4)^2 = \frac{3}{5}$

Again, on the left side we see the answer choices as they appear in the test booklet. Most untrained test-takers will simply read the choices from left to right, as they're presented.

But on the right side we can see the same choices visually divided into columns. When we make a quick vertical scan of those columns, we can note the following things more easily:

- Every choice begins with $x^2 + (y$
- Two choices involve subtracting 4 from y, and two include adding 4 to y.
- Every choice squares the parenthetical expression with y and 4.
- Two choices end with a fraction where 25 is the numerator and 9 is the denominator.
- Two choices end with a fraction involving the numbers 5 and 3.
  - One choice has 5 in the numerator and 3 in the denominator.
  - One choice has 3 in the numerator and 5 in the denominator.

This is helpful, because it lets us know that we can focus our attention on two issues:

1. Whether 4 should be added or subtracted in the parenthetical expression.
2. Whether the final fraction should be $\frac{25}{9}, \frac{5}{3}$, or $\frac{3}{5}$.

(Incidentally, this analysis also makes it easier to notice that squaring is quite important in this question: we can see quickly that each choice has an x expression and a y expression that are both squared, and one choice ends with a fraction $(\frac{5}{3})$ that's squared in two of the other choices $(\frac{25}{9})$ and inverted in the remaining choice $(\frac{3}{5})$. Noticing this kind of thing can often help us figure out how to attack the question in the most efficient, effective way possible. For a complete discussion of this question, take a look at its walkthrough in the SAT Math section of this Black Book, on page 331)

When to Use the Vertical Scan

We can use the vertical scan whenever we notice that the answer choices in a question are highly similar to each other, or whenever we want to reconsider the relationships among the answer choices in light of the answer-choice patterns we've been trained to notice on a particular type of question. (We'll discuss specific answer-choice patterns later, in the parts of this Black Book devoted to the different types of questions you'll see on test day.)

We'll generally find that sets of answer choices on the Math sections and the Writing and Language section of the SAT are the most vulnerable to the vertical scan, but we'll sometimes find that Reading questions can also be successfully attacked with a vertical scan. This is because the Math sections and the Writing and Language section use more question types with answer choices that imitate each other visually, while questions on the Reading section tend to have wrong answers that differ from right answers in other ways.

Now that we've discussed how and when to use vertical scans, you may still be wondering *why* we'd want to use them. As it turns out, they're pretty helpful in a lot of scenarios . . .

Benefits of the Vertical Scan

We've already mentioned that vertical scans can help you note and keep track of the differences among a set of answer choices. But why is that a big deal in the first place?

Once you understand how the SAT actually works (which you'll learn as you go through this Black Book), you'll find that one of the major challenges on test day is simply keeping track of all the relevant details in a question and making sure you never fall for the College Board's repeated tricks.

The vertical scan can help you overcome this challenge in several important ways:

- It can give you a simple way to notice all the options being presented to you, since you're directly comparing the answer choices to each other instead of evaluating each choice individually.

- It can help alert you to the mistakes the College Board is hoping you'll make, by calling your attention to the relationships among the answer choices.

- It can make some answer choice patterns more obvious. (We'll discuss the answer choice patterns for each question type in the corresponding training later in this book.)

- It can help you pinpoint the type of question you're dealing with, because your training will make you aware of the types of answer choices that are featured in different question types. Knowing the rules and patterns of the question you're working on can help you limit your thinking to the kinds of issues that can be relevant to a given question. (For example, on the Writing and Language section, if you can tell that you're working on a Reading Comprehension question, then you know that you don't need to worry about grammar.)

The vertical scan can also help you figure out what a prompt is even asking in the first place, which may not always be obvious when you first encounter a question. This is often possible because the vertical scan makes it easier to notice relationships among the ideas represented in each answer choice in a set. For example, if the differences in a set of answer choices for a Writing and Language question all relate to whether particular words are singular or plural, then you know that the question is testing your understanding of things like subject-verb agreement, which might not have been obvious when you first read the relevant sentence. If the answer choices to a Math question all differ from each other by a factor of 10, then we know that multiplying or dividing by 10 is probably a key element of the ideal approach to the question, which may not have been obvious from the prompt.

Conclusion

By now, you can probably tell that the vertical scan is a very powerful tool in a lot of situations, whether as a stand-alone reading method in some questions, or in combination with the normal line-by-line method of reading answer choices for most questions. Keep it in mind as you continue your training. You'll see many more examples of its use in the question walkthroughs throughout this Black Book, particularly in the Math section and the Writing and Language section.

Part 7: Reading Section Training and Walkthroughs

In this part, we'll finally start tackling a specific test on the SAT, applying all of the training concepts we've discussed so far. Remember that prepping for the SAT Reading test is the best way to lay the foundation for the rest of the SAT: reading carefully and paying attention to details that other people will overlook are key skills throughout the test.

In this part of the Black Book, you'll learn the following:

- the single most important secret of doing well on the SAT Reading section
- why the College Board had to design SAT Reading questions the way they're designed
- the key role that literal reading plays throughout the SAT
- the difference between restatement and demonstration, and why both are critical on test day
- the four reasons why most untrained test-takers never realize how SAT Reading actually works
- how the College Board tries to trick us into thinking subjectively instead of objectively
- why it's so important to consider the precise meaning of each word we encounter
- the key patterns that account for all wrong answers on the SAT Reading section
- the different approaches to reading the passages on test day, and how to find the one that suits you best
- why you shouldn't take notes when you read a passage on test day
- how to deal with passages, paragraphs, and sentences that are hard to follow
- how to recognize (and work around) slang, rhetorical questions, jargon, and other strange expressions
- how mentally removing "comma sandwiches" can help you understand a text better
- specific ideas to keep in mind for decoding the types of text you'll encounter on test day
- a list of terms you'll need to know in order to understand prompts and answer choices fully
- the recommended process for answering SAT Reading questions
- how to handle "best evidence" questions, and why they can often save you time
- how to answer "most nearly means" questions
- why questions about the author's "attitude" still require us to think objectively, and how to do that
- how to approach questions with figures and data
- what "yes-yes-no-no" questions are, and the SAT's unwritten rules for them
- how to remain objective when answering questions about the "central claim" of a passage
- what constitutes "humor" on the SAT
- how to attack questions about paired passages without guessing what an author might say
- how to apply all of these ideas to every Reading question in the first four official SAT Practice Tests
- and more . . .

SAT Reading Training

Education . . . has produced a vast population able to read but unable to distinguish what is worth reading.
G. M. Trevelyan

Overview and Important Reminders for SAT Reading

Students often tell me that Reading questions are their least favorite questions on the SAT. A lot of people think these questions are too subjective to be part of a standardized test—they think that questions about an author's intentions can be answered in more than one way, so it's unfair to use them in multiple-choice tests.

Fortunately, this isn't the case. The answer to an SAT Reading question is every bit as clear and definite as the answer to an SAT Math question. In this section, I'll show you how trained test-takers identify those answers.

But first, I want to say that again, because it's really important. I'll put it in caps, too. And center it, even:

THE ANSWER TO AN SAT READING QUESTION IS ALWAYS AS CLEAR AND DEFINITE AND OBJECTIVELY PREDICTABLE AS THE ANSWER TO AN SAT MATH QUESTION.

If the reading questions required arbitrary interpretation, then the SAT would produce meaningless results, because there would be no objective basis for rewarding one answer choice and punishing the others. And if the results from the SAT were meaningless, then colleges would stop using them. (For more on the role of standardized tests in the admissions process and the implications of that role for us test-takers, check out the article on the purpose of standardized testing at my blog, www.TestingIsEasy.com.)

You see, the main problem with SAT reading is that it requires you to look at a passage in a way that's totally different from the approach you would use in an English class. In the typical English class, you're often rewarded for coming up with any interpretation of a passage that you possibly can; every interpretation that doesn't directly contradict the reading is welcomed with open arms.

But that approach clearly won't work for a multiple-choice question with only one correct answer. So on the SAT, you have to read everything as literally as you possibly can, without adding any of your own interpretation at all. (We'll get into this in a lot more detail below.)

After working with me, most of my students who didn't like SAT Reading to begin with end up changing their minds about Reading questions. Actually, they often end up thinking that the Reading questions are among the easiest ones on the entire test, and I tend to agree with them.

The Big Secret of SAT Reading

In order for the College Board to develop Reading questions that would function properly on a multiple-choice test, it had to overcome a pretty big problem: it needed a way to ask questions about literature that weren't subjective, so that each question would only have one legitimate, objective answer. After all, the College Board has to use the multiple-choice format to make efficient grading of millions of tests possible, and you can't use that format effectively unless one choice for each question is clearly correct, and the other choices are clearly wrong—otherwise each question would be up for debate, and colleges wouldn't be able to rely on the data generated by the test.

So the College Board had to find a way to eliminate interpretation from the process of answering questions about a text. This would allow it to write questions that would ask students to talk about a text while still using the multiple choice format in a valid, meaningful way.

If you think about it, there are really only two ways you can possibly talk about a text without interpreting it—and these two ways of talking about a text are the big secret of the SAT Reading section. They apply to all questions on the Reading Test. I'll put them in italics, because they're really important:

- *restating the text without changing the meaning, and*
- *demonstrating an idea that appears on the page*

In other words, believe it or not, we'll find that the correct answer to every single question on the Reading section of the SAT is spelled out or demonstrated somewhere on the page.

Yes, really.

(At this point, if you've ever taken the SAT before, or ever had any kind of traditional SAT preparation, you're probably shaking your head angrily and cursing me for lying to you about the test. But trust me on this: the correct answers to SAT Reading questions are always restated or demonstrated by relevant ideas from the text, and the incorrect answers are always wrong because they fail to be restated or demonstrated by the text, and/or because they add in ideas that aren't in the text.)

Before we proceed, let me take a moment to give you concrete examples of how restatement and demonstration work on the SAT Reading section.

Restatement

Restatement refers to the idea that two separate pieces of text express the same idea using different words. For an example of this idea, let's start with the following phrase, which appears in the second passage of section 1 in SAT Practice Test #1:

> The notion of gift-givers and gift-recipients being unable to account for the other party's perspective seems puzzling . . . [66-68]

Question 21 from that section asks what "the authors would likely attribute" some data in the graph to. The correct answer is (A), the only one that directly restates an idea from the passage. That choice says "an inability to shift perspective," which directly restates "being unable to account for the other party's perspective" from the sentence above.

The other choices are loosely connected to the text, and test-takers who don't read carefully might even think some of the other choices restate the text. But when we read the other choices carefully, we can find concrete reasons why each one fails to restate the text. (For a complete discussion of this question and its wrong answer choices, see its walkthrough on page 88 in this Black Book.)

Demonstration

The idea of demonstration is a little different from the idea of restatement, but both ideas involve careful reading and a focus on evaluating the literal meaning of a text without interpretation. When a correct answer depends on demonstration, one of two things happens:

1. the correct answer provides an example or scenario that's exactly described in the text, or
2. the text provides an example or scenario that's exactly described in the correct answer

For an example from a real SAT Reading question, look at question 24 from section 1 of SAT Practice Test #4. That question asks what the word "expert" means in context. The word "expert" appears in line 20 of the passage, as part of this sentence:

> dairy animals, on the other hand, are expert protein producers, their udders swollen with milk.

The right answer is choice (C), "capable," even though nothing in the surrounding text specifically *restates* the idea that dairy animals are "capable protein producers." So how do we know that "capable" is the correct answer?

Well, the phrase "their udders swollen with milk" tells us clearly that the dairy animals produce milk. In other words, that phrase *demonstrates* that the animals are able to produce milk, which means they must be "capable protein producers," because "capable" basically means "able to do something." (For a complete discussion of this question, please see its walkthrough on page 153 in this Black Book.)

Again, a *restatement* of the phrase "capable protein producers" might be a phrase like "the dairy animals were able to make proteins in their milk" or "dairy animals could make milk with their udders." But in this case, instead of restating the correct answer, the passage *demonstrated* the correct answer: it just described the dairy animals producing milk. This might seem a like a nitpicky distinction to make, but on certain challenging questions, understanding the difference between restatement and demonstration will help you find the portion of the relevant text that directly supports the correct answer.

Is that Really All there Is?

It might sound a little ridiculous to say that the entire Reading section avoids literary interpretation and focuses on the literalist ideas of restatement and demonstration, but let's think about this from the College Board's standpoint:

1. The College Board needs the SAT to include multiple-choice questions about passages.
2. The College Board needs to avoid any ambiguity and interpretation in order for the SAT to fulfill its role as a legitimate, reliable standardized test. (For more on this, see my article on the purpose of standardized tests at www.TestingIsEasy.com)
3. The only way to discuss a text without interpreting it is to restate it or to demonstrate ideas from it.

All of this leads to one conclusion:

4. The College Board has designed the correct answers on the SAT Reading section so they restate elements of the text, or are demonstrated by elements of the text.

At this point, you might be wondering something very important: if SAT Reading questions really are as simple as I say, then how can so many intelligent people take the SAT every year without ever noticing that the correct answer to each question either says exactly the same thing as the text they're reading, or demonstrates an idea from the text in a literal way?

This is a very good question. There are four reasons why most test-takers never notice how Reading questions work, and you need to know them so you can prevent them from affecting you negatively:

1. Most Test-Takers aren't Even Looking for an Answer Choice to be Stated Directly in the Text.

Most SAT-takers are used to analyzing everything they read the way an English teacher would want, so when they read the passages on the SAT they try to analyze them automatically. In other words, most test-takers wouldn't even notice if an answer choice was restated or demonstrated by the text, because it never occurs to them to look for that. This is just one more way in which most untrained test-takers are their own worst enemies.

---

2. The College Board Deliberately Phrases Questions to Make you Think you Should Use Subjective Interpretation to Find the Answer.

If you've ever seen any real Reading questions from the College Board, you've definitely seen that they use words like "primarily," "probably," "suggests," "likely," and so on, like this:

> The author would likely use the example in line 5 to illustrate . . .

The College Board deliberately phrases questions in this way to mislead you and get you to interpret the text. It wants you to think that two or three answer choices might all be pretty reasonable. So we have to learn to ignore the subjectivity in words like "primarily" and "suggests." When I read a question like "The author uses the phrase 'turtle power' in line 10 primarily to suggest which of the following?" I treat that question as though it said, "Which of the following ideas appears directly in the text near the discussion of 'turtle power' in line 10?"

Here's a simple chart with some similar examples of how we should treat the prompt when it contains phrases that seem subjective to untrained test-takers:

When the prompt says . . .	. . . we should read it as . . .
"Which choice most nearly means . . ."	"Which is the only choice that means the same thing as . . ."
"The author of Passage 2 would most likely respond . . ."	"The author of Passage 2 directly states which opinion . . ."
"Which choice provides the best evidence for . . ."	"Which is the only choice that provides evidence for . . ."

3. We Sometimes Have to be Extremely Particular about the Exact Meanings and Relationships of Words in the Prompt, the Text, and in the Answer Choices.

The College Board is very picky about the specific meanings of phrases. As a result, test-takers often make the mistake of thinking that more than one answer choice can be restated or demonstrated by the passage. One clear example of this from a real SAT question can be found in question 7 on SAT Practice Test #4. The question asks us how the narrator would describe something, and one of the wrong answers includes the phrase "socially beneficial." The passage clearly mentions elements of society, and clearly mentions benefits, but it never actually says the benefits themselves would be social, which is enough to make the choice wrong.

So if you want to make a perfect score on the Reading section, you'll have to learn to *attack* every single phrase that you read, and you'll have to make sure you're only considering *exactly* what each word means, instead of working from your generalized assumptions about what it might mean, or what you think it implies, as you might do in a literature class. The College Board splits hairs when it comes to these things, and if you want to score high you'll have to learn to split them too.

4. Test-Takers are Sometimes Mistaken about What Words Mean.

No matter how strong your vocabulary is, I promise you that there are some words that you use incorrectly—it happens to all of us. Sometimes the differences are subtle. For example, I once had a student who mistakenly thought that "shrewd" had a strong negative connotation. He correctly understood that it involved being clever and intelligent, but incorrectly thought that it indicated a certain type of calculating evil. For this reason, he didn't pick an answer choice with the word "shrewd" since he didn't see anything in the text that indicated negativity, and he missed the question. On the other hand, sometimes the differences are huge, and a little embarrassing—I always thought the word "pied" meant something like "renowned" or "famous," because of the story of the Pied Piper. But it actually describes something with patches of different colors. Needless to say, I drew a complete blank when a test question mentioned the word "pied" and my understanding of that word didn't match with anything on the page. (Don't think that memorizing vocabulary words will help correct these mistakes—memorizing vocab might even contribute to making more of them, because test-takers' actual understanding of memorized vocabulary is often limited. Just know that you might be confronted with unknown vocabulary words at some point.) If you're looking at a question and none of the answer choices seems to be restated or demonstrated by the passage, then the bottom line is that you've made a mistake somewhere.

So those are the four major reasons that most test-takers never realize that the correct answers to Reading questions function by directly restating the relevant portion of the text. I'll list them again briefly, for review:

1. Test-takers aren't even looking for these kinds of ideas in the first place.
2. The College Board deliberately misleads you by using subjective phrasing.
3. You have to be extremely particular about what words actually mean.
4. Sometimes you might have a flawed understanding of a word you think you know.

Now that we've covered the Big Secret Of SAT Reading, which is that the correct answers to all SAT Reading questions must be spelled out on the page, you might be wondering what the wrong answers do.

Well, simply put, the wrong answers are the ones that *aren't* restated or demonstrated by the reading. And the ways that they fail to be restated or demonstrated by the passage are standardized, just like every other important detail of the test, so it can be very beneficial for us to know the various ways that wrong answers tend to relate back to the text on the SAT.

What do Wrong Answers Do?

We've already seen that the right answer to a Reading question on the SAT will restate or demonstrate the ideas from the relevant portion of the text. But what will wrong answers do?

Broadly speaking, wrong answers are wrong because they fail to restate the relevant portion of the text or demonstrate an idea from it. But there are a handful of ways that the College Board creates these wrong answers—that is, there are certain common ways in which wrong answers fail to restate the passage exactly, or to be demonstrated by the passage. And it can be very helpful for us to know what those ways are.

But Wait! Before We Discuss Types of Wrong Answers . . .

Remember as you learn about these answer types that you won't need to classify each wrong answer choice—or any wrong answer choice—on test day, or even when you train for the test. You'll only need to pick the correct answer choice out of the set of answer choices, of course. But we're going to discuss these different types of wrong answer choices because knowing the standardized ways that the College Board tries to trick us will allow us to be ready for them, and avoid falling for them.

In some instances, some of these wrong answer choice types might seem to overlap—there might be a specific answer choice that I see as one type of wrong answer choice, but you see as more of another type of answer choice, for example. That's fine! To some extent, the classifications will vary a little depending on the test-taker's perspective. We don't need to agree on the exact classification for each wrong answer on each test as long as we can reliably separate the right answers from the wrong answers.

A Hypothetical Example

For the purposes of illustration, we'll use a fake question and fake wrong answers. In other words, what you see below did NOT come from a real College Board source. It came from my head. But I constructed it in the same ways that the College Board constructs its wrong answers. And later, I'll demonstrate my methods in action against real questions from the College Board's SAT Practice Tests #1-4 (remember, you should only ever practice with real test questions from the College Board itself).

Okay, so let's pretend our fake sample question reads like this:

> According to the citation, research suggests that Benjamin Franklin invented bifocals because . . .

And let's pretend that the relevant citation is this part of a fake text:

> . . . Researchers have shown that Benjamin Franklin's sister was visually impaired, which might explain the amount of energy that Franklin invested in the invention of bifocals . . .

(By the way, as far as I know, Benjamin Franklin's sister had nothing to do with the invention of bifocals. In fact, I don't even know if he had a sister. It's an example—just go with it.)

Here are some of the various wrong answer types we might see for this kind of question.

Wrong answer type 1: Off by one or two words

This might be one of the most dangerous and sneaky types of wrong answer when it comes to trapping test-takers who know how the test works. For this type of wrong answer, the College Board provides a phrase that mirrors the text exactly—except for one or two words. Even when test-takers know they have to find answer choices that are restated or demonstrated by the passage, they can still fall for these kinds of wrong answers if they're not in the habit of constantly attacking every single word they read.

Example:

> His sister had a congenital vision problem.

In this wrong answer, the ideas of "sister" and "had a vision problem" directly restate the phrase "Franklin's sister was visually impaired" from the fake citation. But the word "congenital" isn't reflected at all in the citation, so this answer choice would be wrong if this were a real SAT question. Remember that you have to look for a textual justification for every concept in every answer choice.

Wrong answer type 2: Barely relevant

This type of wrong answer is a statement that has almost nothing to do with the cited text. These wrong answers can be very tempting to a lot of test-takers, because they don't actually contradict the text—they just say something that might seem to make sense to an untrained test-taker. This wrong answer type exploits your natural tendency to give the benefit of the doubt to anything that doesn't directly contradict the text.

Example:

> He wanted to revolutionize the way society viewed glasses.

This wrong answer has almost nothing to do with anything mentioned in the citation. Once we know that the correct answer must be spelled out directly in the passage, it's usually pretty easy to eliminate these barely relevant choices from consideration—but for untrained test-takers, these kinds of answer choices can often be quite tempting.

Wrong answer type 3: Statements that would be valid literary interpretations in a classroom

The College Board frequently creates wrong answers that would be valid, defensible interpretations of the text in a literature class. Students often fall for these types of wrong answers if they're still mistakenly approaching the test in a subjective, interpretive way, instead of in the objective way that the College Board rewards. These types of wrong answers often involve character analysis, symbolism, or metaphor.

Example:

> Franklin loved his sister and wanted to make her life easier.

In this imaginary example, the answer choice reflects the fact that the text mentions Franklin's sister's eye problems as a motivation for the invention. But the answer choice adds some interpretation of Franklin's character when it speculates that Franklin was motivated by love for his sister and a desire to ease her suffering. While that would certainly be a plausible analysis of the passage in a literature class, it doesn't restate or demonstrate the passage, so it's a wrong answer. Since the text didn't mention Franklin loving his sister and inventing bifocals to make her life easier, we can't assume that he did—for all we know, she worked for him and he just wanted her to be able to do a better job, or he felt pressure from his parents to help her out, or who knows what else.

Wrong answer type 4: Reasonable statements that aren't in the text

Another very common type of wrong answer is one that might seem like a reasonable statement to a reader who already has a general familiarity with the subject, even though the statement itself isn't restated or demonstrated in the passage.

Example:

> He thought that improved vision would help his countrymen to be more productive with their work.

This imaginary example might tempt some untrained test-takers who have learned about Franklin in school, and know that he placed a lot of importance on productivity and effectiveness, even though the relevant text doesn't say anything about that at all. It's especially important to look out for this kind of wrong answer on SAT Reading questions related to science, history, or data, where you might be tempted to rely on your outside knowledge instead of focusing exclusively on the words on the page.

Wrong answer type 5: Direct contradiction

This type of wrong answer directly contradicts something in the citation.

Example:

> His sister's perfect vision served as an inspiration.

Here, the wrong answer choice contradicts the cited fact that the sister has poor vision. This imaginary example might fluster an untrained test-taker, because he wouldn't expect the College Board to use an answer choice that says exactly the opposite of what the text says. People who notice an answer choice like this one will likely get confused and wonder whether they read the passage wrong, then wonder whether they read the prompt or answer choice wrong, and then go back and carefully read everything all over again, while doubting themselves and wondering what they're missing. This kind of time-wasting response is probably exactly why the College Board includes answers choices like this in the first place.

Wrong answer type 6: Confused relationships

This type of wrong answer uses a lot of the ideas mentioned in the citation, but messes up the relationships among them. The College Board includes these types of wrong answers because they want to trap people who remember major concepts from the passage but who don't bother to pay attention to the details—this is just one more example of the ways in which small details play a tremendously important role on the SAT.

Example:

> His sister invested in a cure for his vision problems.

This made-up example mentions the ideas of the sister, the investing, the vision problems, and the idea that the bifocals would correct those problems, but it messes up the relationships among those ideas. Untrained test-takers who don't read carefully often fall for these types of wrong answers.

Wrong answer type 7: Restatement or demonstration of the wrong part of the passage

Some SAT Reading questions will cite a specific line or quotation from the text. The College Board knows that many untrained test-takers won't bother to go back to the original text to verify an answer choice before they pick it, which makes it easy to trick them by presenting an answer choice that's accurately restated or demonstrated by a part of the passage that's not cited in the prompt.

Many untrained test-takers will see a wrong answer like this, vaguely remember that they saw the same idea in the passage, and then pick the choice without ever realizing that the prompt requires them to look elsewhere in the passage. As trained test-takers, we always need to make sure that we're looking at the part of the passage that's relevant to the prompt when we pick an answer choice. This is especially true if we think that two choices both seem to restate the passage accurately—it may well be that one of them is restating the wrong part of the text, which makes it a wrong answer.

Conclusion

These wrong-answer types, or combinations of them, will account for most of the wrong answers you'll encounter in SAT Reading questions. Basically, they all boil down to the idea that wrong answers provide information that differs from the information found in the relevant portion of the text, while the right answer for each question will restate concepts and relationships from the relevant part of the text, or be demonstrated by the relevant part of the text.

(Once again, bear in mind that you don't have to classify the wrong answer choices that you encounter on test day! You only need to pick the correct answer. But we're discussing the types of wrong answer choices here because it will be harder for the College Board to trick you if you already know what kinds of tricky wrong answer choices will appear on the test.)

Now that we've explored the types of wrong answers we're likely to encounter on Reading questions, you're probably eager to see how we actually go about answering questions. But before we get into that stuff, we need to talk about how to go through passages on the SAT Reading section.

How to Handle Passages on the SAT Reading Section

General Ideas for SAT Reading Passages

One of the most common issues people have with Reading questions on the SAT is the issue of actually reading the passages. Another is the question of how to take notes on the passages.

So let's talk about those things. My answers are pretty simple, really:

- You can read the passage in any way you want, as long as your approach leaves you enough time to finish the section. You can even skip reading the passage if you want, and just refer back to portions of the text on a question-by-question basis.

- You shouldn't take any kind of notes on the passage.

Like most good SAT advice, those two ideas probably contradict most of what you may have heard from teachers, tutors, and prep books. So let's explore them a little. (If you haven't already read my previous remarks on "The Big Secret of SAT Reading" on page 58," I'd recommend you go back and do that before proceeding.)

When we talked about correct answer choices for these questions, we indicated that they're restated or demonstrated by elements of the relevant portion of the original text. This is necessary because the College Board needs to have an objective, legitimate reason to say that one choice is correct and the others are incorrect, otherwise there would be tens or hundreds of thousands of test-takers each year trying to challenge questions without clear correct answers. The only real way to do that is to have the correct answer be the only choice that restates or demonstrates the passage.

This means there are always specific words and phrases in the passage that correspond to the correct answer. It also means that, technically, *the only portion of the text you need to read for any question is the specific portion that restates or demonstrates the ideas in the correct answer.*

So, in theory, if it were somehow possible to know in advance which portions of the text were going to restate or demonstrate the key phrases in the right answer, then we could completely avoid reading the rest of the passage and still answer every question correctly.

In other words, there is literally *no test-taking benefit whatsoever* in trying to get an overall impression of the passage, because there will never be a situation in which the only way to find the correct answer to a real SAT question is to make a general inference from the entire text. (To be sure, there are some students who try to draw inferences from the text and still successfully pick the correct answer to every question, but it's not the most efficient approach, and it's never *necessary*. We can always find the answer for every question spelled out somewhere on the page, even if an untrained test-taker would think the question was asking for a general impression of the whole text.)

For this reason, it doesn't really matter which method you use to read the text. All that matters is that you can locate the relevant portion of the text so that you can figure out which choice is being restated or demonstrated as quickly as possible without sacrificing accuracy.

In general, there are three ways to do this, and I recommend you play around with them to see what works best for you. Again, you can mix, match, or modify these approaches as you see fit, so long as you come up with a system that lets you find the relevant portion of the text quickly enough to allow you to complete the entire section within the time limit.

I want to add one very important piece of advice before we discuss these three approaches, though: make sure you read the introduction to each passage on the Reading Test! Before each passage, there will be a bolded statement that says something like this:

> Questions 1-10 are based on the following passage.

Immediately after that, and before the beginning of the passage itself, there will be a brief introduction to the passage that provides the author, title, and year of the work the passage is taken from. That introduction will often contain additional relevant information. It sometimes happens that a prompt or an answer choice will assume you know the material in the introduction; without that knowledge, it may be impossible to see how the right answer is restated or demonstrated by an idea from the passage. So, no matter which approach you take to reading the passage, you should definitely read the brief introduction in full.

With that in mind, let's take a look at the three main ways to approach an SAT Reading passage.

Reading the whole passage at once

The first approach is the old standard of simply reading the passage before attempting the questions. This is by far the most widely used approach. It can definitely work, as long as you don't read too slowly to finish the section before time is called. One note, though—if you read the passage first, don't worry about trying to understand it as an organic whole. *Definitely* don't take notes on it, for reasons we'll get into in a moment. Just give it a thorough once-over. You're going to have to come back to specific parts of it later to verify which answer choices are correct anyway, so just read it once and move on to the questions.

Answering citation questions first before trying to read the passage

The second-most popular approach is to skip reading the passage and just move straight to the questions. On your first pass, you start with two types of questions:

- the questions that have specific line citations, and

- "best evidence" questions.

For each citation question, you go back to the relevant portion of the text, read that portion, and then consider the answer choices. For each "best evidence" question, you either answer the previous question and then the "best evidence" question itself (if the "best evidence" question refers to the previous question), or you just answer the best evidence question (if the "best evidence" question is one of the few that doesn't refer to the previous question). In either case, you use the citations from the answer choices in the "best evidence" question to decide where to look for the answer in the passage. (See "Is there a "best evidence" shortcut?" on page 72 of this Black Book for more thoughts on answering questions in this way.)

When you've finished all the citation questions and "best evidence" questions, you'll generally have a good idea of how the passage is structured. Then you move on to the remaining questions in the section. Many of those questions will mention key concepts that you'll recall from the citation questions and "best evidence" questions, so you'll know where to go back in the passage and locate those portions of the text again. When one of the remaining questions has no citation and also doesn't refer to something that you've already read, you can simply skim the portions of the text that you haven't read yet to find the relevant key terms, and proceed accordingly.

And that brings us to the third type of approach:

Making a mental map

The third general approach to reading passages involves lightly skimming the passage before approaching the questions, in order to construct a rough mental map of where different terms and concepts appear in the passage. I want to stress that, so I'll say it again: in this type of skimming, you're just moving your eyes through the text quickly, NOT really trying to understand the text, but trying to get a rough idea of where various concepts appear in the text so you can use your "map" for later. This way, if a question lacks a citation, you can look at the concepts in the question and the answer choices and recall those concepts from your skimming. This allows you to zero in on the relevant text, read it closely, and find the answer. Of course, you can always re-skim if you need to.

Again, it's important to be aware of these different approaches, and to play around with them during your practice sessions so you can figure out what works best for you. Different students will prefer different approaches based on their personalities and skills.

Why not take notes?

You may be wondering why I'm opposed to the idea of taking notes on the text. The reason is simple, actually: taking notes involves interpreting the text so that you can decide which parts of the passage seem important to you, and then modifying those parts to make them your own. When we interact with a text by making assumptions about what the College Board will ask us, prioritizing words or phrases that seem important to us, or thinking about our reactions to an author's statements, we're straying from the literal meaning of the words on the page, which can hurt our score on the Reading section. As we keep discussing, the correct answer to every single question is spelled out somewhere on the page, so there's no need to interpret what you're reading in any way, including by taking notes.

That's really it for the general approaches to reading SAT passages.

I often hear from students who read this section and then contact me directly to ask what's *really* the one best way to read passages on the SAT. I'll tell you now what I tell those students: *there really, truly is no single best way to read passages on the SAT.* It's possible to use any of the approaches we just discussed and be successful—the key is just trying them all out in practice against real questions, and finding out which one works best for you. Remember that it's okay to tweak one of the approaches if you want, as long as your version of the approach works within the time limit against real SAT questions.

If you've tried all of these approaches and you're still running out of time, the issue probably has more to do with your understanding of how to answer questions in the first place, and less to do with the way you read the passage. In that situation, I'd recommend that you focus on the other aspects of training for the Reading section of the SAT, and that you carefully review your reading practice. It could also help to revisit "Time Management on Test Day" on page 36 of this Black Book.

More Specific Approaches for Different Types of Passages

The College Board likes to incorporate different types of writing in the passages that it uses for the SAT Reading section. When I say this, I'm only talking about the general types of *texts* that appear on the section (such as the way the College Board categorizes its texts into Literary, Scientific, and Historical/Social types)—I'm referring to broader differences in the kinds of passages you'll see:

- The publication dates for the passages have ranged from as early as the 18th century to as late as the 21st century.
- Some passages are written in the third person, some are in the first person, and some even use the second person.
- Some passages use short sentences and a style that we might think of as more "modern," while other passages use much longer sentences, and sometimes don't even follow the rules of punctuation and grammar that you'll need to know for the Writing and Language section of the SAT.

The result of this wide array of different writing styles is that most test-takers will find some passages harder to read than others—in fact, they'll even find some parts of a given passage harder to understand than other parts of the same passage.

Most high school English classes don't ask their students to read such a wide variety of texts as carefully as the SAT requires, so I've found that it's helpful to give my students some specific tactics that will help them navigate any kind of text they'll see on test day.

We'll talk about the individual tactics first, and then we'll talk about how they tend to be useful in different ways on the three different kinds of passages we'll see from the College Board.

Key tactics:

1. Always focus on the easiest questions available, but don't stereotype any particular type of passage.

In "Approach Each Section in Multiple Passes—Probably More than Two." on page 37 of this Black Book, we discussed the importance of investing your time in questions that you find easier before you worry about questions that are harder for you.

On the SAT Reading section, this idea can lead you to save an entire passage's share of questions for later passes, or it can lead you to skip around within the set of questions for one passage before deciding to move on to questions for another passage.

But it's important not to develop the bad habit of assuming that you should always skip certain types of passages or certain types of questions and save them for later passes! As you'll see during your training, and during the walkthroughs of real SAT questions later in this Black Book, the College Board can write questions that are straightforward and relatively obvious about any kind of passage . . . and it can also ask questions that are relatively complex and confusing about any kind of passage. So if you get in the habit of avoiding all questions with figures for as long as possible, or automatically saving any questions about older texts for later, you'll probably miss out on the opportunity to invest your time in easier questions, which could cause you to rush through them later and hurt your score.

2. Use the "bad connection" approach when you encounter parts of a sentence or paragraph that make no sense to you.

A lot of people dislike reading certain kinds of passages because they get frustrated when they don't understand what an author is saying. But, as trained test-takers, we have to remember that our goal on the SAT Reading is NOT to understand entire passages, because no real SAT question will require us to do that. Instead, our goal is always—and only—to try to understand *as much of a text as we need to* in order to figure out which choice is the only one that restates or demonstrates the relevant part of the passage.

So instead of focusing on the parts of a text that you don't understand, which is only likely to cause frustration, you may find that it's surprisingly effective just to ignore the confusing parts of a sentence or a paragraph, and think about the meanings of the parts you do understand. Believe it or not, this can often give you enough information to arrive at a correct answer with certainty; alternatively, it can put you in a position to make a very well informed hunch guess, if you decide to use that kind of guessing. (See "Guessing on the SAT" on page 33 of this Black Book for more on the different approaches to SAT guessing.)

I often compare this approach to the experience of trying to have a phone conversation or a video chat with somebody when there's a bad connection between you—instead of clearly hearing everything the other person says, you can only hear bits and pieces, but those bits and pieces are often enough to allow you to understand most of what the other person is saying. Most high school students are pretty good at communicating in this way when they have to. I recommend you make a conscious attempt to view the challenging parts of a text in the same way: try to focus on the parts you understand better, and use them to figure out which part of the text is relevant to a question because it restates or demonstrates one of the answer choices.

3. Recognize unknown slang expressions or cultural references, and try to understand them from context—if you even need to understand them at all.

In older texts, and in texts that originate from non-American cultures, we may run into slang phrases that have no immediate meaning for us, even if we understand the individual words in the phrase. For example, line 15 on the first passage on the Reading section of SAT Practice Test #2 includes the phrase "has held high carnival," which is a phrase that was popular in the 1800's, but is pretty uncommon now. An untrained test-taker might see that phrase on test day and panic, because he's never heard it, even if he knows the individual words that make it up. But a trained test-taker would realize that the passage was relatively old, and would already be expecting to see some unfamiliar phrases—and she'd know that the meanings of phrases on SAT Reading passages only matter in the first place if we get asked a question about them. As it turns out, question 34 on that Reading test does ask about this phrase, and the correct answer restates the ideas of "overpowering" and "crushing" from the same sentence in the passage—which are words that most test-takers would have no problem with. So it's never actually necessary to understand the phrase "has held high carnival" in order to answer a question correctly in that section. (See the walkthrough for question 34 on page 93 in this Black Book for further explanation.)

On the other hand, consider the phrase "our First Parents" from line 41 of the first passage on the Reading section of SAT Practice Test #4. Some test-takers may get confused by the phrase, since the narrator never mentions his parents—or any other parents, or any other family relations at all—throughout the rest of the passage. But, again, a trained test-taker would know that he didn't need to worry about the phrase unless a prompt or an answer choice touched on it; as it turns out, no question asks about that phrase at all, so it doesn't matter if a test-taker recognizes the reference or not.

4. Recognize rhetorical questions, and realize the "answers" to these questions are almost always obvious, broad, and/or extreme.

You may have heard of rhetorical questions in school, but many teachers don't really address them specifically, so it's important for us to make sure you understand them for the SAT Reading section.

A rhetorical question is a sentence that has the same structure as any other kind of question in English—the subject and verb are usually inverted, and it ends with a question mark, as in the question "where are we?" But writers don't use rhetorical questions because they're trying to get information, which would be the normal reason someone would ask a question. Instead, a rhetorical question is designed to make the reader believe that the answer to the question is so obvious, and so widely agreed upon, that the writer doesn't even need to state the answer to the question.

In modern English, a common example of a rhetorical question in everyday speech might be something like, "Have you ever heard anything so ridiculous in your entire life?" A person who asks that question may not even wait for an answer—she might just say something like, "So my boss asked me if I'm willing to work on Saturday for no pay—have you ever heard anything so ridiculous in your entire life? Of course I told him I'm not available." If a speaker does wait after a rhetorical question like this, it's only so that the listener can agree immediately, not so that the listener can provide new information in response to the question. Nobody who says, "Have you ever heard anything so ridiculous?" is open to a sincere answer like "Yes, actually—I once heard of a guy who used to dress his dogs in three-piece suits and have them walk on their hind legs so he could try to sneak them into movies. One time they made it in and cried all the way through *Muppets In Space*. That's way more ridiculous than your thing."

So a rhetorical question is a "question" that's really more like a statement—it's designed to make the reader feel like the point being raised in the question is obvious and can't be argued with. For this reason, the implied or expected answer to a rhetorical question is usually an extreme or broad statement. As an example, consider these lines from the first Reading passage on SAT Practice Test #4, in which the speaker is talking about whether the North Pole has any benefit:

> Can you eat it? Will it carry you from Gothenburg to Malmo like a railway?

Instead of sincerely asking us whether the North Pole can be eaten, or whether it can get you from place to place, the speaker is using rhetorical questions to show that the North Pole *can't* be eaten under any circumstances, and it can *never* carry you from place to place. Again, these implied responses are broad statements (things like "no," and "never"), and the context makes the author's point clear.

In SAT Reading questions, we'll typically find that rhetorical questions occur more often in older passages, but you can theoretically encounter them in any kind of passage. When you do encounter them, remember that they aren't intended to be sincere requests for information—they're intended to make the reader realize that a particular point is obvious.

5. Don't be afraid to ignore the meanings of academic or technical expressions, especially.

Some of the more technical passages on the SAT will include academic-sounding phrases you've never heard before, which will intimidate a lot of untrained test-takers. As trained test-takers, we need to realize that we can often completely ignore the meanings of these technical expressions, even if they seem like they're extremely important to the passage. For example, one of the Reading passages in SAT Practice Test #3 begins with a sentence that includes this phrase, which sounds pretty scientific:

> pathogenic large ectoparasitic mite *Varroa destructor* (Varroa mites)

. . . but the words "pathogenic" and "ectoparasitic" never appear again in the passage, and no question or answer choice refers to them. We could literally ignore those words and phrases without having any effect on our ability to answer any question on the test.

6. With longer sentences, consider mentally removing phrases in "comma sandwiches," and/or ignoring punctuation altogether.

As you'll see when we talk about the Writing and Language section, "comma sandwich" is my made-up term for a phrase surrounded by commas (or other identical pieces of punctuation, such as parentheses or dashes), which "sandwich" it. (See page 448 for more on comma sandwiches if you want.) For our purposes right now, on the Reading section, it's enough to realize that the phrase inside a "comma sandwich" can usually be removed from the sentence where it appears and considered separately, without altering the meaning of the rest of the sentence, or of the sandwiched phrase itself. We can also think of phrases that are sandwiched between dashes or parentheses in the same way—basically, any phrase surrounded by two matching punctuation marks can be thought of as a "punctuation sandwich," meaning it can be removed and considered separately. This can be useful on test day when you're trying to understand a sentence that spans multiple lines of text.

Let's use the sentence that starts on line 69 of the second Reading passage from SAT Practice Test #2 as an example:

> The model of man on which classical economics is based—an entirely rational and selfish being—is a parody, as John Stuart Mill, the philosopher who pioneered the model, accepted.

If a question required a test-taker to work through parts of that sentence, she might notice these two punctuation sandwiches:

1. —an entirely rational and selfish being—
2. , the philosopher who pioneered the model,

If we remove those two phrases from the original sentence, we get this, which is probably easier to understand:

> The model of man on which classical economics is based is a parody, as John Stuart Mill accepted.

If necessary to answer a question, we could also separately consider the ideas from the punctuation sandwiches that we removed: that the model is one of "an entirely rational and selfish being," and that John Stuart Mill is "the philosopher who pioneered the model."

We may also run into SAT Reading passages that are so old the author doesn't even use the same rules of punctuation that you'd have to follow on the SAT Writing and Language section. If a question requires us to consider a sentence like that, we can often just ignore the punctuation altogether, and still identify the key elements of the text that allow us to find the correct answer with total certainty.

Consider question 41 on the Reading section of SAT Practice Test #1, which refers to lines 72-76 of a passage. That citation includes a single sentence with five semi-colons used in a way that we wouldn't be allowed to use them on the Writing and Language section, and that most English teachers wouldn't reward in class. But if we just read the words in the citation and don't get too distracted by the weird punctuation, we should have no trouble answering the question correctly. (For a more detailed discussion of that question, see the corresponding walkthrough later in this section, on page 96.)

Now that we've discussed some tactics for working through different types of texts, let's talk about some of the ways you may need to use those tactics on the particular "types" of passages that the College Board recognizes: literary, historical/social, and scientific.

Things to keep in mind when reading literary passages

The literary passages on the SAT can sometimes include relatively long, relatively complex sentences, especially if they come from older sources. They may also involve expressions and cultural references that don't make much sense to us, even if we think we understand the individual words that make up the expressions. For these reasons, we may need to be especially prepared to ignore or work around the parts of individual sentences that we don't understand, using the tactics described above.

But there's another difficult aspect of some literary passages: their narrative structures. Unlike the other types of passages on the SAT, the literary passages often depict a story or episode, and many untrained test-takers will feel a strong need to try to understand the structure and flow of the overall narrative. As trained test-takers, we need to remember that the College Board never asks us to understand every part of an entire passage all at once; instead, it can only ask us questions based on individual words and phrases throughout the passage. So if we can't understand the entire sequence of events in a literary passage, there's no need to panic—we may still be able to answer every single question with certainty if we just focus on the portions of sentences and paragraphs that we can understand, and remember our training.

Things to keep in mind when reading passages for history and social studies

Like the literary passages on the SAT, the historical and sociological passages can sometimes come from older sources, and can often describe social situations that don't exist today. This means, once again, that we'll often need to make a deliberate effort to ignore the parts of the passage that don't make sense at first, and focus on the parts we can understand, and the parts that are relevant to the prompts and answer choices that we encounter in the questions.

Some of these passages can include figures, especially when the passages are a bit more academic. As trained test-takers, we need to remember that figure-based questions on the SAT Reading section can sometimes require us to match phrases from answer choices with labels on a figure, and/or with phrases in the passage itself. (See "Reading Graphs, Charts, Tables, and Other Figures on page 44 of this Black Book for more on this.)

Things to keep in mind when reading science passages

Science passages on the SAT are generally modern in terms of style and grammar, which can make them feel more approachable in some ways than the other passages. On the other hand, many untrained test-takers might be intimidated by some of the phrases and concepts that appear in Science passages, because they might involve areas of science that test-takers have never encountered before in class. Of course, as trained test-takers, we know that the SAT Reading section always provides the information we need in order to answer questions with complete certainty, so there's no need to panic if a scientific passage is discussing something unfamiliar.

We also know that technical terms can often be overlooked for SAT purposes because they end up not being relevant to any of the questions in the section, as we discussed above, and as we'll see in the Reading walkthroughs later in this Black Book.

You might think that test-takers who aren't particularly strong in science would have a harder time with scientific passages than people who like science in school—but this isn't always the case! It sometimes happens that untrained test-takers who like science will look at a passage on the SAT and assume they already know what it's trying to say, because it might discuss an area of science that they've already read about. This can be a very dangerous situation, because it can lead some test-takers to rely on outside knowledge, which can cause them to pick answer choices that might seem like true statements in real life, even if they aren't restated or demonstrated directly in the passage.

For more on the ways that issues related to science can appear on the SAT, see "How Science Appears on the SAT" on page 43 of this Black Book.

Critical Technical Terms for the SAT Reading Section

SAT Reading questions often involve certain words that might be unfamiliar for a lot of test-takers. It's important to have a decent grasp on these words if you want to answer every question on the Reading section with total certainty.

I've compiled a brief list of these words below, along with informal explanations of them. I encourage you to review them, even if you already feel that you know most of them. I've found in the past that many students develop slightly incorrect understandings of these kinds of words because most teachers never explicitly cover them.

(Notice that I'm not recommending you memorize these words and definitions exactly as they're laid out here, or that you make flashcards or anything like that. I just want to make sure that you're familiar with these terms, because you'll certainly see some of them on test day. If you read this list through twice and then refer back to it as needed in your training, you'll be in good shape.)

Abstract: "Abstract" is the opposite of "physical" or "concrete." For example, joy is an abstract idea since we can't see or touch it.

Acknowledge: To acknowledge something basically means to mention it.

Address ("address a concern," "address a question," etc.): To address something means to comment on it or respond to it. For example, I could address an issue by making a statement about that issue, or I could address a question by answering it.

Advance a view: To advance a view means to provide support for that view.

Adversarial: An adversarial relationship is one in which two sides work against each other, as adversaries.

Advocate for: To advocate for something means to argue in favor of that thing.

Allude: To allude to something just means to mention or refer to that thing.

Analysis: Analysis is the act of closely examining something in an attempt to understand or explain that thing.

Anomaly: An anomaly is an outlier—a situation or data point that differs from what we'd expect based on past experience.

Anticipate (an objection, a complaint, a criticism, etc.): To anticipate something in a passage means to address it before it's mentioned by someone else. On the SAT, we usually talk about anticipating a negative reaction from a reader who is still reading the passage. The author can "anticipate" that negative comment by responding to that reaction in the passage.

Argument: On the SAT, an argument is typically the position someone takes on an issue, and the support that person provides for her position. For example, in a discussion of school uniforms, an author's argument might be that schools shouldn't require uniforms because students need to learn to make decisions for themselves, and that includes deciding how to dress.

Articulate: To articulate an idea or position means to state it and explain some or all of its details.

Assert: To assert an idea means to state that idea.

Attribute: When used as a verb, to attribute something to someone means to say that the person is responsible for the thing. For example, if I attribute our successful meeting to Amy, I'm saying that Amy is the reason our meeting was successful.

Authority: Technically, an authority is any source of an idea or quote, whether that authority is recognized as an expert or not.

Capture: When we say that a word or phrase captures an idea, we're saying that the phrase expresses that idea.

Challenge: To challenge a statement means to say that you believe the statement isn't correct.

Characterize: To characterize means to describe something, or to be a typical example of something.

Conclusion: A conclusion is a brief summary of an argument that comes at the end of that argument.

Conducive: If a situation is conducive to a result, then the situation makes it easier for that result to happen. For example, we could say that prescription glasses are conducive to better eyesight.

Contend: When an author contends that something is true, the author is stating her argument or position.

Convey: To convey an idea means to express that idea.

Counter: Countering an idea or position involves presenting facts or reasoning that contradict the original idea or position.

Criticism, Criticize, Critique: A critique or criticism is a discussion of a concept, argument, or work of art. The person who writes the critique or criticism is a critic. A critique or criticism doesn't have to be negative .

Depiction: A depiction is just a description of something.

Develop/Development: To develop an argument means to express some or all of the ideas that make up the argument.

Dubious: If a claim is dubious, then people can easily doubt it.

Elaborate: To elaborate on something means to provide more information on it.

Establish: To establish an idea means to mention it for the first time in a given passage.

Evaluate: To evaluate an idea means to consider whether that idea is true.

Examine: To examine something means to consider it closely in an attempt to understand or explain it.

Explicit: Something that is explicit is stated clearly and directly.

Expose: To uncover or reveal, often said of something scandalous or unpleasant.

Highlight: To highlight something means to call attention to that thing.

Illustrate: To illustrate an idea means to describe the idea and/or provide examples of the idea.

Imply/implicit: To imply something is to state it indirectly. "Implicit" is an adjective meaning that something isn't stated directly. (Remember the text will directly restate or demonstrate the correct answer, even if the College Board uses the word "imply.")

Interpret: To interpret means to look for meaning in something beyond what is on the surface. In the context of a passage, to interpret means to find meaning beyond what is directly, literally stated in the passage.

Lament: If an author laments a situation, she's saying that she doesn't like the situation and wishes it would change.

Limitation: A limitation is a weakness or a downside.

Maintain: To maintain a position means to argue in favor of it, sometimes in spite of something that might weaken it.

Motive: A motive is what drives (or "motivates") a person to do something.

Outline: An outline of an argument or position is a relatively simplified description of the argument or position.

Perspective: A perspective can be an opinion or a point of view.

Phenomenon/Phenomena: A phenomenon is a situation or event, often involving something unexplained or misunderstood. "Phenomena" is the plural form of "phenomenon."

Plausible: Something that is plausible is believable, or sounds like it could be true.

Practical/Practicality: A practical idea is one that can be implemented. For example, if we discuss the practicality of a self-flying helicopter, we're talking about whether such a helicopter can actually be created and used in the real world.

Refute: To refute an idea means to prove that the idea isn't correct.

Reinforce: To reinforce an idea means to provide additional support for that idea.

Relate (a story): To relate a story means to tell a story.

Reservations: If someone has reservations about an idea, it means the person doesn't fully support the idea.

Reveal: To reveal an idea just means to show or express that idea.

Skeptic/Skeptical/Skepticism: A skeptic is someone who doesn't believe in a particular idea. The word "skeptical" is the adjective form that describes a skeptic. The word "skepticism" is the noun for the general philosophy of questioning new ideas.

Stance: A stance is a position that someone takes on an issue. For example, an author's stance on the question of changing speed limit laws might be that speed limits are fine as they are, but that existing speed limits just need to be better enforced.

Substantiate: To substantiate a claim or statement means to provide support for that claim or statement.

Summarize: To summarize a topic or story means to touch on all the major points related to it, without covering the details.

Support: To support a statement means to provide information that indicates the statement is valid.

Take a position on: To take a position on an issue means to indicate what your opinion is on that issue.

Tentative: If an argument or position is tentative, then it hasn't been firmly established or decided on yet.

Undermine: To undermine an idea means to provide reasons that the idea isn't correct.

Underscore: To underscore something means to highlight or emphasize it.

The General Process for Answering Reading Questions

Most Reading questions can be answered with a fairly simple process, which we'll discuss now. Later, I'll show you how to answer other types of questions that might seem a bit odd. (Actually, the process we'll use for *all* Reading questions is basically the same process with a few minor, occasional modifications, but I'll present them as unique scenarios because most students have already been taught to see them that way by other tutors or books.)

Don't worry if this process feels uncomfortable or strange when you first read it. In later sections of this Black Book, we'll go through a lot of questions from real SAT Practice Tests together, and you can see the process in action for yourself. You can also watch the videos at www.SATprepVideos.com to get a feel for the process.

For the moment, we're only going to talk about questions with line citations—that is, questions that tell you which part of the text to look at by mentioning a specific word, line, or paragraph. Then we'll cover the modifications for questions without them.

1. Always Read the Brief Introduction to Each Passage!

On the page where each passage starts, there is a brief introduction that appears *below* the bolded statement, but *above* the start of the passage itself, that says something like this:

> Questions 1-10 are based on the following passage.

As we'll see in the walkthroughs of real SAT questions later in this Black Book, the introductions to each passage often contain critical information that identifies the author of the passage and the purpose for which the passage was written. As we discussed earlier, some prompts and answer choices will assume that you know this basic background information about the passage, and there won't be any way to determine that information without investing a few seconds in reading that introduction.

2. Read or Skim the Passage if You Want To. Keep in Mind the Strategies from Our Earlier Discussion on How to Approach Different Types of Passages.

There are a few different ways to approach reading the actual passage, as we discussed in "How to Handle Passages on the SAT" on page 64. Pick whichever approach works for you, whether it's one of the ones I explained, or your own approach that you've tested against real SAT questions.

3. Read the Question, Noting the Citation if There is One. Then Read the Relevant Text.

If the citation is a line citation and the cited line picks up in the middle of a sentence, go back up to the beginning of that sentence and start there. (It may also help to read one or two sentences before or after the cited text, but this isn't always necessary.)

4. Find Three Wrong Answers.

It's generally easiest to find wrong answers first. For one thing, there are three times as many of them; for another, it's usually easier to identify ways that answer choices differ from the text than it is to feel confident that a choice says exactly the same thing as the text. Expect to find that most (and possibly all) of the wrong answers you find will fit into one of the types I talked about in "What do Wrong Answers Do?" on page 61. (But remember that it's not really important to *classify* the wrong answers—it's only important to note that three of the choices aren't literally restated or demonstrated in the text, which means they must be wrong! The classifications we mentioned in the training are just tools to help you organize your thinking.)

If you end up not being able to eliminate three choices, then you're making some kind of mistake. It might be that you've misread the text or the question. It might be that your understanding of some of the words you read is slightly (or very) inaccurate. It's often the case that people who are left with 2 or 3 answer choices that seem to be restated or demonstrated by the text probably aren't being picky enough about sticking to *exactly* what each word on the page means to ensure an accurate restatement or demonstration.

If you end up eliminating all 4 answer choices from consideration, then, again, you've made some kind of mistake, but it might be a different kind of mistake. You may have been referring to the wrong part of the passage; you might also have misread or misunderstood one or more words in the question, passage, or answer choices.

5. Look at the Remaining Answer Choice.

See if the remaining answer choice fits the right answer pattern (in other words, see if it's restated or demonstrated by concepts and relationships from the relevant portion of the text). If it does, that's great.

If you still can't identify one choice that's clearly restated or demonstrated by the passage (and three choices that aren't), then you'll need to consider whether to hunch-guess right away, or skip the question and save it for a later pass. For more on this aspect of SAT-taking, see "Guessing on the SAT," on page 33 of this Black Book, and "Time Management on Test Day" on page 36.

Closing Thoughts on the SAT Reading Process

And that's it, believe it or not—the process for Reading questions typically isn't as complex as the processes for other SAT question types can be.

As I noted above, the simple process we just went through works on a large percentage of SAT Reading questions exactly as described. In a broader sense, it works on all Reading questions. But let's look at some specific, small adjustments we might make if the question isn't exactly a classic line-citation question.

What about Questions Without Citations?

When a question has no citation, very little actually changes in our approach to it. The answer to the question is still going to be spelled out somewhere in the passage, but now we have to figure out where, rather than having the convenience of being told which lines to look at.

Let me say that again: even though there's no specific citation, the answer is still going to be restated or demonstrated *somewhere* on the page. You should NOT try to answer a question with no citation by making a broad inference from the overall passage that isn't directly supported by actual phrases from the text.

The only challenging thing that separates these questions from the ones with citations is that it can sometimes be harder to locate the part of the text that contains the answer.

I generally recommend saving any questions without citations on a particular passage until after you've attempted the questions that have citations for that passage—in other words, I often skip around and do all the citation questions for a passage first, then come back and pick up the more general questions for that passage. I do this because answering the citation questions will typically cause me to go back through most of the text, and I'll often find that the answers to non-citation questions are right there in the citations for other questions. So I can save some time and energy by doing the citation questions first.

Even if answering the citation questions doesn't cause me to read the part of the text that contains the answer to a general question, I can still save a little time because I don't need to re-read or skim those areas of the text I've already seen when I go back to find the answers to the non-citation questions.

Again, the critical thing to remember with non-citation questions is that the answer is always clearly spelled out in black and white somewhere within the passage, even though the question lacks a citation. There is literally never a moment on a real SAT in which the only way to answer a question is to draw a general inference from the overall "feeling" of the text.

What about "Best Evidence" Questions?

The SAT Reading section includes some questions that ask you to identify the text that "provides the best evidence," either for the answer to the previous question, or for a statement in the question itself. Some untrained test-takers will be put off by this question type because it's not commonly used on other standardized tests. But, as trained test-takers, we know that finding the correct answer to these questions will come down to carefully reading the passage without literary interpretation, just as we would for any other SAT Reading question.

We need to keep a few things in mind for questions of this type.

1. As we just discussed, the correct answer will be the part of the text that's directly restated or demonstrated in the question we're being asked about—without literary interpretation, judgment calls, or outside knowledge from the test-taker.

2. The cited text in the correct answer is sometimes sort of a summary of evidence discussed in the paragraph where that citation appears. In other words, you may find that the text immediately before or after the citation repeats or elaborates on the evidence in the citation itself. So don't be put off if some statement of relevant evidence appears just before or after the cited text from the right answer to the "best evidence" question—even though the cited text in the correct answer will provide evidence for the statement in question, there may be some additional relevant evidence that shows up just outside of that cited text. We'll see that in the walkthroughs later in this book.

3. Finally, the correct answer to this type of question is typically pretty straightforward—often, only one of the four choices will seem to have any real connection to the statement in question. But, on the few questions when more than one choice seems plausible at first, we'll always find that only one choice refers to a part of the text that's specifically restated or demonstrated in the correct answer to the relevant question.

Remember—the best way to get comfortable with these "best evidence" questions (and with all SAT questions) is to practice with real questions of this type from the College Board, and review those questions with the walkthroughs later in this Black Book.

Is there a "best evidence" shortcut?

There's something else to keep in mind for this question type as well: when the "best evidence" question asks about the answer to the previous question, the "best evidence" question can sometimes also help us find the answers to *both* questions more quickly and easily.

Of course, one of the four answers for a "best evidence" question must be right—which, as we just discussed, means that the right answer must support the statement in the previous question with no literary interpretation or judgment calls involved.

Once we realize this, we have a potential shortcut for identifying the relevant text when we try to answer the preceding question: we can just look at the answer choices for the "best evidence" question that comes next, and then check those parts of the text to see which one restates or demonstrates an answer to the question we're working on.

For a real-life example of this strategic use for "best evidence" questions, let's consider questions 9 and 10 from the Reading section of SAT Practice Test #1. Question 9 asks why Akira calls his meeting with Chie "a matter of urgency" (line 32). If we check question 10, we can see that it refers back to question 9. This means one of the choices in question 10 MUST be the text that restates or demonstrates the correct answer for question 9. If we want, we can just check those quotations in 10 to find the right answer for 9, instead of looking through the whole passage on our own to try to answer 9. Sure enough, the quotation from choice (B) in question 10 includes this quote:

'. . . I've received word of a position. I've an opportunity to go to America, as dentist for Seattle's Japanese community.'

This quote clearly supports choice (C) from question 9, which says that Akira

has been offered an attractive job in another country.

That means (C) must be the right answer to question 9, and (B) must be the right answer to question 10. (For a complete discussion of these two questions, see their walkthroughs starting on page 83 later in this Black Book.)

Notice that we were able to use this strategy to find the right answer to both questions in less time than it would have otherwise taken to answer just question 9, because we didn't need to go back through the whole passage in order to answer either question.

Of course, you don't have to use this "shortcut" approach if you don't feel like it. Still, you should always make sure that your answer to a "best evidence" question makes sense in connection with your understanding of the question that the "best evidence" question is referring to.

What about "Most Nearly Means" Questions?

Some questions ask you how a word is used in the passage. They often read something like this:

As used in line 14, "plotz" most nearly means . . .

When we deal with these kinds of questions, we need to understand that the College Board isn't just asking us to pick an answer choice with a similar meaning to the word in the prompt, even though untrained test-takers might think that.

Instead, the correct answer to a "most nearly means" question will nearly always restate some part of the relevant text. For example, consider question 3 from the Reading section of SAT Practice Test #1. The right answer is "without mediation," which restates the idea from the text of not using a "go-between." (In fact, the root of the word "mediation" is related to words like "median" and "medium," which signify the idea of being between two things. Of course, you don't have to recognize this etymology in order to find the right answer, but I'm pointing it out here to show how concretely and directly the right answers to this type of question often restate the text).

But in some situations, rather than restate the text, the correct answer might be the only choice that demonstrates the relevant text, or is demonstrated by the relevant text. (See page 59 in this Black Book for more on the difference between restatement and demonstration on the SAT.) As an example of this kind of answer, consider question 2 on the Reading section of SAT Practice Test #3. The relevant text of this question refers to the idea of someone taking a "turn or two up and down" the "length" of a "platform;" the correct answer indicates that the word "turn" most nearly means "short walk." We can tell this choice must be correct because it's the only choice that's demonstrated by the idea of a person going "up and down" the "length" of something, even if the phrase "short walk" doesn't literally restate the phrase "turn . . . up and down [the] length." We'll see more of this idea in the walkthroughs later in this book.

What about "Attitude" Questions?

Sometimes the College Board asks about the author's attitude, or about how a passage might be characterized, and so on. Untrained test-takers are usually tempted to answer these kinds of questions in the same way they would in a literature class: they usually just read the passage and make a subjective assessment of how it makes them feel, and then look for an answer choice that describes their feelings.

But, as we've mentioned repeatedly, the SAT wouldn't be a valid, reliable standardized test if it were based on subjectivity and inference.

So, even for "attitude" questions, the correct answer is going to be spelled out somewhere in the text.

For a real-life example of a question that asks about attitude, let's take a look at question 1 from the Reading section of SAT Practice Test #4. This question asks how the narrator's attitude changes during the passage.

The narrator says that he feels "a vast yearning" in line 2, and also that he doesn't "understand quite what it is that the yearning desires." This idea of not-quite-understanding restates the idea that the narrator is "uncertain[] of his motives," as described in choice (C). Later in the passage, he says he can "now see" that he's on the brink of knowing himself, and that the trip is "both a challenge to [his] egotism and a surrender to it." The idea of the narrator "now see[ing]" what his motives are is the same as saying he "recogni[zes] them," just as described in (C). So every part of choice (C) is restated by the text, which makes (C) correct. (For a complete discussion of this question, see its walkthrough on page 144 later in this Black Book.)

Notice that even though the prompt mentions "attitude," which most untrained test-takers see as a subjective idea, the correct answer was still directly restated by the text in an objective way.

So when you answer these kinds of questions, you're still just going to be looking carefully through the text to match phrases in the text with one of the answer choices—just as you do for all Reading questions, basically.

What about Questions with Figures?

As we discussed earlier in "Reading Graphs, Charts, Tables, and Other Figures" on page 44, the current version of the SAT is designed to incorporate skills related to reading and understanding figures with data. (Notice that I didn't say the SAT rewards us for *interpreting* data—this was a very deliberate choice of words on my part! The SAT Reading section always rewards us for picking answer choices that reflect exactly what's on the page, rather than trying to interpret anything we see and drawing our own conclusions. This important distinction extends to figure-based questions, too.)

When we see questions that refer to figures, we want to keep in mind the basic concepts that we discussed in "Reading Graphs, Charts, Tables, and Other Figures" on page 44 in this Black Book, and combine them with our awareness of the other rules and patterns of the SAT Reading section in order to identify the choice that's exactly restated or demonstrated by what appears on the page.

What about "Purpose" Questions?

Some SAT Reading questions ask you about the purpose of a text, or about the author's reason for doing something. By now, it's probably no surprise that we handle these questions exactly the same way we handle any other SAT Reading question: we look for the answer choice that's restated or demonstrated by the relevant text, rather than trying to read the author's mind or guess her intentions.

As an example of this kind of question, consider question 7 on section 1 of SAT Practice Test #1, which asks us to identify the purpose of a paragraph. Many untrained test-takers will assume incorrectly that the only way to answer the question is to try to guess what the author was thinking when she wrote it—but the right answer, (D), turns out to be the only choice that's directly present in the text. Choice (D) says the purpose is to "analyze a reaction," and we can see the paragraph directly demonstrating this idea when it asks what actions could have been taken by one character to cause another character to react differently. (For a full discussion of this question, see its walkthrough on page 82.)

What about "Yes-Yes-No-No" Questions?

Some questions may follow a pattern that I call "yes-yes-no-no," which includes the following elements:

- The prompt asks a question that can be answered with two opposing responses—usually "yes" or "no."
- Two of the answer choices begin with one of the two opposing responses (like "yes"), followed by a sentence or two explaining why that response could be the correct answer.
- The other two choices begin with the other opposing response (like "no"), followed by a sentence or two explaining why that response could be the correct answer.

There's no need to be especially worried about these questions, but I'm mentioning them here because some of my students are bothered by them before we start working together.

As trained test-takers, we need to remember that *every part of a correct answer choice has to reflect the text,* or else the choice is wrong. This applies to yes-yes-no-no questions, too, which means the following parts of the correct answer must both be valid:

- The "yes" or "no" part of the answer choice must be a correct answer to the question in the prompt, *and*
- the explanation in the choice must be accurately restated or demonstrated by the relevant part of the passage.

For this reason, many trained test-takers find it easier to attack these questions by focusing on the explanation portion of each answer choice, and identifying the explanations that are directly restated or demonstrated by the passage. If only one answer choice has an explanation that's restated or demonstrated by the passage, then we can quickly confirm that the "yes" or "no" at the beginning of that answer choice makes sense as an answer to the prompt, and select that choice.

But, occasionally, two or more of the answer choices will include explanation components that are restated or demonstrated by the passage; in these situations, you'll need to consider whether the correct answer to the first portion of the question should be "yes" or "no." You'll find that only one option is logical in light of the prompt; that option is the correct answer.

For a real-life example of a question with this kind of "yes-yes-no-no" answer choice pattern, let's take a look at question 29 from the Reading section of SAT Practice Test #1. That question asks whether

> the data in the table support the authors' proposed pairing of bases in DNA.

Choice (A) starts with "yes," and then says,

> for each organism, the percentage of adenine is closest to the percentage of thymine, and the percentage of guanine is closest to the percentage of cytosine.

When we look at the table, we can see that the statement that comes after "yes" is supported by that table. But choice (C) contains exactly the same statement as choice (A), except that (C) starts with "no" instead of "yes."

Now that we know the main statements in (A) and (C) are the same, and are supported by the figure, we need to figure out whether the correct answer should begin with "yes" or "no." When we look in the passage to find "the authors' proposed pairing of bases in DNA" as described by the prompt, we can see that lines 34 and 35 say,

> the only pairs of bases possible are: adenine with thymine, and guanine with cytosine.

If the percentage of adenine is closest to the percentage of thymine, then the author's proposed pairing of adenine and thymine would be logically supported: if adenine and thymine are paired together, then we'd expect them to be present in similar amounts. Along the same lines, if the percentage of guanine is closest to the percentage of cytosine, that would support the author's proposed pairing of guanine and cytosine, because if guanine and cytosine are paired together, we'd expect them to be present in similar amounts, too. So the data in the table *do* support the author's proposed pairing, which means "yes" is appropriate, and (A) must be correct. (See the walkthrough for this question on page 91 later in this Black Book if you'd like to read more about it.)

On any given test day, you're relatively unlikely to encounter a yes-yes-no-no question with two or more answer choices whose explanations are restated or demonstrated by the relevant part of the passage, so you usually won't have to worry about figuring out whether "yes" or "no" makes sense as an answer to the prompt. And even if you do see a question like that on test day, you'll find that the yes-no portion of the choices is usually clear once you've identified the choices whose explanations are restated or demonstrated by the passage, as we just saw.

What about "Central Claim" Questions?

You'll occasionally see a question that asks you to identify the "central claim" of a passage, or of some part of a passage. You may also see questions that ask about the "central purpose" or "main idea" of a cited text, and so on. These questions can basically be treated in the same way that any other SAT Reading question can: the correct answer will be the only choice that restates an idea from the relevant part of the text.

As an example, consider question 14 from the Reading section of SAT Practice Test #3. This question asks us for the central idea of the fourth paragraph, which is about public transport. The correct answer, choice (B), says,

> some public transportation systems are superior to travel by private automobile

which is a restatement of the following quotes from the relevant paragraph:

> public transport can be faster, more comfortable, and cheaper than the private automobile . . . In Latin America, China, and India, working people board fast-loading buses . . . [while] sedans and SUVs . . . [are] mired in dawn-to-dusk traffic jams

So we can see that the paragraph restates the idea that public transport can be better than traveling by private automobile. (For a complete discussion of this question, see the corresponding walkthrough on page 128 later in this Black Book.)

What about Summary and Development Questions?

Some questions will ask us to pick the answer choice that summarizes the cited text, or that describes the "development" of the text, or something along those lines. Whenever a prompt seems to be asking for something along these lines, we'll find that the correct answer will still be restated or demonstrated by key elements of the cited text in sequence, just like the correct answer to any other kind of SAT Reading question. In other words, we won't be required to interpret the cited text just because some people view summarizing as an act of interpretation.

For a real-life example of a question that asks about summarizing a text, let's take a look at question 1 from the Reading section of SAT Practice Test #2. The prompt asks us to select the answer choice that summarizes the passage.

The correct answer is (A), which says that

> a character describes his dislike for his new job and considers the reasons why.

This idea directly reflects what we see in lines 6 and 7: "I felt my occupation irksome." It's also demonstrated by the idea that the job is a "nuisance," which we find in line 10. The word "occupation" from the text restates the word "job" from the answer choice, and the speaker "describes his dislike" for the job when he calls it a "nuisance" and says that it's "irksome." In lines 9 through 27, he explains various aspects of the job that make it unpleasant (such as the "closeness, smoke, monotony, and joyless tumult" in lines 19 and 20). He then proceeds to describe his difficult relationship with his boss, and provide reasons why his boss hates him in lines 34 through 48. In short, we see that every part of (A) is directly restated or demonstrated by ideas we can find throughout the passage, just as the prompt requires. As trained test-takers, we see that the other choices seem generally related to the topic of the passage, but none of them simply restates the passage without adding extra ideas that don't appear in the passage, so we know they must be wrong. (For a complete discussion of this question, see the walkthrough on page 102 in this Black Book.)

What about "Humor?"

Sometimes an answer choice will mention the idea of humor or comedy. In order to evaluate these kinds of answer choices along the lines of the SAT, we have to know that the College Board uses these terms in very particular ways that don't really reflect their use in everyday speech.

When the College Board refers to part of a passage as "humorous," "comical," "funny," or anything else along those lines, we should understand that to mean one of two things:

1. either the text can't be true in a literal sense, or

2. the text involves something unexpected or unusual

Let's take a look at question 5 from the Reading section of SAT Practice Test #3 for an example of this idea. This question asks about a story from the passage in which Lady Carlotta sits and works on a sketch while a woman she knows is trapped by an angry boar in a tree nearby, and the text mentions in lines 12-14 that Lady Carlotta has a history of "interfering on behalf of a distressed animal."

The correct answer is (C), which calls the anecdote "a humorous insight into her character." We know the College Board would consider this story "humorous" because it's the opposite of what we would expect from the character, given the information in lines 12-14. (See this question's walkthrough on page 124 later in this Black Book for a full explanation of the rest of the question.)

Again, whether a real person would actually laugh at something doesn't matter on the SAT; all that matters is whether the text describes something that couldn't literally be true, or something that's unexpected. (By the way, if this discussion seems a little odd right now, don't worry—we'll see more examples of these ideas at work in real SAT questions from the College Board in just a bit.)

What about Paired Passages?

Sometimes the College Board asks you questions about two passages at once. These questions often ask how the author of one passage would respond to a statement from the other passage. When this happens, students often worry that they need to read an author's mind, which seems very subjective and unfair.

But we have to remember that every answer to a Reading question is spelled out somewhere in the text, and these questions are no exception, even if they seem to be asking you to guess how an author would feel in a hypothetical situation.

Whenever the SAT asks how an author would feel about something, it must always be true that the author's passage directly states how that author feels about that topic. So if the test asks,

> How would the author of Passage 1 respond to the claim in Passage 2 about banana cream pie?

then it must be the case that Passage 1 directly discusses claims about banana cream pie like the one in Passage 2.

This might sound a little complicated, but it's actually not that difficult in practice. Let's explore a real-life example of an SAT question that asks how the author of one passage would react to something from another passage. We'll take a look at question 38 from the Reading section of SAT Practice Test #4. This question asks how Edmund Burke (the author of Passage 1) would react to the comments in the final paragraph of Thomas Paine's passage, which is Passage 2.

When we look for the remarks in the final paragraph of Passage 2, we see that they say,

> circumstances . . . chang[e] . . . and as government is for the living . . . it is the living only that has any right in [government]. That which may be thought right and found convenient in one age, may be thought wrong and found inconvenient in another.

Since the prompt asks how Burke would react to this idea, there must be some specific wording in Passage 1 to tell us how Burke feels about government changing from one generation to the next. Sure enough, there is: Burke directly contradicts Paine's opinion when Burke says that people aren't

> morally at liberty…to separate and tear asunder the bands of their subordinate community

just because they think there might be a "contingent improvement" (37). (In other words, simply thinking that a change in government might make things better doesn't justify making significant changes to that government.)

So, in short, we see that Paine says people should be able to change aspects of government that used to be "convenient" (77) but are now "inconvenient" (79), while Burke says that people can't just change their government because they think the change might result in an "improvement" (37).

This contradiction between Burke's view and Paine's view is exactly restated in the right answer, (D), which says Burke would react

> with disapproval, because changing conditions are insufficient justification for changing the form of government.

Notice that answering this question with total confidence didn't require us to try to read Burke's mind, nor to make any guesses about how Burke would react to Paine's statements! Passage 1 directly told us exactly how Burke would feel about those statements, and we picked the answer choice that reflected Burke's position. (For a complete discussion of this question, see its walkthrough on page 159 later in this Black Book.)

Also note that we can use this approach whenever an SAT Reading question asks us how someone would respond to a claim, argument, or question—it doesn't only apply to questions that are about two distinct passages. For an example of this idea, see the walkthrough for question 15 on section 1 of SAT Practice Test #1, which appears on page 85 of this Black Book.

Conclusion

Now that we've discussed the best ways to approach every SAT Reading question in the abstract, we'll pause to summarize these ideas on the next page, and then dive in to walkthroughs of every Reading question on the first 4 SAT Practice Tests from the College Board, so you can see these concepts in action against the types of real test questions you'll encounter on test day.

SAT Reading Quick Summary

This is a one-page summary of the major relevant concepts from this section. Use it to evaluate your comprehension or jog your memory. For a more in-depth treatment of these ideas, see the rest of the section.

The Big Secret: The answer to every question comes directly from what's on the page. No interpretation whatsoever is involved.

The rules for Reading on the SAT are simple; the only challenging thing is making sure you follow them all the time, no matter what. Here they are:

- Correct answers are always directly restated or demonstrated in the text—no matter the kind of passage, and no matter the kind of question.

- <u>Details are critical</u>. The difference between right and wrong can be one word.

- There's <u>always exactly one objectively right answer choice per question</u>, and the other choices are objectively wrong. There aren't "good," "better," and "best," choices; there are only totally wrong choices and totally right choices.

Here are the most <u>common wrong-answer patterns</u> you'll see:

- Answer choice contains statements that might seem <u>reasonable, but aren't actually stated in the text.</u>

- Answer choices may mention concepts from the text but <u>confuses the relationships</u> among them.

- Answer choice is <u>barely relevant</u> to the text.

- Answer choice <u>directly contradicts</u> the text.

- Answer choice would be an acceptable <u>literary interpretation</u> if you were in a classroom setting.

Here's the general Reading process:

1. Read the brief passage introduction.
2. Skim, read, or skip the passage (whichever you're most comfortable with, as discussed earlier in this section).
3. Read the question and note any citation, then read the relevant text.
4. Find three wrong answers.
5. Confirm the remaining answer choice.

Special Notes:

- The word "humor" in an answer choice refers to something in the passage that is unexpected or can't be taken literally.

- If you think 2 or more answer choices are equally valid (or that none are valid), then you're overlooking some small detail. Consider skipping the question and coming back to it on a later pass, but make sure you mark an answer for every question on the section before time is called.

- Remember to invest your time in questions that will be easiest for you to answer!

See the many walkthroughs in the next section for demonstrations of these principles.

Reading Question Walkthroughs

Since we've gone through all of the necessary training on the SAT Reading process, it's time to see that process in action against real SAT questions like the ones you'll encounter on test day. (Remember, I recommend that you only prepare with official practice questions, because those are the only questions that are guaranteed to play by the College Board's rules. For more on that, see "Only Work with Questions from the College Board!" on page 18 of this Black Book. You can get real practice tests from the College Board in the College Board's Blue Book, or by downloading them for free from the College Board's website.)

We'll go through every question in the first four SAT Practice Tests from the College Board, starting in just a couple of pages. But first, I'd like to take a second to explain how my walkthroughs for this section are set up. (By the way, if you'd like to see some video demonstrations of these ideas, go to www.SATprepVideos.com for a selection of demonstration videos that are free to readers of this book.)

Sample Reading Walkthrough

The question walkthroughs in this book are laid out in a way that allows us to do the following:

- capture the ideal thought process for attacking individual questions, from initial assessment of the question through consideration of each answer choice

- make it easier to pick and choose specific pieces of information, while also allowing you to read the entire solution easily

- present the walkthroughs so they can stand on their own, while still making it easy to refer back to the relevant parts of the training for more details on key ideas if you want a refresher

- demonstrate how mechanical and repetitive real SAT questions are

Here's a diagram of an example walkthrough, with the elements of the walkthrough explained on the next page:

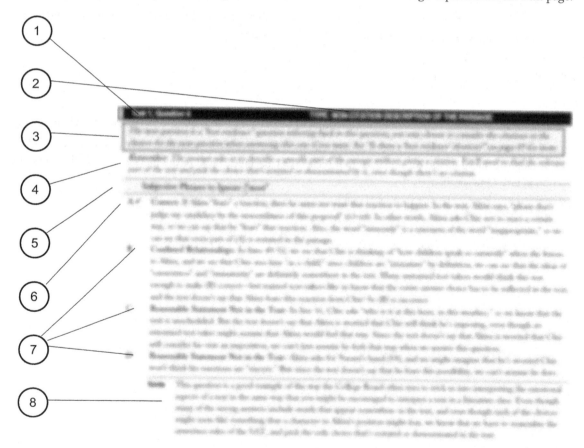

Explanation of Walkthrough Elements

The elements of the walkthrough are presented in a way that reflects the ideal mental process for approaching a new SAT Reading question. First, we quickly get a general impression of what's going on in the question, then we remind ourselves of what the question wants us to do, and finally we consider each answer choice and figure out which common SAT patterns it reflects:

1. This shows the test number and question number of the question being analyzed in the walkthrough. You can use this information to locate the relevant question in one of the editions of the Blue Book, or in the College Board's free online preparation materials.

2. This indicates the type of question, according to our rough classification system. I've deliberately avoided discussing the idea of classifying the questions in detail during your training, because I don't want you to think that classifying a question is a particularly important step in the process of answering that question. At the same time, as you work with more and more official SAT questions from the College Board, you'll naturally begin to notice that some questions are extremely similar to others, and the questions will sort of automatically organize themselves into "types" in your mind, even if you're not trying to categorize them deliberately. So I've included general classifications of each question in the walkthroughs to help show you what kinds of associations a trained test-taker might initially make on reading the prompt for a question. Don't worry if your idea of a question's type doesn't always match exactly with mine! The classification isn't what really matters—all that really matters is that you stay in the habit of answering every question based on a literal reading of the words and figures on the page, and that you pick an answer choice that's restated or demonstrated by the text. Item 4 will tell you more about each type.

3. This tells you whether the following question is a "best evidence" question, which can be useful if you prefer to try to take advantage of the potential "best evidence shortcut" referred to on page 72 of this Black Book. (Remember that you don't have to use this "shortcut" if you don't want to!)

4. This italicized text is a quick reminder of the specific issues that are likely to come up in the question and how you should expect to tackle them, based on the "type" identified in Item 2. See the description of Item 2 above for more.

5. This Item reminds us that we can ignore the kinds of subjective wording that the College Board often uses to try to fool untrained test-takers into interpreting the text. Remember that we should never try to interpret the text or read it subjectively, even though the College Board frequently uses phrases like "most likely" and "would probably." (See "2. The College Board Deliberately Phrases Questions to Make you Think you Should Use Subjective Interpretation to Find the Answer." on page 60 for more on this idea.)

6. The correct answer will be noted with a checkmark icon, and the following explanation will show exactly how the correct answer is restated or demonstrated by the relevant part of the passage.

7. The descriptions of the wrong answers will begin with a brief mention of the overall pattern being followed by the wrong answer, and then a lengthier explanation showing how the answer choice fits that pattern. (Remember to see "What do Wrong Answers Do?" starting on page 61 of this Black Book for an explanation of these patterns.) Please keep in mind that you can still answer a question correctly without classifying or interpreting the wrong answers exactly the same way I do! Ultimately, all that matters is that you realize the wrong answers aren't restated or demonstrated in the relevant part of the text. If I decided to classify something as an example of the "confused relationships" pattern and you think it's a better example of the "off by one or two words" pattern, that's fine. I've just indicated these patterns here to help you see how I'm structuring my thinking as I approach a question.

8. If I feel that something is noteworthy about the question but I can't fit it in the rest of the walkthrough, then I'll note that at the end of the walkthrough. Be sure to pay attention to these notes when they appear, as they'll often contain useful information about what a particular question can teach us generally about future SAT questions.

Note that some walkthroughs are missing some of the Items in this list! If one of the Items above isn't relevant to a particular question, then it's omitted.

Remember that the ultimate goal of these walkthroughs is to help you see how I attack each question, and how I recommend you do the same. But, in the end, what matters most is that you develop an approach for SAT Reading questions that allows you to identify the one correct answer choice that's directly restated or demonstrated on the page, and the three wrong answers that aren't. Feel free to modify my approach as you see fit, as long as your modifications still bring you the results you want.

TEST 1

Test 1, Question 1   TYPE: DESCRIBE THE PASSAGE

ⓘ *The prompt often mentions describing the passage, and usually doesn't include a line citation. The answer must still be restated or demonstrated by some specific part of the text, even if there's no citation. See "What about Questions Without Citations?" p. 72*

Subjective Phrases to Ignore: "best"

A   **Barely Relevant:** Akira and Chie have a conversation, but we can't say they "argue" with one another, because they don't express opposing views on a subject. Further, Akira visits Chie's home, but we can't say he "intrudes" on it. In fact, Chie invites him in by saying "come inside, get out of this nasty night" (37).

B ✓ **Correct:** The text tells us Chie received a surprising request from Akira. Akira asks for Naomi's hand (59), which is a request; afterwards, he says that he can see he has "startled" (73) Chie, which means she's surprised by his request.

C   **Barely Relevant:** This is a classic example of the "barely relevant" answer choice type. The passage doesn't describe any character reminiscing about anything, or anything happening "over the years."

D   **Off by One or Two Words:** The text does mention people doing things unexpectedly, but no one in the text actually "criticizes" anyone else. Even when Chie talks about Akira in lines 84 - 86, she doesn't actually "criticize" him, because she doesn't explicitly say anything bad about him. She only says that Akira "thinks he can marry the Fuji heir and take her to America all in the snap of his fingers."

Test 1, Question 2   TYPE: DESCRIBE THE PASSAGE

ⓘ *The prompt often mentions describing the passage, and usually doesn't include a line citation. The answer must still be restated or demonstrated by some specific part of the text, even if there's no citation. See "What about Questions Without Citations?" p. 72*

Subjective Phrases to Ignore: "best"

A   **Off by One or Two Words:** This passage does mention a traditional practice—that of using a "go-between" (4) to arrange a marriage—but that traditional practice is not carefully analyzed. In order for us to be able to say that this practice was carefully analyzed, there would have to be phrases in the text that describe different aspects of the practice, what they mean, how they work, and so on.

B ✓ **Correct:** The text includes many details, not limited to "he came on a winter's eve" (5), and "Chie heard her soft scuttling footsteps, the creak of the door" (8-9), and "his hands hanging straight down, a black cap in one, a yellow oil-paper umbrella in the other" (26-28). Also, we can certainly describe Akira's conversation with Chie as an "encounter," since it involves two people meeting. Further, Akira refers to the "urgency" (32) of the matter, which is one of many details that demonstrate the discussion is important, or "meaningful." The text restates or demonstrates everything in (B), so it's right.

C   **Literary Interpretation:** Chie asks Akira some questions, but there is nothing in the text to support the idea that the answers to these questions are "definitive." In order to call an answer definitive, there would need to be a phrase like "the question was answered once and for all" or "there would be no further discussion of the issue."

D   **Literary Interpretation:** The text gives us no reason to call the recounting of the story "cheerful," or to call the anecdote "amusing." The text does mention Chie's "amusement" (43), but this answer choice would require the *anecdote* to be *amusing*, not a *character in the anecdote* to be *amused*—and, anyway, Chie's amusement doesn't last throughout the passage. To support the word "amusing" in the answer choice, the narrator would have to say something like "it makes me smile to think of how…" or "Akira standing in the rain was a funny sight," but we don't have anything like that in this passage.

Test 1, Question 3   TYPE: WORD MOST NEARLY MEANS

ⓘ *The prompt includes the phrase "most nearly means" and the choices are usually one- or two-word phrases. The answer is either restated or demonstrated by an idea from the surrounding text. Remember you can work around unknown words, and be ready to guess/skip and focus on other questions if you don't know the words. See "What about "Most Nearly Means" Questions?" on p.73.*

Subjective Phrases to Ignore: "most nearly"

A   ("Akira came <u>frankly</u>, breaking all tradition." (1) "I ask <u>frankly</u> because the use of a go-between takes much time." (64-66)) **Reasonable Statement Not in the Text:** In another context, the word "frankly" could mean the same thing as "directly," because if you're being honest with someone, you could call that being both "frank" and "direct." But the word "frankly" isn't restated or demonstrated by anything in the text, so it's incorrect according to the SAT's rules.

B   ("Akira came <u>confidently</u>, breaking all tradition." (1) "I ask <u>confidently</u> because the use of a go-between takes much time"" (64-66).) **Reasonable Statement Not in the Text:** Being "confident" and being "direct" in dealing with other people are often closely associated, but the idea of "confidence" doesn't restate anything in the relevant part of the passage or follow logically from it, so "confidently" is incorrect.

C ✓ ("Akira came <u>without mediation</u>, breaking all tradition." (1) "I ask <u>without mediation</u> because the use of a go-between takes much time" (64-66).) **Correct:** As trained test-takers, we can see that both cited uses of the word "directly" present the idea of approaching "directly" as the opposite of using a "go-between." We know this because coming "directly" is equated to the idea of "breaking all tradition" (1), while using a go-between is "follow[ing] form;" since "breaking" tradition and "following form" are opposites, the things they're equated to (being direct and using a go-between) must also be opposites. This means the phrase "without _____" needs to mean the opposite of the phrase "using a go-between, and the word "without" means that the underlined phrase needs to mean basically the same thing as "using a go-between." If we already know the word "mediation," we know it does basically mean "using a go-between." If we don't know that already, we may be able to break down the word "mediation," and see that it's related to words like "median" and "medial," which are related to the idea of something being in the center of two other things. A "go-between" is literally someone "between" two other people, which means a "go-between" is literally a type of "mediation," so (C) directly restates an idea from the relevant part of the text, which means it's right.

D ("Akira came <u>with precision</u>, breaking all tradition." (1). "I ask <u>with precision</u> because the use of a go-between takes much time" (64-66).) **Barely Relevant:** The phrase "with precision" doesn't restate or demonstrate any concept from the relevant part of the passage, so this answer choice must be wrong.

| **Test 1, Question 4** | **TYPE: DESCRIBE THE PASSAGE** |

> *The next question is a "best evidence" question referring back to this question; you may choose to consider the citations in the choices for the next question when answering this one if you want. See "Is there a 'best evidence' shortcut?" on page 72 for more.*

ⓘ *The prompt often mentions describing the passage, and usually doesn't include a line citation. The answer must still be restated or demonstrated by some specific part of the text, even if there's no citation. See "What about Questions Without Citations?" p. 72*

Subjective Phrases to Ignore: "most"

A ✓ **Correct:** If Akira "fears" a reaction, then he must not want that reaction to happen. In the text, Akira says, "please don't judge my candidacy by the unseemliness of this proposal" (63-64). In other words, Akira asks Chie not to react a certain way, so we can say that he "fears" that reaction. Also, the word "unseemly" is a synonym of the word "inappropriate," so we can see that every part of (A) is restated in the passage.

B **Confused Relationships:** In lines 49-52, we see that Chie is thinking of "how children speak so earnestly" when she listens to Akira, and we see that Chie sees him "as a child;" since children are "immature" by definition, we can see that the ideas of "earnestness" and "immaturity" are definitely somewhere in the text. Many untrained test-takers would think this was enough to make (B) correct—but trained test-takers like us know that the entire answer choice has to be reflected in the text, and the text doesn't say that Akira fears this reaction from Chie! So (B) is incorrect.

C **Reasonable Statement Not in the Text:** In line 16, Chie asks "who is it at this hour, in this weather," so we know that the visit is unscheduled. But the text doesn't say that Akira is worried that Chie will think he's imposing, even though an untrained test-taker might assume that Akira would feel that way. Since the text doesn't say that Akira is worried that Chie will consider his visit an imposition, we can't just assume he feels that way when we answer this question.

D **Reasonable Statement Not in the Text:** Akira asks for Naomi's hand (59), and we might imagine that he's worried Chie won't think his emotions are "sincere." But since the text doesn't say that he fears this possibility, we can't assume he does.

Note This question is a good example of the way the College Board often tries to trick us into interpreting the emotional aspects of a text in the same way that you might be encouraged to interpret a text in a literature class. Even though many of the wrong answers include words that appear somewhere in the text, and even though each of the choices might seem like something that a character in Akira's position might fear, we know that we have to remember the unwritten rules of the SAT, and pick the only choice that's restated or demonstrated in the text.

| **Test 1, Question 5** | **TYPE: BEST EVIDENCE** |

ⓘ *The answer must restate or demonstrate the relevant statement. See "What about "Best Evidence" Questions?" on page 72.*

Subjective Phrases to Ignore: "best"

A **Barely Relevant:** This text isn't relevant to the correct answer from question 4, or to any answer choice from question 4.

B **Confused Relationships:** This might seem related to (B) from the previous question, but the explanation for that answer choice shows why that answer choice is incorrect, and why this choice is incorrect, too—the text doesn't say that Akira is worried that Chie will think him immature, which is what question 4 requires.

C ✓ **Correct:** As we discussed in the walkthrough for question 4, this text supports the right answer from that question.

D **Confused Relationships:** This choice might seem to be related to choices from question 4, but it doesn't explicitly mention Akira being afraid of anything, so it can't be relevant to either of the two questions.

ⓘ *The prompt often mentions describing the passage, and usually doesn't include a line citation. The answer must still be restated or demonstrated by some specific part of the text, even if there's no citation. See "What about Questions Without Citations?" p. 72*

A   Confused Relationships: Untrained test-takers may be tempted by this answer choice if they get confused and think that Akira wants to marry Chie, rather than Naomi, and then make the further mistake of trying to determine whether Akira is actually in love. Either way, Akira never address Chie with "affection," so this answer choice is wrong.

B   Direct Contradiction: We can't say that Akira addresses Chie with "objectivity," because "objectivity" would involve detachment and/or neutrality by definition, but he shows emotions of his own when he blushes (57), and concern for her emotions when he apologizes for startling her (72-74).

C   Confused Relationships: It is Chie who addresses Akira with amusement—not the other way around—as we see in line 43: "'Congratulations,' Chie said with amusement." Many untrained test-takers will fall for this trap, because they won't be in the habit of looking out for these kinds of wrong answers!

D✓   Correct: We see that Akira addresses Chie "with respect" when he calls her "Madame" and asks for her forgiveness (31), and says "I don't want to trouble you" (39). We can also see that he does not show "utter deference" because he asks to marry her daughter Naomi (59) and says "'without your consent, I must go to America, to secure a new home for my bride'" (69-70), which means that he'll marry Naomi whether Chie gives her consent or not. If he were showing "utter deference" to Chie, then he would do whatever Chie wanted, and wouldn't tell Chie directly that her lack of consent wouldn't stop the marriage from happening.

ⓘ *The prompt asks about the purpose or role of a part of the text. The correct answer must be accurately restated or described by the relevant text, with no interpretation. See "What about "Purpose" Questions?" on p.74.*

A   Literary Interpretation: The first paragraph mentions a "tradition," which can, perhaps, be considered a part of a culture, but no actual culture is even mentioned in this paragraph, much less described. So this answer choice can't be right.

B   Confused Relationships: The first paragraph mentions a "tradition," but it doesn't describe any problems related to that tradition, so we can't say the paragraph is "criticizing" that tradition.

C   Confused Relationships: The paragraph does include two sentences that end in question marks, so we can definitely say that something is being questioned—but there's no evidence in the paragraph that anything has actually been suggested by anyone, so (C) must be wrong.

D✓   Correct: The third sentence in the paragraph asks if Chie "would…have been more receptive" to Akira's request if he had followed tradition. Being "receptive" to something is a kind of reaction to it, which means that asking a question about whether someone "would…have been more receptive" under different circumstances is a way of "analyz[ing] a reaction." After reading the third sentence, we can see that the second sentence ("Was that it?") is asking "Did Chie react the way she did because Akira broke all tradition and approached her without a go-between?" This makes (D) the only choice that's demonstrated in the paragraph, so (D) is correct.

ⓘ *The prompt includes the phrase "most nearly means" and the choices are usually one- or two-word phrases. The answer is either restated or demonstrated by an idea from the surrounding text. Remember you can work around unknown words, and be ready to guess/skip and focus on other questions if you don't know the words. See "What about "Most Nearly Means" Questions?" on p.73.*

Subjective Phrases to Ignore: "most nearly"

A   ("Had he followed <u>appearance</u>—had he asked his mother to speak to his father to approach a go-between—would Chie have been more receptive?") Reasonable Statement Not in the Text: In another context, "appearance" could mean "form," since the physical "appearance" of an object is its "form." But this isn't restated or demonstrated by (A), so (A) is wrong.

B✓   ("Had he followed <u>custom</u>—had he asked his mother to speak to his father to approach a go-between—would Chie have been more receptive?") Correct: The structure of this question—particularly the phrases "had he" and "would have been"—tells us that this question is asking about something Akira did NOT do. To see what he DID do, we need to check the surrounding text. In line 1, we see "Akira came directly, breaking all tradition." So "coming directly" and "breaking all tradition" is what Akira did, and "following form" is what he did NOT do. This means that "following form" must be the same thing as NOT "breaking all tradition," which means "form" must mean the same thing as "tradition" for the purposes of this question. This answer choice is synonymous with "tradition," which makes it correct.

C   ("Had he followed <u>structure</u>—had he asked his mother to speak to his father to approach a go-between—would Chie have been more receptive?") Reasonable Statement Not in the Text: In some other context, "structure" could mean "form," because an object's physical "structure" can be described as its "form." But, as trained test-takers, we know the right answer to an SAT Reading question must either restate a concept from the relevant text or be demonstrated by it, so this is wrong.

D ("Had he followed <u>nature</u>—had he asked his mother to speak to his father to approach a go-between—would Chie have been more receptive?") **Barely Relevant:** The text doesn't restate the idea of "nature," so this can't be right.

| **Test 1, Question 9** | **TYPE: CITATION QUESTION** |

The next question is a "best evidence" question referring back to this question; you may choose to consider the citations in the choices for the next question when answering this one if you want. See "Is there a 'best evidence' shortcut?" on page 72 for more.

ⓘ *The question includes a citation from the text. The answer must be directly restated or demonstrated in the cited text, or in the text closely surrounding the cited text. See the general process for answering SAT Reading questions on p. 71.*

A   **Confused Relationships:** Akira tells Chie he wants "parental approval" (67) from Chie, when he mentions "your [Chie's] consent" to her. He doesn't say anything about his own parents, so we don't know how he feels about their consent; the text only shows us that Akira wants Naomi's mother to approve of him.

B   **Confused Relationships:** The text never tells us that Akira is worried about rejection from Naomi; as discussed in the explanation for choice (A), the text only indicates that Akira is hoping for approval from Naomi's mother, Chie.

C ✔ **Correct:** Akira says to Chie, "I would approach you more properly but I've received word of a position. I've an opportunity to go to America, as a dentist for Seattle's Japanese community" (39-42). We can tell from this sentence that Akira has an offer for a job, and that he considers this offer "attractive," because he calls it an "opportunity," and because we can see that it's potentially "attracting" him to America. We can also tell that he must be outside of America when he says this sentence, because he mentions going "to America," which means the attractive offer is in another country for him. Since every component of (C) is restated explicitly in the text, we know (C) is correct.

D   **Confused Relationships:** As readers, *we* know from the text that Chie is unaware of Akira's feelings for Naomi—for example, her statements in lines 61-62 and 84-86 indicate that she had no prior knowledge of Akira's feelings. But the prompt asks us for the reason that *Akira* says the matter is urgent, and the text doesn't connect Akira's urgency with Chie's lack of knowledge. Instead, Akira clearly says, in lines 64-70, that he doesn't want to take "much time" because his decision will depend on Chie's "consent." So the urgency is related to his time constraints in deciding whether to go to America and be a dentist, NOT to the issue of whether he knows that Chie might have heard about his feelings for Naomi.

Note   This question is a good example of the kind of thing that confuses a lot of untrained test-takers. Each answer choice includes at least one major concept from the text, but only one choice links multiple concepts from the text in a way that directly reflects exactly what the text says. Keep this kind of thing in mind on test day, and always remember that we have to stick to what's spelled out on the page!

| **Test 1, Question 10** | **TYPE: BEST EVIDENCE** |

ⓘ *The answer must restate or demonstrate the relevant statement. See "What about "Best Evidence" Questions?" on page 72.*

Subjective Phrases to Ignore: "best"

A   **Barely Relevant:** This text isn't relevant to the correct answer from question 9 (or, indeed, to any choice from that question).

B ✔ **Correct:** As discussed in the walkthrough for the previous question, this text supports the correct answer for question 9—it shows that the reason for Akira's behavior is that he's been offered a job in America.

C   **Literary Interpretation:** This citation does mention the idea that Akira might stay in Japan, depending on Chie's response to his request—but the specific lines in this citation don't mention the reason for Akira's "urgency" that was mentioned in question 9. So this citation, on its own, doesn't provide the evidence that allows us to answer question 9.

D   **Confused Relationships:** The idea of Akira startling Chie may seem relevant to (D) from question 9. But, as we discussed in the walkthrough for question 9, Akira's "urgency" is related to the job offer he has received, and to his need to decide whether to take Naomi with him to America or to stay and marry her in Japan; the urgency itself has nothing to do with whether Chie was previously aware of Akira's feelings, which is what (D) would require. (D) provides evidence for a choice in the previous question that's irrelevant to the prompt from the previous question, so it's wrong.

| **Test 1, Question 11** | **TYPE: PURPOSE OF CITED TEXT** |

ⓘ *The prompt asks about the purpose or role of a part of the text. The correct answer must be accurately restated or described by the relevant text, with no interpretation. See "What about "Purpose" Questions?" on p.74.*

Subjective Phrases to Ignore: "most likely"

A ✔ **Correct:** The cited text specifically says people "regularly buy presents" (6), and also mentions the "frequent experience of gift-giving" (9), which are both word-by-word restatements of choice (A). When we compare this to the other answer choices, we can see that (A) is correct (see notes for this question).

B   **Barely Relevant:** The text says that "Last year, Americans spent over $30 billion at retail stores in the month of December alone" (3-5). But the text doesn't tell us what they spent previously, so there's no support in the text for us to say whether that number represents a "recent increase" or not.

C   **Wrong Part of the Passage:** The text says in line 14 that "many dread the thought of buying gifts," so a lot of untrained test-takers may fall for (C). But the prompt asked about lines 1-9, and nothing in the passage connects the idea in line 14 to the examples in lines 1-9. (In fact, the sentence in lines 10-13 actually says that some people enjoy gift-giving; we can't argue that line 14 is relevant to the citation without acknowledging that lines 10-13 would have to be relevant in the same way, but this answer choice contradicts line 10-13 lines by making it sound like everyone has anxiety about gift-giving.)

D   **Literary Interpretation:** It's true that a portion of the text names some occasions for gift-giving, such as "weddings, birthdays, anniversaries, graduations, and baby showers" (7-9). But a trained test-taker can tell that (D) is wrong because the text doesn't specifically state whether the authors think the number of special occasions in itself is high or low—there's no phrase in the text that says anything like "the huge number of holidays" or "the few special occasions." Once more, we see the extreme importance of reading the text on the SAT very literally, and keeping in mind the test's unwritten rules!

Note   Notice that the ideas in choices (B) and (D) would both probably be fine in a classroom discussion, but they're both clearly wrong when we read carefully and apply the unwritten rules of the test. To a trained test-taker, (A) is clearly correct because it restates phrases from the passage without contradicting the passage or including ideas that don't appear in the passage, while no other answer choice does that.

Test 1, Question 12   **TYPE: WORD MOST NEARLY MEANS**

ⓘ *The prompt includes the phrase "most nearly means" and the choices are usually one- or two-word phrases. The answer is either restated or demonstrated by an idea from the surrounding text. Remember you can work around unknown words, and be ready to guess/skip and focus on other questions if you don't know the words. See "What about "Most Nearly Means" Questions?" on p.73.*

Subjective Phrases to Ignore: "most nearly"

A   ("This frequent experience of gift-giving can engender <u>unrealistic</u> feelings in gift-givers.") **Reasonable Statement Not in the Text:** Nothing in the text restates the idea of being "unrealistic," which means this choice has to be wrong.

B ✓   ("This frequent experience of gift-giving can engender <u>conflicted</u> feelings in gift-givers.") **Correct:** The feelings that gift-givers experience are described immediately after the citation: we see that "many relish the opportunity to buy presents" (10-11), while "many dread the thought of buying gifts" (14). The idea that many people "relish" buying gifts and many people "dread" buying gifts shows that people have "conflicted" feelings, since the ideas of "relishing" and "dreading" are opposites. (If we don't know that the word "relish" is positive in this sense, we can still tell that the sentence about relishing must be positive because it refers to gift-buying as an "opportunity," rather than using a word like "hassle" or "obligation.")

C   ("This frequent experience of gift-giving can engender <u>apprehensive</u> feelings in gift-givers.") **Confused Relationships:** The idea that people "dread" (14) buying gifts might seem to go along with the idea of "apprehensive" feelings, but the word "apprehensive" doesn't account for the fact that people also "relish" (11) gift-giving and view it as an "opportunity" (11) according to the text, so (C) contradicts that portion of the text.

D   ("This frequent experience of gift-giving can engender <u>supportive</u> feelings in gift-givers.") **Reasonable Statement Not in the Text:** An untrained test-taker might think that being "supportive" is a positive idea that might go along with gift-giving, but the idea of supportiveness isn't explicitly in the text.

Test 1, Question 13   **TYPE: DESCRIBE THE PASSAGE**

The next question is a "best evidence" question referring back to this question; you may choose to consider the citations in the choices for the next question when answering this one if you want. See "Is there a 'best evidence' shortcut?" on page 72 for more.

ⓘ *The prompt often mentions describing the passage, and usually doesn't include a line citation. The answer must still be restated or demonstrated by some specific part of the text, even if there's no citation. See "What about Questions Without Citations?" p. 72*

A   **Off by One or Two Words:** The text does speculate that gift-giving can express something: "perhaps givers believe that bigger…gifts convey stronger signals" (53-55), and "gift-givers may be motivated…to send a 'stronger signal' to their intended recipient" (60-62)—the idea of "signaling" something is a type of expression. But there are still two problems with this choice that make it wrong. First, the text doesn't specifically say that gift-giving is *definitely* a way to send a signal; instead, the text uses words like "perhaps" and "may," showing that the authors aren't sure that self-expression is involved. Second, we need to note the difference between the idea of possibly sending a signal about a relationship and the idea of expressing one's self; "self-expression" generally refers to the idea of using art or language to make a statement about one's ideas or beliefs, etc. For these two reasons, (A) fails to restate the text, and must be wrong.

B   **Barely Relevant:** Lines 41-65 discuss a perceived connection between the cost of a gift and how much that gift is appreciated, but nothing in the text says that gifts in general are always "inexpensive," as (B) would require.

C   **Reasonable Statement Not in the Text:** The text describes in lines 35-37 how "gift-givers have considerable experience acting as both gift-givers and gift-recipients," and says in lines 68-69 that "people slip in and out of these roles [of gift-giver and gift-recipient] every day." But, if we think carefully, like trained test-takers, we see that this isn't the same thing as reciprocity! The passage doesn't specifically describe a situation in which one person receives a gift and then turns around and gives a gift back to the original gift-giver, which is what the word "reciprocate" would have to involve. Furthermore, the text certainly doesn't say that any kind of reciprocating is "required"—or, indeed, that any kind of behavior of any kind is required. Many untrained test-takers will be attracted to this wrong answer because they've been taught that it's polite to give a person a gift if the person gives you one—but, again, the text never says anything about reciprocal gift-giving.

D ✓   **Correct:** (D) directly restates the idea of "build[ing] stronger bonds with one's closest peers" (12-13).

| **Test 1, Question 14** | **TYPE: BEST EVIDENCE** |

ⓘ *The answer must restate or demonstrate the relevant statement. See "What about "Best Evidence" Questions?" on page 72.*

Subjective Phrases to Ignore: "best"

A ✓   **Correct:** As discussed in the walkthrough for question 13, this text directly restates the right answer from 13, which is (D).

B   **Barely Relevant:** This text isn't really relevant to any answer choice from the previous question.

C   **Barely Relevant:** This text isn't really relevant to any choice from the previous question.

D   **Literary Interpretation:** This text is kind of related to the idea of inexpensive gifts from choice (B) in the previous question, but, as discussed in the explanation for that question, choice (B) for that question isn't actually restated in the text. So (B) is wrong for the previous question, and (D) is wrong for this question.

| **Test 1, Question 15** | **TYPE: CITATION QUESTION / PAIRED PASSAGES (see note below!)** |

ⓘ *The question includes a citation from the text. The answer must be directly restated or demonstrated in the cited text, or in the text closely surrounding the cited text. See the general process for answering SAT Reading questions on p. 71. The prompt also asks how someone would respond to a claim or argument. The correct answer restates a position that's already stated in the passage. See "What about Paired Passages?" on p.76. (See the note below!)*

Subjective Phrases to Ignore: "likely"

A ✓   **Correct:** The "social psychologists" from the prompt appear in lines 30-31, in this sentence: "That in itself is not surprising to social psychologists." In order to understand this sentence, we need to know what the word "that" is referring to; when we look at the previous sentence, we see the word "that" refers to the idea of the "deadweight loss" described in lines 28-30. So we now know that the "deadweight loss…is not surprising to social psychologists," according to the text. The word "predictable" in this answer choice is a direct restatement of the idea that something is "not surprising," which is what we just found in the text, so (A) is correct.

B   **Reasonable Statement Not in the Text:** An untrained test-taker might imagine that social psychologists would find the "deadweight loss" "questionable," because it might seem hard to believe that so many people aren't good at giving gifts. But the text doesn't actually restate that idea, so this answer can't be correct.

C   **Reasonable Statement Not in the Text:** An untrained test-taker might imagine that social psychologists would find the deadweight loss "disturbing," because it would mean that gift-giving—something a lot of people seem to enjoy—is actually a waste of money. But the text doesn't say anything about social psychologists being disturbed, so this answer can't be correct.

D   **Barely Relevant:** In order for (D) to be right, the text would need to state specifically that nothing like the deadweight loss had ever happened before, because that's what "unprecedented" means. But the text doesn't do that, so (D) is wrong.

Note   We don't really need to understand what the phrase "deadweight loss" actually means, or why psychologists chose the term "deadweight" in the first place. It's still possible to determine that the "deadweight loss" is unsurprising or predictable from the text. Remember this kind of thing when you run into strange phrasing on test day! For more on this, see our advice on the "bad connection" approach for working around unknown vocabulary on page 66. Also note that I've categorized this as a "paired passage" question even though there's really only one passage involved; I did this because the defining feature of "paired passage" questions is that they ask us to consider how someone would respond to something and the answer is spelled out on the page, which is the case with this question. Remember that it really isn't important to classify a question in your mind, as long as you look for the answer choice that's restated or demonstrated in a literal way in the text. I only include the classifications in these walkthroughs to help you start to see how the College Board repeats the same kinds of tactics over and over.

| **Test 1, Question 16** | **TYPE: CITATION QUESTION** |

The next question is a "best evidence" question referring back to this question; you may choose to consider the citations in the choices for the next question when answering this one if you want. See "Is there a 'best evidence' shortcut?" on page 72 for more.

The question includes a citation from the text. The answer must be directly restated or demonstrated in the cited text, or in the text closely surrounding the cited text. See the general process for answering SAT Reading questions on p. 71.

A   **Barely Relevant:** In order for this to be correct, the text would need to say that people were doing something without really meaning it, but the text doesn't say anything about that in the given citation. As we discuss below in the explanation for (C), the passage does indicate that the assumption is incorrect—but, as trained test-takers, we know that we have to think very carefully and specifically about what words actually mean when we're taking the SAT, and there's an important difference between the idea of being wrong about something and the idea of being insincere. In fact, if we think about it, it's difficult to imagine that an assumption could be insincere: an assumption is something we believe to be true, in our own thoughts—how can we assume something is true, but somehow not really mean it?

B   **Reasonable Statement Not in the Text:** As discussed below in the explanation for choice (C), the passage indicates that the assumption is incorrect. But that doesn't mean that we can call it "unreasonable," as this answer choice would require. The word "unreasonable" means that there's no logical reason for something, but it's very possible for an assumption to be reasonable and still turn out to be wrong in the end; the text doesn't say anything about assuming things without reason. These are the kinds of careful distinctions that trained test-takers look out for on test day.

C✓   **Correct:** The assumption in lines 41-44 is that "gift-givers equate how much they spend with how much recipients will appreciate the gift. (The more expensive the gift, the stronger a gift-recipient's feelings of appreciation)." The text that immediately follows says "such an assumption may be unfounded" (46-47). The word "unfounded" in this context is an exact restatement of the idea of being "incorrect," so (C) is right. (Even if we don't know what the word "unfounded" means, we can still tell from other parts of the passage that researchers believe there's no necessary connection between the cost or size of a gift and the amount of importance that the recipient attaches to the gift. For example, lines 48-50 say the authors believe recipients are "less inclined" to appreciate "the magnitude of a gift than givers assume," and lines 63-65 say, "gift-recipients...may not construe smaller and larger gifts as representing smaller and larger signals of thoughtfulness and consideration." So we can clearly see the text says the assumption is incorrect, even if we might need to work around the word "unfounded" in line 47.)

D   **Direct Contradiction:** As discussed in the explanation for (C), the passage indicates the assumption is incorrect. But the word "substantiated" means something has substance, which is another way to say it's valid or correct. So (D) directly contradicts the right answer, which is something we'll see as a common pattern on the SAT.

| **Test 1, Question 17** | **TYPE: BEST EVIDENCE** |

The answer must restate or demonstrate the relevant statement. See "What about "Best Evidence" Questions?" on page 72.

Subjective Phrases to Ignore: "best"

A   **Literary Interpretation:** This text describes the "assumption" mentioned in the previous question, but it's not relevant to any of the choices in the previous question, so it can't be correct.

B   **Literary Interpretation:** This choice provides general information about the purpose of gift-giving according to some researchers, but it's not relevant to the assumption mentioned in question 16, so it can't be correct.

C✓   **Correct:** This text discusses the idea that gift-givers' assumptions about a correlation between the magnitude of a gift and the recipients' appreciation of the gift may not be valid, as we saw in our walkthrough for 16. So (C) is right.

D   **Literary Interpretation:** This text provides a general explanation for why people are bad gift-givers, but it doesn't specifically address the idea of more expensive gifts being more appreciated by recipients, and whether that idea has merit, so it isn't relevant to a discussion of the assumption in the previous question.

| **Test 1, Question 18** | **TYPE: WORD MOST NEARLY MEANS** |

The prompt includes the phrase "most nearly means" and the choices are usually one- or two-word phrases. The answer is either restated or demonstrated by an idea from the surrounding text. Remember you can work around unknown words, and be ready to guess/skip and focus on other questions if you don't know the words. See "What about "Most Nearly Means" Questions?" on p.73.

Subjective Phrases to Ignore: "most nearly"

A   ("Perhaps givers believe that bigger (i.e. more expensive) gifts <u>transport</u> stronger signals of thoughtfulness and consideration.")
     Reasonable Statement Not in the Text: In another context, "convey" could mean "transport," because both words can describe the act of physically taking an object from one place to another. But the passage doesn't restate or demonstrate the idea of physically moving anything, so this choice can't be correct.

B   ("Perhaps givers believe that bigger (i.e. more expensive) gifts <u>counteract</u> stronger signals of thoughtfulness and consideration.")
     Barely Relevant: Nothing in the relevant text discusses the idea of "counteract[ing]" anything. If you found this answer choice tempting, you may have misread or misunderstood some part of the text on a basic level.

C   ("Perhaps givers believe that bigger (i.e. more expensive) gifts <u>exchange</u> stronger signals of thoughtfulness and consideration.")
     Confused Relationships: This answer choice may be tempting to an untrained test-taker because the word "exchange" is closely

---

related to the idea of giving gifts in general. But the text doesn't restate anything about exchanging signals, so this answer can't be correct.

D ✓ ("Perhaps givers believe that bigger (i.e. more expensive) gifts <u>communicate</u> stronger signals of thoughtfulness and consideration.") Correct: The word "communicate" directly restates the ideas of "signal[ing]...positive attitudes" (57-58), and "send[ing] a 'stronger signal'" (62). This idea of sending a signal is the definition of "communicat[ing]."

Test 1, Question 19 — TYPE: CITATION QUESTION

🛈 *The question includes a citation from the text. The answer must be directly restated or demonstrated in the cited text, or in the text closely surrounding the cited text. See the general process for answering SAT Reading questions on p. 71.*

A ✓ Correct: The citation occurs two sentences after the beginning of a paragraph; the first sentence in the paragraph asks "why...gift-givers assume" (51) something. The next sentence says, "perhaps givers believe that bigger (i.e. more expensive) gifts convey stronger signals of thoughtfulness and consideration" (53-55). Then the citation itself tells us that Camerer and others say, "gift-giving represents a symbolic ritual, whereby gift-givers attempt to signal their positive attitudes toward the intended recipient and their willingness to invest resources in a future relationship" (56-60). So the sentence before the citation tells us something that "givers believe" about gift-giving, and then the cited sentence explains something about what "gift-giving represents;" both of these sentences form an answer to the question of "why" gift-givers assume something. Since the word "explanation" in this answer choice refers to the act of describing why something happens, we can see that the cited text is an explanation of behavior related to gift-giving. So choice (A) is correct.

B Confused Relationships: As discussed above in the explanation for (A), the cited text provides an explanation for an aspect of the previous sentence. Since it's a continuation or extension of an idea from the previous sentence, we can't say this sentence "introduces" any argument, as this choice would require.

C Off by One or Two Words: This choice might be tempting to untrained test-takers because the cited text discusses why "gift-givers may be motivated" (60-61) to make the decisions they make, which definitely goes along with the word "motive" in this answer choice. But (C) says the purpose of the citation is to "question" something, and nothing in the text corresponds to the idea of questioning a motive. If we "question" something, it means we doubt that thing in some way. The text doesn't say anything about doubting the motives of gift-givers; all it discusses is the idea of trying to understand what those motives are. So (C) is wrong.

D Off by One or Two Words: This choice mentions a "conclusion," but no conclusion has been reached at this point in the text; Camerer's statements can't support a conclusion that doesn't exist in the text. The previous sentence starts with the word "perhaps" (53), so it can't be called a conclusion, because the word "perhaps" means the author is only exploring or considering an idea, not putting it forth as a conclusive answer to the question being asked.

Note The word "argument" in (B) is used in the classical, logical sense—meaning a position that a person takes on an issue, rather than a heated disagreement. Even if we didn't recognize this usage of the word "argument," we can still answer this question correctly, because the cited sentence wasn't "question[ing]" or "conclu[ding]" anything, and it wasn't "introduc[ing]" an argument in either the logical sense or in the more commonly used sense —it was only following up on an idea from the previous sentence. (See "Critical Technical Terms for the SAT Reading Section" on page 69 of this Black Book for more terms like "argument" that can be useful on this part of the test.)

Test 1, Question 20 — TYPE: FIGURE

🛈 *The prompt refers to a graph/table/diagram/etc.; carefully note all labels, keys, units, and any other explanatory details. The answer must directly restate some part of the data and/or text. See "Reading Graphs, Charts, Tables, and Other Figures" on p. 44.*

A Confused Relationships: (A) is probably here to trap untrained test-takers who haven't read the passage carefully, because the passage includes the idea of recipients' appreciation (even though the passage actually says there's no strong correlation between a giver's prediction of a recipient's level of appreciation and the actual appreciation felt by the recipient). As trained test-takers, we look at the graph and see that there's no consistent relationship among the bars that represent the givers' perceptions and the recipients' appreciation: the two dark bars show that the givers and recipients are comparatively far apart when it comes to the less expensive gift, while the two light bars show that the givers and recipients are a bit closer together when it comes to more expensive gifts. On top of that, the value for the givers is lower than the value for the receivers when we look at the darker bars, but higher than the value for the receivers for the lighter bars. In short, there's no way we can say that the values for givers are based on the values for receivers when we look at the graph, so this choice must be wrong.

B ✓ Correct: Looking at the bars related to the givers' expectations (which are the two bars to the left in the graph), we can see that the darker bar (relating to a less expensive gift) is smaller than the lighter bar (which relates to a more expensive gift). Since givers expect less appreciation for a less expensive gift and more appreciation for a more expensive gift, we see that givers' prediction of appreciation can be based on the expensiveness of the gift, just as (B) describes, so (B) is right.

C   Reasonable, but not in the Figure: We might imagine that a person giving a gift would allow her own desire for the gift to have an impact on how much she expects someone else to appreciate it. But the graph doesn't contain any information about how much the giver wants the gift, so (C) can't possibly be restated by the figure—which means it must be wrong.

D   Reasonable, but not in the Figure: We might imagine that a person's relationship with the recipient could have an impact on how much he expects the recipient to appreciate the gift. But this graph doesn't contain any information about the relationship between the giver and the receiver, so (D) can't be restated by the text, which means it can't be correct.

Test 1, Question 21   **TYPE: FIGURE**

ⓘ *The prompt refers to a graph/table/diagram/etc.; carefully note all labels, keys, units, and any other explanatory details. The answer must directly restate some part of the data and/or text. See "Reading Graphs, Charts, Tables, and Other Figures" on p.44.*

Subjective Phrases to Ignore: "likely"

A ✓   Correct: The idea of an "inability to shift perspective" is restated multiple times in the text. One example is in lines 28-32: "This 'deadweight loss' suggests that gift-givers are not very good at predicting what gifts others will appreciate. That in itself is not surprising to social psychologists. Research has found that people often struggle to take account of others' perspectives..." Another example appears in lines 66-68: "The notion of gift-givers and gift-recipients being unable to account for the other party's perspective seems puzzling..." The authors make it clear that givers and receivers have different ideas about how much a gift will be appreciated because people in either role fail to understand the perspective of the people in the other role, which is exactly what this choice says.

B   Literary Interpretation: The beginning of this passage mentions the "$30 billion" (4) that Americans spent at retail stores in December of the previous year, and an untrained test-taker might think of that number as evidence of a "materialistic culture" as described in this answer choice. But the text never actually restates the idea of people being materialistic at all, and it certainly gives no evidence to support the word "increasingly" in this choice—in order for the word "increasingly" to be appropriate here, the text would have to show not only that people were materialistic in the first place, but that they were *more* materialistic now than they used to be.

C   Confused Relationships: The text mentions that some people "dread the thought of buying gifts" (14), but the idea of actual opposition to gift-giving doesn't appear in the passage—there's never a point where the authors say something like "some people even think that gift-giving should be abolished entirely," or anything like that. Further, there's nothing in the text that restates the idea that feelings toward gift-giving are "growing," "increasing," or changing in any other kind of way, which is another reason that (C) and (B) must be wrong.

D   Confused Relationships: As we saw in the discussion of choice (A) above, the authors clearly mention that people have a difficult time understanding each other's perspectives when it comes to gift-giving, but this isn't the same thing as saying that they misunderstand each other's intentions. While "intentions" and "perspective" might seem like similar ideas to an untrained test-taker who doesn't bother to consider the passage carefully, trained test-takers will notice the difference between those ideas in the context of the passage: the passage never mentions either gift-givers or recipients attempting to understand the goals or motivations of other people, which is what a discussion of "intentions" would require. We can therefore see that (D) isn't restated anywhere in the passage.

Test 1, Question 22   **TYPE: CITATION QUESTION**

ⓘ *The question includes a citation from the text. The answer must be directly restated or demonstrated in the cited text, or in the text closely surrounding the cited text. See the general process for answering SAT Reading questions on p. 71.*

A   Confused Relationships: The text mentions that the molecule DNA "is a very long chain" (3-4), but it never makes any connection between the length of DNA and whether an organism has a spinal column. Line 3 describes "a very long chain, the backbone of which..." The phrase "of which" refers to the phrase "long chain," which means we are talking about the backbone of a chain, not the backbone of an organism. Line 39 mentions "the phosphate-sugar backbone of our model...," which, again, clearly indicates that the "backbone" being discussed is part of the model, and not part of an organism. Since the text never mentions the spinal column of an organism, (A) can't be restating anything in the text, so it can't be correct.

B ✓   Correct: This answer is correct because it restates the text. In lines 2-4 the text says "the molecule is a very long chain, the backbone of which consists of a regular alternation of sugar and phosphate groups." The word "regular" in this context means that something repeats systematically or predictably, so a "regular alternation of sugar and phosphate groups" is a consistent pattern of sugars alternating with phosphate groups; these are the "repeating units" mentioned in the answer choice. We can also tell that the phrase "main structure" directly reflects the passage because the word "backbone" (3) itself can indicate the main structure of a thing, and because the passage tells us that other things are attached to the sugars in variable ways, which means the sugars and phosphates are the main part of the structure. This idea is repeated in lines 39 and 40 when the "phosphate-sugar backbone" is again described as "completely regular."

C   **Off by One or Two Words:** The words "entirely" and "or" combine to make this choice incorrect. Line 4 says the chain "consists of a regular alternation of sugar and phosphate groups," and line 39 refers to a "phosphate-sugar backbone;" both of these phrases make it clear that the backbone consists of sugars *and* phosphates, not one or the other.

D   **Confused Relationships:** The "backbone" in line 3 is said to consist "of a regular alternation of sugar and phosphate groups." Later on we see that "to each sugar is attached a nitrogenous base" (5). In other words, the backbone is made of sugars and phosphate groups, and nitrogenous bases are things that are attached to the sugars in that backbone. The text makes it clear that the nitrogenous bases aren't even part of the backbone, so we have nothing in the text to say that the word "backbone" as described in the prompt is related to nitrogenous bases being the main structural unit of DNA.

| **Test 1, Question 23** | **TYPE: BEST EVIDENCE** |

ⓘ *The answer must restate or demonstrate the relevant statement. See "What about "Best Evidence" Questions?" on page 72.*

A   **Confused Relationships:** This citation describes a nitrogenous base attaching to a sugar, but that doesn't mean the bases can't *also* pair randomly with other bases, as the student in the prompt claims. So this choice doesn't contradict the student's claim, which means it's not the correct answer.

B   **Confused Relationships:** This citation refers to the sequence of bases "along the chain," not the way that the bases pair with other bases, so it would be possible for the student's claim to be true even if the claim in this answer choice is also true, which means this choice isn't a contradiction of the student's claim.

C   **Confused Relationships:** This citation describes the pairs of nitrogenous bases bonding together, but it doesn't say whether that happens randomly or not, which means this choice doesn't contradict the claim about the bases bonding randomly.

D✓   **Correct:** This citation specifically says that "one member of a pair must be a purine and the other a pyrimidine," which contradicts the claim that the bases pair randomly, because it establishes some rules for the pairing.

| **Test 1, Question 24** | **TYPE: CITATION QUESTION** |

ⓘ *The question includes a citation from the text. The answer must be directly restated or demonstrated in the cited text, or in the text closely surrounding the cited text. See the general process for answering SAT Reading questions on p. 71.*

A   **Confused Relationships:** Lines 1-2 say, "the chemical formula of deoxyribonucleic acid (DNA) is now well established," and lines 16-17 mention that there's "only one chain in the chemical formula." Neither of these phrases expresses the idea that the chemical formula is a "feature of biological interest," which means (A) isn't restating the citation, so (A) is wrong.

B   **Confused Relationships:** Lines 14-15 describe how "two chains are both coiled around a common fiber axis," but this doesn't restate or demonstrate that the axis is a "feature of biological interest" as the prompt requires, so (B) is wrong.

C   **Confused Relationships:** The "X-ray evidence" (18-19) is mentioned in the citation as something that supports the idea of there being two chains in one molecule, but the X-ray evidence itself isn't described in the passage as a feature of biological interest. As we'll see below in the explanation for (D), the two chains themselves are the "feature...of biological interest" in the passage, while the X-ray evidence just indicates that the two chains probably exist.

D✓   **Correct:** Lines 12-14 say that "the first feature of our structure which is of biological interest is that it consists not of one chain, but of two." So we know that the "feature of biological interest" is the fact that the DNA consists of two chains, which is an exact restatement of this answer choice, so we know that (D) is correct.

| **Test 1, Question 25** | **TYPE: PURPOSE OF CITED TEXT** |

ⓘ *The prompt asks about the purpose or role of a part of the text. The correct answer must be accurately restated or described by the relevant text, with no interpretation. See "What about "Purpose" Questions?" on p.74.*

Subjective Phrases to Ignore: "main"

A   **Confused Relationships:** The author mentions "density" and "X-ray evidence" (18-19), and says they suggest "very strongly that there are two" chains. Lines 43-45 mention the idea of carrying "genetical information." But nothing in the text connects the idea of the density and the X-ray evidence *themselves* with the idea of carrying "genetical information."

B   **Confused Relationships:** A "nucleotide" is defined in lines 10-11, and the text makes no further mention of nucleotides or of any alternate hypothesis about the composition of nucleotides, so (B) can't possibly be restating an idea from the text.

C✓   **Correct:** The author mentions "the density" and the "X-ray evidence" (18-19) and he says they suggest "very strongly that there are two" chains. The word "suggests" in this context is a restatement of the phrase "provide support for" in (C), and the "claim about the number of chains" in (C) is the claim that "there are two" in line 19, so we see that (C) and the relevant part of the passage restate each other. This means (C) must be correct.

D   **Off by One or Two Words:** We have to be very careful with (D), because it will fool a lot of untrained test-takers who don't read carefully! The problem with (D) is the word "confirms," because the text only says the combination of the X-ray evidence and density "suggests very strongly" that there are two chains in the structure even though there's only one chain in the formula. This is the kind of small difference in meaning that we trained test-takers are always on the lookout for!

ℹ️ *The question includes a citation from the text. The answer must be directly restated or demonstrated in the cited text, or in the text closely surrounding the cited text. See the general process for answering SAT Reading questions on p. 71.*

Subjective Phrases to Ignore: "implies"

A **Confused Relationships:** The text talks about pairing purines and/or pyrimidines "between the two chains" (28-29). We know the text doesn't talk about whether such a pair would fit in "the space between a sugar and a phosphate group" as (A) requires, because, as we can see in the first paragraph, a sugar and a phosphate group would be *next to each other in one chain* of DNA, but the citation in lines 29-30 is clearly talking about the room necessary to "bridge between the two chains."

B ✓ **Correct:** The text says that a pair consisting of a purine and a pyrimidine can "bridge between the two chains" (28-29), but a "pair...of two purines" wouldn't have enough "room" (29-30). That means a pair of purines must be larger than a purine and a pyrimidine—if two purines can't fit in a space where a purine and a pyrimidine can fit, then the two purines must be bigger than the purine and the pyrimidine. Since (B) directly restates the relevant portion of the text, it's right.

C **Confused Relationships:** This choice makes a comparison between a pair of pyrimidines and a pair of purines, but the cited text only compares the size of a pair of purines to the size of a pair consisting of a purine and a pyrimidine—so we can't make any conclusions about the statement in this answer choice, based on the passage.

D **Confused Relationships:** This choice has the same basic problem we saw in (C). The cited text only compares the size of a pair of purines to a pair consisting of a purine and a pyrimidine, so we can't use that citation to make any conclusions about a statement comparing the size of a pair of pyrimidines to the size of a pair consisting of a purine and a pyrimidine.

ℹ️ *The prompt asks about the purpose or role of a part of the text. The correct answer must be accurately restated or described by the relevant text, with no interpretation. See "What about "Purpose" Questions?" on p.74.*

Subjective Phrases to Ignore: "mainly"

A **Confused Relationships:** The author mentions a "nucleotide" (11), but never says anything about the percentage of molecules of DNA for which the sequences of nucleotides are known, so the word "most" in (A) isn't restating the text.

B **Off by One or Two Words:** The text does say, "any sequence...can fit into the structure" (40-41). But the word "counter" in this context indicates the idea of contradicting something (as in the word "counterattack" or the phrase "counter offer"), and nothing in the text contradicts the idea of the bases occurring in any order. So the word "counter" makes this wrong.

C **In the Wrong Part of the Text:** Many untrained test-takers will fall for this choice because they'll remember reading something about the regularity of the phosphate-sugar backbone in the text, and because they won't bother to go back to the citation and verify what's actually going on in the relevant part of the passage. It's true that the complete regularity of the "phosphate-sugar backbone" is mentioned in lines 39-40, but the prompt cites lines 47-49, which occur later in the paragraph and which talk about the "order of the bases on one of the pair of chains" (45-46). So we can't say the quoted words in the prompt describe the phosphate-sugar backbone, as (C) would require. (See the explanation for (D) below.)

D ✓ **Correct:** Every part of (D) restates an element of the passage that's directly relevant to the citation in the prompt, so (D) is right. To find the relevant part of the text, we should note that the word "exact" in the citation modifies the phrase "order of the bases on the other [chain]" (47-48); the word "specific" in the citation describes the "pairing" (48) of bases on the two chains; the word "complement" describes how one chain of a DNA molecule relates to the other, and is the "feature which suggests how [DNA] might duplicate itself" (50-51). All of this shows that the cited words in the prompt are talking about "how the...molecule might duplicate itself" (50-51) by relying on the way "one chain is...the complement of the other" (49) in terms of the "specific pairing" (48) of the bases, which is restated and demonstrated exactly in (D): "replicate" and "copy" in the choice are synonyms of "duplicate" (51), and the "template" from the choice is the "complement" in line 49.

ℹ️ *The prompt refers to a graph/table/diagram/etc.; carefully note all labels, keys, units, and any other explanatory details. The answer must directly restate some part of the data and/or text. See "Reading Graphs, Charts, Tables, and Other Figures" on p.44.*

A **Confused Relationships:** This is the answer an untrained test-taker could get if he thought guanine and cytosine were purines, instead of adenine and guanine.

B **Confused Relationships:** This answer could be the result of incorrectly thinking cytosine and thymine were purines, instead of adenine and guanine; it could also be the result of misreading the question and thinking it was asking about pyrimidines in yeast DNA, rather than purines.

C ✓ **Correct:** As explained in the Notes section of this walkthrough, we know that adenine and guanine are purines. With that in mind, we can see that yeast has 18.7% guanine and 31.3% adenine, so (C) is correct.

D **Confused Relationships:** (D) could reflect thinking that adenine and thymine were purines, instead of adenine and guanine.

Note This question will confuse a lot of untrained test-takers because the table doesn't mention "purines" anywhere. But, as trained test-takers, we know not to panic if something like this happens, because we know the SAT must provide all the necessary information to answer a Reading question with no interpretation on our part. We might notice the prompt says the answer is "based on the table and passage;" sure enough, if we look in the passage, we see that "adenine and guanine—are purines" (7), which means the correct answer will reflect the percentages of adenine and guanine in yeast according to the table. As trained test-takers, we should also notice that the answer choices contain most possible combinations of two numbers from the row of data that relates to yeast in the table, which clearly indicates the College Board is hoping we'll either misread the table, or misread which bases are purines. When we notice this kind of trap being set, we should be reminded to make sure we read extremely carefully!

| **Test 1, Question 29** | **TYPE: FIGURE** |

The next question is a "best evidence" question referring back to this question; you may choose to consider the citations in the choices for the next question when answering this one if you want. See "Is there a 'best evidence' shortcut?" on page 72 for more.

ⓘ *The prompt refers to a graph/table/diagram/etc.; carefully note all labels, keys, units, and any other explanatory details. The answer must directly restate some part of the data and/or text. See "Reading Graphs, Charts, Tables, and Other Figures" on p.44.*

A ✓ **Correct:** The passage says in lines 34-35 that the only possible base pairs are "adenine with thymine, and guanine with cytosine." This fits with the information in the table, because the percentages for adenine and thymine for any given organism are very close, and the percentages of guanine and cytosine for any given organism are very close. For example, for a chicken, adenine and thymine are 28.0% and 28.4% respectively, while guanine and cytosine are 22.0% and 21.6% respectively. This pattern holds true for all the data, which makes this choice correct.

B **Confused Relationships:** The data do support the "authors' proposed pairings of bases in DNA," but not for the reason described in this answer choice. As discussed in the explanation for choice (A), the percentages of adenine and thymine are close to each other, as well as the percentages of guanine and cytosine; the percentages of adenine and guanine are NOT close to each other, nor are the percentages of cytosine and thymine.

C **Direct Contradiction:** The fact that "the percentage of adenine is closest to the percentage of thymine, and the percentage of guanine is closest to the percentage of cytosine" is true...but it's proof that the data *do* support the "authors' proposed pairings of bases in DNA." The passage says in lines 34-35 that the only possible base pairs are "adenine with thymine, and guanine with cytosine," so, if the authors' argument is correct, we'd expect the percentages of adenine and thymine to be close to each other, and the percentages of guanine and cytosine to be close to each other, just as they are.

D **Confused Relationships:** (D) is wrong for two reasons: the data do support the "authors' proposed pairings of bases in DNA," and the statements about adenine, guanine, cytosine, and thymine in (D) don't reflect the table. See the explanation of (A) above for more details.

Note Many untrained test-takers will be intimidated by this question because the choices each take up 4 lines of text, which will make a lot of people think they need to keep 16 different lines of text in their memories in order to compare the choices and pick the best one. But, as trained test-takers, we should recognize that the choices only differ in two ways: whether they start with "yes" or "no," and whether they pair adenine with thymine or guanine (and cytosine with guanine or thymine). Once we recognize that those are the only differences among the choices, we have a much easier time identifying which combination of those options is correct. (Of course, the high degree of similarity among the choices should also remind us to be even more precise in our reading, because we see that the College Board is trying to set us up to misread some small detail in the choices and pick the wrong one.)

| **Test 1, Question 30** | **TYPE: FIGURE / BEST EVIDENCE** |

ⓘ *The prompt refers to a graph/table/diagram/etc.; carefully note all labels, keys, units, and any other explanatory details. The answer must directly restate some part of the data and/or text. See "Reading Graphs, Charts, Tables, and Other Figures" on p.44. The answer must restate or demonstrate the relevant statement. See "What about 'Best Evidence' Questions?" on page 72.*

A ✓ **Correct:** The answer to question 29 said that percentages of adenine and thymine should be closest to each other, and percentages of guanine and cytosine should be closest to each other. These are the percentages from the table for cytosine and guanine, respectively, in sea urchin DNA, and they're close to each other, so they support the answer to 29.

B **Confused Relationships:** The answer to question 29 said that percentages of adenine and thymine should be closest to each other, and the percentages of guanine and cytosine should be closest to each other. These are the percentages from the table for cytosine and thymine in sea urchin DNA, so they don't give us enough information to support the correct answer to 29.

C **Confused Relationships:** The answer to question 29 said the percentages of adenine and thymine should be closest to each other, and the percentages of guanine and cytosine should be closest to each other. These are the percentages from the table for cytosine and adenine in sea urchin DNA, so they don't give us enough information to support the correct answer to 29.

D   Confused Relationships: The answer to question 29 said that percentages of adenine and thymine should be closest to each other, and the percentages of guanine and cytosine should be closest to each other. These are the percentages from the table for guanine and adenine in sea urchin DNA, so they don't give us enough information to support the right answer to question 29.

Note   One easy way to attack this question (or to check it) is to realize that the previous question depends on the idea of certain pairs of bases appearing in roughly equal amounts, and the correct answer to this question is the only choice that includes two numbers that are roughly equal.

Test 1, Question 31   TYPE: FIGURE

ⓘ *The prompt refers to a graph/table/diagram/etc.; carefully note all labels, keys, units, and any other explanatory details. The answer must directly restate some part of the data and/or text. See "Reading Graphs, Charts, Tables, and Other Figures" on p.44.*

Subjective Phrases to Ignore: "most"

A   Direct Contradiction: When we look at the table, we can see in the column labeled "adenine (%)" that the percentage of adenine in each organism's DNA varies from 26.8% to 33.2%, so we know the percentage varies, and (A) can't be correct.

B   Direct Contradiction: This choice is wrong for the same basic reason that (A) is wrong.

C   Barely Relevant: When we look at the table, we can see in the column labeled "adenine (%)" that the percentage of adenine in each organism's DNA varies from 26.8% to 33.2%, so we know that the percentage varies. But the cited text doesn't explain why the percentage should vary—that text only says that when adenine appears on one chain, its partner must be thymine. This doesn't tell us how much total adenine can appear in the entire chain.

D✓   Correct: When we look at the table, we can see in the column labeled "adenine (%)" that the percentage of adenine in each organism's DNA varies from 26.8% to 33.2%, so we know that the percentage varies. The cited text is directly relevant to this variation because it says that "many different permutations are possible," and looking at the previous sentence shows us that these "permutations" are the "sequence of the pairs of bases." Since the passage tells us there are many different ways to create a sequence of pairs of bases in DNA, we know that the amount of a particular nitrogenous base can vary from one organism to another.

Test 1, Question 32   TYPE: DESCRIBE THE PASSAGE

ⓘ *The prompt often mentions describing the passage, and usually doesn't include a line citation. The answer must still be restated or demonstrated by some specific part of the text, even if there's no citation. See "What about Questions Without Citations?" p. 72*

Subjective Phrases to Ignore: "main"

A   Literary Interpretation: The author describes things like "the procession of the sons of educated men" (10-11) and the fact that "the daughters of educated men have always done their thinking from hand to mouth" (64-66), but the passage never actually refers to anything as a "tradition" (or a "custom," a "habit, or any other equivalent word). Since the author never really mentions a tradition, she can't possibly be "emphasizing" the "value" of a tradition, as this choice would require.

B✓   Correct: The word "urgency" in this answer choice specifically restates the passage's statements that "we are pressed for time" (7-8) and that the audience has "very little time in which to answer" "very important questions" (48-49), and that "the moment is short" (57). The word "issue" in the answer choice refers to the "questions that we have to ask and answer" (50), which "are so important…that they may well change the lives of all men and women forever" (51-53). So we can see that this answer choice directly restates key portions of the passage, which means it must be correct.

C   Reasonable Statement Not in the Text: Many untrained test-takers who read this passage will mentally associate the subject matter with the ideas of discrimination and social inequality, but, as trained test-takers, we know that we have to confine our thinking to the words and phrases that are directly in the text. (C) uses the plural word "divisions," but there's only one division that's even alluded to in the passage, and it isn't presented as an issue of social classes or economic standing, but one of gender: the difference between the educational and professional opportunities for men and women. Further, the author doesn't use any phrases that "highlight…severity," as (C) would require: she never says anything like "and to make this injustice even worse…," or "this discrimination seems even sharper when we consider…."

D   Off by One or Two Words: The "undertaking" mentioned in the answer choice could refer to the idea of "join[ing] the procession" from lines 54-57: "do we wish to join that procession, or don't we? On what terms shall we join that procession? Above all, where is it leading us, the procession of educated men?" But the word "feasibility" in the choice refers to whether something can actually be done, and the author never asks anything like "can we do this?" or "is this possible?" Instead, she asks whether "we wish" (54) to do something. Since the word "feasibility" isn't restated in the passage, (D) must be wrong.

Test 1, Question 33   TYPE: DESCRIBE THE PASSAGE

ⓘ *The prompt often mentions describing the passage, and usually doesn't include a line citation. The answer must still be restated or demonstrated by some specific part of the text, even if there's no citation. See "What about Questions Without Citations?" p. 72*

A ✓   **Correct:** This choice restates the passage because the phrase "educated women" in the answer choice refers to an idea that appears throughout the passage. The author mentions "the procession of the sons of educated men...who have been educated at public schools and universities" (10-13); later, she says, "there...at the tail end of the procession, we go ourselves" (23-24). So the author has established that she's talking about women being educated at universities when she talks about women joining the procession. The phrase "face a decision" in the answer choice directly restates the portion of the passage in which the author asks her readers to decide whether "we wish to join that procession, or don't we? On what terms shall we join that procession? Above all, where is it leading us, the procession of educated men?" (54-57). The phrase "existing institutions" in (A) is a direct reference to the ideas of attending universities, speaking from a pulpit, joining the military, administering justice, and so on, from lines 30-42. Since every part of (A) is directly paralleled in the text, it's right.

B   **Reasonable Statement Not in the Text:** Some untrained test-takers will consider marking (B) because it seems historically plausible to them, and because some parts of the choice do reflect concepts in the passage. The text does mention the idea of women eventually having "positions of influence" (for example, it says they "may...speak from a pulpit" (33-34) or "dress in military uniform" (37-38) in a century or two). The text also mentions women in more traditional roles ("stir[ring] the pot" and "rock[ing] the cradle" (68-69), for example). But the text never says that the "only" way to have influence is to abandon traditional roles, so this choice must be wrong.

C   **Reasonable Statement Not in the Text:** Many untrained test-takers will simply assume that this answer choice is historically true, or at least that it would have seemed true to the author, without noticing that the choice isn't actually restated or demonstrated in the text, which means it must be wrong. The author never actually describes anything that could be called a "grave" or "continuing" effect of men having power, as (C) requires—in fact, the effects that she talks about are the possible future effects of women having power ("where...is it leading us, the procession of the sons of educated men?" (81-83)).

D   **Reasonable Statement Not in the Text:** Just as with (C), many untrained test-takers will assume that the concepts in this answer choice are true without noticing that the choice, on the whole, doesn't actually restate an idea from the passage, even if portions of the choice are similar to concepts mentioned in the passage. The text does describe the idea of "educated women" getting into "positions of power traditionally held by men," as (D) mentions ("we too can leave the house,...make money, administer justice..." (29-32)). And the text does say that some "questions...during this moment...may well change the lives of all men and women for ever" (50-53), which indicates a possible transformation of some kind. But the text never specifically says that the *positions themselves* will be transformed; it only says that people's lives in general *may well* be transformed. In other words, the text doesn't say that the job of being a businessperson or a judge will be different, only that women will do those jobs in addition to men doing them.

❚   Test 1, Question 34   TYPE: PURPOSE OF CITED TEXT

ⓘ *The prompt asks about the purpose or role of a part of the text. The correct answer must be accurately restated or described by the relevant text, with no interpretation. See "What about "Purpose" Questions?" on p.74.*

A   **Reasonable Statement Not in the Text:** Untrained test-takers might assume that a lot of women who are in the same situation together, as described in the explanation for choice (C), would eventually become friendly with one another—and that may well be the case, for all we know from the passage. But the author never actually says anything in the text about growing friendliness, as this answer choice would require. In order for (A) to be right, the text would need to say something like, "we used to be isolated from one another, but now we are increasingly joining together in friendship;" in other words, the text would have to describe some amount of friendliness among the women existing at one point, and then more friendliness existing among the women at a later point. None of that appears in the text.

B   **Reasonable Statement Not in the Text:** Untrained test-takers might assume it would be important for the women in the passage to be candid—that is, honest—with one another. But the author never discusses this idea, so (B) is wrong.

C ✓   **Correct:** Many untrained test-takers may assume that this choice can only be correct if we apply the kind of literary interpretation to the text that would be welcome in a literature class—in other words, if we take exactly the approach that I teach you to *avoid at all costs* when it comes to the SAT! But the correct answer to this question still depends on a literal and objective approach, just like the correct answer to every other question on the SAT. The word "solidarity" refers to a sense of togetherness; the pronoun "we" demonstrates that the speaker is including a set of people in the same group as herself—in other words, that the speaker and her audience are together when it comes to making the decisions in the text. Since the use of the pronoun "we" demonstrates the idea in (C) in a literal way, (C) is right.

D   **Reasonable Statement Not in the Text:** An untrained test-taker might imagine that it would be helpful for the women in the passage to respect each other, but the author never actually says anything about respect when she uses the word "we," so (D) must be wrong. The author does use the word "Madam" (62), and some untrained test-takers might think that's enough to make (D)

---

correct. But the prompt doesn't ask us about the use of the word "Madam," so the role of that word in the text is irrelevant to the question! There's nothing connecting the word "we" to the idea of respect, so (D) must be wrong.

Test 1, Question 35   **TYPE: DESCRIBE THE PASSAGE**

ⓘ *The prompt often mentions describing the passage, and usually doesn't include a line citation. The answer must still be restated or demonstrated by some specific part of the text, even if there's no citation. See "What about Questions Without Citations?" p. 72*

A   **Direct Contradiction:** The author specifically says the bridge shouldn't be used for "dreaming" (7) with the sentence "But not now" (7-8). So she doesn't want to use the bridge as a place for "fanciful reflection," which is a synonym for the idea of dreaming in the context of the passage. (A) was probably included to trap people who remembered reading something about reflecting on the bridge, but who failed to go back and re-check the text before marking an answer.

B ✔ **Correct:** The author says the bridge is "an admirable vantage ground for us to make a survey" (2-3); the phrase "good view" in (B) is a direct restatement of the phrase "admirable vantage point" from the text. She goes on to say "we are here [at the bridge] to consider facts; now we must fix our eyes upon the procession—the procession of the sons of educated men" (8-11). So she says the bridge is a good place to see something, and now that we're here on the bridge, we need to "fix our eyes on the procession...of the sons of educated men." Again, (B) is a word-for-word restatement of the text, so it's right.

C   **Reasonable Statement Not in the Text:** The author mentions that "Westminster and the Houses of Parliament" (6) are nearby, and an untrained test-taker might imagine that "historic episodes" have taken place at these locations—but the passage doesn't mention any historic episodes, so we know that this choice must be wrong.

D   **Literary Interpretation:** This might seem like the kind of thing that a Literature professor would happily accept from a student, but a trained test-taker can easily see that this choice doesn't restate the passage at all: the author never says that the bridge is a symbol, or a metaphor, or any other kind of abstract concept.

Test 1, Question 36   **TYPE: DESCRIBE THE PASSAGE**

The next question is a "best evidence" question referring back to this question; you may choose to consider the citations in the choices for the next question when answering this one if you want. See "Is there a 'best evidence' shortcut?" on page 72 for more.

ⓘ *The prompt often mentions describing the passage, and usually doesn't include a line citation. The answer must still be restated or demonstrated by some specific part of the text, even if there's no citation. See "What about Questions Without Citations?" p. 72*

A   **Barely Relevant:** The author does say something has changed about the procession in recent years, as described below for (D). But she doesn't say anything about the "practical influence" of this procession, so (A) must be wrong.

B   **Barely Relevant:** The word "pageant" (26) might make some untrained test-takers interpret the procession as a "celebration" or a "public" event of some kind, as (B) would require, but nothing in the text actually states that this procession is a "celebrated feature of English public life," so (B) must be wrong.

C   **Off by One or Two Words:** The text describes the men in this procession as the ones who are "ascending those pulpits, preaching, teaching, administering justice, practising [sic] medicine, transacting business, making money" (15-17), which indicates that they seem to have some amount of power and money—but this isn't the same thing as specifically calling them "the richest and most powerful men in England." As trained test-takers, we know that we can't pick an answer choice that mentions "the richest and most powerful men in England" unless the text specifically says something like "no man in England has more money or influence than these men."

D ✔ **Correct:** In describing the procession, the author says, "for the past twenty years or so,...there...we go ourselves" (19-24). If the procession was once just "the sons of educated men" (10-11), but "for the past twenty years or so" women are also in the procession, then the procession must have become less exclusive, because it now includes more types of people. So (D) is clearly demonstrated in the text.

Test 1, Question 37   **TYPE: BEST EVIDENCE**

ⓘ *The answer must restate or demonstrate the relevant statement. See "What about "Best Evidence" Questions?" on page 72.*

Subjective Phrases to Ignore: "best"

A   **Confused Relationships:** This may appear to support choice (C) in the previous question, but the fact that these men have some power and money isn't necessarily the same thing as calling them "the richest and most powerful men in England," so (C) isn't the answer to the previous question, and this choice must be wrong.

B   **Barely Relevant:** This text isn't really relevant to any answer choice from the previous question.

C ✔ **Correct:** This text demonstrates the exact concept from the right answer to question 36, as we just saw in that walkthrough.

D   **Literary Interpretation:** This text may seem to support the correct answer from the previous question, because it describes women doing jobs that used to be only available to men, which seems to be vaguely related to the idea of women joining the procession of educated men. But, as trained test-takers, we always need to think in terms of details, and the previous question asks about the *procession* itself, not about jobs that women might do someday. So this choice doesn't provide evidence that's directly relevant to the correct answer to the previous question, which makes it wrong.

| **Test 1, Question 38** | **TYPE: CITATION QUESTION** |

> *The next question is a "best evidence" question referring back to this question; you may choose to consider the citations in the choices for the next question when answering this one if you want. See "Is there a 'best evidence' shortcut?" on page 72 for more.*

ⓘ *The question includes a citation from the text. The answer must be directly restated or demonstrated in the cited text, or in the text closely surrounding the cited text. See the general process for answering SAT Reading questions on p. 71.*

A **Barely Relevant:** In order for the questions to be "controversial," there would have to be some statement to the effect that at least two sides had strongly differing opinions about the questions, but that isn't in the text. To be "threatening," there would have to be evidence that the questions make people think they're in danger, but that doesn't appear in the text either.

B **Off by One or Two Words:** The text clearly describes the questions as "weighty," because the author says they are "very important" (48), which means the same thing as "weighty." But the text doesn't say these questions are unanswerable—in fact, the author specifically refers to them as "questions that we have to ask and to answer" (50), so there's truly no basis in the text for saying the author thinks they can't be answered. Since part of (B) doesn't restate the passage, (B) is wrong.

C ✓ **Correct:** The author says the questions are "very important" (48), which means the same thing as "momentous," and that "we have very little time in which to answer them" (48-49), which is the same thing as saying they are "pressing." Since this answer choice directly restates the text, it must be correct.

D **Barely Relevant:** In order for the questions to be "provocative" for SAT purposes, there would have to be a statement in the text saying that they provoke strong reactions from people, but that isn't in the text. In order for them to be "mysterious," there would have to be some kind of question or mystery about what the questions are or what they mean, but that doesn't appear in the text either.

| **Test 1, Question 39** | **TYPE: BEST EVIDENCE** |

ⓘ *The answer must restate or demonstrate the relevant statement. See "What about "Best Evidence" Questions?" on page 72.*

Subjective Phrases to Ignore: "best"

A **Literary Interpretation:** This text just explains that the women are "on the bridge" to ask themselves "certain questions." The text doesn't say anything about the nature of those questions, so it can't contain the textual evidence for any of the answer choices in the previous question, which means it has to be wrong.

B ✓ **Correct:** As discussed in the walkthrough for question 38, this text restates the right answer to that question.

C **Literary Interpretation:** This text restates the idea that the questions are "pressing," but it doesn't restate the idea that they are "momentous," which means it doesn't provide evidence of every part of the right answer to the question 38, so it's wrong.

D **Barely Relevant:** This text isn't really relevant to the correct answer from 38, or to any answer choice from that question.

| **Test 1, Question 40** | **TYPE: CITATION QUESTION** |

ⓘ *The question includes a citation from the text. The answer must be directly restated or demonstrated in the cited text, or in the text closely surrounding the cited text. See the general process for answering SAT Reading questions on p. 71.*

Subjective Phrases to Ignore: "most closely"

A **Barely Relevant:** There isn't anything in the text to support the idea that the "sixpence" represents "tolerance." (A) was probably included because the College Board hopes that some untrained test-takers will simply assume that an author who endorses educational equality for women will also generally endorse tolerance, but trained test-takers know the correct answer needs to be restated or demonstrated by the relevant text.

B **Confused Relationships:** The author refers to the sixpence as "brand-new;" this is a direct statement that women have not always had the "sixpence," whatever the sixpence is. But the author never says that "knowledge" is something new for women to have, as (B) would require. So the sixpence must not represent knowledge. (This choice might still be tempting for some untrained test-takers because the text does say that women are now "at the tail end of the procession [of the sons of educated men]" (23-24); that is, women are now being "educated at public schools and universities" (13). So we're told that women have access to more *education* than they previously did—but the text never explicitly says education and knowledge are the same thing! If we think carefully about the meanings of "education" and "knowledge," we see that they describe different things, even if those things might be related: while many educated people do acquire knowledge, it's possible to go through the process of education without gaining knowledge, and it's possible to have knowledge without having been educated.)

C ✓ **Correct:** In lines 70 and 71, the author says that women have a "brand-new sixpence," and that "it falls to us now to go on thinking; how are we to spend that sixpence?" Lines 71-76 then describe different situations in which women should keep thinking about how "to spend that sixpence," including "taking part in" "ceremonies" and "making money out of" "professions." Earlier, in lines 12-17, the author had referred to professions as things that men had always done. Then, in lines 30-32, the author

---

indicated that women "no longer" had to watch from inside the home as men work; women can now "leave the house" and "make money." In short, the "sixpence" of these opportunities is "brand-new," and (C) is the only choice that mentions something else that the author says is new for women. Further, the different ways "to spend that sixpence" are all chances to do different things, and a chance to do something is an "opportunity," as this choice requires.

D   Barely Relevant: There's nothing in the text to support the idea that the "sixpence" represents "perspective." The only mention of something like perspective occurs in the description of the "vantage" in line 2, but the author never says anything to indicate the vantage and the sixpence are connected in her mind—the vantage is never described as new, like the sixpence, nor is the vantage mentioned in connection with the sixpence. So this choice must be wrong.

Note   It might seem tempting to think of this question as a "most nearly means" question, but I've classified it differently for two reasons. The most important one is that the prompt doesn't include the phrase "most nearly means." But it's also worth noting that none of the choices can be plugged directly into the passage without altering the meaning of the original text, as we can do with the right answer to a "most nearly means" question. (The reason for this is that the author is using "sixpence" in a metaphorical or figurative way, while "most nearly means" questions are based on words that are used literally.) But we still use the same process of careful, literal reading to find the answer, regardless of question type, and the right answer is still the only one that's directly, literally restated and/or demonstrated in the text! Keep this kind of thing in mind on test day. It doesn't really matter how you classify a question when you first see it; all that matters is that you stick to the game plan of reading literally and thinking very carefully about what the text says, without considering things that you think the author might be trying to imply. Also note that we were still able to answer this question with this literal-minded approach, even though the specific term mentioned in the prompt is being used figuratively in the passage—in other words, the author isn't literally referring to money when she uses the word "sixpence," but the right answer is still the only one that's demonstrated literally in the text.

Test 1, Question 41   **TYPE: CITATION QUESTION**

🛈 *The question includes a citation from the text. The answer must be directly restated or demonstrated in the cited text, or in the text closely surrounding the cited text. See the general process for answering SAT Reading questions on p. 71.*

Subjective Phrases to Ignore: "mainly"

A   Reasonable Statement Not in the Text: We know that the author thinks something "novel" is happening, because she refers to the "brand-new sixpence" that we discussed in answering the previous question, and "novel" is a synonym for "new." But we know from lines 63-70 that the author says women have always thought in the past, so the list of places to think in lines 72-76 can't reflect something novel, which means (A) is wrong.

B ✓ Correct: The author mentions many different settings where women need to think ("offices," "omnibuses," "standing in the crowd watching Coronations and Lord Mayor's Shows," "the gallery of the House of Commons," "the Law Courts," "at baptisms and marriages and funerals" (72-76)), and then says women must "never cease from thinking." The phrase "critical reflection" in (B) is a direct restatement of the idea of "thinking" from the text; the word "pervasive" in (B) refers to the idea of spreading to many places, which is demonstrated by the author's list of all the places where thinking needs to happen.

C   Reasonable Statement Not in the Text: An untrained test-taker might assume that the author believes the issues of the day are complex, but the author never actually says anything about complexity, sophistication, or any other word with a similar meaning. As trained test-takers, we realize that (C) isn't restating anything from the text, which means it has to be wrong.

D   Reasonable Statement Not in the Text: Many untrained test-takers might assume the author thinks women would enjoy new opportunities, but the cited text doesn't actually say anything about "enjoy[ment]," as (D) would require, so it's wrong.

Note   The prompt for this question cites a sentence whose punctuation would be considered strange by today's standards, but it's still pretty easy to understand the writer's meaning if we ignore the strangeness of the punctuation and focus on the words themselves. Keep this kind of thing in mind on test day when you're confronted by older passages with strange punctuation.

Test 1, Question 42   **TYPE: PURPOSE OF CITED TEXT**

🛈 *The prompt asks about the purpose or role of a part of the text. The correct answer must be accurately restated or described by the relevant text, with no interpretation. See "What about "Purpose" Questions?" on p.74.*

Subjective Phrases to Ignore: "primarily"

A   Reasonable Statement Not in the Text: An untrained test-taker might assume that mining in space would require advances in technology, but the idea of technological advancements isn't explicitly discussed in or around lines 9-17. (For example, the text doesn't specifically say one company's "prospecting telescopes" (12) are an advancement over existing technology, nor that those telescopes are necessary for space-mining; the same issue exists with the other technology mentioned.)

B ✓ **Correct:** The citation begins with the phrase "the forum;" as trained test-takers, we know that we need to figure out which forum is being mentioned. We see that the phrase refers to the "first-of-its-kind forum on mining beyond Earth" (2-3). The phrase "first-of-its-kind" indicates that there was never a forum on space mining before; since we know from the passage that there was one recently, we know that interest in space mining must be growing (from a level of zero interest at one point, to some interest at this point). After this forum appears in the citation, we see a mention of three companies created in 2012 ("Planetary Resources" (11), "Deep Space Industries" (13), and "Golden Spike" (16)) that are all connected to space-mining. These three companies related to space mining are clearly "evidence of...interest in space mining" mentioned in (B); the fact that the companies are new is evidence that the interest is "growing," which is also required by (B). Since every part of (B) points directly to something we see in the passage, we know it's right.

C **Wrong Part of the Passage:** (C) might tempt some untrained test-takers because the text says that "the first space miners won't just enrich themselves" (23-24). But there's nothing in the citation that refers to anything in lines 23 and 24, and the fact that three space mining companies were created in 2012 (which is what appears in the citation) doesn't specifically indicate that there are "large profits to be made from space mining"—in fact, the profits aren't discussed at all in the citation.

D **Confused Relationships:** The cited text never mentions how many ways there are to mine things in space. For all we know from the citation, all three companies plan to use the same method of space mining. Since (D) isn't restated or demonstrated by an idea from the citation, it can't be correct.

| **Test 1, Question 43** | **TYPE: DESCRIBE THE PASSAGE** |

> *The next question is a "best evidence" question referring back to this question; you may choose to consider the citations in the choices for the next question when answering this one if you want. See "Is there a 'best evidence' shortcut?" on page 72 for more.*

ⓘ *The prompt often mentions describing the passage, and usually doesn't include a line citation. The answer must still be restated or demonstrated by some specific part of the text, even if there's no citation. See "What about Questions Without Citations?" p. 72*

A ✓ **Correct:** The text mentions three space mining companies in the third paragraph, and then says "these firms may be meeting earthly demands for precious metals, such as platinum and gold, and the rare earth elements vital for personal electronics, such as yttrium and lanthanum" (18-22). The word "materials" in the choice restates the phrases "precious metals" (19) and "rare earth elements" (20); the phrase "important to Earth's economy" in (A) restates the phrase "earthly demand," as well as the idea of "vital[ity]" (20). Since this choice directly restates elements of Passage 1, it must be right.

B **Confused Relationships:** The text says that space mining firms "may be meeting earthly demands for precious metals, such as platinum and gold" (18-20), and the text does refer to the idea of "enrich[ment]" (24), which could involve the idea of a *person's* or a *company's* level of *wealth* rising. But the text doesn't specifically say that anything will "raise the value" of *metals* "on Earth," which is what the answer choice would require.

C **Off by One or Two Words:** An untrained test-taker might imagine that making space mining a reality would involve the creation of "unanticipated technological innovations" as (C) requires, but that specific idea doesn't actually appear in Passage 1, so (C) can't be correct. Passage 1 does discuss some technology that could be involved in space-mining (24-45), but there's nothing in the text to restate or demonstrate the word "unanticipated"—if anything, the discussion demonstrates that the author is anticipating the technologies already.

D **Reasonable Statement Not in the Text:** An untrained test-taker might assume that scientific understanding of the resources involved in space-mining would evolve, but nothing in the text specifically states that. Since this answer choice doesn't restate anything in the text, it can't be correct.

| **Test 1, Question 44** | **TYPE: BEST EVIDENCE** |

ⓘ *The answer must restate or demonstrate the relevant statement. See "What about "Best Evidence" Questions?" on page 72.*

Subjective Phrases to Ignore: "best"

A ✓ **Correct:** As we discussed in the walkthrough for question 43, choice (A) in 43 restates the text in this choice.

B **Direct Contradiction:** If an untrained test-taker failed to read this text carefully, then this choice might appear to support the correct answer for the previous question. But that answer mentioned "Earth's economy," while this text discusses "an off-planet economy free of any bonds with Earth."

C **Confused Relationships:** This choice might seem to support choice (D) from the previous question in the eyes of an untrained test-taker, but the idea that water from other worlds could be "the most desired commodity" in space isn't specifically the same thing as saying that space-mining "could change scientists' understanding of space resources." If scientists are already saying that water could be a very valuable resource in space, then they already understand this about water—space mining isn't being presented as something that would change that understanding. It would have been true to say that the same resources could have differing values depending on whether they're on Earth or in space, but that isn't what choice (D) from the previous question says, so that choice is wrong, and so is this one.

D Confused Relationships: Untrained test-takers could mistakenly conclude that this choice restates (D) from the previous question, but (as discussed in the explanation for (D) from the previous question) listing different ways that resources in space could be used isn't specifically the same thing as saying that space mining "could change scientists' understanding of space resources." That makes (D) wrong in the previous question, which means this choice has to be wrong.

Test 1, Question 45 — TYPE: WORD MOST NEARLY MEANS

The prompt includes the phrase "most nearly means" and the choices are usually one- or two-word phrases. The answer is either restated or demonstrated by an idea from the surrounding text. Remember you can work around unknown words, and be ready to guess/skip and focus on other questions if you don't know the words. See "What about "Most Nearly Means" Questions?" on p.73.

Subjective Phrases to Ignore: "most nearly"

A ("Within a few decades, these firms may be meeting earthly <u>offers</u> for precious metals, such as platinum and gold…") Direct Contradiction: The passage doesn't say the earth is "offering" any precious metals, or that it could make sense for the firms to "meet" those "offers," which is what this choice would require. In fact, as the explanation for choice (D) shows, "demands" means something like "desires," which is essentially the opposite of "offers."

B ("Within a few decades, these firms may be meeting earthly <u>claims</u> for precious metals, such as platinum and gold…") Confused Relationships: (B) might be tempting to an untrained test-taker, because the idea of "claiming" something for yourself is kind of similar to the idea of "demanding" something, and because some test-takers may be familiar with the term "claim" in the context of mining and prospecting. But there isn't anything in the passage that actually says the Earth is "claiming" any precious metals, or that it could make sense for the firms to "meet" those "claims," as (B) would require.

C ("Within a few decades, these firms may be meeting earthly <u>inquiries</u> for precious metals, such as platinum and gold…") Literary Interpretation: (C) might tempt some untrained test-takers because an "inquiry" is kind of like a "demand" in some contexts: both can involve the idea of asking for or about something. But the text doesn't restate or demonstrate the idea of "inquiring" for precious metals, so (C) is wrong.

D✓ ("Within a few decades, these firms may be meeting earthly <u>desires</u> for precious metals, such as platinum and gold…") Correct: This is the only choice that's demonstrated by concepts from the cited sentence, such as the words "precious" (19) and "vital" (20), both of which have to do with the idea of being wanted, needed, or desired. So (D) is right.

Test 1, Question 46 — TYPE: PURPOSE OF CITED TEXT

The prompt asks about the purpose or role of a part of the text. The correct answer must be accurately restated or described by the relevant text, with no interpretation. See "What about "Purpose" Questions?" on p.74.

A Confused Relationships: This choice might be tempting for an untrained test-taker because the previous paragraph does include a comparison between the worth of gold and water in the desert. But that comparison ends in the previous paragraph, and the cited text doesn't mention gold or deserts at all.

B Confused Relationships: This choice might tempt an untrained test-taker because the previous paragraph does ask a question about the relative worth of gold and water in the desert. But that question is answered in lines 33-34, which is before the citation in the prompt, and the author never says whether the answer to the question was something unexpected or not: "Gold is useless. Water will let you live." Since (B) doesn't restate what appears in the citation, it must be wrong.

C✓ Correct: This answer choice restates exactly what happens in the citation. The "claim" in the "previous paragraph" that's referred to in the answer choice is expressed in this sentence: "'water will let you live'" (34). The "hypothetical examples" of this claim that are required by the answer choice appear in lines 35-40: "Water ice from the moon's poles could be sent to astronauts on the International Space Station for drinking or as a radiation shield" and "splitting water into oxygen and hydrogen makes spacecraft fuel." Since water can be used for drinking, or for a shield, or to make fuel, we see that it would hypothetically help people in space to live, which supports the claim in the previous paragraph. So (C) is right.

D Off by One or Two Words: This paragraph does discuss ways that water could be used in space, which is relevant to the concepts from the previous paragraph, as we just saw in our discussion of (C). But the previous paragraph doesn't make any kind of "proposal," which is what this answer choice would require, so this choice can't be correct.

Test 1, Question 47 — TYPE: DESCRIBE THE PASSAGE

The prompt often mentions describing the passage, and usually doesn't include a line citation. The answer must still be restated or demonstrated by some specific part of the text, even if there's no citation. See "What about Questions Without Citations?" p. 72

A Confused Relationships: Passage 2 says, "it may be difficult to persuade the public that such barren environments are worth preserving" (68-69). That means it could be hard to convince people to worry about environmental concerns in space—but this isn't the same thing as saying space mining will "encourage humanity's reckless treatment of the environment." Encouraging bad treatment of the environment means actively convincing or persuading people to damage the environment, which isn't what the authors describe.

B ✓ **Correct:** The authors say, "space mining seems to sidestep most environmental concerns…But its consequences…merit careful consideration" (54-59). Saying that the consequences of space mining "merit careful consideration" is the same as saying the effect of space mining "should be thoughtfully considered," so this choice is correct.

C **Confused Relationships:** Passage 2 mentions "bringing celestial riches down to Earth" (48-49) and "mineral bounty" that "could enrich us all" (51-52). But it says that these things "are disappearing on Earth," as this choice would require.

D **Direct Contradiction:** Passage 2 mentions "celestial riches" that "no doubt…will make a few billionaires even wealthier" (48), as well as "mineral bounty" (51) and "space's riches" (64). The passage repeatedly connects the ideas of space and wealth, and never says anyone disagrees on the "commercial viability" of space mining.

Test 1, Question 48	TYPE: WORD MOST NEARLY MEANS

ℹ *The prompt includes the phrase "most nearly means" and the choices are usually one- or two-word phrases. The answer is either restated or demonstrated by an idea from the surrounding text. Remember you can work around unknown words, and be ready to guess/skip and focus on other questions if you don't know the words. See "What about "Most Nearly Means" Questions?" on p.73.*

Subjective Phrases to Ignore: "most nearly"

A ✓ ("History suggests that those will be hard lines to <u>maintain</u>, and it may be difficult to persuade the public that such barren environments are worth preserving.") **Correct:** As trained test-takers, we know that we need to understand what the phrase "those…lines" (67) is referring to, since "those…lines" are the things being "held" in the citation from the prompt. We also know that we sometimes need to read the line or two before and after a citation to get some indication of what the citation means. So we'll look back at the previous sentence or two in order to see what the sentence in the citation is talking about, and we'll also look at the rest of the cited sentence. When we look back, we see that "some will argue that space's 'magnificent desolation' is not ours to despoil, just as they argue that our own planet's poles should remain pristine" (60-63), and "others will suggest that glutting ourselves on space's riches is not an acceptable alternative to developing more sustainable ways of earthly life" (63-66). These two ideas—the "argu[ment]" and "suggest[ion]"— seem like they might be "those…lines" mentioned in the cited text. When we look forward from the cited text and read the rest of the sentence after the word "hold," we see this: "and it may be difficult to persuade the public that such barren environments are worth preserving" (68-69). So the two ideas from the previous sentences are about protecting the environment in space, and the cited sentence says it will be hard to "persuade" people "that such barren environments are worth preserving." At this point, we start to see that the idea of it being "difficult" to "persuade" people about "preserv[ation]" is a direct parallel or restatement of the idea that it will be "hard" to "hold" the "lines" about preservation from the previous paragraph. So we can now see that the right answer will be a word that can have the same meaning as the word "persuade" in the context of the sentence. (A) works for this reason: the idea of "maintain[ing]" a line or "maintain[ing]" a position can refer to the idea of putting forth an argument or continuing to believe and support something in the face of opposition or disagreement.

B ("History suggests that those will be hard lines to <u>grip</u>, and it may be difficult to persuade the public that such barren environments are worth preserving.") **Reasonable Statement Not in the Text:** In another context, "grip" and "hold" could both describe physically grasping something. But the text doesn't restate or demonstrate that idea, so (B) can't be right.

C ("History suggests that those will be hard lines to <u>restrain</u>, and it may be difficult to persuade the public that such barren environments are worth preserving.") **Reasonable Statement Not in the Text:** In another context, "restrain" and "hold" could both describe physically stopping someone from doing something, but the passage doesn't restate or demonstrate that idea, so this answer can't be correct.

D ("History suggests that those will be hard lines to <u>withstand</u>, and it may be difficult to persuade the public that such barren environments are worth preserving.") **Direct Contradiction:** Inserting the word "withstand" where the word "hold" appears might give the impression that the authors are suggesting we fight back against the ideas from the previous paragraph, but the rest of the text indicates that the authors are discussing the likelihood of being able to "persuade the public" of the ideas in the previous paragraph, rather than the likelihood of having to fight against those ideas, as (D) might require.

Test 1, Question 49	TYPE: PAIRED PASSAGES

ℹ *The prompt also asks how someone would respond to a claim or argument. The correct answer restates a position that's already stated in the passage. See "What about Paired Passages?" on p.76.*

Subjective Phrases to Ignore: "best"

A **Barely Relevant:** The central claim of Passage 1 is that space mining companies soon "may be meeting earthly demands for precious metals … and [some] rare earth elements" (18-20), and that they will even "build an off-planet economy free of any bonds with Earth, in which the materials extracted and processed from the moon and asteroids are delivered for space-based projects" (25-28). Passage 2 cautions that the consequences of space mining "merit careful consideration" (57-59). In order for Passage 2 to refute Passage 1, it would have to be the case that Passage 2 contained statements that specifically contradicted statements from Passage 1. In this case, that would mean that Passage 2 would have to say that the kinds of mining projects and economies described in Passage 1 weren't going to happen in the first place, since Passage 1 says they *will* happen. Since Passage 2 never directly contradicts a statement in Passage 1, we know this choice is wrong.

B   **Barely Relevant:** The only concrete example or illustration in Passage 2 is a discussion of a situation in which potential space-miners would not want to be regulated (79-83)...but this example doesn't "illustrate" anything that was discussed in Passage 1, as (B) requires! Passage 1 describes some potential directions for space mining and the engineering problems surrounding it, but Passage 1 never specifically indicates that space-mining companies don't want to be regulated.

C   **Barely Relevant:** Passage 2 doesn't argue against the practicality of any proposals from Passage 1, so this choice is wrong. In fact, Passage 1 doesn't actually make any proposals in the first place—it simply discusses the emergence of space mining, and what might come of that. (In order to propose something, as (C) requires, Passage 1 would need to say something like "space-mining companies should aggressively pursue these new opportunities," but there's no such statement in the passage.)

D ✓ **Correct:** The author of Passage 1 writes about different groups "working to make space mining a reality" (8), and then discusses the possible results of space mining, like acquiring "precious metals" (19) and "rare earth elements" (20), and the creation of "an off-planet economy" (25); these could all be called "developments," as the answer choice requires. The authors of Passage 2 then caution that the "consequences" of space mining "merit careful consideration" (57-59), and go on to discuss the possibility that "claims will be disputed, investments risky, and the gains made insecure" (85-87); the word "reservations" indicates that the authors of Passage 2 aren't sure that the developments will be positive, and "reservations" in the answer choice is certainly a literal description of Passage 2's statements about "dispute[s]," "risk[s]," "insecur[ities]," and other possibly negative "consequences" that need to be "careful[ly] consider[ed]" according to the authors. As trained test-takers, we can tell that every word of (D) is directly restated or demonstrated in the two passages, so (D) is right.

| **Test 1, Question 50** | **TYPE: PAIRED PASSAGES** |

> *The next question is a "best evidence" question referring back to this question; you may choose to consider the citations in the choices for the next question when answering this one if you want. See "Is there a 'best evidence' shortcut?" on page 72 for more.*

ⓘ *The prompt also asks how someone would respond to a claim or argument. The correct answer restates a position that's already stated in the passage. See "What about Paired Passages?" on p.76.*

Subjective Phrases to Ignore: "most likely"

A   **Barely Relevant:** The authors of Passage 2 don't reach any conclusions about the "sustainable use of space resources" described in this answer choice; instead, they say that "questions of...[space] stewardship have barely been broached" (76-77), meaning that people haven't even really started asking those questions, let alone figuring out answers to them (note that "stewardship" is the idea of using resources "sustainabl[y]," which is our indication that lines 76-77 are relevant to the answer choice.) This means that the authors of Passage 2 believe we don't know yet what would be consistent, or inconsistent, "with the sustainable use of space resources." Since this choice doesn't reflect what appears in Passage 2, it must be wrong.

B ✓ **Correct:** As trained test-takers, we know that we need to find the portion of Passage 2 that addresses the ideas in lines 18-28 directly, instead of trying to guess what the authors of Passage 2 might say if the authors of these passages ever met, which is what an untrained test-taker would do. Lines 18-28 make it clear that the author of Passage 1 expects space-mining to include the acquisition of "precious metals" and "rare earth elements" and the establishment of "an-off planet economy." We see that the part of Passage 2 that addresses the "off-world economy" is around line 73, and continues to the end of that passage. The second to last paragraph mentions the "off-world economy" (73), then mentions resources that are valuable in orbit and says that "questions of their stewardship have barely been broached—and the...regulatory framework...is fragmentary...." (76-78). The next paragraph mentions "such questions," which lets us know that this paragraph is still discussing the questions from the previous paragraph. The next sentence mentions that one speaker thinks "regulation should be avoided" (83)—that is, the regulation of the off-world economy discussed in this paragraph and the previous paragraph. The following sentence says "but miners have much to gain from a broad agreement on the for-profit exploitation of space" (83-85). The word "but" lets us know the idea after "but" is somehow opposed to what was discussed immediately before the word "but." In other words, the idea of the benefits of a "broad agreement" are opposed to the idea of wanting to "avoid" "regulation," so we can conclude that "broad agreement" refers to the idea of "regulation." Finally, the next sentence says that without "consensus" (85) (which means the same thing as "broad agreement" (84), which in turn refers to the idea of "regulation" (83) of the "off-world economy" (73)) "claims will be disputed, investments risky, and the gains made insecure" (85-87). So the author of Passage 2 says the off-world economy described in Passage 1 will be hard to achieve—there will be "dispute[s],...risk[s],...and... insecur[ity]" (85-87)—without "consensus," or regulation. We can see now that every phrase in (B) is directly restated or demonstrated in Passage 2.

C   **Reasonable Statement not in the Text / Wrong Part of the Passage:** A lot of untrained test-takers will pick this choice. For one thing, an untrained test-taker might imagine that the vision of space mining expressed in lines 18-28 would, indeed, require "technologies that do not yet exist," as (C) describes. Further, the author of Passage 1 uses phrases like "may be" (18), "hope" (24), "in this scenario" (29), "could become" (30), "could be sent" (35), and "could be used" (42-43), all of which indicate that the technologies discussed in the passage might not exist yet. But the prompt asked us what the authors of *Passage 2* would say, and the authors of Passage 2 never say anything about whether space-mining technology already exists!

D   **Direct Contradiction:** The authors of Passage 2 specifically say that "we all stand to gain: the mineral bounty and spin-off technologies could enrich us all" (50-52). They also say that "it is in all of our long-term interests to seek" a "consensus" on the regulation of space mining. They never indicate that space mining will affect Earth's economy in a negative way.

Test 1, Question 51   **TYPE: BEST EVIDENCE**

ℹ️ *The answer must restate or demonstrate the relevant statement. See "What about "Best Evidence" Questions?" on page 72.*

A   **Confused Relationships:** This citation may seem to support (A) from question 50, but the text doesn't say that space mining *will* "despoil" (62) space; instead, it just says we *shouldn't* despoil space. Choice (A) in question 50 would only have been correct if Passage 2 had stated conclusively that future space-mining would definitely result in an unsustainable use of space resources.

B   **Barely Relevant:** This citation talks about the difference between the values of "resources…in orbit" (74) and resources "we prize on Earth" (75-76), but none of the choices in question 50 talk about that difference, so (B) can't be right.

C   **Confused Relationships:** To an untrained test-taker who doesn't read carefully, this citation may seem to contradict the correct answer from the previous question, because the citation describes a miner who wants mining not to be regulated. But the previous question asks what *the authors of Passage 2 think*, not what "one speaker" at a forum thinks. As we saw in our discussion of choice (B) for the previous question, the citation in this answer choice is part of the chain of ideas that helps us determine the correct answer to that question—but this citation, by itself, doesn't say anything that's restated in the correct answer to that question, so it's not the correct answer to this question.

D✓   **Correct:** As we discussed in the walkthrough for the previous question, this citation is the one that ultimately states the authors' opinion, which is that the space-mining economy will be unlikely to succeed without regulations. (For a full explanation of how a trained test-taker knows that the word "consensus" in this citation is equivalent to the "regulations" mentioned in choice (B) of the previous question, see the walkthrough for that question.)

Test 1, Question 52   **TYPE: PAIRED PASSAGES**

ℹ️ *The prompt also asks how someone would respond to a claim or argument. The correct answer restates a position that's already stated in the passage. See "What about Paired Passages?" on p.76.*

Subjective Phrases to Ignore: "implicit"

A✓   **Correct:** The author of Passage 1 explicitly states, "water mined from other worlds could become the most desired commodity" (29-30). Notice that the words "could become" are an indication that water is not currently "the most desired commodity;" instead, water is something that might be more valuable when it's "mined from other worlds." In other words, the author of Passage 1 uses "water mined from other worlds" as an example of a "resource that will be highly valued in space," as the prompt describes, and the words "could become" (30) indicate that water isn't currently that valuable, as this answer choice requires. Similarly, the authors of Passage 2 state this idea when they say, "The resources that are valuable in orbit and beyond may be very different to those we prize on Earth" (74-76). Notice that the phrase "the resources that are valuable in orbit and beyond" from Passage 2 is equivalent to the phrase "resources that will be highly valued in space" from the prompt, and the phrase "may be very different" in Passage 2 is equivalent to the phrase "may be different resources" in this answer choice. For all of these reasons, we can see that this answer choice restates concepts that appear in both passages.

B   **Reasonable Statement Not in the Text:** Some untrained test-takers might assume that space-mining would only make sense economically if materials could be "harvested cheaply" in space, as this answer choice would require—but trained test-takers realize that neither passage says anything about whether mining in space would be "cheap" (or "inexpensive," or any similar term). Since this choice doesn't restate anything in either passage, it must be wrong.

C   **Confused Relationships:** Passage 1 does say that there's "earthly demand for precious metals" and "rare earth elements" (19-20) that could be mined in space, but it still never mentions the idea that these materials will be "highly valued in space," as the prompt describes. Further, Passage 2 never says anything about "precious metals and rare earth elements," as this answer choice would require. Either of these problems by itself would be enough to make this choice wrong.

D   **Barely Relevant:** Passage 1 mentions the idea of bringing things that are already "rare earth elements" (20) back from space, but this answer choice talks about things that aren't currently rare on Earth "*becom[ing]* rare on Earth" (emphasis added). Neither passage discusses the possibility of things "becom[ing] rare on Earth," so this choice can't be correct.

Note   Even though the prompt indicates that something in the correct answer will only be implicit in Passage 1, we were still able to read carefully and determine that Passage 1 actually provides an *explicit* example of the concept in the correct answer choice, so that we could identify the right answer with 100% certainty, without using any kind of interpretation or subjectivity at all. As trained test-takers, we know that sticking to this standard of total objectivity is key to making an elite score on the SAT.

ⓘ *The prompt often mentions describing the passage, and usually doesn't include a line citation. The answer must still be restated or demonstrated by some specific part of the text, even if there's no citation. See "What about Questions Without Citations?" p. 72*

Subjective Phrases to Ignore: "best"

A ✓ **Correct:** The speaker says in lines 6-7, "From the first week of my residence in X—I felt my occupation irksome," and he goes on to describe "the thing itself—the work of copying and translating business-letters" (7-8) as a "nuisance" (10). The word "occupation" in these quotes restates the word "job" in the answer choice, and the fact that the author calls it a "nuisance" and says that it's "irksome" demonstrate his "dislike" for it, as the answer choice requires. In line 9, he calls the work "a dry and tedious task," which gives us one "reason" for his dislike, as (A) also requires; in lines 10-27, he elaborates on various aspects of the job that are unpleasant, and how he could still put up with them if needed. From there, the speaker discusses at length how much he dislikes his employer, which is another reason he dislikes the job; the speaker calls his employer "a hard, grinding, master" (62) and a "tyrant" (64), and in line 67 a voice in his head says that his life is "intolerable," all of which further reinforces the idea that the author dislikes his job, and gives us further reasons for that dislike. Since every part of (A) directly restates something we can find throughout the passage, we know (A) is correct.

B **Literary Interpretation:** The passage does include a description of two different characters: the speaker, and his employer, "Edward Crimsworth" (35). Both of these characters work in the same office, but the text doesn't describe them "compet[ing]" with each other, let alone "increasingly" so, as (B) would require. In order for "competitive" to be correct in the context of SAT Reading, the characters would have to be working or struggling for something that only one of them could have—like a promotion, or a certain office, or the business of a certain client—because that's the literal definition of the word "competitive." To be "increasingly competitive," the text would have to describe this situation as less competitive in the past and more competitive as time goes by. Since those elements aren't present in the text, this choice is wrong.

C **Barely Relevant:** This choice might be tempting to an untrained test-taker, because the author says, "no man likes to acknowledge that he has made a mistake in the choice of his profession…" (1-2). This may seem to go along with (C), but this excerpt is only a general discussion of what "no man likes to acknowledge," and not a specific statement that the speaker himself refuses to acknowledge his mistake—in fact, the rest of the text, starting from line 27, involves the speaker discussing his mistake at length. Further, the text never describes the author doing anything in public, one way or the other.

D **Literary Interpretation:** (D) might tempt an untrained test-taker because it mentions three ideas that seem to go along in a general way with what's in the passage. But, as trained test-takers, we know that for (D) to be right, each of these three ideas must be specifically restated in the text, and in the order that they appear in the answer choice. As it turns out, the idea of "optimism" isn't anywhere in the text. The speaker never says, "I thought everything would go very well," or, "it seemed to me that things would eventually get better," or anything like that. This, by itself, is enough to make the answer choice completely wrong, because we know that every word in a correct answer choice on the SAT Reading section has to be reflected directly in the text. As for the other two emotions in the answer choice, we might say that the line about the speaker's life being "intolerable" (64-67) is an expression of despair, but, even then, the passage doesn't really say anything directly that would allow us to distinguish a feeling of "frustration" as opposed to "despair." Any of these reasons is enough for a trained test-taker to realize that (D) must be wrong.

Note Notice that choices (C) and (D) (and (B) to a lesser extent) would probably be fine in a normal classroom discussion, but they're clearly wrong here, because they don't satisfy the SAT's requirement that the correct answer exactly restate the passage. Keep this kind of thing in mind on test day!

ⓘ *The prompt asks about the purpose or role of a part of the text. The correct answer must be accurately restated or described by the relevant text, with no interpretation. See "What about "Purpose" Questions?" on p.74.*

Subjective Phrases to Ignore: "main"

A **Barely Relevant:** By definition, a "controversy" necessarily involves some kind of disagreement, but the opening sentence doesn't mention a disagreement—instead, it says that all people are similar in that they don't like to admit their mistakes.

B ✓ **Correct:** A lot of test-takers may not fully understand the last four lines of the first sentence, but we can still tell that the first couple of lines say, "no man likes to acknowledge that he has made a mistake in the choice of his profession." This idea of making a mistake in the choice of a profession is related to the concepts we see in the rest of the passage. Furthermore, the next sentence says that the narrator "felt [his] occupation irksome…" (6-7); later, in line 10, he calls his job a "nuisance." So we can see that the beginning of the first sentence is related to the author's mental state, exactly as this answer choice requires, which means (B) is correct.

C **Off by One or Two Words:** The first sentence describes a man who "will row long against wind and tide before he allows himself to cry out, 'I am baffled!' and submits to be floated passively back to land" (3-6). Since the text never describes anyone literally rowing a boat, and since the author inserts this boat image into a description of how he doesn't like his job, this sentence is definitely a "symbolic representation" of a "plight," just as (C) requires. But a trained test-taker can still tell that (C) is wrong—the "plight" being described by the speaker is the speaker's own plight—not the plight of "Edward Crimsworth," as (C) describes! Edward Crimsworth is the speaker's boss, as we can see in lines 62-63 when the narrator describes "Mr. Crimsworth" as "a hard, grinding master." (C) is a classic example of the way the College Board often tries to trick untrained test-takers by including choices that vary only slightly from what appears in the text!

D **Confused Relationships:** The text doesn't actually say anything about the speaker's "intentions," which (D) would require, let alone whether those "intentions" are "good" or not. Further, the text certainly doesn't describe any "malicious conduct" on the part of the narrator. This choice might be tempting to an untrained test-taker who assumes the speaker must be good, and who doesn't realize that Edward Crimsworth (the speaker's malicious employer) is a different person from the speaker.

Test 2, Question 3	TYPE: CITATION QUESTION

ⓘ *The question includes a citation from the text. The answer must be directly restated or demonstrated in the cited text, or in the text closely surrounding the cited text. See the general process for answering SAT Reading questions on p. 71.*

A **Literary Interpretation:** (A) might be tempting for an untrained test-taker who reads the first sentence of this paragraph and thinks that choosing your profession and then admitting that you made a mistake is the same as having "past confidence" and "present self-doubt" as (A) would require. But, as trained test-takers, we know that we need to pay strict attention to details, and we notice that simply choosing a profession isn't the same thing as having "confidence;" for all we know, the speaker may not have had confidence when he selected his profession; in fact, we don't even know what kind of other options he might have had, or whether he had any at all. Similarly, admitting that you were wrong about the job you chose doesn't specifically mean you doubt yourself now—it just means you're aware that you made a mistake. This is the kind of choice that might be accepted as a valid interpretation in a literature class, but that must be wrong on the SAT because it doesn't directly restate concepts from the passage.

B **Confused Relationships:** The speaker describes the "resolution I had taken to become a tradesman" (13-14), but he doesn't actually say what his "expectations" were, as the answer choice would require. That's enough to make the answer choice wrong by itself, but we also see that the speaker never actually mentions a "desire for another job" as described in the answer choice. An untrained test-taker might assume that the author wants another job, since he clearly seems to hate his current job, but, as trained test-takers, we know that we can't simply assume he feels that way, since the text doesn't say so. For all we know, the speaker might think that other jobs would be even worse than his current job.

C ✓ **Correct:** The paragraph begins with a sentence explaining that "no man likes to admit he has made a mistake in the choice of his profession" (1-2); the phrase "no man" begins a universal statement, or a "generalization," as the answer choice requires, and the generalization is clearly about "job dissatisfaction," which the answer choice also requires. The rest of the paragraph from lines 6-33 describes the specifics of the speaker's actual job, as the answer choice further requires. Since every part of the answer choice is directly restated or demonstrated in the text, we know that (C) must be correct.

D **Off by One or Two Words:** The first paragraph does mention a number of factors that the speaker doesn't like, such as "the work of copying and translating" (8), which he calls a "nuisance" (10); it also mentions "the rust and cramp of [his] best faculties" (15), as well as "the closeness, smoke, monotony, and joyless tumult" (19-20) of his office. But the speaker never identifies any alternatives to his current situation, so this choice can't be correct.

Test 2, Question 4	TYPE: PURPOSE OF CITED TEXT

ⓘ *The prompt asks about the purpose or role of a part of the text. The correct answer must be accurately restated or described by the relevant text, with no interpretation. See "What about "Purpose" Questions?" on p.74.*

Subjective Phrases to Ignore: "mainly"

A ✓ **Correct:** We know the narrator is "dismay[ed]," as (A) requires, because we see that he was excluded "from every glimpse of the sunshine of life" (30-31), and his life has become "intolerable" (67), among other things throughout the text.

B **Confused Relationships:** (B) may be tempting for untrained test-takers who make two mistakes: first, they interpret Edward Crimsworth as someone with "sinister thoughts," and, second, they confuse the narrator with Crimsworth. As trained test-takers who know we need to read carefully, we can see that the text doesn't say anything about the narrator having sinister thoughts, which means (B) must be wrong.

C **Literary Interpretation:** An untrained test-taker might read words like "shade" (30) and "darkness" (32) or the remark about feeling like a "plant growing in...a well" (32-33) and assume that the speaker "fear[s]" "confinement" as the choice would require, but the narrator never specifically mentions any fear of any kind, which means this choice must be wrong.

D   Barely Relevant: The narrator does describe his unhappiness with his job at length, but he never says that he's tired or wants rest; as trained test-takers, we know that this means (D) must be wrong.

Test 2, Question 5   TYPE: DESCRIBE THE PASSAGE

ⓘ *The prompt often mentions describing the passage, and usually doesn't include a line citation. The answer must still be restated or demonstrated by some specific part of the text, even if there's no citation. See "What about Questions Without Citations?" p. 72*

Subjective Phrases to Ignore: "mainly"

A   Barely Relevant: Lines 38-48 describe what Crimsworth dislikes about the narrator; that list doesn't say that the narrator has "high spirits" (or a good mood, or a pleasant demeanor, or anything along those lines). As trained test-takers, we know (A) can't be correct, since it doesn't directly restate anything in the text.

B   Literary Interpretation: Lines 38-48 describe what Crimsworth dislikes about the narrator, but the list doesn't mention having a "humble background" (or low beginnings, or a peasant birth, or anything along those lines). (Some untrained—and biased—test-takers might interpret the speaker's reference to his "accent" (38) as some indication of a "humble background," but the speaker never indicates whether a person with that accent is typically viewed as having a "humble background.") Since (B) doesn't restate anything in the passage, we know it must be wrong.

C   Direct Contradiction: Lines 38-48 describe what Crimsworth dislikes about the narrator, but that list doesn't include "rash actions" (or a tendency to act without thinking, or anything along those lines); in fact, the speaker specifically mentions the narrator's "Caution, Tact, [and] Observation [sic]" in line 51, which means that he doesn't act rashly, since "rash" is an antonym for words like "cautious" and "tactful."

D✓   Correct: Lines 38-48 describe what Crimsworth dislikes about the narrator. The word "envy" is mentioned in the list in line 40, and is directly restated by the word "jealousy" in the answer choice. The list culminates with this: "...I knew all that he knew, and, what was worse, he suspected that I kept the padlock of silence on mental wealth in which he was no sharer" (44-48). In other words, the narrator knew everything that his boss knew, AND the narrator also had "mental wealth," or knowledge, in which Crimsworth was "no sharer," which means Crimsworth didn't have some of the knowledge that the narrator had. So Crimsworth envied the narrator's abilities, which Crimsworth also believed to be stronger than Crimsworth's own abilities. This is exactly restated by the answer choice, so we know (D) is correct.

Test 2, Question 6   TYPE: DESCRIBE THE PASSAGE

The next question is a "best evidence" question referring back to this question; you may choose to consider the citations in the choices for the next question when answering this one if you want. See "Is there a 'best evidence' shortcut?" on page 72 for more.

ⓘ *The prompt often mentions describing the passage, and usually doesn't include a line citation. The answer must still be restated or demonstrated by some specific part of the text, even if there's no citation. See "What about Questions Without Citations?" p. 72*

A   Barely Relevant / Confused Relationships: The word "harmless" doesn't restate anything in the text, so (A) can't be right.

B✓   Correct: There is only one point in the text where the narrator indicates what his previous feelings for Crimsworth were. In lines 61-62, he says, "I had long ceased to regard Mr. Crimsworth as my brother." If the narrator "ceased to regard Mr. Crimsworth as [his] brother," then we know that, at one point, the narrator must have regarded Crimsworth as a brother—otherwise, it would be impossible to stop doing so. In this context, the idea of a "sympathetic ally" restates the idea of being viewed "as [a] brother," so choice (B) is correct.

C   Barely Relevant: Nothing in the text supports the idea that the narrator viewed Crimsworth as a "perceptive judge."

D   Reasonable Statement Not in the Text: An untrained test-taker might imagine that an employer who was disliked by an employee could be seen at some point as a "demanding mentor," but the passage doesn't really indicate that Crimsworth is a "mentor," as the answer choice would require; a mentor is a figure who wants to help someone else succeed in a new field. The text does indicate that Crimsworth is "demanding" when the speaker refers to his pay as "hard-earned" (60), but the prompt asks what the narrator thought when he "began working," and the remark about the hard-earned wages is made after the speaker "received [his] first quarter's wages" (57), so there's no way for us to tie the feelings from line 60 back to the beginning of the narrator's employment. (And, again, even if there were a way to relate those feelings to an earlier time, it would still be true that Crimsworth isn't described as a mentor.)

Test 2, Question 7   TYPE: BEST EVIDENCE

ⓘ *The answer must restate or demonstrate the relevant statement. See "What about "Best Evidence" Questions?" on page 72.*

A   Barely Relevant: This text isn't really relevant to any choice from the previous question, so it can't be right.

B   Barely Relevant: This text isn't really relevant to any choice from the previous question, so it can't be right.

C   Confused Relationships: This text might seem to support the notion of Crimsworth as a "rival" as described in (A) from question 6, but it doesn't directly indicate that Crimsworth was "harmless" in the eyes of the narrator, as (A) in 6 would require. Further, this citation isn't relevant to any of the other choices in the previous question, so it must be wrong.

D ✓   Correct: As discussed in the walkthrough for question 6, choice (B) from that question restates the key concept of "brother[hood]" from this citation, which is why (B) is right in question 6 and (D) is right in this question.

ⓘ *The question includes a citation from the text. The answer must be directly restated or demonstrated in the cited text, or in the text closely surrounding the cited text. See the general process for answering SAT Reading questions on p. 71.*

Subjective Phrases to Ignore: "mainly"

A   Barely Relevant: (A) can't be right because the text doesn't describe any hypothetical courses of action; in order for (A) to be right, we'd need to see some kind of phrase like "imagine what might happen if the lynx did one thing but the snake did another," or something similar.

B   Reasonable Statement Not in the Text: Untrained test-takers might think that animals like a "lynx" (53) and a "snake" (55) could be "feroci[ous]," as this answer choice would require, but the text never actually says anything that restates the idea of "ferocity," so a trained test-taker can immediately recognize that this answer choice is incorrect. Further, the text never describes any kind of "resolution," so the answer choice is wrong for that reason, as well.

C   Literary Interpretation: The text never says any particular thing is likely to happen, as (C) would require, so (C) is wrong; further, the text never mentions any kind of "altercation," which is another way to say something like "violent confrontation." (Don't worry if you didn't know the word "altercation"—as we just discussed, you could still tell (C) is wrong by noticing that the text doesn't mention that anything is likely to happen, which means it's wrong no matter what "altercation" means.)

D ✓   Correct: If we know most or all of the words in lines 48-56, then we can understand that the narrator says his "natural sentinels" (53), which are "Caution, Tact, and Observation [sic]" (51), have "lynx-eyes" (53). He also says that Crimsworth's "prowling" and "prying" "malignity" (51-52) can't "baffle" his "sentinels" (53), and that Crimsworth's "malice" can't "steal snake-like" (55) on the "slumber" (55-56) of the narrator's tact. If Crimsworth's "malignity" wants to "baffle" the narrator's "sentinels" (or guards), then we know the guards and the malignity must be adversaries, which means (D) directly restates the concepts at the end of the second paragraph, so (D) must be right. But what if we don't know a lot of the words at the end of the paragraph? We can actually probably still tell that (D) is correct, for two reasons: first, we know the narrator and Crimsworth are adversaries because this idea is mentioned repeatedly throughout the text, and we can see that the "lynx" attributes belong to the narrator and the "snake" attributes belong to Crimsworth; second, we can tell that each of the other choices must be wrong, for the reasons we discussed above.

Note   This question provides a great example of the way a trained test-taker can often work around a lot of unknown vocabulary if she keeps the rules of the test in mind, and refuses to be intimidated by the College Board's attempts to use complex sentences and misleading prompts in an effort to confuse other test-takers. Keep this kind of thing in mind when you run into challenging vocabulary on test day! (See our discussion of the "bad connection" technique on page 66 of this Black Book for more on this.)

The next question is a "best evidence" question referring back to this question; you may choose to consider the citations in the choices for the next question when answering this one if you want. See "Is there a 'best evidence' shortcut?" on page 72 for more.

ⓘ *The prompt often mentions describing the passage, and usually doesn't include a line citation. The answer must still be restated or demonstrated by some specific part of the text, even if there's no citation. See "What about Questions Without Citations?" p. 72*

A   Confused Relationships: An untrained test-taker might think of Crimsworth himself as treacherous because of the end of the second paragraph, but that isn't the same thing as saying that the narrator finds his living quarters to be "treacherous."

B ✓   Correct: At the end of the passage the narrator "was returning to [his] lodgings" (57-58) and says when he looked "towards the window of [his] sitting-room, [he] saw no cheering red gleam" (72-74). "Dreariness" is the same thing as the absence of cheer, so (B) restates the idea of the lack of a "cheering red gleam" in the text.

C   Direct Contradiction: The narrator says he engaged in "speculation as to whether [his] fire would be out" (71-72); if he has to "speculat[e]" about something, then we know that he doesn't know what condition it will be in, since "speculation" requires a lack of knowledge about the future. This is the direct opposite of the word "predictable" in (C), so it's wrong.

D   Confused Relationships: (D) will trap a lot of untrained test-takers who don't make a habit of going back to the text to confirm their answers. In the third paragraph, the narrator does say to himself that his "life is intolerable" (67). But saying his *life* is intolerable isn't the same as saying his *living quarters* themselves are intolerable, which means (D) isn't restated or demonstrated by the text, so it must be wrong.

ⓘ *The answer must restate or demonstrate the relevant statement. See "What about "Best Evidence" Questions?" on page 72.*

A   **Confused Relationships:** This text might seem to be relevant to question 9, but the narrator says his "small bedroom" is "at Mrs. King's Lodgings" (23), not in "Bigben Close" (20), so this citation doesn't describe the narrator's living quarters.

B   **Wrong Part of the Passage:** (B) does mention the narrator's "small bedroom at Mrs. King's Lodgings" (23), but it doesn't describe his living quarters "after a long day of work," as the prompt in question 9 requires, so it isn't relevant to question 9.

C   **Confused Relationships:** This citation does describe what was going through the narrator's mind as he "was returning to [his] lodgings" (58), but it doesn't say anything specific about the narrator's "living quarters," so it isn't relevant to question 9.

D✓   **Correct:** As discussed in the walkthrough for the previous question, this citation restates the idea of cheerlessness or dreariness, which shows that (B) is the correct answer to the previous question.

❚ Test 2, Question 11   **TYPE: DESCRIBE THE PASSAGE**

The next question is a "best evidence" question referring back to this question; you may choose to consider the citations in the choices for the next question when answering this one if you want. See "Is there a 'best evidence' shortcut?" on page 72 for more.

ⓘ *The prompt often mentions describing the passage, and usually doesn't include a line citation. The answer must still be restated or demonstrated by some specific part of the text, even if there's no citation. See "What about Questions Without Citations?" p. 72*

A   **Confused Relationships:** This choice will trap a lot of untrained test-takers who don't read carefully, because the passage repeatedly discusses the role of ethics in economics, but it only mentions a "cost-benefit analysis" (23) once, and it doesn't specifically say that the cost-benefit analysis poses an "ethical dilemma." Since (A) doesn't restate the passage, it's wrong.

B   **Confused Relationships:** The passage repeatedly discusses the idea of ethics in economics, and the last paragraph mentions "psychology" (81, 83), which means that this answer choice will probably attract a lot of untrained test-takers; the reason the choice is wrong is that the passage never mentions a particular "study," let alone a particular "psychology study." It's important to note the difference between the general idea of neurologists studying human psychology, which is clearly mentioned in the last paragraph, and the idea of "describ[ing] a psychology study," which doesn't actually happen in the passage. Being able to notice this kind of distinction and avoid picking the wrong answer here will translate to the difference between a well-trained, high-scoring test-taker, and an untrained test-taker with an average score.

C   **Direct Contradiction:** The author says, "some argue that because the free markets allow for personal choice, they are already ethical" (4-5). So the passage's only explicit mention of ethics in conjunction with the free market describes a view that says free markets *can be* ethical, which contradicts the statement made in this answer choice.

D✓   **Correct:** Near the beginning of the article, the author says, "we need to be clear on what we are talking about" (10) when we talk about issues of ethics and economics; sure enough, the rest of the passage explores different ways to be clear about ethics in the context of economics. Paragraph 3 begins by saying, "there are different views on where ethics should apply when someone makes an economic decision" (11-12). The rest of that paragraph discusses Adam Smith's view on ethics in economics; paragraph 4 discusses Aristotle's views on ethics in economics; paragraph 5 discusses "yet another approach" (45) focusing on "actions themselves" (47). So we can see clearly that this answer choice directly restates what we observe in the passage: "ways of evaluating the ethics of economics" is a restatement of "views on where ethics should apply when someone makes an economic decision" in lines 11-12, and the passage goes on to explore existing views, until the last two paragraphs discuss how new views might emerge in the future.

❚ Test 2, Question 12   **TYPE: DESCRIBE THE PASSAGE**

The next question is a "best evidence" question referring back to this question; you may choose to consider the citations in the choices for the next question when answering this one if you want. See "Is there a 'best evidence' shortcut?" on page 72 for more.

ⓘ *The prompt often mentions describing the passage, and usually doesn't include a line citation. The answer must still be restated or demonstrated by some specific part of the text, even if there's no citation. See "What about Questions Without Citations?" p. 72*

A   **Confused Relationships:** The third paragraph discusses Adam Smith's views on ethics in economics, but the author doesn't say that Smith associates "free markets with ethical behavior," or that this idea "still applies today." (You may remember that lines 4-5 indicate that "some argue that...free markets...are already ethical," but that's still not relevant to this answer choice, because the choice specifically says that *Smith* associated free markets and ethical behavior, while lines 4-5 only say that some unnamed people have claimed this.) Since this choice doesn't restate the passage, we know it's wrong.

B   **Reasonable Statement Not in the Text:** Some untrained test-takers might assume that people who believe in free markets would say "ethics are a secondary concern" after "high profits," as (B) requires, but the author never makes this statement, or even says anything about "high profits" in the passage. Since (B) isn't restated or demonstrated by the text, it's wrong.

C   **Confused Relationships:** Lines 4-5 do mention the idea of free markets being "ethical," and lines 52-56 do mention an example that involves the idea of devaluing currency, but the two ideas aren't connected with each other at all in the text, which means (C) is wrong.

D ✓   Correct: This choice directly restates what we see in lines 4-5: "some argue that because the free markets allow for personal choice, they are already ethical."

Note   (D) is the only choice that restates the passage exactly, so we know it's correct, but let's talk about the mechanics of the argument in the passage, since the College Board has written this prompt to mislead us into thinking we need to understand the structure of the passage. Some test-takers won't know what the phrase "anticipating an objection" means, so let's explore that idea: the author is anticipating that some readers may object that a free marketplace is unethical, and then the author addresses that objection by explaining why some people feel a free marketplace can be ethical. In other words, the author "anticipates" that a reader might dislike the idea of discussing ethics in the context of a free market, so he explains why he thinks it's okay to discuss that, before the reader can voice an objection. But, again, as trained test-takers, we realize that the correct answer to this question must restate the passage, and only (D) does that; being able to realize this allows us to avoid wasting a lot of time and mental energy on figuring out what the prompt is talking about when it mentions anticipating objections. (We can also use the fact that the next question refers back to this question as a way to streamline our thinking even further—as we'll see in a moment, (D) is the only answer choice from this question that's directly restated by any of the answer choices in the next question, which is one more way to realize that (D) must be correct, since the correct answer to the next question must restate one of the answer choices from this question.) For more on the major ideas in this note, see "Critical Technical Terms for the SAT Reading Section" on page 69 of this Black Book, and "Is there a 'best evidence' shortcut?" on page 72.

Test 2, Question 13   TYPE: BEST EVIDENCE

ⓘ *The answer must restate or demonstrate the relevant statement. See "What about "Best Evidence" Questions?" on page 72.*

Subjective Phrases to Ignore: "best"

A ✓   Correct: As we discussed in the walkthrough for question 12, this citation is an exact restatement of (D) from that question; since (D) is the correct answer to the previous question, (A) is the correct answer to this question.

B   Barely Relevant: This citation discusses the need to clarify what ethics in economics really means, but it doesn't mention free markets at all, so it can't restate the right answer to question 12, since 12 focused on the issue of ethics in free markets.

C   Literary Interpretation: This citation discusses Smith's view of selfish behavior, but none of the answer choices in the previous question touches on the idea of selfish behavior in connection with the idea of ethics in free markets, so this choice can't restate the correct answer to the previous question, which means it must be wrong.

D   Literary Interpretation: This citation discusses one way of defining ethics with respect to economics, and it mentions "devalu[ing] a currency," like choice (C) from the previous question. But this citation doesn't mention free markets, so it can't support the correct answer from the previous question; further, as we discussed in the explanation for question 12, the passage never connects the idea of devaluing a currency with the idea of free markets.

Test 2, Question 14   TYPE: WORD MOST NEARLY MEANS

ⓘ *The prompt includes the phrase "most nearly means" and the choices are usually one- or two-word phrases. The answer is either restated or demonstrated by an idea from the surrounding text. Remember you can work around unknown words, and be ready to guess/skip and focus on other questions if you don't know the words. See "What about "Most Nearly Means" Questions?" on p. 73.*

Subjective Phrases to Ignore: "most nearly"

A   ("Others have accepted the ethical critique and <u>lovingly held</u> corporate social responsibility.") Reasonable Statement Not in the Text: In another context, "embraced" could mean "lovingly held," because to "embrace" someone can mean to "hold" that person "lovingly," but this sense of "embrace" doesn't restate any concept from the passage, so it's wrong.

B ✓   ("Others have accepted the ethical critique and <u>readily adopted</u> corporate social responsibility.") Correct: The text says those who "embraced corporate social responsibility" have "accepted the ethical critique" (5-7); this indicates that "embrac[ing]" and "accep[ting]" represent the same idea, and the idea of "readily adopt[ing]" that we see in this answer choice is a restatement of the idea of "accept[ing]," so we can see this choice is correct.

C   ("Others have accepted the ethical critique and <u>eagerly hugged</u> corporate social responsibility.") Reasonable Statement Not in the Text: In another context, "embraced" could mean "eagerly hugged," but it's not restated or demonstrated by the text, so it's wrong here.

D   ("Others have accepted the ethical critique and <u>reluctantly used</u> corporate social responsibility.") Reasonable Statement Not in the Text: An untrained test-taker might imagine that someone trying to make money would dislike the idea of "corporate social responsibility" (7) and would therefore "reluctantly use" it, but there's nothing in the relevant part of the passage that actually indicates anyone who's thinking about corporate social responsibility is reluctant about it. Since we know that the right answer must restate some relevant part of the passage, we can see that this choice must be wrong.

ⓘ *The question includes a citation from the text. The answer must be directly restated or demonstrated in the cited text, or in the text closely surrounding the cited text. See the general process for answering SAT Reading questions on p. 71.*

Subjective Phrases to Ignore: "main"

A   **Barely Relevant:** The fifth paragraph can't be a counterargument to the idea that greed is good, because the paragraph doesn't say anything about greed (or "selfishness," or any other similar word).

B   **Direct Contradiction:** The first sentence of the fifth paragraph says "instead of rooting ethics in character or the consequences of action, we can focus on our actions themselves" (45-47). In other words, the phrase "instead of" indicates that people are doing something different from "rooting ethics in character," which directly contradicts the statement in (B).

C ✓   **Correct:** The third paragraph discusses Adam Smith's approach to ethics in economics; the fourth paragraph discusses Aristotle's approach to ethics in economics; and the fifth paragraph discusses a third approach to ethics in economics—an approach that focuses on "actions themselves" (47). Since (C) directly restates what's going on in the paragraph, it's right.

D   **Confused Relationships:** Lines 45-47 state that the paragraph focuses on "actions themselves" "instead of rooting ethics in character." This answer choice mentions "actions" and "character," but says that one is a result of the other; such a relationship between actions and character isn't stated anywhere in the text, so we know this answer choice is wrong.

ⓘ *The prompt includes the phrase "most nearly means" and the choices are usually one- or two-word phrases. The answer is either restated or demonstrated by an idea from the surrounding text. Remember you can work around unknown words, and be ready to guess/skip and focus on other questions if you don't know the words. See "What about "Most Nearly Means" Questions?" on p.73.*

Subjective Phrases to Ignore: "most nearly"

A ✓   ("Many moral dilemmas arise when these three versions pull in different directions but <u>conflicts</u> are not inevitable.") **Correct:** As trained test-takers, we know the correct answer to this question must be restated or demonstrated in the passage; in this case, the word "conflicts" restates the idea of "pull[ing] in different directions."

B   ("Many moral dilemmas arise when these three versions pull in different directions but <u>mismatches</u> are not inevitable.") **Reasonable Statement Not in the Text:** In another context, "clash" could mean "mismatch;" for example, we can say clothes that "clash" are "mismatched." But the word "mismatch" isn't restated or demonstrated in the text, so (B) is wrong.

C   ("Many moral dilemmas arise when these three versions pull in different directions but <u>collisions</u> are not inevitable.") **Confused Relationships:** This answer choice may tempt some untrained test-takers because "clash" sounds like "crash," and a "crash" can be called a "collision." But, as trained test-takers, we know that we need to read carefully and look for a choice that restates the passage; since the word "collision" isn't restated or demonstrated by the text, this answer can't be correct.

D   ("Many moral dilemmas arise when these three versions pull in different directions but <u>brawls</u> are not inevitable.") **Reasonable Statement Not in the Text:** In another context, "clash" could mean "brawl," but the word "brawl" isn't restated or demonstrated by any word from the text, so we know this choice can't be right.

ⓘ *The answer must restate or demonstrate the relevant statement. See "What about "Best Evidence" Questions?" on page 72.*

Subjective Phrases to Ignore: "best"

A   **Literary Interpretation:** This citation does indicate that "different views" exist on the topic of ethics in economics, but the citation never says that those views share common ground, so it doesn't do what the prompt requires.

B   **Confused Relationships:** This citation tells us about one specific "perspective" (48) regarding ethics in economics, but it doesn't say anything about other perspectives, or about common ground, as the prompt requires, so it's wrong.

C ✓   **Correct:** To understand exactly how fair trade coffee is an example of this common ground, we can note the following: according to the citation, fair trade coffee can "have good consequences" (62-63), which satisfies Adam Smith's idea that he could "justify selfish behavior by the outcome" (21-22), since "consequences" and "outcome" are synonyms in this context; we also see that fair trade coffee can "be virtuous" (63), which satisfies Aristotle's idea that ethics is about "displaying virtues" (32-33); finally, selling fair trade coffee can "be the right way to act in a flawed market" (63-64), which satisfies the idea in the fifth paragraph that ethics can be about "actions themselves" (47). Thus the citation in (C) is a direct restatement of the ideas related to a "common ground" among the ethical approaches in the passage—in fact, the next sentence after the citation in (C) says the previous examples show "common ground" (64) among different ethical approaches.

D   **Barely Relevant:** This citation is a general statement about the way people act, and it isn't really directly related to any concept of "common ground" as required by the prompt.

ⓘ *The question includes a citation from the text. The answer must be directly restated or demonstrated in the cited text, or in the text closely surrounding the cited text. See the general process for answering SAT Reading questions on p. 71.*

A   Confused Relationships: The last paragraph mentions "human quirks" (78), and says researchers are working to "anticipate our decisions in the marketplace more accurately" (82-83), so the ideas of anticipation and quirks are present in the citation. But the "decisions in the marketplace" (82-83) aren't described as "ethical decisions," which (A) would require. (A) is probably here to trick untrained test-takers who mistakenly equate ethical decisions with economic decisions, or who forget to read carefully.

B   Off By One Or Two Words: (B) might tempt some test-takers, because the last paragraph says that "we react in disgust at economic injustice" and also that we "accept a moral law as universal" (85-86). A test-taker who doesn't read carefully might think the word "universal" describes the reaction to economic injustice, but it doesn't—it only describes how we "accept a moral law." The text doesn't mention people "universally" reacting in disgust to economic injustice, so (B) is wrong.

C ✓ Correct: This answer choice restates a concept that appears in multiple places throughout the last paragraph. Lines 83-86 say, "psychology can also help us understand why we react in disgust at economic injustice, or accept a moral law as universal;" these lines restate the idea that an understanding of psychology will help to define ethics in economics, which appears in the answer choice. The passage then says, "the relatively new science of human behavior might also define ethics for us" (86-88), which is an even more direct restatement of this choice. Since (C) restates an idea from the text, it's right.

D   Barely Relevant: The final paragraph never explicitly mentions reforming the free market at all; an untrained test-taker might assume the "economic injustice" in line 85 is related to the free market, but the text never says that, so (D) is wrong.

ⓘ *The prompt refers to a graph/table/diagram/etc.; carefully note all labels, keys, units, and any other explanatory details. The answer must directly restate some part of the data and/or text. See "Reading Graphs, Charts, Tables, and Other Figures" on p.44.*

Subjective Phrases to Ignore: "most strongly"

A ✓ Correct: On the graph that shows "Coffee Profits," we see the values on the vertical axis start with zero at the low end, and then get higher as we move up the axis. The line for fair trade coffee is above the line for regular coffee for all years shown, which means "fair trade coffee consistently earned greater profits than regular coffee earned," as this choice requires.

B   Direct Contradiction: The profits for regular coffee clearly vary from year to year, which is what the word "fluctuate" means. The profits are as low as approximately 23 cents per pound around 2003, and as high as approximately 62 cents per pound in 2008. Many untrained test-takers will fall for this answer choice because the values for *fair trade coffee* remain relatively consistent throughout all the years in the graph, and a lot of people won't spend the extra second or two to go back to the graph and double-check which type of coffee is indicated by the line that doesn't fluctuate.

C   Direct Contradiction: The profits for fair trade coffee appear to be exactly the same in 2004 and 2006, at around 130 cents per pound. This contradicts the claim in (C) that profits for fair trade coffee rose in that time, so the choice must be wrong.

D   Direct Contradiction: When we look at the graph, we see that the two lines never touch each other, which means there was no point on the graph when the quantities represented by the lines were equal to each other, and this choice must be wrong.

ⓘ *The prompt refers to a graph/table/diagram/etc.; carefully note all labels, keys, units, and any other explanatory details. The answer must directly restate some part of the data and/or text. See "Reading Graphs, Charts, Tables, and Other Figures" on p.44.*

A   Direct Contradiction: We can see that the gap between fair trade coffee profits and regular coffee profits was not at its greatest from 2000 to 2002, with fair trade averaging around 130 cents per pound and regular averaging around 40 cents per pound, for a difference of around 90 cents per pound. We can tell, visually, that the two lines representing the profits have the greatest separation between 2002 and 2004, and not between 2000 and 2002.

B ✓ Correct: We can see that the gap between fair trade coffee profits and regular coffee profits was greatest from 2002 to 2004, with fair trade averaging around 130 cents per pound and regular averaging around 23 cents per pound for that whole period, for a difference of around 107 cents per pound throughout the period. This exceeds the difference between the two lines over any other period in the other answer choices, as required by the prompt, so this choice is correct.

C   Direct Contradiction: We can see that the gap between fair trade coffee profits and regular coffee profits was not at its greatest from 2004 to 2005. Fair trade coffee averaged around 130 cents per pound during this time, and regular coffee averaged around 30 cents per pound, for a difference of around 100 cents per pound. This isn't as great as the difference between the two kinds of coffee from 2002 to 2004, so we can see this answer choice isn't correct.

D   Direct Contradiction: We can see that the gap between fair trade coffee profits and regular coffee profits was at its *lowest* in the time period from 2006 to 2008, with a difference of around 70 cents per pound. But the prompt asked for the time period when the difference was *greatest*, so (D) is wrong.

ⓘ The prompt refers to a graph/table/diagram/etc.; carefully note all labels, keys, units, and any other explanatory details. The answer must directly restate some part of the data and/or text. See "Reading Graphs, Charts, Tables, and Other Figures" on p. 44.

A   **Confused Relationships / Reasonable Statement Not in the Text:** This is an idea discussed in lines 18-19, and it might seem like a reasonable belief to a lot of untrained test-takers who don't base their answer on the passage. But the passage doesn't make any connection between what's represented in the graph and the idea of acting on empathy, so (A) is wrong.

B   **Confused Relationships:** The connection between ethics and character is discussed in lines 31-44, but the passage doesn't make any connection between anything in the graph and the idea of character, so this choice must be wrong.

C ✓   **Correct:** The graph shows that profits per pound are higher for fair trade coffee than for regular coffee, and the text directly states that the example of "fair trade coffee" (59) suggests that "ethical economics is still possible" (66), so (C) directly reflects what appears in the passage and the graph, which means it's right.

D   **Confused Relationships:** This choice restates an idea from lines 75-76, but the passage doesn't indicate any connection between the graph and the idea of fearing losses or hoping for gains. Since (D) doesn't satisfy the prompt, it's wrong.

> *The next question is a "best evidence" question referring back to this question; you may choose to consider the citations in the choices for the next question when answering this one if you want. See "Is there a 'best evidence' shortcut?" on page 72 for more.*

ⓘ The prompt often mentions describing the passage, and usually doesn't include a line citation. The answer must still be restated or demonstrated by some specific part of the text, even if there's no citation. See "What about Questions Without Citations?" p. 72

A   **Confused Relationships:** The passage mentions a "study of video-gaming" (7) and a "British study" (16) related to searching online, so it does describe studies of "the use of screen-based technologies" (as described in the prompt) that *have already happened*. But the passage doesn't say the technologies "should be thoroughly studied," which is what (A) would require.

B   **Direct Contradiction:** The passage says that "the human brain is highly plastic; neurons and synapses change as circumstances change" (39-41); further, it says that "when we adapt...we end up with a different brain" (41-43). These are both examples of Passage 1 explicitly stating that the brain is adaptable and flexible, which is the opposite of saying that the brain becomes "increasingly rigid," as this answer choice would require.

C ✓   **Correct:** The passage says "certain cognitive skills are strengthened by our use of computers and the Net" (3-4). The phrase "some positive effects" from this choice restates the idea that "skills are strengthened," so (C) is correct.

D   **Literary Interpretation:** Some untrained test-takers will fall for (D) because they'll try to interpret Passage 1, instead of reading it literally, and they'll assume that the author is generally in favor of people using digital technologies. The text *does* say that "certain cognitive skills are strengthened by our use of computers and the Net" (3-4), but this isn't literally the same thing as saying that anything "should be widely encouraged," which is what (D) would require, so (D) is wrong.

ⓘ The answer must restate or demonstrate the relevant statement. See "What about "Best Evidence" Questions?" on page 72.

Subjective Phrases to Ignore: "best"

A ✓   **Correct:** As we discussed in the walkthrough for the previous question, this citation is restated by (C) in the previous question, which is the correct answer to that question. That makes this choice the correct answer for this question.

B   **Barely Relevant:** This citation doesn't restate any of the answer choices from the previous question, so it can't be the correct answer to this question. Further, this citation might seem to contradict the correct answer for the previous question, because it says that we shouldn't "conclude that the Web is making us smarter" (24-25). But, as trained test-takers, we know that we need to read carefully when we take the SAT, and we realize that the author of Passage 1 still says "certain cognitive skills are strengthened" (3-4), even if screen-based technologies may not be making us smarter overall, so it's still possible for (C) to be the correct answer to the previous question, even if Passage 1 contains the citation in this answer choice.

C   **Confused Relationships:** At first glance, an untrained test-taker might think this citation supported choice (A) from the previous question. But when we read carefully, we see that this citation doesn't actually say that "the use of screen-based technologies" "should be thoroughly studied," which is what choice (A) in the previous question would have required. Instead, this citation simply mentions a number of existing studies, which isn't the same thing as saying that anything should be thoroughly studied. Since the correct answer to the previous question isn't a restatement of this citation, (C) is wrong.

D   **Barely Relevant:** This citation tells us about Patricia Greenfield's conclusions about the use of various media; it can't tell us what the author thinks about "the use of screen-based media," which is what question 22 required. Since the citation in (D) isn't discussing the right person's opinion in the first place (as required by the prompt to question 22), we know that it can't be restated by the correct answer to the previous question, which means it can't be the correct answer to this question.

❶ *The prompt often mentions describing the passage, and usually doesn't include a line citation. The answer must still be restated or demonstrated by some specific part of the text, even if there's no citation. See "What about Questions Without Citations?" p. 72*

A   Literary Interpretation: The passage does mention a study about how "women search for medical information online" (17), but it doesn't actually say anything about the way people feel about their health, so (A) can't be right. (Note that we don't need to know the word "complacent" in order to tell that (A) must be wrong, because the text doesn't say anything about people having any kind of feeling or reaction "about their health" at all, which is what (A) requires. So we can tell that there's no potential meaning of "complacent" that could make (A) correct, because the rest of (A) makes it wrong anyway.)

B ✓ Correct: The last paragraph of Passage 1 says that "our online habits" (45) cause us to "exercis[e] the neural circuits devoted to skimming and multitasking while ignoring those used for reading and thinking deeply" (47-50). The phrase "online habits" in the passage restates the idea of "using the Internet" in the prompt. The phrase "think deeply" in (B) restates the idea of "thinking deeply" from line 50, obviously; the phrase "undermine the ability" in (B) restates the idea of "ignoring" (49) "the neural circuits devoted to" (48) deep thinking, since Passage 1 establishes that the brain gets better at tasks it performs frequently, and worse at tasks that it performs less frequently. Since (B) restates the elements of the relevant part of the passage, we can tell it must be correct.

C   Reasonable Statement Not in the Text: An untrained test-taker might imagine that "becoming adept at using the Internet" could "increase people's social contacts," because it's possible to meet people online. But Passage 1 never says anything about meeting people online, so trained test-takers know (C) can't be correct.

D   Reasonable Statement Not in the Text: Untrained test-takers might imagine that "becoming adept at using the Internet" could "improve people's self-confidence," as (D) would require, because getting better at something often makes people more confident. But the passage doesn't restate that idea at any point, so this answer can't be correct.

❶ *The prompt includes the phrase "most nearly means" and the choices are usually one- or two-word phrases. The answer is either restated or demonstrated by an idea from the surrounding text. Remember you can work around unknown words, and be ready to guess/skip and focus on other questions if you don't know the words. See "What about 'Most Nearly Means' Questions?" on p.73.*

Subjective Phrases to Ignore: "most nearly"

A   ("We know that the human brain is highly <u>creative</u>; neurons and synapses change as circumstances change.") **Reasonable Statement Not in the Text:** Untrained test-takers might waste time trying to decide if (A) is right, because they often try to interpret a passage, and it might make sense to describe the brain as "creative" in some other context. But trained test-takers recognize right away that the passage doesn't restate the idea of creativity at any point, so (A) can't be right.

B   ("We know that the human brain is highly <u>artificial</u>; neurons and synapses change as circumstances change.") **Reasonable Statement Not in the Text:** (B) might be tempting to some untrained test-takers because some people think of "plastic" as an "artificial" substance, or because of some connection between the brain and the idea of "artificial" intelligence. But we can see that the citation doesn't restate the idea of anything being "artificial," "fake," or any similar word, so (B) is wrong.

C ✓ ("We know that the human brain is highly <u>malleable</u>; neurons and synapses change as circumstances change.") **Correct:** This citation says that "the human brain is highly plastic; neurons and synapses change as circumstances change" (39-41). So "neurons and synapses chang[ing] as circumstances change" is an example of the human brain being "highly plastic." In other words, something "chang[ing]" is the same as something being "plastic". Since the word "malleable" can mean something like "able to be changed," we can see that this choice is correct. (If you didn't know the word "malleable" when answering this question, see the note on this question for a way to work around that word.)

D   ("We know that the human brain is highly <u>sculptural</u>; neurons and synapses change as circumstances change.") **Barely Relevant:** The word "sculptural" doesn't restate anything on the page, nor is it demonstrated by the passage, so (D) is wrong.

Note   It's still possible to tell that (C) must be right even if we're not familiar with the word "malleable." If we know the words "creative," "artificial," and "sculptural," and if we know that the correct answer needs to restate the idea of changing in response to something, we can tell (A), (B), and (D) must all be wrong answers. This is a great example of the way that knowing the unwritten rules of the SAT is much more useful than memorizing the meaning of an individual word: "malleable" is unlikely to come up on test-day in a way that requires you to know it in order to answer a question correctly, but the idea of insisting on an answer choice that restates the relevant portion of the passage is something that's relevant to every single SAT Reading question, and can often help you work around any unknown words you see on test-day. Keep this in mind as you decide where to focus your preparation efforts! (Also see our discussion of the "bad connection" approach on page 66 of this Black Book for more on these ideas.)

ⓘ *The prompt often mentions describing the passage, and usually doesn't include a line citation. The answer must still be restated or demonstrated by some specific part of the text, even if there's no citation. See "What about Questions Without Citations?" p. 72*

Subjective Phrases to Ignore: "primarily" "suggest"

A   **Barely Relevant:** Nothing in the text states that Woody Allen had any kind of like or dislike for anything, so (A) isn't restated or demonstrated by anything in the text, which means it's wrong.

B ✓   **Correct:** Lines 60-61 say "experience does not revamp the basic information-processing capacities of the brain," and then the next sentence mentions "speed-reading programs...claim[ing] to do just that," where the phrase "just that" refers back to the idea in the previous sentence about revamping the brain's capacity for processing information. The sentence continues with "but the verdict was rendered by Woody Allen" (63); as trained test-takers, we know that the word "but" in line 63 tells us that Woody Allen must be directly contradicting the claim mentioned earlier—that is, he's directly contradicting the idea that speed-reading programs improve the brain's ability to process information. In the context of Woody Allen reading a "famously long novel...in one sitting," we can understand this to mean that Woody Allen was not able to understand the novel after he read it using speed-reading. Once again, we see that an awareness of the SAT's unwritten rules allows us to find the correct answer to a question with total certainty, even though the wording of the prompt would lead an untrained test-taker to think that the question required subjectivity and interpretation.

C   **Confused Relationships:** Lines 62-65 describe the result of Woody Allen reading War and Peace, and lines 66-69 describe how "multitasking" is a "myth." But the text never mentions anything about Woody Allen's ability to multitask, which means (C) isn't restated or demonstrated by the passage, so it's wrong.

D   **Literary Interpretation:** The text mentions that Woody Allen read War and Peace, which is a "famously long novel" (64). But nothing in the text indicates that Woody Allen regrets anything, so this choice must be wrong.

ⓘ *The prompt often mentions describing the passage, and usually doesn't include a line citation. The answer must still be restated or demonstrated by some specific part of the text, even if there's no citation. See "What about Questions Without Citations?" p. 72*

A   **Reasonable Statement Not in the Text:** An untrained test-taker might imagine that pursuing knowledge involves taking risks, but the text doesn't restate or demonstrate that idea, so (A) must be wrong.

B   **Direct Contradiction:** Right before mentioning "novelists" (79) and "scientists" (80), the author says "accomplished people don't bulk up their brains with intellectual calisthenics" (77-78). So the text actually says "accomplished people" don't "bulk up their brains," which is the opposite of what (B) requires when it talks about "improv[ing]...minds."

C   **Confused Relationships:** Lines 71-77 mention a variety of different tasks related to different fields of study, but the text never says anything about whether people are "curious about other subjects," as (C) requires. If anything, the text says that people like novelists and scientists "immerse themselves in their fields" (79), rather than having any interest in other fields.

D ✓   **Correct:** The text says that accomplished people "immerse themselves in their fields," (78-79), then says that "novelists read lots of novels, [sic] scientists read lots of science" (79-80). We can see the text offers novelists reading novels and scientists reading science as examples of people "immersing themselves in their fields," which directly restates (D).

ⓘ *The prompt asks about the purpose or role of a part of the text. The correct answer must be accurately restated or described by the relevant text, with no interpretation. See "What about "Purpose" Questions?" on p.74.*

Subjective Phrases to Ignore: "primarily"

A   **Reasonable Statement Not in the Text:** Some untrained test-takers might arbitrarily decide that the wording in the citation text is "ornate," and that the concept being illustrated is hard to understand, as the answer choice would require. But, as trained test-takers, we know that it doesn't matter what *we think* about a passage; the only thing that matters is what's explicitly stated in the passage. In order for the word "difficult" to be an acceptable part of the right answer, the text would have to say something like "a lot of people have trouble grasping this," or "even though it might not be easy to comprehend," or something like that. Since none of that appears in the cited text, this choice must be incorrect.

B   **Confused Relationships:** As trained test-takers, we know that this choice must be incorrect because the author doesn't express any "severe opinion about human behavior," as the answer choice would require; all he describes is what "media critics" (83) "assume" (87), and what they assume is never described as "severe" or anything similar to "severe."

C   **Confused Relationships:** The citation does mention "ancient peoples" (85-86), who are necessarily part of "the past," as (C) requires. But the word "nostalgia" in the answer choice doesn't restate anything from the passage, so (C) is wrong.

D ✓   **Correct:** To understand how the author of Passage 2 "criticizes the view of a particular group," as this answer choice requires, we need to consider the other two sentences in the paragraph, because the last sentence is a continuation of thoughts that are begun in those earlier sentences. The word "they" (87) in the citation refers to "media critics" (83), who are the "group" mentioned in the answer choice. The author says, "media critics write as if the brain takes on the qualities of whatever it consumes" (83-84), and then the final sentence provides examples of this general idea that media critics have. We can already tell from the phrase "as if" (83) that the author of Passage 2 doesn't agree with the position of the media critics. Further, the first sentence of the last paragraph says "the effects of consuming electronic media are likely to be far more limited than the panic implies" (81-82), and the "media critics" (83) are presented as an example of the "panic" in that sentence; in other words, there's a "panic" that "implies" something about "the effects of consuming electronic media," and the author says those "effects" are probably "far more limited" than whatever the panic says they are. For these reasons, we know that the author is "criticiz[ing] the view" of the media critics, just as (D) requires, which means (D) is right.

Test 2, Question 29	TYPE: PAIRED PASSAGES / PURPOSE OF CITED TEXT

ⓘ *The prompt also asks how someone would respond to a claim or argument. The correct answer restates a position that's already stated in the passage. See "What about Paired Passages?" on p.76. The prompt also asks about the purpose or role of a part of the text. The correct answer must be accurately restated or described by the relevant text, with no interpretation. See "What about "Purpose" Questions?" on p.74.*

Subjective Phrases to Ignore: "main"

A   **Barely Relevant:** Passage 1 mentions both "video gaming" (7) and "Web browsing," but it doesn't compare brain function between these two groups, and Passage 2 doesn't mention either group at all, so this choice must be wrong.

B   **Barely Relevant:** Passage 1 mentions "skills" (3, 30, 34) in a few places, and the idea of "an experienced Internet user" (18), but it doesn't talk about problem-solving skills or "varying levels of internet experience" at all, as this choice would require; further, Passage 2 doesn't mention any of these topics. Either issue would be enough on its own for this choice to be wrong.

C   **Confused Relationships:** Both passages mention the idea of "studies" (7, 16, 27, 67) but neither mentions "financial support," or even money in general, in any way. Since (C) doesn't restate anything in either passage, it must be wrong.

D✓   **Correct:** Each passage "makes an argument about the effects of electronic media on the brain," exactly as this choice requires, so this choice is correct. In Passage 1, the author takes the following position: "The mental consequences of our online info-crunching are not universally bad. Certain cognitive skills are strengthened by our use of computers and the Net" (1-4). The phrases "online info-crunching" and "our use of computers and the Net" are both references to "types of electronic media" as the answer choice requires; the idea of "mental consequences" and the "strengthen[ing]" of "cognitive skills" are examples of "effects...on the brain," as the answer choice requires. In Passage 2, the author says, "the effects of consuming electronic media are likely to be far more limited than the panic implies. Media critics write as if the brain takes on the qualities of whatever it consumes..." (81-84). The phrase "the effects of consuming electronic media" is almost an exact restatement of the phrase "the effects of electronic media" in the answer choice, and the phrase "as if the brain takes on the qualities..." makes it clear that the effects being discussed are "effects...on the brain," as we see in (D). Since both passages demonstrate exactly what (D) describes, (D) is correct.

Test 2, Question 30	TYPE: PAIRED PASSAGES

ⓘ *The prompt also asks how someone would respond to a claim or argument. The correct answer restates a position that's already stated in the passage. See "What about Paired Passages?" on p.76.*

Subjective Phrases to Ignore: "best"

A   **Barely Relevant:** Passage 2 doesn't mention any "firsthand experiences," so this choice can't possibly be correct, because that part of the choice already fails to describe the reading. Further, Passage 1 doesn't take a "clinical approach" to the question; a clinical approach would require an in-depth explanation of some kind of experiment to measure the impact of electronic media on the brains of patients, or something else along those lines. Either of these issues is enough to make (A) wrong.

B✓   **Correct:** The "conclusions...from the research" that are mentioned in the answer choice appear in lines 9-12, 18-22, and 29-38. After describing these studies, the author of Passage 1 says, "We know that the human brain is highly plastic; neurons and synapses change as circumstances change" (39-41). This answer choice requires Passage 2 to "critique" those conclusions, and the author of Passage 2 does this when he says, "critics of new media sometimes use science itself to press their case, citing research that shows how 'experience can change the brain.' But cognitive neuroscientists roll their eyes at such talk" (51-54). The words "but" and "roll their eyes" demonstrate that the author of Passage 2 is critical of the conclusions discussed in Passage 1, exactly as this choice requires, so we know this is the correct answer.

C   **Barely Relevant:** Nothing in Passage 1 indicates that it's "examin[ing]" anything "in depth," as (C) requires, nor does Passage 2 look at anything from a "high-level view," as (C) also requires. Either issue by itself is enough to make (C) wrong.

D   **Confused Relationships:** Passage 1 discusses the findings of a few studies in lines 9-12, 18-22, and 29-38, as (D) requires, but Passage 2 doesn't *predict* any negative reactions to those findings; instead, Passage 2 itself reacts negatively to those findings. As trained test-takers, we know that this small difference from the text is enough to make (D) completely wrong.

ⓘ *The prompt also asks how someone would respond to a claim or argument. The correct answer restates a position that's already stated in the passage. See "What about Paired Passages?" on p.76.*

Subjective Phrases to Ignore: "most likely"

A   **Confused Relationships:** The first paragraph of Passage 1 does mention a connection between "our use of computers and the Net" and "hand-eye coordination" (3-6), but that passage doesn't say anything about comparing "computer-savvy children" to "their parents," as this answer choice would require. And Passage 2 doesn't mention "hand-eye coordination" at all. Since the concept from this answer choice isn't addressed in either passage, we know this choice must be wrong.

B   **Direct Contradiction:** This is an idea that the authors disagree on. After discussing some benefits of using electronic media, Passage 1 says, "our growing use of the Net" (31) causes "a weakening of our capacity for the kind of 'deep processing' that underpins 'mindful knowledge acquisition, inductive analysis, critical thinking, imagination, and reflection'" (35-38). But the author of Passage 2 tells us that when "critics of new media" say that "'experience can change the brain,'" "cognitive neuroscientists roll their eyes" (51-54); he also says, "The effects of consuming electronic media are likely to be far more limited than the panic implies" (81-82). So we can see that the author of Passage 2 does agree with the statement in this answer choice, but the author of Passage 1 does NOT agree with it. Since the prompt requires the authors to take the same stance on the topic in this choice, we know (B) is wrong.

C ✓   **Correct:** Passage 1 tells us that "use of the Net" (31) has led to development of "visual-spatial skills," but goes on to say that "those gains go hand in hand with a weakening of our capacity for the kind of 'deep processing' that underpins 'mindful knowledge acquisition, inductive analysis, critical thinking, imagination, and reflection'" (34-38). In other words, Passage 1 says that the use of electronic media improves "visual-spatial skills," just as we see in (C), and then lists a lot of skills in other areas that aren't "improved," as (C) further requires. Passage 2 says, "If you train people to do one thing (recognize shapes, solve math puzzles, find hidden words), they get better at doing that thing, but almost nothing else" (71-74). This statement fits exactly with (C)'s statement that "improved...skills" of one kind "do not generalize to improved skills in other areas." As we can see, both passages make statements that are restated by (C), just as the prompt requires, so (C) is right.

D   **Reasonable Statement Not in the Text:** Untrained test-takers might imagine that people would be unlikely to prefer reading on a screen to reading an actual book, and that this imagined preference might somehow be a point of agreement for the two authors. But neither author actually compares the idea of reading books to reading from a screen, so this choice doesn't restate anything in the reading, which means it must be wrong.

ⓘ *The answer must restate or demonstrate the relevant statement. See "What about "Best Evidence" Questions?" on page 72.*

Subjective Phrases to Ignore: "best"

A   **Confused Relationships:** In this citation, the author describes a statement made by "critics of new media" (51). He isn't stating his own opinions, so this text can't possibly show whether the author of Passage 2, himself, agrees or disagrees with anything, including "the claim attributed to Michael Merzenich" as the prompt requires.

B ✓   **Correct:** The "claim attributed to Michael Merzenich in lines 41-43" as described in the prompt says that the brain changes when it adapts to a new cultural phenomenon; the citation in (B) says, "Yes, every time we learn a fact or skill the wiring of the brain changes." These statements directly restate each other, so (B) is right.

C   **Direct Contradiction:** In this citation, the author of Passage 2 acknowledges that "neural plasticity" exists, but then immediately says that doesn't mean "the brain is a blob of clay pounded into shape by experience;" this directly disagrees with "the claim attributed to Michael Merzenich in lines 41-43" as described in the prompt, so (C) can't be correct.

D   **Confused Relationships:** In this citation, the author describes what "media critics write" (83). The author isn't stating his own opinions, so this text can't possibly show what he, himself, agrees with or disagrees with. So (D) is wrong just as (A) is.

Note   The claim attributed to Michael Merzenich in lines 41-43 is "When we adapt to a new cultural phenomenon, including the use of a new medium, we end up with a different brain," so we need to find an answer choice citing text in which the author of Passage 2 expresses the same idea.

ⓘ *The prompt often mentions describing the passage, and usually doesn't include a line citation. The answer must still be restated or demonstrated by some specific part of the text, even if there's no citation. See "What about Questions Without Citations?" p. 72*

A   **Reasonable Statement Not in the Text:** An untrained test-taker might imagine that "equal educational opportunities" could be related to the issues discussed in this passage, but the author never actually says anything about educational opportunities, so (A) can't be right.

B ✓   Correct: (B) directly restates concepts from the passage, so we know it's correct. The phrase "prevented from exerting their positive influence on men" in (B) restates the ideas that "the strong, natural characteristics of womanhood are repressed" (38-39), and that "the feminine element" (17) has been "overpower[ed]" (17), among other similar statements throughout the passage. The phrase "which has led to societal breakdown" in (B) restates lines from the passage like the following: "no one need wonder at the disorganization, at the fragmentary condition of everything [in society]..." (25-26); "and now man...mourns in bitterness that falsehood, selfishness, and violence are the law of life" (53-55). This statement from lines 79-82 also restates the answer choice on its own: "woman's love, if permitted to assert itself...against oppression, violence, and war, would hold all these destructive forces in check." As we can see from these several examples, the author clearly states that society has been destroyed by oppression, violence, war, falsehood, and selfishness, because female nature has been repressed and overpowered, exactly as (B) requires.

C   Literary Interpretation: The text does say "we ask enfranchisement" (61), which is another word for the right to vote. But the text never says anything about particular candidates or elections, which is what the phrase "poor candidates winning important elections" in this answer choice would require, so this choice must be wrong.

D   Confused Relationships: The author mentions that "a man's government, is civil, religious, and social disorganization" (2-3), but she never actually discusses the idea of women being "blocked...from serving as legislators," let alone that circumstance leading to "the creation of unjust laws," which this answer choice would require.

Test 2, Question 34   **TYPE: CITATION QUESTION**

ⓘ *The question includes a citation from the text. The answer must be directly restated or demonstrated in the cited text, or in the text closely surrounding the cited text. See the general process for answering SAT Reading questions on p. 71.*

Subjective Phrases to Ignore: "mainly"

A ✓   Correct: The sentence that contains the phrase "high carnival" (15) goes on to say that the "male element" (15) has been "overpowering the feminine element everywhere" (17). This directly restates the phrase "utter domination of women by men" in this answer choice, so this choice must be correct. Notice that we don't need to be familiar with the phrase "high carnival" to answer this question correctly, because only this answer choice restates an idea from the surrounding text.

B   Literary Interpretation: This choice might be tempting to untrained test-takers, because the word "carnival" might make them think of a fair with rides and games. But nothing in the passage actually restates the idea that the author is describing that kind of carnival, so this choice must be wrong.

C   Off by One or Two Words: The passage does describe bad moral values repeatedly, such as in phrases like "a destructive force, stern, selfish, aggrandizing, loving war, violence, conquest, acquisition, breeding in the material and moral world alike discord, disorder, disease, and death" (4-7). But the word "decline" in this answer choice would require the author to say that moral values are still in the process of getting worse; instead, the author says the situation has been like this "from the beginning" (16), without any sign that things "decline[d]" from a better state. Since the author never says moral values were better at some previous time, we know, as trained test-takers, that the single word "decline" is enough to make this choice wrong. This answer choice is a great example of the extreme importance of making sure that every single word in an answer choice is restated or demonstrated by the relevant portion of the passage! Make sure to keep this in mind on test day!

D   Direct Contradiction: As we discussed for (A), the phrase "high carnival" is immediately followed by a statement about men's power over women, not the other way around. (D) is probably here to trick readers who don't go back to verify their answers with the text, or who assume the text must support the idea of female empowerment since the author is a feminist. This is another example of the importance of relying on exactly what appears on the page, rather than making assumptions!

Test 2, Question 35   **TYPE: DESCRIBE THE PASSAGE**

The next question is a "best evidence" question referring back to this question; you may choose to consider the citations in the choices for the next question when answering this one if you want. See "Is there a 'best evidence' shortcut?" on page 72 for more.

ⓘ *The prompt often mentions describing the passage, and usually doesn't include a line citation. The answer must still be restated or demonstrated by some specific part of the text, even if there's no citation. See "What about Questions Without Citations?" p. 72*

A   Direct Contradiction: The first paragraph says the "soul of humanity" has "struggled for the centuries" (12) through the issues caused by "a man's government" (2); the second paragraph says men have "overpower[ed] the feminine element everywhere" (17) "from the beginning" (16). The phrases "a man's government" and "overpowering the feminine element" from the passage both restate the idea of "the control of society by men" in this answer choice, and the phrases "for the centuries" and "from the beginning" both contradict the idea of this situation being a "relatively recent historical development" as required in the prompt.

B   Confused Relationships: Several portions of the passage refer to ideas like "the spread of war and injustice" as described in the answer choice, such as the "war, violence, conquest, acquisition" (5) brought on by "man's government" (2). But the text doesn't say that these issues only began "relatively recent[ly]," as the prompt requires, so this choice must be wrong.

C   Confused Relationships: The passage mentions "hard iron rule" in "the home" (23-25), which directly restates the idea of the "domination of domestic life" described in this answer choice—but, as with choices (A) and (B), the passage doesn't say that this only began "relatively recent[ly]," as described by the prompt, so this choice must be wrong.

D ✓   Correct: (D) restates something specifically mentioned in the passage as a "recent historical development" as the prompt requires. In lines 19-24, the author says, "we know but little of true manhood and womanhood, of the latter comparatively nothing, for it has scarce been recognized as a power until within the last century." As trained test-takers, we see that the word "it" in that citation refers to the phrase "the latter," which, in turn, refers to "true…womanhood," which is the last thing mentioned by the author in the previous phrase. So the author says womanhood "has scarce been recognized as a power until within the last century." The words "scarce" and "until" indicate that the author considers this recognition to be something that happened not too long ago, and is a "recent historical development" as required by the prompt.

	Test 2, Question 36	TYPE: BEST EVIDENCE

ⓘ *The answer must restate or demonstrate the relevant statement. See "What about "Best Evidence" Questions?" on page 72.*

Subjective Phrases to Ignore: "best"

A   Literary Interpretation: This citation may seem related to (B) from question 35, but it couldn't support (B) as an answer to 35 because it doesn't say that anything "develop[ed]" "relatively recent[ly]," as the prompt for the previous question requires.

B ✓   Correct: As we saw in our discussion of choice (D) for the previous question, this citation restates that choice, which is why (D) was the correct answer to question 35, and (B) is the correct answer to this question.

C   Literary Interpretation: This citation may seem related to (C) from the previous question, but it doesn't say anything about a "relatively recent historical development" as required by the prompt of the previous question, so it can't be the correct answer to this question, and (C) isn't the correct answer to the previous question.

D   Confused Relationships: As we saw with the citations in (A) and (C) above, this choice may seem related to a choice from question 35, but it doesn't mention anything being a "recent historical development," as the prompt for 35 requires.

	Test 2, Question 37	TYPE: WORD MOST NEARLY MEANS

ⓘ *The prompt includes the phrase "most nearly means" and the choices are usually one- or two-word phrases. The answer is either restated or demonstrated by an idea from the surrounding text. Remember you can work around unknown words, and be ready to guess/skip and focus on other questions if you don't know the words. See "What about "Most Nearly Means" Questions?" on p.73.*

Subjective Phrases to Ignore: "most nearly"

A   ("Society is but the reflection of man himself, untempered by woman's thought; the hard iron <u>general guideline</u> we feel alike in the church, the state, and the home.") Reasonable Statement Not in the Text: This might seem like a good choice to an untrained test-taker, because "rule" can mean "general guideline" in some contexts, but the text doesn't restate or demonstrate the idea of a "general guideline," so (A) is wrong. Instead, it describes "the male element…overpowering the feminine element, crushing out all the diviner qualities…" (15-18). Words like "overpowering" and "crushing" in these lines, combined with the description of the rule as "hard iron," don't fit the idea of something as relaxed as a "general guideline."

B ✓   ("Society is but the reflection of man himself, untempered by woman's thought; the hard iron <u>controlling force</u> we feel alike in the church, the state, and the home.") Correct: The passage describes "the male element…overpowering the feminine element, crushing out all the diviner qualities…" (15-18) and says that "man … has undertaken the absolute control of all sublunary matters" (27-30). Phrases like "overpowering" and "absolute control" are restated by the phrase "controlling force" in this answer choice, so we know this choice must be correct.

C   ("Society is but the reflection of man himself, untempered by woman's thought; the hard iron <u>established habit</u> we feel alike in the church, the state, and the home.") Reasonable Statement Not in the Text: "Rule" could mean "established habit" in another context, because something like an "established habit" that has been done regularly for a long time could sometimes be described as a "rule." But nothing in the text actually restates the idea of a "hard iron established habit," so (C) is wrong.

D   ("Society is but the reflection of man himself, untempered by woman's thought; the hard iron <u>procedural method</u> we feel alike in the church, the state, and the home.") Reasonable Statement Not in the Text: A "procedural method" could be called a "rule" in another context. When there is an established procedure for doing something, the specific methods of that procedure can be described as rules. But the passage doesn't restate or demonstrate this idea, so this answer can't be correct.

	Test 2, Question 38	TYPE: CITATION QUESTION

ⓘ *The question includes a citation from the text. The answer must be directly restated or demonstrated in the cited text, or in the text closely surrounding the cited text. See the general process for answering SAT Reading questions on p. 71.*

Subjective Phrases to Ignore: "reasonably" "inferred" "generally"

A   Reasonable Statement Not in the Text: Untrained test-takers might imagine that some people would "praise women who fight for their long-denied rights" as (A) requires. But the text says that the "people" (31) who use the term "the strong-minded" actually "object" (31) to the "demands" (31) of the strong-minded—in other words, people are using the term "strong-minded" to refer to other people whose demands they don't like, and not to people they support. So (A) is wrong.

B   **Reasonable Statement Not in the Text:** Out of context, some untrained test-takers might think the term "the strong-minded" would refer to people "who demonstrate intellectual skill," as this choice would require. But the author doesn't actually say anything about "the strong-minded" being smart or not—she simply says they make some "demands" (32) that some other "people object to" (31). Since this choice doesn't restate anything in the passage, it must be wrong.

C   **Reasonable Statement Not in the Text:** Some untrained test-takers will assume that a passage with this subject matter would talk about women entering male-dominated professions, but the author never says anything about that at all. So this choice can't be restating anything from the passage, which means it must be wrong.

D✓   **Correct:** The text says the "people" (31) who use the term "the strong-minded" (32) "object" (31) to the "demands" (31) of the strong-minded." The text goes on to say that "people" (31) object "because they say 'the right of suffrage will make the women masculine'" (32-34). Since the idea that "the right of suffrage will make the women masculine" is the reason given for "object[ing] to [their] demands" in this sentence, we know the "demands" must be for "the right of suffrage" to be given to women, which restates the idea of "agitat[ing] for the vote for their sex," as required by (D). And we know the phrase "condemn women" from (D) is supported by the text because the text says the people using the term "strong-minded" are people who "object" (31) to those demands, which means they have negative feelings, as the word "condemn" requires.

Note   This question requires us to distinguish among different points of view. The prompt asks about the "intended" use of a term, and we can't find the correct answer to the question unless we realize that the people using the term were people who disagreed with the author of the passage.

❚ Test 2, Question 39   **TYPE: WORD MOST NEARLY MEANS**

ⓘ *The prompt includes the phrase "most nearly means" and the choices are usually one- or two-word phrases. The answer is either restated or demonstrated by an idea from the surrounding text. Remember you can work around unknown words, and be ready to guess/skip and focus on other questions if you don't know the words. See "What about "Most Nearly Means" Questions?" on p.73.*

Subjective Phrases to Ignore: "most nearly"

A   ("Though disfranchised, we have few women in the <u>superior</u> sense; we have simply so many reflections, varieties, and dilutions of the masculine gender.") **Reasonable Statement Not in the Text:** In another context, "best" could mean "superior." For example, in discussing some different applicants for a job, one applicant might appear to be the "best" or "superior" choice. But the passage never restates the idea of the "sense" being "superior," so this answer can't be correct.

B   ("Though disfranchised, we have few women in the <u>excellent</u> sense; we have simply so many reflections, varieties, and dilutions of the masculine gender.") **Reasonable Statement Not in the Text:** In another context, "best" could mean "excellent,". But the passage doesn't restate or demonstrate the idea of excellence, so (B) is wrong.

C✓   ("Though disfranchised, we have few women in the <u>genuine</u> sense; we have simply so many reflections, varieties, and dilutions of the masculine gender.") **Correct:** In the second half of the sentence, the author says, "we have simply...reflections, varieties, and dilutions of the masculine gender." So the author says that, rather than having "women in the best sense," we just have "reflections...of the masculine gender." Since the "masculine gender" refers to men, and men are not women, saying that we have only "reflections...of the masculine gender" is the same as saying we don't have actual or "genuine" women, as this choice requires. For this reason, we can tell this choice must be correct.

D   ("Though disfranchised, we have few women in the <u>rarest</u> sense; we have simply so many reflections, varieties, and dilutions of the masculine gender.") **Reasonable Statement Not in the Text:** An untrained test-taker might think of "rare[ness]" as something related to being the "best," because we might think of things of high quality as being rarer than things of lesser quality. But the passage never restates that idea, so this answer can't be correct.

❚ Test 2, Question 40   **TYPE: DESCRIBE THE PASSAGE**

> *The next question is a "best evidence" question referring back to this question; you may choose to consider the citations in the choices for the next question when answering this one if you want. See "Is there a 'best evidence' shortcut?" on page 72 for more.*

ⓘ *The prompt often mentions describing the passage, and usually doesn't include a line citation. The answer must still be restated or demonstrated by some specific part of the text, even if there's no citation. See "What about Questions Without Citations?" p. 72*

A✓   **Correct:** The text says "and now man himself stands appalled at the results of his own excesses, and mourns in bitterness that falsehood, selfishness, and violence are the law of life" (53-55). The word "lament" in the answer choice directly restates the idea of "mourn[ing]" from the passage, and the phrase "the problems they have created" from the answer choice restates the phrase "the results of his own excesses." Since every part of this answer choice directly restates a portion of the relevant text, we can tell that it must be correct. (See the notes if you weren't sure what the word "lament" means.)

B **Off by One or Two Words:** In lines 31-34 the author mentions the idea of women asking for suffrage, and in line 61 the author, who is a woman, says "we ask woman's enfranchisement," which is synonymous with "call[ing] for woman suffrage" as (B) requires—but the text never describes any man "join[ing]" that call, which makes (B) wrong.

C **Literary Interpretation:** In lines 42-43, the author says "to keep a foothold in society, woman must be as near like man as possible," and some untrained test-takers will be tempted to interpret (C) as though it were related to that citation. But the phrase "as near like man as possible" doesn't reflect something that "men have begun to" think about women, as the prompt would require; instead, the phrase reflects a condition that the writer says women will have to meet in order to have "a foothold in society" (42). So (C) is wrong.

D **Confused Relationships:** In lines 61-66, the author explains that she believes including women in government will improve civic life. But the text never says men have begun to ask women how they would do that—or, indeed, to ask women anything at all. Since this choice doesn't restate anything in the passage, it's wrong.

Note This is another example of a question that can still be answered correctly even if we don't know one of the words in the right answer. In this case, many test-takers won't recognize the word "lament," but they can still tell that (B), (C), and (D) must be wrong if they stick to the rules of the SAT Reading section and insist on looking for a choice that's directly restated or demonstrated by the passage. Since those choices must be wrong, and since we can see that the phrase "problems they have created" from (A) is a direct restatement of "the results of his own excesses" (53-54), we'd still be able to work out that (A) must be right, and "lament" must have a meaning that restates something in the passage. Keep this kind in mind when you're deciding where to focus your test-prep efforts—if you're disciplined in applying your training, you'll often be able to overcome the occasional unknown word with total certainty! See our discussion of the "bad connection" approach on page 66 for more on this.

Test 2, Question 41　　　　　TYPE: BEST EVIDENCE

ⓘ *The answer must restate or demonstrate the relevant statement. See "What about "Best Evidence" Questions?" on page 72.*

Subjective Phrases to Ignore: "best"

A **Confused Relationships:** This citation might seem to support the idea of woman suffrage mentioned in (B) of question 40, but the citation offers the opinion of the author, not of "men," which is what the prompt from question 40 would require.

B ✓ **Correct:** As we saw when we discussed (A) in question 40, this citation directly restates concepts in 40.

C **Confused Relationships:** To an untrained test-taker, this might seem to support the idea of women improving civic life, which appears in (D) in question 40. But the citation offers the opinion of the *author*, not of "men," as the prompt from 40 requires.

D **Confused Relationships:** This citation is related to the idea of woman suffrage mentioned in choice (B) of the previous question, but—as we saw with choices (A) and (C) above—the citation presents the opinion of the author, not of "men," as the prompt of the previous question would require.

Test 2, Question 42　　　　　TYPE: CITATION QUESTION

ⓘ *The question includes a citation from the text. The answer must be directly restated or demonstrated in the cited text, or in the text closely surrounding the cited text. See the general process for answering SAT Reading questions on p. 71.*

Subjective Phrases to Ignore: "primarily"

A **Wrong Part of the Passage:** This passage as a whole does discuss many of the differences between men and women, but the sixth paragraph never actually discusses women in any detail—the phrase "marked in woman" (72) only indicates that some women "often" (72) have the traits that the author associates with "the masculine element" (67). So we can't say the paragraph is "concerned with establishing a contrast between men and women," as (A) requires.

B **Barely Relevant:** The word "spirits" (70) might make (B) tempting to an untrained test-taker, but the sixth paragraph never restates the idea of a contrast between "the spiritual world and the material world," as (B) requires, so it's wrong.

C **Literary Interpretation:** This choice will attract a lot of untrained test-takers who don't read the citation very carefully, because the author does say, "not...all men are hard, selfish, and brutal" (67-69). But, as trained test-takers, we know that we need to read carefully when we evaluate an answer choice; when we do that here, we see that the author never specifically mentions "bad men" as opposed to "good men," which this choice would require. Instead, the author says, "I refer to those characteristics" (71) and "powers" (76), rather than to individual men.

D ✓ **Correct:** The first sentence of the sixth paragraph says, "in speaking of the masculine element...I refer to those characteristics, though often marked in woman, that distinguish what is called the stronger sex" (67-73). So we can clearly see, when we read carefully—like a trained-test-taker would read—that the phrase "the masculine element," which describes masculine "characteristics," isn't the same thing as the population of actual men. It even describes traits that some women can have, as the author says in line 72. This means the author is making a distinction between actual men and the masculine traits that she says are *often*, but not *always*, found in men—which demonstrates the idea in (D).

ⓘ *The question includes a citation from the text. The answer must be directly restated or demonstrated in the cited text, or in the text closely surrounding the cited text. See the general process for answering SAT Reading questions on p. 71.*

Subjective Phrases to Ignore: "mainly"

A   **Wrong Part of the Passage:** The text does describe a scientific device called "the Coriolis Platform" (35-41), but that happens in the fourth paragraph, and the prompt for this question asks about the first paragraph. That means this choice doesn't restate the relevant part of the passage, so it must be wrong. A lot of untrained test-takers will get this question wrong because they'll vaguely remember the passage talking about a "scientific device" as required by the answer choice, but they won't bother to go back and confirm where that discussion occurs in the passage, or they won't read the prompt carefully enough to realize that this question is only talking about the first paragraph. This is a great example of how attention to detail can be the single most important aspect of scoring high on the SAT!

B   **Confused Relationships:** The first paragraph says "internal waves" (3) are "nearly impossible to see" (2), "undetectable" (5), and "hidden" (7), so some untrained test-takers will try to interpret these words and assume incorrectly that these waves might be the subject of a "common misconception," as the answer choice requires. But when we read carefully, as trained-test-takers, we see that the first paragraph doesn't say anything that restates the idea of a "misconception," "mistaken belief," "myth," or any similar kind of word at all, let alone restating the idea that there's any kind of "common," "popular," or "widely held" belief about these waves. Either of these problems by itself would be enough to make (B) wrong.

C ✓   **Correct:** Lines 1-6 describe "internal waves" as "ocean waves," which are a "natural phenomenon," as (C) requires, because the ocean is part of nature. Lines 6-9 explain the "importance" of these waves, as this choice requires, by saying they're "fundamental," which is a synonym for "important." Since this choice directly restates the passage, it must be correct.

D   **Wrong Part of the Passage:** The text does mention a study (21-24), but that's in the third paragraph, and the prompt asks us about the first paragraph. Since this choice describes the wrong part of the passage, it can't be correct. This choice might have been extremely tempting for untrained test-takers who misread the question and thought they needed to describe the main purpose of the entire passage, as opposed to the first paragraph alone, which is what the prompt asked for. Keep this kind of thing in mind on test-day, and always make sure you're referring to the correct part of the passage!

ⓘ *The prompt includes the phrase "most nearly means" and the choices are usually one- or two-word phrases. The answer is either restated or demonstrated by an idea from the surrounding text. Remember you can work around unknown words, and be ready to guess/skip and focus on other questions if you don't know the words. See "What about "Most Nearly Means" Questions?" on p.73.*

Subjective Phrases to Ignore: "closest"

A   ("If we want to have more and more accurate climate models, we have to be able to <u>control</u> processes such as this.") **Reasonable Statement Not in the Text:** In another context, "capture" might mean "control;" for example, if you "capture" an animal, you could be said to "control" that animal. But the passage doesn't restate or demonstrate the idea of "control[ling]" a wave, so (A) is wrong.

B ✓   ("If we want to have more and more accurate climate models, we have to be able to <u>record</u> processes such as this.") **Correct:** This choice restates an idea that's developed throughout the text. The original citation in the prompt appears in a quote from Peacock, and the next sentence after the quote says that Peacock's team "tried to do just that" (20), where the phrase "just that" refers back to the idea of "captur[ing] processes" like internal waves. The next sentence describes "their study, published in November in *Geophysical Research Letters*," which "focused on internal waves" (21-22). If Peacock and his colleagues "tried to do just that"— that is, "capture processes," and the result was a published study about internal waves, that study must be a record of the processes involving internal waves described in the second paragraph. All of this demonstrates the idea of "record[ing]" those processes, so this choice is correct.

C   ("If we want to have more and more accurate climate models, we have to be able to <u>secure</u> processes such as this.") **Reasonable Statement Not in the Text:** In another context, "capture" might mean "secure;" for example, if an army "captures" a location in a military context, we could say it has "secured" that location. But the passage doesn't restate or demonstrate the idea of "secur[ing]" the process described in the passage, so this choice can't be correct.

D   ("If we want to have more and more accurate climate models, we have to be able to <u>absorb</u> processes such as this.") **Confused Relationships:** This choice might be tempting to some untrained test-takers because the text describes how internal waves are involved in the "transfer of heat" (13), and that might make some people think of "absorb[ing]" heat. But nothing in the passage restates or demonstrates the idea of "absorb[ing] processes," as (D) would require, so we know it's incorrect.

The next question is a "best evidence" question referring back to this question; you may choose to consider the citations in the choices for the next question when answering this one if you want. See "Is there a 'best evidence' shortcut?" on page 72 for more.

ⓘ *The prompt often mentions describing the passage, and usually doesn't include a line citation. The answer must still be restated or demonstrated by some specific part of the text, even if there's no citation. See "What about Questions Without Citations?" p. 72*

Subjective Phrases to Ignore: "primarily"

A   Confused Relationships: The text mentions that "some of the largest" internal waves "can reach about 500 meters high" (25-26), but Peacock never says that monitoring these waves will allow scientists to "verify" that, as (A) requires.

B   Confused Relationships: The text does mention "satellite imagery" (5), and Peacock mentions "more accurate climate models" (18), so some untrained test-takers will be fooled into thinking that Peacock is talking about "improving...satellite images," as (B) requires. But Peacock never says anything will improve the quality of satellite images, so (B) must be wrong.

C   Reasonable Statement Not in the Text: Untrained test-takers might imagine that studying "wave analysis" could help people "predict and prevent coastal damage," as the answer choice describes. But if we read carefully and remember that the correct answer has to restate the relevant part of the passage, we see that the passage never actually mentions wave damage at all, or preventing coastal damage caused by waves, or anything like that, so this choice can't be right.

D✓   Correct: As trained-test-takers, we can tell (D) must be right because every part of it restates something that Peacock mentions in the text, just as the prompt requires. The text says Peacock believes "understanding" "these waves" "is crucial to global climate modeling" (13-14); the phrase "the study of such waves" from (D) restates the idea of "understanding" (13) the waves. The word "key" in (D) restates the word "crucial" (14). The phrase "scientific models" from (D) is a reference to "global climate modeling" (14). All of this is basically repeated in lines 17-19 when Peacock says, "if we want to have more and more accurate climate models, we have to be able to capture processes such as this." So (D) is right.

ⓘ *The answer must restate or demonstrate the relevant statement. See "What about "Best Evidence" Questions?" on page 72.*

Subjective Phrases to Ignore: "best"

A   Barely Relevant: This citation makes a general statement about internal waves, but it isn't actually relevant to any answer choice from the previous question, so it can't possibly be correct.

B   Confused Relationships: This citation might seem to support (B) from question 45, because both mention satellite images. But, as we discussed in the explanation for choice (B) from 45, the text never mentions the idea of "improving the quality of satellite images," as (B) would require for that question, so (B) is wrong for question 45 and this choice is wrong for 46.

C✓   Correct: As we saw in our discussion of question 45, lines 17-19 basically repeat the idea mentioned in lines 12-15 that Peacock thinks the study of these waves will impact global climate models, so this citation supports (D) from question 45.

D   Confused Relationships: An untrained test-taker might think this citation supported (C) from question 45, because both texts talk about how tall internal waves can get. But, as we discussed in the explanation for (C) in the previous question, the text never mentions the idea of "verify[ing] the maximum height of such waves," which is what (C) required in the previous question. That means (C) is the wrong answer to question 45, and this is the wrong answer to question 46.

ⓘ *The prompt includes the phrase "most nearly means" and the choices are usually one- or two-word phrases. The answer is either restated or demonstrated by an idea from the surrounding text. Remember you can work around unknown words, and be ready to guess/skip and focus on other questions if you don't know the words. See "What about "Most Nearly Means" Questions?" on p.73.*

Subjective Phrases to Ignore: "most nearly"

A✓   ("The researchers were also able to <u>create</u> a mathematical model that describes the movement and formation of these waves.")
     Correct: This choice is correct because phrases like "the model is" (67) and "[the model] can still help" (68) describe the model existing—that is, they confirm that the model isn't hypothetical, or something planned for the future. If the researchers studied the waves, and those researchers "were...able" to do something to "a mathematical model," and now there is a model "that describes the movement and formation of these waves" (66-67), then it only makes sense to say that the researchers created the model, which makes this choice correct.

B   ("The researchers were also able to <u>solve</u> a mathematical model that describes the movement and formation of these waves.")
     Confused Relationships: This might seem appealing to some test-takers who have heard the phrase "devise a solution," and who think of some connection between the word "devise" and the word "solve." It might also be appealing to test-takers who think there might be a connection between a "mathematical model" and the idea of solving something. But nothing in the text supports the idea that the researchers were able to "solve" a "mathematical model," so this choice is wrong.

C   ("The researchers were also able to <u>imagine</u> a mathematical model that describes the movement and formation of these waves.") **Confused Relationships:** This answer choice might be tempting, because someone who makes a mathematical model needs to use her mind to do that, and when we "imagine" something, we are creating something within our mind as well. But the difference is that when we imagine something, we create it entirely in our heads, while making a mathematical model involves taking actual data from the real world and figuring out how to predict its behavior. Phrases like "the model is" (67) and "[the model] can still help" (68) tell us that the model exists—that is, the model has been created, and isn't just an idea in someone's mind—so this choice can't be correct.

D   ("The researchers were also able to <u>begin</u> a mathematical model that describes the movement and formation of these waves.") **Barely Relevant:** The word "begin" here would indicate the model wasn't finished yet, but the text doesn't restate or demonstrate that idea.

Test 2, Question 48   **TYPE: DESCRIBE THE PASSAGE**

> *The next question is a "best evidence" question referring back to this question; you may choose to consider the citations in the choices for the next question when answering this one if you want. See "Is there a 'best evidence' shortcut?" on page 72 for more.*

ℹ️ *The prompt often mentions describing the passage, and usually doesn't include a line citation. The answer must still be restated or demonstrated by some specific part of the text, even if there's no citation. See "What about Questions Without Citations?" p. 72*

Subjective Phrases to Ignore: "reasonably" "inferred"

A   **Direct Contradiction:** The passage tells us that "internal waves generated in the Luzon Strait" are "some of the largest in the world" (22-25). If these particular waves are some of the largest, then other waves must be smaller, which means these waves don't "reach approximately the same height," as the answer choice would require.

B ✓ **Correct:** The fifth and sixth paragraphs describe how the researchers made a model of the Luzon Strait, and what they learned as a result. The seventh paragraph mentions that "the model" (67) of internal waves developed by Peacock's team "is specific to the Luzon Strait" (67-68), but "it can still help researchers understand how internal waves are generated in other places around the world" (68-70). The phrase "influenced by distinct topographies of different regions" in this choice restates the idea of the model of the waves being "specific" to one place, while the phrase "caused by similar factors" from (B) is demonstrated by the idea that the model "can still help researchers understand...internal waves...around the world" (68-70).

C   **Barely Relevant:** This is a very technical-sounding statement that might intimidate or attract some untrained test-takers, but it doesn't actually restate anything in the text, so we know it's not correct.

D   **Direct Contradiction:** Lines 57-60 describe how "colder, denser water is pushed up over the ridges into warmer, less dense layers above it...generat[ing] an internal wave." So the text says dense water is pushed "up over...ridges" (57-58), which directly contradicts the phrase "over a relatively flat section of ocean floor" in this choice.

Test 2, Question 49   **TYPE: BEST EVIDENCE**

ℹ️ *The answer must restate or demonstrate the relevant statement. See "What about "Best Evidence" Questions?" on page 72.*

Subjective Phrases to Ignore: "best"

A   **Barely Relevant:** This citation isn't relevant to any answer choice from the previous question, so it can't possibly be evidence for the correct answer to that question.

B   **Direct Contradiction:** This citation directly contradicts the statement made in choice (D) from the previous question, and it's not restated by any other choice from that question, so it can't be correct.

C   **Barely Relevant:** Like (A), this citation isn't restated by any answer choice from the previous question, so it can't possibly be evidence for the correct answer to that question.

D ✓ **Correct:** As we showed in the walkthrough for question 48, this citation supports the right answer to 48.

Test 2, Question 50   **TYPE: FIGURE**

ℹ️ *The prompt refers to a graph/table/diagram/etc.; carefully note all labels, keys, units, and any other explanatory details. The answer must directly restate some part of the data and/or text. See "Reading Graphs, Charts, Tables, and Other Figures" on p.44.*

A   **Direct Contradiction:** As discussed in the explanation for choice (D), only the 13°C isotherm shows an increase in depth from 19:12 to 20:24. The 9°C isotherm has a positive slope over that interval, but we have to remember that a *negative* slope correlates to an increase in depth on this graph, because values on the y-axis of the graph *decrease* closer to the top of the graph, as we'll discuss when we evaluate choice (D).

B   **Direct Contradiction:** As discussed in the explanation for choice (D), only the 13°C isotherm shows an increase in depth from 19:12 to 20:24. The 10°C isotherm has a positive slope over that interval, but we have to remember that a *negative* slope correlates to an increase in depth on this graph, because values on the y-axis of the graph *decrease* closer to the top of the graph, as we'll discuss when we evaluate choice (D).

C   Direct Contradiction: As discussed in the explanation for choice (D), only the 13°C isotherm shows an increase in depth from 19:12 to 20:24. The 11°C isotherm has a positive slope over that interval, but we have to remember that a *negative* slope correlates to an increase in depth on this graph, because values on the *y*-axis of the graph *decrease* closer to the top of the graph, as we'll discuss when we evaluate choice (D).

D✓   Correct: The key below the graph shows that the isotherms are represented by different lines, and we can see that the numbers "19:12" and "20:24" both appear near the top right of the graph on the horizontal axis labeled "Time (hours)." The question asks which isotherm "displays an increase in depth" in the given time period, and we can see a label that says "Depth Below Surface" on the vertical axis on the left side of the graph. That axis shows the value of the depth *increasing* as we travel *down* that axis; in other words, the number that is highest on the page is 0, and as you look down the page, the depth-values increase to 40, 80, 120, and so on. So if the question asks for an increase in depth, we actually want to find the line that moves lower down on the page over the given time period—in mathematical terms, we're looking for the line segment with a negative slope during that interval, because that slope indicates depth values *increasing* as we move from left to right. The only isotherm that shows an increase in depth between 19:12 and 20:24 (by moving *down the page*, and having a *negative* slope) is the isotherm represented by the dashed line, 13°C. So we can see this choice must be correct.

Note   Many untrained test-takers will be confused by this question, and will assume incorrectly that an increase in depth should be represented by a line moving up the page, or with a positive slope. But even if we accidentally make a mistake like that, we should still be able to catch that mistake if we remember that we ALWAYS need to check EVERY answer choice before committing to one. If we do that, we'll see that (A), (B), and (C) ALL move up the page between 19:12 and 20:24—since we know that only one choice can be correct, finding three choices that are all apparently "correct" should prompt us to take another look at the question and the graph to figure out where we made a mistake. This is one more example of the importance of remembering your training on test day!

▌ Test 2, Question 51   TYPE: FIGURE

ⓘ *The prompt refers to a graph/table/diagram/etc.; carefully note all labels, keys, units, and any other explanatory details. The answer must directly restate some part of the data and/or text. See "Reading Graphs, Charts, Tables, and Other Figures" on p. 44.*

A   Wrong Part of the Passage: Information about the salinity of the water only appears in the passage, not in the graph—so the graph can't support any statement about the salinity of the water, which means (A) is wrong.

B   Wrong Part of the Passage: Information about the density of the water appears only in the passage, not in the graph. This means the graph can't support any statement about the density of the water, so this choice must be wrong.

C   Direct Contradiction: The graph shows that, at any one time, the bands of water are ordered with the warmest bands on top and the coldest bands below, which contradicts (C)'s statement about "bands of cold water" being "above bands of warmer water."

D✓   Correct: The graph shows that every band of water in the internal wave has a depth greater than 0 at all times, which means they're always under the surface of the water, exactly as the answer choice requires. The passage supports this statement as well when it says "internal waves...do not ride the ocean surface. Instead, they move underwater..." (3-4). So we can see clearly that this choice restates what appears in the graph and in the passage, which means it must be correct.

▌ Test 2, Question 52   TYPE: FIGURE

ⓘ *The prompt refers to a graph/table/diagram/etc.; carefully note all labels, keys, units, and any other explanatory details. The answer must directly restate some part of the data and/or text. See "Reading Graphs, Charts, Tables, and Other Figures" on p. 44.*

A✓   Correct: We can see at several points in the graph (especially around 13:12) that isotherms get pushed down to a depth that's occupied by a colder isotherm for most of the time shown in the graph. In other words, the 13°C isotherm is pushed down to a depth usually occupied by the 11°C or 10°C isotherm at 13:12, and the 11°C isotherm is pushed down to a depth usually occupied by the 10°C isotherm. This shows that the waves affect the "dynamics," or the movement, of the ocean water, as (A) requires.

B   Barely Relevant: The graph doesn't contain any information about the density of water, so the graph can't support a statement about water density, which is what this answer choice would require.

C   Barely Relevant: The graph only contains information about *one* wave—we know this because the title says it shows the changes in depth of isotherms "in an internal wave." So the graph can't support a statement about a "series of deep waves," as (C) requires.

D   Barely Relevant: As we discussed when we analyzed (C), the graph only contains information about one wave, which we know because the title of the graph says it shows the changes in depth of isotherms "in an internal wave." So the graph can't support a statement about the behavior of "multiple waves," as this choice would require.

TEST 3

ℹ️ *The prompt often mentions describing the passage, and usually doesn't include a line citation. The answer must still be restated or demonstrated by some specific part of the text, even if there's no citation. See "What about Questions Without Citations?" p. 72*

Subjective Phrases to Ignore: "best"

A **Confused Relationships:** Lady Carlotta doesn't weigh any positive or negative aspects of anything during the passage, so (A) must be wrong for that reason. Further, to an untrained test-taker, the passage might seem to be about a woman who is beginning a new job, but the woman who seems to start a job as "governess" (36) is called "Lady Carlotta" (1), while her apparent employer, "Mrs. Quabarl" (41), calls her "Miss Hope" (36). In other words, the employer has mistaken Lady Carlotta for someone named Miss Hope, and Miss Hope is the person that the employer has hired. So Lady Carlotta hasn't accepted any job, and is actually just playing along with the mistake made by Mrs. Quabarl. For either reason, (A) is wrong.

B ✓ **Correct:** The passage begins by describing "Lady Carlotta" (1) as she gets off a train. Later, another woman approaches her and calls her "Miss Hope" (36); this situation is restated in the phrase "a stranger who mistakes her for someone else" in the answer choice. For the rest of the passage, Lady Carlotta never tells the woman that her name isn't Miss Hope, which means that Lady Carlotta "does not correct" the stranger, as required by (B).

C **Confused Relationships:** Once Lady Carlotta fails to correct Mrs. Quabarl for calling her "Miss Hope" (36), we can say that Lady Carlotta is impersonating someone else—that is, she's intentionally giving the impression that she's another person, so choice (C)'s idea of "impersonating someone else" definitely appears in the text. Earlier in the text, the narrator describes a situation in which Lady Carlotta "lost the friendship" (22-23) of another woman in a situation that might be interpreted as the result of a vengeful act, which could reflect the idea of "seek[ing] revenge on an acquaintance," as required by the answer choice. But a trained test-taker would notice that these two events involve different people, which means that the idea of Lady Carlotta "impersonat[ing] someone else" *in order to* "seek revenge" is clearly not in the text, so this answer choice is wrong. Notice that a lot of untrained test-takers would fall for this answer choice, because the two main concepts in the choice are present in the text—the problem is that the answer choice relates these two ideas in a way that differs from their relationship in the text. Keep this kind of thing in mind on test day! Choices like this are a large part of the reason why trained test-takers always read carefully, and always consider every answer choice before committing to one.

D **Confused Relationships:** An untrained test-taker might easily fall for (D), because it's the kind of remark that would probably be acceptable in a literature class. But trained test-takers can see that there are several ways in which (D) fails to restate the passage, which means (D) must be wrong. As we discussed in the explanations for (A) and (B), Mrs. Quabarl is not actually Lady Carlotta's employer—Mrs. Quabarl just thinks that Lady Carlotta is someone whom Mrs. Quabarl has already hired as a governess, and Lady Carlotta doesn't tell her otherwise. Another issue is the word "immediate," which would require the dislike to happen instantly; when we look at the lines where the two women meet for the first time (32-40), we don't see any indication that Lady Carlotta dislikes Mrs. Quabarl. Finally, there's no specific indication in the text that Lady Carlotta actually "dislikes" Mrs. Quabarl, as (D) requires; Lady Carlotta does speak "coldly" in line 75, but that isn't specifically the same thing as "dislik[ing]" a person. For any of these reasons, (D) must be wrong, even though it might seem like an acceptable interpretation of the text to an untrained test-taker.

ℹ️ *The prompt includes the phrase "most nearly means" and the choices are usually one- or two-word phrases. The answer is either restated or demonstrated by an idea from the surrounding text. Remember you can work around unknown words, and be ready to guess/skip and focus on other questions if you don't know the words. See "What about "Most Nearly Means" Questions?" on p.73.*

Subjective Phrases to Ignore: "most nearly"

A ("Lady Carlotta stepped out on to the platform of the small wayside station and took a <u>slight movement</u> or two up and down its uninteresting length, to kill time till the train should be pleased to proceed on its way.") **Reasonable Statement Not in the Text:** In another context, "turn" could mean "slight movement;" for example, if you were uncomfortable in your chair, you could "turn" yourself in your chair, which could be called a "slight movement." But the word "its" (3) refers to "the platform of the small wayside station" (2), and Lady Carlotta "took a turn or two up and down its uninteresting length" (2-3). If her "turn or two" (2) took her all the way up and down the length of the platform, then we know it wasn't a "slight movement," which means this choice must be incorrect.

B ("Lady Carlotta stepped out on to the platform of the small wayside station and took a <u>change in rotation</u> or two up and down its uninteresting length, to kill time till the train should be pleased to proceed on its way.") **Reasonable Statement Not in the Text:**

It may be possible to imagine some context in which the phrase "change in rotation" could be substituted for the word "turn." But the passage doesn't restate or demonstrate the idea of a change in rotation.

C ✓ ("Lady Carlotta stepped out on to the platform of the small wayside station and took a <u>short walk</u> or two up and down its uninteresting length, to kill time till the train should be pleased to proceed on its way.") **Correct:** The context says Lady Carlotta "took a turn or two up and down its uninteresting length," where "its" refers to "the platform of the small wayside station." So we need an answer choice that's restated or demonstrated by the idea that her "turn or two" could take her all the way up and down the length of the platform. "Short walk" satisfies this requirement—it makes sense that she could take a "short walk or two" up and down the length of the platform.

D ("Lady Carlotta stepped out on to the platform of the small wayside station and took a <u>course correction</u> or two up and down its uninteresting length, to kill time till the train should be pleased to proceed on its way.") **Reasonable Statement Not in the Text:** In another context, "turn" could mean "course correction;" for example, if you were driving a boat toward an island but you were a little off course, you could "turn" the boat slightly back on course, which could be called a "course correction." But the passage doesn't restate or demonstrate that idea.

| **Test 3, Question 3** | **TYPE: DESCRIBE THE PASSAGE** |

The next question is a "best evidence" question referring back to this question; you may choose to consider the citations in the choices for the next question when answering this one if you want. See "Is there a 'best evidence' shortcut?" on page 72 for more.

ⓘ *The prompt often mentions describing the passage, and usually doesn't include a line citation. The answer must still be restated or demonstrated by some specific part of the text, even if there's no citation. See "What about Questions Without Citations?" p. 72*

Subjective Phrases to Ignore: "most clearly implies"

A ✓ **Correct:** The text says that some of Lady Carlotta's acquaintances had commented on Lady Carlotta's habit of "interfering on behalf of distressed animals" (12-13), saying that such things were "'none of her business'" (14); since someone who gets involved in someone else's business can be called "outspoken," we can see that (A) is correct.

B **Literary Interpretation:** The text never explicitly says that anyone thinks Lady Carlotta is "tactful" (or "polite," "considerate," or any other similar kind of word), which this answer choice would require, so (B) must be wrong.

C **Barely Relevant:** An "ambitious" person is someone who wants to get ahead of others, usually in a social or professional context. Nothing in the text restates the idea that other people find Lady Carlotta "ambitious."

D **Confused Relationships:** The text says in lines 22-23 that Lady Carlotta "lost the friendship" of a certain lady, but losing the friendship of one person doesn't mean that "other people" (as described in the prompt) regard Lady Carlotta as "unfriendly," which is what this answer choice would require.

| **Test 3, Question 4** | **TYPE: BEST EVIDENCE** |

ⓘ *The answer must restate or demonstrate the relevant statement. See "What about "Best Evidence" Questions?" on page 72.*

Subjective Phrases to Ignore: "best"

A ✓ **Correct:** As discussed in the walkthrough for the previous question, the correct answer to question 3 restates the idea of interfering with other people's business, which appears in this citation.

B **Confused Relationships:** To an untrained test-taker, this citation might appear to support choice (D) from the previous question. But if we read carefully, we see that the prompt for the previous question asked how "other people" think of Lady Carlotta. The fact that Lady Carlotta lost the friendship of one single person, as described in the citation, is not the same thing as saying that multiple "other people" see Lady Carlotta as unfriendly. Since this citation is only relevant to a wrong answer for the previous question, it's the wrong answer for this question.

C **Barely Relevant:** This citation isn't really relevant to the correct answer from question 3, nor to any choice from 3.

D **Barely Relevant:** This citation isn't really relevant to the correct answer from question 3, nor to any choice from 3.

| **Test 3, Question 5** | **TYPE: PURPOSE OF CITED TEXT** |

ⓘ *The prompt asks about the purpose or role of a part of the text. The correct answer must be accurately restated or described by the relevant text, with no interpretation. See "What about "Purpose" Questions?" on p.74.*

Subjective Phrases to Ignore: "mainly"

A **Wrong Part of the Passage:** (A) might tempt an untrained test-taker because Lady Carlotta does deceive Mrs. Quabarl about being the governess, Miss Hope, later in the passage. But the cited anecdote itself doesn't involve deception (as the word "foreshadow" would require), so (A) must be wrong.

B **Literary Interpretation:** The cited text shows Lady Carlotta refusing to help a woman stuck in a tree with an "angry boar-pig" (18) underneath it. The idea of "cruelty" isn't literally restated or demonstrated in the citation, because Lady Carlotta isn't described as actively causing actual harm or injury to anyone—among other things, the text doesn't say that the lady in the tree was actually harmed. Furthermore, the cited text doesn't support the idea of "subtlety;" someone who is subtle does something in a way that's not obvious, and the text doesn't say there was anything "not obvious" (or "barely detectable," or any similar kind of idea) about what Lady Carlotta did. An untrained test-taker might decide to interpret Lady Carlotta's behavior as an example of "subtle cruelty," but we trained test-takers notice that there's no actual word or phrase in the citation that restates or demonstrates the idea of cruelty or subtlety, so (B) is wrong.

C ✓ **Correct:** As trained test-takers, we know that one of the College Board's unwritten rules for SAT Reading is that we can call something "humorous" on the SAT if it runs counter to what would be expected in a given situation, or if it involves a word or phrase that can't be taken literally. In this instance, Lady Carlotta works on her "water-colour sketch" (20) while a woman she knows is trapped in a tree by a boar. In other words, instead of intervening herself, which we know is Lady Carlotta's normal behavior (12-15), or going to find help, or reassuring the trapped lady, Lady Carlotta continues working on her picture (19-22). The phrase "insight into her character" is appropriately demonstrated by this portion of the text because lines 11-23 describe Lady Carlotta's general habit of interfering when animals are distressed, and the one time she deviated from this habit. The word "humorous" is okay here because we can see that Lady Carlotta's behavior contradicts her normal behavior, and the College Board will let us say something in a passage is "humorous" if some type of contradiction is present in the text, or if a part of the text can't be taken literally (see "What about "Humor?" on page 75 for more on this.)

D **Confused Relationships:** An untrained test-taker might be tempted by this choice, but the cited text doesn't "explain" anything about why Lady Carlotta did what she did—the text doesn't say Lady Carlotta wanted to teach the other woman a lesson, or that she really wanted to finish the water color sketch, or anything like that. Since the cited text doesn't explain anything about Lady Carlotta's behavior, this choice can't be correct.

Note This question is a great example of the way the College Board uses the idea of "humor" on the SAT! Most readers won't find themselves laughing or smiling when they read the anecdote around lines 14 and 15 in the text, but, as trained test-takers, we know that actual entertainment value has nothing to do with the College Board's idea of "humor." Instead, the College Board will let us call something "humorous" if it reflects some kind of contradiction between what's expected and what actually happens in a passage (like we saw in this question), or a contradiction between the literal meaning of a phrase and its use in the text. See "What about "Humor?""on page 75 for more.)

| **Test 3, Question 6** | **TYPE: WORD MOST NEARLY MEANS** |

ⓘ *The prompt includes the phrase "most nearly means" and the choices are usually one- or two-word phrases. The answer is either restated or demonstrated by an idea from the surrounding text. Remember you can work around unknown words, and be ready to guess/skip and focus on other questions if you don't know the words. See "What about "Most Nearly Means" Questions?" on p.73.*

Subjective Phrases to Ignore: "most nearly"

A ✓ ("...Lady Carlotta was impressively introduced to the nature of the <u>responsibility</u> that had been thrust upon her; she learned that Claude and Wilfrid were delicate, sensitive young people, that Irene had the artistic temperament highly developed, and that Viola was something or other else of a mould equally commonplace among children of that class and type in the twentieth century.") **Correct:** We know that we'll sometimes need to read the sentence or two before or after a citation on the SAT Reading section in order to find the part of the text being restated in the correct answer. In this case, the text says Lady Carlotta was "introduced to the nature of the charge," and then the text says that "she learned" things about the children of the Quabarl mansion, and the next paragraph has Mrs. Quabarl stating her "wish[es]" (62) and "expect[ations]" (68) of Lady Carlotta, along with what Lady Carlotta "must try to" (64) do. These words ("wish," "must," and "expect") indicate Lady Carlotta has a "responsibility" in the eyes of Mrs. Quabarl, as (A) requires, so it's right.

B ("...Lady Carlotta was impressively introduced to the nature of the <u>attack</u> that had been thrust upon her; she learned that Claude and Wilfrid were delicate, sensitive young people, that Irene had the artistic temperament highly developed, and that Viola was something or other else of a mould equally commonplace among children of that class and type in the twentieth century.") **Reasonable Statement Not in the Text:** In another context, a "charge" can be an "attack;" for example, in a battle, a group of soldiers can "charge" a location, which means they "attack" that location. But the passage doesn't restate the idea of Lady Carlotta being involved in an attack, so this answer can't be correct.

C ("...Lady Carlotta was impressively introduced to the nature of the <u>fee</u> that had been thrust upon her; she learned that Claude and Wilfrid were delicate, sensitive young people, that Irene had the artistic temperament highly developed, and that Viola was something or other else of a mould equally commonplace among children of that class and type in the twentieth century.") **Reasonable Statement Not in the Text:** In another context, a "charge" can be a "fee;" for example, on an airplane, there can be a "charge" for a seat with more legroom, which is the same thing as a "fee" the airline charges. But the passage doesn't restate that idea, so this choice can't be correct.

D ("...Lady Carlotta was impressively introduced to the nature of the <u>expense</u> that had been thrust upon her; she learned that Claude and Wilfrid were delicate, sensitive young people, that Irene had the artistic temperament highly developed, and that Viola was something or other else of a mould equally commonplace among children of that class and type in the twentieth century.") **Reasonable Statement Not in the Text:** In another context, a "charge" can be an "expense," just as we saw that it can be a "fee" in the previous answer choice. But the passage doesn't restate that idea, so this answer can't be correct.

| Test 3, Question 7 | TYPE: DESCRIBE THE PASSAGE |

ⓘ *The prompt often mentions describing the passage, and usually doesn't include a line citation. The answer must still be restated or demonstrated by some specific part of the text, even if there's no citation. See "What about Questions Without Citations?" p. 72*

A ✓ **Correct:** At the end of the description of Claude, Wilfrid, Irene, and Viola in lines 56-58, the narrator says that "Viola was something or other else of a mould equally commonplace among children of that class and type in the twentieth century" (58-61). The word "equally" indicates that Viola is like the other children named in the paragraph; the phrase "equally commonplace among children of that class and type" (60) specifically states that all of the named children are "commonplace" compared to "children of that class and type." (A) must be correct, then, because the word "similar" in the choice restates the idea of being "commonplace" (60), and the phrase "many of their peers" restates the phrase "children of that class and type" (60).

B **Direct Contradiction:** This answer choice will trick a lot of untrained test-takers, because lines 53-58 might seem to indicate that the children are "delicate" (56), "sensitive" (57), and "highly developed" (58), so it might seem as though the phrase "unusually creative and intelligent" in the answer choice is a good restatement of those ideas. But trained test-takers who read carefully will see that the word "equally" (59) equates Viola to all of the other named children, and Viola is described as "commonplace" (60), which means all the children are "commonplace," as we discussed in the explanation for choice (A). In other words, what's happening in lines 53-61 is that Mrs. Quabarl is telling Lady Carlotta that the named children are special, but the narrator is saying that all children "of that class and type" (60) are thought by their parents to be "equally" (59) special, which means that the children are actually "commonplace" (60).

C **Reasonable Statement Not in the Text:** An untrained test-taker might allow himself to imagine that children wouldn't want a governess, but this answer choice doesn't restate anything that actually appears in the passage, so (C) can't be correct.

D **Barely Relevant:** This choice is wrong for at least two reasons. First, as we discussed in the explanations for (A) and (B), the text indicates that the children are actually "commonplace" (60), and not exceptional. Second, the statements about the children's supposedly unique attributes don't mention anything in particular about education; instead, we're told that two of the children are "sensitive" (57) and one is "artistic" (57), but neither of these words means the same thing as "educated" anyway. Either of these reasons is enough by itself to make this answer choice wrong.

| Test 3, Question 8 | TYPE: DESCRIBE THE PASSAGE |

ⓘ *The prompt often mentions describing the passage, and usually doesn't include a line citation. The answer must still be restated or demonstrated by some specific part of the text, even if there's no citation. See "What about Questions Without Citations?" p. 72*

Subjective Phrases to Ignore: "implies"

A **Reasonable Statement Not in the Text:** An untrained test-taker might think that a woman who lives in a "mansion" (53) and has a "newly-purchased and expensive car" (84) might like "traditional values," as the answer choice describes. But when Mrs. Quabarl explains how she wants the governess to teach her children in lines 62-69, she doesn't say anything about values or tradition of any kind, which means that this choice doesn't restate anything from the passage, so it can't be correct.

B ✓ **Correct:** Mrs. Quabarl explains how she wishes her governess to educate her children in lines 62-69. She says she wants her children to be "INTERESTED in what they learn," and that they must "feel that they are being introduced to the life-stories of men and women who really lived, not merely committing a mass of names and dates to memory." The word "interested" and the idea of "not merely" memorizing "a mass of facts" both show that Mrs. Quabarl wants her children to be "active[ly] engage[d]" in their educations, as the answer choice requires. (To explain this further, a child can be "taught" (62) without taking any action themselves, like a bored student sitting in a lecture hall and paying no attention to the teacher—the teacher is the one doing the teaching. But a child who is "interested" must actively have an interest in something, by definition, and is mentally engaged with that thing, rather than just memorizing facts about it. So we can see that Mrs. Quabarl favors education that "emphasizes active engagement.")

C **Confused Relationships:** (C) might tempt untrained test-takers because the text says, "Irene had the artistic temperament" (57-58). But the fact that one child out of four is "artistic" doesn't mean that Mrs. Quabarl favors "artistic experimentation" in education, as (C) requires. In fact, when Mrs. Quabarl explains how she wants her governess to teach her children in lines 62-69, she doesn't mention art or experimentation at all. Since the text doesn't restate or demonstrate (C), it's wrong.

D **Direct Contradiction:** Many untrained test-takers will fall for this answer choice, for two reasons: they'll assume that any style of education must involve remembering facts, and they'll notice that the phrase "committing...to memory" appears in lines 67-68. But trained test-takers who read carefully will notice that Mrs. Quabarl specifically says the governess "must try to make them feel like they are not...merely committing a mass of names and dates to memory" (64-68), which means she specifically does not favor "factual retention," which is a direct contradiction of the answer choice.

> *The next question is a "best evidence" question referring back to this question; you may choose to consider the citations in the choices for the next question when answering this one if you want. See "Is there a 'best evidence' shortcut?" on page 72 for more.*

ⓘ *The prompt often mentions describing the passage, and usually doesn't include a line citation. The answer must still be restated or demonstrated by some specific part of the text, even if there's no citation. See "What about Questions Without Citations?" p. 72*

Subjective Phrases to Ignore: "best"

A   **Barely Relevant:** Nothing describing Mrs. Quabarl restates or demonstrates the words "kind" or "selfish," so (A) is wrong.

B ✓ **Correct:** The text says Mrs. Quabarl is "imposingly attired" (34); we can see that this citation matches the word "imposing" in the answer choice, and we can also see that "attire" (clothing) is inherently a superficial or "outward" concept, as the answer choice requires. The text also says Mrs. Quabarl is "magnificent and autocratic" (79), which is another way to restate the idea of being "imposing," but that she only seems that way as long as she's "not seriously opposed" (79-80). Finally, the text says, "the least show of unexpected resistance goes a long way towards rendering [her] cowed and apologetic" (80-82). The word "easily" in the answer choice restates the idea from the text that the "least" (80) amount of defiance is enough to stop her, and the word "resistance" in the text is restated by the word "defied" in the answer choice. For these reasons, we can see that every part of the answer choice restates a concept from the passage, which means this must be the right answer. (Notice that we don't need to understand words like "cowed" or "autocratic" in order to answer this question with total certainty, as long as we work with the words we do know, and stick to the unwritten rules of the test.)

C   **Literary Interpretation:** Mrs. Quabarl seems to be wealthy, since she has a "mansion" (53) and "expensive car" (84), so many untrained test-takers will assume that she's "socially successful," as (C) requires. But trained test-takers will notice the text never actually states that she's successful in any way, socially or not. She's also stern, as when she uses a "tone that admitted of very little argument" (37-38), but a trained test-taker would note that being stern isn't necessarily the same thing as being "bitter." A lot of untrained test-takers might mistakenly interpret the character of Mrs. Quabarl in a way that allows them to mark (C), but trained test-takers know (C) must be wrong because it isn't restated or demonstrated in the passage.

D   **Reasonable Statement Not in the Text:** As we noted in the discussion of (C), Mrs. Quabarl may seem to be wealthy, since she has a "mansion" (53) and "expensive car" (84), but being wealthy doesn't necessarily make her "generous," which is part of what (D) requires. An untrained test-taker might also decide Mrs. Quabarl is "imprudent," as (D) requires, because it might seem unwise to take the wrong person home to watch her children. But the text never specifically uses any word or phrase synonymous with "imprudent" to describe Mrs. Quabarl. So, as trained test-takers, we know (D) must be wrong.

Note   In our analysis, we discussed what was wrong with several aspects of each wrong answer choice—but remember that on test day, you only need one concrete reason to rule out an incorrect choice. As long as you're sure you've found at least one thing that's wrong, you know the entire choice is wrong. We're just being a bit more thorough in our discussion, for training purposes.

ⓘ *The answer must restate or demonstrate the relevant statement. See "What about "Best Evidence" Questions?" on page 72.*

Subjective Phrases to Ignore: "best"

A   **Barely Relevant:** This text isn't really relevant to the correct answer from the previous question, or to any answer choice from that question; an untrained test-taker might view this citation as a sign of bitterness, selfishness, or the state of being imposing, but trained test-takers know that the correct answer to question 9 must directly restate a portion of the passage, and nothing in this citation is directly restated by any of the answer choices for question 9.

B   **Barely Relevant:** Just as we saw with choice (A), an untrained test-taker might arbitrarily decide that Mrs. Quabarl is "imposing," "selfish" or "bitter" on the basis of this citation, but none of the answer choices in question 9 actually restate any concept in this citation, so it can't be relevant to the correct answer for 9, which means it's the wrong answer for 10.

C   **Barely Relevant:** This text isn't really relevant to the correct answer from question 9, or to any choice from that question.

D ✓ **Correct:** As we discussed in the walkthrough for the previous question, this citation provides a lot of the wording that's restated in the correct answer to the previous question, which was (B): "imperfectly self-assured[,]...magnificent and autocratic" (78-79) is restated by "outwardly imposing," while "the least show of resistance...render[s] them apologetic" (80-82) is restated by "easily defied."

Note   As we noted in our discussions of the wrong answers to this question, those wrong answers were snippets of conversation between Lady Carlotta and Mrs. Quabarl. A lot of untrained test-takers might try to read into those bits of conversation and see any number of personality traits, but we have to remember that the correct answer must be directly restated or demonstrated in the text without interpretation, which makes choice (D) the evidence that directly supports choice (B) from the previous question.

Test 3, Question 11 — TYPE: PURPOSE OF CITED TEXT

ℹ️ *The prompt asks about the purpose or role of a part of the text. The correct answer must be accurately restated or described by the relevant text, with no interpretation. See "What about "Purpose" Questions?" on p.74.*

A ✓ **Correct:** The third paragraph mentions a number of problems with public transportation, calling it "a squalid last resort" (21) and "a depressing experience" (25-26) that is often "underfunded, ill-maintained, and ill-planned" (31); these quotes are restated by the word "limitations" in the answer choice. And we can see that public transport is a "practice favored by the author," as the answer choice requires, because line 36-37 say, "public transport can be faster, more comfortable, and cheaper." Since every part of this choice restates something from the relevant part of the passage, we know it's correct.

B **Direct Contradiction:** The first two paragraphs discuss the popularity of public transportation, while the third paragraph actually discusses a number of problems with public transportation, as we just saw in our discussion of (A).

C **Barely Relevant:** The third paragraph does give an overview of some problems with public transportation, but the passage never mentions experts in the field of transportation, nor whether these problems have been addressed by any experts.

D **Off by One or Two Words:** The passage as a whole *does* provide mostly favorable information regarding public transportation, as the answer choice requires, but the third paragraph *does not* actually recommend abandoning public transportation. Even though the third paragraph calls public transportation "a squalid last resort" (21) and "a depressing experience" (25-26), it never specifically says that anyone should stop using this type of transportation, which means that the phrase "advocates for abandoning a practice" in the answer choice doesn't restate any part of the third paragraph, which means (D) must be wrong.

Test 3, Question 12 — TYPE: DESCRIBE THE PASSAGE

> *The next question is a "best evidence" question referring back to this question; you may choose to consider the citations in the choices for the next question when answering this one if you want. See "Is there a 'best evidence' shortcut?" on page 72 for more.*

ℹ️ *The prompt often mentions describing the passage, and usually doesn't include a line citation. The answer must still be restated or demonstrated by some specific part of the text, even if there's no citation. See "What about Questions Without Citations?" p. 72*

A **Reasonable Statement Not in the Text:** Untrained test-takers might assume that environmental impact would be a consideration in choosing between public transportation and private automobiles. But the environmental impact of travel actually isn't mentioned in the passage at all, which means this choice must be wrong.

B **Reasonable Statement Not in the Text:** The author discusses the advantage of "automobile travel in North America" (as mentioned in the prompt) in lines 33-34, where he mentions that cars are a way to reach "your destination more quickly." Some untrained test-takers might assume that speed and convenience are similar concepts where transportation is concerned, but, as trained test-takers, we know that the correct answer must restate a concept from the relevant part of the text, and the passage never explicitly says that cars are more convenient.

C ✓ **Correct:** As we saw for (B), lines 32-34 say, "hopping in a car almost always gets you to your destination more quickly" in North America. The idea that a car gets you somewhere "more quickly" is restated in (C), so (C) is right.

D **Direct Contradiction:** The idea of comparing the cost of public transportation to the cost of using a private car does come up in the fourth paragraph, but it actually says that public transportation can be "cheaper" (37).

Test 3, Question 13 — TYPE: BEST EVIDENCE

ℹ️ *The answer must restate or demonstrate the relevant statement. See "What about "Best Evidence" Questions?" on page 72.*

Subjective Phrases to Ignore: "best"

A **Barely Relevant:** The paragraph that contains this citation is talking about travel "on the planet" (1), not just in North America, as required in the prompt for question 12. That by itself is enough to make this citation irrelevant to question 12, but, even if we overlook that issue, this citation doesn't mention any of the concepts in the choices from question 12.

B **Literary Interpretation:** This citation discusses the unappealing nature of public transportation "in much of North America" (24-25), but it doesn't explicitly mention any actual advantage of the automobile over public transport, as required by 12.

C **Confused Relationships:** Like (B), this citation says that public transportation "in much of North America" (24-25) is depressing, but it doesn't explicitly mention any advantage of the automobile over public transport, as question 12 requires.

D ✓ **Correct:** As we saw in the walkthrough for question 12, (C) in that question restates the idea of cars getting people to their destinations "more quickly" (33-34), and those lines appear in this citation.

Test 3, Question 14 — TYPE: CITATION QUESTION

> *The next question is a "best evidence" question referring back to this question; you may choose to consider the citations in the choices for the next question when answering this one if you want. See "Is there a 'best evidence' shortcut?" on page 72 for more.*

ⓘ *The question includes a citation from the text. The answer must be directly restated or demonstrated in the cited text, or in the text closely surrounding the cited text. See the general process for answering SAT Reading questions on p. 71.*

Subjective Phrases to Ignore: "central"

A   Confused Relationships: This paragraph does discuss positive aspects of public transportation in Europe, but it also mentions similar situations in cities outside of Europe. Further, the paragraph never specifically mentions that places like France, Spain, and Sweden are in Europe; we may know that these are European countries, but the SAT Reading section isn't going to test us on our knowledge of geography, so the passage would need to tell us explicitly that these places were in Europe if the question required us to know that. For all of these reasons, (A) must be wrong.

B ✓ Correct: The text says that "public transport can be faster, more comfortable, and cheaper than the private automobile" (35-37), and then the text gives us concrete examples of systems in "Shanghai" (37), a "provincial French town" (41), etc. The phrase "superior to travel by private automobile" in the answer choice restates the phrase "faster, more comfortable, and cheaper than the private automobile" (36-37); the phrase "some public transportation systems" refers directly to the systems mentioned in Shanghai, France, Spain, Sweden, Latin America, China, and India throughout the fourth paragraph. We can also see examples of this idea in lines 51-52, in which the author says that "sedans and SUVs" can be "mired in dawn-to-dusk traffic jams" in places like Latin America, China, and India, where people use "fast-loading buses." So this choice restates a concept that appears at least twice in the paragraph, which means it must be right.

C   Reasonable Statement Not in the Text: Many untrained test-takers will assume that this choice is correct because the author does seem to believe that North America should imitate the rest of the world when it comes to public transport—but the author never specifically says that! The third paragraph does describe problems with public transportation "in much of North America" (24-25), and the fourth paragraph does describe better public transportation systems in other countries. But, again, the fourth paragraph never actually says that Americans should imitate the public transportation systems of other countries, which is what this answer choice would require, so it's wrong.

D   Off by One or Two Words: A lot of untrained test-takers will fall for this choice because the paragraph says, "from Spain to Sweden, Wi-Fi equipped high-speed trains seamlessly connect with highly ramified metro networks, allowing commuters to work on laptops" (44-46). But the answer choice says "much international public transportation" is made so that people can work on board, and the fourth paragraph only specifically says that "high speed trains" (44-45) have this capability. We can't select an answer choice that says "much international public transportation" allows people to work on board when the fourth paragraph only describes one kind of international public transportation that allows people to work on board.

▌ **Test 3, Question 15**   **TYPE: BEST EVIDENCE**

ⓘ *The answer must restate or demonstrate the relevant statement. See "What about "Best Evidence" Questions?" on page 72.*

Subjective Phrases to Ignore: "best"

A   Barely Relevant: This sentence alone just indicates that public transportation doesn't have to be as bad as described in the third paragraph, but that idea isn't restated by any answer choice from the previous question, so this choice must be wrong.

B ✓ Correct: As we saw in the walkthrough for question 14, this citation is exactly restated by (B) from that question.

C   Reasonable Statement Not in the Text: An untrained test-taker might assume that this positive example of public transportation going well in another country may seem to support choice (C) from the previous question, but a trained test-taker would note that the citation doesn't explicitly say Americans should copy what's done in Shanghai, which is part of why (C) is wrong in question 12, and why this answer choice is wrong.

D   Off by One or Two Words: An untrained test-taker might think this text supports the idea expressed in (D) of question 14, but, as we discussed in the explanation for that choice, (D) is wrong because of the word "much" that appears in it.

▌ **Test 3, Question 16**   **TYPE: WORD MOST NEARLY MEANS**

ⓘ *The prompt includes the phrase "most nearly means" and the choices are usually one- or two-word phrases. The answer is either restated or demonstrated by an idea from the surrounding text. Remember you can work around unknown words, and be ready to guess/skip and focus on other questions if you don't know the words. See "What about "Most Nearly Means" Questions?" on p.73.*

Subjective Phrases to Ignore: "most nearly"

A   ("If you <u>endow</u> the demographers, this transit trend has legs.") Barely Relevant: Nothing in the text restates or demonstrates the idea of "endowing" anything, which would involve the idea of giving a gift to someone.

B   ("If you <u>attribute</u> the demographers, this transit trend has legs.") Confused Relationships: In a different context, "attribute" could mean "credit;" for example, if you "attribute" your grade on a project to your lab partner, you're "crediting" your partner with that grade. But the text surrounding line 58 doesn't restate or demonstrate the idea of attribution, so (B) is wrong.

C ✓ ("If you <u>believe</u> the demographers, this transit trend has legs.") Correct: The text says, "if you credit the demographers, this transit trend has legs;" then, it goes on to give some demographic information to support the idea that the transit trend will continue, because it mentions demographic concepts like "Millenials" (59) who "now outnumber baby boomers" (60-61), and who "tend to favor cities" (61) and are "more willing than their parents to ride buses and subways" (62-63). The paragraph goes on to mention other demographic groups ("teenagers" (68), "seniors" (74), etc.) and to show that they're trending towards being "more likely to use transit" (75). So the text says that if the demographic numbers are accurate, then the transit trend will keep going. This demonstrates that "if you believe the demographers, this transit trend has legs," which means (C) is right.

D   ("If you <u>honor</u> the demographers, this transit trend has legs.") **Barely Relevant:** To "honor" the demographers would mean to give them some kind of public award, or to respect or uphold their wishes, or something along those lines. The passage doesn't restate or demonstrate this idea, so this answer can't be correct.

	Test 3, Question 17	TYPE: WORD MOST NEARLY MEANS

ⓘ *The prompt includes the phrase "most nearly means" and the choices are usually one- or two-word phrases. The answer is either restated or demonstrated by an idea from the surrounding text. Remember you can work around unknown words, and be ready to guess/skip and focus on other questions if you don't know the words. See "What about "Most Nearly Means" Questions?" on p. 73.*

Subjective Phrases to Ignore: "most nearly"

A   ("The 'Millenials,' who reached adulthood around the turn of the century and now outnumber baby boomers, tend to <u>indulge</u> cities over suburbs, and are far more willing than their parents to ride buses and subways.") **Barely Relevant:** As trained test-takers, we can tell that the passage doesn't restate or demonstrate the idea of indulging cities, whatever that would mean, which means this choice must be wrong.

B ✓   ("The 'Millenials,' who reached adulthood around the turn of the century and now outnumber baby boomers, tend to <u>prefer</u> cities over suburbs, and are far more willing than their parents to ride buses and subways.") **Correct:** We can see that (B) directly reflects the idea that Millenials are "more willing" (62) to engage with "buses and subways" (62-63), which the previous paragraph presents as essential elements of city life.

C   ("The 'Millenials,' who reached adulthood around the turn of the century and now outnumber baby boomers, tend to <u>resemble</u> cities over suburbs, and are far more willing than their parents to ride buses and subways.") **Reasonable Statement Not in the Text:** In another context, "favor" could mean "resemble;" for example, if you physically "resemble" your mother, someone could say you "favor" your mother. But nothing in the passage restates that idea.

D   ("The 'Millenials,' who reached adulthood around the turn of the century and now outnumber baby boomers, tend to <u>serve</u> cities over suburbs, and are far more willing than their parents to ride buses and subways.") **Barely Relevant:** Nothing in the relevant text restates or demonstrates the idea of anyone "serv[ing]" a city (or anything else, for that matter).

	Test 3, Question 18	TYPE: BEST EVIDENCE

ⓘ *The answer must restate or demonstrate the relevant statement. See "What about "Best Evidence" Questions?" on page 72.*

Subjective Phrases to Ignore: "best"

A   **Confused Relationships:** This citation mentions the idea of riding "buses and subways" (62-63), but it doesn't say anything about "personal electronic devices" as required by the prompt, so it can't be the correct answer.

B ✓   **Correct:** This citation says that "iPads, MP3 players, Kindles, and smartphones," which are all examples of "personal electronic devices" as required by the prompt, are part of why millennials "are far more willing than their parents to ride buses and subways" (62-63). It goes on to say, "you can get some serious texting done when you're not driving, and earbuds offer effective insulation from...commuting annoyances," which directly demonstrates that people can use "personal electronic devices" on "public transportation," as the prompt describes. So (B) is right.

C   **Barely Relevant:** This citation explains that fewer teenagers have a driver's license than previously, but it doesn't specifically say anything about using "personal electronic devices" on "public transportation" as required by the prompt. So (C) is wrong.

D   **Barely Relevant:** This citation explains that home prices in older neighborhoods are going up, but it doesn't specifically say anything about "personal electronic devices" on "public transportation" as mentioned in the prompt.

	Test 3, Question 19	TYPE: FIGURE

ⓘ *The prompt refers to a graph/table/diagram/etc.; carefully note all labels, keys, units, and any other explanatory details. The answer must directly restate some part of the data and/or text. See "Reading Graphs, Charts, Tables, and Other Figures" on p. 44.*

A ✓   **Correct:** The first figure shows that 10.7% of public transportation passengers in the U.S. are students, and 6.7% are retired, which means that more students than retirees are using public transportation, so this choice is correct.

B   **Direct Contradiction:** The first figure shows that 72% of public transportation passengers are employed, and 6.4% are unemployed. These numbers are not "roughly the same," as the answer choice would require, so this choice is incorrect.

C   **Barely Relevant:** The first figure shows that 72% of public transportation passengers in the U.S. are employed outside the home, and 2.0% are homemakers. This doesn't support the claim in the answer choice, so (C) isn't the correct answer. (Actually, the data in the figure don't show how likely an individual from a particular occupation is to use public transportation. For example, even though homemakers represent only 2.0% of passengers, it might be the case that 100% of homemakers use public transportation, while only 80% of people employed outside the home use it, and there might be a much larger population of people employed outside the home in US cities than homemakers. In other words, the pie chart tells us the likelihood that a randomly selected person on public transportation would have one of the occupations in the chart; it does NOT tell us the likelihood that a person who has one of the occupations would use public transportation. For this reason, the data in the pie chart is irrelevant to the statement in this answer choice.)

D   **Barely Relevant:** Nothing in the pie chart actually indicates how "often" people in the different groups use public transportation: for example, it might be that unemployed people generally use public transit 6 times every day, while employed people only use it twice per day; on the other hand, it might be that unemployed people only use public transit an average of once per week. Either way, the chart would look the same, because it only shows the percentage of the passenger population in each occupation, without reflecting the frequency of use at all. For that reason, the chart is irrelevant to the statement in this answer choice, which means this choice must be wrong.

| Test 3, Question 20 | TYPE: FIGURE |

ⓘ *The prompt refers to a graph/table/diagram/etc.; carefully note all labels, keys, units, and any other explanatory details. The answer must directly restate some part of the data and/or text. See "Reading Graphs, Charts, Tables, and Other Figures" on p.44.*

Subjective Phrases to Ignore: "suggest"

A ✓ **Correct:** The first figure shows that the majority of public transportation passengers are employed outside the home, and the second figure shows that the purpose of most public transportation trips is work-related;. So we see that this choice directly restates the information in the charts, which means it must be correct.

B   **Confused Relationships:** The first figure shows the majority of public transportation passengers are employed outside the home, but the second figure doesn't reflect (B) for two reasons: first, it doesn't include any data about "run[ning] errands," as (B) would require; second, even if there were some information about errands, or even if we broke the unwritten rules of the SAT and assumed that "errands" refers to "personal business," "shopping," and "social" trips, it would still be true that the majority of trips must be for the purpose of work, according to the chart. Either reason is enough to make (B) wrong.

C   **Reasonable Statement not in the Data:** Some untrained test-takers might simply assume that people who mostly travel for work would be less likely to use transit on the weekends, but the data don't distinguish between people traveling during the week or on weekends, and they don't contain information about using private cars. Further, there's no way to know from the data if the majority of people who use transit for work-related purposes generally work on the weekends. In short, there's nothing in the provided information that would allow us to draw a conclusion relevant to (C), so it must be wrong.

D   **Barely Relevant:** The provided figures don't contain any information about whether passengers stop using public transportation once they can afford cars, so (D) must be wrong, because it doesn't restate anything present in the data.

| Test 3, Question 21 | TYPE: DESCRIBE THE PASSAGE |

ⓘ *The prompt often mentions describing the passage, and usually doesn't include a line citation. The answer must still be restated or demonstrated by some specific part of the text, even if there's no citation. See "What about Questions Without Citations?" p. 72*

Subjective Phrases to Ignore: "best"

A   **Confused Relationships:** Nothing in the text ever specifically says the experiment was "prove[d] unworkable," as (A) would require. Instead, as described in the explanation for (D), something unexpected happens and the experiment is modified. We know that if the phrase "proves unworkable" isn't restated or demonstrated by any part of the passage, then (A) is wrong.

B   **Confused Relationships:** The text doesn't start by describing a "new discovery" or a "theory" being "reconsider[ed]," both of which would be required by this answer choice. Instead, Ken Dial is challenged "to come up with new data" (8) related to an unsettled question about how birds evolved the ability to fly. Further, Ken Dial "designed [the] project to see what clues might lie in how baby game birds learned to fly" (9-11)—he didn't "adapt" a "classic study" as this answer choice would require. Any of these reasons by itself is enough to make the answer choice incorrect.

C   **Confused Relationships:** The text never says that any "anomaly is observed" (or that any "outlier is noted," or "unusual result is obtained," or any other synonymous phrase like that), as (C) would require. Some untrained test-takers might want to interpret Terry Dial's statement that "instead of flying up to their perches, the baby Chukars were using their legs" (36-38) as an "anomaly," but an anomaly isn't just something that people didn't know about already—it's specifically something that differs from other collected data. In this case, the Chukars haven't been observed doing anything besides using their legs, so using their legs can't be described as an anomaly. These are exactly the kinds of small, specific details that trained test-takers always have to look out for! Further, the passage doesn't describe anyone comparing the results of the experiment with "previous findings," which is another thing (C) would require. Any of these flaws is enough to make (C) wrong.

D ✓ **Correct:** As trained test-takers, we can tell (D) must be right because every phrase in (D) matches up directly with a portion of the passage. The text does describe a "study," as (D) requires, "to come up with new data on the age-old ground-up-tree-down

---

debate" (8-9), in which Ken Dial "designed a project to see what clues might lie in how baby game birds learned to fly" (9-11). There was an "unexpected finding" (which is also a required part of the answer choice) when, "instead of flying up to their perches, the baby Chukars were using their legs" (36-38)—we know this was unexpected because of the phrase "instead of flying up to their perches," (36-37) and also because the passage calls it "the 'aha' moment" (41) and says it "opened up a world of possibilities" (43), which means it must have been unexpected. We also know that this observation came "during the early phase" of the study, which is another thing the answer choice requires, because it comes right after the paragraph where Ken shows his laboratory where "the birds' first hops and flights would be measured." In other words, the study hadn't even started at that point. We also see that "the study [was] modified in response to this finding," as (D) says, when "Ken came up with a series of ingenious experiments" (45-46) to observe the way the birds got around. Finally "the results [were] interpreted and evaluated" (which is the last component of (D) that we haven't satisfied yet) in the rest of the passage (48-76), which discusses exactly what the birds did "with their wings to help them scramble up otherwise impossible slopes" (58-59), and how "the Dials came up with a viable origin for the flapping flight stroke of birds...and an aerodynamic function for half-formed wings" (71-75) by identifying the WAIR technique (60). Since every part of (D) is directly restated or demonstrated in the passage, we know it's right.

| Test 3, Question 22 | TYPE: WORD MOST NEARLY MEANS |

ⓘ *The prompt includes the phrase "most nearly means" and the choices are usually one- or two-word phrases. The answer is either restated or demonstrated by an idea from the surrounding text. Remember you can work around unknown words, and be ready to guess/skip and focus on other questions if you don't know the words. See "What about "Most Nearly Means" Questions?" on p.73.*

Subjective Phrases to Ignore: "most nearly"

A ✓ ("So when a group of graduate students <u>dared</u> him to come up with new data on the age-old ground-up-tree-down debate, he designed a project to see what clues might lie in how baby game birds learned to fly.") **Correct:** The text says when the students "challenged" him to come up with new data, "he designed a project" (9). So when he was "challenged" to do something, the result was that he tried to do it. This demonstrates the idea of being "dared," so (A) is right.

B ("So when a group of graduate students <u>required</u> him to come up with new data on the age-old ground-up-tree-down debate, he designed a project to see what clues might lie in how baby game birds learned to fly.") **Barely Relevant:** As discussed in the explanation for choice (A), when the students "challenged" Ken Dial, he responded by trying to do what they "challenged" him to do. But there's no evidence in the text that the students "required" him to do that, as opposed to "dar[ing]" him—nothing says that the students had any authority over Ken, or that he'd be punished in some way if he didn't attempt the experiment, which is what the idea of a requirement would involve. For that reason, (B) must be wrong.

C ("So when a group of graduate students <u>disputed with</u> him to come up with new data on the age-old ground-up-tree-down debate, he designed a project to see what clues might lie in how baby game birds learned to fly.") **Barely Relevant:** In another context, the idea of "disput[ing] with" someone could be similar to the idea of "challeng[ing]" them on something; for example, if someone makes a claim you don't agree with, you could "dispute with" them over the claim. But the passage doesn't restate or support that idea.

D ("So when a group of graduate students <u>competed with</u> him to come up with new data on the age-old ground-up-tree-down debate, he designed a project to see what clues might lie in how baby game birds learned to fly.") **Confused Relationships:** In another context, "compete with" could mean "challenge," but the citation doesn't indicate that the graduate students are "competing with" Ken Dial to come up with new data, as this answer choice would require. For that to be true, the text would have to say something about the students also trying come up with new data on their own, but that isn't in the passage, so (D) is wrong.

| Test 3, Question 23 | TYPE: DESCRIBE THE PASSAGE |

The next question is a "best evidence" question referring back to this question; you may choose to consider the citations in the choices for the next question when answering this one if you want. See "Is there a 'best evidence' shortcut?" on page 72 for more.

ⓘ *The prompt often mentions describing the passage, and usually doesn't include a line citation. The answer must still be restated or demonstrated by some specific part of the text, even if there's no citation. See "What about Questions Without Citations?" p. 72*

Subjective Phrases to Ignore: "best"

A ✓ Correct: The prompt tells us we need to focus on the part of the text that describes how Dial "[set] up his research," which is the first paragraph of the passage. First, some "graduate students challenged him to come up with new data on the age-old ground-up-tree-down debate" (7-9). We probably don't know what the "ground-up-tree-down debate" is, and it's not really explained in the main passage. But, as trained test-takers, we know that we need to read the introductory text before the passage; when we read the intro, we can see that the debate has to do with how birds evolved the ability to fly. According to the intro, "the ground-up theory assumes they were fleet-footed ground dwellers that captured prey by leaping and flapping their upper limbs. The tree-down theory assumes they were tree climbers that leapt and glided among branches." So we see in the first paragraph that Dial has been challenged to come up with new data on this debate, and, in response, "he designed a project to see what clues might lie in how baby game birds learned to fly" (9-11). If he is going to observe how baby birds learn to fly in hopes of coming up with new data for the debate about how birds evolved the ability to fly, then he must think that "the acquisition of flight in young birds" (which is the same concept as "how baby game birds learn to fly" in lines 10-11) will teach him something about "the acquisition of flight in their evolutionary ancestors" (which is the same thing as the ground-up-tree-down debate). Since (A) is clearly restated and demonstrated in the text, we know it's right.

B   Barely Relevant: The passage describes how Dial saw that young ground birds would "jump up like popcorn" (4), but the text never indicates that this jumping was a "recent evolved behavior"—in fact, there's nothing in the passage at all about when the jumping behavior evolved. Since this choice makes statements that aren't restated in the passage, it can't be right.

C   Confused Relationships: In the second paragraph a "local rancher" (14-15) told Dial to "give [the birds] something to climb on" (22-23). This reminded Dial that wild birds "preferred to rest on ledges, low branches, or other elevated perches" (26-27), "so he brought in some hay bales for the Chukars to perch on" (29-30). So we can see that Dial never "assumed" the young birds wouldn't need perches, which is what the answer choice would require in order to satisfy the prompt; instead, he just forgot that ground birds like to perch, and, once he was reminded, he brought something in for them to perch on. There's no indication in the text at all that Dial thought about the likelihood of birds perching in a controlled setting as opposed to the likelihood of wild birds perching, as this answer choice would require, so we know this choice is wrong.

D   Barely Relevant: Untrained test-takers may misunderstand the last paragraph and think that it describes two types of predecessors evolving separately and in parallel, as this answer choice requires. But if we read carefully, we see that the passage says WAIR is observed across multiple species (62), and that it explains aspects of evolution that were poorly explained by both the ground-up and tree-down theories (70-76)—in other words, WAIR indicates that the predecessors to birds seem to have evolved using *both* their lower and upper bodies together, as Ken Dial describes in lines 41-42. So the idea of two parallel evolutions isn't actually mentioned anywhere in the text, which means this choice can't be correct.

Test 3, Question 24   **TYPE: BEST EVIDENCE**

ⓘ *The answer must restate or demonstrate the relevant statement. See "What about "Best Evidence" Questions?" on page 72.*

Subjective Phrases to Ignore: "best"

A   Confused Relationships: Untrained test-takers might think this text seems to support (B) from question 23, but no part of the text mentions that the birds' behavior evolved recently, which means (B) must be wrong in 23, and (A) is wrong here.

B ✓   Correct: As we discussed in the walkthrough for question 23, this citation exactly restates the assumption Dial made, which is why (A) is correct in that question, and (B) is correct here.

C   Barely Relevant: This citation describes the "controlled research setting" mentioned in choice (C) from the previous question, but the text never says that young birds in such a setting don't need perches the way birds in the wild do, which is what (C) would require in question 23, so this answer choice can't be evidence for the correct answer to 23.

D   Barely Relevant: This text isn't really relevant to the correct answer from question 23, or to any choice from that question.

Test 3, Question 25   **TYPE: PURPOSE OF CITED TEXT**

ⓘ *The prompt asks about the purpose or role of a part of the text. The correct answer must be accurately restated or described by the relevant text, with no interpretation. See "What about "Purpose" Questions?" on p.74.*

Subjective Phrases to Ignore: "mainly"

A   Wrong Part of the Passage: The first paragraph tells us Dial's motivation in undertaking the project—some graduate students challenged him to find new data for an ongoing debate (6-11). The second paragraph doesn't discuss Dial's motivations; instead, it describes an early adjustment he made in the experiment based on input from the rancher. A lot of untrained test-takers will fall for this wrong answer choice, especially if they accidentally count the intro to the passage as the first paragraph, and mistakenly think that line 1 is the beginning of the second paragraph! Always remember your training, and remember that the College Board is out to trick you in any way that it can.

B   Off by One or Two Words: The second paragraph does describe a difference between the original laboratory setting and field research: in the lab, Dial initially neglected to give the birds perches, but in the wild the birds prefer "to rest on ledges, low branches, or other elevated perches where they were safe from predators" (26-28). But this answer choice says the anecdote underscores "certain differences between laboratory and field research," and the absence of a perch is only *one* difference. This small detail—that the plural word "differences" in the answer choice doesn't fit with the idea of only one difference being mentioned in lines 12-32—is enough to make this answer choice wrong. We always need to maintain this kind of attention to detail when we're taking the SAT!

C ✓   Correct: We know the rancher provided an "unanticipated piece of information," as the answer choice requires, because the rancher told Dial, "they hate to be on the ground! Give them something to climb on!" (22-23), and we're told that this advice "at first...seemed unnatural" (23-24). We know the information "influenced Ken Dial's research," as (C) requires, because, after Dial heard this information, "he brought in some hay bales for the Chukars to perch on" (29-30), and then the Chukar's interactions with the hay bales in the next paragraph provided the insight that led to the documentation of WAIR, as described later in the passage. Since every part of (C) restates something in the passage, we know it's right.

D   **Confused Relationships:** The local rancher mentioned in the prompt does tell Ken Dial to "give [the birds] something to climb on" (22-23), and it's true that the climbing behavior later demonstrated by the birds is key to the observation of WAIR later in the text. But there are two problems with (D). First, it says the rancher is a "key contributor" to a theory, but the text never says that the rancher theorizes about anything—it only says that he told Dial to get some perches. Second, the theory mentioned in the answer choice is the "tree-down theory," but that theory is obviously older than Dial's research, because paragraph 1 tells us that Dial is doing his research in the first place to see if he can learn anything about the tree-down theory, which means the tree-down theory must pre-date the research, and the rancher appears too late in the passage to be a contributor to that pre-existing theory. Either of these reasons is enough to make (D) wrong.

▌ Test 3, Question 26   TYPE: CITATION QUESTION

ⓘ *The question includes a citation from the text. The answer must be directly restated or demonstrated in the cited text, or in the text closely surrounding the cited text. See the general process for answering SAT Reading questions on p. 71.*

A   **Confused Relationships:** The passage mentions "flight" (50), and it mentions "perches" (27), but it never mentions Dial teaching birds to fly to their perches, whether before or after the "'aha' moment'" in the prompt, so (A) must be wrong.

B   **Confused Relationships:** The passage mentions that the Dials were "filming the birds" (46), but the passage never says whether the birds stopped hopping in the first place, which is something (B) would require. Furthermore, the passage never mentions whether the Dials tried to watch videos to find out why the birds no longer hopped. So we can see this choice definitely fails to restate the text, and must be wrong.

C✓ **Correct:** After the description of the "aha" moment in line 41, the next thing Dial did was come up with a "series of ingenious experiments, filming the birds as they raced up textured ramps tilted at increasing angles" (46-48). The word "observing" in the answer choice restates the word "filming" in line 46; the phrase "dealt with" from (C) can describe the idea of "rac[ing] up" (47); the phrase "gradually steeper inclines" from (C) restates the phrase "tilted at increasing angles" (46-47). So we can see that every part of (C) restates an element of the passage, which means it's right.

D   **Reasonable Statement Not in the Text:** An untrained test-taker might make the mistake of assuming that Dial would consult with other researchers after his "aha" moment, because that probably seems like the kind of thing a lot of scientists would do, but the text never says whether Dial did that or not. Since the idea in this answer choice doesn't appear anywhere in the text, the choice must be wrong.

▌ Test 3, Question 27   TYPE: DESCRIBE THE PASSAGE

ⓘ *The prompt often mentions describing the passage, and usually doesn't include a line citation. The answer must still be restated or demonstrated by some specific part of the text, even if there's no citation. See "What about Questions Without Citations?" p. 72*

A   **Confused Relationships:** The text mentions "Formula One racing" (54), which might make an untrained test-taker assume the birds are going very fast. But the text doesn't say that speed is what gave the birds traction on the ramp; instead, as described in the explanation for (B), the position of their wings did that. Since (A) doesn't restate the passage, it's wrong.

B✓ **Correct:** The passage says that the birds "aimed their flapping down and backward, using the force not for lift but to keep their feet firmly pressed against the ramp" (50-52); Dial compares this action to a "spoiler on the back of a race car" (53). Then the passage says that "spoilers...push...cars downward...increasing traction and handling," and "the birds were doing the very same thing with their wings" (55-58). So we can see in the text that the birds flap their wings "down and backward," which is a particular "position" as required by the answer choice, and that this position acts like a spoiler, and spoilers push cars downward to increase traction. In other words, the position of the flapping wings increases traction, just as the answer choice and the prompt require, so we can see that this choice must be correct.

C   **Confused Relationships:** This answer choice might be tempting to untrained test-takers who noticed the mention of "wings" (49) and "feet" (52) in the passage, or who may have misread the phrase "wing-assisted" (60) and thought it said something like "wing-alternating." But the text never mentions the idea of alternating wing and foot movement, which (C) would require, so we know (C) must be wrong.

D   **Confused Relationships:** Hopping is mentioned earlier in the passage (lines 6 and 19), but not at all in the discussion of running up the ramps (45-76). (D) may appeal to an untrained test-taker who remembered hopping came up somewhere in the passage, but who didn't remember where or why, and didn't go back to check the role of hopping in the passage.

▌ Test 3, Question 28   TYPE: WORD MOST NEARLY MEANS

ⓘ *The prompt includes the phrase "most nearly means" and the choices are usually one- or two-word phrases. The answer is either restated or demonstrated by an idea from the surrounding text. Remember you can work around unknown words, and be ready to guess/skip and focus on other questions if you don't know the words. See "What about "Most Nearly Means" Questions?" on p.73.*

A   ("Ken called the technique WAIR, for wing-assisted incline running, and went on to <u>portray</u> it in a wide range of species.")
Barely Relevant: "Portray" would mean something like "depict" or "present," and there's no evidence that Dial "depicted" or "presented" WAIR "in a wide range of species," so (A) must be wrong.

B ✓   ("Ken called the technique WAIR, for wing-assisted incline running, and went on to <u>record</u> it in a wide range of species.")
Correct: The text says Ken Dial "went on" (61) to do something "in a wide range of species" (61-62). The phrase "went on" means that he continued doing something he had previously done. Earlier, the passage tells us that Dial recorded WAIR in the Chukars when it says he was "filming the birds as they raced up textured ramps" (46-47). So it makes sense to say that Ken "went on" to film WAIR in a wide range of other species. We can see that the passage demonstrates the idea of recording WAIR, which means (B) must be right.

C   ("Ken called the technique WAIR, for wing-assisted incline running, and went on to <u>publish</u> it in a wide range of species.")
Confused Relationships: Untrained test-takers might accidentally associate the words "document" and "publish," because scientists publish documents all the time. But no part of the passage restates the idea that Dial "published" WAIR; instead, we see that he published research that discussed WAIR.

D   ("Ken called the technique WAIR, for wing-assisted incline running, and went on to <u>process</u> it in a wide range of species.")
Confused Relationships: This choice is similar to (C), in that both choices involve words that an untrained test-taker might carelessly associate with the idea of a document; in this case, it's possible to document a process—that is, to take detailed notes on the way something is done. But there's nothing in the passage that restates the idea of processing anything, let alone the idea of Dial "process[ing]" WAIR "in a wide range of species." So we can see this choice must be wrong.

| **Test 3, Question 29** | **TYPE: DESCRIBE THE PASSAGE** |

The next question is a "best evidence" question referring back to this question; you may choose to consider the citations in the choices for the next question when answering this one if you want. See "Is there a 'best evidence' shortcut?" on page 72 for more.

ⓘ *The prompt often mentions describing the passage, and usually doesn't include a line citation. The answer must still be restated or demonstrated by some specific part of the text, even if there's no citation. See "What about Questions Without Citations?" p. 72*

A   **Confused Relationships:** Lines 4-6 describe how young ground birds hop along behind their parents, so this choice will definitely attract some test-takers who think that the "gliding animals" mentioned in the prompt are birds. But we see that the passage never says that young ground birds are "gliding animals" in the first place—in fact, lines 72-73 explicitly describe the "flight stroke of birds" as "something gliding animals don't do," which must mean that birds and gliding animals are separate things. All of this means that (A) isn't restated or demonstrated by the text, so it must be wrong. (See note!)

B   **Direct Contradiction:** The text says in lines 72-74 that the "flapping flight stroke of birds" is "something gliding animals don't do." In other words, the text specifically describes a difference between the way birds move and the way gliding animals move, which means that this choice contradicts the passage, so it can't be right.

C   **Confused Relationships:** The text describes how ground birds "preferred to rest on…elevated perches" and "only used the ground for feeding and traveling" (26-29). But the prompt asks about "gliding animals," and the text says ground birds are different from "gliding animals," as we discussed in (A) and (B). So lines 26-29 aren't relevant to this question, which means (C) doesn't restate anything from the passage, so it must be wrong.

D ✓   **Correct:** The passage says young birds use a "flapping...stroke" (72), and that "gliding animals" (72-73) don't do that. Since "gliding animals" don't make a flapping stroke at all, they must not make a flapping stroke for the "climbing" described in (D). Because (D) restates concepts and relationships from the text, we know it must be correct.

Note   The key realization that's necessary to answer this question is the fact that "gliding animals" and "birds" are two different groups of things, as we can see in lines 72-73, and as we discussed when considering choice (A) above. Most untrained test-takers will have problems with this question because they'll assume that birds are gliding animals, rather than paying attention to the details on the page and looking for an answer choice that exactly restates the passage. Keep this kind of thing in mind on test day!

| **Test 3, Question 30** | **TYPE: BEST EVIDENCE** |

ⓘ *The answer must restate or demonstrate the relevant statement. See "What about "Best Evidence" Questions?" on page 72.*

A   **Confused Relationships:** This citation might appear to support (A) from question 29, but, as discussed in the explanation for that choice, this text actually refers to ground birds, not gliding animals, which means it's not relevant to question 29.

B   Confused Relationships: This citation might appear to support (C) from question 29, but, as discussed in the explanation for that choice, this citation actually refers to ground birds, not gliding animals, which means it's not relevant to question 29.

C   Literary Interpretation: This citation describes what ground birds do to climb steep slopes, but question 29 asks about gliding animals, and we know from our discussion of question 29 that gliding animals aren't birds, so (C) must be wrong.

D✓   Correct: As we saw when we discussed question 29, this citation explicitly indicates that birds and "gliding animals" are two different types of things, and that gliding animals don't flap like birds do. This explains why (D) is the correct answer to question 29, and also provides the key realization that we discussed in the notes for question 29.

Test 3, Question 31   TYPE: WORD MOST NEARLY MEANS

🛈 *The prompt includes the phrase "most nearly means" and the choices are usually one- or two-word phrases. The answer is either restated or demonstrated by an idea from the surrounding text. Remember you can work around unknown words, and be ready to guess/skip and focus on other questions if you don't know the words. See "What about "Most Nearly Means" Questions?" on p.73.*

Subjective Phrases to Ignore: "most nearly"

A   ("It seems to us incontestable that our <u>average</u> happiness, above all that of women, requires that they never aspire to the exercise of political rights and functions.") **Reasonable Statement Not in the Text:** In another context, "common" could mean "average," because both words can describe something normal or standard. But the passage doesn't restate or demonstrate that idea, so (A) can't be correct.

B✓   ("It seems to us incontestable that our <u>shared</u> happiness, above all that of women, requires that they never aspire to the exercise of political rights and functions.") **Correct:** The cited sentence refers to "us" and "our common happiness." The words "us" and "our" are plural, which means the speaker is talking about something that belongs to the speaker and to someone else, which necessarily demonstrates that the happiness is "shared," as (B) requires.

C   ("It seems to us incontestable that our <u>coarse</u> happiness, above all that of women, requires that they never aspire to the exercise of political rights and functions.") **Reasonable Statement Not in the Text:** In some other context, "common" could mean "coarse," because both words can describe something unrefined. But the passage doesn't restate or demonstrate that idea, so (C) is wrong.

D   ("It seems to us incontestable that our <u>similar</u> happiness, above all that of women, requires that they never aspire to the exercise of political rights and functions.") **Barely Relevant:** In another context, the words "common" and "similar" could be somewhat related; for example, if we say a trait is common to two people, then the people are "similar." But the two words aren't really synonymous in any context. More importantly, the passage doesn't restate this idea, so (D) is wrong.

Test 3, Question 32   TYPE: DESCRIBE THE PASSAGE

🛈 *The prompt often mentions describing the passage, and usually doesn't include a line citation. The answer must still be restated or demonstrated by some specific part of the text, even if there's no citation. See "What about Questions Without Citations?" p. 72*

Subjective Phrases to Ignore: "inferred"

A   Reasonable Statement Not in the Text: An untrained test-taker might personally feel that "running a household and raising children," as described in the prompt, are "rewarding for men as well as for women," as (A) would require. But, as trained test-takers, we see that the authors never comment on the idea of men performing these duties, so (A) is wrong.

B   Reasonable Statement Not in the Text: An untrained test-taker might assume the authors of Passage 1 would think that "running a household and raising children" aren't as "valu[able] for society" as the "roles performed by men," as (B) requires. But the authors never specifically compare the value of these two sets of responsibilities. They only say there's a "division of powers" (31-32); they never mention what men's duties and roles are, and they never compare the values of societal roles.

C✓   Correct: The prompt doesn't provide a line citation for us to consider, but it does refer to "running a household and raising children," which is a restatement of the phrases "the cares of the home" (29-30) and "the many duties of motherhood" (26-27). The sentence that contains those words appears in lines 25-30. This sentence mentions women being "summon[ed]...to gentle occupations" (29) and being "set...apart from strenuous habits and onerous duties" (28). The phrase "activities that are difficult or unpleasant" from this answer choice restates the idea of "strenuous habits" and "onerous duties," and the idea from the answer choice that women have "very few" of these activities restates the idea of women being "set apart" (27) from them. (Further, the authors say that women's "occupations" (29) are "gentle" (29), which is another indication that they consider these tasks not to be "difficult or unpleasant"—if we can't tell from the context that "strenuous" and "onerous" are negative concepts, then we can still tell that (C) must be right if we can notice that "gentle" is the opposite of "difficult or unpleasant.") For these reasons, we see that (C) clearly restates the relevant part of the passage, so it's right.

D   Reasonable Statement Not in the Text: An untrained test-taker might assume that the domestic skills mentioned in the prompt are "similar to" the skills of "run[ning] a country or business," as this answer choice would require, but the passage never actually describes the skills of running countries or businesses. So (D) doesn't restate the passage, and must be wrong.

ℹ️ *The answer must restate or demonstrate the relevant statement. See "What about "Best Evidence" Questions?" on page 72.*

Subjective Phrases to Ignore: "best"

A   **Barely Relevant:** This citation doesn't say anything about how the authors view "running a household and raising children" as described in the prompt for the previous question, so it must be wrong.

B   **Literary Interpretation:** This citation makes a general statement about the role women play in society, but it doesn't say anything about how the authors view "running a household and raising children," as discussed in question 32, so (B) is wrong.

C ✓ **Correct:** As discussed in the walkthrough for the previous question, this citation includes the sentence in which the authors state that the "many duties of motherhood" and "the cares of the home" are not "strenuous" or "onerous."

D   **Literary Interpretation:** This citation discusses the general idea that each sex should have its own "powers" and "functions," but it doesn't specifically address domestic chores and responsibilities, as the citation in (C) does.

ℹ️ *The prompt often mentions describing the passage, and usually doesn't include a line citation. The answer must still be restated or demonstrated by some specific part of the text, even if there's no citation. See "What about Questions Without Citations?" p. 72*

A   **Barely Relevant:** The author mentions "happiness" (75, 78), as (A) does, but she doesn't mention "financial security," as (A) also requires. And she doesn't connect either idea to the "progress" of "society" mentioned in the prompt. So (A) is wrong.

B   **Barely Relevant:** The author never explicitly mentions the idea of "social rules," or any similar phrase, as (B) requires.

C   **Reasonable Statement Not in the Text:** Untrained test-takers might assume that the author believes women should "replace men as figures of power and authority," because she doesn't agree that women should be left uneducated or without particular legal rights. But she never actually discusses the idea of women "replac[ing] men" in any way, as this answer choice would require, so we know this choice must be wrong.

D ✓ **Correct:** The prompt doesn't provide a line citation, but it does mention the idea of "society" "progress[ing];" when we locate the part of the passage that discusses societal progress, we see that the first paragraph of Passage 2 discusses concepts like "progress" (44) and "mankind" (57), so the correct answer is likely to restate concepts from this area of the text. When we look at the opening of the first paragraph, we see that the author says that if women are not "prepared by education to become the companion of man" (43-44), they will "stop the progress of knowledge and virtue" (44-45); the paragraph goes on to describe how "virtues spring" (55) from a consideration of the "moral and civil interest of mankind" (56-57), but that the way women are currently "educat[ed]...shuts [them] out" from understanding those kinds of things. The idea of women being "prepared by education" (43) restates the idea of "receiving an education" from the answer choice; the idea of women's education making them "the companion of man" (43-44) is restated by the phrase "comparable to that of men" in the answer choice. The idea of "societ[al]...progress" from the prompt is restated by the phrases in the first paragraph relating to "the progress of knowledge and virtue" (44-45) and "the moral and civil interest of mankind" (56-57). Every part of this answer choice is restated by the text, so we know this choice is correct.

ℹ️ *The prompt includes the phrase "most nearly means" and the choices are usually one- or two-word phrases. The answer is either restated or demonstrated by an idea from the surrounding text. Remember you can work around unknown words, and be ready to guess/skip and focus on other questions if you don't know the words. See "What about "Most Nearly Means" Questions?" on p.73.*

Subjective Phrases to Ignore: "most nearly"

A   ("And how can woman be expected to co-operate...unless freedom strengthen her <u>motive</u> till she comprehend her duty, and see in what manner it is connected with her real good?") **Reasonable Statement Not in the Text:** In another context, "reason" and "motive" could be synonyms. For example, someone's "motive" for committing a crime is the "reason" that person committed the crime. But the passage doesn't restate that idea, so this answer can't be correct.

B   ("And how can woman be expected to co-operate...unless freedom strengthen her <u>sanity</u> till she comprehend her duty, and see in what manner it is connected with her real good?") **Reasonable Statement Not in the Text:** In another context, "reason" could mean "sanity." But the context doesn't restate or support that idea, so this answer can't be correct.

C ✓ ("And how can woman be expected to co-operate...unless freedom strengthen her <u>intellect</u> till she comprehend her duty, and see in what manner it is connected with her real good?") **Correct:** The text mentions "strengthen[ing]" a person's "reason" until the person can "comprehend" something. If strengthening "reason" makes someone more able to comprehend things, then that "reason" must be the same thing as an "intellect," because "intellect" is the thing that lets us understand something. This concept of "intellect" is also restated by the word "knowledge" in line 45, and the idea of "education" (43, 52) is the same thing as the idea of "strengthen[ing]...intellect."

D ("And how can woman be expected to co-operate...unless freedom strengthen her <u>explanation</u> till she comprehend her duty, and see in what manner it is connected with her real good?") Reasonable Statement Not in the Text: "Reason" and "explanation" could be interchangeable in another context. For example, we can say that someone who is giving a "reason" for her decision is giving an "explanation" for that decision. But the text doesn't restate the idea of "strengthen[ing]" an "explanation," as this choice would require, so we know this choice must be wrong.

| **Test 3, Question 36** | TYPE: DESCRIBE THE PASSAGE |

The prompt often mentions describing the passage, and usually doesn't include a line citation. The answer must still be restated or demonstrated by some specific part of the text, even if there's no citation. See "What about Questions Without Citations?" p. 72

A ✓ **Correct:** The author of Passage 2 says men are "allowed to judge for themselves respecting their own happiness" (74-75), and that man (meaning the entire male gender) is "the exclusive judge" (78-79); later, the author says women are "den[ied]...civil and political rights" (86). The phrase "society's leaders" in the prompt restates the idea that men are the "exclusive judges" who can "deny...rights" to women, and the phrase "privileged one gender over the other" restates the idea that men are "allowed to judge for themselves" while women are "den[ied]...rights," so this choice must be right.

B **Literary Interpretation:** The author of Passage 2 mentions the idea of "stop[ping] the progress of...virtue" (44-45), and untrained test-takers might assume that this answer choice restates that idea. But *stopping* the "progress" of a thing is NOT, strictly speaking, the same idea as *reducing* that thing, as this answer choice would require. Stopping the progress of virtue just means that virtue won't increase or expand—it doesn't mean that existing virtue will be reduced. So, as trained-test-takers, we can tell this must be a wrong answer.

C **Barely Relevant:** The author mentions "happiness" (75, 78), but she doesn't mention any "arguments" over what happiness *is*, as this answer choice would require. She only says that if men can "judge for themselves respecting their own happiness" (74-75), then women should be able to as well—but, again, this isn't the same thing as saying that a particular group has "caused arguments" about anything, so this choice must be wrong.

D **Direct Contradiction:** As we discussed in the explanation for choice (A), the author says that men have "civil and political rights" that women don't have, which is the opposite of "equality for all people" as described in this choice.

| **Test 3, Question 37** | TYPE: BEST EVIDENCE |

The answer must restate or demonstrate the relevant statement. See "What about "Best Evidence" Questions?" on page 72.

Subjective Phrases to Ignore: "best"

A **Literary Interpretation:** To an untrained test-taker, this citation may appear to support choice (B) from the previous question. But, as discussed in the explanation for that choice, this text says unequal education will "stop the progress of...virtue" (44-45), and not "reduc[e]...virtue," as described in that answer choice.

B **Barely Relevant:** This citation is generally related to the idea that everyone should get the same education men get in order for education to be worthwhile, but it doesn't actually say anything about the "freedoms granted by society's leaders," as described in the prompt for the previous question.

C **Barely Relevant:** As we saw with choice (B) above, the actual cited text for this choice doesn't say anything about society's leaders, so it can't be relevant to the prompt for the previous question.

D ✓ **Correct:** As we discussed in the walkthrough for question 36, this citation is the beginning of the part of Passage 2 that discusses how men can "judge for themselves" (74), while women are "den[ied]...civil and political rights" (86).

| **Test 3, Question 38** | TYPE: PURPOSE OF CITED TEXT |

The prompt asks about the purpose or role of a part of the text. The correct answer must be accurately restated or described by the relevant text, with no interpretation. See "What about "Purpose" Questions?" on p.74.

A **Reasonable Statement Not in the Text:** Some untrained test-takers might imagine that the author of Passage 2 would see the authors of Passage 1 as unqualified to comment on gender issues. But the author of Passage 2 never actually discusses the "qualifications" of the authors of Passage 1, as this answer choice would require.

B **Direct Contradiction:** The author of Passage 2 doesn't dispute the assertion from Passage 1 in lines 61-65. In fact, she says that a "glimpse" (60) of the "truth" (60) actually "seemed to open" (60-61) when they made that assertion. So she agrees with the assertion, rather than "disput[ing]" it, which is what this choice would require.

C ✓ **Correct:** After the author of Passage 2 refers to the other authors' statement, she says, "If so, on what does your constitution rest?" (65-66) The author follows up on this rhetorical question by saying that "a parity of reasoning" (68) will show that the "rights...of woman" (65-66) will also "bear discussion" (67). The phrase "if so" at the beginning of this rhetorical question indicates that the author of Passage 2 doesn't agree with the point she's just quoted from Passage 1, and the phrase "by a parity of reasoning" demonstrates that the author of Passage 2 thinks the authors of Passage 1 have applied their reasoning incorrectly, just as this answer choice requires.

D   Direct Contradiction: In lines 61-65, the author of Passage 2 cites the opening of Passage 1, not the "concluding declarations" of Passage 1; further, the text surrounding lines 61-65 doesn't address any of the concepts in the conclusion of Passage 1 beyond the general fact that both passages are about the way women should be treated in a society, so we can't say that the author of Passage 2 "validates" those "concluding declarations," as this answer choice would require.

ⓘ *The prompt also asks how someone would respond to a claim or argument. The correct answer restates a position that's already stated in the passage. See "What about Paired Passages?" on p.76.*

Subjective Phrases to Ignore: "best"

A ✓   Correct: There are several ways to show that this choice is correct, but one of the easiest might be to point out that the authors of Passage 1 repeatedly say that it's better for everyone if women are confined to "gentle occupations and the cares of the home" (29-30), and that women should "never aspire to...political rights" (23). But Passage 2 asks the authors of Passage 1 to "consider...whether...[it's] inconsistent and unjust to subjugate women" (72-76), and says, "Do you not act [like a tyrant] when you...deny[]...civil and political rights" to "women?" (85-86) In this way, among others, the author of Passage 2 "strongly challenges" Passage 1, just as (A) requires. (The word "strongly" is demonstrated by the text because she compares the other authors to "tyrants" (81) eager to "crush reason" (83), among other things, which are inherently strong statements.)

B   Off by One or Two Words: Untrained test-takers might be tempted by (B) because they know that the two authors disagree, so it may seem like we should be able to say the author of Passage 2 "draws alternative conclusions" from those of the authors of Passage 1, as (B) requires. But (B) also requires the author of Passage 2 to draw conclusions from the evidence *in Passage 1*, and there's no indication that the author of Passage 2 is considering any of that "evidence." In fact, the author of Passage 2 says in lines 42-47 that her "argument is built on [the] simple principle" that women must be educated, or else progress will stop; we can see that this "simple principle" doesn't appear anywhere in Passage 1.

C   Barely Relevant: The authors of Passage 1 don't actually make any proposal at all, as (C) would require. They aren't *proposing* that there be a "division of powers" (31-32) between the sexes; they're saying *there already is one,* and explaining why that division is a good thing in their opinion. Since the first passage doesn't present any proposal, (C) can't be correct.

D   Direct Contradiction: As we discussed in the explanation for choice (A), the author of Passage 2 strongly disagrees with the authors of Passage 1; she doesn't just restate their argument in different terms, as this answer choice would require.

ⓘ *The prompt also asks how someone would respond to a claim or argument. The correct answer restates a position that's already stated in the passage. See "What about Paired Passages?" on p.76.*

Subjective Phrases to Ignore: "most likely"

A   Direct Contradiction: The authors of Passage 1 refer to "the assignment [women] have received" (20), and says that "nature...divided the functions of the two sexes" (33-34). He also says women have "peaceful inclinations" (26) which "summon them to gentle occupations and the cares of the home" (30). So the author of Passage 1 says women are "inclin[ed]" to certain tasks, and these tasks are "divided" from what men do; since the word "inclinations" (26) means the same thing as "natural preferences" in this answer choice, we can see that the author of Passage 1 thinks women don't prefer the same things that men do. The author of Passage 2 doesn't specifically discuss the "natural preferences" of men or women; she just says it's "unjust" to allow men "to judge for themselves respecting their own happiness" (74-75), but to "subjugate women" (76). Since the authors of one passage disagree with the statement in (A), and the other passage doesn't address the statement at all, (A) can't be right.

B   Confused Relationships: The author of Passage 2 does discuss education, women, and society, which are all concepts in this answer choice, but the authors of Passage 1 never say anything about women needing education, nor about education being related to women's role in society, so (B) is wrong.

C   Confused Relationships: The authors of Passage 1 mention "mutual happiness" (15) and "common happiness" (21-22), but they never *compare* the happiness of one gender to the happiness of another gender, as this answer choice would require. Meanwhile, the author of Passage 2 says that only men can "judge for themselves respecting their own happiness" (74-75) while women are "subjugate[d]" (76) and "den[ied]...rights" (86). So the first authors don't discuss the relative happiness of two individual genders, and the second author says that only men can choose to do what makes them happy, while women have no rights. For these reasons, we can see this choice must be wrong.

D ✓   Correct: The authors of Passage 1, referring to women, say, "half the human race is excluded...from any participation in government...and...have no direct influence or representation" (1-6). This idea is restated by (D)'s statement that women had "fewer rights than men did." The author of Passage 2 also agrees with this idea when she says "all women" are "den[ied]...civil and political rights" (86) that men enjoy. Since both authors agree with this statement, just as the prompt requires, (D) is correct.

ⓘ *The prompt also asks how someone would respond to a claim or argument. The correct answer restates a position that's already stated in the passage. See "What about Paired Passages?" on p.76.*

Subjective Phrases to Ignore: "most likely"

A ✔ **Correct:** The last paragraph of Passage 2 says that "denying [women] civil and political rights" (86) makes the authors of Passage 1 like "tyrants" (81) who "crush reason" (83). But the authors of Passage 1 say women should "never aspire to...political rights" (23), and that women have "peaceful inclinations" (26) which lead them to "gentle occupations and the cares of the home" (29-30) and that women shouldn't "change the assignment they have received" (20). So the authors of Passage 1 clearly say women are "naturally suited" for domestic life, and not for "the exercise of civil and political rights," as (A) requires.

B **Reasonable Statement Not in the Text:** The author of Passage 2 mentions that women, like men, have "the gift of reason" (79-80), but the authors of Passage 1 never say anything about whether men and women have the same level of reasoning ability, as this answer choice would require, so we know this choice must be wrong.

C **Direct Contradiction:** The authors of Passage 1 say that women are meant for the "duties of motherhood" (27) and the "gentle occupations and the cares of the home" (29-30). So they believe women *do* need to "remain confined to their traditional family duties," which is the opposite of what this choice says. This choice might attract a particular type of untrained test-taker who overlooks the word "not" in the choice, but, as trained-test-takers, we know that we always need to read each choice carefully, specifically so we don't fall for these kinds of traps.

D **Direct Contradiction:** The authors of Passage 1 say the "exclusion...decreed against women" (13-14) has become "a law" (16) for "all Societies" (16); they further say that women should "never aspire to...political rights and functions" (23-24), and that this kind of separation is "the wish[] of nature" (25). The phrase "principles of natural law" in the answer choice restates the idea of looking to the "wishes of nature" in determining "a law" of "exclusion" for women in "all Societies." But Passage 1 says this kind of natural law *should* be considered when discussing gender roles, which exactly contradicts (D). As we saw with (C) above, many untrained test-takers will accidentally pick (D) because they misread it and overlook the word "not."

ⓘ *The prompt asks about the purpose or role of a part of the text. The correct answer must be accurately restated or described by the relevant text, with no interpretation. See "What about "Purpose" Questions?" on p.74.*

A **Reasonable Statement Not in the Text:** An untrained test-taker might assume that the researchers are "hopeful," but the text doesn't actually express this idea, so this choice isn't restating the paragraph. For example, the paragraph doesn't say anything like "we expect to have favorable results" or "this research will probably be beneficial" or anything like that.

B **Reasonable Statement Not in the Text:** Untrained test-takers might imagine that researchers question whether their research will actually be useful, as this answer choice would require. But, as we saw with (A), the idea in (B) isn't actually stated anywhere in the passage. For example, the paragraph doesn't say anything like "we are not sure that we will see improvement in the near future."

C ✔ **Correct:** The first sentence of the third paragraph says the researchers "suspect" (19) that some bee colonies aren't getting the nutrients they need, and the rest of the paragraph elaborates on the details of what they suspect. The verb "suspect" in the text specifically refers to the idea of thinking that something is likely to be correct, but realizing that you still don't know for sure that it's correct, exactly as this answer choice requires. The things being "postulate[d]" (21, 35) throughout the rest of the text are the ideas that make up the "hypothesis" referred to in the answer choice. So, as we can see, the words "can," "may," and "could" in this paragraph, along with the words "suspect" and "postulate," all show that the authors aren't sure that what they say is true—those words express the idea that something *might* be true, but the speaker doesn't know with certainty. This is reflected in the phrase "tentative tone" from the answer choice. Since every part of this answer choice is demonstrated by the relevant portion of the passage, we know this choice must be right.

D **Confused Relationships:** Some untrained test-takers might assume the researchers are "skeptical of claims" that pyrethrums are in mono-crops, as this choice would require, because most untrained test-takers don't know that the correct answer to an SAT Reading question has to be spelled out in the text. But, as trained-test-takers, we know (D) can't be right because the passage never actually addresses any claims that mono-crops have pyrethrums—there's no way for the researchers to address a claim that doesn't even appear in the passage. (The text says the researchers suspect "bees...which are fed mono-crops are nutritionally deficient" (19-21), and that the bees' "problem is a diet deficient in anti-mite toxins" (21-22). The text then says the mono-crop diets are deficient in "pyrethrums, and possibly other nutrients" (22-23). So "pyrethrums" appear in the text as an example of what's *missing* from the mono-crops, not what's "inherent" in them, as (D) would require.)

ⓘ *The question includes a citation from the text. The answer must be directly restated or demonstrated in the cited text, or in the text closely surrounding the cited text. See the general process for answering SAT Reading questions on p. 71.*

A   **Direct Contradiction:** All of the major concepts in this answer choice appear in the text, but the relationships among those concepts are presented differently in the answer choice from the way they were presented in the passage. The text says that bees with mites can have a "secondary infection with fungi, bacteria or viruses" (5). But the text also says that pyrethrums are "insecticides with anti-mite activity" (12). The text never says anything about being "likely to develop a secondary infection" as a result of "being exposed to both pyrethrums and mites," as this answer choice would require. In fact, we would expect that bees with pyrethrums in their diets would NOT have any mites, and would AVOID any "secondary infection." That's the opposite of what this choice says, so we know this choice must be wrong.

B   **Direct Contradiction:** Like (A), this choice contains several individual concepts that appear somewhere in the passage, but in a way that misrepresents their relationships in the passage. The text actually says that "nutritionally deficient bees may be further weakened" (31-32) if they're exposed to "insecticides...to fight mite infestation" (33-35). So (B)'s statement that "beekeepers...need to increase...insecticides to prevent mite infestations" contradicts an idea expressed in the passage.

C ✓   **Correct:** The text says that "without...feeding on the pyrethrum producing plants, bee colonies are susceptible to mite infestations" (24-28). In other words, feeding on the pyrethrum plants is what keeps bee colonies from being susceptible to mite infestations, exactly as this choice says. So this choice is correct.

D   **Confused Relationships:** As discussed in the explanation for choice (C), the text says that *bees,* not humans, can be at risk of getting varroa mites. The text does mention humans getting scabies from mites in lines 16-17, but that discussion isn't related to varroa mites, and the text doesn't say that nutrition plays any role in the process of humans getting mites. Since this choice doesn't restate anything from the passage, we know it must be a wrong answer.

Test 3, Question 44 — TYPE: BEST EVIDENCE

ⓘ *The answer must restate or demonstrate the relevant statement. See "What about "Best Evidence" Questions?" on page 72.*

A   **Confused Relationships:** This citation might appear to support (A) from the previous question, but that choice mentions being exposed to pyrethrums as well as mites, and this citation doesn't address how pyrethrums would impact the bees. This text also elaborates on the mite infestations from choice (C), but, again, doesn't include information about pyrethrums.

B   **Confused Relationships:** This citation might seem to support choice (D) from the previous question, but that choice talks about humans getting varroa mites, whereas this citation mentions humans getting scabies.

C   **Confused Relationships:** This citation includes some ideas from choice (B) in the previous question, but it doesn't discuss the use of pesticides, as (B) would have required.

D ✓   **Correct:** As discussed in the explanation for (C) in question 43, the citation in this choice says bees are less likely to get mite infestations when they eat plants that produce pyrethrums, which is what (C) restated in question 43.

Test 3, Question 45 — TYPE: DESCRIBE THE PASSAGE

ⓘ *The prompt often mentions describing the passage, and usually doesn't include a line citation. The answer must still be restated or demonstrated by some specific part of the text, even if there's no citation. See "What about Questions Without Citations?" p. 72*

A   **Barely Relevant:** The text never mentions an increase in any kind of population (whether of bees, plants, mites, or anything else), so there's no way this choice can be restating anything from the passage, which means it must be a wrong answer.

B   **Reasonable Statement Not in the Text:** An untrained test-taker might imagine that insecticides could harm some "beneficial...bacteria," as this answer choice would require, but the text never mentions the idea of beneficial bacteria, which means this choice can't be correct.

C   **Confused Relationships:** The text talks about some bees being "nutritionally deficient" (20-21) and their diets being "deficient in anti-mite toxins" (21-22), but it never talks about insecticides destroying the bees' "food source," as this answer choice would require. This choice might have been tempting if an untrained test-taker misread the text and thought that the bees were eating the mites, instead of eating the plants with anti-mite properties.

D ✓   **Correct:** The text says some kinds of bees "may be further weakened" (32) when they're exposed to "commercially produced insecticides" (33). The phrase "further harm the health" in the answer choice restates the idea of the bees being "further weakened" (32), while the phrase "some bees" in the answer choice refers to the "immunocompromised or nutritionally deficient bees" in line 28. Since (D) restates the relevant portion of the passage, we know it must be correct.

Test 3, Question 46 — TYPE: BEST EVIDENCE

ⓘ *The answer must restate or demonstrate the relevant statement. See "What about "Best Evidence" Questions?" on page 72.*

A   **Confused Relationships:** This text might appear to support choice (C) from the previous paragraph if an untrained test-taker thought the text was saying that the bees *eat* the varroa mites, instead of being infested by them.

B   **Barely Relevant:** This text isn't really relevant to any choice from the previous question, so it can't possibly be correct.

C ✓   **Correct:** As we saw in our discussion of (D) in question 45, this citation indicates that insecticides can harm bees in some situations, exactly as that choice restated.

D   **Barely Relevant:** This citation talks about part of an experiment related to mites and bees, instead of "commercially produced pesticides" as described in the prompt of question 45, so it can't really be relevant to any choice for 45.

❚ Test 3, Question 47   **TYPE: WORD MOST NEARLY MEANS**

ⓘ *The prompt includes the phrase "most nearly means" and the choices are usually one- or two-word phrases. The answer is either restated or demonstrated by an idea from the surrounding text. Remember you can work around unknown words, and be ready to guess/skip and focus on other questions if you don't know the words. See "What about "Most Nearly Means" Questions?" on p.73.*

Subjective Phrases to Ignore: "most nearly"

A   ("We further <u>make an unfounded assumption</u> that the proper dosage necessary to prevent mite infestation may be better left to the bees, who may seek out or avoid pyrethrum containing plants depending on the amount necessary to defend against mites and the amount already consumed by the bees, which in higher doses could be potentially toxic to them.") **Direct Contradiction:** The text says, "the proper dosage...may be better left to the bees," and says this is because "higher doses could be...toxic." So the original version of the sentence gives a reason for allowing the bees to determine the dose: it seems like it might be a way to avoid toxic levels of pyrethrums. Since the idea of letting the bees determine the dose is based on something, it can't be called "unfounded," which means this choice must be wrong.

B ✓   ("We further <u>put forth an idea or claim</u> that the proper dosage necessary to prevent mite infestation may be better left to the bees, who may seek out or avoid pyrethrum containing plants depending on the amount necessary to defend against mites and the amount already consumed by the bees, which in higher doses could be potentially toxic to them.") **Correct:** The text after the word "postulate" expresses (or "puts forth") an idea, just as this answer choice requires—the idea that "the proper dosage...may be better left to the bees." That idea isn't being put forth without any foundation, as (A) would require; the idea isn't being "question[ed]," as (C) would require; finally, the idea isn't being stated as a conclusion, as (D) would require. See the analyses of those answer choices for more.

C   ("We further <u>question a belief or theory</u> that the proper dosage necessary to prevent mite infestation may be better left to the bees, who may seek out or avoid pyrethrum containing plants depending on the amount necessary to defend against mites and the amount already consumed by the bees, which in higher doses could be potentially toxic to them.") **Confused Relationships:** This choice might be tempting to some untrained test-takers who don't read carefully, because the researchers are putting forth a theory of theirs. But they don't "question" that theory (or any theory), so this choice can't be correct. In order to "question" the theory, they would have to show that they doubt it in some way, or don't have faith in it, but that idea isn't stated or demonstrated in the text.

D   ("We further <u>conclude based on firm evidence</u> that the proper dosage necessary to prevent mite infestation may be better left to the bees, who may seek out or avoid pyrethrum containing plants depending on the amount necessary to defend against mites and the amount already consumed by the bees, which in higher doses could be potentially toxic to them.") **Direct Contradiction:** The cited text contains the word "may" on lines 36 and 37 and the phrase "could...potentially" on line 41. This means the speakers aren't sure that what they're saying is true. If they were "conclud[ing] based on firm evidence," as (D) says, then they'd be sure that what they were saying was true, and wouldn't use words like "may," "could," and "potentially."

❚ Test 3, Question 48   **TYPE: PURPOSE OF CITED TEXT**

ⓘ *The prompt asks about the purpose or role of a part of the text. The correct answer must be accurately restated or described by the relevant text, with no interpretation. See "What about "Purpose" Questions?" on p.74.*

A   **Off by One or Two Words:** The fourth paragraph describes an experiment that *could be done,* not one that *has been done.* We know this because the authors use the phrases "can...be tested" (42) and "could...be introduced" (47). These phrases indicate that the "test[ing]" and "introduc[ing]" have not actually happened yet. If these events had happened already, then the text would need to use phrases like "were tested" and "were introduced." If (A) had begun with the words "summarize an experiment that could confirm...," then it would have described the paragraph accurately. As it stands, though, (A) is wrong.

B ✓   **Correct:** The fourth paragraph begins by describing how a "hypothesis" (42) could be "tested by a trial" (42). The idea of "testing" a "hypothesis" is restated by the word "experiment" in this answer choice. The paragraph also mentions one group of bees eating "pyrethrum producing plants, as well as...clover" (44-46) while another group of bees would eat "only the clover" (46-47). This is restated by the phrase "different diets" in the answer choice. The paragraph describes noting the "effects of the mite parasites" (49) on the two groups, which is restated by the idea of investigating the bees' "susceptibility to mite infestations," as mentioned in the answer choice. Finally, we can see that the word "propose" in the answer choice accurately reflects the use of phrases like "can...be tested" (42) and "could...be introduced" (47), both of which demonstrate that the authors are talking about something that might be done, not something that they've already done.

C   Barely Relevant: As discussed in the explanation for (B), the fourth paragraph describes an experiment that involves feeding two sets of bees two different diets. The paragraph doesn't mention anything about analyzing honey, so (C) can't be correct.

D   Barely Relevant: The third paragraph doesn't describe an experiment, as (D) requires. It expresses a hypothesis regarding honeybees, but it doesn't say anything about testing that hypothesis. Further, as we saw in the explanation for (B), the fourth paragraph describes an experiment that *could* be done—not a "likely outcome" of an unfinished experiment.

Test 3, Question 49   **TYPE: DESCRIBE THE PASSAGE**

ⓘ *The prompt often mentions describing the passage, and usually doesn't include a line citation. The answer must still be restated or demonstrated by some specific part of the text, even if there's no citation. See "What about Questions Without Citations?" p. 72*

Subjective Phrases to Ignore: "unstated assumption"

A ✓   Correct: The fourth paragraph mentions one group of bees eating "pyrethrum producing plants, as well as...clover" (44-46) and another group of bees eating "only the clover" (46-47). If one group is eating "pyrethrum producing plants" and clover, while the other group is eating "only the clover," then we know the group that eats clover isn't eating any "pyrethrum producing plants." So clover must not produce pyrethrums, and this choice is correct.

B   Barely Relevant: The only time the word "Chrysanthemum" appears in the text is when the authors mention a few pyrethrums whose names all begin with "Chrysanthemum" (9-10). But the text never says that one of those plants is the same thing as "clover," or that clover is a member of the Chrysanthemum genus, so this choice can't be correct.

C   Reasonable Statement Not in the Text: The text mentions that clover is "a typical bee food source" (45), so an untrained test-taker might assume clover would need to be "located near wild-type honeybee colonies," as described in (C). But the text never says anything about where clover is located, so (C) isn't restated or demonstrated by the passage, and it's wrong.

D   Direct Contradiction: In describing the experiment, the researchers specifically say that the "controls" (46) should be "offered only the clover" (46-47), so this choice directly contradicts the relevant portion of the passage.

Note   Notice that the correct answer choice restates an idea expressed directly in lines 44-47. As trained test-takers, we always look for the correct answer to restate a concept that appears on the page somewhere, even if the prompt is deliberately worded in a way that will mislead untrained test-takers into thinking they should interpret the passage. Keep this kind of thing in mind on test day!

Test 3, Question 50   **TYPE: FIGURE**

ⓘ *The prompt refers to a graph/table/diagram/etc.; carefully note all labels, keys, units, and any other explanatory details. The answer must directly restate some part of the data and/or text. See "Reading Graphs, Charts, Tables, and Other Figures" on p.44.*

A   Direct Contradiction: The table shows that 0 percent of colonies *without* colony collapse disorder were infected by all four pathogens. But the prompt asks about colonies *with* colony collapse disorder, so (A) isn't right, even though it will trick a lot of untrained test-takers who accidentally look at the wrong cell in the table because they don't remember to read carefully.

B ✓   Correct: The center column is labeled "Colonies with colony collapse disorder (%)," which means it contains data relevant to the idea of the "percent of colonies with colony collapse disorder" as described in the prompt. The bottom row has a label in the far-left cell that says "All four pathogens," which is exactly restated in the prompt. When we find the cell at the intersection of the center column and the last row, we see that the value is 77, which means that 77 percent of colonies with colony collapse disorder were infected by all four pathogens, exactly as this answer choice requires.

C   Confused Relationships: The table shows that 83 percent of colonies with colony collapse disorder were infected by a virus called "IAPV," but the prompt doesn't mention IAPV by itself, so this choice isn't correct.

D   Confused Relationships: The table shows that 100 percent of colonies with colony collapse disorder were infected by a virus called "KBV," and 100 percent of colonies with colony collapse disorder were infected with a fungus called "*Nosema ceranae*." But neither of these pathogens is mentioned in the prompt, so this choice isn't correct.

Test 3, Question 51   **TYPE: FIGURE**

ⓘ *The prompt refers to a graph/table/diagram/etc.; carefully note all labels, keys, units, and any other explanatory details. The answer must directly restate some part of the data and/or text. See "Reading Graphs, Charts, Tables, and Other Figures" on p.44.*

A   Direct Contradiction: The column on the right is labeled "Colonies without colony collapse disorder (%)," so we know it contains data relevant to the idea of a "percentage of honeybee colonies without colony collapse disorder" from the prompt. The numbers in this column tell us what percentage of colonies without colony collapse disorder were infected with each of the pathogens in the column on the far left. The pathogen called "IAPV," which appears in this answer choice, corresponds to the number 5 in the column on the right, which is NOT the "highest percentage" as required in the prompt—so this can't be the correct answer. This answer choice might attract some untrained test-takers who misread the prompt and think they should find the *lowest* percentage in the column, rather than the highest one.

B   **Barely Relevant:** As we discussed in our explanation of (A), the column on the right is the one we need to pay attention to for this question. The pathogen called "KBV" corresponds to the number 76 in this column, which is NOT the highest percentage in this column, so this choice isn't the correct answer.

C   **Direct Contradiction:** The pathogen called "*Nosema apis*" corresponds to the number 48 in the right-hand column, which isn't the highest percentage in this column, so we know this must be a wrong answer. (See the explanation for (A) to learn how we know the right-hand column is the key one in this question.)

D✓   **Correct:** The highest number in the right-hand column is 81, which corresponds to the pathogen called "*Nosema ceranae*," so that's the correct answer. (See the explanation of (A) for more details on the reason we know that the right-hand column is important in this question.)

Test 3, Question 52   **TYPE: FIGURE**

ⓘ *The prompt refers to a graph/table/diagram/etc.; carefully note all labels, keys, units, and any other explanatory details. The answer must directly restate some part of the data and/or text. See "Reading Graphs, Charts, Tables, and Other Figures" on p.44.*

A   **Barely Relevant:** As we discuss in the explanation for (D), the table doesn't provide any information about "varroa mites," as required in the prompt, so the "Yes/No" portion of the answer must be "No." Further, as trained test-takers, we know that the table doesn't show that any specific thing actually "*caused* the colonies to undergo colony collapse disorder" (emphasis added), which is what this answer choice would require. (For one thing, the column on the right shows that some percentage of the colonies *without* colony collapse disorder *were* infected with each of the four pathogens.) Either of these reasons by itself would be enough to make this a wrong answer.

B   **Off by One or Two Words:** As discussed in the explanation for (D) below, the table doesn't provide any information about varroa mites, so the "Yes/No" portion of the correct answer must be "No." (B) might still be tempting to a lot of untrained test-takers, because the statement after the word "yes" is true...but, again, that statement isn't directly related to varroa mites, as the prompt requires, so (B) is wrong.

C   **Confused Relationships:** This choice might be tempting to a lot of untrained test-takers, because the "no" portion of the choice is correct, and the statement after "no" is also accurate, in the sense that it reflects the data. But the prompt asks about information related to *varroa mites,* and this answer choice says something about *bacteria.* In other words, the statement in this choice after the word "no" is a true statement about the graph, but it isn't relevant to the prompt, so this choice is wrong.

D✓   **Correct:** In order for the data in the table to provide support for a claim about "infection with varroa mites," as the prompt requires, the table would have to give us some information on bees infected with varroa mites—this means we'd have to see at least one label on the table that was related to varroa mites, and we don't see anything like that. This answer choice directly restates that situation, and correctly begins with "no," so we know that it must be the correct answer.

TEST 4

Test 4, Question 1   **TYPE: AUTHOR'S ATTITUDE**

The next question is a "best evidence" question referring back to this question; you may choose to consider the citations in the choices for the next question when answering this one if you want. See "Is there a 'best evidence' shortcut?" on page 72 for more.

ⓘ The prompt asks about the author's tone or attitude; the correct answer must be directly restated or demonstrated by a specific part of the passage. See "What about "Attitude" Questions?" on p.73.

A   **Reasonable Statement Not in the Text:** An untrained test-taker might imagine that someone traveling to the North Pole could have an attitude that shifts from "fear" to "excitement," but the passage doesn't actually restate or demonstrate that idea, so (A) is wrong.

B   **Confused Relationships:** The narrator seems to doubt the value of his trip to the North Pole when he says he doesn't know why he is "so intent" on going there, and asks "what good is it!" (28-29), but he never mentions doubting his *abilities,* which is what this choice would require. Further, while we might argue in an English class that the narrator has become confident of his motives ("what I do is both a challenge to my egotism and a surrender to it" (59-61)), he never discusses the idea of being confident in his *abilities,* as (B) requires. Either of these problems by itself would be enough to make (B) wrong.

C✓   **Correct:** In the beginning of the passage, the narrator says he feels a "vast yearning" (2) but he does "not understand quite what it is that the yearning desires" (6), which is restated by the phrase "uncertainty of his motives" in this answer choice. Later, he says, "what I am on the brink of knowing, I now see, is not an ephemeral mathematical spot but myself" (56-57) and, "what I do is both a challenge to my egotism and a surrender to it" (59-61). In other words, he now sees why he's doing what he's doing, which is restated by the phrase "recognition of [his motives]" in this answer choice. Since every part of (C) restates a concept directly from the passage, we can tell it must be the correct answer.

D   **Confused Relationships:** The narrator does have "disdain" for something, but it's not the North Pole, as this answer choice would require; instead, it's the doctor ("The doctor was right, even though I dislike him" (57-58)). Further, by the end of the passage we could say that he "appreciates" his *motivation* for going to the North Pole—that is, he understands and recognizes what his motivation is—but the text doesn't restate the idea of an appreciation of *the North Pole itself*, as this answer choice requires. Either of these issues would be enough by itself to make this choice wrong.

Test 4, Question 2	**TYPE: BEST EVIDENCE**

ⓘ *The answer must restate or demonstrate the relevant statement. See "What about "Best Evidence" Questions?" on page 72.*

Subjective Phrases to Ignore: "best"

A   **Barely Relevant:** This citation isn't really relevant to the correct answer from question 1 (or to any answer choice from question 1, for that matter) so it can't be the correct answer to this question.

B   **Barely Relevant:** Like (A), this citation isn't really relevant to the correct answer from question 1, or to any answer choice from question 1, so it must be a wrong answer to this question.

C   **Barely Relevant:** Just as with (A) and (B), this choice isn't really relevant to any answer choice from question 1.

D✓   **Correct:** As we discussed in our walkthrough of question 1, this citation is directly restated by the right answer from 1.

Note   This is a good example of a situation that sometimes arises on "best evidence" questions, which we can exploit when we notice it. If we compare the choices for this question to the choices for question 1, we see that the only choices that are relevant to each other are (C) from question 1 and (D) from this question, which means those two choices must be right, since the right answer to each question must be relevant to the right answer of the other question. Keep this kind of thing in mind on test day! For more on this kind of approach, see "Is there a "best evidence" shortcut?" on page 72 of this Black Book.

Test 4, Question 3	**TYPE: WORD MOST NEARLY MEANS**

ⓘ *The prompt includes the phrase "most nearly means" and the choices are usually one- or two-word phrases. The answer is either restated or demonstrated by an idea from the surrounding text. Remember you can work around unknown words, and be ready to guess/skip and focus on other questions if you don't know the words. See "What about "Most Nearly Means" Questions?" on p.73.*

Subjective Phrases to Ignore: "most nearly"

A   ("My emotions are complicated and <u>unable to be authenticated</u>.") **Reasonable Statement Not in the Text:** An untrained test-taker might assume that "unable to be authenticated" and "not readily verifiable" would be synonyms in any context, but nothing in the text restates the idea of "authenticat[ion]," so (A) can't be correct.

B   ("My emotions are complicated and <u>likely to be contradicted</u>.") **Barely Relevant:** Nothing in the passage indicates that the narrator's "emotions" (1) are "likely to be contradicted," as (B) would require, so we know (B) must be wrong.

C   ("My emotions are complicated and <u>without empirical support</u>.") **Reasonable Statement Not in the Text:** The passage doesn't mention the idea of "empirical support," or any phrase that could be synonymous with it, in connection with the narrator's "emotions" (1), as this answer choice would require, so this choice can't be correct.

D✓   ("My emotions are complicated and <u>not completely understood</u>.") **Correct:** The narrator says he "feel[s]" (2) a "yearning" (2), but says he "do[es] not understand quite what it is that the yearning desires" (5-6); the phrase "not completely understood" in this answer choice directly restates this idea, so we know this choice must be right.

Note   Even if we don't know the words "authenticated" or "empirical" from the answer choices, we can still be certain that (D) is correct if we can recognize that "not completely understood" restates part of the relevant text without going beyond what's stated in the text. Keep this kind of thing in mind on test day!

Test 4, Question 4	**TYPE: CITATION QUESTION**

ⓘ *The question includes a citation from the text. The answer must be directly restated or demonstrated in the cited text, or in the text closely surrounding the cited text. See the general process for answering SAT Reading questions on p. 71.*

Subjective Phrases to Ignore: "mainly"

A   **Confused Relationships / Reasonable Statement Not in the Text:** The text says the author's "destiny has worked in secret" (11), but it doesn't say anything about a *side of the narrator himself* being kept hidden or secret, as this answer choice would require. This answer choice might be tempting to some untrained test-takers, because the narrator calls himself "a dangerous madman" (59), which might seem like something a person would want to keep hidden in real life, but the narrator never actually says he's trying to hide that. Since (A) doesn't restate the passage, we know it must be wrong.

B   Reasonable Statement Not in the Text: An untrained test-taker might imagine someone described as a "scientist" in the introduction to the passage would think "in a methodical and scientific manner," as this answer choice would require, but that idea isn't actually restated in lines 10-13 or the surrounding text, so we know (B) must be wrong.

C ✓ Correct: The narrator says that "the machinery of [his] destiny has worked in secret" (10-11) and that "its clockwork has moved exactly toward this time and place and no other" (12-13), and that he's being "carried helplessly" (15). These ideas are exactly restated by the phrase "influenced by powerful and independent forces," just as this answer choice requires, so we know it's the right answer.

D   Literary Interpretation: The cited text describes how "the machinery of [his] destiny has worked in secret," but it doesn't say anything about the narrator actually "prepar[ing] for his expedition," as this choice would require. So the narrator is describing how some mysterious force was at work in his life, not how he himself was deliberately preparing for anything, which means this choice doesn't restate the relevant portion of the passage.

| Test 4, Question 5 | TYPE: DESCRIBE THE PASSAGE |

The next question is a "best evidence" question referring back to this question; you may choose to consider the citations in the choices for the next question when answering this one if you want. See "Is there a 'best evidence' shortcut?" on page 72 for more.

ⓘ *The prompt often mentions describing the passage, and usually doesn't include a line citation. The answer must still be restated or demonstrated by some specific part of the text, even if there's no citation. See "What about Questions Without Citations?" p. 72*

A ✓ Correct: In discussing his trip to the North Pole, the narrator says that "nobody has succeeded in this thing, and many have died" (20-21), so (A) directly restates the relevant portion of the passage, which means (A) is right.

B   Literary Interpretation: Untrained test-takers might expect that explorers heading for the North Pole would make "surprising discoveries," because that sounds like the kind of interpretation of a text that would probably be acceptable in a literature class. But the text doesn't actually restate that idea, so this choice can't be correct.

C   Barely Relevant: There's nothing in the passage about anyone not being able to *determine the location* of the North Pole, which is what this answer choice would require. The text does describe people not being able to *get to* the North Pole, but it doesn't describe people not knowing where the Pole is. The text also says the North Pole is "precisely identical" (45) to all the points around it, but, again, that doesn't specifically mean that no one knows where it is. (For example, you can know exactly where one blade of grass is in a giant field, even though that blade of grass looks just like all the other blades of grass.) As trained test-takers, we know that we always need to read extremely carefully and literally on the SAT Reading test, and this answer choice is a good example of why that's important.

D   Reasonable Statement Not in the Text: The other explorers might have had motivations that were different from those of the narrator, for all we know, but the motivations of other explorers aren't actually discussed in the passage, so (D) is wrong.

| Test 4, Question 6 | TYPE: BEST EVIDENCE |

ⓘ *The answer must restate or demonstrate the relevant statement. See "What about "Best Evidence" Questions?" on page 72.*

Subjective Phrases to Ignore: "best"
___

A ✓ Correct: As we saw in the walkthrough for question 5, this citation restates the correct answer from that question.

B   Barely Relevant: This citation isn't really relevant to the correct answer from question 5, or to any answer choice from question 5, so it can't possibly be the correct answer to this question.

C   Confused Relationships: To an untrained test-taker, this citation may appear to support choice (D) from the previous question, because untrained test-takers might be tempted to assume that other explorers are trying to please the "Danish ministers" (31). But this citation only describes why "Danish ministers" (31) think polar expeditions are "beneficial" (33); it doesn't say anything about the motivations of the explorers themselves, which is what the prompt of the previous question required. For that reason, this citation is irrelevant to question 5, which means it can't be the right answer to question 6.

D   Barely Relevant: Like (B), this citation isn't relevant to any answer choice from question 5, so it must be wrong.

| Test 4, Question 7 | TYPE: AUTHOR'S ATTITUDE |

ⓘ The prompt asks about the author's tone or attitude; the correct answer must be directly restated or demonstrated by a specific part of the passage. See "What about "Attitude" Questions?" on p.73.

Subjective Phrases to Ignore: "best"
___

A   Off by One or Two Words: The passage does restate the idea that the expedition is "inevitable" when it talks about "destiny...mov[ing] exactly toward this time and place" (11-13). But the passage doesn't restate the idea that the narrator sees his expedition as "immoral," which is what this answer choice would require. To be "immoral," one must break some kind of moral rule or taboo, and that isn't described in the text, so we know this choice is wrong.

B ✓ Correct: We know that the narrator sees his expedition as "absurd," as this choice requires, because he says that what you would find at the North Pole is "exactly nothing" (44) and that "no one but a Swedish madman could take the slightest interest in it" (48-49). We also know that the narrator sees his expedition as "necessary," which is also required by the answer choice, because he says the Pole "must...be sought for" (36-37), and the word "must" literally indicates necessity. Since every part of this answer choice restates the passage, we can tell it must be the correct answer.

C   **Confused Relationships:** The phrase "socially beneficial" doesn't restate any idea from the passage, which is enough to make the entire answer choice wrong. It is the *Danish ministers,* not the narrator, who think that the expedition is good "to the soul's eternal well-being" (33), but that isn't actually the same thing as being "socially beneficial;" the word "social" refers to a society, which is necessarily a group of people, whereas "the soul" is something that belongs to only one person. Further, the narrator does say that his "yearning" (2) was "not underst[ood]" (5-6), but that isn't the same thing as saying that the *expedition itself* was "misunderstood," which is what this answer choice would require when we combine it with the prompt. Any of these reasons would be enough by itself to make (C) fail to restate the passage, which makes it incorrect.

D   **Reasonable Statement Not in the Text:** An untrained test-taker might think that a trip taken by a scientist is probably "scientifically important," as this answer choice would require, but the text doesn't restate the idea of any scientific importance being connected to the expedition.

	Test 4, Question 8	TYPE: CITATION QUESTION

ⓘ *The question includes a citation from the text. The answer must be directly restated or demonstrated in the cited text, or in the text closely surrounding the cited text. See the general process for answering SAT Reading questions on p. 71.*

Subjective Phrases to Ignore: "most nearly implies"

A   **Confused Relationships / Reasonable Statement Not in the Text:** The "it" in the cited text refers back to "North Pole" (29), not to the balloon. The balloon itself isn't being discussed in this citation, so this choice can't restate anything in the relevant portion of the passage, which means it must be a wrong answer.

B   **Confused Relationships / Reasonable Statement Not in the Text:** The text does mention cities, and also the North Pole, which are both elements of this answer choice. But the text never actually says that the North Pole is "farther away" than those cities are, even if some untrained test-taker might be tempted to assume it is. The text also doesn't say whether those two places are "cities" as this answer choice would require, nor whether they're "usually reached by train." Any of these issues by itself would be enough to make this choice wrong.

C   **Barely Relevant / Reasonable Statement Not in the Text:** The passage doesn't say anything about what people do or don't think about when they travel from one place to another, so the passage doesn't restate or demonstrate (C).

D✓   **Correct:** When he asks "what good" (29) the Pole is, and then asks rhetorical questions about the Pole that show it to be useless, the narrator is saying that reaching the Pole has no value for humanity, as (D) requires.

> **Note**   The phrase "What good is it!" (29) is a rhetorical question, as are the two questions after it. If you didn't understand the meanings of these questions, review the discussion of rhetorical questions on page 66 of this Black Book.

	Test 4, Question 9	TYPE: WORD MOST NEARLY MEANS

ⓘ *The prompt includes the phrase "most nearly means" and the choices are usually one- or two-word phrases. The answer is either restated or demonstrated by an idea from the surrounding text. Remember you can work around unknown words, and be ready to guess/skip and focus on other questions if you don't know the words. See "What about "Most Nearly Means" Questions?" on p.73.*

Subjective Phrases to Ignore: "most nearly"

A   ("No one but a Swedish madman could <u>accept responsibility for</u> it.") **Reasonable Statement Not in the Text:** The idea of "accept[ing] responsibility" might be tempting for some untrained test-takers, because the speaker does say in line 21 that he "freely willed this enterprise," which means his trip to the North Pole is voluntary . But the word "it" in this sentence doesn't refer to the *voyage* to the North Pole, as this choice would require—see the explanation of (D) for more details.

B   ("No one but a Swedish madman could <u>possess little regard for</u> it.") **Direct Contradiction:** The citation describes the narrator taking interest in the North Pole; having interest in something is the opposite of "possess[ing] little regard" for that thing, so this choice must be wrong. (Notice that this choice means basically the same thing as the cited text if we ignore the context of the passage and forget the SAT's unwritten rules, which say that the correct answer to a "most nearly means" question must either restate the relevant part of the text or be demonstrated by the relevant part of the text. This is another reminder of the critical importance of referring back to the text when you select an answer!)

C   ("No one but a Swedish madman could <u>pay no attention to</u> it.") **Direct Contradiction:** The text describes the narrator taking interest in the North Pole; having interest in something is the opposite of "pay[ing] no attention" to that thing.

D✓   ("No one but a Swedish madman could <u>have curiosity about</u> it.") **Correct:** When we insert this phrase into the original text, we can see that the idea of "hav[ing] curiosity about" the North Pole restates the idea of "seek[ing] out...knowledge" from earlier in the text. Notice that the word "it" in the citation refers to the phrase "North Pole," from line 29. Untrained test-takers would be unlikely to spend the necessary time to trace the meaning of "it" all the way back through the text to line 29. But if you don't do that, you might easily think the word "it" refers to the general idea of the expedition, which would make it difficult to answer this question correctly. Further, if a trained test-taker didn't realize that the word "it" is referring all the way back to line 29, she probably also wouldn't realize that the phrases "seek out and know everything" (38) and "lust for knowledge" (40) are relevant to the citation, which could be a problem because those are the phrases that restate (D).

| Note | We know the "Swedish madman" (48) is the narrator himself: the introductory text tells us he's "Swedish," and he calls himself a "dangerous madman" in line 59. Remember the importance of reading the introductions to the passages you encounter on test day! (See "1. Always Read the Brief Introduction to Each Passage!" on page 71.) |

Test 4, Question 10 — TYPE: WORD MOST NEARLY MEANS

ⓘ The prompt includes the phrase "most nearly means" and the choices are usually one- or two-word phrases. The answer is either restated or demonstrated by an idea from the surrounding text. Remember you can work around unknown words, and be ready to guess/skip and focus on other questions if you don't know the words. See "What about "Most Nearly Means" Questions?" on p. 73.

Subjective Phrases to Ignore: "most nearly"

A ✓ ("The wind is still from the south, <u>carrying</u> us steadily northward at the speed of a trotting dog.") **Correct:** When we look at the relevant text, it's clear that the narrator is in a balloon and the "wind" is physically "carrying" him "steadily northward" (50-51); in lines 14-15, he even says "I am carried helplessly."

B ("The wind is still from the south, <u>affecting</u> us steadily northward at the speed of a trotting dog.") **Barely Relevant:** Nothing in the passage restates the idea of the wind "affecting" the narrator in a particular direction at a particular speed; in fact, it doesn't make much sense in English to say that someone is affected at a particular speed, so the text can't be restating or demonstrating the idea in (B).

C ("The wind is still from the south, <u>yielding</u> us steadily northward at the speed of a trotting dog.") **Barely Relevant:** Nothing in the citation restates the idea of "yielding" the narrator, so this choice must be wrong.

D ("The wind is still from the south, <u>enduring</u> us steadily northward at the speed of a trotting dog.") **Confused Relationships:** (D) will appeal to a lot of untrained test-takers, for two reasons: first, in another context, "enduring" could mean "bearing," because to "bear" something can mean to "go through" or "endure" it; second, it's probably true that going to the North Pole would require some level of "endurance." But, as trained-test-takers, we know (D) is wrong because the passage doesn't restate or demonstrate the idea of the wind "enduring" the narrator.

Test 4, Question 11 — TYPE: CITATION QUESTION

ⓘ The question includes a citation from the text. The answer must be directly restated or demonstrated in the cited text, or in the text closely surrounding the cited text. See the general process for answering SAT Reading questions on p. 71.

Subjective Phrases to Ignore: "best"

A **Direct Contradiction:** (A) will attract a lot of untrained test-takers who misread this sentence: "the 2010 census certainly did not turn up evidence of a middle-class stampede to the nation's cities" (3-5). It's true that the phrase "sizable growth in the number of middle-class families moving" in (A) directly restates the phrase "a middle-class stampede" from the passage, but the word "demonstrated" in (A) contradicts the phrase "certainly did not turn up" in the passage, so (A) is wrong.

B **Literary Interpretation:** This choice will trap a lot of untrained test-takers because it comes very close to restating the passage, but doesn't actually restate it. The passage does say "that raw census numbers are an ineffective blunt instrument" (12-13), but then it discusses "a closer look at the results" (13-14) while discussing trends in more detail. This answer choice, on the other hand, says that the entire "2010 census is not a reliable instrument," instead of drawing a distinction between "raw" census numbers and the insight we can gain from "a closer look at the results," which is what the passage does. As trained-test-takers, we know that this small difference is enough to make the entire answer choice wrong.

C ✓ **Correct:** The text says that "demographic inversion is not a proxy for population growth" (32-33), which can only be true if demographic inversion and population growth are "distinct phenomena," as the first half of this answer choice requires. In order to determine if the second half of the answer choice restates the passage, we have to know what "demographic inversion" means. As trained test-takers, we know that these kinds of unusual terms on the SAT are often defined in a reading passage itself, or in the intro text before the passage—sure enough, when we check the intro text we see that "demographic inversion is...the rearrangement of living patterns throughout a metropolitan area." Armed with that definition, we can see that lines 16-27 describe groups of people moving among metropolitan areas including "central cities" (16) and "suburbs" (18); since both of those terms are plural and the author is speaking in general terms, we can tell that "demographic inversion is evident in many American cities," just as (C) requires. Since every part of (C) restates the passage, we can tell it must be the correct answer.

D **Direct Contradiction:** Lines 5-11 say that some cities grew in population while others shrank, so we can't say that "population growth in American cities has been increasing since roughly 2000," as (D) would require. Further, the first sentence of the passage says, "we are not witnessing the abandonment of the suburbs," and line 18 describes "the settlement of immigrant groups in suburbs," which doesn't support the idea that "suburban populations have decreased," as (D) would also require. Either of these issues would be enough by itself to make (D) wrong.

Test 4, Question 12   **TYPE: DESCRIBE THE PASSAGE**

ℹ️ *The prompt often mentions describing the passage, and usually doesn't include a line citation. The answer must still be restated or demonstrated by some specific part of the text, even if there's no citation. See "What about Questions Without Citations?" p. 72*

A   **Confused Relationships:** "Unemployment" (25) is mentioned in the first paragraph, but nothing in the passage says that the unemployed moved away from central-city areas, as the prompt requires.

B   **Literary Interpretation:** The passage describes "the settlement of immigrant groups in suburbs" (17-18), which might lead untrained test-takers to think this choice is correct—but there are still two reasons why this choice fails to restate the passage. First, while the text says immigrants "often" (18) settled "many miles distant from downtown" (19), it doesn't say they moved *from* downtown *to* the suburbs, as this question would require. For example, they may have come from other countries straight to the suburbs and never lived near the city center. Second, the phrase "often...many miles from downtown" leaves open the possibility that some immigrants settled in places that *weren't* far from downtown, and nothing in the text specifically indicates the actual number of immigrants who did or didn't settle at particular distances "away from central-city areas," as the prompt requires. Any of these issues on its own would be enough to make this choice wrong.

C   **Confused Relationships:** "Young professionals" (26) are mentioned in the first paragraph, but nothing in the passage says they moved away from central-city areas. In fact, the text says, "not many young professionals moved to new downtown condos in the recession years" (25-27), so, if anything, it talks about how many of them moved *to* central-city areas, not *away from* them.

D✓   **Correct:** The text says one of the "most powerful demographic events of the past decade" (14-15) was the "movement of African Americans out of central cities (180,000 of them in Chicago alone)" (16-17). In this context, it's clear that "powerful" means something along the lines of involving "substantial numbers" (9), which goes along with the phrase "in large numbers" from the prompt; further, the use of the word "alone" in the phrase "in Chicago alone" indicates clearly that similar numbers of African-Americans moved out of other central-city areas as well, as the prompt requires. (As we discussed for (B), note that the other "powerful demographic event[...]" from the passage involves immigrants—but the immigrants aren't described as having moved *from* cities *to* suburbs, as African Americans are said to have done. This small but crucial difference is the reason (D) is right and (B) is wrong.)

Test 4, Question 13   **TYPE: WORD MOST NEARLY MEANS**

ℹ️ *The prompt includes the phrase "most nearly means" and the choices are usually one- or two-word phrases. The answer is either restated or demonstrated by an idea from the surrounding text. Remember you can work around unknown words, and be ready to guess/skip and focus on other questions if you don't know the words. See "What about "Most Nearly Means" Questions?" on p.73.*

Subjective Phrases to Ignore: "closest"

A✓   ("...it can occur in cities that are growing, those whose numbers are <u>static</u>, and even in those undergoing a modest decline in size.") **Correct:** Lines 33-35 describe three kinds of cities: "cities that are growing, those whose numbers are flat, and...those undergoing a modest decline in size." If cities "whose numbers are flat" are different from cities that are "growing" or "declining," which is what the citation says, then these cities must not be changing in size. Since the word "static" restate the idea of "not changing," we know this must be the correct answer.

B   ("...it can occur in cities that are growing, those whose numbers are <u>deflated</u>, and even in those undergoing a modest decline in size.") **Reasonable Statement Not in the Text:** In another context, "deflated" could be a synonym for "flat," because something like a tire, when deflated, can be called "flat." But nothing in the passage restates the idea of letting the air out of anything, or anything similar, so this choice must be wrong.

C   ("...it can occur in cities that are growing, those whose numbers are <u>featureless</u>, and even in those undergoing a modest decline in size.") **Reasonable Statement Not in the Text:** In another context, "featureless" could be a synonym for "flat," because terrain that is flat can be called "featureless." But, as with (B), nothing in the passage restates the idea of not having features, so we know (C) is wrong.

D   ("...it can occur in cities that are growing, those whose numbers are <u>obscure</u>, and even in those undergoing a modest decline in size.") **Barely Relevant:** This answer choice may be tempting for untrained test-takers who don't like the other choices and aren't sure what "obscure" means, but nothing in the passage restates the idea of the numbers being hard to determine or refer to, which is what "obscure" means.

Test 4, Question 14   **TYPE: DESCRIBE THE PASSAGE**

The next question is a "best evidence" question referring back to this question; you may choose to consider the citations in the choices for the next question when answering this one if you want. See "Is there a 'best evidence' shortcut?" on page 72 for more.

ⓘ *The prompt often mentions describing the passage, and usually doesn't include a line citation. The answer must still be restated or demonstrated by some specific part of the text, even if there's no citation. See "What about Questions Without Citations?" p. 72*

Subjective Phrases to Ignore: "best"

A   **Reasonable Statement Not in the Text:** The text does say some cities "simply are not producing enough revenue" (40-41); an untrained test-taker might think that "tax increases" could be used to address this problem, as this answer choice states, but the passage itself never restates that idea, so we know this can't be the correct answer.

B ✓ **Correct:** The text describes "enormous fiscal problems" (36-37), which is directly restated by the phrase "economic hardship" from (B). The text then says these problems are often "the result of...obligations" (37-38), which is restated by the phrase "due to promises made" from (B). Finally, the phrase "the past two decades" (39) is restated by the phrase "past years" in the answer choice. Since every part of (B) restates the passage, we can tell it must be the correct answer.

C   **Barely Relevant:** The text never describes "greater overall prosperity" in cities, nor does it describe "an increased inner-city tax base" in those cities; both of these elements would have to be present in the text in order for (C) to be correct.

D   **Confused Relationships:** A lot of untrained test-takers will fall for this answer choice, because the text does say that American cities "simply are not producing enough revenue" (40-41), which restates the idea of "insufficient revenue" from the answer choice; the text also says, "there are scarcely any factories at all" (83-84), which goes along with the idea of a "decrease in manufacturing," as the answer choice describes. But, as trained test-takers, we know that *every* part of the answer choice needs to restate the passage—and we can see that the phrase "due to" in the answer choice doesn't reflect the passage at all! In other words, the passage discusses insufficient revenues and a lack of manufacturing, but it doesn't say that the second situation *caused* the first one, as this answer choice would require.

| **Test 4, Question 15** | **TYPE: BEST EVIDENCE** |

ⓘ *The answer must restate or demonstrate the relevant statement. See "What about 'Best Evidence' Questions?" on page 72.*

Subjective Phrases to Ignore: "best"

A ✓ **Correct:** As we saw in the walkthrough for question 14, choice (B) directly restates the text in this citation, which is why (B) is the correct answer to that question and (A) is the correct answer to this one.

B   **Literary Interpretation:** This citation does refer to the "problem" (44) faced by American cities, but it doesn't describe that problem, and choice (B) from question 14 isn't restating any part of this citation.

C   **Literary Interpretation:** This text does discuss a potential result of the "fiscal crisis" (45), but it doesn't describe that fiscal crisis, as the prompt of question 14 requires, so this answer choice isn't relevant to the correct answer to question 14.

D   **Barely Relevant:** This citation isn't really relevant to any choice from 14, so it can't be evidence for the right answer.

| **Test 4, Question 16** | **TYPE: DESCRIBE THE PASSAGE** |

The next question is a "best evidence" question referring back to this question; you may choose to consider the citations in the choices for the next question when answering this one if you want. See "Is there a 'best evidence' shortcut?" on page 72 for more.

ⓘ *The prompt often mentions describing the passage, and usually doesn't include a line citation. The answer must still be restated or demonstrated by some specific part of the text, even if there's no citation. See "What about Questions Without Citations?" p. 72*

Subjective Phrases to Ignore: "implies"

A   **Confused Relationships:** This answer choice confuses several ideas that appear in the passage. It seems to mix up the "movement of African Americans out of central cities" (16) and the "settlement of immigrant groups in suburbs" (18), neither of which is the same as the "flight of minority populations to the suburbs" described in this answer choice (note, especially, that the passage never says whether "immigrants" or "African Americans" are necessarily "minorities" in the population from the passage). Further, these migrations as described in the text were reflected in the "2010 census" (3), and the text never relates them to what was happening in 1974, as this answer choice would require.

B   **Direct Contradiction:** The text says in "the urban America of 1974" (65), "virtually every city...had a factory district" (66-68). It's true that the text later says, "there are scarcely any factories at all" (83-84), but that change is noted "in the past decade" (80), not in 1974, as this answer choice would require. (Notice that the introductory text says the article was copyrighted in 2013, and also that the article contains numerous references to events as late as 2011 that happened in the past, so "the past decade" in this passage is well past 1974.)

C ✓ **Correct:** Lines 58-63 describe Burgess's "four-zone structure" referred to in this answer choice, and line 65 says Burgess "was right about the urban America of 1974;" in other words, what Burgess said about the four-zone structure was still accurate in 1974, exactly as (C) requires. So we know (C) is right, since it directly restates the relevant part of the text.

D   Direct Contradiction: The text before the passage defines demographic inversion as "the rearrangement of living patterns throughout a metropolitan area," but lines 64-71 say that living patterns in 1974 were still the same as they were in 1925, and nothing in the passage indicates that demographic inversion was going on in 1974. Since (D) contradicts the passage, it's wrong.

| **Test 4, Question 17** | **TYPE: BEST EVIDENCE** |

ⓘ *The answer must restate or demonstrate the relevant statement. See "What about "Best Evidence" Questions?" on page 72.*

Subjective Phrases to Ignore: "best"

A   Literary Interpretation: This citation provides background on the man who first described the "four-zone structure" mentioned in choice (C) from question 16. But it doesn't say anything about whether that structure was relevant to American cities in 1974, so it can't support the correct answer from question 16.

B   Literary Interpretation: This citation establishes that Burgess defined the "four-zone structure" mentioned in choice (C) from question 16. But, like (A), it doesn't say whether that structure was relevant to American cities in 1974, so it can't support the correct answer from question 16.

C ✓   Correct: As we saw in our discussion for question 16, the right answer for 16 directly restates this citation.

D   Literary Interpretation: This text provides a detail about the "four-zone structure" mentioned in choice (C) from question 16. But it doesn't say anything about whether that structure was relevant to American cities in 1974, so it can't support the correct answer from question 16.

| **Test 4, Question 18** | **TYPE: WORD MOST NEARLY MEANS** |

ⓘ *The prompt includes the phrase "most nearly means" and the choices are usually one- or two-word phrases. The answer is either restated or demonstrated by an idea from the surrounding text. Remember you can work around unknown words, and be ready to guess/skip and focus on other questions if you don't know the words. See "What about "Most Nearly Means" Questions?" on p.73.*

Subjective Phrases to Ignore: "closest"

A ✓   ("Virtually every city in the country had a downtown, where the commercial life of the metropolis was <u>carried out</u>...") **Correct:** As trained test-takers, we know that we occasionally need to read the sentence or two before or after a citation to see what's going on in the relevant part of the text. When we do that, we see that the sentence before the cited sentence says, "Burgess was right…." At this point, we should wonder what Burgess said, because it's clearly related to the ideas in the citation from the prompt. Looking at the previous paragraph, we see Burgess wrote about "a central business district" (59). This "central…district" restates the idea of a "downtown" (66), and Burgess said the central downtown district was used for "business." When we insert the phrase from (A), the cited sentence says the "commercial life…was carried out" in the downtown, which restates Burgess's claim about the central district being used for business.

B   ("Virtually every city in the country had a downtown, where the commercial life of the metropolis was <u>supervised</u>...") **Reasonable Statement Not in the Text:** An untrained test-taker might *assume* that "commercial life" would be "supervised" by the government or some similar entity, but the passage doesn't restate that idea, so this answer can't be correct.

C   ("Virtually every city in the country had a downtown, where the commercial life of the metropolis was <u>regulated</u>...") **Reasonable Statement Not in the Text:** Just as with (B), some untrained test-taker might *assume* that some aspect of commercial life would be "regulated" by the government or some other agency, but the passage doesn't restate or demonstrate that idea, so (C) is wrong.

D   ("Virtually every city in the country had a downtown, where the commercial life of the metropolis was <u>inhibited</u>...") **Barely Relevant:** Nothing in the passage indicates that "commercial life" was obstructed, prevented, or made difficult in the downtown area, which is what the word "inhibited" would require, so this choice must be wrong.

| **Test 4, Question 19** | **TYPE: FIGURE / PAIRED PASSAGES** |

ⓘ *The prompt refers to a graph/table/diagram/etc.; carefully note all labels, keys, units, and any other explanatory details. The answer must directly restate some part of the data and/or text. See "Reading Graphs, Charts, Tables, and Other Figures" on p.44. The prompt also asks how someone would respond to a claim or argument. The correct answer restates a position that's already stated in the passage. See "What about Paired Passages?" on p.76.*

Subjective Phrases to Ignore: "most likely"

A   Reasonable Statement not in the Figure / Barely Relevant: An untrained test-taker might assume that the author would think that a chart showing population data would be "excellent evidence," as this answer choice would require. But chart 1 shows data about the types of metropolitan areas that people lived in at one point in time, in 2010; the passage, on the other hand, discusses changes in the geographical distributions of different types of populations ("African Americans" (16), "immigrant groups" (18), "affluent residents" (20), "young professionals" (26)) over a period of time that roughly includes the twentieth century and the first decade or so of the twenty-first century. The chart can't indicate anything at all about these different demographic groups, because the labels on the chart indicate the data is broken down by sizes of metropolitans areas, and not in terms of the four zones (58-59) mentioned in the passage, nor in terms of the demographic groups mentioned in the passage. The chart also can't indicate anything about a change over time because the title tells us it's only relevant to the year 2010. So we can tell this chart is basically irrelevant to the arguments in the passage.

B ✓ **Correct:** In lines 5-11, the author describes "raw census numbers" (12-13) as "an ineffective blunt instrument" (13); he goes on to say that "a closer look at the results" (13-14) reveals information about the changes in numbers of people in different demographic groups within the data, which he explores throughout the rest of the first paragraph. The word "crude" in this choice restates the word "blunt" from line 13, and the idea of the chart not being "informative," as described in (B), restates the idea of census numbers not being an effective instrument (13). The phrase "possibly accurate" is acceptable in (B) because the author never says anything one way or the other about whether particular statistics are reliable or not, so there's no reason for us to think that he would find any particular statistic to be reliable or unreliable; the author's issue isn't with the reliability of any particular statistic, but with whether those statistics are specific enough to be useful in the discussion from the passage. (Note that Chart 1 draws on the type of census data the author mentions in lines 12-13.)

C **Barely Relevant:** In lines 5-11, the author describes "raw census numbers" (12-13) like those in chart 1 as "an ineffective blunt instrument," as we've discussed above for (B), so there's no reason to think he would call this chart "compelling;" the idea of a particular statistic or piece of data being "compelling" (or "moving," or "important," or any other, similar kind of word) doesn't appear anywhere in the passage, so (C) can't be correct.

D **Confused Relationships:** In lines 5-11 the author describes "raw census numbers" (12-13) like those in chart 1 as "an ineffective blunt instrument," so we know that he doesn't think it's a good idea to use those numbers when trying to understand demographic inversion. But the author isn't arguing that people who would consider such data are wrong to do so, and there's no reason to think that the data in the chart itself represents any particular "perspective," as (D) would require. For these reasons, (D) doesn't reflect what's stated on the page, which means it must be wrong.

Test 4, Question 20   TYPE: FIGURE

ⓘ *The prompt refers to a graph/table/diagram/etc.; carefully note all labels, keys, units, and any other explanatory details. The answer must directly restate some part of the data and/or text. See "Reading Graphs, Charts, Tables, and Other Figures" on p. 44.*

A ✓ **Correct:** The white columns represent growth in the years 2000-2010, and the light grey columns represent growth in the 1990s; we can see that every white column in each group is smaller than the light grey column in that group, so it must be true that growth from 2000-2010 was less than growth from 1990-2000 for all metropolitan areas, as (A) requires.

B **Direct Contradiction:** The growth in small metro areas in the years 2000-2010 was 10.3%, but the growth in large metro areas in the years 2000-2010 was 10.9%, which is the opposite of what this answer choice would require.

C **Direct Contradiction:** The growth in small metro areas in the years 2000-2010 was 10.3%, but the growth in small metro areas in the 1980s was only 8.8%, so we can see that small metro areas grew more (as a percentage) from 2000-2010 than they did in 1980-1990. More importantly, since the growth rate is *positive* for each time period, the chart doesn't show any "decline in the population" at all, which this answer choice would require. (Decline in population would mean a *negative* growth rate, which doesn't appear anywhere in Chart 2.) Either reason is enough to make (C) wrong.

D **Direct Contradiction / Off by One or Two Words:** The growth in large metro areas in the years 2000-2010 was 10.9%, and the growth in non-metro areas in the years 2000-2010 was 4.5%. These numbers aren't "roughly equal," as this answer choice would require. This answer choice was probably placed here to trick untrained test-takers who might misread the answer choice and think it was saying that the growth rates for large metro areas were similar to those for small metro areas from 2000-2010, because that statement would have been true.

Test 4, Question 21   TYPE: FIGURE

ⓘ *The prompt refers to a graph/table/diagram/etc.; carefully note all labels, keys, units, and any other explanatory details. The answer must directly restate some part of the data and/or text. See "Reading Graphs, Charts, Tables, and Other Figures" on p. 44.*

Subjective Phrases to Ignore: "suggests"

A **Barely Relevant:** This choice is irrelevant to the chart for multiple reasons. For one thing, the chart doesn't provide information about where people moved from or where they moved to; it only tells us the rate at which the population grew in different sizes of metropolitan areas. If population grew in an area, then we don't know whether people moved to that area, or whether a lot of babies were born there, or fewer people died, or whether something else caused the population to grow. Further, the chart only mentions metropolitan areas and non-metropolitan areas; it doesn't mention "suburban areas" or "urban areas," which is what the answer choice talks about. For these reasons, this choice is irrelevant to the prompt.

B **Direct Contradiction:** Chart 2 shows that the growth rate in small metro areas was 13.1% in the 1990s, which is higher than 8.8%, the growth rate for small metro areas in the 1980s.

C **Barely Relevant:** The chart doesn't provide information about where people moved from or to, as we mentioned in our discussion of choice (A). Further, the chart shows population growth for all types of areas in the 1990s, rather than showing a decline in one area and an increase in another.

D ✓   Correct: The light grey columns represent the 1990s and the dark grey columns represent the 1980s, and the light grey column in each group is larger than the dark grey column in each group. We know the graph represents "the US population as a whole," as (D) requires, because the title over both charts says they relate to the "United States Population."

Test 4, Question 22   **TYPE: DESCRIBE THE PASSAGE**

ⓘ *The prompt often mentions describing the passage, and usually doesn't include a line citation. The answer must still be restated or demonstrated by some specific part of the text, even if there's no citation. See "What about Questions Without Citations?" p. 72*

A ✓   Correct: The phrase "medical breakthrough" in this answer choice restates the idea that ATryn (the drug discussed in the passage) is "the world's first transgenic animal drug" (72). The passage presents the "background" of the creation of this drug, as this answer choice requires, in lines 5-8, 19-21, 24-25, 31-34, 56-58, and more.

B   Literary Interpretation: The passage mentions the work that led to the creation of the drug ATryn, but it doesn't "evaluate" any "research," as this answer choice would require: it never actually describes the process as good or bad or flawed or perfect or anything like that. Further, the goats that produce ATryn aren't really a "scientific discovery," as (B) describes—it's not like the goats existed in the universe already, and some scientists found them under a rock or on a new planet or something, in the way that an explorer would discover a new territory. Instead, scientists worked for years to *invent* the process for creating ATryn in goat udders. This is more appropriately called a "medical breakthrough," as described in (A).

C   Literary Interpretation: The passage describes the process of scientists learning to create transgenic animals, but it doesn't just "summarize the findings" of a single "project," as this answer choice would require. "Summariz[ing] the findings" would be like skipping to the end of all the work and explaining what the researchers learned; instead, the passage goes into detail and tracks the development of the idea of transgenic drugs through decades of experimentation in paragraphs 2 and 3, until "ATryn hit the market in 2006" (71). Further, the passage describes multiple projects being done over a long period, rather than "a long-term research project," as this answer choice would require.

D   Literary Interpretation: The passage does "explain the development" of a *specific way* to make a *specific drug*, but it doesn't explain the development of an entire "branch of scientific study," as this choice would require. A "branch of scientific study" would be something broader, like the process of "edit[ing] the genomes of animals" (1-2) in general, but the passage doesn't explain how that area of study was developed; instead, the passage focuses on editing genes in goats.

Note   Choices (B), (C), and (D) could all be tempting to untrained test-takers who haven't learned to read very carefully at all times. These choices all make statements that would probably be acceptable in a typical classroom discussion about this passage—but, when we look closely, we see that they don't actually restate the passage, and only (A) can be correct. Keep this kind of thing in mind on test day!

Test 4, Question 23   **TYPE: AUTHOR'S ATTITUDE**

ⓘ The prompt asks about the author's tone or attitude; the correct answer must be directly restated or demonstrated by a specific part of the passage. See "What about "Attitude" Questions?" on p.73.

Subjective Phrases to Ignore: "best"

A   Reasonable Statement Not in the Text: An untrained test-taker might assume that some people would be "apprehensi[ve]" about "turn[ing] animals into living pharmaceutical factories" (10-11), as this answer choice would require, but nothing in the passage actually states that the author feels this way.

B   Direct Contradiction: "Ambivalence" would mean that the author has mixed feelings about pharming, which isn't supported by the passage; in order for this choice to be correct, we'd either have to see indications of multiple, contradicting emotions, or we'd need to see the author explicitly say something like "I'm not sure what to think about pharming" or "it's difficult to decide whether pharming is good or bad overall." Since none of that appears in the text, we know (B) is wrong.

C ✓   Correct: The word "appreciation" in this answer choice indicates that the author has positive feelings for pharming, which is indicated in the passage when the author calls pharming a "consequential application" (6) "that save[s] human lives" (7-8), and says that the company that developed ATryn is "delivering on this dream" (8).

D   Reasonable Statement Not in the Text: An untrained test-taker might imagine that "turn[ing] animals into living pharmaceutical factories" (10-11) could be called "astonishing," as this answer choice would require, but nothing in the passage actually says the author is "astonish[ed]," "awe-struck," or anything similar.

Test 4, Question 24   **TYPE: WORD MOST NEARLY MEANS**

ⓘ *The prompt includes the phrase "most nearly means" and the choices are usually one- or two-word phrases. The answer is either restated or demonstrated by an idea from the surrounding text. Remember you can work around unknown words, and be ready to guess/skip and focus on other questions if you don't know the words. See "What about "Most Nearly Means" Questions?" on p.73.*

Subjective Phrases to Ignore: "most nearly"

A   ("Dairy animals, on the other hand, are <u>knowledgeable</u> protein producers, their udders swollen with milk.") **Reasonable Statement Not in the Text:** In another context, "knowledgeable" could be a synonym for "expert," because "experts" are "knowledgeable" about a certain subject. But nothing in the passage restates the idea that the goats consciously know anything about making milk, so this choice can't be correct.

B   ("Dairy animals, on the other hand, are <u>professional</u> protein producers, their udders swollen with milk.") **Literary Interpretation:** It's true that many "professional[s]" are "expert[s]," but these two ideas aren't really identical—for example, not all experts are professionals, and plenty of people who are paid to do something aren't very good at their professions. But nothing in the passage restates or demonstrates the idea that the goats are paid to produce milk, as (B) requires.

C ✓   ("Dairy animals, on the other hand, are <u>capable</u> protein producers, their udders swollen with milk.") **Correct:** The text equates being "expert protein producers" with having "their udders swollen with milk." The word "capable" indicates an ability to do something, and the relevant portion of the text indicates that goats are able to produce milk, which is a source of protein, so this choice must be correct. (It might be argued that test-takers can't be expected to know that "milk" and "protein" are synonyms for the purposes of this passage; if we look at lines 28-29, though, we see that the author explicitly states that "human proteins" are present in the goats' milk.)

D   ("Dairy animals, on the other hand, are <u>trained</u> protein producers, their udders swollen with milk.") **Barely Relevant:** Nothing in the passage states that the goats were trained to produce protein. The passage later describes how scientists genetically modified goats to produce a particular substance, but even that process doesn't involve actually *training* the goat to do anything new, because the passage never says the goat is aware of the proteins it's producing. Further, in lines 20-21 of the passage, the goats are already described as "protein producers," before they undergo the modifications in lines 54-70, which is another way we know that those modifications can't be thought of as "training," according to the passage.)

Test 4, Question 25	**TYPE: DESCRIBE THE PASSAGE**

The next question is a "best evidence" question referring back to this question; you may choose to consider the citations in the choices for the next question when answering this one if you want. See "Is there a 'best evidence' shortcut?" on page 72 for more.

ⓘ *The prompt often mentions describing the passage, and usually doesn't include a line citation. The answer must still be restated or demonstrated by some specific part of the text, even if there's no citation. See "What about Questions Without Citations?" p. 72*

Subjective Phrases to Ignore: "suggest"

A   **Reasonable Statement Not in the Text:** Untrained test-takers might imagine that the studies described in the beginning of the third paragraph could be "expensive," and that the expense could be a limiting factor, as (A) would require. But the text never says that was the case, so (A) is wrong.

B ✓   **Correct:** The text says that "throughout the 1980's and '90s" (31), the "work was merely gee-whiz, scientific geekery, lab-bound thought experiments come true" (35-36). In other words, the work was never expected to produce anything that real people would actually use; even if we don't recognize that the slang expression "gee-whiz" in this context indicates that the work had no practical application, the phrase "lab-bound," in particular, still reinforces the idea that the results of the work were never intended to be practical outside the lab, exactly as this answer choice says.

C   **Reasonable Statement Not in the Text:** After the text mentions the discovery of the anticoagulant ATryn, there isn't really any further discussion of the "studies" (31) in the 1980s and 1990s, which might lead some untrained test-takers to consider marking this answer choice. But, as trained test-takers, we know that this answer choice can't be correct, since the passage doesn't actually tell us that the studies were stopped after ATryn was developed.

D   **Direct Contradiction:** The text clearly states that the "studies" (31) done in the 1980s and 1990s involved other animals besides the "cows, goats, and sheep" mentioned in the answer choice, such as "mice,...pigs,...and rabbits" (33).

Test 4, Question 26	**TYPE: BEST EVIDENCE**

ⓘ *The answer must restate or demonstrate the relevant statement. See "What about "Best Evidence" Questions?" on page 72.*

Subjective Phrases to Ignore: "best"

A   **Confused Relationships:** This part of the text might seem to an untrained test-taker as though it supports choice (A) from question 25, because they both describe something as "expensive." But choice (A) from question 25 says the "transgenic studies" themselves were expensive, while the text from this answer choice says "mak[ing] these compounds on an industrial scale" (17-18) is "expensive" (17). We know from the previous sentence that the phrase "these compounds" refers to "enzymes, hormones, clotting factors, and antibodies" (14). So we can see that (A) from question 25 doesn't restate the passage, which is why (A) is the wrong answer for question 25, and this choice is the wrong answer for this question.

B   **Literary Interpretation:** This citation gives some general background information on the "studies" (31) mentioned in question 25. But it doesn't tell us about the studies themselves, so it can't support the correct answer from question 25, which means it can't be the correct answer for this question.

C ✓ Correct: As we saw in the walkthrough for question 25, the answer to that question restates this citation.

D Barely Relevant: This text isn't really relevant to any answer choice from question 25.

> *The next question is a "best evidence" question referring back to this question; you may choose to consider the citations in the choices for the next question when answering this one if you want. See "Is there a 'best evidence' shortcut?" on page 72 for more.*

ⓘ *The prompt often mentions describing the passage, and usually doesn't include a line citation. The answer must still be restated or demonstrated by some specific part of the text, even if there's no citation. See "What about Questions Without Citations?" p. 72*

A ✓ Correct: The text says antithrombin is a "an anticoagulant that can…prevent…blood clots" (39-40) by "sidling up to clot-forming compounds and escorting them out of the bloodstream" (44), which is directly restated by (A).

B Direct Contradiction: The text says some people have a genetic mutation "that *prevents them from making* antithrombin" (45-46) (emphasis mine); it doesn't say that the genetic mutation *leads* to antithrombin.

C Confused Relationships: The text says researchers pair "the antithrombin gene with a promoter" (62-63); it doesn't say the antithrombin itself *is* the promoter, as this answer choice would require.

D Direct Contradiction: The passage tells us specifically that antithrombin isn't naturally present in goats' mammary glands: lines 54-68 explain the complicated process scientists had to execute to get the goats to produce antithrombin by embedding human genes in the goats. None of that would have been necessary if antithrombin already "occur[red] naturally in goats' mammary glands," as this answer choice would require.

ⓘ *The answer must restate or demonstrate the relevant statement. See "What about "Best Evidence" Questions?" on page 72.*

Subjective Phrases to Ignore: "best"

A Literary Interpretation: This citation makes a broad statement about substances like antithrombin that are produced by our bodies and are useful in medicine. But it doesn't say anything about antithrombin in particular, so it can't support the correct answer from question 27.

B ✓ Correct: As we discussed in the walkthrough for question 27, this citation restates the right answer to that question.

C Direct Contradiction: A lot of untrained test-takers might misread this citation and pick (B) for 27, because they think this citation is talking about people who produce antithrombin, instead of people who can't produce it. But, when we read carefully, we see that this choice isn't restated by (B) in question 27, or by any other choice in 27, so it's wrong.

D Literary Interpretation: This citation provides some details about the process of causing goats to produce antithrombin, but it doesn't say anything about antithrombin itself, so it can't restate the correct answer from question 27.

ⓘ *The question includes a citation from the text. The answer must be directly restated or demonstrated in the cited text, or in the text closely surrounding the cited text. See the general process for answering SAT Reading questions on p. 71.*

A Confused Relationships: The text says the "female goats" in line 59 had modified eggs "injected…directly" (58) into them, and that a portion of the "kids" (60) resulting from these injections "proved to be transgenic" (60-61). These "transgenic females" (66) eventually had udders that "filled with milk containing antithrombin" (66-68). So the "female goats" in line 59 were the *mothers* of the transgenic goats who produced antithrombin, not the goats who produced antithrombin themselves.

B ✓ Correct: When talking about the "kids [who] were born" (60) from the "female goats" in line 59, the text says that "*some of them* proved to be transgenic" (60-61) (emphasis mine). Later, we read that the "transgenic females" (66) from this group "lactated…milk containing antithrombin" (68). So we know that being "transgenic" in the context of this paragraph is the same thing as being "born with the antithrombin gene" as described in (B). If only "some of" the kids in line 60 were transgenic, then, logically, some of them must NOT have been transgenic, and the ones that weren't transgenic "were not born with the antithrombin gene," just as this answer choice requires.

C Direct Contradiction: The text clearly states that microinjection had already "produced GloFish and AquAdvantage salmon" (55-56), so microinjection must have been used on other animals previously, which is the opposite of what this answer choice would require.

D Confused Relationships: The passage says eggs injected with the gene for human antithrombin were implanted into the goats from line 59, but it doesn't say the cells of those goats "already contained genes usually found in humans" before the injection, as this choice would require.

ⓘ *The prompt asks about the purpose or role of a part of the text. The correct answer must be accurately restated or described by the relevant text, with no interpretation. See "What about "Purpose" Questions?" on p.74.*

A   Barely Relevant: Nothing in the text surrounding the word "promoter" (63) indicates that the author is discussing an "abstract concept," as this answer choice would require. Instead, we're told in practical terms that a promoter is a sequence of DNA with a specific, predictable effect on a gene's activity.

B   Barely Relevant: The parentheses in lines 63-64 don't mention any kind of "hypothesis," nor any "theory," "untested assumption," "possible explanation," or any other kind of phrase that could be restated by the word "hypothesis," as this answer choice would require, so we know this choice must be wrong.

C   Barely Relevant: The information in parentheses doesn't say anything to make any claim clearer; in fact, there's not even a "claim" in the surrounding text that could be "clarified," as (C) requires; the surrounding text just describes a series of events.

D✓   Correct: The parenthetical information in lines 63-64 explains what a "promoter" is. Explaining what a term means is the same thing as "defin[ing]" that term, just as this answer choice requires, so we know (D) is correct.

| **Test 4, Question 31** | **TYPE: CITATION QUESTION** |

ⓘ *The question includes a citation from the text. The answer must be directly restated or demonstrated in the cited text, or in the text closely surrounding the cited text. See the general process for answering SAT Reading questions on p. 71.*

A   Reasonable Statement Not in the Text: An untrained test-taker might imagine that a technique used to inject genes into eggs would require a large financial investment, but nothing in the text discusses how much money GTC invested in microinjection, so we know this choice must be wrong.

B   Literary Interpretation: The text does say GTC "can collect more than a kilogram of medicine from a single animal" (74-76), but it never says that this amount represents an increase in production over a previous amount of milk *that GTC produced in its parlors,* as this answer choice would require.

C   Confused Relationships: The text says that ATryn is "liquid gold" (71) "for GTC" (70-71), NOT for dairy farmers! Nothing in the text says transgenic goats will be valuable for dairy farmers, or even that dairy farmers will ever own any transgenic goats.

D✓   Correct: The text says, "ATryn hit the market in 2006" (71), which means GTC is selling ATryn. Since GTC is selling ATryn, ATryn is "financially beneficial" for GTC, just as this answer choice requires, because selling a thing involves receiving money for it, which is one way to benefit financially.

| **Test 4, Question 32** | **TYPE: DESCRIBE THE PASSAGE** |

ⓘ *The prompt often mentions describing the passage, and usually doesn't include a line citation. The answer must still be restated or demonstrated by some specific part of the text, even if there's no citation. See "What about Questions Without Citations?" p. 72*

A   Direct Contradiction: If we know the word "brevity," then we can see that that the text contradicts it. The passage says the "state ought not to be...taken up for a...temporary interest" (19-23), and that it needs to exist for at least "many generations" (31) in order to reach its goals; these statements indicate that the contract that sustains a society can't be brief, as this answer choice would require. If you're not familiar with the word "brevity," see the note at the end of our discussion of this question.

B   Literary Interpretation: An untrained test-taker might think that a contract between a person and society could be quite complex and rigid, and some test-takers may be especially drawn to the idea of "rigidity" mentioned in (B) if they don't read carefully, and think the author is completely against the idea of changing the government. But in the first paragraph the author discusses the idea of the "defects or corruptions" (5) and the "faults of the state" (8), and says they should be addressed with "due caution" (5-6); in other words, the author says there can be problems with the government, and those problems can be addressed in a particular way. So the author doesn't say the social contract must never change, as the word "rigidity" requires. (See note below.)

C   Barely Relevant: Nothing in the text indicates that the contract is "precis[e]," as this answer choice would require; the author never says anything like, "the contract explains exactly what can be done by either party," or anything like that.

D✓   Correct: The text tells us the contract between a person and society is "serious," as this choice requires, because it says people should approach the state's problems with "pious awe and trembling solicitude" (9), and this partnership is not a "low concern" (22) but something that should be looked on with "reverence" (25). We can also see the contract has "permanence," as (D) requires, because Burke says it's not "perishable" (27), and is not "to be dissolved" (19). So (D) is right.

Note   Many test-takers will be unfamiliar with words like "brevity" and "rigidity" in this set of answer choices; they may also have trouble with the phrasing of the passage in general. But it may still be possible to determine that (D) is right, if we remember our training and focus on the words we do know. In this question, most test-takers will be able to tell that the words in (D) are the noun forms of the words "serious" and "permanent;" from there, if we can catch key phrases in the passage like "the evils of inconstancy" (1), "consecrated" (4), "pious awe" (9), "reverence" (25), and the ideas about the contract existing between the dead, the living, and the unborn, then we may be able to realize that the author is calling the contract both serious and permanent. As trained test-takers, we know there can only be one right answer, and it must restate or demonstrate concepts directly on the page. Once we realize (D) must be right, it doesn't matter if there are words in other choices that we don't know. So if you run into unfamiliar words and complex sentences on test day, remember you may still be able to work around them if you keep your training in mind! (See our discussion of the "bad connection" approach on page 66 of this Black Book for more.)

	Test 4, Question 33	TYPE: WORD MOST NEARLY MEANS

ⓘ *The prompt includes the phrase "most nearly means" and the choices are usually one- or two-word phrases. The answer is either restated or demonstrated by an idea from the surrounding text. Remember you can work around unknown words, and be ready to guess/skip and focus on other questions if you don't know the words. See "What about "Most Nearly Means" Questions?" on p.73.*

Subjective Phrases to Ignore: "most nearly"

A   ("...we have consecrated the <u>style of living</u>, that no man should approach to look into its defects or corruptions but with due caution...") **Barely Relevant:** Nothing in the passage restates the idea of a "style of living," as (A) would require.

B   ("...we have consecrated the <u>position in life</u>, that no man should approach to look into its defects or corruptions but with due caution...") **Reasonable Statement Not in the Text:** In another context, "state" could mean "position in life," as (B) would require. For example, someone discussing her job or place in a community could say "it took me years to get to this state," or something along those lines. But nothing in the citation or the surrounding text restates the idea of a position in life.

C   ("...we have consecrated the <u>temporary condition</u>, that no man should approach to look into its defects or corruptions but with due caution...") **Reasonable Statement Not in the Text:** In another context, "state" could mean "temporary condition;" for example, someone who was just in an accident and temporarily disoriented could be said to be "in a state of shock." But nothing in the citation or the surrounding text restates the idea of a "temporary condition," so (C) can't be right.

D✓ ("...we have consecrated the <u>political entity</u>, that no man should approach to look into its defects or corruptions but with due caution...") **Correct:** The text says, "we have consecrated the state, that no man should approach to look into its defects or corruptions but with due caution" (3-6) and people "should approach to the faults of the state as to the wounds of a father" (8-9); as a result of this, we should "look with horror on those children of their country who are prompt rashly to hack that aged parent in pieces" (10-12). In other words, because we know we should be very careful and respectful when we try to fix the state (which is like a father), we should be horrified when other people hack up their country (which is like a parent). This line of reasoning treats "state" and "country" as two equivalent ideas; since a "country" is a "political entity," we know that "state" is also being used to describe a "political entity," so this choice must be correct.

	Test 4, Question 34	TYPE: WORD MOST NEARLY MEANS

ⓘ *The prompt includes the phrase "most nearly means" and the choices are usually one- or two-word phrases. The answer is either restated or demonstrated by an idea from the surrounding text. Remember you can work around unknown words, and be ready to guess/skip and focus on other questions if you don't know the words. See "What about "Most Nearly Means" Questions?" on p.73.*

Subjective Phrases to Ignore: "most nearly"

A✓ ("...but the state ought not to be considered as nothing better than a partnership agreement in a trade of pepper and coffee, calico or tobacco, or some other such <u>petty</u> concern, to be taken up for a little temporary interest, and to be dissolved by the fancy of the parties.") **Correct:** The text says that a "low concern" is something that is "to be taken up for a little temporary interest" (23-24). So we can see that "low" is being used here to refer to something relatively unimportant or minor, which means "petty" is correct.

B   ("...but the state ought not to be considered as nothing better than a partnership agreement in a trade of pepper and coffee, calico or tobacco, or some other such <u>weak</u> concern, to be taken up for a little temporary interest, and to be dissolved by the fancy of the parties.") **Reasonable Statement Not in the Text:** In another context, "low" could mean something like "weak" or "sickly," like in the expression "to feel low." But nothing in the passage restates the idea of a "weak concern," as this choice would require, so we know it's wrong.

C   ("...but the state ought not to be considered as nothing better than a partnership agreement in a trade of pepper and coffee, calico or tobacco, or some other such <u>inadequate</u> concern, to be taken up for a little temporary interest, and to be dissolved by the fancy of the parties.") **Reasonable Statement Not in the Text:** If we read carefully, we see there's nothing in the passage that restates the idea that something is insufficient or lacking, which is what choice (C) would require. The words "little" and "temporary" do appear, but the word "inadequate" would also require the idea of some minimum required threshold not being met, and the passage doesn't mention anything like that.

D   ("...but the state ought not to be considered as nothing better than a partnership agreement in a trade of pepper and coffee, calico or tobacco, or some other such <u>depleted</u> concern, to be taken up for a little temporary interest, and to be dissolved by the fancy of the parties.") **Reasonable Statement Not in the Text:** The word "low" could mean "depleted" in another context; for example, if your financial resources are depleted, you could say you're "low" on cash. But nothing in the passage restates the idea of depletion,

---

so this choice can't be correct.

Test 4, Question 35 — TYPE: DESCRIBE THE PASSAGE

ⓘ *The prompt often mentions describing the passage, and usually doesn't include a line citation. The answer must still be restated or demonstrated by some specific part of the text, even if there's no citation. See "What about Questions Without Citations?" p. 72*

Subjective Phrases to Ignore: "most reasonably"

A   **Direct Contradiction:** Paine states repeatedly that historical precedents should be ignored by people who make decisions about society, as described in the explanation for (D) below.

B   **Reasonable Statement Not in the Text:** Many untrained test-takers will be tempted by this choice because they'll assume that historical precedents might be hard to understand, and they'll assume that Paine would agree with their assumptions. But Paine doesn't say anything about whether it's "difficult...to comprehend" "historical precedents," as this answer choice and the prompt describe, so this choice can't be correct.

C   **Direct Contradiction:** As we'll discuss in the explanation for choice (D) below, Paine doesn't think "human progress" comes from "historical precedent," which this answer choice and the prompt would require; instead, he thinks historical precedent should be ignored when living people decide how to govern themselves.

D✓   **Correct:** Paine states repeatedly that historical precedents are "barely relevant to current political decisions," as this answer choice requires. He says this most clearly at the end of the passage: "That which may be thought right...in one age, may be thought wrong...in another" (76-79). This statement clearly expresses the idea that a historical decision may not be relevant at a later time, exactly as this answer choice requires.

Test 4, Question 36 — TYPE: PAIRED PASSAGES

The next question is a "best evidence" question referring back to this question; you may choose to consider the citations in the choices for the next question when answering this one if you want. See "Is there a 'best evidence' shortcut?" on page 72 for more.

ⓘ *The prompt also asks how someone would respond to a claim or argument. The correct answer restates a position that's already stated in the passage. See "What about Paired Passages?" on p.76.*

Subjective Phrases to Ignore: "most likely"

A   **Confused Relationships:** This answer choice would require Paine to compare the people of his own time to the people who came before him, but Paine never actually does that. In fact, Paine says that "every age and generation" (41) has the same right to "act for itself" (41-42); he specifically contradicts the idea that people of one era or another would have different reactions to a "partnership across generations," as described in this answer choice.

B✓   **Correct:** Paine states repeatedly that there's no meaningful connection among different generations, as (B) requires, when he asks rhetorically "what possible obligation...can exist between them" (67-68), and then essentially repeats the question in more detail by asking again "what rule or principle can be laid down, that two nonentities, the one out of existence, and the other not in, and who never can meet in this world, that the one should control the other to the end of time (68-72)?" Notice that the word "obligation" (67), in context, restates the idea of a "politically meaningful link[]."

C   **Wrong Part of the Passage:** Burke, and NOT Paine, is the one who says that the goals of a government would be hard to accomplish in a single generation (30-31). Paine never says anything about whether anything "could be accomplished within a single generation," as this answer choice describes; instead, he only says that no living group of people should feel obligated to follow the ideas of people who are dead.

D   **Confused Relationships:** Paine's position is NOT that we can't know the thoughts of the dead; it's that dead people's opinions don't matter, because dead people aren't affected by what we do today. Or, as he puts it, "the circumstances of the world are continually changing, and the opinions of men change also; and as government is for the living, and not for the dead, it is the living only that has any right in it" (73-76). (Notice that the phrase "the opinions of men change also" is NOT a support for (D), because Paine never specifically says the opinions of dead people change in unpredictable ways, which is what (D) requires; instead, he's saying that the opinions of living people will be different from the opinions of dead people, which is why the living should govern themselves, instead of being stuck with rules made by people who are no longer alive.)

Test 4, Question 37 — TYPE: BEST EVIDENCE

ⓘ *The answer must restate or demonstrate the relevant statement. See "What about "Best Evidence" Questions?" on page 72.*

Subjective Phrases to Ignore: "best"

A   **Literary Interpretation:** This citation says each generation must be "free to act for itself," but that isn't specifically the same thing as saying that different generations have no "politically meaningful links," as described in the correct answer to 36.

B   **Literary Interpretation:** This citation says that "governing beyond the grave" is "ridiculous," but, as we saw with (A), that isn't the same thing as saying different generations have no "politically meaningful links," as described in the answer to 36.

C Literary Interpretation: This text says that "the living...are to be accommodated," but, once more, that isn't the same thing as saying that different generations have no "politically meaningful links," as described in the correct answer to question 36. The cited text doesn't make any specific reference to political links among generations.

D✓ Correct: As we discussed in the walkthrough for question 36, this text supports (B) from that question. It differs from the other choices because it explicitly mentions "obligation[s]" (67), which are the "politically meaningful links" in (B).

| **Test 4, Question 38** | **TYPE: PAIRED PASSAGES** |

The next question is a "best evidence" question referring back to this question; you may choose to consider the citations in the choices for the next question when answering this one if you want. See "Is there a 'best evidence' shortcut?" on page 72 for more.

ⓘ *The prompt also asks how someone would respond to a claim or argument. The correct answer restates a position that's already stated in the passage. See "What about Paired Passages?" on p.76.*

Subjective Phrases to Ignore: "best" "most likely"

A Confused Relationships: The last paragraph of Passage 2 does describe "new events," as this answer choice would require, when it says, "the circumstances of the world are continually changing" (73-74). But neither author talks about anything "enhanc[ing] existing partnerships," as this answer choice would also require, so this choice cannot be correct.

B Wrong Part of the Passage: Paine is the one who talks about the "inevitab[ility]" of "changing circumstances" when he says, "the circumstances of the world are continually changing" (73-74). But Burke doesn't mention the idea that change is inevitable, as (B) would require, so, as trained-test-takers, we know that we can't say what his reaction to that idea would be.

C Confused Relationships: As trained-test-takers, we know that, in order for this choice to be correct, Burke would have to say something to the effect that he would always be skeptical until he saw some proof that government could be changed for the better. But Burke never says anything like that, so (C) must be wrong. Burke says people shouldn't change a government without "caution" (6), but that isn't the same thing as saying that no government has ever been changed successfully.

D✓ Correct: The prompt refers to "Paine's remarks in the final paragraph," and those remarks say that "circumstances... chang[e]...and as government is for the living...it is the living only that has any right in [government]. That which may be thought right and found convenient in one age, may be thought wrong and found inconvenient in another." (73-79); in other words, Paine says that things change as time goes by, so people should be able to change parts of their government that used to be "convenient" (77) but are now "inconvenient" (79). So we need to look for something in the text where Burke offers an opinion about who can or can't change government, and under what circumstances those changes can happen. When we do that, we find that Burke directly contradicts Paine's opinion by saying that people aren't "morally at liberty...to separate and tear asunder the bands of their subordinate community" (35-38) "on their speculations of a contingent improvement" (36-37). The idea of people doing something "at their pleasure" or "on their speculations of a contingent improvement" restates "changing conditions" from the answer choice (an "improvement" must be a "change"), the phrase "not being morally at liberty" to do something restates the idea of "insufficient justification" from the answer choice (if people aren't at liberty to do something for a certain reason, that reason must be "insufficient justification" to do that thing), and "separat[ing] and tear[ing] asunder the bands of their subordinate community" restates the idea of "changing the form of government" from the answer choice. For all of these reasons, we can see that (D) exactly describes the way Burke disapproves of Paine's idea of rejecting older forms of government simply because things have changed since those forms of government were established.

Note In my opinion, this is one of the most difficult SAT Reading questions from the College Board. It isn't hard because the right answer isn't directly restated or demonstrated in the text—as always, the right answer is spelled out on the page. This question is a little more challenging because the language is a bit more dense and difficult to understand for most test-takers. So if you struggled with this question but not with most of the other Reading questions, don't let it get to you. If you encounter a challenging question like this on test day, your best strategy may be to skip it, answer the dozens of easier questions first, and only come back to this one if you have time. For more on this idea, see "Time Management on Test Day" on page 36 of this Black Book. And for more advice on how to work through more complicated texts on test day, see "More Specific Approaches for Different Types of Passages" on page 65.

| **Test 4, Question 39** | **TYPE: BEST EVIDENCE** |

ⓘ *The answer must restate or demonstrate the relevant statement. See "What about "Best Evidence" Questions?" on page 72.*

Subjective Phrases to Ignore: "best"

A Literary Interpretation: This citation says the state is "consecrated," but it doesn't specifically mention anything about "changing the form of government," as we saw in (D) from question 38, so it can't be the right answer to this question.

B Literary Interpretation: This citation says people should address problems in the state "with pious awe and trembling solicitude," but, like (A), it doesn't mention "changing the form of government," so it can't support (D) from question 38.

C   Barely Relevant: This text describes the scope of the "partnership" between a person and society, but it doesn't mention anything about "changing the form of government," so (D) from the previous question isn't a restatement of this citation.

D ✓   Correct: As we saw in the walkthrough for question 38, evidence for the right answer to 38 appears in this citation.

Test 4, Question 40   TYPE: PAIRED PASSAGES

ⓘ *The prompt also asks how someone would respond to a claim or argument. The correct answer restates a position that's already stated in the passage. See "What about Paired Passages?" on p.76.*

Subjective Phrases to Ignore: "best"

A ✓   Correct: Burke says in Passage 1 that people can only consider changing the government "with due caution" (5-6), and that a government is a "partnership...in all perfection" (28-29), a "partnership...between those who are living, those who are dead, and those who are to be born" (31-34). Paine repeatedly says just the opposite, such as when he says that dead people "ha[ve] no longer any authority in directing...how...government shall be organized, or how administered" (61-63), and when he says, "government is for the living, and not for the dead" (75).

B   Confused Relationships: Passage 2 doesn't discuss any particular approach to a specific problem, so this choice can't be correct. Passage 1 and Passage 2 simply express two opposite opinions on whether people should feel obligated to respect the opinions of dead people from earlier generations when deciding whether to change their government.

C   Direct Contradiction: As we discussed in the explanation for (A), the ideas in Passage 2 directly contradict the ideas in Passage 1. Passage 2 doesn't provide any support for any ideas in Passage 1, as this answer choice would require.

D   Direct Contradiction: (D) has essentially the same problem as (C). The ideas in Passage 2 directly contradict the ideas in Passage 1, so Passage 2 doesn't exemplify an attitude promoted in Passage 1, which means (D) is wrong.

Test 4, Question 41   TYPE: PAIRED PASSAGES

ⓘ *The prompt also asks how someone would respond to a claim or argument. The correct answer restates a position that's already stated in the passage. See "What about Paired Passages?" on p.76.*

Subjective Phrases to Ignore: "main"

A   Barely Relevant: No specific political struggle is discussed in either passage, nor does either passage suggest a particular way to resolve anything, as this answer choice would require; instead, each passage discusses the general concept of whether people should consider the opinions of previous generations when deciding whether to change their governments.

B ✓   Correct: Passage 1 and Passage 2 express opposite viewpoints, but both viewpoints are connected to discussions of the relationship between people and their governments, as (B) requires. For example, Burke says in Passage 1, "we have consecrated the state, that no man should approach to look into its defects…" (3-5), while Paine says in Passage 2, "government is for the living, and not for the dead, it is the living only that has any right in it" (75-76).

C   Barely Relevant: Both passages discuss the concept of political change, but neither specifically talks about that change being "rapid," as (C) requires.

D   Barely Relevant: Neither passage says that governments have duties to their citizens, or that governments owe anything to their citizens, or anything similar, so we know this choice must be wrong.

Test 4, Question 42   TYPE: DESCRIBE THE PASSAGE

ⓘ *The prompt often mentions describing the passage, and usually doesn't include a line citation. The answer must still be restated or demonstrated by some specific part of the text, even if there's no citation. See "What about Questions Without Citations?" p. 72*

Subjective Phrases to Ignore: "main"

A   Off by One or Two Words: The passage mentions the "Little Ice Age" (3) and says it occurred during the "Holocene, a period that stretches from 10,000 years ago to the present" (13-14). But the passage doesn't mention any other "periods" in "Earth's recent geologic history," as this answer choice would require, so it can't be correct.

B   Literary Interpretation: Radiocarbon analysis is mentioned twice in the passage (lines 20 and 55), but the passage doesn't actually "explain" any "methods" that are "use[d] in radiocarbon analysis," as this answer choice would require.

C ✓   Correct: The first paragraph says, "a powerful volcano erupted somewhere" (1-2), and this began "the Little Ice Age" (3). Then, the second paragraph describes how we know that this same "powerful volcano" (5) from the first paragraph "erupted somewhere in the world, sometime in the Middle Ages" (5-6). The third paragraph goes on to explain how scientists "strengthened the link between the mystery eruption and the onset of the Little Ice Age" (18-19). Line 35 says that the powerful volcano looks like it might be Samalas, and the following paragraphs go into detail about why Samalas seems to be the volcano that triggered the Little Ice Age. So we can see clearly that the idea of a volcano triggering the Little Ice Age, and the idea that the volcano was probably Samalas, are discussed throughout the passage, which means (C) is right.

D   Confused Relationships: Volcanic glass is mentioned in the second paragraph and then again in the last paragraph, but the passage never mentions how that glass "forms," as (D) would require.

The next question is a "best evidence" question referring back to this question; you may choose to consider the citations in the choices for the next question when answering this one if you want. See "Is there a 'best evidence' shortcut?" on page 72 for more.

ⓘ *The prompt often mentions describing the passage, and usually doesn't include a line citation. The answer must still be restated or demonstrated by some specific part of the text, even if there's no citation. See "What about Questions Without Citations?" p. 72*

A   Wrong Part of the Passage: The *last* paragraph explains why Quilotoa probably wasn't responsible for the Little Ice Age, and this could be the "criticism of a scientific model" mentioned in the answer choice. But this discussion of Quilotoa happens at the *end* of the passage, so we can't say that the focus of the passage shifts *from* Quilotoa and *to* something else, as (A) would require; by the time Quilotoa gets discussed, the passage is essentially over. Further, the passage doesn't say the theory about Samalas is "new," which (A) would also require. Any of these issues is enough to make (A) completely wrong.

B ✓   Correct: The "recorded event" in (B) is "the Little Ice Age" (3). The "likely cause" in (B) is the eruption of Samalas; we see that "Lavigne and colleagues...think they've identified" (33-34) Samalas as the cause, and the following paragraphs have a variety of types of evidence to "strengthen[] the case that Samalas was responsible" (76-77). So we can clearly see that the concepts in (B) are restated and demonstrated in the text, and they appear in the order required by the prompt and by (B).

C   Confused Relationships: Ice core samples and measuring sulfates are both mentioned briefly near the beginning of the passage (line 7), and then again near the end (lines 74 and 64), so it makes no sense to say the focus shifts from one to the other, since both appear in the same parts of the passage. On top of that, the passage never mentions any "new" ways of measuring sulfates, so (C) can't be right for that reason, either.

D   Confused Relationships: Just as we saw with the concepts in (C), we see that radiocarbon dating and volcanic glass are both mentioned at multiple points throughout the passage, so we can't say the passage shifts from one to the other. Further, the idea of the passage itself "examin[ing] volcanic glass," as this answer choice would require, isn't actually present in the text. The text mentions that "Lavigne's team examined...volcanic glass" (71-72), but the phrasing of this answer choice would require the text itself to "examin[e]" the subject of volcanic glass, which doesn't happen: the text never describes or explains anything about volcanic glass, which is what the idea of "an examination of volcanic glass" in this choice would require.

ⓘ *The answer must restate or demonstrate the relevant statement. See "What about "Best Evidence" Questions?" on page 72.*

Subjective Phrases to Ignore: "best"

A ✓   Correct: This citation is the only one that mentions both elements from (B) in question 43.

B   Barely Relevant: This citation isn't really relevant to any choice from 43, so it can't be the right answer to this question.

C   Barely Relevant: Like (B), this text isn't relevant to any choice from question 43, so we know this choice must be wrong.

D   Confused Relationships: This citation does mention "radiocarbon analyses," which is an idea that appears in (D) from the previous question. But it doesn't mention anything about the volcanic glass, which is the other concept that appears in (D). Since this text doesn't provide evidence to support (D) in 43, (D) is a wrong answer to 43 and this is the wrong answer to 44.

ⓘ *The prompt asks about the purpose or role of a part of the text. The correct answer must be accurately restated or described by the relevant text, with no interpretation. See "What about "Purpose" Questions?" on p.74.*

Subjective Phrases to Ignore: "most likely"

A   Reasonable Statement Not in the Text: (A) might tempt an untrained test-taker who incorrectly assumed that the phrase "is written in" literally described scientists writing things by hand in polar ice cores. But nothing in the text around this citation even mentions any scientists at all, let alone the idea that scientists are doing anything "hands-on," as (A) requires.

B   Confused Relationships: As we saw in our discussion of (A), the second paragraph says that evidence of an eruption "is written in" (6) ice cores, but it never literally describes scientists actually writing about anything.

C   Reasonable Statement Not in the Text: Untrained test-takers might imagine that scientists think their work is important, but nothing in the entire passage mentions any "sense of importance" felt by the scientists.

D ✓   Correct: We know that evidence of the explosion is in the ice cores, and that scientists can read that evidence, because the text says, "these cores suggest" something about the volcanic explosion. Logically, if the cores can "suggest" something, then the cores must contain some "evidence" that "can be interpreted by scientists," as this choice requires.

The next question is a "best evidence" question referring back to this question; you may choose to consider the citations in the choices for the next question when answering this one if you want. See "Is there a 'best evidence' shortcut?" on page 72 for more.

ⓘ *The prompt often mentions describing the passage, and usually doesn't include a line citation. The answer must still be restated or demonstrated by some specific part of the text, even if there's no citation. See "What about Questions Without Citations?" p. 72*

Subjective Phrases to Ignore: "most probably"

A ✓ **Correct:** Line 35 says "Indonesia's Samalas" is thought to be "the volcano in question" (34) that started the Little Ice Age. Lines 61-62 refer to this idea when they identify "an Indonesian volcano" (61) as the possible "source of the eruption" (62); line 63 continues this idea and refers to an "equatorial eruption." Line 67 further reinforces the idea of an "equatorial source." These lines together show clearly that Samalas is "in Indonesia," and "near the equator," as (A) requires.

B **Barely Relevant:** "The Arctic region" in this answer choice is mentioned in line 65, but only as a place where "sulfate appear[ed]" (64-65), not as a place where the eruption happened, which is what the prompt is asking about.

C **Barely Relevant:** "The Antarctic region" in this choice is mentioned in line 66, right after the "Arctic region" we discussed in (B). Again, this region is described as a place where "sulfate appears" (64-65), not as a place where the eruption happened.

D **Confused Relationships:** A volcano in Ecuador is mentioned in lines 69-70, but that paragraph goes on to say that "shards of volcanic glass from this volcano ... didn't match the...glass found in polar ice cores" (72-74), and that this ultimately "strengthens the case that Samalas was responsible" (76-77) for the "medieval volcanic eruption" referred to in the prompt.

ⓘ *The answer must restate or demonstrate the relevant statement. See "What about "Best Evidence" Questions?" on page 72.*

Subjective Phrases to Ignore: "best"

A **Literary Interpretation:** This text only says the volcano erupted "somewhere on Earth" (2), but doesn't specify any particular location on Earth.

B **Barely Relevant:** This citation discusses the idea of a volcano erupting, but it doesn't say anything about the location of that volcano, so it can't be relevant to the previous question.

C **Barely Relevant:** This text provides some details about the scale of the eruption, but, just as we saw with (B), it doesn't mention where the volcano erupted.

D ✓ **Correct:** As we saw in our discussion of question 46, this text restates both the idea of the volcano being in Indonesia, and the idea of it being near the equator, exactly as (A) requires in question 46.

ⓘ *The question includes a citation from the text. The answer must be directly restated or demonstrated in the cited text, or in the text closely surrounding the cited text. See the general process for answering SAT Reading questions on p. 71.*

Subjective Phrases to Ignore: "implies"

A **Barely Relevant:** Nothing around line (68)—or anywhere else in the passage—mentions whether eruptions "occur frequently," as (A) would require, or infrequently.

B **Wrong Part of the Passage:** A lot of untrained test-takers will pick this choice, because *part* of the text *does* says that "a powerful volcano" (1) was responsible for "a centuries-long cold snap known as the Little Ice Age" (2-3), and that statement is directly restated by this answer choice. But, as trained test-takers, we know that the correct answer has to be related to the citation in the prompt according to the unwritten rules of the SAT Reading section. And we can see there's no connection between lines 1-3 and the phrase "another possible candidate" as referred to in the prompt and in line 68, because those two parts of the text are separated by multiple paragraphs, and they don't share any kind of common phrase or pronoun to connect them. So lines 1-3 can't be used to support an answer to a question about line 68 in this case.

C ✓ **Correct:** The prompt cites line 68, which is the beginning of a sentence, and that sentence ends by saying that "Ecuador's Quilotoa" (69-70) is estimated to have erupted "between 1147 and 1320" (70-71). The rest of the passage makes it clear this timeframe is part of the "Middle Ages," as required by (C). So (C) precisely reflects the fact that scientists know about Quilotoa, which erupted during the Middle Ages, just as Samalas is thought to have done, according to the passage.

D **Barely Relevant:** This passage does mention that a caldera "now sits atop the volcano" (45-46), and the phrase "the volcano" clearly refers back to Samalas in line 38. There's no connection between this idea and the phrase "another possible candidate" in line 68, and nothing in the passage states that "other volcanoes" also have large calderas, as this choice would require.

ⓘ *The answer must restate or demonstrate the relevant statement. See "What about "Best Evidence" Questions?" on page 72.*

A   Barely Relevant: This text tells us that finding the volcano responsible for the eruption is difficult, but it doesn't say anything specific about Quilotoa, so it can't "support" any kind of "claim" about Quilotoa, as (A) would require.

B   Barely Relevant: This text gives us details about some effects of the eruption, but it doesn't say anything specific about Quilotoa, so, like (A), it can't be relevant to the question in the prompt.

C   Barely Relevant: Just like (A) and (B), this text doesn't say anything specific about Quilotoa, so it can't be relevant to the question in the prompt. Instead, this text just talks about what the researchers did with the caldera on Samalas.

D ✓ Correct: This citation tells us that the "volcanic glass from this volcano" (72) wasn't a match with "the glass found in polar ice cores" (74). The phrase "this volcano" clearly refers back to "Quilotoa" (70) from the previous sentence, so we know that the glass in the cores doesn't match the glass from Quilotoa. The next sentence after the citation says that this situation "further strengthens the case that Samalas was responsible" (76-77) for the "Little Ice Age," which supports the claim that Quilotoa was *not* responsible for it, as the prompt requires. Note that the claim that Samalas (and therefore not Quilotoa) was responsible is in lines 76-78, but *the evidence to support that claim* appears in line 71-75, as (D) requires.

| Test 4, Question 50 | TYPE: FIGURE |

ⓘ *The prompt refers to a graph/table/diagram/etc.; carefully note all labels, keys, units, and any other explanatory details. The answer must directly restate some part of the data and/or text. See "Reading Graphs, Charts, Tables, and Other Figures" on p.44.*

A   Confused Relationships: The asterisk beneath the figure tells us that the dashed line at 0 represents the "1961-1990 average temperature," and the prompt asks us to find the "greatest below-average...variation." But this choice represents one of the greatest *above-average* temperature variations.

B   Barely Relevant: (B) reflects an approximate time when the temperature was only slightly below the average on the graph.

C ✓ Correct: The greatest temperature variation below the dashed line occurs a little to the left of the hash mark on the horizontal axis that corresponds to 1700 CE, and the only choice in that range is 1675 CE. (Of course, there's no label on the hash mark that corresponds to 1700 CE, but we can still tell that 1700 CE must be the value of the hash mark, because the mark is exactly halfway between 1600 CE and 1800 CE.)

D   Confused Relationships: As we discussed for choice (C), the point on the graph that corresponds to the greatest below-average variation from the dashed line is just to the left of the hash mark that indicates the year 1700 CE. Notice that this answer choice would correspond to a point a little to the *right* of 1700 CE. This choice is probably here because the College Board wants to trick untrained test-takers who realize the correct answer is near 1700 CE, but don't pay enough attention to realize that the answer should be a little *less than* 1700 CE, instead of a little *more than* 1700 CE.

| Test 4, Question 51 | TYPE: FIGURE |

ⓘ *The prompt refers to a graph/table/diagram/etc.; carefully note all labels, keys, units, and any other explanatory details. The answer must directly restate some part of the data and/or text. See "Reading Graphs, Charts, Tables, and Other Figures" on p.44.*

A   Direct Contradiction: The figure shows that 1150 was still during the hottest part of the Medieval Warm Period, and not the beginning of the Little Ice Age, as the prompt requires.

B ✓ Correct: The passage says, "the cold summers and ice growth began abruptly between 1275 and 1300 C.E." (23-24), and line 19 indicates that this was the "onset of the Little Ice Age." The figure shows that temperatures started to decline from their highest point in the Medieval Warm Period right around the same time.

C   Barely Relevant: The graph shows the Little Ice Age was already underway by 1500 CE, and the text doesn't say anything in particular about that date, so neither source indicates this is the "onset of the Little Ice Age" as described in the prompt.

D   Barely Relevant: This choice is similar to (C) in the sense that the graph shows that by 1650 CE the Little Ice Age was already underway, and the passage doesn't say anything in particular about that date.

Note   The "onset of the Little Ice Age" would be the time when temperatures started to drop, because "the onset" means "the start" or "the beginning." So the right answer to this question doesn't have to be a time when temperatures are already low—it only needs to be a time when temperatures are starting to decline, or get lower. Both the passage and the figure support the idea that temperatures began lowering a little before 1300 CE, which is why (B) is correct.

| Test 4, Question 52 | TYPE: FIGURE |

ⓘ *The prompt refers to a graph/table/diagram/etc.; carefully note all labels, keys, units, and any other explanatory details. The answer must directly restate some part of the data and/or text. See "Reading Graphs, Charts, Tables, and Other Figures" on p.44.*

A ✓ Correct: The figure shows the greatest cooling during the Little Ice Age around 1700 CE, and it shows the temperature peaks of the Medieval Warm Period before 1300. This is a difference of 400 years, which is accurately described as "hundreds of years" in the answer choice.

B   **Barely Relevant:** The *passage* indicates a likely connection between a volcanic eruption and the Little Ice Age, but the prompt asked us to consider only "the data in the figure." This figure doesn't contain any information at all about volcanic eruptions, so this choice can't be correct.

C   **Barely Relevant:** As we saw with (B), the concepts in (C) are only mentioned in the passage. The figure doesn't contain any information about pyroclastic flows, so this choice can't be "supported by the data...in the figure," as the prompt requires.

D   **Barely Relevant:** Again, as with (B) and (C), we see that this choice discusses concepts that don't appear anywhere in the figure, so this choice must be wrong.

Part 8: Math Section Training and Walkthroughs

In part 7, we just saw how to attack the SAT Reading section by relying on literal reading and objectivity, and by remembering the important differences between the SAT and a normal test or discussion in a high school setting. Now, we'll build on this foundation in order to address the SAT Math sections. You'll see how we combine our awareness of the test's unique design with our existing math knowledge and our reading skills, allowing us to find correct answers quickly and efficiently.

In this part, you'll learn the following:

- why the SAT Math sections are unlike the math tests you take in high school
- why the SAT Math sections had to be designed in a particular way to make their results useful for colleges
- the single biggest secret of the design of the SAT Math sections
- the two critical components of success on the SAT Math sections
- all of the basic math ideas that you'll need on test day
- the two key ideas related to statistical sampling that the College Board allows itself to test
- the ways that variables, coefficients, exponents, and constants can affect the output of a function
- what backsolving is, why it helps some test-takers a lot, and how to apply it in ways most people aren't aware of
- why it's so important to consider every answer choice on the SAT Math section—and how it can save you time
- the uses of rounding and estimation that aren't obvious to most untrained test-takers
- the unwritten rules of the SAT Math sections
- why formulas matter much less on test day than most people would expect
- why every real SAT Math question can potentially be answered in under 30 seconds
- the hidden patterns of SAT Math sections, and how they can help you attack and check questions efficiently
- the 3 major types of approaches to an SAT Math question, along with the advantages and drawbacks of each
- the recommended 7-step "Math Path" for attacking questions quickly and effectively on test day
- how the SAT's provided diagrams can sometimes be used to answer questions with total certainty at a glance
- how to deal with "grid-in" questions
- how to work through Roman numeral questions
- why it can be important not to think about "showing your work" on test day
- why the "order of difficulty" really doesn't exist
- how to apply these concepts to every math question from the first four Official SAT Practice Tests.
- and more . . .

SAT Math Training

The essence of mathematics is not to make simple things complicated, but to make complicated things simple.
S. Gudder

Overview and Important Reminders for SAT Math

The Math questions on the SAT are a very mixed bag. The current version of the SAT features several different types of math; almost everything you could study in high school math is on there except calculus, advanced trig, and advanced statistics. On top of that, an individual question can combine concepts from any of those areas, which often makes the questions hard to classify.

Some test-takers cover all the basics of SAT Math before they reach high school, and some take geometry as seniors and never even have classes in algebra. For the first type of person, SAT Math concepts are almost forgotten; for the second type, they're just barely familiar.

In short, nobody I've ever met has felt completely comfortable with all the math on the SAT when they began training, for a variety of reasons. Don't let it bother you!

But that's not all—mastering the key mathematical concepts that can appear on the SAT still won't guarantee a high score. In fact, you probably know some people who are "math geniuses" who still don't make perfect scores on the SAT Math section. You might even be one of those people yourself.

For those people—and for most test-takers, actually—there's something missing when it comes to SAT Math. There's a key idea that they haven't realized yet.

What idea is that? It's the fact that the SAT Math test isn't primarily a math test . . . at least, not in the sense that you're probably used to. You need more than just mathematical knowledge to do well on the SAT Math Section. Think of it as a bunch of problem-solving exercises. Actually, the better you get at SAT Math, the more you'll come to realize it's just a game—and the more you come to see it as a game, the better you'll get at it.

The truth is that SAT Math is primarily a test of your knowledge and application of mathematical definitions and properties, and your ability to identify patterns and "shortcuts" that most untrained test-takers won't be looking for. The calculations themselves generally aren't complicated—even on so-called "hard" questions—as you'll see when we go through some real test questions. The main thing that really makes SAT Math questions difficult is figuring out what they're asking you to do in the first place.

So trained test-takers do better on "SAT Math" partly because they focus on looking for the most efficient ways to set problems up, rather than automatically relying on formulas. Unfortunately, most test-takers never realize how different SAT Math is from school math, so they spend too much time trying to find complicated solutions to the problems on the SAT, as though the SAT were like a regular math test in high school. This is very frustrating, and results in lower scores. It's like trying to cook a soufflé with a hammer.

Studying this Black Book will help you use the techniques that trained test-takers use to score well on SAT Math. More importantly, you'll come to see the SAT "Math" test for what it really is: a reading and problem-solving test that happens to involve numbers!

The Big Secret of SAT Math

Before we go any further, it's important that you be in the right frame of mind when you approach SAT Math questions. As I've mentioned a couple of times so far, most SAT Math questions aren't really "math" questions at all, at least not in the way you probably think of math questions. You need to understand why this is.

Put yourself in the College Board's position for a moment. If you're the College Board, your goal is to provide colleges and universities with useful, reliable data on their applicants' abilities. It wouldn't really make sense to have those applicants take a traditional test of advanced math, for two reasons:

- Not all applicants will have taken the same math classes, so a traditional test wouldn't be able to distinguish students who had never had a chance to learn a certain type of math from students who had learned it and were bad at it.

- More importantly, the high school transcript already does a pretty good job of indicating a student's ability to answer traditional math questions.

So a traditional test of advanced math wouldn't let the College Board provide very useful data to colleges and universities. And it wouldn't make any sense to come up with a traditional test of *basic* math, either, because far too many test-takers would do very well on that, and the results would be largely meaningless.

The College Board's solution to this problem is actually kind of clever. They make sure that SAT Math questions only cover relatively basic math topics, but they cover those topics in non-traditional ways. In this way, the College Board can be fairly certain that every test-taker has the potential to answer every question correctly—but only by thinking creatively, which keeps the results of the test interesting for colleges and universities.

In fact, let me say that last part again, in all caps, and centered, because it's super important:

SAT MATH QUESTIONS TEST RELATIVELY BASIC MATH IDEAS IN STRANGE WAYS.

That idea is the thing that most test-takers don't realize. It's the thing that causes so many people to spend so much time practicing math for the SAT with so little result. The way to get better at SAT Math isn't to learn advanced math, because most SAT Math isn't very advanced. The way to get better is to learn to take apart SAT Math questions so you can understand which basic ideas are involved in each question.

For this reason, you'll often find that the most challenging SAT Math questions can't be solved with any of the formulas you normally use in math class. In general, SAT Math questions avoid formal solutions. If anything, you might even say that answering SAT Math questions is kind of a creative process, because we never know exactly what the next question will involve, even though we can know the general rules and principles underlying its design.

The Two Critical Components of SAT Math Success

Since the SAT Math section is all about basic math ideas presented in strange ways, there are two key areas of knowledge we'll need to do well on the test:

- Basic knowledge of arithmetic, geometry, trigonometry, and algebra (including some basic graph-related ideas), and

- a thorough understanding of the SAT's unwritten rules, patterns, and quirks.

So you will need *some* math knowledge, of course, but you won't need anything like calculus or advanced trig or stats, and you won't have to memorize tons of formulas. Like I keep saying (and will continue to say), it's much more important to focus on how the test is designed than to try to memorize formulas.

In a moment we'll go through the Math Toolbox, which is a list of math concepts that the SAT is allowed to incorporate when it makes up questions. After that, we'll get into the SAT's unwritten rules of math question design.

SAT Math Toolbox

In a moment, we'll talk about how to attack the SAT Math section from a strategic perspective. But first, it's important to make sure we know all the mathematical concepts the SAT is allowed to test (don't worry, there aren't that many of them).

This concept review is designed to be as quick and painless as possible—our goal here isn't to learn all of these ideas from scratch, but to review them on the assumption that you've already learned most of them in a classroom setting at some point. If you feel that you'd like a little more of an explanation for a certain topic, the best thing to do is find somebody who's good at math (a teacher, parent, or friend) and ask them to spend a little time explaining any problem areas to you.

The ideas in this Toolbox might seem easier to you than the actual SAT Math section. That's because the difficulty in SAT Math usually comes from the setup of each problem, not from the concepts that the problem involves. The concepts in this review are the same concepts you'll encounter in your practice and on the real test, but the real test often makes questions look harder than they really are by combining and disguising the underlying concepts in the questions.

For SAT Math, it's not that important to have a *thorough* understanding of the underlying concepts. All you need is a quick, general familiarity with a few relatively basic ideas. So that's all we'll spend time on.

Please note that this list is similar in some ways to lists of math concepts provided by the College Board, but my list is organized a little differently and presents the material in more discrete units. In addition, my list explains things in plainer language, omits some concepts that are redundant in College Board sources, and makes fewer assumptions about what you already know, making it easier to study. (This is also a good time to point out that the College Board provides some math questions that *don't* appear in official full-length SATs—instead, they appear in practice materials that are meant to sharpen your general math skills. These College Board math questions that appear outside of an official SAT Practice Test are often significantly more advanced and more challenging than real SAT Math questions will be, and I recommend you avoid them. The College Board probably provides these additional practice questions in an attempt to make untrained test-takers believe that the SAT Math section covers more challenging concepts than it really does. So stick to the SAT Math questions you encounter in official SAT Practice Tests from the College Board!)

As you're going through this list, you may see concepts that aren't familiar. Before you let yourself get confused, make sure you've read this list through TWICE. You'll probably find that a lot of your confusion clears itself up on the second reading. You may also see concepts that seem very familiar, basic, and boring. I would still recommend that you read through the whole list TWICE. A lot of the critical subject matter on the SAT Math *is* pretty basic and boring, and it's helpful to review that material so that you're completely comfortable with it.

Also, please try to remember that the material in the Math Toolbox is pretty dry and technical, and that it shouldn't be the focus of the proper strategic approach to the SAT. It's just a set of basic ideas that need to be refreshed before we get into the stuff that's more important from a test-taking perspective.

Properties of Integers

An **integer** is any number that can be expressed without a fraction, decimal, percentage sign, or symbol.

Integers can be **positive** or **negative**.

Zero is an integer.

> These numbers are integers: $-99, -6, 0, 8, 675$
>
> These numbers are NOT integers: $\pi, 96.7, \frac{3}{4}$

There are **even** integers and there are **odd** integers.

Only integers can be odd or even—a fraction or symbolic number is neither odd nor even.

Integers that are even can be divided by 2 without having anything left over.

Integers that are odd have a remainder of 1 when they're divided by 2.

> These are even integers: $-6, 4, 8$
>
> These are odd integers: $-99, 25, 671$

Some integers have special properties when it comes to addition and multiplication:

Multiplying any number by 1 leaves the number unchanged.

Dividing any number by 1 leaves the number unchanged.

Multiplying any number by 0 results in the number 0.

Adding 0 to any number leaves the number unchanged.

Subtracting 0 from any number leaves the number unchanged.

It's impossible, for purposes of SAT Math, to divide any number by 0.

Word Problems

SAT **word problems** are typically simple descriptions of real-life situations.

An SAT word problem about a real-life situation might look like this: "Joe buys two balloons for three dollars each, and a certain amount of candy. Each piece of the candy costs 25 cents. Joe gives the cashier ten dollars and receives 25 cents in change. How many pieces of candy did he buy?"

To solve SAT word problems, we sometimes have to transform them into math problems. These are the steps we follow to make that transformation:

- Note all the numbers given in the problem, and write them down on scratch paper.
- Identify key phrases and translate them into mathematical symbols for operations and variables. Use these to connect the numbers you wrote down. After the word problem has been translated into numbers and symbols, solve it like any other SAT Math problem.

In the phrase "two balloons for three dollars each," the *each* part means we have to *multiply* the two balloons by the three dollars in order to find out how much total money was spent on the two balloons. $2 \times \$3.00 = \$6.00$. Six dollars were spent on the two balloons if they cost three dollars each. The sentence "Joe gives the cashier ten dollars and receives 25 cents in change" tells us that we need to *subtract* 25 cents from 10 dollars to find out the total cost of the balloons and candy—that's $\$10.00 - \$0.25 = \$9.75$. If the total cost was $\$9.75$ and the balloons were $\$6.00$, then the cost of the candy must have been $\$9.75 - \$6.00$, or $\$3.75$. If Joe spent $\$3.75$ on candy, and each piece of candy cost 25 cents, then we can *divide* $\$3.75$ by 25 cents to get $\frac{\$3.75}{\$0.25}$, or 15. So Joe bought 15 pieces of candy.

Word problems on the SAT Math section can also occasionally avoid calculations altogether, and be based more heavily on the kinds of careful reading we need to do on the other parts of the SAT. Remember that careful reading is always the single most important skill on every section of the SAT!

Number Lines

A **number line** is a simple diagram that arranges numbers from least to greatest.
The positions on a number line can be labeled with actual numbers or with variables.

This number line shows all the integers from −6 to 4:

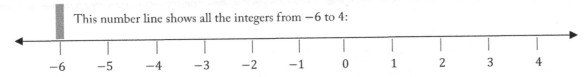

On the SAT, number lines are drawn to scale and the tick marks are spaced evenly unless the question notes otherwise.
To determine the distance between two numbers on a number line, just subtract the number to the left from the number to the right.

On the number line above, the distance between 1 and 3 is two units, which is the same thing as saying that $3 - 1 = 2$.

A number's **absolute value** is the distance of that number from zero on the number line.

−4 and 4 both have an absolute value of 4. We signify the absolute value of a number with vertical lines on either side of the number: $|-4| = |4| = 4$

Rounding

SAT Math questions will occasionally ask you to **round** an answer to the nearest whole number, or to the nearest hundredth, or something along those lines. Rounding is a way to make a number a little less accurate, but a little simpler and "cleaner."
To round a number to the nearest whole, for example, we report the value as the whole number closest to the original value.

When we round 64.31 to the nearest whole number, we end up with 64, because 64 is the whole number that is closest to 64.31.

We can also round to the nearest tenth, hundredth, etc.

When we round 7.691 to the nearest tenth, we end up with 7.7, because 7.7 is the "nearest tenth" to 7.691.

When we round 35.376 to the nearest hundredth, we end up with 35.38, because 35.38 is the "nearest hundredth" to 35.376.

By convention, when a number is halfway between two values it might be rounded to, the number is rounded up.

When we round 7.5 to the nearest whole number, we end up with 8, because 7.5 is equally close to 7 and 8, and when the value we want to round is equally close to two possibilities, we round up.

Basic Operations

You'll have to do basic operations (**addition**, **subtraction**, **multiplication**, **division**) with integers, fractions, and decimals. These are examples of basic operations on integers:

$$3 + 4 = 7 \qquad\qquad 5 - 2 = 3$$

$$3 \times 7 = 21 \qquad\qquad 8 \div 4 = 2$$

These are examples of basic operations on fractions:

$$\frac{1}{2} + \frac{3}{2} = 2 \qquad\qquad \frac{4}{3} - \frac{2}{3} = \frac{2}{3}$$

$$\frac{3}{2} \times \frac{1}{2} = \frac{3}{4} \qquad\qquad \frac{7}{4} \div \frac{1}{4} = 7$$

(We discuss performing basic operations on fractions in more detail in "Fractions and Rational Numbers" on page 170.) These are examples of basic operations on decimals:

$$2.3 + 3.19 = 5.49 \qquad\qquad 9.3 - 6.3 = 3$$

$$1.24 \times 3.5 = 4.34 \qquad\qquad 8.7 \div 10 = 0.87$$

Squares and Square Roots

To **square** a number, multiply the number by itself.

Five squared is five times five, or 5×5, or 25.

To find the **square root** of a number, find the amount that has to be multiplied by itself in order to generate the number.

> The square root of 25 is the amount that yields 25 when it's multiplied by itself. As we just saw, 5 squared is equal to 25. So a square root of 25 is 5.

When you square any number, the result is always positive. This is because a positive number times a positive number gives a positive result, and so does a negative number times a negative number.

A **radical expression** uses the $\sqrt{}$ symbol to indicate the square root of a given number.

> $\sqrt{7}$ is a radical expression that indicates the square root of 7.

Radical expressions on the SAT are always positive.

Fractions and Rational Numbers

A **fraction** is a special type of number that represents parts of a whole.

Fractions are written this way:

$$\frac{\text{[number of parts being described in the situation]}}{\text{[number of parts that the whole is divided into]}}$$

The number above the fraction bar is called a **numerator**.

The number under the fraction bar is called a **denominator**.

> Imagine that we're sharing a six-pack of soda cans. I really like soda, so I drink five of the cans. In this situation, I've had five of the six cans that make up the six-pack—I've had $\frac{5}{6}$ of the six-pack.

When the numerator of a fraction is less than the denominator, the value of the fraction is less than 1.

When the numerator of a fraction is greater than the denominator, the value of the fraction is greater than 1.

> $\frac{1}{2}$ is equal to one half, which is less than 1. $\frac{6}{3}$ is equal to 2, which is greater than 1.

Any integer can be thought of as having the denominator 1 already underneath it.

> 7 is the same thing as $\frac{7}{1}$.

A **reciprocal** is what you get if you switch the numerator and the denominator of a fraction.

> The reciprocal of $\frac{2}{3}$ is $\frac{3}{2}$. The reciprocal of 7 is $\frac{1}{7}$. (Remember that all integers can be thought of as having the denominator 1.)

To multiply two fractions, first multiply their numerators and write that amount as the numerator of the new fraction; then, multiply their denominators and write that amount as the denominator of the new fraction.

$$\frac{4}{7} \times \frac{9}{13} = \frac{36}{91}$$

To divide fraction a by fraction b, we actually multiply fraction a by the RECIPROCAL of fraction b.

$$\frac{4}{7} \div \frac{9}{13} = \frac{4}{7} \times \frac{13}{9} = \frac{52}{63}$$

Fraction a is equal to fraction b if you could multiply the numerator in a by a certain number to get the numerator in b, and you could also multiply the denominator in a by the same number to get the denominator of b.

$\frac{3}{5}$ is equal to $\frac{18}{30}$ because $3 \times 6 = 18$ and $5 \times 6 = 30$. Here's another way to write this: $\frac{3}{5} \times \frac{6}{6} = \frac{18}{30}$. Note that $\frac{6}{6}$ is the same thing as 1 (six parts of a whole that's divided into six parts is the same thing as the whole itself). So all we really did here was multiply $\frac{3}{5}$ by 1, since $\frac{6}{6} = 1$, and we know that doing this will give us an amount equal to $\frac{3}{5}$.

We can **reduce a fraction** when the numerator and denominator can both be evenly divided by the same number—we divide the numerator and denominator by that number. The resulting reduced fraction is equal in value to the original fraction.

The fraction $\frac{15}{25}$ can be reduced because both 15 and 25 can be evenly divided by 5. When we divide the numerator and denominator by 5, we get $\frac{3}{5}$. The reduced fraction $\frac{3}{5}$ is equal to the original fraction $\frac{15}{25}$.

For more on fractions, see the discussion of factors and multiples below.

Factors

The **factors** of a number x are the positive integers that can be multiplied by each other to generate that number x.

The number 10 has the factors 5 and 2, because $5 \times 2 = 10$. It also has the factors 10 and 1, because $1 \times 10 = 10$.

Common factors, as the name suggests, are factors that two numbers have in common.

The number 10 has the factors 1, 2, 5, and 10, as we just saw. The number 28 has the factors 1, 2, 4, 7, 14, and 28. So the common factors of 10 and 28 are 1 and 2, because both 1 and 2 can be multiplied by positive integers to get both 10 and 28.

Prime numbers

A **prime number** is a number that has exactly two factors: 1 and itself.

17 is a prime number because there are no positive integers besides 1 and 17 that can be multiplied by other integers to generate 17. (Try to come up with some—you won't be able to.)

24 is NOT a prime number because there are positive integers besides 1 and 24 that can be multiplied by other integers to generate 24. For example, 2, 3, 4, 6, 8, and 12 can all be multiplied by other integers to generate 24.

All prime numbers are positive.
The only even prime number is 2.
1 is NOT a prime number because it has only one factor (itself), while prime numbers must have exactly two factors.

Multiples

The **multiples** of a number x are the numbers you get when you multiply x by 1, 2, 3, 4, 5, and so on.
The multiples of 4 are 4, 8, 12, 16, 20, 24, 28, 32, 36, 40, 44, 48, 52, and so on.

Order of Operations (PEMDAS)

When an expression involves multiple types of operations, the rules of math require us to perform them in a certain order, called the **order of operations**. Many students learn the proper order by memorizing the acronym **PEMDAS**, which stands for Parentheses, Exponents, Multiplication, Division, Addition, Subtraction.

This is the order in which we must perform the operations in an expression. Any PEMDAS operations that don't appear in an expression are omitted when we evaluate that expression.

Imagine we have to evaluate the following expression: $1 + (9 - 3) \times 7 - 6^2 \div 2$

PEMDAS tells us that we first do the operation within the *P*arentheses:

$$1 + (9 - 3) \times 7 - 6^2 \div 2$$

Next, we address the *E*xponent expression:

$$1 + 6 \times 7 - 6^2 \div 2$$

Then we do any *M*ultiplication in the equation:

$$1 + 6 \times 7 - 36 \div 2$$

Then we do the *D*ivision:

$$1 + 42 - 36 \div 2$$

Next we do any *A*ddition:

$$1 + 42 - 18$$

Finally, we do any *S*ubtraction that might be in the equation:

$$43 - 18$$

That gives us the simplified value of the expression:

$$25$$

Ratios, Proportions, and Percentages

Ratios, proportions, and percentages are all ways to express a relationship between two numbers.

A **ratio** is often written as a pair of numbers with a colon between them.

> If you make 5 dollars for every 1 dollar Bob makes, then the ratio of *your pay* to *Bob's pay* is 5 : 1.

A **proportion** is usually written as a fraction, with a number in the numerator compared to the number in the denominator.

> If you make 5 dollars for every 1 dollar Bob makes, then your pay can be compared to Bob's pay with the proportion $\frac{5}{1}$. (Or, if we wanted to compare Bob's pay to your pay, that proportion would be $\frac{1}{5}$.)

A **percentage** is a special proportion where one number is compared to 100.

To determine a percentage, first compare two numbers with a proportion, and then divide the top number by the bottom number and multiply the result by 100.

> If Bob makes 1 dollar for every 5 dollars you make, then the proportion that compares Bob's pay to your pay is $\frac{1}{5}$. If we divide 1 by 5 and multiply by 100, we see that Bob makes 20% of what you make, because $\frac{1}{5} \times 100 = 20$.

If the relationship between two quantities is the kind where increasing one quantity results in a consistent increase in the other quantity, then we say those two quantities **vary directly** or are **directly proportional**.

> If I make 1 dollar for every 5 dollars you make, then when I make 4 dollars you make 20 dollars—increasing my pay to 4 leads to an increase in your pay to 20. That means our two rates of pay are in direct proportion.

If two quantities are related so that increasing one consistently decreases the other, then we say those two quantities **vary indirectly** or are **inversely proportional**.

> If we have two quantities x and y set up so that $xy = 20$, then x and y are inversely proportional—every time one increases, the other one decreases, and vice-versa. So if x starts out as 10 and y starts out as 2, changing x to 5 means we have to change y to 4—as one value decreases, the other increases.

Converting among Fractions, Decimals, and Percentages

Because fractions, decimals, and percentages are all ways to express a portion of a whole unit, it can be helpful to know how to express the same value as a fraction, decimal, or percentage.

To make a fraction into a decimal, divide the numerator by the denominator (feel free to use your calculator if you're working on the section that allows you to do that). Remember that your decimal expression will be less than 1 if the numerator is smaller than the denominator, and greater than 1 if the numerator is larger than the denominator.

> For example, $\frac{3}{16} = 3 \div 16 = 0.1875$.

To make a fraction into a percentage, divide the numerator by the denominator, then multiply by 100 and add a percent symbol.

> For example, $\frac{3}{5} = 3 \div 5 = 0.6 = 60\%$.

To make a percentage into a fraction, just give the original percentage a denominator of 100, and then simplify if necessary.

> For example, 47% is the same as $\frac{47}{100}$.

To make a percent value into a decimal expression, just divide the original percentage by 100.

> For example, 3% is the same as 0.03, because $3 \div 100 = 0.03$.

To make a decimal into a percentage, we multiply the original decimal expression by 100 and then add the percent sign.

> For example, 0.895 is the same as 89.5%.

Making a decimal value into a fraction can be a little more complicated, and it doesn't come up very often on the SAT, although the ability to think of a decimal in terms of a roughly equivalent fraction can be helpful sometimes when we're approximating (for example, you probably wouldn't need to know how to convert 0.78 into a fraction, but it may be useful to realize that 0.78 is approximately $\frac{3}{4}$ or $\frac{4}{5}$).

Toward that end, it helps to be able to recognize some decimal expressions and their equivalent fractions:

- $0.1 = \frac{1}{10}$
- $0.2 = \frac{1}{5}$
- $0.\overline{3} = \frac{1}{3}$
- $0.\overline{6} = \frac{2}{3}$
- $0.\overline{1} = \frac{1}{9}$
- $0.25 = \frac{1}{4}$
- $0.5 = \frac{1}{2}$
- $0.75 = \frac{3}{4}$

Remember that you can use your calculator or long division to confirm the fraction equivalent of a decimal expression if you need to for some reason.

> For example, if you see the value 0.125, and you think it's equal to $\frac{1}{8}$, then you can just divide 1 by 8 on a calculator and make sure you're right.

Distance = Rate × Time ($d = rt$)

(This discussion of the distance formula, $d = rt$, includes some relatively basic ideas. But the concepts behind the distance formula can appear on the SAT in different forms, so read this carefully even if you feel comfortable with the distance formula.)

A **rate** is a ratio that tells us how often one event happens in relation to another event happening. Rates are usually (but not always) expressed in terms of time. For example, if someone walks at a rate of 3 miles per hour, then that person walks 3 miles every time 1 hour passes.

To find the distance traveled by an object, we can multiply the rate at which the object travels by the time that the object spends traveling at that rate. As we just saw, this relationship is expressed by the distance formula, $d = rt$.

> What is the distance covered by a car traveling at 60 miles per hour for 2 hours?
>
> $d = rt$ (distance formula)
>
> $d = (60)(2)$ (plug in $r = 60$ and $t = 2$)
>
> $d = 120$ (simplify)
>
> So a car traveling at 60 miles per hour for 2 hours will cover 120 miles.

We can use the same formula to find out how long an object takes to cover a certain distance in a given time:

> How long does it take a car traveling at 40 miles per hour to go 10 miles?
>
> $d = rt$ (distance formula)

$$10 = (40)t \qquad \text{(plug in } d = 10 \text{ and } r = 40)$$
$$\frac{10}{40} = t \qquad \text{(divide both sides by 40)}$$
$$\frac{1}{4} = t \qquad \text{(reduce)}$$

So a car traveling at 40 miles per hour will cover 10 miles in $\frac{1}{4}$ hours.

We can also use this formula to find out the speed of an object that covers a certain distance in a given time.

How fast does a car travel if it covers 200 miles in 4 hours?

$$d = rt \qquad \text{(distance formula)}$$
$$200 = r(4) \qquad \text{(plug in } d = 200 \text{ and } t = 4)$$
$$50 = r \qquad \text{(divide both sides by 4)}$$

So a car that goes 200 miles in 4 hours travels at an average speed of 50 miles per hour.

The same relationship can be used to discuss the rates at which other processes happen, not just the rate of movement of an object. We just use the variables in the following way:

- We make d equal to the total amount of whatever ends up getting done
- We make r equal to the rate at which that activity gets done
- We make t equal to the amount of time it takes to get that activity done.

Brandon can mow 14 lawns in a week. How long will it take him to mow 168 lawns?

$$d = rt \qquad \text{(distance formula)}$$
$$168 = (14)t \qquad \text{(plug in } d = 168 \text{ and } r = 14)$$
$$\frac{168}{14} = t \qquad \text{(divide both sides by 14)}$$
$$12 = t \qquad \text{(reduce)}$$

So it will take Brandon 12 weeks to mow 168 lawns.

(Notice in the example above that the d value was equal to the total number of lawns that got mowed, and the r or "rate" value was the number of lawns Brandon could mow in a week.)

Maritza can write 3 chapters of her book in one month. How many chapters can she write in eight months?

$$d = rt \qquad \text{(distance formula)}$$
$$d = (3)(8) \qquad \text{(plug in } r = 3 \text{ and } t = 8)$$
$$d = 24 \qquad \text{(simplify)}$$

So Maritza can write 24 chapters in eight months. (Notice in this example above that the d value was equal to the total number of chapters Maritza wrote, and the r or "rate" value was the number of chapters Maritza could write in a month.)

Discounts and taxes

Some SAT word problem involves calculating a **discount** and/or **tax** on some item in a store. When we encounter these problems, we must make sure that we're applying the discount and/or tax to the correct number.

Sven sees a rocking horse for sale for $150. The store is offering a 25% discount on everything in the store. There is a 10% sales tax that applies to the discounted price of any item in the store. How much does Sven pay for the rocking horse?

The original price of the rocking horse is $150. To find the price of the rocking horse after the store-wide 25% discount, we multiply $150 by 0.75, because 100% − 25% = 75% = 0.75. We find that $150 × 0.75 = $112.50. Now we have to calculate the sales tax, which is based on the *discounted price* of the item. To find the price of the rocking horse after the 10% sales tax, we multiply $112.50 by 1.1, because

$100\% + 10\% = 110\% = 1.1$. We find that $\$112.50 \times 1.1 = \$123.75$, so the final price that Sven pays is $\$123.75$.

Notice that we can't simply apply a discount of 15% based on the idea of subtracting 25% and then adding 10%! The 25% is calculated from the *original* price, while the 10% is based on the *discounted* price, so the percentages can't be combined like this.

Unit conversion

On the SAT, we occasionally encounter questions that require us to convert data from one unit of measure to another unit of measure.

Joe has 500 grams of sugar. If there are 1000 grams in a kilogram and approximately 0.45 kilograms in a pound, about how many pounds of sugar does Joe have?

First, we convert from grams to kilograms. We are told that 1000 grams corresponds to 1 kilogram, and we want to figure out how many kilograms 500 grams corresponds to. So we set up an equation using these ratios:

$$\frac{1000\text{ g}}{1\text{ k}} = \frac{500\text{ g}}{x\text{ k}} \qquad \text{(set ratios equal to one another)}$$

$$1000x = 500 \qquad \text{(cross-multiply)}$$

$$x = \frac{1}{2} \qquad \text{(divide both sides by 1000)}$$

So 500 grams is equal to $\frac{1}{2}$ kilogram, or 0.5 kilograms. Now we need to convert kilograms to pounds. We are told that 0.45 kilograms corresponds to approximately 1 pound, and we want to figure out how many pounds 0.5 kilograms corresponds to. So we set up an equation using these ratios:

$$\frac{0.45\text{ k}}{1\text{ lb}} = \frac{0.5\text{ k}}{x\text{ lb}} \qquad \text{(set ratios equal to one another)}$$

$$0.45x = 0.5 \qquad \text{(cross-multiply)}$$

$$x \approx 1.11 \qquad \text{(divide both sides by 0.45)}$$

So 500 grams is equal to approximately 1.11 pounds.

Note that we can be expected to know the relationships between common, everyday units like minutes, hours, and days—there are 60 minutes in an hour and 24 hours in a day, for example—but any relevant information about more obscure units will be provided by the College Board.

Imaginary Numbers

Imaginary numbers involve the imaginary quantity i or the square root of a negative number. The quantity i represents the square root of -1. The following numbers are all imaginary:

$$\sqrt{-7},\ 14i,\ i$$

To manipulate expressions and calculations involving i, just treat i like any regular variable, except that i^2 always becomes -1. See the following examples:

$$3i + i = 4i$$

$$2i \times 5i = 10i^2 = 10(-1) = -10$$

Real Numbers

On the SAT, a **real number** is any number that doesn't involve i or the square root of a negative number. The following numbers are all real:

$$\sqrt{5},\ 19,\ \pi,\ -4$$

Complex Numbers

A **complex number** is an expression with both a real component and an imaginary component, like the following:

$$4 + i$$

$$6 - 3i$$

As with imaginary numbers, we can perform operations with complex numbers by treating i like any other variable, and plugging in -1 for i^2, as in the following example:

$3i(2 + i)$	(initial example expression)
$6i + 3i^2$	(distribute $3i$)
$6i + 3(-1)$	(substitute $i^2 = 1$)
$6i - 3$	(simplify)

Complex conjugates

For our purposes, the **complex conjugate** of a complex number is another complex number whose real component is identical but whose imaginary component has the opposite sign but is otherwise identical.

For example, if we're given the imaginary number $5 + 2i$, then its complex conjugate is $5 - 2i$.

Complex conjugates don't come up very often on the SAT Math section. When they do, it's usually in the context of allowing us to remove the imaginary component of a complex denominator. To do this, we take the fraction with the complex denominator and multiply it by a fraction whose numerator and denominator are both equal to the complex conjugate of the denominator of the first fraction, like this:

$\dfrac{9}{5+2i}$	(initial example expression with complex denominator)
$\dfrac{9}{5+2i} \times \dfrac{5-2i}{5-2i}$	(multiply by $\dfrac{5-2i}{5-2i}$, which is equal to 1)
$\dfrac{45-18i}{25-4(i^2)}$	(distribute 9 in the numerator; multiply $5 + 2i$ and $5 - 2i$ in the denominator)
$\dfrac{45-18i}{25-4(-1)}$	(substitute $i^2 = -1$)
$\dfrac{45-18i}{25+4}$	(simplify)
$\dfrac{45-18i}{29}$	(simplify)

Set Notation

In the context of SAT Math, a **set** is a group of specific things—usually a group of numbers. In set notation, there are curly braces on either end of the set, and commas between the elements of the set.

The set of positive integers less than 4 is as follows: $\{1, 2, 3\}$

The set of numbers that satisfy the equation $x^2 - 5x - 14 = 0$ is as follows: $\{-2, 7\}$

Algebra

For our purposes, **algebra** is the process of using variables like x to stand for unknown numbers in mathematical expressions, and then manipulating those expressions to find the values of one or more of those unknown numbers.

Using equations

On the SAT, an **equation** is a statement that involves an algebraic expression and an equals sign.

$5x = 20$ is an equation, because it involves the algebraic expression $5x$ and an equals sign.

Solving an equation means figuring out the value of the variable in the equation. We solve equations just like you learned in algebra class—by performing the same operations on both sides of the equation until we're left with a value for the variable.

Here's an example of solving for x in an algebraic equation:

$5x = 20$	(example equation)
$\dfrac{5x}{5} = \dfrac{20}{5}$	(divide both sides by 5)

$$x = 4 \qquad \text{(simplify)}$$

On the SAT, it can often be useful to **cross-multiply**. When we encounter an equation on the SAT with one fraction on either side of the equals sign, we can multiply the denominator of each side by the numerator of the other side and end up with two expressions that must be equal. Let's look at an example without variables first:

Imagine the equation $\frac{9}{15} = \frac{3}{5}$. We know this equation is true because we can reduce $\frac{9}{15}$ to $\frac{3}{5}$ by dividing the numerator and denominator of $\frac{9}{15}$ by 3. Notice that when we cross multiply—that is, multiply the numerator on the left side of the equation by the denominator on the right side of the equation, and vice-versa—we end up with two expressions that are equal to each other: $9 \times 5 = 3 \times 15,$ or $45 = 45.$

This can be a handy shortcut when dealing with an equation involving variables, if the equation has one fraction on each side:

$$\frac{12}{x} = \frac{20}{5} \qquad \text{(given equation)}$$

$$12(5) = 20(x) \qquad \text{(cross-multiply)}$$

$$60 = 20x \qquad \text{(simplify)}$$

$$3 = x \qquad \text{(divide both sides by 20)}$$

Solving an equation for one variable "in terms of" another variable means isolating the first variable on one side of the equation.

What if we have the equation $4n - 7 = 2a$, and we want to solve for n in terms of a?

$$4n - 7 = 2a \qquad \text{(original equation)}$$

$$4n = 2a + 7 \qquad \text{(add 7 to both sides to isolate the term involving } n\text{)}$$

$$n = \frac{2a + 7}{4} \qquad \text{(divide by 4 to isolate } n \text{ completely)}$$

Sometimes you'll have a system of equations. A **system of equations** contains two or more equations with the same variables.

A solution to a system of equations is a set of values that creates a valid statement when plugged into each equation in the system. The easiest way to solve a system of equations algebraically is usually to solve one equation in terms of one variable, like we just did before. Then we substitute that value in the second equation and solve.

Imagine that we need to solve the following system of equations, finding an (x, y) pair that satisfies both equations:

$$x + y = 5$$

$$2x - y = 7$$

First, we'll isolate the y in the first equation, giving us that equation in terms of y. We can do that by subtracting x from both sides, which gives us $y = 5 - x$. Now that we know y is the same thing as $5 - x$, we just plug in $5 - x$ wherever y appears in the second equation:

$$2x - (5 - x) = 7 \qquad \text{(plug } y = 5 - x \text{ into second equation)}$$

$$2x - 5 + x = 7 \qquad \text{(distribute negative sign)}$$

$$3x - 5 = 7 \qquad \text{(simplify)}$$

$$3x = 12 \qquad \text{(add 5 to both sides)}$$

$$x = 4 \qquad \text{(divide both sides by 3)}$$

Now that we know x is 4, we just plug that back into either original equation, and we'll be able to solve for y:

$$4 + y = 5 \qquad \text{(plug } x = 4 \text{ into first equation)}$$

$$y = 1 \qquad \text{(subtract 4 from both sides)}$$

So the solution to the system of equations above is $x = 4$ and $y = 1$ or $(4, 1)$.

When we graph a system of equations, each solution to the system is a point of intersection of the two graphs. This is the graph of the system of equations from the example above:

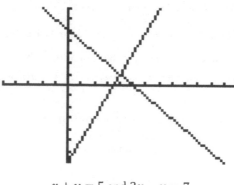

$$x + y = 5 \text{ and } 2x - y = 7$$

The point of intersection in the graph is $(4, 1)$, the solution of the system of equations.

Inequalities

On the SAT, **inequalities** are statements that show a particular amount is greater than or less than a second amount. They use these symbols:

- The symbol $<$ means "less than."
- The symbol $>$ means "greater than."
- The symbol $\leq$ means "less than or equal to."
- The symbol $\geq$ means "greater than or equal to."
- The phrase "from 0 to 10, inclusive," means that 0 and 10 are included in the range.
- The phrase "from 0 to 10, exclusive," means that 0 and 10 are *not* included in the range.

You solve an inequality the same way you solve an equation, with one difference: when you multiply by -1 to solve for a variable, you have to switch the direction of the inequality symbol:

$$-\frac{x}{4} \leq 10 \qquad \text{(example inequality)}$$

$$-x \leq 10(4) \qquad \text{(multiply both sides by 4)}$$

$$-x \leq 40 \qquad \text{(simplify)}$$

$$x \geq -40 \qquad \text{(multiply by } -1 \text{ and switch direction of inequality symbol)}$$

When we graph an inequality, we end up with a shaded region on the side of the line that contains all the points that are solutions to the inequality.

This is the graph of $y \leq 2x - 5$. The shaded region represents all the (x, y) coordinates that are solutions of the inequality.

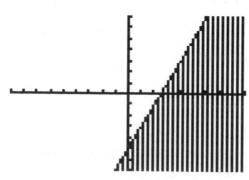

We can check whether a particular point is a solution of an inequality by plugging that point into that inequality. If the result is a valid statement, then the point is a solution of the inequality.

Is the point $(10, 2)$ a solution for $y \leq 2x - 5$?

$$y \leq 2x - 5 \qquad \text{(given inequality)}$$

$$2 \leq 2(10) - 5 \qquad \text{(plug in } (10, 2))$$

$$2 \leq 20 - 5 \qquad \text{(simplify)}$$

$$2 \leq 15 \qquad \text{(simplify)}$$

Plugging $(10, 2)$ into the inequality gives us a valid statement. So $(10, 2)$ is a solution of $y \leq 2x - 5$.

We've already discussed systems of equations in this toolbox. We can also have a **system of inequalities**. When we graph a system of inequalities, the solution region will be the set of points in the coordinate plane that satisfy both inequalities.

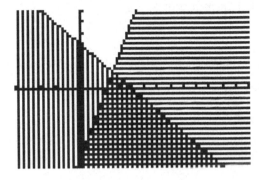

The above graph represents the following system of inequalities:

$$y \leq 4 - x$$

$$y \leq 3x - 6$$

The bottom-middle area of the graph where the two shaded regions overlap is the solution region of this system of inequalities. Each of the points in that double-shaded region satisfies both inequalities.

We can check whether a particular point is a solution to a system of inequalities by plugging that point into each of the inequalities in the system. If the point satisfies all the inequalities, then the point is a solution to the system of inequalities. If the point fails to satisfy all the inequalities, then the point isn't a solution to the system of inequalities.

Is the point $(2, 1)$ a solution for the following system of inequalities?

$$y \leq 4 - x$$

$$y \leq 3x - 6$$

First, let's plug $(2, 1)$ into the first inequality.

$$y \leq 4 - x \qquad \text{(first inequality)}$$

$$1 \leq 4 - 2 \qquad \text{(plug in } (2, 1))$$

$$1 \leq 2 \qquad \text{(simplify)}$$

When we plug $(2, 1)$ into the first inequality, we get a valid statement. So $(2, 1)$ is a solution of the first inequality. Now let's plug $(2, 1)$ into the second inequality.

$$y \leq 3x - 6 \qquad \text{(first inequality)}$$

$$1 \leq 3(2) - 6 \qquad \text{(plug in } (2, 1))$$

$$1 \leq 6 - 6 \qquad \text{(simplify)}$$

$$1 \leq 0 \qquad \text{(simplify)}$$

When we plug $(2, 1)$ into the second inequality, we get an invalid statement. So $(2, 1)$ isn't a solution of the second inequality, and it isn't a solution of the system of inequalities.

Exponents

An **exponent** of a number is what we get when we multiply the number by itself a certain number of times.

> a^3 is an example of an exponential expression. It's equal to $a \times a \times a$. The 3 in this example is the "exponent," and the a is called the "base."

Exponents can be positive or negative.

When an exponent is positive, we multiply the base by itself as many times as the exponent indicates, just like we did in the above example.

When an exponent is negative, we treat it just like a positive exponent EXCEPT that we take the reciprocal of the final amount, as demonstrated in the following example:

> $$a^5 = a \times a \times a \times a \times a$$
>
> $$a^{-5} = \frac{1}{a^5}$$

We can multiply exponent expressions by each other when the bases are identical. To do that, we just add the exponents:

> $$(a^2)(a^3) = (a \times a)(a \times a \times a) = a \times a \times a \times a \times a = a^5$$
>
> $$(a^7)(a^{-4}) = a^3$$

We can also divide exponent expressions when they have the same base. For that we just subtract the exponents:

> $$\frac{a^8}{a^2} = a^6$$

We can raise exponential expressions to other exponents by multiplying the first exponent by the second one:

> $$(a^4)^5 = a^{20}$$

When we raise a number to a fractional exponent, the denominator of the fraction denotes the root of the base in the expression:

> $$a^{\frac{1}{2}} = \sqrt{a}$$
>
> $$a^{\frac{1}{3}} = \sqrt[3]{a}$$

When fractional exponents include numerators other than 1, the numerator determines the exponent to which the base is raised, and the denominator indicates the root of the expression to be taken.

> $$a^{\frac{5}{3}} = \sqrt[3]{(a^5)} = \left(\sqrt[3]{a}\right)^5$$

a raised to the $\frac{5}{3}$ exponent is equal to the cube root of a raised to the fifth power. Notice that it doesn't matter whether the cube root of a is found first and the result is raised to the fifth power, or a is raised to the fifth power and the cube root of the result is found; the value of the expression is the same either way.

Note that raising any number to an exponent of zero gives you the number 1.

> $$a^0 = 1$$

Growth and decay

Questions on the SAT will occasionally involve using exponents to calculate **growth** and **decay**. Often, these problems involve money that grows by earning interest, but they can also involve substances other than money, and the amount of that substance can decay (shrink) rather than grow.

If answering a growth or decay question requires the use of a formula, then that formula will be provided, and it will look something like this:

$$\textbf{\textit{amount of substance}} = \textbf{\textit{initial amount of substance}}(\textbf{\textit{rate of growth or decay}})^{\textbf{\textit{amount of time}}}$$

When you plug values into each of the three components on the right hand side of the formula, you will get the amount of the substance after a given period of time at the provided rate of growth or decay.

If the question were related to money, the result might be the amount of money that results from depositing an initial amount of money for a certain number of years at a given interest rate. If the question were about radioactive decay, the result might be the amount of an element that remains after a certain number of years if the amount of the substance decreases by a given percentage each year, and so on.

Either way, the test will provide a formula in the question if a formula is necessary; otherwise, you might be asked a question that requires a basic understanding of how a growth or decay formula works, as we've discussed in this section and will see in the relevant walkthroughs later in this book.

Polynomials

On the SAT, a **polynomial** is an expression that includes multiple terms, at least one of which contains a variable.

The following are examples of polynomials:

$$5x + 3$$

$$x^2 - 2x + 9$$

$$4ab^2 + 5a$$

Remember that a **variable** is a letter, like x or a, that's used to represent a value. In different expressions, a variable can have different values. For example, in one expression, x can be equal to 100, while in another expression, x can be equal to 12.

A **constant** is a number like 3 or 11 or 716.9234 that has a set, defined value that can't change. The constant 7 is always equal to 7, regardless of the expression where the 7 appears.

A **coefficient** is a constant that appears immediately before a variable in a polynomial to indicate that the variable is being multiplied by the amount of the coefficient. So in the expression $8 + 2y$, we know that 8 is a constant, y is a variable, and 2 is the coefficient of y.

When we write a polynomial, we list the terms in decreasing order of the exponent of the variable. That sounds complicated, so let's look at an example:

$$x^4 + 3x^3 + 5x^2 - 2x + 4 = 0$$

We started with the x-term raised to the fourth power, then followed with the one raised to the third power, then the one that was squared, then the x-term without an exponent (which is the same as x^1), then the constant with no x-term (which as the same as an x^0 term, since any number raised to the power of zero is equal to 1).

The **degree** of a variable in a polynomial refers to the highest exponent to which that variable is raised in the expression. So $x^3 + 5x^2 - x - 7$ is a third-degree polynomial, because the highest exponent of an x-term in the polynomial is 3.

Operations on polynomials

Polynomials can be added, subtracted, multiplied, and divided, but sometimes there are special considerations.

When we add or subtract polynomials, we simply combine like terms.

Let's add the polynomials $5x + 3$ and $x^2 - 2x + 9$:

$$5x + 3 + x^2 - 2x + 9 \qquad \text{(original expression)}$$

$$x^2 + (5x - 2x) + (3 + 9) \qquad \text{(group like terms)}$$

$$x^2 + 3x + 12 \qquad \text{(simplify)}$$

As you can see, we combined the following kinds of terms:

- x^2 terms (there was only one, in this case)

- the x terms ($5x$ and $-2x$)

- the constants (3 and 9)

Notice that you can only add or subtract like terms during this process.

Let's add the polynomials $2x^3 + 4x^2$ and $x + 7$:

$$2x^3 + 4x^2 + x + 7 \qquad \text{(given expression)}$$

In this case, nothing can be combined, because there are no like terms. So we just write the sum as shown above.

We can multiply a polynomial by another quantity by multiplying each term in the polynomial by that quantity.

$$3y(5x + 6) \qquad \text{(given expression)}$$

$$(3y \times 5x) + (3y \times 6) \quad \text{(multiply the } 3y \text{ by } 5x \text{ and by 6)}$$

$$15xy + 18y \quad \text{(multiply)}$$

Note that multiplying one term by each of two or more terms in parentheses is called **distribution**.

$$3(x + 7) \quad \text{(given expression)}$$

$$3x + 21 \quad \text{(distribute the 3)}$$

A **binomial** is a polynomial with two terms.

We can multiply one binomial by another binomial using the **FOIL** technique, which you've probably encountered in your math classes. "FOIL" stands for *F*irst, *O*uter, *I*nner, *L*ast, and the technique works as we see in the following example.

Let's multiply $2x + 5$ by $x - 1$:

$$(2x + 5)(x - 1)$$

First, we multiply the first two terms of each polynomial together (the "F" in FOIL stands for "first"). That gives us $2x(x)$, or $2x^2$.

Next, we multiply the outer two terms together (the "O" in FOIL stands for "outer"). That gives us $2x(-1)$, or $-2x$.

Next, we multiply the two inner terms together (the "I" in FOIL stands for "inner"). That gives us $5(x)$, or $5x$.

Last, we multiply the last two terms of each polynomial together (the "L" in FOIL stands for "last"). That gives us $5(-1)$, or -5.

Now that we have all the terms, we simply add them together (combing like terms, as always):

$$2x^2 + (-2x) + 5x + (-5)$$

$$2x^2 + 3x - 5$$

On the SAT, we can also divide a polynomial by another quantity if each term of the polynomial has a factor in common with the quantity we're dividing by. Simply divide each term of the polynomial individually.

Let's divide $14ab + 2b$ by $2b$:

$$\frac{14ab + 2b}{2b} \quad \text{(given expression—note that } 2b \text{ is a factor of both terms in the numerator)}$$

$$\frac{14ab}{2b} + \frac{2b}{2b} \quad \text{(rewrite as the sum of two fractions with a common denominator)}$$

$$7a + 1 \quad \text{(simplify)}$$

Factoring polynomials

On the SAT, factoring polynomials means taking a polynomial and breaking it into two expressions that can be multiplied together to get the original polynomial.

On the SAT, there are three possible factoring situations you'll need to be able to recognize:

- common factors
- FOIL in reverse
- difference of squares

Recognizing **common factors** involves noticing that each term in a polynomial has a common factor that can be factored out.

If we have a polynomial like $(3x + 9)$, we can see that both $3x$ and 9 are divisible by 3. That means we can divide a 3 out of each term in the polynomial and end up with the factors 3 and $(x + 3)$, because $3(x + 3) = 3x + 9$.

One way to factor polynomials is to do **FOIL in reverse**. This might sound intimidating, but it gets easy when you're used to it.

Suppose we're asked to factor the expression $6x^2 - 7x - 3$ into two binomials. We'll need to reverse-FOIL the expression. We can see the product of the first terms of each polynomial will have to be $6x^2$. So we'll just pick two x terms to try out, like $3x$ and $2x$:

$$(3x+?)(2x+?)$$

We also know the last terms will have to multiply together to equal -3, so they must be either -1 and 3 or 1 and -3. We'll just try one pair (reverse-FOILing often involves some trial and error).

$$(3x + 1)(2x - 3)$$

Then we multiply out our binomials to see if we've reverse-FOILed correctly:

$(3x + 1)(2x - 3)$	(our guess for the factorization)
$6x^2 - 9x + 2x - 3$	(FOIL the two binomials)
$6x^2 - 7x - 3$	(simplify)

In this case, we got it right on the first try; if you don't, of course, you can look at what didn't work and try other pairs of factors. Problems like this on the SAT aren't too common, and the factors usually aren't too hard to figure out. This gets a lot easier with a little bit of practice.

A **difference of squares** is a special case in factoring binomials. You can recognize a difference of squares because both terms in the binomial will be squares, and the second term will be subtracted from the first (this is why it's called a "difference" of squares; this special factoring shortcut doesn't work when the squares are added together). When we see this situation, the two factors are always the following:

- the square root of the first term *plus* the square root of the second term
- the square root of the first term *minus* the square root of the second term

$$4x^2 - 25 = (2x + 5)(2x - 5)$$

Remember 1 is square, and x^2 equals $1x^2$. So an expression like $x^2 - 9$ is a difference of squares, with factors of $(x + 3)$ and $(x - 3)$.

"Zeros" of a polynomial function

The SAT sometimes asks us about the **zeros** of a function that involves a polynomial. The term "zero of a polynomial" refers to a value of a variable (usually x) that makes the polynomial expression equal to zero.

We can see that $x = 1$ is a zero of the polynomial $x^2 + 2x - 3$:

$x^2 + 2x - 3$	(given polynomial)
$(1)^2 + 2(1) - 3$	(plug in $x = 1$)
$1 + 2 - 3$	(simplify)
0	(simplify)

Another way to find the zeros of a polynomial involves factoring it. Once we know the factors of a polynomial, we can set them each equal to zero to find the zeros of the polynomial (because if any of the factors equals zero, then the whole expression must equal zero).

$x^2 + 2x - 3 = 0$	(original polynomial, set equal to zero)
$(x + 3)(x - 1) = 0$	(factor expression by reverse-FOIL)
$x + 3 = 0$ or $x - 1 = 0$	(identify the 2 possibilities to make the original expression equal 0)
$x = -3$ or $x = 1$	(solve to find the two zeros of the original polynomial)

We've found that $x = -3$ and $x = 1$ are both zeros of the polynomial, because the factors are $(x + 3)$ and $(x - 1)$; if either of those factors is equal to zero, then the whole expression must equal zero. Note that we can also work in the other direction: if we know that -3 is a zero of a polynomial, then we know that one factor of that polynomial is $(x - (-3))$, or $(x + 3)$. Similarly, if we know that 1 is a zero of a polynomial, then we know that $(x - 1)$ is a factor of that polynomial.

Another way to find the zeros of a polynomial function is to use a graphing calculator. When we graph a function, the zeros of that function are the points where the graph of the function touches or crosses the x-axis:

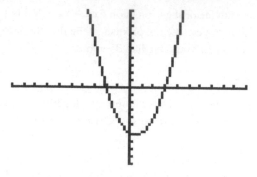

The above is the graph of $f(x) = x^2 - x - 6$. The graph crosses the x-axis at $x = -2$ and $x = 3$, so we know the zeros of the function are $x = -2$ and $x = 3$, and the factors are $x + 2$ and $x - 3$.

Completing the square

Sometimes it can be useful to rewrite a polynomial expression as an equivalent polynomial that includes a squared binomial, which is a technique called "completing the square." This is especially true in the context of equations for circles, parabolas, lines, and other conic sections, because completing the square allows us to produce standard versions of those equations that can give us useful information about key features of the conic section.

We complete the square by adding the same amount to both sides of a given equation so that one side becomes a polynomial expression that can be expressed as the square of a binomial; we then reverse-FOIL that expression so that we can write it as the square of a binomial, and then finish the process by re-isolating the other variable.

Let's complete the square so that we can create an expression of the equation $y = x^2 + 6x + 15$ that involves a squared binomial.

$y = x^2 + 6x + 15$ (original polynomial, not expressed as the square of a binomial)

$y - 15 = x^2 + 6x$ (subtract the constant on the right side from both sides)

$y - 15 + 9 = x^2 + 6x + 9$ (find half the coefficient of x, square the result, and add that number to both sides of the equation)

$y - 6 = (x + 3)^2$ (simplify on the left side of the equation, and reverse-FOIL the right side of the equation to generate the squared binomial)

$y = (x + 3)^2 + 6$ (add or subtract any constants on the left to both sides, as necessary, to isolate y again)

So when we complete the square with the equation $y = x^2 + 6x + 15$, the result is $y = (x + 3)^2 + 6$.

Polynomial long division

This is similar to the long division you may have learned in elementary school or middle school, but it involves polynomials instead of constants.

(NOTE: This is a relatively obscure math concept that only appears rarely on the SAT! If you're struggling with it, you may find that it's not worth the trouble to keep working on it too much: there's a good chance you won't see it at all on test day, and, even if you do, it's still possible to get a perfect or near-perfect SAT Math score if you miss one question on the Math section. It may also be possible to answer a question that seems to involve polynomial long division without actually doing the polynomial long division, as we'll see in the walkthrough for question 15 on section 3 of SAT Practice Test #2 on page 269 later in this book.)

The steps of polynomial long division are essentially the same as the steps of regular long division. The best way to explain them is probably with an example:

Let's divide $6x - 15$ by $x + 2$. In this case, $6x - 15$ is the numerator, and $x + 2$ is the denominator. First, we set up our work like this:

$$x + 2 \overline{)6x - 15}$$

Next, we figure out how many times the *first* term in the denominator can go into the *first* term in the numerator. In this case, that means figuring out how many times x goes into $6x$. We write in that number above the numerator, and we write in the result of multiplying the denominator by that number below the numerator. In this case, x goes into $6x$ exactly 6 times, so we write in 6 above the numerator. $x + 2$ multiplied by 6 equals $6x + 12$, so we write in $6x + 12$ below the numerator:

$$\begin{array}{r} 6 \\ x+2\overline{)6x-15} \\ 6x+12 \end{array}$$

Now we subtract the number below the numerator from the numerator, and write the result below.

$$\begin{array}{r} 6 \\ x+2\overline{)6x-15} \\ -(6x+12) \\ \hline 0-27 \end{array}$$

(Notice that $6x$ and 12 are both positive numbers, but we <u>subtract</u> those numbers from the numbers directly above them to find that $6x + 12$ subtracted from $6x - 15$ equals -27.)

Next, we see whether the first term in the denominator can go into the first term in the number we just found. If it can, we repeat the process again until the result of our subtraction is 0, or until we find that the first term in the denominator can no longer go into the first term at the bottom of our work.

In this case, the variable x can't go into the constant -27, so -27 becomes part of the remainder. We make a fraction with -27 as the numerator and the original denominator as the denominator, and we add the result to the number above the numerator.

$$6 + \frac{-27}{x+2} \ or \ 6 - \frac{27}{x+2}$$

So the result when we divide $6x + 15$ by $x + 2$ is $6 - \frac{27}{x+2}$.

This topic is particularly awkward to explain, so you may want to read it through slowly another couple of times, thinking about each step and matching up the description of the step with the relevant work in the example.

The Remainder Theorem

The Remainder Theorem says that when we divide a polynomial function $p(x)$ by $x - c$, the remainder is equal to $p(c)$. This probably sounds complicated in the abstract, so let's look at an example:

The Remainder Theorem tells us that dividing $p(x) = x^3 - 5$ by $x - 2$ results in a remainder of 3, because $p(2) = 3$.

Note that you probably don't need to know the Remainder Theorem on test day, because it comes up very, very rarely, and even when it does come up, you can generally work around it—and, if you do ever need it, you'll only need to know the very basic application we've covered here.

Solving Quadratic Equations by Factoring

A quadratic equation is an equation that involves three terms:

- one term is a variable expression raised to the power of 2.
- one term is a variable expression not raised to any power.
- one term is a constant.

$x^2 + 3x = -2$ is a quadratic equation because it involves a term with x squared, a term with x, and a constant.

One way to answer SAT questions that involve quadratic equations is by factoring. See the discussion of factoring polynomials above if you need a refresher on that general idea. (Graphing and the quadratic formula are two other ways to answer SAT questions that involve quadratic equations, in case you were wondering.)

To solve a quadratic equation by factoring, we have to make one side of the equation equal to zero, and then factor the other side of the equation (the quadratic part).

$x^2 + 3x = -2$ \hspace{2cm} (given quadratic equation)

$$x^2 + 3x + 2 = 0 \qquad \text{(add 2 to both sides to make right side equal to 0)}$$

$$(x + 1)(x + 2) = 0 \qquad \text{(reverse-FOIL left side of equation)}$$

Now that we know $(x + 1)(x + 2) = 0$, what else do we know? We know that one of those two factors has to equal zero—either $x + 1 = 0$ or $x + 2 = 0$. How do we know this? Remember that the only way to multiply two numbers and get zero is if one of the numbers is zero. So if we can multiply $x + 1$ by $x + 2$ and get zero, then either $x + 1$ is zero or $x + 2$ is zero.

Once we've factored, we solve for the variable by creating two small sub-equations in which each factor is set equal to zero.

$$x + 1 = 0 \ \text{ or } \ x + 2 = 0$$

$$x = -1 \quad \text{ or } \ x = -2$$

So in the equation $x^2 + 3x = -2$, x can equal either -1 or -2.

Quadratic equations can have multiple solutions, as we've just seen.

Quadratic formula

The general quadratic equation is $ax^2 + bx + c = 0$. As we've discussed elsewhere, it's sometimes possible to determine the value of x in such a quadratic equation through different types of factoring—but those approaches aren't always easy to apply.

We can *always* find the solutions to a quadratic equation using the quadratic formula, which is as follows, given the general quadratic format of $ax^2 + bx + c = 0$:

$$x = \frac{-b \pm \sqrt{b^2 - 4ac}}{2a}$$

Find the solutions to the equation $3x^2 + 10x - 2 = 0$.

$$x = \frac{-b \pm \sqrt{b^2 - 4ac}}{2a} \qquad \text{(quadratic equation)}$$

$$x = \frac{-(10) \pm \sqrt{(10)^2 - 4(3)(-2)}}{2(3)} \qquad \text{(plug in } a = 3, b = 10, \text{ and } c = -2)$$

$$x = \frac{-10 \pm \sqrt{124}}{6} \qquad \text{(simplify)}$$

$$x = \frac{-10 \pm 2\sqrt{31}}{6} \qquad \text{(factor } \sqrt{4} \text{ out of the expression under the radical)}$$

$$x = \frac{-5 \pm \sqrt{31}}{3} \qquad \text{(reduce)}$$

So the two solutions are $x = -\frac{5}{3} + \frac{\sqrt{31}}{3}$ and $x = -\frac{5}{3} - \frac{\sqrt{31}}{3}$.

(Notice in the example above that we find the a, b, and c values by comparing the given equation to the general quadratic equation. In this case, when we compare the given equation $3x^2 + 10x - 2 = 0$ to the general quadratic equation $ax^2 + bx + c = 0$, we can see that $a = 3$, $b = 10$, and $c = -2$.)

Functions

Concepts related to functions appear frequently on the SAT. Make sure you're thoroughly comfortable with the material in this section before test day, and see the question walkthroughs later in this Black Book for examples of how these concepts are tested in real questions.

A **function** is a type of equation that allows us to enter one value (often called x) and generate another value (often called y, or $f(x)$). The values we enter into the function can be referred to as **inputs** or **x-values** (if the function is written in terms of x).

The values generated by the function can be referred to as **outputs** or **y-values** (if the function is written in terms of y) or $f(x)$ values (if the function is called f and written in terms of x-values).

There are many different ways we can write a function, but one of the most common ways we'll encounter on the SAT is probably by using $f(x)$:

$$f(x) = x + 3$$

Even though the most common way that functions are expressed on the test is in terms of f and x, any other two letters can also be used, as in the following examples:

$$g(h) = h + 3$$

$$E(\theta) = \theta + 3$$

$$r(N) = N + 3$$

All of these functions express the same relationship; they just use different letters as variables.

In the example function above, the function $f(x)$ is equal to $x + 3$. In other words, for any x-value that we enter into the function above, we find $f(x)$ by adding 3 to the x-value. For example, entering $x = 8$ will produce an $f(x)$ value of 11. We could write this in the following way: $f(8) = 11$.

The expression in parentheses immediately after the f is the thing we'll be plugging into the function:

- If the expression in parentheses after the f is a variable, such as x, then we're using it to represent the idea of *any* expression being plugged into the function.
- If the expression in parentheses after the f is a specific value, such as 8, then the notation describes the idea of that specific value being plugged into the function.

$$f(x) = x + 3 \qquad \text{(equation defining function } f\text{)}$$
$$f(8) = 8 + 3 \qquad \text{(plug in } x = 8\text{)}$$
$$f(8) = 11 \qquad \text{(add 3 and 8 to find } f(8)\text{)}$$

The **domain** of a function is the set of numbers on a number line where the function can be evaluated.

In the function $f(x) = x^3 + 4$, the domain is all the numbers on the number line, because we can plug any value from the number line in for x and get a result for $f(x)$.

In the function $f(x) = \sqrt{x}$, the domain is only those numbers that can have a real square root. Negative numbers don't have real square roots, so the domain for the function $f(x) = \sqrt{x}$ is the set of non-negative numbers.

The **range** of a function is the set of numbers that $f(x)$ can come out equal to.

The function $f(x) = x^3 + 4$ has a range of negative infinity to positive infinity—by plugging in the right value for x, we can get any number we want as $f(x)$.

The function $f(x) = \sqrt{x}$ has a range of only non-negative numbers, because there is no way to put in any number as x and get a number for $f(x)$ that's negative. (Remember that a radical expression is never negative on the SAT.)

A function is **undefined** when the function includes a fraction whose denominator is equal to 0.

The function $f(x) = \frac{1}{x-3}$ is undefined at $x = 3$ because $f(3) = \frac{1}{(3)-3}$ which is equal to $\frac{1}{0}$.

Nested functions

To take the concept of a function a step farther, let's look at the idea of using the output from one function as the input for another function. We'll call this a **nested function**.

Let's imagine that we have one function called $f(x)$, and another function called $g(x)$. Function $f(x)$ will be equal to $x^2 + x + 2$, and function $g(x)$ will be equal to $\frac{x}{3} - 1$:

$$f(x) = x^2 + x + 2 \qquad \text{(definition of } f(x)\text{)}$$

$$g(x) = \frac{x}{3} - 1 \qquad \text{(definition of } g(x)\text{)}$$

We can evaluate an expression like $f(g(x))$ by plugging x into $g(x)$ first, and then taking the result and plugging it into $f(x)$. Let's follow that process to find $f(g(9))$.

$$g(x) = \frac{x}{3} - 1 \qquad \text{(definition of } g(x)\text{)}$$

$$g(9) = \frac{(9)}{3} - 1 \qquad \text{(plug } x = 9 \text{ into } g(x))$$

$$g(9) = 2 \qquad \text{(simplify)}$$

So we see that $g(9) = 2$. Now we plug 2 into $f(x)$.

$$f(x) = x^2 + x + 2 \qquad \text{(definition of } f(x))$$

$$f(2) = (2)^2 + (2) + 2 \qquad \text{(plug in } x = 2 \text{ into } f(x))$$

$$f(2) = 8 \qquad \text{(simplify)}$$

So by finding $g(9)$, then plugging that value into $f(x)$, we find that $f(g(9)) = 8$.

Linear functions

The xy-coordinate plane has 4 quadrants numbered $I, II, II,$ and IV.

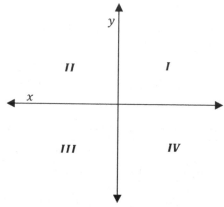

The **origin** is the point where the x-axis and y-axis intersect. The coordinate pair that corresponds to the origin is $(0, 0)$.

A **point** can be plotted on the xy-coordinate plane in (x, y) notation if we make the x number the horizontal separation between the point (x, y) and the origin $(0, 0)$, and then we make the y value the vertical separation between (x, y) and $(0, 0)$.

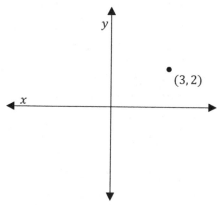

The above graph shows the point $(3, 2)$ on the xy-coordinate plane. (Notice in the graph above that point $(3, 2)$ is 3 units to the right of the origin and 2 units above the origin.)

A **linear function** is a function whose (x, y) value pairings form a straight line when they're plotted as points on a graph.

$f(x) = x - 1$ is linear, because all the (x, y) pairings that it generates form a straight line when plotted on a graph.

Here are some (x, y) pairings for the function $f(x) = x - 1$:

x	y
-2	-3
-1	-2
0	-1
1	0
2	1
3	2

When we plot the (x, y) pairings from a linear function, we can see they fall in a straight line:

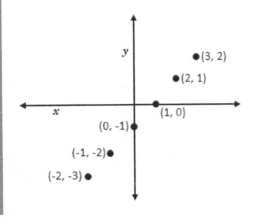

As you can see, we've only plotted six specific points based on the (x, y) coordinates we got for six specific values of x. But we can see that the domain for $f(x) = x - 1$ must be all numbers from negative infinity to infinity, because any x value we plug in will result in a defined y value. So we can draw a line connecting these plotted points, and the line will represent all possible (x, y) pairs that satisfy $f(x) = x - 1$.

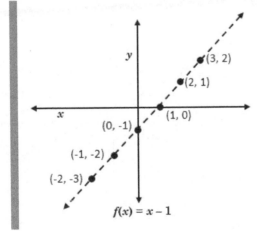

The **slope** of a function is a fraction that expresses a measurement of how far up or down the line travels for a given distance that it travels from left to right:

- The number of units traveled up goes in the numerator of the slope fraction. (A negative number in the numerator indicates that the line travels down as it goes from left to right, and a zero in the numerator—in other words, a slope of zero—indicates that the line is horizontal.)
- The number of units traveled from left to right is the denominator of the slope fraction.

For this reason, the slope fraction is often described as "rise over run"—the number of units traveled up (the "rise"), divided by the number of units traveled from left to right (the "run").

If the slope of a line is $\frac{1}{3}$, then the line travels 1 unit up for every 3 units it travels from left to right, because the numerator, or "rise," is 1, and the denominator, or "run," is 3.

This means we can calculate the slope between two points on a function graph by finding the vertical distance between them, and dividing it by the horizontal distance between them:

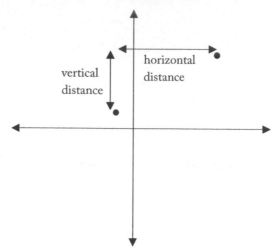

The vertical distance between the two points is the difference between the y-values of the points, and the horizontal distance between them is the difference between the x-values.

> The slope between the points $(5, 3)$ and $(19, 8)$ is equal to $\dfrac{8-3}{19-5}$, or $\dfrac{5}{14}$.

By convention, we take the values from the left-most point and subtract them from the values of the right-most point, but it doesn't actually matter which order you subtract in, as long as you use the same order for coordinates in the numerator and denominator, and you keep track of any minus signs.

> If we switch the order of subtraction for the points from the previous example, we get $\dfrac{3-8}{5-19}$, or $\dfrac{-5}{-14}$, which is still equal to $\dfrac{5}{14}$.

As we discussed earlier, a line with positive slope is slanted upward as we read from left to right, and a line with a negative slope is slanted downward as we read from left to right:

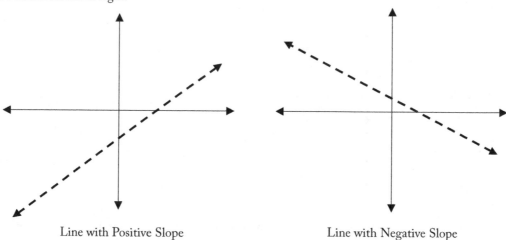

Line with Positive Slope   Line with Negative Slope

The **y-intercept** is the y-value of the function where $x = 0$, and is also the point where the graph of the function crosses the y-axis. Two linear functions with the same slope and different y-intercepts are **parallel**.

Two lines are **perpendicular** when their slopes are the negative reciprocals of one another.

> 2 and $-\dfrac{1}{2}$ are examples of perpendicular slopes

The slope of a **horizontal** line is 0, because the "rise" is always zero, and 0 divided by any number is 0.

The slope of a **vertical** line is **undefined**, because the "run" is always zero, and any number divided by 0 is undefined.

You'll never have to draw your own graph of a linear function on the SAT, because the formatting of the test makes that impossible. Instead, you might have to use your understanding of graphs to figure out a value, or to pick one graph out of several others as the correct graph of a particular function. (Your calculator may come in handy for that—see the walkthroughs later in this Black Book for examples of this idea in action.)

Note that an **x-intercept** of a function is a point where the graph of the function crosses the x-axis, which is also a point where the y-value of the function is equal to 0.

Slope-intercept form

We can easily find the slope of a line when the function equation for the line is in something called **slope-intercept form**, which looks like this:

$$y = mx + b$$

The variables in slope-intercept form represent the following aspects of the graph:

- y and x represent the values in an (x, y) coordinate pair of any point on the graph

- m represents the slope, often in fraction form

- b represents the y-intercept

So when a line is in slope-intercept form, the coefficient of x is the slope of the line.

> For the function $y = 4x - 7$, the slope of the line is 4, and the y-intercept is $(0, -7)$.
>
> For the function $y = \frac{x}{5} + 1$, the slope is $\frac{1}{5}$, and the y-intercept is $(0, 1)$. (Remember that $\frac{x}{5}$ is the same as $\frac{1}{5}x$.)

Point-slope form

When we know the slope of a line, m, and a point on that line, (x_1, y_1), we can create an equation for that line using **point-slope form**, which looks like this:

$$y - y_1 = m(x - x_1)$$

> For the line with slope $m = 2$ that contains the point $(1, 6)$, an equation using point-slope form is $y - 6 = 2(x - 1)$.

Evaluating a function

When we evaluate a function like $f(x)$, we determine the output when we plug in a certain x value. The two most common ways to evaluate a function are:

- to plug an x value into the function itself, or

- to look at a graph of the function and see which y value corresponds to a certain x value.

We'll look at both methods.

> We can evaluate $f(x) = 2x + 4$ when $x = 5$ by plugging 5 into the given function:
>
> $f(x) = 2x + 4$ (given function)
>
> $f(5) = 2(5) + 4$ (plug in $x = 5$)
>
> $f(5) = 14$ (simplify)
>
> So if we evaluate $f(x) = 2x + 4$ when $x = 5$, we find that $f(5) = 14$.
>
> Below is the graph of $g(x)$:
>
>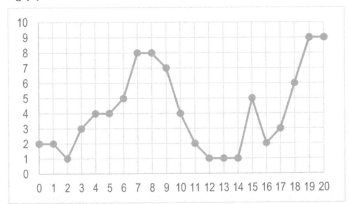
>
> We can evaluate $g(5)$ by finding the value of $g(x)$ when $x = 5$. We can see that when $x = 5$, the y-value on the graph is 4. So we know that $g(5) = 4$.
>
> (Notice that when we have a graph of $g(x)$, we can evaluate $g(x)$ without actually knowing what expression $g(x)$ is equal to.)

An **equivalent form** of a function or equation is basically another way to write the same function or equation. Both forms of the function or equation will be satisfied by the exact same set of (x, y) coordinates, which means they produce identical graphs. Any function or equation can have many different equivalent forms.

$y = (x + 4)(x - 1)$ and $y = x^2 + 3x - 4$ are equivalent forms of the same equation, because they're both satisfied by the same sets of (x, y) coordinates, and both produce the same graph, which looks like this:

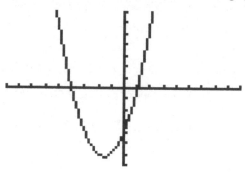

Quadratic functions

A **quadratic function** is a function where the x variable has an exponent of 2.

$y = x^2$ is a quadratic function.

Quadratic functions are NEVER linear—in other words, the graph of a quadratic function is always a curve.

The SAT never requires you to draw a graph by hand. It will only ask you to use given graphs to answer questions, or to identify which answer choice correctly graphs a given function.

Quadratic functions always extend infinitely in some direction (up, down, left, right, or a combination).

The graph of $y = x^2$ extends up infinitely, and looks roughly like this:

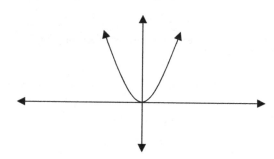

The graph of $y = -(x^2)$ extends down infinitely, and looks roughly like this:

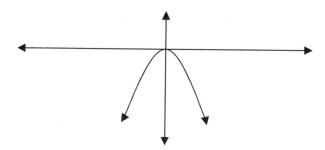

Note that in the context of a discussion of functions on the SAT, the "direction" of the graph of a quadratic equation is really just a question of its range. When the range extends to negative infinity, the graph "opens down." When the range extends to positive infinity, the graph "opens up."

When a quadratic function "opens down," its highest point or **maximum value** is the (x, y) pair that has the greatest y value.

When a quadratic function "opens up," its lowest point or **minimum value** is the (x, y) pair that has the lowest y value.

Sometimes you'll be asked to find the "zeros" of a quadratic function. Quadratic functions are a kind of polynomial functions, so this process is the same as finding zeros of a polynomial, as discussed earlier in this Toolbox.

Geometric Notation

The SAT likes to use what it calls "geometric notation" to describe lines, rays, angles, and so on. You've probably seen this notation in your classes, but don't worry if you haven't—it's not hard to learn.

$\overline{AB}$ describes the distance from A to B.

$\overleftrightarrow{AB}$ describes the line that goes through points A and B (the arrows indicate an infinite extension into space in both directions).

$\overline{AB}$ describes the line segment with endpoints A and B (the lack of arrowheads on the symbol indicates that the given segment doesn't continue on to infinity).

$\overrightarrow{AB}$ describes the ray with endpoint A that goes through B and then continues on infinitely.

$\overrightarrow{BA}$ describes the ray with B for an endpoint that goes through A and continues on infinitely.

$\angle ABC$ describes the angle with point B as a vertex that has point A on one leg and point C on the other.

$\angle ABC = 60°$ indicates that the measure of the angle with point B as a vertex and with point A on one leg and point C on the other is 60 degrees.

$\triangle ABC$ describes the triangle with vertices A, B, and C.

$\square ABCD$ describes the quadrilateral with vertices A, B, C, and D.

$\overline{AB} \perp \overline{BC}$ indicates that the line segments $\overline{AB}$ and $\overline{BC}$ are perpendicular to each other.

$\overline{AB} \parallel \overline{BC}$ indicates that the line segments $\overline{AB}$ and $\overline{BC}$ are parallel to each other.

Angles in the Plane

Degrees are the units that we use to measure how "wide" or "big" an angle is.

This is a 45-degree angle:

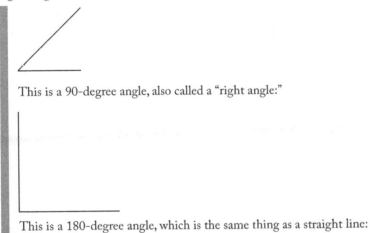

This is a 90-degree angle, also called a "right angle:"

This is a 180-degree angle, which is the same thing as a straight line:

Congruent angles are just angles with the same measures. So if one angle has a measure of 30° and another angle has a measure of 30°, those two angles are congruent.

Sometimes angles have special relationships. Three types of special relationships that appear often on the SAT are vertical angles, supplementary angles, and complementary angles.

Vertical angles are the pairs of angles that lie across from each other when two lines intersect. In a pair of vertical angles, the two angles have the same degree measurements as each other.

Angles $\angle ABC$ and $\angle DBE$ are a pair of vertical angles, so they have the same degree measurements as each other. Angles $\angle ABD$ and $\angle CBE$ are also a pair of vertical angles, so they have the same measurements as each other as well.

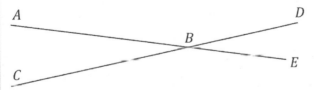

Supplementary angles are pairs of angles whose measurements add up to 180 degrees. When supplementary angles are next to each other, they form a straight line.

$\angle ABC$ and $\angle ABD$ are a pair of supplementary angles, because their measurements together add up to 180 degrees—together, they form the straight line CD.

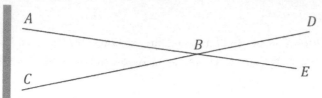

Complementary angles describe angles who measures add up to 90°.

In the figure below, $\angle AXB$ and $\angle BXC$ are complementary, because the sum of the measures of the two angles is 90°.

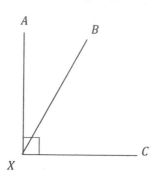

A **transversal** is the result when a line crosses two parallel lines, as we can see in the diagram below.

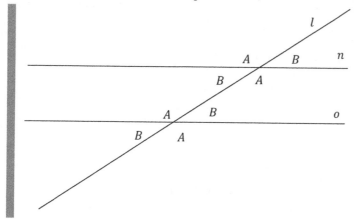

In the above diagram,

- n and o are parallel
- all angles labeled A are equal to one another
- all angles labeled B are equal to one another
- $A + B = 180°$

We can see that each angle labeled A lies across from another angle labeled A, and that each pair of angles labeled A is a set of vertical angles. Similarly, each angle labeled B lies across from another angle labeled B, and each pair of angles labeled B is a set of vertical angles.

Also, because lines n and o are parallel, we know that that line l crosses line n at the same angle that line l crosses line o. For this reason, we know that the angles labeled A in the top intersection are equal to the angles labeled A in the bottom intersection, and also that the angles labeled B in the top intersection are equal to the angles labeled B in the bottom intersection.

There are special terms for the relationships among the various angles created by a transversal, but we don't need to know those on the SAT, beyond what we've already discussed in this section.

Triangles

The SAT loves to ask about **triangles**.

The sum of the measures of the angles in any triangle is 180 degrees.

In any triangle, the longest side is always opposite the biggest angle, and the shortest side is always opposite the smallest angle.

In an **equilateral triangle**, all the sides are the same length, and all the angles measure 60 degrees each.

In the equilateral triangle ΔEQI below, all the sides are of equal length, and all the angles are 60 degrees.

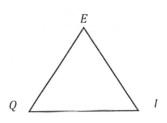

In an **isosceles triangle**, two of the three sides are the same length, and two of the three angles are the same size as each other.

In the isosceles triangle $\triangle ISO$ below, side $\overline{IS}$ is the same length as side $\overline{SO}$. Also, $\angle SIO$ and $\angle SOI$ have the same degree measurement as each other.

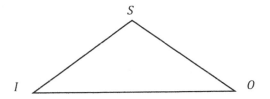

A **right triangle** is a triangle that includes a ninety-degree angle as one of its three angles.

A special relationship exists between the measurements of the sides of a right triangle: If you take the lengths of the two shorter sides and square them, and then add those two squares together, the resulting amount is the square of the length of the longest side.

In the right triangle below, $a^2 + b^2 = c^2$.

The expression of this relationship, $a^2 + b^2 = c^2$, is called the "**Pythagorean Theorem.**"

A "**Pythagorean triple**" is a set of three numbers that can all be the lengths of the sides of the same right triangle. Memorizing four of these sets will make your life easier on the SAT.

$\{3, 4, 5\}$ is a Pythagorean triple because $3^2 + 4^2 = 5^2$

$\{1, 1, \sqrt{2}\}$ is a Pythagorean triple because $1^2 + 1^2 = \sqrt{2}^2$

$\{1, \sqrt{3}, 2\}$ is a Pythagorean triple because $1^2 + \sqrt{3}^2 = 2^2$

$\{5, 12, 13\}$ is a Pythagorean triple because $5^2 + 12^2 = 13^2$

When we multiply each number in a Pythagorean triple by the same number, we get another Pythagorean triple.

If we know $\{3, 4, 5\}$ is a Pythagorean triple, then we also know $\{6, 8, 10\}$ is a Pythagorean triple, because $\{6, 8, 10\}$ is what we get when we multiply every number in $\{3, 4, 5\}$ by 2.

In a $\{1, 1, \sqrt{2}\}$ right triangle, the angle measurements are 45°, 45°, 90°.
In a $\{1, \sqrt{3}, 2\}$ right triangle, the angle measurements are 30°, 60°, 90°.

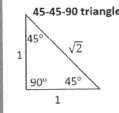

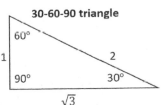

Two triangles are **similar triangles** if they have all the same angle measurements.

Between two similar triangles, the relationship between any two corresponding sides is the same as between any other two corresponding sides.

Triangles ΔABC and ΔDEF below are similar. Side $\overline{AB}$ has length 8, and side $\overline{DE}$ has length 24, so every side measurement in ΔDEF must be three times the corresponding side in ΔABC.

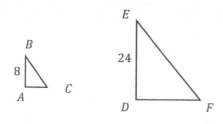

The formula for the **area of a triangle** is given in the front of every real SAT Math section. That formula is $A = \frac{1}{2}bh$, which means that the area of a triangle is equal to one half the length of the base of the triangle multiplied by the height of the triangle.

In every triangle, the length of each side must be less than the sum of the lengths of the other sides. (Otherwise, the triangle wouldn't be able to "close," because the longest side would be too long for the other two sides to touch.)

You can see in this diagram that the longest side is longer than the two shorter sides combined, which means the two shorter sides are too far apart to connect and "close" the triangle.

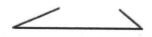

Points and Lines

A unique **line** can be drawn to connect any two **points**.

Between any two points on a line, there is a **midpoint** that is halfway between the two points.

Any three or more points may or may not fall on the same line. If they do, we say the points are **collinear**.

We can find the **distance between any two points** on the xy-coordinate plane as long as we know the coordinates of each point. We can use the distance formula to find the distance between the point (x_1, y_1) and (x_2, y_2). That formula looks like this:

$$\sqrt{(x_2 - x_1)^2 + (y_2 - y_1)^2}$$

We can also avoid memorizing a formula by just understanding the distance between the two points as the hypotenuse of a right triangle. We can then determine the lengths of the two sides of that right triangle, and use them to find the length of the hypotenuse. (This is ultimately what the distance formula does, but I find that test-takers tend to make more mistakes trying to memorize a complicated formula than they do just sketching out the right triangle as we'll see in the example.)

Imagine that we're trying to find the distance between $(1, 3)$ and $(5, 6)$.

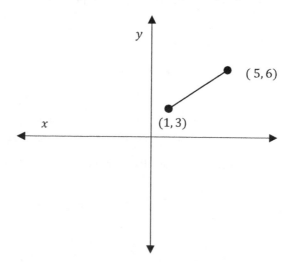

Let's zoom in on that line segment, and draw in the sides of the triangle.

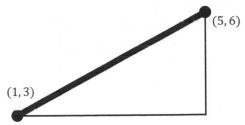

The vertical distance between the two points is the difference between their y-coordinates, which is $6 - 3$, or 3. This is the length of the vertical leg. The horizontal distance between the two points is the difference between their x-coordinates, which is $5 - 1$, or 4. This is the length of the horizontal leg. Let's add those lengths to the diagram.

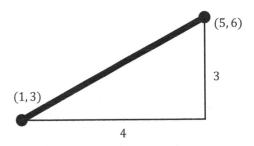

Now let's plug these numbers into the Pythagorean theorem to find the length of the hypotenuse.

$a^2 + b^2 = c^2$ (Pythagorean theorem)

$4^2 + 3^2 = c^2$ (plug in the two side lengths)

$16 + 9 = c^2$ (square the two side lengths)

$25 = c^2$ (simplify)

$5 = c$ (take square root of both sides)

So the distance between $(1, 3)$ and $(5, 6)$ is 5.

Parallelograms

A parallelogram is a four-sided figure where both pairs of opposite sides are parallel to each other.
In a parallelogram, opposite angles are equal to each other, and the measures of all the angles added up together equal 360.
In $\square$ $ABCD$ below, all the interior angles taken together equal 360°, and opposite angles have equal measurements.

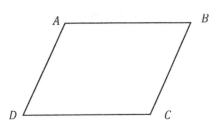

Rectangles

Rectangles are special parallelograms where all the angles measure 90°. In a rectangle, if you know the lengths of the sides then you can always figure out the length from one corner to the opposite corner by using the Pythagorean theorem.

In the rectangle below, all angles are right angles, and we can use the Pythagorean theorem to determine that the diagonal $\overline{AC}$ must have a length of 13, since $5^2 + 12^2 = 13^2$.

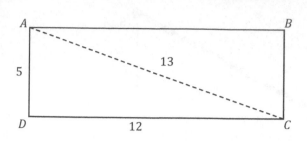

Squares

Squares are special rectangles where all the sides have equal length.

Area

The **area** of a two-dimensional figure is the amount of two-dimensional space that the figure covers.

Area is always measured in square units.

All the area formulas you need for the SAT appear in the beginning of each Math section, so there's no need to memorize them—you just need to know how to use them.

Perimeters (Squares, Rectangles, Circles)

The **perimeter** of a two-dimensional object is the sum of the lengths of its sides, or, for a circle, the distance around the circle.

To find the perimeter of a non-circle, just add up the lengths of its sides.

The perimeter of a circle is called the circumference—see the section on circles for more information.

Other Polygons

The SAT might give you questions about special polygons, like pentagons, hexagons, octagons, and so on.

The sum of the angle measurements of any polygon can be determined with a simple formula: Where s is the number of sides of the polygon, the sum of the angle measurements is $(s - 2) \times 180$.

> A triangle has 3 sides, so the sum of its angle measurements is given by $(3 - 2) \times 180$, which is the same thing as 1×180, which is the same thing as 180. So the angles in a triangle add up to 180 degrees.

> A hexagon has 6 sides, so the sum of its angle measurements is $(6 - 2) \times 180$, or 4×180, which is 720. So all the angles in a hexagon add up to 720 degrees.

To find the perimeter of any polygon, just add up the lengths of the sides.

To find the area of a polygon besides a triangle, parallelogram, or circle, just divide the polygon into smaller triangles, polygons, and/or circles and find the areas of these pieces. A real SAT math question involving this concept will always lend itself to this solution nicely.

Circles

A circle is the set of points in a particular plane that are all equidistant from a single point, called the **center**.

> Circle O has a center at point O, and consists of all the points in one plane that are 5 units from the center:

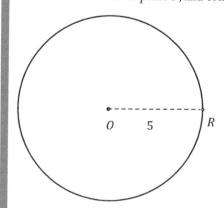

A **radius** is a line segment drawn from the center point of a circle to the edge of the circle.

> In circle O above, $\overline{OR}$ is a radius because it runs from the center of the circle (O) to the edge of the circle at point R.

All the radii of a circle have the same length, since all the points on the circle are the same distance from the center point.

A **diameter** is a line segment drawn from one edge of a circle, through the center of the circle, all the way to the opposite edge.

$\overline{LR}$ is a diameter of circle O because it starts at one edge of the circle, stretches through the center of the circle, and stops at the opposite edge of the circle.

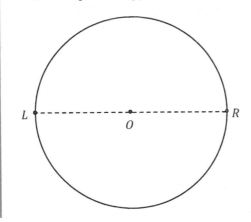

Because a diameter can be broken into two opposite radii, a diameter always has a length equal to twice the radius of the circle. A diameter of a circle is the longest line segment that can be drawn through the circle.

The perimeter of a circle is called the **circumference**.

The formulas for area of a circle ($A = \pi r^2$) and circumference of a circle ($C = 2\pi r$) appear in the beginning of all real SAT Math sections, so there's no need to memorize them if you don't already know them. (In each formula, r represents the radius of the circle.)

A **tangent** is a line that intersects a circle at only one point. A tangent is perpendicular to the radius ending at the shared point.

Circle O has a tangent line $\overline{TS}$ that intersects the circle at point R, and is perpendicular to radius OR.

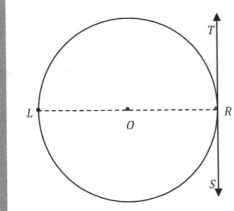

An **arc** is a portion of a circle that is measured in degrees, like an angle. We can measure an arc by drawing radii to the endpoints of the arc, and then measuring the angle formed by the radii at the center of the circle.

Circle O has a 90° arc $\overset{\frown}{PR}$, whose measure we can find by measuring the angle formed by radius PO and radius RO.

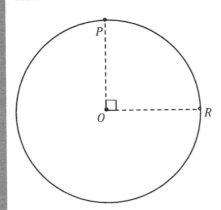

Two points on the circumference of a circle can define two different arcs. One arc is the shorter distance between the two points, while the other arc is the longer distance between the two points. The context in the problem often makes it clear which arc is relevant to the question. When the context isn't sufficient, we can use the term **minor arc** to refer to the arc that covers the shorter distance between the two points, and **major arc** to refer to the arc that covers the longer distance between the two points.

Minor arc $\widehat{YZ}$ measures 135°. Major arc $\widehat{YZ}$ measures 225°.

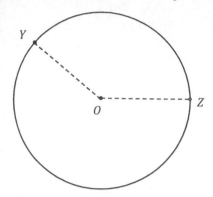

A **central angle** is an angle whose vertex is the center of a circle and whose sides are radii of that circle

In the previous figure, $\angle YOZ$ is a central angle whose measure is 135°.

A **chord** is a line segment whose ends are points on the circumference of a circle. Note that a diameter is a chord that passes through the center of the circle.

$\overline{ST}$ is a chord on circle O. $\overline{DE}$ is a diameter of circle O, because $\overline{DE}$ is a chord that passes through the center of circle O.

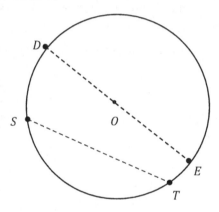

An **inscribed angle** is an angle created by two chords that meet on one end to form a vertex. We can "move" the vertex of an inscribed angle anywhere along the circumference the circle, and the measure of the inscribed angle will remain unchanged as long as the other endpoints of the angle don't move.

$\angle FGH$ is an inscribed angle in circle O. $\angle FKH$ is another inscribed angle in circle O. $\angle FGH$ and $\angle FKH$ have the same degree measure because they are inscribed angles of the same circle, and they share the endpoints F and H.

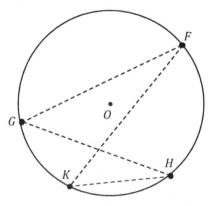

The degree measure of an inscribed angle is half the degree measure of a central angle with the same endpoints.

The angle measure of $\angle FGH$ is half the angle measure of $\angle FOH$ because $\angle FGH$ is an inscribed angle in circle O and $\angle FOH$ is a central angle in circle O and they share the endpoints F and H.

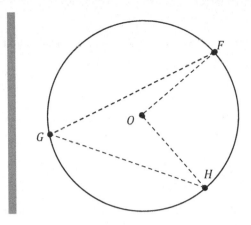

A **sector** is a portion of a circle defined by the center of the circle and two points on the circle, kind of like a slice of pizza. We can find the area of a sector by finding the area of the entire circle, and then multiplying by the fraction of the circle represented by the sector.

Let's find the area of the shaded sector. Circle O has a radius of 4, so the area of circle O is πr^2, or $\pi(4)^2$, or 16π. The shaded sector has a central angle of $135°$, so the sector represents $\frac{135°}{360°}$ of the total area of the circle. That means the area of the sector is $16\pi \times \frac{135°}{360°}$, or 6π.

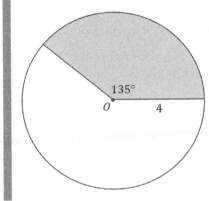

The **standard equation for a circle** with a center at the origin and a radius of r is $x^2 + y^2 = r^2$

The above equation is for a circle with a center at the origin. A circle whose center isn't at the origin can be expressed like this:

$$(x - h)^2 + (y - k)^2 = r^2$$

The circle described by the above equation will have a center at (h, k).

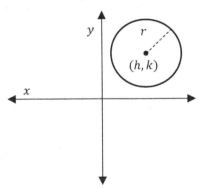

Sometimes, to get an equation for a circle into the above form, we'll need to complete the square. See the section on completing the square under "Polynomials" earlier in this Toolbox on page 181 for more information.

Solid Geometry

On the SAT, solid geometry may involve cubes, rectangular solids, prisms, cylinders, cones, spheres, or pyramids.

All necessary volume formulas will be given to you, so there's no need to memorize them.

The surface area of a solid is the sum of the areas of its faces (except for spheres or other "rounded" solids, whose surface areas won't be tested on the SAT unless a question provides a formula for finding their surface areas).

Statistics

The **mean** or **arithmetic mean** of a set of numbers is the result you get when you add all the numbers together and then divide by the number of things that you added.

> The average of $\{4, 9, 92\}$ is 35, because $\frac{4+9+92}{3} = 35$.

The **median** of a set of numbers is the number that appears in the middle of the set when all the numbers in the set are arranged from least to greatest.

> The median of $\{4, 9, 92\}$ is 9, because when we arrange the three numbers from least to greatest, 9 is in the middle.

If there is an even number of elements in the set, then the median of that set is the arithmetic mean of the two numbers in the middle of the set when the elements of the set are arranged from least to greatest.

> The median of $\{4, 9, 11, 92\}$ is 10, because the number of elements in the set is even, and 10 is the average of the two numbers in the middle of the set (which are 9 and 11).

The **mode** of a set of numbers is the number that appears most frequently in the set.

> The mode of $\{7, 7, 23, 44\}$ is 7, because 7 appears more often than any other number in the set.

The **range** of a set of numbers is the difference between the highest number in the set and the lowest number in the set.

> The range of $\{7, 7, 23, 44\}$ is 37: 44 is the largest number in the set, 7 is the smallest, and $44 - 7 = 37$.

On a graph that shows a set of data points, the **line of best fit** is a line that demonstrates the trend in the data. In the sample figure below, the points represent actual data, while the dashed line demonstrates the *trend* in the data:

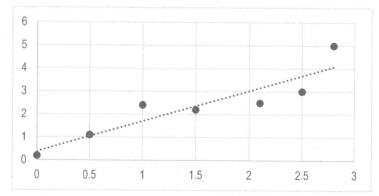

On the SAT, you'll never have to calculate a line of best fit, but you will need to understand that the line of best fit shows us the overall trend in the data—it doesn't represent *actual* data.

The closer the slope of a line of best fit is to 1, the stronger the **positive association** is between the x and y variables.

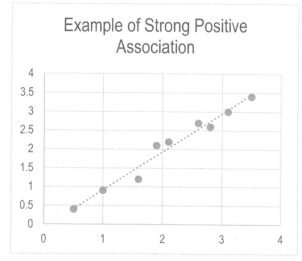

The closer the slope of a line of best fit is to -1, the stronger the **negative association** is between the x and y variables.

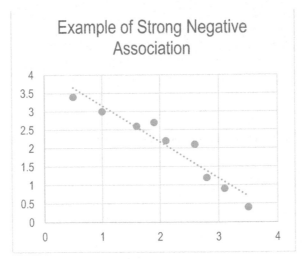

Example of Strong Negative Association

An **outlier** is a data point that doesn't follow the trend established by the other data points in the set. In a set of numbers, an outlier can simply be a number that is significantly greater than or less than the other numbers in the set.

In the set {4,5,5,7,7,8,9,31}, 31 is an outlier.

Probability

The **probability** of an event is a fraction from 0 to 1 that describes how likely the event is to happen. If the fraction is closer to 1, the event is more likely to happen; if the fraction is closer to 0, the event is less likely to happen.

To determine the fraction, you first calculate the total number of possible outcomes and place this number in the denominator of the fraction; then, you determine the number of outcomes that satisfy the event's requirements, and place this number in the numerator of the fraction.

The probability of rolling a 3 on a normal 6-sided die is $\frac{1}{6}$. There are 6 possible outcomes, so 6 goes in the denominator of the fraction. Out of those 6 outcomes, we only want one—the one where a 3 comes up—so 1 goes in the numerator.

The probability of rolling an odd number on a normal 6-sided die is $\frac{3}{6}$. Again, there are 6 possible numbers we might roll, so 6 is our denominator. But now, since we want any odd number, the numbers 1, 3, and 5 all satisfy the requirements of our event, so there are 3 possible outcomes that we'll be happy with—that means 3 goes in the numerator. (Notice that we can reduce the probability to $\frac{1}{2}$.)

Probability fractions can be manipulated just like any other fractions.

To find the probability of two or more events happening in a sequence, we just find the probability of each event by itself, and then multiply them by each other.

The probability of rolling double-sixes on two normal 6-sided dice is $\frac{1}{36}$, because the probability of rolling a six on either die is $\frac{1}{6}$, and $\frac{1}{6} \times \frac{1}{6} = \frac{1}{36}$.

Trigonometry

The trigonometry that you need on the SAT is relatively basic and limited. The most important things you need to know are the three basic trigonometric ratios.

You've probably learned the three basic ratios in math class with the acronym "SOHCAHTOA."

"SOH" stands for Sine = Opposite / Hypotenuse

"CAH" stands for Cosine = Adjacent / Hypotenuse

"TOA" stands for Tangent = Opposite / Adjacent

Given a right triangle:

The **hypotenuse** is the side that's opposite the right angle.

The **opposite** side is the side across from the angle whose sine, cosine, or tangent we're evaluating.

The **adjacent** side is the side that's next to the angle we're evaluating (the one that isn't the hypotenuse).

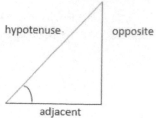

You can use these ratios to solve for the lengths of sides or the measure of angles.

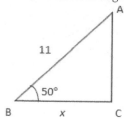

In the figure above, we're given the measure of an angle and the length of the hypotenuse. We can set up an expression for x, the adjacent side length, because we know that the cosine of an angle is equal to the length of the adjacent side divided by the length of the hypotenuse.

In this example, $cos\ 50° = \frac{x}{11}$, so that means $11(cos\ 50°) = x$.

In the context of trigonometry, you may see angles measured in degrees or radians. **Radians** are just another way to measure the size of an angle, and are usually expressed using π. $360° = 2\pi$ radians.

When you use your calculator to evaluate trigonometric expressions, always make sure your calculator is in the correct mode! If the expression uses degrees, your calculator should be in degree mode. If the expression uses radians, your calculator should be in radian mode.

The Unit Circle

The unit circle is a mathematical construct at the heart of trigonometry. It has many interesting applications in mathematical theory, but we're not concerned with those applications for the purposes of the SAT Math section. In fact, questions on the SAT don't require us to know anything about the unit circle—still, it sometimes happens that understanding the unit circle will allow us to answer a question more quickly. For these reasons, our discussion of the unit circle will be limited to the following:

1. giving a formal definition of the unit circle

2. explaining how the various trig functions can be evaluated for a given angle on the unit circle

3. explaining the difference between measuring angles in radians and degrees

The unit circle is a circle drawn in the xy-coordinate plane with its center at $(0, 0)$ and a radius of 1 unit. The unit circle therefore passes through the points $(1, 0)$, $(0, 1)$, $(-1, 0)$, and $(0, -1)$:

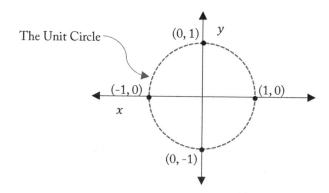

We can use the unit circle to determine the trig values for a given angle by taking the following steps.

1. Lay the angle over the unit circle in the following way:

   a. the vertex of the angle goes on the point $(0, 0)$

   b. one leg of the angle extends along the positive portion of the x-axis.

   c. the angle's other leg opens upward, counter-clockwise. If the angle is greater than $180°$, then it opens past the point $(-1, 0)$ and towards the point $(0, -1)$.

2. Note the point where the leg from part (c) intercepts the unit circle:

- The cosine of the angle is the *x*-coordinate of the point in Step 2.
- The sine of the angle is the *y*-coordinate of the point in Step 2.
- All other trig values for the angle can be calculated from the sine and cosine.

Let's see how we could find the trig values for a 60° angle using the unit circle. To do this, we start by imagining that we're placing the angle over the unit circle in the way we just described:

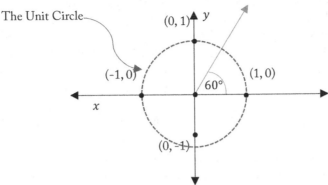

The *x*-coordinate of the point of intersection is the angle's cosine, and the *y*-coordinate of the point of intersection is the angle's sine. As we can see, the sine of a 60° angle is approximately 0.866, and the cosine is 0.5. These two values allow us to determine the value of tangent for the angle as well:

$$\text{Tangent } 60° = (\text{sine } 60°/\text{cosine } 60°) \approx \frac{0.866}{0.5} \approx 1.732$$

Conclusion

We've just covered all the math concepts that the College Board will allow itself to cover on the SAT. As I mentioned at the beginning of the Toolbox, it's important to keep in mind that simply knowing these concepts is not enough to guarantee a good score on the SAT. It's much more important to focus on the design of the SAT Math section and learn to take apart challenging questions.

The Basics of Surveys and Sampling

Some SAT Math questions may discuss surveys and samples from a basic scientific standpoint, so it's important for you to have a simple understanding of how those things work.

Scientists test a sample of something when they want to know some information about a larger whole, but they don't have the time or resources to test the entire whole. The basic idea behind sampling is that we assume the properties of the sample are roughly the same as the properties of the whole.

For example, if we want to know what the water is like in a certain lake, then we might dip a bucket in the lake, and test the water in the bucket—in this case, the lake would be the "whole," and the water in the bucket would be the "sample."

As another example, if we wanted to know the opinions of the people in a whole state, we might survey the opinions of a hundred people who live in that state. Here, the state would be the "whole," and the hundred people we asked would be the "sample."

The potential issue with sampling a whole, from a scientific standpoint, is that we have to make sure the sample has a good chance of representing the attributes of the whole, or else the results we get from the sample won't be reliable indicators of what's going on with the whole.

Again, let's use the example of trying to sample the water in a lake. If we just fill a bucket with lake water while we're standing on the shore, is the water in the bucket likely to be an accurate representation of all the water in the entire lake? Well, probably not—we might expect that water at different depths in the lake would have different properties, for one thing; if the lake is pretty large, then we might also expect that different regions of the lake might be affected differently by forces like weather, pollution, currents, and so on. So if we really wanted to get an accurate representation of the entire lake, we might decide to sample multiple bucketfuls of lake water from a variety of depths and locations in the lake.

Or, again, if we're taking a survey of the opinions of the people in a state, then we might decide that we need to contact a large number of the inhabitants of the state; we might also decide to contact people in different parts of the state, at different times of day, and so on, to give ourselves the best chance of interacting with a sample of the state that would accurately represent the whole state. On the other hand, if we only survey ten people who are all standing in line for the same movie at the same time, then we'd run a risk of having a very biased sample, since all of our survey respondents would be likely to have similar interests and daily routines, which means there would be a good chance we'd be leaving out a lot of other people with different interests and routines, who might have different opinions.

As you might imagine, the statistical principles of sampling have been worked out by mathematicians to a fairly high degree of precision, and the general principles and formulas related to sampling have been more or less settled for a while now. But the SAT won't ask you to know any of those formulas or statistical processes. All you'll really need to know are the following two ideas:

- A sample should include as many different parts of the whole as possible, to maximize the chance that it will accurately reflect the whole.

- Larger samples are generally more reliable than smaller samples.

If you understand those two ideas, you'll be able to handle any questions on the SAT that relate to the reliability of samples.

Special Technique: Understanding how Variables, Coefficients, Exponents, and Constants can Affect a Function

The College Board generally includes a few questions per test that ask us to identify the role of a particular variable or constant in a function that models a real-life situation. For example, a question might tell you that the cost, C, to rent a car for d days is represented by the function $C = 45d + 10$. Then the question might ask what a particular part of that function model represents, such as the number 45 in this example.

In this section, we'll discuss the most effective ways to answer these kinds of questions. We'll start with a little background on the math ideas involved, and then we'll address SAT-specific issues that will be relevant on test day.

Math Background

Before we can discuss the ways that different parts of a function interact, we need to have a quick discussion about the basic differences among variables, coefficients, and constants. You may have covered some of these topics in your math classes, but we need to discuss them as precisely as we can, so I'll go through a quick refresher now to make sure we're on the same page. We'll use the example function we just mentioned for reference:

$$\overset{\text{Variable}}{C} = 45\overset{\text{Variable}}{d} + \underset{\text{Constant}}{10}$$
$$\underset{\text{Coefficient}}{}$$

- A **variable** is a placeholder (typically represented by a letter like x or y) that can have different values in a function. In the example above, C and d are variables; the rest of the function demonstrates the relationship that must exist between any valid (C, d) pair that satisfies the function.

- A **coefficient** is a numerical value that's multiplied by a variable. In the example above, the number 45 is a coefficient; it indicates that the value represented by d in this function is multiplied by 45. (Remember that even when a function model includes a term like $\frac{x}{4}$, we can think of that as the variable x multiplied by a coefficient of $\frac{1}{4}$, because $\frac{x}{4} = \frac{1}{4}x$.)

- A **constant** is a numerical value that's added to (or subtracted from) an expression. In the example above, the number 10 is a constant; it indicates that we add 10 to the expression $45d$ in this function.

The Effects of Variables, Coefficients, and Constants on Function Models

We'll see questions on test day that provide us with functions that model the behavior of real-life situations, such as a function for determining the cost of a project for a business, or a function that tells us how much interest will be earned on a deposit in a bank. In a moment, we'll talk about test-specific considerations for these kinds of function-modeling questions. Right now, I want to talk about general concepts that apply when we try to create functions to model the real world.

As we did before, I'll focus this discussion on the individual aspects of variables, coefficients, and constants. Let's get started.

The role of variables in function models

A variable in a function model takes the place of a real-world quantity; the whole purpose of a function model is to show us the unchanging relationship among real-world quantities that are represented by variables.

Function models are often written so that they seem to have a clear "output" variable, and one or more clear "input" variables. The output variable is usually isolated on one side of the equation, and the input variable(s) can be found on the other side of the equation, along with any necessary coefficients and constants that show us how the input variable can be used to produce the output variable.

Let's take another look at our previous example formula for the cost in dollars of renting a car, $C = 45d + 10$, where the variables correspond to the following real-world values:

- C is the cost of the rental, in dollars
- d is the number of days that the car is rented

We can see that this formula is telling us that we can find the overall cost of renting the car if we multiply the number of days (d) by 45, and then add that result to the number 10. In this case, the function is expressed in a format that isolates C on one side of the equation, so the output variable is C (the overall cost of the rental) and the input variable is d (the number of days of the rental).

I'll repeat this because it's important: as we continue to explore how function modeling works, we want to keep in mind that functions use numbers and mathematical relationships to demonstrate the unchanging relationships among variables; the variables themselves can represent any numbers that satisfy the function, but the parts of the function that show the relationships among the variables don't change.

The role of coefficients in function models

Coefficients in a function are used to indicate that we need to take a particular value and multiply or divide it by a consistent amount.

Coefficients often indicate a consistent, repeated increment, such as a daily, monthly, or yearly increase in a number. In our example function that models the cost of a car rental, $C = 45d + 10$, the coefficient 45 is multiplied by the variable d. So for every additional day of the car rental, the cost in dollars, C, increases by 45.

The role of constants in function models

Constants are used to reflect scenarios in which a value always needs to be adjusted up or down by a certain unchanging amount. For this reason, constants are often used to represent things like one-time costs in a model involving money. In our example function that models the cost of a car rental, $C = 45d + 10$, the constant 10 represents a one-time cost charged by the car rental company. This means the car rental company will add a single $10 charge to the cost of a car rental no matter how long the rental is—whether the car is rented for 1 day or 20 days, the one-time $10 charge will be part of the cost.

A Few More Examples of Function Models with Variables, Coefficients, and Constants

Let's take a quick look at a few more examples of function models so you can see these ideas at work in other situations.

Cost of an international phone call

The cost of an international phone call could be modeled by the function $P = 2m + 3$, where P represents the cost of the phone call in dollars and m is the length of the call in minutes. We multiply the variable m by the coefficient 2, and then add the result to the constant 3 to find the value of the variable P. In plain English, this model tells us that the cost of an international phone call is $3 to start plus an additional $2 per minute—so a 5-minute phone call will cost 13 dollars, because $2(5) + 3 = 13$.

Number of members joining a new gym

The number of members joining a new gym in its first month of business could be modeled by the function $M = 5d$, where M represents the total number of members and d is the number of days since the gym has opened. We multiply the variable d by the coefficient 5, and the result is the number of members the gym has, M. In plain English, this model tells us that in its first month of business, a new gym adds 5 new members every day—so, after 9 days, the gym will have 45 members, because $5(9) = 45$.

True temperature compared to measured temperature

The temperature of a room could be modeled by the function $T = r - 10$, where T represents the true temperature of the room and r is the temperature reading given by a faulty thermometer in the room. We subtract the constant 10 from the variable r, and the result is the true temperature of the room, T. In plain English, this model tells us that a faulty thermometer gives us a reading that's 10 degrees warmer than the actual temperature of the room—so when the thermometer shows a reading of 81 degrees, the temperature in the room is actually 71 degrees, because $(81) - 10 = 71$.

Exponents in Function Models Generally Show Compounded Change over Time

Sometimes, function models on the SAT will involve **exponents**. These exponents often appear in function models that represent growth or decay, such as the growth of an interest-earning bank account, or the decay of a radioactive material.

The Logical Basis for Exponents

As an example of how exponents can be used in these situations, let's imagine that someone deposits $100 in a bank account, and every year that deposit will grow by 7%. To find the amount of money in the account after one year, we multiply the original deposit of $100 by 107%, which is equal to 1.07. The result is $107, because $100(1.07) = 107.

If we wanted to find the amount of money in the account after 2 years, then we'd multiply the number that we just found by 1.07 again: another year has passed, which means the amount in the account increases by another 7%. So we multiply the original deposit of $100 by 1.07 to represent the first year of growth, and then we multiply by 1.07 *again* to represent the second year of growth. The result is $100(1.07)(1.07)$, which is equal to $114.49.

Notice that after two years, we found the interest with the expression $100(1.07)(1.07)$, which is the same as $100(1.07)^2$. The amount in the account after 3 years would be $100(1.07)^3$, and the amount in the account after 10 years would be $100(1.07)^{10}$, and so on. The exponent tells us how many times to multiply the percentage of growth (or decay) by the original amount, which shows how long the growth or decay has been going on.

So, on the SAT, exponents in function models that represent growth or decay will indicate the amount of time that the growth or decay has been going on.

Function Models with Exponents Produce Curved Lines

Let's return to the example of the bank account that starts with a balance of $100 and grows by 7% each year. As we saw above, the new balance after the first year is $107, which means that the total change in the balance after the first year was $7. After the second year, the balance has increased from $107 to $114.49, which means that the change in the balance from the end of the first year to the end of the second year was $7.49 . . . which is a different amount of change than we saw after the first year alone! In other words, the exponential nature of the change causes the actual amount of the difference to be different for each new time period. (This happens because an exponential function involves multiplying by an amount that's always changing: in our example, we multiply 1.07 by 100 in the first year and then multiply 1.07 by 107 in the second year, and so on.)

So the influence of an exponent on a function model is to create a different amount of change in the function for each new time period, because exponential change involves multiplying by an amount that changes over time.

This means that the graphs of functions with exponential components will involve curved lines instead of straight lines when the horizontal axis is evenly divided. The curve of these graph reflects the fact that the amount of change is different for each time period, instead of being the same, as we'd see in a function without an exponent.

As long as we understand that, and we understand what's been discussed in this section, we should be able to handle any real SAT practice question involving a function model and an exponent.

Applying this Knowledge on Test Day

Questions about function models usually show up in the multiple-choice portion of the SAT Math test. The prompt typically describes some kind of real-life situation, provides a function to model that real-life situation, and then asks a question like:

- "What does h represent in the function?"
- "What is the meaning of the value 12 in this equation?"

For SAT Math Questions Without Graphs

If the question is text-based, then all you need to remember is the stuff we've talked about so far:

- Variables are placeholders to represent numbers that can be plugged into the function to produce a result.
- Coefficients indicate that a variable is always multiplied by the same amount; they often apply when we're modeling something connected to recurring costs, consistent ratios, and so on.
- Constants indicate that an expression needs to be adjusted up or down by a fixed, one-time amount. They're often used to model things like one-time costs or a starting value.
- Exponents in function models on the SAT are used to model growth or decay, which will often be in the context of money accruing interest in a bank, or a radioactive substance decaying. The exponent will tell us how many times to multiply the original amount by the rate of growth or decay, based on the amount of time of the growth or decay.

Using these ideas and their underlying concepts will allow you to understand how the relationships among the variables in the function are being used to model the situation described in the prompt. For examples of how this approach can be used on test day, see the walkthroughs for the following questions:

- SAT Practice Test #1, section 3, question 4 (our walkthrough is on page 234 of this Black Book)
- SAT Practice Test #1, section 4, question 15 (our walkthrough is on page 322 of this Black Book)
- SAT Practice Test #2, section 3, question 3 (our walkthrough is on page 254 of this Black Book)
- SAT Practice Test #2, section 4, question 1 (our walkthrough is on page 344 of this Black Book)

For SAT Math Questions that Include Graphs

Of course, if the question involves graphs, then you'll need to consider the way that variables, coefficients, constants, and exponents can affect the graph of a function model.

Graphs of Linear Function Models

Let's discuss those ideas in the context of the car rental function we analyzed earlier in this article. That function was $C = 45d + 10$, and it tells us the cost, C, in dollars of renting a car for d days.

When we graph that function, we get the following (note that the scales on the two axes are different from one another):

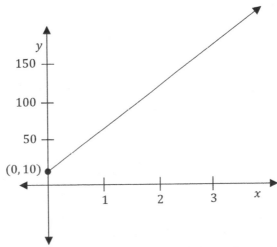

We might notice that the function $C = 45d + 10$ looks a lot like the slope-intercept form of a function, $y = mx + b$. In fact, if we substitute y for C and x for d, to reflect the idea that we've graphed C on the vertical axis and d on the horizontal axis, we get $y = 45x +$

10. This lets us see right away that the slope of the line is 45, and the y-intercept is $(0, 10)$. (For more on slope-intercept form, see "Slope-intercept form" on page 191 in the Math Toolbox in this Black Book.)

(We'll find that function models on the SAT are often written in $y = mx + b$ form, or can be easily rewritten in that form. That makes determining the slope and y-intercept quick and easy. But function modeling questions on the SAT don't just ask for the slope or y-intercept of a function. Instead, they ask what that slope or y-intercept *represents*.)

In this example:

- d is the input variable, so d-values are plotted on the horizontal axis of the graph,

- C is the output variable, so C-values are plotted on the vertical axis of the graph,

- 45 is the slope of the line, which represents the daily increase in the cost of the rental—each day, the cost increases by $45—and

- 10 is the y-intercept, which represents the one-time cost applied to each rental, without considering the daily rate—each rental includes a charge of $10, regardless of length.

Graphs of Function Models with Exponents

As we noted previously, real SAT Math questions that ask us to analyze the graph of a function model that involves an exponent will include a curved line, rather than straight line like the one we just saw in the graph above. On the SAT, questions that test this concept are generally more direct than questions that might ask about the elements of a linear graph; questions about exponential graphs rely almost totally on the fact that exponential change involves a curve. So there's not much point in us dissecting a made-up example of the graph of an exponential model in the same way that we just dissected the graph of a linear model, or in the way that your math or science teachers might cover the graphs of exponential functions in school. Instead, I'll just refer you to question 15 on section 4 of SAT Practice Test #4 as one example of how the SAT Math sections test whether you know that exponential functions produce curved graphs.

As you can see from that question, one way to find the right answer involves knowing that the function $y = ax^b$ would create a *curve* that decreased from left to right under the conditions in the prompt, because it would involve a negative exponent. (For more on this question, including a calculator-based approach that would require even less math knowledge than just knowing that exponential functions create curved graphs, see its walkthrough on page 412 of this Black Book.)

Conclusion

We need to get comfortable understanding which specific components of function models correspond to the different aspects of the real-life situations modeled by those functions. This concept will definitely come up on test day in a variety of ways.

Please review this section carefully until it feels comfortable—and most importantly, make sure to review the selected SAT practice questions listed above, and to work through other real SAT practice questions from the College Board that involve function modeling to see how these ideas will appear on the test.

Special Technique: Backsolving

One common tactic for trying to beat multiple-choice math questions in school is called "backsolving," which is basically what you do when you take numbers from the answer choices and plug them into the prompt to see which choice makes the prompt valid, instead of setting up a formal algebraic solution and then arriving at one of the answer choices on your own.

Many test-takers are aware that backsolving exists, but most don't realize the extent to which we can use it on this test, so I strongly recommend that you pay attention to this section, even if you think you're already familiar with backsolving!

There are two main kinds of backsolving that we can do:

- Backsolving when there are no variables in the answer choices
- Backsolving when the answer choices include variables

Backsolving when there are No Variables in the Answer Choices

This type of backsolving is useful on some questions that ask for the value of a variable in a given expression. We can often just take the numbers from the answer choices and plug them into the given equation to see which one makes a true statement.

You can see an example of this type of backsolving in SAT Practice Test #1, section 3, question 1. This question gives us an expression involving x and k, tells us that $k = 3$, and then asks for the value of x. One way to approach this question is to plug in the given k-value, then set x equal to each answer choice in turn—the answer choice that creates a true statement in the prompt is the correct answer. To see the full solution, read the walkthrough of this question on page 232.

Here are a few more examples of official SAT questions whose solutions can involve this type of backsolving:

- SAT Practice Test #1, section 3, question 9 (our walkthrough is on page 238 of this Black Book)
- SAT Practice Test #1, section 4, question 8 (our walkthrough is on page 316 of this Black Book)
- SAT Practice Test #1, section 4, question 11 (our walkthrough is on page 319 of this Black Book)

Backsolving when the Answer Choices Include Variables

This type of backsolving can get a little more complicated, but it's still a valuable tactic on some questions. When the answer choices are expressions involving variables, we can pick an arbitrary value to plug in for the variable in the expressions from the answer choices, and see which expression gives the result that the question is looking for.

You can see an example of this type of backsolving in SAT Practice Test #1, section 3, question 5. That question gives us an expression involving x and y and asks us to pick the choice with an equivalent expression. One way to solve this question is as follows:

1. Choose arbitrary values for x and y.
2. Plug these arbitrary values into the original expression from the prompt, and determine the numerical value of the expression.
3. Plug the same x- and y-values into each expression in the choices, and determine the numerical values of each expression.
4. See which choice yields the same numerical value as the expression in the prompt. That choice is the right answer.

(For the full solution to this question, read its walkthrough on page 234 in this Black Book.)

There are two things we must keep in mind when backsolving like this:

1. **Any value we decide to pick for the variable must meet the requirements given in the question.**

   For example, if the question says x must be greater than 6, then we have to pick a value greater than 6 for x; we can't pick 5. If the question requires a negative integer, then we pick a negative integer. And so on. You get the idea—if the number we use to backsolve doesn't meet the requirements given by the prompt, then our conclusions won't be reliable. This might seem like a silly thing to point out, but I bet you'd be surprised how many times I've seen trained test-takers miss a question because they accidentally tried to backsolve with a number that didn't meet the written requirements of the prompt.

2. **We should generally avoid picking numbers that are likely to result in false positives.**

   Depending on how a question is set up, and on what number we decide to use for backsolving, it can sometimes happen that more than one answer choice will give us a result that matches the result from the expression in the prompt, just by sheer coincidence, even when two expressions aren't algebraically equivalent. I call these coincidental matches "false positives."

To understand how we might get a false positive, consider the following algebraic expressions:

$$x \qquad\qquad 2x \qquad\qquad x^3$$

If we plugged 0 into these expressions as x, we'd get the same result for all three, even though the expressions themselves aren't algebraically equivalent for all values of x. If we plugged 1 into all three expressions as x, then the first and third expressions would produce the same result as one another. On the other hand, if we plugged in 2, 3, 4, 5, or most other numbers, we'd get three different results from the three different expressions.

Generally speaking, we're more likely to produce false positives on the SAT Math sections when we backsolve with 0, 1, -1, or any number that appears in the question, so we should avoid picking those numbers when we backsolve.

But don't worry too much if you accidentally do create a false positive in your backsolving. You can fix the problem by picking another value to backsolve with, and then plugging that value into each answer choice. The correct choice will be the only one whose value matches the value from the prompt no matter which valid number is used to backsolve. (By the way, the odds are usually pretty small that you could pick two numbers in a row that would coincidentally give you a false positive when you backsolve with them.)

Since running into a false positive means you'll have to do all your backsolving work again with different numbers, you can potentially save time on test day by avoiding false positives in the first place. Again, the easiest way to prevent these kinds of issues is to make a habit of avoiding 0, 1, -1, and any number from the question when we pick an arbitrary number for backsolving.

Here are a few more examples of official SAT questions that can be backsolved, and that have variable expressions in the choices:

- SAT Practice Test #1, section 3, question 13 (my walkthrough is on page 243 of this Black Book)
- SAT Practice Test #2, section 3, question 12 (my walkthrough is on page 266 of this Black Book)
- SAT Practice Test #2, section 4, question 22 (my walkthrough is on page 359 of this Black Book)

Catching and Fixing Common Mistakes by Evaluating Every Answer Choice

As trained test-takers, we understand the importance of avoiding small mistakes on the SAT, and we know that the College Board often designs wrong answers to attract people who make those mistakes. There are two major types of mistakes that a test-taker could be likely to make when backsolving, and there's a single technique that can help us eliminate both.

The first mistake is to backsolve with a number that happens to have a unique property relative to the question, and results in more than one answer seeming to be correct. We discussed ways to avoid this situation in general above, but it can still come up on some questions even if you don't backsolve with -1, 0, or 1, or a number in the question. If there are two or three answer choices that coincidentally all work out to the same result during your backsolving, then you run the risk of accidentally selecting a wrong answer.

The second type of potential mistake is to make a small error in your calculations while you're backsolving. As you might imagine, this can easily cause an incorrect answer to seem correct (or vice-versa) if you don't realize your mistake.

We can greatly reduce the likelihood of both kinds of mistakes by making sure that we *always evaluate all the answer choices whenever we backsolve!* This will give us a better chance of noticing when more than one answer choice seems to work out to the target value. For example, if a trained test-taker is working through a backsolving solution and finds that (B) seems to be correct, she doesn't just stop working on the question and pick (B) as her answer! She continues to evaluate (C) and (D). If she finds that more than one choice results in the desired value, then she knows she needs to re-evaluate her work. It might be that she's picked a number that results in a false positive, or it might just be that she's miscalculated. In either case, one of the best ways to try to find the correct answer is to retry the backsolving with a different number plugged in. If the initial mistake was choosing a bad number, then choosing a new number will usually solve the problem, because it's unlikely that two different numbers will result in the same false positives; if the initial mistake was a miscalculation, then the test-taker will often avoid the mistake on a second approach with new values.

It's very important to commit to the idea of testing out every answer choice whenever you backsolve! This is why you'll always see me go through every answer choice whenever I use a backsolving approach in the walkthroughs in this Black Book.

What if none of the answer choices seems to work?

Of course, another type of error in the backsolving process could lead us to think that all of the answer choices are wrong, if we make a mistake when we're working with the choice that's actually correct. When this happens, we do basically the same thing we would do if we thought all the choices were wrong for any other question on the SAT: we realize that we must have made a mistake, and we decide whether it makes more sense to try again, skip the question for the time being, or guess on it.

As always, it's important to remember that our mistake might be a simple miscalculation, but it could also be something else. We might have misread something, or we might even have been wrong to think the question could be backsolved in the first place.

Conclusion

Backsolving can be a very useful technique, and it can be applied in a lot of different ways on real SAT Math questions from the College Board. The best way to get more comfortable with backsolving is to see it in action before trying it yourself, so make sure you read this Black Book's walkthroughs of the listed example questions for examples of both types of backsolving.

Make sure you keep the possibility of backsolving in mind when we discuss the Math Path in a few pages.

Rounding and Estimating on the Math Sections

Rounding and estimating are useful skills on the SAT Math sections, and the opportunities to apply them generally fall into two categories:

- questions whose prompts specifically mention rounding or estimating
- questions with answer choices that allow a trained test-taker to determine the correct answer with total confidence by using estimation, even though the prompt doesn't mention this possibility.

Let's take a look at both kinds of situations.

Questions Whose Prompts Specifically Mention Rounding or Estimating

SAT Math questions occasionally refer to the idea of approximating or estimating a number. There are two ways we can choose to answer these kinds of questions:

- We can calculate the exact answer to the question and then pick the answer choice that's closest to it
- We can roughly estimate the correct answer from the beginning, and pick the answer choice that's closest to our rough estimation.

The first approach is probably pretty self-explanatory: since the process of estimating involves arriving at a number that's close to a real value without actually matching it, we just figure out the exact answer to the question and then pick the answer choice that's closest to it. This approach is often easiest for test-takers who aren't comfortable with concepts like rounding, or with doing quick calculations in their heads.

The second approach is to estimate an answer like the question describes. The process of estimating on the SAT usually involves the following steps:

- Note the general level of detail and exactness in the prompt and the answer choices, to get an idea of how precise you need to be when you do your estimating. If the choices are numbers that are far apart from each other, like 2, 30, 170, and 300, then you can probably estimate pretty loosely and still find the correct answer. On the other hand, if there are smaller relative gaps between the numbers (such as with the numbers 10, 25, 35, and 40), then you may need to be a little more precise with your rounding.
- Round off the relevant numbers so you're dealing with only one or two digits of non-zero numbers (for example, round the number 12,477 to 12,000 or 10,000, depending on the precision required by the question). If a question involves percentages, then consider rounding the percentages to the nearest 10 or 25 (for example, round 79% to 75% or 80%, depending on the context of the question).
- Do the calculations required in the question with the rounded numbers from the previous step. For example, if a question initially asks you to estimate 53% of $17,854, then you might be able to identify the correct answer by calculating 50% of $18,000, and identifying the only answer choice that's close to the result, $9,000.
- Pick the answer choice that's close to the result you got from working with your rounded numbers. If more than one answer choice seems to be close to your estimated result, then there are two possibilities—either you performed your calculations incorrectly, or you weren't precise enough when you rounded.

For examples of how rounding can appear on test day, see the walkthroughs for the following questions:

- SAT Practice Test #1, section 4, question 10 (my walkthrough is on page 318 of this Black Book)
- SAT Practice Test #1, section 4, question 12 (my walkthrough is on page 320 of this Black Book)
- SAT Practice Test #1, section 4, question 22 (my walkthrough is on page 329 of this Black Book)
- SAT Practice Test #1, section 4, question 25 (my walkthrough is on page 334 of this Black Book)

As you become familiar with this general process of rounding and calculating as a rough way to identify the correct answers to questions, you'll begin to realize that this approach can sometimes be successfully applied even when the College Board doesn't specifically mention it, which leads us to our next topic . . .

Questions that Allow a Trained Test-Taker to Find the Right Answer through Estimation, even though the Prompt doesn't Mention this Possibility

As trained test-takers, we'll notice that it's sometimes possible to use rounding and estimation to eliminate all of the wrong answer choices on an SAT Math question without actually doing the calculation that the question seems to be asking us to do, allowing us to identify the correct answer with total certainty in pretty short order.

In other words, based on the context of a given question, we can sometimes tell for sure that one of the answer choices is right, without doing the math that most untrained test-takers would do to approach the question. This can be useful for two reasons:

- It can save us the time and frustration of doing the calculation that the question seems to be asking for.

- It can often give us a very high degree of confidence that we're right, because the techniques for ruling out some answer choices are often more simple than the calculation we would have to do otherwise.

There are potentially many different scenarios that might allow us to rule out an answer choice, because official SAT Math questions can combine basic math concepts in a wide variety of ways, as we've discussed. But the most common way to rule out answer choices is to use estimation or rounding and determine that the correct answer must be above or below a certain value. Once we know that the correct answer must fall within a certain range (or outside of a certain range, depending on the question), we can sometimes rule out some of the answer choices if they're too small or too large.

Practice SAT #1, section 4, question 3 is one example of a real SAT practice question from the College Board that allows us to rule out three wrong answer choices without doing the math that seems to be required by the question. The relevant diagram doesn't include a note that says it isn't drawn to scale, we so we know the diagram must be drawn exactly to scale. The question asks for the measure of ∠2, and we can see that the measure of ∠2 is clearly larger than 90°. Three choices are smaller than 90°, so we can rule them out. The only remaining choice is the correct answer. (For a detailed discussion of this question, see its walkthrough on page 313 in this Black Book.)

We can see a similar use of this general technique in this Black Book's walkthroughs for the following questions, among others:

- SAT Practice Test #1, section 4, question 7 (my walkthrough is on page 315 of this Black Book)
- SAT Practice Test #2, section 4, question 2 (my walkthrough is on page 345 of this Black Book)
- SAT Practice Test #2, section 4, question 3 (my walkthrough is on page 346 of this Black Book)

Of course, you won't be able to use this technique on every question you see on test day. In fact, you probably won't be able to apply it more than a few times on any one test. But it's still a good idea to keep this kind of approach in mind, because it will save you a lot of time and hassle when you do get the opportunity to use it. As you continue to read through this Black Book and practice on your own, you'll continue to improve your instincts for figuring out the best way to approach a given question. And if you do accidentally try a technique like this on a question where it can't be used, you'll find that you've only lost a couple of seconds, and you can continue working on a different approach to the question.

Unwritten Rules of SAT Math

The rules for SAT Math problems are pretty much the same whether you're looking at multiple choice questions or student-produced response questions, and whether the question allows the use of a calculator or not.

SAT Math Rule 1: You Need to Know the Words in Order to be Certain of the Answer.

On the Reading section and the Writing and Language section of the SAT, you can usually "fake" your way past a few exotic words in a particular question by using the "bad connection" technique, as we discuss in the Reading section training of this Black Book. But if an SAT Math question asks you about the number of zeros a function has, then there's typically no way to answer the question without knowing what zeros and functions are, because SAT Math questions typically don't provide you with context in the way that questions on the rest of the SAT might. You pretty much have to know the terminology, which is why we discussed all the concepts in the Math Toolbox. If you're practicing with real SAT questions from the College Board and you run into a math term you're not familiar with and it keeps you from answering a question with confidence, then it's a good idea to make sure you learn what the term means, because there's a chance you could see it again on test day. (Sometimes we only need a general understanding of the term, as we see in question 23 on section 4 of SAT Practice Test #4. In that question, we need to understand the term "standard deviation" from the answer choices. As you can see in the walkthrough for that question on page 417 of this Black Book, you don't actually have to be able to calculate standard deviation, or even have a detailed understanding of the concept—but you still need a rough idea of what the term means in order to answer the question correctly.)

SAT Math Rule 2: Formulas aren't as Important as you Probably Think.

While the SAT Math section does occasionally require you to use a memorized formula in order to answer a question with confidence, you'll find that most of the difficulty you encounter on the SAT Math section is related to things like reading carefully and making sure you avoid small errors in calculation. Also remember that the test provides a resource box at the beginning of each Math section, which contains a lot of the formulas that might be relevant to questions you encounter in the section—in fact, that resource box contains every formula related to area or volume that the SAT can require you to know. So if you're looking at a real SAT question that asks you to work with the area or volume of a figure, then there must be some way to work out the answer without using any area or volume formulas besides the ones in that box.

SAT Math Rule 3: SAT Calculations are Relatively Easy.

All SAT Math content is relatively "easy" in the way that most high school students think of easy math.

In advanced high school math problems, the solution to a single problem might involve complex graphs, trigonometric expressions, fraction bars, and π; complex problems tend to have complex answers.

On the SAT, the solution is much more likely to be a plain old number like 2, because the actual calculations that we do for an SAT Math question are usually basic (such as multiplying two single-digit integers or using algebra to isolate a variable). The most challenging part of an SAT Math question will typically be figuring out what the prompt is asking you to do in the first place; actually doing the proper calculations usually isn't too hard after that.

(If that sounds a little confusing right now, don't worry—it'll make a lot more sense after we look at some examples of real SAT Math questions together in a few pages.)

SAT Math Rule 4: The Figures are Usually Accurate . . . and you can Use this Fact in Ways that Often Surprise Untrained Test-Takers.

The College Board does tell us that every drawing or diagram is done to scale EXCEPT when the test specifically says otherwise. What the College Board doesn't point out is that you can often identify the correct answer to a question with a diagram just by noticing that all but one of the answer choices are obviously too large or too small to fit with the scale of the diagram. As one example of this kind of question, consider question 6 on section 3 of Practice SAT Test #2—you can see the walkthrough for that question on page 257 of this Black Book.

Even if it's not possible to answer a question outright based on a diagram, we can still use this rule as a way to verify that our calculations are probably correct: if our final answer doesn't make sense within the scale of a given diagram, then we know that we must have made a mistake. We'll see several examples of these kinds of questions in the SAT Math walkthroughs later.

SAT Math Rule 5: Limited Subject-Matter.

In the Math Toolbox, we went over every single mathematical concept you'll need for test day. You'll probably find that you're familiar with most of them, if not all of them, and the rest are relatively straightforward to learn. Once you know these concepts, you can rest assured that they will be enough to answer *every single real SAT Math question*, even if that might not seem to be the case when you first read the question. In fact, we'll often find that what actually makes a challenging question hard is the process of figuring out how the question relates back to the limited list of relatively basic math concepts that the College Board allows itself to cover on the SAT.

SAT Math Rule 6: 30 Seconds or Less.

Perhaps the most important rule of all, from a strategic perspective, is that EVERY SINGLE REAL SAT MATH QUESTION can be answered in less than 30 seconds if we find the most efficient possible solution.

But this doesn't mean that you're going to get the question wrong if it takes you longer, or even that you should be trying to answer each question in under 30 seconds! It just means that you aren't going about answering the question in the easiest way if your solution takes you longer than half a minute. When you're looking for a way to solve the problem, just remember that answering every single question can be simple, no matter how complicated the question may seem at first. When we run into questions we can't figure out at first—which is guaranteed to happen to everyone—we need to train ourselves so that our instincts are to look for ways to make things simpler, not more complex.

SAT Math Rule 7: Questions Provide all Necessary Information to Find a Correct Answer with Total Certainty . . . Even if one of the Choices Says, "The Value cannot be Determined from the Information Given."

In order for the SAT Math sections to serve their purpose and generate reliable data on test-takers' performance every year, the answer to each question has to be totally objective and beyond dispute—just as we saw with the Reading section, and just as we'll see in the Writing and Language section. That means each SAT Math question must include all the information necessary for a test-taker to choose the correct answer choice with total certainty, no matter how much it might sometimes seem like the only way to find the answer is with a lucky guess.

And this rule still holds true even if one of the answer choices says something like "The value cannot be determined from the information given." If the correct answer is that the value cannot be determined from the given information, then the question must provide enough information for us to be sure that the "cannot be determined" answer is correct—in other words, there will still be a concrete reason based on the information provided that the value the question asks for can't be determined.

So the key thing to keep in mind is that the SAT Math section will never, ever present you with a question that can't be answered with total certainty.

(By the way, don't worry too much about SAT Math questions that include a choice saying the prompt doesn't provide enough information for a definitive answer. They only appear rarely—in fact, it's likely that you won't see a single question like this on any one test. I just wanted to address them specifically because I know that some students are especially nervous about them, even though they have zero impact on most people's scores since they usually don't show up on test day. If you do see a question like that, don't get thrown off. Just remember that it still follows the rule about only having one answer choice that's mathematically valid.)

SAT Math Rule 8: Wrong Answers are There for a Reason.

The College Board doesn't just randomly generate the wrong answers that it offers you on every multiple-choice question; instead, each wrong answer is the result of certain mistakes that the College Board thinks untrained test-takers will make on a particular question.

Imagine that you try to solve an SAT Math question and end up with the number 15 as your answer. Then you look at the answer choices and see that they only include 10, 12, 18 and 24. In that case, you'd know right away that you had made a mistake on the question, and you'd be able to start over and try to solve the question correctly. From the College Board's standpoint, this would be like letting you get away with a free mistake, because you'd be able to realize you'd done something wrong, and you'd have a chance to fix it.

To keep that from happening, the College Board does its best to include wrong answers that try to anticipate the mistakes you're likely to make. So to continue the example above, if the College Board realized that a common mistake on that question would result in test-takers thinking 15 was the correct answer, then the College Board would make 15 one of the wrong answer choices. That way students who thought 15 was the answer would probably mark that answer and move on, never realizing they had made a mistake.

This might seem mean-spirited on the part of the College Board, but we can actually use it to our advantage as trained test-takers. Since the College Board tries to come up with wrong answers to tempt us into making mistakes—and since it has to do this in standardized, repetitive ways, just like everything else it does—then we can learn to use the concepts and relationships that appear in the answer choices to get an idea of what the question is actually asking about.

This will make a lot more sense after we talk about common patterns that we'll encounter in the answer choices, and after we go through some solutions to real SAT Math questions together. We'll cover some of those common patterns starting on the next page, and then we'll go through hundreds of questions from official SAT Practice Tests later in this Black Book.

Hidden Test Design Patterns of SAT Math Questions

Most of the hidden patterns on the SAT Math section have to do with using the answer choices to help you determine the most efficient ways to answer questions and check your work (remember that small mistakes can kill your chances of a good score, even if you have a very good grasp of math!).

Many students are surprised to find out that the patterns we're about to discuss appear reliably and consistently in real SAT Math questions from the College Board, because the patterns often have very little to do with actual math concepts—they're mostly related to the test-design principles required by the standardization of the test. So before we get into these patterns, I'd like to take a moment to remind you why they're a part of the SAT.

As we discussed in "The "Big Secrets" of the SAT: Simplicity, Repetition, Weirdness, and Details" on page 14 of this Black Book, it's important to remember that the SAT isn't a normal test. It has a very specific purpose and must, therefore, follow very specific rules to make sure that questions are designed to test the same skills in the same underlying ways, without actually repeating the questions word-for-word. It's also important to remember that the SAT is predominantly a multiple-choice test, and that the multiple-choice format only requires a test-taker to separate right answers from wrong answers, rather than requiring you to provide correct answers on your own. This means that the relationships among right answers and wrong answers must remain constant for all real SAT tests, because changing those relationships would involve changing the nature of the multiple-choice questions and breaking the standardization rules of the test.

So you'll definitely want to keep these things in mind as we discuss the patterns in the SAT Math section, and as you encounter real SAT Math questions in the future.

You'll find that some of the answer-choice patterns on an SAT Math question can be easily identified before you start working on a question, such as the "Halves and Doubles" pattern or the "Opposites" pattern. On the other hand, some patterns can only be identified after you've started working on a question, such as the "Right Approach, Wrong Step" pattern. We'll discuss the pre-solution patterns first, and then tackle the post-solution patterns.

Pre-Solution Patterns

These patterns reflect relationships in the answer choices that we can notice before we've even tried to attack the question.

Hidden pattern 1: Halves and doubles

Very often, one of the wrong answer choices will be twice as much as the right answer, or half as much as the right answer. This is especially true when the problem involves multiplying or dividing an amount by 2, but we'll often observe this pattern even on questions where answering the question has nothing to do with multiplying or dividing by 2. If you solve a problem and get an answer like 18, a wrong answer choice like 36 or 9 might make you more confident that you're probably right.

But remember that this pattern is an indication that you're *probably* right, not a confirmation that you're *definitely* right! Also, it's important not to get it backwards—in the same hypothetical example, the right answer might be 36 or 9, and the wrong answer might be 18, rather than the other way around. Be very aware of this useful pattern, but don't rely on it exclusively to pick an answer. For this reason, if you notice that some answer choices are half as much as other choices, then you should be especially on guard against any mistakes that might cause you to be off by a factor of 2 while you plan your attack on the question.

Hidden pattern 2: "Opposites"

You'll sometimes encounter answer choices that are opposites of other choices for the same question. For example, a question might have choices like 9 and -9, or $\frac{1}{3}$ and $-\frac{1}{3}$.

Untrained test-takers commonly lose track of negative signs when they're doing their calculations, which can cause them to come up with an answer that's the opposite of the correct answer. So you'll commonly see two answer choices that are opposites of one another, and the correct answer is slightly more likely to be one of those two choices than it is to be an answer choice whose opposite isn't present in the other choices.

But these types of opposites aren't the only "opposites" that you should look out for on test day! You might also see any of the following kinds of opposites:

- a pair of choices that are reciprocals of one another, such as $\frac{r}{k}$ and $\frac{k}{r}$
- a pair of choices that include commonly confused concepts, such as sine and cosine
- a pair of choices that could be thought of as complements or supplements of one another, such as 35° and 55°, or 20% and 80%

For the purposes of this pattern, any pair of answer choices like this can be thought of as "opposites," because they all reflect an attempt by the College Board to get us to confuse two concepts that might seem easily interchangeable if we aren't paying close enough attention.

If you see this pattern in a set of answer choices, you should be especially careful to double-check your work for any mistake that could result in choosing the "opposite" of the correct answer. Such mistakes could involve things like multiplying an expression by -1 instead of 1, or going in the wrong direction on a number line, or confusing the numerator and denominator of a fraction, and so on.

As with any pattern in the answer choices, seeing a pair of opposites doesn't guarantee that one of the opposites is correct, but noticing this pattern can often help alert you to potential mistakes that you'll want to avoid while you figure out your solution. You'll see several examples of how this pattern can influence our thinking in the question walkthroughs later in this Black Book.

Hidden pattern 3: The first and last terms in a series are often wrong answers.

Sometimes the answer choices in a math question will include a series. These series might be pretty easy to recognize in some cases, such as 7, 8, 9, 10. In other cases, the series might be less obvious, and it might be related to a concept in the question: if the question is talking about dividing some quantity by 4, then the answer choices might contain the series 3, 12, 48, because each number in the series is one fourth of the next number in the series.

The College Board seems to include series in the answer choices when it hopes that you'll make a mistake and repeat a step in the solution one time too many or too few, ending up with one of the wrong answers in the series. In other words, if a question involves finding the perimeter of a triangle with sides of 5 units each, then the answer choices might include the series 10, 15, 20, because the College Board is hoping you'll either add 5 one time too few (ending up with 10) or one time too many (ending up with 20).

For this reason, when a series is involved in the answer choices, we'll typically find that the correct answer isn't the first or last number in the series. The College Board seems to like to put the correct answer near the middle of the series in order to allow you to make a mistake in either direction and still find a wrong answer that reflects your mistake.

Remember, as with the other patterns in this section, that this isn't an unbreakable rule. So I'm not saying that we'll never, ever find the right answer at the beginning or the end of a series; sometimes we will. I'm just saying that it's more common to find it in one of the middle positions of a series, and that it helps to be aware of that. Again, we'll see examples of how to use this pattern in the walkthroughs later in this section.

Hidden pattern 4: Wrong answers try to imitate right answers.

The College Board likes to create wrong answers that incorporate elements of correct answers, probably in an attempt to make it harder for you to eliminate answer choices on the basis of a partial solution. In other words, if you're working on a question where the answer choices are all algebraic expressions, and you figure out that the right answer should include the expression $2r$ along with some other stuff, then you'll often find that a majority of the answer choices include $2r$. This way, the College Board can try to force you to figure out the rest of the question in order to identify the correct answer.

While this can be an annoying thing for the College Board to do, you'll find that you can actually use it to your advantage in many cases: after you think you've solved a question, if you see that the wrong answers seem to include a lot of the elements in common with the choice that you like, then you can often take that as a good sign that you've thought about the question correctly. (Notice I said, "typically," and not "always!")

Similarly, if you're having trouble deciding how to start attacking a question, then an expression or idea that appears often in the answer choices can give you a hint about how to set up your solution! For example, if most or all of the choices involve dividing by 3, that's a strong hint that a correct solution will involve dividing by 3; if most or all of the choices include a radical expression, that's a strong hint that a correct solution will involve finding the square root of something.

Noticing this kind of imitation among the answer choices can also help remind you to stay sharp and avoid any mistakes related to the common elements of the choices, because the answer choices indicate that the College Board is expecting untrained test-takers to make those kinds of mistakes! So, for example, if you see that some answer choices involve adding 4 and some involve subtracting 4, then you know that the College Board expects some test-takers to get confused on how to handle the number 4 in their solution—which lets you know that you should pay special attention to that issue.

We'll see several examples of this, and of the other SAT Math patterns, when we go through some questions from real SAT tests in a few pages.

Post-Solution Patterns

These patterns are just as useful for trained test-takers as the pre-solution patterns are, but they can usually only be identified with certainty after we've done some calculations for a particular question. (We should also note that, on some questions, any of the pre-solution patterns we just discussed might only really be noticeable after you've finished the solution, so they can all be thought of as potential post-solution patterns too, depending on the circumstances.)

Hidden pattern 5: Right approach, wrong step.

One of the ways that the SAT will try to confuse you is by giving you a problem that involves multiple steps, and making one of the wrong answers a number that you'd get if you attempted a valid solution but then accidentally stopped after one of the earlier steps, before your solution was complete. For example, a problem might ask you to find the price for erasers by giving you the prices for different combinations of pencils and erasers. The problem might require you to figure out the price of pencils in order to find the price for erasers, and one of the wrong answers would be the price of pencils.

Because this type of wrong answer is actually a number that you find in the process of solving the math problem, seeing it can reassure you that you've approached the question correctly —but you can usually only realize that this kind of wrong answer is present after you've already gone through a few steps of a valid approach to the question.

This wrong answer pattern is an important reminder that you always need to read SAT Math questions carefully, to be sure that the answer you select is actually what the question asks for, and not just a number you find on the way to the real answer!

Hidden pattern 6: The right answer to the wrong question.

This answer choice pattern takes advantage of situations where the test-taker gets mixed up about what the question is asking, either through careless reading or through losing track of the steps in a question.

A classic example of this type of choice is when a question about the *area* of a figure includes an answer choice that's the *perimeter* of the figure. In this case, we can imagine that a test-taker who gets caught up in executing the solution to the question might not realize that he mixed up area and perimeter when he read the question. The answer he ends up with seems right to him, *but it's the right answer to the wrong question.*

Other examples of this kind of thing could include an answer choice that provides the y-intercept of a graph when the question asked for the x-intercept, or an answer choice that provides the mean of a set of numbers instead of the median, and so on.

Of course, when you think an answer choice is following this pattern, you should check to make extra sure that you've identified the answer choice that actually reflects what the prompt is asking for.

Don't worry if this sounds a little vague right now. We'll see several examples of it when we go through real SAT questions from the College Board in a few pages.

Understanding the Major Types of Approaches to SAT Math Questions

As we'll see repeatedly in the various walkthroughs in this Black Book, one of the most important aspects of approaching the SAT like a trained test-taker is the realization that the SAT doesn't really test the same skills and knowledge that get tested in high school and college, which means that we'll often find that the most effective way to approach an SAT question is very different from the kinds of approaches you can use on questions in school.

This idea is perhaps most important on the Math sections of the SAT, because we'll often find that the types of formulas and techniques we might use in a math class can't be applied at all to an SAT Math question. In fact, we'll see that most SAT Math questions can be successfully approached in more than one way, and some of the most effective approaches for a particular question might include some combination of trial and error, graphing something on your calculator, noting the scale on a diagram, or even just remembering the definition of a term, and so on.

As it turns out, there are three general types of ways to approach SAT Math questions, and it can be useful for you to be aware of all of them, even though you'll only need to come up with one successful approach for each question you see on test day. These three general types of approaches are the following:

- concrete approaches
- abstract approaches
- test-smart approaches

Let's explore each type in more detail, and see some examples of them.

Concrete Approaches

Generally speaking, concrete approaches to an SAT Math question involve the idea of actually testing out or observing specific mathematical situations that are described in a question, and then picking the answer choice that fits with what you've observed in your test. Concrete approaches can include things like the following, which we'll discuss in more detail below:

- backsolving
- trial and error
- calculator graphing

Using a concrete approach can often allow you to find a correct answer to an SAT Math question even if you don't completely remember or understand all the details of the math concepts that appear in the question.

One reason that SAT Math questions often lend themselves to concrete approaches is that the test's format means the College Board can't check your work in the way that a teacher might check it in class—your answer sheet only reflects your final answer to a question, not the process that you used to get there. So, for example, if a question asks you to find the zeros of a function, the College Board has no way of knowing whether you found the correct answer through a formal mathematical approach, or by graphing the function on your calculator and tracing it to find the x-intercepts, which is much faster for most people. So when you're trying to decide how to attack a question, remember that the SAT doesn't expect you to follow the same rules that you might have to follow in Math class.

Concrete approaches can also be especially well suited to multiple-choice questions, because questions in that format often provide us with a set of answer choices that we can test against the prompt to see which one is valid, instead of requiring us to generate answers on our own; most test-takers find it easier to check whether a choice could be correct than to go through the mental work of finding a correct answer completely on their own. So, for example, if a multiple-choice question asks us to find the possible solutions to a quadratic equation, it's often easier to plug in the values from each answer choice to find the choice that works, rather than formally working out the algebra, as you'd have to do in a math class.

For these reasons, concrete approaches to SAT Math questions are often attractive to test-takers who lack confidence in their math abilities. But there is a potential drawback to concrete approaches: they generally take longer than other kinds of approaches, because they typically involve working through every single answer choice to make sure we've identified the correct one with no false positives (see the article "Special Technique: Backsolving" on page 211 of this Black Book for more details on this idea). Concrete solutions also tend to require a test-taker to do more calculations than the other approaches require, even if the calculations we use for concrete approaches are less advanced than the math ideas we'd apply in abstract or test-smart solutions.

With that in mind, let's discuss the three major types of concrete approaches in a little more detail.

Backsolving

Backsolving is the process of testing concrete values against an algebraic expression in a question's prompt, which allows us to identify the correct answer choice without actually going through a formal algebraic solution. (Backsolving is probably one of the most well-known "tricks" for multiple-choice math questions, but most test-takers don't realize all the ways backsolving can be applied, or all the ways it can go wrong if you're not careful. The best-known form of backsolving is probably the process of plugging a number from each answer choice back into an algebraic expression from the prompt to see which choice results in a valid statement, instead of formally solving that algebraic expression. But we can also sometimes use backsolving even when the answer choices are all algebraic expressions themselves. That's why I included an entire article on how to backsolve correctly on page 211, and I strongly recommend you read it.)

Trial and error

Trial and error (which is also sometimes called the "guess-and-check" approach) is similar to backsolving, but we use it in situations where we can't just test out answer choices to identify the correct one. Instead, we make up our own values to test against the prompt, and then adjust our next guess up or down based on the results of testing out the previous guess; we repeat this process until we make a guess that checks out to be the correct answer to the question.

Calculator graphing

Many questions on the SAT Math section address topics like the x- and y-intercepts of functions, or other aspects of a function that can be easily read off the screen of a graphing calculator if we input the function from the prompt.

Now that we've discussed some concrete approaches to SAT Math questions, we can talk about approaching questions in more abstract ways.

Abstract

Abstract approaches to SAT Math questions involve applying generalized mathematical reasoning, rather than working out specific instances of a given situation, as we'd do in a concrete approach. Abstract approaches usually require less time to execute than concrete approaches do—in fact, we'll sometimes find that we can apply an abstract approach without actually writing down any calculations at all. The trade-off for this speed improvement over concrete approaches is that abstract approaches generally require a test-taker to be a little more comfortable with math as an academic subject.

There are two common types of abstract approaches, which we'll discuss here in order to give you a sense of how abstract approaches work in general:

- understanding equations
- definitions and attributes

Understanding equations

Some SAT Math questions ask us about equations in a way that allows us to find the correct answer by thinking about the relationships among the components in the equation without actually calculating anything in the equation. (Remember that formulas and functions are also basically types of equations.) See "Special Technique: Understanding how Variables, Coefficients, Exponents, and Constants can Affect a Function" on page 207 for more details on these concepts, or see the second solution in the walkthrough for question 4 on section 3 of SAT Practice Test #4, which is on page 295 of this Black Book.

Definitions and attributes

Sometimes the key to approaching a question in an abstract way lies in the specific definitions or attributes of a mathematical concept, and keeping these definitions and attributes in mind allows us to see the right answer right away, often without picking up our pencils or calculators. To see this kind of solution in action, review the third solution in the walkthrough for question 28 on section 4 of SAT Practice Test #1, which is on page 337 of this Black Book.

****

As I mentioned above, abstract approaches are faster than concrete approaches but require a bit more confidence with math as a subject. But some questions allow for approaches that are even faster; I call this last type of approach a "test-smart" approach.

Test-Smart

A test-smart approach to an SAT Math question is one in which we combine our knowledge of math (and possibly some basic calculations) with an awareness of the limitations of the SAT's design and patterns. This can sometimes let us see quickly that the correct answer to a question must have a particular type of appearance (such as including an x-term with a negative coefficient) or be in a particular range of the number line, and that only one choice fits that requirement, which means it must be correct. Some test-smart solutions are so quick that we can't even really list out steps for them, because the act of noticing the possibility of the test-smart solution reveals the answer to the question. For an example of this kind of test-smart approach, consider the third solution in the walkthrough of question 12 on section 3 of SAT Practice Test #1, which starts on page 242 of this Black Book.

****

Now that we've discussed the major types of approaches to SAT Math questions, let's consider an example of a real SAT question from the College Board that can be approached in each of these three ways.

An Example of an Official SAT Question that Allows all 3 Types of Approaches: SAT Practice Test #1, Section 3, Question 6

This question asks about the yearly increase in a boy's height, given a formula to estimate the boy's growth. My walkthrough for this question starts on page 235 of this Black Book.

- The first solution in my walkthrough is a concrete one, in which we plug in two numbers that differ by 1 unit for the boy's age, then note the difference in the boy's height at the two ages.

- My second solution is abstract: we analyze the given formula and think about how the output of the formula changes when the boy's age increases by 1.

- Finally, in my third solution, we realize a certain characteristic that the correct answer must have, and we see that only one answer choice has that characteristic, so we know that choice must be correct. This approach to this question is only possible because the College Board chose the set of answer choices in a way that allowed us to recognize a key difference among the choices.

Conclusion and Progression

As you may have noticed in the example we just saw, I generally tend to organize my walkthroughs for SAT Math questions so that concrete approaches are presented before abstract approaches, and test-smart approaches are presented last of all. To be clear, it's not that every question lends itself easily to all three types of solutions; it's just that, in general, I present the more concrete solutions first, and then transition into more abstract solutions last.

I do this because I want my readers to have the best chance of understanding each approach and how they relate to each other. Concrete approaches are generally the easiest types of approaches for most people to understand; abstract approaches basically involve realizing in a general way what the concrete approaches are showing us in specific instances. Finally, test-smart approaches represent a level of applied abstract thinking that combines math principles with the design of the SAT. By generally handling more concrete approaches for a given question earlier than more abstract approaches, the walkthroughs can help test-takers who don't feel comfortable with the higher-level approaches develop the kind of confident understanding of the test that allows them to come up with faster solutions on test day.

The Recommended Math Path

Now that we've explained the rules and patterns that you'll find on the SAT Math section, we can look at the process that I recommend for those questions. I call it the "Math Path," mostly because that rhymes.

The Math Path is a set of guidelines to help us figure out how to attack tough questions. You won't need to use it on every question, and you can modify it as you keep practicing. I'm teaching it to you because it's a good way to keep all the elements of SAT Math questions in mind. If you practice with these ideas, you'll find that implementing them becomes second nature, and you won't need to make a point of always following every single step on every single question.

Here's a high-level list of the seven steps, and then I'll go into each step in more detail:

1. Read the prompt carefully and identify what the prompt is asking for.
2. Consider diagrams, if there are any.
3. Read and analyze the answer choices, if there are any.
4. Think about which areas of math might be involved.
5. Look for a 30-second solution.
6. Carry out your solution.
7. Re-check your work, paying attention to post-solution patterns. Consider using a different approach to re-solve the question.

Now let's take a closer look at each step.

1. Read the Prompt Carefully and Identify what the Prompt is Asking For.

This might sound kind of strange, but if you asked me to pick the single mistake that costs people the most points on the Math part of the SAT, I'd say it's the mistake of not reading carefully.

In fact, we should really think of the entire SAT, including the Math sections, as an extended test of reading skills. Most of what we do on the Math sections will depend on our ability to notice key phrases and details in each question—which, ultimately, comes down to our ability to read what's on the page and catch what it actually says.

(By the way, because of the way SAT Math works, if you know the meanings of every word and concept in a particular question, then you know enough math to be able to answer that question. Trust me on this—we'll see proof of it as we continue.)

At some point, the prompt will indicate the exact thing that will make up the correct answer. (This will usually, but not always, appear in the last sentence of the prompt.) We need to make sure we know what the question is asking us to figure out because this will determine and direct all our other decisions as we work on the question.

We must always keep in mind what the question is actually asking for! We'll often find that the College Board deliberately tries to confuse untrained test-takers with wrong-answer choices that reflect the values of expressions that are still relevant to the question, even if they aren't the expressions we were asked to find. (For example, a question might mention the variables x and y, and then ask us for the value of y, while providing a wrong answer that reflects the value of x instead.)

In high school math classes, we often don't need to make a special effort to keep our minds focused on what a question is asking for, because most math classes give you homework and tests that involve batches of questions all asking you to do basically the same thing for each question. But on the SAT Math section, it's unlikely that two consecutive questions would ask you to solve the same kind of problem, so it's very important that we always make sure we know what a question is asking us to do. Never lose sight of that.

2. Consider Diagrams, if there are Any.

There are two questions you should always ask yourself when an SAT Math question includes a diagram:

1. **Are any dimensions of the diagram left out of the diagram itself but included in the text underneath it?**
   Any dimensions that are left out of the diagram itself but included in the text of the question will probably be the basis for the first step in the solution to the question. For example, in question 18 on section 3 of SAT Practice Test #3, the diagram itself only shows two isosceles triangles whose angle measurements are labeled with variables; when we look below the diagram, we see in the prompt that y is 75, and that $18 - z = 2y$. These two pieces of information are the first things we need to consider when finding the most efficient approach to the question—see the walkthrough for this question on page 289 of this Black Book if you'd like the rest of the solution.

2. **Is the diagram drawn to scale?**
   If a diagram is drawn to scale, we can sometimes (but not always!) answer the question just by looking at the diagram itself and using its scale to eliminate choices that are obviously too large or too small. As one example of this kind of situation, consider question 6 on section 3 of SAT Practice Test #2. In that question, we can tell from the scale of the diagram that only (D) can possibly be correct. (For more on this question, see its walkthrough on page 257. We'll also see this idea at work in other SAT Math walkthroughs later in this Black Book.)

---

3. Read and Analyze the Answer Choices, if there are Any.

Most untrained test-takers ignore the answer choices in a Math question until they're basically done with the question. They typically read a question, try to figure out the answer on their own, and look for that answer (or a similar answer) in the answer choices. Now, if you could successfully do that for every question over the course of an entire test without making a single mistake, it's true that you wouldn't miss any questions. But so many questions become so much easier to answer when we consider the answer choices as part of the question from the very beginning.

Remember that the College Board likes to play little "games" in the answer choices of the SAT Math sections. We talked about some of those games a few pages ago when we covered the hidden patterns of these answer choices. For example, the wrong answers will sometimes include elements of the right answer, or sometimes they'll form a series, and so on. In some cases, simply noting that all the answer choices are one-digit numbers can be enough to help you realize how to approach a question.

So after you read the prompt and any diagrams, look over the answer choices and see what kind of options the SAT is giving you. Try to figure out why the test is presenting the answer choices that way—look at the values in the choices, but also look at the *relationships among those values*, and try to think about how those relationships might be important to the question.

I said earlier that it's important to remember that every SAT Math question can be answered in less than 30 seconds each if we're really on our game. Often, a large part of finding these extremely fast solutions involves thinking about how the answer choices relate to the question from the very beginning, because noticing some of these relationships can help us realize that it's possible to attack a question in a way that's different from how we would be forced to attack the question in a traditional math class.

So remember to think of the entire question, including the answer choices, as one big system of ideas. We'll see several examples of how this works when we look at some real SAT questions from the College Board in a few pages.

Make a quick mental note of the similarities, differences, and other relationships among the answer choices.

The College Board wants untrained test-takers to be able to find answer choices that reflect likely mistakes in attacking the question. Sometimes, the College Board provides wrong answers that reflect simple mistakes in reading or calculation; other times, the mistakes may reflect more fundamental errors, like confusing the definitions of "mean" and "median."

As we just discussed, we'll often find it useful to compare a question's answer choices to one another *before we start trying to figure out how to answer the question*. There are multiple reasons for this:

- Noting the *similarities* in the answer choices can help us realize which math concepts are likely to be involved in the ideal approach to the question. For example, if all the choices are algebraic expressions with two variables, then we know that a valid solution to the question must ultimately result in an expression with two variables. If all the answer choices are phrases from the same row or column in a chart, then we know that row or column is critical to answering the question. We'll see several examples of this kind of thing in the walkthroughs in a few pages.

- Noting the *differences* can help us realize what kinds of simple mistakes the College Board thinks an untrained test-taker would be likely to make. For example, if two answer choices contain fractions that are reciprocals of one another, then we know the College Board probably thinks that some test-takers will make a small mistake that causes them to switch the numerator and denominator of the correct fraction. Again, we'll see examples of these kinds of issues in the walkthroughs.

- Noting other relationships can make us aware of the best ways to approach a question, and help alert us to specific issues for that question. For example, if you notice the halves-and-doubles pattern in the answer choices, then you should be aware that the question might involve multiplying or dividing by 2.

(For more on this idea of comparing answer choices to one another, please see The Vertical Scan: A Key Tactic for Trained Test-Takers" on page 54 of this Black Book.)

4. Think about which Areas of Math Might be Involved.

Now that you've read the question and the answer choices, and considered the diagram if there is one, you should have a pretty good idea of which specific math terms and concepts are mentioned in the question.

Many test-takers overlook the fact that the solution to a question can only involve concepts that are immediately related to the concepts in the question. (This idea sounds kind of obvious once it's pointed out, but it's something that people often don't realize on their own: everything in math proceeds in a step-by-step fashion, with each step building on the previous one.)

When most people get stumped on the SAT Math section, they panic and try to call to mind every single math concept they know in the hope that one of those concepts will miraculously reveal the answer. This usually doesn't work, because it overwhelms the test-taker and prevents him from focusing on the specific issues related to the question. So instead of panicking and mentally flailing around, we want to narrow our focus and confine our thought process to two types of ideas:

- the concepts mentioned directly in the question, and

- the concepts that are directly related to the concepts mentioned in the question.

For example, if an SAT Math question involves words like "degrees" and "radius" and "center," then it must be a question about circles, and the SAT is only allowed to ask us about a limited set of circle-related concepts (look back at the SAT Math Toolbox in this Black Book if you don't remember what they are). That means that the solution to the question must somehow involve those circle-related concepts, so we should focus our attention on them.

If necessary, identify the "bridge" concepts that connect what the prompt is asking for to the ideas you've found in the question.

In some situations, the math concepts that you've noticed in the question may not directly address what the prompt asked you to find in the first place. For example, the prompt may have asked you about the y-intercepts of two different functions, without explicitly reminding you that the y-intercepts of a function appear where x in the function is set equal to zero. In this scenario, the "bridge" concept would be the idea of setting x equal to zero in order to find the y-intercept: coming up with an effective solution to the question requires you to remember the bridge concept and realize that it's relevant.

If we wanted to be really technical, we could say that every single SAT Math question involves a bridge concept in the sense that solving every question requires us to realize something that's not directly spelled out on the page. But in many cases, the bridge concept is fairly obvious. For example, if a question gives us an algebraic equation and asks us to solve for a variable, then the bridge concept is the idea that we can transform the equation in a series of steps that each involve modifying both sides of the equation in the same way, until the variable is isolated on one side of the equation. Most test-takers don't need to be reminded of a bridge concept like that, because they automatically know that they can solve for a variable in that way.

But we'll sometimes find that the bridge concepts are less obvious, and we may need to spend a few seconds trying to identify the concept that relates the ideas in the prompt (and/or the diagram) to the answer choices.

Note things to look out for!

As trained test-takers, we know that one of the most important aspects of maximizing our score on a standardized test is the idea of avoiding mistakes (or catching them and correcting them after we've made them).

The Math sections of the SAT will provide us with a lot of opportunities to make small mistakes like the following:

- confusing the numerator and denominator of a fraction
- solving for the wrong variable in a question that involves more than one variable
- simplifying a fraction incorrectly
- misreading the label on an axis of a graph
- . . . and so on.

These kinds of mistakes can easily cause us to miss questions even when we fully understand what they're asking us to do.

So one of the easiest and most straightforward ways to improve your SAT Math score is to get in the habit of identifying the aspects of a question that might cause you to make a mistake . . . *before* you make the mistake, so you can avoid it in the first place.

Again, one of the best ways to do this is to pay attention to answer choice patterns (if a question has answer choices, of course). For example, if you notice that two choices are opposites, then there's a good chance that some untrained test-takers might misunderstand the question in a way that causes them to pick the opposite of the right answer. You can also notice potential pitfalls in a question when you read the prompt—for example, if a question mentions more than one variable, then you know that it's important to keep the variables separate in your mind, and to remember which variable (if any) the prompt is asking you about, because some untrained test-takers will make the mistake of finding the wrong variable.

5. Look for a 30-Second Solution.

In this step, we try to use everything we've already figured out to help us string together the right basic math ideas that will let us connect the prompt to the correct answer choice. And don't forget—the best solutions will take you less than 30 seconds to work out.

If you can't think of a fast, efficient way to find the correct answer with total certainty, then consider saving the question for a later pass, as we discussed earlier in this Black Book, in the section called "Time Management on Test Day" on page 36; if you've already passed on the question multiple times, or if you only have a few minutes left on the section, then consider guessing.

Of course, as I said before, you can still get the question right even if you can't find a solution in under 30 seconds. But it's a good idea to get in the habit of looking for fast, simple solutions, because most of the difficulty that people have on the SAT Math section comes from not catching small details in a question, and wasting a lot of time and effort pursuing unnecessarily complicated solutions as a result.

6. Carry Out Your Solution.

After you have read the prompt, the diagram, and the answer choices, and thought about what the College Board is presenting to you and how it fits with what you know about the design of the SAT, and decided on a straightforward solution, you've finally earned the right to go ahead and solve the problem. IF YOU TRY TO SOLVE THE PROBLEM WITHOUT GOING THROUGH THE EARLIER STEPS, THERE'S A VERY GOOD CHANCE YOU'LL JUST BE WASTING YOUR TIME.

This is one more way that SAT Math questions differ from the math questions you encounter in school. In school, the questions on a math test are basically just like the questions you've been doing for homework and the questions your teacher has been doing in lectures, so you build up a kind of instinctive, automatic approach to school math, in which you memorize formulas and then automatically apply certain formulas in certain situations.

But that won't work on the SAT Math section, where questions are often specifically written so that formulas are of little help. If you read a math question on the SAT and dive right into it without thinking about it first, you're probably doing something wrong, and you'll probably end up choosing the wrong answer. Don't try to solve the problem until you've read it and thought about how it fits the SAT's patterns and rules.

7. Re-check Your Work, Paying Attention to Post-Solution Patterns. Consider Using a Different Approach to Re-solve the Question.

Checking your work is critical, because one of the easiest ways to lose points on the SAT Math section is to make a small mistake even though you fully understand the question.

One of the best ways to guard against mistakes is to look at all the choices you think are wrong and see if you can figure out why some of them were included. In other words, if you can figure out the mistakes that the College Board wanted you to make for some of the wrong choices, then there's a pretty good chance that you've handled the question correctly. But if you look back over the wrong answers and you don't have any idea why any of them are there, that can be a sign that you misunderstood the question, and you may have fallen for one of the test's tricks. Be especially on the lookout for hidden patterns like the ones we talked about.

Another good way to check your work is to see if you can figure out a different way to arrive at the same result you found originally. For example, if you originally found a y-intercept for a function by graphing it on your calculator, then you could re-confirm that value by plugging it in for y in the original function and making sure that $x = 0$ in the resulting equation.

Of course, another way to check your work is just to re-do exactly the same steps you've already completed, which is what most people do when they check their work in a math class. This approach can be effective, but it's not my favorite way to guard against errors: many people will have a hard time identifying small mistakes they've just made if they go back through their work only a few seconds later, because they're still in the same frame of mind that they were in when they made the mistake. This is why I prefer to approach a question in a different way when I'm checking for mistakes, rather than just walking back through the same steps I used in my initial approach. On the SAT, these alternative approaches can often include things like considering patterns in the answer choices, using a calculator to backsolve, and so on.

If you're fully satisfied that you know why your answer is right (ideally including understanding why at least one or two of the other answer choices are present as wrong answers), then you can mark your answer and move on to the next question. If you're not completely sure that you've figured out the correct answer, consider saving the question until a later pass, as we discussed in "Time Management on Test Day" on page 36. If you decide that it's time to guess on the question, remember the ideas we discussed in "Guessing on the SAT" on page 33.

Closing Thoughts on the SAT Math Path

You shouldn't try to solve SAT Math questions without reading them carefully and setting them up first, taking into account all of the aspects of the SAT's design that make these questions different from traditional math questions. Taking a few seconds to get your bearings will make answering the question a lot easier. Remember to keep the solution to every problem as simple as possible, and remember that you don't have to find formulaic approaches in most cases.

It may feel like the process we've just gone over is pretty long or complicated, especially for questions that seem obvious when you first look at them. But it's important to remember that you don't have to use this process on every question—only on the ones that you can't figure out at first. And you can modify the process as you see fit, depending on the question and your own preferences.

The important thing is to be aware of all the elements involved in the Math Path and try to implement them in your practice sessions, so they can become second nature when you see challenging questions on the test, which will allow you to use these ideas naturally, when you need them, instead of turning the Math Path into a rote system that you force yourself to follow even when you can answer a question without it.

I'll list the steps here one more time for reference:

1. Read the prompt carefully and identify what the prompt is asking for.
2. Consider diagrams, if there are any.
3. Read and analyze the answer choices, if there are any.
4. Think about which areas of math might be involved.
5. Look for a 30-second solution.
6. Carry out your solution.
7. Re-check your work, paying attention to post-solution patterns. Consider using a different approach to re-solve the question.

As I said, this process will allow you to break down any official SAT Math question you run into on test day, and figure out the most effective and efficient way to attack it. But I know from experience that some readers will have lingering questions about some aspects of the process, so we'll address those below.

What about Grid-In Questions?

Many students wonder if the student-produced response questions (or "grid-in" questions) require a different approach from the multiple-choice questions. For the most part, the Math Path process that we just discussed is the process I would follow for the grid-in questions (with the obvious exception that we won't have any answer choices to consider in deciding how to attack the question).

There are a few special considerations we should keep in mind for the grid-in questions, though.

If the question refers to the possibility of multiple solutions, make sure you understand why.

The grid-in format allows the College Board to ask more open-ended math questions, which is one of the reasons it exists on the SAT in the first place. So be aware that you might see questions that allow more than one valid solution. Such a question will often use a phrase like "one possible value," as in, "If x has a value between 3.9 and 4, what is one possible value of x?"

If you realize that you're dealing with a question that refers to the possibility of more than one valid response, make sure you can figure out why. In other words, if you can only think of one possible answer for such a question, then you've probably misunderstood it in some fundamental way, which means there's a very good chance that the answer you're thinking of is wrong.

I'm not saying that you actually need to work out more than one solution in order to know that you've got the question right! I'm just saying that you need to understand where other solutions might come from.

For example, consider Question 31 on Section 4 of SAT Practice Test #3. The prompt asks us for "one possible value of x." When we look at the question, we should be able to tell that the value of x could change because the prompt allows for the possibility of spending $11, $12, $13, or $14, and each of those levels of spending could result in a different value for x. On the other hand, if we read the phrase "one possible value" in the prompt and couldn't understand how the question might have more than one solution, then we'd know that we misunderstood the question. (See my walkthrough of this question on page 399 of this Black Book for more.)

Don't be afraid to guess, but don't expect much to come of it.

Of course, you should never leave a question blank on the SAT. On the other hand, since there are thousands of possible ways to fill out the answer for each grid-in question, the chance of guessing right is relatively small.

If you do decide to guess on a grid-in question, make that decision as quickly as you can so you don't waste any more time on the question than necessary. If you have a rough idea of what the answer might be, guess that—but if you don't have a clue, I would recommend guessing either 0 or 1, if those answers seem to have any chance of being right, just because I feel like I see those answers appearing slightly more frequently than any other individual number. But the advantage of that, if there even is one, is extremely slight, and your chance of being correct on a random guess is basically zero anyway.

How Should We Approach Roman Numeral Questions?

For a trained test-taker, the best approach to a Roman numeral question isn't really any different from the best approach to any other SAT Math question. The only small difference is that we evaluate each individual Roman numeral to see which ones are valid, and then pick the choice that accurately reflects our findings, instead of considering which individual answer choice is correct right away. Just as with any SAT question, it's extremely important to pay attention to small details and to insist on finding an answer choice that fits exactly with our understanding of the question.

If you'd like to see these ideas in action against real test questions that involve Roman numerals, take a look at this Black Book's walkthroughs of the following questions:

- Question 11 on Section 3 of SAT Practice Test #3 (page 283 of this Black Book)
- Question 15 on Section 3 of SAT Practice Test #3 (page 287 of this Black Book)
- Question 26 on Section 4 of SAT Practice Test #2 (page 363 of this Black Book)

Avoid Decimal Expressions Unless a Question Uses Them.

In high school and college math classes, we're often encouraged to use decimal values rather than fractions. For instance, we might write 0.8 instead of $\frac{4}{5}$. But on the SAT, it's usually a bad idea to express things in terms of decimals, unless the answer choices are also in decimal form. When we work with decimals, we often miss opportunities to simplify and reduce expressions that are much easier to see when we keep everything in fraction form.

For instance, if a question involves multiplying $\frac{4}{5}$ by $\frac{5}{6}$, then using fractions might help me see right away that the 5's cancel out and I'm left with $\frac{4}{6}$, which is the same thing as $\frac{2}{3}$. If I had to multiply those fractions with a calculator, I might not immediately recognize that the answer simplifies to $\frac{2}{3}$. I'd probably lose time, and I'd also run the risk of hitting the wrong key or something. In general, we'll have a much better chance of finding the shortest possible solution if we get in the habit of avoiding decimal expressions on the SAT.

It's Not School Math—Your Work Doesn't Matter!

Lots of test-takers experience significant difficulty on the SAT Math section for a reason that might seem strange to a lot of people: they try to approach each question in a formalized way that would satisfy a math teacher.

But by now we know that the SAT doesn't reward the same things that school rewards. The SAT Math section is no exception.

The bottom line is that the SAT doesn't care what kind of work you do to arrive at the answer that you choose. The SAT only cares if the answer that you choose is correct. That's it.

This fact has two very important implications for us as test-takers. First, it means that we can, and should, get in the habit of looking for the fastest, most direct route to the answer, even if that route doesn't involve solving a formal equation (or writing anything down at all!). Second, it means that we have to make sure we don't make any small mistakes in our solution that might lead us to mark the wrong answer even if our overall approach is formally sound, because the College Board will never know what our approach was. For the College Board, a wrong answer is a wrong answer no matter how solid the approach to the question was, and a right answer is a right answer no matter what you did to arrive there (as long as you don't cheat, of course).

In the parts of this book where I provide solutions to real SAT Math questions from the College Board, you'll often see that the approach I recommend wouldn't be acceptable to most math teachers, because it's not formal. This isn't because I'm not good at math; it's because I'm very, very good at *SAT Math*, and in SAT Math we have no obligation to use a formal approach. In fact, we're usually better off avoiding formal math whenever possible, because the most efficient approaches to many questions involve taking advantage of the flaws in the SAT's design, as we'll see in the walkthroughs.

So try to get in the habit of finding the most direct approach to a question that you possibly can, and remember that the only thing that matters to the College Board is that you mark the correct answer without cheating!

Ignore the So-Called "Order of Difficulty."

Test-takers are often encouraged to believe that the questions on the SAT Math section get harder as the section goes on. But I would recommend ignoring that idea.

At this point, I'm sure you're starting to realize that every SAT question deserves our full attention and respect on test day, because it's very easy to make small mistakes in our approach and end up choosing the wrong answer even if we fully understand all the concepts in a question. At the same time, you're probably also beginning to see that it's often possible to find very efficient solutions if we're aware of the test's design limitations, even when a question might seem challenging to most untrained test-takers.

When we combine those two ideas, we see that we should always expect test questions to try to trick us into small mistakes, and we should always be on the lookout for easier ways to answer every question. Once we're in that frame of mind, worrying about the so-called "order of difficulty" makes no sense. Every question becomes both an opportunity to find a clever solution and a challenge to make sure we avoid small mistakes.

(By the way, when I work with students who are trying to score a perfect 800 on the SAT Math section but who might be missing a few questions per test, I find that they often miss questions in the first half of a section because of small mistakes—usually because they've been incorrectly taught that those questions are always "easy" and that they don't have to worry so much about them.)

So here's the bottom line: you should ignore the idea of an order of difficulty, because it serves no purpose. Instead, treat each question as a separate event. Don't be afraid of any questions, and don't take any for granted either.

SAT Math Quick Summary

This is a one-page summary of the major relevant concepts. Use it to evaluate your comprehension or jog your memory. For a more in-depth treatment of these ideas, see the rest of the section.

The Big Secret: SAT Math tests relatively simple things in relatively strange ways.

- The concepts in the SAT Math section must be limited because of standardization. No calculus or advanced stats—just <u>arithmetic, algebra, geometry, and basic trig</u>. Refer to the SAT Math Toolbox if necessary.
- Focus on the <u>definitions and properties</u> of the concepts in each question, not primarily on formulas. The College Board provides all the formulas related to area and volume that you'll be required to use.
- SAT Math is usually simpler than it looks, and each question can be done in <u>30 seconds or less</u> if you find the fastest solution. If your solution is very complicated, you're probably doing the question wrong.
- Look for shortcuts, things that cancel out, equivalent terms, etc. Leave expressions as fractions and radicals when possible (instead of converting to decimals) for easier canceling and substitution.
- Diagrams are assumed to be to scale unless the question says otherwise. Taking a close look can often help to eliminate wrong answers or even point to the right one without doing any actual math.
- Assuming you know the math in the Math Toolbox of this Black Book, every question contains all the information you need to answer it, even if it doesn't seem like that. <u>If you understand every word in the question, then you know enough to figure out the right answer.</u>

Some common wrong answer patterns include choices that are:

- half or double the right answer
- in a series with the right answer
- a number that you get on an earlier step of the right approach to the question
- the right answer to the wrong question
- similar in appearance to the right answer

I recommend a step-by-step process called the Math Path for questions that are hard to figure out. Here's a simplified version:

1. Read the question carefully, and consider the words in the question. This is the most important step.
2. Consider any diagrams—scale, missing dimensions, etc.
3. Consider answer choices (if there are any)—relationships with each other and with the question.
4. Which areas of math are involved? What can the SAT test in those areas? (Math Toolbox.)
5. In light of steps 1 - 4, look for a solution—ideally one that would take 30 seconds or less.
6. Execute your solution.
7. Check your work with the answer choices and/or alternate solutions. Remember that "carelessness" costs most people more points than any other single thing does.

Remember:

- Always think about the question as a whole system of ideas—prompt, diagrams, answer choices, and so on—before you actually start solving it.
- Ignore the idea of an "order of difficulty." You can make careless mistakes on any question, and every question has a simple, direct solution.

See the walkthroughs in this Black Book for demonstrations of all these ideas.

Math Question Walkthroughs

Now that we've thoroughly discussed the right approach to the SAT Math section in general terms, we'll go through all the SAT Math questions in the first four SAT Practice Tests from the College Board, so you can see the approach in action against official SAT questions. (See "Only Work with Questions from the College Board!" on page 18 of this Black Book for details on why official questions are so important, and where to get them for free if you want. And if you'd like to see some video demonstrations of these ideas, go to www.SATprepVideos.com for a selection of demonstration videos that are free to readers of this book.)

First, we'll look at all the walkthroughs from section 3 (the no-calculator section) of the first four official SAT Practice Tests. Then, we'll look at all the walkthroughs from section 4 (the calculator section) of the same four tests.

Sample Math Walkthrough

My SAT Math walkthroughs are roughly similar to the SAT Reading walkthroughs we saw earlier in this Black Book, though the Math ones have a few more components. As with the Reading walkthroughs, you don't need to worry about copying my approach exactly when you attack a question on your own. Instead, the walkthroughs are presented in a format that lets us do the following:

- show the ideal thought process for attacking a question, from the initial assessment, through one or more solutions, ending with checking the result and observing any relevant post-solution patterns in the answer choices (but remember that you only need to find one solution on test day! I just show multiple solutions to help you understand that SAT Math questions can be attacked in a variety of ways)

- allow you to focus on the specific information you're interested in for a particular question, while also letting you read through the entire walkthrough easily if you prefer

- present each walkthrough so it can stand on its own as a full explanation of the question, while still making it easy to refer back to relevant parts of the training for more details if you want a refresher

- show how simple the reasoning and calculations are for most SAT Math questions, and how important it is to avoid small mistakes

Here's a diagram of a sample walkthrough, with the key elements of the walkthrough explained on the next page:

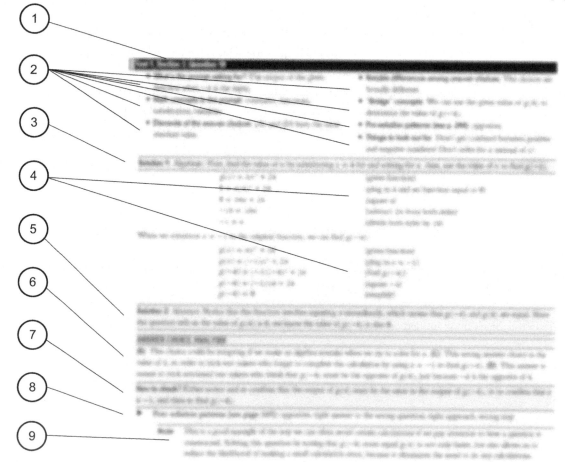

Explanation of Walkthrough Elements

The elements of the walkthrough are presented in an order that reflects the "Math Path" from page 223 of this Black Book:

1. This shows the test number and question number of the question being analyzed in the walkthrough. You can use this information to locate the relevant question in one of the editions of the Blue Book, or in the College Board's free online practice materials.

2. This area of the walkthrough reflects steps 1-4 of the "Math Path" on page 223 of this Black Book; in other words, this part of the walkthrough shows the kinds of things that a trained test-taker might notice initially, while she was deciding on the best way to attack the question. This part of the walkthrough reflects the following ideas:

   - the specific thing that the prompt is actually asking for

   - the math concepts in the prompt, diagram, and/or answer choices

   - the notable differences among the answer choices (you could choose to use a vertical scan to pick these out, as described on page 54 of this Black Book)

   - the patterns in the answer choices that might be observable before we attempt a solution

   - a list of potential mistakes and pitfalls to look out for before we begin our solution

3. This Item reflects step 5 in the "Math Path" on page 223 of this Black Book. It names the first solution that the walkthrough will explore. It begins with a simple one- or two-word description of the type of solution that's being discussed (such as "backsolving" or "graphing"), and then proceeds to a one- or two-sentence description of the steps that would be taken for the solution. As you become more comfortable with SAT Math, you may be able to understand the entire solution just from this Item. (In Item 4, this simple description will be fleshed out at length.)

4. In this Item, which reflects step 6 in the "Math Path" on page 223 of this Black Book, we spell out the specific steps for the solution in Item 3. These steps allow you to follow along with the exact process that would lead to the answer to the question according to the approach in Item 3.

5. Here you'll find a different potential solution to the question from the one in Item 3, also reflecting step 5 in the "Math Path" on page 223 of this Black Book. Just like the description in Item 3, this description will begin with a one- or two-word rough classification of the type of solution being proposed (such as "abstract" or "test-smart"), followed by a one- or two-sentence description of the solution. If necessary, this Item will be followed by another set of relevant steps, just as Item 4 provides the steps for the solution in Item 3. Note that you only need to find one solution on test day! We just go through multiple solutions in the walkthroughs so you can come to understand how each question can be attacked in multiple ways.

6. After all the possible solutions are presented, along with their various steps, Item 6 discusses the wrong answer choices, and indicates likely errors that might have led to some of them.

7. This Item provides a quick indication of a way to check over our work in order to catch any mistakes we might have made.

8. This Item notes any answer choice patterns that might only be noticeable after we've executed a solution. Items 6, 7, and 8 all reflect Step 7 in the "Math Path" on page 223 of this Black Book.

9. If I feel that something is noteworthy about the question but I can't fit it in the rest of the walkthrough, then I'll note that at the end of the walkthrough. Be sure to pay attention to these notes when they appear, as they'll often contain useful information about what a particular question can teach us generally about future SAT questions.

Note that some walkthroughs are missing some of the items in this list! If one of the Items above isn't relevant to a particular question, then it's omitted.

Remember that the ultimate goal of these walkthroughs is to help you see multiple ways that I might attack each question, and how I recommend you do the same. Also notice that the walkthroughs always begin by pointing out all the key details of the question that will help you figure out the most efficient solution to apply—this is very important to keep in mind on test day!

As always, feel free to modify my approach as you see fit, as long as your modifications still bring you the results you want.

- **What's the prompt asking for?** The value of x.
- **Math concepts in the prompt:** fractions, substitution, algebra
- **Elements of the answer choices:** They're all small numbers, most are single-digit numbers.
- **Concepts in the answer choices:** small integers

- **"Bridge" concepts:** In order to find x, we need to make it the only variable in the equation. We can make x the only variable if we sub in $k = 3$. This will allow us to solve for x.
- **Pre-solution patterns (see p. 217):** halves and doubles
- **Things to look out for:** Don't switch k and x in your mind!

Solution 1: Substitute $k = 3$ and solve for x.

$$\frac{x-1}{3} = k \qquad \text{(original equation)}$$

$$\frac{x-1}{3} = 3 \qquad \text{(plug in } k = 3\text{)}$$

$$x - 1 = 9 \qquad \text{(multiply both sides by 3)}$$

$$x = 10 \qquad \text{(add 1 to both sides)}$$

So we can see that (D) is correct.

Solution 2: Substitute $k = 3$ and then backsolve each answer choice as x.

$$\frac{x-1}{3} = k \qquad \text{(original equation)}$$

$$\frac{x-1}{3} = 3 \qquad \text{(plug in } k = 3\text{)}$$

Now we can test each answer choice:

$$\frac{2-1}{3} = 3 \qquad \text{(plug in } x = 2 \text{ to test choice (A))}$$

$$\frac{1}{3} \neq 3 \qquad \text{(simplify)}$$

$\frac{1}{3}$ doesn't equal 3, so (A) can't be correct.

$$\frac{4-1}{3} = 3 \qquad \text{(plug in } x = 4 \text{ to test choice (B))}$$

$$1 \neq 3 \qquad \text{(simplify)}$$

1 doesn't equal 3, so (B) can't be correct.

$$\frac{9-1}{3} = 3 \qquad \text{(plug in } x = 9 \text{ to test choice (C))}$$

$$\frac{8}{3} \neq 3 \qquad \text{(simplify)}$$

$\frac{8}{3}$ doesn't equal 3, so (C) can't be correct.

$$\frac{10-1}{3} = 3 \qquad \text{(plug in } x = 10 \text{ to test choice (D))}$$

$$3 = 3 \qquad \text{(simplify)}$$

3 equals 3, so (D) is correct.

ANSWER CHOICE ANALYSIS

(A): This is half of (B). **(C):** This is 1 less than the right answer, for people who forget the numerator is $x - 1$. (In other words, this is the value of $x - 1$, but the prompt asks for x).

How to check? Rework the algebra carefully. Plug in the correct answer to make sure it fits.

- **What's the prompt asking for?** The sum of $(7 + 3i) + (-8 + 9i)$
- **Math concepts in the prompt:** basic operations, imaginary numbers

- **Elements of the answer choices:** All choices contain -1 or 15 as the first term, then either $+12i$ or $-6i$.
- **"Bridge" concepts:** Adding the two expressions will require us to combine like terms.
- **Pre-solution patterns (see p. 217):** wrong answers try to imitate right answers
- **Things to look out for:** Don't overlook the negative sign! Don't add imaginary expressions to real expressions!

Solution 1: Combine like terms and simplify.

$(7 + 3i) + (-8 + 9i)$	(original equation)
$7 + 3i - 8 + 9i$	(distribute positive sign to $(-8 + 9i)$)
$-1 + 12i$	(simplify)

So we can see that (A) is correct.

ANSWER CHOICE ANALYSIS

(B): This is the result if we subtract $9i$ instead of adding $9i$. **(C):** This is the result if we add 8 instead of subtracting 8. **(D):** This is the result if we make both of the mistakes from the (B) and (C).

How to check? Carefully re-do the arithmetic. Consider the real integers and imaginary numbers separately.

Note The question tells us that i is the root of -1, but the answer would be the same if i were a regular variable. The choices give us every possible combination of the following: either -1 or 15 for the first term, and either $12i$ or $-6i$ for the second term. Also notice that we needed to distribute the positive sign in front of the binomial $(-8 + 9i)$ so we could remove the parentheses from around that binomial.

Test 1, Section 3, Question 3

- **What's the prompt asking for?** An expression for the total number of messages sent by both people.
- **Math concepts in the prompt:** algebraic modeling, basic operations, variables
- **Elements of the answer choices:** Two have the expression mp; two have m and p separately.
- **Notable differences among answer choices:** Two choices have 4 and 5; one choice has the sum of 4 and 5, and one has the product of 4 and 5.
- **Pre-solution patterns (see p. 217):** wrong answers try to imitate right answers
- **Things to look out for:** Don't confuse addition and multiplication! Don't confuse which person is represented by which variable!

Solution 1: Concrete approach: Pick numbers for m and p, determine number of text messages, then see which answer choice has the same values when you plug in the numbers you picked.

Let $m = 3$ and $p = 7$.

If Armand sent 3 text messages per hour for 5 hours, he sent 3×5 messages, or 15 text messages. If Tyrone sent 7 text messages per hour for 4 hours, he sent 7×4 messages, or 28 text messages. So the "total number of messages sent by Armand and Tyrone" in this case would be $15 + 28$, or 43. Now let's plug $m = 3$ and $p = 7$ into the expressions from the answer choices:

A $9mp = 9(3 \times 7) = 9(21) = 189$
B $20mp = 20(3 \times 7) = 20(21) = 420$
C ✓ $5m + 4p = 5(3) + 4(7) = 15 + 28 = 43$
D $4m + 5p = 4(3) + 5(7) = 12 + 35 = 47$

Only (C) gives us the correct number of text messages, so (C) is correct.

Solution 2: Abstract: Translate the text into algebra directly.

If "Armand sent m text messages each hour for 5 hours," then he must have sent $5m$ text messages—that's five hours spent texting at m texts per hour. If "Tyrone sent p text messages each hour for 4 hours," then he must have sent $4p$ text messages—that's four hours spent texting at p texts per hour. To find the total number of text messages that Armand and Tyrone both sent, we add the number of texts one sent to the number of texts the other sent. That gives us choice (C), $5m + 4p$.

ANSWER CHOICE ANALYSIS

(A): This is the result if we add 4 and 5 and then multiply the result by m and p. **(B):** This is the result if we multiply 4 and 5 and then multiply the result by m and p. **(D):** This is the result if we think Armand spent 4 hours texting and Tyrone spent 5 hours texting, instead of the other way around.

How to check? Reconsider each element of the answer choices to make sure that they're all supported by the text. Try an approach that you didn't try above.

- **What's the prompt asking for?** The role of 108 in the equation from the prompt.
- **Math concepts in the prompt:** algebraic modeling, basic operations, variables
- **Elements of the answer choices:** (C) and (D) relate to a rate.
- **Notable differences among answer choices:** (A) and (B) don't discuss a rate.
- **Concepts in the answer choices:** algebraic modeling, rates

- **"Bridge" concepts:** A rate involves a ratio (note the similarity in the terms "rate" and "ratio"). If 108 isn't involved in some kind of ratio in the formula, then it can't play a role related to rates in the formula.
- **Pre-solution patterns (see p. 217):** wrong answers try to imitate right answers
- **Things to look out for:** Make sure not to switch P and d in your mind!

Solution 1: Abstract: Carefully read the prompt and think about how the numbers in the prompt and the equation relate to each other. Then consider each answer choice in light of the information in the prompt.

When we look at the answer choices, we see the following:

(A) describes the repairs happening "within 108 days." The word "within" would seem to suggest some kind of inequality relationship—it says the period of repair will be less than or equal to 108. Since the prompt describes an "equation" and nothing in the prompt says anything about Kathy repairing phones in less than a certain number of days, we know the idea of an inequality can't relate to this prompt, so (A) must be wrong.

(B) seems like it could make sense. The prompt does describe Kathy "receiv[ing] a batch of phones each week," which matches up with the idea of "start[ing] each week" with a certain number of "phones to fix." We can also see from the prompt that the function would involve subtracting a number from 108 in order to determine how many phones Kathy has left each day; this is consistent with the idea that 108 is the number of phones at the beginning of each week. Of course, as trained test-takers, we know that we always need to consider every answer choice before committing to one.

(C) can't be right because it describes something happening at a certain "rate...per hour," but the prompt doesn't give us any information that would let us determine what Kathy does in an average hour. We don't know if she works on the phones around the clock, or for 3 hours a day, or what. Further, if the idea of "108 per hour" were relevant to the prompt and the formula, then we'd expect to see the number 108 multiplied by a number of hours in the formula, but we don't see 108 being multiplied by anything in the formula, and we don't see a variable representing the number of hours Kathy spends working on an average day.

(D) can't be right either. If 108 were the number of phones being repaired on an average day, then the formula would need to involve multiplying 108 by the number of days. Instead, the formula multiplies the number of days by 23.

Now that we've considered the answer choices, we can see clearly that (B) is the only one that reflects the ideas in the prompt.

Solution 2: Abstract: Carefully read the prompt and think about how the numbers in the prompt and the equation relate to each other. Then determine the role of 108 in the function on your own.

We know from the prompt that Kathy starts each week with a certain number of phones to fix, and then she works on those phones until she gets another batch of phones the next week. Nothing in the prompt suggests that the value representing the initial number of phones will need to be multiplied or divided by anything—especially not by the number of days, which is represented by d according to the prompt. Further, it makes sense that the number of phones needing repairs should have something subtracted from it as each day goes by, because more phones are repaired each day in the week according to the prompt, so fewer phones should need repairs.

Once we realize the ideas in the previous paragraph, we should realize that the number 108 must represent the number of phones that need repair at the beginning of the week, since 108 is the only number in the formula that isn't multiplied by anything, and it has another number subtracted from it. So we can see that (B) is correct.

How to check? We can consider the other answer choices and confirm that none of them make sense, and only (B) is possible.

- **What's the prompt asking for?** An expression equivalent to the one in the prompt.
- **Math concepts in the prompt:** operations on polynomials, PEMDAS
- **Elements of the answer choices:** All choices have at least one component that involves a power of 2. All choices have at least one expression with x-squared. All choices have at least one expression with y-squared. Two choices involve subtracting $6y^2$.

- **Notable differences among answer choices:** Two choices involve two terms, while one choice includes only one term, and one choice includes three terms. Two choices include only positive values, and two include negative values.
- **"Bridge" concepts:** We can simplify this expression by carefully adding and subtracting the coefficients of expressions with matching variable components.
- **Pre-solution patterns (see p. 217):** halves and doubles; wrong answers try to imitate right answers

- **Things to look out for:** Don't forget to distribute the negative sign! Don't misread the variable expressions or their exponents!

Solution 1: Algebra: Distribute the negative sign, then carefully combine like algebraic terms.

$$(x^2y - 3y^2 + 5xy^2) - (-x^2y + 3xy^2 - 3y^2)$$ (original equation)

$$x^2y - 3y^2 + 5xy^2 + x^2y - 3xy^2 + 3y^2$$ (distribute the negative sign)

$$2x^2y + 2xy^2$$ (simplify)

Solution 2: Concrete: Assign values to x and y. Evaluate the prompt and each answer choice. The choice whose value matches the value of the prompt will be correct.

Let $x = 2$ and $y = 4$.

$$(x^2y - 3y^2 + 5xy^2) - (-x^2y + 3xy^2 - 3y^2)$$ (original equation)

$$((2)^2(4) - 3(4)^2 + 5(2)(4)^2) - (-(2^2)(4) + 3(2)(4)^2 - 3(4)^2)$$ (plug in $x = 2$ and $y = 4$)

$$(16 - 48 + 160) - (-16 + 96 - 48)$$ (exponents and multiplication)

$$(128) - (32)$$ (simplify)

$$96$$ (subtract)

When $x = 2$ and $y = 4$, the equation in the prompt equals 96. So when we plug those same values into the answer choices, the correct answer should also be equal to 96.

A $4x^2y^2 = 4(2)^2(4)^2 = 256$

B $8xy^2 - 6y^2 = 8(2)(4)^2 - 6(4)^2 = 256 - 96 = 160$

C ✓ $2x^2y + 2xy^2 = 2(2)^2(4) + 2(2)(4)^2 = 32 + 64 = 96$

D $2x^2y + 8xy^2 - 6y^2 = 2(2)^2(4) + 8(2)(4)^2 - 6(4)^2 = 32 + 256 - 96 = 192$

Only choice (C) gives us the result we got by plugging $x = 2$ and $y = 4$ into the expression from the prompt.

ANSWER CHOICE ANALYSIS

(A): This is the result if we think the terms from (C) can somehow be combined to create a single x^2y^2 term. **(B):** This is the result if we don't distribute the minus sign to each term in the second set of parentheses. **(D):** This is the result if we only distribute the minus sign to the first term in the second set of parentheses, but not to the other two terms.

How to check? If we realize the correct answer must not have a y-squared term, and must include $2x^2y$, then we know (C) is right.

Test 1, Section 3, Question 6

- **What's the prompt asking for?** The boy's estimated yearly height increase.
- **Math concepts in the prompt:** basic operations, formulas, variables
- **Elements of the answer choices:** Three answer choices involve decimals.

- **Notable differences among answer choices:** One answer choice is an integer.
- **Concepts in the answer choices:** decimals
- **"Bridge" concepts:** If we increase a by 1 unit, we can observe the change in h.
- **Things to look out for:** Don't confuse h and a!

Solution 1: Concrete: Choose two values for a that differ by 1 unit, then plug in each value and see which answer choice corresponds to the change in h.

We'll plug in $a = 3$ and $a = 4$ to see how much the boy's height increases from year 3 to year 4.

$h = 3a + 28.6$ (original equation)
$h = 3(3) + 28.6$ (plug in $a = 3$)
$h = 37.6$ (simplify)

Now we'll plug in $a = 4$.

$h = 3(4) + 28.6$ (plug in $a = 4$)
$h = 40.6$ (simplify)

When $a = 3$, $h = 37.6$. When $a = 4$, $h = 40.6$. So the yearly increase in height is equal to $40.6 - 37.6$, or 3, and (A) is correct.

Solution 2: Abstract: Analyze the model in the prompt and figure out how a change in a would impact the output $h(a)$.

The question tells us that a is equal to the boy's age. So if the boy is 2 years old, then $a = 2$, and if the boy is 3 years old, then $a = 3$, and so on. The question asks for the "estimated increase…of a boy's height each year." In other words, when one year passes, roughly how much does the boy's height increase?

The given equation tells us h, the boy's height. This means we need to think about what happens to h when a increases by 1. The variable a has a coefficient of 3, and the term $3a$ is added to 28.6. So when we increase a, we're increasing the number that gets multiplied by 3—in other words, every time a increases by 1, the value for h in the estimation formula must go up by 3. That's the same as saying that each year, the boy's height increases by 3 inches, so (A) is correct.

Solution 3: Test-smart: Consider the answer choices and notice that only one of them relates back to the model in a way that could be relevant to the prompt.

As trained test-takers, we know the correct answer to this question must be a number that relates directly to the concepts in the prompt, and especially in the modeling function for $h(a)$. When we read carefully, we see that the prompt is ultimately asking for "the estimated increase, *in inches*, of...height each year" (emphasis mine), and that the function model is also given in terms of "height h...*in inches*, in terms of...age a in years*" (emphasis mine)—in other words, the prompt is asking us for a number that's in the same terms and units as the numbers in the original function, which means we don't need to think about any kind of conversion or anything like that.

With that in mind, when we notice that (A) is the only choice that's directly present in the function, and that all the other choices result from dividing numbers in the function by other numbers in the prompt (see answer choice analysis below), we can quickly ask ourselves whether there's any reason to think that dividing or converting any number in the original function seems necessary. When we realize that no such dividing or conversion is necessary, we know that the correct answer must be the only number that doesn't involve dividing or converting, so (A) must be correct. (Again, this is a very test-smart approach, and it relies on a good level of familiarity with the design of the SAT Math sections. If you don't feel comfortable trying to approach this question in this way, you can always use one of the other approaches in this explanation.)

ANSWER CHOICE ANALYSIS

(B): This is an approximation of $\frac{28.6}{5}$. This choice might be tempting if we thought we should divide the constant 28.6 by 5, the upper end of the age range, but there's nothing in the prompt that indicates we should do that. **(C):** This is an approximation of $\frac{28.6}{3}$, which was probably put here to trap people who try to approach the question by isolating a for some reason, and end up dividing 28.6 by 3. But nothing in the question would suggest that we should divide anything to answer the prompt. **(D):** This is half of the constant 28.6, which appears in the prompt, but there's no reason to think that dividing the constant in half would be relevant to a yearly change in h.

How to check? Try an alternate approach above.

Test 1, Section 3, Question 7

- **What's the prompt asking for?** An equation that isolates P.
- **Math concepts in the prompt:** algebra, exponents, fractions, cross-multiplication
- **Elements of the answer choices:** Every choice is an equation with P on one side. All choices involve multiplying something by m.
- **Notable differences among answer choices:** (A) and (B) include compound fractions, while (C) and (D) include simple fractions, The fractions in (A) and (B) are the reciprocals of each other. The fractions in (C) and (D) are the reciprocals of each other.

- **Concepts in the answer choices:** compound fractions, reciprocals
- **"Bridge" concepts:** In order to isolate P, we'll need to follow the principles of algebra and perform the same steps on both sides of the equation, until P is alone on one side.
- **Pre-solution patterns (see p. 217):** opposites; wrong answers try to imitate right answers
- **Things to look out for:** Don't switch the numerators and denominators of the fractions as you work through your solution! Don't overlook any details of the large compound fraction in the prompt!

Solution 1: Perform the algebra directly on the original formula from the prompt, isolating P.

$$m = \frac{\left(\frac{r}{1200}\right)\left(1+\frac{r}{1200}\right)^N}{\left(1+\frac{r}{1200}\right)^N - 1}P \qquad \text{(original equation)}$$

$$m\left(\left(1+\frac{r}{1200}\right)^N - 1\right) = \left(\frac{r}{1200}\right)\left(1+\frac{r}{1200}\right)^N P \qquad \text{(multiply both sides by } \left(1+\frac{r}{1200}\right)^N - 1)$$

$$m\frac{\left(1+\frac{r}{1200}\right)^N - 1}{\left(\frac{r}{1200}\right)\left(1+\frac{r}{1200}\right)^N} = P \qquad \text{(divide both sides by } \left(\left(\frac{r}{1200}\right)\left(1+\frac{r}{1200}\right)^N\right))$$

The result is the same as the expression in (B), so (B) is correct.

Solution 2: Consider the answer choices first, and compare each one to the original formula from the prompt.

Facebook.com/TestingIsEasy   Youtube.com/TestingIsEasy

When we compare the answer choices to the expression in the prompt and to each other, we see that we have essentially two options to consider:

1. whether the correct answer should involve a compound fraction (like (A) and (B) do), or a "simplified" fraction (like (C) and (D) do), and
2. which expression(s) should go in the numerator of the correct answer, and which expression(s) should go in the denominator.

We can notice that the fraction $\left(\frac{r}{1200}\right)$ appears in four places: the prompt, choice (A), choice (B), and choice (C). The inverse of the fraction (which is $\left(\frac{1200}{r}\right)$) appears in (D). If there's some way to manipulate the fraction in the prompt and arrive at only $\left(\frac{r}{1200}\right)$, the only way to do that is probably going to involve some kind of simplifying or canceling. Now, we need to ask ourselves: does it make sense to think that we can simplify the fraction from the prompt and arrive at $\left(\frac{r}{1200}\right)$? Simplifying and reducing fractions involves dividing the numerator and denominator by a common amount; if we're going to arrive at $\left(\frac{r}{1200}\right)$ after doing that, then we'd need to try dividing both parts of the fraction by $\left(1 + \frac{r}{1200}\right)^N$, since that's the only thing being multiplied by $\left(\frac{r}{1200}\right)$ in the numerator in the prompt. And an untrained test-taker may be tempted to try this, because $\left(1 + \frac{r}{1200}\right)^N$ does appear in the denominator of the prompt...but it doesn't appear by itself, and it doesn't appear as a quantity being multiplied by another quantity, so we can't divide the numerator and the denominator by $\left(1 + \frac{r}{1200}\right)^N$ in this case! A lot of untrained test-takers will simply overlook the − 1 in the denominator because they don't read carefully enough, and incorrectly assume the fraction can be simplified. This mistake would lead them to either (C) or (D).

Once we realize that the fraction from the prompt can't be simplified, we only have to figure out whether (A) or (B) is correct. The only difference between the two choices is that (A) involves multiplying m by the fraction from the prompt, while (B) involves multiplying m by the *reciprocal* of the fraction in the prompt. As trained test-takers, we know that we can only isolate P if we multiply both sides of the equation by the *reciprocal* of the coefficient of P (which is the same thing as dividing by the coefficient of P), which is what we see in (B)—so (B) must be correct.

ANSWER CHOICE ANALYSIS

(A): The compound fraction in this answer choice is the reciprocal of the compound fraction in the correct answer to trick people who forget that dividing by a fraction is the same thing as multiplying by the reciprocal of the fraction. **(C):** This wrong answer choice combines the mistakes made in (A) and (D). **(D):** You could easily arrive at this wrong answer by ignoring the −1 in the denominator of the original equation, and then thinking you could cancel out the fractions that are raised to the power of N.

Test 1, Section 3, Question 8

- **What's the prompt asking for?** The value of $\frac{4b}{a}$.
- **Math concepts in the prompt:** algebra, cross-multiplication
- **Elements of the answer choices:** All the answer choices are small numbers.
- **Notable differences among answer choices:** One choice is zero, while the other three are positive integers.

- **"Bridge" concepts:** We can apply algebraic transformations to the equation in the prompt to find a value for $\frac{4b}{a}$.
- **Pre-solution patterns (see p. 217):** halves and doubles; the first and last terms in a series are often wrong answers
- **Things to look out for:** Don't confuse b and a! Don't confuse the numbers 2 and 4 from the prompt and the answer choices!

Solution 1: Concrete: Choose values for a and b such that $\frac{a}{b} = 2$, and then evaluate $\frac{4b}{a}$.

Let $a = 6$ and $b = 3$.	(Note that $\frac{a}{b} = \frac{6}{3} = 2$)
$\dfrac{4b}{a}$	(given equation)
$\dfrac{4(3)}{6}$	(plug in $a = 6$ and $b = 3$)
2	(simplify)

So we can see that (C) is correct.

Solution 2: Abstract: Use algebra to manipulate the original equation until $\frac{4b}{a}$ is isolated on one side of the equation.

$$\frac{a}{b} = 2 \qquad \text{(original equation)}$$

$$a = 2b \qquad \text{(multiply both sides by } b\text{)}$$

$$1 = \frac{2b}{a} \qquad \text{(divide both sides by } a\text{)}$$

$$2 = \frac{4b}{a} \qquad \text{(multiply both sides by 2)}$$

Again, we can see that (C) is correct.

How to check? Note that the correct answer follows both of the patterns we would expect choices to usually follow: it's involved in a halves-and-doubles relationship with (B) and (D); it's neither first nor last in the series $1, 2, 4$; and it's neither first nor last in the series $0, 2, 4$. This adherence to the common patterns of the SAT Math section doesn't guarantee that (C) is correct, but it strongly suggests that (C) is likely to be correct, just as we think it is.

Note Any of the wrong answers might be tempting if an untrained test-taker made a range of basic mistakes, such as accidentally stopping at the next-to-last step in Solution 2 and thinking that the question was asking for the value of $\frac{2b}{a}$, which would lead to choosing (B) incorrectly.

Test 1, Section 3, Question 9

- **What's the prompt asking for?** A solution to the system in the prompt.
- **Math concepts in the prompt:** algebra, system of equations
- **Elements of the answer choices:** every choice is a set of (x, y) pairs with single-digit numbers as the value for each variable. two choices have -6 as the y-value.
- **Notable differences among answer choices:** Choice (A) has two negative numbers, while the other choices have positive x-values and negative y-values.

- **Concepts in the answer choices:** coordinate pairs
- **"Bridge" concepts:** The correct answer must be an (x, y) pair that can be plugged into both equations.
- **Pre-solution patterns (see p. 217):** wrong answers try to imitate right answers
- **Things to look out for:** Don't confuse x and y!

Solution 1: Concrete: Substitute each answer choice into the equations to see which choice satisfies both. Be sure to test every answer choice if you use this approach!

$3x + 4y = -23$	$2y - x = -19$	(original equations)
$3(-5) + 4(-2) = -23$	$2(-2) - (-5) = -19$	(plug in $(-5, -2)$ from (A))
$-23 = -23$	$1 \neq -19$	(simplify)

Choice (A) is a solution for the first equation, but not for the second equation.

$3x + 4y = -23$	$2y - x = -19$	(original equations)
$3(3) + 4(-8) = -23$	$2(-8) - (3) = -19$	(plug in $(3, -8)$ from (B))
$-23 = -23$	$-19 = -19$	(simplify)

Choice (B) is a solution for both equations.

$3x + 4y = -23$	$2y - x = -19$	(original equations)
$3(4) + 4(-6) = -23$	$2(-6) - (4) = -19$	(plug in $(4, -6)$ from (C))
$-12 \neq -23$	$-16 \neq -19$	(simplify)

Choice (C) isn't a solution for either equation.

$3x + 4y = -23$	$2y - x = -19$	(original equations)
$3(9) + 4(-6) = -23$	$2(-6) - (9) = -19$	(plug in $(9, -6)$ from (D))
$3 \neq -23$	$-21 \neq -19$	(simplify)

Choice (D) isn't a solution for either equation. Now that we've tried each answer choice, we can see that (B) is correct.

Solution 2: Algebraic: Combine the equations, solve for one variable, and use that value to solve for the other variable.

If we multiply the second equation by two, and then subtract that equation from the first equation, we can isolate the x term.

$$3x + 4y = -23$$
$$\underline{- \; -2x + 4y = -38}$$
$$5x \qquad = 15 \qquad \text{(subtract one equation from the other)}$$
$$x \qquad = 3 \qquad \text{(divide both sides by 5)}$$

Now that we know $x = 3$, we can plug that value in to either equation and solve for y. Let's use the second equation (I'm not picking the second equation for any particular reason—you could use either equation).

$$2y - x = -19 \qquad \text{(second equation)}$$
$$2y - 3 = -19 \qquad \text{(plug in } x = 3\text{)}$$
$$2y = -16 \qquad \text{(add 3 to both sides)}$$
$$y = -8 \qquad \text{(divide both sides by 2)}$$

So $x = 3$ and $y = -8$, which gives us the coordinate pair $(3, -8)$, meaning (B) is correct.

Solution 3: Algebraic: Isolate x or y in one equation, plug the resulting expression into the other equation, solve that equation for one variable, and then use it to find the value of the other variable.

Let's solve for x in the second equation, since the x in the second equation doesn't have a coefficient and that might make our algebra easier:

$$2y - x = -19 \qquad \text{(second equation)}$$
$$2y = -19 + x \qquad \text{(add } x \text{ to both sides)}$$
$$2y + 19 = x \qquad \text{(add 19 to both sides)}$$

Now that we have a value for x, we can plug that value in for x in the first equation:

$$3x + 4y = -23 \qquad \text{(first equation)}$$
$$3(2y + 19) + 4y = -23 \qquad \text{(plug in } x = 2y + 19 \text{)}$$
$$6y + 57 + 4y = -23 \qquad \text{(distribute the 3)}$$
$$10y + 57 = -23 \qquad \text{(simplify)}$$
$$10y = -80 \qquad \text{(subtract 57 from both sides)}$$
$$y = -8 \qquad \text{(divide both sides by 10)}$$

Now that we have a value for y, we can plug that into either equation and solve for x. Let's use the first equation, for no particular reason:

$$3x + 4y = -23 \qquad \text{(first equation)}$$
$$3x + 4(-8) = -23 \qquad \text{(plug in } y = 8 \text{)}$$
$$3x - 32 = -23 \qquad \text{(simplify)}$$
$$3x = 9 \qquad \text{(add 32 to both sides)}$$
$$x = 3 \qquad \text{(divide both sides by 3)}$$

So $x = 3$ and $y = -8$, which gives us the coordinate pair $(3, -8)$, and we know (B) is right.

ANSWER CHOICE ANALYSIS

(A): This choice works in the first equation from the prompt, but not the second one. Some test-takers will choose this incorrectly because they don't test things out thoroughly enough when they backsolve. **(C):** This choice doesn't satisfy either equation in the prompt. **(D):** This choice doesn't satisfy either equation in the prompt.

How to check? Plug the values you found back into the original equations and re-verify that they work.

Test 1, Section 3, Question 10

- **What's the prompt asking for?** The output of the given function when -4 is the input.
- **Math concepts in the prompt:** constants, functions, substitution, variables
- **Elements of the answer choices:** (A) and (D) have the same absolute value.

- **Notable differences among answer choices:** The choices are broadly different.
- **"Bridge" concepts:** We can use the given value of $g(4)$ to determine the value of $g(-4)$.
- **Pre-solution patterns (see p. 217):** opposites
- **Things to look out for:** Don't get confused between positive and negative numbers! Don't solve for a instead of x!

Solution 1: Algebraic: First, find the value of a by substituting $x = 4$ for and solving for a. Then, use the value of a to find $g(-4)$.

$$g(x) = ax^2 + 24 \qquad \text{(given function)}$$
$$8 = a(4)^2 + 24 \qquad \text{(plug in 4 and set function equal to 8)}$$
$$8 = 16a + 24 \qquad \text{(square 4)}$$
$$-16 = 16a \qquad \text{(subtract 24 from both sides)}$$
$$-1 = a \qquad \text{(divide both sides by 16)}$$

When we substitute $a = -1$ in the original function, we can find $g(-4)$:

$$g(x) = ax^2 + 24 \qquad \text{(given function)}$$

$$g(x) = (-1)x^2 + 24 \quad \text{(plug in } a = -1)$$
$$g(-4) = (-1)(-4)^2 + 24 \quad \text{(find } g(-4))$$
$$g(-4) = (-1)16 + 24 \quad \text{(square } -4)$$
$$g(-4) = 8 \quad \text{(simplify)}$$

So we can see that (A) is correct.

Solution 2: Abstract: Notice that the function involves squaring x immediately, which means that $g(-4)$ and $g(4)$ are equal. Since the question tells us the value of $g(4)$ is 8, we know the value of $g(-4)$ is also 8, and that (A) is correct.

ANSWER CHOICE ANALYSIS

(B): This choice could be tempting if we make an algebra mistake when we try to solve for a. **(C):** This wrong answer choice is the value of a, in order to trick test-takers who forget to complete the calculation by using $a = -1$ to find $g(-4)$. **(D):** This answer is meant to trick untrained test-takers who think that $g(-4)$ must be the opposite of $g(4)$, just because -4 is the opposite of 4.

How to check? Either notice and re-confirm that the output of $g(4)$ must be the same as the output of $g(-4)$, or re-confirm that a is -1, and then re-find $g(-4)$.

▶ **Post-solution patterns (see page 218):** opposites; right answer to the wrong question; right approach, wrong step

Note This is a good example of the way we can often avoid certain calculations if we pay attention to how a question is constructed. Solving this question by noting that $g(-4)$ must equal $g(4)$ is not only faster, but also allows us to reduce the likelihood of making a small calculation error, because it eliminates the need to do any calculations.

Test 1, Section 3, Question 11

- **What's the prompt asking for?** The price for a pound of beef when it was equal to the price of a pound of chicken.
- **Math concepts in the prompt:** algebra, algebraic modeling, formulas, variables
- **Elements of the answer choices:** Each choice is a price between $2.60 and $3.35.

- **Notable differences among answer choices:** Three of the choices are less than $3, while one isn't. Three of the choices end in 5, while one ends in 0.
- **Concepts in the answer choices:** The first answer choice is the sum of the two numbers in the function for b.
- **"Bridge" concepts:** Some value of x causes b and c to be equal. We have to find that value of x, and then see what b and c are equal to for that value of x.

Solution 1: Concrete: Plug each choice into both equations from the prompt. See which one creates the same x-value in both equations.

$$b = 2.35 + 0.25x \quad \text{(equation for the price of beef)}$$
$$2.60 = 2.35 + 0.25x \quad \text{(plug in } b = 2.60 \text{ from choice (A))}$$
$$0.25 = 0.25x \quad \text{(subtract 2.35 from both sides)}$$
$$1 = x \quad \text{(divide both sides by 0.25)}$$
$$c = 1.75 + 0.40x \quad \text{(equation for the price of chicken)}$$
$$2.60 = 1.75 + 0.40x \quad \text{(plug in } c = 2.60)$$
$$0.85 = 0.40x \quad \text{(subtract 1.75 from both sides)}$$
$$2.125 = x \quad \text{(divide both sides by 0.40)}$$

At these prices, the x-values are different from each other, so the beef and chicken were $2.60 per pound at different times, which means (A) must be wrong.

$$b = 2.35 + 0.25x \quad \text{(equation for the price of beef)}$$
$$2.85 = 2.35 + 0.25x \quad \text{(plug in } b = 2.85 \text{ from choice (B))}$$
$$0.50 = 0.25x \quad \text{(subtract 2.35 from both sides)}$$
$$2 = x \quad \text{(divide both sides by 0.25)}$$
$$c = 1.75 + 0.40x \quad \text{(equation for the price of chicken)}$$
$$2.85 = 1.75 + 0.40x \quad \text{(plug in } c = 2.85)$$
$$1.10 = 0.40x \quad \text{(subtract 1.75 from both sides)}$$
$$2.75 = x \quad \text{(divide both sides by 0.40)}$$

At these prices, the x-values are different from each other, so the beef and chicken were $2.85 per pound at different times, which means (B) must be wrong.

$$b = 2.35 + 0.25x \quad \text{(equation for the price of beef)}$$
$$2.95 = 2.35 + 0.25x \quad \text{(plug in } b = 2.95 \text{ from choice (C))}$$
$$0.60 = 0.25x \quad \text{(subtract 2.35 from both sides)}$$

$$2.4 = x \quad \text{(divide both sides by 0.25)}$$
$$c = 1.75 + 0.40x \quad \text{(equation for the price of chicken)}$$
$$2.95 = 1.75 + 0.40x \quad \text{(plug in } c = 2.95\text{)}$$
$$1.20 = 0.40x \quad \text{(subtract 1.75 from both sides)}$$
$$3 = x \quad \text{(divide both sides by 0.40)}$$

At these prices, the x-values are different from each other, so the beef and chicken were \$2.95 per pound at different times, which means (C) must be wrong.

$$b = 2.35 + 0.25x \quad \text{(equation for the price of beef)}$$
$$3.35 = 2.35 + 0.25x \quad \text{(plug in } b = 3.35 \text{ from choice (D))}$$
$$1.00 = 0.25x \quad \text{(subtract 2.35 from both sides)}$$
$$4 = x \quad \text{(divide both sides by 0.25)}$$
$$c = 1.75 + 0.40x \quad \text{(equation for the price of chicken)}$$
$$3.35 = 1.75 + 0.40x \quad \text{(plug in } c = 3.35\text{)}$$
$$1.60 = 0.40x \quad \text{(subtract 1.75 from both sides)}$$
$$4 = x \quad \text{(divide both sides by 0.40)}$$

At these prices, the x-values are both 4, so the beef and chicken were \$3.35 per pound at the same time: 4 weeks after July 1. We can see that (D) is correct.

Solution 2: Algebraic: Set the functions for b and c equal to each other, find x, then use that value of x to find b and c.

$$2.35 + 0.25x = 1.75 + 0.40x \quad \text{(set equations equal to one another)}$$
$$0.6 + 0.25x = 0.40x \quad \text{(subtract 1.75 from both sides)}$$
$$0.6 = 0.15x \quad \text{(subtract 0.25x from both sides)}$$
$$60 = 15x \quad \text{(multiply both sides by 100)}$$
$$\frac{60}{15} = x \quad \text{(divide both sides by 15)}$$
$$4 = x \quad \text{(reduce)}$$

Now that we know the x-value that makes the equations equal to one another, we can plug $x = 4$ into either equation to find out what the price of beef was when it was equal to the price of chicken. We'll plug the value into the first equation for no particular reason (either one would work).

$$b = 2.35 + 0.25x \quad \text{(equation for the price of beef)}$$
$$b = 2.35 + 0.25(4) \quad \text{(plug in } x = 4\text{)}$$
$$b = 3.35 \quad \text{(simplify)}$$

So we can see again that (D) is correct.

Solution 3: Test-smart: Notice that (A) is the sum of \$2.35 and \$0.25, which are the two quantities in the b function. Realize you can easily work out the first few possible values of the b function, and see which one could also be a value of the c function.

We know from the prompt that the correct answer must be a possible value of both the b function and the c function. Since we're used to the idea of mentally comparing the quantities in the answer choices to the quantities in the prompt, we might notice that (A) is the sum of \$2.35 and \$0.25 from the prompt—in other words, (A) is the value of b after the first week, when $x = 1$. That might make us realize that we could quickly mentally determine which other answer choices could also possibly be values of b, since each possible value of b would involve adding \$0.25 to \$2.35 a certain number of times—and since the choices aren't much larger than \$2.35 in the first place, we know we wouldn't have to think about adding \$0.25 dozens of times or anything.

We can see that (B) is \$0.25 more than (A), so (B) could also potentially be a value of b. But (C) is only \$0.10 more than (B), so (C) can't be a value of b. (D), on the other hand, is \$0.50 more than (B), which means it could also be a value of b, since \$0.50 is exactly twice as much as \$0.25. So we can see that (A), (B), and (D) could all be values of b. Now the question is this: which of those values could also be a value of c? Well, we can do a similar kind of mental calculation to determine that: \$1.75 + \$0.40 is \$2.15. Adding \$0.40 again gives us \$2.55. Adding \$0.40 again gives us \$2.95. Adding \$0.40 again gives us \$3.35. So the only possible value of b in the choices that can also be a possible value of c is \$3.35, which means (D) must be correct.

ANSWER CHOICE ANALYSIS

(A): This choice is the sum of the two values in the b function. It's the value of b when $x = 1$. **(B):** This is the value of b when $x = 2$. **(C):** This is the value of c when x is 3. **(D):** Correct: this is the value of both b and c when x is 4.

How to check? Re-verify that (D) is possible for both functions when $x = 4$, and that no other value is possible for both functions.

▶ Post-solution patterns (see page 218): right approach, wrong step

---

- **What's the prompt asking for?** A point on the line that goes through the origin and has a slope of $\frac{1}{7}$.

- **Math concepts in the prompt:** linear functions, origin, slope, xy-coordinate plane

- **Elements of the answer choices:** Each choice has at least one value that's a multiple of 7.

- **Notable differences among answer choices:** (A) and (B) are the only choices with an x-value that's less than their y-values. (C) is the only choice with an x-value equal to its y-value. (D) is the only choice with an x-value larger than its y-value.

- **Concepts in the answer choices:** slopes greater than, equal to, or less than 1

- **"Bridge" concepts:** Since the line in the prompt goes through the origin and the slope is $\frac{1}{7}$, the correct answer needs to have (x, y) values in a $7:1$ ratio, because the denominator in the slope fraction corresponds to the horizontal component of the slope, and the numerator corresponds to the vertical component of the slope.

- **Pre-solution patterns (see p. 217):** halves and doubles; wrong answers try to imitate right answers

- **Things to look out for:** Don't confuse rise and run! Don't confuse x and y!

Solution 1: Algebraic: Construct an equation for the line in the prompt, then see which choice has values that satisfy the equation.

We can use $y = mx + b$ to define a straight-line function, where m is the slope and b is the y-intercept. The prompt tells us that the line has a slope of $\frac{1}{7}$, and the lines passes through the origin, so the y-intercept must be 0. When we plug those values into $y = mx + b$ we end up with $y = \frac{1}{7}x + 0$, or $y = \frac{1}{7}x$.

Now that we have an equation for the line, we can plug in the pairs of (x, y) coordinates from the answer choices to see which one is on the line:

$$y = \frac{1}{7}x \qquad \text{(equation for the line)}$$
$$7 = \frac{1}{7}(0) \qquad \text{(plug in } (0, 7) \text{ from choice (A))}$$
$$7 \neq 0 \qquad \text{(simplify)}$$

The coordinate pair $(0, 7)$ isn't on the line $y = \frac{1}{7}x$, so (A) must be wrong.

$$7 = \frac{1}{7}(1) \qquad \text{(plug in } (1, 7) \text{ from choice (B))}$$
$$7 \neq \frac{1}{7} \qquad \text{(simplify)}$$

The coordinate pair $(1, 7)$ isn't on the line $y = \frac{1}{7}x$, so (B) must also be wrong.

$$7 = \frac{1}{7}(7) \qquad \text{(plug in } (7, 7) \text{ from (C))}$$
$$7 \neq 1 \qquad \text{(simplify)}$$

The coordinate pair $(7, 7)$ isn't on the line $y = \frac{1}{7}x$, so (C) must be wrong, too.

$$2 = \frac{1}{7}(14) \qquad \text{(plug in } (14, 2) \text{ from (D))}$$
$$2 = 2 \qquad \text{(simplify)}$$

The coordinate pair $(14, 2)$ is on the line $y = \frac{1}{7}x$, so (D) is correct.

Solution 2: Diagramming: Sketch an xy-plane and roughly plot the points from each answer choice, along with a line that goes through the origin and has a slope of $\frac{1}{7}$. The correct answer will be the one whose point is on the line. Note that the wrong answers are pretty far away from the line once we actually sketch them out:

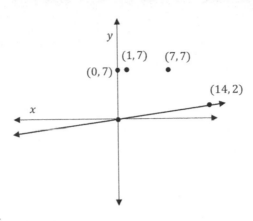

We can see that (D) is the correct answer.

Solution 3: Test-smart: Note that the correct answer choice must have an x-value larger than its y-value, so only (D) can be correct.

If the line goes through the origin, then the point $(0, 0)$ must be on the line, because $(0, 0)$ is the origin. If the slope is $\frac{1}{7}$, then for every 1 unit the line travels upward, it must travel 7 units to the right. The x-coordinate of any point measures how far the point is from the y-axis, and the y-coordinate measures how far the point is from the x-axis. So if a line through the origin travels 1 unit up for every 7 units it travels to the right, then the x-coordinate must always be larger than the y-coordinate. Only (D) has an x-coordinate larger than the y-coordinate, so only (D) can be correct.

ANSWER CHOICE ANALYSIS

(A): This point would lie on the line if the y-intercept were 7. Instead, the prompt says the line passes through the origin, and the slope is $\frac{1}{7}$. **(B):** This point would lie on the line if the slope were 7, not $\frac{1}{7}$. **(C):** This point would lie on the line if the slope were $\frac{7}{7}$, not $\frac{1}{7}$.

How to check? Once we realize that the line in the prompt is much closer to horizontal than vertical, it becomes clear that only (D) can be correct when we re-check the details of our approach.

> **Note**   Many test-takers will waste unnecessary time on this question. But we can quickly tell (D) is right if we stand back and consider how the choices relate to the prompt. We should remember to look out for these kinds of opportunities! The College Board could have made this question much more challenging by including more than one choice near the line in the prompt, or by making the y-intercept of the line something other than zero.

Test 1, Section 3, Question 13

- **What's the prompt asking for?** The choice equal to the expression in the prompt when x is greater than 3.

- **Math concepts in the prompt:** algebra, compound fractions, inequalities, polynomials

- **Elements of the answer choices:** Every choice includes 5, which is the sum of 3 and 2 from the expression in the prompt.

- **Notable differences among answer choices:** (A) and (B) have fraction bars, and are reciprocals of one another. (A), (B), and (D) include x^2, while (C) doesn't. (C) is the only choice without the number 6. (C) is also the numerator in (A) and the denominator in (B). (D) is the denominator in (A) and the numerator in (B).

- **Concepts in the answer choices:** polynomials

- **"Bridge" concepts:** Algebra and PEMDAS will allow us to transform the expression in the prompt into one of the answer choices.

- **Pre-solution patterns (see p. 217):** opposites; wrong answers try to imitate right answers

- **Things to look out for:** Don't confuse the numerator and denominator! Make sure you cancel correctly if you decide to cancel something!

Solution 1: Concrete: Choose a number for x that's bigger than 3, and then plug it into every expression in the whole question. The correct answer will be the answer choice that ends up having a value equal to the value of the expression in the prompt.

Let's plug in $x = 5$ (we could pick any number for x that's larger than 3. I just like 5, for no particular reason):

$$\frac{1}{\frac{1}{x+2} + \frac{1}{x+3}}$$ (original equation)

$$\frac{1}{\frac{1}{5+2}+\frac{1}{5+3}}$$

(plug in $x=5$, because 5 is bigger than 3)

$$\frac{1}{\frac{1}{7}+\frac{1}{8}}$$

(simplify)

$$\frac{1}{\frac{1}{7}\left(\frac{8}{8}\right)+\frac{1}{8}\left(\frac{7}{7}\right)}$$

(change to least common denominators)

$$\frac{1}{\frac{8}{56}+\frac{7}{56}}$$

(simplify)

$$\frac{1}{\frac{15}{56}}$$

(simplify)

$$\frac{56}{15}$$

(simplify)

Now let's plug $x=5$ into the expressions from the answer choices to see which one equals $\frac{56}{15}$:

$$\frac{2x+5}{x^2+5x+6}$$

(original expression from (A))

$$\frac{2(5)+5}{5^2+5(5)+6}$$

(plug in $x=5$)

$$\frac{15}{56}$$

(simplify)

This expression doesn't have the same value as the expression from the prompt when we plug in $x=5$, so (A) can't be correct.

$$\frac{x^2+5x+6}{2x+5}$$

(original expression from (B))

$$\frac{5^2+5(5)+6}{2(5)+5}$$

(plug in $x=5$)

$$\frac{56}{15}$$

(simplify)

This expression has the same value as the expression from the prompt when we plug in $x=5$, so (B) seems to be correct. Since we're trained test-takers and we know that one of the best ways to avoid small mistakes on the SAT Math section is to check every answer choice for every question, we'll check the other answer choices to make sure we haven't made a mistake:

$$2x+5$$

(original expression from (C))

$$2(5)+5$$

(plug in $x=5$)

$$15$$

(simplify)

This expression doesn't have the same value as the expression from the prompt when we plug in $x=5$, so (C) can't be correct.

$$x^2+5x+6$$

(original expression from (D))

$$5^2+5(5)+6$$

(plug in $x=5$)

$$56$$

(simplify)

This expression doesn't have the same value as the expression from the prompt when we plug in $x=5$, so (D) is wrong, too. We can see now that (B) is, indeed, right.

Solution 2: Algebraic: Manipulate the expression in the prompt until it matches one of the expressions in the answer choices.

None of the answer choices has a fraction in the denominator, so we'll have to figure out a way to get the fractions out of the denominator. We need to put the two fractions in terms of the same denominator to do this:

$$\frac{1}{\frac{1}{x+2}+\frac{1}{x+3}}$$

(original equation)

$$\frac{1}{\frac{1}{x+2}\left(\frac{x+3}{x+3}\right)+\frac{1}{x+3}\left(\frac{x+2}{x+2}\right)}$$

(put each fraction in terms of the least common denominator)

$$\frac{1}{\frac{x+3}{x^2+5x+6}+\frac{x+2}{x^2+5x+6}}$$ (multiply)

$$\frac{1}{\frac{2x+5}{x^2+5x+6}}$$ (add the fractions in the denominator)

$$\frac{x^2+5x+6}{2x+5}$$ (simplify)

The result is the same as the expression from (B), so we know (B) must be correct.

Solution 3: Test-smart: Note that the correct answer must be greater than 1, and must be a fraction. Only (B) meets those conditions.

The original expression in the prompt is a compound fraction whose numerator is 1, and each of the sub-fractions in the denominator also has a numerator of 1. Meanwhile, the denominators of the sub-fractions must each be larger than 1, because they involve adding x to 2 and 3, and x itself is already larger than 1, since $x > 3$ according to the question. When we combine all of these ideas, we see that the fraction in the prompt is the reciprocal of a fraction that's less than 1:

- Each of the sub-fractions in the denominator of the main fraction must be less than 1 by itself, because we have to get a number that's less than 1 if we divide 1 by a number larger than itself. In fact, each sub-fraction must be less than $\frac{1}{2}$, because each sub-fraction involves dividing 1 by a number that's larger than 3. So the two sub-fractions must add up to a number less than 1, because each of them is less than $\frac{1}{2}$.

- This means that, when we evaluate the main fraction, we'll be dividing 1 by a number that's smaller than 1, which is the same thing as multiplying 1 by a number that's larger than 1 (see the calculations for choice (B) in solution 1 for an example of this).

So, again, we know that the fraction in the prompt must have a value greater than 1. We also know that there's no way to simplify the fraction in the prompt so that it's no longer a fraction, because the denominator of the fraction involves adding other fractions that don't have a common denominator (again, see the calculations for choice (B) in solution 1 for an example of this).

When we look at the answer choices, we see that only (B) would result in a fraction that must be more than 1, given that x is a number larger than 3, so we know (B) is correct. (If this test-smart solution is a little intimidating for you, don't worry—the other solutions work just as well, of course.)

ANSWER CHOICE ANALYSIS

(A): This is the reciprocal of the correct answer, to trap test-takers who make a mistake in dealing with the compound fraction in the prompt. **(C):** This is the denominator of the correct answer. **(D):** This is the numerator of the correct answer.

How to check? We can choose an alternate approach, or notice that the correct answer must be a fraction larger than 1 when $x > 3$.

Test 1, Section 3, Question 14

- What's the prompt asking for? The value of $\frac{8^x}{2^y}$.

- **Math concepts in the prompt:** algebra, exponents, fractions, variables

- **Elements of the answer choices:** Apart from (D), each of the choices has an exponent of 2 as a base

- **Notable differences among answer choices:** (D) indicates that the correct answer cannot be determined.

- **Concepts in the answer choices:** exponents with different bases, powers of 2

- **"Bridge" concepts:** If there's a ratio that must exist between x and y, then we pick the answer choice that matches it. If there's no definite ratio between x and y, we'll pick (D).

- **Pre-solution patterns (see p. 217):** halves and doubles

- **Things to look out for:** Don't forget that a large number of (x, y) pairs will satisfy the equation in the prompt! Don't switch x and y! Remember we can only pick (D) if we have a concrete reason to do so—we can't just pick it because we don't know how to answer the question!

Solution 1: Concrete: Come up with values that satisfy the equation in the prompt, and then plug them into the ratio. Make sure to test multiple pairs of (x, y) values to test whether (D) is correct as well.

If $3x - y = 12$, then $3x$ is more than 12. Let's think of numbers we can multiply by 3 that give us a little more than 12. Well, 12 itself is 3×4, so let's try 3×5, or 15. If $x = 5$, that gives us this:

$$3x - y = 12$$ (original expression)

$$15 - y = 12 \quad \text{(result when we plug in } x = 5)$$
$$15 = 12 + y \quad \text{(add } y \text{ to both sides)}$$
$$3 = y \quad \text{(subtract 12 from both sides)}$$

So when $x = 5$, $y = 3$. Let's plug those values into $\frac{8^x}{2^y}$.

$$\frac{8^x}{2^y} \quad \text{(expression from the prompt)}$$

$$\frac{8^5}{2^3} \quad \text{(substitute } x = 5 \text{ and } y = 3)$$

$$\frac{8^5}{8} \quad \text{(simplify } 2^3)$$

$$8^4 \quad \text{(divide the numerator and denominator by 8)}$$

At this point we may notice that our answer doesn't look like any of the answer choices. We know that (C) must be wrong, because 8^2 can't equal 8^4. We also know (B) can't be right, because raising 4 to the fourth power can't give us the same result as raising 8 to the fourth power, since 4 and 8 are different numbers. So that leaves us with (A) to consider: can 8^4 equal 2^{12}? Yes, because 8 is equal to 2^3, and when we substitute 2^3 for 8, we get $(2^3)^4$, which is the same as 2^{12}. This means we also know (D) is wrong, because we've found that the value of $\frac{8^x}{2^y}$ can be determined from the information given.

To make sure that the ratio of x to y is constant for all values of x and y that satisfy the prompt, and not just the result of picking $x = 5$, let's think of another (x, y) pair for which $3x - y = 12$. Let's set x equal to 7 (just to pick a value at random that isn't already in the question) and see what y would equal then:

$$3x - y = 12 \quad \text{(original expression)}$$
$$21 - y = 12 \quad \text{(result when we plug in } x = 7)$$
$$21 = 12 + y \quad \text{(add } y \text{ to both sides)}$$
$$9 = y \quad \text{(subtract 12 from both sides)}$$

So when $x = 7$, $y = 9$. Let's plug that into $\frac{8^x}{2^y}$:

$$\frac{8^x}{2^y} \quad \text{(expression from prompt)}$$

$$\frac{8^7}{2^9} \quad \text{(substitute } x = 7 \text{ and } y = 9)$$

$$\frac{8^7}{(2^3)(2^3)(2^3)} \quad \text{(express } 2^9 \text{ as to } 2^3 2^3 2^3 \text{ make simplifying easier)}$$

$$\frac{8^7}{(8)(8)(8)} \quad \text{(express } 2^3 \text{ as 8 to make simplifying easier)}$$

$$\frac{8^7}{8^3} \quad \text{(express } (8)(8)(8) \text{ as } 8^3 \text{ to make simplifying easier)}$$

$$8^4 \quad \text{(divide the numerator and denominator by } 8^3, \text{ or } 2^9)$$

$$2^{12} \quad \text{(express } 8^4 \text{ as } 2^{12}, \text{ as we did before)}$$

So we can see that the ratio holds true for different (x, y) pairs, and (A) must be correct.

Solution 2: Abstract: Recognize that the numerator and denominator of the expression $\frac{8^x}{2^y}$ involve two different powers of 2, because 8 can be expressed as 2^3. Express the ratio in terms of a common base, simplify, and compare to the equation in the prompt.

Let's plug in 2^3 for 8 and see what we get:

$$\frac{(2^3)^x}{2^y} \quad \text{(plug in } 2^3 \text{ for 8)}$$

$$\frac{2^{3x}}{2^y}$$
(simplify 2^{3^x})

From there, we can make a further algebraic simplification:

$$2^{3x-y}$$
(simplify $\frac{2^{3x}}{2^y}$)

At this point, we can realize that the expression in the exponent is equal to the left-hand side of the equation in the prompt, which means the exponent must be equal to 12 (remember that the prompt tells us $3x - y = 12$).

$$2^{12}$$
(substitute 12 for $3x - y$)

This means, again, that 2^{12} must be the correct answer, so (A) is correct.

Note (B), (C), or (D) could all tempt an untrained test-taker who was unclear on the properties of exponents, and made an algebra mistake as a result. Also, the College Board could have made this question more difficult by using powers of 3 or of some other larger number, or by making the equation in the prompt less obviously related to the ratio.

Test 1, Section 3, Question 15

- **What's the prompt asking for?** The two possible values for c, given that $a + b = 8$.
- **Math concepts in the prompt:** algebra, FOIL, polynomials, variables
- **Notable differences among answer choices:** Every choice except (D) has one value that's a multiple of 3 and one value that's a multiple of 5. (A) and (D) both have prime numbers. (B) and (C) both include a multiple of 7 and a multiple of 2. No two answer choices share a number. The two terms in choice (B) add up to one of the terms in choice (D), and the two terms in (C) add up to one of the terms in (D).
- **Concepts in the answer choices:** multiples of 2, multiples of 3, multiples of 5, multiples of 7, prime numbers
- **"Bridge" concepts:** If we figure out the possible values of a and b, we can use them in the FOIL process to determine possible values of c.
- **Things to look out for:** Don't confuse the values of a and b with the values of c!

Solution 1: Algebraic: Determine the possible values of a and b according to FOIL, and then determine the possible values of c.

For this solution, we need to find the possible values of a and b, and then plug them into the left-hand side of the equation so that we can find possible values for c. If we used FOIL on the expression on the left-hand side of the equation, we would see that $(ax)(bx)$ must equal $15x^2$, since ax and bx correspond to the "First" term in the FOIL process, and $15x^2$ is their product. Since $(ax)(bx) = 15x^2$, we know the following:

$(ax)(bx) = 15x^2$ (the definition of the "First" part of FOIL)

$abx^2 = 15x^2$ (multiply ax and bx)

$ab = 15$ (divide both sides by x^2)

So we know that the product of a and b must be 15. We also know from the prompt that the sum of a and b is 8. And if a and b are two numbers that add up to 8 and multiply out to 15, the only possible values for a and b are 5 and 3...but we still don't know which variable is 5 and which one is 3.

Let's plug those possible values into the equation, use FOIL, and see what we get:

$(ax + 2)(bx + 7) = 15x^2 + cx + 14$ (original equation)

$abx^2 + 2bx + 7ax + 14 = 15x^2 + cx + 14$ (FOIL left side)

$abx^2 + 2bx + 7ax = 15x^2 + cx$ (subtract 14 from both sides)

At this point we can isolate cx if we remember that $15x^2$ is equal to abx^2:

$2bx + 7ax = cx$ (subtract abx^2 from left and $15x^2$ from right, since $abx^2 - 15x^2$)

$2b + 7a = c$ (divide both sides by x to isolate c)

Now we can find the possible values of x when we plug in the two possible combinations of values for a and b:

$2(3) + 7(5) = c$ (plug in $(3, 5)$ to find one possible combination of (a, b) values)

$6 + 35 = c$ (simplify $2(3)$ and $7(5)$)

$41 = c$ (add 6 and 35)

$2(5) + 7(3) = c$ (plug in $(5, 3)$ as the other possible combination of (a, b) values)

$$10 + 21 = c \qquad \text{(simplify 2(5) and 7(3))}$$
$$31 = c \qquad \text{(add 10 and 21)}$$

So the two possible values for c are 41 and 31, which means (D) is correct.

ANSWER CHOICE ANALYSIS

(A): These are the only possible values for a and b, given that ab must be 15 and $a + b = 8$. (Note that we don't know whether a or b is 3 or 5 individually, but we do know that one must be 3 and one must be 5.) **(B):** These are the two coefficients of x during the FOIL process when $a = 5$ and $b = 3$. **(C):** These are the two coefficients of x during the FOIL process when $a = 3$ and $b = 5$.

How to check? We can observe the relationships among the answer choices to re-trace the process of solving the question and make sure we're correct. We can re-trace the calculation carefully.

▶ Post-solution patterns (see page 218): right approach, wrong step

Test 1, Section 3, Question 16

- **What's the prompt asking for?** The value of t
- **Math concepts in the prompt:** algebra, inequalities, positive/negative, squares and square roots

- **"Bridge" concepts:** We can use algebra to determine the value of t that satisfies both statements in the prompt.

Solution 1: Algebraic: Solve the equation in the prompt to find the possible values of t, then mark the value that's greater than zero.

$$t^2 - 4 = 0 \qquad \text{(given equation)}$$
$$t^2 = 4 \qquad \text{(add 4 to both sides)}$$
$$t = 2 \text{ or } t = -2 \qquad \text{(take square root of both sides)}$$

Given that $t > 0$, we know $t = 2$.

How to check? Re-work the question carefully.

Note   This question is relatively easy, and has the same influence on your score as any other question in this section. Trained test-takers know that it's very important to answer these kinds of questions correctly. We also want to answer them as quickly as possible (without sacrificing accuracy!) so we can take the time we save and invest it in other questions. For more on these ideas, see "Time Management on Test Day" on page 36 of this Black Book.

Test 1, Section 3, Question 17

- **What's the prompt asking for?** The value of x in the diagram
- **Math concepts in the prompt:** congruent angles, similar triangles, transversals
- **Math concepts in the diagram:** similar triangles, vertical angles are congruent
- **"Bridge" concepts:** We can see from the diagram that ABE and BDC are similar triangles, since angles D and E are

congruent, and the two angles at B are also congruent. This will allow us to determine the ratio between any two corresponding sides of the two triangles; from there, we can find the value of x by comparing it to the length of DC.

- **Things to look out for:** Don't assign values from the prompt to the wrong parts of the diagram!

Solution 1: Geometric: Determine the ratio between two corresponding sides of the triangles, and then use that ratio to determine x by comparing it to DC.

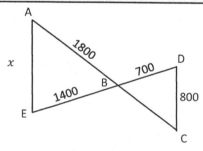

Given that $\angle AEB$ is equal to $\angle BDC$, and $\angle ABE$ is equal to $\angle DBC$ (since they're vertical angles), $\triangle ABE$ must be congruent to $\triangle BCD$.

Side EB corresponds to side BD, and the ratio of EB to BD is $\frac{1400}{700}$, which reduces to $\frac{2}{1}$. So side AE must be twice as long as side DC. Since DC is 800 feet long, the value of x must be 2 times 800, or 1600.

Solution 2: Geometric: Determine the ratio between BD and DC, and apply that ratio to BE and x, since BE corresponds to BD in the same way that x corresponds to DC.

Once we understand that the two triangles are congruent—as discussed in the previous solution—we can set up a ratio of side lengths like this:

$$\frac{DC}{BD} = \frac{AE}{EB}$$ (set up ratio)

$$\frac{800}{700} = \frac{x}{1400}$$ (plug in values from diagram)

$$800 \times 1400 = 700x$$ (cross multiply)

$$x = \frac{800 \times 1400}{700}$$ (divide both sides by 700)

$$x = 800 \times 2$$ (reduce)

$$x = 1600$$ (simplify)

So, again, we see that 1600 is the correct answer.

How to check? Try one of the alternate approaches above, or compare the value of x to other lengths in the diagram to ensure that x makes triangle ABE similar to triangle BDC, since we know the diagram is drawn to scale.

Test 1, Section 3, Question 18

- **What's the prompt asking for?** The value of x
- **Math concepts in the prompt:** systems of equations

- **"Bridge" concepts:** We can use algebra or trial and error to determine values of x and y that satisfy both equations.
- **Things to look out for:** Don't confuse x and y in your algebra!

Solution 1: Algebra: Combine the two equations to isolate y, and then use y to find x.

If we subtract the first equation from the second equation, we'll be able to isolate y:

$$x + 2y = -25$$
$$- \quad x + y \ = -9$$
$$\overline{\qquad\quad y = -16}$$ (subtract one equation from the other)

Now we can plug $y = -16$ into either equation and solve for x.

$$x + y = -9$$ (first equation from the prompt)
$$x + (-16) = -9$$ (plug in $y = -16$)
$$x = 7$$ (add 16 to both sides)

So the correct answer is 7.

Solution 2: Algebra: Isolate x in one of the equations, and plug the definition of x into the other equation, then solve for x.

$$x + y = -9$$ (first equation from the prompt)
$$x = -9 - y$$ (subtract y from both sides)

Now we can plug $x = -9 - y$ into the other equation:

$$x + 2y = -25$$ (second equation from the prompt)
$$-9 - y + 2y = -25$$ (plug in $x = -9 - y$)
$$y = -16$$ (combine like terms and add 9 to both sides)

As we saw in the last solution, we can now plug $y = -16$ into either equation and solve for x.

$$x + y = -9$$ (first equation from the prompt)
$$x + (-16) = -9$$ (plug in $y = -16$)
$$x = 7$$ (add 16 to both sides)

So the correct answer is 7.

Solution 3: Test-smart: Note that y must be -16, then determine x from the first equation and check it in the second equation.

The difference between $x + y$ and $x + 2y$ is that the second equation includes one more y than the first equation. So if $x + y$ equals -9, and $x + 2y$ equals -25, then adding another y must be the same as subtracting 16, because one more y changes the result from -9 in the first equation to -25 in the second equation. So we know that $y = -16$. We can solve for x by plugging $y = -16$ into the first equation—we'll see that x equals -9 plus 16, or $x = 7$. We can plug these values into the second equation to check our work:

$$x + 2y = -25$$ (second equation from the prompt)
$$(7) + 2(-16) = -25$$ (plug in $x = 7$ and $y = -16$)
$$-25 = -25$$ (simplify)

So the correct answer is 7.

How to check? Re-check the values of x and y. Be very careful not to mark down the value of y, since the question asked for x!

Note   This is a great example of the way that we can often avoid more detailed calculations if we keep our eyes out for opportunities to use mental math, such as identifying that y must be equal to the difference between -9 and -25.

Test 1, Section 3, Question 19

- **What's the prompt asking for?** The cosine of $(90 - x)$ degrees.
- **Math concepts in the prompt:** complementary angles, fractions, right triangles, trigonometry

- **"Bridge" concepts:** We can use SOHCAHTOA or the unit circle to relate the sine of one angle to the cosine of its complement.
- **Things to look out for:** Don't confuse sine and cosine! Don't get confused between x and the complement of x!

Solution 1: SOHCAHTOA: Sketch a right triangle like the one in the prompt. Use it to find the cosine of the complement of x.

Let's sketch the right triangle described in the prompt:

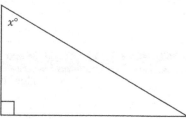

We know that $\sin x° = \frac{4}{5}$. We know from SOHCAHTOA that $Sine = \frac{Opposite}{Hypotenuse}$, so the opposite side must have a length of 4, and the hypotenuse must have a length of 5. Let's add those values to the diagram:

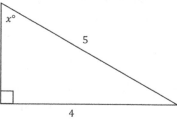

We need to find the cosine of $(90° - x°)$. We know that the sum of the measures of the angles in a triangle is $180°$. In the diagram above, we know that the angle between the legs of the triangle has a measure of $90°$, and another angle has a measure of $x°$. This means the remaining angle must have a measure of $180° - 90° - x°$, which is the same thing as $90° - x°$. Since the question is asking for the cosine of $(90° - x°)$, we now know that the question is asking for the cosine of the unlabeled angle in our diagram. We know from SOHCAHTOA that $Cosine = \frac{Adjacent}{Hypotenuse}$, so the cosine of $(90° - x°)$ is $\frac{4}{5}$, according to our diagram:

So the correct answer is $\frac{4}{5}$.

Solution 2: Unit circle: Sketch an angle with a sine of $\frac{4}{5}$ on the unit circle, then determine the cosine of that angle's complement.

Let's sketch an angle on the unit circle with a measure of $x°$ and sine of $\frac{4}{5}$ (not to scale):

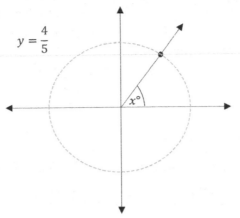

Now let's add in the angle that would correspond to $(90° - x°)$ and see what happens:

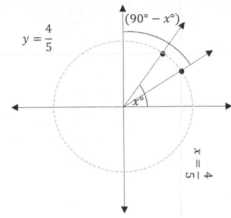

We can see in the sketch that when we start from $90°$ and travel $x°$ *back* towards the positive part of the x-axis, we end up intercepting the unit circle at a point with an x-coordinate of $\frac{4}{5}$, just as the first angle opens up from the x-axis and intercepts the unit circle at a point with a y-coordinate of $\frac{4}{5}$.

Since the cosine of an angle can be defined as the x-coordinate of the point where the angle intercepts the unit circle, and since the angle indicated by $(90° - x°)$ intercepts the unit circle at a point with an x-coordinate of $\frac{4}{5}$, we know the cosine of $(90° - x°)$ is $\frac{4}{5}$.

Solution 3: Abstract: Use your knowledge of the properties of complementary angles to determine that the cosine of the complement of x is equal to the sine of x. As trained test-takers, we may be familiar with the property of sine and cosine that says the sine of an acute angle is equal to the cosine of its complement, in which case we would know immediately that the answer is $\frac{4}{5}$.

But don't worry if you didn't remember that property when you saw this question, or if your teacher never taught it to you. You could still use one of the other two approaches we just described. Further, it's probably not worthwhile from an SAT perspective to spend a significant amount of time learning that property of sine and cosine, because the College Board won't ask you a question that can only be answered if you've memorized that property—you'll always be able to use solutions similar to 1 and 2 above.

How to check? Use an alternate approach above to verify the result.

Note We never actually have to find the value of x in order to answer this question—in fact, without a calculator, it's impossible for most test-takers to find x in this question—but it's still possible to answer this question with total certainty. Also, the College Board could have made this question more difficult by asking for another trig value related to the complement of x, but it chose not to do that. This is one more example of how the College Board often makes the calculation for a question very straightforward once we find the most simple approach.

Test 1, Section 3, Question 20

- **What's the prompt asking for?** The value of x
- **Math concepts in the prompt:** algebra, squares and square roots, variables

- **"Bridge" concepts:** We can use algebra to combine the equations in the prompt and determine x.
- **Things to look out for:** Don't confuse a and x! Don't make mistakes when dealing with simplifying radical expressions!

Solution 1: Algebra: Multiply both sides of the first equation by 2, then set $10\sqrt{2}$ equal to $\sqrt{2x}$ and solve for x.

$$a = 5\sqrt{2} \qquad \text{(first equation from prompt)}$$
$$2a = 10\sqrt{2} \qquad \text{(multiply both sides by 2)}$$

Now we have two different expressions that are equal to $2a$, so we can set them equal to each other:

$$10\sqrt{2} = \sqrt{2x} \qquad \text{(both expressions equal to } 2a\text{)}$$
$$100(2) = 2x \qquad \text{(square both sides)}$$
$$100 = x \qquad \text{(divide both sides by 2)}$$

So the correct answer is 100.

How to check? Plug your value for x back into the prompt and make sure it works.

TEST 2 – SECTION 3

Test 2, Section 3, Question 1

- **What's the prompt asking for?** The value of $10x + 3$
- **Math concepts in the prompt:** addition, algebra, variables
- **Elements of the answer choices:** integers

- **"Bridge" concepts:** The variable in the prompt has a specific value, which will allow us to determine the value of $10x + 3$.
- **Things to look out for:** Don't misread any of the expressions in the prompt!

Solution 1: Basic algebra: Solve for x in the first equation, and then plug that value into $10x + 3$ to find the answer.

$$5x + 6 = 10 \qquad \text{(original equation)}$$
$$5x = 4 \qquad \text{(subtract 6 from both sides)}$$
$$x = \frac{4}{5} \qquad \text{(divide both sides by 5)}$$

Now we can plug $x = \frac{4}{5}$ into $10x + 3$.

$$10x + 3 \qquad \text{(given equation)}$$
$$10\left(\frac{4}{5}\right) + 3 \qquad \text{(plug in } x = \frac{4}{5}\text{)}$$
$$8 + 3 \qquad \text{(multiply)}$$
$$11 \qquad \text{(add)}$$

So we can see that (C) is correct.

Solution 2: More advanced algebra: Note that we can find $5x$ with quick mental math by subtracting 6 from both sides of the given equation, then use that value to find $10x + 3$.

Note that once we find the value of $5x$, we can save ourselves some algebra by just doubling $5x$ and adding 3:

$$5x = 4 \qquad \text{(result of subtracting 6 from original equation)}$$
$$10x = 8 \qquad \text{(multiply both sides by 2)}$$
$$10x + 3 = 11 \qquad \text{(add 3 to both sides)}$$

So we can see that (C) is correct.

Solution 3: Another advanced algebraic approach: Double the value of $5x + 6$ and then subtract 9 to find $10x + 3$.

$$5x + 6 = 10 \qquad \text{(original equation)}$$
$$10x + 12 = 20 \qquad \text{(multiply both sides by 2)}$$
$$10x + 3 = 11 \qquad \text{(subtract 9 from both sides)}$$

So we can see that (C) is correct.

ANSWER CHOICE ANALYSIS

(A): This is the value of $5x$, which we found as part of Solution 1 and Solution 2. **(B):** This is the difference between $10x + 12$ (which we found as part of Solution 3) and $10x + 3$ (which is what the prompt asks for). **(D):** This is the value of $10x + 12$, which we found as part of Solution 3. Like (A) and (B), it could potentially represent a step in a particular approach to the question.

How to check? Try an alternate approach above, and/or re-read the prompt carefully and make sure your value for $10x + 3$ makes sense in the context of the rest of the question.

▶ Post-solution patterns (see page 218): right approach, wrong step

Test 2, Section 3, Question 2

- **What's the prompt asking for?** An (x, y) pair that satisfies both equations in the prompt.
- **Math concepts in the prompt:** addition, algebra, coordinate pairs, equations, subtraction, systems of equations, variables, zero
- **Elements of the answer choices:** coordinate values, integers, negative numbers
- **Notable differences among answer choices:** (A) is the only choice with the value 3. All four choices have at least one instance of 2 or -2.

- **Concepts in the answer choices:** coordinate pairs, opposites
- **"Bridge" concepts:** Some combination of x and y values can be plugged into the given equations to cause both equations to be true.
- **Pre-solution patterns (see p. 217):** opposites; wrong answers try to imitate right answers
- **Things to look out for:** Don't confuse x and y! Don't confuse positive and negative numbers! Don't confuse addition and subtraction in any algebra you do!

Solution 1: Substitution: Isolate x in one of the equations to define x in terms of y. Plug that definition of x into the other equation and solve that equation for y. Then plug the y-value into either equation and solve for x.

$x + y = 0$	(first equation from the prompt)
$x = -y$	(subtract y from both sides)

Now we can plug $x = -y$ into the second equation.

$3x - 2y = 10$	(second equation from the prompt)
$3(-y) - 2y = 10$	(plug in $x = -y$)
$-5y = 10$	(simplify)
$y = -2$	(divide both sides by -5)

Now we can plug $y = -2$ into either equation to solve for x, and we'll have both values in the (x, y) coordinate pair. We'll use the first equation because it looks more straightforward—but either one would work.

$x + y = 0$	(first equation from the prompt)
$x + (-2) = 0$	(plug in $y = -2$)
$x = 2$	(add 2 to both sides)

So the correct answer is $(2, -2)$, or (B).

Solution 2: Adding equations: Multiply the top equation by 2 and add it to the bottom equation, isolating x. Solve for x and use the x-value to find the y-value in either equation.

$2x + 2y = 0$	
$+ \quad 3x - 2y = 10$	(multiply the first equation by 2, then add the equations)
$5x \qquad = 10$	
$x \qquad = 2$	(divide both sides by 5)

Now we can plug $x = 2$ into either equation to solve for y, and we'll have both values in the (x, y) coordinate pair. Again, we'll use the first equation because it looks more straightforward—but either one would work.

$x + y = 0$	(first equation from the prompt)
$(2) + y = 0$	(plug in $x = 2$)
$y = -2$	(subtract 2 from both sides)

So the correct answer is $(2, -2)$, which is (B).

Solution 3: Backsolving: Take each (x, y) pair from the answer choices and plug it into the equations in the prompt to see which choice is valid in both equations.

Choice (A): $(3, -2)$

$x + y = 0$	(first equation from the prompt)
$(3) + (-2) = 0$	(plug in $x = 3$ and $y = -2$ from choice (A))
$1 = 0$	(simplify)

This isn't a true statement, so (A) can't be correct. Now let's try the values from (B):

$x + y = 0$	(first equation from the prompt)
$(2) + (-2) = 0$	(plug in $x = 2$ and $y = -2$ from choice (B))
$0 = 0$	(simplify)

The (x, y) coordinate pair from (B) makes a true statement in the first equation; now let's try it in the second equation:

$3x - 2y = 10$	(second equation from the prompt)
$3(2) - 2(-2) = 10$	(plug in $x = 2$ and $y = -2$ from choice (B))
$10 = 10$	(simplify)

This is also a true statement. So we can see that plugging the coordinate pair $(2, -2)$ into both equations creates true statements in each of them, which means (B) is correct, assuming that we haven't made any mistakes in our approach. As trained test-takers, we know that we always need to check *every* answer choice when we backsolve, to help make sure that we haven't made any mistakes. So let's check the remaining two choices, starting with (C):

$x + y = 0$	(first equation from the prompt)
$(-2) + (2) = 0$	(plug in $x = -2$ and $y = 2$ from choice (C))
$0 = 0$	(simplify)

The $(x. y)$ coordinate pair from (C) makes a true statement in the first equation; now let's try it in the second equation:

$3x - 2y = 10$	(second equation from the prompt)
$3(-2) - 2(2) = 10$	(plug in $x = -2$ and $y = 2$ from choice (C))
$-10 = 10$	(simplify)

This isn't a true statement, so (C) can't be correct, since it doesn't satisfy both equations. Now let's check (D):

$x + y = 0$	(first equation from the prompt)
$(-2) + (-2) = 0$	(plug in $x = -2$ and $y = -2$ from choice (D))
$-4 = 0$	(simplify)

This isn't a true statement, so (D) can't be correct. We can confirm that (B) is right.

ANSWER CHOICE ANALYSIS

(A): These are the coefficients of the terms on the left side of the second equation. **(C):** These are the opposites of the coordinate values in the correct answer. This choice might be tempting to an untrained test-taker who confused x and y. **(D):** This choice might be tempting if you made an algebra error involving positive and negative signs.

How to check? Try an alternate approach above, and/or re-read the prompt carefully and re-check your work, paying careful attention to the issues described above.

Test 2, Section 3, Question 3

- **What's the prompt asking for?** The role of the number 12 in the given function.
- **Math concepts in the prompt:** addition, function modeling, multiplication, variables
- **Elements of the answer choices:** integers, sentences
- **Notable differences among answer choices:** (A) and (C) are the only choice that include the idea of something happening "per hour" (note that "every hour" has the same meaning as "per hour" within the context of (C)). They're also the only two choices with a dollar sign. (B) is the only choice that mentions the idea of a minimum number.

- **Concepts in the answer choices:** function modeling, inequalities, multiplication
- **"Bridge" concepts:** Each number or variable in a function model plays a specific role in describing the relationships of the other numbers or variables.
- **Pre-solution patterns (see p. 217):** wrong answers try to imitate right answers
- **Things to look out for:** Don't misread the function model! Don't misread the answer choices!

Solution 1: Function modeling: Read the prompt and carefully analyze the concepts in the function model, comparing them to the choices to determine which one could possibly describe the model accurately.

(A) says the number 12 tells us the company charges $12 per hour per landscaper. Well, if that were true, then for every hour that 1 landscaper worked, the company would charge $12 times the number of hours the landscaper worked—so if 1 landscaper worked 3 hours, then the company would charge $36, since $12 \times 3 = \$36$. Since h represents the number of hours worked, that would be the same as $12h$. But that only accounts for 1 landscaper! What if there were 2 landscapers? If 2 landscapers worked for 3 hours, then the company would charge $36 *for each landscaper,* if (A) is right—which would be $72. Since h represents the number of hours worked, and n represents the number of landscapers, that would be the same as $12hn$, which is the same as $12nh$ from the prompt. So it seems to make sense that 12 would represent the number of dollars per hour that the company charges for each landscaper. Of course, as trained test-takers, we know that we need to consider every choice before committing to one, so let's check out the other choices.

(B) doesn't make sense because the prompt tells us that n represents the number of landscapers, but we don't have any reason to believe that n has to be at least 12. Further, if (B) were correct, then it wouldn't make any sense to multiply the number of landscapers (n) by the lowest acceptable number of landscapers, which is what $12nh$ would involve.

(C) would only make sense if n had to be equal to one fixed number, because (C) doesn't take into account the number of workers. For example, if (C) were true, then the cost of a 6-hour landscaping job would be the same whether it involved 1 landscaper, or 10 landscapers, or 100 landscapers, which doesn't make sense in the context of the provided expression used to estimate the cost of the job—the expression from the prompt will increase as the number of workers (n) increases, not just as the number of hours (h) increases. So this choice is wrong.

(D) has a problem that's similar to the problem with (B). The prompt tells us that h represents the total number of hours it will take n landscapers to complete the job, but we don't have any reason to believe that h must be equal to 12.

Now that we've considered all the choices, we can see (A) is right.

Test 2, Section 3, Question 4

- **What's the prompt asking for?** An expression that's equivalent to the one in the prompt.
- **Math concepts in the prompt:** addition, algebra, exponents, multiplication, variables
- **Elements of the answer choices:** algebraic expressions, exponents, integers
- **Notable differences among answer choices:** (A) and (C) involve squaring an expression in parentheses, while (B) and (D) involve raising expressions in parentheses to the fourth power. (A) and (B) incorporate $3a$ and $2b$, while (C) and (D) incorporate $9a$ and $4b$.

- **Concepts in the answer choices:** binomial expansion, exponents, FOIL
- **"Bridge" concepts:** One of the answer choices contains an expression that can be algebraically expanded to result in an expression equal to the one in the prompt.
- **Pre-solution patterns (see p. 217):** wrong answers try to imitate right answers
- **Things to look out for:** Don't make a mistake when squaring a binomial expression—remember FOIL! Don't misread any of the exponents in the prompt or in the answer choices!

Solution 1: Backsolving: Use algebra to expand each of the answer choices and see which one matches the expression in the prompt. Pay particular attention to the coefficients.

For choice (A):

$(3a^2 + 2b^2)^2$	(original expression)
$(3a^2 + 2b^2)(3a^2 + 2b^2)$	(re-written to make FOIL easier)
$9a^4 + 6a^2b^2 + 6a^2b^2 + 4b^4$	(FOIL)
$9a^4 + 12a^2b^2 + 4b^4$	(simplify)

This expression matches the expression in the prompt, which means (A) is correct, assuming we haven't made a mistake in our approach. Of course, as trained test-takers, we know that we have to consider every answer choice before picking one, to help make sure we haven't made any mistakes. So let's take a look at (B):

$(3a + 2b)^4$	(original expression)

(To make the algebra a little easier here, we'll square $3a + 2b$, and then square the result of that again, because that's easier for most people than raising the expression to the fourth power all at once.)

$((3a + 2b)(3a + 2b))^2$	(re-written to make FOIL easier)
$(9a^2 + 6ab + 6ab + 4b^2)^2$	(FOIL)
$(9a^2 + 12ab + 4b^2)^2$	(simplify)

At this point, we can see that if we squared this trinomial, the first term would be $81a^4$, which doesn't appear anywhere in the expression from the prompt, so choice (B) can't be correct. Let's try (C):

$(9a^2 + 4b^2)^2$	(original expression)
$(9a^2 + 4b^2)(9a^2 + 4b^2)$	(re-written to make FOIL easier)
$81a^4 + 36a^2b^2 + 36a^2b^2 + 16b^4$	(FOIL)
$81a^4 + 72a^2b^2 + 16b^4$	(simplify)

Just like (B), this expression doesn't match the expression in the prompt, so (C) can't be correct. Let's take a look at (D):

$(9a + 4b)^4$	(original expression)

To make the algebra a little easier here, we'll square $9a + 4b$, and then square the result:

$((9a + 4b)(9a + 4b))^2$	(re-written to make FOIL easier)
$(81a^2 + 36ab + 36ab + 16b^2)^2$	(FOIL)
$(81a^2 + 72ab + 16b^2)^2$	(simplify)

We can see that if we squared this trinomial, the first term would have a coefficient much larger than 9, which wouldn't match what appears in the prompt (in fact, the coefficient would be 6561). So choice (D) can't be correct.

Solution 2: Test-smart: Realize that each answer choice will produce a different set of coefficients when it's expanded, and only one set of coefficients matches the ones in the prompt.

(A) The first term will be $9a^4$, which matches the first term in the expression from the prompt. So (A) could be correct.

(B) The first term will be $81a^4$, which doesn't match the first term in the expression from the prompt. So (B) can't be correct.

(C) The first term will be $81a^4$, which doesn't match the first term in the expression from the prompt. So (C) can't be correct.

(D) The first term will be $6561a^4$, which doesn't match the first term in the expression from the prompt. So (D) can't be correct. (Even if we're not comfortable calculating 81^2, we can see the result would be much more than 9, which means the first term for this choice can't match the first term in the prompt.)

After finding the first term in each expression, we're confident that only (A) can be correct. (Note that if more than one answer choice produced a first term that matched the first term in the prompt, then we would have needed to check the second term, and so on—but the College Board designed this question so the answer choices would only require us to find the first term.)

ANSWER CHOICE ANALYSIS

(B): This might be tempting if we got confused about the properties of exponents. **(C):** This might be tempting if we tried to use a reverse-FOIL process and forgot to take the square root of the coefficients. **(D):** This combines the errors from (B) and (C).

How to check? Try an alternate approach above. Pay particular attention to the values of the coefficients that would result from the answer choice you've chosen.

Test 2, Section 3, Question 5

- **What's the prompt asking for?** The value of k under the given conditions.
- **Math concepts in the prompt:** addition, coefficients, equations, square roots, subtraction, variables, zero
- **Elements of the answer choices:** integers
- **Notable differences among answer choices:** The choices form a series that runs from 2 to 5.
- **Concepts in the answer choices:** series

- **"Bridge" concepts:** Some combination of values for the variables in the prompt will make the equation in the prompt true.
- **Pre-solution patterns (see p. 217):** halves and doubles; the first and last terms in a series are often wrong answers
- **Things to look out for:** Don't forget that k must be positive! Don't confuse x and k! Don't make small mistakes in any algebra you do!

Solution 1: Algebra: Substitute 7 for x and then find the possible value for k that's positive.

$\sqrt{2k^2 + 17} - x = 0$	(original expression)
$\sqrt{2k^2 + 17} - 7 = 0$	(plug in $x = 7$)
$\sqrt{2k^2 + 17} = 7$	(add 7 to both sides)
$2k^2 + 17 = 49$	(square both sides)
$2k^2 = 32$	(subtract 17 from both sides)
$k^2 = 16$	(divide both sides by 2)
$k = 4$ or $k = -4$	(take square root of both sides)

The prompt told us $k > 0$, so the answer is $k = 4$, or (C).

Solution 2: Backsolving: Substitute 7 for x and then plug each answer choice in for k to see which choice makes the equation valid.

$\sqrt{2k^2 + 17} - x = 0$	(original expression)
$\sqrt{2k^2 + 17} - 7 = 0$	(plug in $x = 7$)

Now we can plug in the value from each answer choice and see which one creates a valid statement.

$\sqrt{2k^2 + 17} - 7 = 0$	
$\sqrt{2(2)^2 + 17} - 7 = 0$	(plug in $k = 2$ from choice (A))
$\sqrt{25} - 7 = 0$	(simplify under the radical)
$-2 = 0$	(simplify)

This isn't a valid statement, so (A) can't be correct. Now let's try (B):

$$\sqrt{2k^2 + 17} - 7 = 0$$

$$\sqrt{2(3)^2 + 17} - 7 = 0 \qquad \text{(plug in } k = 3 \text{ from choice (B))}$$

$$\sqrt{35} - 7 = 0 \qquad \text{(simplify under the radical)}$$

$$\sqrt{35} = 7 \qquad \text{(add 7 to both sides)}$$

This isn't a valid statement, so (B) can't be correct. Let's try (C):

$$\sqrt{2k^2 + 17} - 7 = 0$$

$$\sqrt{2(4)^2 + 17} - 7 = 0 \qquad \text{(plug in } k = 4 \text{ from choice (C))}$$

$$\sqrt{49} - 7 = 0 \qquad \text{(simplify under the radical)}$$

$$0 = 0 \qquad \text{(simplify)}$$

This is a valid statement, so (C) is correct, assuming we haven't made a mistake in our approach. As trained test-takers, we know that we always need to be on the lookout for any small mistakes we might have made, especially when we're backsolving, and one of the best ways to find any small mistakes is to check every answer choice. So let's take a look at (D):

$$\sqrt{2k^2 + 17} - 7 = 0$$

$$\sqrt{2(5)^2 + 17} - 7 = 0 \qquad \text{(plug in } k = 5 \text{ from choice (D))}$$

$$\sqrt{67} - 7 = 0 \qquad \text{(simplify under the radical)}$$

$$\sqrt{67} = 7 \qquad \text{(add 7 to both sides)}$$

This isn't a valid statement, so (D) can't be correct. After checking each choice, we're sure that (C) is correct.

> **Note** (C) follows two common patterns for right answers on the SAT Math section, just as we might expect: it's not the first or last number in the series 2, 3, 4, 5, and it's involved in the halves-and-doubles relationship between 2 and 4. This doesn't guarantee that (C) is correct, but it strongly suggests that we've thought about the question correctly.

ANSWER CHOICE ANALYSIS

(A): This choice would be true if x were equal to 5, not 7.

Test 2, Section 3, Question 6

- **What's the prompt asking for?** The value of p.
- **Math concepts in the prompt:** coordinate plane, coordinate values, lines, parallel lines
- **Math concepts in the diagram:** coordinate values, parallel lines, slope, x-intercepts, y-intercepts
- **Elements of the answer choices:** integers

- **Notable differences among answer choices:** (A) and (B) are the opposites of numbers that appear in the diagram, while (C) and (D) are twice as much as (A) and (B), respectively.
- **"Bridge" concepts:** If we know a line's slope and at least one point on the line, we can determine all other points on the line. Parallel lines have identical slopes.
- **Pre-solution patterns (see p. 217):** halves and doubles
- **Things to look out for:** Don't confuse the axes!

Solution 1: Formulaic algebra: Determine the slope of line l, and then use that information to find the value of p, given that $(0, -4)$ is a point on line k.

We know that the slope of a line is the difference between the y-values of two points on the line divided by the difference between the corresponding x-values of those points (in other words, the "rise" of the line over the "run" of the line). Let's start by finding the slope of l:

$$\frac{2 - 0}{0 - (-5)} \qquad \text{(difference between the } y\text{-values divided by the difference between the } x\text{-values)}$$

$$\frac{2}{5} \qquad \text{(simplify)}$$

Now let's create a similar expression for line k and set the slope equal to $\frac{2}{5}$. Then we can solve for p:

$$\frac{0 - (-4)}{p - 0} = \frac{2}{5} \qquad \text{(difference between the } y \text{ values divided by the difference between the } x \text{ values, set equal to } \frac{2}{5})$$

$$\frac{4}{p} = \frac{2}{5} \qquad \text{(simplify)}$$

$$20 = 2p \qquad \text{(cross multiply)}$$

$$10 = p \qquad \text{(divide both sides by 2)}$$

We can see that (D) is correct.

Solution 2: Algebraic reasoning: Remember that slope is a way to describe the relationship between horizontal and vertical changes in a line. Note that the y-intercept of line l is twice as far from the origin as the y-intercept of line k, and realize that the x-intercept of line k must also be twice as far from the origin as the x-intercept of line l, because the lines are parallel.

The distance from the origin to the x-intercept for line l is 5, so the distance from the origin to the x-intercept for line k must be 10, as we just discussed in describing this solution. This means that (D) must be correct.

Solution 3: Test-smart: Remember the diagram must be drawn to scale. Note that only (D) makes sense in the context of the scale.

When we look at the distance from the origin straight down to $(0, -4)$, we can see that it's less than half of the distance from the origin to $(p, 0)$ (remember that we know the diagram is to scale!). Only (D) offers a choice that's more than twice as long as 4 (which is the the distance from the origin to $(0, -4)$), so (D) must be correct.

ANSWER CHOICE ANALYSIS

(A): This choice is half of (C). **(B):** This choice is half of the correct answer. It's probably here because some test-takers will incorrectly think p should be the same distance from the origin as the distance from the origin to the x-intercept of line l. **(C):** This choice is twice as much as the distance from the origin to the y-intercept of line k, for test-takers who accidentally double the wrong number, or who apply the scale of the diagram incorrectly.

Test 2, Section 3, Question 7

- **What's the prompt asking for?** The value of $a - b$.
- **Math concepts in the prompt:** equations, exponents of exponents, fractions, systems of equations, variables
- **Elements of the answer choices:** integers
- **Notable differences among answer choices:** (C) is the only choice that appears in the prompt. (A) and (C) are the only pair of choices that differ from each other by a factor of 2, which could be relevant because the prompt involves division and contains the number 2. (B), (C), and (D) form a series in which each number is 2 more than the one before it, which could be relevant because the prompt contains the number 2.
- **"Bridge" concepts:** When we divide two exponent expressions with the same base, it's the same as leaving the base unchanged and subtracting the exponent in the denominator from the exponent in the numerator to find the exponent of

the quotient. If x is greater than 1, then x^{16} must be greater than x and also greater than 1, which means the numerator in the fraction must be larger than its denominator. We're only told that $a + b$ is 2; we're not told whether a or b is positive, negative, or zero. That means either variable could potentially be any kind of number for all we know before we try our solution, as long as they add up to 2. It may be possible to find the value of $a - b$ without finding the individual values of a or b.

- **Pre-solution patterns (see p. 217):** halves and doubles; the first and last terms in a series are often wrong answers
- **Things to look out for:** Don't confuse a and b! Don't arbitrarily pick numbers for $a, b,$ or x that violate the rules in the prompt! Don't forget how to handle exponents of exponents! Don't accidentally fill in the value of a or b as your answer!

Solution 1: Backsolve: For each answer choice, test an a-value and a b-value in the prompt so that $a + b = 2$ and $a - b$ is equal to the value in the answer choice you're testing. The choice that produces a valid equation in the prompt is the correct answer.

$$\frac{x^{a^2}}{x^{b^2}} = x^{16} \qquad \text{(original equation)}$$

$$\frac{x^{5^2}}{x^{-3^2}} = x^{16} \qquad \text{(plug in } a = 5 \text{ and } b = -3, \text{ because } 5 + (-3) = 2 \text{ and } 5 - (-3) = 8. \text{ Any } (a, b) \text{ pair where } a + b = 2 \text{ and } a - b = 8 \text{ will work for this test.)}$$

$$\frac{x^{25}}{x^9} = x^{16} \qquad \text{(simplify)}$$

$$x^{16} = x^{16} \qquad \text{(simplify)}$$

This is a valid statement, so (A) is correct, assuming we haven't made any mistakes. Of course, as trained-test-takers, we always check every answer choice when we backsolve, so we can help make sure we haven't made any mistakes. So let's take a look at (B):

$$\frac{x^{a^2}}{x^{b^2}} = x^{16} \qquad \text{(original equation)}$$

$$\frac{x^{8^2}}{x^{-6^2}} = x^{16} \qquad \text{(plug in } a = 8 \text{ and } b = -6, \text{ because } 8 + (-6) = 2 \text{ and } 8 - (-6) = 14. \text{ Any } (a, b) \text{ pair where } a + b = 2 \text{ and } a - b = 14 \text{ will work for this test.)}$$

$$\frac{x^{64}}{x^{36}} = x^{16} \qquad \text{(simplify)}$$

$$x^{28} = x^{16} \qquad \text{(simplify)}$$

This isn't a valid statement, so (B) isn't correct. Now let's check (C):

$$\frac{x^{a^2}}{x^{b^2}} = x^{16} \qquad \text{(original equation)}$$

$$\frac{x^{9^2}}{x^{-7^2}} = x^{16} \qquad \text{(plug in } a = 9 \text{ and } b = -7, \text{ because } 9 + (-7) = 2 \text{ and } 9 - (-7) = 16. \text{ Any}$$
$$(a, b) \text{ pair where } a + b = 2 \text{ and } a - b = 16 \text{ will work for this test.)}$$

$$\frac{x^{81}}{x^{49}} = x^{16} \qquad \text{(simplify)}$$

$$x^{32} = x^{16} \qquad \text{(simplify)}$$

This isn't a valid statement, either, so (C) isn't correct. Finally, we'll check (D):

$$\frac{x^{a^2}}{x^{b^2}} = x^{16} \qquad \text{(original equation)}$$

$$\frac{x^{10^2}}{x^{-8^2}} = x^{16} \qquad \text{(plug in } a = 10 \text{ and } b = -8, \text{ because } 10 + (-8) = 2 \text{ and } 10 - (-8) = 18.$$
$$\text{Any } (a, b) \text{ pair where } a + b = 2 \text{ and } a - b = 18 \text{ will work for this test.)}$$

$$\frac{x^{100}}{x^{64}} = x^{16} \qquad \text{(simplify)}$$

$$x^{36} = x^{16} \qquad \text{(simplify)}$$

This isn't a valid statement, so (D) is wrong. Since (A) is the only choice that worked out when we tested them all, (A) is right.

Solution 2: Formal algebra: Use $a + b = 2$ to isolate a and define it in terms of b, and then plug that definition in for a in the first equation. Solve the first equation for b and then use the value of b to find the value of a. Then find the value of $a - b$.

$$a + b = 2 \qquad \text{(second equation from prompt)}$$
$$a = 2 - b \qquad \text{(subtract } b \text{ from both sides)}$$

Now we can plug $a = 2 - b$ into the other equation from the prompt:

$$\frac{x^{(2-b)^2}}{x^{b^2}} = x^{16} \qquad \text{(original equation with } 2 - b \text{ plugged in for } a)$$

$$\frac{x^{4-4b+b^2}}{x^{b^2}} = x^{16} \qquad \text{(use FOIL to expand } (2 - b)^2)$$

$$x^{4-4b} = x^{16} \qquad \text{(get rid of the denominator by subtracting } b^2 \text{ from each exponent)}$$

$$4 - 4b = 16 \qquad \text{(simplify)}$$

$$-4b = 12 \qquad \text{(subtract 4 from both sides)}$$

$$b = -3 \qquad \text{(divide both sides by } -4)$$

Now we plug $b = -3$ into either equation and solve for a. We'll pick the second one because the algebra will be more straightforward:

$$a + b = 2 \qquad \text{(second equation from prompt)}$$
$$a = 2 - b \qquad \text{(subtract } b \text{ from both sides to isolate } a)$$
$$a = 2 - (-3) \qquad \text{(plug in } b = -3)$$
$$a = 5 \qquad \text{(simplify)}$$

Finally, we can use $a = 5$ and $b = -3$ to find $a - b$:

$$5 - (-3) = 8 \qquad \text{(plug in } a = 5 \text{ and } b = -3 \text{ to find } a - b.)$$

So we can see (A) is right.

ANSWER CHOICE ANALYSIS

(B): This is the value of the exponent of the x-term on the right side of the given equation minus 2. **(C):** This is double the right answer. It's also the exponent of the x-term on the right side of the given equation. **(D):** This is the exponent of the x-term on the right side of the given equation plus 2.

How to check? Try an alternate approach above; verify that your values for a and b make the first equation true.

Test 2, Section 3, Question 8

- **What's the prompt asking for?** The greatest possible value of n under the circumstances in the question.
- **Math concepts in the prompt:** algebra, angles, inequalities, multiplication, regular polygons, variables
- **Elements of the answer choices:** integers
- **Notable differences among answer choices:** The choices form a series from 5 to 8, with each choice being one more than the choice before it.
- **Concepts in the answer choices:** integers, series

- **"Bridge" concepts:** The number of sides in a regular polygon must be an integer, since a polygon can't have a fractional number of sides.
- **Pre-solution patterns (see p. 217):** the first and last terms in a series are often wrong answers
- **Things to look out for:** Don't get confused between "greater than" and "less than!" Don't get confused by "greatest number" and "smallest number!"

Solution 1: Backsolving: Try each answer choice in the equation to determine the corresponding A-value for each answer choice. If a choice results in an A-value below 50, eliminate it from consideration, because the prompt specifies that the exterior angle must be greater than 50°. The correct answer will be the remaining choice with the highest value.

For choice (A), which is 5:

$nA = 360$	(original equation)
$5A = 360$	(plug in $n = 5$ from (A))
$A = \frac{360}{5}$	(divide both sides by 5)
$A = 72$	(simplify)

When we use the value from (A), the angle measure is 72°, which is greater than 50°, so we know that 5 is one possible number of sides that satisfies the prompt. Let's check the remaining choices, starting with (B). From choice (B):

$nA = 360$	(original equation)
$6A = 360$	(plug in $n = 6$ from (B))
$A = \frac{360}{6}$	(divide both sides by 6)
$A = 60$	(simplify)

When we use the value from (B), the angle measure is 60°, which is also greater than 50°, so we know that 6 also satisfies the prompt. Let's keep checking the other choices. From choice (C):

$nA = 360$	(original equation)
$7A = 360$	(plug in $n = 7$ from (C))
$A = \frac{360}{7}$	(divide both sides by 7)
$A = 51\frac{3}{7}$	(simplify)

When we use the value from (C), the angle measure is greater than 50°, so we know 7 satisfies the prompt as well. Let's check (D):

$nA = 360$	(original equation)
$8A = 360$	(plug in $n = 8$ from (D))
$A = \frac{360}{8}$	(divide both sides by 8)
$A = 45$	(simplify)

When we use the value from (D), the angle measure is less than 50°, so this choice can't be right.

Now that we've checked every answer choice, we can see that a regular polygon with exterior angles greater than 50° can have no more than 7 sides, since 7 was a valid number in our testing but 8 was not.

Solution 2: Abstract: Realize that n and A are indirectly proportional—that is, *higher* values of n must correlate with *lower* values of A, so the right answer will be an n-value that allows for an A-value that's close to 50 but not less than 50. Plug $A = 50$ into the given equation. Since A must be greater than 50, the right answer must be the *highest* choice that's *less than* the resulting n-value.

$nA = 360$	(given equation)
$n(50) = 360$	(plug in $A = 50$)
$n = \frac{360}{50}$	(divide both sides by 50)
$n = 7\frac{1}{5}$	(simplify)

So when $A = 50, n = 7\frac{1}{5}$. We know that as A increases, n must decrease, because A and n are indirectly proportional. So since A must be greater than 50, we know n must be less than $7\frac{1}{5}$. The question asks for the greatest number of sides the polygon can have—in other words, the greatest value for n. The greatest possible n value less than $7\frac{1}{5}$ is 7, so choice (C) is correct.

Solution 3: Algebra: Isolate A in the given equation and write a new inequality using the fact that $A > 50$. Solve the new inequality for n and pick the corresponding answer choice.

$nA = 360$	(original equation)
$A = \frac{360}{n}$	(divide both sides by n)
$A = \frac{360}{n}$, and $50 < A$	(introduce the inequality that $50 < A$)
$50 < \frac{360}{n}$	(if $50 < A$ and $A = \frac{360}{n}$, then $50 < \frac{360}{n}$)
$50n < 360$	(multiply both sides by n)
$n < \frac{360}{50}$	(divide both sides by 50)
$n < 7\frac{1}{5}$	(simplify)

So n must be less than $7\frac{1}{5}$, which means (C) is correct, since the prompt asked us for the largest possible number that satisfies the prompt, and 7 is the largest possible number of sides that's less than $7\frac{1}{5}$.

ANSWER CHOICE ANALYSIS

(D): This choice might have been tempting if an untrained test-taker misread the question and thought she needed to find the choice that would result in an exterior angle *less* than 50 degrees.

How to check? Try an alternate approach above, or see what happens to A when n is 1 more than the value you've chosen for the correct answer (if you have the right answer, any n-value greater than the one you've chosen should cause A to go below 50).

Test 2, Section 3, Question 9

- **What's the prompt asking for?** The value of $a + b$ under the circumstances in the prompt.
- **Math concepts in the prompt:** addition, coordinate values, graphing in the xy-coordinate plane, intersecting lines, point-slope format, slope
- **Elements of the answer choices:** integers, negative numbers
- **Notable differences among answer choices:** (A) and (D) are the only pair of opposites in the answer choices. (B) is the sum of (A) and (C). (A) and (B) are positive, while (C) and (D) are negative.
- **"Bridge" concepts:** If a point is at the intersection of two lines, then the point lies on both lines, which means the (x, y) values for the point must satisfy the equations for both lines.
- **Things to look out for:** Don't get confused as to which points in the prompt are on a line together! Don't confuse the x-axis and the y-axis!

Solution 1: Algebra: Use the definition of slope to determine the slope of the second line, then use slope-intercept format to define both lines. Isolate y in the equations for both lines and then set the two definitions of y equal to each other to find the y-value of the point where the two lines intersect, and then use the y-value in one of the line equations to determine the x-value of the point of intersection. Finally, add the x- and y-values.

We know that the slope of a line is the difference between the y-values of two points on that line divided by the difference between the two corresponding x-values of those points. Let's start by finding the slope of the second line:

$\frac{1-2}{2-1}$	(difference between y-values divided by the difference between x-values)
-1	(simplify)

Now that we know the slope of the second line is -1, we can find the y-intercept of the second line by plugging its slope into the slope-intercept format, along with the coordinates of one valid point from the line:

$y = mx + b$	(slope-intercept formula)
$y = -x + b$	(plug in $m = -1$ for the slope that we just found)
$2 = -1 + b$	(plug in the coordinate pair $(1, 2)$, since we know it's a valid point on the second line)
$3 = b$	(add 1 to both sides to find b, the y-intercept of the second line)

Now that we know $m = -1$ and $b = 3$, we can plug those values into $y = mx + b$ and create an equation for the second line:

$y = mx + b$	(slope-intercept formula)

$$y = -x + 3 \qquad \text{(plug in } m = -1 \text{ and } b = 3)$$

With a similar process, we can use the first line's slope and a point on the first line to create an equation for that line, using the slope-intercept formula:

$$y = mx + b \qquad \text{(slope-intercept formula)}$$
$$y = 2x + b \qquad \text{(plug in } m = 2 \text{ as the slope for the first line, according to the prompt)}$$
$$8 = 2 + b \qquad \text{(plug in the coordinate pair } (1,8) \text{, since we know it's a valid point on the first line)}$$
$$6 = b \qquad \text{(subtract 2 from both sides)}$$

Now that we know $m = 2$ and $b = 6$, we can plug those values into $y = mx + b$ and create an equation for the line:

$$y = mx + b \qquad \text{(slope-intercept formula)}$$
$$y = 2x + 6 \qquad \text{(plug in } m = 2 \text{ and } b = 6)$$

Now that we have equations for both lines, we can set the y-value from the first line's equation equal to the y-value from the second line's equation, and find the x-value of the point of intersection—in other words, the x-value that's valid on both lines:

$$2x + 6 = -x + 3 \qquad \text{(the expressions for the } y\text{-values from the two equations, set equal to one another)}$$
$$3x + 6 = 3 \qquad \text{(add } x \text{ to both sides)}$$
$$3x = -3 \qquad \text{(subtract 6 from both sides)}$$
$$x = -1 \qquad \text{(divide both sides by 3)}$$

Since we know that $x = -1$ is the x-value of the point of intersection, we can plug in $x = -1$ into either equation to solve for the y-value of the point of intersection. We'll use the equation of the second line (not for any particular reason—you could do this with the equation for either line):

$$y = -x + 3 \qquad \text{(equation for the second line)}$$
$$y = -(-1) + 3 \qquad \text{(plug in } x = -1)$$
$$y = 4 \qquad \text{(simplify)}$$

Now we know the point of intersection (which the prompt called (a, b)) is $(-1, 4)$. At this point, we have what we need to find $a + b$:

$$a + b \qquad \text{(value we need to find)}$$
$$-1 + 4 \qquad \text{(plug in } a = -1 \text{ and } b = 4)$$
$$3 \qquad \text{(simplify)}$$

So we can see that (B) is correct.

Solution 2: Diagramming: Read the prompt carefully and create an accurate diagram that satisfies the description in the prompt. Note the point of intersection in the two lines you've drawn, and add the x- and y-coordinates for the point of intersection.

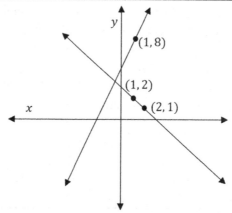

This approach won't be appealing to test-takers who don't feel like they can diagram the solution carefully enough to be sure of the correct answer. On the other hand, some people find that actually plotting the points helps them see that the second line's slope of -1 makes it predictable and easy to graph, and makes it possible to tell for sure that the point of intersection is $(-1, 4)$.

Let's take a closer look at how using the diagram can help us figure out that the lines intersect at $(-1, 4)$. We'll start by looking at the line that contains the point $(1, 8)$. The prompt tells us that the line that contains the point $(1, 8)$ has slope 2. We know that a line with slope 2 moves 2 units up every time it moves 1 unit to the right—because the line has a "rise" of 2 over a "run" of 1. Well, the diagram shows us that the point of intersection is to the left of the point $(1,8)$, so we're interested in finding out about points on the line to the left of $(1, 8)$. Because we're moving left instead of right, we'll move *down* 2 and *left* 1. When we move down 2 and left 1, we end up at the point $(0,6)$. This point lies on the y-axis, but the diagram seems to show a point of intersection to the left of the y-axis—so let's move left again to find another point. When we do that, we end up at $(-1, 4)$. That seems like it could be the point of intersection on the diagram, so let's take a look at the other line, figure out a few more points, and see what we come up with.

The other line in the diagram runs through $(1, 2)$ and $(2, 1)$. Again, the point of intersection is to the left of these points, so let's figure out what some of the points to the left are. To move from the rightmost point, $(2,1)$, to the other point, $(1,2)$, we would move up 1 unit and left 1 unit. So to find more points to the left on this line, we can keep moving up 1 unit and left 1 unit. Starting at $(1, 2)$, we can move up 1 and left 1 to get to $(0, 3)$. From there, we can move up 1 and left 1 again to get to $(-1, 4)$. At this point, we've found that both lines contain $(-1, 4)$. That means they intersect at $(-1, 4)$.

The question says the lines intersect at (a, b), and asks for the value of $a + b$. If the point $(-1, 4)$ corresponds to (a, b), then $a + b = -1 + 4 = 3$. So (B) is right.

Solution 3: Test-smart: Note that (B) is the only choice that's the sum of two other choices, and note that the sum of the x- and y-coordinates is 3 for both points given on the second line. Test other points on this line (sketch the line if you need to) to determine that every point on the second line has an x- and y-coordinate pair that adds to 3. That means the sum of the x- and y- coordinates of every point on the second line—including the point of intersection with the first line—is 3, so (B) must be correct.

ANSWER CHOICE ANALYSIS

(A): This is the value of the y-coordinate of the point of intersection, but the question asked for the sum of the x- and y-coordinates of that point. Untrained test-takers would be likely to pick this choice if they correctly executed the algebraic approach above, found y, and then forgot what the question was actually asking for. **(B):** This is the correct answer. Note that we identified this choice as the only one that was the sum of two other choices, which ends up making sense from a test-design standpoint, because the College Board wants to give untrained test-takers the chance to forget to complete the question and select a choice that reflects only one coordinate. **(C):** This is the value of the x-coordinate of the point of intersection. Like (A), this choice is probably here to trap test-takers who correctly executed most of a valid approach to the question, but forgot what the question was actually asking for. **(D):** This is the opposite of (A).

Test 2, Section 3, Question 10

- **What's the prompt asking for?** The choice that would create a graph whose y-values would always be at least -1.
- **Math concepts in the prompt:** graphing equations, inequalities, range of a function
- **Elements of the answer choices:** absolute value, algebraic expressions, equations, exponents, integers
- **Notable differences among answer choices:** (A) is the only choice with absolute-value brackets. (B) and (C) are the only choices that involve squaring something. (D) is the only choice that involves cubing something.

- **Concepts in the answer choices:** equations, absolute value, squaring, cubing, graphing equations
- **"Bridge" concepts:** Every equation has a set of possible y-values (this is called a "range," but we don't need to know that term to answer this question). One choice has an equation that can't generate y-values that are less than -1.
- **Pre-solution patterns (see p. 217):** wrong answers try to imitate right answers
- **Things to look out for:** Don't confuse "greater than or equal to" with "less than or equal to!" Don't misread any of the small differences among the answer choices.

Solution 1: Diagramming: Use your knowledge of graphing and transformations to sketch a graph of each answer choice, and select the one that never goes below $y = -1$. (If you're not familiar with this kind of graphing, try one of the other three solutions below.)

(A) $y = |x| - 2$

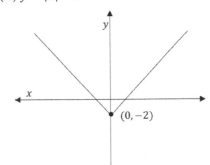

(0, −2)

(B) $y = x^2 - 2$

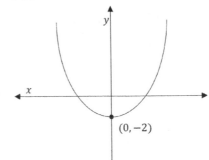

(0, −2)

(C) $y = (x - 2)^2$

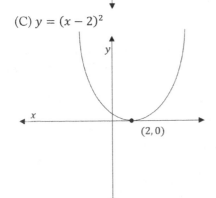

(2, 0)

(D) $y = x^3 - 2$

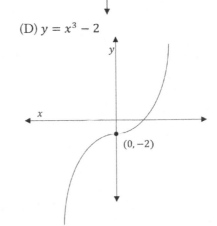

(0, −2)

When we roughly sketch the graphs of each of the equations, we see that only (C) never goes below $y = -1$, so (C) is right.

Solution 2: Abstract: Consider the attributes of each answer choice as they would relate to the values of y.

(A) The lowest value for y that could be generated by this equation would happen when $x = 0$, because the lowest possible value for an absolute value is 0. When $x = 0$ in this expression, $y = -2$, which is less than -1, so this choice can't be correct, because the prompt specifies that y can't be less than -1.

(B) The lowest y-value that this equation could generate would happen when $x = 0$, because the lowest possible value for x^2 would occur when $x = 0$. When $x = 0$ in this equation, $y = -2$, so this choice can't be correct either.

(C) The lowest value for y that this equation could generate would happen when $x = 2$, because the lowest possible value for $(x - 2)^2$ would occur when the amount being squared is 0, and the amount being squared would equal 0 when x is 2. When $x = 2$, in this equation, $y = 0$. So this choice is correct, assuming we haven't made a mistake in our approach, because the value of y can't be less than 0, which means it must always be greater than -1. Of course, as trained test-takers, we know that we always have to test every choice, because that's one of the best ways to make sure we haven't made a small mistake somewhere. With that in mind, let's take a look at (D).

(D) This graph can't generate a lowest possible value for y, because any negative x-value will result in a negative value for x^3, and therefore a negative value for y; furthermore, the larger the absolute value of the negative number that we use for x, the lower the value of y drops. For example, when $x = -2$ in this equation, $x^3 = -8$ and $y = -10$; when $x = -3$, $x^3 = -27$ and $y = -29$; when $x = -10$, $x^3 = -1000$ and $y = -1002$. So (D) contains an infinite number of points whose y-value is less than -1.

So we can see that (C) is the only choice that would satisfy the prompt, which means it must be correct.

Solution 3: Concrete: Since only one of the answer choices is unable to produce y-values that are less than -1, we could try testing a y-value that's less than -1 (such as $y = -2$) in each answer choice; if only one choice fails the test, then that choice is correct.

For choice (A):

$y = \|x\| - 2$	(equation from (A))
$-2 = \|x\| - 2$	(plug in $y = -2$)
$0 = \|x\|$	(add 2 to both sides)

This results in an expression that can be true, so (A) can't be correct, because $y = -2$ is valid for (A), and the prompt directs us to find the function whose y-values can't go below $y = -1$. So let's test (B):

$y = x^2 - 2$	(equation from (B))
$-2 = x^2 - 2$	(plug in $y = -2$)
$0 = x^2$	(add 2 to both sides)
$0 = x$	(take square root of both sides)

A y-value of -2 results in an expression that can be true for choice (B) as well, so (B) can't be correct, for the same reason that (A) couldn't. Let's try (C) next:

$y = (x - 2)^2$	(equation from (C))
$-2 = (x - 2)^2$	(plug in $y = -2$)
$\sqrt{-2} = x - 2$	(take square root of both sides)
$\sqrt{-2} + 2 = x$	(add 2 to both sides)

The square root of a negative number can't appear on a graph in the xy-plane, which means that this choice doesn't result in a real expression when $y = -2$, so (C) can be correct, assuming we haven't made any mistakes in our approach. Let's test (D) as a way to help make sure our thinking is correct:

$y = x^3 - 2$	(equation from (D))
$-2 = x^3 - 2$	(plug in $y = -2$)
$0 = x^3$	(add 2 to both sides)
$0 = x$	(take cube root of both sides)

As with (A) and (B), the result is an expression that can be true, so (D) can't be the correct answer.

Since (C) is the only choice that can't produce a y-value of -2, we know that (C) must be correct.

Solution 4: Test-smart: The question basically asks which equation never has a y-value less than -1. We might notice that the right side of the equations in (A), (B), and (D) involve 2 subtracted from an x-term, and that if we plug $x = 0$ into each of those equations, the right side becomes $0 - 2$, and the result for each is $y = -2$. So (A), (B), and (D) are wrong, and from there we can see that the lowest value for (C) will be $y = 0$ when $x = 2$, so (C) is correct.

ANSWER CHOICE ANALYSIS

(A): This choice would generate an acceptable graph if not for the "-2" component, and is probably here for test-takers who misread the choice or the prompt. **(B):** This has an issue similar to what we see in (A); it may also be here to trick people who try to apply their knowledge of formal math and forget the difference between the domain (horizontal) shift in (C) and the range (vertical) shift in (B). (See note below.)

How to check? Try an alternate approach above.

Note This question will cause many untrained test-takers to assume that they need to be familiar with the formal rules for graphing different kinds of functions. But, as we just saw, it's completely possible to answer this question with perfect confidence even without already knowing those rules, as long as we remember to take advantage of the opportunities provided to us by the multiple-choice structure of the test.

Test 2, Section 3, Question 11

- **What's the prompt asking for?** The answer choice that's equivalent to the expression in the prompt.
- **Math concepts in the prompt:** addition, complex numbers, fractions, i, subtraction
- **Elements of the answer choices:** fractions, imaginary numbers, integers
- **Notable differences among answer choices:** (A) and (B) both involve $\frac{3}{8}$ and $\frac{5i}{2}$. (C) and (D) both involve $\frac{7}{34}$ and $\frac{23i}{34}$. (A) and (C) both involve subtraction, while (B) and (D) both involve addition.
- **Concepts in the answer choices:** addition, fractions, imaginary numbers, subtraction
- **Pre-solution patterns (see p. 217):** wrong answers try to imitate right answers; opposites
- **Things to look out for:** Don't misread the choices, especially with respect to plus and minus signs! Don't make mistakes when you square i, or divide -1 by i!

Solution 1: Imaginary numbers: Eliminate the imaginary component in the denominator: multiply the fraction by $\frac{8-2i}{8-2i}$ and simplify.

$\dfrac{3-5i}{8+21}$	(original expression)
$\dfrac{3-5i}{8+2i} \times \dfrac{8-2i}{8-2i}$	(multiply by $\dfrac{8-2i}{8-2i}$ to get rid of imaginary component in denominator)
$\dfrac{24-6i-40i+10i^2}{64-16i+16i-4i^2}$	(FOIL the numerators and denominators)
$\dfrac{24-6i-40i+10(-1)}{64-16i+16i-4(-1)}$	(plug in $i^2 = -1$)
$\dfrac{14-46i}{68}$	(simplify)
$\dfrac{7-23i}{34}$	(divide through by 2 to simplify)

This expression is equivalent to the expression in (C), so (C) is correct.

Solution 2: Test-smart: Go through each answer choice and consider it in light of the prompt, to see which choice fits.

When we notice the similarities and differences among the answer choices (as described above), we might realize that the issue of identifying the correct answer can be reduced to answering two questions:

1. Should the correct answer involve fractions with different denominators (like in (A) and (B)), or fractions with identical denominators (like in (C) and (D))?
2. Should the correct answer involve subtracting fractions (like in (A) and (C)), or adding fractions (like in (B) and (D))?

If we spend a few seconds considering these issues, we can reliably identify the answer without necessarily doing any calculations.

For the first question, we should know, as trained test-takers, that we would be breaking the basic rules of math if we took the fraction in the prompt and "broke it up" so that the two numbers on the left-hand side of the numerator and the denominator went into the first fraction in (A) or (B), and the two numbers on the right-hand side of the numerator and denominator went into the second fraction in (A) or (B). When we modify fractions to create equivalent fractions, we have to do that by multiplying or dividing both the numerator and denominator of the original fraction by equivalent amounts. The result of this kind of modification would be some kind of fraction expression with common denominators, which is what we see in choices (C) and (D).

For the second question, we'd need to think a little bit about what the formal approach to this question might be. As we saw in solution 1, the formal approach to a question like this would be to multiply the numerator and denominator of the fraction in the prompt by $8 - 2i$, because this will result in a difference of squares in the denominator, which will ultimately lead to a single real number in the denominator (again, see the steps in solution 1 for a demonstration of this idea). So what will happen when we multiply the *numerator* by $8 - 2i$? Well, as we saw in solution 1, the result will be an expression in the numerator that involves subtracting one number from another—we may be able to realize that subtraction will be involved without actually doing the FOIL process ourselves.

Since we now know the correct answer must involve expressions with a common denominator, and it must involve subtracting one thing from another, we know that only (C) can possibly be correct.

As with all test-smart solutions, don't be discouraged if you couldn't see this solution right away! The important lesson to learn from this example is that the College Board often designs answer choices to SAT Math questions in such a way that only the correct answer demonstrates key features that can be identified beforehand. Keep this in mind as you train, because it can save you a lot of time and work even if you're only able to put it into practice a few times per test.

ANSWER CHOICE ANALYSIS

(A): This choice might be tempting for an untrained test-taker who was unclear on the properties of fractions, and incorrectly thought that it was okay to separate a complex number from the denominator into two denominators: one with the real component of the original fraction, and one with the imaginary component. **(B):** This choice has problems similar to the problems in (A). **(D):** This choice might be tempting if we make a mistake involving positive and negative signs.

How to check? Try an alternate approach above.

▶   Post-solution patterns (see page 218): opposites

Test 2, Section 3, Question 12

- **What's the prompt asking for?** The answer choice that accurately expresses F in terms of R and N.
- **Math concepts in the prompt:** algebra, defining variables, equations, variables, formula modeling
- **Elements of the answer choices:** algebraic expressions, equations, fractions, integers
- **Notable differences among answer choices:** (A) and (B) have RN in the numerator, while (C) and (D) only have N in the numerator. (A) and (D) have $R - 1$ in the denominator, while (B) and (C) have $1 - R$ in the denominator.

- **Concepts in the answer choices:** fractions, multiplication, variables
- **"Bridge" concepts:** Every algebraic equation with multiple variables can be algebraically manipulated to isolate any single variable.
- **Pre-solution patterns (see p. 217):** wrong answers try to imitate right answers
- **Things to look out for:** Don't make small mistakes in your algebra! Make sure you pay specific attention to the differences among the choices we identified above! Don't confuse the variables!

Solution 1: Algebra: Manipulate the equation in the prompt until you've isolated F on one side of the equation, and then pick the answer choice that matches the form of the equation you've found.

$$R = \frac{F}{N+F}$$ (original equation)

$$R(N + F) = F$$ (multiply both sides by $N + F$)

$$RN + RF = F$$ (distribute R)

$$RN = F - RF$$ (subtract RF from both sides)

$$RN = F(1 - R)$$ (factor out F from the right-hand side of the equation)

$$\frac{RN}{1-R} = F$$ (divide both sides by $1 - R$ to isolate F)

Since this expression matches (B), we can see (B) is correct.

Solution 2: Concrete: Pick arbitrary values for F and N, and then use those values to determine a corresponding R-value. Then take these values for $F, R,$ and N, and plug them into each answer choice; the choice that produces a valid statement will be right.

$$R = \frac{F}{N+F}$$ (original equation)

$$R = \frac{2}{3+2} \qquad \text{(plug in } F = 2 \text{ and } N = 3, \text{ as arbitrary values)}$$

$$R = \frac{2}{5} \qquad \text{(simplify to find the } R\text{-value when } F = 2 \text{ and } N = 3)$$

Now we can plug $F = 2$, $N = 3$, and $R = \frac{2}{5}$ in to each answer choice, and see which choice makes a valid statement. We'll start with (A):

$$F = \frac{RN}{R-1} \qquad \text{(equation from (A))}$$

$$2 = \frac{\frac{2}{5}(3)}{\frac{2}{5} - 1} \qquad \text{(plug in } F = 2, N = 3, \text{ and } R = \frac{2}{5})$$

$$2 = \frac{\frac{6}{5}}{-\frac{3}{5}} \qquad \text{(simplify)}$$

$$2 = -2 \qquad \text{(simplify)}$$

This statement is invalid, so (A) can't be correct. Let's try (B) now:

$$F = \frac{RN}{1-R} \qquad \text{(equation from (B))}$$

$$2 = \frac{\frac{2}{5}(3)}{1 - \frac{2}{5}} \qquad \text{(plug in } F = 2, N = 3, \text{ and } R = \frac{2}{5})$$

$$2 = \frac{\frac{6}{5}}{\frac{3}{5}} \qquad \text{(simplify)}$$

$$2 = 2 \qquad \text{(simplify)}$$

This statement is valid, so (B) could be correct, assuming that we haven't made any mistakes in our approach, and also assuming that we didn't accidentally choose arbitrary values for F and N that result in more than one answer choice seeming to be valid. (See "Special Technique: Backsolving" on page 211 of this Black Book for more on issues related to backsolving and false positives.) Let's keep checking the choices to make sure we've correctly identified the only one that's a valid expression of F in terms of R and N. Here's what we get for (C):

$$F = \frac{N}{1-R} \qquad \text{(equation from (C))}$$

$$2 = \frac{3}{1 - \frac{2}{5}} \qquad \text{(plug in } F = 2, N = 3, \text{ and } R = \frac{2}{5})$$

$$2 = \frac{3}{\frac{3}{5}} \qquad \text{(simplify)}$$

$$2 = 5 \qquad \text{(simplify)}$$

This statement is invalid, so (C) can't be correct. Finally, we'll check (D):

$$F = \frac{N}{R-1} \qquad \text{(equation from (D))}$$

$$2 = \frac{3}{\frac{2}{5} - 1} \qquad \text{(plug in } F = 2, N = 3, \text{ and } R = \frac{2}{5})$$

$$2 = \frac{3}{-\frac{3}{5}} \qquad \text{(simplify)}$$

$$2 = -5 \qquad \text{(simplify)}$$

This statement is invalid, so (D) can't be correct, either. Only (B) resulted in a valid statement, so only (B) can be correct.

How to check? Try an alternate approach above, paying specific attention to the differences among the answer choices that we identified above.

Note   Any of the wrong answers might be tempting if we make simple errors in algebra. Remember SAT Math is just as much a test of your ability to pay attention to small details as a test of math knowledge!

- **What's the prompt asking for?** The sum of the possible values of m in the given equation.
- **Math concepts in the prompt:** addition, algebra, quadratic equations, variables, zero
- **Elements of the answer choices:** integers, negative numbers, radical expressions
- **Notable differences among answer choices:** (A) is the opposite of (D) and (B) is the opposite of (C). (A) and (B) are negative; (C) and (D) are positive. (B) and (C) involve radical expressions, while (A) and (D) do not.
- **"Bridge" concepts:** m can have multiple values in the given equation because the equation is quadratic.
- **Pre-solution patterns (see p. 217):** opposites; wrong answers try to imitate right answers
- **Things to look out for:** Don't make small algebra mistakes! Don't confuse positive and negative numbers, since the answer choices are clearly trying to get you to do that!

Solution 1: Algebra: Use the quadratic formula to identify the possible values of m, and add them to find the correct answer. (We could also try using reverse-FOIL to find the values of m, but if we try that it becomes clear pretty quickly that it's not possible.)

The quadratic formula is based on the general quadratic equation $ax^2 + bx + c = 0$. In this instance, the given equation is $2m^2 - 16m + 8 = 0$, so $a = 2, b = -16, c = 8,$ and $x = m$.

$$x = \frac{-b \pm \sqrt{b^2 - 4ac}}{2a}$$ (quadratic formula)

$$m = \frac{-(-16) \pm \sqrt{(-16)^2 - 4(2)(8)}}{2(2)}$$ (plug in $a = 2, b = -16, c = 8,$ and $x = m$)

$$m = \frac{16 \pm \sqrt{192}}{4}$$ (simplify)

$$m = \frac{16 \pm 8\sqrt{3}}{4}$$ (factor $\sqrt{64}$ out of the expression under the radical if you notice that 64 is a factor of 192; otherwise, factor $\sqrt{4}$ out three times)

$$m = 4 \pm 2\sqrt{3}$$ (reduce)

The m values that satisfy $2m^2 - 16m + 8 = 0$ are $4 + 2\sqrt{3}$ and $4 - 2\sqrt{3}$. The sum of these two values is $4 + 2\sqrt{3} + 4 - 2\sqrt{3}$, or 8, so (D) is correct.

ANSWER CHOICE ANALYSIS

(A): This is the opposite of the correct answer, presumably here for people who get the signs switched while trying to apply the quadratic formula.

How to check? Carefully reconsider your work, paying attention to the differences among the choices that we identified above.

- **What's the prompt asking for?** The choice that models a 13% annual decay of 325 grams after t years.
- **Math concepts in the prompt:** decay, function modeling, percentages
- **Elements of the answer choices:** equations, exponents, function modeling, multiplication
- **Notable differences among answer choices:** (A) and (B) both have 325 as the number immediately after the equals sign, while (C) has 0.87 after the equals sign, and (D) has 0.13 after the equals sign. (A) has 0.87 in parentheses raised to an exponent of t, while (B) has 0.13 in parentheses raised to an exponent of t, and both (C) and (D) have 325 in parentheses raised to an exponent of t.
- **Concepts in the answer choices:** exponents, function modeling, PEMDAS, variables
- **"Bridge" concepts:** If something decreases by 13%, that's the same thing as saying there's 87% of it left, since $100\% - 13\% = 87\%$. Finding 87% of a number is the same thing as multiplying that number by 0.87. Raising a number to an exponent of t is the same as multiplying the number by itself t times.
- **Pre-solution patterns (see p. 217):** wrong answers try to imitate right answers
- **Things to look out for:** Make sure you determine whether 0.13 or 0.87 should be in the correct answer! Make sure you correctly determine whether the number 325 itself should be raised to an exponent.

Solution 1: Algebra: Use algebra to model the decay, and pick the answer choice that matches your model.

If the initial amount of the radioactive substance is 325 grams, then it makes sense that the function would be based on that value. So let's start with that idea, and we'll fill in the rest as we go:

$$f(t) = 325\ldots$$

If the substance decays at 13 percent each year, then we know that we'll have 87 percent of it at the end of the first year, because $100\% - 13\% = 87\%$. So it makes sense that 325 would be multiplied by 0.87, because we'll have 87% of the starting amount after a year. So let's add that idea to our function model:

$$f(t) = 325 \times 0.87...$$

Now, the expression above only accounts for one year of decay, because we'd have 87% of the original 325 after the first year. But how could we account for the fact that the prompt told us to pick the model that shows how much would be left after t years, and not just after one year? Let's think about what's going to happen with each passing year. We know that after one year, we'll have 87% of our starting amount. What happens the second year? Well, at the beginning of the second year, we'll be starting with a sample that's 87% of the first year's size, and then that sample will continue to decay, leaving us with an amount at the end of year two that's 87% of what it was at the beginning of year two...which was only 87% of what it was at the beginning of year one. So with each year that passes, we're multiplying our remaining amount by 0.87 again to account for another year's worth of decay.

This idea of multiplying 0.87 by itself a certain number of times is the same as the idea of raising 0.87 to an exponent. And what exponent should we raise it to? Well, we're re-doing this multiplication by 0.87 with each new year that passes, so we'll need to multiply 0.87 by itself every year. If t years pass, then we'll multiply 0.87 by itself t times, which is the same thing as raising 0.87 to the exponent of t. So let's add that to our function and see what we've got:

$$f(t) = 325 \times (0.87)^t$$

So we can see that (A) is correct.

Solution 2: Test-smart: Consider each of the differences among the answer choices that we noted above, and pick the answer choice with the appropriate options.

When we note the similarities and differences among the answer choices that are described above, we see that we can identify which choice must be correct if we can figure out the answers to the following questions:

1. Should the correct answer involve the number 0.87 (like in (A) and (C)), or the number 0.13 (like in (B) and (D))?
2. Should the number 325 be raised to an exponent of t (like in (C) and (D)), or should some other number be raised to an exponent of t?

Once we figure out the answers to those questions, we'll be able to identify the answer choice that has the correct features.

For the first issue, we should realize that the numbers 0.87 and 0.13 are being multiplied by the number 325, and then ask ourselves what that's supposed to represent. The prompt asks for the "remaining amount" after the substance decays at a rate of 13%. So should we be multiplying the original amount by 13% to see what's left, or multiplying by 87% to see what's left? The answer is 87%—for the reasons we discussed in solution 1, we'll have 87% of something left after 13% of it is removed, so the correct function will need to multiply the amount of the original sample by 87%.

For the second issue, we need to think about what the t exponent represents. The t exponent indicates that we're multiplying a certain quantity by itself t times—in other words, we're multiplying that quantity by itself one time for every year, since t is the number of years. If the sample exists for 2 years, then we multiply that amount by itself twice; if the sample exists for 7 years, then we multiply that amount by itself 7 times; and so on. So which number should we be multiplying by itself? Should it be the size of the original sample? It doesn't make sense to multiply the original sample by the size of the original sample again and again, because nothing in the prompt describes anything similar to that—if we start with a sample size of 325 grams, why would we keep multiplying that sample by 325 every year after the first year? Just from simple estimating, we can tell that multiplying 325 by itself for the second year would result in a number bigger than 90,000 grams (since 300×300 is 90,000), which definitely doesn't go along with the idea of the sample size decaying. So we can tell that the amount being raised to an exponent shouldn't be 325. (And if we follow reasoning similar to what we described in solution 1, we can also see why the percentage left over after each year's decay *should* be multiplied by itself for every year of decay...but we don't need to understand that fully for this approach. We just need to realize that it doesn't make sense to multiply 325 by itself repeatedly, given the context of the question.)

Since we now know that the correct answer should involve 0.87, and should avoid raising 325 to an exponent, we can see that (A) must be correct, since it's the only choice with those features.

ANSWER CHOICE ANALYSIS

(B): This choice would tempt someone who forgot that, when a thing decays by 13%, there's 87% left. **(C):** This choice confuses the relationship between the initial amount and the rate of decay. **(D):** This choice combines the errors from (B) and (C).

How to check? Try an alternate approach above, paying particular attention to the differences among the answer choices that we noted as you confirm your answer.

Test 2, Section 3, Question 15

- **What's the prompt asking for?** The choice that contains an expression equivalent to the expression in the prompt.
- **Math concepts in the prompt:** addition, algebraic expressions, fractions, subtraction, variables

- **Elements of the answer choices:** algebraic expressions, fractions, integers
- **Notable differences among answer choices:** (A) is the only choice in which every number is in either the numerator or

denominator of a fraction. (A) and (B) are the only choices without a variable. (A), (B), and (C) all have a 2 in the numerator of a fraction, while (D) has 17 in the numerator.

- **Concepts in the answer choices:** addition, fractions, subtraction, variables

- **Pre-solution patterns (see p. 217):** wrong answers try to imitate right answers
- **Things to look out for:** Make sure you determine whether 5 should be part of the fraction! Don't make a mistake when you consider canceling x! Make sure you accurately determine whether 17 or 2 should be in the numerator of the fraction!

Solution 1: Concrete: Pick an arbitrary value for x and evaluate the original fraction using that x-value. Then use that x-value to evaluate each answer choice, and pick the choice whose value matches the expression in the prompt.

$$\frac{5x-2}{x+3}$$ (original expression)

$$\frac{5(7)-2}{7+3}$$ (plug in $x = 7$ as an arbitrary value)

$$\frac{33}{10}$$ (simplify to find the value of the fraction when $x = 7$)

Now we can plug $x = 7$ into the expressions from the other answer choices and see which one is equal to $\frac{33}{10}$. We'll start with (A):

$$\frac{5-2}{3}$$ (expression from (A))

$$1$$ (simplify)

This expression isn't equal to $\frac{33}{10}$, so (A) can't be equal to the fraction from the prompt, which means it can't be right. Let's try (B):

$$5 - \frac{2}{3}$$ (expression from (B))

$$4\frac{1}{3}$$ (simplify)

This expression isn't equal to $\frac{33}{10}$, so (B) can't be correct, either. Now, let's try (C):

$$5 - \frac{2}{x+3}$$ (expression from (C))

$$5 - \frac{2}{7+3}$$ (plug in $x = 7$)

$$5 - \frac{2}{10}$$ (simplify)

$$4\frac{8}{10}$$ (simplify)

When $x = 7$, this expression isn't equal to $\frac{33}{10}$, so (C) can't be correct. Finally, we'll test (D):

$$5 - \frac{17}{x+3}$$ (expression from (D))

$$5 - \frac{17}{7+3}$$ (plug in $x = 7$)

$$5 - \frac{17}{10}$$ (simplify)

$$3\frac{3}{10}$$ (simplify)

This expression is equal to $\frac{33}{10}$ when $x = 7$, so (D) is correct.

Solution 2: Algebra: Use polynomial long division to divide $5x - 2$ by $x + 3$.

Page 270 Facebook.com/TestingIsEasy Youtube.com/TestingIsEasy

$$x+3{\overline{\smash{\big)}\,5x-2}}$$
$$\underline{-(5x+15)}$$
$$-17$$

With 5 above the division.

After performing polynomial long division, we can see that $\frac{5x-2}{x+3} = 5 - \frac{17}{x+3}$. (Be sure to review polynomial long division in the Toolbox if you're uncomfortable with that approach, and remember that it's never necessary to know polynomial long division in order to get a perfect or near-perfect score on the SAT Math section. Also, notice that in Solution 1 we were able to answer this question without using polynomial long division at all.)

ANSWER CHOICE ANALYSIS

(A): This choice might be tempting if an untrained test-taker incorrectly thought she could eliminate the x-terms and leave the rest of the fraction unchanged for some reason. **(B):** This choice might be tempting if an untrained test-taker incorrectly tried to separate the initial expression into $\frac{5x}{x} - \frac{2}{3}$, and then canceled the x-es on the left side of the expression.

How to check? Try an alternate approach above.

Test 2, Section 3, Question 16

- **What's the prompt asking for?** One possible number of $250 bonuses according to the prompt.
- **Math concepts in the prompt:** division, inequalities
- **Things to look out for:** Don't make any small mistakes with your arithmetic! Don't forget that there has to be at least one $750 bonus!

Solution 1: Concrete arithmetic: Determine the number of possible $250 bonuses, assuming that one $750 bonus is given.

If one $750 bonus is awarded, that leaves $3000 - $750, or $2250.

Now we can divide $2250 by $250 to figure out how many $250 bonuses might have been awarded: $\frac{\$2250}{\$250} = 9$
So one possible number of $250 bonuses is 9.

How to check? Carefully re-check the work you've done, including re-checking your reading of the prompt. Note that the prompt uses the phrase "one possible number" because the number of bonuses could have been 3, 6, or 9 bonuses of $250, depending on the number of $750 bonuses given.

Test 2, Section 3, Question 17

- **What's the prompt asking for?** The value of b under the circumstances in the prompt.
- **Math concepts in the prompt:** quadratic equations, variables, algebra, multiplication, exponents, constants
- **"Bridge" concepts:** Since $a, b,$ and c are constants, we know that some set of values for $a, b,$ and c will make the equation in the prompt valid for all x-values.
- **Things to look out for:** Don't make mistakes in your algebra! Don't confuse $a, b,$ and c!

Solution 1: Algebra: Simplify the equation on the left until it has one x^2 term, one x-term, and one integer without a variable. The coefficient of the x-term will be the value of b in the original equation.

$2x(3x+5) + 3(3x+5) = ax^2 + bx + c$	(original equation)
$6x^2 + 10x + 9x + 15 = ax^2 + bx + c$	(distribute)
$6x^2 + 19x + 15 = ax^2 + bx + c$	(simplify)

We can see that the coefficient of x is 19, so $b = 19$.

How to check? Re-read the prompt carefully to make sure you've provided the value that the question was asking for, and carefully re-check your work to make sure there are no mistakes in the arithmetic or the algebra.

Test 2, Section 3, Question 18

- **What's the prompt asking for?** The length of CE under the circumstances in the prompt and the diagram.
- **Math concepts in the prompt:** intersection, length of a line, parallel lines
- **Math concepts in the diagram:** parallel lines cut by a transversal, vertical angles
- **"Bridge" concepts:** Angles CBD and ABE must be the same size, since they're vertical angles. The angle at C must be the same size as the angle at E, since CD and AE are parallel and CE is a straight line. The angle at A must be the same size as the angle at D, since CD and AE are parallel, and AD is a straight line. The two triangles must be similar, since their angle measurements are the same. If two triangles are similar,

then pairs of corresponding sides have lengths in a constant ratio to one another.

- **Things to look out for:** Don't provide the length of the wrong segment! Don't get confused about which pairs of sides correspond to one another!

Solution 1: Geometry: Determine the ratio of AB to BD, and apply that ratio to BC and BE to determine the length of BC. Then add the length of BC to the length of BE to get CE.

$\overline{AB}$ is twice as long as $\overline{BD}$, so $\overline{EB}$ must be twice as long as $\overline{BC}$. Since $\overline{EB}$ is 8 units long, $\overline{BC}$ must be 4 units long. So $\overline{CE}$ must have a length of 4 units plus 8 units, which means it's 12 units long. That means the correct answer is 12.

Solution 2: Geometry: Determine the ratio of AB to BE, and apply that ratio to BD and BC to find BC. Then add the length of BC to the length of BE to get CE.

The ratio of $\overline{AB}$ to $\overline{EB}$ is $\frac{10}{8}$. The ratio of $\overline{BD}$ to $\overline{BC}$ is $\frac{5}{x}$. We can set these ratios equal to one another and solve for x.

$$\frac{10}{8} = \frac{5}{x}$$ (ratios of corresponding sides set equal to one another)

$$10x = 40$$ (cross multiply)

$$x = 4$$ (divide both sides by 10)

So the length of $\overline{BC}$ must be 4 units long. That means $\overline{CE}$ must have a length of 4 units plus 8 units, or 12 units.

How to check? Carefully re-read the prompt and re-check your work. Make sure you've provided the value of CE, and not of some other line segment! Use the scale of the diagram to help you confirm visually that CB is 4 units, and CE must be 12.

Test 2, Section 3, Question 19

- **What's the prompt asking for?** The value of a under the circumstances in the prompt.
- **Math concepts in the prompt:** algebra, center of a circle, fractions, π, radians, xy-coordinate plane
- **Math concepts in the diagram:** circles, coordinate values, square roots, xy-coordinate plane,

- **"Bridge" concepts:** A radian measures the size of an angle by comparing it to the unit circle. The circle in the diagram is NOT the unit circle, since $(\sqrt{3}, 1)$ is on the circle.
- **Things to look out for:** Don't forget that the question is asking for a in the fraction from the prompt—the question isn't asking us to measure AOB in degrees!

Solution 1: Algebra/Trigonometry: We can make $\overline{OA}$ the hypotenuse of a triangle, then use the Pythagorean Theorem to find the length of that hypotenuse. When we know all the side lengths, we can find the measure of $\angle AOB$ in radians. Then we can find a.

Let's sketch our triangle with $\overline{OA}$ as the hypotenuse:

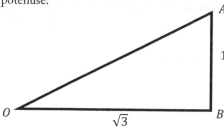

Now we can use the Pythagorean Theorem to find the length of the hypotenuse:

$a^2 + b^2 = c^2$ (Pythagorean Theorem)

$\sqrt{3}^2 + 1^2 = c^2$ (plug in the side lengths from the coordinates)

$3 + 1 = c^2$ (simplify)

$4 = c^2$ (simplify)

$2 = c$ (take the square root of both sides)

So the length of the hypotenuse is 2. We can add that value to our diagram:

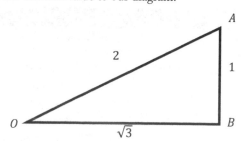

We know from SOHCAHTOA that $sine = \frac{opposite}{hypotenuse}$, so $\sin AOB = \frac{1}{2}$, which means that the measure of $\angle AOB$ is $30°$. We can convert $30°$ to radians by multiplying by $\frac{\pi}{180}$, since π radians equals $180°$. That gives us $30° \times \frac{\pi}{180} = \frac{\pi}{6}$. The question asked for the value of a if the measure of $\angle AOB$ is $\frac{\pi}{a}$, so 6 is the answer.

Solution 2: Formal: We can use geometry and algebra to compare the given angle to the unit circle, which should allow us to express the size of AOB in radians, and determine the value of a. (If you're not comfortable with the unit circle, remember that you can use one of the other solutions in this walkthrough.)

If we've studied the unit circle, we know that a $30°$-angle intercepts the unit-circle at the point $(\frac{\sqrt{3}}{2}, \frac{1}{2})$. We can see from the diagram that A lies on the point $(\sqrt{3}, 1)$, which means the x-value and y-value of A are both exactly twice as much as the x-value and y-value of the point on the unit circle that corresponds to a $30°$-angle. This means that $\angle AOB$ must be a $30°$-angle, since line segment OA has the same orientation as the hypotenuse of a $30°$-angle on the unit circle. Since a $30°$ angle corresponds to $\frac{\pi}{6}$ radians, we know $a = 6$.

Solution 3: Test-smart: We know the that diagram must be drawn exactly to scale, because there isn't any note to say that the diagram *isn't* drawn to scale. We know that a whole circle has 2π radians of arc, which means that a quarter circle has $\frac{1}{4}$ of that, or $\frac{\pi}{2}$ radians of arc. We can see from the diagram that $\angle AOB$ is some portion of the of the top right quarter of the circle. Clearly that portion is less than half of that quarter circle, and it appears to be more than a quarter of the quarter circle—we can confirm that by drawing a line on the diagram to bisect the larger angle in the upper right quarter of the circle, like this:

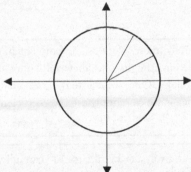

So $\angle AOB$ is less than $\frac{1}{2}$ but more than $\frac{1}{4}$ of the quarter circle, which means it must be $\frac{1}{3}$ of the arc of the upper right quarter of the circle. That means the measure of the angle is $\frac{1}{3}$ of $\frac{\pi}{2}$, or $\frac{1}{3} \times \frac{\pi}{2}$, or $\frac{\pi}{6}$. Again, we see that $a = 6$.

Solution 4: Test-smart: Once we realize that $\overline{OA}$ can be the hypotenuse of a triangle with sides $\sqrt{3}$ and 1, we might recognize that $\sqrt{3}$ and 1 are the side lengths of a $30°$-$60°$-$90°$ triangle with hypotenuse 2. Then we can see that $\angle AOB$ is the smallest angle, the $30°$ angle. We can convert $30°$ to radians as discussed in the previous solutions to find that the measure of $\angle AOB$ is $\frac{\pi}{6}$. So $a = 6$.

How to check? Pay careful attention to what the question is actually asking for, and make sure you didn't make any calculation mistakes. Also re-consider your answer in light of the scaled diagram.

Test 2, Section 3, Question 20

- **What's the prompt asking for?** The value of $\frac{a}{b}$ if the system of equations is valid for an infinite set of (x, y) pairs.

- **Math concepts in the prompt:** addition, constants, fractions, systems of equations, variables

- **"Bridge" concepts:** Both equations are in the standard format for a line. The prompt tells us a and b are values that allow the system to have "infinitely many solutions." Since the equations are linear—that is, they produce straight lines when graphed—we know a and b make the system work for all possible values of x and their corresponding y-values, and not just for a limited number of (x, y) pairs.

- **Things to look out for:** Make sure you find the value of $\frac{a}{b}$, not $\frac{b}{a}$, nor the value of a or b individually! Don't try to find the value of $\frac{x}{y}$ instead of the value of $\frac{a}{b}$!

Solution 1: System of equations: Multiply the top equation by 5 in order to make the constants in both equations equivalent. Determine the value of a by setting $5ax$ equal to $2x$ and solving for a; determine the value of b by setting $5by$ equal to $8y$ and solving for b. Then use those values to find $\frac{a}{b}$.

$$ax + by = 12 \qquad \text{(first equation from the prompt)}$$

$$5ax + 5by = 60 \qquad \text{(multiply both sides of the first equation by 5 to make 60 the constant)}$$

Now that both equations involve setting the sum of an x-term and y-term equal to 60, we know that the expressions $5ax + 5by$ and $2x + 8y$ are both equal to 60, and equal to each other. Since the system has an infinite number of solutions, we know that the x-terms in the two expressions must be equal to each other, and the y-terms must be equal to each other. That allows us to find the value of a by setting the x-terms equal to each other, and to find the value of b by setting the y-terms equal to each other:

$$5ax = 2x \qquad \text{(set the x-expressions from each equation equal to each other)}$$

$$a = \tfrac{2}{5} \qquad \text{(divide both sides by $5x$ to isolate a)}$$

$$5by = 8y \qquad \text{(set the y-expressions from each equation equal to each other)}$$

$$b = \tfrac{8}{5} \qquad \text{(divide both sides by $5y$ to isolate b)}$$

Now that we've found values for a and b individually, we can find $\frac{a}{b}$:

$$\frac{\frac{2}{5}}{\frac{8}{5}} \qquad \text{(substitute $a = \tfrac{2}{5}$ and $b = \tfrac{8}{5}$ into $\tfrac{a}{b}$)}$$

$$\frac{2}{8} \qquad \text{(simplify)}$$

$$\frac{1}{4} \qquad \text{(simplify)}$$

So we can see that $\frac{1}{4}$ is the value of $\frac{a}{b}$.

Solution 2: Test-smart: Since the system has infinitely many solutions and both equations describe lines, we know that both equations must describe the same line (if they were two different straight lines, they could only have one point in common at most, which means they would only have one solution, not infinitely many). Once we realize that, we see that the prompt is actually asking for the ratio of the coefficient of x to the coefficient of y. This means we can simply use the coefficients of the x- and y-terms in the bottom equation as a and b, to arrive at an answer of $\frac{1}{4}$.

How to check? Try an alternate approach above—as always, make sure to read carefully, and make sure you provided the value of $\frac{a}{b}$, and not some on-the-way answer!

TEST 3 – SECTION 3

Test 3, Section 3, Question 1

- **What's the prompt asking for?** The variable that should be changed to reflect a more expensive brand of paint.
- **Math concepts in the prompt:** function modeling, units, variables, word problems
- **Elements of the answer choices:** algebraic expressions
- **Notable differences among answer choices:** Each choice is one of the four variables in the expression from the prompt.
- **Concepts in the answer choices:** function modeling, variables
- **Things to look out for:** Read carefully and make sure you don't confuse the variables!

Solution 1: Critical reading: Read the prompt carefully and determine which variable could be related to the cost of the paint.

The prompt says K is a constant with units of dollars per square feet. It makes sense that a more expensive brand of paint would raise the cost per square foot. Also, K is the only variable with any direct connection with money. These facts indicate (C) is right.

How to check? Carefully re-read the prompt and make sure you've marked the choice that you meant to mark.

Test 3, Section 3, Question 2

- **What's the prompt asking for?** The value of $6r + 3$.
- **Math concepts in the prompt:** algebra, arithmetic
- **Elements of the answer choices:** integers
- **Notable differences among answer choices:** (D) is 3 more than (C), which may be relevant because the question asks for a value that involves adding 3. (A) is one-sixth of (C), which

may be relevant because the prompt asks for an expression that involves multiplying something by 6. (A) is also one-third of 18, which may be relevant because the prompt mentions a quantity multiplied by 3 to produce 18.

- **Things to look out for:** Make sure you find $6r + 3$, instead of just finding r! Don't make any small mistakes in your algebra or arithmetic!

Solution 1: Algebra: Find r, and then use r to find $6r + 3$.

$$3r = 18 \qquad \text{(first equation in the prompt)}$$
$$r = 6 \qquad \text{(divide both sides by 3)}$$

Now we can plug $r = 6$ into $6r + 3$.

$$6r + 3 \qquad \text{(second equation in the prompt)}$$
$$6(6) + 3 \qquad \text{(plug in } r = 6)$$
$$39 \qquad \text{(simplify)}$$

Choice (D) is correct.

Solution 2: Algebra: Multiply $3r$ by 2 and add 3 in order to find $6r + 3$.

If $3r = 18$, then $6r$ must must be twice as much as 18, or 36. So $6r + 3$ equals $36 + 3$, or 39.

Solution 3: Test-smart: Note the relationships among the answer choices and identify (D) as the correct answer.

As trained test-takers, when we note the relationships among the answer choices, we can see that the College Board is clearly trying to bait us to make small mistakes on this question. We see that (A) is the value of r, for test-takers who forget what the prompt was asking for. We also see that (D) is 3 more than (C), and (C) is twice as much as 18, one of the numbers from the prompt. When we realize this, we can see that (C) corresponds to $6r$, and (D) must be equal to $6r + 3$. (For this approach, it helps to be able to multiply 18 by 2 in your head. If you're not comfortable doing that, then another approach to this question is probably more ideal for you.)

ANSWER CHOICE ANALYSIS

(A): This is the value of r. **(C):** This is the value of $6r$, not $6r + 3$.

How to check? Try an alternate approach above, paying careful attention to the relationships among the choices we noted above.

Test 3, Section 3, Question 3

- **What's the prompt asking for?** An equivalent expression for $a^{2/3}$
- **Math concepts in the prompt:** fractional exponents, variables
- **Elements of the answer choices:** algebraic expressions, exponents, fractions, integers, radical expressions
- **Notable differences among answer choices:** (A) and (B) are both square-root expressions, while (C) and (D) involve the cube-root. (A) and (B) both have exponents that involve 3, while (C) and (D) both have exponents that involve 2. (A) and (C) both have fractional exponents, while (B) and (D) both have integers for exponents.
- **Concepts in the answer choices:** cube roots, exponents, fractional exponents, square roots, variables
- **Pre-solution patterns (see p. 217):** wrong answers try to imitate right answers
- **Things to look out for:** Don't confuse square roots with cube roots! Don't pick an expression whose exponent is the reciprocal of the correct exponent!

Solution 1: Algebra: Using your knowledge of fractional exponents, identify the correct answer choice.

This question appears to be a direct test of whether we understand how fractional exponents work. As trained test-takers, we simply need to recognize automatically that $a^{x/y}$ is equal to $\sqrt[y]{a^x}$, which means (D) is correct. (If we were allowed to use a calculator on this question, then there are ways we could test the choices with arbitrary values to find out which expression was equal to the prompt; since we can't use a calculator, we just have to know what a fractional exponent is in this case. See the section on fractional exponents in the "Exponents" part of the Math Toolbox on page 180 if you need a refresher on how they work.)

ANSWER CHOICE ANALYSIS

(A): This is equal to $a^{(1/3)(1/2)}$. **(B):** This is equal to $a^{3/2}$. **(C):** This is another expression that is equal to $a^{(1/3)(1/2)}$.

How to check? Carefully re-read the question and re-examine your thought process to make sure you've picked the right choice.

Test 3, Section 3, Question 4

- **What's the prompt asking for?** The choice with an equation that reflects the facts in the prompt.
- **Math concepts in the prompt:** variables, word problems
- **Elements of the answer choices:** algebraic expressions, equations, fractions, integers
- **Notable differences among answer choices:** Each choice involves 30, 2, and x. (A) and (B) involve multiplication, while (C) involves division and (D) involves addition. (B) and (C) both use 2 to modify the x-term: (B) multiplies 2 by x, (C) divides x by 2.
- **Concepts in the answer choices:** algebra, arithmetic
- **Pre-solution patterns (see p. 217):** opposites; wrong answers try to imitate right answers
- **Things to look out for:** Don't confuse multiplication and division! Don't misread the prompt and get confused about which number is represented by x!

Solution 1: Algebra: Write your own equation for the situation in the prompt and then compare your equation to the ones in the answer choices to find the correct answer.

If the number of $1776 - 1849$ states is 30, and 30 is twice the number of $1850 - 1900$ states, or x, then it must be true that $2x = 30$, so (B) is correct.

Solution 2: Concrete: Read the prompt and note that the value of x must be 15; then pick the answer choice that creates a true equation when $x = 15$.

For choice (A):

$$30x = 2$$ (expression from (A))

$$x = \frac{1}{15}$$ (divide both sides by 30)

This expression doesn't result in $x = 15$, so this choice can't be correct. Now let's try (B):

$$2x = 30$$ (expression from (B))
$$x = 15$$ (divide both sides by 2)

This expression results in $x = 15$, so this choice can be correct, assuming we haven't made any mistakes in our approach. As trained test-takers, we know we should try the other choices to see if any other choice produces an x-value equal to 15, because doing that will help us realize if we've stumbled on a false positive. Here's what we get for (C):

$$\frac{x}{2} = 30$$ (expression from (C))

$$x = 60$$ (multiply both sides by 2)

This doesn't result in $x = 15$, so (C) can't be correct. Now let's try (D):

$$x + 30 = 2$$ (expression from (D))
$$x = -28$$ (subtract 30 from both sides)

This doesn't result in $x = 15$ either, so (D) can't be right. Since x is only equal to 15 in the expression from (B), (B) must be right.

Solution 3: Test-smart: Compare each answer choice to the prompt and identify the choice that accurately reflects the prompt.

(A) would mean that if we multiply the number of $1850 - 1900$ states by 30, the result would be 2. This doesn't reflect the information in the prompt.

(B) would mean that if we double the number of $1850 - 1900$ states, the result would be 30. This is directly supported by the information in the prompt.

(C) would mean that if we divide the number of $1850 - 1900$ states by 2, the result would be 30. This doesn't reflect the information in the prompt. In fact, it's the opposite of what the prompt says.

(D) would mean that if we add the number of $1850 - 1900$ states to 30, the result would be 2. This doesn't reflect the prompt.

When we consider each choice, we can see that (B) is correct.

ANSWER CHOICE ANALYSIS

(A): This might be the result if an untrained test-taker made a mistake converting the relationships in the prompt to a mathematical expression. **(C):** This choice might be tempting if a test-taker mixed up the time periods and thought that twice as many states joined between 1850 and 1900, not the other way around.

How to check? Try an alternate approach above. Be sure to re-read the prompt and be certain which group of states is represented by x!

Test 3, Section 3, Question 5

- **What's the prompt asking for?** The value of $\frac{x}{5}$.
- **Math concepts in the prompt:** algebra, equations, fractions, reciprocals, variables
- **Elements of the answer choices:** fractions, integers
- **Notable differences among answer choices:** (C) is one-fifth of (A), which may be relevant since the prompt involves dividing x by 5. (D) is the inverse of (C), which may be relevant since the prompt mentions the reciprocals $\frac{5}{x}$ and $\frac{x}{5}$.

- **Concepts in the answer choices:** reciprocals
- **Pre-solution patterns (see p. 217):** opposites; wrong answers try to imitate right answers
- **Things to look out for:** Don't pick an answer that represents x by itself! Don't make small mistakes in your algebra and arithmetic!

Solution 1: Cross-multiplication: Cross-multiply the given equation and solve for x; then use x to find $\frac{x}{5}$.

$$\frac{5}{x} = \frac{15}{x+20}$$ (given equation)

$$5(x + 20) = 15x \qquad \text{(cross-multiply)}$$
$$5x + 100 = 15x \qquad \text{(distribute the 5)}$$
$$100 = 10x \qquad \text{(subtract } 5x \text{ from both sides)}$$
$$10 = x \qquad \text{(divide both sides by 10 to find } x)$$

Now we can plug $x = 10$ into $\dfrac{x}{5}$:

$$\frac{x}{5} \qquad \text{(given expression)}$$
$$\frac{10}{5} \qquad \text{(plug in } x = 10)$$
$$2 \qquad \text{(simplify)}$$

So we can see the answer is (C).

Solution 2: Inversion: Invert the two fractions in the given equation, and then multiply the expression on the left by $\dfrac{3}{3}$ and solve for x; use x to find $\dfrac{x}{5}$.

$$\frac{x}{5} = \frac{x+20}{15} \qquad \text{(inverted given equation)}$$
$$\frac{3x}{15} = \frac{x+20}{15} \qquad \text{(multiply left side by } \tfrac{3}{3})$$
$$3x = x + 20 \qquad \text{(multiply both sides by 15)}$$
$$2x = 20 \qquad \text{(subtract } x \text{ from both sides)}$$
$$x = 10 \qquad \text{(divide both sides by 2)}$$

Now that we know $x = 10$, we can plug that value into $\dfrac{x}{5}$ and find that the answer is (C), 2, as we did in the previous solution.

Solution 3: Test-smart / Backsolving: Test the answer choices against x in the equation, noting from the relationships among the answer choices that x is likely to be 10; then find $\dfrac{x}{5}$.

For choice (A):

$$\frac{x}{5} = 10 \qquad \text{(value of given expression if (A) is correct)}$$
$$x = 50 \qquad \text{(multiply both sides by 5)}$$
$$\frac{5}{x} = \frac{15}{x+20} \qquad \text{(given equation)}$$
$$\frac{5}{50} = \frac{15}{50+20} \qquad \text{(plug in } x = 50)$$
$$\frac{1}{10} = \frac{15}{70} \qquad \text{(simplify)}$$
$$70 = 150 \qquad \text{(cross multiply)}$$

This doesn't result in a true statement, so (A) can't be correct. Now let's try (B):

$$\frac{x}{5} = 5 \qquad \text{(value of given expression if (B) is correct)}$$
$$x = 25 \qquad \text{(multiply both sides by 5)}$$
$$\frac{5}{x} = \frac{15}{x+20} \qquad \text{(given equation)}$$
$$\frac{5}{25} = \frac{15}{25+20} \qquad \text{(plug in } x = 25)$$
$$\frac{1}{5} = \frac{1}{3} \qquad \text{(simplify)}$$

This doesn't result in a true statement either, so (B) can't be correct. Let's take a look at (C):

$$\frac{x}{5} = 2 \qquad \text{(value of given expression if (C) is correct)}$$

$$x = 10 \qquad \text{(multiply both sides by 5)}$$

$$\frac{5}{x} = \frac{15}{x+20} \qquad \text{(given equation)}$$

$$\frac{5}{10} = \frac{15}{10+20} \qquad \text{(plug in } x = 10\text{)}$$

$$\frac{1}{2} = \frac{1}{2} \qquad \text{(simplify)}$$

This results in a true statement, so (C) is right, assuming we haven't made any mistakes in our approach. Let's take a look at (D):

$$\frac{x}{5} = \frac{1}{2} \qquad \text{(value of given expression if (D) is correct)}$$

$$x = \frac{5}{2} \qquad \text{(multiply both sides by 5)}$$

$$\frac{5}{x} = \frac{15}{x+20} \qquad \text{(given equation)}$$

$$\frac{5}{\frac{5}{2}} = \frac{15}{\frac{5}{2} + 20} \qquad \text{(plug in } x = \frac{5}{2}\text{)}$$

$$\frac{10}{5} = \frac{15}{\frac{5}{2} + \frac{40}{2}} \qquad \text{(simplify)}$$

$$2 = \frac{15}{\frac{45}{2}} \qquad \text{(simplify)}$$

$$2 = \frac{30}{45} \qquad \text{(simplify)}$$

$$2 = \frac{2}{3} \qquad \text{(simplify)}$$

This doesn't result in a true statement, so (D) must be wrong. Since only (C) resulted in a valid statement, (C) must be correct.

ANSWER CHOICE ANALYSIS

(A): This is the value of x. **(B):** This is half the value of x. **(D):** This is $\frac{5}{x}$.

How to check? Try an alternate approach above—make sure you've found $\frac{x}{5}$, and not just x!

▶ Post-solution patterns (see page 218): right approach, wrong step

Test 3, Section 3, Question 6

- **What's the prompt asking for?** The value of $x - y$ under the conditions in the prompt.
- **Math concepts in the prompt:** algebra, arithmetic, coordinate pairs, systems of equations, word problems
- **Elements of the answer choices:** integers, negative numbers
- **Notable differences among answer choices:** (B) and (D) are opposites, which may be relevant because the prompt involves subtraction, and subtracting the same numbers in different orders will give opposite results. (B) is twice as much as (C), which may be relevant because the College Board often likes to include a choice that's half or twice as much as the right answer.
- **Concepts in the answer choices:** opposites
- **Pre-solution patterns (see p. 217):** opposites; wrong answers try to imitate right answers
- **Things to look out for:** Don't find x or y instead of $x - y$! Don't find $y - x$ instead of $x - y$! Don't make small mistakes in your algebra and arithmetic!

Solution 1: One variable at a time: Define x in terms of y by isolating x in one of the equations, and then plug that definition in for x in the other equation; solve the second equation for y, and then use the value of y to find x. Finally, find $x - y$.

$$2x - 3y = -14 \qquad \text{(first equation)}$$

$$2x = 3y - 14 \qquad \text{(add } 3y \text{ to both sides)}$$

$$x = \frac{3y - 14}{2} \qquad \text{(divide both sides by 2 to isolate } x \text{ and define it in terms of } y\text{)}$$

Now that we know x is equal to $\frac{3y-14}{2}$, we can plug that value into the second equation and solve for y:

$$3x - 2y = -6 \qquad \text{(second equation)}$$

$$3\left(\frac{3y-14}{2}\right) - 2y = -6 \qquad \text{(plug in } x = \frac{3y-14}{2})$$

$$3(3y-14) - 4y = -12 \qquad \text{(multiply both sides by 2)}$$

$$9y - 42 - 4y = -12 \qquad \text{(distribute the 3)}$$

$$5y = 30 \qquad \text{(simplify and add 42 to both sides)}$$

$$y = 6 \qquad \text{(divide both sides by 5)}$$

Now we can plug $y = 6$ into the either equation and solve for x. We'll use the first equation to do that (you could also use the second if you prefer—they'll both ultimately reach the same result):

$$2x - 3y = -14 \qquad \text{(first equation)}$$

$$2x - 3(6) = -14 \qquad \text{(plug in } y = 6)$$

$$2x - 18 = -14 \qquad \text{(simplify)}$$

$$2x = 4 \qquad \text{(add 18 to both sides)}$$

$$x = 2 \qquad \text{(divide both sides by 2)}$$

Now that we know $x = 2$ and $y = 6$, we can find $x - y$:

$$x - y \qquad \text{(given expression)}$$

$$2 - 6 \qquad \text{(plug in } x = 2 \text{ and } y = 6)$$

$$-4 \qquad \text{(simplify)}$$

So we can see that (C) is correct.

Solution 2: Adding equations: Note that you can add the two equations to find $5x - 5y$, and then divide through the resulting equation by 5 to find $x - y$.

$$
\begin{array}{l}
\ 2x - 3y = -14 \\
+\ \underline{\ 3x - 2y = \ -6\ } \\
\ 5x - 5y = -20
\end{array}
\qquad \text{(add the given equations)}
$$

$$x - y = -4 \qquad \text{(divide both sides by 5)}$$

Again, we see that (C) is correct.

ANSWER CHOICE ANALYSIS

(A): This is the value of $5x - 5y$, which we find if we add the two equations as described above, on the way to finding the value of $x - y$. A lot of untrained test-takers will add the two equations and then choose (A) without remembering what the question really asked for. **(B):** This is twice as much as the correct answer, which is a pattern the College Board often follows when designing wrong answers. This choice is also the difference between the numbers -14 and -6 from the prompt, which might tempt an untrained test-taker who didn't read the prompt carefully and thought the top equation was $3x - 3y = -14$, and the bottom equation was $2x - 2y = -6$; making that reading mistake could lead you to subtract one equation from the other incorrectly and arrive at -8. **(D):** This choice could result from a similar misreading to the one we discussed in (B), except that a test-taker would need to misread the top equation as $2x - 2y$ and the bottom equation as $3x - 3y$.

How to check? Try an alternate approach above. Note the similarities and differences among the answer choices and make sure you haven't misread the prompt!

▶ Post-solution patterns (see page 218): right approach, wrong step

---

Test 3, Section 3, Question 7

- **What's the prompt asking for?** The answer choice that must be a factor of $f(x)$.
- **Math concepts in the prompt:** factors of polynomials, functions, polynomials, reading data from a table
- **Math concepts in the diagram:** (x, y) pairings, x-intercepts, y-intercepts
- **Elements of the answer choices:** algebraic expressions, integers

- **Notable differences among answer choices:** Each choice begins with an x and a minus sign, and the following number is an integer ranging from 2 to 5.
- **Pre-solution patterns (see p. 217):** the first and last terms in a series are often wrong answers
- **Things to look out for:** Don't misread the table!

Solution 1: Algebra: Read the table to decide which choice must be a factor of $f(x)$, using your knowledge of polynomials and factors.

As trained test-takers, we need to know that a factor of a polynomial is an expression that can be multiplied by another expression to result in the original polynomial, just as a factor of an integer is an integer that can be multiplied by another integer to generate the original integer. On the SAT, factors of polynomials are often expressions that begin with a single variable and then add or subtract a number—we might be reminded of this when we look at the choices and see they all start with x and then subtract an integer from x.

We also need to remember that factors of polynomials are related to graphing and the zeros of functions (your math teacher may call these things "roots" of the function instead of "zeros"—for our purposes, the two terms are interchangeable). When we graph a polynomial function (which is a function with a form like $f(x) = ax^2 + bx + c$, where a, b, and c are constants), the points on the x-axis where the graph crosses the axis are the zeros of the function. As coordinate pairs on the x-axis, they represent places where the y-value of the function is zero, and these points correspond to factors of the polynomial being graphed, because the value of the entire polynomial is zero when the value of any factor is zero.

All of this means that if $f(x)$ for this function is 0 when $x = 4$, as the table shows, then we know that $x - 4$ is a factor of the polynomial. We know this because the expression $x - 4$ has a value of 0 when $x = 4$; this value of zero would cause the entire polynomial to have a value of zero when $x = 4$, which matches the information in the table. So (C) must be correct.

ANSWER CHOICE ANALYSIS

(B): This choice would attract an untrained test-taker who got confused and thought that the zeros of a polynomial function were indicated by the y-intercept of the graph, not by the x-intercepts of the graph. This choice could also trick a test-taker who correctly understood factors of polynomials, but simply switched the two columns in his mind.

How to check? Re-read the prompt and the answer choices, being careful not to make any small mistakes.

Test 3, Section 3, Question 8

- **What's the prompt asking for?** The expression for the slope of the line in terms of c and d.
- **Math concepts in the prompt:** coordinate values, lines, slope, slope-intercept format, zero
- **Elements of the answer choices:** algebraic expressions, fractions, integers
- **Notable differences among answer choices:** Each choice includes a numerator with one of the variables either being subtracted from 4 or having 4 subtracted from it, with the denominator being the other variable. 4 appears in every answer choice, as well as in the equation from the prompt.
- **Concepts in the answer choices:** order of subtraction, slope
- **Pre-solution patterns (see p. 217):** opposites; wrong answers try to imitate right answers
- **Things to look out for:** Don't confuse c and d! Don't confuse the order of subtraction with 4!

Solution 1: Concrete: Sketch a diagonal line with a y-intercept of 4 to be $y = kx + 4$, and then pick an arbitrary point on that line to be (c, d). Finally, pick the answer choice that expresses k in terms of c and d.

The line $y = kx + 4$ must have a y-intercept of $(0, 4)$. Here's one example of what that line could be, with an arbitrary point as (c, d):

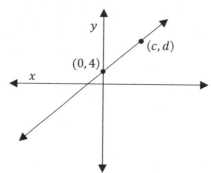

We know that the slope of a line is the difference between the y-values of two points on the line divided by the difference between the two corresponding x-values. In this case, the two points we have to work with are $(0, 4)$ and (c, d):

$$\frac{d-4}{c-0}$$

(difference between y-values divided by difference between x-values)

$$\frac{d-4}{c}$$

(simplify the denominator)

So the correct answer is (A).

Solution 2: Abstract: Think about the properties of slope, lines, and intercepts, and pick the answer choice that correctly relates c and d to the slope of $y = kx + 4$.

As we noted when we considered the answer choices, the question presents us with the opportunity to pick a choice representing every combination of the following two elements:

- either c or d in the denominator
- the other variable in the numerator, either being subtracted from 4 or having 4 subtracted from it

We can use our knowledge of slope to figure out which combination of those elements is the appropriate one for this question.

When we try to figure out which variable belongs in the denominator, we should remember that a slope fraction is, by definition, the ratio of the vertical change in a line to the horizontal change in the line (or, in other words, the "rise" over the "run"). So which variable corresponds to the horizontal change in the line? That must be c, since c is the horizontal coordinate of point (c, d). So c belongs in the denominator.

Now we need to figure out whether the numerator should be $d - 4$, or $4 - d$. As trained test-takers, we know that we have to keep the coordinates for each point in the slope fraction in a consistent order when we construct the fraction; in this case, that means the fraction could either be constructed as $\frac{d-4}{c-0}$ (with the (c, d) coordinates first), or as $\frac{4-d}{0-c}$ (with the (c, d) coordinates last), but not as $\frac{4-d}{c-0}$, for example. If we placed the (c, d) coordinates last in the subtraction, as choices (C) and (D) would indicate, then we'd end up with *negative c* in the denominator, because we'd be subtracting c from 0. But that isn't what we see in the choices! Every choice has c or d in the denominator without a negative sign, which means that the (c, d) variables must come first in both the numerator and the denominator. So $d - 4$ must be the expression in the correct version of the numerator, and (A) is right.

ANSWER CHOICE ANALYSIS

(B): This would be the result if we thought c was the y-value and d was the x-value. **(C):** This would be the result if we switched the order of the y-values when finding the slope fraction. **(D):** This would be the result if we made the mistakes from (B) and (C).

How to check? Try an alternate approach above. Make sure to consider the answer choices carefully, since the College Board is clearly baiting us to make a small mistake in structuring the slope fraction.

Test 3, Section 3, Question 9

- **What's the prompt asking for?** A value of k that causes the system not to have a solution.
- **Math concepts in the prompt:** constants, systems of equations, variables
- **Elements of the answer choices:** fractions, integers
- **Notable differences among answer choices:** (A) and (B) are the opposites of (D) and (C), respectively. The numbers 5 and 7 appear in the prompt and in the denominators of the answer choices. The numbers 12 and 16 appear in the numerators of the answer choices, and both 12 and 16 are the products of two numbers in the system of equations from the prompt.
- **Concepts in the answer choices:** fractions, opposites

- **"Bridge" concepts:** A system of equations has no solutions if no set of values exists that's valid for the variables in every equation in the system. Since we want a situation in which no set of (x, y) values satisfies both equations, we must be looking for a value of k that causes the lines represented by the equations NOT to intersect one another. If two lines in the same plane never intersect, then they MUST be parallel lines. Parallel lines have identical slopes.
- **Pre-solution patterns (see p. 217):** opposites; wrong answers try to imitate right answers
- **Things to look out for:** Don't make any small mistakes in your algebra and arithmetic! Make sure you correctly determine whether the right answer is positive or negative!

Solution 1: Algebra: Determine a value of k that causes the two lines in the prompt to have identical slopes, since lines with identical slopes are parallel to each other, and parallel lines don't intersect, which means no single (x, y) point would be valid for both equations.

First, we'll find the slope of the first line, using $y = mx + b$ format (you could also just use your knowledge of the standard equation for a line to determine the slope and skip this step):

$$kx - 3y = 4 \qquad \text{(first equation)}$$

$$-3y = -kx + 4 \qquad \text{(subtract } kx \text{ from both sides)}$$

$$y = \frac{kx}{3} - \frac{4}{3} \qquad \text{(divide both sides by } -3)$$

So we can see the slope of the first equation is $\frac{k}{3}$, since that's the coefficient of x when the line is in slope-intercept format. Now we'll find the slope of the second line (or, again, you can use your knowledge of the standard equation of a line for this if you want):

$$4x - 5y = 7 \qquad \text{(second equation)}$$

$$-5y = -4x + 7 \qquad \text{(subtract } 4x \text{ from both sides)}$$

$$y = \frac{4x}{5} - \frac{7}{5} \qquad \text{(divide both sides by } -5)$$

The slope of the second equation is $\frac{4}{5}$, which is the coefficient of x when the line is in slope-intercept format. Now we just need to find the value of k that will make those two slopes equal to each other:

$$\frac{k}{3} = \frac{4}{5}$$ (set slopes equal)

$$5k = 12$$ (cross multiply)

$$k = \frac{12}{5}$$ (divide both sides by k)

So we can see that (A) is correct.

Solution 2: Test-smart: Realize that the correct answer must be positive and have 5 as a denominator.

In order for these equations to have no solution, the graphs of these equations must never touch. That means those graphs need to be parallel—in other words, their slopes have to be equal. We can see that the slope of the line in the bottom equation is $\frac{4}{5}$ (you can also put that equation in $y = mx + b$ form to see the slope if you need to). So the slope of the line in the top equation must also be $\frac{4}{5}$.

If we're familiar with the standard equation for a line, we know that the slope of the top line must be $\frac{k}{3}$ (or, again, we can put that equation in $y = mx + b$ form to see the slope as well). In order for $\frac{k}{3}$ to have a value of $\frac{4}{5}$, as we know it must, the value of k must be a positive fraction with a denominator of 5. Only (A) fits that description, so (A) must be correct.

ANSWER CHOICE ANALYSIS

(B): This would be the result if we multiplied the top equation by 4, and then divided the constant in the top equation by the constant in the bottom equation for some reason. **(C):** This would be the result if we made the mistake from (B) and also mixed up a negative sign somewhere along the way. **(D):** This is the opposite of the correct answer.

How to check? Try an alternate approach above. Note that the similarities and differences among the answer choices make it clear that College Board is hoping you'll make a simple mistake in your reading or calculation, so make sure you don't fall for those traps!

Test 3, Section 3, Question 10

- **What's the prompt asking for?** The length of $\overline{AB}$.
- **Math concepts in the prompt:** algebra, graphing lines, graphing parabolas, points of intersection, variables
- **Elements of the answer choices:** integers

- **Notable differences among answer choices:** The answer choices form a series from 10 to 16, with each choice being 2 more than the choice before it.
- **Things to look out for:** Don't make a mistake with the order of operations! Don't confuse x and y!

Solution 1: Algebra: Find the two possible values of x when $y = 25$ in the first equation, and then use those values to determine the length of $\overline{AB}$.

$$y = (x - 11)^2$$ (equation of parabola)
$$25 = (x - 11)^2$$ (plug in $y = 25$)
$$5 = x - 11 \text{ or } -5 = x - 11$$ (take square root of both sides)
$$16 = x \quad \text{or} \quad 6 = x$$ (add 11 to both sides)

So $\overline{AB}$ connects $(6, 25)$ and $(16, 25)$. The y-coordinates of the two points are the same, so the distance between the points is the difference between their x-coordinates. That means $\overline{AB}$ is 10 units long, because $16 - 6 = 10$, and (A) is correct

---

Solution 2: Test-smart: Realize that the correct answer must be twice the square root of 25.

If we're familiar with the idea of transforming graphs of conic sections, we can see that the parabola in the prompt would be the same shape as the standard parabola, which is given by $y = x^2$; the only difference between the parabola in the prompt and the standard parabola is that the one in the prompt would be shifted 11 units to the right of the standard parabola.

This means that the line $y = 25$ will intersect the parabola at points that are the same vertical distance from the vertex of the parabola as they would be on the standard parabola, and the number of horizontal units separating these two points of intersection from the vertex will be equal to the square-root of the height of the line, since the y-coordinate of any point on the standard parabola is equal to the square of its x-coordinate.

Since the points of intersection of the line and the parabola are both 5 units away from the vertex, horizontally, we know that the number of units between them must be 10, because $5 + 5 = 10$.

(If this explanation didn't make sense to you because you're not familiar with the idea of transforming the standard parabola in the xy-coordinate plane, don't worry! You could always use solution 1 above to answer this question.)

ANSWER CHOICE ANALYSIS

(B): This is twice as much as 6, the x-coordinate for one of the points of intersection. **(C):** This is what we would get if we plugged $x = 25$ into $x - 11$ for some reason. **(D):** This is the x-coordinate for one of the points of intersection.

How to check? Try an alternate approach above.

▶ Post-solution patterns (see page 218): the first and last terms in a series are often wrong answers

Test 3, Section 3, Question 11

- **What's the prompt asking for?** The choice that includes the Roman numerals with true statements.
- **Math concepts in the prompt:** angle measurements, congruent angles, equations, intersecting lines, variables
- **Math concepts in the diagram:** diagram not drawn to scale, line geometry, vertical angles
- **Elements of the answer choices:** Roman numerals

- **Notable differences among answer choices:** (A), (B), and (C) contain every possible combination of two of the three Roman numerals. (D) gives us the possibility of choosing all three Roman numerals.
- **Pre-solution patterns (see p. 217):** wrong answers try to imitate right answers
- **Things to look out for:** Don't confuse the different variables and angles! Don't assume the diagram is drawn to scale!

Solution 1: Algebra / Geometry: Use your knowledge of vertical angles to determine which pairs of angles must equal one another.

We know that $y = u$, because they represent the angle measures of vertical angles. The prompt also says that $x + y = u + w$, and if we subtract y and u from each side of that equation, we're left with $x = w$.

From there, we know that $x = t$ and $w = z$, because those statements each involve pairs of vertical angles.

So at this point we've established the following:

$$y = u$$
$$x = w = t = z$$

So I and III are definitely true statements.

But what about II? Is there any way we can show that y and w are equal? Well, since y is equal to u and the other four angles are all equal to each other, showing that y and w were equal would be the same thing as showing that all six angles are equal. Is there any way we can show that all six angles must be equal? It turns out that there isn't—there's no property of angles that would allow us to say for certain that the y and u angles are the same size as all the other angles. That means II doesn't have to be true, which makes (B) correct.

How to check? Carefully re-check your assumptions. Make sure you haven't misread any of the Roman numerals or the answer choices.

Test 3, Section 3, Question 12

- **What's the prompt asking for?** The value of d under the circumstances in the question.
- **Math concepts in the prompt:** constants, coordinate values, graphing parabolas, parabolas, quadratic equations, vertex of a parabola
- **Elements of the answer choices:** algebraic expressions, integers, negative numbers

- **Notable differences among answer choices:** Each choice is some negative coefficient multiplied by a.
- **"Bridge" concepts:** The x-coordinate of a vertex that points up or down must be halfway between the x-coordinates of the points where the vertex crosses the x-axis.
- **Things to look out for:** Don't confuse a with x or y! Don't make small mistakes in your algebra and arithmetic!

Solution 1: Algebra: Determine the x-intercepts of the parabola, and use that to find the x-coordinate of the vertex of the parabola. Use the x-coordinate of the vertex to find y in terms of a.

$$y = a(x - 2)(x + 4) \qquad \text{(equation from the prompt)}$$
$$0 = a(x - 2)(x + 4) \qquad \text{(set } y = 0 \text{ to find } x\text{-intercepts)}$$

We can see that $y = 0$ when either of the expressions in parentheses equals 0, which ends up being when $x = 2$ or $x = -4$. If the parabola crosses the x-axis at $x = 2$ and $x = -4$, then the x-coordinate of the vertex must be halfway between those two points, at $x = -1$. We can plug in $x = -1$ to find the corresponding y-value.

$$y = a(x - 2)(x + 4) \qquad \text{(equation from the prompt)}$$
$$y = a((-1) - 2)((-1) + 4) \qquad \text{(plug in } x = -1)$$
$$y = a(-3)(3) \qquad \text{(simplify)}$$
$$y = -9a \qquad \text{(simplify)}$$

So the vertex is at $(-1, -9a)$, which means $d = -9a$.

ANSWER CHOICE ANALYSIS

(B): This is the result if we plug in $x = 0$ instead of $x = -1$. **(C):** This is the result if we plug in $x = 1$ instead of $x = -1$.

How to check? Carefully reconsider your approach, and make sure not to make any small mistakes with your algebra or arithmetic.

Test 3, Section 3, Question 13

- **What's the prompt asking for?** The value of a that makes the equation in the prompt true.
- **Math concepts in the prompt:** algebra, constants, equations, fractions, variables
- **Elements of the answer choices:** integers, negative numbers
- **Notable differences among answer choices:** (A) and (B) are the opposites of (D) and (C), respectively.
- **Pre-solution patterns (see p. 217):** opposites
- **Things to look out for:** Don't get overwhelmed by the complexity of the expressions in the question! Don't confuse a with x! Don't make small mistakes in your algebra and arithmetic!

Solution 1: Algebra: Multiply both sides of the equation by $ax-2$, and then simplify.

$\dfrac{24x^2+25x-47}{ax-2} = -8x - 3 - \dfrac{53}{ax-2}$	(given equation)
$\dfrac{24x^2+25x+6}{ax-2} = -8x - 3$	(add $\dfrac{53}{ax-2}$ to both sides)
$24x^2 + 25x + 6 = (ax-2)(-8x-3)$	(multiply both sides by $ax-2$)
$24x^2 + 25x + 6 = -8ax^2 - 3ax + 16x + 6$	(FOIL the right side)
$24x^2 + 9x = -8ax^2 - 3ax$	(subtract $16x + 6$ from both sides)
$24x + 9 = -8ax - 3a$	(divide both sides by x)

At this stage, we can notice that the only way for this equation to be valid for all possible values of x is for the x terms on either side of the equation to be equal, and for the constants on either side to be equal. That means $24x$ is equal to $-8ax$, and $9x$ is equal to $-3a$. Since that's the case, it must be true that a is the same thing as -3, which means (B) is correct.

Solution 2: Test-smart: Set x equal to 1 to make the calculations easier, and then backsolve for a with the values from the choices.

$\dfrac{24x^2+25x-47}{ax-2} = -8x - 3 - \dfrac{53}{ax-2}$	(given equation)
$\dfrac{24(1)^2+25(1)-47}{a(1)-2} = -8(1) - 3 - \dfrac{53}{a(1)-2}$	(plug in $x = 1$ to make it easier to identify a)
$\dfrac{2}{a-2} = -11 - \dfrac{53}{a-2}$	(simplify)

Now we can plug in the values from the answer choices to see which one results in a valid statement. Let's start with (A):

$\dfrac{2}{a-2} = -11 - \dfrac{53}{a-2}$	(value of given equation when $x = 1$)
$\dfrac{2}{(-16)-2} = -11 - \dfrac{53}{(-16)-2}$	(plug in $a = -16$ from (A))
$\dfrac{2}{-18} = -11 + \dfrac{53}{18}$	(simplify)
$0 = -11 + \dfrac{55}{18}$	(add $\dfrac{2}{18}$ to both sides)
$11 = \dfrac{55}{18}$	(add 11 to both sides)

This isn't a valid statement, so (A) can't be correct. Now, let's try (B):

$\dfrac{2}{a-2} = -11 - \dfrac{53}{a-2}$	(value of given equation when $x = 1$)
$\dfrac{2}{(-3)-2} = -11 - \dfrac{53}{(-3)-2}$	(plug in $a = -3$ from (B))
$\dfrac{2}{-5} = -11 + \dfrac{53}{5}$	(simplify)
$0 = -11 + \dfrac{55}{5}$	(add $\dfrac{2}{5}$ to both sides)

$$11 = \frac{55}{5}$$ (add 11 to both sides)

$$11 = 11$$ (reduce fraction)

This is a valid statement, so (B) could be correct, assuming that we didn't accidentally choose an arbitrary value for x that creates a false positive (that is, that causes more than one value for a to produce a true statement). The best way to be sure we haven't done that is to make sure we check all the answer choices, so we'll keep going. Here's what we get when we check (C):

$$\frac{2}{a-2} = -11 - \frac{53}{a-2}$$ (value of given equation when $x = 1$)

$$\frac{2}{(3)-2} = -11 - \frac{53}{(3)-2}$$ (plug in $a = 3$ from (C))

$$2 = -11 - 53$$ (simplify)

$$2 = -64$$ (simplify)

This isn't a valid statement, so (C) can't be correct. Now we'll check (D):

$$\frac{2}{a-2} = -11 - \frac{53}{a-2}$$ (value of given equation when $x = 1$)

$$\frac{2}{(16)-2} = -11 - \frac{53}{(16)-2}$$ (plug in $a = 16$ from (D))

$$\frac{2}{14} = -11 - \frac{53}{14}$$ (simplify)

$$0 = -11 - \frac{55}{14}$$ (subtract $\frac{2}{14}$ from both sides)

$$11 = -\frac{55}{14}$$ (add 11 to both sides)

This isn't a valid statement, so (D) can't be correct, either. This means we've successfully identified (B) as the correct answer.

ANSWER CHOICE ANALYSIS

(C): This is the opposite of the correct answer. **(D):** This is the opposite of (A).

How to check? Try an alternate approach above.

Test 3, Section 3, Question 14

- **What's the prompt asking for?** The answer choice with the solutions to the given equation.
- **Math concepts in the prompt:** quadratic equations, solutions to equations
- **Elements of the answer choices:** algebraic expressions, integers, negative numbers, radical expressions
- **Notable differences among answer choices:** (A) and (B) begin with the number -2, while (C) and (D) begin with the number -6. (A) and (C) end with $\sqrt{2}$, while (D) ends with $6\sqrt{2}$ and (B) ends with $\frac{\sqrt{30}}{3}$
- **Concepts in the answer choices:** solutions to quadratic equations
- **Pre-solution patterns (see p. 217):** opposites; wrong answers try to imitate right answers
- **Things to look out for:** Don't make mistakes in your algebra and arithmetic!

Solution 1: Quadratic formula: Apply the quadratic formula to the equation in the prompt.

The quadratic formula is based on the polynomial $ax^2 + bx + c = 0$. In this instance, the given equation is $3x^2 + 12x + 6 = 0$. We may notice we can make things easier on ourselves by dividing both sides of the equation by 3, which gives us $x^2 + 4x + 2 = 0$. So, for our purposes, $a = 1$, $b = 4$, and $c = 2$:

$$x = \frac{-b \pm \sqrt{b^2 - 4ac}}{2a}$$ (quadratic formula)

$$x = \frac{-(4) \pm \sqrt{(4)^2 - 4(1)(2)}}{2(1)}$$ (plug in $a = 1$, $b = 4$, and $c = 2$)

$$x = \frac{-4 \pm \sqrt{8}}{2}$$ (simplify)

$$x = \frac{-4 \pm 2\sqrt{2}}{2}$$ (factor $\sqrt{4}$ out of the expression under the radical)

$$x = -2 \pm \sqrt{2}$$ (reduce)

We can see that (A) is correct.

Solution 2: Backsolve: Test each answer choice in the equation from the prompt.

$$3x^2 + 12x + 6 = 0$$ (given equation)

$$x^2 + 4x + 2 = 0$$ (divide both sides by 3 to simplify our work)

$$(-2 + \sqrt{2})^2 + 4(-2 + \sqrt{2}) + 2 = 0$$ (plug in $x = -2 + \sqrt{2}$ from (A))

$$4 - 4\sqrt{2} + 2 - 8 + 4\sqrt{2} + 2 = 0$$ (simplify)

$$0 = 0$$ (simplify)

We see that plugging in $x = -2 + \sqrt{2}$ results in a true statement. Now let's plug in $x = -2 - \sqrt{2}$, the other solutions from (A):

$$x^2 + 4x + 2 = 0$$ (given equation, divided by 3 to simplify our work)

$$(-2 - \sqrt{2})^2 + 4(-2 - \sqrt{2}) + 2 = 0$$ (plug in $x = -2 - \sqrt{2}$ from (A))

$$4 + 4\sqrt{2} + 2 - 8 - 4\sqrt{2} + 2 = 0$$ (simplify)

$$0 = 0$$ (simplify)

We can see that both $x = -2 + \sqrt{2}$ and $x = -2 - \sqrt{2}$ are solutions for the given equation, so (A) appears to be correct. Let's check the other answer choices to make sure we haven't made a mistake:

$$x^2 + 4x + 2 = 0$$ (given equation, divided by 3 to simplify our work)

$$(-2 + \frac{\sqrt{30}}{3})^2 + 4(-2 + \frac{\sqrt{30}}{3}) + 2 = 0$$ (plug in $x = -2 + \frac{\sqrt{30}}{3}$ from (B))

$$4 - 4\frac{\sqrt{30}}{3} + \frac{30}{9} - 8 + 4\frac{\sqrt{30}}{3} + 2 = 0$$ (simplify)

$$\frac{30}{9} - 2 = 0$$ (simplify)

We can see that plugging in $x = -2 + \frac{\sqrt{30}}{3}$ doesn't result in a true statement, so (B) is incorrect. We don't need to check $x = -2 - \frac{\sqrt{30}}{3}$, because (B) can't be correct if plugging in $x = -2 + \frac{\sqrt{30}}{3}$ doesn't result in a true statement. Now let's check (C):

$$x^2 + 4x + 2 = 0$$ (given equation, divided by 3 to simplify our work)

$$(-6 + \sqrt{2})^2 + 4(-6 + \sqrt{2}) + 2 = 0$$ (plug in $x = -6 + \sqrt{2}$ from (C))

$$36 - 12\sqrt{2} + 2 - 24 + 4\sqrt{2} + 2 = 0$$ (simplify)

$$16 - 8\sqrt{2} = 0$$ (simplify)

$$16 = 8\sqrt{2}$$ (add $8\sqrt{2}$ to both sides)

$$2 = \sqrt{2}$$ (divide both sides by 8)

We can see that plugging in $x = -6 + \sqrt{2}$ doesn't result in a true statement, so (C) is incorrect. We don't need to check $x = -6 - \sqrt{2}$, because (C) can't be correct if plugging in $x = -6 + \sqrt{2}$ doesn't result in a true statement. Now let's check (D):

$$x^2 + 4x + 2 = 0$$ (given equation, divided by 3 to simplify our work)

$$(-6 + 6\sqrt{2})^2 + 4(-6 + 6\sqrt{2}) + 2 = 0 \qquad \text{(plug in } x = -6 + 6\sqrt{2} \text{ from (D))}$$

$$36 - 72\sqrt{2} + 72 - 24 + 24\sqrt{2} + 2 = 0 \qquad \text{(simplify)}$$

$$86 - 48\sqrt{2} = 0 \qquad \text{(simplify)}$$

$$86 = 48\sqrt{2} \qquad \text{(add } 48\sqrt{2} \text{ to both sides)}$$

$$43 = 24\sqrt{2} \qquad \text{(divide both sides by 2)}$$

We can see that plugging in $x = -6 + 6\sqrt{2}$ doesn't result in a true statement, so (D) is incorrect. We don't need to check $x = -6 - 6\sqrt{2}$, because (D) can't be correct if plugging in $x = -6 + 6\sqrt{2}$ doesn't result in a true statement.
We can see that only the values in (A) result in valid statements when plugged into the given equation, so (A) must be correct.

How to check? Carefully re-check the work you've done to find the correct answer—pay particular attention to applying the quadratic formula to make sure you don't end up with the wrong result.

Test 3, Section 3, Question 15

- **What's the prompt asking for?** The choice with the Roman numerals that reflect statements that must be true.
- **Math concepts in the prompt:** equations, fractions, function modeling, multiplication, PEMDAS
- **Elements of the answer choices:** Roman numerals, sentences
- **Notable differences among answer choices:** Each of the individual Roman numerals appears by itself once in the answer choices. The only possible combination of Roman numerals in the choices is the combination of I and II.
- **Pre-solution patterns (see p. 217):** wrong answers try to imitate right answers
- **Things to look out for:** Make sure you don't misread the prompt, the Roman numerals, or the answer choices! Make sure you don't confuse C and F! Make sure not to invert the fraction $\frac{5}{9}$ incorrectly.

Solution 1: Concrete: Test each Roman numeral by picking arbitrary values and plugging them into the equation from the prompt.

$$C = \frac{5}{9}(F - 32) \qquad \text{(given equation)}$$

$$100 = \frac{5}{9}(F - 32) \qquad \text{(plug in } C = 100, \text{ as an arbitrary value)}$$

$$100 = \frac{5}{9}F - \frac{160}{9} \qquad \text{(distribute } \frac{5}{9}\text{)}$$

$$900 = 5F - 160 \qquad \text{(multiply both sides by 9)}$$

$$1060 = 5F \qquad \text{(add 160 to both sides)}$$

$$212 = F \qquad \text{(divide both sides by 5 to find } F \text{ when } C = 100)$$

Now we know that when $C = 100$ the value of F is 212. We can use these numbers as a starting point to test the three statements in the prompt. Here's what we get when we test numeral I:

$$C = \frac{5}{9}(F - 32) \qquad \text{(given equation)}$$

$$C = \frac{5}{9}(213 - 32) \qquad \text{(plug in } F = 213 \text{ as a value 1 degree Fahrenheit more than 212)}$$

$$C = \frac{5}{9}(181) \qquad \text{(simplify)}$$

$$9C = 5(181) \qquad \text{(multiply both sides by 9)}$$

$$9C = 905 \qquad \text{(simplify)}$$

$$C = \frac{905}{9} \qquad \text{(divide both sides by 9)}$$

$$C = 100\frac{5}{9} \qquad \text{(change to mixed fraction)}$$

We can see that increasing the temperature by 1 degree Fahrenheit (from 212 to 213) resulted in an increase in Celsius of $\frac{5}{9}$ degrees (from 100 to $100\frac{5}{9}$). So the statement in I is true. Now, let's test the statement in II:

$$C = \frac{5}{9}(F - 32) \qquad \text{(given equation)}$$

$$101 = \frac{5}{9}(F - 32) \qquad \text{(plug in } C = 101 \text{ as a value 1 degree Celsius more than 100)}$$

$$101 = \frac{5}{9}F - \frac{160}{9} \qquad \text{(distribute } \frac{5}{9} \text{)}$$

$$909 = 5F - 160 \qquad \text{(multiply both sides by 9)}$$

$$1069 = 5F \qquad \text{(add 160 to both sides)}$$

$$\frac{1069}{5} = 213\frac{4}{5} = 213.8 = F \qquad \text{(divide both sides by 5)}$$

When we increased the temperature by 1 degree Celsius, the temperature in Fahrenheit increased by 1.8 degrees. So the statement in II is true.

We've already seen that a temperature increase of 1 degree Celsius results in a temperature increase of 1.8 degrees Fahrenheit, not $\frac{5}{9}$ degrees Fahrenheit—so we know the statement in III isn't correct.

Statements I and II must be true, so (D) is the correct answer.

Solution 2: Abstract: Study the relationships in the equation from the prompt and determine the relative impact of increasing C or F individually. (Refer to the article called "Special Technique: Understanding how Variables, Coefficients, Exponents, and Constants can Affect a Function" on page 207 of this Black Book if you need a refresher on these ideas.)

Let's start by looking at Statement I. When we increase F by 1 degree, we increase the value of the expression $(F - 32)$ by 1 degree. That expression is then multiplied by $\frac{5}{9}$ to produce C. So increasing F by 1 degree causes C to be increased by 1 degree multiplied by $\frac{5}{9}$, which is the same as $\frac{5}{9}$ of a degree. That means statement I is true.

Now let's consider Statement II. When we increase C by 1 degree, the expression on the right of the equation also needs to increase by 1 degree in order for the equation to remain true. The expression on the right involves multiplying the expression in parentheses by $\frac{5}{9}$. (We should also remember that the result of multiplying a fraction by its reciprocal is always 1.) In order to raise the value of the entire right-hand side of the equation by 1, we'll need to increase F by an amount that's the reciprocal of $\frac{5}{9}$, which is what the value of $(F - 32)$ is going to be multiplied by in the equation. The reciprocal of $\frac{5}{9}$ is $\frac{9}{5}$. $\frac{9}{5}$ is equal to $\frac{18}{10}$, which is equal to 1.8. So Statement II is true.

We know that Statement III must be false for a couple of reasons. First of all, the reasoning from our analysis of Statement I shows us that when the temperature increases by a certain amount in degrees Fahrenheit, the temperature increases by a *smaller* amount in degrees Celsius. So we wouldn't expect an increase of $\frac{5}{9}$ degree Fahrenheit to result in an increase of more than $\frac{5}{9}$ degree Celsius. Also, only one answer choice says that Statement III is true, and that choice omits Statements I and II. After we double-check our reasoning to make sure that Statements I and II really are true, we can be even more confident that III must be false.

With all of that in mind, we know that (D) is the correct answer.

How to check? Try an alternate approach above. Make sure to read the statements accurately, since they're phrased in similar ways!

Test 3, Section 3, Question 16

- **What's the prompt asking for?** One possible value for x in the given equation.
- **Math concepts in the prompt:** algebra, arithmetic, equations, exponents, order of operations

- **Things to look out for:** Don't make any small mistakes in algebra and arithmetic!

Solution 1: Algebra: Manipulate the expression algebraically until you can determine one possible value for x.

$$x^3(x^2 - 5) = -4x \qquad \text{(given equation)}$$

$$x^2(x^2 - 5) = -4 \qquad \text{(divide both sides by } x\text{)}$$

$$x^4 - 5x^2 = -4 \qquad \text{(distribute } x^2\text{)}$$

$$x^4 - 5x^2 + 4 = 0 \qquad \text{(add 4 to both sides)}$$

$$(x^2 - 4)(x^2 - 1) = 0 \qquad \text{(reverse FOIL)}$$

Now we know that either $x^2 - 4$ must equal zero or $x^2 - 1$ must equal zero. Now we'll need to consider each of these factors separately. We'll start with $x^2 - 4$:

$x^2 - 4 = 0$	(set one factor equal to zero)
$x^2 = 4$	(add 4 to both sides)
$x = 2$ or $x = -2$	(take square root of both sides)

So 2 and -2 both make this factor equal to zero—but the prompt says that $x > 0$! That means only the value we found that's greater than 0 can work. So, out of the two possible values for x that we just found, only 2 is a possible correct answer. Now we'll consider the other factor, $x^2 - 1$:

$x^2 - 1 = 0$	(set the other factor equal to zero)
$x^2 = 1$	(add 1 to both sides)
$x = 1$ or $x = -1$	(take square root of both sides)

We can see that 1 and -1 both make this second factor equal to zero—but remember (again) that the prompt says that $x > 0$! This means that -1 can't be a correct answer. We now know that either 1 or 2 can be a correct answer to this question. (Notice that earlier in our algebra we factored x out of both sides of the equation, which means $x = 0$ would be a possible solution to the original equation—except, again, the prompt says $x > 0$, so 0 can't be a correct answer either.)

Solution 2: Test-smart: Try testing arbitrary values for x, and note that the number 1 is valid for x.

It might occur to us that testing $x = 1$ would be relatively easy, so we could give that a shot and see what happens.

$x^3(x^2 - 5) = -4x$	(given equation)
$(1)^3((1)^2 - 5) = -4(1)$	(plug in $x = 1$)
$1(-4) = -4(1)$	(simplify)
$-4 = -4$	(simplify)

We see that plugging in $x = 1$ produces a valid result, and 1 is greater than 0, as the prompt requires. So 1 is an acceptable answer.

How to check? Carefully re-test the value you've chosen for x in the original equation from the prompt.

Test 3, Section 3, Question 17

- **What's the prompt asking for?** The value of x in the given equation.

- **Math concepts in the prompt:** algebra, arithmetic, equations, fractions
- **Things to look out for:** Don't misread the equation! Don't make small mistakes in algebra and arithmetic!

Solution 1: Algebra: Isolate x on one side of the given equation to find the value of x.

$\frac{7}{9}x - \frac{4}{9}x = \frac{1}{4} + \frac{5}{12}$	(given equation)
$\frac{3}{9}x = \frac{1}{4} + \frac{5}{12}$	(simplify)
$\frac{3}{9}x = \frac{3}{12} + \frac{5}{12}$	(multiply $\frac{1}{4}$ by $\frac{3}{3}$)
$\frac{3}{9}x = \frac{8}{12}$	(simplify)
$\frac{1}{3}x = \frac{2}{3}$	(simplify fractions)
$x = 2$	(multiply both sides by 3)

So we can see that x is 2.

How to check? Take the value you found for x and plug it into the original equation to make sure the equation is valid.

Test 3, Section 3, Question 18

- **What's the prompt asking for?** The value of x in the given diagram.
- **Math concepts in the prompt:** arithmetic, equations, isosceles triangles, variables
- **Math concepts in the diagram:** diagram not drawn to scale, external angles, isosceles triangles
- **"Bridge" concepts:** Isosceles triangles have two equal angles, and supplementary angles add up to 180°.
- **Things to look out for:** Don't confuse $x, y,$ and z! Note that the diagram isn't drawn to scale! Don't assume the two long line segments in the diagram are parallel! Don't assume that y and z are vertical angles!

Solution 1: Algebra / Geometry: Apply the information from the prompt to the diagram, then use geometric principles to find x.

The prompt tells us that both triangles are isosceles triangles. The hash marks on the sides of the triangles in the diagram tell us that the two marked sides of each triangle are equal to each other in length, which also means that the two unlabeled angles in the triangle on the left are equal to each other in size, and the two unlabeled angles in the triangle on the right are equal to each other in size.

The sum of the measures of the three angles in a triangle is 180. The prompt tells us that $180 - z = 2y$, which means that the two unlabeled angles in the triangle on the right must add up to $2y$; since the two angles are equal in size, the measure of each angle must be y. The prompt also tells us that $y = 75$, so the measure of each unlabeled angle in the triangle on the right is 75°. Let's add that information to the diagram:

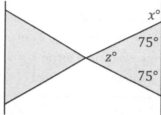

We also know that the top 75° angle and the angle whose measure is $x°$ are supplementary angles, which means they add up to 180°, because they result in a straight line when they're placed next to each other:

$$75° + x° = 180° \qquad \text{(definition of supplementary angles)}$$

$$x° = 105° \qquad \text{(subtract 75° from both sides)}$$

So we can see that the correct answer is 105.

How to check? Take your value of x and plug it into the diagram to make sure it fits the given angle measurements and relationships.

Note It's possible to answer this question without determining any new information about the triangle on the left. Keep this kind of thing in mind on test day: you may not always need to consider every aspect of a diagram or figure.

Test 3, Section 3, Question 19

- **What's the prompt asking for?** The number of calories in a hamburger under the conditions in the prompt.
- **Math concepts in the prompt:** algebra, arithmetic, word problems
- **Things to look out for:** Don't confuse hamburgers and fries in the question! Don't misread the prompt! Don't make small mistakes in algebra and arithmetic!

Solution 1: Algebra: Create an equation that relates the number of calories in a hamburger to the number 1700, then solve for the number of calories in the hamburger.

For our system of equations, I'll let h represent the number of the calories in a hamburger, and f represent the number of calories in an order of fries. Then, following the relationships described in the prompt, I can write these equations:

$$h = f + 50 \qquad \text{(this equation says a hamburger has 50 more calories than fries)}$$

$$2h + 3f = 1700 \qquad \text{(this equation says that 2 hamburgers and 3 fries have 1700 calories)}$$

Now we can use this system of questions to solve for h and answer the question. The easiest way to do this is probably just to take the first equation, which defines h in terms of f, and plug that definition for h in the second equation:

$$2h + 3f = 1700 \qquad \text{(second equation)}$$

$$2(f + 50) + 3f = 1700 \qquad \text{(plug in } h = f + 50 \text{ from first equation)}$$

$$5f + 100 = 1700 \qquad \text{(distribute the 2 and simplify)}$$

$$5f = 1600 \qquad \text{(subtract 100 from both sides)}$$

$$f = 320 \qquad \text{(divide both sides by 5)}$$

Now that we know the value of f, we can plug $f = 320$ into either equation to solve for h:

$$h = f + 50 \qquad \text{(first equation)}$$

$$h = 320 + 50 \qquad \text{(plug in } f = 320\text{)}$$

$$h = 370 \qquad \text{(simplify)}$$

So the answer is 370, because that's how many calories are in a hamburger.

Solution 2: Guess and check: Pick arbitrary numbers for the caloric value of the hamburgers, and test them against the word problem until you arrive at a value that satisfies the prompt.

Since we know that 2 hamburgers and 3 orders of fries add up to 1700 calories, we can try to start guessing and checking by beginning with numbers that are roughly one-fifth of 1700 (because 2 hamburgers and 3 orders of fries add up to 5 items).

One-fifth of 1700 is 340. We know that 340 can't be the actual number of calories in a hamburger, because 340 was our estimate based on the idea that each of the 5 items had an equal number of calories, which isn't actually true. So we don't need to bother checking 340 as the answer. But what if we check the possibility of 350 as the number of calories in a hamburger?

If a hamburger had 350 calories, then an order of fries would have 300 calories, according to the prompt. If we add up the number of calories in 2 hamburgers and 3 orders of fries, we get this: $2(350) + 3(300) = 700 + 900 = 1600$. This number is 100 less than the number indicated in the prompt, so 350 can't be the number of calories in the hamburger. It's too low.

So we need to increase the size of our next guess—but by how much? Well, our original guess for the caloric values of the 5 items was too low by 100 calories, which means that each item was an average of 20 calories too low. So what if we guess 20 calories higher?

That would result in a guess of 370 calories per hamburger, which would mean each order of fries had 320 calories, and the total number of calories in 2 hamburgers and 3 orders of fries would be $2(370) + 3(320) = 740 + 960 = 1700$. This is the total number of calories that the prompt mentions, so we know that each hamburger does, indeed, have 370 calories.

How to check? Try an alternate approach above, paying close attention to the issues noted above.

Test 3, Section 3, Question 20

- **What's the prompt asking for?** $\sin F$
- **Math concepts in the prompt:** ratios, right angles, similar triangles, triangles, word problems
- **"Bridge" concepts:** The sine of an angle in a right triangle can be expressed as the ratio between the side of the triangle opposite the angle and the hypotenuse of the triangle, which

means we can determine $\sin F$ if we know the ratio of length $\overline{DE}$ to $\overline{DF}$.

- **Things to look out for:** Don't confuse the different vertices and line segments named in the prompt! Don't confuse sine with other trig functions!

Solution 1: Diagramming: Construct a diagram that matches the prompt, and use it to find $\sin F$.

If we recognize that a right triangle with a hypotenuse of 20 and side length of 16 is a multiple of a 3-4-5 Pythagorean triple, then we know the missing side length is 12. If not, we can still use the Pythagorean Theorem to find the missing side length.

$$a^2 + b^2 = c^2 \qquad \text{(Pythagorean Theorem)}$$

$$16^2 + b^2 = 20^2 \qquad \text{(plug in the hypotenuse length and given side length from prompt)}$$

$$256 + b^2 = 400 \qquad \text{(simplify)}$$

$$b^2 = 144 \qquad \text{(subtract 256 from both sides)}$$

$$b = 12 \qquad \text{(take the square root of both sides)}$$

So the missing side length is 12. Let's make a diagram with the information we know so far.

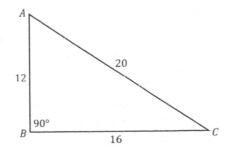

The prompt tells us that triangle DEF is similar to triangle ABC, and that vertex F corresponds to vertex C. If the triangles are similar, then $\sin F$ will be equal to $\sin C$, because sine is a ratio of side-lengths, and similar triangles have a constant ratio between lengths of corresponding sides. We know from SOHCAHTOA that $\sin C$ is equal to the opposite side over the hypotenuse, or $\frac{12}{20}$, which we can reduce to $\frac{3}{5}$. So the correct answer is $\frac{3}{5}$.

How to check? Carefully re-check the value you've found in the context of your diagram and the prompt to make sure everything fits. Remember that the College Board likes to try to confuse us with small details.

TEST 4 – SECTION 3

Test 4, Section 3, Question 1

- **What's the prompt asking for?** The answer choice that can be equal to zero for some value of x.
- **Math concepts in the prompt:** algebra, zero
- **Elements of the answer choices:** absolute value, algebraic expressions, integers
- **Notable differences among answer choices:** (A) and (D) begin with $x - 1$, while (B) begins with $x + 1$ and (C) begins with $1 - x$. (A) ends with -1, while all the other choices end with $+1$.

- **Concepts in the answer choices:** absolute value, algebra, arithmetic
- **Pre-solution patterns (see p. 217):** opposites; wrong answers try to imitate right answers
- **Things to look out for:** Don't forget order of operations when you're dealing with absolute value! Don't misread the answer choices, which are all very similar to each other!

Solution 1: Algebra: Set each choice equal to zero and try to solve for x. The choice that makes this possible will be right.

For choice (A):

$$|x - 1| - 1 = 0 \qquad \text{(expression from (A) set equal to 0)}$$

$$|x - 1| = 1 \qquad \text{(add 1 to both sides)}$$

$$x - 1 = 1 \text{ or } x - 1 = -1 \qquad \text{(account for absolute value)}$$

$$x = 2 \text{ or } x = 0 \qquad \text{(add 1 to both sides)}$$

The expression from (A) is equal to 0 when x equals 2 or 0, so (A) is right, assuming we haven't made any mistakes in our approach. As trained test-takers, we know it's always important to consider each choice before picking one, so let's keep going and check (B):

$$|x + 1| + 1 = 0 \qquad \text{(expression from (B) set equal to 0)}$$

$$|x + 1| = -1 \qquad \text{(subtract 1 from both sides)}$$

We know that the absolute value of an expression can never be negative, so (B) can't be correct, because it would require an absolute value expression to be equal to negative one. Now let's take a look at (C):

$$|1 - x| + 1 = 0 \qquad \text{(expression from (C) set equal to 0)}$$

$$|1 - x| = -1 \qquad \text{(subtract 1 from both sides)}$$

(C) has the same problem (B) had: it would require an absolute value expression to equal -1, which is impossible. Now, let's try (D):

$$|x - 1| + 1 = 0 \qquad \text{(expression from (D) set equal to 0)}$$

$$|x - 1| = -1 \qquad \text{(subtract 1 from both sides)}$$

Again, we know the absolute value of an expression can't be negative, so (D) can't be right. This shows that (A) is, indeed, correct.

Solution 2: Test-smart: Notice that the right answer must involve *subtracting* a number from the absolute-value expression in order to get a result of zero, because absolute-value expressions can't be negative, and the only option in the choices for arriving at a value of zero when starting from a non-negative number is to subtract. Pick the only choice that fits this requirement, which is (A).

How to check? Try an alternate approach above. Especially notice that the correct answer must end in subtracting something from the absolute-value expression, because we can't add a positive number to an absolute value expression and get zero.

Note Any of the wrong answer choices could have been tempting if we thought it was possible for an absolute value expression to equal -1.

Test 4, Section 3, Question 2

- **What's the prompt asking for?** The value of $f(-2)$.

- **Math concepts in the prompt:** algebra, arithmetic, constants, functions, variables
- **Elements of the answer choices:** integers, negative numbers
- **Notable differences among answer choices:** (A) and (B) are negative, while (C) and (D) are positive. (B) and (D) are numbers that appear in the prompt, while (A) and (C) are not.
- **Things to look out for:** Don't confuse x and b! Don't make small mistakes in your algebra and arithmetic!

Solution 1: Algebra: Set $f(6)$ equal to 7 and solve to find b; then use b to find $f(-2)$.

$$f(x) = \frac{3}{2}x + b \qquad \text{(original function)}$$

$$f(6) = \frac{3}{2}(6) + b \qquad \text{(plug in } x = 6\text{)}$$

$$7 = \frac{3}{2}(6) + b \qquad \text{(plug in } f(6) = 7, \text{ since the prompt tells us this statement is true)}$$

$$7 = 9 + b \qquad \text{(simplify)}$$

$$-2 = b \qquad \text{(subtract 9 from both sides)}$$

Now that we know $b = -2$, we can find $f(-2)$:

$$f(x) = \frac{3}{2}x - 2 \qquad \text{(original function with } b = -2\text{)}$$

$$f(-2) = \frac{3}{2}(-2) - 2 \qquad \text{(plug in } x = -2 \text{ to find } f(-2)\text{)}$$

$$f(-2) = -3 - 2 \qquad \text{(multiply } \frac{3}{2} \text{ by } -2\text{)}$$

$$f(-2) = -5 \qquad \text{(simplify)}$$

So we can see that (A) is correct.

ANSWER CHOICE ANALYSIS

(B): This is the value of b, but the questions asks for $f(-2)$. **(D):** This is the value of $f(6)$.

How to check? Carefully reconsider your reading and your calculations. Try to identify a couple of mistakes that could lead an untrained test-taker to one of the wrong answers.

Test 4, Section 3, Question 3

- **What's the prompt asking for?** The value of y.
- **Math concepts in the prompt:** algebra, arithmetic, coordinate pairs, fractions, systems of equations
- **Elements of the answer choices:** integers
- **Notable differences among answer choices:** (A) is half of (B), and (C) is half of (D). (C) is 6 times as much as (A), and (D) is 6 times as much as (B). This may be relevant since the first equation in the prompt involves a ratio of 6.
- **Pre-solution patterns (see p. 217):** halves and doubles
- **Things to look out for:** Don't confuse x and y! Don't make small mistakes in your algebra and arithmetic!

Solution 1: Algebra: Isolate x in the top equation to define it. Plug the definition of x into the second equation, and solve it for y.

First, we'll isolate x in the first equation:

$$\frac{x}{y} = 6 \qquad \text{(first equation)}$$

$$x = 6y \qquad \text{(multiply both sides by } y\text{)}$$

Now we can plug $x = 6y$ into the second equation, and use it to solve for y:

$$4(y + 1) = x \qquad \text{(second equation)}$$

$$4(y + 1) = 6y \qquad \text{(plug in } x = 6y\text{)}$$

$$4y + 4 = 6y \qquad \text{(distribute the 4)}$$

$$4 = 2y \qquad \text{(subtract } 4y \text{ from both sides)}$$

$$2 = y \qquad \text{(divide both sides by 2)}$$

So we can see that (A) is correct.

Solution 2: Backsolving: Test each answer choice as the value of y in both equations; the choice that produces the same x-value in both equations will be the correct answer.

For choice (A):

$$\frac{x}{y} = 6 \qquad\qquad \text{(first equation)}$$

$$\frac{x}{2} = 6 \qquad\qquad \text{(plug in } y = 2 \text{ from (A))}$$

$$x = 12 \qquad\qquad \text{(multiply both sides by 2)}$$

We can see that plugging the value from (A) into the first equation as y gives us an x-value of 12. Now, we need to see which x-value results when we plug $y = 2$ into the second equation:

$$4(y + 1) = x \qquad\qquad \text{(second equation)}$$

$$4(2 + 1) = x \qquad\qquad \text{(plug in } y = 2 \text{ from (A))}$$

$$12 = x \qquad\qquad \text{(simplify)}$$

We got the same x-value in both equations when we plugged in $y = 2$, so (A) must be right, assuming we haven't made any mistakes in our calculations. Since one of the best ways to verify that we haven't made any small mistakes like that is to check the other choices, let's move on to (B):

$$\frac{x}{y} = 6 \qquad\qquad \text{(first equation)}$$

$$\frac{x}{4} = 6 \qquad\qquad \text{(plug in } y = 4 \text{ from (B))}$$

$$x = 24 \qquad\qquad \text{(multiply both sides by 4)}$$

So plugging the value from (B) into the first equation gives us $x = 24$. Now let's try the second equation:

$$4(y + 1) = x \qquad\qquad \text{(second equation)}$$

$$4(4 + 1) = x \qquad\qquad \text{(plug in } y = 4 \text{ from (B))}$$

$$20 = x \qquad\qquad \text{(simplify)}$$

We got different x-values for the two equations, so (B) can't be correct. Now let's try (C):

$$\frac{x}{y} = 6 \qquad\qquad \text{(first equation)}$$

$$\frac{x}{12} = 6 \qquad\qquad \text{(plug in } y = 12 \text{ from (C))}$$

$$x = 72 \qquad\qquad \text{(multiply both sides by 12)}$$

When we plug the value from (C) into the first equation, we get $x = 72$. Now let's try the second equation:

$$4(y + 1) = x \qquad\qquad \text{(second equation)}$$

$$4(12 + 1) = x \qquad\qquad \text{(plug in } y = 12 \text{ from (C))}$$

$$52 = x \qquad\qquad \text{(simplify)}$$

We got different x-values for the two equations, so (C) can't be correct. Finally, let's consider (D):

$$\frac{x}{y} = 6 \qquad\qquad \text{(first equation)}$$

$$\frac{x}{24} = 6 \qquad\qquad \text{(plug in } y = 24 \text{ from (D))}$$

$$x = 144 \qquad \text{(multiply both sides by 24)}$$

Plugging the y-value from (D) into the first equation gave us $x = 144$. Now let's see if the second equation gives us the same x-value:

$$4(y + 1) = x \qquad \text{(second equation)}$$

$$4(24 + 1) = x \qquad \text{(plug in } y = 24 \text{ from (D))}$$

$$100 = x \qquad \text{(simplify)}$$

So (D) can't be correct, because we got different x-values for the two equations. Our testing has shown us that (A) must be right.

ANSWER CHOICE ANALYSIS

(B): This is twice as much as (A). **(C):** This is the value of x, but the question asks for the value of y. **(D):** This is twice as much as (C).

How to check? Try an alternate approach above. Try to figure out how an untrained test-taker might make a mistake that could lead to one or more of the wrong answers.

Test 4, Section 3, Question 4

- **What's the prompt asking for?** The expression that's equivalent to $f(-3x)$.
- **Math concepts in the prompt:** algebra, arithmetic, functions, variables
- **Elements of the answer choices:** algebraic expressions, exponents, integers
- **Notable differences among answer choices:** (A) begins with $-6x$, while (B) and (C) both begin with $6x$, and (D) begins with $6x^2$. (A) and (C) end with -5, while (B) ends with $+5$ and (D) ends with $-15x$.
- **Concepts in the answer choices:** algebra, variables, exponents
- **Pre-solution patterns (see p. 217):** opposites; wrong answers try to imitate right answers
- **Things to look out for:** Don't overlook the negative signs in the prompt! Don't make small mistakes in your algebra and arithmetic!

Solution 1: Algebra: Plug $-3x$ into $f(x)$ to find $f(-3x)$.

$$f(x) = -2x + 5 \qquad \text{(given function)}$$

$$f(-3x) = -2(-3x) + 5 \qquad \text{(plug in } (-3x) \text{ for } x \text{ to find } f(-3x))$$

$$f(-3x) = 6x + 5 \qquad \text{(simplify)}$$

So we can see that (B) is right.

Solution 2: Abstract: Notice that the correct answer must end in $+5$, and that only one answer choice fits that requirement.

When we compare the choices to the prompt, we might notice that what we're putting into the $f(x)$ function will first be multiplied by -2, and then have 5 added to it. Since the prompt asks about plugging in a value that involves a variable without a separate constant, there's no way that plugging in $-3x$ can result in a change to the constant in the $f(x)$ expression.

This means that the correct answer must end in $+5$, just as the original $f(x)$ expression does. Only (B) satisfies that requirement, so (B) must be correct.

ANSWER CHOICE ANALYSIS

(A): This is the result if we make an error with a negative sign. **(C):** This is the result if we make an error with a negative sign. **(D):** This is the result if we multiply each term in the function by $-3x$.

How to check? Try an alternate approach above. Try to figure out how an untrained test-taker could arrive at some of the wrong answers, and make sure you haven't made any mistakes yourself.

Test 4, Section 3, Question 5

- **What's the prompt asking for?** The answer choice that's equivalent to the expression in the prompt.
- **Math concepts in the prompt:** algebra, arithmetic, FOIL, multiplying binomials
- **Elements of the answer choices:** algebraic expressions, exponents, integers
- **Notable differences among answer choices:** (A) is the only choice that involves the number 45. (B) and (C) both begin with $24x^2$ and end with $+3$, but (C) includes the term $18x$. (D) begins with $18x^2$.
- **Concepts in the answer choices:** polynomials
- **Pre-solution patterns (see p. 217):** wrong answers try to imitate right answers
- **Things to look out for:** Don't make small mistakes in your algebra and arithmetic!

Solution 1: Algebra: Multiply out the expression in the prompt and select the answer choice that's equivalent to it.

$$3(2x + 1)(4x + 1) \qquad \text{(given expression)}$$

$$3(8x^2 + 2x + 4x + 1) \qquad \text{(FOIL)}$$

$$3(8x^2 + 6x + 1) \qquad \text{(simplify)}$$

$$24x^2 + 18x + 3 \qquad \text{(distribute the 3)}$$

So we can see that (C) must be correct.

Solution 2: Test-smart: Note that the right answer must involve three terms, and pick the only choice that satisfies that requirement.

As trained test-takers, we know that FOILing two binomials will normally result in an expression with one x^2-term, one x-term, and one constant. (The only exception to this general rule would be a situation where we were FOILing the factors in a difference of squares; those factors would each have to involve the same x-term and constants with the same absolute value but opposite signs, such as $(2x - 7)(2x + 7)$, which would result in an expression without an x-term when it was FOILed out.)

Multiplying the FOILed-out expression by 3 won't add any extra terms or cancel out any terms, so the correct answer must still involve three terms. Only (C) is an expression with three terms, so it must be correct!

ANSWER CHOICE ANALYSIS

(A): This is the result if we make a couple of different algebra errors and think the expression is equal to $3(3x)(5x)$, but then leave out an x when we combine those terms. The coefficient would also be equal to the result if we tried to evaluate the expression in the prompt with x set equal to 1. **(B):** This is the result if we forget to include the x-term when we do FOIL.

How to check? Try an alternate approach above, and try to figure out how untrained test-takers could make small mistakes that would lead them to one or more of the wrong answers.

Test 4, Section 3, Question 6

- **What's the prompt asking for?** The choice that must be true according to the equation in the prompt.
- **Math concepts in the prompt:** algebra, arithmetic, fractions, multiple variables
- **Elements of the answer choices:** algebra, fractions
- **Notable differences among answer choices:** (A) and (B) both define $\frac{a}{b}$, while (C) defines $\frac{a+b}{b}$ and (D) defines $\frac{a-2b}{b}$. (B) and (C) both end in $\frac{10}{7}$, while (A) ends in $\frac{-4}{7}$ and (D) ends in $\frac{-11}{7}$.

- **Concepts in the answer choices:** algebraic expressions, fractions
- **Pre-solution patterns (see p. 217):** wrong answers try to imitate right answers
- **Things to look out for:** Don't confuse a and b! Don't assume that you must find a and b individually! Don't make any small mistakes with your algebra and arithmetic, especially when it comes to subtraction and negative numbers!

Solution 1: Formal algebra: Manipulate the given equation until you arrive at an equation that matches one of the answer choices.

$$\frac{a-b}{b} = \frac{3}{7} \qquad \text{(given equation)}$$

$$\frac{a}{b} - \frac{b}{b} = \frac{3}{7} \qquad \text{(separate into two fractions with a common denominator)}$$

$$\frac{a}{b} = \frac{3}{7} + 1 \qquad \text{(add 1 to both sides, since } \frac{b}{b} = 1\text{)}$$

$$\frac{a}{b} = \frac{10}{7} \qquad \text{(rewrite 1 as } \frac{7}{7} \text{ and simplify)}$$

So the correct answer is (B).

Solution 2: Test-smart algebra: Realize the given equation allows us to set b equal to 7 and find a easily, which allows us to know $\frac{a}{b}$.

Since both sides of the original equation consist of a single fraction each, we can set the numerators of the fractions equal to each other, and we can also set the denominators of each fraction equal to each other. When we do that, we get this:

$$\frac{a-b}{b} = \frac{3}{7} \qquad \text{(given equation)}$$

$$a - b = 3 \quad \text{and} \quad b = 7 \qquad \text{(set numerators equal to each other and denominators equal to each other)}$$

Now that we know $a - b = 3$ when $b = 7$, we can tell a must equal 10, since $10 - 7 = 3$. So $\frac{a}{b}$ must equal $\frac{10}{7}$, and (B) is right.

ANSWER CHOICE ANALYSIS

(A): This would be true if $\frac{a+b}{b}$ were equal to $\frac{3}{7}$. **(C):** This choice could tempt an untrained test-taker who found the right answer but didn't read carefully when looking at the answer choices.

How to check? Try an alternate approach above. Try to identify small mistakes that could lead to some of the wrong answers.

Test 4, Section 3, Question 7

- **What's the prompt asking for?** The statement that best describes how Amelia's running changes between week 4 and week 16.
- **Math concepts in the prompt:** constant increase, word problems
- **Elements of the answer choices:** decimals, integers, sentences
- **Notable differences among answer choices:** Each choice talks about the amount by which Amelia increases the length of her longest run, so we can focus more of our attention on the second line of each choice, since the first line of each choice is identical. (A), (B), and (D) discuss changes made "every week," while (C) discusses changes made "every 3 weeks." (B) and (C) both involve an increase

of 2 miles, but each choice would have that increase made in a different period of time. (C) and (D) are actually reciprocals if we read carefully: 2 miles every 3 weeks is $\frac{2}{3}$ miles/week, while 1.5 miles per week is equal to $\frac{3}{2}$ miles/week. (A) and (B) are actually reciprocals if we read carefully: 0.5 miles/week is the same thing as $\frac{1}{2}$ miles/week, which is the reciprocal of 2 miles/week.

- **Concepts in the answer choices:** rate of increase
- **Pre-solution patterns (see p. 217):** opposites; wrong answers try to imitate right answers
- **Things to look out for:** Don't misread the choices, which are all very similar to one another! Don't make small mistakes in your arithmetic, especially as they relate to fractions and their reciprocals!

Solution 1: Arithmetic: Determine the change in distance from 8 miles to 26 miles, and divide that by the change in time from 4 weeks to 16 weeks.

$$\frac{26-8}{16-4}$$ (increase in distance divided by number of weeks)

$$\frac{3}{2}$$ (simplify to find the change per week)

$\frac{3}{2}$ equals 1.5, and we know the change is on a per-week basis, since we divided the change by the number of weeks. So (D) is right.

Solution 2: Backsolving: Begin with a distance of 8 miles in week 4, and then apply each change from each answer choice to determine which choice results in a distance of 26 miles in week 16.

There are 12 weeks from week 4 to week 16. Here are the results that Amelia would have in week 16 if she made each of the changes described in the answer choices:

For choice (A):

Week 4	8	Week 11	11.5
Week 5	8.5	Week 12	12
Week 6	9	Week 13	12.5
Week 7	9.5	Week 14	13
Week 8	10	Week 15	13.5
Week 9	10.5	Week 16	14
Week 10	11		

For choice (B):

Week 4	8	Week 11	22
Week 5	10	Week 12	24
Week 6	12	Week 13	26
Week 7	14	Week 14	28
Week 8	16	Week 15	30
Week 9	18	Week 16	32
Week 10	20		

For choice (C):

Week 4	8	Week 13	14
Week 7	10	Week 16	16
Week 10	12		

For choice (D):

Week 4	8	Week 11	18.5
Week 5	9.5	Week 12	20
Week 6	11	Week 13	21.5
Week 7	12.5	Week 14	23
Week 8	14	Week 15	24.5
Week 9	15.5	Week 16	26
Week 10	17		

Only (D) results in a 26 mile run after 12 weeks, so (D) is correct.

ANSWER CHOICE ANALYSIS

(C): This choice could be tempting if an untrained test-taker misunderstood the $\frac{3}{2}$ he found doing the algebraic solution.

How to check? Try an alternate approach above. Also try to figure out how test-takers could make small mistakes that might lead to some of the wrong answers.

▶ Post-solution patterns (see page 218): opposites

Test 4, Section 3, Question 8

- **What's the prompt asking for?** A line parallel to the line in the given equation
- **Math concepts in the prompt:** algebra, equations, parallel lines, slope, slope-intercept format
- **Elements of the answer choices:** algebraic expressions, integers
- **Notable differences among answer choices:** The choices frequently use 3 and 2 as coefficients for x and y, and (A) uses 6 as a coefficient, which is the product of 3 and 2. The choices are all in the standard format for a line, while the equation in the prompt is in slope-intercept format.

- **Concepts in the answer choices:** equations of lines, standard format of a line
- **"Bridge" concepts:** Two lines in a plane are parallel if they have identical slopes and different y-intercepts.
- **Pre-solution patterns (see p. 217):** opposites; wrong answers try to imitate right answers
- **Things to look out for:** Don't make small mistakes in your algebra and arithmetic, especially with respect to positive and negative numbers!

Solution 1: Algebra: Identify the answer choice with the same slope as the original equation, possibly by converting all the lines in the answer choices to slope-intercept form, or by converting the line in the original expression to the standard form.

For choice (A):

$$6x + 2y = 15 \qquad \text{(equation from (A))}$$

$$2y = -6x + 15 \qquad \text{(subtract } 6x \text{ from both sides)}$$

$$y = -3x + \frac{15}{2} \qquad \text{(divide both sides by 2)}$$

The slope of this equation is -3, so (A) is right, as long as we haven't made any mistakes or miscalculations. As trained test-takers, we know that one of the best ways to make sure we haven't made any small mistakes like that is to check every choice. So let's try (B) now:

$$3x - y = 7 \qquad \text{(equation from (B))}$$

$$-y = -3x + 7 \qquad \text{(subtract } 3x \text{ from both sides)}$$

$$y = 3x - 7 \qquad \text{(multiply both sides by } -1)$$

The slope of this equation is 3, not -3, so (B) isn't correct. Now let's try (C):

$$2x - 3y = 6 \qquad \text{(equation from (C))}$$

$$-3y = -2x + 6 \qquad \text{(subtract } 2x \text{ from both sides)}$$

$$y = \frac{2}{3}x - 2 \qquad \text{(divide both sides by } -3)$$

The slope of this equation is $\frac{2}{3}$, not -3, so (C) isn't correct, either. Now let's try (D):

$$x + 3y = 1 \qquad \text{(equation from (D))}$$

$$3y = -x + 1 \qquad \text{(subtract } x \text{ from both sides)}$$

$$y = -\frac{1}{3}x + \frac{1}{3} \qquad \text{(divide both sides by 3)}$$

The slope of this equation is $-\frac{1}{3}$, not -3, so (D) isn't correct. This means that (A) is, indeed, the right answer.

ANSWER CHOICE ANALYSIS

(B): This line would have a slope that was the opposite of the slope in the prompt. **(C):** This choice has a coefficient of -3 for the y-term in its current form, which might trick some test-takers who were looking to match the slope of -3 from the prompt, and didn't read this answer choice carefully enough. **(D):** This line would have the reciprocal of the slope in the prompt.

How to check? Carefully review your reading, algebra, and arithmetic; try to figure out how an untrained test-taker could make small mistakes that would lead to some of the wrong answers.

Test 4, Section 3, Question 9

- **What's the prompt asking for?** The set of possible values of x when a is 2.
- **Math concepts in the prompt:** algebra, arithmetic, PEMDAS, solution sets, square roots, substitution
- **Elements of the answer choices:** integers, sets
- **Notable differences among answer choices:** (A) includes both options from (C) and (D). (A), (B), and (C) contain factors of the number in (D).
- **Concepts in the answer choices:** sets

- **"Bridge" concepts:** The square root of a number can be positive or negative, but a radical expression like $\sqrt{5x}$ refers to the positive square root of $5x$.
- **Pre-solution patterns (see p. 217):** wrong answers try to imitate right answers
- **Things to look out for:** Avoid small mistakes in your algebra and arithmetic! Don't forget that the choices show us there can potentially be more than one value for x! Don't forget that a radical expression like $\sqrt{3}$ is positive by definition!

Solution 1: Algebra: Using the given value of a, square both sides of the equation and solve for x, keeping in mind that a radical expression must be positive.

$$\sqrt{x - a} = x - 4 \qquad \text{(original equation)}$$

$$\sqrt{x - 2} = x - 4 \qquad \text{(plug in } a = 2)$$

$$x - 2 = x^2 - 8x + 16 \qquad \text{(square both sides)}$$

$$0 = x^2 - 9x + 18 \qquad \text{(subtract } x \text{ from both sides and add 2 to both sides)}$$

$$0 = (x - 6)(x - 3) \qquad \text{(reverse FOIL)}$$

So $x^2 - 9x + 18 = 0$ when $x = 6$ or when $x = 3$. Many untrained test-takers will assume that this makes (A) right, but we still need to verify which values of x allow the square-root expression from the prompt to be positive. (Remember that an expression under a radical must be positive!) We see which values make the original equation true by plugging $x = 6$ and $x = 3$ back into that original equation to see what we get. Here's what we get when we test $x = 3$:

$$\sqrt{x - a} = x - 4 \qquad \text{(original equation)}$$

$$\sqrt{x - 2} = x - 4 \qquad \text{(plug in } a = 2)$$

$$\sqrt{3 - 2} = 3 - 4 \qquad \text{(plug in } x = 3)$$

$$1 = -1 \qquad \text{(simplify)}$$

This isn't a valid statement, so $x = 3$ isn't part of the solution set for the original equation. Now let's test $x = 6$:

$$\sqrt{x - a} = x - 4 \qquad \text{(original equation)}$$

$$\sqrt{x - 2} = x - 4 \qquad \text{(plug in } a = 2)$$

$$\sqrt{6 - 2} = 6 - 4 \qquad \text{(plug in } x = 6)$$

$$2 = 2 \qquad \text{(simplify)}$$

This is a valid statement, so $x = 6$ is part of the solution set. Since only $x = 6$ makes the given equation true when $a = 2$, (D) is right.

Solution 2: Backsolving: Substitute the numbers in each answer choice for x; the correct answer choice will be the one that contains all valid solutions for x that appear in the answer choices.

$$\sqrt{x - a} = x - 4 \qquad \text{(given equation)}$$

$$\sqrt{3 - 2} = 3 - 4 \qquad \text{(plug in } a = 2 \text{ from the prompt and } x = 3 \text{ from (A))}$$

$$1 = -1 \qquad \text{(simplify)}$$

This doesn't result in a true statement, so (A) isn't correct. Notice that we don't need to plug in $x = 6$ to test (A), because if plugging in $x = 3$ doesn't result in a true statement, then (A) can't be correct. Let's take a look at (B).

$$\sqrt{x - a} = x - 4 \qquad \text{(given equation)}$$

$$\sqrt{2 - 2} = 2 - 4 \qquad \text{(plug in } a = 2 \text{ from the prompt and } x = 2 \text{ from (B))}$$

$$0 = -2 \qquad \text{(simplify)}$$

This doesn't result in a true statement, so (B) isn't correct. We don't need to look at (C), because we already tested $x = 3$ when we looked at choice (A), and we found that plugging in that value didn't result in a true statement. So let's look at (D).

$$\sqrt{x - a} = x - 4 \qquad \text{(given equation)}$$

$$\sqrt{6 - 2} = 6 - 4 \qquad \text{(plug in } a = 2 \text{ from the prompt and } x = 6 \text{ from (D))}$$

$$2 = 2 \qquad \text{(simplify)}$$

We can see that when we plug in $x = 6$, the result is a true statement—so (D) is correct.

ANSWER CHOICE ANALYSIS

(A): This might be tempting to an untrained test-taker who tried a formal algebraic approach but didn't realize that plugging 3 into the original equation would result in an invalid statement, as we saw in solution 1. **(B):** This might be tempting if we thought the x-term on the right side of the equation was an x-squared term. **(C):** This might be tempting if we got confused about whether plugging 3 or 6 into the original equation resulted in an invalid statement.

How to check? Try an alternate approach above; also, try to figure out how the College Board was trying to trick you with some of the wrong answers.

Test 4, Section 3, Question 10

- **What's the prompt asking for?** The value of t.
- **Math concepts in the prompt:** algebra, arithmetic, fractions
- **Elements of the answer choices:** fractions, integers
- **Notable differences among answer choices:** (B) is the only choice that's not a fraction. (A) and (C) both involve 11, but (A) has it in the denominator, while (C) has it in the numerator. (D) contains 55, which is the product of 5 and 11, which appear in other choices. This may be relevant because working with fractions often involves multiplying.
- **Concepts in the answer choices:** fractions
- **Pre-solution patterns (see p. 217):** wrong answers try to imitate right answers
- **Things to look out for:** Don't confuse the numerators and denominators in the fractions! Don't make small mistakes in your algebra and arithmetic!

Solution 1: Backsolving: Test each answer choice in the prompt to see which choice creates a valid equation.

For choice (A):

$$\frac{t+5}{t-5} = 10 \qquad \text{(given equation)}$$

$$\frac{\frac{45}{11}+5}{\frac{45}{11}-5} = 10 \qquad \text{(plug in } t = \frac{45}{11} \text{ from (A))}$$

$$\frac{45}{11} + 5 = 10\left(\frac{45}{11} - 5\right) \qquad \text{(multiply both sides by } \frac{45}{11} - 5\text{)}$$

$$\frac{45}{11} + 5 = \frac{450}{11} - 50 \qquad \text{(distribute the 10)}$$

$$\frac{45}{11} + \frac{55}{11} = \frac{450}{11} - \frac{550}{11} \qquad \text{(multiply 5 and 50 by } \frac{11}{11} \text{ in order to have a common denominator for all terms)}$$

$$\frac{100}{11} = -\frac{100}{11} \qquad \text{(simplify)}$$

This isn't a valid statement, so (A) can't be correct. Now let's try (B):

$$\frac{t+5}{t-5} = 10 \qquad \text{(given equation)}$$

$$\frac{5+5}{5-5} = 10 \qquad \text{(plug in } t = 5 \text{ from (B))}$$

The expression on the left involves dividing by zero, which yields an undefined value that can't be equal to 10. So (B) can't be correct, either. Now let's try (C):

$$\frac{t+5}{t-5} = 10 \qquad \text{(given equation)}$$

$$\frac{\frac{11}{2}+5}{\frac{11}{2}-5} = 10 \qquad \text{(plug in } t = \frac{11}{2} \text{ from (C))}$$

$$\frac{11}{2} + 5 = 10\left(\frac{11}{2} - 5\right) \qquad \text{(multiply both sides by } \frac{11}{2} - 5\text{)}$$

$$\frac{11}{2} + 5 = \frac{110}{2} - 50 \qquad \text{(distribute the 10)}$$

$$\frac{11}{2} + \frac{10}{2} = \frac{110}{2} - \frac{100}{2} \qquad \text{(multiply 5 and 50 by } \frac{2}{2} \text{ in order to have a common denominator for all terms)}$$

$$\frac{21}{2} = \frac{10}{2} \qquad \text{(simplify)}$$

This isn't a valid statement, so (C) can't be right. Finally, let's try (D):

$$\frac{t+5}{t-5} = 10 \qquad \text{(given equation)}$$

$$\frac{\frac{55}{9}+5}{\frac{55}{9}-5} = 10 \qquad \text{(plug in } t = \frac{55}{9} \text{ from (D))}$$

$$\frac{55}{9} + 5 = 10\left(\frac{55}{9} - 5\right) \qquad \text{(multiply both sides by } \frac{55}{9} - 5\text{)}$$

$$\frac{55}{9} + 5 = \frac{550}{9} - 50 \qquad \text{(distribute the 10)}$$

$$\frac{55}{9} + \frac{45}{9} = \frac{550}{9} - \frac{450}{9} \qquad \text{(multiply 5 and 50 by } \frac{9}{9} \text{ in order to have a common denominator for all terms)}$$

$$\frac{100}{9} = \frac{100}{9} \qquad \text{(simplify)}$$

This is a valid statement, so (D) is correct.

Solution 2: Algebra: Manipulate the expression to solve for t.

$$\frac{t+5}{t-5} = 10 \qquad \text{(given equation)}$$

$$t + 5 = 10(t - 5) \qquad \text{(multiply both sides by } t - 5\text{)}$$

$$t + 5 = 10t - 50 \qquad \text{(distribute the 10)}$$

$$t + 55 = 10t \qquad \text{(add 50 to both sides)}$$

$$55 = 9t \qquad \text{(subtract } t \text{ from both sides)}$$

$$\frac{55}{9} = t \qquad \text{(divide both sides by 9)}$$

So we can see that (D) is right.

ANSWER CHOICE ANALYSIS

(A): This reflects a mistake with a negative sign in the algebra of solution 2 above, which could cause you to subtract 5 from 50 instead of adding 5 to 50. **(B):** This reflects the mistake of thinking that plugging in 5 would create a denominator of 1 instead of 0 in solution

1. **(C):** This reflects an algebra mistake in solution 2 above that would cause us to arrive at $55 = 10t$, resulting in the statement $\frac{55}{10} = t$, which simplifies to $\frac{11}{2} = t$.

How to check? Try an alternate approach above, and/or note some of the ways that the College Board could be trying to trick you into choosing one of the wrong answers, as discussed in the answer choice analysis above.

Test 4, Section 3, Question 11

- **What's the prompt asking for?** The number of ordered pairs that satisfy the system in the prompt.
- **Math concepts in the prompt:** algebra, arithmetic, FOIL, multiple variables, systems of equations
- **Elements of the answer choices:** integers, words or phrases, zero
- **Notable differences among answer choices:** (A), (B), and (C) form a series in which each choice is one more than the previous choice.
- **Concepts in the answer choices:** infinity, zero
- **"Bridge" concepts:** The number of (x, y) pairs that satisfy the system is the same thing as the number of points where the graphs of the two equations intersect, because the coordinates of any point of intersection will be a pair of (x, y) values that lie on both equations. Since the top equation is a straight line, and the bottom equation is a function as well, and since all functions must pass the vertical line test, we know that any points of intersection between the two equations must have different x-values.

- **Pre-solution patterns (see p. 217):** opposites; the first and last terms in a series are often wrong answers
- **Things to look out for:** Don't confuse x and y! Don't confuse the numbers in the answer choices with potential values for x or y themselves—the answer choices reflect the number of solutions, not the values involved in those solutions! Don't make small mistakes in your algebra and arithmetic!

Solution 1: Algebra: Since each point of intersection must have a unique x-value, solve for all possible x-values by plugging the definition of y from the bottom equation into the top equation, then solving the top equation to find all possible values of x. Finally, pick the answer choice that accurately reflects the possible number of (x, y) pairings that satisfy the system.

$x = 2y + 5$	(top equation)
$x = 2\big((2x - 3)(x + 9)\big) + 5$	(plug in $y = (2x - 3)(x + 9)$ from the bottom equation)
$x = 2(2x^2 + 15x - 27) + 5$	(FOIL)
$x = (4x^2 + 30x - 54) + 5$	(distribute the 2)
$x = 4x^2 + 30x - 49$	(simplify)
$x = \dfrac{-30 \pm \sqrt{30^2 - 4(4)(-49)}}{2(4)}$	(apply the quadratic formula)
$x = \dfrac{-30 \pm \sqrt{900 - (16)(-49)}}{8}$	(simplify)

At this stage, an untrained test-taker might be wondering how to finish solving for x, given that we can't use calculators for this section. But a trained test-taker realizes that the prompt isn't asking for the specific x-values and y-values that satisfy the system; the prompt is only asking *how many* pairs of those values exist!

When we look at the last step of our solution, we can see that there are two real values of x that would satisfy the system, because the number under the radical will be positive, and the denominator doesn't result in any undefined values. Further, we can see that there must be *two* values for x: the one that results from adding the value of the radical expression to -30, and the one that results from subtracting the value of the radical expression from -30.

Again, each of these x-values must have a single y-value that corresponds to it, so there must be two (x, y) points that represent solutions to both systems, which means (C) is correct.

Solution 2: xy-plane: Note that the first equation is a line, and the second equation is a parabola. Roughly sketch the graphs of each to determine how many points of intersection they have, possibly by plotting individual (x, y) points for each equation.

First, let's plug some x-values into the first equation to generate some ordered pairs for that line. I'll pick the x-values $-2, 0,$ and 2, for no particular reason:

$x = 2y + 5$	(first equation)
$(-2) = 2y + 5$	(plug in $x = -2$)
$-7 = 2y$	(subtract 5 from both sides)

$$-\frac{7}{2} = y \qquad \text{(divide both sides by 2)}$$

So $\left(-2, -\frac{7}{2}\right)$ is one ordered pair on the line $x = 2y + 5$. Now let's plug in $x = 0$:

$$(0) = 2y + 5 \qquad \text{(plug in } x = 0\text{)}$$

$$-5 = 2y \qquad \text{(subtract 5 from both sides)}$$

$$-\frac{5}{2} = y \qquad \text{(divide both sides by 2)}$$

We see that another ordered pair on the line $x = 2y + 5$ is $\left(0, -\frac{5}{2}\right)$. Finally, we'll plug in $x = 2$:

$$(2) = 2y + 5 \qquad \text{(plug in } x = 2\text{)}$$

$$-3 = 2y \qquad \text{(subtract 5 from both sides)}$$

$$-\frac{3}{2} = y \qquad \text{(divide both sides by 2)}$$

So a third ordered pair on this line is $\left(2, -\frac{3}{2}\right)$.

Now let's find some points on the graph of the second equation. Again, for no particular reason, I'll pick the x-values $-2, 0$, and 2:

$$y = (2x - 3)(x + 9) \qquad \text{(second equation)}$$

$$y = (2(-2) - 3)((-2) + 9) \qquad \text{(plug in } x = -2\text{)}$$

$$y = (-7)(7) \qquad \text{(perform operations in parentheses)}$$

$$y = -49 \qquad \text{(simplify)}$$

So one ordered pair on $y = (2x - 3)(x + 9)$ is $(-2, -49)$. Now let's try plugging in $x = 0$:

$$y = (2(0) - 3)((0) + 9) \qquad \text{(plug in } x = 0\text{)}$$

$$y = (-3)(9) \qquad \text{(perform operations in parentheses)}$$

$$y = -27 \qquad \text{(simplify)}$$

We can see that $(0, -27)$ is another ordered pair on the parabola $y = (2x - 3)(x + 9)$. Finally, let's plug in $x = 2$:

$$y = (2(2) - 3)((2) + 9) \qquad \text{(plug in } x = 2\text{)}$$

$$y = (1)(11) \qquad \text{(perform operations in parentheses)}$$

$$y = 11 \qquad \text{(simplify)}$$

So a third ordered pair on the parabola $y = (2x - 3)(x + 9)$ is $(2, 11)$.

We now have the following ordered pairs for the two given equations:

$x = 2y + 5$	$\left(-2, -\frac{7}{2}\right)$	$\left(0, -\frac{5}{2}\right)$	$\left(2, -\frac{3}{2}\right)$
$y = (2x - 3)(x + 9)$	$(-2, -49)$	$(0, -27)$	$(2, 11)$

Let's sketch those ordered pairs and see what we come up with.

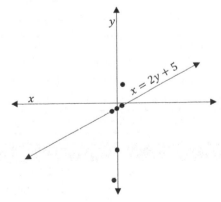

After plotting the points we found, we can easily see the form of the line $x = 2y + 5$. But we may need a few more points to tell what's going on with $y = (2x - 3)(x + 9)$, so we can see how many points of intersection exist. Let's try plugging in $x = -10$ and $x = 10$:

$$y = (2x - 3)(x + 9) \quad \text{(second equation)}$$
$$y = (2(-10) - 3)((-10) + 9) \quad \text{(plug in } x = -10\text{)}$$
$$y = (-23)(-1) \quad \text{(perform operations in parentheses)}$$
$$y = 23 \quad \text{(simplify)}$$

This means $(-10, 23)$ is a fourth ordered pair on the parabola $y = (2x - 3)(x + 9)$. Now let's plug in $x = 10$:

$$y = (2(10) - 3)((10) + 9) \quad \text{(plug in } x = 10\text{)}$$
$$y = (17)(19) \quad \text{(perform operations in parentheses)}$$
$$y = 323 \quad \text{(simplify)}$$

So $(10, 323)$ is another ordered pair on the line $y = (2x - 3)(x + 9)$.

Let's add $(-10, 23)$ and $(10, 323)$ to our diagram. (Note that $(10, 323)$ wouldn't fit on our diagram because the y-value is so high, but it's enough for our purposes to see that the point would be significantly above the line $x = 2y + 5$.)

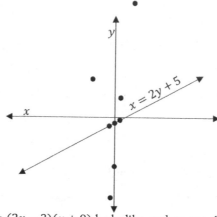

Now we can start to see what the parabola $y = (2x - 3)(x + 9)$ looks like, and we can sketch that line in our diagram, roughly connecting the points from left to right:

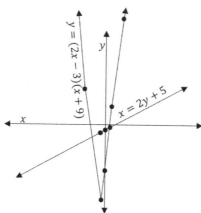

So $y = (2x - 3)(x + 9)$ looks like a parabola that crosses the line $x = 2y + 5$ twice, which means that (C) is correct. (We can also see that if we plugged x-values into $y = (2x - 3)(x + 9)$ with higher absolute values than our test numbers, the corresponding y-values would always get larger, which shows that the graph of $y = (2x - 3)(x + 9)$ would never come back to intersect $x = 2y + 5$ again.)

ANSWER CHOICE ANALYSIS

(A): This choice would tempt an untrained test-takers if she thought the graphs of the two equations would never intersect, or if she didn't realize that the quadratic formula shows there are two real solutions for x in the system. **(D):** This choice might be tempting if an untrained test-taker thought the two functions were equivalent, which would require him not to notice that one equation has only an x-term and a constant, while the other would have an x^2 term as well, which means they can't be equivalent to each other.

How to check? Try an alternate approach above. Try to identify the mistakes that might lead to one or more of the wrong answers.

Test 4, Section 3, Question 12

- **What's the prompt asking for?** The amount that each person paid under the conditions in the prompt.

- **Math concepts in the prompt:** algebra, algebraic modeling, arithmetic, percentages, word problems

- **Elements of the answer choices:** algebraic expressions, decimals
- **Notable differences among answer choices:** (C) is half of (D), which may be especially relevant here because the question talks about two people splitting a cost evenly. (C) and (D) both contain the quantity 1.2.

- **Concepts in the answer choices:** addition, multiplication, variables
- **Pre-solution patterns (see p. 217):** halves and doubles
- **Things to look out for:** Don't forget to account for the cost of both sandwiches! Don't forget to apply the tip to the entire cost! Don't make any small mistakes in your algebra or arithmetic!

Solution 1: Algebra: Come up with your own expression for the price paid by each person, and then pick the answer choice that contains an equivalent expression.

If the cost of Ken's sandwich was x dollars, and the cost of Paul's sandwich was a dollar more than the cost of Ken's sandwich, then Paul's sandwich must have cost $x + 1$ dollars. So the cost of both sandwiches was $x + x + 1$ dollars, or $2x + 1$ dollars.

The prompt says they paid a 20% tip. If they paid 100% of the bill plus a 20% tip, they must have paid 120% of the cost of the sandwiches. We can express that total cost as $1.2(2x + 1)$.

Finally, the prompt says Ken and Paul split the total, so we divide our expression by 2 to find the amount paid by each: $\frac{1.2(2x+1)}{2}$.

Unfortunately, none of the answer choices is a fraction, so we'll have to manipulate our expression further to see if we can make it identical to one of the choices. One obvious way to try to do that is to simplify our expression so it's no longer a fraction:

$$\frac{1.2(2x+1)}{2} \qquad \text{(our fraction that expresses the cost that Ken and Paul each paid)}$$

$$\frac{2.4x+1.2}{2} \qquad \text{(distribute the 1.2 in the numerator)}$$

$$1.2x + 0.6 \qquad \text{(divide the terms in the numerator by 2 to cancel the denominator)}$$

Now we can see that our expression is equivalent to (C), so (C) is correct.

Solution 2: Concrete/Backsolving: Pick an arbitrary number for x and then determine the price paid by each person based on that value for x. Then plug the same x-value into each answer choice; the correct choice will be the one that has the same concrete value as the one you found for the situation described in the prompt.

Let's arbitrarily assume that Ken's sandwich was $5. That means Paul's sandwich was $6, and the total cost of both sandwiches was $11. If they added a 20% tip, that tip would be 0.2×11, or $2.20. Adding the tip to the cost of the sandwiches gives us a total cost of $13.20. Once they split this cost, they'd each pay $6.60.

Now let's plug $x = 5$ into the answer choices to see which one gives us $6.60. Choice (A) would give us the following:

$$0.2x + 0.2 \qquad \text{(expression from (A))}$$
$$0.2(5) + 0.2 \qquad \text{(plug in } x = 5\text{)}$$
$$1.2 \qquad \text{(simplify)}$$

This isn't equal to $6.60, so (A) isn't correct. Now, let's try (B):

$$0.5x + 0.1 \qquad \text{(expression from (B))}$$
$$0.5(5) + 0.1 \qquad \text{(plug in } x = 5\text{)}$$
$$2.6 \qquad \text{(simplify)}$$

This isn't equal to $6.60 either, so (B) isn't correct. Let's try (C) now:

$$1.2x + 0.6 \qquad \text{(expression from (C))}$$
$$1.2(5) + 0.6 \qquad \text{(plug in } x = 5\text{)}$$
$$6.6 \qquad \text{(simplify)}$$

This is equal to $6.60, which was the cost we found for each person before we looked at the answer choices, so (C) is correct—assuming, of course, that we haven't accidentally picked an arbitrary value for x that results in a false positive. As trained test-takers, we know that we need to guard against this, so we should check every choice when we backsolve. So let's take a look at (D):

$$2.4x + 1.2 \qquad \text{(expression from (D))}$$
$$2.4(5) + 1.2 \qquad \text{(plug in } x = 5\text{)}$$
$$13.2 \qquad \text{(simplify)}$$

This isn't equal to $6.60, so (D) isn't correct. We can see that (C) is, indeed, the correct answer.

Solution 3: Test-smart: Consider each answer choice in light of the discussion in the prompt, and pick the choice whose elements accurately reflect the situation described in the prompt.

The prompt tells us x is the cost of Ken's sandwich, and that Paul's sandwich cost a dollar more than Ken's. So we know that the total cost of both sandwiches was more than $2x$, which means that each person must have paid more than x just for the sandwiches.

If Ken and Paul split the cost of *both* sandwiches, it doesn't make sense that each one would only pay 0.2 times the cost of Ken's sandwich—so (A) must be wrong. Choice (B) must be wrong for a similar reason: the coefficient of x needs to be more than 1.

Choice (C) looks like it could make sense. If they split the cost of 2 sandwiches that cost x dollars, and added a 20% tip, the result would be $1.2x$ each. Since one sandwich costs an extra dollar, they would need to split that dollar, which would be an additional 50 cents each—plus a 20% tip on that extra dollar, which works out to an extra 10 cents each on top of the original extra 50 cents each. So each person would pay $1.2x + 0.6$, just as (C) says.

Choice (D) doesn't make sense because if each person pays $2.4x$, that means they're each paying for more than the cost of 2 of Ken's sandwiches. The 1.2 in this expression also indicates that each person is paying the extra dollar for Paul's sandwich *and* the 20% tip on that extra dollar. After we think about (C), we can see that (D) is actually the total amount that the two pay, not the price that each one of them pays, as the prompt requires. (D) would be tempting for a test-taker who used algebra to find the full cost of the meal and then forgot to divide by 2.

We can see that (C) is the only choice that can make sense here, so it must be right.

ANSWER CHOICE ANALYSIS

(A): This could be the result if an untrained test-taker made an algebra error while calculating only the tip that Ken and Paul paid. **(B):** This could be the result if someone made an algebra error calculating half the cost of one sandwich, plus the tip. **(D):** This is the total cost of the sandwiches and tip, but the question asks for the amount each person paid—in other words, half of this total cost.

How to check? Try an alternate approach above, and/or identify the mistakes the College Board wants you to make that would lead you to the wrong answers.

▶ Post-solution patterns (see page 218): right approach, wrong step

Test 4, Section 3, Question 13

- **What's the prompt asking for?** The value of k in the given scenario.
- **Math concepts in the prompt:** algebra, arithmetic, coordinate points, functions, graphing functions, intersecting in the xy-plane, opposites, word problems, x-intercepts
- **Math concepts in the diagram:** coordinate values, graphing functions, intersecting in the xy-plane, variables
- **Elements of the answer choices:** fractions, integers

- **Notable differences among answer choices:** All four choices form a series in which each choice is twice as much as the one before it. (B) and (D) are reciprocals.
- **Concepts in the answer choices:** fractions, reciprocals
- **Pre-solution patterns (see p. 217):** halves and doubles; the first and last terms in a series are often wrong answers
- **Things to look out for:** Don't make small mistakes in your algebra and arithmetic! Don't confuse x-intercepts and y-intercepts! Don't confuse x- and y-values in the diagram!

Solution 1: Algebra: Plug $y = 0$ into either equation to find the value of k that satisfies that equation.

$f(x) = 8x^2 - 2$	(first function)
$0 = 8x^2 - 2$	(plug in $y = 0$)
$2 = 8x^2$	(add 2 to both sides)
$\frac{1}{4} = x^2$	(divide both sides by 8)
$\frac{1}{2} = x$ or $-\frac{1}{2} = x$	(take square root of both sides)

Since the diagram is written so that k is positive, we can see that (B) is correct.

Solution 2: Backsolving: Take each answer choice and plug it into one of the given equations, along with $y = 0$; the correct answer will be the one that makes the equation valid.

For choice (A):

$f(x) = 8x^2 - 2$	(first function)
$0 = 8\left(\frac{1}{4}\right)^2 - 2$	(plug in $y = 0$ and $x = \frac{1}{4}$ from (A))
$0 = 8\left(\frac{1}{16}\right) - 2$	(simplify)
$0 = \frac{1}{2} - 2$	(simplify)
$0 = -\frac{3}{2}$	(simplify)

This isn't a valid statement, so (A) can't be correct. Now let's take a look at (B):

$$0 = 8\left(\frac{1}{2}\right)^2 - 2 \qquad \text{(plug in } y = 0 \text{ and } x = \frac{1}{2} \text{ from (B))}$$

$$0 = 8\left(\frac{1}{4}\right) - 2 \qquad \text{(simplify)}$$

$$0 = \frac{8}{4} - 2 \qquad \text{(simplify)}$$

$$0 = 0 \qquad \text{(simplify)}$$

This is a valid statement, so (B) is correct, assuming we haven't made any mistakes in our approach. As trained test-takers, we know that one of the best ways to be sure we haven't made any errors is to keep checking the rest of the choices. So let's try (C):

$$0 = 8(1)^2 - 2 \qquad \text{(plug in } y = 0 \text{ and } x = 1 \text{ from (C))}$$
$$0 = 8(1) - 2 \qquad \text{(simplify)}$$
$$0 = 6 \qquad \text{(simplify)}$$

This isn't a valid statement, so (C) can't be right. Finally, we'll test (D):

$$0 = 8(2)^2 - 2 \qquad \text{(plug in } y = 0 \text{ and } x = 2 \text{ from (D))}$$
$$0 = 8(4) - 2 \qquad \text{(simplify)}$$
$$0 = 30 \qquad \text{(simplify)}$$

This isn't a valid statement either, so (D) must be wrong. This means (B) is, indeed, correct.

ANSWER CHOICE ANALYSIS

(A): This is the value of k^2, not k. **(D):** This is the y-intercept of $g(x)$ and the absolute value of the y-intercept of $f(x)$.

How to check? Try an alternate approach above. Also, try to identify likely mistakes that would lead an untrained test-taker to a wrong answer.

Test 4, Section 3, Question 14

- **What's the prompt asking for?** The value of a when the expression in the prompt is in the form $a + bi$.
- **Math concepts in the prompt:** arithmetic, fractions, imaginary numbers
- **Elements of the answer choices:** fractions, integers
- **Notable differences among answer choices:** The number 3 appears as an integer in (C), and as the denominator in (B) and (D). 3 is also the difference between the numerators of (B) and (D).
- **Concepts in the answer choices:** fractions
- **"Bridge" concepts:** In order to convert the given expression to the $a + bi$ form, we need to find a way to get rid of the denominator in the given expression without changing the value of the given expression. We can do this by multiplying the numerator and denominator of the original fraction by a quantity that will result in a product fraction without an imaginary component in the denominator—in other words, we multiply the original fraction by a fraction whose numerator and denominator are both equal to the conjugate of the denominator of the original fraction. (See the solution below.)
- **Pre-solution patterns (see p. 217):** wrong answers try to imitate right answers
- **Things to look out for:** Don't make small mistakes in your arithmetic!

Solution 1: Conjugate: Multiply the given fraction by the fraction $\frac{3+2i}{3+2i}$ and then simplify.

$$\frac{8-i}{3-2i} \qquad \text{(given expression)}$$

$$\frac{8-i}{3-2i} \times \frac{3+2i}{3+2i} \qquad \text{(multiply by } \frac{3+2i}{3+2i} \text{)}$$

$$\frac{24+16i-3i-2i^2}{9-4i^2} \qquad \text{(FOIL)}$$

$$\frac{24+13i-2(-1)}{9-4(-1)} \qquad \text{(substitute } -1 \text{ for } i^2\text{)}$$

$$\frac{26+13i}{13} \qquad \text{(simplify)}$$

$$\frac{26}{13} + \frac{13i}{13} \qquad \text{(separate fractions with common denominators)}$$

$$2 + i \qquad \text{(reduce)}$$

We see the fraction in the prompt is equal to $2 + i$. The prompt asked for the value of the a term when we express $2 + i$ in the form $a + bi$; in this case, a corresponds to 2 in the value that we found, while b would be 1. Since the value of a is 2, (A) is correct.

(B): This would be the result if an untrained test-taker thought he could just delete the terms involving i. **(C):** This is the value of a from only the denominator in the prompt, rather than from an expression that's equivalent to the entire fraction.

How to check? Carefully re-check your reading and your calculations. Try to identify mistakes that an untrained test-taker might have made that would lead him to some of the wrong answers.

Test 4, Section 3, Question 15

- **What's the prompt asking for?** The solutions for x in the given quadratic equation.
- **Math concepts in the prompt:** constants, quadratic equations
- **Elements of the answer choices:** algebraic expressions, equations, exponents, fractions, negative numbers, radical expressions
- **Notable differences among answer choices:** (A) and (B) both begin with $\frac{k}{4}$, while (C) and (D) both begin with $\frac{k}{2}$. (A) and (C) both include the expression $2p$, while (B) and (D) both include the expression $32p$. The denominator of the second fraction in (C) is 2, while the denominator of the corresponding fraction in all the other choices is 4.
- **Concepts in the answer choices:** quadratic solutions
- **Pre-solution patterns (see p. 217):** wrong answers try to imitate right answers
- **Things to look out for:** Make sure you correctly determine whether the denominator under k should be 4 or 2! Make sure you correctly determine whether p should have a coefficient of 2 or 32!

Solution 1: Pure algebra: Convert the given equation into a quadratic equation, and then solve for x using the quadratic formula. Pick the answer choice that matches the expression you find.

$$x^2 - \frac{k}{2}x = 2p \qquad \text{(original equation)}$$

$$x^2 - \frac{k}{2}x - 2p = 0 \qquad \text{(subtract } 2p \text{ from both sides to set up an application of the quadratic formula)}$$

$$x = \frac{-(-\frac{k}{2}) \pm \sqrt{(-\frac{k}{2})^2 - 4(1)(-2p)}}{2(1)} \qquad \text{(insert } a = 1, b = -\frac{k}{2}, \text{ and } c = -2p \text{ into the quadratic formula)}$$

$$x = \frac{(\frac{k}{2}) \pm \sqrt{\frac{k^2}{4} + 8p}}{2} \qquad \text{(simplify)}$$

At this point, we may be starting to realize that our expression looks broadly similar to what we see in the answer choices, but it doesn't match exactly. One big difference between our expression and the answer choices is that our expression is all contained in only one fraction, while the choices all include two fractions. So let's address that issue first, and see where we stand after that:

$$x = \frac{(\frac{k}{2}) \pm \sqrt{\frac{k^2}{4} + 8p}}{2} \qquad \text{(our quadratic expression in one fraction)}$$

$$x = \frac{\frac{k}{2}}{2} \pm \frac{\sqrt{\frac{k^2}{4} + 8p}}{2} \qquad \text{(break the numerator into two fractions with a common denominator)}$$

$$x = \frac{k}{4} \pm \frac{\sqrt{\frac{k^2}{4} + 8p}}{2} \qquad \text{(simplify the first fraction by dividing } \frac{k}{2} \text{ by 2 to get } \frac{k}{4} \text{)}$$

Now our expression looks a bit more like the answer choices, but it's still a little bit different from them: our expression has $\frac{k^2}{4}$ in the second numerator, while every answer choice has k^2 in that position. We can address this issue by multiplying the numerator and denominator of the second fraction by an amount that will result in the k-related part of the expression being simply k^2. We might think at first that we need to multiply the second fraction by $\frac{4}{4}$ to get rid of the fraction in our k-term, but that would be ignoring the fact that the k-term is part of a radical expression. So, instead, we'll multiply the second fraction by $\frac{\sqrt{4}}{2}$! (Notice that this is the same as multiplying by 1, since $\sqrt{4}$ is equal to 2.) Multiplying by $\frac{\sqrt{4}}{2}$ will allow us to multiply everything under the radical in the second numerator by 4, and multiply the second denominator by 2 without changing the overall value of the expression. The result is $x = \frac{k}{4} \pm \frac{\sqrt{k^2+32p}}{4}$, which matches the expression in (B). So we can see that (B) is the correct answer.

How to check? Carefully re-check your work, and try to identify small mistakes that might lead an untrained test-taker to one of the wrong answers.

Test 4, Section 3, Question 16

- **What's the prompt asking for?** The maximum height of an object that can fit between the top shelf and the middle shelf in the diagram.
- **Math concepts in the prompt:** height, parallel lines, word problems
- **Math concepts in the diagram:** coefficients, labeled dimensions in a diagram, scale, triangles, variables

- **Things to look out for:** Don't make small mistakes in your trig, algebra, or arithmetic! Don't make the question harder than it is! Remember that there may not be a specific formula for many questions on the SAT Math section! Don't assume that the triangle needs to be equilateral—we know the diagram is drawn to scale, and the triangle looks equilateral, but it's probably possible to answer the question without assuming an equilateral triangle!

Solution 1: Geometry: Note that the side of one triangle is given in terms of x, and compare that length to the height of 18 inches to determine a height that corresponds to the $3x$ portion of the triangle's side between the top shelf and the middle shelf.

The entire length of the left side of the triangle is $x + 3x + 2x$, or $6x$. The maximum height of the bottle takes up as much vertical space as the $3x$ portion of the side of the triangle takes up. If the vertical space occupied by the $6x$ triangle side length is 18 inches, then a $3x$ portion of that side length must correspond to half of that vertical space, since $3x$ is half of $6x$. This would be a height of $\frac{18}{2}$ inches, or 9 inches. So 9 is the correct answer.

How to check? Carefully re-check your reading of the prompt and the diagram, along with your calculations.

Test 4, Section 3, Question 17

- **What's the prompt asking for?** The cosine of y degrees.
- **Math concepts in the prompt:** cosine, decimals, degrees, sine, triangles

- **Math concepts in the diagram:** right triangles
- **Things to look out for:** Don't confuse sine and cosine! Don't confuse x and y!

Solution 1: SOHCAHTOA: Assign relative lengths to the legs of the triangle, based on the given sine of x; use those lengths to determine the cosine of y.

We know from SOHCAHTOA that the sine is equal to $\frac{Opposite}{Hypotenuse}$. If the sine of $x°$ is 0.6, or $\frac{6}{10}$, then the ratio of the opposite side to the hypotenuse must be 6 to 10. We can add those values to the diagram:

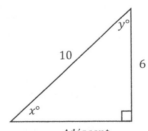

We also know from SOHCAHTOA that the cosine is equal to $\frac{Adjacent}{Hypotenuse}$. We see that the ratio of the length of the side adjacent to y to the length of the hypotenuse is $\frac{6}{10}$. So the answer is $\frac{6}{10}$, or 0.6.

Solution 2: Abstract trigonometry: Recognize that the cosine of y will be exactly the same fraction as the sine of x.

As we discussed in solution 1, we know from SOHCAHTOA that the sine of an angle is equal to the ratio $\frac{Opposite}{Hypotenuse}$, while the cosine of an angle is equal to the ratio of $\frac{Adjacent}{Hypotenuse}$; we also know that the side *opposite* x is also the side *adjacent* to y. This means that the value of the ratio for cosine y will be equal to the value of the ratio for sine x.

How to check? Try an alternate approach above.

Test 4, Section 3, Question 18

- **What's the prompt asking for?** A real value of x that makes the given equation true.
- **Math concepts in the prompt:** equations, real numbers, third-degree polynomials, zero

- **Things to look out for:** Don't make any small mistakes in your algebra or arithmetic!

Solution 1: Algebra: Factor the expression on the left-hand side, set the product of the factors equal to zero, and then find the real-number solution.

The first impulse for most test-takers who see this question will be to try to reverse-FOIL the expression on the left side of the equation. But test-takers who try that will find that it won't work for a variety of reasons. So we need to get creative when it comes to factoring this equation. Let's think—is there anything at all that we can factor out of the expression on the left?

We could try factoring out an x from the first three terms. Let's see where that gets us.

$$x^3 - 5x^2 + 2x - 10 = 0 \qquad \text{(given equation)}$$
$$x(x^2 - 5x + 2) - 10 = 0 \qquad \text{(factor an } x \text{ out of the first three terms)}$$

Well, that doesn't seem too helpful. We might try to reverse FOIL the expression in the parentheses, but that will end up being another dead end. Let's think of another way to factor the original expression.

We might notice that we can factor an x^2 out of the first two terms. We can also factor a 2 out of the last two terms:

$$x^3 - 5x^2 + 2x - 10 = 0 \qquad \text{(given equation)}$$
$$x^2(x - 5) + 2(x - 5) = 0 \qquad \text{(factor out } x^2 \text{ and 2)}$$

Now it looks like we're on to something, because we have two different terms, x^2 and 2, each multiplied by the same expression in parentheses, $(x - 5)$. At this point there are two ways that we can come up with the correct answer:

1. We can look at the equation we have and notice that when $(x - 5)$ is equal to 0, the whole expression is equal to 0, which means that $x = 5$ is a real-value solution.
2. The other way is to see that we can rewrite the expression above as the product of two polynomials, like this: $(x^2 + 2)(x - 5) = 0$. When we do that, we can see that the expression will equal 0 when $(x - 5)$ is equal to 0, which means again that $x = 5$ is the real-value solution to the equation.

(Notice that the expression will also be equal to 0 when $(x^2 + 2)$ is equal to 0, but that only happens when $x = \pm i\sqrt{2}$, which includes i and therefore is not a real value. The question asks for a real value, which means that only $x = 5$ is correct.)

Solution 2: Concrete: Test different values for x until you find a real value that satisfies the equation. Use the results from previous guesses to determine whether the next guess should be higher or lower.

A lot of test-takers might not feel comfortable trying to factor the expression in the prompt. As trained test-takers, when we look at the prompt, we note that the numbers in the expression are relatively small, and that two of them are factors of the third one; all of this suggests that it might be possible for us to guess-and-check our way to the value of x that satisfies the equation.

So let's try guessing $x = 1$ first, to see if that's correct. If it's not, we may be able to figure out whether we should guess higher or lower than 1 as a value of x:

$$x^3 - 5x^2 + 2x - 10 = 0 \qquad \text{(given equation)}$$
$$(1)^3 - 5(1)^2 + 2(1) - 10 = 0 \qquad \text{(plug in } x = 1)$$
$$-12 \neq 0 \qquad \text{(simplify)}$$

Okay, that didn't work. It looks like we need to try guessing with a larger number, because plugging in $x = 1$ left us in the position of having to subtract 10 from a number that was smaller than 10, which resulted in a negative value instead of the zero that we needed to make the equation valid. Since 2 is more than 1, we'll try guessing $x = 2$. Let's take a look at that:

$$x^3 - 5x^2 + 2x - 10 = 0 \qquad \text{(given equation)}$$
$$(2)^3 - 5(2)^2 + 2(2) - 10 = 0 \qquad \text{(plug in } x = 2)$$
$$8 - 20 + 4 - 10 = 0 \qquad \text{(simplify)}$$
$$-18 \neq 0 \qquad \text{(simplify)}$$

That didn't work, and it resulted in a value on the left-hand side of the equation that was even further from 0 than the result we got when we tried $x = 1$. So now what?

It may occur to us at this point that the last two terms in the expression on the left-hand side would add up to 0 if $x = 5$. With nothing else to try, I might as well consider making x be 5 and testing that:

$$x^3 - 5x^2 + 2x - 10 = 0 \qquad \text{(given equation)}$$
$$(5)^3 - 5(5)^2 + 2(5) - 10 = 0 \qquad \text{(plug in } x = 5)$$
$$125 - 125 + 10 - 10 = 0 \qquad \text{(simplify)}$$
$$0 = 0 \qquad \text{(simplify)}$$

So we can see that the equation in the prompt is valid when $x = 5$, which means 5 is the correct answer.

Solution 3: Test-smart: Remember that the College Board often leaves us with easier ways to approach questions if we pause to look for them. Notice that the last half of the left-hand expression is $2x - 10$, which is zero if $x = 5$; then, notice that the first half of the expression is $x^3 - 5x^2$, which is also zero if $x = 5$. Another way to notice this is to see that x^3 would be equal to $5x^2$, and $2x$ would be equal to 10, if x were equal to 5. So plugging in $x = 5$ makes the whole equation true. Since 5 is a real number, as the prompt requires, it must be the correct answer to the question.

How to check? Try an alternate approach above. Be especially careful not to make any small mistakes in your reading or your work!

Note Solving this question either requires us to notice something pretty quickly about the equation, or to play around with factoring for a while. If you encounter a question like this on test day, and you don't quickly come up with a good way to attack the question, then you should probably skip it and only return to it after answering the other questions in the section.

Test 4, Section 3, Question 19

- **What's the prompt asking for?** The value of x, given that (x, y) is a solution to the system of equations in the prompt.
- **Math concepts in the prompt:** algebra, arithmetic, coordinate values, systems of equations
- **Things to look out for:** Don't confuse x and y! Don't make small mistakes in your algebra and arithmetic!

Solution 1: Algebra (substitution): Define y in one equation in terms of x, then plug that definition in for y in the other equation and find x.

$$-3x + 4y = 20 \qquad \text{(first equation)}$$

$$4y = 3x + 20 \qquad \text{(add } 3x \text{ to both sides)}$$

$$y = \frac{3}{4}x + 5 \qquad \text{(divide both sides by 4 to define } y \text{ in terms of } x)$$

Now we can plug $y = \frac{3}{4}x + 5$ into the second equation and solve for x:

$$6x + 3y = 15 \qquad \text{(second equation)}$$

$$6x + 3(\tfrac{3}{4}x + 5) = 15 \qquad \text{(plug in } y = \tfrac{3}{4}x + 5)$$

$$6x + \frac{9}{4}x + 15 = 15 \qquad \text{(distribute the 3)}$$

$$6x + \frac{9}{4}x = 0 \qquad \text{(subtract 15 from both sides)}$$

So we can see that x must equal 0 for this equation to be valid. We don't need to find the corresponding y-value, because the question only asked for the x-value—which means the correct answer is 0.

Solution 2: Algebra (multiplication and addition): Multiply the top equation by -3 and the bottom equation by 4, and then add the equations together and divide through to solve for x.

Since the question asks us to solve for x, it might occur to us to try to add the equations together in a way that lets us cancel out the y-values. One way to do that would involve multiplying the top equation by -3, and the bottom equation by 4. That would give us the following equations, which we could then add together:

$$
\begin{aligned}
9x - 12y &= -60 \qquad &\text{(multiply both sides of the top equation by } -3) \\
+\ 24x + 12y &= 60 \qquad &\text{(multiply both sides of the bottom equation by 4)} \\
\hline
33x &= 0 \qquad &\text{(add both equations to eliminate } y\text{-terms)} \\
x &= 0 \qquad &\text{(divide both sides by 33)}
\end{aligned}
$$

So we can see that x must equal 0 for the (x, y) solution that makes both equations valid, which means the right answer is 0.

How to check? Try an alternate approach above, and/or plug your value for x back into both equations and make sure that the the y-value for both equations is the same.

Test 4, Section 3, Question 20

- **What's the prompt asking for?** The value of k in the situation described in the prompt.
- **Math concepts in the prompt:** arithmetic, constant rate, distance, negative numbers, temperature, word problems

- **Things to look out for:** Don't confuse the distances and temperatures in the prompt! Don't forget that the question is asking for a k-value that describes every 10-kilometer change in altitude, NOT every 1-kilometer change in altitude! Don't make any small mistakes in your algebra and arithmetic!

Solution 1: Algebra: Set up a ratio that compares the change in altitude to the change in temperature, and use that to determine k (remembering that k corresponds to a change in altitude of 10km, not 1km).

The distance between a layer of atmosphere 50 kilometers from Earth and a layer of atmosphere 80 kilometers from Earth is 30 kilometers, because $80 - 50 = 30$. If the temperature decreases by $k°$ every 10 kilometers, then the temperature will decrease by $3k$ over the space of 30 kilometers, because $\frac{30}{10} = 3$.

The prompt tells us that the temperature is $-5°C$ at 50 kilometers from Earth, and $-80°C$ at 80 kilometers from Earth. So the temperature difference is $-80 - (-5)$, or $-75°$ over 3 of those 10 kilometers stretches. That means the value of k is $\frac{75}{3}$, or 25, because the temperature decreases 25° for every 10 kilometers up from the Earth's surface we travel.

How to check? Carefully reconsider the prompt and your work. Remember you're looking for a constant to reflect a change of 10km, not 1km!

Note Remember that the question asks for the decrease in temperature, so there's no need to include a negative sign in your answer, because the wording of the question already indicates that the number in the answer is being subtracted. In other words, -25 is an INCORRECT answer for this question because a decrease of -25 would be the same thing as adding 25.

TEST 1 - SECTION 4

Test 1, Section 4, Question 1

- **What's the prompt asking for?** The interval where the graph is only increasing, then only decreasing.
- **Math concepts in the prompt:** decreasing values on a graph, increasing values on a graph
- **Math concepts in the diagram:** axis labels, decreasing slope, increasing slope, plotting values
- **Elements of the answer choices:** Each choice represents a range on the x-axis.

- **Concepts in the answer choices:** ranges on an axis or number line
- **"Bridge" concepts:** One of the ranges in the choices corresponds to a region of the graph where the value is increasing first, and then immediately decreasing.
- **Things to look out for:** Don't look at the wrong region of the graph when considering an answer choice! Don't get confused between increasing and decreasing!

Solution 1: Test-smart: Consider each choice, and choose the one with a region showing an increase, followed by a decrease.

A   shows an *increasing* heartrate followed by an *unchanging* heartrate.
B ✓   shows an *increasing* heartrate followed by a *decreasing* heartrate.
C   shows a *decreasing* heartrate followed by an *increasing* heartrate.
D   shows an *unchanging* heartrate followed by and *increasing* heartrate followed by an *unchanging* heartrate.
Only choice (B) provides what the question asks for, so (B) is correct.

Solution 2: Graph-first: Consider the graph and find a region where the value is increasing and then decreasing, then choose the answer choice that reflects that range.

The prompt asks us to find a part of the graph that shows the heartrate increasing and then decreasing. When we scan the graph from left to right, we can see that the only place on the graph where the rate is increasing and then immediately decreasing, with nothing else in the middle, is the kind of "mountain-peak" shape right in the middle of the graph. When we look at the part of the x-axis that's taken up by that peak, we see that it corresponds to the 40-to-60 minute interval, so we know (B) is correct.

ANSWER CHOICE ANALYSIS

(A): This range starts out showing an increasing heart rate, but after the increase, the heart rate doesn't increase or decrease. **(C):** This answer choice is there to trap test-takers who confuse the concepts of increasing and decreasing in the prompt.

How to check? Carefully re-work the question, keeping in mind the various ways that the prompt, diagram, and answer choices could be misread.

Test 1, Section 4, Question 2

- **What's the prompt asking for?** The value of y, given that $x = 5$.
- **Math concepts in the prompt:** algebra, multiplication, substitution, variables
- **Notable differences among answer choices:** (A) is the only single-digit number. (A) and (B) are the only multiples of 3. (B) and (C) are the only multiples of 5. (D) is the only prime number.

- **Concepts in the answer choices:** multiples of 3, multiples of 5
- **"Bridge" concepts:** We can use algebra to find k from the information in the prompt, and then use k to answer the question.
- **Things to look out for:** Don't confuse the various values of y and x! Don't accidentally stop working when you find the value of k!

Solution 1: Algebra: Use the information from the prompt to solve for k, then set up a new equation with the value of k, and with x equal to 5, and solve for y.

$$y = kx \quad \text{(equation from the prompt)}$$
$$24 = k(6) \quad \text{(plug in } y = 24 \text{ and } x = 6 \text{ from the prompt)}$$
$$4 = k \quad \text{(divide both sides by 6 to find } k)$$

Now let's use the value of k to find the value of y when $x = 5$:

$$y = kx \quad \text{(equation from the prompt)}$$
$$y = (4)(5) \quad \text{(plug in } k = 4 \text{ and } x = 5)$$
$$y = 20 \quad \text{(simplify)}$$

So we can see that (C) is correct.

Solution 2: Mental math: Observe that k must be 4, which means y must be 20 when x is 5.

Note that the College Board has given us relatively easy numbers to work with for this question—most test-takers can probably divide 24 by 6 in their heads to determine that k is 4, and then realize that 4×5 is 20, and the answer is (C). Of course, when you take this kind of mental approach to a question, you have to be extremely careful that you're not misreading or miscalculating!

ANSWER CHOICE ANALYSIS

(B): This choice might be tempting if we made an algebra mistake and thought that $k = 3$. **(D):** This choice is one less than the value of y when x was 6. It's probably here to trap test-takers who think that the value of y should be reduced by one unit (from 24 to 23) if the value of x is reduced by one unit (from 6 to 5).

How to check? Try an alternate approach above.

> **Note** Once you realize that $k = 4$, and that all of the answer choices are whole numbers, you can tell that the right answer must be a multiple of 4. Only choice (C) is a multiple of 4, so (C) must be correct.

Test 1, Section 4, Question 3

- **What's the prompt asking for?** The measure of angle 2 if angle 1 is 35 degrees.
- **Math concepts in the prompt:** angle measurements, parallel lines
- **Math concepts in the diagram:** parallel lines, supplementary angles, transversals, vertical angles
- **Elements of the answer choices:** three of the choices end in 5
- **Notable differences among answer choices:** Only (D) is greater than 90 degrees.

- **Concepts in the answer choices:** acute angles, complementary angles, congruent angles, obtuse angles, supplementary angles
- **"Bridge" concepts:** When we add the measure of angle 1 to the diagram, we can use our knowledge of angles to determine the size of angle 2.
- **Pre-solution patterns (see p. 217):** complements or supplements, halves and doubles
- **Things to look out for:** Don't get confused about which angle is indicated by the 2 on the diagram! Don't confuse supplementary and complementary angles!

Solution 1: Geometry: Use the diagram to determine that angle 2 must form a straight line with an angle the same size as angle 1, so angle 2 must have a measure of 145 degrees.

We can see from the diagram that angle 2 makes a straight line with another angle, and that other angle has the same size as angle 1. In other words, the measure of angle 2 and the measure of angle 1 add up to 180°. So the measure of angle 2 must be equal to 180° minus the measure of angle 1, or $180° - 35°$, or 145°.

Solution 2: Test-smart: Remember that the diagram is drawn to scale, and that angle 2 is clearly greater than 90°, and note that (D) is the only choice that's greater than 90°, so it must be correct.

ANSWER CHOICE ANALYSIS

(A): This choice might tempt an untrained test-taker if he thought angle 2 should be equal to angle 1 for some reason. **(B):** This choice is the complement of 35, rather than the supplement, for people who mistakenly think the two angles should add up to 90° instead of 180°. **(C):** This choice might be tempting if we thought that angle 2 should be twice as big as angle 1 for some reason.

How to check? Remember the diagram is drawn to scale. Visually confirm that 145 seems to be the only plausible size for angle 2.

▶ Post-solution patterns (see page 218): right answer to the wrong question

Test 1, Section 4, Question 4

- **What's the prompt asking for?** The value of $8x$.
- **Math concepts in the prompt:** addition, algebra, converting text to algebra
- **Elements of the answer choices:** All choices are even.
- **Notable differences among answer choices:** (A) and (B) are single-digit numbers. (C) and (D) are double-digit numbers.
- **Concepts in the answer choices:** Choice (C) is 10 more than choice (B), and the prompt talks about one number being 10 more than another number. (C) is 8 times as much as (A), which may reflect the $8x$ relationship in the prompt.
- **"Bridge" concepts:** We can translate the prompt into algebra and then transform the information we have into an equation that gives us the value of $8x$.
- **Things to look out for:** Don't confuse the value of $8x$ with the value of x!

Solution 1: Algebra: Convert the information from the prompt into an equation. Find x from that equation, and then find $8x$.

If $16 + 4x$ is 10 more than 14, then $16 + 4x$ must equal 24. We can use that information to solve for x, and then multiply the result by 8 to get $8x$:

$16 + 4x = 24$	(equation derived from the prompt)
$4x = 8$	(subtract 16 from both sides)
$x = 2$	(divide both sides by 4)
$8x = 16$	(multiply both sides by 8 to find $8x$)

So we can see that (C) is correct.

Solution 2: Algebra: Convert information from the prompt into an equation, then find $8x$ directly, without finding x first.

$16 + 4x = 24$	(equation derived from the prompt)
$4x = 8$	(subtract 16 from both sides)
$8x = 16$	(multiply both sides by 2 to find $8x$)

So, again, we see that (C) is correct.

Solution 3: Test-smart: Note that the prompt refers to the idea of $8x$, and that a lot of test-takers will make the mistake of finding x and forgetting what the question asked for. Consider the answer choices and see that (A) and (C) reflect this $8x$ relationship, and test $x = 2$ and $8x = 16$ to confirm that (C) is correct.

ANSWER CHOICE ANALYSIS

(A): This is the value of x, but the question asks for the value of $8x$. **(B):** This would be the value of x if we set $4x$ equal to 24 for some reason. **(D):** This would be the value of $8x$ if we thought x was equal to 10 for some reason.

How to check? Note the answer-choice patterns, and try an alternate approach above.

▶ Post-solution patterns (see page 218): right approach, wrong step

Test 1, Section 4, Question 5

- **What's the prompt asking for?** The graph that shows a strong negative association between d and t.
- **Math concepts in the prompt:** data analysis, negative associations, strength of associations
- **Notable differences among answer choices:** The points in (A) and (D) both generally slope down from left to right. (A) has a wider band of points than the other choices. (B) is the only one whose points form a generally horizontal band. (C) is the only one whose points generally slope upward.
- **Concepts in the answer choices:** negative slope, positive slope, strength of associations, zero-slope
- **Pre-solution patterns (see p. 217):** wrong answers try to imitate right answers
- **Things to look out for:** Make sure to check every answer choice before committing!

Solution 1: Data analysis: Consider each choice to see which one shows the "strong negative association" required in the prompt.

As trained test-takers, we know that a "negative association" between two variables means that one variable decreases while the other increases. This would result in a negative slope if the variables were plotted against each other in the xy-coordinate plane. Only choice (D) shows data with a clearly negative slope, so (D) is correct.

(A): This graph shows a weak negative association. **(B):** This graph shows a weak positive association. **(C):** This graph shows a strong positive association.

How to check? Re-read the prompt and the choices carefully to make sure (D) is right.

Test 1, Section 4, Question 6

- **What's the prompt asking for?** The number of 1mg doses in 2 decagrams.
- **Math concepts in the prompt:** converting units, word problems
- **Math concepts in the diagram:** grams in a decagram, milligrams in a gram
- **Elements of the answer choices:** All of the choices involve the digit 2 and at least two zeros.
- **Notable differences among answer choices:** Each choice has a different number of zeros. (A) is the only choice that's less than 1.

- **Concepts in the answer choices:** multiplying by powers of 10, dividing by powers of 10
- **"Bridge" concepts:** Unit conversion will allow us to convert from decagrams to milligrams.
- **Pre-solution patterns (see p. 217):** opposites; the first and last terms in a series are often wrong answers
- **Things to look out for:** Don't be off by a factor of 10! Don't convert in the wrong direction! Since milligrams are smaller than decagrams, the correct answer should be larger than 1.

Solution 1: Arithmetic: Use the information in the table to convert from decagrams to milligrams.

2 decagrams	(original expression of given amount)
20 grams	(multiply by 10 since 1 decagram $=$ 10 grams)
20,000 milligrams	(multiply by 1,000 since 1 gram $=$ 1,000 milligrams)

So (D) is correct.

Solution 2: Arithmetic: Use rough estimation to determine the necessary scale of the correct answer, and see if more than one answer choice is in that range. If only one choice is in that range, then it must be correct.

As soon as we realize that 1 gram is equal to a thousand milligrams, and that decagrams are bigger than grams, we know the answer must be more than 2,000, which means only (D) can be correct.

ANSWER CHOICE ANALYSIS

(A): This is the result of dividing 2 by 1000, which is something a test-taker might do if she didn't read the prompt carefully, and/or if she accidentally pressed the "divide" button on her calculator instead of the "multiply" button at some point. **(C):** This is the result of multiplying 2 by 1000, which might be tempting if an untrained test-taker accidentally forgot to account for the difference between decagrams and grams.

How to check? Try an alternate approach above. Also, re-read the prompt and the answer choices carefully to make sure you're not off by a factor of 10, 100, or 1000.

Note In this case, the correct answer was the last number in a series. As trained test-takers, we know that if we see a mathematical series in the answer choices, the right answer is likely not to be the first or last number in that series—but we also know this isn't a hard and fast *rule*. It's just a general tendency. Sometimes the correct answer will be the first or last number in a series! When that happens, we should re-check our work one last time to make sure the question really is breaking from the normal pattern.

Test 1, Section 4, Question 7

- **What's the prompt asking for?** An appropriate label for the vertical axis in the diagram.
- **Math concepts in the prompt:** addition, axis labels, bar graphs
- **Math concepts in the diagram:** reading bar graphs
- **Elements of the answer choices:** Each choice has the same phrase before the parentheses
- **Notable differences among answer choices:** Each has a different power of ten in a parenthetical expression.

- **Concepts in the answer choices:** powers of ten
- **"Bridge" concepts:** We can add the values indicated by the bars in the graph, compare them to the chart, and determine the correct answer.
- **Pre-solution patterns (see p. 217):** the first and last terms in a series are often wrong answers
- **Things to look out for:** Don't be off by a factor of 10! Don't add the values in the bar graph incorrectly!

Solution 1: Data: Add the numbers in the chart; compare them to the information in the prompt to determine the appropriate label.

$9 + 5 + 6 + 4 + 3.5$	(values from each bar in the graph)
27.5	(simplify)

Now we divide the total number of installations by the number of units represented in the graph to find out how many installations each unit represents:

$$\frac{27,500}{27.5} = 1,000$$ (divide the number of installations by the total number of units on the graph, which is 27.5)

Each unit is equal to 1,000 installations, so (C) is correct.

Solution 2: Test-smart: Use mental math to determine whether any of the answer choices are much too large or much too small to make sense in the context of the question.

If (D) were right, then the first bar alone would count for 90,000 installations, which is far more than the prompt allows. We can also quickly rule out (B), because if (B) were right, the bars could only represent a few thousand installations, not 27,500. (A) must be wrong too, because the units in (A) are even smaller than the units in (B). This means (C) must be right.

How to check? Try an alternate approach above. Re-consider the question, being extra careful to make sure you've chosen the correct power of ten.

Test 1, Section 4, Question 8

- **What's the prompt asking for?** The value of n that satisfies the prompt.
- **Math concepts in the prompt:** absolute value, addition, algebra, subtraction, variables, zero
- **Notable differences among answer choices:** (A) and (B) are both integers with unique properties relative to the question. (A) and (B) are the only integers mentioned in the prompt. (C) is the only choice with an integer that's not in the prompt. (D) indicates that no other choice is correct.
- **Concepts in the answer choices:** logical impossibility, properties of 1, properties of zero

- **"Bridge" concepts:** This question wants us to think about the properties of absolute value, addition, and zero, which means we also need to consider the properties of negative and positive numbers.
- **Pre-solution patterns (see p. 217):** halves and doubles
- **Things to look out for:** Don't get confused on which parts of the expression are in the absolute value brackets! If you set up an equation, make sure to handle the absolute value brackets correctly!

Solution 1: Backsolve: Substitute each of the first three answer choices for n in the prompt, and see if any of them work.

For choice (A):

$\lvert n - 1 \rvert + 1 = 0$	(equation from the prompt)
$\lvert 0 - 1 \rvert + 1 = 0$	(plug in the value from (A))
$1 + 1 = 0$	(find absolute value)
$2 \neq 0$	(simplify)

We see that choice (A) can't be correct. Now, let's take a look at choice (B):

$\lvert 1 - 1 \rvert + 1 = 0$	(plug in the value from (B))
$0 + 1 = 0$	(find absolute value)
$1 \neq 0$	(simplify)

Choice (B) can't be right, either. Let's consider (C):

$\lvert 2 - 1 \rvert + 1 = 0$	(plug in the value from (C))
$1 + 1 = 0$	(find absolute value)
$2 \neq 0$	(simplify)

Choice (C) must also be wrong.

In this case, since (A), (B), and (C) aren't right, we know (D) must be correct—NOT because of any process of elimination, but because (D) specifically says that no value of n satisfies the equation, and we've just seen in our testing that this is true.

Solution 2: Algebraic: Set up an equation based on the prompt, and solve for n.

$\lvert n - 1 \rvert + 1 = 0$	(equation from the prompt)
$\lvert n - 1 \rvert = -1$	(subtract 1 from both sides)

No value of n can satisfy this equation, because an absolute value can never be negative, so (D) must be correct.

Solution 3: Abstract: Consider the properties of absolute value and zero, and figure out what kind of absolute value can be added to 1 to produce zero.

We can't add a positive number to an absolute value expression and get 0, because an absolute value expression can never be negative. So, again, (D) must be correct.

ANSWER CHOICE ANALYSIS

(A): This choice might be tempting if we thought that $|0 - 1|$ was equal to -1 instead of 1. **(B):** This choice might be tempting if we forgot to add 1 to $|1 - 1|$. **(C):** This choice might be tempting if we thought absolute values were negative instead of positive.

How to check? Try one of the alternate approaches above, being sure to read carefully and think closely about the properties of the concepts in the question.

Test 1, Section 4, Question 9

- **What's the prompt asking for?** An equation that defines t in terms of a
- **Math concepts in the prompt:** addition, algebraic modeling, defining variables, multiplication, variables
- **Elements of the answer choices:** Every answer choice is an equation that defines t in terms of a fraction that includes a.
- **Notable differences among answer choices:** (A) is the only choice that involves subtracting 1,052 from a. (A), (B), and (C) all have a denominator of 1.08, while (D) has a denominator of $a + 1{,}052$. (C) is the only choice that involves subtracting a from 1,052. (B) and (D) are the only choices

that involve adding a to 1,052. (B) and (D) are reciprocals of each other.
- **Concepts in the answer choices:** addition, fractions, reciprocals, subtraction
- **"Bridge" concepts:** Algebraic transformation of the formula in the prompt will allow us to isolate t.
- **Pre-solution patterns (see p. 217):** wrong answers try to imitate right answers
- **Things to look out for:** Don't make mistakes with addition and subtraction in your algebra! Don't make mistakes with multiplication and division in your algebra!

Solution 1: Algebra: Use algebra to isolate t in the equation in the prompt.

$$a = 1052 + 1.08t \qquad \text{(formula for speed of sound, from the prompt)}$$

$$a - 1052 = 1.08t \qquad \text{(subtract 1,052 from both sides)}$$

$$\frac{a - 1052}{1.08} = t \qquad \text{(divide both sides by 1.08)}$$

So we can see that (A) is right.

Solution 2: Concrete: Assign a value to t in the prompt and find the corresponding value of a. Then use those two values to test all the expressions in the answer choices.

Let $t = 5$, as an arbitrary value for testing purposes.

$$a = 1052 + 1.08t \qquad \text{(formula for speed of sound, from the prompt)}$$
$$a = 1052 + 1.08(5) \qquad \text{(plug in } t = 5\text{)}$$
$$a = 1057.4 \qquad \text{(simplify to find } a \text{ when } t = 5\text{)}$$

Now let's plug $a = 1057.4$ into the equations in the answer choices to see which one gives us a t-value of 5.

$$t = \frac{a - 1052}{1.08} \qquad \text{(equation from (A))}$$

$$t = \frac{1057.4 - 1052}{1.08} \qquad \text{(plug in } a = 1057.4\text{)}$$

$$t = 5 \qquad \text{(simplify)}$$

When we plug $a = 1057.4$ into the equation from (A), we get $t = 5$, which matches our arbitrary testing value of $t = 5$. So choice (A) is correct, assuming we haven't made any small mistakes in our approach. As trained test-takers, we know that checking all the answer choices is usually the best way to make sure we haven't made any small mistakes, so let's keep going through the other choices. We'll check (B) next:

$$t = \frac{a + 1052}{1.08} \qquad \text{(equation from (B))}$$

$$t = \frac{1057.4 + 1052}{1.08} \qquad \text{(plug in } a = 1057.4\text{)}$$

$$t \approx 1953.15 \qquad \text{(simplify)}$$

When we plug $a = 1057.4$ into the equation from (B), we get $t \approx 1953.15$. So choice (B) is incorrect. Now let's check (C):

$$t = \frac{1052 - a}{1.08} \qquad \text{(equation from (C))}$$

$$t = \frac{1052 - 1057.4}{1.08} \qquad \text{(plug in } a = 1057.4\text{)}$$

$$t = -5 \qquad \text{(simplify)}$$

When we plug $a = 1057.4$ into the equation from (C), we get $t = -5$, which is the opposite of our arbitrary testing value of $t = 5$. So choice (C) is wrong, too. Now, let's take a look at (D):

$$t = \frac{1.08}{a+1052} \qquad \text{(equation from (D))}$$

$$t = \frac{1.08}{1057.4+1052} \qquad \text{(plug in } a = 1057.4\text{)}$$

$$t \approx 0.000512 \qquad \text{(simplify)}$$

When we plug $a = 1057.4$ into (D), we get $t \approx 0.000512$. So (D) is wrong, and we can see that (A) is, indeed, right.

Solution 3: Test-smart: Note that isolating t must involve subtracting 1,052 from both sides, and then pick the only choice that involves that idea.

When we consider isolating t in the equation $a = 1052 + 1.08t$, we should notice that the first step will be subtracting 1052 from both sides. That means we'd expect the answer to involve subtracting 1052. Only (A) involves subtracting 1052, so (A) is right.

ANSWER CHOICE ANALYSIS

(B): This choice might be tempting if we made an algebra mistake and added 1,052 instead of subtracting it. **(C):** This choice might be tempting if we made an algebra mistake and added 1,052 instead of subtracting it, and also got confused about the sign of a. **(D):** This is the reciprocal of the mistake in (B).

How to check? Try an alternate method above, and/or compare the details of each answer choice (minus signs, etc.) to the prompt.

▶ Post-solution patterns (see page 218): opposites

Test 1, Section 4, Question 10

- **What's the prompt asking for?** The temperature that comes "closest" to corresponding to a speed of 1,000 feet per second—in other words, the t-value that most nearly corresponds to an a-value of 1000.
- **Math concepts in the prompt:** addition, algebraic modeling, variables
- **Notable differences among answer choices:** (A), (B), and (D) form a series in which each choice is 2 more than the previous one. (B), (C), and (D) form a series in which each choice is 1 more than the previous one. (C) is the only choice that's odd.

- **Concepts in the answer choices:** series
- **"Bridge" concepts:** Some value for t in the prompt corresponds to an a-value of 1000. We'll need to test the function in some way to find that t-value.
- **Pre-solution patterns (see p. 217):** the first and last terms in a series are often wrong answers
- **Things to look out for:** Don't confuse t and a! If you test values, make sure you test all of them!

Solution 1: Graphing: Use a calculator to graph the function from the prompt, and then use the trace function to see which input corresponds to the output that's closest to 1000.

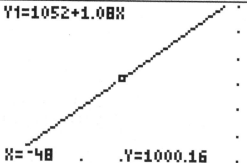

So we can see that x is -48 when y is basically 1000, which means (B) is correct. (Don't be put off by the small decimal difference in the y-value from this example. The important thing to realize is that when we get the tracing cursor as close to $y = 1000$ as possible, the x-value is clearly "closest" to -48, so we can see that (B) is right.

Solution 2: Backsolving: Use a calculator to test each answer choice in the function from the prompt. The choice that produces an a-value "closest to 1000" (as the prompt says) is the correct answer.

For choice (A):

$$a = 1052 + 1.08t \qquad \text{(formula from the prompt)}$$
$$a = 1052 + 1.08(-46) \qquad \text{(plug in } t\text{-value from (A))}$$
$$a = 1002.32 \qquad \text{(solve with calculator)}$$

This value isn't equal to our target value of $a = 1000$. It's somewhat close to 1000, but other choices might be closer, so let's check the rest of them, starting with (B):

$$a = 1052 + 1.08t \qquad \text{(formula from the prompt)}$$
$$a = 1052 + 1.08(-48) \qquad \text{(plug in } t\text{-value from (B))}$$
$$a = 1000.16 \qquad \text{(solve with calculator)}$$

This value is pretty close to 1000—definitely closer than the value we got from (A). Let's check (C) next:

$$a = 1052 + 1.08t \qquad \text{(formula from the prompt)}$$
$$a = 1052 + 1.08(-49) \qquad \text{(plug in } t\text{-value from (C))}$$
$$a = 999.08 \qquad \text{(solve with calculator)}$$

This a-value is also pretty close to 1000, but not as close as the a-value we found for (B). Let's finish our testing by checking (D):

$$a = 1052 + 1.08t \qquad \text{(formula from the prompt)}$$
$$a = 1052 + 1.08(-50) \qquad \text{(plug in } t\text{-value from (D))}$$
$$a = 998 \qquad \text{(solve with calculator)}$$

When we compare the choices, we see that the value from (B) gives us a speed closest to 1,000 feet per second, so (B) is right.

Solution 3: Algebra: Set a equal to 1,000, then solve for t. The choice that is closest to the resulting t-value is the correct answer.

$$a = 1,052 + 1.08t \qquad \text{(given formula)}$$
$$1,000 = 1,052 + 1.08t \qquad \text{(plug in } a = 1,000)$$
$$-52 = 1.08t \qquad \text{(subtract 1,052 from both sides)}$$
$$-48.148 \approx t \qquad \text{(divide both sides by 1.08)}$$

The resulting t-value is closest to $-48°F$ from choice (B), so (B) is correct.

How to check? Try an alternate approach above.

Note   Any of the wrong answer choices might have been tempting if we made a mistake reading the graph on our calculator or entering values into our calculator.

Test 1, Section 4, Question 11

- **What's the prompt asking for?** An answer choice that doesn't satisfy the inequality in the prompt.
- **Math concepts in the prompt:** inequalities, multiplication, subtraction, variables
- **Notable differences among answer choices:** (A), (B), and (C) form a series in which each choice is one less than the choice before. (A) and (B) have numbers that aren't present in the inequality from the prompt, while (C) and (D) have numbers present in that inequality.
- **Concepts in the answer choices:** negative numbers, series
- **Pre-solution patterns (see p. 217):** the first and last terms in a series are often wrong answers
- **Things to look out for:** Don't accidentally mark an answer that IS a valid solution to the inequality! Don't make a mistake with the inequality sign!

Solution 1: Algebra: Isolate x in the inequality, then mark the answer choice that falls outside the range of x you've identified.

$$3x - 5 \geq 4x - 3 \qquad \text{(inequality from question)}$$
$$3x - 2 \geq 4x \qquad \text{(add 3 to both sides)}$$
$$-2 \geq x \qquad \text{(subtract } 3x \text{ from both sides)}$$

We can see that any number less than or equal to -2 is valid for the equation. Only -1 falls outside of this range, so (A) is correct.

Solution 2: Backsolving: Test each choice in the inequality and select the choice that's NOT a valid solution for the inequality.

For choice (A):

$$3x - 5 \geq 4x - 3 \qquad \text{(inequality from the prompt)}$$
$$3(-1) - 5 \geq 4(-1) - 3 \qquad \text{(plug in } -1 \text{ from (A))}$$
$$-8 \geq -7 \qquad \text{(simplify)}$$

This is an untrue statement, so the value in (A) doesn't satisfy the inequality, which means (A) is correct, assuming we haven't made any mistakes in our approach. As trained test-takers, we know that one of the best ways to make sure we haven't made a mistake in our backsolving is to backsolve every single answer choice—and this is especially true for a question like this, in which more than one choice should actually satisfy the inequality in the prompt! So let's continue, and take a look at choice (B):

$$3x - 5 \geq 4x - 3 \qquad \text{(inequality from the prompt)}$$
$$3(-2) - 5 \geq 4(-2) - 3 \qquad \text{(plug in } -2 \text{ from (B))}$$
$$-11 \geq -11 \qquad \text{(simplify)}$$

This is a true statement, so the value in (B) satisfies the inequality...which means (B) is WRONG, because the prompt asked for an answer choice that's NOT valid in the inequality. Now, let's try (C):

$$3x - 5 \geq 4x - 3 \qquad \text{(inequality from the prompt)}$$
$$3(-3) - 5 \geq 4(-3) - 3 \qquad \text{(plug in } -3 \text{ from (C))}$$
$$-14 \geq -15 \qquad \text{(simplify)}$$

Just as with (B), this is also a true statement, so (C) satisfies the inequality, which means (C) is wrong. Finally, let's test (D):

$$3x - 5 \geq 4x - 3 \qquad \text{(inequality from the prompt)}$$
$$3(-5) - 5 \geq 4(-5) - 3 \qquad \text{(plug in } -5 \text{ from (D))}$$
$$-20 \geq -23 \qquad \text{(simplify)}$$

This is a true statement, so the value in (D) satisfies the inequality, which means (D) is wrong. So we see that (A) is, indeed, right.

How to check? Try an alternate approach above.

Test 1, Section 4, Question 12

- **What's the prompt asking for?** The integer value that's closest to the average number of seeds from the chart.
- **Math concepts in the prompt:** arithmetic mean, histogram
- **Math concepts in the diagram:** bar graph, horizontal axis, vertical axis

- **Elements of the answer choices:** The answer choices form a series from 4 through 7.
- **Pre-solution patterns (see p. 217):** the first and last terms in a series are often wrong answers

Solution 1: Concrete: Determine the total number of seeds and the total number of apples. Use those numbers to find the average.

To find the average number of seeds per apple, we divide the total number of seeds by the total number of apples. We know there are 12 apples, because the title on the histogram says so. Now, let's find out how many seeds there are.

The chart tells us that 2 apples have 3 seeds, 4 apples have 5 seeds, 1 apple has 6 seeds, 2 apples have 7 seeds, and 3 apples have 9 seeds. If we add all of that up, we get this: $(2 \times 3) + (4 \times 5) + (1 \times 6) + (2 \times 7) + (3 \times 9) = 73$. There are 73 seeds and 12 apples, so the average number of seeds per apple is $\frac{73}{12}$, or approximately 6.1. So (C) is correct, since the prompt asked us to pick the answer choice that's "closest" to the average.

ANSWER CHOICE ANALYSIS

(A): This is the number of apples in the group with the most apples (apples with five seeds). **(B):** This is the number of seeds in each apple in the group with the most apples (apples with five seeds).

How to check? Carefully re-consider the histogram and make sure 6 makes sense as the average of the data.

Test 1, Section 4, Question 13

- **What's the prompt asking for?** The category that accounts for roughly 19% of the respondents.
- **Math concepts in the prompt:** percentages, reading diagrams
- **Math concepts in the diagram:** tabulated data
- **Elements of the answer choices:** (A) and (B) mention females. (C) and (D) mention males. (A) and (C) mention geometry. Only (B) mentions Algebra II. Only (D) mentions Algebra I.

- **Concepts in the answer choices:** reading from a table
- **"Bridge" concepts:** Carefully reading the table will let us find the category accounting for roughly 19% of the total.
- **Pre-solution patterns (see p. 217):** wrong answers try to imitate right answers
- **Things to look out for:** Don't misread the table! Don't make a mistake when you calculate the percentages!

Solution 1: Data: Determine the percentages of respondents represented in each category mentioned in an answer choice. Mark the answer choice that reflects the category representing roughly 19% of the respondents. (Notice that we only have to check values that appear in the answer choices because one of the answer choices must be correct.)

To find what percent of the total respondents belongs to a given category, we take the value of that category and divide it by the total number of respondents, which is 310 (we know 310 is the total number of respondents because it appears in the bottom-right-hand cell of the table from the prompt, in a position that indicates that 310 is both the total when the male and female students are added together, and the total when the students in each math class are added together). When we calculate those percentages, we get:

	Algebra I	Geometry	Algebra II	Total
Female		$\frac{53}{310} \approx 17\%$	$\frac{62}{310} = 20\%$	150
Male	$\frac{44}{310} \approx 14\%$	$\frac{59}{310} \approx 19\%$		160
Total				310

We can see that males taking Geometry account for approximately 19 percent of all survey respondents, so (C) is correct.

Solution 2: Percentage: Calculate 19% of 310. Mark the choice corresponding to the appropriate category according to the table.

The total number of respondents is 310. 19% of 310 is 310×0.19, or 58.9. The category with the number of students closest to 58.9 is males taking geometry, which has 59 students. We can confirm that $\frac{59}{310} \approx 19\%$, so (C) is correct.

ANSWER CHOICE ANALYSIS

(A): This choice features the right math course but the wrong gender. **(B):** This category accounts for 20% of survey respondents, which is close to 19%, and might tempt untrained test-takers who tried to estimate, but then didn't notice that the right answer should be *less than* 62, because the estimation that leads to 62 is based on deliberately rounding up the percentage of 310 that the prompt asks for. **(D):** This choice features the right gender but the wrong math course.

How to check? Try an alternate approach from above, making sure not to read the wrong column or row of data.

Test 1, Section 4, Question 14

- **What's the prompt asking for?** The choice that indicates the aspect of the data that will be changed the most if the 24-inch measurement is discarded.
- **Math concepts in the prompt:** mean, median, range, reading tables
- **Math concepts in the diagram:** data points
- **Notable differences among answer choices:** (A), (B), and (C) are aspects of the data, while (D) indicates that all three aspects will change to the same extent. (A) and (B) are types of averages, while (C) isn't.
- **Concepts in the answer choices:** mean, median, range
- **"Bridge" concepts:** A single outlier will potentially impact different aspects of a data-set to different extents; we need to determine which aspect is affected the most in this case.
- **Things to look out for:** If you add up all the values in the table, make sure not to make a calculation mistake! Don't confuse mean, median, and/or range!

Solution 1: Concrete: Consider the data once with the 24-inch measurement and once without that measurement, then determine which aspect of the data changes the most without the measurement.

The following calculation gives the mean length (which could also be called the "average" length) if we include the 24-inch fish:

$$\frac{8 + 9 + 9 + 9 + 10 + 10 + 11 + 11 + 12 + 12 + 12 + 12 + 13 + 13 + 13 + 14 + 14 + 15 + 15 + 16 + 24}{21} \approx 12.5$$

(Again, the above is the result when we divide the sum of all the lengths by the number of lengths.)

The median is the number in the middle when the values are listed from least to greatest. In 21 measurements, the 11th measurement is the one in the middle. In this case, the 11th measurement is 12 inches, so the median is 12 when the 24-inch fish is still considered.

The range is the difference between the largest number and the smallest number in the dataset. In this case, the range is $24 - 8$, or 16.

Now let's do the same calculations with the 24-inch measurement removed. Here's the mean of those lengths, which we get by dividing the sum of all the remaining lengths by the number of remaining lengths:

$$\frac{8 + 9 + 9 + 9 + 10 + 10 + 11 + 11 + 12 + 12 + 12 + 12 + 13 + 13 + 13 + 14 + 14 + 15 + 15 + 16}{20} = 11.9$$

When there are an even number of values in a dataset, the median is the average of the two numbers in the middle. In a list of 20 measurements, the 10th and 11th measurements are the ones in the middle. In this case, the 10th and 11th both have values of 12, so their average is 12, which means the median is 12 when we don't consider the 24-inch fish.

Without the 24-inch measurement, the range of the dataset is $16 - 8$, or 8.

So here are the mean, median, and range, both with and without the 24-inch measurement included:

	With 24-inch measurement	Without 24-inch measurement
Mean	12.5	11.9
Median	12	12
Range	16	8

(Of course, you don't need to make this table for yourself. I'm just putting it in here to help present what we've found.)

We can see that the biggest change is in the range, so (C) is the correct answer.

Solution 2: Abstract: Consider the properties of mean, median, and range, and determine which will be most affected by removing the 24-inch measurement.

Let's think about mean, median, and range. The mean of a group of numbers is the average—it's the result when we add up all the numbers and divide by the number of numbers. In a group of 21 numbers, where the average is roughly around 12 (which we can roughly guess from looking at the values in the chart), the impact of the 24-inch value won't be very large when we remove it, since 24 inches differs from the average by about 12 units, and the impact of that change of 12-or-so units is being divided across a set of 20 numbers. This means the impact of removing the number 24 from the set won't be very large—probably somewhere around a unit or less, since 12 divided by 20 is less than 1.

The median of a group of numbers is the number in the middle when those numbers are listed in order from least to greatest. Removing the largest number from the list will slightly shift the "middle" of the list toward the lower end of the list. In this case, the effect of the change is nothing, because several numbers in the middle of the dataset are 12, and removing the largest number from the original dataset ends up meaning that we average 12 and 12 to find the median, which is still 12.

The range is calculated using only two values: the biggest number in the dataset, and the smallest number. If the biggest number in the group is removed, then there can be a big impact on the range, especially if there's a big difference between the number being removed the next-largest number. In this case, the next-largest number in the set is 16, which is 8 less than the biggest number before we remove it; this means that removing the largest number from this set will have the effect of changing the range by a value of 8.

So we can see that the range will have the largest change when the 24-inch fish is removed.

Don't feel bad if this approach seems a little too conceptual to you! You could always use an approach more like solution 1. I went through this conceptual, abstract way of looking at the question to help you start to see that SAT Math questions can often be attacked in multiple ways, and many of the alternative ways will involve thinking in terms of abstract ideas.

How to check? Consider an alternate approach above.

Note Any of the wrong answers could have been tempting if we didn't have a clear understanding of mean, median, mode, and range. This question is a great example of an item with a lot of small details for an untrained test-taker to mess up, even though the math concepts involved are fairly simple. When we trained test-takers see a question like this, we know that we need to make sure we lock down the right answer as efficiently as possible, so we can take the time we save on this question and invest it in questions that are more challenging for us.

Test 1, Section 4, Question 15

- **What's the prompt asking for?** The significance of the C-intercept on the given graph.
- **Math concepts in the prompt:** axis intercepts
- **Math concepts in the diagram:** graphing in a plane
- **Notable differences among answer choices:** Each choice describes a different value that can potentially be determined from the graph.

- **Concepts in the answer choices:** reading a 2-dimensional graph, slope, y-intercept, function modeling
- **Things to look out for:** Make sure to read the answer choices and the graph carefully!

Solution 1: Backsolve: Consider the choices first, comparing each one to the graph to determine which one describes the role of the C-intercept in the graph.

(A) makes sense as the right answer to the question, because the C-intercept represents the idea that a customer is paying \$5 at $h = 0$, even before the boat is used, which is what an "initial cost" would be.

(B), on the other hand, doesn't make any sense, for several reasons. For one thing, nothing about the labels on the axes would indicate that a combination of information about those axes (which is what a coordinate point represents) should tell us anything about a number of boats, as (B) requires; all that any point can tell us is the cost at a particular time. More obviously, the title of the figure mentions "renting *a* boat" (emphasis mine), and the text underneath the figure also specifically says that the graph shows the cost of "renting *a* boat" (emphasis mine), which means the graph is only relevant to the idea of renting one single boat. So (B) makes no sense.

(C) can't be right, either, because it would mean the boat rental was 5 hours long, since the C-intercept is 5. But the h-axis of the graph clearly indicates that boats can be rented for any period of time from 0 to 5 hours, so this choice doesn't make sense.

And one way to tell that (D) must also be wrong is to figure out the hourly increase in cost and then compare that number to the value of the C-intercept. We can tell from the graph that the cost is \$8 after 1 hour, and \$11 after 2 hours, which means the hourly change in cost is \$3. \$3 isn't the value of the C-intercept, so (D) can't be right. So we can see that (A) must be correct.

Solution 2: Abstract: Consider the graph first, and then pick the answer choice that accurately describes the intercept.

The C-intercept is the point where the graph of the function crosses the C-axis. The label tells us that the C-axis represents the total cost in dollars of renting a boat. The h-axis represents the number of hours the boat is rented.

Where the graph crosses the C-axis, the h-value is 0, by definition. In other words, at the point represented by the C-intercept, the boat has been rented for zero hours, in a sense—but we can still see that this zero-hour cost of renting the boat is a number besides zero. In other words, from the instant that you start renting this boat—at zero hours of boat rental—you'll owe 5 dollars already, before you even start paying for any time spent in the boat.

So it makes sense to say that the C-intercept is the "initial cost" of renting the boat, as choice (A) indicates, because it's the cost a renter pays who hasn't spent any time in the boat yet.

(C): This choice might be tempting because the C-intercept is 5 and the horizontal axis, which shows how many hours the boat is rented, features values up to 5. **(D):** This choice describes the slope of the graph, not the C-intercept.

How to check? Try an alternate approach above, and/or identify the aspects of the graph reflected in each of the answer choices.

Note   Don't be thrown off by the way the College Board calls the vertical axis of the table the "C-axis" instead of the "y-axis." Remember that we can use any variables we want when we define a function or label a graph, but that the standard is to use the horizontal axis for the independent or "input" variable (time, in this case) and the vertical axis for the dependent or "output" variable (cost). If you felt that you needed to guess on this question, it would help to notice that the text in (A) uses the word "initial," which refers to the beginning of something, and seems especially appropriate here because the C-intercept is the "start" of the data if we read the graph from left to right. (This isn't a coincidence, of course—the intercept represents the initial cost because it tells us the cost when $h = 0$.) See "The Effects of Variables, Coefficients, and Constants on Function Models" on page 207 of this Black Book for more on these concepts.

Test 1, Section 4, Question 16

- **What's the prompt asking for?** The relationship between h and C
- **Math concepts in the prompt:** functions with 2 variables, relationship between variables
- **Math concepts in the diagram:** axes with different labeling frequencies, graphing in a plane
- **Notable differences among answer choices:** (A), (B), and (C) all begin with C, while (D) begins with h. (A), (B), and (C) all include 5, while (D) doesn't. (B) is the only choice that involves the number 4. (B), (C), and (D) all involve the number 3. (B) is the only choice with a fraction. (B) and (C) both involve adding 5, while (A) and (D) don't.

- **Concepts in the answer choices:** addition, fractions, slope, variables, y-intercept
- **"Bridge" concepts:** The arrangement of points on the graph can be compared to the equations in the answer choices to see which choice would generate the graph.
- **Pre-solution patterns (see p. 217):** wrong answers try to imitate right answers; opposites
- **Things to look out for:** Don't confuse C and h! Don't misread the labeling on the graph! If you graph the answer choices, make sure you check them all! Don't forget that the spacing between the units is different on the two axes!

Solution 1: Backsolve: Compare each answer choice to the graph and see which one fits every aspect of the graph.

(A) would have a point at $(0, 0)$, but the graph doesn't have a point at $(0, 0)$, so this choice can't be right.

(B) would have a slope of $\frac{3}{4}$. But for every 3 units the line travels up, it only travels 1 unit across, which means the slope is 3, not $\frac{3}{4}$. (This choice might be tempting if an untrained test-taker failed to read the scale of the graph carefully.)

(C) has a slope of 3, which matches the graph, because for every 3 units the line travels up the C-axis, the line travels 1 unit across the h-axis. (C) also has a C-intercept at $(0, 5)$, which is reflected in the graph as well. So we can see this choice is correct. But, as trained test-takers, we should always be in the habit of considering every answer choice to help us make sure we haven't made a small mistake. So let's take a look at (D).

(D) would have a point at $(0, 0)$, just like (A) would. But the graph doesn't have a point at $(0, 0)$, so both (A) and (D) must be wrong, and we can confirm that (C) is correct.

Solution 2: Graphing / Backsolving: Graph each answer choice and see which one matches the graph in the question.

Since we're graphing the equations in these answer choices for the purpose of comparing them, we have to make sure that we've set up the units on our axes to reflect the scale of the axes in the graph from the question. This means that every tick-mark on the vertical graph should be 1 unit, while 1 unit on the horizontal axis should be four tick-marks across, just like in the SAT's graph. When we set the axes like that, the graph of (A) looks like this:

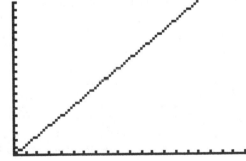

Since this graph doesn't have the same y-intercept or slope as the graph in the question, we know (A) must be wrong. Now, let's take a look at the graph for (B):

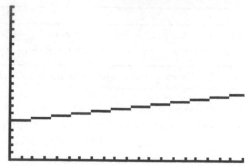

This graph has the same intercept on the vertical axis as the graph from the question does, but the slope doesn't match the graph from the question when we pay attention to the units on the axes. Here's what the graph from (C) looks like on our calculator:

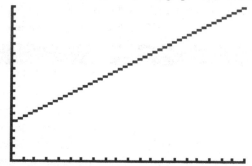

This graph has the same intercept on the vertical axis as the graph in the question does. The slope of this graph also matches the slope of the graph in the question. So (C) is the correct answer, assuming that we haven't made any mistakes. Let's check (D) next, to help make sure we haven't made any mistakes:

This graph clearly has a different slope and different intercept-point on the vertical axis from what we see in the graph from the question, so (D) must be wrong. So we know that (C) must be correct.

Solution 3: Abstract: Observe the key aspects of the graph (slope and intercept) and pick the choice that reflects them accurately.

The slope of the graph is the "rise" over the "run," by definition—in other words, the slope can be expressed as a fraction whose numerator is the vertical separation between two points, and whose denominator is the horizontal separation between those two points. So we can find the slope of this graph by comparing the vertical and horizontal separations of two points from the graph.

We can see that one clearly labeled point on the graph is at $(0, 5)$ and another is at $(1, 8)$. The rise between those two points is the difference between their C values, which is $8 - 5$, or 3. The run between those two points is the difference between their h values, which is $1 - 0$, or 1. So the rise over run is $\frac{3}{1}$, or 3, which means the slope of the line is 3.

The C-intercept is the point where the function crosses the C-axis. We can see that the function crosses the C-axis at $(0, 5)$.

Using the slope-intercept format for a line (also known as the $y = mx + b$ format), we can plug in 3 for m and 5 for b, since m represents the slope of a line, and b represents the intercept of the vertical axis. This gives us $y = 3x + 5$.

But in the graph in the question, the vertical axis is the C-axis, and the horizontal axis is the h-axis, so we'd need to substitute C for y, and h for x, in order to get our equation to resemble the answer choices. That gives us $C = 3h + 5$, so (C) is correct.

Solution 4: Slope: Since each choice has a unique slope, determine the slope in the graph and pick the choice that matches it.

As we mentioned in solution 1, the slope of the graph in the question is 3 (see solution 3 above for details if you'd like).

Only (C) has a slope of 3, so (C) must be right. (Choice (D) might appear to have a slope of 3 at first, but we have to remember that the slope-intercept format requires the variable for the vertical axis to be isolated on one side of the equation, so we have to put that equation in terms of C. When we do that, we get $C = \frac{1}{3}h$, and we see that the slope of the line in (D) is $\frac{1}{3}$.)

ANSWER CHOICE ANALYSIS

(A): This choice might be tempting if mix up the C-intercept and the slope, and somehow combine them into one term. **(B):** This choice might be tempting if we don't realize that 4 horizontal units on the graph correspond to 1 hour, not 4 hours. **(D):** This choice might be tempting if we confuse h with C and forget to account for the C intercept.

How to check? Try an alternate method above.

▶ Post-solution patterns (see page 218): opposites

Test 1, Section 4, Question 17

- **What's the prompt asking for?** The x-value that corresponds to the lowest y-value on the graph.
- **Math concepts in the prompt:** minimum of a graph, reading a function graph
- **Math concepts in the diagram:** graphing a function, scale
- **Notable differences among answer choices:** (A), (B), and (C) are all negative, while (D) is positive. (B) and (D) are opposites.

- **Concepts in the answer choices:** negative numbers
- **"Bridge" concepts:** The minimum is the lowest point on the function; since it is a point, it must have an x-value and y-value associated with it.
- **Pre-solution patterns (see p. 217):** wrong answers try to imitate right answers; opposites
- **Things to look out for:** Don't confuse x- and y-values!

Solution 1: Graph-first: Look at the graph, identify the minimum, and choose the x-value that corresponds to the minimum.

We can see that the lowest point on the graph is the point near the bottom left. If we count carefully from the origin, we can see that the x-value for that minimum point is at $x = -3$. (We can tell that each square in the grid of this graph is 1 unit wide and 1 unit tall because of the labels at $(0, 1)$ and $(1, 0)$.) So (B) is right.

Solution 2: Choices-first: Look at the answer choices, and then find the y-values that correspond to each, and mark the choice that corresponds to the lowest y-value.

A   at $x = -5$, the y-value is 2.
B ✓ at $x = -3$, the y-value is -2.
C   at $x = -2$, the y-value is around -0.5.
D   at $x = 3$, the y-value is 5.

So the choice with the lowest y-value is (B), which means (B) is correct.

ANSWER CHOICE ANALYSIS

(A): This is the lowest x-value on the graph. **(C):** This wrong answer is the y-value of the minimum, but the question asked for its x-value. This is exactly the kind of wrong answer that often trips up a test-taker who doesn't pay close enough attention to a question. **(D):** This is the opposite of the correct answer, which is a common pattern for the College Board to use, as we've seen.

How to check? Try an alternate approach above.

▶ Post-solution patterns (see page 218): opposites; right answer to the wrong question

Note Many untrained test-takers will be put off by the strange appearance of this function, because they can't figure out an equation for it. But as trained test-takers, we need to realize that it isn't always necessary to know the equation for a function when we answer an SAT question about the function. Further, a trained test-taker would be able to predict that (B) was likely to be right just from seeing the answer choices: three of the four choices are negative, which would suggest that the correct answer is likely to be negative, and -3 is the only one of those choices that also has its opposite in the set of answer choices.

Test 1, Section 4, Question 18

- **What's the prompt asking for?** The answer choice that reflects the relationship between a and b, given that $(0, 0)$ is a valid (x, y) pair for both inequalities.
- **Math concepts in the prompt:** addition, inequalities, negative numbers, systems of algebraic statements
- **Notable differences among answer choices:** (A), (B), and (C) all include inequalities, while (D) is an equation. (C) has absolute value brackets, while the other choices don't. (D) involves a negative sign, while the other choices don't.

- **Concepts in the answer choices:** absolute value, inequalities, negative numbers, variables
- **"Bridge" concepts:** When we plug $(0, 0)$ into the statements from the prompt, we should be able to transform those statements algebraically and arrive at one of the answer choices.
- **Pre-solution patterns (see p. 217):** wrong answers try to imitate right answers
- **Things to look out for:** Don't confuse a and b! Don't make mistakes with the inequality signs!

Solution 1: Picking numbers: Plug in $x = 0$ and $y = 0$ from the prompt, and then pick arbitrary numbers for a and b that make both statements true; see which choice reflects those values.

When we plug in $(0, 0)$ from the prompt, we get these statements:

$$0 < a$$
$$0 > b$$

Now we can choose values for a and b that satisfy these inequalities, and then we can see which choice correctly describes the relationship between the numbers we pick for a and b.

If we make a equal to 5 and b equal to -3, then the above inequality statements are true. Now we can check the choices to see which one indicates a correct relationship between an a-value of 5 and a b-value of -3.

At this point, both (A) and (C) accurately describe the relationship between our a-value of 5 and our b-value of -3. So now what?

As trained test-takers, we know that these number-picking approaches can sometimes result in false positives, given the numbers that we've picked. In these situations, we need to pick new numbers that will only make it possible for one answer choice to be acceptable. Let's try to think of a way to do that.

The difference between the statements in (A) and (C) is related to absolute value, which refers to the distance of a particular number from 0 on the number line. When we randomly chose an a-value of 5 and b-value of -3, we ended up picking an arrangement where the absolute value of a was larger than the absolute value of b. So let's try to do something different this time around: let's try to pick an a-value with a smaller absolute value than the b-value.

What if we make a equal to 3, and b equal to -5? These values still work for a and b in the prompt, because a is still positive and b is still negative. And these values still make (A) correct. What about (C)? With these new numbers, we can see that the absolute value of a would NOT be greater than the absolute value of b, even though our a- and b-values still satisfy the prompt. That means (C) is wrong, and (A) is right.

Solution 2: Algebra: Plug in $x = 0$ and $y = 0$ in the statements in the prompt, and then combine the resulting expressions.

$y < -x + a$	(original inequalities)
$y > x + b$	
$0 < -0 + a$	(plug in $(0, 0)$ for each inequality)
$0 > 0 + b$	
$0 < a$	(simplify each inequality)
$0 > b$	

So we can see that a is greater than 0, and b is less than 0. If we want, we can combine these two relationships and write the following:

$$b < 0 < a$$

That means b must be less than a, which is also the same thing as saying that a must be greater than b. So (A) is right.

ANSWER CHOICE ANALYSIS

(B): This might be tempting if we make an algebra mistake or confuse a and b. **(C):** This relationship is true for some values of a and b, but not for all, so we can't say that it "must be true," as the prompt requires. **(D):** As with (C), this relationship *can* be true—for example, when b has the same absolute value as a—but we can't say it "must be true," as the prompt requires.

How to check? Try an alternate approach above.

▶ Post-solution patterns (see page 218): opposites

Test 1, Section 4, Question 19

- **What's the prompt asking for?** The number of salads sold
- **Math concepts in the prompt:** translating words into algebra, word problem
- **Notable differences among answer choices:** (B), (C), and (D) form a series where each choice is 6 more than the previous choice. (A) is noticeably lower than the other choices.
- **Concepts in the answer choices:** series

- **"Bridge" concepts:** If we translate the prompt into algebra, we can determine the numbers of salads and drinks that were sold.
- **Pre-solution patterns (see p. 217):** the first and last terms in a series are often wrong answers
- **Things to look out for:** Don't confuse salads and drinks!

Solution 1: Algebra: Translate the prompt into an algebraic expression and solve for the number of salads.

The question gives us information about the revenue from a lot of salads and drinks that were sold on a given day. Let's use the variable s to represent the number of salads sold, and d to represent the number of drinks sold.

The salads sell for "$6.50 each." We can represent the revenue from selling salads with the expression "$6.50s$," because each salad represents $6.50, and multiplying the price of each salad by the number of salads must give us the total revenue from salads. Similarly, drinks sell for "$2.00 each," so we can represent the revenue from drinks with the expression "$2.00d$," which multiplies the price of each drink by the number of drinks sold.

We know from the prompt that 209 total items were sold in one day, so the equation $s + d = 209$ indicates that 209 is the sum of the number of salads sold and the number of drinks sold.

We also know that the total revenue from the salads and drinks was $836.50, so we can represent the total revenue from both salads and drinks that day with the equation $6.50s + 2.00d = \$836.50$, which says that $836.50 is the sum of the revenue from salads and the revenue from drinks.

So now we have the following system of equations:

$$s + d = 209 \qquad \text{(this equation says the total number of things sold was 209)}$$
$$6.50s + 2.00d = \$836.50 \qquad \text{(this equation says the total revenue was \$836.50)}$$

The prompt asks us for the number of salads sold that day, which is represented by s.

The easiest way to find s in this case is probably to solve for d in one equation, and then plug that definition for d into the other equation, and solve for s. So let's start by isolating d in the first equation:

$$s + d = 209 \qquad \text{(first equation)}$$
$$d = 209 - s \qquad \text{(subtract } s \text{ from both sides to isolate } d\text{)}$$

Then we plug the result into the other equation:

$$6.50s + 2.00d = \$836.50 \qquad \text{(second equation)}$$
$$6.50s + 2.00(209 - s) = \$836.50 \qquad \text{(plug in } d = 209 - s \text{ from the other equation)}$$
$$6.50s + 418 - 2s = \$836.50 \qquad \text{(distribute 2.00)}$$
$$4.50s + 418 = \$836.50 \qquad \text{(simplify)}$$
$$4.50s = \$418.50 \qquad \text{(subtract 418 from both sides)}$$
$$s = 93 \qquad \text{(divide both sides by 4.50)}$$

So we can see that the number of salads sold was 93, which means (B) is correct.

Solution 2: Backsolving: Try each answer choice as the number of salads in the situation from the prompt, and see which one fits.

(A) If the food truck sold 77 salads at $6.50, then it sold 132 drinks at $2.00, for total revenue of $764.50, which doesn't match up with the revenue number from the prompt, so (A) isn't correct.

(B) If the food truck sold 93 salads at $6.50, then it sold 116 drinks at $2.00, for total revenue of $836.50. This matches the revenue from the prompt, so we can see that (B) is correct, assuming that we haven't made any small mistakes in our approach. Let's keep checking the other answer choices, to help make sure that we haven't done anything wrong.

(C) If the food truck sold 99 salads at $6.50, then it sold 110 drinks at $2.00 for total revenue of $863.50. This revenue number looks similar to the number in the prompt, but it actually has two of the digits reversed! This is one more example of the importance of careful reading on the SAT Math section.

(D) If the food truck sold 105 salads at $6.50, then it sold 104 drinks at $2.00, for total revenue of $890.50. This doesn't match the revenue from the prompt, so (D) is wrong.

Only choice (B) produces the revenue mentioned in the prompt, so we can see that (B) is correct.

ANSWER CHOICE ANALYSIS

(A): If this choice were the number of sodas, then (D) would be the number of salads that would need to be sold in order to generate a total revenue of $836.50; the problem is that (A) and (D) don't add up to 209, as the prompt requires. These two choices are probably placed here for test-takers who try to backsolve the question but don't remember that the total number of items sold has to be 209. **(C):** This is close to the value we'd get if we divided $836.50 by $8.50, the total cost of a salad and a drink. **(D):** (see discussion of (A).)

How to check? Try an alternate approach above.

Test 1, Section 4, Question 20

- **What's the prompt asking for?** An expression of the original price of the laptop in terms of p.
- **Math concepts in the prompt:** algebra, discounts, division, multiplication, percentages, word problems
- **Notable differences among answer choices:** (A) and (C) involve multiplying p by a coefficient, while (B) and (D) involve dividing p. (A) and (B) involve the number 0.88, while (C) and (D) involve the expression (0.8)(1.08).

- **Concepts in the answer choices:** division, multiplication, variables
- **Pre-solution patterns (see p. 217):** wrong answers try to imitate right answers
- **Things to look out for:** Don't confuse multiplication and division! Don't confuse the final price and the original price!

Solution 1: Concrete: Choose an arbitrary price for the computer, determine p based on that price, and then see which answer choice is equivalent to the computer's price when you sub in your value for p.

Let's say the laptop was originally priced at $1,000. A 20 percent discount off of $1,000 would reduce the price to $800. To calculate the result when an 8 percent tax is added to the discounted price, we multiply the discounted price by 1.08. That gives us 800×1.08, or 864, as the price with tax. So the final price, after the discount and with the tax added, would be $864. Now let's see which answer choice produces an original price of $1,000 when p = 864. (We can use our calculators for this, of course.)

A $0.88p = 0.88(864) = 760.32$

B $\frac{p}{0.88} = \frac{864}{0.88} \approx 981.82$

C $(0.8)(1.08)p = (0.8)(1.08)864 \approx 746.50$

D ✓ $\frac{p}{(0.8)(1.08)} = \frac{864}{(0.8)(1.08)} = 1000$

Only choice (D) gives us the correct result of 1000 when $p = 864$, so (D) is right.

Solution 2: Abstract: Translate the prompt into algebra and simplify your expression until it matches one of the answer choices.

The prompt says the store gave a 20 percent discount off the original price of the laptop. If you get a 20 percent discount, then you're paying 80 percent of the original price. So we can find the price after the 20 percent discount if we multiply the original price by 0.8.

Next, the prompt mentions adding 8 percent sales tax to this discounted price. Some untrained test-takers might want to multiply by 0.08, but that would only give us the 8 percent sales tax alone, not the full price (the full price includes the discounted price *plus* the 8 percent sales tax). To get the price plus the 8 percent tax, we need to multiply the number we just found by 1.08.

So to account for the 20 percent discount and the increase in price from the 8 percent sales tax, we multiply the original price by both 0.8 and 1.08. Note that this is how we find p from the original price—but we need an expression that gives us the original price in terms of p!

To answer the question in the prompt, we can start by writing an equation that expresses the relationship between the original price of the laptop and the p that we just found (I'll use L to represent the original price of the laptop):

$$L(0.8)(1.08) = p$$

In order to find the original price, L, in terms of p, we'll need to use algebra to isolate L on one side of the equation:

$L(0.8)(1.08) = p$ (equation we just came up with to relate L and p)

$L = \frac{p}{(0.8)(1.08)}$ (divide both sides by $(0.8)(1.08)$ to isolate L)

We can see that when we find the original price of the laptop in terms of p, our expression looks just like (D), so (D) is right.

Solution 3: Abstract / Backsolving: Consider each of the answer choices and compare them to the prompt to see which one accurately reflects the concepts in the prompt.

(A) would give us 88 percent of the final price, p. This might seem appropriate to some untrained test-takers, since the prompt tells us to drop the price by 20 percent and then raise it by 8 percent. But this choice actually combines two separate errors. First, it would have us multiply the *final price*, p, by 0.88, to account for the discount and the sales tax. But we would multiply the *original price* by a decimal expression to get the *final price*, which means we need to *divide* the final price by a decimal expression to get the original price. (Remember that the prompt asks for an expression that represents the original price in terms of the final price.) Second, the question asks for an expression that accounts for a 20 percent discount off the original price, and then 8 percent sales tax *based on that discounted price*. We can't add back 8 percent of the *original price* to account for an 8 percent sales tax on the *discounted price*, which is what this choice would have us do.

(B) This choice correctly includes the idea of dividing the *final price* by the decimal expression to get the *original price*, so it avoids one of the errors from (A). But this choice still includes the other error from (A): the decimal expression 0.88 isn't an acceptable way to combine the 20% discount and the 8% sales tax on that discounted price, as we saw in our discussion of (A).

(C) This choice involves multiplying by 0.8, which would reflect the idea of a 20 percent discount (because when a price is discounted by 20 percent, you're paying 80 percent of the original price). This choice also includes multiplying by 1.08, which would reflect the idea of paying 8 percent sales tax on whatever price you're multiplying by—in this case, the discounted price. But this choice makes one of the mistakes we saw in (A): it would have us multiply the *final price*, p, by $(0.8)(1.08)$, to account for the discount and the sales tax. But we would need to multiply the *original price* by a decimal expression to get the *final price*, not the other way around. In fact, if p represented the original price of the laptop, then this expression would give us the final price of the laptop—but the prompt tells us that p represents the *final price* of the laptop, and we need an expression involving p to represent the *original price*.

(D) This choice appropriately includes the idea of using 0.8 to reflect the 20% discount, and 1.08 to reflect the 8% sales tax on the discounted price. This choice also appropriately shows that we need to *divide* p by 0.8 and 1.08 to find the original price of the laptop—see our discussion of (A) for more on that. This choice represents the original price of the computer in terms of the final price, p, so it's correct. (Take a look at the earlier solutions if you're having trouble conceptualizing this.)

ANSWER CHOICE ANALYSIS

(See Solution 3 above.)

How to check? Try an alternate approach above, and/or re-consider each aspect of your choice to be sure that it makes sense in the context of the prompt.

Test 1, Section 4, Question 21

- **What's the prompt asking for?** The probability that a person who recalled a dream is in Group Y, the group of people who observed later bed times.
- **Math concepts in the prompt:** probability, reading data in a table
- **Math concepts in the diagram:** data analysis, sub groups of data
- **Elements of the answer choices:** Every choice involves a fraction.
- **Notable differences among answer choices:** (A) and (B) have 100 as the denominator, while (C) and (D) each have unique denominators. (A) and (D) are both unsimplified, while (B) and (C) can't be further reduced. (B) and (C) both have 79 as the numerator, while (A) and (D) both have unique numerators.

- **Concepts in the answer choices:** fractions
- **"Bridge" concepts:** One of the answer choices is a fraction that reflects the probability described in the prompt. Remember that the denominator of a probability fraction is the total number of possible outcomes, and the numerator is the number of outcomes we're targeting.
- **Pre-solution patterns (see p. 217):** wrong answers try to imitate right answers
- **Things to look out for:** Make sure you properly define the numerator and denominator!

Solution 1: Probability: Translate the concepts from the prompt into a numerator and denominator, and select the answer choice that matches the fraction you've constructed.

The denominator of the probability fraction will be the number of possible outcomes. In this case, the possible outcome is choosing any person who recalled at least 1 dream. So the denominator will be the number of people who recalled at least 1 dream, which is $28 + 57 + 11 + 68$, or 164. (Notice that "at least 1 dream" includes people who recalled 1 to 4 dreams, as well as people who recalled 5 or more dreams.)

To find the numerator, we need to determine the number of desired outcomes. The question says we want to know the likelihood that a person who recalled at least 1 dream also belonged to Group Y. The number of people who recalled at least 1 dream and who belonged to Group Y is $11 + 68$, or 79.

So the numerator is 79, and the denominator is 164, which means the probability is $\frac{79}{164}$. So (C) is correct.

Solution 2: Test-smart: Observe the differences and similarities among the answer choices, compare them to the prompt and the diagram, and observe that only one answer choice has an acceptable denominator, so it must be correct.

Notice that once we realize the denominator must be 164, we know (C) is correct, because only (C) has a denominator of 164. (It's true that the denominator might still have been simplified or reduced once we figured out the numerator, but, in this case, none of the other denominators are factors of 164, so none of those other answer choices could be right. In other words, once we realize that 164 is a valid denominator, we know that (C) is the only choice that can possible follow from that realization.)

ANSWER CHOICE ANALYSIS

(A): This is the probability that a person in Group Y had at least 5 dreams. **(B):** This is the probability that a person in Group Y had at least 1 dream. **(D):** This is the probability that a person chosen from both groups had at least 1 dream.

How to check? Try an alternate approach above.

Test 1, Section 4, Question 22

- **What's the prompt asking for?** The best approximation of "the rate of change in the annual budget for agriculture/natural resources in Kansas from 2008 to 2010."
- **Math concepts in the prompt:** approximation, average, rate of change, sub-groupings of data
- **Math concepts in the diagram:** data in a table, sub-groupings of data
- **Elements of the answer choices:** Each choice is a yearly rate involving a number of dollars in the millions.

- **Notable differences among answer choices:** (D) is the only choice that's greater than $100,000,000.
- **"Bridge" concepts:** We can calculate the average rate of change in those parts of the budget from 2008 to 2010 by dividing the budget difference from those years by the number of years.
- **Pre-solution patterns (see p. 217):** halves and doubles
- **Things to look out for:** Make sure you consider the numbers from the right parts of the budget! Make sure you divide the total by the right number of years!

Solution 1: Data: Identify the correct sub-grouping of budget data in the table, and subtract the 2008 values from the 2010 values. Then divide that difference by the number of years from 2008 to 2010, and pick the answer choice that's closest to the result.

$$\frac{488,106,000-358,708,000}{2} = 64,699,000$$ (budget for agriculture/natural resources for 2008 subtracted from the number for 2010, all divided by 2, which is the number of years from 2008 to 2010)

This number works out to roughly $65,000,000, which is what choice (B) says, so (B) is correct.

Solution 2: Data estimation: Follow the data solution mentioned above, but note that the difference between 488,106,000 and 358,708,000 is roughly 130,000,000; when we divide this number by 2, we arrive at 65,000,000.

We may notice when we compare 488,106,000 and 358,708,000 that the two numbers are roughly $130,000,000 apart, which works out to about a $65,000,000 difference per year. So, again, we can see that (B) is correct.

ANSWER CHOICE ANALYSIS

(D): This is double the correct answer, which might tempt an untrained test-taker who forgot to divide the difference in the budget by the number of years, which was 2.

How to check? Carefully re-work the problem. Note that the correct answer fits both the halves-and-doubles pattern and the right-approach-wrong-step pattern, which strongly suggests (but does NOT guarantee!) that (B) is correct.

▶ Post-solution patterns (see page 218): right approach, wrong step

Note Any of the wrong answers could potentially be tempting if an untrained test-taker misread the table or looked at the wrong range of years. Remember that critical reading is the most important skill on the entire SAT, including the Math sections!

Test 1, Section 4, Question 23

- **What's the prompt asking for?** The name of the program whose 2007 and 2010 budgets are in the ratio that's closest to the ratio of the 2007 and 2010 budgets of the human resources program.
- **Math concepts in the prompt:** data sub-groups, ratio, reading data from a table
- **Math concepts in the diagram:** data sub-groups
- **Elements of the answer choices:** Each answer choice is the name of one of the programs in the diagram.

- **"Bridge" concepts:** We can determine the ratio of the 2007 and 2010 numbers for the human resources program. We can then determine the same 2007: 2010 ratio for each of the programs in the answer choices, and the correct answer will be the choice whose ratio is closest to the ratio for the human resources program.
- **Things to look out for:** Don't compare the data from the wrong years! Don't reverse the years in the ratio! Don't accidentally use data from the wrong programs!

Solution 1: Concrete data: Determine the ratio of the 2007 budget to the 2010 budget for the human resources department. Then determine the ratios of the 2007 budgets to the 2010 budgets for each answer choice. The answer choice with the ratio that's closest to the ratio for the human resources department will be the correct answer.

The ratio of the human resources budget in 2007 to the same budget in 2010 is $\frac{4,051,050}{5,921,379}$, or approximately 0.68.

(A): the ratio of the agriculture/natural resources budget in 2007 to the same budget in 2010 is $\frac{373,904}{488,106}$, or approximately 0.77

(B): the ratio of the education budget in 2007 to the same budget in 2010 is $\frac{2,164,607}{3,008,036}$, or approximately 0.72.

(C): the ratio of the highways and transportation budget in 2007 to the same budget in 2010 is $\frac{1,468,482}{1,773,893}$, or approximately 0.83.

(D): the ratio of the public safety budget in 2007 to the same budget in 2010 is $\frac{263,463}{464,233}$, or approximately 0.57.

The closest ratio is in choice (B), so (B) is correct.

Solution 2: Data estimation: Approximate the ratio of the human resources budgets from 2007 and 2010. Then make the same approximation for the 2007 and 2010 budgets for each choice. If only one choice has an approximation that's very close to the approximation for the human resources department, then that choice is correct.

If we look at the human resources budget, we see that its 2007 budget was about $4,000,000,000 and its 2010 budget was about $6,000,000,000. That's roughly a 4: 6 ratio, which is the same thing as a 2: 3 ratio.
- The budget in (A) increased from around $400,000,000 to around $500,000,000, which is roughly a 4: 5 ratio.
- The budget in (B) increased from around $2,000,000,000 to around $3,000,000,000, which is roughly a 2: 3 ratio.

- The budget in (C) increased from around $1,500,000,000 to around $1,800,000,000, which is roughly a 15 : 18 ratio, or a 5 : 6 ratio.
- The budget in (D) increased from around $250,000,000 to around $450,000,000, which is roughly a 25 : 45 ratio, or a 5 : 9 ratio.

So we can see that the ratio of the 2007 education budget to the 2010 education budget was approximately 2 : 3. This is the ratio closest to the one we found for the human resources budget, which was also around 2 : 3. So (B) is right.

How to check? Try an alternate approach above.

Note We know the College Board designs SAT Math questions so they can be answered quickly if we use the most efficient approach. In this case, that instinct should lead us to expect that the College Board might have created the table so that the right answer could be found quickly through approximation, instead of requiring us to determine the precise ratios for each answer choice—and, as we saw in Solution 2, that's exactly what the College Board did. This question would have been harder if the ratios had been more difficult to approximate (such as by making the ratio $\frac{14}{17}$ or something), and/or if the ratios for the wrong answers had been closer to the ratio in the right answer.

Test 1, Section 4, Question 24

- **What's the prompt asking for?** The equation of a circle with center $(0, 4)$ and a radius with an end at $\left(\frac{4}{3}, 5\right)$.
- **Math concepts in the prompt:** circles, graphing, radius
- **Elements of the answer choices:** Every choice is an equation for a circle with a 4 in the y-expression and a fraction on the right-hand side.
- **Notable differences among answer choices:** (A) and (C) involve subtracting 4 from y. (B) and (D) involve adding 4 to y. (A) and (B) include the fraction $\frac{25}{9}$. (C) has the fraction $\frac{5}{3}$. (D) has the fraction $\frac{3}{5}$.
- **Concepts in the answer choices:** algebra, equations for circles, fractions, variables

- **"Bridge" concepts:** A radius has two endpoints: the center of its circle, and some point on the circle itself. This means the prompt is telling us the circle passes through $\left(\frac{4}{3}, 5\right)$. If we wanted to, we could apply the distance formula to determine the length of the radius (because the radius must reach from $(0, 4)$ to $\left(\frac{4}{3}, 5\right)$).
- **Pre-solution patterns (see p. 217):** opposites; wrong answers try to imitate right answers
- **Things to look out for:** Make sure you're clear on whether 4 should be added to y or subtracted from it! Make sure you're clear on which fraction should appear in the correct answer!

Solution 1: Calculator: If your calculator can graph circles, then graph each answer choice; the correct answer will be the one that goes through $\left(\frac{4}{3}, 5\right)$, and has a center at $(0, 4)$.

Choice (A):

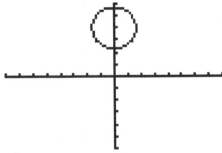

We can see that the center of the circle is at $(0, 4)$, and it definitely seems like this circle could include the point $\left(\frac{4}{3}, 5\right)$—if we start at the origin and move right until we're a little past the line that indicates 1 unit, then move up 5 units, it looks like we'll be right on the top/right part of the circle. We should check the other choices, though, to see if any other choices look like they could be right too. Let's look at (B):

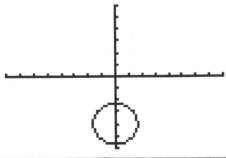

The center of this circle definitely isn't at $(0, 4)$, so we know this choice must be wrong. Let's take a look at (C):

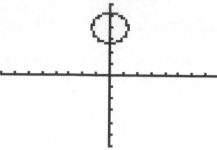

We can see that the center of the circle is at $(0, 4)$. But if we start at the origin and move right until we're a little past the line that indicates 1 unit, then move up 5 units, we'll definitely be a little above and to the right of the circle. In other words, this circle doesn't include the point $(\frac{4}{3}, 5)$, so (C) must be wrong. Let's take a look at (D):

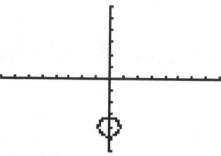

The center of this circle definitely isn't at $(0, 4)$, so we know this choice must be wrong too. After graphing the equation from each answer choice, we can see that only (A) can be right.

Solution 2: Circles/distance: If you know how an equation for a circle works, then you can use the distance formula to determine the length of the radius and select the answer choice that correctly describes the center and radius of the circle.

We can find the length of the radius by calculating the distance between the center at $(0, 4)$ and radius endpoint $(\frac{4}{3}, 5)$.

The distance formula is just a way to use the Pythagorean theorem to find the distance between two points. If we feel confident using the distance formula directly, we can do that. If not, we can sketch the points and make the distance between them the hypotenuse of a right triangle. We can then determine the lengths of the two legs of that right triangle, and use them to find the length of the hypotenuse—which is the distance we're looking for.

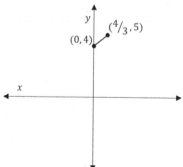

Let's zoom in on that line segment, and draw in the sides of the triangle.

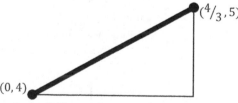

The vertical distance between the two points is the difference between their y-coordinates, which is $5 - 4$, or 1. This is the length of the vertical leg. The horizontal distance between the two points is the difference between their x-coordinates, which is $\frac{4}{3} - 0$, or $\frac{4}{3}$. This is the length of the horizontal leg. Let's add those lengths to the diagram:

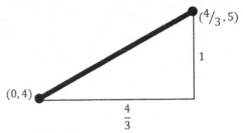

(0, 4)

$\frac{4}{3}$

1

$(^4/_3, 5)$

Now let's plug these numbers into the Pythagorean theorem to find the length of the hypotenuse.

$$a^2 + b^2 = c^2 \qquad \text{(Pythagorean theorem)}$$

$$1^2 + \left(\frac{4}{3}\right)^2 = c^2 \qquad \text{(plug in the two side lengths)}$$

$$1 + \frac{16}{9} = c^2 \qquad \text{(square the two side lengths)}$$

$$\frac{25}{9} = c^2 \qquad \text{(convert 1 to } \frac{9}{9} \text{ and simplify)}$$

$$\frac{5}{3} = c \qquad \text{(take square root of both sides)}$$

So the distance between $(0, 4)$ and $(\frac{4}{3}, 5)$ is $\frac{5}{3}$, which means the length of the radius is $\frac{5}{3}$.

The prompt gave us the center of the circle, and we found the length of the radius. We can plug these values into the standard equation for a circle, which is $(x - h)^2 + (y - k)^2 = r^2$, where the center is at (h, k) and r is the radius. So the equation for the circle described in the prompt is $(x - 0)^2 + (y - 4)^2 = \frac{5^2}{3}$, which simplifies to $x^2 + (y - 4)^2 = \frac{25}{9}$. That means (A) is correct.

Solution 3: Test-smart: Knowing that the correct answer passes through $(\frac{4}{3}, 5)$, find the choice that's valid when $x = \frac{4}{3}$ and $y = 5$.

$$x^2 + (y - 4)^2 = \frac{25}{9} \qquad \text{(equation from (A))}$$

$$\left(\frac{4}{3}\right)^2 + (5 - 4)^2 = \frac{25}{9} \qquad \text{(plug in } x = \frac{4}{3} \text{ and } y = 5\text{)}$$

$$\frac{16}{9} + 1 = \frac{25}{9} \qquad \text{(simplify)}$$

$$\frac{25}{9} = \frac{25}{9} \qquad \text{(simplify)}$$

The point $(\frac{4}{3}, 5)$ is valid in this equation, which means it's on the graph of this circle, so (A) could be correct as far as we can tell right now. We need to consider the other choices, to make sure no other choices are valid for $(\frac{4}{3}, 5)$. So let's check out (B) now:

$$x^2 + (y + 4)^2 = \frac{25}{9} \qquad \text{(equation from (B))}$$

$$\left(\frac{4}{3}\right)^2 + (5 + 4)^2 = \frac{25}{9} \qquad \text{(plug in } x = \frac{4}{3} \text{ and } y = 5\text{)}$$

$$\frac{16}{9} + 81 = \frac{25}{9} \qquad \text{(simplify)}$$

$$\frac{745}{9} = \frac{25}{9} \qquad \text{(simplify)}$$

This isn't a true statement, so $(\frac{4}{3}, 5)$ isn't on the graph of the circle in (B), which means (B) can't be correct. Next we evaluate (C):

$$x^2 + (y - 4)^2 = \frac{5}{3} \qquad \text{(equation from (C))}$$

$$\left(\frac{4}{3}\right)^2 + (5 - 4)^2 = \frac{5}{3} \qquad \text{(plug in } x = \frac{4}{3} \text{ and } y = 5\text{)}$$

$$\frac{16}{9} + 1 = \frac{5}{3} \qquad \text{(simplify)}$$

$$\frac{25}{9} = \frac{5}{3} \qquad \text{(simplify)}$$

This isn't a true statement either, so $(\frac{4}{3}, 5)$ doesn't satisfy this equation, and (C) can't be correct. Next, we take a look at (D):

$$x^2 + (y + 4)^2 = \frac{3}{5} \qquad \text{(equation from (D))}$$

$$\left(\frac{4}{3}\right)^2 + (5 + 4)^2 = \frac{3}{5} \qquad \text{(plug in } x = \frac{4}{3} \text{ and } y = 5\text{)}$$

$$\frac{16}{9} + 81 = \frac{3}{5} \qquad \text{(simplify)}$$

$$\frac{745}{9} = \frac{3}{5} \qquad \text{(simplify)}$$

Once more, we see that $\left(\frac{4}{3}, 5\right)$ isn't on the graph of this circle, so (D) can't be correct.

We've now verified that $\left(\frac{4}{3}, 5\right)$ is only on the graph of the circle described by the equation in (A), so only (A) can be correct.

ANSWER CHOICE ANALYSIS

(B): This circle would have the correct radius, but the center would be at $(0, -4)$ instead of at $(0, 4)$. **(C):** This circle would have the correct center, but the radius would be the square root of what the prompt requires. **(D):** This choice combines the mistake from (B) with an incorrect radius.

How to check? Try an alternate approach above.

▶ Post-solution patterns (see page 218): opposites

Note   Once more, we see that the College Board has made this question much easier than it could have been, as long as we remember our training and look for approaches that will take less than 30 seconds and/or involve calculators. We can quickly tell that (A) is correct if we realize that the correct answer must pass through $\left(\frac{4}{3}, 5\right)$, because (A) is the only choice that does that. The College Board could have made this question harder by having more than one answer choice that was valid for the point $\left(\frac{4}{3}, 5\right)$, which would have prevented us from testing that single point to find the correct answer.

Test 1, Section 4, Question 25

- **What's the prompt asking for?** The approximate number of seconds that have passed when the ball hits the ground.
- **Math concepts in the prompt:** addition, algebra, function modeling, multiplication, negative numbers, variables
- **Elements of the answer choices:** The answer choices form a series from 3.5 to 5.0, with each choice being 0.5 more than the choice before it.

- **"Bridge" concepts:** When the ball "hit(s) the ground" as described in the prompt, its height must be zero, since height is measured from the ground. This means the question is asking for the t-value that corresponds to an h-value of zero.
- **Pre-solution patterns (see p. 217):** the first and last terms in a series are often wrong answers
- **Things to look out for:** Don't make algebra mistakes when working with the function equation! Don't confuse h and t!

Solution 1: Algebra: Set $h = 0$ and solve for t.

When the ball has hit the ground, the height, h, is zero, so we can answer this question by finding t when h is zero:

$$h = -4.9t^2 + 25t \qquad \text{(original equation)}$$
$$0 = -4.9t^2 + 25t \qquad \text{(plug in } h = 0\text{)}$$
$$4.9t^2 = 25t \qquad \text{(add } 4.9t^2 \text{ to both sides)}$$
$$4.9t = 25 \qquad \text{(divide both sides by } t\text{)}$$
$$t = \frac{25}{4.9} \approx 5 \qquad \text{(divide both sides by 4.9 to approximate } t \text{ when } h \text{ is zero.)}$$

This shows us that the correct answer is (D), since the question asked for the approximate number of seconds at which h is 0.

Solution 2: Backsolve: Substitute each answer choice for t and see which one results in an h-value of zero.

For choice (A):

$$h = -4.9t^2 + 25t \qquad \text{(original equation)}$$
$$h = -4.9(3.5)^2 + 25(3.5) \qquad \text{(plug in } t = 3.5 \text{ from (A))}$$
$$h = 27.475 \qquad \text{(simplify)}$$

We can see that the height of the ball is 27.475 meters after 3.5 seconds, so (A) isn't correct. So now let's try (B):

$$h = -4.9(4.0)^2 + 25(4.0) \qquad \text{(plug in } t = 4.0 \text{ from (B))}$$
$$h = 21.6 \qquad \text{(simplify)}$$

So, after 4.0 seconds, the height of the ball is 21.6 meters, which means (B) isn't correct. Now let's look at (C):

$$h = -4.9(4.5)^2 + 25(4.5)$$ (plug in $t = 4.5$ from (C))
$$h = 13.275$$ (simplify)

After 4.5 seconds, the height of the ball is 13.275 meters, so (C) isn't correct. Now, let's take a look at (D):

$$h = -4.9(5.0)^2 + 25(5.0)$$ (plug in $t = 5.0$ from (D))
$$h = 2.5$$ (simplify)

After 5.0 seconds the height of the ball is 2.5 meters. At this point, it's important to remember that the question asks for an *approximate* value of t, and this 2.5 value is much closer to 0 than the values produced by the other choices, so (D) must be correct.

Solution 3: Graphing: Graph the equation in the prompt and see which answer choice is close to a t-value that corresponds to an h-value of zero on the graph.

When we graph the function on our calculators, we get this:

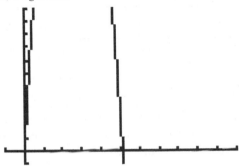

Remember that we're looking for the point where the graph crosses the horizontal axis, because that's the point at which its height is zero. In this case, we can clearly see that this happens right around the 5th tick-mark from the origin, which is where x equals 5. So, again, we see that (D) is right.

How to check? Try an alternate approach above.

Note Any of the wrong answer choices might have been tempting if an untrained test-taker made a mistake reading the graph or entering values into the calculator. Further, this question doesn't follow the general pattern of avoiding the first and last number in a mathematical series in the answer choices. Remember: patterns like these aren't hard-and-fast "rules"—they're just general observations that give us an extra weapon to use when we approach a question!

Test 1, Section 4, Question 26

- **What's the prompt asking for?** The number of pears produced by Type B trees.
- **Math concepts in the prompt:** percentages, word problems
- **Elements of the answer choices:** Each choice is a number between 100 and 200.
- **Notable differences among answer choices:** (A), (B), and (C) are all less than 144, the number in the prompt. Only (D) is greater than 144.

- **"Bridge" concepts:** If Type A produced 20% more pears than Type B, then we know that Type A produced 120% of what Type B produced.
- **Things to look out for:** Don't confuse A and B! Don't confuse the 20% relationship! Saying that Type A produced 120% of Type B is NOT the same thing as saying that Type B produced 80% of Type A!

Solution 1: Algebra: Translate the text into an algebraic expression of the percentage relationship between Type A and Type B, and then solve that expression for the number of pears produced by Type B.

If Type A trees produce 20 percent more pears than Type B trees, then the number of pears, a, produced by Type A trees must be 120% of the number of pears, b, produced by Type B trees. We can express this relationship with the expression $a = 1.2b$.

The prompt tells us that Type A trees produced 144 pears. Let's plug that value in for a, and then solve for b:

$$a = 1.2b$$ (original equation)
$$144 = 1.2b$$ (plug in $a = 144$)
$$120 = b$$ (divide both sides by 1.2)

So we can see that (B) is correct.

Solution 2: Backsolve: Go through each answer choice and see which choice makes Type A 120% of Type B.

Since Type A trees produce 20 percent more pears than Type B trees, we should be able to multiply the Type B value by 1.2 to come up with the Type A value. Let's multiply each answer choice by 1.2 to see which one matches the 144 pears mentioned in the prompt:

A		$115 \times 1.2 = 138$
B	✓	$120 \times 1.2 = 144$
C		$124 \times 1.2 = 148.8$
D		$173 \times 1.2 = 207.6$

We can see that (B) matches the target of 144, so (B) must be correct.

ANSWER CHOICE ANALYSIS

(A): This is a rounded version of the result if we incorrectly assume Type B must be 80% of Type A, because $0.8 \times 144 = 115.2$. A test-taker would need to make two mistakes to arrive at this choice: First, he'd have to confuse the relationship between Type A and Type B, and then he'd have to make the mistake of thinking that rounding was acceptable in this context—we can't round on this question because the prompt doesn't say anything about rounding, approximation, estimation, or anything like that. **(C):** This is the result if we accidentally subtract 20 from the quantity for Type A, instead of calculating an amount for Type B that would result in Type A being 20% more than Type B. **(D):** An untrained test-taker could reach this answer by making two mistakes: First, she'd misread the prompt and think Type B was 120% more than Type A, instead of the other way around; then, she'd have to round 120% of 144 to 173. As we saw for (A), rounding isn't okay here since the prompt doesn't mention rounding, approximation, etc.

How to check? Try an alternate approach above, and/or consider each of the wrong answers and confirm for yourself why they must be wrong.

▶   Post-solution patterns (see page 218): opposites

> **Note**   This is a relatively straightforward question, and it provides us a good opportunity to see several of the College Board's favorite principles of question design in one place. Each of the wrong answer choices is deliberately calculated to reflect a mistake that a test-taker would be likely to make under stress, even if he understands all the concepts in the question. Keep this kind of thing in mind on test day, and remember that you always need to proceed carefully and check your work!

Test 1, Section 4, Question 27

- **What's the prompt asking for?** A "reasonable approximation" of the number of earthworms in the field.
- **Math concepts in the prompt:** estimation, reading tables, word problems
- **Math concepts in the diagram:** reading data from a table
- **Elements of the answer choices:** Each choice involves the number 15 followed by a certain number of zeros.
- **Notable differences among answer choices:** Choices (A) through (D) form a series in which each choice is 10 times as much as the choice before it.
- **Concepts in the answer choices:** multiplying by 10

- **"Bridge" concepts:** One way to approximate the number of worms would be to multiply the number of regions by the estimated average number of worms in each region.
- **Pre-solution patterns (see p. 217):** the first and last terms in a series are often wrong answers, wrong answers try to imitate right answers
- **Things to look out for:** Don't mis-count the number of zeros in the answer choice you pick! Don't confuse the number of earthworms in the TABLE with the number of earthworms in the ENTIRE FIELD!

Solution 1: Approximation: Note the text, the answer choices, and the table, and realize that there are 10 regions in the table, and that 150 is a rough average of the numbers in the table. Then figure out the portion of the field represented in the table.

The table gives us information about 10 randomly selected regions of the field, each being 1 square meter. The number of earthworms in each of those 10 regions is around 150, so we'll use 150 as an approximate number of earthworms in each square meter of the field.

We're asked for an approximation of the number of earthworms in the entire field. The entire field is 10 meters by 10 meters, so the area of the field is $10m \times 10m$, or $100m^2$. If a region with an area of 1 square meter contains around 150 earthworms, then a region with an area of 100 square meters should contain 15,000 earthworms, because $100 \times 150 = 15,000$. So (C) is right.

Solution 2: Calculation/approximation: Calculate the actual number of earthworms in the table and the portion of the field represented in the table, and then estimate the number of earthworms in the whole field and select the nearest answer choice.

When we add up all the earthworms indicated in the table, we see that the figure tells us there are 1471 earthworms total in ten regions of 1 square meter each. We're asked for an approximation of the number of earthworms in the entire field. The entire field is 10 meters by 10 meters, so the area of the field is $10m \times 10m$, or $100m^2$. If 10 square meters of the field contain 1471 earthworms, then a region with an area of 100 square meters should contain approximately 14,710 earthworms, since 100 is 10 times as much as 10, and $10 \times 1471 = 14,710$. This is approximately 15,000 earthworms, so (C) is correct.

ANSWER CHOICE ANALYSIS

(A): This is an approximation of the average number of earthworms in each of the regions in the table—in other words, the average of all the numbers that appear in the table. **(B):** This is an approximation of the total number of earthworms IN THE TABLE, but this choice is wrong because the question asked us to approximate the total number of earthworms IN THE FIELD. **(D):** This wrong answer choice could reflect the error of thinking that the field was 100 times larger than the sample in the table, rather than 10 times larger; it could also reflect the error of miscounting or misreading the number of zeros in the answer choice. This choice reflects a common trick that the College Board often tries to play when the answer choices in a question form a series: by giving us a choice that reflects the error of going one step beyond the correct answer (in terms of multiplying by 10 too many times), the College Board seems to be trying to increase the likelihood of anticipating all the mistakes that a test-taker would be likely to make.

How to check? Try an alternate approach above. Carefully reconsider the number of times that 150 should be multiplied by 10, and carefully recount the number of zeros in your answer choice to make sure you haven't made a mistake.

▶ Post-solution patterns (see page 218): right approach, wrong step; right answer to the wrong question

> **Note** Many untrained test-takers will miss this question because they'll forget that the area represented in the table is only one-tenth of the area of the entire field. This is a great example of how important it is to read extremely carefully, and to pay attention to what's going on in the answer choices—in this case, the relationships among the choices indicate clearly that the College Board expects us to be off by a factor of ten, which should remind a trained test-taker to triple-check her answer before committing to it.

Test 1, Section 4, Question 28

- **What's the prompt asking for?** The quadrant that does NOT contain a solution for the system of inequalities in the prompt.
- **Math concepts in the prompt:** algebraic systems, graphing inequalities, inequalities, quadrants of the xy-coordinate plane
- **Math concepts in the diagram:** quadrants of the xy-coordinate plane
- **Notable differences among answer choices:** (A), (B), and (C) are different quadrants of the xy-coordinate plane, while (D) says every quadrant contains a valid solution to the system of inequalities in the prompt. No choice singles out the first quadrant.

- **Concepts in the answer choices:** quadrants of the xy-coordinate plane
- **"Bridge" concepts:** Every possible (x, y) solution for the system of inequalities in the prompt can be plotted in the xy-coordinate plane. If we figure out which regions of the plane satisfy the system, then we can tell which quadrant, if any, contains zero solutions.
- **Things to look out for:** Don't forget which quadrant is which! Don't mistake greater-than signs for less-than signs! Don't forget to switch the direction of the inequality sign as you do your algebra, if necessary!

Solution 1: Calculator: Graph the inequalities in the prompt and observe which regions of the xy-coordinate plane contain solutions to the system.

When we graph the inequalities from the prompt, we get this:

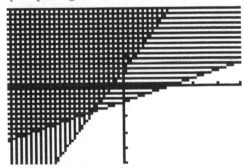

By definition, the solutions to the system of inequalities are the (x, y) points that satisfy both inequalities. In the graph, the solutions to one inequality are indicated with horizontal shading, while the solutions to the other inequality are indicated with vertical shading; the area with both vertical and horizontal shading is the area with solutions to the system of both inequalities. We can see that the region of solutions to both inequalities never comes into the fourth quadrant, so (C) is the correct answer.

Solution 2: Backsolving: Test one or two points in each quadrant to see which points satisfy both equations, and use the results to help you figure out which quadrants can have solutions to the system.

Choice (A) says that quadrant II contains no solutions to the system. Let's pick a point in quadrant II and see if that point could satisfy both inequalities from the prompt. I'll use $(-4, 4)$ because it's in quadrant II, the numbers are relatively small, and I noticed that x will be divided by 2 in the second inequality, so it might be a little easier to start out with an x-value that's divisible by 2:

$$y > 2x + 1 \qquad \text{(first inequality)}$$
$$4 > 2(-4) + 1 \qquad \text{(plug in the point } (-4, 4))$$

$$4 > -7 \qquad \text{(simplify)}$$

So $(-4, 4)$ is a solution for the first inequality. Let's try that point in the second inequality:

$$y > \frac{1}{2}x - 1 \qquad \text{(second inequality)}$$

$$4 > \frac{1}{2}(-4) - 1 \qquad \text{(plug in the point } (-4, 4))$$

$$4 > -3 \qquad \text{(simplify)}$$

We can see that the point $(-4, 4)$ is a solution for the system of inequalities, which means quadrant II does contain at least one solution for the system. So (A) is wrong.

Choice (B) says that quadrant III contains no solutions to the system. Let's pick a point in quadrant III and see what we come up with. I'll use $(-4, -4)$:

$$y > 2x + 1 \qquad \text{(first inequality)}$$

$$-4 > 2(-4) + 1 \qquad \text{(plug in the point } (-4, -4))$$

$$-4 > -7 \qquad \text{(simplify)}$$

So $(-4, -4)$ is a solution for the first inequality. Let's try that point in the second inequality:

$$y > \frac{1}{2}x - 1 \qquad \text{(second inequality)}$$

$$-4 > \frac{1}{2}(-4) - 1 \qquad \text{(plug in the point } (-4, -4))$$

$$-4 > -3 \qquad \text{(simplify)}$$

We can see that the point $(-4, -4)$ is not a solution for the system of inequalities. But we can't simply conclude from this that (B) is wrong, because the fact that $(-4, -4)$ isn't a solution doesn't mean this entire quadrant contains no solutions.

Let's try to think of a point in quadrant III that could be a solution to the system of inequalities. When we look at the point we just tested, we might notice that there are y-values that would be greater than or equal to the value on the right side of both inequalities. For example, -2 is greater than or equal to both -7 and -3. So let's plug in $(-4, -2)$ and see what happens with our inequalities:

$$y > 2x + 1 \qquad \text{(first inequality)}$$

$$-2 > 2(-4) + 1 \qquad \text{(plug in the point } (-4, -2))$$

$$-2 > -7 \qquad \text{(simplify)}$$

So $(-4, -2)$ is a solution for the first inequality. Now let's look at the second inequality:

$$y > \frac{1}{2}x - 1 \qquad \text{(second inequality)}$$

$$-2 > \frac{1}{2}(-4) - 1 \qquad \text{(plug in the point } (-4, -2))$$

$$-2 > -3 \qquad \text{(simplify)}$$

We can see that the point $(-4, -2)$ is actually a solution for the system of inequalities, which means quadrant III does contain at least one solution for the system. So (B) is wrong.

Choice (C) says that quadrant IV contains no solutions to the system. Let's pick a point in quadrant IV and see how it performs in our system of inequalities. I'll use $(4, -4)$:

$$y > 2x + 1 \qquad \text{(first inequality)}$$

$$-4 > 2(4) + 1 \qquad \text{(plug in the point } (4, -4))$$

$$-4 > 9 \qquad \text{(simplify)}$$

So $(4, -4)$ isn't a solution for the first inequality. Let's try to think of a point that could be a solution for the first inequality. Any y-value in quadrant IV must be negative, so the value on the left side of the first inequality will always be negative. Can we choose an x-value in quadrant IV that will make the expression on the right side of the first inequality less than or equal to a negative number? We can't, actually. The value on the right will always involve adding 1 to a number that's 2 times a positive number—because in quadrant IV, x is always positive! When we double a positive number and add 1, the result is always positive.

In quadrant IV, the y-value on the left side of the first inequality will always be negative, and the value on the right side of the inequality will always be positive, so the value on the left can't ever be greater than or equal to the value on the right. That means there's no value in quadrant IV that satisfies the first inequality, which in turn means that there is no point in quadrant IV that satisfies the system of inequalities. So (C) is correct.

We can see that (D) is wrong because we just found that quadrant IV contains no solutions to the system of inequalities.

Solution 3: Properties and definitions: Consider the properties of x and y in each quadrant, and how those properties relate to the inequalities in the prompt.

The defining properties of the four quadrants are the types of x- and y-values that can exist for points in each quadrant. Both values in quadrant I must be positive, and both values in quadrant III must be negative. In quadrant II, the x-value is negative while the y-value is positive; in quadrant IV, the y-value is negative and the x-value is positive. When we consider these attributes in light of the inequalities from the prompt, we eventually arrive at the realization we had towards the end of the last solution: when x is positive, the first inequality must always have a positive value on the right-hand side, which means the first inequality can never be true when y is negative and x is positive. Since that's the case, the quadrant with negative y-values and positive x-values (which is quadrant IV) can't contain a solution to the first inequality, which means (C) must be correct.

How to check? Try an alternate approach above.

Test 1, Section 4, Question 29

- **What's the prompt asking for?** The choice that contains a statement that must be true about $p(x)$.
- **Math concepts in the prompt:** functions, polynomials
- **Elements of the answer choices:** (A), (B), and (C) all say that some expression with x is a factor of $p(x)$.
- **Concepts in the answer choices:** dividing polynomials, factors and zeros of polynomials, remainders
- **"Bridge" concepts:** A polynomial is an expression that combines variables and numbers. A polynomial can serve as a function if we set the polynomial equal to a different variable

and then evaluate the polynomial for a given value—in this question, we're told that applying the p polynomial to an input of 3 gives a result of -2. A factor of a polynomial is an expression that causes the polynomial to equal zero when the factor is set equal to zero.

- **Pre-solution patterns (see p. 217):** wrong answers try to imitate right answers
- **Things to look out for:** Don't confuse something that CAN be true with something that MUST be true!

Solution 1: Backsolving: Consider the choices to see what we can conclude about factors of $p(x)$. (See the note below!)

For (A), we can see that if $x - 5$ were a factor of $p(x)$, then that would mean that $p(5)$ would equal zero. But knowing the value of $p(3)$ doesn't tell us anything about what $p(5)$ is, so this choice can't be correct.

(B) has the same problem as (A): knowing the value of $p(3)$ doesn't tell us anything about what $p(2)$ is when we're dealing with a function that isn't linear, so this choice can't be correct.

(C) has the same problem as (A) and (B): knowing the value of $p(3)$ doesn't tell us anything about what $p(-2)$ is—and, again, we can't say whether $x + 2$ is a factor of $p(x)$ without knowing $p(-2)$—so this choice can't be right.

(D) may be difficult to conceptualize if you're not previously familiar with graphing polynomials or with the Remainder Theorem (see note), but if we know that we've eliminated the other choices with good reason—which we have—then we can mark (D) with confidence.

Normally we like to find a concrete reason to select the correct answer, rather than just eliminating the wrong answers and picking what's left over! But, in this case, if we understand factors of functions, we can be confident that there is no information in the question to support (A), (B), or (C), so even if we don't totally understand what (D) says, we can mark (D) and move on. (See the note below for more on this.)

How to check? Carefully reconsider your work. Also consider the concepts discussed in the note below.

Note The College Board's official "explanation" for this question relies on a concept called the Remainder Theorem, though the College Board never uses that term. (You can see our *very* brief description of the Remainder Theorem on page 185 of this Black Book to get the essential information you might arguably need on the SAT, or search the concept online for a more detailed explanation.) But the most important lesson to be drawn from this question isn't that you need to know the Remainder Theorem for the SAT! In fact, what this question really demonstrates is that the College Board often designs its questions and "explanations" so that untrained test-takers will be intimidated into thinking the math on the test is much more advanced than it actually is. This question will probably frustrate a lot of untrained test-takers, because many of them will assume, incorrectly, that they need more information about $p(x)$. But trained test-takers can actually take advantage of the small amount of information offered in the prompt: we can easily see that we must not have enough information to say that any particular term is a factor of $p(x)$, since the prompt didn't say anything about a p-value being equal to 0, which is what happens when we find the p-value that corresponds to a factor of $p(x)$. That means only one of the choices is directly related to the concepts in the prompt, so it must be the only choice that can follow logically from the prompt, which means it's the only choice that can be correct. In short, we see that it's possible to answer this question with total certainty even if you've never heard of the Remainder Theorem, and even if you don't feel comfortable with the complicated algebra in the College Board's "explanation"—in fact, our walkthrough doesn't even require you to pick up a pencil or turn on your calculator. Still, if you run into a question that challenges you on test day, consider saving it for a later pass—don't let a harder question

Test 1, Section 4, Question 30

- **What's the prompt asking for?** The choice that produces the same graph as the one in the diagram, *and* uses the coordinates of point *A* as constants.

- **Math concepts in the prompt:** constants, coordinates of a point, equivalent equations, graphing in the xy-coordinate plane, vertex of a graph

- **Math concepts in the diagram:** graphing in the xy-coordinate plane, different scales for different axes of a graph, parabolas, polynomial functions

- **Elements of the answer choices:** Each choice is a function that sets y equal to an expression involving x.

- **Notable differences among answer choices:** (A) includes the idea of factoring the expression in the diagram into binomial expressions with the numbers 3 and -5, while (B) has a similar appearance to (A) but reverses the signs on the numbers in (A). (C) involves factoring a portion of the expression in the diagram, and includes the numbers -2 and -15. (D) is the only answer choice with a squared term, and (D) includes the numbers -1 and -16.

- **Concepts in the answer choices:** algebraic constants, factoring, multiplying binomials

- **"Bridge" concepts:** A point in the xy-coordinate plane has coordinates that define it in terms of x and y. An equation in terms of x and y can be written in a variety of equivalent ways, which would all produce the same set of (x, y) solutions, and therefore produce the graph in the xy-coordinate plane.

- **Pre-solution patterns (see p. 217):** opposites; wrong answers try to imitate right answers

- **Things to look out for:** Don't confuse the signs on numbers in the answer choices! Don't misread the coordinates of point *A*!

Solution 1: Backsolving: Consider the answer choices and identify the one that contains the coordinates for point *A*.

Let's look at each answer choice in turn:

(A) The constants in this equation are 3 and 5. There's no combination of a positive or negative 3 and a positive or negative 5 that could make a coordinate pair for *A* on the graph. In other words, *A* isn't at $(3, 5)$, $(-3, 5)$, $(3, -5)$, or $(-3, -5)$.

(B) The constants in this equation are also 3 and 5, so this choice can't work for the same reason that choice (A) couldn't work.

(C) The constants in (C) are 2 and 15. There's no combination of a positive or negative 2 and a positive or negative 15 that could make a coordinate pair to describe point *A* on the graph. We can see that the y-coordinate of point *A* is near -15, so that might make this choice tempting for some test-takers—but the x-coordinate is clearly not 2 or -2, so (C) must be wrong.

(D) The constants in this equation are 1 and 16. We can see that the x-coordinate of point *A* is 1, so that part of this equation works, and the y-coordinate of *A* appears to be a little less than -15, so -16 seems like it fits that coordinate as well.

Since $(1, -16)$ is the location of *A*, and no combination of the constants in (A), (B), or (C) contains 1 and 16, we know that choice (D) is correct.

Solution 2: Graph-first: Look at *A* on the graph, and then identify the answer choice that contains the coordinates for that point.

We can see that the x-coordinate of point *A* is 1, and the y-coordinate is a little less than -15. The only choice with a constant of 1 is (D), and (D) also includes -16. Once we realize that, we can verify that point *A* has coordinates $(1, -16)$, so (D) is right.

ANSWER CHOICE ANALYSIS

(A): This choice is an equivalent expression for the equation in the diagram, using the reverse-FOIL type of factoring. But this choice doesn't allow us to identify the coordinates of the vertex as constants in the expression. It's probably here for test-takers who misread or misunderstand the requirements of the prompt, and think it's okay just to find an equivalent equation, without noticing that two other choices are also equivalent to the equation in the diagram. **(B):** This is similar to (A), but the factoring is done incorrectly, with the opposites of the correct constants (that is, -3 appearing where $+3$ should appear, and $+5$ appearing where -5 should appear). This choice is probably here for test-takers who make the mistake of thinking that reverse-FOIL is the only way to factor a quadratic expression, and then make the further mistake of doing that factoring incorrectly. **(C):** This is an equivalent expression to the one in the diagram, but it refers to the numbers 2 and 15, which aren't the coordinates of point *A*. **(D):** This choice is an equivalent expression to the one in the diagram, and it's the only choice that allows us to identify the coordinates of *A* from the expression itself.

How to check? Re-confirm that the prompt asked us for an expression that allows us to identify the coordinates of *A*, and re-confirm that *A* is at $(1, -16)$ in the diagram.

▶   Post-solution patterns (see page 218): right answer to the wrong question

Note   This question might seem challenging, but as we can see in the solution above, it's actually a lot quicker and easier than it appears.

Test 1, Section 4, Question 31

- **What's the prompt asking for?** One possible value for the amount of time that it could take Wyatt to husk 72 dozen ears of corn.
- **Math concepts in the prompt:** inequalities, rate of completion, word problems

- **"Bridge" concepts:** The number of tasks that can be completed in one hour will allow us to determine the number of hours required for a larger number of tasks.
- **Things to look out for:** Don't make mistakes in your arithmetic! Don't misread the numbers in the prompt!

Solution 1: Range-first: Determine the number of hours necessary for the task, using both the maximum and minimum rates, and then record an answer in the range you've discovered.

If Wyatt husks 12 dozen ears of corn per hour, then he can husk 72 dozen ears of corn in $\frac{72}{12}$ hours, or 6 hours. If Wyatt husks 18 dozen ears of corn per hour, then he can husk 72 dozen ears of corn in $\frac{72}{18}$ hours, or 4 hours. So Wyatt can husk 72 dozen ears of corn in any amount of time from 4 hours to 6 hours.

Solution 2: Rate-first: Arbitrarily choose an hourly rate within the range defined in the prompt, and then use that rate to determine the number of hours that would be required to complete 72 dozen ears at the rate that you've chosen.

Wyatt can husk from 12 to 18 dozen ears of corn per hour. Let's assume he husks 15 dozen ears of corn per hour, as an arbitrary number between 12 dozen and 18 dozen. At 15 dozen per hour, he would husk 72 dozen ears of corn in $\frac{72}{15}$ hours, or 4.8 hours. So we know that 4.8 hours is one possible amount of time it could take Wyatt to husk 72 dozen ears of corn.

How to check? Try an alternate approach above, and/or reconfirm your arithmetic and your reading.

Test 1, Section 4, Question 32

- **What's the prompt asking for?** The largest possible number of boxes that can be added to the truck without exceeding the weight limit for the bridge.
- **Math concepts in the prompt:** inequalities, solving for a variable, translating text into algebra, variables, word problems

- **"Bridge" concepts:** We can write an algebraic inequality that expresses the relationship between x and the quantities in the prompt, and then use it to determine the highest possible value of x.
- **Things to look out for:** Don't confuse the numbers in the prompt when you create your algebraic inequality!

Solution 1: Algebra: Translate the concepts from the prompt into an algebraic statement and then find the acceptable value for x.

The prompt says that the combined weight of the truck, driver, and boxes must be less than the bridge's posted weight limit of 6000 pounds. We know that the weight of the truck and driver is 4500 pounds. The weight of the boxes is 14 pounds per box, and the number of boxes is x. So the weight of all the boxes can be expressed as $14x$ pounds, which indicates that we're multiplying 14 pounds by the number of boxes. Further, the weight of the truck, driver, and boxes can be expressed as $4500 + 14x$.

Now we need to find out the maximum number of boxes that will keep the total below 6000 pounds. Let's set the expression we just found equal to 6000, and then we can round down the number of boxes to keep the total below 6000:

$$4500 + 14x = 6000 \quad \text{(total weight of truck, driver, and boxes set equal to 6000)}$$

$$14x = 1500 \quad \text{(subtract 4500 from both sides)}$$

$$x = \frac{1500}{14} \quad \text{(divide both sides by 14)}$$

$$x \approx 107.14 \quad \text{(calculate)}$$

So when there are approximately 107.14 boxes, the total weight of the truck, driver, and boxes is *equal* to 6000 pounds. But the prompt asked us for the highest number of boxes that would let us stay *below* 6000 pounds total. We can find this by rounding 107.14 down to 107 boxes, so 107 is the answer.

Solution 2: Guess-and-check: Try various values for x and test them against the concepts in the prompt until you find the maximum value for x.

If we guess that there are 100 boxes, then we could find the total weight like this: $4500 + 14(100) = 5900$.

With that guess, we're 100 pounds shy of the weight limit, which means we can add more boxes. Let's try adding 5 more, which would give us this calculation: $4500 + 14(105) = 5970$.

We're still under the limit of 6000 pounds by 30 pounds. We'll try adding 2 boxes, which gives us this: $4500 + 14(107) = 5998$.

At this point, we're very close to the 6000 pound limit. In fact, we can see that if we add even one more 14-pound box, we'll push the weight over the limit. So 107 boxes is the maximum number of boxes under the conditions in the prompt.

Solution 3: Arithmetic: Without formally translating the values from the prompt into algebra, work through the concepts in the prompt until you identify the maximum value for x.

We know the maximum allowed weight is 6000 pounds, and the truck and driver account for 4500 pounds. That leaves a maximum of 1500 pounds for all the boxes. If we divide 1500 by 14, we'll get the maximum number of boxes that could make up that 1500 pounds—the result is about 107.14. If around 107.14 boxes would make the total weight equal to 6000 pounds, and we need to be *under* the weight limit, then we should round down to 107 boxes.

So adding 107 boxes to the truck and driver gives us the maximum weight without going over the 6000 pound limit. We can test this by verifying that 108 boxes would cause us to exceed the limit of 6000 pounds, while 107 boxes are still under the limit.

How to check? Try an alternate method above. You can also try testing your value for x, and then testing $x + 1$ to make sure that your value for x is the highest possible value that satisfies the prompt.

Test 1, Section 4, Question 33

- **What's the prompt asking for?** A fraction comparing the number of players sold in 2008 to the number in 2011.
- **Math concepts in the prompt:** fractions, reading data from a graph
- **"Bridge" concepts:** The graph shows the values for 2008 and 2011. We can construct a fraction comparing these two numbers.

- **Things to look out for:** Don't misread the chart and choose the wrong numbers for 2008 and 2011! Don't switch the numerator and denominator when you construct your fraction!

Solution 1: Arithmetic: Read the data off the graph and construct the fraction from the relevant numbers.

100 million portable media players were sold in 2008, and 160 million portable media players were sold in 2011. We can compare those two numbers with the fraction $\frac{100,000,000}{160,000,000}$. This fraction can be reduced to $\frac{10}{16}$, or $\frac{5}{8}$. (Notice that we could also enter $.625$, which is the decimal equivalent of $\frac{5}{8}$.)

How to check? Re-check the graph to make sure you've combined the right numbers to create the fraction; re-check the prompt to make sure the numbers are in the right parts of the fraction.

Test 1, Section 4, Question 34

- **What's the prompt asking for?** The total number of 30-minute slots available for Tuesday and Wednesday.
- **Math concepts in the prompt:** multiplication, word problems, number of minutes in an hour

- **Things to look out for:** Make sure you don't make any small mistakes in your multiplication! Make sure you've read the prompt carefully, and have accurately understood the number of days and hours involved, and the amount of time for each time-slot.

Solution 1: Arithmetic: Read the prompt carefully and multiply the appropriate numbers by one another to determine the number of 30-minute slots in two full days.

30 minutes is half an hour, and there are two half-hours in every hour, by definition. If the station plays 24 hours per day, then they play 48 half-hour slots in one day, because 48 is equal to 24×2. So Tuesday and Wednesday each have 48 half-hour slots, and those two days together have 96 total half-hour slots, because $48 + 48 = 96$. So the right answer is 96.

How to check? Re-read the prompt and re-work the arithmetic to make sure that everything is correct.

Test 1, Section 4, Question 35

- **What's the prompt asking for?** The diameter of the base of the cylinder, in yards.
- **Math concepts in the prompt:** diameter, formulas from the beginning of the math section (right circular cylinders, volume)
- **Math concepts in the diagram:** height, right circular cylinders

- **"Bridge" concepts:** We can find the formula for the volume of a right-circular cylinder at the beginning of the math section; we can then plug in the given information to determine the radius of the cylinder, and use the radius to find the diameter.
- **Things to look out for:** Don't confuse radius and diameter!

Solution 1: Geometry: Use the formula for the volume of a right-circular cylinder to find the radius from the height and the volume; then use the radius to find the diameter.

$V = \pi r^2 h$	(area for volume of a right circular cylinder, provided at beginning of section)
$72\pi = \pi r^2(8)$	(plug in 8 for the height and 72π for volume, from the prompt)
$9 = r^2$	(divide both sides by 8π)
$3 = r$	(take square root of both sides to find the radius)

So the radius of the base of the cylinder is 3 yards—but the prompt asks for the diameter, not the radius! We have to remember that the diameter is twice the length of the radius, so the right answer is 6.

How to check? Carefully re-read the prompt and re-consider your calculations to make sure you've answered correctly. Also note that the diagram is drawn to scale, and compare the value you found for the diameter to the diagram to make sure it's plausible.

Test 1, Section 4, Question 36

- **What's the prompt asking for?** The value of x for which $h(x)$ is undefined.
- **Math concepts in the prompt:** algebra, functions, undefined functions, variables
- **"Bridge" concepts:** A function is undefined for a particular input when the input would result in a value of zero for the denominator of a fraction in the function. The value of x that causes $(x - 5)^2 + 4(x - 5) + 4$ to be equal to zero will be the value that causes $h(x)$ to be undefined.
- **Things to look out for:** Don't make any mistakes in your algebra! Don't make the mistake of thinking that x should be zero, instead of finding the x-value that makes the denominator equal to zero!

Solution 1: Algebra: Set the expression in the denominator equal to zero and solve for x.

Values in a function are undefined when the denominator of the function is equal to zero. So let's set the denominator equal to zero and solve for x:

$$(x - 5)^2 + 4(x - 5) + 4 = 0 \qquad \text{(denominator from function set equal to zero)}$$
$$x^2 - 10x + 25 + 4x - 20 + 4 = 0 \qquad \text{(square } (x-5) \text{ and distribute the 4)}$$
$$x^2 - 6x + 9 = 0 \qquad \text{(simplify)}$$
$$(x - 3)^2 = 0 \qquad \text{(reverse FOIL)}$$
$$x - 3 = 0 \qquad \text{(take square root of both sides)}$$
$$x = 3 \qquad \text{(add 3 to both sides)}$$

So the function is undefined when $x = 3$, which means 3 is the answer to the question.

Solution 2: Calculator: Graph $h(x)$ on your calculator and then determine the point on the graph where $h(x)$ is undefined.

When we graph this function, we get this:

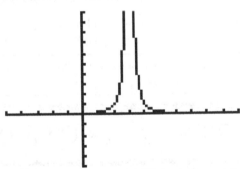

As we can see, the graph is undefined where $x = 3$. (We can also confirm this by looking at the table of values on our calculator.)

How to check? Plug $x = 3$ back into the original expression to confirm that it makes the denominator equal to 0; try an alternate approach above; re-read the prompt and re-check your arithmetic.

Test 1, Section 4, Question 37

- **What's the prompt asking for?** The value of x in Jessica's algebraic expression.
- **Math concepts in the prompt:** compound interest, function models, translating text into algebra, variables, word problems
- **"Bridge" concepts:** Since the expression in the prompt models the situation in the prompt, each number or variable in that expression must correspond to a number or concept elsewhere in the prompt.
- **Things to look out for:** Don't confuse different parts of the model expression in the prompt!

Solution 1: Functions: Carefully re-read the prompt and figure out how each component of the expression corresponds to the situation described in the prompt.

The given expression for calculating the value after t years is $\$100(x)^t$. The $\$100$ is Jessica's initial deposit, and t is the number of years that the account has been accruing interest. The only value unaccounted for in the function so far is the 2 percent interest rate that the account earns. The decimal equivalent of 2 percent is 0.02…but x in this expression isn't equal to 0.02! If we were to multiply $\$100$ by 0.02, then we'd end up with a number of dollars in the account that's less than $\$100$, since we'd be multiplying $\$100$ by a number smaller than 1. So x must be a value that causes the expression to be larger than $\$100$.

When we think about it, we realize that x actually needs to be 1.02, to reflect the idea that we're adding the 2 percent (which is reflected in the 0.02) to the amount in the account (which is reflected in the number 1, indicating 100%). So it makes sense that $x = 1.02$, which means that, every year, the balance should be multiplied by 1.02 to reflect the interest added that year. So the right answer is 1.02.

How to check? Reconsider each component of the expression and its role.

Test 1, Section 4, Question 38

- **What's the prompt asking for?** The difference between the amount that Tyshaun's deposit will have earned after two years, and the amount Jessica's deposit will have earned at that time (rounded to the nearest cent).
- **Math concepts in the prompt:** compound interest, function modeling, subtraction

- **"Bridge" concepts:** We can determine the interest earned by each person's deposit after 10 years if we plug the relevant numbers into the model; after that, we can take the amount earned by Jessica and subtract it from the amount earned by Tyshaun to determine the answer to the question.

Solution 1: Arithmetic: Using a calculator, determine the amount earned by Tyshaun's deposit after 10 years, and then determine the amount earned by Jessica's deposit after 10 years, and subtract the smaller number from the larger number.

First, let's find the value of Jessica's account after 10 years of earning 2 percent interest on her $100 deposit:

$\$100(1.02)^t$	(expression for interest on Jessica's $100 investment—see the explanation for question 37 for more)
$\$100(1.02)^{10}$	(plug in $t = 10$)
$\approx \$121.8994$	(simplify)

Now, let's find the value of Tyshaun's account after 10 years of earning 2.5 percent interest on his $100 deposit. We'll need to modify our expression for calculating Jessica's balance so that it reflects Tyshaun's interest rate; we can do this by changing the 1.02 in Jessica's expression to 1.025, to reflect the idea of the balance at the end of the year being 102.5% of what it was at the beginning of the year:

$\$100(1.025)^t$	(expression for interest earned on Tyshaun's $100 investment)
$\$100(1.025)^{10}$	(plug in $t = 10$)
$\approx \$128.0085$	(simplify)

The prompt asks how much more money Tyshaun's deposit earns than Jessica's deposit does, so let's find the difference between the two amounts, and round to the nearest penny, as the prompt requires: $128.0085 - $121.8994 $\approx$ $6.11. So the answer is $6.11.

How to check? Reconsider every step in the process to make sure you've followed through correctly—pay particular attention to whichever kinds of small mistakes you tend to make more often.

TEST 2 – SECTION 4

Test 2, Section 4, Question 1

- **What's the prompt asking for?** The choice with the function that accurately models the musician's earnings based on downloads and streaming.
- **Math concepts in the prompt:** function modeling, variables, word problems
- **Elements of the answer choices:** algebraic expressions, decimals
- **Notable differences among answer choices:** (A) and (B) both have 0.002 as the coefficient of d and 0.09 as the coefficient of s, while (C) and (D) both have 0.09 as the coefficient of d

and 0.002 as the coefficient of s. (A) and (C) both involve adding the two variable expressions, while (B) and (D) involve subtracting one from the other.

- **Concepts in the answer choices:** decimals, multiplication, variables
- **Pre-solution patterns (see p. 217):** wrong answers try to imitate right answers
- **Things to look out for:** Don't confuse s and d! Don't misread the answer choices!

Solution 1: Algebraic: Read the prompt carefully and construct the correct model. Pick the answer choice that matches your model.

If the musician earns $0.09 each time the song is downloaded, and the song is downloaded d times, then she must earn a total of $0.09d$ for downloaded songs, because that expression represents the idea of multiplying 9 cents by the number of downloads. If the musician earns $0.002 each time the song is streamed, and the song is streamed s times, then she must earn a total of $0.002s$ for streamed songs, because that expression reflects the idea of multiplying the number of streams by $0.002.

So the total for both downloaded and streamed songs must be the sum of those two expressions, which would look like this: $0.09d + 0.002s$. That means the correct answer must be (C).

Solution 2: Test-smart: Consider the similarities and differences among the answer choices in light of the concepts in the prompt, and pick the answer choice that accurately reflects the prompt.

When we compare the answer choices to one another, we can see that they represent every possible combination of two options:

1. Either 0.002 is the coefficient of d (like in (A) and (B)), or it's the coefficient of s (like in (C) and (D)), and 0.09 is the coefficient of the other variable.
2. Either the two variable expressions are added together (like in (A) and (C)), or the s expression is subtracted from the d expression (like in (B) and (D)).

So we can determine which choice is correct by figuring out which of the above options should appear in the correct answer.

For the first issue, we can tell that d should be multiplied by $0.09, because the prompt says she earns "$0.09 each time the song is downloaded," and we know that d represents the number of downloads. In this context, the phrase "each time" indicates that $0.09 should be multiplied by the number of downloads.

For the second issue, we can tell that the two expressions should be added together, because the word "and" in line 3 of the prompt indicates that the two numbers combine to give us the total amount earned.

Since only one choice reflects the idea of multiplying 0.09 by d and adding that to the s expression, we know (C) must be right.

ANSWER CHOICE ANALYSIS

(A): This is the result if we switch the amount of money the musician earns from a downloaded song with the amount of money the musician earns from a streamed song. **(B):** This choice combines the mistakes from (A) and (D). **(D):** This is the result if we think that the money the musician makes from streamed songs takes away from the money the musician makes from downloaded songs.

How to check? Try an alternate approach above. Remember to read the prompt and the answer choices carefully.

▶ Post-solution patterns (see page 218): opposites

Test 2, Section 4, Question 2

- **What's the prompt asking for?** The number of inspected lightbulbs if the factory produces 20,000 bulbs.
- **Math concepts in the prompt:** ratios, word problems
- **Elements of the answer choices:** integers

- **Notable differences among answer choices:** The choices form a series from 300 to 450, with each number being 50 more than the one before it.
- **Pre-solution patterns (see p. 217):** the first and last terms in a series are often wrong answers
- **Things to look out for:** Make sure you're not off by 50!

Solution 1: Ratios: Construct an equation that equates the relationship between 7 and 400 to the relationship between the correct answer and 20,000. Then solve to find the correct answer.

The phrase "at this rate" in the prompt indicates that we need to determine the rate of inspection for the 400 lightbulbs produced, and then extend that rate to account for the production of 20,000 lightbulbs. We can do that by setting up equivalent ratios in an equation.

One of the ratios in our equation needs to represent the idea that 7 lightbulbs out of 400 are checked, which can look like this: $\frac{7}{400}$. The other ratio needs to represent the idea that we don't yet know how many lightbulbs out of 20,000 will need to be checked. That ratio can look like this, with the x representing the unknown number of tested lightbulbs: $\frac{x}{20000}$

Then we can set those ratios equal and solve for x:

$\frac{7}{400} = \frac{x}{20000}$ (create equation to show that the ratio of 7 lightbulbs inspected per 400 lightbulbs produced is equal to the ratio of x bulbs inspected per 20,000 lightbulbs produced)

$140000 = 400x$ (cross-multiply)

$350 = x$ (divide both sides by 400)

So we can see the correct answer is (B).

Solution 2: Arithmetic: Note that 400 times 50 is 20,000, which means that 7 times 50 will be the correct answer to the question.

400 times 50 equals 20,000, so the right answer must be 7 times 50, or 350, because the ratio between the number of lightbulbs being checked in both situations must be the same as the ratio between the number of lightbulbs being produced in both situations.

Solution 3: Test-smart: Realize that the correct answer must be a multiple of 7, and that only (B) qualifies.

The question doesn't ask for an approximate value, so we know the correct answer must be exact—not rounded off or approximated. We can also see that the prompt doesn't involve fractions, and that each of the answer choices ends in a zero, which means that finding the correct answer in one of the traditional ways will involve multiplying 7 by an integer (see solutions 1 and 2 above for examples). If we notice that only choice (B) is a multiple of 7, then we know that (B) must be correct.

How to check? Try an alternate approach above.

▶ Post-solution patterns (see page 218): the first and last terms in a series are often wrong answers

Test 2, Section 4, Question 3

- **What's the prompt asking for?** The value of m in the given equation when l is 73.
  Math concepts in the prompt: addition, algebra, function modeling, multiplication, word problems
- **Elements of the answer choices:** decimals, integers

- **Notable differences among answer choices:** (A) and (C) are the only choices that are integers, while (B) and (D) are both decimal numbers.
- **Things to look out for:** Don't confuse l and m!

Solution 1: Algebra: Set l equal to 73 in the given equation and solve for m.

$l = 24 + 3.5m$	(original equation from the prompt)
$73 = 24 + 3.5m$	(plug in $l = 73$)
$49 = 3.5m$	(subtract 24 from both sides)
$14 = m$	(divide both sides by 3.5 to find m when l is 73)

So we can see the answer is (A).

Solution 2: Estimation: Note that m must be less than one-third the value of l. Only one choice satisfies this requirement.

If we compare the choices to one another, and to the numbers in the prompt, we may realize that we can think about the structure of the function to figure out roughly how m relates to l. When we do that, we can see that m must always be less than one-third of l, because we find l after multiplying m by a number that's bigger than 3, and then adding 24 to that product. So when l is 73, m must be a number that's less than one-third of 73.

We see that only (A) is less than one-third of 73, so it must be right. (We can roughly estimate that one-third of 73 must be slightly less than 25, since 73 is slightly less than 75 and one-third of 75 is 25.)

ANSWER CHOICE ANALYSIS

(B): This is the result if we add 24 to 73 and end up dividing 97 by 3.5, instead of dividing 49 by 3.5. **(C):** This is the value we were given for l. **(D):** This is the result an untrained test-taker would get after confusing l and m—in other words, if we set m equal to 73 and then solve for l, we arrive at this choice.

How to check? Try an alternate approach above, making especially sure that you're not confusing l and m!

Test 2, Section 4, Question 4

- **What's the prompt asking for?** The amount earned by the performer when 20 people attend.
- **Math concepts in the prompt:** arithmetic, direct proportionality, ratios
- **Elements of the answer choices:** integers
- **Notable differences among answer choices:** (A), (B), and (D) form a series in which each choice is $\frac{1}{2}$ of the choice before it.
- **"Bridge" concepts:** Since the relationship between earnings and attendees is "directly proportional" according to the

prompt, we know there must be a consistent ratio (or proportion) between the number of attendees and the amount of money.

- **Pre-solution patterns (see p. 217):** halves and doubles; the first and last terms in a series are often wrong answers
- **Things to look out for:** Make sure you're not off by a factor of 2! Make sure you don't set up the proportion incorrectly by comparing the wrong pairs of numbers!

Solution 1: Algebra: Set up an equation with 2 proportions: one comparing 8 to 120, and the other comparing 20 to x. Solve for x.

The phrase "directly proportional" in the prompt indicates that we can extend the given rate of dollars earned per attendee to account for the money earned when there are 20 attendees. We can do that by setting up equivalent ratios in an equation.

One of the ratios in our equation needs to represent the idea that 120 dollars are earned when there are 8 attendees. That ratio can look like this: $\frac{120}{8}$. The other ratio needs to represent the idea that we don't yet know how many dollars are earned when 20 people attend. That ratio can look like this, with the x representing the unknown number of dollars: $\frac{x}{20}$

Then we can set those ratios equal and solve for x:

$\frac{120}{8} = \frac{x}{20}$	(proportions of earnings to attendees set equal to one another)
$2400 = 8x$	(cross-multiply)
$300 = x$	(divide both sides by 8)

So we can see that (C) is correct.

Solution 2: Arithmetic: Note that 20 is 8 × 2.5, and then multiply $120 by 2.5 to find the correct answer.

We may be able to do the mental calculation that 20 is two-and-a-half times 8, and realize the correct answer must likewise be two-and-a-half times 120, which was the number of dollars corresponding to 8 in the prompt. 2.5 × 120 is 300, so (C) is correct.

Solution 3: Test-smart: Compare the answer choices to the prompt. Notice that (A), (B), and (D) are all multiples of $120 . . . but that 20 isn't a multiple of 8, so the correct answer can't be a multiple of $120, which means (C) must be correct.

ANSWER CHOICE ANALYSIS

(A): This choice is twice as much as (B). **(B):** This is the result if we make an algebra mistake and end up setting 2400 equal to $5x$ instead of $8x$. **(D):** This is the result if we make an algebra mistake and end up setting 2400 equal to $10x$ instead of $8x$.

How to check? Try an alternate approach above.

▶   Post-solution patterns (see page 218): the first and last terms in a series are often wrong answers

Test 2, Section 4, Question 5

- **What's the prompt asking for?** The performer's profit when 8 people attend the show.
- **Math concepts in the prompt:** percentages, word problems
- **Elements of the answer choices:** decimals
- **Notable differences among answer choices:** (A) and (C) are the only two choices that add up to $120. This may be relevant because, as trained test-takers, we can expect that the College Board will likely make one of the wrong answers correspond to the costs of the performance instead of the profit. (A) and (B) are both less than half of $120, while (C) and (D) are more than half of $120. This could be relevant because the question tells us that the costs are less than 50% of the earnings, which means that the profit must be more than 50%.

- **"Bridge" concepts:** If the costs are 43% of the earnings, then the profit must be 57% of the earnings, because 43% + 57% = 100%. Finding 57% of a number is the same as multiplying it by 0.57.
- **Pre-solution patterns (see p. 217):** complements or supplements
- **Things to look out for:** Don't forget that you're looking for the profit, not the cost! Don't make any small mistakes in your multiplying!

Solution 1: Arithmetic: Multiply $120 by 0.57 to find the correct answer.

As we noted in the "bridge" concepts above, the performer's profit will be 57% of the money earned, because 100% − 43% = 57%. So we can answer this question by finding 57% of the amount earned for 8 people. That calculation looks like this: 120 × 0.57 = 68.4 So we can see that (C) must be correct.

Solution 2: Test-smart estimation: Realize that the correct answer must be more than $60 but less than $72.

The performer's profit is 57% of the money earned, which means that the profit must be between 50% and 60%, because 57 is between 50 and 60. 50% of $120 would be $60, so the answer must be more than $60, which eliminates (A) and (B). 60% of $120 would be $72, so the answer must be less than $72, which eliminates (D). This leaves only (C), so (C) must be right.

ANSWER CHOICE ANALYSIS

(A): This is 43% of the money earned, which the prompt tells us goes to the performer's *costs*. The question asks for the performer's *profit*. **(B):** This is $100 − $43, which we might find if we confuse the percent sign in the prompt with a dollar sign. **(D):** This is $120 − $43, which we might find if we confuse the percent sign in the prompt with a dollar sign and also mix up the percentage calculation with the dollar calculation.

How to check? Try an alternate approach above. Be sure to read carefully and verify that the prompt asks for the profit, not the cost.

▶   Post-solution patterns (see page 218): complements or supplements, right answer to the wrong question

Test 2, Section 4, Question 6

- **What's the prompt asking for?** The value of $2x + 7$.
- **Math concepts in the prompt:** addition, algebra, multiplication, variables, word problems
- **Elements of the answer choices:** integers, negative numbers

- **Notable differences among answer choices:** (A) is the only negative number, while (B), (C), and (D) are positive. (C) is the only number that also appears in the prompt.
- **Things to look out for:** Don't make mistakes in your algebra! Don't misread the prompt when you're setting up your algebraic solutions! Don't accidentally mark the value of x!

Solution 1: Algebra: Use algebra to determine the value of x according to the prompt, and then use x to answer the question.

We can translate the first sentence in the prompt into an equation that allows us to determine the value of x. To do that, we move through the sentence, phrase by phrase, translating each phrase into a mathematical expression. The phrase "4 times the number x" is equivalent to the expression $4x$; the phrase "is added to 12" is equivalent to $+\ 12$; the phrase "the result is 8" is equivalent to an equals sign followed by the number 8. So the first sentence can be expressed in the equation $4x + 12 = 8$, which we can solve for x:

$$4x + 12 = 8 \quad \text{(first equation described in the prompt)}$$
$$4x = -4 \quad \text{(subtract 12 from both sides)}$$
$$x = -1 \quad \text{(divide both sides by 4)}$$

Now we can plug $x = -1$ into the second expression described in the prompt. (In that expression, "2 times x" is equivalent to $2x$, and "is added to 7" is equivalent to $+\ 7$, so the entire expression is equivalent to $2x + 7$.)

$$2x + 7 \quad \text{(second expression described in the prompt)}$$
$$2(-1) + 7 \quad \text{(plug in } x = -1\text{)}$$
$$5 \quad \text{(simplify to find } 2x + 7 \text{ when } x = -1\text{)}$$

So the correct answer is (B).

Solution 2: Arithmetic: Note that x must be -1, and then use that value to answer the question.

We may be able to do mental math and realize that x is equal to -1, just by realizing that $12 - 4$ is 8, which means that the x described in the prompt must be -1. (Noticing that -1 is one of the answer choices would also help reassure us that our mental math was correct, because, as trained test-takers, we know that the College Board often likes to include wrong answers that reflect values we have to find on the way to answering a question correctly, such as the value of x in this case.)

Once we realize that x is -1, we can do a little more mental math and realize that 5 is the answer to the prompt, so (C) must be correct.

ANSWER CHOICE ANALYSIS

(A): This is the value of x, and a lot of untrained test-takers will pick this answer because they're able to find x correctly but unable to remember that the question didn't ask us to find x. This is why it's so important to keep in mind what the question is asking for! **(B):** This is the correct answer. **(C):** This is the sum of choices (A) and (D). **(D):** This is the result if we accidentally add *positive* 2 to 7, instead of adding negative 2, as the prompt requires. Let this be a reminder that we always have to double-check basic things like arithmetic and the sign of a number!

How to check? Try an alternate approach above.

▶   Post-solution patterns (see page 218): opposites; right approach, wrong step

---

Test 2, Section 4, Question 7

- **What's the prompt asking for?** The form of the equation that displays the x-intercepts of the graph as constants or coefficients.
- **Math concepts in the prompt:** algebra, equivalent equations, exponents, functions, parabolas, zeros of a function
- **Elements of the answer choices:** algebraic expressions, equations, exponents, integers
- **Notable differences among answer choices:** (A) and (C) both include the integers 6 and 8, which also appear in the prompt; on the other hand, (B) and (D) each have integers unique to them.

- **Concepts in the answer choices:** equations, exponents, FOIL
- **"Bridge" concepts:** When two equations are equivalent, by definition, the same set of (x, y) coordinates satisfies both equations. The x-intercepts of a function are the x-values of the function when y equals zero; these are also called the zeros of the function.
- **Pre-solution patterns (see p. 217):** wrong answers try to imitate right answers
- **Things to look out for:** Don't make any small mistakes in your reading, algebra, or arithmetic!

Solution 1: Graphing: Graph the function in the prompt and see where its x-intercepts are; then pick the answer choice that displays the x-intercepts.

When we graph the equation from the prompt, we get this:

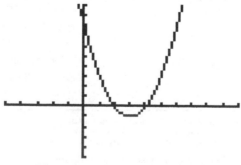

As we can see, the x-intercepts are $x = 2$ and $x = 4$. The only choice that includes both of these numbers is (D), so (D) is right.

Solution 2: Algebra: Determine the zeros of the function in the prompt by using the reverse-FOIL technique, and then pick the answer choice that matches them.

$$y = x^2 - 6x + 8 \qquad \text{(original equation)}$$
$$y = (x - 2)(x - 4) \qquad \text{(reverse FOIL)}$$

So $y = 0$ when $x = 2$ or when $x = 4$, which means the graph has x-intercepts at $x = 2$ and $x = 4$. This means (D) must be right.

How to check? Try an alternate approach above.

Test 2, Section 4, Question 8

- **What's the prompt asking for?** The value of k under the given conditions
- **Math concepts in the prompt:** algebra, multiplication, subtraction, variables, word problems
- **Elements of the answer choices:** integers, zero

- **Notable differences among answer choices:** (B) and (C) add up to (D), which may be relevant because the question discusses the idea of losing points—one or more of these choices may reflect a number we need to find on the way to finding the correct answer.
- **Things to look out for:** Don't misread the prompt! Don't make any small mistakes in your algebra or arithmetic!

Solution 1: Algebraic modeling: Create an expression for the number of points a player has in terms of k, and then plug in the given values from the prompt and solve for k.

For this approach, we need to create an equation that reflects the situation described in the prompt. Let's have t equal the number of uncompleted tasks, and s equal the player's score. The prompt says a player "loses 2 points" for "each...task" that's not completed; the idea of 2 points for each uncompleted task can be expressed as $2t$, and the idea of losing those points can be expressed as subtraction. So that leaves us with the idea that a score starts as k, and then loses 2 points per uncompleted task, to arrive at a final score of s. That equation would be $k - 2t = s$.

We can use this to figure out the value of k when t is 100 and s is 200, as the prompt describes:

$$k - 2t = s \qquad \text{(equation based on information in the prompt)}$$
$$k - 2(100) = 200 \qquad \text{(plug in } t = 100 \text{ and } s = 200\text{)}$$
$$k - 200 = 200 \qquad \text{(simplify)}$$
$$k = 400 \qquad \text{(add 200 to both sides)}$$

So we can see that (D) is correct.

Solution 2: Arithmetic: Note that each failed task accounts for a 2-point loss, and realize we can find the correct answer if we multiply 100 by 2 and add that to 200.

$$(100 \times 2) + 200 = 400$$

Again, we see that (D) must be correct.

Solution 3: Backsolving: Test each answer choice as the starting number of points in the game, either by using an algebraic model or by simply working through the situation in the prompt with basic arithmetic. The correct choice will be the one that results in a score of 200 points after 100 tasks are failed.

$$0 - (100 \times 2) = -200 \qquad \text{(result of (A))}$$
$$150 - (100 \times 2) = -50 \qquad \text{(result of (B))}$$
$$250 - (100 \times 2) = 50 \qquad \text{(result of (C))}$$
$$400 - (100 \times 2) = 200 \qquad \text{(result of (D))}$$

Only the value from (D) results in a score of 200, so (D) must be correct.

Solution 4: Test-smart: Notice that the right answer must be more than 200, and can't end in 50, which means (D) is the only possible answer.

When we read the prompt, we realize the starting score must be larger than 200, because the prompt tells us we subtract something from the starting score and still end up with 200 points left. We can also realize the correct answer must not end in 50, because the number of tasks is 100, and the final score is 200, which means the number of points lost must be a multiple of 100, and no multiple of 100 can end in 50.

The only choice that's larger than 200 and reflects a number of lost points that's a multiple of 100 is (D), so (D) must be correct.

ANSWER CHOICE ANALYSIS

(A): This choice is probably here to trap untrained test-takers who make the mistake of thinking that "common sense" should apply to word problems on the SAT. A lot of people who play video games would expect that the score for a game would start at 0, because that's how most games work, but 0 doesn't satisfy the requirements in the prompt, so it must be wrong. **(B):** This is the result if we add 100 and 200 from the prompt and divide by 2 from the prompt. **(C):** This is the difference between (D) and (B).

How to check? Try an alternate approach above. Make sure you've read the prompt carefully!

Test 2, Section 4, Question 9

- **What's the prompt asking for?** The system of inequalities that accurately reflects the prompt.
- **Math concepts in the prompt:** addition, algebra, multiplication, systems of inequalities, word problems
- **Elements of the answer choices:** algebraic expressions, fractions, inequalities, integers
- **Notable differences among answer choices:** (A) and (B) both compare the sum of x and y to 45, while (C) and (D) compare $x + y$ to 2,400. (A) and (D) both compare the expression $40x + 65y$ to 2,400, while (C) compares it to 45,

and (B) doesn't have the expression. (B) is the only choice with a fraction. (D) is the only choice without the number 45.

- **Concepts in the answer choices:** addition, fractions, inequalities, multiplication, systems of inequalities
- **"Bridge" concepts:** The prompt tells us about two limits on what the forklift can carry. The right answer must accurately reflect both limits.
- **Pre-solution patterns (see p. 217):** wrong answers try to imitate right answers
- **Things to look out for:** Don't misread the prompt! Don't misread the choices, which contain very similar elements!

Solution 1: Algebra: Write out 2 inequality expressions that reflect the prompt. Find the choice that matches what you've written.

The total weight of the 40-pound boxes must be the number of 40-pound boxes times 40, which is reflected in the expression $40x$. Similarly, the total weight of the 65-pound boxes must be the number of 65-pound boxes times 65, or $65y$. The total weight of all of the 40-pound boxes and the 65-pound boxes can be expressed as $40x + 65y$. The prompt tells us that this total amount must be less than or equal to 2400, so we can write $40x + 65y \leq 2400$.

The prompt also tells us that the total number of boxes must be less than or equal to 45, so we can say that $x + y \leq 45$.

Only choice (A) includes both of the inequality statements we arrived at, so (A) must be correct.

Solution 2: Backsolving: Compare each answer choice to the prompt to see which one accurately reflects it.

If we compare (A) to the ideas in the prompt, we see that it reflects them, as we discussed in solution 1.

When we compare (B) to the ideas in the prompt, one of the first issues we're likely to notice is that (B) involves fractions, but there's nothing in the prompt that indicates we should be dividing a number of boxes by the weight of a box, so (B) can't be correct.

(C) can't be correct for multiple reasons; one of them is that the second inequality compares the sum of the number of 40-pound boxes (which is x) and the number of 65-pound boxes (which is y) to the number 2,400, which isn't reflected in the prompt. The prompt says 2,400 is related to weight, not to the number of boxes.

(D) can't be correct for the same reason that (C) can't be correct, among other things—it includes the same inaccurate statement comparing the sum of x and y to the weight in the prompt.

So we can see that (A) must be correct.

Solution 3: Test-smart: Consider the similarities and differences among the choices that we noted above, and decide which elements should appear in the correct answer.

When we compare the answer choices to one another, we see that the choices are offering the following options, as we noted earlier in our discussion of this question:

- Two choices ((A) and (D)) compare the sum of $40x$ and $65y$ to 2,400, while (C) compares that sum to 45.
- One choice (choice (B)) involves fractions.
- Every choice except (D) includes one inequality that involves the number 45. (D) involves two inequality statements that relate variable expressions to the number 2,400.

If we figure out how to resolve each of these issues, we can figure out which choice is correct.

For the first issue, it makes sense to compare $40x$ and $65y$ to 2,400, since all of those numbers are related to weight in the prompt.

For the second issue, it doesn't make any sense to divide x or y by anything, because the prompt doesn't discuss the idea of dividing anything by the weights of the different kinds of boxes.

For the third issue, it makes sense that the sum of x and y should be compared to 45, since all of those concepts are related to numbers of boxes in the prompt.

The only answer choice that satisfies all of these requirements is (A), so we know (A) is right.

ANSWER CHOICE ANALYSIS

(C): This is just like the correct answer, except the values on the right side of the two inequalities are switched—this could be the result of a test-taker who understood the question but was careless in writing down the two equations.

How to check? Try an alternate approach above.

- **What's the prompt asking for?** The value of $f(g(3))$.
- **Math concepts in the prompt:** nested functions, functions, inputs and outputs of functions
- **Elements of the answer choices:** integers
- **Notable differences among answer choices:** All of the choices are numbers that appear in the prompt.
- **"Bridge" concepts:** None of the choices indicates that we don't have enough information to answer the question; as trained test-takers, we know this means it must be possible to use the given information to answer the question. When we see nested function notation like $f(g(3))$, we know that we need to work from the inside out to evaluate the expression.
- **Pre-solution patterns (see p. 217):** halves and doubles
- **Things to look out for:** Don't confuse f and g! Make sure to evaluate the parts of $f(g(3))$ in the correct order!

Solution 1: Algebra: Relying on the given information and the notation conventions, evaluate $g(3)$ first; then find the f-value that corresponds to the value of $g(3)$.

The prompt tells us that $g(3) = 2$, so $f(g(3)) = f(2) = 3$. That means (B) is right.

ANSWER CHOICE ANALYSIS

(A): This is the value of $g(3)$, but the question didn't ask us to stop working after we found $g(3)$! Instead, we're supposed to take this value and plug it into function f, so we can find $f(g(3))$. **(C):** This is $f(3)$, not $f(g(3))$. **(D):** This is $g(f(3))$, not $f(g(3))$.

How to check? Re-read the prompt carefully to make sure you haven't made any small mistakes in comprehension or execution!

▶ Post-solution patterns (see page 218): right approach, wrong step

- **What's the prompt asking for?** The choice "closest" to the number of days it will take Tony to read the novel.
- **Math concepts in the prompt:** division, estimation, reading data from a table, word problems
- **Math concepts in the diagram:** reading data from a table
- **Elements of the answer choices:** integers
- **Notable differences among answer choices:** We may be able to come up with a quick, accurate estimation of the answer, since (C) is the only two-digit choice, and (D) is the only three-digit choice.
- **Things to look out for:** Don't misread the rows of data in the table! Don't make the mistake of thinking that all of the information in the table must be relevant!

Solution 1: Data: Using the relevant data in the table, determine which choice is closest to the number of days it will take Tony to read the 349,168 words in the novel.

If Tony reads 250 words per minute, and he spends 3 hours reading per day, then he'll read $3 \times 60 \times 250$ words per day, or 45,000 words per day.

Now that we know the number of words that Tony can read in a day, we can find the number of days it will take to read the 349,168 words in the novel. To do this, we divide the number of words in the book by the number of words read each day, so we see it will take Tony $\frac{349,168}{45,000}$ days to read the novel, which is approximately 7.76 days. Since (B) is closest to 7.76, (B) is right.

Solution 2: Backsolving estimation: Go through each answer choice and determine the number of words Tony would be able to read for each choice; the correct answer is the choice that comes closest to allowing Tony to read 349,168 words.

If Tony reads for 3 hours per day, and he can read 250 words per minute, and he spends 6 days reading, as choice (A) calls for, then Tony will read $3 \times 60 \times 250 \times 6$ words, or 270,000 words in that time. This is significantly less than the number of words in the novel, so Tony won't finish the novel in 6 days.

If Tony spends 8 days reading, as (B) calls for, then he'll read $3 \times 60 \times 250 \times 8$ words, or 360,000 words. This is just a little bit more than the 349,168 words in the novel. This looks like it could be the right answer, since the prompt tells us we're looking for the answer choice with the closest approximation of the number of days that Tony's reading will take. Of course, as trained test-takers, we know that we always need to consider each answer choice before committing to one, so let's take a look at (C) and (D).

If Tony spends 23 days reading, as (C) calls for, then he'll read $3 \times 60 \times 250 \times 23$ words, or 1,035,000 words.

Finally, if Tony spends 324 days reading, as (D) calls for, then he'll read $3 \times 60 \times 250 \times 324$ words, or 14,580,000 words. 360,000 words is the value closest to the 349,168 words in the novel, so (B) is correct.

ANSWER CHOICE ANALYSIS

(C): This is the approximate number of *hours* it would take Tony to read the novel. **(D):** This is approximately the novel's average number of words per page.

How to check? Try an alternate approach above. Pay special attention to the table to make sure you used the right numbers!

- **What's the prompt asking for?** The answer choice that accurately describes the set of years when the landfill is at capacity or above capacity.
- **Math concepts in the prompt:** function modeling, inequalities, multiplication, rate, word problems
- **Elements of the answer choices:** inequalities, integers
- **Notable differences among answer choices:** (C) is the only choice that doesn't include the number 325,000, and the only choice that does include 150,000. (A) is the only choice that doesn't involve multiplying 7,500 by y. (A) involves subtraction, while (D) involves addition; (B) and (C) don't involve addition or subtraction. Every choice except (A) involves multiplication. (D) is the only choice that involves 175,000.

- **Concepts in the answer choices:** addition, function modeling, inequalities, multiplication, subtraction
- **Pre-solution patterns (see p. 217):** wrong answers try to imitate right answers
- **Things to look out for:** Don't misread the prompt—for example, don't get confused between the numbers 7,500 and 175,000! Don't misread the answer choices!

Solution 1: Algebra: Write out an inequality based on the prompt, and pick the answer choice that matches your expression.

If the landfill already has 175,000 tons of trash as of January 1, 2000, and every year another 7500 tons is added, then we can say that the total amount of trash in the landfill is equal to $175,000 + 7500y$, where y is the number of years after January 1, 2000.

If the capacity of the landfill is 325,000 tons, then the landfill must be at or above capacity when $175,000 + 7500y \geq 325000$.

So we can see that (D) must be correct.

How to check? Carefully re-check your work, paying particular attention to your reading, and to the similarities and differences among the answer choices that we noted above.

Test 2, Section 4, Question 13

- **What's the prompt asking for?** The factor that "makes it least likely that a reliable conclusion can be drawn."
- **Math concepts in the prompt:** sample sizes, surveys
- **Elements of the answer choices:** words or phrases
- **Notable differences among answer choices:** (A) and (B) both mention the concept of size. (D) is the only choice that mentions a location.

- **Concepts in the answer choices:** population size, sample size
- **Things to look out for:** Make sure to read the prompt carefully, especially the phrase "least likely…that a reliable conclusion can be drawn!" Make sure not to confuse the statistical terms in the answer choices!

Solution 1: Data reasoning: Compare the terms in the answer choices to the prompt and select the choice that accurately describes a factor that makes a reliable conclusion least likely.

To answer this question, we need to remember the basic ideas related to sample sizes that we discussed in "The Basics of Surveys and Sampling" on page 206. With those ideas in mind, let's consider each of the choices to see which choice describes something that might contribute to the survey being inaccurate.

Choice (A) could be an appealing answer choice at first, because we know that a small sample size can make a study less reliable in general. The question does refer to the idea of 117 people being used to represent "a certain large town," but we don't have any indication of how many people actually live in the town.

Choice (B) mentions the population size, which is the number of people in the town itself, in this case. As we mentioned when we talked about choice (A), the question doesn't actually tell us what the population size is.

Choice (C) refers to the fact that 7 people refused to answer the survey. But this relatively small number of people who refused to answer doesn't affect the reliability of the survey, especially because the survey isn't asking about any kind of behavior that might be similar to the idea of refusing to answer a question. (As an example of a situation in which this choice might have been more relevant, we can imagine if the survey had been focused on determining people's privacy preferences rather than their sports-watching preferences, then the idea of refusing to answer a survey might have arguably been linked to the subject of the survey.)

Choice (D) could be relevant to the validity of the survey, because the survey was conducted in one place at one time, and the particular time and place chosen would probably prevent the sample from reflecting the different types of people in the "large town." For example, people who answer a survey at a restaurant on Saturday will be people who like the particular kind of food at the restaurant and who are available on Saturday; the survey would end up excluding people who don't like restaurants, or don't like a particular cuisine, or who work on Saturdays, and so on. As we discussed in "The Basics of Surveys and Sampling" on page 206 of this Black Book, surveys are generally more reliable when the people doing the survey make an effort to represent the entire population in their sample as much as possible.

Now that we've seen all of the answer choices, we might be a little torn between (A), (B), and (D). (D) is an attractive answer choice for the reasons we just discussed, but (A) and (B) might also seem somewhat plausible, especially since we don't know what the population size actually is. But this uncertainty about (A) and (B) should lead us to realize they can't be correct, for two reasons.

1. Since we don't know what the population size actually is, we can't possibly know if the sample size is appropriate (not to mention that the SAT would never require us to know the advanced statistical formulas for determining the relationship between confidence in a survey and the number of respondents as compared to the size of the population).
2. We can only talk about a small sample size *in relation to the size of a population*, which means that (A) and (B) are kind of the same answer——in other words, if a study is designed in such a way that the sample size is too small relative to the overall size of the town, we can also think of this situation as the population size being too large relative to the sample size.

So we don't have enough information to say that (A) or (B) make the survey unreliable, and we don't have any reason to think (C) is a problem either. (D), on the other hand, points to a clear issue with the survey: asking one group of people in one location at one particular time makes it unlikely that the survey is a good representation of the population of the whole town. Thus we can see that (D) is the only choice that can be correct.

How to check? Re-read the entire question and make sure you haven't missed any small details.

Test 2, Section 4, Question 14

- **What's the prompt asking for?** The year when 550 billion was the best approximation of the number of miles traveled.
- **Math concepts in the prompt:** approximation, line of best fit, reading data from a graph
- **Math concepts in the diagram:** axis labels, data points, titles of graphs
- **Elements of the answer choices:** integers
- **Notable differences among answer choices:** (A), (B), and (C) form a series in which each choice is 3 years later than the choice before it. This may be relevant because 2000 is one of the labeled years on the horizontal axis, and the years 1997 and 2003 both differ from that year by the same amount, which suggests that the College Board might be trying to get us to misread the graph and end up 3 years away from 2000 in the wrong direction.
- **Pre-solution patterns (see p. 217):** the first and last terms in a series are often wrong answers
- **Things to look out for:** Make sure not to misread the number of miles in the prompt! Make sure not to read data from the wrong row and column on the table!

Solution 1: Data interpretation: Read the graph to determine the year in which approximately 550 billion miles were traveled, then find the corresponding answer choice.

The line of best fit crosses the horizontal line representing 550 billion miles between the years 2000 and 2005 (note that 2005 is halfway between 2000 and 2010, even if it's not specifically labeled). The only choice in the range between 2000 and 2005 is (C), which is the correct answer.

Solution 2: Backsolving: Check each year in the answer choices against the graph, and pick the year that corresponds to approximately 550 billion miles.

(A) The line of best fit shows a value between 450 billion and 500 billion in 1997, so (A) isn't correct.
(B) The line of best fit shows a value of 500 billion in 2000, so (B) must be wrong.
(C) The line of best fit shows a value very close to 550 billion in 2003, so (C) is correct, assuming we haven't misread or misunderstood anything in our approach.
(D) The line of best fit shows a value greater than 600 billion in 2008, so (D) can't be correct.

ANSWER CHOICE ANALYSIS

(A) As noted above, this choice is probably here to confuse untrained test-takers who realize correctly that the line of best fit crosses the 550 billion level at a point that's around 3 years away from 2000, but then accidentally subtract 3 years from 2000, instead of adding 3 years, and choose 1997 instead; alternatively, this choice could be here to trap test-takers who mis-read the prompt or the graph, and end up choosing an approximation for when the line reaches the level corresponding to 450 billion. (B) This choice corresponds to the year when the number of miles traveled by air passengers in Country X was estimated to be 500 billion, not 550 billion. Some test-takers might accidentally choose (B) if they mixed up the horizontal line on the graph representing 500 billion with the horizontal line on the graph representing 550 billion.

How to check? Review the prompt, the graph, and the answer choices to make sure you haven't made any small mistakes!

Note Any of the wrong answer choices could be tempting for a test-taker who misreads the graph.

Test 2, Section 4, Question 15

- **What's the prompt asking for?** The nearest approximation of the Earth's speed as it travels around the Sun, in miles per hour.
- **Math concepts in the prompt:** distance = (rate)(time), word problems
- **Elements of the answer choices:** integers

- **Notable differences among answer choices:** (C) is half of (D). As trained test-takers, we know this may be relevant because the College Board often likes to present us with wrong answers that are half as much or twice as much as right answers.
- **"Bridge" concepts:** There are 24 hours in a day and roughly 365 days in a year. We'll need to express one year in terms of hours so we can find the final answer in terms of miles per hour, as the prompt requested. The "speed" referred to in the prompt is the same concept as "rate" in the $d = rt$ formula. We can apply $d = rt$ to the given information, which will allow us to determine the rate of travel.
- **Things to look out for:** halves and doubles

Solution 1: Algebra: Convert one year into hours, and then substitute the given distance and time in the $d = rt$ formula, and solve for r, which corresponds to the speed of travel in miles per hour.

One year is equal to 365 days, and each day is equal to 24 hours—so one year is equal to 365×24 hours, or 8,760 hours.

The prompt tells us that in one year, the Earth travels 580,000,000 miles. So the Earth travels 580,000,000 miles in 8,760 hours, which means we can figure out the speed in miles per hour if we divide the number of miles by the number of hours. When we do that, we see that the Earth travels at $\dfrac{580,000,000}{8,760}$ miles per hour, or approximately 66,000 miles per hour. So (A) is correct.

Test 2, Section 4, Question 16

- **What's the prompt asking for?** The probability that a randomly selected person who passed the exam did NOT take a course.
- **Math concepts in the prompt:** probability, reading data from a table, surveys
- **Math concepts in the diagram:** data labels, reading data from a table
- **Elements of the answer choices:** fractions
- **Notable differences among answer choices:** (A) and (B) both have 25 as a denominator, while (C) and (D) both have 200 as a denominator. (B) and (D) both have 7 in the numerator, while (A) and (C) have numerators that are unique to them. (A) and (B) would add up to $\dfrac{25}{25}$, or 1. This may be relevant because, as trained test-takers, we know that the College Board often likes to present the complement of a correct answer as one of the incorrect answers when a question involves fractions or percentages.
- **Concepts in the answer choices:** fractions
- **"Bridge" concepts:** To construct a probability fraction, we need two numbers: the total number of possible outcomes will be the denominator, and the number of outcomes we're interested in will be the numerator.
- **Pre-solution patterns (see p. 217):** complements or supplements
- **Things to look out for:** Make sure you read the prompt carefully! Make sure you determine both the denominator and numerator of the probability fraction correctly!

Solution 1: Probability: Construct the probability fraction on your own, then compare your result to the choices to find the answer.

The desired outcome is choosing a student who passed the exam but didn't take the review course, and the table shows that 7 people passed the exam but didn't take the course, so we know the numerator of our probability fraction will be 7.

The number of possible outcomes is the number of students who passed the exam, which is $18 + 7$, or 25, according to the table. So the denominator of our probability fraction is 25.

This means the probability fraction is $\dfrac{7}{25}$, so (B) is correct.

Solution 2: Backsolving: Consider each answer choice in light of the prompt, paying special attention to the key differences we noted above, and pick the choice that matches the prompt and the data.

When we compare the answer choices to one another and to the prompt, we see that there are basically two issues we need to resolve if we want to identify the correct answer:

1. Should the denominator be 25, or 200?
2. Should the numerator be 18, 7, or 25?

For the first issue, we need to decide whether the total number of possible outcomes described in the prompt is 25 or 200 (since we know, as trained-test-takers, that the denominator of a probability fraction reflects the total number of possible outcomes). 200 is the sum of every number in the table, so it would reflect the idea of including both people who passed the exam and who didn't, as well as including people who took a course and people who didn't. The prompt, on the other hand, describes "one of the surveyed graduates who passed the bar exam" being chosen at random, so the denominator should only reflect "the surveyed graduates who passed the bar exam." Those students are the ones in the left-hand column of the table, which includes the numbers 18 and 7, which add up to 25. So we can see that 25 should be the denominator.

For the second issue, we know from the prompt that the numerator of the probability fraction should be the number of people who passed the bar exam but "who did <u>not</u> take the review course." That number is 7, so the numerator should be 7. So (B) is right.

ANSWER CHOICE ANALYSIS

(A): This is the probability that a person chosen from those who passed the bar *did* take the course. **(C):** This is the probability that a person chosen *from the entire group* passed the bar, with or without the course. **(D):** This is the probability that a person chosen *from the entire group* passed the bar without taking the course.

How to check? Re-read the prompt and the data carefully, and reconsider your choice, especially in light of the patterns noted above.

▶ Post-solution patterns (see page 218): opposites

Test 2, Section 4, Question 17

- **What's the prompt asking for?** The "best approximat[ion]" of the atomic weight of the unknown element.
- **Math concepts in the prompt:** approximation, percentages
- **Elements of the answer choices:** integers
- **Notable differences among answer choices:** (D) is the only choice that's *more* than 40, which is relevant because the question tells us the answer must be 20% LESS than 40. (C)

and (D) are both multiples of (A), which may be relevant since finding a percentage involves multiplication.

- **"Bridge" concepts:** Looking for a number that's 20% less than a given quantity is the same thing as finding 80% of the given quantity. Finding 80% of a quantity is the same thing as multiplying that quantity by 0.8.
- **Things to look out for:** Don't find a number that's 20% MORE than 40!

Solution 1: Percentages: Find the number that 20% less than 40, and pick the corresponding answer choice.

A number that is 20% less than 40 is the same thing as a number that is 80% of 40, because $100\% - 20\% = 80\%$. The decimal equivalent of 80% is 0.8. So we can find the answer to this question by multiplying 40 and 0.8, which looks like this: $40 \times 0.8 = 32$. This means the answer is (C).

Solution 2: Test-smart: Note that (B) is too small to be the right answer, and (D) is too large.

(B) is half of 40, and half of something is less than 80% of it, so (B) can't be right. (A) is even less than (B), so (A) can't be right, either. (D) is more than 40, but the prompt told us the unknown element is 20% *less* than the weight of calcium, so (D) is wrong, too. This leaves (C) as the only choice that can possibly be right.

ANSWER CHOICE ANALYSIS

(A): This represents 20% of the weight of calcium itself, not a value that's 20% less than the weight of calcium. **(B):** This is the result when we divide the weight of calcium by 2. **(D):** This would be the atomic weight of an element 20% heavier than calcium, not lighter.

How to check? Try an alternate approach above.

Test 2, Section 4, Question 18

- **What's the prompt asking for?** An explanation for the difference between median and mean in the data.
- **Math concepts in the prompt:** mean, median, surveys
- **Elements of the answer choices:** sentences
- **Notable differences among answer choices:** (B) and (C) express opposite concepts from one another.
- **Concepts in the answer choices:** averages, data sets

- **"Bridge" concepts:** The median is the number in the center of the dataset when the values are listed from least to greatest. The mean is the result when we add every value in the dataset together, and then divide by the number of values.
- **Pre-solution patterns (see p. 217):** opposites
- **Things to look out for:** Don't confuse the definitions of mean and median! Don't confuse the numbers in the prompt! Don't misread the answer choices!

Solution 1: Reasoning: Come up with a situation in which the mean value is higher than the median, and then pick an answer choice that reflects the situation you've come up with.

The mean of a set of numbers is the average of those numbers—the result when we add up all the numbers, and divide that sum by the number of numbers. The median is the number in the middle when all the numbers in the group are ordered from smallest to largest.

In order for the mean to be significantly larger than the median, there must be some numbers in the set that are pulling the mean up—in other words, the difference between the larger numbers and the mean must be larger than the difference between the smaller numbers and the mean.

For example, imagine that the county only had three homes, with the following prices:

- $246,000
- $125,000
- $124,000

The mean of this group of numbers is $165,000, while the median is only $125,000. As we can see in this small example, it's only possible to have the mean be so much higher than the median because the difference between the largest value and the median is over 100 times larger than the difference between the smallest value and the median (ie, a difference of $121,000 as compared to a difference of $1,000).

So a mean that's significantly larger than the median must indicate that there must be a small number of large values in the group, so that the average is increased without shifting the median out of the range of relatively smaller values.

This matches with (C)—a few homes valued much more than the rest would pull up the mean, but still allow for a lower median.

Solution 2: Backsolving: Consider each situation in the answer choices and determine whether it could be relevant to the prompt.

If (A) were true, then we'd expect the mean and median to be closer to one another. For example, if the prices were $115,000, $120,000, $125,000, 128,000, and $130,000, then the mean value would be $123,600 and the median value would be $125,000. We can see that the mean and median would be relatively close to each other in this case.

If (B) were true, we would expect the mean to be lower than the median—the few lower values would drag down the mean, but the price in the middle of the group would still be relatively high. For example, if the prices were $25,000, $30,000, $125,000, 128,000, and $130,000, then the mean value would be $87,600 and the median value would be $125,000.

If (C) were true, then we would expect the mean to be higher than the median—the few higher values would pull up the mean, but the price in the middle of the group would still be relatively low. This is the situation described in the prompt, so (C) is correct. For example, if the prices were $115,000, $120,000, $125,000, $230,000, and $235,000, the mean value would be $165,000 and the median value would be $125,000, as described in the prompt.

If (D) were true, then we wouldn't necessarily be able to make a determination about the median and mean. A couple of low home prices could still drag the mean down, and a couple of very high home prices could still pull the mean up. A lack of either high or low home prices could result in a mean that's close to the median value. A situation like the one in (D) *could* match the situation described in the prompt, but it could *also* match situations very different from the one in the prompt—so (D) can't be correct.

How to check? Re-read the prompt and your answer carefully, and make sure you haven't made any small mistakes that could cause you to pick the opposite of the right answer, since the College Board was clearly anticipating that kind of a mistake when it came up with choices (B) and (C).

Test 2, Section 4, Question 19

- **What's the prompt asking for?** The median number of siblings in the survey.
- **Math concepts in the prompt:** medians, reading data from a table, surveys, word problems
- **Math concepts in the diagram:** data labels, reading data from a table
- **Elements of the answer choices:** integers, zero

- **Notable differences among answer choices:** The answer choices form a series from 0 to 3, with each choice being 1 more than the one before it.
- **Pre-solution patterns (see p. 217):** halves and doubles; the first and last terms in a series are often wrong answers
- **Things to look out for:** Don't misread the data from the table! Don't forget the definition of median, as opposed to mean or mode!

Solution 1: Data analysis: Consider the numbers of children in each row of the table in order to determine the number of siblings that would fall in the center of the dataset if all of the students were listed individually.

The information above the table tells us that 300 students from each of two schools were surveyed. In a group of 600 values (remember, there were 300 students from each school), the median is the average of the 300th value and 301st value when the values are ordered from smallest to largest.

Now we need to figure out which values from the table would actually be the 300th and 301st when the values are listed. Of course, we don't have the time to write out all 600 values in order and then count 300 positions down through that list, so we'll need to think of something a little more clever.

We can see from the table that 260 students have 0 siblings (because the first row says that 120 Lincoln students and 140 Washington students have 0 siblings, and 120 + 140 = 260). So if we made a list of numbers of siblings for all 600 students, then the 1st value through the 260th values would all be 0's. The table also tells us that 190 students have 1 sibling (again, because 80 Lincoln students and 110 Washington students add up to 190 students overall), so the next 190 positions after the first 260 must all be 1's—in other words, the 261st value through the 450th value must be 1.

Since that group of positions includes the 300th and 301st position, we know that the 300th and 301st values must both be 1, which means their average is 1, which means the median number of siblings for all 600 students is 1. So (B) is correct.

How to check? Carefully reconsider both your reading and your reasoning. Remember that the College Board likes to design questions in ways that make it easy for test-takers to get confused about small details.

Note Any of the wrong answer choices could be tempting for a test-taker who misreads the table.

Test 2, Section 4, Question 20

- **What's the prompt asking for?** The choice that "most accurately compares the expected total number of students with 4 siblings at the two schools."
- **Math concepts in the prompt:** data extrapolation, reading data from a table, surveys, word problems
- **Math concepts in the diagram:** data labels, reading data from a table
- **Elements of the answer choices:** sentences
- **Notable differences among answer choices:** (B) and (C) are opposites of one another. (A) says the two values would be equal. (C) and (D) both say that the number at Washington school would be larger, but they disagree about the extent of the difference. (D) mentions the number 900, which is the difference between the two school populations according to the text under the table.
- **Concepts in the answer choices:** data extrapolation
- **"Bridge" concepts:** The text under the table tells us the number of students who attend each school. We can use that information to extrapolate an expected number of students with 4 siblings for each school.
- **Pre-solution patterns (see p. 217):** wrong answers try to imitate right answers
- **Things to look out for:** Don't confuse the two school names when they appear in the prompt, diagram, and answer choices! Don't confuse the answer choices, which are highly similar to one another in some cases!

Solution 1: Data extrapolation: Note that the sample in Lincoln school is $\frac{1}{8}$ the total population of that school, while the sample in Washington is $\frac{1}{11}$ the total population of that school, according to the information below the figure. Use this information along with the table to extrapolate expected numbers of students with 4 siblings from each school, and then compare them.

$\dfrac{300}{2400} = \dfrac{10}{L}$ (proportion of surveyed Lincoln students to total Lincoln students, set equal to the proportion of surveyed Lincoln students with 4 siblings to the expected total number of Lincoln students with 4 siblings)

$300L = 24000$ (cross-multiply)

$L = 80$ (divide both sides by 300 to find the total number of expected Lincoln students with 4 siblings)

$\dfrac{300}{3300} = \dfrac{10}{W}$ (proportion of surveyed Washington students to total Washington students, set equal to proportion of surveyed Washington students with 4 siblings to the expected total of Washington students with 4 siblings)

$300W = 33000$ (cross-multiply)

$W = 110$ (divide both sides by 300 to find the total number of expected Washington students with 4 siblings)

So Washington is expected to have 30 more students with 4 siblings than Lincoln has, because $110 - 80 = 30$, so (C) is right.

Solution 2: Test-smart: Noting the similarities and differences among the choices described above, determine which school should have a higher expected number by comparing their populations. Then, if necessary, determine the size of the difference in expected numbers.

When we compare and contrast the concepts in the choices, we can see that the College Board is basically giving us three things to consider when we select an answer:

1. Are the expected numbers of students with 4 siblings at each school equal to each other?
2. If they're not equal, than which school has a higher expected number of students with 4 siblings?
3. If one school has a higher expected number of students with 4 siblings, how much higher is that number than the number at the other school?

So let's think about those issues.

We can see from the figure that the surveys at each school involved the same number of students (300 in each case), and that the same number of people in each survey indicated having 4 siblings (10 surveyed students at each school had 4 siblings). At this point, a lot of untrained test-takers would assume (A) is correct, but there's a key piece of information below the figure, which indicates (A) must be wrong: we're told that Lincoln School has 2400 students, and Washington School has 3300 students. This means the results in the bottom row of the table represent different portions of the schools' populations…which means that we'd expect the number of students with 4 siblings to be different at each school.

So now we need to figure out which school should have the higher number of expected students with 4 siblings. Well, since the sample size at each school was 300 students, we can see that the sample at the smaller school (Lincoln) would represent a larger share than the sample at the bigger school (Washington). (See the calculations in solution 1 above for an example of how this works.) That means Washington would be expected to have more students with 4 siblings than Lincoln has.

Since there are two choices that indicate Washington has more students with 4 siblings, the last thing we need to figure out is *how many* more of those students are expected to be at Washington. If we want, we could figure this out by doing the calculations from solution 1, but we can also be a little bit more efficient in our approach if we compare the options in the answer choices to the information in the prompt. We see that (C) says Washington has 30 more of the students, and (D) says Washington has 900 more of them. Since 900 is a significantly larger number than 30, we can probably tell which of the two numbers could possibly be correct through a little mental math and estimation, rather than through doing actual calculations.

The easiest way to tell that 900 is much too large to be correct is probably just to notice that it's wildly out of proportion to the scale indicated in the figure and the surrounding information. The figure shows us there are 14 times as many expected students with 0 siblings at Washington as there are students with 4 siblings, and there are an additional 11 times as many expected students with 1 sibling (we can see this because 140 is 14 times as much as 10, and 110 is 11 times as much as 10). So if there were 900 students at Washington with 4 siblings (let alone the idea of 900 *more* students than the number at Lincoln), then there would have to be 900×14 Washington students with 0 siblings, and another 900×11 Washington students with 1 sibling—this would work out to tens of thousands of other students also being at Washington. But we can see that Washington only has 3,300 students, so there's no way to fit all of those other students into that number.

The only conclusion we can reach is that the number 900 in (D) is much too large. This means (C) must be correct.

ANSWER CHOICE ANALYSIS

(A): This choice may be tempting because the number of students in the table with 4 siblings each is equal for both schools—but one school has more students than the other. **(B):** This choice might tempt an untrained test-taker who confused the names of the schools. **(D):** This would be the result if we squared the difference between the number of students with four siblings at the two schools for some reason.

How to check? Try an alternate approach above. Make sure you read the data, prompt, and answer choices very carefully, since it would be easy to confuse the two schools' data!

Note   Pay attention to the way that the College Board chose to make this question challenging! As we saw in solution 2, it's possible to answer this question correctly using only estimation and considering the options in the answer choices; the College Board even gives us a variety of numbers that are multiples of 10 to make the mental aspect of the math easier. But the key piece of information in the question is the fact that Lincoln and Washington have different numbers of students, and this fact is hidden underneath the table, in a position where a lot of untrained test-takers will overlook it. Once again, we see that the College Board has chosen to make the reading comprehension aspect of an SAT Math question more challenging than the actual calculations that are involved in answering the question. Keep this kind of thing in mind on test day!

Test 2, Section 4, Question 21

- **What's the prompt asking for?** An inequality that reflects the relationship between y and x, according to the situation in the prompt.
- **Math concepts in the prompt:** inequalities, variables, word problems
- **Elements of the answer choices:** algebraic expressions, inequalities, integers, negative numbers

- **Notable differences among answer choices:** (D) is the only choice that involves two inequality signs.
- **Concepts in the answer choices:** inequalities
- **Pre-solution patterns (see p. 217):** wrong answers try to imitate right answers; opposites
- **Things to look out for:** Don't confuse x and y! Remember it may not be relevant that x is greater than 100, since none of the choices refers to 100!

Solution 1: Algebra: Come up with your own expression to describe the relationship between x and y, then find the answer choice that matches your expression.

Since the estimate, which is x, must be within 10 hours of the actual number of hours to complete the project, which is y, we might start by thinking about subtracting x from y, because doing that would show us how far apart x and y are from each other. Then, we need to show that the distance between x and y is less than 10. When we put all of that together, we get something like $y - x < 10$.

When we compare this expression to the answer choices, though, we notice something we haven't accounted for yet: the only choice that involves subtracting x from y (which is choice (D)) also compares the difference between those two values to -10, which is something we haven't thought about yet.

So now we need to ask ourselves: should we compare the difference between y and x to -10 as well as 10? This idea of negative numbers is potentially interesting for us, because we know that subtracting *larger* numbers from *smaller* numbers results in negative values, but that isn't something we really considered when we first set up our inequality. What would happen, for example, if the initial estimate x were 300 hours, and the actual time to completion y were 40 hours? Then $y - x$ would be -260; this is still below 10, but it definitely fails the requirement in the prompt of having x be within 10 hours of y.

At this point we can see that we need to include a reference to -10 so that we can account for situations where y is the smaller number, to make sure that y and x are still within 10 units of each other on a number line. So now we can see that $-10 < y - x < 10$ makes sense, and (D) must be correct.

Solution 2: Concrete: Pick numbers for x and y that should satisfy the relationship in the prompt, and test those values against the answer choices. If more than one choice works, then pick numbers for x and y that should NOT work, and eliminate any choices for which those numbers do work.

Let's assume the manager estimates that the project will take 105 hours to complete, and the project ends up taking 110 hours to complete. So, in this scenario, $x = 105$ and $y = 110$. Now we can plug our numbers into each choice and see what happens.

For choice (A):

$x + y < 10$	(expression from (A))
$105 + 110 < 10$	(plug in $x = 105$ and $y = 110$)
$215 < 10$	(simplify)

This isn't a valid statement, so (A) can't be correct. Now let's take a look at (B):

$y > x + 10$	(expression from (B))
$110 > 105 + 10$	(plug in $x = 105$ and $y = 110$)
$110 > 115$	(simplify)

This isn't a valid statement either, so (B) can't be right. Let's try (C):

$y < x - 10$	(expression from (C))
$110 < 105 - 10$	(plug in $x = 105$ and $y = 110$)
$110 < 95$	(simplify)

This isn't a valid statement, so (C) can't be correct. Let's test (D) and see what happens:

$-10 < y - x < 10$	(expression from (D))
$-10 < 110 - 105 < 10$	(plug in $x = 105$ and $y = 110$)
$-10 < 5 < 10$	(simplify)

This is a valid statement, so (D) could be correct.

Since we only found one answer choice that resulted in a valid statement, we know choice (D) is correct.

How to check? Try an alternate approach above.

Test 2, Section 4, Question 22

- **What's the prompt asking for?** The choice accurately expressing r^2 in terms of the other variables.
- **Math concepts in the prompt:** algebra, exponents, fractions, function modeling, isolating variables, multiplication, variables
- **Elements of the answer choices:** algebraic expressions, exponents, fractions, integers
- **Notable differences among answer choices:** (A), (C), and (D) all have I in the numerator, while (B) has it in the denominator. (A) and (B) have P in the numerator, while (C) and (D) have it in the denominator. (A), (B), and (D) have 4π in the denominator, while (C) has 4π in the numerator. The fractions in (B) and (C) are reciprocals of each other.
- **Concepts in the answer choices:** fractions, variables
- **Pre-solution patterns (see p. 217):** opposites; wrong answers try to imitate right answers
- **Things to look out for:** Don't make any small mistakes in your algebra!

Solution 1: Algebra: Manipulate the equation in the prompt until you've isolated r^2 on one side of the equation, and pick the answer choice that matches the expression you've come up with.

$I = \dfrac{P}{4\pi r^2}$	(given formula)
$Ir^2 = \dfrac{P}{4\pi}$	(multiply both sides by r^2)
$r^2 = \dfrac{P}{4\pi I}$	(divide both sides by I to isolate r^2, as the prompt requires)

Thus (B) is right.

Solution 2: Test-smart: Note that the correct answer must involve a numerator with only P.

We may notice that the equation in the prompt tells us that I is the result when P is divided by $4\pi r^2$. This means, in other words, that $I, 4, \pi,$ and r must be "factors" of P, in a sense. (If this seems hard to grasp, think about a similar situation with the number 210. We could say that $2 = \dfrac{210}{(3)(5)(7)}$, and this shows us that 2, 3, 5, and 7 can all be multiplied together to give us 210.)

If $I, 4, \pi,$ and r can all be multiplied together to produce P, then isolating any one of those variables besides P must result in an equation with the isolated variable on one side, and a fraction on the other side that involves P alone in the numerator, with the other "factors" of P in the denominator. (B) is the only choice with P alone in the numerator, and the other "factors" in the denominator, so we know (B) must be correct.

How to check? Try an alternate approach above. Pay careful attention to the quantities that go in the numerator and denominator, since (B) and (C) are reciprocals of one another.

▶ Post-solution patterns (see page 218): opposites

Note Any of the wrong answer choices could be tempting if an untrained test-taker made an algebra mistake.

Test 2, Section 4, Question 23

- **What's the prompt asking for?** The relative distances of Observer A and Observer B from the antenna.
- **Math concepts in the prompt:** fractions, algebra, exponents, function modeling, isolating variables, multiplication
- **Elements of the answer choices:** fractions
- **Notable differences among answer choices:** The choices form a series, with each being $\frac{1}{4}$ of the one before it.

- **"Bridge" concepts:** The formula relates intensity to distance, and the prompt gives us the relative difference in two intensities. This will allow us to determine the relative distance of the two observers.
- **Pre-solution patterns (see p. 217):** the first and last terms in a series are often wrong answers
- **Things to look out for:** The answer choices are clearly anticipating the possibility that you'll be off by a factor of 4, so make sure not to make that mistake!

Solution 1: Concrete: Pick two arbitrary I-values so that one is 16 times the other (say, $I = 16$ for Observer A and $I = 1$ for Observer B). Then find the corresponding r-values of those I-values, and compare these r-values to determine the right answer.

First we find the r-value that corresponds to an I-value of 16:

$$I = \frac{P}{4\pi r^2} \qquad \text{(given formula)}$$

$$16 = \frac{P}{4\pi r^2} \qquad \text{(set } I \text{ equal to 16)}$$

$$64\pi r^2 = P \qquad \text{(multiply both sides by } 4\pi r^2)$$

$$r^2 = \frac{P}{64\pi} \qquad \text{(divide both sides by } 64\pi)$$

$$r = \sqrt{\frac{P}{64\pi}} \qquad \text{(take square root of both sides)}$$

$$r = \frac{1}{8}\sqrt{\frac{P}{\pi}} \qquad \text{(simplify to find } r \text{ when } I = 16)$$

So when $I = 16$, the radius for Observer A is $\frac{1}{8}\sqrt{\frac{P}{\pi}}$. Now let's find the r-value when $I = 1$:

$$I = \frac{P}{4\pi r^2} \qquad \text{(given formula)}$$

$$1 = \frac{P}{4\pi r^2} \qquad \text{(set } I \text{ equal to 1)}$$

$$4\pi r^2 = P \qquad \text{(multiply both sides by } 4\pi r^2)$$

$$r^2 = \frac{P}{4\pi} \qquad \text{(divide both sides by } 4\pi)$$

$$r = \sqrt{\frac{P}{4\pi}} \qquad \text{(take square root of both sides)}$$

$$r = \frac{1}{2}\sqrt{\frac{P}{\pi}} \qquad \text{(simplify to find } r \text{ when } I = 1)$$

So when $I = 1$, $r = \frac{1}{2}\sqrt{\frac{P}{\pi}}$ for Observer B.

In this example, the distance of Observer A from the radio antenna was $\frac{1}{8}\sqrt{\frac{P}{\pi}}$, and the distance of Observer B from the radio antenna was $r = \frac{1}{2}\sqrt{\frac{P}{\pi}}$. Now we can compare those distances to see which answer choice accurately reflects the distance of Observer A as a fraction of the distance of Observer B:

$$\frac{\frac{1}{8}\sqrt{\frac{P}{\pi}}}{\frac{1}{2}\sqrt{\frac{P}{\pi}}}$$ (ratio of Observer A's distance to Observer B's distance)

$$\frac{\frac{1}{8}}{\frac{1}{2}}$$ (cancel like terms)

$$\frac{1}{4}$$ (simplify)

So the ratio of the Observer A distance to the Observer B distance is $\frac{1}{4}$, and (A) is correct.

Solution 2: Abstract: Note that any change in r is squared in the formula, and figure out what kind of change in r would result in one observer seeing an intensity that was 16 times brighter than the intensity seen by other observer.

The formula in the prompt involves squaring r, but doesn't involve squaring I. This means that linear changes in I will go along with exponential changes in r. In this case, we can see that a change that makes I be 16 times bigger will go along with a change that makes r be 4 times bigger, since the r term is squared and 4 squared is equal to 16.

Further, since the r-term is in the denominator on the right side, the correct answer will be the *reciprocal* of 4, which is $\frac{1}{4}$. So we can see that when the term on the left side of the formula is multiplied by 16, that change corresponds to the r-term on the right side being multiplied by $\frac{1}{4}$. When the r-term on the right side of the formula is multiplied by $\frac{1}{4}$, that term is squared and becomes equivalent to multiplying the r-term by $\frac{1}{16}$. Since that r-term is in the denominator, this is the same as dividing the term on the right side of the formula by $\frac{1}{16}$. When the right side of the equation is divided by $\frac{1}{16}$, that's the same as the right side being multiplied by 16, just as the left side of the formula was multiplied by 16. Once more, this confirms that the right answer is (A), $\frac{1}{4}$.

Don't worry if this approach doesn't make any sense to you! You could always use the approach in solution 1. But if this kind of thing does make sense to you, then you can answer this question in seconds, without calculating anything. (This idea of determining the corresponding linear change for an exponential change doesn't come up frequently on the SAT, and it's never the only way to solve an official SAT Math question, so it's really not worth worrying about if you don't feel comfortable with it.)

ANSWER CHOICE ANALYSIS

(B), (C), and (D) could all be the result of making mistakes in algebra or arithmetic that might involve multiplying or dividing by 4 the wrong number of times, or possibly squaring incorrectly.

How to check? Try an alternate approach above.

Test 2, Section 4, Question 24

- **What's the prompt asking for?** The radius of the circle in the equation from the prompt.
- **Math concepts in the prompt:** addition, algebra, circles, exponents, subtraction, variables
- **Elements of the answer choices:** integers
- **Notable differences among answer choices:** (C) is the square of (A), and (D) is the square of (B). This is probably relevant because the equation in the prompt involves squaring values,

and because we may know that the general format for the equation of a circle involves squaring.

- **Concepts in the answer choices:** squaring
- **Things to look out for:** Make sure you consider whether the correct answer should be a square number or not, since the answer choices clearly indicate that issue is relevant! Make sure you don't get confused as to whether 2 or 3 should be in the correct answer, since the answer choices are clearly set up to encourage you to make a mistake on that!

Solution 1: Calculator: Graph the circle on your graphing calculator and find the diameter of the circle, then divide the diameter by 2 to find the radius.

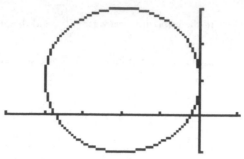

When we look at the graph of the circle, we can see that the circle measures 4 units across, which means the diameter of the circle is 4, and the radius is 2. So (A) is correct.

Solution 2: Algebra: Manipulate the given equation by completing the square until it has the form of a center-radius circle equation, and use that to determine the radius of the circle.

$x^2 + y^2 + 4x - 2y = -1$	(given expression)
$(x^2 + 4x) + (y^2 - 2y) = -1$	(group terms with the same variables)
$(x^2 + 4x + 4) + (y^2 - 2y + 1) = -1 + 4 + 1$	(Find half the coefficient of x, square it, and add it inside the parentheses with the x-terms. Do the same with the coefficient of y inside the parentheses with the y-terms. Add the resulting values on the right side of the equation.)
$(x + 2)^2 + (y - 1)^2 = 4$	(reverse-FOIL each expression in parentheses)

Now that we have a standard equation for a circle, we know that $4 = r^2$, and that $r = 2$.

ANSWER CHOICE ANALYSIS

(C): This is the value of r squared, or the length of the diameter. **(D):** This is the square of (B).

How to check? Carefully re-check your algebra from when you completed the square.

▶ Post-solution patterns (see page 218): right approach, wrong step

Test 2, Section 4, Question 25

- **What's the prompt asking for?** The statement that must be true about the slope of the graph of f.
- **Math concepts in the prompt:** algebra, linear functions, inequalities, slope, x-intercepts, y-intercepts, zero
- **Elements of the answer choices:** sentences
- **Notable differences among answer choices:** (A) and (B) are opposites of one another.
- **Concepts in the answer choices:** slope, undefined fractions

- **"Bridge" concepts:** If $a + b = 0$ and a isn't equal to b, then we know that a and b must be opposite numbers (such as 2 and -2, or -30 and 30, something like that). Coordinate values that have one coordinate equal to zero must lie on one of the axes, which means $(a, 0)$ is the x-intercept, and $(0, b)$ is the y-intercept.
- **Pre-solution patterns (see p. 217):** opposites
- **Things to look out for:** Don't confuse the different kinds of slope!

Solution 1: Diagramming: Sketch an xy-coordinate plane. Choose numbers for a and b that satisfy the prompt, and then connect them with a line. Use the line to answer the question.

If $a + b = 0$, then we can subtract b from both sides to see that $a = -b$. If $a \neq b$, then neither number can be zero. That means a and b are opposites of one another, like 5 and -5. We'll arbitrarily use $a = 5$ and $b = -5$. Let's sketch the points $(5, 0)$ and $(0, -5)$, and then draw a line through them:

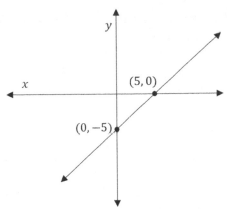

The resulting line has a positive slope, so (A) is correct.

Solution 2: Abstract: Think about the properties a line must have if it passes through two intercepts as described in the prompt.

As we discussed above, the logical implication of the concepts in the prompt is that the line must pass through one axis with a positive intercept on that axis, and the other axis with a negative intercept on that axis. So it could pass through the positive part of the x-axis and the negative part of the y-axis, or it could pass through the positive part of the y-axis and the negative part of the x-axis.

Either arrangement would cause the line to rise as it moves from left to right, which means the slope must be positive, so (A) must be correct.

ANSWER CHOICE ANALYSIS

(B): This might be tempting if we misread the prompt and thought that $a = b$ and $a \neq 0$ **(C):** This might be tempting if we misread the prompt and thought the points were $(a, 0)$ and $(b, 0)$. **(D):** This might be tempting if we misread the prompt and thought the points were $(0, a)$ and $(0, b)$.

How to check? Try an alternate approach above, being very careful not to confuse the different types of slope.

▶ Post-solution patterns (see page 218): opposites

Test 2, Section 4, Question 26

- **What's the prompt asking for?** The choice with the set of Roman numerals whose options are equal to 1.
- **Math concepts in the prompt:** function graphs, xy-coordinate planes
- **Math concepts in the diagram:** function graphs, scale, xy-coordinate planes
- **Elements of the answer choices:** Roman numerals

- **Notable differences among answer choices:** Every choice includes III.
- **"Bridge" concepts:** Using the graph, we can determine the y-values that correspond to each x-value in the Roman numerals.
- **Pre-solution patterns (see p. 217):** wrong answers try to imitate right answers
- **Things to look out for:** Don't confuse the x- and y-values of the function! Don't misread the graph!

Solution 1: Backsolving: Go through each Roman numeral and determine whether its value is 1 by using the graph. Pick the answer choice that correctly indicates which Roman numerals have values of 1.

For Roman numeral I, we find $f(-4)$ by counting four units to the left from the origin, to arrive at $x = -4$, and then looking up from that point to see the y-value of the function where $x = -4$. We see that the y-value is 1, so we know that $f(-4) = 1$.

For Roman numeral II, we find $f\left(\frac{3}{2}\right)$ by counting over $\frac{3}{2}$ units to the right from the origin, to arrive at $x = \frac{3}{2}$, and then we look up to see the y-value of the function where $x = \frac{3}{2}$; in fact, the y-value of the function is $y = 1$ for all x-values from $x = 1$ to $x = 3$, as we can see from the part of the function that tracks horizontally for two units. So we see the y-value is 1, and we know $f\left(\frac{3}{2}\right) = 1$.

For Roman numeral III, we already saw in our analysis of Roman numeral II that $f(3) = 1$.

So all the Roman numeral values are equal to 1, and (D) is correct.

How to check? Carefully re-read the entire question and make sure you haven't overlooked any small details.

Test 2, Section 4, Question 27

- **What's the prompt asking for?** The answer choice that correctly compares the average rates of change for the temperature in the two samples.

- **Math concepts in the prompt:** rate of change, reading data from a graph, word problems

- **Math concepts in the diagram:** axis labels, legends on a graph, multiple data sets in one graph, rate of change, reading data from a graph
- **Elements of the answer choices:** sentences
- **Notable differences among answer choices:** (A) and (B) both begin with the phrase "In every 10-minute interval, the magnitude of the rate of change of…". (A) says the insulated sample has a greater rate of change, while (B) says the non-insulated sample does. (C) and (D) both begin with "In the intervals from 0 to 10 minutes and from 10 to 20 minutes, the rates of change of temperature of the…". Both choices also have the phrase "whereas in the intervals from 40 to 50 minutes and from 50 to 60 minutes, the rates of change of temperature of the…". (C) says the insulated sample has a larger rate of change in the first intervals and the non-insulated sample has a larger rate of change in the last intervals, while (D) says the non-insulated sample has a larger rate of change in the first intervals and the insulated sample has a larger rate of change in the last samples.

- **Concepts in the answer choices:** axis labels, legends on a graph, multiple data sets in one graph, rate of change, reading data from a graph
- **"Bridge" concepts:** The rate of change is another term for the slope of a line or curve. Since the time axis is labeled in constant increments from left to right, and the temperature axis is labeled with constant increments from bottom to top, we can just look at the different separations between the data points to determine quickly which points have more vertical change distributed over the same horizontal change.
- **Pre-solution patterns (see p. 217):** opposites; wrong answers try to imitate right answers
- **Things to look out for:** Don't confuse the words "insulated" and "non-insulated!" Don't get overwhelmed by the large blocks of text in the answer choices—as we noted above, large portions of text are re-used in multiple answer choices! Focus on the differences among the choices! Don't confuse the rate-of-change of a dataset with the actual average value of the dataset!

Solution 1: Test-smart / backsolving: Consider the similarities and differences among the answer choices that we noted above, and determine which option in the answer choices accurately reflects the graph.

When we consider the similarities and differences among the choices, we see that the choices essentially present us with two issues to resolve—in other words, we'll be able to tell which choice is correct if we can figure out the answers to these two questions:

1. Are the relative magnitudes of the changes in each interval always greater for one sample than for the other, as (A) and (B) indicate, or are they greater for one sample in the intervals from 0 to 20 minutes, and greater for the other sample in the intervals from 40 to 60 minutes, as (C) and (D) indicate?
2. Which sample has the larger rate of change for any particular interval?

For the first issue, we can compare the changes in the heights of the dots to the changes in the heights of the boxes, and see that the height-change in the first two dots is much larger than the height-change for the first two boxes; on the other hand, the last several dots have no height-change, while the last several boxes have some height-change as we read from left to right. So (A) and (B) must both be wrong, because we've seen that the changes in magnitude are larger for the dots in some cases, and larger for the boxes in other cases.

For the second issue, we can note, again, that the height-change is much larger for the first two dots than it is for the first two boxes. This means that the change in the non-insulated sample was much larger for the interval from 0 to 10 than it was for the insulated sample, which is what (D) says, so (D) must be right. (Notice that at this point we can focus on the interval from 0 to 10 minutes because we've eliminated (A) and (B), and the two remaining choices make conflicting statements about that interval.)

How to check? Carefully re-check your reading of the prompt, the data, and the answer choices. Pay special attention to the items that we noted above in "things to look out for!"

▶ Post-solution patterns (see page 218): opposites

Test 2, Section 4, Question 28

- **What's the prompt asking for?** An equation of the line that passes through B and D in the graph.
- **Math concepts in the prompt:** center of a square, coordinate values, equations of lines, squares, word problems, xy-coordinate plane
- **Math concepts in the diagram:** axis labels, coordinate values, squares, xy-coordinate plane
- **Elements of the answer choices:** algebraic expressions, equations, fractions, integers, negative numbers

- **Notable differences among answer choices:** (A) and (B) have the number -3 as the first number in the choice, while (C) and (D) have $-\frac{1}{3}$. (A), (B), and (D) all have -1 as the last number in the choice, while only (C) has $+4$. (B) is the only choice with an expression in parentheses.
- **Concepts in the answer choices:** slope, parenthetical expressions, linear equations, $y = mx + b$
- **Pre-solution patterns (see p. 217):** wrong answers try to imitate right answers
- **Things to look out for:** Don't make any mistakes when dealing with negative numbers! Don't misread the coordinates of (C) and (E) in the prompt! Don't invert your slope fraction by accident!

Solution 1: Geometry / algebra: Use the graph and the information in the prompt to determine the coordinates of B and D. Use the coordinates of B and D to find the slope between them. Use the slope and the coordinates of one of the points to construct an equation for the line, and then put that line in slope-intercept format and pick the answer choice that matches it.

Point B, the top corner of the square, is at $(-1, 6)$. We can also see that Point D, the lowest corner of the square, is at $(3, -6)$.

Now that we know the coordinates of B and D, we can find the equation of the line that passes through the two points. We'll start by finding the slope.

We know that the slope of a line is the difference between the y values of two points on the line divided by the difference between the corresponding x-values of those points. So let's find the slope of the line through B and D:

$$\frac{-6-6}{3-(-1)}$$ (difference between the y-values of B and D divided by the difference between their x-values)

$$\frac{-12}{4}$$ (simplify)

$$-3$$ (simplify)

Now that we know the slope of the line between those points is -3, we can use the coordinates of one of the points and the slope to find the y-intercept of the equation in slope-intercept form (since all of the answer choices are basically in slope-intercept form):

$y = mx + b$ (slope-intercept form)
$6 = -3(-1) + b$ (plug in $(-1, 6)$ and $m = -3$)
$6 = 3 + b$ (simplify)
$3 = b$ (subtract 3 from both sides)

Now we can plug $m = -3$ and $b = 3$ into $y = mx + b$ to find the equation of the line in slope-intercept form:

$y = mx + b$ (slope-intercept form)
$y = -3x + 3$ (plug in $m = -3$ and $b = 3$)

This equation doesn't look like any of the answer choices—but if we read carefully, we'll see that only choice (B) isn't exactly in slope-intercept form. Let's distribute the -3 in (B) and see what happens:

$y = -3(x - 1)$ (equation from (B))
$y = -3x + 3$ (distribute -3)

We can see now that the equation we found is equal to the equation in (B), so (B) is the correct answer.

Solution 2: Test-smart: Recognize that the line must pass through E, since E is the center of the square. Also note that the coordinates of E only satisfy one answer choice, so that choice must be the correct answer.

The coordinates of E are $(1, 0)$. We can plug these coordinates into each choice to see which line contains E. We'll start with (A):

$y = -3x - 1$ (equation from (A))
$0 = -3(1) - 1$ (plug in $(1, 0)$)
$0 = -4$ (simplify)

We get an invalid statement when we plug $(1, 0)$ into the expression from (A), so (A) can't be right. Now we'll try (B):

$y = -3(x - 1)$ (equation from (B))
$0 = -3(1 - 1)$ (plug in $(1, 0)$)
$0 = 0$ (simplify)

We get a valid statement when we plug $(1, 0)$ into the expression from (B), so (B) is correct, assuming that we haven't made any mistakes in our reasoning or calculating. Let's keep checking the other choices. We'll do (C) next:

$y = -\frac{1}{3}x + 4$ (equation from (C))

$0 = -\frac{1}{3}(1) + 4$ (plug in $(1, 0)$)

$0 = 3\frac{2}{3}$ (simplify)

We get an invalid statement when we plug $(1, 0)$ into the expression from (C), so (C) can't be correct. Finally, we'll check (D):

$y = -\frac{1}{3}x - 1$ (equation from (D))

$0 = -\frac{1}{3}(1) - 1$ (plug in $(1, 0)$)

$0 = -1\frac{1}{3}$ (simplify)

We get an invalid statement when we plug $(1, 0)$ into the expression from (D), so (D) can't be correct.

After checking each answer choice, we can be confident that (B) is correct.

Solution 3: Test-smart: Remember the diagram is drawn to scale. Note that each answer choice has a different y-intercept. Connect points B and D with a straight line and determine the y-intercept of $\overline{BD}$; then, pick the choice with the appropriate y-intercept.

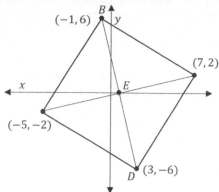

We can see that the y-intercept of $\overline{BD}$ is halfway between point B and point E, which means it's 3. The only choice with a y-intercept of 3 is (B), so (B) must be correct. (Notice that we need to distribute the -3 to get choice (B) into $y = mx + b$ format.)

Solution 4: Graphing: Use your calculator to graph each line in the answer choices and compare them to the diagram to determine which equation could be the correct answer.

If we sketch in a line that passes through points B and D, we can see that such a line will cross the x-axis a little to the right of the origin. So the graph of the correct answer will also show a line that crosses the x-axis a little to the right of the origin. Let's start by graphing the equation from (A):

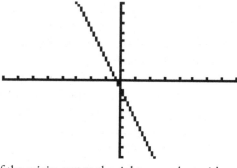

This line crosses the x-axis a little to the *left* of the origin, not to the right, so we know it's wrong. Let's check out the graph of (B):

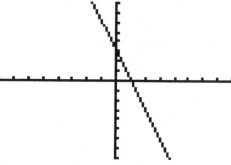

This line crosses the x-axis a little to the right of the origin. This looks like it could be the correct answer, but we should check the other graphs to see what we find. Here's the graph of (C):

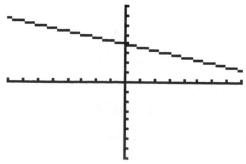

This line crosses the x-axis much farther to the right of the origin than the line we need to find would cross it, so this choice can't be correct. Let's look at (D):

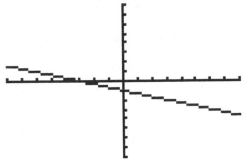

Like the graph of (A), this line crosses the x-axis to the *left* of the origin, not to the right, so we know it's wrong. After graphing each answer choice, we can see that only (B) could be correct, so the right answer is (B).

ANSWER CHOICE ANALYSIS

(A): This choice has the same slope as the correct answer, but not the same y-intercept. **(C)**: This choice has the reciprocal of the slope of the correct answer. **(D)**: This choice has the reciprocal of the slope of the correct answer.

How to check? Try an alternate approach above.

Test 2, Section 4, Question 29

- **What's the prompt asking for?** The values of a and b such that the system in the prompt has exactly two real solutions.
- **Math concepts in the prompt:** algebra, constants, exponents, systems of equations, variables
- **Elements of the answer choices:** algebraic expressions, equations, integers, negative numbers
- **Notable differences among answer choices:** (A) and (B) both have a equal to -2, while (C) has a equal to $+2$, and (D) has a equal to 4. (B) and (C) both have b equal to 4, while (A) has b equal to 2 and (D) has b equal to 3. (D) is the only choice with 3 in it; every other number in the choices appears more than once.
- **Concepts in the answer choices**: equations, variables
- **"Bridge" concepts:** In order for the system of variables to have two real solutions, it must be the case that a and b are numbers that cause there to be two (x, y) pairs that make both equations in the prompt true. Since one equation in the

prompt is $y = 3$, it must be the case that both (x, y) pairs that are solutions to the system have y equal to 3. Given the way the question is written, it may be possible for a and b to have several different values that would satisfy the system; still, as trained test-takers, we know that each question can only have one correct answer. So it must be the case that only one of the choices has a valid pair of a- and b- values, even though it may be possible for us to come up with other valid pairs of a- and b-values that don't appear in the answer choices. For this reason, if we try to come up with a- and b- values on our own to answer the question, there's no guarantee that our values will be reflected in the answer choices.

- **Pre-solution patterns (see p. 217):** opposites; wrong answers try to imitate right answers
- **Things to look out for:** Don't confuse a and b with x and y! Don't confuse a with b! Don't misread the numbers in the choices!

Solution 1: Test-smart / backsolving: Try each answer choice in the system of equations and determine which choice creates exactly two values of x that satisfy the system.

For choice (A):

$$y = ax^2 + b \qquad \text{(second equation in the system)}$$

$$y = -2x^2 + 2 \qquad \text{(plug in } a = -2 \text{ and } b = 2 \text{ from (A))}$$

$$3 = -2x^2 + 2 \qquad \text{(plug } y = 3 \text{ from the first equation into the second equation)}$$

$$3 + 2x^2 = 2 \qquad \text{(add } 2x^2 \text{ to both sides)}$$

$$2x^2 = -1 \qquad \text{(subtract 3 from both sides)}$$

$$x^2 = -\frac{1}{2} \qquad \text{(divide both sides by 2)}$$

$$x = \sqrt{-\frac{1}{2}} \qquad \text{(take the square root of both sides)}$$

The square root of a negative number can't be a real number, so (A) can't be correct, because there are no real solutions to the system using the values from (A). Now let's try (B):

$$y = ax^2 + b \qquad \text{(second equation in the system)}$$

$$y = -2x^2 + 4 \qquad \text{(plug in } a = -2 \text{ and } b = 4 \text{ from (B))}$$

$$3 = -2x^2 + 4 \qquad \text{(plug } y = 3 \text{ from the first equation into the second equation)}$$

$$3 + 2x^2 = 4 \qquad \text{(add } 2x^2 \text{ to both sides)}$$

$$2x^2 = 1 \qquad \text{(subtract 3 from both sides)}$$

$$x^2 = \tfrac{1}{2} \qquad \text{(divide both sides by 2)}$$

$$x = \tfrac{1}{4} \quad \text{and} \quad x = -\tfrac{1}{4} \qquad \text{(take the square root of both sides)}$$

The values from (B) resulted in a system of equations with exactly two real solutions, so (B) is correct, assuming we haven't made any mistakes in our approach. As trained test-takers, we know that one of the best ways to guard against small errors in a situation like this is to check every answer choice before moving on to the next question, so let's keep going and take a look at (C):

$$y = ax^2 + b \qquad \text{(second equation in the system)}$$

$$y = 2x^2 + 4 \qquad \text{(plug in } a = 2 \text{ and } b = 4 \text{ from (C))}$$

$$3 = 2x^2 + 4 \qquad \text{(plug } y = 3 \text{ from the first equation into the second equation)}$$

$$-1 = 2x^2 \qquad \text{(subtract 4 from both sides)}$$

$$-\tfrac{1}{2} = x^2 \qquad \text{(divide both sides by 2)}$$

$$\sqrt{-\tfrac{1}{2}} = x \qquad \text{(take the square root of both sides)}$$

The square root of a negative number can't be a real number, so (C) can't be correct, because it doesn't generate any real solutions for the system of equations. Now let's take a look at (D):

$$y = ax^2 + b \qquad \text{(second equation in the system)}$$

$$y = 4x^2 + 3 \qquad \text{(plug in } a = 4 \text{ and } b = 3 \text{ from (D))}$$

$$3 = 4x^2 + 3 \qquad \text{(plug } y = 3 \text{ from the first equation into the second equation)}$$

$$0 = 4x^2 \qquad \text{(subtract 3 from both sides)}$$

$$0 = x^2 \qquad \text{(divide both sides by 4)}$$

$$0 = x \qquad \text{(take the square root of both sides)}$$

0 is a real number, but the prompt asked for values of a and b that result in "exactly two" real solution, and 0 is only one solution, so (D) can't be correct. Only the values from (B) resulted in a system of equations with exactly two real solutions, so (B) is right.

Solution 2: Test-smart / graphing: Use a calculator to graph the system of equations with each pair of a- and b-values, and pick the answer choice that creates graphs that intersect each other in exactly two places.

When we graph the system of equations using $a = -2$ and $b = 2$ from choice (A), we get this:

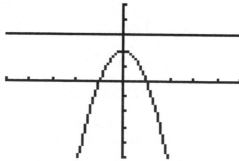

As we can see, there are no points of intersection in the xy-plane when we use the a- and b-values from (A), so (A) can't be correct. When we graph the system of equations using $a = -2$ and $b = 4$ from choice (B), we get this:

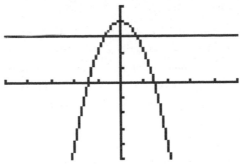

As we can see, there are two points of intersection in the xy-plane when we use the a- and b-values from (B), so (B) is right. Let's check the remaining choices to help make sure we haven't made a mistake. When we graph the system of equations using $a = 2$ and $b = 4$ from choice (C), we get this:

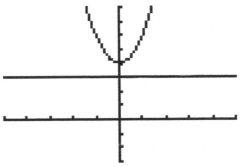

As we can see, there are no points of intersection in the xy-plane when we use the a- and b-values from (C), so (C) can't be correct. When we graph the system of equations using $a = 4$ and $b = 3$ from choice (D), we get this:

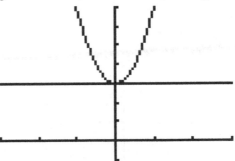

As we can see, there is one point of intersection in the xy-plane when we use the a- and b-values from (D), so (D) can't be correct After we test each answer choice, we can see that only the values from (B) result in two points of intersection for the graphs, which means that (B) is correct.

ANSWER CHOICE ANALYSIS

(C): This choice might be tempting to someone who makes an error involving a positive or negative sign.

How to check? Try an alternate approach above.

▶ Post-solution patterns (see page 218): opposites

Test 2, Section 4, Question 30

- **What's the prompt asking for?** The area of the square in square inches.
- **Math concepts in the prompt:** hexagons, radical expressions, regular polygons, squares
- **Math concepts in the diagram:** hexagons, regular polygons, squares
- **Elements of the answer choices:** integers, radical expressions
- **Notable differences among answer choices:** (A) and (B) are both integers, while (C) and (D) include $\sqrt{3}$. (C) is one-sixth of the number $384\sqrt{3}$, which is the only number in the prompt; this may be relevant because the question involves a hexagon, which is a six-sided figure. (D) is one-fourth of the number in (C), which may be relevant because the question asks for the area of a square, which is a four-sided figure.
- **Concepts in the answer choices:** square roots
- **"Bridge" concepts:** As trained test-takers, we know that the College Board can't require us to use any area formulas besides the ones that appear in the information panel at the beginning of each math section on the SAT! (See p.215 for more on that.) Since the area of a hexagon isn't one of the formulas in that information panel, we know it must be possible to answer this question without knowing a formula

for the area of a hexagon. The College Board can require us to answer questions that involve the areas of triangles, rectangles, and circles, which means there must be some way to describe a hexagon in those terms in order to answer the question. The easiest approach is probably to subdivide the hexagon into six equilateral triangles with a common point at the center of the hexagon. The recurrence of $\sqrt{3}$ is a hint that we should think this way, because $\sqrt{3}$ comes up frequently in questions related to 30-60-90 triangles—in fact, those special right triangles are even mentioned in the information panel at the start of every SAT math section.

- **Pre-solution patterns (see p. 217):** wrong answers try to imitate right answers
- **Things to look out for:** Don't be intimidated if you don't know a formula for the area of a hexagon!

Solution 1: Geometry: Sub-divide the hexagon into 30-60-90 special right triangles of equal size. Find the hypotenuse of one of those triangles, which will be the same length as a, the side-length of the square. Use a to find the area of the square.

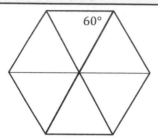
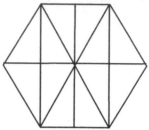

As we can see from the diagrams above, the hexagon can be divided into 6 equilateral triangles, and each of those equilateral triangles can be divided into two special 30-60-90 triangles of equal area. So the hexagon contains twelve special 30-60-90 triangles of equal area. The total area of the hexagon is given as $384\sqrt{3}$, so the area of each of the twelve 30-60-90 triangles must be $\frac{384\sqrt{3}}{12}$, or $32\sqrt{3}$, since $\frac{384\sqrt{3}}{12} = 32\sqrt{3}$.

We know that 30-60-90 triangles have side lengths with the following ratios (this information appears at the beginning of each official SAT Math section, in case you need a reminder on test day):

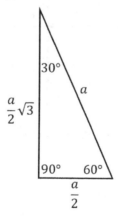

Now we can combine the formula for the area of a triangle with the side-length ratios of 30-60-90 triangles to find a:

$$\frac{1}{2}bh = 32\sqrt{3}$$
(area of a triangle set equal to $32\sqrt{3}$)

$$\frac{1}{2}\left(\frac{a}{2}\right)\left(\frac{a}{2}\sqrt{3}\right) = 32\sqrt{3}$$
(plug in $b = \frac{a}{2}$ and $h = \frac{a}{2}\sqrt{3}$)

$$\frac{a^2}{8}\sqrt{3} = 32\sqrt{3}$$
(simplify)

$$\frac{a^2}{8} = 32$$
(divide both sides by $\sqrt{3}$)

$$a^2 = 256$$
(multiply both sides by 8)

$$a = 16$$
(take the square root of each side)

Now that we know a is 16, we can square 16 to get the area of the square with a side of length a. $16^2 = 256$, so (A) is right.

ANSWER CHOICE ANALYSIS

(B): This is the result of dividing $384\sqrt{3}$ by 6 to get $64\sqrt{3}$ (which would be the area of each equilateral triangle in the diagram above), and then accidentally squaring $\sqrt{3}$ and multiplying it by 64 for some reason. **(C):** This choice reflects the mistake of thinking the area of the hexagon is 6 times the area of the square. **(D):** This choice reflects the mistake of multiplying a by $\sqrt{3}$ instead of squaring it for some reason.

How to check? Carefully reconsider your reading and your work. Note the thought processes that could lead to the wrong answers and make sure you haven't made any mistakes in your own thought process.

▶ Post-solution patterns (see page 218): right approach, wrong step

Test 2, Section 4, Question 31

- **What's the prompt asking for?** The number of years it will take for the beach to erode 21 feet.
- **Math concepts in the prompt:** constant rate, word problems
- **Things to look out for:** Read the prompt carefully!

Solution 1: Arithmetic: Divide 21 by 1.5 to determine the number of years it will take for the beach to erode 21 feet at the rate of 1.5 feet per year.

$$\frac{21}{1.5} = 14 \text{ , so we can see that the answer is } 14.$$

How to check? Carefully re-read the prompt and re-check your arithmetic.

Test 2, Section 4, Question 32

- **What's the prompt asking for?** The value of h under the conditions in the prompt.
- **Math concepts in the prompt:** hours and minutes, variables, word problems
- **"Bridge" concepts:** One hour is 60 minutes.
- **Things to look out for:** Don't make the common mistake of thinking an hour is 100 minutes!

Solution 1: Algebra: Set up an equation relating h to 450 and solve for h.

$$h + 30 = 450 \qquad \text{(equation relating } h \text{ to 450 in minutes)}$$
$$h = 420 \qquad \text{(subtract 30 from both sides)}$$

If h hours is equal to 420 minutes, then h must equal 7, because there are 60 minutes in an hour, and $\frac{420}{60} = 7$. So the correct answer is 7.

Solution 2: Arithmetic: Subtract 30 from 450 to find the number of minutes that must be accounted for in h hours, and then divide this number by 60 to find h.

If "h hours and 30 minutes" is 450 minutes, then "h hours" by itself must be 420 minutes, because $450 - 30 = 420$. Since one hour is 60 minutes, and $420 = 60(7)$, we know that h hours must be 7 hours, so the answer to the question is 7.

How to check? Try an alternate approach above.

Test 2, Section 4, Question 33

- **What's the prompt asking for?** The value of b under the given circumstances.
- **Math concepts in the prompt:** algebra, coordinate values, exponents, functions, xy-coordinate plane
- **"Bridge" concepts:** When x is 3 and y is 6, there can only be one value of b that satisfies the equation.
- **Things to look out for:** Don't confuse x or y with b! Don't make small mistakes in algebra or arithmetic!

Solution 1: Algebra: Plug the coordinates $(3, 6)$ into the equation from the prompt and solve for b.

$$f(x) = 3x^2 - bx + 12 \qquad \text{(given equation)}$$
$$6 = 3(3)^2 - b(3) + 12 \qquad \text{(plug in } (x = 3) \text{ from the prompt)}$$
$$6 = 39 - 3b \qquad \text{(use PEMDAS and simplify)}$$
$$0 = 33 - 3b \qquad \text{(subtract 6 from both sides)}$$
$$3b = 33 \qquad \text{(add } 6b \text{ to both sides)}$$
$$b = 11 \qquad \text{(divide both sides by 3)}$$

So we can see that b is 11.

How to check? Plug the values you found back into the original expression to make sure the result is valid. Carefully re-read the prompt and re-check your work to make sure you haven't made any small mistakes!

Test 2, Section 4, Question 34

- **What's the prompt asking for?** The number of hours Laura spend in the lab.
- **Math concepts in the prompt:** addition, word problems

- **Things to look out for:** Don't confuse Doug and Laura! Don't make small mistakes in your arithmetic or algebra!

Solution 1: Algebra: Set up an equation that relates Doug's time to Laura's time, and to the number 250. Then solve to find how much time Doug spent.

Let D represent the number of hours Doug spent in the lab, and let L represent the number of hours Laura spent in the lab. That lets us write and solve the following system of equations:

$D + L = 250$	(equation showing Doug and Laura spent a combined 250 lab hours)
$D = L + 40$	(equation showing Doug spent 40 more hours than Laura)
$L + 40 + L = 250$	(plug $D = L + 40$ into the first equation)
$2L = 210$	(subtract 40 from both sides)
$L = 105$	(divide both sides by 2)

So we can see that Laura spent 105 hours in the lab, and the correct answer is 105.

Solution 2: Arithmetic: Test various numbers for Doug's time to determine which number satisfies the setup in the prompt.

If we want to try a guess-and-check approach like this, we might decide to start by seeing what happens when we imagine Doug and Laura spending an equal amount of time in the lab, and then we can adjust our guesses from there.

If they spent an equal amount of time in the lab, then they would have each spent 125 hours in the lab, because 125 is half of 250. But we know that Doug spent 40 more hours than Laura, according to the prompt—does that mean we should add 40 to 125 to find Doug's hours? If we do that, we'd get 165 hours for Doug…which might sound like the right answer at first, but we have to remember that Doug and Laura still need to combine for 250 hours, so if Doug spends 165 hours, then Laura spends 85 hours, because 250 − 165 = 85. That would mean that Doug actually spent 80 more hours in the lab than Laura did. This contradicts the prompt, so it can't be right.

So let's review what we've found so far: when we imagine Doug spending 125 hours, he spends 0 hours more than Laura, which is 40 extra hours less than the prompt asks us for; when we imagine Doug spending 165 hours, he spends 80 hours more than Laura, which is 40 extra hours more than the prompt asks us for. So what if we try guessing a number of hours for Doug that's exactly in the middle of 125 and 165? That number would be 145. If Doug spends 145 hours at the lab, then Laura spends 105 hours at the lab, because 250 − 145 = 105. And we can see that 105 is 40 less than 145, just as the prompt requires.

So we can tell that Doug spends 145 hours at the lab, and Laura spends 105 hours, which means the answer is 105.

How to check? Try an alternate approach above. Remember to read carefully, and remember to find Laura's time, not Doug's!

Test 2, Section 4, Question 35

- **What's the prompt asking for?** The size of Jane's initial deposit under the circumstances in the question.
- **Math concepts in the prompt:** algebra, function modeling, understanding parts of a function, variables, word problems

- **"Bridge" concepts:** Since we're not told how much money is in the account or how long Jane has been putting money in it, we won't be able to work out Jane's initial deposit through algebra. This means there must be some way to determine Jane's initial deposit by considering only the information we've been given.

Solution 1: Function modeling: Consider each component of the model and compare it to the situation described in the prompt to determine which part of the model must correspond to the initial deposit.

As trained test-takers, we know that every component of the function model in the prompt must correspond to something described in words in the prompt. So one way to approach this question is to figure out what role is being played by each of these elements, and see which one corresponds to the idea of an initial investment. The function has the following expressions as elements: a, 18, t, and 15. So let's figure out what each one represents.

- The function explicitly tells us that a is the amount of money Jane has after her t weekly deposits, so a can't correspond to the initial investment—further, it would be impossible to grid the letter a into the answer sheet anyway.
- 18 is multiplied by t in the function, so let's consider those two elements together. We're told that t refers to the number of weeks that Jane has had the account, so we can see that the function involves multiplying 18 by the number of weeks the account has existed. But there's no reason why the function should relate the amount of money in the account to the idea of multiplying the initial investment by the number of weeks the account has existed, so we can see that 18 must not tell us anything about the initial investment. In fact, 18 must represent the "fixed amount" that was deposited "each week" after the account was opened, according to the prompt.
- 15 is a number that the function adds to the $18t$ expression in order to find a.

Facebook.com/TestingIsEasy   Youtube.com/TestingIsEasy

We've already figured out that $18t$ represents the idea of depositing 18 dollars every week as a fixed amount of money. We can also realize that a, the amount in the account, must be equal to the sum of the fixed weekly deposits and the initial deposit, because those are the only two sources of money going into the account. Since $18t$ represents the weekly deposits of \$18, we know that 15 must represent the initial deposit. So the correct answer is 15.

How to check? Carefully re-read the prompt and re-check your conclusion.

Test 2, Section 4, Question 36

- **What's the prompt asking for?** The length of minor arc $\overarc{LN}$ in the diagram.

- **Math concepts in the prompt:** arcs, center of a circle, circles, circumference, geometry, intersection, line segments, minor arcs, tangents

- **Math concepts in the diagram:** angle measurements, arcs, center of a circle, circles, circumference, geometry, intersection, line segments, minor arcs, tangents

- **"Bridge" concepts:** In order to find the length of minor arc $\overarc{LN}$, we'll need to know the measure of angle $\angle LON$; then we can use that to find the portion of the circle's circumference that's taken up by minor arc $\overarc{LN}$.

- **Things to look out for:** Don't confuse the positions and/or labels of the points in the diagram! Don't forget what you've been asked to find—don't fill in an answer that's on the way to finding the right answer!

Solution 1: Geometry: Determine the measure of angle $\angle LON$, and then compare that measure to 360 degrees to determine the portion of the circle occupied by minor arc $\overarc{LN}$.

We know that $\angle OLM$ is a right angle, because $\overline{LM}$ is tangent to circle O and $\overline{OL}$ is a radius of circle O. We also know that $\angle ONM$ is a right angle, because $\overline{NM}$ is tangent to circle O and $\overline{ON}$ is a radius of circle O.

The four interior angles of quadrilateral $OLMN$ must add up to $360°$, because the interior angles of all quadrilaterals add up to $360°$. So we can find the measure of $\angle LON$ by subtracting the three known angle measures from $360°$: $360° - 60° - 90° - 90° = 120°$. Let's add the values we've found to the diagram:

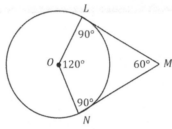

If $\angle LON = 120°$, which is one third of the $360°$ in circle, then minor arc $\overarc{LN}$ must be one third of the circumference of circle O. Since circle O has a circumference of 96, minor arc $\overarc{LN}$ must have a circumference of $\frac{96}{3}$, or 32. So the right answer is 32.

How to check? Reconsider your reading and calculations. Pay special attention to the scale of the diagram, and note that minor arc $\overarc{LN}$ looks like one-third of the circle, and $\angle LON$ looks twice as large as $\angle LMN$; both of these facts are consistent with the idea that minor arc $\overarc{LN}$ takes up 120 degrees of arc, which would mean the length of the arc is one-third of 96, making 32 the right answer.

Test 2, Section 4, Question 37

- **What's the prompt asking for?** The number of plants two years from now if $K = 4000$, rounded to the nearest whole number.

- **Math concepts in the prompt:** addition, function modeling, multiplication, order of operations, rounding, sub-scripts, variables, word problems

- **"Bridge" concepts:** To find the number of plants two years from now, we'll need to repeat the process of finding "next year's" number of plants twice—in other words, we'll have to

find the number of plants "next year" once first, and then use that number as the number of plants "this year" so we can find the number of plants for the year after next year.

- **Things to look out for:** Don't get confused by the process of repeating the formula twice to find the number of plants two years from now! Don't make small mistakes in your arithmetic or algebra!

Solution 1: Algebra: Plug $K = 4000$ into the equation from the prompt to find the number of plants next year. Repeat the process to find the number of plants 2 years into the future. (Notice that the given information says the environment "currently has 3000 of these plants," so we know that $N_{this\ year} = 3000$.)

$$N_{next\ year} = N_{this\ year} + 0.2\left(N_{this\ year}\right)\left(1 - \frac{N_{this\ year}}{K}\right) \qquad \text{(given formula)}$$

$$N_{next\ year} = 3000 + 0.2(3000)\left(1 - \frac{3000}{4000}\right)$$ (plug in $N_{this\ year} = 3000$ and $K = 4000$)

$$N_{next\ year} = 3000 + (600)\left(\frac{1}{4}\right)$$ (simplify)

$$N_{next\ year} = 3150$$ (simplify)

So next year there will be 3150 plants. To find the number of plants two years from now, we'll plug in $N_{this\ year} = 3150$ and $K = 4000$:

$$N_{next\ year} = N_{this\ year} + 0.2\left(N_{this\ year}\right)\left(1 - \frac{N_{this\ year}}{K}\right)$$ (given formula)

$$N_{next\ year} = 3150 + 0.2(3150)\left(1 - \frac{3150}{4000}\right)$$ (plug in $N_{this\ year} = 3000$ and $K = 4000$)

$$N_{next\ year} = 3150 + (630)(0.2125)$$ (simplify)

$$N_{next\ year} = 3283.875$$ (simplify)

So the number of plants in 2 years, rounded to the nearest whole number, will be 3284, which means 3284 is the right answer.

How to check? Carefully re-read the prompt and re-check your work.

Test 2, Section 4, Question 38

- **What's the prompt asking for?** The number of plants that need to be supported in order for next year's number of plants to be 3360 if this year's number of plants is 3000.
- **Math concepts in the prompt:** addition, function modeling, multiplication, order of operations, sub-scripts, variables, word problems

- **Things to look out for:** Don't confuse the number of plants this year with the number of plants next year! Don't make small mistakes in your algebra or arithmetic!

Solution 1: Algebra: Using the values from the prompt, plug in 3000 as the number of plants for this year and 3360 as the number of plants for next year, and find K under those conditions.

$$N_{next\ year} = N_{this\ year} + 0.2\left(N_{this\ year}\right)\left(1 - \frac{N_{this\ year}}{K}\right)$$ (given formula)

$$3360 = 3000 + 0.2(3000)\left(1 - \frac{3000}{K}\right)$$ (plug in $N_{this\ year} = 3000$ and $N_{next\ year} = 3360$)

$$3360 = 3000 + (600)\left(1 - \frac{3000}{K}\right)$$ (simplify)

$$3360 = 3000 + 600 - \frac{1{,}800{,}000}{K}$$ (distribute)

$$3360 = 3600 - \frac{1{,}800{,}000}{K}$$ (simplify)

$$-240 = -\frac{1{,}800{,}000}{K}$$ (subtract 3600 from both sides)

$$-240K = -1{,}800{,}000$$ (multiply both sides by K)

$$K = 7500$$ (divide both sides by -240)

So we can see that the number of supported plants needs to be 7500.

How to check? Carefully re-read the prompt and re-check your work, making sure you haven't made any small mistakes in your algebra or arithmetic!

TEST 3 – SECTION 4

Test 3, Section 4, Question 1

- **What's the prompt asking for?** The point on the graph that corresponds to finishing lunch and continuing the hike.
- **Math concepts in the prompt:** distance, time, word problems, reading a line graph

- **Math concepts in the diagram:** axis labels, distance, time, line graphs
- **Elements of the answer choices:** times

- **Notable differences among answer choices:** (A) and (C) both end in : 40, while (B) ends in : 10 and (D) ends in : 00. (B) and (C) both begin with 1:, while (A) begins with 12: and (D) begins with 2:.
- **"Bridge" concepts:** Since the graph shows distance against time, the period when Marilyn has stopped will look like a horizontal line—during that period, the distance is unchanged, since Marilyn isn't moving.

- **Pre-solution patterns (see p. 217):** wrong answers try to imitate right answers
- **Things to look out for:** Don't confuse the different times in the answer choices! Don't misinterpret the different features of the graph!

Solution 1: Reading data / Backsolving: Compare each answer choice to the graph and determine which choice could represent the time that Marilyn resumes movement.

(A) The graph shows a general upward trend around 12 : 40 P.M. which indicates that Marilyn is moving farther from her camp and hasn't taken a 30 minute break.

(B) Right after 1: 10 P.M. the graph goes flat—which indicates that this is the time that Marilyn *started* her 30 minute lunch break, not the time she *finished* the break, which is what the prompt asked for.

(C) At 1: 40 P.M. the graph starts to move up again after remaining flat since around 1: 10 P.M. This is consistent with the idea of Marilyn finishing a 30 minute break at 1: 40 P.M. and beginning to hike again, so (C) looks to be correct, assuming that we haven't made any mistakes in our approach.

(D) At 2: 00 P.M. the graph changes from trending upward to trending downward. This might seem like an important point on the graph, but this change doesn't have anything to do with stopping for a 30 minute break. The change from the line increasing to the line decreasing indicates that Marilyn stopped moving farther from camp, and started moving closer to camp.

After considering each choice, we can see that (C) is right.

How to check? Re-check your reading of the prompt and the graph to make sure you've come to the right conclusion.

Test 3, Section 4, Question 2

- **What's the prompt asking for?** The probability that a person randomly selected from the table is *either* a female under 40, *or* a male who's 40 or older.
- **Math concepts in the prompt:** either-or, probability, random selection, reading data from a table
- **Math concepts in the diagram:** data labels, rows and columns
- **Elements of the answer choices:** fractions

- **Notable differences among answer choices:** Each choice is a fraction with 25 as the denominator. Only choice (C) has a numerator that's in the table.
- **Things to look out for:** Don't forget which types of people the question asked us to identify! Don't misread the answer choices!

Solution 1: Reading data / probability: Construct a probability fraction to answer the question by adding the number of females under 40 to the number of males who are 40 or older.

We know the numerator of a probability fraction should reflect the number of possible desired outcomes, and the desired outcome in this case is *either* a female under age 40, *or* a male age 40 or older. The table tells us there are 8 females under age 40, and 2 males age 40 or older, so the numerator of the probability fraction should be 8 + 2, or 10. The number of possible outcomes is the total number of people in the contest, which is 25. So the denominator of our probability fraction is 25, making the probability $\frac{10}{25}$, and (B) is right.

ANSWER CHOICE ANALYSIS

(A): This is the result if we divide the number of females under 40 by the number of males 40 or older to find the numerator of the probability fraction, instead of adding them. **(C):** This is the probability of randomly selecting a female from the entire group. **(D):** This is the result if we multiply the number of females under 40 by the number of males 40 or older to find the numerator of the probability fraction, instead of adding them.

How to check? Carefully re-read the prompt and re-check the table to make sure you haven't made any small mistakes.

Test 3, Section 4, Question 3

- **What's the prompt asking for?** The statement that most accurately reflects the graph.
- **Math concepts in the prompt:** data trends, reading line graphs, word problems
- **Math concepts in the diagram:** axis labels, line graphs
- **Elements of the answer choices:** sentences

- **Notable differences among answer choices:** (A) and (B) are opposite statements. (C) is the only statement that describes a year between 1997 and 2009.
- **Concepts in the answer choices:** decreasing trends, flat trends, increasing trends
- **Pre-solution patterns (see p. 217):** opposites

- **Things to look out for:** Don't misread the years in the prompt and the answer choices!

Solution 1: Reading line graphs / backsolving: Compare each answer choice to the line graph. The correct answer will be the one that accurately reflects the behavior of the graph.

(A) Sales generally decreased from 2000 on, so this statement isn't correct.

(B) Sales increased from 1997 to 2000, so this statement isn't correct.

(C) We can see that the sales increased each year from 1997 to 2000. After 2000, sales seem to decrease just about every year, with the exception of the period from 2003-2004, when sales seem to have increased slightly. We can accurately describe that as "generally" decreasing after 2000, so this choice is correct.

(D) As we saw in the discussion of the other answer choices, sales increased from 1997 to 2000, and then generally decreased afterward. We can't accurately say that sales "generally remained steady" from 1997 to 2009.

How to check? Carefully re-read the prompt, the answer choices, and the graph, to make sure your conclusion is valid.

Test 3, Section 4, Question 4

- **What's the prompt asking for?** The choice that defines f in terms of n, based on the table.
- **Math concepts in the prompt:** defining functions, linear functions, reading data from a table
- **Math concepts in the diagram:** inputs and outputs of a function
- **Elements of the answer choices:** equations, integers
- **Notable differences among answer choices:** Each choice begins with an n expression, and then subtracts an integer

from it. The choices form a type of "series" in which the coefficient of n increases from 1 to 4, and the integer being subtracted increases from 3 to 6.

- **Pre-solution patterns (see p. 217):** the first and last terms in a series are often wrong answers
- **Things to look out for:** Don't confuse the inputs and outputs in the table! Avoid small mistakes in algebra and arithmetic!

Solution 1: Backsolving: Test each answer choice against the values in the table; the correct answer will be the only one that produces the appropriate output for every one of the inputs.

For choice (A):

$$f(n) = n - 3 \qquad \text{(function from (A))}$$

$$f(1) = 1 - 3 = -2 \qquad \text{(plug in } n = 1)$$

The function in (A) matches the value in the table when $n = 1$. Let's try $n = 2$:

$$f(2) = 2 - 3 = -1 \qquad \text{(plug in } n = 2)$$

The function in (A) doesn't match the value in the table when $n = 2$, so (A) can't be correct, because the correct answer needs to describe every pairing of n and $f(n)$ from the table. Let's analyze (B) now:

$$f(n) = 2n - 4 \qquad \text{(function from (B))}$$

$$f(1) = 2(1) - 4 = -2 \qquad \text{(plug in } n = 1)$$

The function in (B) matches the value in the table when $n = 1$. Let's try $n = 2$.

$$f(2) = 2(2) - 4 = 0 \qquad \text{(plug in } n = 2)$$

The function in (B) doesn't match the value in the table when $n = 2$, so (B) can't be right, for the same reason (A) wasn't right. Now we'll need to take a look at (C):

$$f(n) = 3n - 5 \qquad \text{(function from (C))}$$

$$f(1) = 3(1) - 5 = -2 \qquad \text{(plug in } n = 1)$$

The function in (C) matches the value in the table when $n = 1$, so let's try $n = 2$:

$$f(2) = 3(2) - 5 = 1 \qquad \text{(plug in } n = 2)$$

The function in (C) matches the value in the table when $n = 2$, so let's try $n = 3$:

$$f(2) = 3(3) - 5 = 4 \qquad \text{(plug in } n = 3)$$

The function in (C) matches the value in the table when $n = 3$, so let's try $n = 4$:

$$f(2) = 3(4) - 5 = 7 \qquad \text{(plug in } n = 4)$$

The function in (C) matches all the values in the table, so (C) must be correct, assuming we haven't made any mistakes in our approach. Let's try (D) to help make sure we haven't made a mistake:

$$f(n) = 4n - 6 \qquad \text{(function from (D))}$$

$$f(1) = 4(1) - 6 = -2 \qquad \text{(plug in } n = 1)$$

The function in (D) matches the value in the table when $n = 1$, so let's try $n = 2$:

$$f(2) = 4(2) - 6 = 2 \qquad \text{(plug in } n = 2)$$

The function in (D) doesn't match the value in the table when $n = 2$, so (D) can't be right. We can tell now that (C) must be right.

Solution 2: Test-smart: Note that the outputs in the table increase by 3 with every 1-unit increase in the inputs, which means the slope of the correct answer must be 3; pick the answer choice with a slope of 3.

If we notice that $f(n)$ increases by 3 every time n increases by 1, then we know that the slope must be 3, because slope is the ratio of vertical change to horizontal change, by definition. Only the function in (C) has a slope of 3, so (C) must be correct.

ANSWER CHOICE ANALYSIS

(A): This might be tempting if we only check the first $(n, (f(n))$ pair. **(B):** This might be tempting if we only check the first $(n, (f(n))$ pair. **(D):** This might be tempting if we only check the first $(n, (f(n))$ pair.

How to check? Try an alternate approach above.

Test 3, Section 4, Question 5

- **What's the prompt asking for?** The choice with the closest approximation for the number of juniors and seniors inducted this year.
- **Math concepts in the prompt:** approximation, percentages, word problems
- **Elements of the answer choices:** integers
- **Notable differences among answer choices:** (B) is the sum of (C) and (D), which may be relevant because the question asks us to consider two groups together. (A) is approximately twice as much as (B), which may be relevant since we know the College Board likes to include numbers that are half as much or twice as much as the right answer, and since the prompt specifically asks us to approximate.
- **Pre-solution patterns (see p. 217):** halves and doubles
- **Things to look out for:** Don't confuse the juniors and seniors when you're finding your percentages!

Solution 1: Arithmetic: Add 7% of 562 and 5% of 602, and pick the answer choice that's closest to the result.

$$562(0.07) + 602(0.05) = 69.44$$

The choice that's closest to this result is (B), so (B) is correct. (Note that the word "closest" in the prompt tells us we'll need to do some rounding when we pick the correct answer.)

Solution 2 plan: Estimation: Find 7% of 500 and 5% of 600, add them, and pick the answer choice that's closest to the result.

We can estimate that 7% of 500 is 35 and 5% of 600 is 30. If we add those numbers together and get 65, we can see that only (B) is close enough to be correct.

ANSWER CHOICE ANALYSIS

(A): This is 12% of the junior and senior classes combined. **(C):** This is 7% of 562, which is the number of juniors who were inducted. **(D):** This is 5% of 602, which is the number of seniors who were inducted.

How to check? Try an alternate approach above; also, note that multiple patterns in the choices suggest (B) is likely to be correct.

▶ Post-solution patterns (see page 218): halves and doubles; right approach, wrong step

---

Test 3, Section 4, Question 6

- **What's the prompt asking for?** The sum of the given polynomials.
- **Math concepts in the prompt:** adding polynomials, algebra, arithmetic
- **Elements of the answer choices:** algebraic expressions, exponents, integers
- **Notable differences among answer choices:** (A) and (B) involve squaring the first x-term, while (C) and (D) involve raising the first x-term to the fourth power and squaring the second x-term. (A) and (C) involve subtracting the second x-term, while (B) and (D) involve adding it.
- **Pre-solution patterns (see p. 217):** opposites; wrong answers try to imitate right answers
- **Things to look out for:** Don't misread the answer choices or the expressions in the prompt! Don't make small mistakes in algebra and arithmetic!

Solution 1: Algebra: Add the two polynomials and find the answer choice that reflects your result.

$$3x^2 - 5x + 2$$
$$+ \quad \underline{5x^2 - 2x - 6}$$
$$8x^2 - 7x - 4$$

(add the two polynomials from the prompt)

So we can see the correct answer is (A).

ANSWER CHOICE ANALYSIS

(B): This is the result if we mix up the minus signs on the x-terms. **(C):** This is the result of thinking that adding the polynomials means we have to add the exponents of the terms that involve variables. **(D):** This combines the mistakes from (B) and (C).

How to check? Reconsider your reading and your calculations. Be especially sure that you haven't misread the answer choices or the initial expressions in the prompt.

▶ Post-solution patterns (see page 218): opposites

Test 3, Section 4, Question 7

- **What's the prompt asking for?** The value of w in the given equation.
- **Math concepts in the prompt:** algebra, arithmetic, equations, fractions
- **Elements of the answer choices:** fractions
- **Notable differences among answer choices:** (A) is a reciprocal of (D), and (B) is a reciprocal of (C). (A) and (D) involve 20, which is the product of 4 and 5 from the prompt; these

choices also involve 9, which would be the result of multiplying the two 3's in the prompt. (B) and (C) involve 4 and 5, two numbers that appear in the prompt.

- **Pre-solution patterns (see p. 217):** opposites; wrong answers try to imitate right answers
- **Things to look out for:** Don't accidentally pick the reciprocal of the correct answer! Don't make small mistakes in your algebra and arithmetic!

Solution 1: Algebra: Solve for w in the given equation.

$$\frac{3}{5}w = \frac{4}{3}$$

(given equation)

$$9w = 20$$

(cross multiply)

$$w = \frac{20}{9}$$

(divide both sides by 9)

So we can see that the correct answer is (D).

Solution 2: Backsolving: Test each answer choice against the original equation; pick the choice that results in a valid equation.

For choice (A):

$$\frac{3}{5}w = \frac{4}{3}$$

(given equation)

$$\frac{3}{5}\left(\frac{9}{20}\right) = \frac{4}{3}$$

(plug in $w = \frac{9}{20}$ from (A))

$$\frac{27}{100} = \frac{4}{3}$$

(simplify)

$$0.27 = 1.333$$

(decimal approximation using calculator)

This value doesn't result in a valid statement, so (A) can't be correct. Now we'll take a look at (B):

$$\frac{3}{5}w = \frac{4}{3}$$

(given equation)

$$\frac{3}{5}\left(\frac{4}{5}\right) = \frac{4}{3}$$

(plug in $w = \frac{4}{5}$ from (B))

$$\frac{12}{25} = \frac{4}{3}$$

(simplify)

$$0.48 = 1.333$$

(decimal approximation using calculator)

This value doesn't result in a valid statement, so (B) can't be correct. Now we'll test (C):

$$\frac{3}{5}w = \frac{4}{3}$$

(given equation)

$$\frac{3}{5}\left(\frac{5}{4}\right) = \frac{4}{3}$$

(plug in $w = \frac{5}{4}$ from (C))

$$\frac{15}{20} = \frac{4}{3} \qquad \text{(simplify)}$$

$$0.75 = 1.333 \qquad \text{(decimal approximation using calculator)}$$

This value doesn't result in a valid statement either, so (C) can't be correct. Let's try (D):

$$\frac{3}{5}w = \frac{4}{3} \qquad \text{(given equation)}$$

$$\frac{3}{5}\left(\frac{20}{9}\right) = \frac{4}{3} \qquad \text{(plug in } w = \frac{20}{9} \text{ from (D))}$$

$$\frac{60}{45} = \frac{4}{3} \qquad \text{(simplify)}$$

$$1.333 = 1.333 \qquad \text{(decimal approximation using calculator)}$$

This is the only answer choice whose value results in a valid statement, so (D) must be correct.

ANSWER CHOICE ANALYSIS

(A): This is the reciprocal of the correct answer. **(B):** This is the result if we cross multiply incorrectly and make an additional algebra error so that we end up solving for w in the equation $15w = 12$. **(C):** This is the result if we cross multiply incorrectly and end up solving for w in the equation $12w = 15$.

How to check? Try an alternate approach above. Be especially sure that you haven't accidentally chosen the reciprocal of the correct answer, since the test is clearly trying to bait you into doing that!

▶ Post-solution patterns (see page 218): opposites

Test 3, Section 4, Question 8

- **What's the prompt asking for?** The role of the number 0.56 in the given function.
- **Math concepts in the prompt:** averages, function modeling, word problems
- **Elements of the answer choices:** sentences
- **Notable differences among answer choices:** (A) mentions a "total" number, while (B), (C), and (D) mention an "average" number. (C) mentions a yearly "increase," while (D) mentions a "difference."
- **Concepts in the answer choices:** averages, estimation
- **Pre-solution patterns (see p. 217):** wrong answers try to imitate right answers
- **Things to look out for:** Don't confuse averages with totals! Don't confuse rates of change with concrete quantities! Don't misread the answer choices!

Solution 1: Reading comprehension: Compare the choices to the prompt to determine which choice could reflect the role of 0.56.

The prompt tells us that x represents the number of years since 2000. We can see that y must increase by 0.56 every time x increases by 1, because y is the result when $0.56x$ is added to 27.2. Since y represents the average number of students per classroom, it makes sense to say that the average number of students per classroom increases by 0.56 each year. So (C) is right.

ANSWER CHOICE ANALYSIS

(A): It doesn't make much sense to say that the "total number of students" could be less than one, which is what this choice says. **(B):** This is the meaning of the number 27.2, which appears in this choice as a constant, meaning we'll always be adding the incremental extra students in the $0.56x$ expression to this base number of average students from the beginning of the time period being modeled in the function. Remember that the prompt tells us that $x = 0$ corresponds to data for the year 2000, and when $x = 0$, the value of the equation is 27.2 **(D):** This choice describes the difference between the outputs of the equation when $x = 10$ and when $x = 0$; there's no reason to think it should be equal to 0.56. In fact, we can see that each year, x increases by 1, which means the value of the expression increases by 0.56 each year—so after 10 years, the average number of students per classroom definitely increases by more than 0.56.

How to check? Carefully re-consider the answer choices in light of the prompt to make sure you haven't overlooked or misread anything in reaching your conclusion.

Test 3, Section 4, Question 9

- **What's the prompt asking for?** The choice that's closest to the distance Nate will walk in 4 minutes.
- **Math concepts in the prompt:** distance, rate, time, word problems
- **Elements of the answer choices:** integers, units
- **Notable differences among answer choices:** (D) is twice as much as (C), which may be relevant because the College Board often likes to include a wrong answer that's half as much or twice as much as the right answer.
- **Concepts in the answer choices:** distance
- **"Bridge" concepts:** 1 minute = 60 seconds
- **Pre-solution patterns (see p. 217):** halves and doubles

- **Things to look out for:** Don't accidentally find the distance walked in 1 minute! Don't make small mistakes in your algebra and arithmetic!

Solution 1: $d = rt$: Determine the rate at which Nate walks, and extrapolate the distance he would walk in 4 minutes at that rate.

There are 60 seconds in a minute, so 4 minutes is the same as 240 seconds. With that in mind, we can create an equation that sets two ratios equal to each other: the ratio of 25 to 13.7, and the ratio of the unknown distance to 240. (We'll call the unknown distance d.) Then we can solve for d:

$$\frac{25}{13.7} = \frac{d}{240}$$ (ratios of distance to time set equal, with d as the unknown distance)

$$6000 = 13.7d$$ (cross-multiply)

$$437.956 \approx d$$ (divide both sides by 13.7 to find d)

The value we found is approximately equal to 450, so (B) is correct.

Solution 2: Test-smart / Estimation: Note that 13.7 seconds is a little less than $\frac{1}{4}$ of a minute, which means Nate walks a little more than 100 meters in a minute, which means he walks a little more than 400 meters in 4 minutes, so only (B) can be right.

ANSWER CHOICE ANALYSIS

(A): This is the result if we invert one of the fractions before we cross multiply, or if we cross multiply incorrectly. **(C):** This is the result if we assume there are 100 seconds in a minute, rather than 60 seconds in a minute. **(D):** This is twice as much as (C).

How to check? Try an alternate approach above. Carefully re-check your reading and calculations.

▶ Post-solution patterns (see page 218): right approach, wrong step

Test 3, Section 4, Question 10

- **What's the prompt asking for?** The weight in newtons of a 90 kg mass on Mercury, according to the table.
- **Math concepts in the prompt:** function modeling, reading data from a table, unit conversion, word problems
- **Math concepts in the diagram:** column labels, units
- **Elements of the answer choices:** integers
- **Notable differences among answer choices:** Choice (C) is roughly four times as much as (A), and choice (D) is roughly four times as much as choice (B). This may be relevant because the value in the table that corresponds to Mercury is a little less than 4.
- **Things to look out for:** Don't misread the table and use a value for the wrong planet! Don't make small mistakes in your algebra and arithmetic! Don't confuse the variables in the function from the prompt!

Solution 1: Algebra / data: Use the data from the table and the formula in the prompt to determine W when m is 90 and g is 3.6.

The chart tells us g on Mercury is equal to 3.6. Let's plug that into the given formula, along with the mass from the prompt:

$$W = mg$$ (given formula)
$$W = (90)(3.6)$$ (plug in $m = 90$ and $g = 3.6$)
$$W = 324$$ (simplify)

So we see the right answer is (D).

Solution 2: Test-smart: Note that the formula and the table indicate the W for every planet will be at least 3 times its mass in kilograms, which means (D) is the only answer choice that can possibly be correct.

ANSWER CHOICE ANALYSIS

(A): This is the result an untrained test-taker would reach if she accidentally divided 90 by 3.6, instead of multiplying by 3.6. **(B):** This is approximately equal to $90 - 3.6$. **(C):** This is approximately equal to $90 + 11.1$ or $90 + 10.7$.

How to check? Try an alternate approach above. Be especially careful not to make any small mistakes in your algebra, since the College Board is clearly hoping you'll do that!

▶ Post-solution patterns (see page 218): opposites

Test 3, Section 4, Question 11

- **What's the prompt asking for?** The planet that would cause an object to weigh 170 newtons if the same object weighs 150 newtons on Earth.
- **Math concepts in the prompt:** algebra, arithmetic, function modeling, reading data from a table, unit conversion, variables, word problems
- **Math concepts in the diagram:** data labels, units
- **Elements of the answer choices:** words or phrases
- **Things to look out for:** Don't misread the data in the table or confuse the names of the planets! Don't make small mistakes in your algebra and arithmetic! Don't assume you can

estimate, because the g values for Saturn and Uranus are close   to one another!

Solution 1: Algebra / Data: Use the formula in the prompt to determine the object's mass. Then set W equal to 170 and m equal to the mass, and solve for g; the correct answer will be the planet whose g value is the result you find.

The chart tells us that g on Earth is equal to 9.8. We can use that to find the mass of the object from the prompt:

$W = mg$	(given formula)
$150 = m(9.8)$	(plug in $W = 150$ and $g = 9.8$ from the prompt)
$15.3 \approx m$	(divide both sides by 9.8 to find the mass of the object from the prompt)

Now we can plug the object's mass into the $W = mg$ formula and set the weight equal to 170:

$W = mg$	(given formula)
$170 = (15.3)g$	(plug in $W = 170$ from prompt, $m = 15.3$ from previous calculations)
$11.11 \approx g$	(divide both sides by 15.3)

Our value of approximately 11.11 for g is very close to Saturn's value for g on the chart, so (B) is correct.

How to check? Carefully re-check your reading and your work to make sure you haven't made a small mistake.

Note   We could potentially arrive at any of these wrong answer choices if we use the wrong value from the chart and/or make an algebra mistake in our solution.

Test 3, Section 4, Question 12

- **What's the prompt asking for?** The graph that could represent a function with five zeros.
- **Math concepts in the prompt:** function graphing, functions, zeros of a function
- **Elements of the answer choices:** diagrams
- **Notable differences among answer choices:** Each choice has a graph with the same shape shifted higher or lower.

- **Concepts in the answer choices:** function graphing
- **"Bridge" concepts:** The zeros of a function graph are the points where the graph intercepts the x-axis.
- **Pre-solution patterns (see p. 217):** wrong answers try to imitate right answers
- **Things to look out for:** Don't miscount the number of x-intercepts!

Solution 1: Graphing: Pick the choice whose graph has five x-intercepts.

The graph in (D) crosses the x-axis 5 times, so (D) is correct.

How to check? Carefully re-read the prompt and re-count the x-intercepts in the choices to make sure you're right.

Note   Any of the wrong answers could be tempting if an untrained test-taker thinks that "zeros" are places where a graph switches from going up to going down or vice-versa—and forgets to check all the choices.

Test 3, Section 4, Question 13

- **What's the prompt asking for?** The choice whose expression correctly defines v in terms of $h, t,$ and k.
- **Math concepts in the prompt:** algebra, arithmetic, function modeling, variables, word problems
- **Elements of the answer choices:** algebraic expressions, equations, fractions, integers
- **Notable differences among answer choices:** (A) and (C) involve adding k, while (B) and (D) involve subtracting it. (A) is the only choice without a fraction. (B) has the entire right-

hand side of the equation as a fraction, while (C) and (D) both have a fraction with h and k in the numerator, and t in the denominator. (A) and (C) involve subtracting $16t$, while (D) involves adding $16t$.

- **Pre-solution patterns (see p. 217):** wrong answers try to imitate right answers
- **Things to look out for:** Don't make small mistakes in your algebra and arithmetic! Don't misread the equations in the prompt and in the answer choices!

Solution 1: Backsolving: Pick arbitrary values for $t, v,$ and k, and plug them into the equation in the prompt to find a corresponding h-value. Then take your values for $h, k, t,$ and v, and test them in each answer choice; the correct answer will be the one that makes a valid equation with those values.

Let's use $t = 2, v = 3,$ and $k = 5$, arbitrarily:

$h = -16t^2 + vt + k$	(given equation)
$h = -16(2)^2 + (3)(2) + 5$	(plug in $t = 2, v = 3,$ and $k = 5$)
$h = -64 + 6 + 5$	(simplify)
$h = -53$	(simplify to find h when $t = 2, v = 3,$ and $k = 5$)

So when $t = 2$, $v = 3$, and $k = 5$, we now know that $h = -53$. We can plug these values into the answer choices to see which one results in a valid statement. Here's what we get for choice (A):

$$v = h + k - 16t \qquad \text{(expression from (A))}$$
$$3 = -53 + 5 - 16(2) \qquad \text{(plug in } t = 2, v = 3, k = 5, \text{ and } h = -53)$$
$$3 = -80 \qquad \text{(simplify)}$$

This isn't a valid statement, so (A) can't be correct. Now let's try (B):

$$v = \frac{h - k + 16}{t} \qquad \text{(expression from (B))}$$
$$3 = \frac{-53 - 5 + 16}{2} \qquad \text{(plug in } t = 2, v = 3, k = 5, \text{ and } h = -53)$$
$$3 = \frac{-42}{2} \qquad \text{(simplify)}$$
$$3 = -21 \qquad \text{(reduce)}$$

This isn't a valid statement, so (B) can't be correct. Let's take a look at (C):

$$v = \frac{h + k}{t} - 16t \qquad \text{(expression from (C))}$$
$$3 = \frac{-53 + 5}{2} - 16(2) \qquad \text{(plug in } t = 2, v = 3, k = 5, \text{ and } h = -53)$$
$$3 = \frac{-48}{2} - 32 \qquad \text{(simplify)}$$
$$3 = -56 \qquad \text{(simplify)}$$

This isn't a valid statement, so (C) can't be correct. Let's consider (D):

$$v = \frac{h - k}{t} + 16t \qquad \text{(expression from (D))}$$
$$3 = \frac{-53 - 5}{2} + 16(2) \qquad \text{(plug in } t = 2, v = 3, k = 5, \text{ and } h = -53)$$
$$3 = \frac{-58}{2} + 32 \qquad \text{(simplify)}$$
$$3 = 3 \qquad \text{(simplify)}$$

This is the only answer choice that produced a valid statement, so (D) must be correct.

Solution 2: Algebra: Manipulate the given equation until v is isolated, and then pick the answer choice that's equivalent to the definition of v that you've found.

$$h = -16t^2 + vt + k \qquad \text{(given equation)}$$
$$h + 16t^2 = vt + k \qquad \text{(add } 16t^2 \text{ to both sides)}$$
$$h + 16t^2 - k = vt \qquad \text{(subtract } k \text{ from both sides)}$$
$$\frac{h + 16t^2 - k}{t} = v \qquad \text{(divide both sides by } t)$$

At this point, the expression we've found for v doesn't look quite like any of the answer choices. (B) is the only answer choice that expresses v as one fraction with nothing added to or subtracted from it...but (B) isn't equal to the fraction we found, which means it must be wrong. So one of the other answer choices must be correct, which means we need to find another way to express v either as a fraction with some value added to it or subtracted from it (like (C) or (D)), or with no fraction at all (like (A)).

(A) doesn't look like a good choice because our current expression for v involves subtracting k, not adding k, and the rules of math don't allow us to cancel out the t in the denominator for the entire expression that we found above, which is what (A) seems to involve.

(C) doesn't look like a good choice because our expression for v involves adding $16t^2$, and it doesn't make sense that we could turn adding $16t^2$ into subtracting $16t$, which is what this choice would require.

(D) is right because the expression we found, $\frac{h + 16t^2 - k}{t}$, is equivalent to $\frac{h - k}{t} + \frac{16t^2}{t}$, which is equivalent to $\frac{h - k}{t} + 16t$.

How to check? Try an alternate approach above.

Test 3, Section 4, Question 14

Facebook.com/TestingIsEasy   Youtube.com/TestingIsEasy

- **What's the prompt asking for?** The c-value for h hours of phone use, according to the prompt.
- **Math concepts in the prompt:** rate, units, variables, word problems
- **Elements of the answer choices:** decimals, equations, fractions, integers

- **Notable differences among answer choices:** (B) is the only choice that involves addition; (A) involves only multiplication, while (C) and (D) involve division.
- **"Bridge" concepts:** There are 60 minutes in an hour.
- **Pre-solution patterns (see p. 217):** opposites; wrong answers try to imitate right answers
- **Things to look out for:** Don't confuse multiplication, addition, and/or division!

Solution 1: Concrete: Pick an arbitrary value for h and calculate the corresponding cost. Then use the same h-value along with the c-value you just found, and test each answer choice to find the one that's valid with those values.

Let's say arbitrarily that $h = 3$. There are 60 minutes in an hour, so there must be 180 minutes in 3 hours, because $60 \times 3 = 180$. If the cost of using the telephone is \$0.20 per minute, then using the phone for 180 minutes must cost \$36, because $180 \times \$0.20 = \$36$. So when $h = 3$, we see that $c = 36$. Let's plug those two values into the expressions from the answer choices and see which one results in a valid statement. We'll start with choice (A):

$$c = 0.20(60h) \qquad \text{(expression from (A))}$$
$$36 = 0.2(60(3)) \qquad \text{(plug in } h = 3 \text{ and } c = 36)$$
$$36 = 36 \qquad \text{(simplify)}$$

This results in a valid statement, so (A) could be correct, assuming that we haven't made any small mistakes in our approach, and assuming that we haven't accidentally chosen an arbitrary h-value that results in false positives in the answer choices. As trained test-takers, we know that it's necessary to check all of the answer choices when we backsolve, so we can try to minimize the chance of making those kinds of mistakes. So let's check the other answer choices, starting with (B):

$$c = 0.20h + 60 \qquad \text{(expression from (B))}$$
$$36 = 0.20(3) + 60 \qquad \text{(plug in } h = 3 \text{ and } c = 36)$$
$$36 = 60.6 \qquad \text{(simplify)}$$

This isn't a valid statement, so (B) can't be correct. Now let's check (C):

$$c = \frac{60h}{0.20} \qquad \text{(expression from (C))}$$
$$36 = \frac{60(3)}{0.20} \qquad \text{(plug in } h = 3 \text{ and } c = 36)$$
$$36 = 900 \qquad \text{(simplify)}$$

This isn't a valid statement either, so (C) can't be right. Let's take a look at (D):

$$c = \frac{0.20h}{60} \qquad \text{(expression from (D))}$$
$$36 = \frac{0.20(3)}{60} \qquad \text{(plug in } h = 3 \text{ and } c = 36)$$
$$36 = 0.01 \qquad \text{(simplify)}$$

This isn't a valid statement, so (D) can't be correct. Since (A) is the only choice that works for the valid pair of h- and c-values we found from the prompt, we know (A) must be correct.

Solution 2: Abstract: Consider the prompt and create an algebraic model to describe the cost c for h hours of phone use.

We know that the cost of using the phone is \$0.20 per minute, so we'll have to multiply that cost by the time spent on the phone to find the total cost of a phone call. But that cost is measured in minutes, and we have to come up with an equation that models the total cost in *hours*, not minutes. There are 60 minutes in an hour, so if we multiply h by 60, we'll have the amount of time spent on the phone measured in minutes. That means we can find the cost c of a phone call by multiplying the number of hours h spent on the phone by 60, and also by the per-minute cost of the call. That way, we're multiplying the number of minutes spent on the phone by the per-minute cost of using the phone. The result is $c = h(60)(0.2)$, which is equal to the correct answer we see in choice (A).

Solution 3: Abstract: Consider the similarities and differences among the answer choices in light of the concepts in the prompt, in order to identify the answer choice that correctly relates c, h, 60, and 0.2.

When we compare the answer choices, we see that we can identify the correct answer choice if we're able to answer two questions:
- What should we do with 60—add it (like in (B)), multiply it by h (like in (A) or (C)), or divide h by 60 (like in (D))?
- Should we multiply h by 0.20 (like in (A), (B), and (D)), or divide h by 0.20, like in (C)?

For the first issue, we need to think about the relationship of the number 60 to the rest of the question. 60 doesn't appear in the prompt, but the prompt does include the ideas of a cost "per minute" and a cost "for h <u>hours</u>," and we know that one hour contains 60 minutes. So the 60 is clearly supposed to be related to the idea of converting hours into minutes. Now, do we convert hours into minutes through multiplication, division, or addition? If we think about it, we'll realize that we have to multiply the number of hours by 60 in order to arrive at the number of minutes: 1 hour is 60 minutes, 2 hours is 120 minutes, and so on. So the correct answer should involve multiplying 60 and h. (As trained test-takers, we can also see that this makes sense from a test-design standpoint: the idea of multiplying 60 appears more times in the answer choices than any other way to deal with 60, which suggests, but doesn't guarantee, that multiplying 60 is the right thing to do.)

For the second issue, we need to determine whether 0.20 should be multiplied by h, or whether h should be divided by 0.20. We know that the question says every minute costs $0.20, so this $0.20 cost should be multiplied by the amount of time spent on the phone; since h represents that time, we should be multiplying 0.20 by h (don't worry that h is in hours and the cost is per minute—that discrepancy is taken care of when we multiply $0.20h$ by 60, as we discussed above). (This idea of multiplying 0.20 also makes sense from a test-design standpoint, since three of the four answer choices involve it. As trained test-takers, we know that this suggests, but doesn't guarantee, that multiplying by 0.20 is correct.)

So we should multiply h by both 60 and 0.20, which means (A) must be correct.

How to check? Try an alternate approach above. Pay particular attention to the issue of multiplying or dividing, since the College Board is clearly trying to confuse us with those concepts in this question.

Test 3, Section 4, Question 15

- **What's the prompt asking for?** The choice with an appropriate conclusion for the provided information.
- **Math concepts in the prompt:** data analysis, population size, random selection, study design

- **Elements of the answer choices:** sentences
- **Things to look out for:** Don't misread the prompt or the answer choices!

Solution 1: Reading Comprehension: Compare each choice to the situation described in the study and pick the one that's restated or demonstrated in the text, as you would for a Reading question or a Writing and Language question.

(A) seems like an appropriate conclusion at first. The prompt mentions that people with poor eyesight who received treatment X had significantly improved eyesight, and the statement in (A) essentially restates this, just as we'd see in the right answer to a question from the Reading or Writing and Language sections. The word "likely" confirms that we can't be certain treatment X will improve the eyesight of every person with poor eyesight—it's just that such a result is probable. Of course, as trained test-takers, we know that we need to consider every choice before committing to one, so we'll do that now.

(B) doesn't make sense, because the prompt doesn't say anything about comparing the effects of treatment X to the effects of any other treatment; it only says that X worked better "compared to those who did not receive" it. So (B) makes a statement that's irrelevant to the prompt, just as we might see in the wrong answer to a Reading question, which means (B) must be wrong.

(C) makes a stronger claim than what we see in the actual prompt. The prompt very clearly says the people in the study were "people with poor eyesight," but this choice says treatment X will work for "anyone who takes it." This difference makes (C) wrong (it's not true that every single person has poor eyesight, so the prompt doesn't demonstrate or restate the claim in (C)).

(D) has a problem similar to the one in (C), because it doesn't restrict itself to a claim about "people with poor eyesight," as the prompt does.

After considering each choice and applying the same techniques we'd apply against SAT Reading questions, we see (A) is right.

How to check? Pay strict attention to the wording of each answer choice!

Test 3, Section 4, Question 16

- **What's the prompt asking for?** The value of x that causes the sum of $f(x)$ and $g(x)$ to be zero.
- **Math concepts in the prompt:** evaluating functions, function graphing, zero
- **Math concepts in the diagram:** axis labels, function graphing, parabolas
- **Elements of the answer choices:** integers, negative numbers, zero

- **Notable differences among answer choices:** The answer choices form a series from -3 to 0, with each choice being one more than the choice before it.
- **"Bridge" concepts:** If $f(x) + g(x) = 0$, then we know that $f(x)$ and $g(x)$ must be opposite numbers, like -5 and 5.
- **Pre-solution patterns (see p. 217):** the first and last terms in a series are often wrong answers
- **Things to look out for:** Don't misread the graphs! Make sure you note the units on the xy-plane!

Solution 1: Reading graphs: Look at the graph to determine the x-coordinate for which $f(x)$ and $g(x)$ are opposite numbers.

We can see that $f(-2) = -2$ and $g(-2) = 2$, so $f(x) + g(x) = 0$ when $x = -2$. This is what (B) says, so (B) is correct.

Solution 2: Backsolving: Consider each x-coordinate in the choices. Find the one for which $f(x)$ and $g(x)$ are opposite numbers.

A $f(-3) = -1$ and $g(-3) = -1$, so when $x = -3$, $f(x) + g(x) = -2$.

B ✓ $f(-2) = -2$ and $g(-2) = 2$, so when $x = -2$, $f(x) + g(x) = 0$.

C $f(-1) = -1$ and $g(-1) = -1$, so when $x = -1$, $f(x) + g(x) = -2$.

D $f(0) = 2$ and $g(0) = -9$, so when $x = 0$, $f(x) + g(x) = -7$.

We can see that (B) is the only choice that satisfies the prompt, so it's correct.

ANSWER CHOICE ANALYSIS

(A): This is where $f(x) - g(x) = 0$, not where $f(x) + g(x) = 0$. **(C):** This is another place where $f(x) - g(x) = 0$, not where $f(x) + g(x) = 0$. **(D):** This is where the sum of the x-coordinates is 0.

How to check? Try an alternate approach above. Make sure your eyes correctly track the graphs relative to the x-values in the choices.

Test 3, Section 4, Question 17

- **What's the prompt asking for?** The choice that describes the change in supply that would result from a price increase of $10.
- **Math concepts in the prompt:** algebra, arithmetic, corresponding changes in variables, function modeling, reading comprehension, word problems
- **Elements of the answer choices:** integers, sentences, units
- **Notable differences among answer choices:** (A) is the only choice that says the quantity will decrease. (A) and (B) are opposite statements.

- **Pre-solution patterns (see p. 217):** opposites; the first and last terms in a series are often wrong answers; wrong answers try to imitate right answers
- **Things to look out for:** Don't misread the formulas in the prompt! Don't misread the answer choices! Don't confuse the functions or variables! Don't make small mistakes in your algebra and arithmetic!

Solution 1: Concrete: Pick two arbitrary numbers for P so that one is $10 more than the other. Plug both numbers into $S(P)$ and pick the answer choice that describes the $S(P)$ of the higher P relative to the lower P.

We'll arbitrarily find the supply when $P = 5$, and then find the supply when $P = 15$, as examples of two prices that differ by $10:

$$S(P) = \tfrac{1}{2}P + 40 \qquad \text{(given function for supply of a product)}$$

$$S(5) = \tfrac{1}{2}(5) + 40 \qquad \text{(plug in } P = 5\text{)}$$

$$S(5) = 42.5 \qquad \text{(simplify to find } S(5)\text{)}$$

Now let's increase P to 15 and see what happens:

$$S(P) = \tfrac{1}{2}P + 40 \qquad \text{(given function for supply of a product)}$$

$$S(15) = \tfrac{1}{2}(15) + 40 \qquad \text{(plug in } P = 15\text{)}$$

$$S(15) = 47.5 \qquad \text{(simplify to find } S(15)\text{)}$$

So when we increased P by 10, the quantity supplied increased by 5, from 42.5 to 47.5. This reflects choice (B), so (B) is correct.

Solution 2: Algebraic: Consider the $S(P)$ formula to see what will happen when P is increased by 10, and pick the answer choice that reflects that change.

When we consider the $S(P)$ formula, we see that it begins by finding one-half of the P value, and then it adds a constant value (which is 40). This means that any change in P will be cut in half when it affects $S(P)$, so increasing P by 10 will result in increasing $S(P)$ by 5, since 5 is half of 10. This is what (B) says, so we know (B) is correct. (Don't worry if you're not comfortable with this kind of solution! You'll never see a question on test day that can only be solved in this way—you'll always be able to use a concrete approach like Solution 1 to answer a question like this if you prefer.)

ANSWER CHOICE ANALYSIS

(A): This is how the quantity of the product supplied changes when the price of the product is decreased by $10. **(C):** This is double the correct answer. **(D):** This is the result if we add the 10 from the prompt to the 40 in the equation for $S(P)$.

How to check? Try an alternate approach above.

▶   Post-solution patterns (see page 218): opposites

Test 3, Section 4, Question 18

- **What's the prompt asking for?** The price at which the supply and the demand will be equal.
- **Math concepts in the prompt:** algebra, arithmetic, corresponding changes in variables, function modeling, reading comprehension, word problems

- **Elements of the answer choices:** integers
- **Things to look out for:** Don't misread the prompt! Avoid small mistakes in your algebra and arithmetic!

Solution 1: Algebra: Set $S(P)$ equal to $D(P)$ and solve for P. Then pick the answer choice that reflects your result.

$$\tfrac{1}{2}P + 40 = 220 - P \qquad (S(P) \text{ and } D(P) \text{ functions from prompt set equal to each other})$$

$$\tfrac{3}{2}P + 40 = 220 \qquad (\text{add } P \text{ to both sides})$$

$$\tfrac{3}{2}P = 180 \qquad (\text{subtract 40 from both sides})$$

$$P = 120 \qquad (\text{multiply both sides by } \tfrac{2}{3} \text{ to find } P \text{ so that } S(P) = D(P))$$

This reflects choice (B), so (B) is correct.

Solution 2: Backsolving: Try each number in the answer choices as P for both equations in the prompt. Pick the answer choice that generates equal values for $S(P)$ and $D(P)$.

For choice (A):

$S(P) = \tfrac{1}{2}P + 40$	$D(P) = 220 - P$	(given equations)
$S(90) = \tfrac{1}{2}(90) + 40$	$D(90) = 220 - 90$	(plug in $P = 90$ from (A))
$S(90) = 85$	$D(90) = 130$	(simplify)

The functions aren't equal when $P = 90$, so (A) can't be correct.

$S(P) = \tfrac{1}{2}P + 40$	$D(P) = 220 - P$	(given equations)
$S(120) = \tfrac{1}{2}(120) + 40$	$D(120) = 220 - 120$	(plug in $P = 120$ from (B))
$S(120) = 100$	$D(120) = 100$	(simplify)

The functions are equal when $P = 120$, so (B) seems to be correct, assuming we haven't made any small mistakes in our calculations. Let's keep checking the other choices:

$S(P) = \tfrac{1}{2}P + 40$	$D(P) = 220 - P$	(given equations)
$S(133) = \tfrac{1}{2}(133) + 40$	$D(133) = 220 - 133$	(plug in $P = 133$ from (C))
$S(133) = 106.5$	$D(133) = 87$	(simplify)

The functions aren't equal when $P = 133$, so (C) can't be correct. Let's check (D):

$S(P) = \tfrac{1}{2}P + 40$	$D(P) = 220 - P$	(given equations)
$S(155) = \tfrac{1}{2}(155) + 40$	$D(155) = 220 - 155$	(plug in $P = 155$ from (D))
$S(155) = 117.5$	$D(155) = 65$	(simplify)

The functions aren't equal when $P = 155$, so (D) can't be correct.

Only the value from (B) made the two functions equal, so (B) must be correct.

ANSWER CHOICE ANALYSIS

(A): This choice might seem correct if we forget to multiply P by $\tfrac{1}{2}$ in the equation for $S(P)$.

How to check? Try an alternate approach above. Make sure you haven't misread or miscalculated anything.

Test 3, Section 4, Question 19

Facebook.com/TestingIsEasy   Youtube.com/TestingIsEasy

- **What's the prompt asking for?** The approximate number of acres that would be covered by 48 ounces of graphene.
- **Math concepts in the prompt:** ratios, units, word problems
- **Elements of the answer choices:** integers
- **Notable differences among answer choices:** (A), (B), and (C) form a series in which each choice is 100 more than the previous one. (D) is three times as much as (C), which may be relevant because the prompt mentions the quantity $\frac{1}{3}$.
- **Pre-solution patterns (see p. 217):** the first and last terms in a series are often wrong answers
- **Things to look out for:** Don't misread the prompt! Don't make small mistakes in your arithmetic!

Solution 1: Unit conversion: Determine how many acres an ounce can cover, and then multiply that amount by 48.

One ounce can cover $9\frac{1}{3}$ acres, because $7 \times \frac{4}{3} = 9\frac{1}{3}$. If one ounce can cover $9\frac{1}{3}$ acres, then 48 ounces must cover 448 acres, because $48 \times 9\frac{1}{3} = 448$. This is roughly equivalent to (C).

Solution 2: Estimation: Note that 7 football fields is approximately 10 acres, which means that 48 ounces will cover approximately 480 acres. The only choice that's close to 480 acres is (C), so we know that (C) is correct.

ANSWER CHOICE ANALYSIS

(A): This is roughly the result of dividing the number of football fields by $\frac{4}{3}$ acres, instead of multiplying by $\frac{4}{3}$ acres. **(B):** This is roughly the number of football fields—not acres—covered by 48 ounces of graphene. **(D):** This is roughly the result of multiplying the number of football fields by 4, instead of by $\frac{4}{3}$.

How to check? Try an alternate approach above.

Test 3, Section 4, Question 20

- **What's the prompt asking for?** The difference between Michael's actual heart rate and the line of best fit for the swim that took 34 minutes.
- **Math concepts in the prompt:** line of best fit, reading data from a graph, scatterplot
- **Math concepts in the diagram:** axis labels, line of best fit, reading data from a graph, scatterplot
- **Elements of the answer choices:** integers
- **Notable differences among answer choices:** The choices form a series from 1 to 4, with each choice being 1 more than the choice before it.
- **Pre-solution patterns (see p. 217):** the first and last terms in a series are often wrong answers
- **Things to look out for:** Don't misread the scatterplot or look at the wrong x-coordinate!

Solution 1: Reading data: Find the point for the swim that was 34 minutes, and determine how far down it is from the line of best fit. (Note the axis labels to determine the number of units represented by one rectangle in the grid.)

The data for the swim that took 34 minutes is represented by the black dot on the vertical line labeled 34. The line of best fit crosses that vertical line at 150 beats per minute. The black dot representing Michael's actual heartrate for that swim is at the intersection of the vertical line labeled 34 and the horizontal line immediately below the horizontal line representing 150 beats per minute.

If we look at the units along the vertical axis, we can see that each horizontal line represents 2 more beats per minute than the horizontal line immediately below it. For example, if we look at the horizontal line representing 140 beats per minute, and then we count each horizontal line as we move our eyes up the figure, we'll find the horizontal line representing 150 beats per minute is 5 horizontal lines above the horizontal line representing 140 beats per minute.

So the horizontal line immediately below the horizontal line representing 150 beats per minute must represent a value of 148 beats per minute. That's 2 beats per minute less than the heartrate predicted by the line of best fit, so (B) is correct.

ANSWER CHOICE ANALYSIS

(A): This would be correct if moving up one horizontal line on the graph meant an increase of 1 beat per minute, instead of 2 beats per minute. **(D):** This would be correct if moving up one horizontal line on the graph meant an increase of 4 beats per minute, intead of 2 beats per minute.

How to check? Carefully re-read the prompt and the scatterplot to make sure you haven't made a mistake.

Test 3, Section 4, Question 21

- **What's the prompt asking for?** The choice that would result in exponential growth.
- **Math concepts in the prompt:** exponential growth
- **Elements of the answer choices:** decimals, integers, percentages, sentences
- **Notable differences among answer choices:** (A), (B), and (C) all involve percentage increases, while (D) involves only addition. (B) and (D) each involve adding $100 per year. (A) and (B) both refer to percentages of the initial amount of the

investment, while (C) refers to a percentage of the current amount in the account.

- **"Bridge" concepts:** Exponential growth refers to a situation in which the size of the increase from year to year is an ever-increasing quantity.

- **Pre-solution patterns (see p. 217):** wrong answers try to imitate right answers

- **Things to look out for:** Don't forget the difference between exponential and linear growth! Don't misread the choices!

Solution 1: Abstract: Consider each answer choice to determine the one that would result in exponential growth.

We know that exponential yearly growth refers to the idea of an annual increase that's always larger in size than the increase from the previous year. For example, if something increases by 2 units one year, and then by 4 units the next year, and then by 8 units, and so on, it's demonstrating exponential growth. A different kind of growth would be linear growth, in which the size of the increase for a given time period is always the same—if something increases by 2 units one year, and then by 2 units the next year, and then again by 2 units the following year, and so on, then it's showing linear growth. With that in mind, let's consider the choices.

(A) describes a situation in which the same amount is always being added to the account, because 2% of the initial deposit will always be the same amount, since the initial deposit is a one-time transaction that can never change in size. So this describes linear growth, and it's not the right answer.

(B) also describes a situation with linear growth, since the sum of "1.5% of the initial savings and $100" will always be the same amount of money every year. So this isn't right, either.

(C) does describe exponential growth, because the amount being added will be larger every year: we'd always add 1% *of the current value of the account*, not of the initial deposit. In other words, if we started with $10,000 in the account, then after one year the account would be worth $10,100, since 1% of $10,000 is $100. At the end of the second year, the account would increase by $101, because 1% of $10,100 is $101, so the balance after two years would be $10,201. The increase for the third year would be an increase of $102.01, because that's 1% of $10,201, so the balance after year 3 would be $10,303.01. So each year, the percentage being added to the account would reflect the constantly growing balance of the account, resulting in exponential growth. This means (C) is correct, assuming we haven't misread anything in the question.

(D) is another example of linear growth, because the amount being added to the account would be unchanging (in this case, $100). So we can see that (C) is correct.

How to check? Re-read the prompt and the answer choices to make sure that you've chosen the correct answer.

Test 3, Section 4, Question 22

- **What's the prompt asking for?** The value of x in the situation from the prompt.
- **Math concepts in the prompt:** addition, algebra, percentages

- **Elements of the answer choices:** integers
- **Things to look out for:** Don't misread the prompt! Don't make small mistakes in algebra and arithmetic!

Solution 1: Algebra: Create an equation that expresses x in terms of 855 and the other two numbers, and then solve for x.

Let's create 2 equations based on the information in the prompt. Since the other two numbers are grouped together in the prompt, we can actually represent the sum of those two numbers with one variable, y.

First, we need to express the idea that x and y can be added together to equal 855. We can do that like this: $x + y = 855$. Next, we need to express the idea that x is 50% more than y. Saying that x is 50% more than y is the same thing as saying that x is 150% of y, which is the same thing as writing this equation: $x = 1.5y$. We can use these two equations to solve for x.

First, we'll manipulate one of the equations to isolate y, and then we'll plug that definition of y into the other equation:

$$x + y = 855 \qquad \text{(equation that relates } x \text{ and } y \text{ to 855)}$$

$$y = 855 - x \qquad \text{(subtract } x \text{ from both sides)}$$

Now we'll plug this into our other equation and solve for x:

$$x = 1.5(855 - x) \qquad \text{(plug } y = 855 - x \text{ into the other equation)}$$

$$x = 1,282.5 - 1.5x \qquad \text{(distribute the 1.5)}$$

$$2.5x = 1,282.5 \qquad \text{(add } 1.5x \text{ to both sides)}$$

$$x = 513 \qquad \text{(divide both sides by 2.5)}$$

So the correct answer is (B).

Solution 2: Backsolving: Test each answer choice as the value of x to determine the choice that fits the situation in the prompt.

As we did in the other solution, we need to come up with equations to represent the relationships described in the prompt. We'll use the same equations we found in the first part of solution 1:

Facebook.com/TestingIsEasy   Youtube.com/TestingIsEasy

1. $x + y = 855$
2. $x = 1.5y$

Now we can plug in the values from the answer choices to see which one produces a valid result. We'll start with (A):

$$570 = 1.5(y)$$ (plug the value from (A) into the second equation)

$$380 = y$$ (divide both sides by 1.5)

Next, we plug the given x value and the y-value we just found into the first equation:

$$570 + 380 = 855$$ (plug the result into the first equation)

$$950 = 855$$ (simplify)

This isn't a valid statement, so (A) can't be correct. Let's look at (B):

$$513 = 1.5(y)$$ (plug the value from (B) into the second equation)

$$342 = y$$ (divide both sides by 1.5)

Next, we plug the given x-value and the y-value we just found into the first equation:

$$513 + 342 = 855$$ (plug the result into the first equation)

$$855 = 855$$ (simplify)

This is a valid statement, so (B) could be right. Still, as trained test-takers, we know that we always need to consider each choice, especially when we're backsolving—that's the best way to make sure we've avoided any small mistakes. So let's check (C) next:

$$214 = 1.5(y)$$ (plug the value from (C) into the second equation)

$$142.66666 \approx y$$ (divide both sides by 1.5)

Next, we plug the given x-value and the y-value we just found into the first equation:

$$214 + 142.66666 \approx 855$$ (plug the result into the first equation)

$$356.66666 \approx 855$$ (simplify)

This isn't a valid statement, so (C) can't be correct. Let's look at (D):

$$155 = 1.5(y)$$ (plug the value from (D) into the second equation)

$$103.333333 \approx y$$ (divide both sides by 1.5)

Next, we plug the given x-value and the y-value we just found into the first equation:

$$155 + 103.333333 \approx 855$$ (plug the result into the first equation)

$$258.333333 \approx 855$$ (simplify)

This isn't a valid statement, so (D) can't be correct. Now that we've checked each answer choice, we can see that (B) is right.

ANSWER CHOICE ANALYSIS

(A): This would be the value of y if we incorrectly thought x was 50% of the sum of the other two numbers—not 50% *more than* the sum of the other two numbers.

How to check? Try an alternate approach above.

Test 3, Section 4, Question 23

- **What's the prompt asking for?** The value of k under the conditions in the question.
- **Math concepts in the prompt:** acute angles, algebra, arithmetic, cosine, sine, word problems

- **Math concepts in the diagram:** acute angles, figure not drawn to scale
- **Elements of the answer choices:** decimals
- **Things to look out for:** Don't confuse a and b! Avoid small mistakes in your trig, algebra, and arithmetic!

Solution 1: Trig / Algebra: Observe that a and b must add up to 90 degrees, and then use that information to combine the given equations into one equation, and solve for k.

The question tells us that the sine of a and the cosine of b are identical. If we're familiar with trig, we may realize that this means a and b are complementary angles, which means they add up to 90° by definition. If we do realize this, then we can set up an equation that relates both k expressions to 90, and then solve for k (but if you didn't realize that a and b must be complementary, don't worry—you can still try solution 2, which I'll demonstrate below):

$(4k - 22) + (6k - 13) = 90$ (Set the sum of the measures of the angles equal to 90)

$10k - 35 = 90$ (simplify)

$10k = 125$ (add 35 to both sides)

$k = 12.5$ (divide both sides by 10 to find k)

So we can see that (C) is correct.

Solution 2: Backsolving: Try each answer choice as k in both equations from the prompt. The correct choice will be the one that creates values for a and b such that $sin(a) = cos(b)$.

For choice (A):

$a = 4k - 22$ $b = 6k - 13$ (given equations)

$a = 4(4.5) - 22$ $b = 6(4.5) - 13$ (plug in value from (A))

$a = -4$ $b = 14$ (simplify)

$sin(-4) \approx -0.070$ $cos(14) \approx 0.970$ (find sine and cosine, respectively)

This k value doesn't cause $sin(a°)$ to equal $cos(b°)$, so (A) can't be correct. Let's take a look at (B):

$a = 4k - 22$ $b = 6k - 13$ (given equations)

$a = 4(5.5) - 22$ $b = 6(5.5) - 13$ (plug in value from (B))

$a = 0$ $b = 20$ (simplify)

$sin(0) \approx 0$ $cos(20) \approx 0.940$ (find sine and cosine, respectively)

This k value doesn't cause $sin(a°)$ to equal $cos(b°)$, so (B) can't be correct, either. Now, let's take a look at (C):

$a = 4k - 22$ $b = 6k - 13$ (given equations)

$a = 4(12.5) - 22$ $b = 6(12.5) - 13$ (plug in value from (C))

$a = 28$ $b = 62$ (simplify)

$sin(28) \approx 0.469$ $cos(62) \approx 0.469$ (find sine and cosine, respectively)

This k-value causes $sin(a°)$ to equal $cos(b°)$, so (C) is correct, assuming we haven't made any small mistakes. Let's check (D) next:

$a = 4k - 22$ $b = 6k - 13$ (given equations)

$a = 4(21.5) - 22$ $b = 6(21.5) - 13$ (plug in value from (D))

$a = 64$ $b = 116$ (simplify)

$sin(64) \approx 0.899$ $cos(116) \approx -0.438$ (find sine and cosine, respectively)

This k value doesn't cause $sin(a°)$ to equal $cos(b°)$, so (D) can't be right. Only (C) causes $sin(a°)$ to equal $cos(b°)$, so (C) is right.

ANSWER CHOICE ANALYSIS

(A): This is the result of ignoring the first equation in the prompt, setting the definition of a equal to the definition of b, and then solving for k and taking the absolute value of that result for some reason. **(C):** This is the result of making an algebra error and thinking $10k + 35 = 90$, instead of $10k - 35 = 90$. **(D):** This is the result of thinking the sum of a and b is 180, instead of 90.

How to check? Try an alternate approach above, or re-check your work to make sure you haven't made a mistake somewhere.

| Test 3, Section 4, Question 24

- **What's the prompt asking for?** The number of students in the class.
- **Math concepts in the prompt:** addition, division, remainders, word problems
- **Elements of the answer choices:** integers
- **Notable differences among answer choices:** (A), (B), and (D) form a series in which each choice is 5 more than the one before it.

- **Pre-solution patterns (see p. 217):** the first and last terms in a series are often wrong answers
- **Things to look out for:** Don't confuse the quantities in the prompt! Don't make small mistakes in your algebra and arithmetic!

Solution 1: Algebra: Create a system of equations that relates the quantities in the prompt to the number of students, and then solve for the number of students.

Let's have x represent the number of students. We can use the information in the prompt to create two equations that relate x to n, the amount of solution:

1. $n = 3x + 5$ This equation reflects the fact that the amount of solution would allow every student to have 3 milliliters of solution, with 5 milliliters left over.
2. $n = 4x - 21$ This equation shows that the amount of solution necessary to give every student 4 milliliters would require 21 more milliliters than Mr. Kohl currently has.

We can set these equations equal to one another and solve for x to find the number of students:

$$3x + 5 = 4x - 21 \qquad \text{(equations set equal to one another)}$$
$$3x + 26 = 4x \qquad \text{(add 21 to both sides)}$$
$$26 = x \qquad \text{(subtract } 3x \text{ from both sides)}$$

So the correct answer is (D).

Solution 2: Backsolving: Consider each answer choice and identify the one that fits the description in the prompt.

We can figure out how much of the solution Mr. Kohl has in each scenario from the prompt if we multiply the number of students by the amount of solution in each answer choice, and then add 5 mL (in the case of giving out 3 mL) or subtract 21 mL (in the case of giving out 4 mL). Let's start with (A):

$$(16 \times 3) + 5 = 53 \qquad \text{(number of students in (A) times 3 mL per student, plus 5 mL left over)}$$

We can see that if each of 16 students gets 3 mL, and there are 5 mL left over, then there must be 53 mL of solution. Let's see what happens when each student gets 4 mL and Mr. Kohl is 21 mL short, as described in the prompt:

$$(16 \times 4) - 21 = 43 \qquad \text{(number of students in (A) times 4 mL per student, minus 21 mL short)}$$

When we plug in the value from (A), we get two different quantities of solution for n, so (A) must be wrong. Let's check (B):

$$(21 \times 3) + 5 = 68 \qquad \text{(number of students in (B) times 3 mL per student, plus 5 mL left over)}$$

So if each of 21 students gets 3 mL, and there are 5 mL left over, then there must be 68 mL of solution. Let's see what happens when each student gets 4 mL and Mr. Kohl is 21 mL short:

$$(21 \times 4) - 21 = 63 \qquad \text{(number of students in (B) times 4 mL per student, minus 21 mL short)}$$

So plugging in the value from (B) gave us two different results for the two scenarios in the prompt, which means (B) must also be wrong. Let's check (C):

$$(23 \times 3) + 5 = 74 \qquad \text{(number of students in (C) times 3 mL per student, plus 5 mL left over)}$$

If each of 23 students gets 3 mL, and there are 5 mL left over, then there must be 74 mL of solution. Let's see what happens when each student gets 4 mL and Mr. Kohl is 21 mL short:

$$(23 \times 4) - 21 = 71 \qquad \text{(number of students in (C) times 4 mL per student, minus 21 mL short)}$$

So, just as with (A) and (B), plugging in the value from (C) gave us two different results, meaning (C) is wrong. Let's try (D):

$$(26 \times 3) + 5 = 83 \qquad \text{(number of students in (D) times 3 mL per student, plus 5 mL left over)}$$

If each of 26 students gets 3 mL, and there are 5 mL left over, then there must have been 83 mL of solution originally. Let's see what happens when each student gets 4 mL and Mr. Kohl is 21 mL short:

$$(26 \times 4) - 21 = 83 \qquad \text{(number of students in (D) times 4 mL per student, minus 21 mL short)}$$

Plugging in the value from (D) gives us the same beginning amount of solution for each situation in the prompt, so (D) is right.

Solution 3: Test-smart: Think about what happens when each student gets an extra milliliter, and figure out which answer choice makes sense as a result.

When each student gets 3 milliliters, there are 5 extra milliliters. When each student gets 4 milliliters, Mr. Kohl is short by 21 milliliters. So giving one extra milliliter per student causes Mr. Kohl to go from 5 extra milliliters to being short 21 milliliters. That means a 26 milliliter difference results from giving each student 1 extra milliliter, so there must be 26 students. Thus (D) is correct.

ANSWER CHOICE ANALYSIS

(A): This could be the result if an untrained test-taker created two equations to represent the relationships described in the prompt as we did in solution 1 above, and then made a mistake trying to subtract one equation from the other. **(B):** This could be the result if someone tried solution 1 above, but overlooked the "+5."

How to check? Try an alternate approach above.

Test 3, Section 4, Question 25

- **What's the prompt asking for?** The choice with the closest approximation of the volume of the silo.
- **Math concepts in the prompt:** right circular cones, right circular cylinders, units, word problems
- **Math concepts in the diagram:** height, measurement labels, radius, right circular cylinders and cones
- **Elements of the answer choices:** decimals
- **Notable differences among answer choices:** (D) is the sum of (A) and (B), which may be relevant because the volume of the silo is the sum of the volumes of different shapes.

- **"Bridge" concepts:** As trained test-takers, we know the College Board can only ask us to find the volumes of shapes that appear in the information panel at the beginning of every SAT Math section (see p. 215 for more on that). So it must be possible to find the volume of the silo by adding the volumes of the cylinder and cones in the diagram.
- **Things to look out for:** Don't confuse the dimensions in the diagram! Don't make a mistake in applying the formulas from the information panel! Don't make small mistakes in your algebra and arithmetic!

Solution 1: Geometry: Feed the measurements from the diagram into the formulas from the information panel to determine the volumes of the components of the silo, then add those volumes together to find the volume of the whole silo.

Let's start by finding the volume of the cylinder, using the formula supplied by the College Board at the beginning of each SAT Math section:

$V = \pi r^2 h$ (volume for a cylinder from the beginning of the section)

$V = \pi(5)^2(10)$ (plug in $r = 5$ and $h = 10$)

$V = 250\pi$ (simplify)

$V \approx 785.4$ (simplify to find the volume of the cylinder)

Now let's find the volume of one of the cones on the silo, using the formula supplied at the beginning of each SAT Math section:

$V = \frac{1}{3}\pi r^2 h$ (volume for a right circular cone from the beginning of the section)

$V = \frac{1}{3}\pi(5)^2(5)$ (plug in $r = 5$ and $h = 10$)

$V = \frac{125}{3}\pi$ (simplify)

$V \approx 130.9$ (simplify to find the volume of one of the cones)

We also need to add the volume of the other cone; since both cones are listed with the same dimensions, we can just add the volume of the cone twice. That gives us this calculation: $785.4 + 130.9 + 130.9 = 1047.2$. So (D) is correct.

ANSWER CHOICE ANALYSIS

(A): This is the volume of the two conical parts of the silo. **(B):** This is the volume of just the cylindrical part of the silo. **(C):** This is the volume of the cylindrical part of the silo plus the volume of only one of the conical parts of the silo.

How to check? Re-check your reading and your work to make sure you haven't made any small mistakes. Also note that (A) represents the combined volumes of the cones, while (B) represents the volume of the cylinder, and (D) is the sum of those numbers—this is a common pattern among the answer choices when an SAT question requires us to follow multiple steps on the way to the right answer.

▶ Post-solution patterns (see page 218): right approach, wrong step

---

Test 3, Section 4, Question 26

- **What's the prompt asking for?** The choice that could be the value of k.
- **Math concepts in the prompt:** graphing lines, origin, word problems, xy-coordinate plane

- **Elements of the answer choices:** integers, zero
- **Notable differences among answer choices:** (A), (B), and (C) form a series in which each choice is 4 more than the choice

before it. (B), (C), and (D) form a series in which each choice is twice as much as the choice before it.

- **"Bridge" concepts:** A line that passes through the origin has a y-intercept of 0 by definition. The slope of a line that passes through the origin is directly reflected in the ratio of the y-coordinate of any point on the line to its corresponding x-coordinate.

- **Pre-solution patterns (see p. 217):** halves and doubles; the first and last terms in a series are often wrong answers

- **Things to look out for:** Don't confuse the two points in the prompt! Don't confuse the order of the coordinates in the points from the prompt! Don't make small mistakes in your algebra and arithmetic!

Solution 1: Slope / algebra: Set up an equation in which 2 has the same relationship to k that k has to 32, and then solve for k.

$$\frac{2}{k} = \frac{k}{32}$$ (proportion based on information in prompt)

$$64 = k^2$$ (cross multiply)

$$8 = k \text{ or } -8 = k$$ (take the square root of both sides)

k could be 8 or -8, but only 8 appears in the answer choices, so (C) is correct.

Solution 2: Backsolving / Sketching: Try each value from the answer choices as k, and then pick the choice that causes $(2, k)$ and $(k, 32)$ to lie on a straight line through the origin.

Here's a rough sketch of the points created by (A):

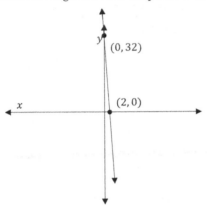

Here's a rough sketch of the points created by (B):

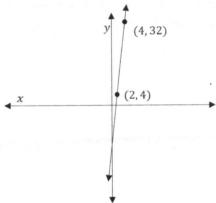

Here's a rough sketch of the points created by (C):

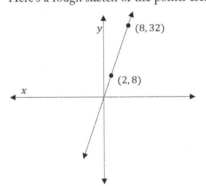

Here's a rough sketch of the points created by (D):

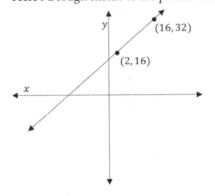

After making a rough sketch of the points created by using each answer choice, we can see that (C) is correct.

ANSWER CHOICE ANALYSIS

(A): This is the sum of the two k-values we found in solution 1. This choice might also be tempting if an untrained test-taker knew the origin was at $(0, 0)$, and thought the number zero might be relevant somehow. **(B):** This is half the correct answer, and also the slope of the line. **(D):** This is double the correct answer.

How to check? Try an alternate approach above, and/or sketch a quick diagram of the points you've come up with to make sure they lie on a straight line that goes through the origin. Make sure you've read carefully and avoided making any small mistakes!

Test 3, Section 4, Question 27

- **What's the prompt asking for?** The value of p under the conditions in the question.

- **Math concepts in the prompt:** area, dimensions, percentages, rectangles, word questions

- **Elements of the answer choices:** integers

- **Things to look out for:** Don't misread the prompt! Don't   increasing with decreasing!
  confuse the changes to the height and width! Don't confuse

Solution 1: Backsolving: Try each answer choice as the value of p in the situation described in the prompt; the correct answer choice will be the one that makes the statements in the prompt true.

Let's imagine a rectangle that is 10 units long by 20 units wide. We can multiply the length and the width according to description in the prompt, using the value of p in each answer choice, to see which one decreases the original area by 12%.

We can find the original area of the rectangle by multiplying the length by the width. So the original rectangle has an area of 10×20, or 200. We want to find the answer choice that decreases that area by 12%, which is the same as multiplying the area by $(100\% - 12\%)$, or 88%, or 0.88. That means the final area of the rectangle in our example will be 200×0.88, or 176.

The prompt tells us that we will increase the length by 10%. We chose a length of 10 for our rectangle, so increasing the length by 10% gives us a length of $10 \times 110\%$, which is the same as 10×1.1, or 11. We need to multiply that increased length by the width of the rectangle *decreased* by p percent. We will use the p value in each answer choice, and multiply the resulting width by our increased length of 11. Whichever choice gives us an area of 176 will be the correct answer. Let's start by looking at (A):

$11 \times 20(100\% - 12\%)$ (increased length multiplied by 12% less than original width)

$11 \times 20(0.88)$ (simplify)

193.6 (simplify)

When we plug in the value from (A), we get an area of 193.6, not 176, so (A) is wrong. Let's check (B):

$11 \times 20(100\% - 15\%)$ (increased length multiplied by 15% less than original width)

$11 \times 20(0.85)$ (simplify)

187 (simplify)

When we plug in the value from (B), we get an area of 187, not 176, so (B) is wrong. Now let's check (C):

$11 \times 20(100\% - 20\%)$ (increased length multiplied by 20% less than original width)

$11 \times 20(0.80)$ (simplify)

176 (simplify)

When we plug in the value from (C), we get an area of 176. This matches the area we found when we decreased the original area by 12%, so (C) is correct. Let's check (D) as well, to help make sure we haven't made any mistakes:

$11 \times 20(100\% - 22\%)$ (increased length multiplied by 22% less than original width)

$11 \times 20(0.78)$ (simplify)

171.6 (simplify)

Plugging in the value from (D) gives us 171.6, not 176, so (D) is wrong. After checking each choice, we see that (C) is right.

Solution 2: Geometry / Algebra: Set up an equation that relates the dimensions and percentage changes in the prompt to p and a 12% decrease in area, and then solve for p.

We should know that the formula for the area of a rectangle is $A = lw$, or area equals length times width. (If you've forgotten this formula, you can find it at the beginning of the math section in your booklet on test day.)

The prompt says that the length of the rectangle was increased by 10 percent. Increasing something by 10% is the same as multiplying that value by 110%, or 1.10. The prompt also tells us that the width of the rectangle is decreased by p percent. That's the same as multiplying the width by $100\% - p\%$, which can also be written as $1 - p$.

So the area of the original rectangle was equal to its length times its width, or lw. But now the length has been multiplied by 1.10 and the width has been multiplied by $1 - p$. So we can use the following expression to represent the new area:

$$(1.10)l(1 - p)w$$

The prompt then tells us that the impact of the changes we just discussed is to decrease the area of the triangle by 12%. Decreasing the area by 12% is the same as multiplying the area by $100\% - 12\%$, or 88%, or 0.88. So we can use the following expression to represent the area of the rectangle decreased by 12%:

$$(0.88)lw$$

The prompt tells us that both of these situations describe the area of the same rectangle—so we can set these two expressions equal to each other, and then solve for p.

$(1.10)l(1 - p)w = (0.88)lw$ (expressions we found set equal to each other)

$1.10(1 - p) = 0.88$ (divide both sides by lw)

$$1 - p = 0.8 \qquad \text{(divide both sides by 1.10)}$$

$$1 = p + 0.8 \qquad \text{(add } p \text{ to both sides)}$$

$$0.2 = p \qquad \text{(subtract 0.8 from both sides)}$$

$$0.2 \times 100 = 20\% \qquad \text{(convert to percentage)}$$

We can see that $p = 20$, which means (C) is correct.

ANSWER CHOICE ANALYSIS

(A): This might be the result if someone set up an equation that forgot to account for the 10% increase in length, or if he thought he could just decrease the width by the 12 percent mentioned in the prompt. **(D):** This is the sum of the percentages in the prompt.

How to check? Try an alternate approach above. Make sure you've read carefully and avoided small mistakes!

Test 3, Section 4, Question 28

- **What's the prompt asking for?** The expression that represents the population estimate t years from now.
- **Math concepts in the prompt:** function modeling, percentage decrease, word problems
- **Elements of the answer choices:** decimals, exponents, fractions, integers
- **Notable differences among answer choices:** (A) and (B) involve raising 0.1 to an exponent, while (C) and (D) raise 0.9 to an exponent. (A) and (C) include an exponent of $20t$, while (B) and (D) each have an exponent of $\frac{t}{20}$.
- **Pre-solution patterns (see p. 217):** wrong answers try to imitate right answers
- **Things to look out for:** Make sure you don't misread the prompt! Don't make small mistakes in your algebra or arithmetic!

Solution 1: Algebra: Come up with an expression that fits the prompt, then pick the choice that matches your expression.

The prompt describes a situation in which the population decreases by a fixed percentage every 20 years, starting from a population of 50,000. We can start to model this with an exponential expression that multiplies the starting population by the percentage of the remaining population, which would look like this: $50{,}000 \times 0.9$

(You may be wondering why we're multiplying by 0.9 instead of 0.1. The reason is that the prompt says the population decreases by 10 percent, which means that every year the remaining population is 90 percent of what it was previously. Multiplying a number by 0.9 gives us 90% of that number, which is what we want in this case, since the prompt told us to model the remaining population of the city over time, not the number of people who've left the city over time.)

The next thing we need to do is reflect the idea that this multiplication by 0.9 happens on a regular basis. We can do that by raising it to an exponent to show that it's repeated. But what exponent should we raise it to? We can't raise it to the number of years that pass, because the prompt says the multiplication by 0.9 happens "every 20 years," not every year. So, for example, in 20 years the multiplication should happen one time, in 40 years it should happen twice, and so on. This is reflected in the idea of dividing the number of years by 20.

So we need to raise our existing expression to an exponent that reflects dividing the number of years by 20. Since the number of years is t according to the prompt, $\frac{t}{20}$ reflects the idea of dividing the number of years by 20. Raising our existing expression to the exponent of $\frac{t}{20}$ gives us this: $50{,}000(0.9)^{\frac{t}{20}}$

So we can see that the correct answer is (D).

Solution 2: Concrete: Pick an arbitrary number of years to test. Work out the correct population according to the engineer's assumptions, and then find the choice that produces the correct result when you plug in the number of years you've chosen as t.

Let's figure out the population after 60 years—that's three 20-year periods. After the first 20 years, the population of 50,000 would have decreased by 10%. When something decreases by 10%, what's left over is 90% of the original amount. So after 20 years, the population is $50{,}000 \times 0.9$, or 45,000. After another 20 years, the population decreases by an additional 10%, so the population is is $45{,}000 \times 0.9$, or 40,500. After the final 20 years, the population decreases by an additional 10%, so the population is $40{,}500 \times 0.9$, or 36,450.

Now we can plug in $t = 60$ for each choice and see which expression yields a population of 36,450. Let's start with (A):

$$50{,}000(0.1)^{20t} \qquad \text{(expression from (A))}$$

$$50{,}000(0.1)^{20(60)} \qquad \text{(plug in } t = 60\text{)}$$

$$\approx 0 \qquad \text{(simplify—the result is a tiny number that rounds to zero)}$$

This choice doesn't produce a value of 36,450, so it can't be correct. Let's try (B) next:

$$50,000(0.1)^{\frac{t}{20}}$$ 　　　　　(expression from (B))

$$50,000(0.1)^{\frac{60}{20}}$$ 　　　　　(plug in $t = 60$)

$$50$$ 　　　　　(simplify)

This choice doesn't produce a value of 36,450, so it can't be correct. Let's evaluate (C) now:

$$50,000(0.9)^{20t}$$ 　　　　　(expression from (C))

$$50,000(0.9)^{20(60)}$$ 　　　　　(plug in $t = 60$)

$$\approx 0$$ 　　　　　(simplify—the result is a tiny number that rounds to zero)

This choice doesn't produce a value of 36,450, so it can't be correct. Let's take a look at (D) now:

$$50,000(0.9)^{\frac{t}{20}}$$ 　　　　　(expression from (D))

$$50,000(0.9)^{\frac{60}{20}}$$ 　　　　　(plug in $t = 60$)

$$36,450$$ 　　　　　(simplify)

This is the only choice that produces a value of 36,450, so (D) is correct.

ANSWER CHOICE ANALYSIS

(A): This choice includes two mistakes: thinking we should multiply by 0.1 to model a decrease of 10%, and thinking that multiplying t by 20 is the right way to model the idea of doing something once every 20 years. **(B):** This choice includes only the first mistake we discussed for (A). **(C):** This choice includes only the second mistake we discussed for (A).

How to check? Try an alternate approach above. Make sure you pay close attention to the prompt and the answer choices!

Test 3, Section 4, Question 29

- **What's the prompt asking for?** The answer choice that's closest to the probability that a randomly selected right-handed student is female.
- **Math concepts in the prompt:** algebra, arithmetic, probability, reading data from a table, word problems
- **Math concepts in the diagram:** data labels, incomplete data

- **Elements of the answer choices:** decimals
- **Things to look out for:** Don't misread the prompt! Don't make small mistakes in arithmetic when you include the information from the prompt and then extrapolate from it! Don't accidentally find the probability of a randomly chosen female being right-handed!

Solution 1: Algebra: Create a system of equations that relates the information from the text to the empty cells in the table, and then use algebra to find the missing data. Finally, construct a probability fraction to describe the likelihood that a randomly chosen right-handed student is female.

We can create 2 equations based on the information in the prompt, and then use them to start filling in the table. I'll let f be the number of left-handed females, and m be the number of left-handed males. We know from the prompt and from the table that there are 18 left-handed students, so we can write the following equation to show that the left-handed females and the left-handed males add up to 18:

$$f + m = 18.$$

But we can also use the information in the prompt to write an equation relating the number of right-handed students to the number 122, because the prompt tells us there are 5 times as many right-handed female students as left-handed ones (which means that there are $5f$ right-handed female students), and 9 times as many right-handed male students as left-handed ones (so there are $9m$ right-handed male students). So we can write the following equation to show that the total number of right-handed students is 122:

$$5f + 9m = 122.$$

Now we can use these equations to solve for f and m. We'll start by isolating f in one of the equations to isolate it, and then we'll plug that into the other equation:

$$f + m = 18$$ 　　　　　(first equation)

$$f = 18 - m$$ 　　　　　(subtract m from both sides to define f in terms of m)

Now we can plug $f = 18 - m$ into the second equation:

$5f + 9m = 122$	(second equation)
$5(18 - m) + 9m = 122$	(plug in $f = 18 - m$)
$90 - 5m + 9m = 122$	(distribute the 5)
$90 + 4m = 122$	(simplify)
$4m = 32$	(subtract 90 from both sides)
$m = 8$	(divide both sides by 4)

Now we can plug $m = 8$ into either equation to solve for f. Let's use the first equation:

$f + m = 18$	(first equation)
$f + 8 = 18$	(plug in $m = 8$)
$f = 10$	(subtract 8 from both sides)

Now we know that there are 10 left-handed female students. The prompt tells us that there are 5 times as many right-handed female students as left-handed female students, so there must be 50 right-handed female students. We also know that there are 8 left-handed male students. The prompt tells us there are 9 times as many right-handed male students as left-handed male students, so there must be 72 right-handed male students. We can add this information to the chart from the prompt to check our work:

Handedness

Gender	Left	Right
Female	10	50
Male	8	72
Total	18	122

Finally, we need to construct our probability fraction. The desired outcome in the fraction is a right-handed female student, so the value in the numerator of our probability fraction will be 50. The total number of possible outcomes will be the total number of right-handed students according to the prompt, so the denominator of our probability fraction will be 122. This means the probability of picking a female student at random from the group of right-handed students is $\frac{50}{122}$.

When we look at the choices, we see that none of them are in the same form as the probability fraction we just created. But when we divide 50 by 122, we see the result is approximately 0.410, which means (A) is correct.

ANSWER CHOICE ANALYSIS

(B): This is the probability of selecting a right-handed female from all the students, not just from the right-handed students. **(D):** This is the ratio of the number of all left-handed students to the number of right-handed male students.

How to check? Carefully re-read the prompt and re-check your algebra and your probability fraction to make sure you haven't made any small mistakes. Try to determine the potential mistakes that could lead to some of the wrong answers.

Test 3, Section 4, Question 30

- **What's the prompt asking for?** The choice that's true in light of the situation in the prompt.
- **Math concepts in the prompt:** algebra, arithmetic, constants, systems of equations
- **Elements of the answer choices:** fractions, integers, sentences
- **Notable differences among answer choices:** (A), (B), and (C) form a kind of series in which the number at the end of the sentence is twice as much as it is in the previous choice. (B) is the opposite of (D), since (B) involves subtracting $\frac{1}{2}$, and (D) involves adding $\frac{1}{2}$.
- **Concepts in the answer choices:** defining one variable in terms of another
- **Pre-solution patterns (see p. 217):** halves and doubles; opposites; the first and last terms in a series are often wrong answers
- **Things to look out for:** Don't confuse b and c! Don't confuse x and y! Don't make small mistakes in algebra and arithmetic!

Solution 1: Algebra: Use the information from the prompt to express b in terms of c, and then use algebra to solve the system of equations to find x in terms of y.

The prompt tells us that b is c minus $\frac{1}{2}$, which can also be expressed like this: $b = c - \frac{1}{2}$. We can plug this value for b into the first equation in the system.

$$3x + b = 5x - 7 \qquad \text{(first equation)}$$

$$3x + c - \frac{1}{2} = 5x - 7 \qquad \text{(plug in } b = c - \frac{1}{2}\text{)}$$

$$c - \frac{1}{2} = 2x - 7 \qquad \text{(subtract } 3x \text{ from both sides)}$$

$$c = 2x - \frac{13}{2} \qquad \text{(add } \frac{1}{2} \text{ to both sides)}$$

Now we have a value for c in terms of x that we can plug into the second equation.

$$3y + c = 5y - 7 \qquad \text{(second equation)}$$

$$3y + 2x - \frac{13}{2} = 5y - 7 \qquad \text{(plug in } c = 2x - \frac{13}{2}\text{)}$$

$$2x - \frac{13}{2} = 2y - 7 \qquad \text{(subtract } 3y \text{ from both sides)}$$

$$2x = 2y - \frac{1}{2} \qquad \text{(add } \frac{13}{2} \text{ to both sides)}$$

$$x = y - \frac{1}{4} \qquad \text{(divide both sides by 2)}$$

Now that we've found x in terms of y, we can see that (A) is correct.

Solution 2: Algebra / picking numbers: Pick an arbitrary number for x and use it to find b; then, use that b to find c, and find the corresponding y. Pick the answer choice that accurately relates the y-value you found to the arbitrary x-value you selected. Use the information from the prompt to express b in terms of c, then use algebra to solve the system of equations to find x in terms of y.

Let's say that $x = 4$, and use that value to solve for b in the first equation.

$$3x + b = 5x - 7 \qquad \text{(first equation)}$$
$$3(4) + b = 5(4) - 7 \qquad \text{(plug in } x = 4\text{)}$$
$$12 + b = 20 - 7 \qquad \text{(multiply)}$$
$$b = 1 \qquad \text{(simplify and subtract 12 from both sides)}$$

The prompt tells us that b is c minus $\frac{1}{2}$, which can also be expressed like this: $b = c - \frac{1}{2}$. Let's plug our b-value into that expression.

$$b = c - \frac{1}{2} \qquad \text{(relationship from prompt)}$$

$$1 = c - \frac{1}{2} \qquad \text{(plug in } b = 1\text{)}$$

$$\frac{3}{2} = c \qquad \text{(add } \frac{1}{2} \text{ to both sides)}$$

We can now use the c-value to find the value of y in the second equation.

$$3y + c = 5y - 7 \qquad \text{(second equation)}$$

$$3y + \frac{3}{2} = 5y - 7 \qquad \text{(plug in } c = \frac{3}{2}\text{)}$$

$$\frac{3}{2} = 2y - 7 \qquad \text{(subtract } 3y \text{ from both sides)}$$

$$\frac{17}{2} = 2y \qquad \text{(add 7 to both sides)}$$

$$\frac{17}{4} = y \qquad \text{(divide both sides by 2)}$$

$$y = 4\frac{1}{4} \qquad \text{(rewrite } \frac{17}{4} \text{ as mixed number)}$$

When we started out, we chose an x-value of 4. We ended up finding out that the corresponding y-value would be $4\frac{1}{4}$. The relationship between these two values is reflected accurately by (A), so (A) is correct.

 Facebook.com/TestingIsEasy　　　Youtube.com/TestingIsEasy

Solution 3: Test-smart: Note that the two given equations are identical except that the top one has x and b where the bottom one has y and c. Use this information, along with the information from the prompt that b is c minus $\frac{1}{2}$, to figure out how x relates to y.

When we read the equations closely, we see that their structures are very similar; the only differences are that the second equation substitutes y for x, and c for b. This suggests that we'll be able to reason out the relationship of x and y if we take into account the relationship between b and c that we're given in the prompt, and the structures of the equations themselves.

It will probably help to simplify the two equations if we can; we can do that by isolating b and c in each equation. When we do that, we get $b = 2x - 7$ in the top equation, and $c = 2y - 7$ in the bottom equation.

At this point, we can start to see that if c is 0.5 more than b, it must be the case that this half-unit difference is reflected on the right-hand sides of the two equations; the difference can't affect the value of 7, which is a constant, so it must be spread evenly to each x in the $2x$ term, which means each x must be 0.25 less than y. So we can see that (A) is correct. (If you're not comfortable with this abstract solution, remember that you can just use a more concrete solution, like either of the first two we discussed above.)

Test 3, Section 4, Question 31

- **What's the prompt asking for?** One possible value of x under the circumstances in the prompt.
- **Math concepts in the prompt:** inequalities, word problems

- **Things to look out for:** Don't confuse the prices for adult and student tickets! Don't make small mistakes in your arithmetic!

Solution 1: Arithmetic: Test values for x until you find one that fits the concepts in the prompt.

1 adult ticket is $3.
1 adult ticket and 1 student ticket is $3 + $2, or $5.
1 adult ticket and 2 student tickets is $3 + $4, or $7.
1 adult ticket and 3 student tickets is $3 + $6, or $9.
1 adult ticket and 4 student tickets is $3 + $8, or $11.

So Chris can buy 4 student tickets and 1 adult ticket and spend at least $11 but not more than $14, which means 4 is an acceptable answer.

How to check? Carefully re-check your work and look for small mistakes in your arithmetic.

Test 3, Section 4, Question 32

- **What's the prompt asking for?** The mean age of the presidents in the table at the beginning of their terms, rounded to the nearest tenth.
- **Math concepts in the prompt:** reading data from a table, average (arithmetic mean)
- **Math concepts in the diagram:** data labels

- **Things to look out for:** Don't misread the numbers in the table! Don't make any mistakes with your calculator or your arithmetic when you add the ages of the presidents! Don't divide by the wrong number when you find the average! Don't forget to round the result to the nearest tenth!

Solution 1: Arithmetic mean: Add up the ages in the table and divide them by 12 to find the mean age. Round to the nearest tenth as required in the prompt.

$$\frac{57 + 62 + 58 + 58 + 59 + 58 + 62 + 55 + 68 + 51 + 50 + 65}{12} \approx 58.583333$$

The question asks for the answer rounded to nearest tenth, so 58.6 is the correct answer.

How to check? Carefully look over your work and make sure to look out for the issues we noted above!

Test 3, Section 4, Question 33

- **What's the prompt asking for?** The value of b under the conditions in the prompt.
- **Math concepts in the prompt:** algebra, distributed negative signs, quadratic expressions, word problems

- **Things to look out for:** Avoid small mistakes in your algebra and arithmetic! Don't confuse a, b, and c!

Solution 1: Algebra: Simplify the given expression until it fits the quadratic format mentioned in the prompt, and then find b in that quadratic expression.

$(-3x^2 + 5x - 2) - 2(x^2 - 2x - 1)$	(given expression)
$-3x^2 + 5x - 2 - 2x^2 + 4x + 2$	(distribute the -2)
$-5x^2 + 9x$	(simplify)

b is the coefficient of the x-term, according to the prompt, so $b = 9$, which means 9 is the correct answer.

Test 3, Section 4, Question 34

- **What's the prompt asking for?** The fraction of the circle's area represented by the sector marked off by AOB.
- **Math concepts in the prompt:** area, center of a circle, central angles, circles, fractions, radians

- **Things to look out for:** Don't make mistakes in your trigonometry and arithmetic! Don't forget that a full circle represents 2π radians of arc!

Solution 1: Trigonometry / geometry: Determine the fraction of 2π radians that's represented by $\frac{5\pi}{4}$ radians.

$$\frac{\frac{5\pi}{4}}{2\pi} \qquad \text{(divide } \frac{5\pi}{4} \text{ by } 2\pi\text{)}$$

$$\frac{5\pi}{4} \times \frac{1}{2\pi} \qquad \text{(rewrite, since dividing by } 2\pi \text{ is the same as multiplying by the reciprocal of } 2\pi\text{)}$$

$$\frac{5\pi}{8\pi} \qquad \text{(simplify)}$$

$$\frac{5}{8} \qquad \text{(cancel } \pi\text{)}$$

So the correct answer is $\frac{5}{8}$.

How to check? Carefully re-check your reading, trig, and arithmetic to make sure you haven't made any small mistakes!

Test 3, Section 4, Question 35

- **What's the prompt asking for?** The lowest possible value for the 11th rating that will still allow an average of at least 85 for the first 20 ratings.
- **Math concepts in the prompt:** averages, inclusive ranges, word problems

- **"Bridge" concepts:** If the average of the first 10 ratings is 75, then the total number of points across those 10 ratings is 750, because $\frac{750}{10} = 75$.
- **Things to look out for:** Don't misread the prompt and confuse the 20th with the 10th or the 11th! Don't confuse the average rating received so far (75) with the average after 20 ratings (85)!

Solution 1: Arithmetic reasoning: Realize that the highest possible ratings for the 12th to the 20th ratings will allow the lowest possible value for the 11th rating, which means we can write an equation to find the 11th ranking.

If we want to know the lowest possible 11th rating that will allow an average of 85 for 20 ratings, then it makes sense that the 12th through 20th ratings would need to be as high as possible. The prompt tells us that the highest possible rating is 100, so we'll imagine that the 12th, 13th, 14th, 15th, 16th, 17th, 18th, 19th, and 20th ratings are all 100—that means there would be 9 ratings of 100, for a total of 900 points coming in from the 12th through 20th ratings when the first 20 ratings are averaged.

We also know that the first 10 ratings must account for 750 points. With this in mind, we can construct an equation that will relate the existing 750 points to the 11th rating and to the 900 possible points from future ratings, to find an average of 85 after 20 ratings.

We know that finding an average in this case involves adding together all the points received over 20 ratings, which we can express as $750 + x + 900$, where x is the 11th rating. We also know that finding an average in this case would involve dividing by the 20 total ratings, which would cause our expression to look like this: $\frac{750 + x + 900}{20}$.

Finally, we need to set this average expression equal to 85, according to the prompt. That allows us to create the following equation: $\frac{750 + x + 900}{20} = 85$

Now we can solve this equation for x:

$$\frac{750 + x + 900}{20} = 85 \qquad \text{(expression we just found)}$$

$$750 + x + 900 = 1700 \qquad \text{(multiply both sides by 20)}$$

$$x + 1650 = 1700 \qquad \text{(simplify)}$$

$$x = 50 \qquad \text{(subtract 1650 from both sides)}$$

So the lowest possible 11th rating would be 50, which means 50 is the correct answer.

How to check? Carefully re-check your reading and your work to make sure you haven't made any mistakes.

Note   Notice that the 12th through 20th ratings represents 9 ratings, not 8. Some test-takers might reason that $20 - 12 = 8$, but if we count out the rankings—12th, 13th, 14th, 15th, 16th, 17th, 18th, 19th, and 20th—we can see there are 9.

Test 3, Section 4, Question 36

- **What's the prompt asking for?** The maximum possible value of b under the conditions in the question.
- **Math concepts in the prompt:** coordinate values, systems of inequalities, word problems, xy-coordinate plane
- **"Bridge" concepts:** Each inequality in the prompt will result in a line that divides the xy-coordinate plane, and the valid solutions to the inequality will be the set of points on the line or below it. The lines of the two inequalities will intersect at exactly one point in the xy-coordinate plane. The point of intersection will be the highest point in the xy-coordinate plane that satisfies both inequalities.

- **Things to look out for:** Don't confuse x and y! Don't misread the inequalities as equations! Don't misread the directions of the inequalities! Don't make small mistakes in your algebra and arithmetic!

Solution 1: Algebraic reasoning: Find the point of intersection of the two lines in the given inequalities. The y-coordinate of that point will be the correct answer.

$5x = -15x + 3000$	(set inequalities equal to find the x-coordinate of the point of intersection)
$20x = 3000$	(add $15x$ to both sides)
$x = 150$	(divide both sides by 20)

Now let's plug $x = 150$ into either equation to solve for y. We'll use the second equation here, for no particular reason:

$y = 5x$	(second equation)
$y = 5(150)$	(plug in $x = 150$)
$y = 750$	(simplify)

So the largest y-value that satisfies the system of inequalities is 750. Since this y-value corresponds to b in the (a, b) notation from the prompt, the answer is 750.

Solution 2: Calculator graphing: Graph both inequalities and use the trace function to identify the (x, y) coordinates of the highest point that satisfies both inequalities. The y-value will be the correct answer.

This is what we see when we graph the two inequalities:

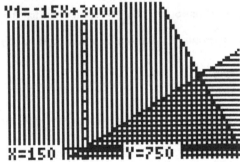

If we use the trace function on the calculator, we can see that the highest b value in the point described would be 750, so the correct answer is 750.

How to check? Carefully re-check your reading and your work. Consider sketching a diagram of the two inequalities to make sure that your value for b makes sense.

Test 3, Section 4, Question 37

- **What's the prompt asking for?** The average number of shoppers waiting to make a purchase.
- **Math concepts in the prompt:** algebra, equations, function modeling, rate, word problems

- **Things to look out for:** Don't confuse the numbers that are specific to question 37 with the numbers from the explanation of Little's law! Don't get nervous because you've never heard of Little's law! Don't make small mistakes in your reading, algebra, and arithmetic!

Solution 1: Algebra: Apply Little's law as provided in the prompt to the given numbers to determine the average number of shoppers waiting in line.

In order to use Little's law, we first need to know the r-value. The prompt tells us that r is the number of "shoppers per minute." But the prompt for this question refers to "84 shoppers per hour," so we'll need to adjust the number 84 to reflect the average number of shoppers per *minute*. We do this by dividing 84 by 60, since there are 60 minutes in an hour. That gives us a fraction equal to $\frac{84}{60}$ shoppers per minute, or 1.4 shoppers per minute, as r. Now we can use this value to apply Little's law to the situation in the prompt:

$N = rT$ (Little's law, provided in the prompt)

$N = (1.4)(5)$ (plug in $r = 1.4$ and $T = 5$, both from the prompt)

$N = 7$ (simplify to find N)

So we can see the answer is 7.

How to check? Carefully re-check your reading, algebra, and arithmetic to make sure you haven't made any small mistakes. Also consider your result in light of the example given in the prompt.

Test 3, Section 4, Question 38

- **What's the prompt asking for?** The percentage difference between the average number of shoppers at any one time in the original store and in the new store.
- **Math concepts in the prompt:** algebra, arithmetic, equations, function modeling, percentage difference, rate, unit conversion, word problems

- **"Bridge" concepts:** There are 60 minutes in an hour.
- **Things to look out for:** Don't confuse the numbers for the new store and the old store! Don't get nervous because you've never heard of Little's law! Don't make small mistakes in your reading, algebra, and arithmetic! Don't find the percentage decrease in the wrong direction!

Solution 1: Algebra: Determine the number of new shoppers per minute and then use Little's law to determine the average number of shoppers at any one time in the new store (the N-value). Then find the percentage decrease from the old store's N-value to the new store's N-value.

90 shoppers per hour is equal to 1.5 shoppers per minute, because there are 60 minutes in an hour, and $\frac{90}{60} = 1.5$. We can use this r-value to find N for the new store:

$N = rT$ (Little's law, provided in the prompt)

$N = (1.5)(12)$ (plug in $r = 1.5$ and $T = 12$ for the new store)

$N = 18$ (simplify)

So we can see there are 18 shoppers in the new store on average.

Now we can find out what percentage 18 is of 45, since the prompt tells us that the N for the original store was 45:

$\frac{18}{45}$ (proportion of average number of shoppers at new store to average number of shoppers at original store)

0.4   (divide)

40%   (convert to percentage)

So we know that 18 is 40% of 45...but the prompt asked us "what percent *less than*" the old N this new N is, so we need to subtract 40% from 100% to find the answer. $100\% - 40\% = 60\%$, so the correct answer is 60. (In other words, N for the new store is 60% less than N for the original store.)

How to check? Reconsider your reading and your calculations. Be especially careful of the "things to look out for" noted above!

TEST 4 – SECTION 4

Test 4, Section 4, Question 1

- **What's the prompt asking for?** The number of movies Julie rented online this month.
- **Math concepts in the prompt:** algebra, arithmetic, word problems
- **Elements of the answer choices:** integers

- **Notable differences among answer choices:** The answer choices form a series from 1 to 4, in which each choice is 1 more than the choice before it. (B) is half of (D).
- **Pre-solution patterns (see p. 217):** halves and doubles; the first and last terms in a series are often wrong answers

- **Things to look out for:** Don't misread the prompt! Don't make small mistakes in your algebra and arithmetic!

Solution 1: Backsolving: Try each answer choice as the number of movie rentals; the choice that leads to a monthly cost of $12.80 is the correct answer.

$9.80 + $1.50 = $11.30	(cost of 1 movie rental as stated in (A))
$9.80 + $1.50 + $1.50 = $12.80	(cost of 2 movie rentals as stated in (B))
$9.80 + $1.50 + $1.50 + $1.50 = $14.30	(cost of 3 movie rentals as stated in (C))
$9.80 + $1.50 + $1.50 + $1.50 + $1.50 = $15.80	(cost of 4 movie rentals as stated in (D))

We can see that (B) results in the correct monthly total, so (B) is right.

Solution 2: Algebra: Create an equation that relates the price Jill paid to the base price and the cost of each movie rental, then solve the equation to find the number of movie rentals.

Since we're trying to figure out the number of movies Jill rented, let's call the number of movies x. We know that x, the number of movies, is being multiplied by $1.50, since the prompt tells us that Jill pays $1.50 for every movie she watches. The expression $1.50x$ reflects this idea of multiplying the number of movies by $1.50. The prompt also tells us that Jill pays a monthly fee of $9.80 in addition to the $1.50x$; we can add this to our expression and write $9.80 + $1.50x$.

Finally, we know that we can set this expression equal to $12.80, and solve for x:

$12.80 = $9.80 + $1.50x$	(equation based on info from the prompt)
$3.00 = $1.50x$	(subtract $9.80 from both sides)
$2 = x$	(divide both sides by $1.50)

So we can see that (B) is correct.

Solution 3: Test-smart: Notice that $12.80 is $3 more than $9.80, and that 3 is twice as much as 1.5, so the answer must be (B).

How to check? Try an alternate approach above; also, carefully re-check your reading and your calculations to make sure you haven't made a small mistake.

Test 4, Section 4, Question 2

- **What's the prompt asking for?** The expression that represents the number of words per minute that Donald expects to hit after m months.
- **Math concepts in the prompt:** algebra, arithmetic, rates, variables, word problems
- **Elements of the answer choices:** algebraic expressions, integers
- **Notable differences among answer choices:** Every choice except (B) involves the number 180; (B) involves the number 225. Every choice except (A) includes the expression $5m$; (A) includes the expression $180m$. Every choice except (D) includes the idea of adding two values; (D) has us subtract $5m$ from 180. (A) and (D) can both be seen as "opposites" of (C), because (A) switches the positions of the two integers in the expression from (C), and (D) switches the sign of the second expression in (C).
- **Pre-solution patterns (see p. 217):** wrong answers try to imitate right answers; opposites
- **Things to look out for:** Make sure you correctly identify whether 180 or 225 should be in the correct answer! Make sure you correctly identify whether 5 or 180 should be multiplied by m! Make sure you correctly identify whether the two parts of the expression should be added or subtracted!

Solution 1: Concrete: Pick an arbitrary value for m and find Donald's speed for that m-value according to the prompt. Then take your m-value and plug it into each choice. The right answer will match the speed you originally found for your m-value.

Let's try to figure out Donald's speed after 3 months, according to the prompt. His speed should be 15 words faster than it originally was, since the prompt says he gains 5 words with each passing month, and $3 \times 5 = 15$. Since his current speed is 180 words per minute, his speed per minute after 3 months should be 195, because $180 + 15 = 195$.

So if we make $m = 3$, then the expression in the correct answer should work out to be 195. Let's see which choice is equal to 195 when we plug in $m = 3$:

A	$5 + 180(3) = 545$
B	$225 + 5(3) = 240$
C ✓	$180 + 5(3) = 195$
D	$180 - 5(3) = 165$

Only choice (C) gives us 195 when $m = 3$, so (C) must be correct.

Solution 2: Algebra: Write out your own expression to model Donald's projected typing speed after m months, and then find the answer choice that's equivalent to your expression.

The prompt tells us Donald's current speed is 180 word per minute, and it says that he hasn't started practicing to increase that speed yet, so it make sense that 180 would be his starting speed. For that reason, we'll make our expression of his speed start with 180, and then add some further information to show his increase in speed every month.

After one month, his speed should be 5 words faster than it was when he started, according to the prompt. After two months, his speed should be 10 words faster than it was when he started. So for every additional month, his speed should be another 5 words faster than it was the previous month; this means his improvement of 5 extra words per month can be expressed as $5m$.

So it makes sense to say that his writing speed after m months would be $180 + 5m$, which reflects the idea of an initial speed of 180, and then subsequent improvements of 5 words with each passing month. This is the expression in (C), so (C) is right.

Solution 3: Test-smart: Compare each choice to the situation from the prompt, paying particular attention to the similarities and differences among the answer choices we noted above, and think about how they relate to the prompt.

As trained test-takers, we can see that the answer choices present us with the following issues to resolve:

1. Should we multiply m by 180 (like in (A)), or by 5 (like in (B), (C), and (D))?
2. Should we include the number 225, like in (B), or can we write the correct expression with just 180, 5, and m, like in the other answer choices?
3. Should we add two expressions to find the correct answer (like in (A), (B), and (C)), or subtract $5m$, like (D)?

For the first issue, it makes sense that m should be multiplied by something related to Donald's monthly increases, since m represents the number of months that Donald has practiced. This tells us that we should multiply m by 5, since Donald improves by 5 additional words every month. It makes no sense to multiply the number of months by the number of words Donald could type at the beginning of his practice, which is what (A) would do.

For the second issue, there's no reason to think that 225 should be involved in the correct expression for Donald's typing speed! 225 is mentioned as the requirement for becoming a court reporter, but the numbers related to Donald's starting speed and his monthly improvement don't include the number 225.

For the third issue, it makes sense that the expression for Donald's typing speed should increase every month, and should be higher than his starting speed, which is 180 words per minute. So we should be adding the two expressions that make up Donald's typing speed, and not subtracting one from the other.

So we can see that the correct answer should involve multiplying m by 5, and adding that to 180. (C) is the only choice that includes all of these elements, so (C) must be right. (See the other solutions above if you'd like further explanation of why (C) is correct from a mathematical perspective.)

ANSWER CHOICE ANALYSIS

(A): This would be the result if Donald's initial typing speed were 5 words per minute and he improved by 180 words per month, instead of the other way around. **(B):** 225 words per minute is the requirement for being a court reporter, but there's no reason for that number to be involved in the expression that describes Donald's speed after each month. (B) might trick untrained test-takers who didn't read the prompt carefully. **(D):** This would be the result if Donald decreased his typing speed by 5 words per month.

How to check? Try an alternate approach above; also, try to figure out mistakes that untrained test-takers could make that would lead them to some of the wrong answers.

▶ Post-solution patterns (see page 218): opposites

Test 4, Section 4, Question 3

- **What's the prompt asking for?** The weight of each slice, in ounces.
- **Math concepts in the prompt:** fractions, unit conversions, word problems
- **Elements of the answer choices:** integers
- **Notable differences among answer choices:** Choices (A), (C), and (D) form a series in which each number is twice the number before it. Choices (A), (B), and (C) form a series in which each choice is 2 more than the one before it.
- **Pre-solution patterns (see p. 217):** halves and doubles
- **Things to look out for:** Make sure you don't make a mistake that causes you to be off by 2, or by a factor of 2, since the College Board has clearly positioned some wrong answers to take advantage of that kind of mistake! Don't misread the prompt!

Solution 1: Arithmetic: Convert 3 pounds into ounces, then follow the steps in the prompt to find the number of ounces per slice.

A 3-pound pizza weighs 48 ounces, because one pound is 16 ounces and $3 \times 16 = 48$. After the pizza is sliced in half, each half weighs 24 ounces, because $\frac{48}{2} = 24$. When each 24-ounce half is sliced in thirds, each slice weighs 8 ounces, because $\frac{24}{3} = 8$. So (C) is right.

ANSWER CHOICE ANALYSIS

(A): This is the result if we divide by 2 one time too many. **(B):** This is the weight of *one-fourth* of half the pizza, not *one-third* of half the pizza. **(D):** This is the weight of one-third of the *whole* pizza, not one-third of *half* the pizza.

How to check? Noting that the answer choices are clearly trying to encourage you to make small mistakes in your calculations, reconsider your reading and your work carefully to make sure you haven't made any such mistakes.

Test 4, Section 4, Question 4

- **What's the prompt asking for?** The approximate number of students who could be expected to prefer October.
- **Math concepts in the prompt:** percentages, projections, random sampling, sample sizes, surveys, word problems
- **Elements of the answer choices:** integers

- **Elements of the answer choices:** Every choice but (C) ends in 0, while (C) ends in 5; this may be useful when we try to estimate to solve the question.
- **Things to look out for:** Don't confuse the numbers 90 and 225 in the prompt! Don't make small mistakes in your reading or arithmetic!

Solution 1: Statistics / arithmetic: Since Nick's sample showed that 25.6% of people preferred October, find 25.6% of 225 to predict the approximate number of people in the whole class who will also prefer October, based on the sample.

Remember that 25.6% is equal to 0.256. Since $225 \times 0.256 = 57.6$, we want to pick the choice that's closest to 57.6, which is (B).

Solution 2: Test-smart / estimation: Reason that 25.6% is approximately one-fourth, and find the only choice that's really close to one-fourth of 225.

We may not be able to determine one-fourth of 225 right away, but we'll probably find it easier to estimate if we think of 225 as the sum of 200 and 25. One-fourth of 200 is 50, and one-fourth of 24 (which is close enough to 25 for estimation purposes) is 6, so one-fourth of 225 is roughly 56. The choice that's closest to 56 is (B), so (B) is right.

(This estimation is also close to (A), but bear in mind that actually *slightly more* than 25% of those surveyed preferred October, and also that we used one fourth of 24 in our approximation, instead of 25, so our estimate would be a little lower than the real calculation.)

ANSWER CHOICE ANALYSIS

(A): This might trick an untrained test-taker who accidentally rounded 57.6 down to 50.

How to check? Try an alternate approach above. Make sure you haven't made any mistakes in your reading or arithmetic!

Test 4, Section 4, Question 5

- **What's the prompt asking for?** The volume, in milliliters, of the given object.
- **Math concepts in the prompt:** arithmetic, ratios, word problems
- **Elements of the answer choices:** decimals, integers
- **Notable differences among answer choices:** (A) and (B) are "reciprocals" of each other in the sense that (A) is equal to one-eighth, which is the reciprocal of 8. (B) and (D) are "opposites" with respect to the prompt because (B) is the result when 24 is divided by 3, and (D) is the result when 24 is multiplied by 3. (Choice (A) might also be seen as an "opposite" in this sense, because it represents the result when 3 is divided by 24.) These relationships may be relevant because the prompt seems to involve a ratio between grams and milliliters, and some untrained test-takers can be expected to

reverse the ratio accidentally. (C) and (D) are both multiples of 3, which may be relevant because the prompt involves ratios and the number 3. (B) is one-third of 24, while (C) is 3 less than 24 and (D) is 3 times 24; these relationships may be relevant because the prompt involves the numbers 3 and 24.

- **Concepts in the answer choices:** division, multiplication, opposite ratios, subtraction
- **Pre-solution patterns (see p. 217):** opposites
- **Things to look out for:** Don't invert the ratio involved in finding the correct answer—the College Board is clearly trying to set us up to make that mistake! Make sure you identify whether you should be subtracting, multiplying, or dividing the numbers 3 and 24!

Solution 1: Arithmetic: Read the prompt carefully to verify which numbers should be divided or multiplied, and then divide 24 by 3 to find the number of milliliters.

Let's use d to represent density, m to represent mass, and v to represent volume. The prompt says that the density of an object is equal to its mass divided by its volume. We can express that relationship like this:

$$d = \frac{m}{v}$$ (provided formula for density)

The prompt gives us the density and mass of the object, which we can plug into the formula we created from the prompt:

$$3 = \frac{24}{v}$$ (plug in $d = 3$ and $m = 24$)
$$3v = 24$$ (multiply both sides by v)
$$v = 8$$ (divide both sides by 3)

So we can see that (B) is right.

ANSWER CHOICE ANALYSIS

(A): This is the reciprocal of the correct answer, for untrained test-takers who end up reversing the correct ratio. **(C):** This is the mass *minus* the density, not the mass *divided by* the density, for untrained test-takers who make a simple mistake in arithmetic or in using their calculators. **(D):** This is the mass *times* the density, not *divided by* the density, for people who make an algebra or arithmetic mistake in trying to execute the solution we demonstrated above.

How to check? Carefully re-read the prompt and re-check your calculations, keeping in mind that the College Board clearly expects you to make a mistake related to division.

▶ Post-solution patterns (see page 218): opposites

Test 4, Section 4, Question 6

- **What's the prompt asking for?** The number of hours that Angelica worked last week.

- **Math concepts in the prompt:** algebra, arithmetic, word problems

- **Elements of the answer choices:** integers

- **Notable differences among answer choices:** (A) is half of (D), which may be relevant because we know, as trained test-takers, that the College Board often includes wrong answers that are twice as much or half as much as correct answers. (A) is 11 less than (B), and the numbers in (A) and (B) add up to 59,

which is relevant because the prompt talks about two quantities that differ by 11 and add up to 59. (D) is 11 less than 59, which may be relevant because the prompt includes the numbers 59 and 11.

- **Pre-solution patterns (see p. 217):** halves and doubles; opposites

- **Things to look out for:** Don't forget that the question is asking for Angelica's hours, not Raul's! Don't make small mistakes in your algebra or arithmetic!

Solution 1: Algebra: Set up a system of equations that relates Angelica's hours to Raul's hours and to the total number of hours, then solve to find Angelica's hours.

We'll let r equal the number of hours Raul worked, and a equal the number of hours Angelica worked. The prompt tells us Raul worked 11 more hours than Angelica, which we can express with the equation $r = a + 11$.

The prompt also tells us they worked a total of 59 hours together, which allows us to write this equation: $r + a = 59$.

Now we can solve this system of equations for a to find the number of hours Angelica worked. One way to do that is to plug the definition of r from our first equation, which was $r = a + 11$, into the second equation. Then we can solve for a:

$r + a = 59$	(second equation from the system)
$a + 11 + a = 59$	(plug $r = a + 11$ into the second equation)
$2a + 11 = 59$	(simplify)
$2a = 48$	(subtract 11 from both sides)
$a = 24$	(divide both sides by 2 to find a)

So we can see that (A) is correct.

Solution 2: Test-smart / backsolving: Note that (A) and (B) must represent the hours worked by the two people in the prompt, and pick the choice that corresponds to Angelica's hours.

As trained test-takers, we know that the College Board often likes to include wrong answers that represent "on-the-way" calculations that might be used to help find the final answer to the question; the College Board is hoping that we'll forget what the question actually asked us to find, and pick an answer with a value that's relevant to the question but different from what the prompt actually asked for.

So when a prompt involves two separate numbers with a specific relationship, and we're asked to provide only one of the numbers, we'll often find that one of the wrong answers represents the other number described in the prompt.

In this case, then, we'd expect the answer choices to include a pair of numbers that differ by 11 and add up to 59. One of those numbers will represent the hours worked by Angelica, and the other number will represent the hours worked by Raul. Sure enough, (A) and (B) fit that pattern. Once we notice that, we can simply make sure that we pick the one representing Angelica's hours, since that's what the prompt asked for. This allows us to identify (A) as the correct answer without doing any real calculation.

Solution 3: Test-smart: Notice that if Angelica and Raul worked a total of 59 hours, and Angelica worked fewer hours than Raul did, then Angelica must have worked fewer than half of the 59 hours. Only (A) is less than half of 59, so (A) is right.

ANSWER CHOICE ANALYSIS

(B): This is the number of hours Raul worked. **(C):** This choice might be tempting because 40 hours is a typical work week in many societies. **(D):** This would be correct if Raul *alone* worked 59 hours, but it says that Raul and Angelica worked 59 hours *combined*.

How to check? Try an alternate approach above.

▶ Post-solution patterns (see page 218): opposites; right answer to the wrong question

---

- **What's the prompt asking for?** The proportion of movies that are comedies with a PG-13 rating.
- **Math concepts in the prompt:** proportions, reading data from a table, word problems
- **Math concepts in the diagram:** addition, data labels, reading data from a table
- **Elements of the answer choices:** fractions
- **Notable differences among answer choices:** (A) and (D) have denominators of 25, while (B) has a denominator of 50 (which is twice as much as 25) and (C) has a denominator of 11. (A) and (C) both have 2 as their numerators. The numerators of (A) and (B) add up to the numerator in (D). The denominator in (C) is the numerator in (D).
- **Concepts in the answer choices:** proportions
- **Pre-solution patterns (see p. 217):** opposites; wrong answers try to imitate right answers
- **Things to look out for:** Make sure you pick the right numbers for the numerator and denominator, because the College Board is clearly giving us the chance to make a mistake!

Solution 1: Proportions: Carefully read the prompt and construct a proportion reflecting it; find the choice that equals your fraction.

The numerator of the proportion will be the number of movies that are comedies and have a PG-13 rating. In the "Comedy" column, we can see in the second row that there were 4 PG-13 comedies. So the numerator of our proportion is 4.

The denominator of the proportion will be the number of movies, which is 50.

That makes our proportion $\frac{4}{50}$. That specific fraction isn't in the answer choices, but if we reduce the fraction it becomes $\frac{2}{25}$, which is choice (A). So (A) is right.

ANSWER CHOICE ANALYSIS

(B): This is the proportion of movies that are comedies, not just comedies with a PG-13 rating. **(C):** This is the proportion of PG movies that are dramas. **(D):** This is the proportion of movies that are rated PG-13, not just comedies rated PG-13.

How to check? Identify the types of mistakes that would lead untrained test-takers to wrong answers, and make sure you avoid them.

▶ Post-solution patterns (see page 218): opposites

- **What's the prompt asking for?** The choice that MUST be true about the line in the prompt.
- **Math concepts in the prompt:** lines, word problems, xy-coordinate plane
- **Elements of the answer choices:** sentences, zero
- **Notable differences among answer choices:** The choices cover every kind of slope a line can have.
- **Concepts in the answer choices:** negative slope, positive slope, undefined slope, zero slope
- **Pre-solution patterns (see p. 217):** opposites
- **Things to look out for:** Don't misread the prompt! Don't confuse the quadrants in the xy-coordinate plane! Don't confuse the different kinds of slope!

Solution 1: Diagramming: Sketch some lines that conform to the prompt. Try to sketch lines whose slopes are positive, negative, undefined, and zero, while still containing points in the indicated quadrants. Pick the choice that corresponds to your results.

If we try to sketch a variety of graphs with lines that avoid the first quadrant while passing through the others, they'll all end up looking something like these:

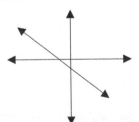 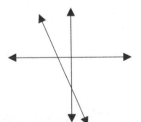 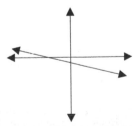

As we can see, these lines all have negative slopes, and there's no way to draw a line that hits every quadrant except I without making the line slope down as it moves from left to right, which means it must have a negative slope. So (D) is correct.

Solution 2: Abstract: Consider the properties of the different kinds of slope with respect to the prompt; pick the appropriate choice.

Quadrant I is the top-right quadrant, which means that any line traveling up and to the right infinitely (remember that all lines are infinite!) would have to cross into Quadrant I eventually. So if a line never crosses into Quadrant I, it can't have a positive slope.

Similarly, if a line is going to cross into more than two quadrants, then it can't be a vertical or horizontal line, because a vertical or horizontal line can never cross through more than two quadrants.

So we know that the line in the prompt must not have a positive slope, a zero slope (which would correspond to a horizontal line), or an undefined slope (which would correspond to a vertical line). The only other kind of slope is negative, so (D) is right.

How to check? Try an alternate approach above. Try to identify mistakes that could lead an untrained test-taker to pick a wrong answer, and make sure you haven't made those mistakes yourself.

▶ Post-solution patterns (see page 218): opposites

Test 4, Section 4, Question 9

- **What's the prompt asking for?** The choice that's closest to the probability that the chosen voter was from the Midwest region.
- **Math concepts in the prompt:** data labels, estimation, probability, random selection, reading data from a table, word problems
- **Math concepts in the diagram:** data labels, reading data from a table
- **Elements of the answer choices:** decimals
- **Notable differences among answer choices:** (B) and (D) add up to 1, which may be relevant because the prompt is asking us to find the probability of a particular outcome, and we know the College Board likes to provide us with the complement to the correct answer when that's possible.
- **Concepts in the answer choices:** complements
- **Pre-solution patterns (see p. 217):** complements or supplements
- **Things to look out for:** Make sure we identify the correct probability, since the College Board seems to be trying to get us to identify the wrong one! Don't misread the table! Don't confuse the parts of your probability fraction!

Solution 1: Statistics: Construct the correct probability fraction by using the table to identify the appropriate values for the denominator and numerator. Pick the answer choice that's closest to your probability fraction.

The numerator of the probability fraction will be the desired outcome—a voter from the Midwest region who was 18 to 44 years old in 2012. We can see that in the column titled "18 to 24" and the column titled "25 to 44," for the row titled "Midwest," there are 3,453 and 11,237 voters respectively, for a total of 14,690 voters. So the numerator of our probability fraction is 14,690.

The denominator of the probability fraction will be the number of possible outcomes. In this case we are selecting from voters who were 18 to 44 years old in 2012. We can see that in the column titled "18 to 24" and the column titled "25 to 44," for the row titled "Total," there are 14,766 and 47,896 voters respectively, for a total of 62,662 voters. So the denominator of our probability fraction is 62,662.

That makes our probability fraction $\frac{14,690}{62,662}$. That option isn't in the answer choices—in fact, the answer choices are all decimal approximations of the probability. So we'll need to divide out the fraction to obtain the equivalent decimal, which is about 23.44%. Thus (B) is correct.

Solution 2: Estimation: Note that the Midwest data for voters 18-24 is approximately one-fourth of the total for the 18-24 column, and the Midwest data for voters 25-44 is approximately one-fourth of the total for the 25-44 column, which means the Midwest data for voters 18-44 must be approximately one-fourth of the total data for voters 18-44. That means the right answer must be (B), 0.25.

ANSWER CHOICE ANALYSIS

(C): Some untrained test-takers might hurry through this question and mistake the number 0.4 for the quantity one-fourth, which would lead them to pick this answer choice. **(D):** This choice is the complement of the correct answer, meaning that it represents the rough probability that a voter aged 18-44 is NOT from the Midwest region. This kind of wrong answer choice frequently appears in SAT questions that involve probability.

How to check? Try an alternate approach above. Identify ways that an untrained test-taker might accidentally arrive at one of the wrong answers, and make sure you haven't made any of those mistakes yourself.

▶ Post-solution patterns (see page 218): opposites

Note Any of the wrong answers might be tempting for someone who misreads the table.

Test 4, Section 4, Question 10

- **What's the prompt asking for?** The life expectancy of the animal with the longest gestation period.
- **Math concepts in the prompt:** reading data from a scatterplot
- **Math concepts in the diagram:** data labels, reading data from a scatterplot
- **Elements of the answer choices:** integers
- **Notable differences among answer choices:** (B) is half of (C).
- **Pre-solution patterns (see p. 217):** halves and doubles
- **Things to look out for:** Don't confuse the axes on the scatterplot! Don't accidentally find the data for the animal with the shortest gestation period!

Solution 1: Reading data: Identify the point that represents the longest gestation period, and pick the answer that represents the life-expectancy-value for that point.

The gestation period is measured along the horizontal axis. The point on the scatterplot that is farthest to the right shows a gestation period of 60 days, and corresponds to a life expectancy of 3 years, so (A) is the answer.

ANSWER CHOICE ANALYSIS

(B): This choice might tempt an untrained test-taker who incorrectly identifies the horizontal line that the right-most point is on. **(C):** This choice might trick someone who thinks he can only pick a data point labeled with a capital letter, and thinks point C is farthest to the right. **(D):** This choice could trick someone who thought point D was farthest to the right.

How to check? Carefully re-read the prompt and the data, and re-check your conclusion.

Test 4, Section 4, Question 11

- **What's the prompt asking for?** The choice that corresponds to the animal with the greatest ratio of life expectancy to gestation.
- **Math concepts in the prompt:** ratios, reading data from a scatterplot

- **Math concepts in the diagram:** data labels, reading data from a scatterplot
- **Things to look out for:** Don't reverse the ratio described in the prompt! Don't confuse the labels on the axes! Don't accidentally find the answer choice with the lowest ratio instead of the highest!

Solution 1: Concrete: Find the values for life expectancy and gestation for each labeled point in the scatterplot, and determine the ratios for each point. Pick the answer choice that corresponds to the highest ratio.

(A) Point A corresponds to a life expectancy of 7 years and a gestation period of around 22 days, so the ratio of life expectancy to gestation period is around $\frac{7}{22}$, or 0.318.

(B) Point B corresponds to a life expectancy of 8 years and a gestation period of around 44 days, so the ratio of life expectancy to gestation period is around $\frac{8}{44}$ or 0.181.

(C) Point C corresponds to a life expectancy of 8 years and a gestation period of around 51 days, so the ratio of life expectancy to gestation period is around $\frac{8}{51}$ or 0.157.

(D) Point D corresponds to a life expectancy of 10 years and a gestation period of around 51 days, so the ratio of life expectancy to gestation period is around $\frac{10}{51}$ or 0.196.

We can see that choice (A) has the highest ratio, so (A) is correct.

Solution 2: Abstract: Identify the attributes of the point with the highest ratio. Then find the point with those characteristics.

We can see on the chart that life expectancy is reflected in the vertical position of a point, and gestation period is represented in the horizontal position. This means that the point with the highest ratio of life expectancy to gestation will have the highest ratio of vertical separation from the origin to horizontal separation from the origin. This is another way of saying that the slope of the line from the origin to any given point is, literally, an indication of the ratio of life expectancy to gestation for that point.

This means that if we drew in lines from the origin to each individual point, the point whose line had the steepest slope would be the desired answer to this question. That would be point A, so (A) is correct.

ANSWER CHOICE ANALYSIS

(C): This is the choice with the lowest ratio of life expectancy to gestation period, which is the opposite of what the prompt asked for. **(D):** This is the choice with greatest life expectancy, as opposed to the greatest ratio of life expectancy to gestation period, which might trick untrained test-takers who didn't read the prompt carefully.

How to check? Try an alternate approach above. Also try to figure out what kinds of small mistakes would lead an untrained test-taker to some of the wrong answers, and make sure you're not making similar mistakes.

Test 4, Section 4, Question 12

- **What's the prompt asking for?** The answer choice that could define function f.
- **Math concepts in the prompt:** graphing functions, word problems, xy-coordinate plane, x-intercepts
- **Elements of the answer choices:** algebraic expressions, equations, exponents, integers
- **Notable differences among answer choices:** (A) and (B) both include $(x - 3)$, while (C) and (D) both include $(x + 3)$. (A) and (C) both include $(x + 1)$ and $(x - 1)$, while

(B) includes $(x - 1)^2$ and (D) includes $(x + 1)^2$.
(A) and (C) both have three parenthetical expressions, while (B) and (D) each have only two, with one squared.

- **Pre-solution patterns (see p. 217):** opposites; wrong answers try to imitate right answers
- **Things to look out for:** Make sure you correctly identify whether the correct answer should include 3 or -3! Make sure you correctly identify whether the answer should involve squaring an expression—and, if so, which expression!

Solution 1: Algebra: Given the information in the prompt, determine the factors of f and pick the corresponding answer choice.

By definition, an x-intercept of a function is a point on its graph where plugging in a given x-value produces a y-value of 0.

So if a function has an x-intercept at $x = -3$, then we know that plugging in $x = -3$ must cause the function to have a y-value of zero. In the context of the choices for this question, a function with an x-intercept at $x = -3$ would have to include $(x + 3)$ as a factor, because plugging $x = -3$ into that factor makes that factor equal to 0, which in turn would result in multiplying the value of the function by 0.

Similarly, an x-intercept at $x = -1$ indicates that $(x + 1)$ is a factor, and an x-intercept at $x = 1$ indicates that $(x + -1)$, which is the same as $(x - 1)$, is a factor. The only choice with all of these elements is (C), so (C) is correct.

Solution 2: Backsolving / Graphing: Graph each choice on a calculator; find the one with intercepts at $x = -3, x = -1$, and $x = 1$.

Graph of (A):

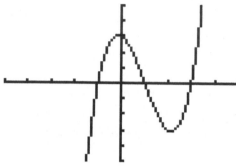

(A) has x-intercepts at $x = -1, x = 1$, and $x = 3$, so it can't be correct. Now let's try (B):

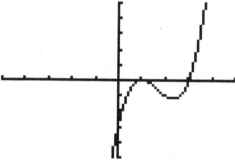

(B) has x-intercepts at $x = 1$ and $x = 3$, so it can't be correct. Now let's try (C):

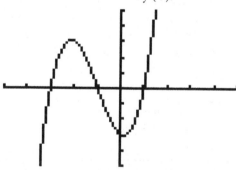

(C) has x-intercepts at $x = -3, x = -1$, and $x = 1$, so it's correct, assuming we haven't made mistakes in our reading or calculator usage. As trained test-takers, we know that we always need to consider every answer choice before we pick one, so let's try (D) now:

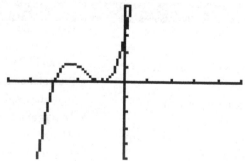

(D) has x-intercepts at $x = -3$ and $x = -1$, so it can't be right. After looking at the graph of each choice, we see that (C) is right.

ANSWER CHOICE ANALYSIS

(A): This choice has an x-intercept at 1, -1, and 3, instead of -3, which will trick a lot of people who don't read carefully.

How to check? Try an alternate approach above. Make sure not to misread the prompt or choices, since they have similar numbers!

Test 4, Section 4, Question 13

- **What's the prompt asking for?** The choice that best describes the relationship in the data from the table.
- **Math concepts in the prompt:** reading data from a table, relationships among data points, word problems
- **Math concepts in the diagram:** data labels, reading data from a table
- **Elements of the answer choices:** words or phrases
- **Notable differences among answer choices:** (A) and (C) both include the idea of something getting larger as time goes by. (B) and (D) both include the idea of something getting smaller as time goes by. (A) and (B) both include the idea of linear change, while (C) and (D) both include the idea of exponential change.
- **Concepts in the answer choices:** exponential change, linear change
- **Pre-solution patterns (see p. 217):** wrong answers try to imitate right answers
- **Things to look out for:** Don't confuse linear and exponential change! Don't confuse increasing and decreasing! Don't misread the prompt or the choices!

Solution 1: Data: Read the table and determine the choice that accurately describes the change reflected in the data.

We can see that the time always increases by the same amount as we read down through the rows on the table: 5 weeks. The population also increases over each 5-week interval. So we know that the correct answer must involve increasing numbers...the issue is just whether the growth is linear or exponential.

As we can see, the increase in each population number over any given 5-week period is a factor of 10 over the previous value. This isn't linear growth, because linear growth features growth by a constant *amount*, not growth by a constant *ratio*. Growth by a constant *ratio* is exponential growth, so (C) is correct.

How to check? Carefully re-read the question and re-evaluate your conclusion.

Test 4, Section 4, Question 14

- **What's the prompt asking for?** The choice that reflects the difference between the interest compounded at 5% and the interest compounded at 3%.
- **Math concepts in the prompt:** algebra, arithmetic, exponents, fractions, function modeling, word problems
- **Elements of the answer choices:** algebraic expressions, exponents, fractions, integers
- **Notable differences among answer choices:** Choices (A) and (D) both involve subtraction. (A) involves subtracting 3 from 5 in the numerator of the expression from the prompt, while (D) involves two entire expressions like the one in the prompt. (B) and (C) both involve division. (B) involves dividing 5 by 3 in the numerator of the expression from the prompt, while (D) involves dividing two entire expressions like the one in the prompt.
- **Concepts in the answer choices:** division, function modeling, PEMDAS, subtraction
- **Pre-solution patterns (see p. 217):** wrong answers try to imitate right answers
- **Things to look out for:** Make sure you determine whether the correct answer should involve subtraction or division! Make sure you determine whether the correct answer choice should involve a single expression like the one from the prompt, or two expressions like the one in the prompt! Don't make any mistakes in your reading!

Solution 1: Concrete / Backsolving: Use your calculator to determine the difference between the amount generated at 5% and the amount generated at 3%, and then use your calculator to find the answer choice that gives the same result.

$$1000\left(1 + \frac{5}{1,200}\right)^{12} \approx \$1051.16 \qquad \text{(result when } r = 5)$$

$$1000\left(1 + \frac{3}{1,200}\right)^{12} \approx \$1030.42 \qquad \text{(result when } r = 3)$$

$$\$1051.16 - \$1030.42 = \$20.74 \qquad \text{(difference between the above results)}$$

Now that we know the difference should come out to $20.74, we can evaluate each choice to see which one matches that value:

$$1000\left(1 + \frac{5-3}{1,200}\right)^{12} \approx \$1020.18 \qquad \text{(result from (A))}$$

$$1000\left(1 + \frac{\frac{5}{3}}{1,200}\right)^{12} \approx \$1016.79 \qquad \text{(result from (B))}$$

$$\frac{1000\left(1+\frac{5}{1,200}\right)^{12}}{1000\left(1+\frac{3}{1,200}\right)^{12}} \approx 1.02 \qquad \text{(result from (C))}$$

$$1000\left(1+\frac{5}{1,200}\right)^{12} - 1000\left(1+\frac{3}{1,200}\right)^{12} \approx \$20.74 \qquad \text{(result from (D))}$$

Since (D) is the only choice that matches the correct value, we know (D) must be correct.

Solution 2: Test-smart / Algebra: Find the right answer by comparing the choices to each other and to the prompt.

When we look at the structures of the choices, we see that only (D) would involve subtracting one interest expression from the other one...which is the only way to find the difference between them, since subtraction is literally the process of finding a difference between two things. This means (D) must be right. ((A) might seem tempting to some untrained test-takers who don't consider all of the choices, because it does involve subtracting 3 from 5 before raising a number to an exponent, but simply raising 2 to an exponent will give a different result from what the prompt asked for, as we can see if we look back at solution 1 above.)

How to check? Try an alternate approach above.

> **Note**   Each wrong answer could trick a test-taker who tried to construct her own algebraic expression to satisfy the prompt, instead of simply working backwards from the provided expressions as we did above.

Test 4, Section 4, Question 15

- **What's the prompt asking for?** The choice with a scatterplot that reflects the equation in the prompt.
- **Math concepts in the prompt:** algebra, coefficients, equations, negative exponents, scatterplots
- **Elements of the answer choices:** diagrams
- **Notable differences among answer choices:** (A) and (B) both show a decreasing trend, while (C) shows an increasing one. (B) and (C) both involve exponential change, while (A) involves linear change. (D) is the only choice that doesn't show any particular trend.
- **Concepts in the answer choices:** decreasing trends, exponential change, increasing trends, linear change
- **Pre-solution patterns (see p. 217):** opposites; wrong answers try to imitate right answers
- **Things to look out for:** Don't confuse a and b! Don't forget that a is positive and b is negative!

Solution 1: Calculator / concrete: Pick values for a and b that conform to the prompt, and use your calculator to graph $y = ax^b$. Determine what kind of trend the graph indicates, and then pick the answer choice that reflects the same kind of trend.

Here's the graph of $y = 5x^{-3}$, which has a positive coefficient for x and a negative exponent, as the prompt requires:

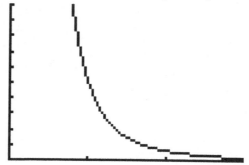

We see a "curving" downward trend as we move from left to right, which matches the curving downward trend in (B), so (B) is right.

Solution 2: Algebra: Identify the algebraic concepts in the equation in the prompt, and pick the choice that reflects those concepts.

We may be able to look at the prompt and realize that the negative exponent b will mean that y gets exponentially smaller as x gets larger, which will cause the graph to have a non-linear, downward trend as we move from left to right. So (B) is right.

But don't be nervous if you didn't realize this right away! You could always try a concrete approach like solution 1 above.

ANSWER CHOICE ANALYSIS

(A): This choice shows a negative *linear* relationship, but the prompt describes a negative *exponential* relationship. Exponential relationships involve curved lines when the x-axis is marked off at constant intervals, like the x-axes in the answer choices. **(C):** This choice shows a *positive* exponential relationship, but the prompt describes a *negative* exponential relationship. This will trick some untrained test-takers who misread the prompt.

How to check? Try an alternate approach above. Note that the similarities among (A), (B), and (C) suggest—but don't guarantee!—that (B) is right, since it's the only choice that incorporates two elements from other choices.

- **What's the prompt asking for?** The choice describing the number of days for which the total price from Store B will be less than or equal to the total price from Store A.
- **Math concepts in the prompt:** function modeling, less than or equal to, reading data from a table, total cost, word problems, algebra
- **Math concepts in the diagram:** data labels, rates, reading data from a table
- **Elements of the answer choices:** algebraic expressions, inequalities, integers
- **Notable differences among answer choices:** (A) and (B) both use the number 6, while (C) and (D) both use the number

7.3. (A) and (C) both say x is less than or equal to a number, while (B) and (D) both say x is greater than or equal to a number.

- **Concepts in the answer choices:** inequalities
- **Pre-solution patterns (see p. 217):** wrong answers try to imitate right answers
- **Things to look out for:** Make sure you correctly identify whether the correct answer should involve 6 or 7.3! Make sure you correctly identify whether x should be greater than or less than the number in the right answer! Avoid small mistakes in your algebra, arithmetic, or reading! Don't confuse the stores!

Solution 1: Backsolving: Notice the similarities and differences among the answer choices and test the costs at Store A and Store B for three kinds of x-values: one value less than 6, one value between 6 and 7.3, and one value greater than 7.3. Use the results of your testing to determine the correct answer choice.

First let's test both stores when $x = 5$, since 5 is less than 6, and we know that we want to test a value that's less than 6:

$B = 600 + (25 + 80)(5)$	(cost from Store B when $x = 5$)
$B = 1125$	(simplify)
$A = 750 + (15 + 65)(5)$	(cost from Store A when $x = 5$)
$A = 1150$	(simplify)

So when $x = 5$, we see that Store A has a higher cost. Now let's try $x = 7$, since we need to test a value between 6 and 7.3:

$B = 600 + (25 + 80)(7)$	(cost from Store B when $x = 7$)
$B = 1335$	(simplify)
$A = 750 + (15 + 65)(7)$	(cost from Store A when $x = 7$)
$A = 1310$	(simplify)

When $x = 7$, Store B has a higher cost than Store A. Finally, let's try $x = 8$, since we also need to test a value greater than 7.3:

$B = 600 + (25 + 80)(8)$	(cost from Store B when $x = 8$)
$B = 1440$	(simplify)
$A = 750 + (15 + 65)(8)$	(cost from Store A when $x = 8$)
$A = 1390$	(simplify)

Just as with $x = 7$, we see that Store B has a higher cost when $x = 8$. So our testing shows that the cost of using Store B was only less than the cost of using Store A when we tested an x-value less than 6. (A) is the only choice that fits that result, so (A) is right.

Solution 2: Algebra: Using the model in the prompt and the cost information in the table, create an inequality stating that the modeled cost of Store B is less than or equal to the modeled cost of Store A, and solve for x.

When we find the two stores' values for M, W, and K in the table and plug them into the equation from the prompt, we see that the cost expression for store A is $750 + (15 + 65)x$, and the cost expression for store B is $600 + (25 + 80)x$. Now that we've figured out those expressions, we can use algebra to set Store B's expression less than or equal to the expression for Store A, and solve for x:

$600 + (25 + 80)x \leq 750 + (15 + 65)x$	(cost from Store B set less than or equal to cost from Store A)
$600 + 105x \leq 750 + 80x$	(simplify)
$600 + 25x \leq 750$	(subtract $80x$ from both sides)
$25x \leq 150$	(subtract 600 from both sides)

$$x \leq 6 \qquad \text{(divide both sides by 25)}$$

We see the cost for Store B is less than or equal to the cost for Store A when the number of days is 6 or fewer. So (A) is right.

ANSWER CHOICE ANALYSIS

(B): This choice could trick someone who confused Store A and Store B, or who made an algebra mistake in solution 2 that resulted in changing the direction of the inequality sign.

How to check? Try an alternate approach above. Also try to figure out what kinds of small mistakes would lead an untrained test-taker to some of the wrong answers, and make sure you're not making similar mistakes.

Test 4, Section 4, Question 17

- **What's the prompt asking for?** The choice that describes what would be revealed by the slope of a graph plotting total cost against number of days.
- **Math concepts in the prompt:** function modeling, graphing data, reading data from a table, xy-coordinate plane
- **Math concepts in the diagram:** data labels, reading data from a table
- **Elements of the answer choices:** sentences
- **Notable differences among answer choices:** (A) and (B) talk about the total cost of something, while (C) and (D) talk about total daily costs. (A) and (C) talk about the cost of the project, while (B) talks about the cost of materials, and (D) talks about the cost of tools.
- **Pre-solution patterns (see p. 217):** wrong answers try to imitate right answers
- **Things to look out for:** Make sure you identify whether the slope is related to a total overall cost, or to a total daily cost! Make sure you identify whether the slope is related to the cost of the project altogether, or only to the costs for the materials or the rental! Don't confuse slope with other attributes of the graph of a line!

Solution 1: Test smart / Algebra: Consider the differences among the answer choices that we noted above, and determine which choice reflects the slope of the line described in the prompt.

(A) doesn't make sense as the correct answer, because slope is a ratio of one kind of change to another kind of change, by definition; the cost of the project isn't a ratio, so (A) can't be correct. Further, the prompt tells us the total cost of the project is y, and y can't be a slope in this context.

(B) has one of the same problems that (A) had: the idea of a total cost doesn't go along with the idea of a ratio in this case.

(C) is wrong because the total daily cost of the project won't be reflected in the slope alone, since the change reflected in the slope will be related to the way the rental costs increase with each day of renting, but the "total daily cost" would also take into account the one-time cost of buying the materials.

(D) is correct because the word "daily" accurately reflects the idea that the cost will change with each day. This makes sense, because the slope is the relationship between one kind of change and another kind of change—in this case, the change in the amount of time (the number of days of the rental) and the change in the cost of renting the tools. Also, the phrase "rental costs of the tools" clarifies that the slope only tells us about the way the rental cost of the tools changes depending on how many days the rental lasts; the slope doesn't tell us anything about the materials costs, which are fixed and therefore don't change from day to day.

ANSWER CHOICE ANALYSIS

See solution 1 above.

How to check? Carefully review your reading and assumptions.

Test 4, Section 4, Question 18

- **What's the prompt asking for?** The largest number of full glasses Jim can pour from a gallon container.
- **Math concepts in the prompt:** diameter, division, height, right circular cylinders, word problems
- **Elements of the answer choices:** integers
- **Notable differences among answer choices:** (A), (B), and (D) form a series in which each choice is 2 more than the previous choice. (B), (C), and (D) form a series in which each choice is 1 more than the previous choice.
- **Pre-solution patterns (see p. 217):** halves and doubles; the first and last terms in a series are often wrong answers
- **Things to look out for:** Don't confuse the diameter, height, and radius! Remember the question is asking for whole glasses, and not asking you to include the last partial glass that can be poured! Avoid small mistakes in your geometry, arithmetic, or reading!

Solution 1: Geometry: Determine the volume of each glass in cubic inches, and then divide the number of cubic inches in a gallon by the number of cubic inches in each glass, and ignore the partial glass.

The formula for the volume of a cylinder is normally given in terms of r, the radius of the cylinder; that's how it appears at the beginning of each SAT Math section. Since the prompt gave us the diameter of each drinking glass as 3 inches, we'll have to divide that number in half to find the radius of each glass. Once we realize the radius is 1.5 inches, we can plug that number in for r in the volume formula for cylinders, along with the 6-inch height from the prompt:

$V = \pi r^2 h$ (formula for the volume of a right circular cylinder, as given at the start of each SAT Math section)

$V = \pi(1.5)^2 6$ (plug in $r = 1.5$ and $h = 6$)

$V \approx 42.412$ (simplify to find the volume of one cylindrical drinking glass)

Now we know the volume of each glass of milk is approximately 42.412 cubic inches. We can divide the number of cubic inches in a gallon (which we're given in the prompt) by the number of cubic inches in each glass to find out how many full glasses we can pour from one gallon of milk: $\frac{231}{42.412} \approx 5.447$.

A lot of untrained test-takers will think of this as 6 glasses, because they'll forget what the prompt actually asked them for! We were asked to provide the number of *full* glasses Jim can pour from one gallon—not the number of glasses with milk in them—and he can only pour 5 full glasses; he doesn't have enough milk in the gallon to fill a 6th glass. So (C) is correct.

ANSWER CHOICE ANALYSIS

(D): This would trick an untrained test-taker who forgot that he couldn't count 5.447 glass as 6 glasses according to the prompt.

How to check? Carefully re-check your reading and calculations, especially the part of the prompt that says the glasses must be full.

Test 4, Section 4, Question 19

- **What's the prompt asking for?** The least possible value of $3p + 2$.
- **Math concepts in the prompt:** algebra, arithmetic, inequalities
- **Elements of the answer choices:** integers
- **Notable differences among answer choices:** (B), (C), and (D) form a series in which each choice is one less than the choice before it.

- **Pre-solution patterns (see p. 217):** halves and doubles; the first and last terms in a series are often wrong answers
- **Things to look out for:** Don't find the least possible value of $3p - 2$ instead of $3p + 2$! Don't make small mistakes in your algebra and arithmetic!

Solution 1: Algebra: Find an inequality to describe p by itself, then use it to find the least possible value of $3p + 2$.

$3p - 2 \geq 1$ (inequality given in the prompt)

$3p \geq 3$ (add 2 to both sides)

$p \geq 1$ (divide both sides by 3)

If p is greater than or equal to 1, then $3p$ must be greater than or equal to 3, which means $3p + 2$ must be greater than or equal to 5. So the answer is (A).

Solution 2: Faster algebra: Note that $3p + 2$ is 4 more than $3p - 2$, and add 4 to both sides of the given inequality to find the least possible value of $3p + 2$.

When we add 4 to both sides of the inequality in the prompt, we get $3p + 2 \geq 5$, which means (A) must be correct.

ANSWER CHOICE ANALYSIS

(B): This is the least possible value of $3p$, which might trick someone who didn't read the prompt carefully. **(C):** This choice could trick someone who made an algebra mistake and thought the least possible value of p was zero. **(D):** This is the least possible value of p itself, and also of $3p - 2$.

How to check? Try an alternate approach above. Make sure you've read the prompt carefully.

▶   Post-solution patterns (see page 218): right approach, wrong step

Test 4, Section 4, Question 20

- **What's the prompt asking for?** The answer choice whose graph indicates a yearly doubling in biomass.
- **Math concepts in the prompt:** constant rate, defined terms, graph modeling, word problems
- **Elements of the answer choices:** diagrams
- **Notable differences among answer choices:** (A), (B), and (C) all show an increasing trend over time, while (D) shows a flat trend over time. (A) and (D) show a linear trend, while (C)

shows an exponential trend, and (B) shows a trend that's partly linear and partly step-wise.

- **Concepts in the answer choices:** exponential trends, flat trends, increasing trends, linear trends, step-wise trends
- **Pre-solution patterns (see p. 217):** wrong answers try to imitate right answers
- **Things to look out for:** Make sure you're thinking of the right kind of trend to show an annual doubling!

Solution 1: Data / Test-smart: Note the differences among the choices above. Pick the one that shows an annual doubling.

(A), (B), and (C) all have y-values at $x = 2$ that are twice as much as the y-values at $x = 1$...but only (C) indicates that its y-value at $x = 0$ was $y = \frac{1}{2}$, which is what an annual doubling would require in order to generate a y-value of 1 at $x = 1$. So (C) is right.

ANSWER CHOICE ANALYSIS

(A): This shows constant or linear growth, not yearly doubling. It would produce a y-value of 3 instead of 4 at $x = 3$, for example.

How to check? Re-read the prompt and the answer choices. Identify the mistakes that untrained test-takers might be likely to make, and make sure that you're not making any similar mistakes.

Test 4, Section 4, Question 21

- **What's the prompt asking for?** The number of points that would be above the line $y = x$ if the data were presented as a scatterplot.
- **Math concepts in the prompt:** axis labels, graphing lines, scatterplots, xy-coordinate plane
- **Math concepts in the diagram:** axis labels, bar graphs, keys
- **Elements of the answer choices:** integers

- **Notable differences among answer choices:** All four choices form a series in which each choice is one more than the choice before it.
- **Pre-solution patterns (see p. 217):** halves and doubles; the first and last terms in a series are often wrong answers
- **Things to look out for:** Don't accidentally find the number of points below the line! Don't confuse the x-axis and the y-axis! Avoid small mistakes reading the data or the prompt!

Solution 1: Concrete / diagramming: Sketch out an xy-plane with the data points from the graph scattered on it. Then sketch the line $y = x$ on your diagram, and count the number of data points above that line.

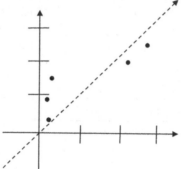

The dashed line is the line $y = x$. Three data points appear above that line, so (C) must be correct.

Solution 2: Abstract: Recognize that a point above the line $y = x$ must have a y-coordinate that's greater than its x-coordinate, and then count the number of points on the graph that would satisfy that requirement.

According to the prompt, our graph would have the 2000 values on the horizontal axis, and the 2010 values on the vertical axis. So the points whose 2010 values were higher than their 2000 values would be above the line $y = x$. Those points would be the ones whose light-shaded bars are taller than their dark bars in the provided graph: biofuels, geothermal, and wind. Since there would be three of these points, (C) is correct.

ANSWER CHOICE ANALYSIS

(B): This is the number of data points that appear below the line, for people who misread the prompt or flip the axes.

How to check? Try an alternate approach above.

▶ Post-solution patterns (see page 218): opposites

Test 4, Section 4, Question 22

- **What's the prompt asking for?** The choice that best approximates the percent decrease in wood power from 2000 to 2010.
- **Math concepts in the prompt:** approximation, percent decrease, reading data from a bar graph
- **Math concepts in the diagram:** axis labels, bar graphs, keys
- **Elements of the answer choices:** integers, percentages
- **Notable differences among answer choices:** (A) differs from (B) by 5%, and (C) differs from (D) by 5%. This suggests

that it might be possible to misread the data in some way that makes it likely for a test-taker to be off by 5%.
- **Concepts in the answer choices:** percentages
- **Things to look out for:** Make sure you compare the values in the correct order when you calculate the percentage decrease! Make sure you consider the data for wood power, and not for another type of power! Don't make any small mistakes in your reading or calculations!

Solution 1: Concrete: Determine the actual percentage decrease of wood power from 2000 to 2010 using the data in the table and the definition of "percentage decrease." Then mark the corresponding answer choice.

To find the percentage decrease in consumption from 2000 to 2010, we divide the difference in consumption for those years by the amount of consumption in 2000. That calculation looks like this:

$$\frac{2.25 - 2.00}{2.25} \approx 0.11 = 11\%$$

So the answer is (B).

Solution 2: Estimation / test-smart: Note that the decrease is roughly 0.25 compared to a starting value of 2.25, which means the decrease is slightly more than 10% of the starting value. Then pick the only choice that's slightly more than 10%, which is (B).

How to check? Try an alternate approach above.

Test 4, Section 4, Question 23

- **What's the prompt asking for?** The choice whose statement accurately reflects the provided data.
- **Math concepts in the prompt:** reading data from tables, word problems
- **Math concepts in the diagram:** data labels, reading data from tables
- **Elements of the answer choices:** sentences
- **Notable differences among answer choices:** Each choice makes a statement about the standard deviations of the temperatures for City A and City B. (A) says that standard deviation is larger for City A. (B) says the standard deviation is larger for City B. (C) says the two standard deviations are equal, and (D) says the two standard deviations can't be determined from the given information.
- **Concepts in the answer choices:** standard deviation
- **Pre-solution patterns (see p. 217):** wrong answers try to imitate right answers
- **Things to look out for:** Don't make any small mistakes in your reading or calculations! Don't confuse City A and City B!

Solution 1: Properties and definitions: Standard deviation relates to how much the data in a set deviates from the average value of the set. Calculate the average of each set of data and see which set of data deviates the most from the average.

We can find the average of each set of data by adding up the values in each set and dividing by the number of values.

$$\frac{(80\times3)+(79\times14)+(78\times2)+(77\times1)+(76\times1)}{21} \approx 78.81° \quad \text{(Average temperature for City A)}$$

$$\frac{(80\times6)+(79\times3)+(78\times2)+(77\times4)+(76\times6)}{21} \approx 77.95° \quad \text{(Average temperature for City B)}$$

We can see that the values in the set for City B vary much more from their average than the values in the set for City A. In City A, the average was just below 79°, and 14 of the data points were also 79°. On the other hand, in City B, the average was just below 78°, and only 2 of the data points were also at 78°—with 6 data points at 80° and 6 data points at 76°.

So we can clearly see that the data for City B deviates more from its average than the data for City A deviates from its average, which means City B has the greater standard deviation, and (B) is correct.

Solution 2: Abstract / Estimation: Observe the differences in the frequencies of temperature readings, and pick the choice reflecting that difference.

We see that the temperatures measured in City A tended to stay closer to around 79°, while the temperatures measured in City B varied—or "deviated"—more from their mean of around 78°. So the standard deviation was greater in City B, and (B) is correct.

ANSWER CHOICE ANALYSIS

(A): This choice might trick an untrained test-taker who confused City A and City B.

How to check? Try an alternate approach above. Also try to figure out what kinds of small mistakes would lead an untrained test-taker to some of the wrong answers, and make sure you're not making similar mistakes.

Note Even if we aren't exactly sure what "standard deviation" means, we've got a good shot at figuring out enough about the term to be able to answer this question anyway. We probably know that "standard" means something like "regular" or "normal," and "to deviate" from something means "to be different" from that thing, or "to move away" from it. This suggests that "standard deviation" means something like "being different from the normal thing." (Of course, this definition isn't exactly precise, and might not be very helpful in a math classroom. But we'll see how this kind of definition can be useful on this question, and how this general type of thinking can be helpful on the rest of the SAT.) Now let's think about the data in the question and the answer choices. We can see that the data for City A are mostly pretty close to 79, as we discussed in solution 2—they don't "deviate" much from that "standard" value. On the other hand, the data for City B aren't so close to one value—in fact, more than half of the data points are either the highest possible value (80 degrees) or the lowest possible value (76 degrees). So it makes sense to say that the data for City B "deviate" from a "standard" value more than the data for City A, which probably means the standard deviation of the temperatures for City B is greater than that of City A, which means (B) must be right. Also notice that the College Board could have made this question much more challenging by making the data sets for the two cities more similar. If the data sets had been more similar, we might have actually had to calculate the standard deviation for each set to find the right answer. But the question was intentionally designed so that calculations wouldn't be necessary, and anyone with a general understanding of the term "standard deviation" could find the correct answer.

Test 4, Section 4, Question 24

- **What's the prompt asking for?** The radius of the circle.
- **Math concepts in the prompt:** arcs, diameters, π, radii
- **Math concepts in the diagram:** circles, diameters, labeled points
- **Elements of the answer choices:** integers
- **Notable differences among answer choices:** The choices form a series in which each choice is twice as much as the choice before it.

- **Pre-solution patterns (see p. 217):** halves and doubles; the first and last terms in a series are often wrong answers
- **Things to look out for:** Don't confuse arc $\overset{\frown}{ADB}$ with the circumference of the whole circle! Don't make small mistakes in your geometry or calculations! Be especially careful about a mistake that could cause you to be off by a factor of 2, since the College Board is clearly hoping you'll make a mistake like that!

Solution 1: Geometry: Determine the circumference of the circle, and use that to find the radius.

Arc $\overset{\frown}{ADB}$ must be a semi-circle, because it starts at one end of the circle's diameter and stops at the other end of the diameter. If the semi-circle has a length of 8π, then the full circumference of the circle must be twice as long, or 16π. Knowing this circumference allows us to find the radius using the formula $C = 2\pi r$, which appears at the beginning of each SAT Math section, in case you don't remember it. Let's apply the formula now:

$$C = 2\pi r \qquad \text{(formula relating circumference to radius)}$$
$$16\pi = 2\pi r \qquad \text{(plug in } C = 16\pi\text{)}$$
$$8 = r \qquad \text{(divide both sides by } 2\pi \text{ to find } r\text{)}$$

So we can see that (C) is correct.

Solution 2: Scale / test-smart: Note that the diagram is drawn to scale and that 8π is roughly 24 or 25, and then pick the answer choice that would result in a radius being drawn to the same scale as the arc.

When we visually compare the length of the diameter to the length of the given arc, we may be able to tell that the diameter would have a length in the range of 15 or 20 units; this would indicate that the radius has a length of probably a little less than 10 units or so. Only (C) is in that range, so it must be correct.

ANSWER CHOICE ANALYSIS

(A): This is half of (B). **(B):** This is half of the correct answer. This choice could be tempting for someone who got confused about the relationship between the radius of a circle and the diameter of a circle. **(D):** This is the length of the diameter of the circle.

How to check? Try an alternate approach above. Also try to figure out what kinds of small mistakes would lead an untrained test-taker to some of the wrong answers, and make sure you're not making similar mistakes.

▶ Post-solution patterns (see page 218): right answer to the wrong question; right approach, wrong step

Test 4, Section 4, Question 25

- **What's the prompt asking for?** The choice with a polynomial divisible by $2x + 3$.
- **Math concepts in the prompt:** algebra, arithmetic, dividing polynomials, polynomials
- **Elements of the answer choices:** algebraic expressions, equations, integers
- **Notable differences among answer choices:** (C) and (D) are "opposites" in the sense that (C) involves multiplying f by 2 and g by 3, while (D) involves multiplying f by 3 and g by 2.

(A) is the only choice without coefficients. (B) is similar to (C) in that both involve multiplying g by 3, but (B) doesn't multiply f by anything.

- **Concepts in the answer choices:** adding functions, multiplying functions
- **Pre-solution patterns (see p. 217):** wrong answers try to imitate right answers
- **Things to look out for:** Don't confuse f and g! Don't make any small mistakes in your algebra or arithmetic!

Solution 1: Test-smart / backsolving: Assign an arbitrary value to x, and use that x-value to find $f(x)$, $g(x)$, and $2x + 3$. Use the values of those expressions to identify the choice with a value that could be evenly divided by the value you found for $2x + 3$.

I'll arbitrarily decide to test $x = 5$. When I plug it into $f(x)$ and $g(x)$, and into $2x + 3$, I get the following results:

$$f(x) = 2(5)^3 + 6(5)^2 + 4(5) = 420 \qquad \text{(plug } x = 5 \text{ into } f(x))$$

$$g(x) = (5)^2 + 3(5) + 2 = 42 \qquad \text{(plug } x = 5 \text{ into } g(x))$$

$$2(5) + 3 = 13 \qquad \text{(plug } x = 5 \text{ into } 2x + 3)$$

Now I can plug these values for $f(x)$ and $g(x)$ into each of the answer choices, and see which one results in a number that can be evenly divided by 13, since 13 is the value of $2x + 3$ when $x = 5$. The results of this testing are below:

(A) $f(x) + g(x) = 420 + 42 = 462$ $\qquad \frac{462}{13} \approx 35.538$

(B) $f(x) + 3g(x) = 420 + 3(42) = 546$ $\qquad \frac{546}{13} = 42$

(C) $2f(x) + 3g(x) = 2(420) + 3(42) = 966$ $\qquad \frac{966}{13} \approx 74.308$

(D) $3f(x) + 2g(x) = 3(420) + 2(42) = 1344$ $\qquad \frac{1344}{13} \approx 103.385$

Only (B) can be divided evenly when $x = 5$, so (B) is correct, since the right answer must divide evenly for all values of x.

How to check? Carefully reconsider your reading and your calculations to make sure you haven't made any small mistakes.

Note The College Board includes another approach to this question in its explanations, but in my experience, that approach isn't something most test-takers will be comfortable attempting to execute on test day. The solution we just discussed is a great example of how we can use backsolving to work around a lot of complicated algebra and reliably arrive at the correct answer.

Test 4, Section 4, Question 26

- **What's the prompt asking for?** The choice that indicates the Roman numerals whose statements MUST be true.
- **Math concepts in the prompt:** absolute value, inequalities, negative numbers, opposites, Roman numeral questions, variables, zero
- **Elements of the answer choices:** Roman numerals

- **Notable differences among answer choices:** Roman numeral I must be true, since each choice includes it.
- **Pre-solution patterns (see p. 217):** wrong answers try to imitate right answers
- **Things to look out for:** Don't confuse x and y! Don't forget that it might be possible for either x or y to be positive or negative!

Solution 1: Concrete: Pick different sets of x-values and y-values that satisfy the prompt, and determine which Roman numerals are true with the values you've picked. Pick the choice that indicates the Roman numerals whose statements must always be true.

Let's say $y = 3$ and $x = 2$. This satisfies the prompts' requirements, since $-3 < 2 < 3$. We'll check each Roman numeral in turn:

$$|x| < y \qquad \text{(statement from Roman numeral I)}$$
$$|2| < 3 \qquad \text{(plug in } x = 2 \text{ and } y = 3)$$

We can see that this makes a true statement. After only testing one value, we can't say for sure yet that Roman numeral I *must* be true, but it's true in this case. Let's test the other statements:

$$x > 0 \qquad \text{(statement from Roman numeral II)}$$
$$2 > 0 \qquad \text{(plug in } x = 2)$$

Again, we can see that this makes a true statement, but we can't say for sure yet that Roman numeral II *must* be true in every case. Let's test Roman numeral III:

$$y > 0 \qquad \text{(statement from Roman numeral I)}$$
$$3 > 0 \qquad \text{(plug in } y = 3)$$

Once more, we can see that this makes a true statement, but we can't say for sure yet that Roman numeral III must always be true. Let's try each statement again with $y = 3$ and $x = -2$ to see what else we can learn:

$$|x| < y \qquad \text{(statement from Roman numeral I)}$$
$$|-2| < 3 \qquad \text{(plug in } x = -2 \text{ and } y = 3)$$

We see that this makes a true statement again, just as it did last time. In fact, when we look at the answer choices, we can see that each choice includes Roman numeral I, so we know that this statement must always be true. Let's focus on the next two statements:

$$x > 0 \qquad \text{(statement from Roman numeral II)}$$
$$-2 > 0 \qquad \text{(plug in } x = -2)$$

When we plug in $x = -2$, or any negative x-value, this statement will be false. So we know that II will not be part of the correct answer. Let's test Roman numeral III again:

$$y > 0 \qquad \text{(statement from Roman numeral I)}$$

We used the same y-value as before, so we know this statement will be true again. If we think about, in order for it to be true that $-y < x < y$, the y-value must *always* be positive. If y were negative, then $-y$ would be *greater than* y, and $-y < x < y$ wouldn't be true. So statement III must always be true. We already saw that statement I must be true as well, so (C) is the correct answer.

Solution 2: Abstract: Think about the properties of x and y from the prompt, and then determine which Roman numerals must be true based on those properties. It may be possible to ignore I in this analysis, since I is true in every answer choice.

When we consider the choices, we see that Roman Numeral I must be correct, no matter what, because it's in every choice. That allows us to focus on II and III.

II says, essentially, that x must be positive. But if we think about it, we see this isn't necessarily true—x can be a negative number as long as it's more than $-y$. For example, as we saw in solution 1, the statement from the prompt is true if $y = 3$ and $x = -2$. So we can tell that II doesn't have to be true.

III says that y has to be positive. If we think about this, we can see that it must be true, in at least two ways. For one thing, the inequality from the prompt indicates that $-y$ must be less than y, which can only be true if y is positive; for another thing, we know that Roman numeral I is true because it's part of every answer choice, and it would also require y to be positive, since y is presented as a number that's greater than the absolute value of x, and absolute values can't be negative.

So we can tell that I and III are both correct, which means the correct answer is (C).

How to check? Try an alternate approach above.

Note   This question relies much more heavily on mathematical properties and abstract concepts than it does on calculations or formulas, which means that a lot of untrained test-takers will struggle here, even though the ideas involved are actually pretty simple. Keep this kind of thing in mind as you continue your preparation!

Test 4, Section 4, Question 27

- **What's the prompt asking for?** The role of the number 61 in the equation from the prompt.
- **Math concepts in the prompt:** algebra, arithmetic, axis labels, equations, line of best fit, reading data from scatterplots, scatterplots, variables
- **Math concepts in the diagram:** axis labels, data points, line of best fit, reading data from scatterplots
- **Elements of the answer choices:** integers, sentences
- **Notable differences among answer choices:** (B), (C), and (D) view 61 as a percentage, while (A) views 61 as a number of dollars. (C) and (D) mention percentages of the national average, while (B) mentions a percentage of the highest cost. (C) and (D) are "opposites" in the sense that (C) mentions being below 61%, and (D) mentions being at least 61%.
- **Concepts in the answer choices:** percentages
- **Pre-solution patterns (see p. 217):** opposites; wrong answers try to imitate right answers
- **Things to look out for:** Don't confuse percentages with costs! Don't confuse the idea of being below a number with the idea of being at least as much as a number! Don't make small mistakes in your reading!

Solution 1: Abstract: Consider the differences among the answer choices described above in relation to the given scatterplot, and pick the answer choice that correctly describes the role of 61 in the equation from the prompt.

(A) must be wrong because the labeling on the figure clearly indicates that the graph doesn't provide any information about monthly costs in dollars, as this choice would require. It's also wrong because it draws a conclusion about the "lowest…cost in the United States," but the graph only provides data about "several large US cities."

(B) is also wrong, because it differs from the details of the figure—the figure says that the data on the graph is expressed as a "percent of national *average* cost" (emphasis added) while (B) talks about the "% of the *highest* housing cost" (emphasis added). (B) also has the same issue that (A) does in terms of the phrase "lowest…cost in the United States" being used when the prompt says the data only reflects "several large US cities," rather than the entire country. These small differences in wording are enough to make this choice wrong (note that this is exactly the kind of difference we might expect to see in a wrong answer on a Reading question or a Writing and Language question).

(C) will be tempting for a lot of untrained test-takers, but, as trained test-takers, we need to make sure that we understand what the line of best fit represents. The line of best fit represents a *trend* in data—not *actual* data. So even though the lowest y-value on the line of best fit is 61, it only represents a *trend* in relative housing cost; the actual data could be above or below the line of best fit. But this choice says, "costs were never below" 61% of the national average, which is something we can't know from the graph…again, because the line of best fit only tells us about trends, not about the housing costs of individual cities, or individual people in those cities.

(D) is the correct answer because the phrase "likely at least 61%" matches with the idea of averaging costs that we see in the figure and the prompt. We can see from both the equation and the line of best fit that the lowest theoretical population density (basically where $x = 0$) would probably have an average cost at least 61% of the national average—again, according to the trend indicated by the line of best fit. We know that the "average" of a set of costs represents roughly the middle or dominant value in those costs, and that any value from that set is "likely" to be at least as high as the average value from that set, by definition. In this case, that means that the housing cost when $x = 0$ would likely be at least 61% of the national average. Since this choice reflects that situation, we know it's correct.

How to check? Try to figure out what kinds of small mistakes would lead an untrained test-taker to some of the wrong answers, and make sure you're not making similar mistakes.

Note This is extremely similar to a data-based question that we might see on other sections of the test. Let this be one more reminder that careful, accurate reading is the most important skill on the entire SAT! See "Reading Graphs, Charts, Tables, and Other Figures" on page 44 for more on attacking this kind of question.

Test 4, Section 4, Question 28

- **What's the prompt asking for?** The choice with an equivalent expression for f that shows the lowest possible value of f as a coefficient or constant.
- **Math concepts in the prompt:** algebra, coefficients, constants, equivalent expressions, function definitions, functions, minimum value of a function
- **Elements of the answer choices:** algebraic expressions, exponents, integers

- **Notable differences among answer choices:** (A) and (B) include the number 24. (C) and (D) both include the number 1. (B) is the only choice that includes the number 2 as a coefficient or constant, while (D) is the only choice that includes the number 25.
- **"Bridge" concepts:** The minimum value of a parabola that opens up is the vertex of that parabola.
- **Pre-solution patterns (see p. 217):** wrong answers try to imitate right answers

Solution 1: Graphing: Graph the given equation on your calculator and note the lowest point of the function. Then pick the answer choice with a value that reflects the lowest point.

When we graph the function, we get this:

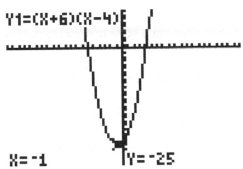

We can use the trace function on the calculator to tell that the lowest possible value of the function is $y = -25$. Since (D) is the only choice that includes this number, (D) is correct.

Solution 2: Algebra: Convert the given equation into vertex form, and pick the answer choice that matches.

The vertex form of a quadratic equation is $y = a(x - h)^2 + k$, where (h, k) is the vertex. We can convert the given function into vertex form by FOILing that expression, then completing the square.

$f(x) = (x + 6)(x - 4)$	(given function)
$f(x) = x^2 + 2x - 24$	(FOIL)
$f(x) + 24 = x^2 + 2x$	(add 24 to both sides of the equation)
$f(x) + 24 + 1 = x^2 + 2x + 1$	(Find half the coefficient of x, square it, and add that value to both sides.)
$f(x) + 24 + 1 = (x + 1)^2$	(rewrite the expression on the right as the square of a binomial)
$f(x) = (x + 1)^2 - 25$	(subtract 25 from both sides)

This form of the function matches (D), so (D) is correct.

How to check? Try an alternate approach above. Also try to figure out what kinds of small mistakes would lead an untrained test-taker to some of the wrong answers, and make sure you're not making similar mistakes.

Test 4, Section 4, Question 29

- **What's the prompt asking for?** The average of $x, y,$ and z in terms of m.
- **Math concepts in the prompt:** algebra, arithmetic mean, variables

- **Elements of the answer choices:** algebraic expressions, integers
- **Notable differences among answer choices:** (B), (C), and (D) form a series in which each answer choice is $m + 7$ more than the choice before it. (B) is one-third of (D), which may be relevant because the prompt mentions finding the average of three numbers, which will involve dividing by 3.

- **Pre-solution patterns (see p. 217):** halves and doubles; the first and last terms in a series are often wrong answers
- **Things to look out for:** Make sure you find the average of the numbers, and not their sum! Don't make any small mistakes in your reading, algebra, or arithmetic! Don't forget that $x, y,$ and z are described in terms of averages in the prompt!

Solution 1: Algebra: Separately determine the given values of $x, y,$ and z in terms of m, according to the prompt. Add these three expressions and divide them by 3 to find the average of $x, y,$ and z in terms of m.

$$x = \frac{m+9}{2} \qquad y = \frac{2m+15}{2} \qquad z = \frac{3m+18}{2}$$
($x, y,$ and z according to the prompt)

$$\frac{m+9}{2} + \frac{2m+15}{2} + \frac{3m+18}{2} = \frac{6m+42}{2} = 3m + 21$$
(sum of $x, y,$ and z)

$$\frac{3m+21}{3} = m + 7$$
(sum of $x, y,$ and z divided by 3)

So we can see that (B) is correct.

Solution 2: Concrete: Assign an arbitrary value to m and use that value to find $x, y,$ and z according to the prompt, as well as the expressions in the answer choices. Finally, average $x, y,$ and z, and pick the answer choice whose value matches the average.

I'll let $m = 4$, just as an arbitrary value for testing purposes. That lets us determine the following values for $x, y,$ and z:

$$x = \frac{m+9}{2} = \frac{(4)+9}{2} = \frac{13}{2}$$
(plug $m = 4$ into the definition of x from the prompt to find x when m is 4)

$$y = \frac{2m+15}{2} = \frac{2(4)+15}{2} = \frac{23}{2}$$
(plug $m = 4$ into the definition of y from the prompt to find y when m is 4)

$$z = \frac{3m+18}{2} = \frac{3(4)+18}{2} = \frac{30}{2} = 15$$
(plug $m = 4$ into the definition of z from the prompt to find z when m is 4)

$$\frac{\frac{13}{2} + \frac{23}{2} + 15}{3}$$
(add values of $x, y,$ and z and divide by 3 to find their average when m is 4)

$$\frac{\frac{36}{2} + 15}{3}$$
(simplify the numerator)

$$\frac{18 + 15}{3}$$
(simplify the numerator)

$$\frac{33}{3}$$
(simplify the numerator)

$$11$$
(simplify further to find the average when $m = 4$)

Now we need to test $m = 4$ in the answer choices to see which one matches the value of 11 that we just found:

A $m + 6 = 4 + 6 = 10$
B ✓ $m + 7 = 4 + 7 = 11$
C $2m + 14 = 8 + 14 = 22$
D $3m + 21 = 12 + 21 = 33$

We can see that (B) is correct.

ANSWER CHOICE ANALYSIS

(C): This is double the right answer, which is a common type of wrong answer on SAT Math sections. **(D):** This is the sum of $x, y,$ and z in terms of m, probably included to trick untrained test-takers who forget that the prompt asked us to find the average of those variables, not their sum.

How to check? Try an alternate approach above. Also try to figure out what kinds of small mistakes would lead an untrained test-taker to some of the wrong answers, and make sure you're not making similar mistakes.

▶   Post-solution patterns (see page 218): right approach, wrong step

Test 4, Section 4, Question 30

- **What's the prompt asking for?** The value of k in the given scenario.
- **Math concepts in the prompt:** constants, functions, solutions to a function, xy-coordinate plane

- **Math concepts in the diagram:** graphing functions, xy-coordinate plane

- **"Bridge" concepts:** $f(x) = k$ is a horizontal line; the solutions in the question must be points where $f(x) = k$ crosses the function graph in the prompt.
- **Elements of the answer choices:** integers, negative numbers, zero
- **Notable differences among answer choices:** (A) and (C) are opposites.
- **Pre-solution patterns (see p. 217):** opposites
- **Things to look out for:** Don't make any small mistakes in your reading, algebra, or arithmetic!

Solution 1: Graphing / abstract: Note that the $f(x) = k$ must be a horizontal line, and pick the value for k that results in a horizontal line that intersects the function in three places.

   A line at $f(x) = -3$ would cross the function in three places: at roughly $x = -1$, roughly $x = 0$, and roughly $x = 1.5$. The other k-values in the choices don't result in lines that would cross the function on the graph in three places, so (D) is right.

How to check? Carefully reconsider your reading and your reasoning.

Note   Many test-takers would assume this question must be hard because it involves a third-degree polynomial and graphing, but all we need to realize is that $f(x) = k$ is a horizontal line, and the solutions in the question must be points where $f(x) = k$ crosses the function graph in the prompt. We never need to manipulate the function in the prompt at all.

Test 4, Section 4, Question 31

- **What's the prompt asking for?** The number of gallons of water in the pool after 70 minutes.
- **Math concepts in the prompt:** arithmetic, constant rates, word problems
- **Things to look out for:** Don't forget that there were already 600 gallons of water in the pool before the hose was turned on! Don't make small mistakes in your arithmetic!

Solution 1: Arithmetic: Determine the amount of water that comes out of the hose after 70 minutes, and add that amount to the 600 gallons that were already in the pool.

   Since we're told that 8 gallons of water are added to the pool every minute for 70 minutes, we can find the number of gallons added to the pool if we multiply 8 by 70, which gives us 560. But don't forget the original 600 gallons!
   When we add 560 to 600, we get 1160 gallons in the pool, so the answer is 1160.

How to check? Carefully re-check your reading and your calculations.

Test 4, Section 4, Question 32

- **What's the prompt asking for?** The increase in millimeters of mercury that corresponds to an increase in 1 year of age, according to the given model.
- **Math concepts in the prompt:** algebra, arithmetic, fractions, function models, word problems
- **Things to look out for:** Don't confuse P and x! Don't be intimidated if you've never heard of the scientific terms in the prompt—you don't need to know what they mean in order to answer the question! Don't make small mistakes in reading, algebra, or arithmetic!

Solution 1: Concrete: Pick an arbitrary value for x and find the corresponding value of P; then, find the corresponding P-value when x is increased by 1. The change in P is the answer to the question.

I'll arbitrarily pick 20 as my first value for x. When $x = 20$, $P = \frac{(20)+220}{2} = \frac{240}{2} = 120$.

When $x = 21$, $P = \frac{(21)+220}{2} = \frac{241}{2} = 120.5$.

So increasing x from 20 to 21 led to an increase in P from 120 to 120.5, which is an increase of 0.5. That means the answer is 0.5.

Solution 2: Algebra / abstract: Note that any increase in x is divided by 2 in the formula, which means that increasing x by 1 will increase P by 0.5, so the answer is 0.5.

How to check? Try an alternate approach above.

Test 4, Section 4, Question 33

- **What's the prompt asking for?** The number of feet (to the nearest hundredth) in 75 Roman digits, given the length of a Roman digit described in the prompt.
- **Math concepts in the prompt:** rounding fractions, unit conversions, word problems
- **Things to look out for:** Don't confuse pes, feet, digits, and inches! Don't misread or mis-key the values related to the *pes* unit and the digit unit! Don't make any small mistakes in your reading or arithmetic as you convert! Don't forget that we divide when converting to larger units, and multiply when converting to smaller units! Don't forget that the question is

asking for the number of feet, not the number of inches!   and not to the nearest tenth or whole number!

Don't forget to round your answer to the nearest hundredth,

Solution 1: Arithmetic: Convert 75 digits to *pes*, convert that number of *pes* to inches, and then convert the inches to feet.

We can find the number of *pes* in 75 digits by dividing the number of digits by 16, since the prompt tells us that there are 16 digits in one *pes*. That conversion would look like this:

$$\frac{75}{16} = 4.6875 \quad \text{(divide 75 digits by 16 to find the number of \textit{pes} in 75 digits)}$$

Next, we can find the number of inches in 4.6875 *pes* by multiplying the number of *pes* by 11.65, since the prompt tells us that each *pes* is equal to 11.65 inches. That equation would look like this:

$$4.6785 \times 11.65 \approx 54.609 \quad \text{(multiply 4.6785 \textit{pes} by 11.65 to find the number of inches in 4.6785 \textit{pes})}$$

Now we know that 75 digits is equal to approximately 54.609 inches. Since there are 12 inches in a foot, we can divide 54.609 by 12 to find the approximate number of feet represented by 54.609 inches: $\frac{54.609}{12} \approx 4.551$ feet.

So, to the nearest hundredth of a foot, 75 digits is equal to 4.55 feet.

Solution 2: Faster arithmetic: Find the number of inches in 75 digits, and then convert the inches to feet. (This approach uses a ratio to find the answer a little more quickly than we did in the last solution.)

We can find the number of inches in 75 digits by setting up an equation between the ratio of digits to inches in one *pes*, and the ratio of 75 digits to an unknown number of *pes*. That equation would look like this:

$$\frac{16}{11.65} = \frac{75}{x} \quad \text{(equate ratio of digits in one \textit{pes} to inches, and ratio of 75 digits to an unknown number of \textit{pes})}$$

$$16x = 873.75 \quad \text{(cross multiply)}$$

$$x \approx 54.609 \quad \text{(divide both sides by 16 to find the number of inches in 75 digits)}$$

So 75 digits is equal to approximately 54.609 inches. Since there are 12 inches in a foot, we can divide 54.609 by 12 to find the approximate number of feet represented by 54.609 inches: $\frac{54.609}{12} \approx 4.551$ feet.

Again, we can see that, to the nearest hundredth of a foot, 75 digits is equal to 4.55 feet.

How to check? Carefully re-check your reading and your calculations.

<hr>

Test 4, Section 4, Question 34

- **What's the prompt asking for?** The number of additional male bats that must be tagged so three-fifths of the bats in the study are male, under the circumstances in the prompt.
- **Math concepts in the prompt:** fractions, ratios, scientific studies, word problems

- **Things to look out for:** Don't confuse the components of the ratio! Don't confuse male and female bats! Don't forget about the extra 100 female bats that are tagged after the initial tagging! Don't make any small mistakes in your reading, algebra, or arithmetic!

Solution 1: Algebra: Write an equation that relates the number of male bats, the number of female bats, the necessary additional male bats, and the desired proportion of male bats; then, solve to find the number of additional male bats that must be tagged.

We know that the prompt is asking us for the proportion of male bats to "the total number of bats in the study," so we'll need to create a fraction with the final number of male bats in the numerator, and the total number of tagged bats in the denominator.

We know that the initial number of male bats is 240; let's use x to indicate the number of additional male bats, since that's part of what the prompt is asking for. So the total number of male bats at the end of the tagging will be $240 + x$.

The total number of bats will have to include all the male bats and all the female bats in both rounds of tagging. That works out to $240 + 160 + 100 + x$, where x is the number of additional male bats being tagged, as we discussed above. So the ratio of male bats to total bats after all the tagging can be expressed as $\frac{240+x}{240+160+100+x}$. Now we can set that equal to $\frac{3}{5}$ and solve for x:

$$\frac{3}{5} = \frac{240+x}{240+160+100+x} \quad \text{($\frac{3}{5}$ set equal to ratio of male bats to total bats, as required in the prompt)}$$

$$\frac{3}{5} = \frac{240+x}{500+x} \quad \text{(simplify)}$$

$$1500 + 3x = 1200 + 5x \quad \text{(cross multiply)}$$

$$1500 = 1200 + 2x \qquad \text{(subtract } 3x \text{ from both sides)}$$

$$300 = 2x \qquad \text{(subtract 1200 from both sides)}$$

$$150 = x \qquad \text{(divide both sides by 2)}$$

So we can see that 150 is correct.

Solution 2: Arithmetic: Note that 240 male bats and 160 female bats already add up to a proportion in which three-fifths of the bats are male; in this proportion, there are 50% more male bats than female bats. To maintain this proportion after 100 more female bats are added, we need to add a number of male bats that's 50% more than the 100 female bats added—so we'll need 150 more male bats. Again, we see that the answer is 150.

How to check? Try an alternate approach above. Also carefully reconsider your reading and calculating.

Test 4, Section 4, Question 35

- **What's the prompt asking for?** The ratio of the pressure of the faster fluid to the pressure of the slower fluid.
- **Math concepts in the prompt:** algebra, arithmetic, constants, exponents, fractions, function modeling, ratios, word problems

- **Things to look out for:** Don't get overwhelmed if you've never heard of the technical terms in the question! You don't need to know what they mean in order to answer the question correctly. Don't confuse the variables in the expression! Don't reverse the ratio! Don't make any small mistakes in your reading, algebra, or arithmetic!

Solution 1: Concrete: Pick an arbitrary value for v and find the corresponding q-value; then, find the q-value that corresponds to a v-value that's 1.5 times your original v-value. The answer to the question is the ratio of the second q-value to the first q-value.

Let's arbitrarily pick a v-value of 4 to start:

$$q = \tfrac{1}{2}nv^2 \qquad \text{(given formula)}$$

$$q = \tfrac{1}{2}n(4)^2 \qquad \text{(plug in } v = 4)$$

$$q = 8n \qquad \text{(simplify to find } q \text{ when } v = 4)$$

Now let's do the same thing with a v-value that's 1.5 times our original v-value, as the prompt requires. In our case, that would be a new v-value of 6:

$$q = \tfrac{1}{2}nv^2 \qquad \text{(given formula)}$$

$$q = \tfrac{1}{2}n(6)^2 \qquad \text{(plug in } v = 6 \text{ for the second } v\text{-value)}$$

$$q = 18n \qquad \text{(simplify to find } q \text{ when } v = 6)$$

Now we can see that the ratio of the dynamic pressure of the faster fluid to the dynamic pressure of the slower fluid is $\frac{18n}{8n}$, which is equal to $\frac{9}{4}$, so the answer is $\frac{9}{4}$.

Solution 2: Abstract / algebra: Note that part of the process for finding q involves squaring the value of v. This means that any change in v will result in the square of that change happening to q, so multiplying v by 1.5 will result in multiplying the q-value by 1.5^2, which is the same thing as $\frac{3}{2} \times \frac{3}{2}$, which is the same thing as $\frac{9}{4}$. So, again, the correct answer is $\frac{9}{4}$.

How to check? Try an alternate approach above.

Test 4, Section 4, Question 36

- **What's the prompt asking for?** One possible integer value of x, given the situation in the prompt.
- **Math concepts in the prompt:** arcs, centers of circles, circles, integers, multiple possible solutions, radii, ranges of values
- **Math concepts in the diagram:** arcs, centers of circles, circles, degree measurements of angles, labeled points, radii, variables

- **Things to look out for:** Don't forget that the diagram is NOT drawn to scale! Don't forget that there might be more than one possible correct answer! Don't forget the difference between radius and diameter! Don't confuse the length of the radius with the length of the arc! Don't forget that you need to find a possible *integer* value for x! Don't make any small mistakes in your geometry, algebra, arithmetic, or reading!

Solution 1: Geometry: Assign a length of 10 to the radius and determine the circumference of the circle. After that, determine the range of values for the portion of the circle that would be represented by an arc of 5 to 6 units. Then find the corresponding proportion of 360 to determine a corresponding value for x; if your x-value isn't an integer, then round it to the nearest integer and re-test that x-value to see if it allows for an arc length between 5 and 6.

$C = 2\pi r$	(formula for circumference)
$C = 2\pi 10$	(plug in $r = 10$ from the prompt)
$C \approx 62.832$	(calculate circumference)
$\dfrac{5}{62.832} \approx 0.0796$	(approximate minimum proportion of circle represented by arc $\overset{\frown}{AB}$)
$\dfrac{6}{62.832} \approx 0.0955$	(approximate maximum proportion of circle represented by arc $\overset{\frown}{AB}$)

So x can be between approximately 7.96% of 360 and 9.55% of 360°, which means it's between approximately 28.656° and 34.38°. The question asks for an integer value of x, so correct answers would be 29, 30, 31, 32, 33, or 34.

How to check? Carefully reconsider your reading and your calculations.

Test 4, Section 4, Question 37

- **What's the prompt asking for?** The proper value for r in the model for the stock price.
- **Math concepts in the prompt:** algebra, arithmetic, constant rate, exponents, function modeling, percentage decrease, price, word problems

- **Things to look out for:** Don't confuse $r, t,$ and V! Don't forget that percentage decrease is calculated from the starting amount, not from the ending amount! Don't forget that we divide by 100 when converting a percentage to a decimal! Don't make any small mistakes in your reading or arithmetic!

Solution 1: Concrete: Find the price of the stock after it decreases by 28 percent three times. Set that price as V in the given model, set t equal to 3, and solve for r.

When something decreases by 28%, what's left is 72%, because $100\% - 28\% = 72\%$. We can find the result of a number decreasing by 28% three times if we multiply the original number by 72% three times. So after three weeks, the $360 stock would have decreased by 28% three times, which means we could find its new value by multiplying $360 by 0.72 three times:
$$\$360(0.72)(0.72)(0.72) = \$134.36928.$$

Let's use those ideas to find r:

$V = 360(r)^t$	(given equation)
$134.36928 = 360(r)^3$	(plug in $V = 134.36928$ and $t = 3$ to reflect the values we just used)
$0.373248 = r^3$	(divide both sides by 360)
$0.72 = r$	(take cube root of both sides)

So we can see that r is 0.72, which is the same as the 72% value we just discussed. So the right answer is 0.72.

Solution 2: Abstract / algebra: Carefully read the prompt and note that r corresponds to the idea of decreasing by 28%, and repeating this decrease every week. Since decreasing a number by 28% is the same thing as finding 72% of the number, and finding 72% of a number is the same thing as multiplying by 0.72, we know that r is 0.72.

How to check? Try an alternate approach above.

Test 4, Section 4, Question 38

- **What's the prompt asking for?** The price that the analyst expects the stock to have after three weeks.
- **Math concepts in the prompt:** algebra, arithmetic, constant rate, exponents, function modeling, percentage decrease, price, word problems

- **Things to look out for:** Don't confuse $r, t,$ and V! Don't forget that percentage decrease is calculated from the starting amount, not the ending amount! Don't forget that we divide by 100 when converting a percentage to a decimal! Don't make any small mistakes in your reading or arithmetic! Don't forget to round to the nearest dollar like the prompt requires!

Solution 1: Concrete: Multiply $360 by 0.72 to find the price of the stock after it has decreased by 28% the first time. Then take that new price and multiply by 0.72 again to find the price after the stock has decreased by 28% a second time. Finally, multiply this new price by 0.72 a third time, to find the price after it has decreased by 28% for the third time. Remember to round to the nearest dollar.

$$\$360(0.72)(0.72)(0.72) = \$134.36928$$

After we round this value to the nearest dollar as the prompt requires, the answer is $134.

Solution 2: Algebra: Using the formula from the prompt, set r equal to 0.72 and t equal to 3, and find V. Remember to round!

$$V = 360(r)^t \qquad \text{(given equation)}$$
$$V = 360(0.72)^3 \qquad \text{(plug in } r = 0.72 \text{ and } t = 3\text{)}$$
$$V = 134.36928 \qquad \text{(calculate)}$$

Again, we have to round this value to $134 to satisfy the prompt.

How to check? Try an alternate approach above.

Part 9: Writing and Language Section Training and Walkthroughs

By now, we've addressed the Reading and Math sections of the SAT. We've seen how those sections are designed in a way that rewards careful reading and attention to detail above all. We've also seen that the SAT Reading section requires very little outside knowledge beyond the meanings of terms like "argument" and "undermine," while the SAT Math sections require a bit of subject-matter knowledge that you've probably learned in school. Now we'll turn our attention to the Writing and Language section, which requires us to know some basic principles of grammar, style, and punctuation. But, just as with the other sections, we'll find that the best way to attack this section is to stay focused on careful reading, attention to detail, and SAT-specific strategies that let us exploit the weaknesses inherent in the test's design.

In this part of the SAT Prep Black Book, you'll learn the following:

- the most important secret of the SAT Writing and Language section
- the two major groups of questions on this section
- how demonstration and restatement, which we discussed for the SAT Reading section, apply here as well
- all about the specific types of questions within each group, and how to approach them
- the specific grammatical rules that appear on the SAT—many of which might seem outdated to a lot of teachers
- the unwritten rules that shape this section
- the hidden patterns that often appear among answer choices, and how to use them on test day
- how to recognize intervening phrases and work around them
- two key phrases that are used in a unique way in the prompts for questions on this section, and what they mean
- how to use "parallelism" to determine which choice is correct when the rules of grammar alone aren't enough
- the recommended process for answering questions on this section
- and more . . .

SAT Writing and Language Training

Thus I got into my bones the essential structure of the ordinary British sentence, which is a noble thing.
Winston Churchill

Overview and Important Reminders for the SAT Writing and Language Section

Before we dive into the two major question groups on this section, we need to clear up a few misconceptions that often keep people from doing as well on the SAT Writing and Language section as they could.

Let's get started.

The Big Secrets of SAT Writing and Language

There are two big secrets on the SAT Writing and Language section, because the question types on this section fall into two major groups, each with its own rules and its own big secret. These groups are my own personal classifications, not official classifications from the SAT, so you won't see them listed or described this way on the actual SAT.

The names of the groups are pretty self-explanatory:

- Reading Comprehension questions
- Grammar/Style/Punctuation questions

We'll get into the details of each group shortly, but first let's talk about each group's big secret.

The Big Secret of Reading Comprehension Questions

The big secret of the Reading Comprehension questions on the SAT Writing and Language section is that they work a lot like the questions from the Reading section of the SAT: each question has one clear, definite, right answer . . . and three clear, definite, wrong answers. And we can always find the right answer through a plain, literal reading of the text, with no literary interpretation or judgment calls.

(Remember that this is very different from what most students encounter in a classroom setting, as we discussed in the Reading training. In most English or Literature classrooms, almost any interpretation is accepted as long as it's vaguely connected to the text.)

But there are a few minor differences between the Reading section on the one hand, and the Reading Comprehension questions on the Writing and Language section on the other hand. We need to be aware of them if we want to maximize our performance on test day.

Demonstration vs restatement

The first difference is that questions on the Writing and Language part of the test generally depend a little more on literal demonstration, rather than on restatement. (To be clear, you'll still see some questions on the Writing and Language section that do depend on restatement, just as you'll see some question on the Reading section that depend on demonstration. But the balance is shifted a little more towards demonstration on this part of the SAT, just as it's shifted a little more towards restatement on the Reading part.)

Remember our definitions of restatement and demonstration from our discussion of the SAT Reading section:

- Restatement refers to the idea of two different phrases using synonymous wording to express the same idea, often with parallel structures. For example, if one part of a passage says,

  Arbor Day was Kate's favorite holiday every year,

  and an answer choice says,

  Kate always preferred Arbor Day to all other official celebrations,

  then we can say those two phrases *restate* each other: each phrase expresses the idea that Arbor Day is Kate's favorite holiday, using synonymous wording.

- Demonstration refers to a situation in which one phrase provides an example of a situation described in another phrase. If a prompt asks whether to include a sentence that says

  To me, the worst part about living in a haunted house is getting pranked by ghosts in the shower.

  and an answer choice says that the sentence

  provides an opinion about a negative aspect of life in a haunted house,

  then we can say that the sentence *demonstrates* the idea from the answer choice, even though the two phrases aren't synonymous restatements of each other. In other words, the sentence and the answer choice don't express precisely the same idea, but the sentence demonstrates the idea from the answer choice by providing an example of it. The answer choice describes the sentence accurately and literally in a way that isn't open to interpretation.

(For more on this topic, see the discussion of restatement and demonstration starting on page 59 in this Black Book.)

More sub-types with specific rules

The other difference we need to keep in mind between questions for the Writing and Language section and questions on the Reading section is that questions on this section depend a little more on specific rules and processes for each sub-type, and a little less on one broad rule that will apply to every question. We'll start covering the rules for those sub-types on page 431.

The Big Secret of Grammar/Style/Punctuation Questions

The big secret of the Grammar/Style/Punctuation questions is that they don't quite follow the rules and conventions that many educated people follow when they write or speak in American English today. Instead, these questions follow the rules that the College Board has decided they should follow, which might loosely be described as the rules that governed standard written American English in the early-to-mid 20th century. (We'll cover exactly what those rules are later in this section, in the Grammar/Style/Punctuation Toolbox starting on page 435.)

Most untrained test-takers don't realize this. Whenever they come across a new Grammar/Style/Punctuation question, they just try to identify the choice that sounds best to *them*, the way they would phrase things if they were writing or talking in school.

This is a huge mistake. By now we should realize that the SAT doesn't care what seems right to you, or to me, or to anybody else who doesn't write the SAT. So instead of looking at an SAT question and answering based on what sounds good to us, we should be answering based on what the test consistently rewards. That's all. What you and I think sounds good or bad isn't important if it disagrees with the College Board's standards.

Let me say that again: when you're faced with a Grammar/Style/Punctuation question, you should immediately ask yourself which answer satisfies the College Board's rules and patterns for that type of question.

When we talked about the Reading section earlier in this Black Book, we said that one of the biggest reasons people struggle with those questions is that they're used to classroom discussions in which almost any interpretation of a text has some value, while the SAT Reading section only rewards a literal reading of each text. Well, a lot of test-takers have a similar issue when it comes to Grammar/Style/Punctuation questions, because most English teachers have very loose standards for grammar and writing style. This means that most test-takers find the College Board penalizes them for things that their English teachers would accept.

For example, many people are taught in school that a comma can be placed almost anywhere in a sentence, whether to indicate that a reader would take a breath at that point in the sentence if it were being read out loud, or just to break up a lot of text, or for any number of other reasons. But Grammar/Style/Punctuation questions don't reward us for using commas like that—instead, they have their own rigid rules about comma usage. Similarly, many test-takers would also naturally use apostrophes and pronouns in ways the College Board doesn't reward. Again, we'll cover the College Board's rules for these things in the Grammar/Style/Punctuation Toolbox starting on page 435.

(By the way, don't be nervous if you don't know what a pronoun is, or if there are other technical grammatical terms you're not familiar with! In a few pages, I'll explain the terms that will help you understand how the SAT operates. And remember that the SAT itself will never require us to know the name of a grammatical concept in order to answer a question correctly.)

Conclusion

Just as we learned to attack the questions on the Reading section in a systematic and dependable way—even though they mostly ask us to do things we don't normally do in school—we can learn to beat SAT Writing and Language questions in a reliable way. As before, we'll use an approach that's tailored to the repetitive patterns and issues that come up in this part of the test. We'll see that most of the questions in the SAT Writing and Language section test only a handful of concepts over and over again; they just do it in a way that's different from what we see in school. (By now, that should be no surprise :))

Now that we've addressed some of the important preliminary issues with the SAT Writing and Language section, let's talk about the different major types of questions that can appear on the section.

SAT Writing and Language Question Groups

As we discussed earlier, I generally encourage test-takers to think of the questions on the SAT Writing and Language section as falling into two major groups:

1. Reading Comprehension questions
2. Grammar/Style/Punctuation questions

Training yourself to recognize the attributes of these groups of questions will make it easier for you to focus on the concepts that might be tested in a question. This, in turn, will make the SAT Writing and Language section easier to approach.

Don't get stressed out at the thought of learning to recognize these groups! It'll become second nature pretty quickly, and it's not really something that can lead you to a wrong answer if you do it wrong; it'll usually just save you some time if you do it right. As I said, it's more about helping you focus your mind on the specific tricks the College Board is trying to play on you with a given question.

Now let's talk about each group in more detail, and about some of the major issues that the SAT will test with them.

Reading Comprehension Questions

Reading Comprehension questions on the Writing and Language test are relatively easy to spot because most questions with prompts will primarily focus on reading comprehension (as opposed to questions that simply offer a set of answer choices without a prompt, which usually focus on grammar, style, and/or punctuation).

The correct answers to these questions generally reward the same kind of literal approach to the text, prompt, and answer choices that we've already seen in the Reading section: either they plainly demonstrate the concepts and relationships from the prompt, or the relevant text plainly demonstrates the concept described in the correct answer choice.

As you might imagine, we'll also find that the wrong-answer choices on these kinds of questions are frequently similar to the types of wrong answers we'll encounter on the Reading section: some wrong answers will directly contradict the relevant text, some will confuse the relationships among concepts from the text, some will be largely irrelevant, and so on.

There are a few different specific forms that these questions frequently take. We'll look at them now.

"Best accomplishes X"

Some questions will ask which answer choice best accomplishes a goal of the author, such as providing an example that's similar to one in the text, or supporting the author's primary claim. We'll find that the correct answer is always the only one that plainly and directly demonstrates the idea required by the prompt.

We can see a real-life example of this question type in question 2 from the Writing and Language section of SAT Practice Test #3. The prompt of the question asks which answer choice "provides the most appropriate introduction to the passage." The title of the passage is "Shed Some Light on the Workspace," and we can see that the passage repeatedly discusses the ideas of "artificial lighting" and "natural lighting" in work settings. (B) is the correct answer because it's the only choice that actually mentions an idea from the passage: it mentions natural light, while the other choices mention things like temperature, energy loss, and accommodations for workers, which aren't mentioned in the passage. (For a more complete discussion of this question, see its walkthrough on page 504 of this Black Book.)

Notice that the College Board didn't include more than one choice that mentioned lighting in the workplace, which would require us to choose the "best" one—instead, only one choice was even related to the topic of the passage, which made that choice clearly right and the others clearly wrong. Remember that on a real SAT question there will always be a clear, objective reason that the right answer is right and the wrong answers are wrong!

Transition words (and phrases)

There are a lot of instances in SAT Writing and Language passages in which you'll see what I call "transition words." (This isn't a formal grammatical concept—it's just an easy way to think about this idea in the context of the SAT.)

"Transition words" are just words that indicate some type of relationship between the idea before the transition and the idea after the transition. Here are some examples of the kinds of words I'm talking about:

- likewise
- therefore
- however
- for instance
- nevertheless
- furthermore
- previously
- although

The SAT likes to ask us to select the transition that reflects the appropriate connection between the idea in the previous sentence and the idea in the sentence in question. For example, the SAT would consider this underlined transition word to be ACCEPTABLE:

My brother likes to watch most sports on TV. However, he doesn't enjoy watching tennis.

In this case, the word "however" appropriately indicates that the second sentence provides information which is unexpected based on the information in the first sentence, or somehow opposed to the idea in the first sentence: the first sentence says my brother likes to watch most sports on TV, but the second sentence says he doesn't like to watch a particular sport.

But a transition word like the following would be UNACCEPTABLE on the SAT Writing and Language section:

*My brother likes to watch most sports on TV. Therefore, he doesn't enjoy watching tennis.

The word "therefore" would indicate that the information in the second sentence is the logical result of the information in the first sentence, but that isn't the case here.

We always need to make sure that we choose the transition word that correctly demonstrates the relationship between the previous sentence and the given sentence.

For a real-life example of this question type, we can look at question 9 from the Writing and Language section of SAT Practice Test #1. That question gives us four options to start a sentence that provides nutritional information about Greek yogurt. We can see that the previous sentence provides other nutritional information about Greek yogurt. In this case, the correct transition word is choice (A), "also," because the relevant sentence provides more information that is similar to the information in the previous sentences.

Choice (B), "in other words," is wrong, because the relevant sentence isn't a restatement of the information from the previous sentence. Choice (C), "therefore," is also wrong, because the sentence isn't a logical conclusion based on the information from the previous sentence. Finally, (D), "for instance," is wrong, because the sentence isn't an example of a concept in the previous sentence.

We can see that the correct answer clearly reflects the relationship between the information in the previous sentence and the information in the given sentence, and the wrong answers all fail to do that. (For a more detailed discussion of this question, see its walkthrough on page 468 of this Black Book.)

Sentence or paragraph placement

Some questions will ask where a sentence or paragraph should be placed. In a question like this, the College Board wants sentences and paragraphs to appear in a sequence that makes them refer to each other in a logical order, and that arranges events in a logical order.

For example, if one sentence says,

> My neighbor had a dog named Snowflake.

then that sentence needs to come before a sentence that says,

> That dog would follow her everywhere.

It wouldn't make sense to use the word "that" to refer to the dog unless a previous sentence had already introduced the idea of the dog, and it wouldn't make sense to use the pronoun "her" to refer to my neighbor unless my neighbor has already been mentioned.

Also, if one sentence refers to something in another sentence, then the College Board will want those sentences to appear as close to each other as possible. Let's look at a real-life example: question 5 from the Writing and Language section of SAT Practice Test #1. That question asks about the correct placement for sentence 5, which says,

> If it is improperly introduced into the environment, acid-whey runoff can pollute waterways, depleting the oxygen content of streams and rivers as it decomposes.

In its original placement, that sentence describes the difficulties associated with getting rid of acid-whey—but it appears after sentences 3 and 4, which tell us about the solution to that problem.

The idea of the acid whey being "difficult to dispose of" doesn't appear until the end of sentence 2. Only (C) allows us to put sentence 5 immediately after sentence 2. This placement lets us put the sentence that describes the difficulty of disposing acid whey immediately *after* the sentence that introduces the idea of that difficulty, and immediately *before* the sentences with solutions for the difficulty. It makes sense to the College Board that we'd provide additional information about a problem after that problem has been introduced, but before the solution to that problem has been discussed, instead of just jumping around from briefly describing a problem to mentioning its solutions and then going back to broader implications of the problem, which is what the original version of the paragraph does. (C) allows the ideas in the paragraph to be grouped together and presented in a logical order, so (C) is right. (For a more detailed discussion of this question, see its walkthrough on page 466 of this Black Book.)

Vocabulary in context

Some questions on the SAT Writing and Language section will include an underlined word or phrase, and three alternatives for that word or phrase in the answer choices. There won't be any punctuation involved, or different forms of the same word—just four different words or phrases (the original, plus three alternatives) with somewhat similar meanings.

The words in the answer choices will often be words you could probably use interchangeably in a classroom discussion, but their specific meanings won't be quite the same, and one will clearly be a better choice than the others when you think carefully about the meaning of each word and the sentence where it will be inserted.

Typically, these words and phrases aren't unusual or exotic—they tend to be words that test-takers are familiar with, but whose precise meanings might not be something the average test-taker normally pays close attention to.

The key to answering these questions correctly is to think in a precise way about what each relevant word actually means, and what it can be used to describe. For a real-life example, look at question 40 on the Writing and Language section of SAT Practice Test #3 from the College Board. That question asks us whether the word "decreed," "commissioned," "forced," or "licensed" is the best word to use in a sentence about museum officials having paintings made.

All of these words might seem to be vaguely appropriate to a situation that involves creating new works of art, but we know by now that the SAT isn't satisfied if we just pick an answer choice that's vaguely appropriate. Instead, we need to think about what each word actually means, and how it fits into the given context.

The first choice describes the officials "decree[ing]" the paintings. Does that really make sense? We might know that a decree is a kind of official statement or command, but does it make sense to say that officials "decree" an object directly? If we're familiar with the use of "decree" as a verb, we may realize that it's usually related to creating a new rule, rather than a physical object, and it's often followed by the word "that," as in "the Mayor decreed that today would be a holiday." So "decreed" isn't an appropriate fit for the sentence in question 40. (Keep reading to see what we might need to do with this question if we don't know the word "decreed," or any of the other words in the answer choices.)

How about "commissioned?" This means something like "requested that an artist create a new work for pay," which fits exactly with the situation described in the rest of the paragraph—note that the text says the artist was "chosen" for the "task" of creating the paintings.

What about the word "forced?" This word has some of the same issues that we saw with the word "decreed:" the passage doesn't describe the museum officials using some kind of royal force or power to get something done. When they "chose" Zakirov to be the painter, there's no indication that they threatened him in order to get him to paint the cats, or made him do anything against his will.

Finally, let's consider the word "licensed," which is loosely related to the idea of art, but not directly relevant to the passage. When an artwork is "licensed," an existing piece of art is allowed to be used for a new purpose by the person who owns the rights to it. So we can see that "licensed" makes no sense in this context.

As we said before, if you just skimmed these answer choices, or if you heard any of them used in this context in a classroom discussion, you might think any of them could be adequate. But if you take the time to think carefully about each one, you'll find that only (B) can make sense. (For more on this question, see its walkthrough on page 522 in this Black Book.)

So when you see a question like this, be sure to check the context, including the sentences before and after the one in question, to see which key phrases you can find to determine your answer.

And if you run into a question with words you don't know, you may well be able to work around them. In the example we just used, for instance, some test-takers might not know the word "decreed." But if they have decent ideas of the meanings of the other three words and they insist on finding a good match, they can realize that "commissioned" exactly restates the concepts from the paragraph, which means it must be correct, no matter what the word "decreed" means—remember that there can only be one answer choice that fits the relevant text, and that choice must be correct.

Figure

The SAT Writing and Language section includes figure questions that are very similar to the ones we saw in the Reading section, and we answer them in basically the same way: we use the principles discussed in the section of this Black Book called "Reading Graphs, Charts, Tables, and Other Figures" on page 44 to evaluate the graph or table that's cited in the prompt, and then we pick the answer choice that reflects the data accurately.

As an example of this kind of question, let's consider question 12 from the Writing and Language section of SAT Practice Test #1. That question asks for the choice that "most accurately and effectively represents the information in the graph." Only one choice actually reflects the information in the graph, and that's the correct answer, choice (B). The other choices all directly contradict the information presented in the graph. (For a complete discussion of this example question, see its walkthrough on page 469 of this Black Book.)

Including or excluding a phrase or sentence

Sometimes the question will tell you that the author is considering including or excluding a phrase or sentence. The prompt might refer to a sentence already in the passage and say the author is considering deleting or keeping that sentence, or the prompt might present a new sentence and ask whether the sentence should be added. In either situation, you'll see two answer choices that say the sentence should be included in the text and two answer choices that say the sentence shouldn't be included in the text, and each choice will include a comment about the role of the sentence in the text.

There are three rules we can use to find the correct answer to this type of question. We'll often find that we only need to consider the first rule, because that rule is often enough by itself to allow us to identify the right answer with certainty. In some cases, though, we'll need to consider the other rules as well. Let's discuss these three rules in order of importance.

The first rule: plain, literal description of the sentence's role in the text

Before we discuss the first rule, I want to make it clear that we have to apply it by *ignoring* the part of each answer choice that says whether the sentence should be included in the text (such as the words "yes," "no," "added," or "deleted.") For the first rule, we'll *only* focus on what each choice says about the role of the sentence in the text.

With that in mind, the first rule is that the relationship between the sentence and the rest of the text will be plainly and literally restated or demonstrated by the correct answer. So remember not to interpret anything when considering the comment—you're just looking for choices that plainly describe what the sentence or phrase is doing, relying on the same principle of careful reading that we'll use throughout the SAT.

(Also remember that, when we apply this rule, we're only thinking about how the comment in the answer choice describes *the sentence referred to in the prompt*. In other words, if the sentence mentioned in the prompt says something like "There are lots of role models who live good lives," and then the following sentences list the names of those role models, then it's not true to say that the sentence in the prompt "provides examples relevant to the argument in the passage." In this made-up scenario, *the sentence itself* doesn't provide any examples at all—it only mentions that examples exist. The actual examples are mentioned in *other* sentences. This kind of distinction is very important, because we'll often see wrong answers that accurately describe other sentences in the paragraph, or describe the paragraph as a whole, or even describe ideas found elsewhere in the passage—but we must focus only on the sentence or phrase that the prompt is actually asking about. We can see an example of this concept in action in choice (C) from question 6 on section 2 of SAT Practice Test #1. That choice says that the sentence in question "continues the explanation of how acid whey can be disposed of safely." Earlier sentences in the passage do continue that explanation, but the sentence in question does not—so we know that (C) is wrong. For a complete discussion of that question, see its walkthrough on page 466 of this Black Book.)

As we said before, on most questions about whether a sentence should be included in a paragraph, you'll only need to consider the rule we just discussed in order to answer the question. In other words, when you eliminate all the answer choices that don't accurately describe the relationship of the sentence to the rest of the text, only one choice will remain, and it will be the right answer.

We can see this first rule in action when we look at question 28 from the Writing and Language section of SAT Practice Test #1. The sentence mentioned in the prompt is the last sentence in a paragraph that "explain[s] [what] coworking spaces are," and that last sentence is the only sentence in the paragraph that says anything about "launching a new coworking business," or about the cost of anything. The only choice that accurately describes the relationship of the sentence to the rest of the text is (C), so (C) is the right answer to the question. (C) mentions the idea of a "loosely related detail," accurately describing the relationship of the sentence in the prompt to the rest of the paragraph. (For a full discussion of this question, see its walkthrough on page 476 of this Black Book.)

Now, sometimes you'll find that *two* choices have comments that accurately, literally describe the relationship of the prompt sentence to the paragraph, which means the first rule won't be enough to allow you to find the correct answer by itself. In that case, you'll need to apply the second rule of this question type to the remaining choices.

The second rule: follow all the other rules for Reading Comprehension questions on this section

Any sentence still under consideration after we apply the first rule must follow all the broader standards of ideal sentences and paragraphs on the SAT Writing and Language test. Those standards are basically the following:

- DO include relevant details and examples
- DO include introductions for ideas that appear in the next sentence
- DO include a transition between ideas that are different
- DO include a transition between paragraphs
- DO include phrases that reflect relationships present in the text
- DON'T include irrelevant ideas that aren't obviously connected to the text or don't get explained or discussed elsewhere.

So if there's more than one answer choice left after we apply the first rule, then the correct answer will be the one that correctly says to include or exclude the sentence based on the standards we just listed.

We can see the second rule in action on question 6 from the Writing and Language section of SAT Practice Test #1. The underlined sentence from that question tells us that conservation efforts related to the environmental impact of producing Greek yogurt are "well worth the effort."

Only choices (B) and (D) for that question pass the first test we described above:

- Choice (B) says the underlined sentence

  > fails to support the main argument of the passage as introduced in the first paragraph

  When we look back to the first paragraph, we can see that the main argument introduced there is that Greek yogurt

  > has grown enormously in popularity in the United States since it was first introduced

  So it's correct to say, as (B) does, that the underlined sentence doesn't support the idea of Greek yogurt getting increasingly popular in the United States, because the underlined sentence doesn't even mention the idea of Greek yogurt being popular. So (B) passes our first test for questions of this type, because the relationship between the sentence in the prompt and the rest of the passage demonstrates that what (B) says is true.

- Choice (D) says that the underlined sentence

  > sets up the argument in the paragraph for the benefits of Greek yogurt.

  The underlined sentence says that the conservation methods associated with the production of Greek yogurt are "well worth the effort," and then the following sentences explain why Greek yogurt is healthy. The underlined sentence introduces the idea that there's something good about Greek yogurt—that it's "worth . . . effort"—and the following sentence tells us specifically what's good about it. So (D) accurately describes the relationship between the underlined sentence and the text as well.

Now, when we consider the SAT's standards for ideal paragraphs and sentences, as we just discussed, we can see that we should choose to include the underlined sentence: it introduces the ideas in the next sentence of the passage, instead of discussing irrelevant concepts that aren't referred to elsewhere in the passage. So, as trained test-takers, we know (D) must be right, since (D) is the choice that says we should include the sentence. (By the way, the question we just talked about is one of the trickier questions of this type that the College Board has published. For a full explanation of that question, see its walkthrough on page 466 of this Black Book.)

There's one more rule to keep in mind, and it doesn't come up very often at all.

The third rule: don't contradict data

The third rule is just that any sentence that gets included in a passage must not contradict any figure or data that appears in the passage. For an example of this rule, see question 32 from the Writing and Language section of SAT Practice Test #6. It asks about a sentence that seems to support the main point of the paragraph, as choice (A) from that question says—except that the sentence contradicts some data in a figure that's part of the passage. So (C), which points out this contradiction, is the right answer.

Including or excluding a figure

Very rarely, a question of this type might ask you whether to include or exclude a graph or other figure, rather than a sentence or phrase. All the rules for this kind of question are still the same: you'll need to pick the answer choice that accurately describes the role of the figure in the passage, and if more than one choice passes that test, then you should pick the choice that says to include or exclude the figure for reasons that are consistent with the broader rules of ideal sentences and paragraphs on the SAT.

Now that we've discussed the various kinds of reading comprehension questions you'll encounter on the SAT Writing and Language section, let's move on to the next major question group.

Grammar/Style/Punctuation Questions

These questions test your ability to identify the form of a phrase or sentence that follows the SAT's rules for written American English.

These questions can often test rule-based concepts like proper verb conjugations, the proper use of punctuation, the formation of possessives, and so on. They also sometimes offer us more than one answer choice that's grammatically acceptable, and require us to indicate which one sounds the most appropriate according to the SAT. (I know that may sound like a pretty subjective exercise, and like exactly the kind of thing the SAT would never ask. But we'll find that the correct answers to these questions are just as predictable as the correct answer to any other SAT question, because the SAT consistently rewards the same attributes in the correct answers to Writing and Language questions.)

You'll typically (but not always) be able to identify these grammar/style/punctuation questions because of the following attributes:

- The question won't have a separate prompt—it's just a list of answer choices.
- The first answer choice will be "NO CHANGE."

An individual grammar/style/punctuation question can cover multiple areas of grammar, style, and punctuation, but don't worry—most questions will only cover one or two topics each, and we'll find that the topics tested on the SAT are relatively simple.

Since grammar/style/punctuation questions on the SAT Writing Test are all about picking the answer choice that follows the rules and patterns for ideal phrases and sentences as determined by the College Board, we'll need to do two things:

- learn the College Board's standards for style, grammar, and punctuation, and
- get familiar with the way the College Board tests those standards in real SAT practice questions.

We'll take care of the first step by reviewing the Grammar/Style/Punctuation Toolbox, which is a collection of all the major rules and patterns you'll need to know to understand the College Board's standards for grammar, style, and punctuation. Once we've learned all the relevant information from that toolbox, we'll jump right in to the various test design elements that the College Board uses on the Writing and Language section.

Grammar/Style/Punctuation Toolbox

Whether you feel totally comfortable with grammar and writing style as general concepts, or you can't wait to be done with all your English classes and never read a book or write a sentence again, I strongly recommend that you read this entire toolbox *twice*.

(Even if you think you already have a perfect understanding of modern English grammar, I want to remind you gently that the SAT will probably disagree with you on at least a few issues.)

Remember—we need to be fully comfortable with the College Board's rules and standards for English grammar, which aren't necessarily the same as the rules and standards that you're used to, or the rules and standards that your teachers prefer.

(Of course, the grammar rules on the SAT have much in common with the grammar rules that most people use, but we know by now that the SAT is a test of *details*, and there are a number of details we need to pay special attention to if we want to be able to pick the correct answer on the SAT Writing and Language section consistently.)

Also, because of the ways that different parts of a sentence interact with each other, there will be some overlap among the concepts we talk about, so don't worry if some of these ideas run together a little bit in your mind. As long as you can understand the right answer when you're practicing, you're in good shape.

If you're feeling confused at any point as you read through any one of these topics, just do your best and keep reading through the material. I'll follow up with examples when necessary, and the examples will tend to clear things up. It's often a lot harder to understand a description of these issues than it is just to look at an example and see what we're talking about. So, again, just keep at it, even if things don't seem clear right away.

This is also a good time for me to bring up the importance of the question walkthroughs you'll see after this training. We'll cover a lot of stuff in this training section, but you'll really get the best sense of how to beat SAT Writing and Language questions by following along in your copy of the official SAT Practice Tests with the walkthroughs in this Black Book. That way, you can see all of this material in action, which will really help you recognize these concepts when you see them on test day.

And after that, of course, the most important thing is always for you to do some real practice SAT Writing and Language questions on your own after you've learned the material in this Black Book.

(Before we jump in, I'd like to mention that the SAT will never test you on specific grammatical terms like "participle," "pronoun," "conjugation," and so on, so don't worry if you can't keep those terms straight—or if you've never even heard of them. Instead, the SAT tests you on its principles of grammar and style by having you choose the form of a phrase that it considers superior within the context of a passage. So you'll never see direct questions about grammatical terminology on the SAT—we only discuss these terms here to make the training and walkthroughs easier to understand.)

Important note:

In this section, I'll show you a lot of different sample sentences—some with errors, some without. To keep things clear, the examples with errors will have an asterisk (*) at the beginning of the example.

So if you see an example that begins with an asterisk, you'll know that it shows something you should *avoid* on the SAT Writing and Language section.

Nouns

Nouns are the first parts of speech that babies learn, because nouns are the things you can point to. A baby can point to its mother and say, "mommy," because the word "mommy" describes an actual, physical thing. The most basic nouns are things you can point at like a baby would, such as the following:

- apple
- bicycle
- toy

- umbrella
- watch
- computer

- shoe
- train
- mall

- sign
- book
- car

Any object you can touch or point to is a noun.

But there are other types of nouns as well. Some nouns represent ideas, like "happiness" or "fatalism." These nouns are things that you can't point at. But don't worry—you can usually recognize them by their endings.

If a word ends in "-ness," "-ism," "-hood," "-ology," or anything similar, it's probably a noun, like "quickness," "cubism," "brotherhood," and "cardiology."

Nouns can be either **singular** or **plural**. The plural form of a noun is usually formed with the suffix "-s" or the suffix "-es," but there are some special nouns that form their plurals differently. "Shoe," "box," and "mouse" are all singular nouns, and "shoes," "boxes," and "mice" are the plural forms of those nouns.

Verbs

Verbs are the second-most basic class of words. A verb is an action. Verbs are things you can do—the word *do* is a verb itself.

One way to test whether a word is a verb is to try to think of a sentence that places that word immediately after the word "cannot." If you can do that with the word, then that word is a verb. Here are some examples of verbs:

- run
- do

- make
- swim

- cook
- imagine

- follow
- think

You can see that any of these words can be placed into a logical sentence after the word "cannot," as in the following examples:

I cannot run far.

He cannot do that for very long.

They cannot make a sports car.

We cannot swim here.

A verb takes different forms, called "conjugations," depending on who is doing the action described by the verb, and the time period of the action the described by the verb. For the purposes of the SAT, we only care about two aspects of a conjugation:

- whether a verb-form is singular or plural (which is called the verb's "number"), and
- whether a verb's action takes place in the present, past, or future (which is called the verb's "tense")

Singular versus plural verbs

Like nouns, verbs have singular and plural forms. Singular forms of verbs often end in "-s," while plural forms often do not.

Rhonda <u>drives</u> to the dentist.

My friends <u>drive</u> downtown.

In these sentences,

- The singular noun "Rhonda" requires the singular verb form "drives."
- The plural noun "friends" requires the plural verb form "drive."

Here's the verb "to speak" conjugated in the present tense. Note that the form used with "he," "she," and "it" ends in "-s":

I speak	we speak
you speak	you speak
he/she/it speaks	they speak

In many cases, the singular and plural forms of a verb are identical, as we see in the following examples:

I like biscuits.   We like biscuits.

Both of these examples would be acceptable on the SAT because "like" can be both a singular verb-form and a plural verb-form, which means it can be acceptably paired with both the singular pronoun "I" and the plural pronoun "we."

A verb must always agree in number with the noun or nouns that it modifies, as we see below:

Monica and Alex enjoy the theater.

The previous example would be acceptable on the SAT because "Monica and Alex" is a plural subject, and "enjoy" is a plural verb-form that modifies that plural subject. But the following example would be unacceptable on the SAT:

*Monica and Alex enjoys the theater.

This would be unacceptable on the SAT because "enjoys" is a singular verb-form that might seem, at first, like it correctly agrees with the noun "Alex." But in this sentence, "enjoys" actually has to agree with the plural noun phrase "Monica and Alex," because the sentence tells us that Monica and Alex *both* enjoy the theater.

Mixing singular verbs with plural nouns (and plural verbs with singular nouns) is a common error on the SAT Writing and Language section. Always check to see which noun a verb is supposed to agree with!

Tenses of verbs

As we discussed before, verbs describe actions. We have three basic **tenses** to describe when the action of a verb takes place: past, present, and future. We change the form of a verb to indicate its tense. Consider the following:

- "Love" is a present-tense verb-form, indicating that the action of loving my grandmother is going on right now:

  I love my grandmother.

- "Will love" is a future verb-form that indicates the loving has not started yet, but will happen later:

  I will love my children very much when I have them.

- "Loved" is a past-tense verb-form, indicating that the act of loving has already finished:

  I loved my pet goldfish.

On the SAT Writing and Language Section, verb tenses should indicate actions in a sequence that's logically possible; if a question requires you to consider the tense of a verb, make sure you pick an answer choice that doesn't create an impossible sequence of events in the context of the passage.

Verb-forms as nouns

The "–ing" and "to" forms of verbs can function as nouns:

Singing is a lot of fun.

I like to sing.

In the previous examples, "singing" and "to sing" both act like nouns:

- "Singing" is the subject of the verb-form "is."
- "to sing" is the object of the verb-form "like."

Misleading verb forms in the answer choices

Sometimes, the SAT uses a question's answer choices to try to confuse us about the proper form of a verb. There's a real-life example of this issue in question 19 from the Writing and Language section of SAT Practice Test #4, involving this phrase:

the minute amounts of residue falling within such limits <u>have</u> no negative impact.

The choices include three singular verb forms: two are different present-tense forms, and one is in the past tense. To an untrained test-taker, it might seem like we need to figure out which tense is appropriate. But, in reality, the noun that should go with the verb is the plural noun "amounts." This plural noun needs a plural verb form, and the only choice with a plural verb form is the correct answer, (A). (Notice also that it was easier to find the answer in this example after we mentally removed the intervening phrase

> of residue falling within such limits

which left us with this:

> The minute amounts <u>have</u> no negative impact

For a complete discussion of this question, please see its walkthrough on page 531 in this Black Book. For more on the College Board's use of intervening phrases, see "The Intervening Phrase" on page 456 later in this Black Book.)

Adjectives and adverbs

Adjectives are single words that describe nouns. You'll usually find an adjective right before the noun it describes, or as part of a list of other adjectives describing that noun, as in this example:

> Bowser is a tiny dog.

- In this sentence, the word "tiny" is an adjective that describes the noun "dog."

If you want to modify a word that isn't a noun, then you'll need to use the **adverb** form of the adjective. The adverb form of an adjective almost always ends in "-ly." Consider this example:

> I quickly ran across the street to see what was happening.

- In this sentence, the adverb "quickly" is used to modify the verb "ran."

On the SAT, you'll sometimes see UNACCEPTABLE sentences that involve adjectives modifying words that are not nouns, or adverbs modifying words that are nouns. Watch out for this! The following sentence would be unacceptable on the SAT Writing and Language section:

> *I walked slow through the halls so no one would hear me.

- In the above sentence, the adjective "slow" is being incorrectly used to modify the verb "walked," which is not a noun. We should use the adverb form "slowly."

This would be an ACCEPTABLE sentence on the SAT Writing and Language section:

> I walked slowly through the halls so no one would hear me.

In the above sentence, the adverb "slowly" is correctly being used to modify the verb "walked."

Pronouns

Pronouns are a particular type of noun that we use to refer to a noun that has already been mentioned in a conversation. These are pronouns:

- I
- you
- he
- she

- it
- we
- they
- me

- him
- her
- us
- them

- one
- who
- which
- that

(**NOTE:** The words "that" and "which" are special types of pronouns called "**relative pronouns**." Both words can also be used in other ways that aren't related to pronouns, depending on the context. Don't worry about those other usages right now—just know that the words "that" and "which" are often, but not always, pronouns.)

When we have a sentence like

> Thomas wants to know why he has to do the dishes.

the word "he" lets us know that we're still talking about the person that was recently mentioned. It would sound strange to say,

> Thomas wants to know why Thomas has to do the dishes.

so we use the pronoun "he" in place of the second "Thomas."

When a pronoun appears on the SAT, it must agree in number with the noun it's replacing:

> Last week I saw an antique car. <u>It</u> was over 100 years old.

- In the above example, the singular pronoun "it" is correctly used to refer to the singular noun "car."

Let's look at an example that breaks this rule, and would be UNACCEPTABLE on the SAT:

> *Last week I saw an antique car. At over 100 years old, <u>they</u> were in great shape.

- The second sentence above incorrectly uses the plural pronoun "they" to refer to the singular noun "car."

Subjects and objects

The thing that performs the action is called the "**subject**" of the sentence (or the subject of the verb). If there's a noun that receives the action in the sentence, that noun is called the "**object**" in the sentence (or the object of the verb). Consider this example:

> John grabbed the pencil.

In the above sentence,

- the word "John" is the subject, because "John" is the thing doing the action—in this case, the action is described by the verb "grabbed."
- the word "pencil" is the object of the verb "grabbed," because "pencil" is the thing receiving the action of being grabbed.

Some pronouns are **subject pronouns**, and some are **object pronouns**.

The following pronouns are examples of subject pronouns, since they can be used to replace words that serve as subjects of verbs:

- I
- you
- he
- she
- it
- we
- they
- what
- who

The following pronouns are examples of object pronouns, since they can be used to replace words that serve as objects of verbs:

- me
- you
- him
- her
- it
- us
- them
- what
- whom

Notice that the words "you," "it," and "what" each have identical subject and object forms.

Subject pronouns can only be used as subjects; they must be the thing in the sentence that does an action.

Object pronouns can only be used as objects; they must be the thing in a sentence that receives an action.

So the following would be ACCEPTABLE sentences on the SAT Writing and Language section:

> He gave her a present.
>
> They sent a letter to us.

In the above sentences,

- "He" and "they" are subject pronouns that are doing the actions in the sentences.
- "Her" and "us" are object pronouns that are receiving the actions in the sentences.

The following sentences would be UNACCEPTABLE on the SAT Writing and Language section:

> *He gave she a present.
>
> *Them sent a letter to us.

In the above sentences,

- "She" is a subject pronoun that can't properly receive the action of the verb "gave."
- "Them" is an object pronoun that can't properly do the action of the verb "sent."

Who versus whom

You'll occasionally see SAT Writing and Language questions that require you to choose between "who" and "whom." We've already seen that "who" is a subject pronoun and "whom" is an object pronoun, and we'll need to keep this distinction in mind for this type of question. For example, you may see a sentence like this:

> This is the man <u>who</u> taught me how to ride a bike.

Then, you may have to decide whether "who" or "whom" (or something else) is appropriate in the underlined space. In the sentence above, "who" is the correct choice, because it's used to describe something or someone doing an action. Here, the word "who" refers to "the man," and "the man" does the action indicated by the word "taught."

The word "whom" describes someone who's being acted upon, as we see in the following sentence:

He is also the man <u>whom</u> I accidentally hit with my bike before I knew how to ride it.

In this sentence,

- the word "whom" is correct because it refers to "the man," someone receiving an action
- "the man" receives the action of being "hit with my bike."

Here's another way to think about it that's simpler for some people. It involves turning a sentence into a question, and then figuring out how that question would be answered. Let's take a look. Imagine you need to evaluate a sentence like this:

This is the man <u>who</u> taught me how to ride a bike.

Turn it into a question:

*(Who/whom) taught me how to ride a bike?

Then answer it with a pronoun:

<u>He</u> taught me how to ride a bike.

- If you'd use the word "he" to answer the question, then "who" is the proper form in the original sentence.
- If you'd use the word "him" to answer the question, then "whom" is the proper form in the original sentence (you can remember this because both "whom" and "him" end in "m").

Let's try it with our other sentence from before:

He is also the man <u>whom</u> I accidentally hit with my bike before I knew how to ride it.

Turn it into a question:

*(Who/whom) did I accidentally hit with my bike?

Then answer it with a pronoun:

I hit <u>him</u> with my bike.

Since we'd answer the question with "him," we know the proper form in the original sentence is "whom."

So remember that "who" corresponds with "he," and "whom" corresponds with "him" (again, you can remember that because both "whom" and "him" end with the letter "m"). Of course, if the sentence mentions a girl or a woman, you can just mentally switch out "she" for "he," and "her" for "him," or you can always think in terms of female pronouns if you prefer. I just prefer to teach it in terms of "he" and "him" because "him" and "whom" both end in "m," which usually makes it easier for students to remember.

We can still use this approach when a question involves a plural noun; we just use "they" or "them" to answer the question:

- "they" functions like "he" or "who." It refers to nouns that perform actions (note that each word ends in a vowel sound).
- "them" functions like "him" or "whom." It refers to nouns that receive actions (note that all three words end in "m").

Let's look at an example with a plural noun this time. Imagine we had to choose the correct version of this sentence:

*Those are the kids to (who/whom) I gave all my toys.

When we read that, we might ask ourselves,

To (who/whom) did you give all your toys?

The answer to this question would be

I gave all my toys to <u>them</u>.

Because I'd answer with "them," I know that the correct form in the original sentence is "whom:"

Those are the kids to <u>whom</u> I gave all my toys.

There's an example of this in question 30 on the Writing and Language section of SAT Practice Test #1. The original sentence says,

*the most valuable resources…are actually the people <u>whom use</u> them.

We have the option of changing "whom" to "who." We can see that "who" is correct, because the sentence describes "people" doing the action in the verb "use." Since the noun being described by who/whom is *doing* an action in this case, not *receiving* the action, we know that we need the subject form "who," as in (D).

If we wanted to turn the sentence into a "who/whom" question, we would say,

> Who use(s) them?

The answer would be

> They use them.

Since we know that "they" corresponds to "who," we can again see that the "who" form is needed, which we find in (D). (Incidentally, we also know that we need the plural form "use" to agree with the plural noun "people," which is why (D) is right, and not (C)—see this question's full walkthrough on page 476 in this Black Book for more on that.)

Personal pronouns

Personal pronouns are pronouns that can be used to replace a noun that describes a person. The ones that can sometimes cause trouble on the SAT Writing and Language section are usually the pronouns "who," "whom," and "one." When a pronoun is used in place of a noun that describes a person, that pronoun must be a personal pronoun.

The following would be an ACCEPTABLE sentence on the SAT Writing and Language section:

> This is my aunt, who got me interested in physics.

In the above sentence, the word "who" is a personal pronoun that takes the place of the personal noun "aunt."
The following would be an UNACCEPTABLE sentence on the SAT Writing and Language section:

> *This is my aunt that got me interested in physics.

In this sentence, the word "that" isn't a personal pronoun, so it can't refer to "aunt" on the SAT Writing and Language section.

Pronoun ambiguity

On the SAT Writing and Language section, we can only use a pronoun if that pronoun could only be referring to a single, specific noun phrase. If it's unclear which noun is being referred to by a pronoun, then we're not allowed to use that pronoun on the SAT Writing and Language section. We can see a real-life example of an SAT question involving pronoun ambiguity in question 5 from the Writing and Language section of SAT Practice Test #2.

That question asks us to choose from among four answer choices that many test-takers would find to be more or less equally appealing. But three of those answer choices involve a pronoun (either "them" or "their"). In context, it isn't clear what those pronouns would refer to—plural nouns in the sentence include "materials," "formats," and "e-books." Since it wouldn't be clear what "them" or "their" would refer to, we have to pick the one choice that avoids pronoun ambiguity by not including any pronouns—the correct answer, choice (D). (For a complete discussion of that question, see its walkthrough on page 485 in this Black Book.)

Possession

Luckily, the SAT's rules for **possessives** are actually pretty simple, even if they arguably differ from today's common usage.
There are three things you need to know if you want to form possessives on the SAT.
First, you need to know how possessive pronouns are formed. Most people are comfortable with these possessive pronouns:

- my
- his
- her

The ones that sometimes cause trouble tend to be these:

- your
- its
- whose
- their

People often mix up those possessive pronouns with these contractions:

- The possessive pronoun "your" is confused with the contraction "you're," which is short for "you are."
- The possessive pronoun "its" is confused with the contraction "it's," which is short for "it is."
- The possessive pronoun "whose" is confused with the contraction "who's," which is short for "who is."
- The possessive pronoun "their" is confused with the contraction "they're," which is short for "they are."

So here's the rule to remember: *possessive pronouns contain no apostrophes.* If you're in a position where you have to choose between "your" and "you're," or "its" and "it's," or "whose" and "who's," or "their" and "they're," remember that the form with the apostrophe is a contraction involving a form of the verb "to be," and the other form is possessive. Whenever you see these contractions in a sentence or an answer choice, imagine them in their "un-contracted" state, and you should be able to tell if they're appropriate:

- "You're" with an apostrophe can always be read as "you are"
- "It's" with an apostrophe can always be read as "it is"
- "Who's" with an apostrophe can always be read as "who is"
- "They're" with an apostrophe can always be read as "they are"

Many people are unsure about sentences like these:

> *She sat in the car and honked <u>it's</u> horn.

> *<u>Who's</u> house is this?

But if we imagine the contractions in their "un-contracted" forms, the grammatical errors become a lot more obvious:

> *She sat in the car and honked <u>it is</u> horn.

> *<u>Who is</u> house is this?

When you get into the habit of reading "you're" as "you are," "it's" as "it is," "who's" as "who is," and "they're" as "they are," you won't be tricked by that kind of sentence.[2]

The second thing to remember about possessives is that a PLURAL noun ending in "-s" will ALWAYS form its possessive with a single apostrophe, and nothing more. Consider the following examples:

> This toy belongs to the cats. It is the <u>cats'</u> toy.

> Those are the <u>girls'</u> bikes. Those bikes belong to the girls.

> That lawn mower belongs to the neighbors. It is the <u>neighbors'</u> lawn mower.

In each of these three situations, there's a plural noun that ends in "-s:"

- cats
- girls
- neighbors

To form a possessive for each of those plural words, you just add an apostrophe, and don't change anything else:

- cats'
- girls'
- neighbors'

So that's the second rule: to form the possessive of a plural noun ending in "-s," just add an apostrophe to the end.

The third rule is that EVERY OTHER KIND OF NOUN forms its possessive with an apostrophe AND an "s." That's right: except for pronouns, and for plural nouns ending in "-s," every noun on the SAT forms its possessive with an apostrophe and an "s."

Here are a few examples of words that get an apostrophe and an "s" on the SAT. Note that many of these possessive forms differ from modern usage (including the things your teachers might write):

> This ball belongs to my dog. It is my <u>dog's</u> ball.

> The game belongs to the children. It is the <u>children's</u> game.

> The abacus has wooden beads. They are the <u>abacus's</u> wooden beads.

> The geese live on a pond. It is the <u>geese's</u> pond.

So let's do a quick review of the three possessive rules you need to know for the SAT:

1. Possessive pronouns like "your," "their," "whose," and "its" NEVER include apostrophes.
2. The possessive form of a plural noun ending in "-s" is formed by adding an apostrophe and nothing else.
3. The possessive form of EVERY OTHER KIND OF NOUN is formed by adding an apostrophe and an "-s," no matter what letter or sound the base noun ends in.

Once you learn these rules and see them in action on some real SAT practice questions, they'll become second nature.

For a real-life example of a question involving possessives, take a look at question 19 from the Writing and Language section of SAT Practice Test #1. The relevant text says,

---

[2] One more bonus mistake: People sometimes confuse the word "there," which indicates a place, with the possessive pronoun "their," which indicates that something belongs to a group of people. In this case, the easiest thing to remember is probably that the word "there" has a spelling similar to the spellings of "here" and "where," and all of those words are related to physical positions.

So, one more time, just to be clear:

The word "their" is a possessive pronoun and indicates that a group of people own something: "They invited me to <u>their</u> house."

The word "they're" is always interchangeable with the phrase "they are:" "They said <u>they're</u> going to decide tomorrow."

The word "there" has a similar spelling to "here" and "where," and indicates position: "The car isn't here; it's over <u>there</u>."

> *soot particles facilitate melting by darkening snow and ice, limiting <u>it's</u> ability to reflect the Sun's rays.

We need to choose from among "it's," "its," "there," and "their" for the correct text in the underlined portion. When we look at the context, we see that the "ability to reflect the Sun's rays" belongs to "snow and ice." Since we're talking about the idea of "snow and ice" possessing something (an "ability"), and since "snow and ice" is plural, we know that we need a plural possessive pronoun here. The only choice with a plural possessive pronoun is (D), "their," which is the correct answer. (For a more detailed look at that question, please take a look at its walkthrough on page 472 in this book.)

Singular vs plural

One of the broadest and most common issues that comes up on the SAT Writing and Language section is the distinction between the singular and plural forms of different kinds of words. This can come up in a lot of ways, and you should learn to keep a sharp eye out for all of them. For example, you might see the singular word "it" used incorrectly to refer to a plural noun. You might even see an incorrect sentence that says something like

> *My brother and my sister both want to be a dentist.

when the correct version would be

> My brother and my sister both want to be dentists.

since two people can't become a single dentist.

This idea of the difference between singular and plural forms has already come up in this Toolbox in other situations, and we'll see plenty more of it in the walkthroughs later in this Black Book—it's just such a common issue that I wanted to call it to your attention here. Always remember to be on the lookout for issues related to the difference between singular and plural forms of words, especially in the context of verbs and pronouns.

Prepositional idioms

The word **"idiom"** can have two different meanings. In a loose sense, the "idiom of a language" is the natural way that native speakers of that language communicate. In a stricter sense, an idiom is an individual phrase that's considered to be grammatically correct for reasons that can't be predicted or explained by a grammatical rule. In other words, this second type of idiom is an expression that's simply right because it's right, even though it has no detectable similarity to any other correct phrase.

This second type of idiom is the type I'm referring to when I talk about idioms on the SAT. Let's consider a quick example. You're probably familiar with this phrase:

> to fall in love

Most speakers of American English are familiar with the phrase "fall in love"—we hear the phrase repeated in movies, songs, and everyday conversation. But why aren't the following forms acceptable?

> *to fall *with* love

> *to fall *to* love

There's no logical reason for one of those phrases to be acceptable while the other two aren't: love isn't a physical substance or location, so people can't literally fall "in" love any more than they can literally fall "to" love or "with" love. The correct version of this idiomatic phrase just uses the preposition "in" because that's how speakers of American English have used it for a long time.

In other words, if you weren't already familiar with this phrase and you had to pick which preposition to use with it, there would be no rule you could follow that would predict the right answer. You'd just have to guess and hope you were right. And that's what makes this phrase's use of "in" truly idiomatic in the strict sense: it's a one-of-a-kind expression in the sense that it doesn't follow any rule that applies to any other use of the word "in."

Luckily, on the SAT there will only be a limited number of questions that ask about things that are strictly idiomatic.

These questions will often involve prepositional phrases you've probably heard before, like "to fall in love." **Prepositions** are typically short words like "in," "at," "to," "by," "with," "for," and so on. (Not all short words are prepositions, but prepositions are usually short words.) Many languages use prepositions idiomatically, and English is one of them. Here are a few more phrases that depend on idiomatic usage of prepositions, with those prepositions underlined:

> to be <u>on</u> time

> to jump <u>to</u> a conclusion

> to depend <u>on</u> something

> to be all <u>for</u> something

In these phrases, the only way to know which preposition is correct is to be familiar with each phrase beforehand. If you've never heard the phrase before, then there's really no way to predict the correct preposition to go with it.

Some students have asked me if they should try to memorize a list of idioms in the hope that something from the list might show up on test day, but the odds are very much against that being a good investment of your time. The energy you'd spend on memorizing the list would definitely be better spent somewhere else, for the following reasons:

- There are untold thousands of idioms in English, and there doesn't seem to be any restriction on the idioms the SAT occasionally tests.

- You probably already know a lot of idioms if you've been speaking American English for a while.

- There aren't very many SAT Writing and Language questions that rely on idioms anyway.

So if you see a question that seems to be asking about an idiom, you should go with your gut instinct about which version of the phrase sounds right to you, and move on to other questions that don't rely on idioms. There's no penalty for being wrong on the SAT, and there's no point in wasting time trying to figure something out that literally can't be figured out, because it doesn't follow any rules by definition.

Remember that most SAT Writing and Language questions *do* follow rules and patterns, so you should be able to answer almost every SAT Writing and Language question on test day with certainty and confidence if you know the test's rules. If you feel like you're encountering lots of idiomatic phrases (in the strict sense) when you practice with official SAT questions from the College Board, then you're misunderstanding or misreading the questions, and you should carefully review the training and walkthroughs in this part of this Black Book.

(By the way, a lot of test-prep resources like to describe almost any acceptable word usage as "idiomatic," using the loose sense of the term. This is basically like saying that something is correct because it's correct—which isn't very helpful if you're trying to learn *why* a phrase is acceptable or unacceptable. Look out for that, and avoid test-prep resources that "explain" questions in that way. On the SAT, the only strictly idiomatic phrases you'll encounter are similar to the ones with prepositions, which we just discussed. When talking about SAT Writing and Language questions, this Black Book will only use the word "idiomatic" in its strict sense, to describe the few correct answers on this section that can't be predicted by rules.)

Question 25 from the Writing and Language section of SAT Practice Test #1 asks about an idiom that involves a preposition. The sentence in the question is this:

> *It was during this during this time that I read an article <u>into</u> coworking spaces.

This sentence could be corrected as follows:

> It was during this during this time that I read an article <u>about</u> coworking spaces.

So the right answer is (B), which creates the strictly idiomatic phrase "article about coworking spaces." As we just discussed, there's no rule we could follow to figure out that answer if we saw that question on test day; we'd either have to be familiar with the appropriate usage beforehand, or make the best guess we could and then move on to other questions. (For a more complete discussion of this question, see its walkthrough on page 475 of this Black Book.)

Conjunctions

Conjunctions are words that link ideas to each other, like the following:

- and
- but
- yet
- either
- or
- nor
- because
- neither

On the SAT Writing and Language section, two or more ideas that are linked by a conjunction must appear in the same form. (This is one example of something called "parallelism," which we'll discuss later in "Special Technique: Considering Parallelism When Answering Writing and Language Questions" on page 458.)

So the following sentence would be ACCEPTABLE on the SAT Writing and Language section:

> Samantha likes singing, dancing, and acting.

In the above sentence, the words "singing," "dancing," and "acting" are connected by the conjunction "and," and they're all in the same form (the "-ing" form), so this would be a good sentence on the SAT Writing and Language section.

But the following sentence would be UNACCEPTABLE on the SAT Writing and Language section:

> *Samantha likes to sing, dancing, and acting.

In the above sentence, the phrases "to sing," "dancing," and "acting" are all connected with the conjunction "and," but they're not all in the same form (one is in the "to" form, and two are in the "-ing" form), so this wouldn't be a good sentence on the SAT Writing and Language section.

Correlative conjunctions

Correlative conjunctions are sets of words that typically appear in the same sentence together, like the common expressions "either . . . or" and "neither . . . nor."

When we see the first word or phrase in a pair of correlative conjunctions, we typically expect to see the other word or phrase from that pair later in that same sentence.

The following are some common examples of correlative conjunction pairs:

- both . . . and
- either . . . or
- just as . . . so
- neither . . . nor
- no sooner . . . than
- not only . . . but (also)
- whether . . . or

The following would be ACCEPTABLE uses of correlative conjunctions on the Writing and Language section of the SAT:

> I have <u>neither</u> the time <u>nor</u> the energy to do a jigsaw puzzle with you.

> I don't know <u>whether</u> to leave <u>or</u> stay.

> <u>Not only</u> is that my favorite chair, <u>but</u> it's <u>also</u> a family heirloom.

(Note that in the case of the correlative conjunction "not only . . . but (also)," the word "also" doesn't *always* appear; when it does appear, it doesn't have to follow the word "but" immediately.)

The following would be UNACCEPTABLE uses of correlative conjunctions on the Writing and Language section of the SAT:

> *I have <u>neither</u> the time <u>as well as</u> the energy to do a jigsaw puzzle with you.

> *I don't know <u>whether</u> to leave <u>but</u> stay.

> *<u>Not only</u> is that my favorite chair, <u>or</u> it's a family heirloom.

Remember that you don't necessarily have to know the term "correlative conjunction" when you take the SAT; you just have to be able to recognize this issue when it comes up, and pick the choice that causes constructions like "either . . . or" to be used correctly.

Phrases

A **phrase** is a group of words that serves a particular function in a sentence; it usually functions like a part of speech.

A phrase can include one or more words.

Phrases are referred to by the functions they fulfill within their sentences. There are "noun phrases," "verb phrases," "prepositional phrases," "adverbial phrases," et cetera. Let's identify some of the phrases in the following sentence:

> The cat who lives next door likes my pineapple plant.

In the above sentence,

- "The cat" is a noun phrase.
- "lives next door" is a verb phrase.
- "the cat who lives next door" is a noun phrase that includes the noun phrase "the cat" and the verb phrase "lives next door."
- "likes my pineapple plant" is a verb phrase
- "my pineapple plant" is a noun phrase.

(There are other phrases that could be said to exist in this sentence, but you get the idea.)

Don't worry if this idea doesn't make a lot of sense right now! The SAT doesn't actually test your knowledge of phrases, or your ability to pull phrases out of a sentence. We're only covering this idea so that when I say, "the noun phrase such-and-such" in this toolbox and in the walkthroughs later in this book, you'll have some idea what I'm talking about.

Clauses

A **clause** is a group of words that includes a subject noun phrase, a verb phrase, and, if necessary, an object noun phrase. This is an example of a clause:

> This pizza recipe requires cheese.

In the clause above,

- "This pizza recipe" is the subject noun phrase.
- "requires" is the verb phrase.
- "cheese" is the object noun phrase.

Dependent and independent clauses

A clause can be either "independent" or "dependent."

An **independent** clause *can* stand on its own as a complete sentence—in fact, the term "independent clause" means it can exist *independently* as a sentence, without "depending" on another clause. Here's an example of an independent clause:

> I collect wombats.

In the independent clause above, which CAN stand alone as a sentence,

- "I" is a noun phrase
- "collect" is a verb phrase
- There's no conjunction at the beginning of the sentence
- (The clause also includes the object noun phrase "wombats," but clauses in general don't require object phrases.)

A **dependent** clause generally begins with one of the following words or phrases:

• after	• even though	• so that	• whether
• although	• if	• than	• which/whichever
• and	• in order that	• that	• while
• as	• once	• though	• who/whom/whose
• because	• provided that	• unless	• whoever/
• before	• rather than	• until	whomever/
• but	• since	• where/	whosever
• even if	• so	wherever	• why

Most of the words and phrases in this list are **conjunctions** or **relative pronouns**, but you won't need to know those terms on test day, because the SAT Writing and Language section doesn't require us to know the names of grammatical concepts. Just be aware that we might refer to a "conjunction" or a "relative pronoun" in the walkthroughs later in this book when we discuss dependent clauses that appear in real practice SAT questions, and that all you need to know is that those kinds of words often introduce dependent clauses.

(You may have heard of the acronym FANBOYS as a way to remember the set of words in the list above that are thought to appear most commonly in written American English: "for," "and," "nor," "but," "or," "yet," and "so." But you don't really need to memorize the above list, nor the acronym FANBOYS. Instead, you can just read through the above list a couple of times. After you start to work with real practice SAT Writing and Language questions and read through the walkthroughs in this Black Book, you'll get comfortable with spotting dependent clauses.)

A dependent clause CANNOT stand on its own as a complete sentence, as we see in the following example:

> *and now I only eat mushrooms from Japan

In the dependent clause above, which CANNOT stand alone as a sentence,

- "I" is a noun phrase
- "only eat" is a verb phrase
- "and" is a conjunction
- ("mushrooms from Japan" is another noun phrase, serving as the object of the verb "eat," but clauses don't have to include object nouns.)

We can also have a sentence that includes both a dependent clause and an independent clause, like the following:

> You have to sleep more because you study too much.

In the sentence above,

- "You have to sleep more" is an independent clause: it's a clause with a noun phrase ("you") and a verb phrase ("have to sleep more"), and it doesn't start with a conjunction.
- "because you study too much" is a dependent clause, since it's a clause with a noun phrase ("you") and a verb phrase ("study too much"), and it starts with the conjunction "because."

On the SAT Writing and Language section, every correctly written sentence must contain at least one independent clause.

When dependent clauses appear before independent clauses in a sentence, a comma is placed after the dependent clause. When an independent clause appears before a dependent clause, no comma is necessary—unless the dependent clause begins with a form of "which" or "who." Consider the following examples:

> Until I heard the explosion, I was playing video games in the dark.
>
> I was playing video games in the dark until I heard the explosion.
>
> The explosion was caused by my great-aunt, who was making gravy.

In the first example sentence above, the dependent clause "until I heard the explosion" appears before the independent clause "I was playing video games in the dark," so the clauses are separated by a comma. In the second example sentence, the order is reversed, so no comma is necessary. In the third example sentence, the dependent clause begins with "who," so we separate that clause from the independent clause with a comma.

Sentence fragments

For the purposes of the SAT Writing and Language section, any group of words that doesn't include an independent clause is a **sentence fragment**. The SAT will never require you to know the phrase "sentence fragment" in order to answer a question correctly, but you *will* be required to avoid answer choices that would result in sentence fragments. Here are some examples of sentence fragments:

*The very best time for some hot chocolate and a nap.

*Although we were never able to agree about the best way to fry and eat an entire package of candy bars.

The first example above is a sentence fragment because it doesn't include a verb phrase. The second example above is a sentence fragment because it's a clause that starts with "although," which makes it a dependent clause, and it doesn't also include an independent clause.

Clauses and commas

Independent clauses CAN be separated from each other by a period or a semi-colon. They CANNOT be separated from each other by a comma. The following example is UNACCEPTABLE on the SAT, because it uses a comma to separate two independent clauses:

*I have not yet begun to fight, time is on my side.

In the UNACCEPTABLE sentence above,

- "I have not yet begun to fight" is an independent clause including the subject pronoun "I" and the verb-form "have begun."
- "time is on my side" is an independent clause including the subject noun "time" and the verb-form "is."

(By the way, this UNACCEPTABLE use of a comma to join two independent clauses is called a "**comma splice**." As with other technical terms in this Toolbox, you won't be required to know the term "comma splice" on test day. But it will be helpful to remember the term when reading the walkthroughs of official SAT Writing and Language questions later in this book.)

The following sentence solves the problem from the previous example by separating the independent clauses with a semi-colon instead of a comma:

I have not yet begun to fight; time is on my side.

The following would be equally acceptable on the SAT Writing and Language section, because it allows each independent clause from the original example to stand alone as its own sentence:

I have not yet begun to fight. Time is on my side.

Colons, semicolons, and commas

You'll see several questions on test day that involve the proper use of colons, semicolons, and commas. The rules for using colons and semicolons on the SAT Writing and Language section are fairly straightforward, so we'll cover them first. Commas, on the other hand, are used in a wider variety of ways on the test, and proper comma usage on the SAT differs from the usage that's allowed by most teachers. Since it will take us a little more time and effort to explore commas, we'll do that after we get colons and semicolons out of the way.

Colons on the SAT Writing and Language section

A colon is used after an independent clause to introduce one or more examples of the idea in the independent clause, or to provide a further explanation of the idea in the independent clause. Everything that appears in a sentence leading up to a colon must be able to stand on its own as a complete sentence. The following examples show ACCEPTABLE colon usage on the SAT because, in each case, the part of the sentence leading up to the colon could stand on its own as a complete sentence, and what comes after the colon is an example or further explanation related to the idea mentioned before the colon:

I brought two of my favorite books on the train: *Anna Karenina* and *The Little Engine That Could.*

Sarah hadn't really liked dogs before she met Mr. Scruffles: when she was in kindergarten, a neighbor's Cocker Spaniel tricked her out of a turkey sandwich, and she never got over it.

Semicolons on the SAT Writing and Language section

A semicolon is used to join two independent clauses; in other words, a semicolon can be used on the SAT anywhere a period is used between two sentences. This usage results in a sentence that includes two groups of words that could each be sentences on their own, as in the following example:

Some days are colder than others; I've always preferred days when it snows.

The example above is ACCEPTABLE on the SAT because a semi-colon is used to separate the independent clause "some days are colder than others" from the independent clause "I've always preferred days when it snows."

On the SAT Writing and Language section, we can't use a semicolon to join an independent clause to a dependent clause, nor to join two dependent clauses to each other.

Commas on the SAT Writing and Language section

Commas can appear in a variety of ways on test day. We should approach questions that involve comma placement with the attitude that it's better to *avoid* commas unless we have an actual, concrete reason to use one. In other words, if a phrase would be acceptable without commas, then the College Board wants us to leave out commas.

It's also very important that you read the walkthroughs at the end of this training section so you can see what these comma placement questions are actually like.

The acceptable comma usage that we need to be aware of on the SAT Writing and Language section falls into the following main categories:

1. commas used to divide items in a list of three or more things (including the so-called "Oxford comma," which we'll discuss in a moment)
2. commas with quotations or speech
3. commas between dependent clauses and independent clauses
4. "comma sandwiches," which show that the sandwiched phrase could be removed from a sentence without creating any grammatical issues or changing the meaning of the rest of the sentence

We'll discuss each of these uses in more detail now.

Commas in a list of three or more things

On the SAT, if we have a list of three or more items, then a comma is placed after each item, and the word "and" appears before the last item in the list. For example, the following sentence is ACCEPTABLE on the SAT Writing and Language section:

> Thomasina had always liked falcons, ravens, eagles, and cardinals.

But the following sentence would be UNACCEPTABLE on the SAT Writing and Language section, because it omits the comma before the word "and:"

> *Thomasina had always liked falcons, ravens, eagles and cardinals.

(You may have heard someone call the comma that appears before the word "and" in these kinds of lists the "Oxford comma." If you've never heard that term, don't worry about it—you don't need to know it on the SAT. I only mention it because it has become fashionable in the last few years to omit the Oxford comma in some types of writing. It's important to remember that the College Board REQUIRES the Oxford comma on the SAT Writing and Language section, even if your teachers might prefer you to avoid it in school.)

Also note that the College Board doesn't want us to use both a comma and the word "and" if we're only dealing with a list of two items. In other words, if a list only includes two things, then we should join those two things with the word "and;" there should NOT be a comma before or after the "and" in that case.

Commas with quotations or statements

If a reported statement from a person or publication is enclosed in quotation marks and introduced by a word like "said," "commented," or "remarked," then a comma must be inserted before the space that comes before the opening quotation mark:

> The master said, "A gentleman knows neither sorrow nor fear."

But if a reported statement is preceded by a phrase like "said that" or "reported that," then no comma appears:

> The master said that "a gentleman knows neither sorrow nor fear."

Lastly, if a quotation appears in the middle of a sentence without ending punctuation of its own, then a comma appears before the closing quotation mark:

> My coach used to say, "defense wins championships," but he also said, "the best defense is a good offense," so I never really understood what he meant.

"Comma sandwiches"

"Comma sandwich" isn't a technical grammatical term, of course. It's something I made up to help test-takers remember a useful concept. As the name implies, a "comma sandwich" is a phrase "sandwiched" between two commas (or between a comma and a period, if the end of the comma sandwich is also the end of the sentence). This particular type of phrase isn't a complete sentence or a part of a list. Instead, it's a descriptive phrase that provides additional information about something in a sentence.

When a comma sandwich is used properly on the SAT Writing and Language section, the entire sandwiched phrase can be removed, leaving behind a complete sentence, without changing the meaning of the rest of the sentence.

Let's look at a couple of examples of this so you can actually see what I'm talking about. In these examples, I'll underline the "comma sandwich:"

The man next door, who told us we could borrow his lawn mower, was always very helpful.

In the above sentence, removing the comma sandwich gives us this:

The man next door was always very helpful.

Here's another example. Imagine we start with this sentence:

The orange shirt, which is the one I wanted to wear, isn't clean right now.

Removing the comma sandwich gives us this:

The orange shirt isn't clean right now.

In each case, we see that, when the commas and the phrase between them are removed, what's left is still a complete sentence. Let's look at our two examples again, this time with UNACCEPTABLE comma placement:

*The man next door, who told us we, could borrow his lawn mower was always very helpful.

Removing the phrase between the commas in the above sentence would leave us with the following, which would be UNACCEPTABLE on the SAT:

*The man next door could borrow his lawn mower was always very helpful.

Here's another example of an UNACCEPTABLE use of commas on the SAT:

*The orange shirt, which is the one I wanted to wear isn't clean, right now.

Removing the phrase between the commas would give us this UNACCEPTABLE fragment:

*The orange shirt right now.

(Note that in cases where three commas are potentially involved in comma sandwiches, all the normal rules apply, and we must be able to remove either comma sandwich—or both comma sandwiches—and leave behind an acceptable sentence with the same core meaning.)

There are a few different ways that the SAT might test us on comma sandwiches. We might see something like the previous examples where the whole sandwich is underlined, or there might be an underlined segment that only overlaps with a portion of the comma sandwich.

For a real-life example of the comma sandwich, take a look at question 33 from the Writing and Language section of SAT Practice Test #2. In this example, choices (B) and (C) create bad comma sandwiches that, when removed, leave behind an incoherent sentence fragment. For example, if you selected (B) and then eliminated the phrase "or removed from," you would be left with a sentence that includes this grammatically UNACCEPTABLE phrase:

*a good model of how carbon can be sequestered the atmosphere

The right answer to this question is (D), which creates the comma sandwich "or removed." When we take out that comma sandwich, we're left with this grammatically ACCEPTABLE phrase:

a good model of how carbon can be sequestered from the atmosphere

(For a more complete discussion of this question, see its walkthrough on page 498 in this Black Book.)

No comma sandwich when a profession is indicated immediately before a name

We'll sometimes find that a passage mentions a person's occupation immediately before the person's name, instead of after the person's name with the help of a phrase like "who is a." When the profession is mentioned immediately before the name, the SAT doesn't allow us to use a comma sandwich. So, for example, these phrases would be ACCEPTABLE on the Writing and Language section:

We read about famous astronaut Buzz Aldrin in class.

My favorite song is *Hungarian Rhapsody #2* by composer Ferenc Liszt.

When the profession is mentioned immediately after the name, a comma sandwich is needed:

> Buzz Aldrin, a famous astronaut, was the subject of an article we read.

> Ferenc Liszt, a composer, created some of my favorite music.

(By the way, the comma sandwiches in the last two sentences are examples of "appositives." An **appositive** is a descriptive phrase that can't stand alone on its own, inserted after the phrase it's describing, usually in some kind of comma sandwich. You don't need to know the word "appositive" on test day, but you might run into it when reading an explanation for a test item. If you do, you can basically just remember that an appositive is a kind of comma sandwich.)

Comma sandwiches at the beginning or end of a sentence

Of course, if a sandwiched phrase appears at the very beginning of a sentence, then the initial comma is omitted, because we can't start a sentence with a comma.

Similarly, if a sandwiched phrase appears at the very end of a sentence, then the final comma is omitted, because we can't include a comma immediately next to a period, exclamation point, or question mark.

We can see an example of a comma sandwich that appears at the end of a sentence in question 24 from the Writing and Language section of SAT Practice Test #3. The correct answer to that question involves deleting the underlined phrase, which causes the sentence to end in this comma sandwich:

> a chemical that causes fruit to ripen and eventually rot.

(For a complete discussion of that question—which involves a few other grammatical issues—see its walkthrough on page 515 in this Black Book.)

Other "punctuation sandwiches"

One last note: you may see the "comma sandwich" concept on the test with dashes or parentheses around the sandwiched phrase, instead of commas. These other "punctuation sandwiches" function just like "comma sandwiches" on the SAT.

No commas after conjunction expressions (unless a comma sandwich is involved)

Some people will be tempted to use commas by default after conjunction phrases, especially "and," "unless," and "such as." But we're not allowed to use commas after these expressions on the SAT (unless the comma is part of a comma sandwich), so the following sentences would be UNACCEPTABLE on the SAT Writing and Language section, for example:

> *The Senator picked up the phone and, ordered a pizza.

> *Unless, this time will be different, I don't think playing canasta is a good idea.

> *Jerry has always had a problem with dogs, such as, Pomeranians and Malamutes.

Instead, these versions would be ACCEPTABLE on the SAT:

> The Senator picked up the phone and ordered a sandwich.

> Unless this time will be different, I don't think playing canasta is a good idea.

> Jerry has always had a problem with dogs, such as Pomeranians and Malamutes.

Of course, it's possible to insert a comma sandwich immediately after a conjunction expression:

> The Senator picked up the phone and, with tears in his eyes, ordered a sandwich.

Dashes

A dash is a punctuation mark that looks like an elongated hyphen (—). On the SAT Writing and Language section, dashes can only be used in two scenarios:

1. to create a punctuation sandwich as described on page 450
2. to function as a colon would, by providing an example or explanation of a concept expressed in a group of words that could be a sentence on their own (see page 447 for a description of the proper usage of colons on the SAT)

Dangling participles

A **participle** is a special verb-form. On the SAT, the only participle we need to worry about is a verb form that ends in "-ing." A phrase that begins with a participle can be called a "participial phrase." They're often used at the beginning of a sentence. When these participles are used in standard written American English, they are always understood to refer to the first noun phrase in the independent clause in the sentence. Consider this example:

> Screaming for help, the mailman ran away from the angry dog.

In the sentence above,

- "screaming" is a participle
- "screaming for help" is the participial phrase (beginning with the participle "screaming," an "–ing" word)
- "the mailman ran away from the angry dog" is the independent clause (remember that an independent clause has a subject noun phrase and main verb phrase)

We know this participle was used correctly because the word "screaming" describes the word "mailman," which is what makes sense in context. The following sentence, on the other hand, would be completely UNACCEPTABLE on the SAT:

> *Screaming for help, the dog chased the mailman down the street.

What's wrong with the above sentence? We still have a participial phrase ("screaming for help") and an independent clause ("the dog chased the mailman down the street"), but the problem is that the participle in this sentence can't describe the first noun phrase in the independent clause, which is "the dog." This sentence is no good because the dog can't scream. Only the mailman can scream.

(In the next section, we'll talk about descriptive phrases that *don't* begin with "–ing" verbs. On the SAT Writing and Language section, those phrases modify the noun phrase *closest to the descriptive phrase.* It's a little bit of a nitpicky distinction to make, but it doesn't come up very often—and it will be a lot more intuitive once we see some examples in the training and in the walkthroughs.)

Phrase proximity

When a phrase on the SAT Writing and Language section describes or refers back to another phrase, the College Board wants us to keep those two phrases as close to each other as possible, to keep the meaning clear. (The exception to this situation is the type of participial phrase we just talked about in the previous section.) Let's look at a couple of examples.

This is an example of poor phrase placement on the SAT Writing and Language section:

> *Tomorrow I'll get that report done, which is when it's due.

This is an example of good phrase placement on the SAT Writing and Language section:

> I'll get that report done tomorrow, which is when it's due.

The phrase "which is when it's due" refers to the word "tomorrow," so the College Board would want the word "tomorrow" to be moved over so the two phrases are next to each other.

Here's another example of poor phrase placement on the SAT:

> *As the event coordinator, flower arrangements are the main thing John worries about.

This is an example of good phrase placement on the SAT:

> As the event coordinator, John mainly worries about flower arrangements.

According to the rules of the SAT, the first version of the sentence makes it sound like "flower arrangements" are the event coordinator, since they come immediately after the phrase "as the event coordinator." The word "John" could refer to the event coordinator, so "John" needs to be positioned right next to the phrase "as the event coordinator."

You can see an example of this issue in question 21 from the Writing and Language section of SAT Practice Test #2. In this question, the underlined portion is an entire sentence, and the main difference among the choices is the placement of this phrase:

> dotted with pin-sized knobs.

In three of the answer choices, the phrase "dotted with pin-sized knobs" appears next to "another visitor," which would mean that the visitor is the one "dotted with pin-sized knobs." Only the correct answer, (D), places this phrase right after "drawers," to make it clear that the "drawers" are what are "dotted with pin-sized knobs." (See the walkthrough for this question on page 493 of this Black Book for more on that question.)

So remember—if a phrase refers back to another phrase in this way on the SAT Writing and Language section, then we want to put those phrases right next to each other if we can.

(Again, note that in this section we're talking about a descriptive phrase that *does not* begin with a verb form that ends in "–ing," also a called a "participle." When the descriptive phrase *does not* start with the "–ing" form of a verb, that descriptive phrase modifies the closest noun phrase, as we discussed in this section. When the descriptive phrase *does* start with the "–ing" form of a verb, that phrase modifies the first noun phrase in the independent clause of the sentence it's in, as we discussed in the previous section on participles. This will probably make more sense when we encounter it in the walkthroughs later in this Black Book.)

Confused homophones

A **homophone** group is a group of words or phrases that have the same pronunciation, but different meanings and spellings. The College Board occasionally likes to test your awareness of these groups by requiring you to choose which homophone is appropriate in a given context.

Some frequently confused homophones are listed below.

"then" and "than"

- "Then" is an adverb used to indicate a time when something occurred, as in this sentence:

  > Then it happened.

  The word "then" can also be used to signal the second half of a conditional statement with the word "if," as in this sentence:

  > If it keeps raining then we'll need to wear boots when we go outside.

  We can remember that "then" is related to time expressions because it has a spelling that's very similar to the word "when."

- "Than" is used when we're comparing two things, as in the sentence:

  > This dog is nicer than that one.

"there," "their," and "they're"

We discussed this homophone group earlier, when we talked about possessive pronouns on page 441. As a refresher, we should remember that "there" indicates location (and has a spelling very similar to "where"), while "their" is a possessive pronoun and "they're" is always short for "they are."

"its" and "it's"

We also discussed this homophone group earlier, when we talked about possessive pronouns on page 441. To review, we should remember that "its" is a possessive pronoun and "it's" is always short for "it is."

"your" and "you're"

This is another homophone group we discussed earlier, when we talked about possessive pronouns on page 441. We should remember that "your" is a possessive pronoun and "you're" is always short for "you are."

Homophones that are confused relatively rarely could include groups like "cite," "site," and "sight," or "fair" and "fare," each of which appear in official SAT practice tests from the College Board. It's unlikely that you'll see these particular homophones being tested when you take the SAT, but the College Board could decide to test you on some other group of rarely confused homophones.

Redundancy

Redundancy is an important concept in SAT Writing and Language questions. Basically, we want to avoid answer choices in grammar/style/punctuation questions that would cause the passage to restate something clearly stated somewhere else in the immediate context.

For example, imagine we have a choice between these two sentences:

> *We went to a nearby diner not far from here.

> We went to a nearby diner.

The SAT would reward the second sentence, because the first sentence contains the phrase "not far from here," which redundantly expresses the same idea as the word "nearby;" when we say that something is "nearby," it already means that the thing isn't far away.

Here's another example:

> *John always chose the aisle seat every time he flew.

> John chose the aisle seat every time he flew.

In this example, the second sentence would be ACCEPTABLE on the SAT. The original sentence already contains the phrase "every time he flew," so the word "always" isn't necessary, and the SAT would reward you for avoiding it in this situation.

Notice that the example about the seat requires us to notice more of the sentence than the example about the diner did, because the sentence about the seat included more words between the redundant phrases.

The SAT likes to look for opportunities to separate important phrases from one another on the Writing and Language section, to decrease the likelihood that test-takers will notice the key elements in a question. This is why it's always important to pay attention!

Still, our job won't be to read through every single sentence in every single SAT Writing and Language passage and look out for redundant phrases, so please don't try to do that—it would be far too time-consuming. Instead, when we see an answer choice that allows us to get rid of a phrase (or part of a phrase) altogether, we just need to remember to take a look at the immediate context and see whether that phrase is redundant and should be removed.

There's a real-life example of this kind of redundancy in question 21 from the Writing and Language section of SAT Practice Test #1. That question refers to this text:

> the pattern…may repeat <u>itself again</u>, with harmful effects on the Arctic ecosystem.

Choice (A) leaves the underlined phrase alone, but this is redundant because "repeat" in the immediate context already expresses the idea of something happening "again." (B) changes the underlined phrase to "itself," which is correct because it avoids the redundancy from the other answer choices without creating any new problems. (C) changes the underlined phrase to "itself, with damage and," but this is redundant because "harmful effects" in the immediate context already expresses the idea of "damage." Finally, (D) changes the underlined phrase to "itself possibly," but this is redundant because "may" in the immediate context already expresses the idea of something "possibly" happening. So the correct answer is the only one that doesn't repeat an idea from the immediate context of the underlined phrase. (For more on this question, see its walkthrough on page 473 in this Black Book.)

Questions that ask us to join two sentences

On the SAT Writing and Language section, we'll occasionally see a question with a prompt that says something like this:

> Which choice most effectively combines the underlined sentences?

The relevant part of the passage will usually show two entire consecutive sentences underlined, and each choice will be a single sentence. The right answer to this kind of question will be the choice that does the following:

1. maintains the original meaning of the two sentences in the context of the passage, and
2. conforms to all the College Board's style, grammar, and punctuation guidelines as discussed in this Toolbox—especially those related to phrase proximity, transition words, logical order, and finding the shortest grammatically acceptable way to express a set of ideas (this is a test-design rule we'll discuss in the next section).

For an example of a question that requires us to consider all of these elements at once, take a look at question 23 on section 2 of SAT Practice Test #3 from the College Board. It asks us to combine these two sentences:

> 1-MCP lengthens storage life by three to four times when applied to apples.
>
> This extended life allows producers to sell their apples in the off-season, months after the apples have been harvested.

Choice (A) is correct. It starts with the phrase "when applied to apples," which provides context for the next idea that appears in the sentence, "1-MCP lengthens storage life." The idea that 1-MCP lengthens storage life logically completes the explanation of what happens when "1-MCP" is "applied to apples." The next phrase, "allowing producers to sell their apples in the off-season," tells us the effect of the lengthened storage life immediately after the idea of lengthened storage life is mentioned. Finally, the phrase "months after the apples have been harvested" appears immediately after the phrase it modifies, "the off-season." So this answer is correct because it presents the ideas from both sentences in logical order, and places modifying phrases next to the ideas they modify. (For a discussion of the problems with the wrong answers in that question, take a look at its walkthrough on page 514 in this Black Book.)

Note that the SAT Writing and Language section sometimes also includes questions that involve underlined text that includes parts of two sentences. These questions could potentially also involve "joining two sentences," but they tend to be a little simpler than the question type we just discussed, which typically involves two entire sentences being underlined.

Conclusion

That concludes the grammar, style, and punctuation issues you'll need to know for the Writing and Language section of the SAT. If you've only read them through once, I strongly recommend again that you go back through and read them one more time—the concepts will probably feel much more comfortable and familiar after that.

It also concludes our overview of the main types of questions you'll encounter on the Writing and Language section on test day. Now we're ready to focus on the rules and patterns the College Board will try to use against us.

Unwritten Test Design Rules for the SAT Writing and Language Section

We've discussed the College Board's rules and standards for grammar on the SAT Writing section, but there are also a few global test design rules that apply to grammar/style/punctuation questions on this part of the SAT. We'll look at those now.

Rule 1: Shorter is Better, All Else Being Equal

This is an idea that overlaps with some of what we've already talked about, but it's worth mentioning on its own: in questions of style on the SAT Writing and Language section, shorter is better, all else being equal.

This would be an example of an unnecessarily long sentence on the SAT Writing and Language section:

> *If I were the one who had the choice about going, I would choose to stay home.

This would be an improved version of the sentence, according to the SAT:

> If it were up to me, I would stay home.

Technically speaking, there isn't anything grammatically *wrong* with the first choice: all the words in the sentence agree grammatically with the words they should agree with. But the SAT Writing and Language section would prefer the second version, because it's the shorter version and also has no other issues of its own.

(I want to make it clear that shortness has nothing to do with grammar in real life! It's just something the College Board has arbitrarily decided to reward on the SAT Writing and Language section.)

We can see a real-life example of this "shorter is better" principle in question 14 on the Writing and Language section of SAT Practice Test #4. In this question, (A) and (D) are both grammatically acceptable according to the College Board, but (D) is correct because it's the shortest choice. (Incidentally, (B) and (C) are wrong because they're both redundant, which we discussed in the section of the Grammar/Style/Punctuation Toolbox about redundancy on page 452.)

Rule 2: Don't Make Trouble

When Writing and Language questions require us to consider grammar, style, and/or punctuation, it's important to remember that the correct answer choice must do more than just fix any mistakes in the underlined portion of the passage—it also has to avoid creating new mistakes.

Sometimes untrained test-takers will zero-in on one particular problem in the underlined portion of a passage and then pick the first answer choice that gets rid of that problem—but that choice could create problems of its own! The correct answer choice can't just fix the original mistake; it must not have ANY mistakes. So it's important to consider each answer choice in its entirety before settling on an answer.

Rule 3: No Special Consideration for "NO CHANGE"

Don't be afraid to select "NO CHANGE" on a grammar/style/punctuation question if you think the original version of the phrase is correct according to the rules and patterns of the SAT Writing and Language section.

A lot of people start to worry if they think they've chosen "NO CHANGE" too many times (or too few times). But that answer choice isn't any more or less likely to be correct than any other answer choices are.

On school tests, teachers often use trick answer choices that are rarely right, like "none of the above," to make multiple-choice questions seem harder. But the SAT doesn't do that with the "no change" answer choice. On some test days the "no change" choice is correct a little more often than other answer choices are, and on some days it's correct a little less often. So there's no magic number of times that this kind of answer choice has to be correct.

Hidden Answer Choice Patterns of the SAT Writing and Language Section

Now let's take a look at the hidden answer choice patterns we need to be aware of on the Writing and Language section.

Hidden Pattern 1: Wrong Answers Tend to Imitate Elements of Right Answers

We'll often find that phrases from the correct answer to a question are repeated in some of the incorrect answers, because the College Board wants to trick you by making the wrong answers imitate the right answers. This means that you can often get an idea of which elements of an answer choice are likely to be correct by seeing which ones are repeated more often throughout the answer choices.

For a real-life example, take a look at question 4 from the Writing and Language section of SAT Practice Test #1. Each choice includes only the words "scientists and," with different punctuation (or no punctuation) after each word. Together, the four choices have the following attributes:

- 3 of the 4 choices have no punctuation after "and"
- 2 of the 4 choices have a comma after "scientists"
- 1 of the 4 choices has a semi-colon after "scientists"
- 1 of the 4 choices has a colon after "scientists"
- 1 of the 4 choices has a comma after "and"

So the most common attributes are having no punctuation after "and" and a comma after "scientists." We would expect the correct answer to have one or both of these attributes as well, based on this hidden answer choice pattern. And, in fact, the correct answer is (C), the only choice that has the two most common features among the four answer choices.

(You may remember that the answer choices in certain SAT Math questions feature similar patterns, and for similar reasons. Just like in the Math section, it's important to remember that I'm NOT saying that an answer choice will ALWAYS be correct if it includes all the most popular attributes from the other choices! I'm just saying that this happens often, and it's something we should be aware of as we work on SAT Writing and Language questions. Even though this answer choice pattern worked very well on this question, an answer choice pattern alone is NEVER the basis for deciding that one choice must be correct over the others.)

Hidden Pattern 2: Functionally Identical Answer Choices

As you go through the SAT Writing and Language section, you'll find many questions in which two or three of the choices are basically the same, in the context of the question.

Because there can only be one correct answer for every SAT question, if you find two or three choices that are effectively the same, then they must all be wrong, since they can't all be right. This can be a helpful pattern to notice, especially if you're having trouble picking out a correct answer otherwise.

You can see an example of this concept in question 8 from the Writing and Language section of SAT Practice Test #3.

In this example, the underlined phrase from the passage is "each year." The next two choices to replace this are the phrases "every year" and "per year." In context, all three of these answer choices are functionally identical, since "each year," "every year," and "per year" all have the same meaning here. So each choice is a phrase indicating that something happens yearly, followed by a period.

Since these choices are all basically the same, and they can't all be right, we know as trained test-takers that they must all be wrong. The only answer choice that's different is the correct answer, (D), which would have us delete the phrase completely.

(Incidentally, this is an example of a question that tests the "redundancy" issue we talked about on page 452. Since the sentence already includes the word "annual," the phrases in the first three answer choices are considered redundant by the College Board.)

The Intervening Phrase

The SAT will use a few different tactics to try to trick you into not noticing that a verb is conjugated incorrectly. One of these is something I call the "intervening phrase."

Just as the name suggests, the intervening phrase is a phrase that the SAT sticks between a noun and its verb. The test does this because it's hoping you'll get confused and think the verb should agree with a word in the intervening phrase, instead of agreeing with the main noun that actually does the action of the verb.

We can see a real-life example of this issue in question 36 on the Writing and Language section of SAT Practice Test #3, which refers to this sentence:

> *Yet some of the earliest known works of art, including paintings and drawings tens of thousands of years old found on cave walls in Spain and France, <u>portrays</u> animals.

We need to choose the correct form of the verb "portrays."

When we identify and mentally remove the intervening phrase "including paintings and drawings tens of thousands of years old found on cave walls in Spain and France," we're left with a much more manageable version of the sentence:

> *Yet some of the earliest known works of art <u>portrays</u> animals.

We can further simplify the sentence by removing the intervening phrase "of art," which leaves us with this:

> *Yet some of the earliest known works <u>portrays</u> animals.

This makes it obvious that the verb form in the underlined portion of the sentence needs to agree with the plural noun "works." Only one answer choice includes a plural verb form—choice (C), "portray," which is correct.

Intervening phrases can also cause problems for untrained test-takers even when verb conjugations aren't directly involved. For example, consider question 27 from the Writing and Language section of SAT Practice Test #2. That question refers to a phrase from the following long, complicated sentence:

> *A recent study by two professors at the University of California, Santa Cruz, Chris Wilmers and James Estes, <u>suggests, that</u> kelp forests protected by sea otters can absorb as much as twelve times the amount of carbon dioxide from the atmosphere as those where sea urchins are allowed to devour the kelp.

That sentence includes the following intervening phrases, among others:

- "by two professors at the University of California, Santa Cruz, Chris Wilmers and James Estes,"
- "protected by sea otters"
- "of carbon dioxide from the atmosphere"
- "as those where sea urchins are allowed to devour the kelp"

When we mentally remove those intervening phrases, we end up with this much less complicated sentence:

> *A recent study <u>suggests, that</u> kelp forests can absorb as much as twelve times the amount.

This version of the sentence makes it much easier to see that choice (D) is correct, and that no punctuation is appropriate between "suggests" and "that." (For a full discussion of this question, see its walkthrough on page 495 in this Black Book.)

So when you read a sentence on the SAT Writing and Language section, it can be very helpful to ignore these intervening phrases and focus on the core relationships in the sentence to make sure the appropriate words agree with one another, and that punctuation is used in ways that the College Board accepts. We'll see several examples of this in a few pages when we look at solutions to real SAT questions.

(Note, by the way, that many intervening phrases will appear in comma sandwiches, as we discussed earlier in this Black Book when we talked about acceptable use of colons, semicolons, and commas on the SAT Writing and Language section, beginning on page 447.)

The College Board's Unique Phrasing

I've received a fair number of questions from students on a couple of phrases that the College Board uses often on the Writing and Language part of the SAT, so I wanted to make sure I explained them to you briefly. The two phrases are the following:

- "set up"
  The College Board uses the phrase "set up" to mean, essentially, "introduce" or "begin discussing."

- "blur the focus"
  On the SAT, "blurring the focus" of a paragraph or passage means introducing an idea that's not present in the rest of the paragraph or passage.

Keep these special phrases in mind on test day.

Special Technique: Considering Parallelism When Answering Writing and Language Questions

The term "parallelism" is used much too loosely by most people when it comes to standardized test prep, in my opinion, but it's actually useful on SAT Writing and Language questions if you understand what it really means, and you use it in the proper context.

Ultimately, in order to use parallelism as a tool to beat the SAT, we should think of it as the idea of looking at the text surrounding the underlined portion when we're trying to find clues about what to do with the underlined portion. This often helps on the Writing and Language section because the test sometimes does us a favor by using ideal style and punctuation in a part of the passage that's near the part we're being asked to fix.

That probably sounds confusing, so let's look at an example.

Question 1 on the Writing and Language section of SAT Practice Test #3 asks us about the underlined phrase "healthier, and more." Our other options, from the answer choices, are the following:

- "healthy, and more"

- "healthier, and they are"

- "healthier, being more"

At first, just from looking at this sentence, we might have trouble deciding which choice is correct. At least two of the choices are grammatically acceptable, technically speaking, outside the context of the SAT.

But if we look at the rest of the sentence, we can see that it includes an earlier comparison: "employees are happier." Once we see this comparison, and we realize that the underlined phrase continues that comparison, we know as trained test-takers that the rest of the sentence should use the same structure—so the SAT wants us to pick "healthier, and more." Only this option results in the comparative forms of "healthy" and "productive"—"healthier" and "more productive"—to match the comparative form "happier" from earlier in the sentence. This means (A) is the correct answer.

Unfortunately, it's not possible to use this technique on every single question, simply because the SAT doesn't structure its texts in a way that makes that possible. Depending on the context, though, we might use this technique to determine something like the appropriate form of a verb, or even the right punctuation for a phrase, as long as something in the surrounding text is similar and there's an answer choice to match it.

Of course, you shouldn't double-check every sentence in every passage for these kinds of parallel structures—that would take up a lot of time, for one thing, and the test doesn't include parallelism on every question, as we just discussed. Instead, keep this parallelism idea in mind for situations where more than one answer choice seems equally good—it may be that the correct answer becomes clear when you compare the underlined phrase to other phrases in the surrounding text, as we just did in the example above.

How to Read Passages on the SAT Writing and Language Section

In "How to Handle Passages on the SAT" on page 64, we talked about the best ways to read passages on the SAT Reading section. I said there were three main ways to approach those passages—reading, skimming, or skipping—and that you should experiment with them and pick the approach you're most successful with.

But my advice for the passages on the SAT Writing and Language section is different, because this section is structured differently.

For the SAT Writing and Language section, my recommendation is that you just start reading the passage from the very beginning (including the title). Every time you see a number with a square around it in the text, finish the sentence, and then look to the right of the text to find the question that corresponds to the numbered square. In most cases, you'll be able to answer that question based on the text you've read so far; you may sometimes need to read a little further, especially if a question involves one of the following elements:

- parallelism (which we discussed on page 458)

- placing a set of sentences in the right order (discussed on page 432)

- redundancy (see page 452)

- the option to include or exclude a phrase or sentence (see page 433)

- "setting up" a sentence or idea, or "blurring the focus" of a text (see page 457)

- transition words (see page 431)

You'll get used to this general approach as you go through the walkthroughs in this book, and do some practice of your own.

The General Process for Answering SAT Writing and Language Questions

Now that we've learned all the basics, let's take a look at the general process I recommend for answering this type of question.

1. Read the Passage until You Come to a Part of the Passage that Corresponds to a Question.

The questions will appear to the right of the passage, and they'll correspond to a number in a box that will appear in or immediately after the passage. When you come to a question, finish the sentence you're on, then stop reading the passage and shift your attention to the question.

2. Carefully Read the Prompt (if There is One) and the Answer Choices, and Determine which Type of Question it is. Consider Doing a Vertical Scan to Make Sure You Note the Similarities and Differences among the Answer Choices.

Not all questions will have a prompt; some will only offer four answer choices as possible versions of an underlined portion of the text. Either way, read the prompt if there is one, and carefully read the answer choices. Determine whether you're dealing with a grammar/style/punctuation question or a reading comprehension question, and consider doing a vertical scan to get an even stronger idea of the possibilities being presented in the answer choices, and the mistakes the College Board thinks an untrained test-taker is likely to make.

3a. For Grammar/Style/Punctuation questions, Look for Any of the Relevant Issues We Discussed in the Grammar/Style/Punctuation Toolbox.

Look at the words in the underlined portion, and see how they relate to the other words in the surrounding text. Do pronouns agree in number with the words they relate to? Are verbs in the right number and tense? Are possessives formed correctly? Are periods, commas, colons, and semicolons in the right place according to the SAT's grammar rules?

Consider all the answer choices. Are any choices functionally equivalent in the context of the passage, and therefore both wrong? Do some elements in the answer choices appear more often than others? (See "The Vertical Scan: A Key Tactic for Trained Test-Takers" on page 54 of this Black Book for more on this kind of analysis, as well as the Writing and Language walkthroughs starting on page 462 for examples of this technique in action.)

3b. For Reading Comprehension questions, Look for Any of the Relevant Issues We Discussed in the Section on Reading Comprehension Question Types.

There are several different issues we talked about regarding reading comprehension questions in SAT Writing and Language, but they generally have to do with finding an answer choice that directly demonstrates or reflects the concepts and relationships in the prompt, answer choices, and/or passage.

4. Find the Right Answer, or Eliminate Three Wrong Answers.

Sometimes you can immediately see which concept the question is testing, and you can tell that a particular answer choice is correct. If not, you should still be able to start eliminating wrong-answer choices based on the issues we discussed for that question type. For example, on a grammar/style/punctuation question, you might be able to tell that an answer choice has a verb in the wrong tense, or a comma in the wrong place; on a reading comprehension question, you might be able to see that an answer choice differs from the passage in a way that is unacceptable for that question type. No matter what, make sure to consider all the answer choices and identify the one correct choice that follows the rules and patterns of the SAT Writing and Language section, and the three wrong choices that break those rules and patterns.

5. Take a Second Look to Reconsider the Question, the Answer Choices, and the Passage.

Now that you've chosen a correct answer, take another look at the question, answer choices, and passage to make sure you haven't overlooked or misread anything. Did you miss an intervening phrase between a subject and its verb? Did you refer back to the wrong sentence in a paragraph? Always remember that the SAT is trying to trick you into making a small mistake on every single question. Stay on your toes.

6. Mark Your Answer Choice and Move On.

Once you've gone through the process and double-checked your answer, mark your choice and move on. Keep going through the passage until you reach the next question.

SAT Writing and Language Quick Summary

This is a one-page summary of the major concepts you'll need to know for the SAT Writing and Language section. Use it to evaluate your comprehension or jog your memory. For a more in-depth treatment of these ideas, see the rest of this section.

The Big Secrets: There are 2 main groups of SAT Writing and Language question types:

1. **Reading comprehension questions**

   The Reading Comprehension questions require careful, literal reading, and finding the answer choice that's restated or demonstrated by the relevant text. They're similar to questions on the SAT Reading section.

2. **Grammar/Style/Punctuation questions.**

   The Grammar/Style/Punctuation questions reward us for applying the College Board's standards for grammar, style, and punctuation, rather than relying on your own sense of what sounds good to you personally.

Reading Comprehension questions will tend to include a prompt. Their answer choices will express substantially different ideas. They may involve the following concepts:

- picking the answer choice that best accomplishes a task described in the prompt
- choosing the transition word that appropriately relates the given sentence to the previous sentence
- placing a sentence or paragraph in the appropriate place in the paragraph or passage
- choosing to include or not include a sentence in the passage
- choosing a word or phrase whose meaning is appropriate in context
- picking the statement that is consistent with the information in a provided figure

Grammar/Style/Punctuation questions will tend NOT to include a prompt. Their answer choices will generally express very similar ideas in slightly different ways. Common issues for these kinds of questions include:

- agreement in tense and number between/among verbs and nouns
- idiomatic usage of prepositions
- parallel structures of phrases
- avoiding redundancy and unnecessary length
- proper use of commas, semicolons, and colons

… and similar topics, all of which are covered in the Grammar/Style/Punctuation Toolbox from earlier in this section.

Here's the general SAT Writing and Language process:

1. Read the passage until you come to a question.
2. Carefully read the prompt (if there is one) and the answer choices and determine whether the question is primarily based on reading comprehension or on grammar/style/punctuation.
3. Look for any of the issues we discussed in the training for Reading Comprehension questions or Grammar/Style/Punctuation questions, as appropriate.
4. Find the right answer, or eliminate three wrong answers.
5. Take another look at the question, answer choices, and passage.
6. Mark your answer choice and move on.

Go through the SAT Writing and Language walkthroughs in this Black Book, and follow along with the SAT Practice Tests from the College Board.

If you want a more detailed description of the SAT rules for grammar, style, and punctuation, see the Grammar/Style/Punctuation Toolbox from this section.

Writing Question Walkthroughs

Now that we've discussed everything you need to know in order to tackle the Writing and Language section on the SAT, we'll show this approach in action against all the Writing and Language questions from the first four SAT Practice Tests released by the College Board. (See "Only Work with Questions from the College Board!" on page 18 of this Black Book for details on why official questions are so important, and where to get them for free if you want. And if you'd like to see some video demonstrations of these ideas, go to www.SATprepVideos.com for a selection of demonstration videos that are free to readers of this book.)

Sample Writing Walkthroughs

There are actually two types of SAT Writing and Language walkthroughs, reflecting the two general groups of SAT Writing and Language questions we identified on page 431: one type of walkthrough for Reading Comprehension questions, and one for Grammar/Style/Punctuation questions. The walkthroughs for Reading Comprehension questions look more or less similar to the walkthroughs for SAT Reading questions, and should be self-explanatory for that reason. The walkthroughs for Grammar/Style/Punctuation questions look like this:

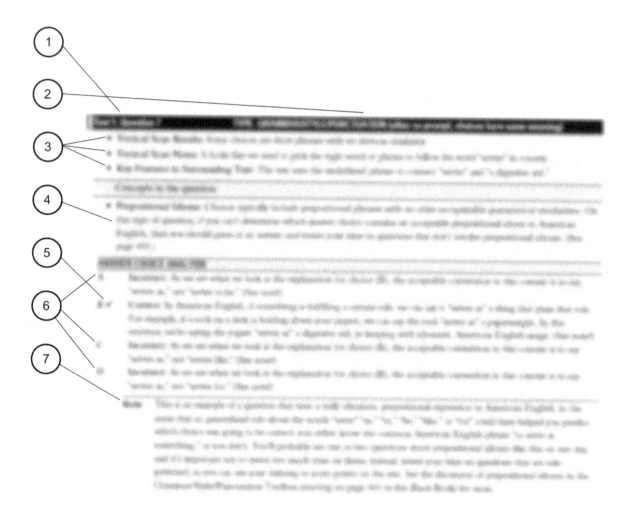

Explanation of Walkthrough Elements

The elements of the walkthrough are presented in an order that reflects "The General Process for Answering SAT Writing and Language Questions" on page 460 of this Black Book, as we can see when referring to the diagram above:

1. This shows the test number and question number of the question being analyzed in the walkthrough. You can use this information to locate the relevant question in one of the editions of the Blue Book, or in the College Board's free online practice materials.

2. This Item indicates whether the question is a Reading Comprehension question, or a Grammar/Style/Punctuation question, and how we know that. See page 431 for more on that distinction.

3. For Grammar/Style/Punctuation questions, this Item reflects the attributes of the question that a trained test-taker would notice when he first read it:

   - the results of a vertical scan of the choices (see page 54 of this Black Book for more on that)
   - the relevant features of the surrounding text, which might reveal phrases that should be paralleled in the correct answer, or phrases that must agree grammatically with the underlined phrase in the question

4. This Item reflects the Grammar/Style/Punctuation concepts that might be relevant to this question, based on the observations we made in Item 3.

5. The correct answer will be indicated with a check-mark icon, and the explanatory text will show how the correct answer follows the College Board's rules as discussed in our training for the Writing and Language section.

6. For each of the three wrong answers, the walkthrough will explain how they fail to satisfy the College Board's requirements.

7. If I feel that something is noteworthy about the question but I can't fit it in the rest of the walkthrough, then I'll note that at the end of the walkthrough. Be sure to pay attention to these notes when they appear, as they'll often contain useful information about what a particular question can teach us generally about future SAT questions.

Note that some walkthroughs are missing some of the items in this list! If one of the Items above isn't relevant to a particular question, then it's omitted.

Remember that the ultimate goal of these walkthroughs is to show you how I recommend you diagnose a question and evaluate the answer choices to find the correct answer. As always, you should feel free to modify this approach if you want, as long as your modifications still bring you the results you're looking for.

TEST 1

- **RC Question sub-type:** Vocabulary In Context. (Choices include words or short phrases that have vaguely similar but not identical meanings. Most or all of the choices will seem vaguely appropriate, but only one choice will be correct when we think very carefully and specifically about the word means and how it can be used. See page 432.)

ANSWER CHOICE ANALYSIS

A   ("Given these solutions as well as the many health benefits of the food, the advantages of Greek yogurt <u>outdo</u> the potential drawbacks of its production.") **Pattern:** Same ballpark. **Incorrect:** The word "outdo" means to perform some task better than someone else in the context of a competition. But the "solutions" and "benefits" aren't in competition with anything; they just count for more than the "drawbacks," so this choice is incorrect.

B   ("Given these solutions as well as the many health benefits of the food, the advantages of Greek yogurt <u>defeat</u> the potential drawbacks of its production.") **Pattern:** Same ballpark. **Incorrect:** The word "defeat" means to beat someone else in a contest. But the "solutions" and "benefits" aren't in a contest against anyone or anything; they just count for more than the "drawbacks," so this choice is incorrect.

C   ("Given these solutions as well as the many health benefits of the food, the advantages of Greek yogurt <u>outperform</u> the potential drawbacks of its production.") **Pattern:** Same ballpark. **Incorrect:** The word "outperform" means to do or perform some task better than someone else in the context of a competition. But the "solutions" and "benefits" aren't in competition with anything; they just count for more than the "drawbacks," so this choice is incorrect.

D ✓   ("Given these solutions as well as the many health benefits of the food, the advantages of Greek yogurt <u>outweigh</u> the potential drawbacks of its production.") **Correct:** To "outweigh" something means to carry more weight or importance than that thing. That's what's happening in this sentence—the "benefits" and "advantages" of the yogurt count for more than the "drawbacks," so this choice is correct.

- **RC Question sub-type:** Best Accomplishes X. (The prompt describes a goal of the author, and asks us which choice achieves that goal. The correct answer choice will plainly and directly demonstrate the task described in the prompt. See page 431.)
- **Subjective phrases to be ignored:** "most"

ANSWER CHOICE ANALYSIS

A   **Pattern:** Largely irrelevant. **Incorrect:** This detail mentions people making their own yogurt at home, but that isn't a "relevant detail" in the context of this paragraph—the paragraph doesn't say anything about other ways to make Greek yogurt, or foods people can make at home, or anything like that. (Note that "acid whey" and Greek yogurt are two different things—the first sentence of this paragraph tells us acid whey is "a by-product" of Greek yogurt.)

B ✓   **Pattern:** Correct. This detail mentions converting acid whey into gas for "electricity production," which is an example of one of the "number of uses for acid whey" mentioned earlier in this sentence. This answer choice demonstrates the idea of a "relevant detail" as described in the prompt, so it's correct.

C   **Pattern:** Largely irrelevant. **Incorrect:** This detail mentions that sweet whey is a better food additive for people, but that isn't a "relevant detail" in the context of this paragraph—the paragraph doesn't say anything about sweet whey, or food additives for humans, or anything along those lines.

D   **Pattern:** Largely irrelevant. **Incorrect:** The rest of the paragraph doesn't say anything about what's important for cows to eat, or anything else along those lines, so this choice doesn't demonstrate the idea of a "relevant detail."

- **Vertical Scan Results:** Some choices have different forms of the same base word.
- **Vertical Scan Notes:** We need to choose from "can pollute," "could have polluted," and "has polluted," and also from "waterways" and "waterway's."
- **Key Features in Surrounding Text:** As trained test-takers, we know that we often need to consider other verbs in the surrounding text when a question asks us for the right form of a verb. In this case, the other verb phrase in the sentence includes the present-tense verb "is." Also, with respect to the issue of whether "waterway" should be plural or possessive, we can see that nothing in the text indicates that there's one "waterway" that possesses anything, and the text mentions two types of waterways ("stream" and "rivers").

Concepts in the question:

- **Parallelism:** Choices include options that would ignore a parallel structure in the surrounding text. The correct answer choice should match phrasing in the surrounding text when possible. (See page 458.)
- **Plural/Possessive/Contraction:** Choices include the same noun ending in "-s" with or without an apostrophe before or after the "-s." Remember the three rules for forming possessives. Think of contractions in their uncontracted forms ("you're" = "you are"). (See page 441.)
- **Verb Tense/Conjugation:** Choices include different forms of the same verb. Look at the surrounding text to find each verb's subject. Also, look for other verbs that could indicate the proper tense for the verbs in the answer choices. (See page 437.)

ANSWER CHOICE ANALYSIS

A ✓   **Correct:** The word "if" indicates we're talking about what might happen in a possible scenario, which goes along with the word "can." We can also see that "pollute" needs to be in a present-tense form, since the first half of the sentence has the verb phrase "if it is," which is also in that kind of form. Further, the text mentions the impact of the runoff on "streams and rivers," which is a plural phrase describing types of waterways, so it makes sense that we'd use the plural form "waterways," not the possessive form "waterway's."

B   **Incorrect:** The text doesn't indicate that anything belongs to a waterway, or that there's a reason to use a contraction of the phrase "waterway is," so "waterway's" can't be correct.

C   **Incorrect:** As we discussed for (A), the verb "pollute" needs to be in a present-tense form, but the verb form in this choice would describe something that could possibly have happened in the past.

D   **Incorrect:** The phrase "has polluted" would describe something that definitely happened in the past, but the context doesn't support that form of the verb, as we discussed for (A). Further, the text doesn't indicate that anything belongs to a waterway, as we discussed for (B).

Answer choice patterns (see page 455): Wrong answers incorporate elements of the right answer.

Test 1, Question 4   **TYPE: GRAMMAR/STYLE/PUNCTUATION (often no prompt; choices have similar meanings)**

- **Vertical Scan Results:** Same words, different punctuation.
- **Vertical Scan Notes:** We need to choose from a semicolon, colon, or comma after "scientists," and from a comma or no punctuation after "and."
- **Key Features in Surrounding Text:** The part of the sentence before "and" can't stand on its own as a sentence, which is important to consider when we're deciding how to punctuate it.

Concepts in the question:

- **Colons:** Choices include one or more colons. A colon can be placed after a set of words that could be a sentence on their own, and before a demonstration or example of the idea before the colon. (See page 447.)
- **Commas:** Choices include one or more commas. On the Writing and Language section, commas can be used to separate things in a list of three or more, to form a comma sandwich, or to introduce an independent clause after a dependent clause. (See pages 448-450.)
- **Dependent and Independent Clauses:** Answer choice(s) would incorrectly use a dependent or independent clause. An independent clause can stand alone as a sentence: it has a main subject/verb pair. A dependent clause is introduced by a conjunction or relative pronoun. (See page 445.)
- **Semi-colons:** Choices include one or more semicolons. Semi-colons can be used to separate two sets of words that could each stand on their own as a full sentence. (See page 447.)

ANSWER CHOICE ANALYSIS

A   **Incorrect:** There shouldn't be a semi-colon after "scientists," because semi-colons can only be used on the SAT to join two independent clauses. In this case, what would come before the semi-colon and what would come after the semi-colon in this sentence aren't independent clauses.

B   **Incorrect:** There can't be a colon after "scientists" here, because what would come before the colon can't stand on its own as a complete sentence, and because what would come after the colon isn't an example or explanation of what would come before it.

C ✓   **Correct:** The word "scientists" is the second thing in a list of three things, so it should be followed by a comma and the word "and" according to the SAT's rules, just as (C) provides.

D   **Incorrect:** As we discussed in the Writing and Language training portion of this Black Book, the SAT doesn't allow us to use a comma after the word "and." (The only exception would involve a comma sandwich that was inserted at that point in a sentence, but this choice wouldn't create a valid comma sandwich, so it's still wrong.)

Answer choice patterns (see page 455): Wrong answers incorporate elements of the right answer.

- **RC Question sub-type:** Sentence or paragraph placement. (The prompt asks us where a sentence should go in a paragraph, or where a paragraph should go in the passage. The correct order will reflect a logical chronology, and/or will allow for pronouns in the sentences to refer to nouns in a logical way, and/or will place related concepts near one another. See page 432.)
- **Subjective phrases to be ignored:** "most"

ANSWER CHOICE ANALYSIS

A **Pattern:** Causes text to introduce an idea that has already been discussed. **Incorrect:** In its current position, sentence 5 talks about acid-whey runoff being a problem *after* the solution to that problem has already been mentioned in sentence 3.

B **Pattern:** Causes text to refer to an idea that hasn't been mentioned yet. **Incorrect:** If sentence 5 is placed after sentence 1, then sentence 5 will talk about improper disposal of acid-whey before the text even says (in sentence 2) that disposing of acid-whey is hard.

C ✓ **Pattern:** Correct. Sentence 5 should be placed after sentence 2 because sentence 2 introduces the idea that acid whey is "difficult to dispose of." Sentence 5 then explains what can happen if "acid-whey runoff" is "improperly introduced into the environment," which provides more information about why disposing of acid-whey is hard. Then sentence 3 talks about ways "to address the problem of disposal," which makes sense once we place sentence 5 before sentence 3.

D **Pattern:** Causes text to introduce an idea that has already been discussed. **Incorrect:** If sentence 5 is placed after sentence 3, then sentence 5 will talk about why improper disposal of acid-whey runoff is a problem *after* the idea of solving that problem has already been mentioned in sentence 3. Further, sentence 3 mentions that "farmers have found a number of uses for acid whey," and sentence 4 gives a couple of examples of those uses; if sentence 5 were placed after sentence 3, then sentence 5 would separate a sentence that mentions solutions from another sentence that gives examples of those solutions.

- **RC Question sub-type:** Including/excluding a phrase/sentence. (The question asks whether a sentence should be included in the passage. The correct choice will include a comment that plainly describes the role of the phrase or sentence in the passage. Sentences that should be included will follow broad College Board standards for ideal sentences and paragraphs—including consistency with any figures in the passage—while sentences that shouldn't be included will not follow those standards. See page 433.)

ANSWER CHOICE ANALYSIS

A **Pattern:** Direct contradiction. **Incorrect:** This sentence *does* provide a transition from the previous paragraph, which directly contradicts what (A) says. The underlined sentence restates the idea of "conservation methods" from the previous paragraph, and then introduces the idea that doing work to produce Greek yogurt is "well worth the effort," which is discussed in the current paragraph.

B **Pattern:** Direct contradiction. **Incorrect:** You could make the argument that this description of the sentence is accurate—simply saying that that it's "worth it" to put up with costly conservation methods in order to produce Greek yogurt doesn't *directly* support the main argument of the passage as introduced in the first paragraph, which is that Greek yogurt has "grown enormously in popularity" in the U.S. After all, it could be worth dealing with the difficulty associated with Greek yogurt production even if Greek yogurt had grown in popularity in other parts of the world, and not the U.S., or if the yogurt's popularity had always been high and simply remained constant in the U.S. during that time period. But, as trained test-takers, we know that the College Board will want us to follow its broader rules for ideal sentences and paragraphs, and we just saw in our analysis of choice (A) that the underlined sentence provides a transition from the previous paragraph, which is something the College Board rewards. So the sentence belongs in the paragraph, which means (B) isn't right—let's take a look at the remaining choices.

C **Pattern:** Confused concepts. **Incorrect:** The underlined sentence doesn't explain how whey can be disposed of safely, as this choice would require, so this choice is incorrect. (Note that the sentence describes conservation methods related to Greek yogurt as "costly," "time-consuming," and "worth it," but it doesn't actually explain how the whey is disposed.)

D ✓ **Pattern:** Correct. This choice describes the role of the underlined sentence in the text, because this sentence says that Greek yogurt is worth the effort involved in its production, and the rest of the paragraph provides examples to support this idea. Also, the paragraph concludes with a statement that the yogurt should continue to be made, an idea that is introduced or "set up" by the underlined sentence. Notice again that (B) and (D) both describe the sentence accurately, but we know that the College Board's broader rules for ideal sentences and paragraphs require us to include a sentence like this one that creates a transition from the previous paragraph and also introduces ideas that appear later in this paragraph.

- **Vertical Scan Results:** Some choices are short phrases with no obvious similarity.
- **Vertical Scan Notes:** It looks like we need to pick the right word or phrase to follow the word "serves" in context.
- **Key Features in Surrounding Text:** The text uses the underlined phrase to connect "serves" and "a digestive aid."

Concepts in the question:

- **Prepositional Idioms:** Choices typically include prepositional phrases with no other recognizable grammatical similarities. On this type of question, if you can't determine which answer choice contains an acceptable prepositional idiom in American English, then you should guess at an answer and invest your time in questions that don't involve prepositional idioms. (See page 443.)

ANSWER CHOICE ANALYSIS

A **Incorrect:** As we see when we look at the explanation for choice (B), the acceptable convention in this context is to say, "serves as," not "serves to be." (See note!)

B ✓ **Correct:** In American English, if something is fulfilling a certain role, we can say it "serves as" a thing that plays that role. For example, if a rock on a desk is holding down your papers, we can say the rock "serves as" a paperweight. In this sentence, we're saying the yogurt "serves as" a digestive aid, in keeping with idiomatic American English usage. (See note!)

C **Incorrect:** As we see when we look at the explanation for choice (B), the acceptable convention in this context is to say "serves as," not "serves like." (See note!)

D **Incorrect:** As we see when we look at the explanation for choice (B), the acceptable convention in this context is to say "serves as," not "serves for." (See note!)

Note This is an example of a question that tests a truly idiomatic prepositional expression in American English, in the sense that no generalized rule about the words "serve" "as," "to," "be," "like," or "for" could have helped you predict which choice was going to be correct; you either know the common American English phrase "to serve as something," or you don't. You'll probably see one or two questions about prepositional idioms like this on test day, and it's important not to invest too much time on them; instead, invest your time on questions that are rule-governed, so you can use your training to score points on the test. See the discussion of prepositional idioms in the Grammar/Style/Punctuation Toolbox (starting on page 443 in this Black Book) for more.

Test 1, Question 8   TYPE: GRAMMAR/STYLE/PUNCTUATION (often no prompt; choices have similar meanings)

- **Vertical Scan Results:** Some choices have different forms of the same base word.
- **Vertical Scan Notes:** It looks like we need to decide which form of the word "contain" is correct, and whether the word "it" should appear before "contains."
- **Key Features in Surrounding Text:** The context tells us three things about Greek yogurt: "it is an excellent source of calcium and protein, serves [as] a digestive aid, and [blank] few calories…" So the other verbs in this list, "is" and "serves," appear in the form that ends in "-s".

Concepts in the question:

- **Commas:** Choices include one or more commas. On the Writing and Language section, commas can be used to separate things in a list of three or more, to form a comma sandwich, or to introduce an independent clause after a dependent clause. (See pages 448-450.)
- **Parallelism:** Choices include options that would ignore a parallel structure in the surrounding text. The correct answer choice should match phrasing in the surrounding text when possible. (See page 458.)
- **Verb Tense/Conjugation:** Choices include different forms of the same verb. Look at the surrounding text to find each verb's subject. Also, look for other verbs that could indicate the proper tense for the verbs in the answer choices. (See page 437.)

ANSWER CHOICE ANALYSIS

A **Incorrect:** The previous phrase in the list, "serves [as] a digestive aid," doesn't include the word "it," so this portion of the text shouldn't include the word "it" either. (The structure of the sentence uses the word "it" immediately after the colon to apply to all the verbs in the following list: "is," "serves," and "contains." So we shouldn't repeat "it" before "contains," just as it's not repeated before "serves.").

B **Incorrect:** The other verbs in this list ("is" and "serves") appear in the present-tense form, ending in "-s," as opposed to a form that ends in "-ing." The form of "contain" should match those verbs, because it appears in parallel with them in the list in this sentence.

C ✓ **Correct:** As we noted for (B), the form of "contain" should match "is" and "serves," because it appears in parallel with those verbs in the list in this sentence. Also, the word "it" shouldn't appear before "contains," as we discussed for (A).

D **Incorrect:** (D) has essentially the same problem (B) has—it doesn't match the form of the parallel verbs "is" and "serves."

Answer choice patterns (see page 455): Wrong answers incorporate elements of the right answer.

- **RC Question sub-type:** Transition phrase. (The choices include words or phrases showing a transition from the previous sentence, like "however," "instead of," "for example," etc. The transition phrase must reflect the relationship between the previous sentence and the sentence where the transition phrase appears. See page 431.)

ANSWER CHOICE ANALYSIS

A ✓   **Pattern:** Correct. The previous sentence tells us Greek yogurt is "slightly lower in sugar and carbohydrates than conventional yogurt," which gives us nutritional information. The sentence we're introducing also provides nutritional information about Greek yogurt by telling us about the protein it contains. The word "also" appropriately reflects the fact that both sentences provide similar information.

B   **Pattern:** Confused concepts. **Incorrect:** "In other words" would be appropriate if this sentence restated the same information from the previous sentence, but that's not the case—this sentence provides us with information about the protein in yogurt, which is the same *kind* of information as we saw in the previous sentence, but not the *same information.*

C   **Pattern:** Confused concepts. **Incorrect:** "Therefore" would be appropriate if this sentence provided some conclusion based on the information in the previous sentence, but that's not the case.

D   **Pattern:** Confused concepts. **Incorrect:** "For instance" would be appropriate if this sentence provided an example of a concept mention in the previous sentence, but that's not the case.

- **RC Question sub-type:** Vocabulary In Context. (Choices include words or short phrases that have vaguely similar but not identical meanings. Most or all of the choices will seem vaguely appropriate, but only one choice will be correct when we think very carefully and specifically about the word means and how it can be used. See page 432.)

ANSWER CHOICE ANALYSIS

A ✓   ("… Greek yogurt contains slightly more protein per serving, thereby helping people stay <u>satiated</u> for longer periods of time.") **Correct:** To be "satiated" means to be satisfied, in the sense of no longer having a craving or a desire. (We may be able to guess that the words "satiated" and "satisfied" are similar if we notice that they both have the same root.) The text demonstrates the idea that Greek yogurt keeps people from feeling hungry after they eat it, so this choice is correct.

B   ("… Greek yogurt contains slightly more protein per serving, thereby helping people stay <u>fulfilled</u> for longer periods of time.") **Pattern:** Same ballpark. **Incorrect:** The word "fulfilled" refers to a metaphorical idea of having achieved some kind of goal. But the text doesn't specifically discuss the idea of anyone doing that. This choice might tempt some untrained test-takers because it sounds like "fill," and food that satisfies hunger can be called "filling." But "fulfill" has a different meaning that refers more to a person's mental well-being, and it doesn't apply here—this is an important reminder that we must always read carefully on the SAT, and not fall for answer choices that just seem vaguely relevant!

C   ("… Greek yogurt contains slightly more protein per serving, thereby helping people stay <u>complacent</u> for longer periods of time.") **Pattern:** Same ballpark. **Incorrect:** To be "complacent" means to be satisfied with what you've got in such a way that you stop working to hold on to it. Nothing in the text indicates that eating yogurt would make people "complacent."

D   ("… Greek yogurt contains slightly more protein per serving, thereby helping people stay <u>sufficient</u> for longer periods of time.") **Pattern:** Confused concepts. **Incorrect:** If something is "sufficient," then it's enough for whatever use you have in mind for it. This version of the sentence would call *the people themselves* "sufficient," not the yogurt, which makes no sense, since the sentence doesn't indicate what anyone would be using yogurt-eaters for.

- **Vertical Scan Results:** Similar phrases with different short words and/or punctuation.
- **Vertical Scan Notes:** We need to decide whether a comma should appear after "it," and whether the word "so," or "therefore" (or neither word) should appear before "farmers."
- **Key Features in Surrounding Text:** The phrase "because consumers…sell it" can't stand on its own as a sentence. Also, the word "because" already explains the relationship between the part of the sentence ending with "it," and the part beginning with "farmers."

Concepts in the question:

- **Colons:** Choices include one or more colons. A colon can be placed after a set of words that could be a sentence on their own, and before a demonstration or example of the idea before the colon. (See page 447.)
- **Commas:** Choices include one or more commas. On the Writing and Language section, commas can be used to separate things in a list of three or more, to form a comma sandwich, or to introduce an independent clause after a dependent clause. (See pages 448-450.)

- **Dependent and Independent Clauses:** Answer choice(s) would incorrectly use a dependent or independent clause. An independent clause can stand alone as a sentence: it has a main subject/verb pair. A dependent clause is introduced by a conjunction or relative pronoun. (See page 445.)
- **Redundancy:** Answer choices and/or surrounding text could combine to repeat the same concept unnecessarily. We should avoid words or phrases that directly repeat ideas in the immediate context. (See page 452.)

ANSWER CHOICE ANALYSIS

A   **Incorrect:** See Note below.

B ✓   **Correct:** See Note below. All we need in this position is a comma to show that the dependent clause starting with "because" is being attached to the beginning of the independent clause starting with "farmers," which is what (B) provides.

C   **Incorrect:** See Note below.

D   **Incorrect:** The phrase shouldn't include a colon because what would come before the colon can't stand on its own as a complete sentence, and the words coming after the colon wouldn't be an explanation or example of the words before it, as the SAT would require. Either of these issues would be enough to tell us a colon isn't acceptable here.

Answer choice patterns (see page 455): Wrong answers incorporate elements of the right answer.

Note   The phrase shouldn't include the word "therefore" or "so," because the sentence begins with the word "because." The word "because" already expresses the relationship between the part of the sentence before the comma and the part after the comma, which makes a word like "therefore" or "so" redundant.

| **Test 1, Question 12** | **TYPE: READING COMPREHENSION (usually has a prompt; choices have different meanings)** |

- **RC Question sub-type:** Figure. (The prompt requires us to read a figure in order to find an answer that reflects the data in the figure. The correct answer will be directly supported by the information in the figure. Remember to read carefully and check for details such as column headings, axis-labels, legends, and so on. See pages 44-51.)
- **Subjective phrases to be ignored:** "most"

ANSWER CHOICE ANALYSIS

A   **Pattern:** Confused concepts. **Incorrect:** 20 degrees is the lowest number that the average daily *high* can reach. (If we look at the graph, we can see that the average daily high is represented by the dashed line, which never goes lower than 20.) But the text refers to "daily low temperatures," so this choice is wrong.

B ✓   **Pattern:** Correct. When we read the text we can see that the correct answer needs to tell us how low the "average daily low temperatures can drop." We can see that the "average daily low" is represented by the solid black line on the chart. The lowest that the solid black line gets on the graph is right around 12 degrees Fahrenheit, which makes (B) correct.

C   **Pattern:** Direct contradiction. **Incorrect:** The lowest average daily low on the graph is 12 degrees, which happens in early March. Around December 13 the graph shows an average daily low of 19 degrees.

D   **Pattern:** Direct contradiction. **Incorrect:** The graph never shows a temperature of 10 degrees Fahrenheit at any time. Even if we wonder whether the lines just before or after 12 degrees on the graph might dip down to around 10 degrees, the temperature certainly doesn't "stay there for months," as (D) would require. (D) may be tempting because it mentions the lowest temperature on the vertical axis of the graph, but a day at that temperature doesn't appear on the graph.

| **Test 1, Question 13** | **TYPE: GRAMMAR/STYLE/PUNCTUATION (often no prompt; choices have similar meanings)** |

- **Vertical Scan Results:** Similar phrases with different short words and/or punctuation.
- **Vertical Scan Notes:** It looks like we need to decide whether there should be a comma after "summer," and whether the phrase after "summer" should be the word "following," or any one of those phrases starting with "and" and ending in "follows."
- **Key Features in Surrounding Text:** The words "thawing" and "evidence" are already mentioned in the first sentence of the paragraph.

Concepts in the question:

- **Redundancy:** Answer choices and/or surrounding text could combine to repeat the same concept unnecessarily. We should avoid words or phrases that directly repeat ideas in the immediate context. (See page 452.)

ANSWER CHOICE ANALYSIS

A ✓   **Correct:** As trained test-takers, we know that if the shortest answer choice is grammatically acceptable to the College Board, then the College Board will credit it as the correct answer.

B   **Incorrect:** This choice repeats the idea of "thawing" unnecessarily, so it's redundant.

C   **Incorrect:** This choice repeats the idea of "thawing" unnecessarily, so it's redundant.

D   **Incorrect:** This choice repeats the idea of "evidence" unnecessarily, so it's redundant.

Test 1, Question 14   TYPE: READING COMPREHENSION (usually has a prompt; choices have different meanings)

- **RC Question sub-type:** Transition phrase. (The choices include words or phrases showing a transition from the previous sentence, like "however," "instead of," "for example," etc. The transition phrase must reflect the relationship between the previous sentence and the sentence where the transition phrase appears. See page 431.)

ANSWER CHOICE ANALYSIS

A   **Pattern:** Direct contradiction. **Incorrect:** "For example" would be appropriate if this sentence provided an example of something discussed in the previous sentence, but that's not the case. The previous sentence says the ice sheet usually starts thawing "in late summer," but this sentence describes the thawing happening "by mid-July, the earliest date on record."

B ✓   **Pattern:** Correct. The previous sentence tells us that thawing usually starts "in late summer" after "several weeks of higher temperatures." But then this sentence says in 2012, "virtually the entire Greenland Ice Sheet underwent thawing by mid-July, the earliest date on record." The word "however" appropriately reflects the idea that what's discussed in this sentence is not what one would expect, given the information in the previous sentence. Notice that even if we didn't know mid-July came before "late summer," the phrase "the earliest date on record" tells us that what this sentence describes is different from what "typically" happens, as described in the previous sentence.

C   **Pattern:** Direct contradiction. **Incorrect:** "As such" would be appropriate if this sentence made a further statement that was based on the ideas in the previous sentence, but that's not the case, as we saw in our discussion of (A) and (B).

D   **Pattern:** Direct contradiction. **Incorrect:** "Moreover" would be appropriate if this sentence made a further statement that was a continuation of the ideas in the previous sentence, but that's not the case.

Test 1, Question 15   TYPE: GRAMMAR/STYLE/PUNCTUATION (often no prompt; choices have similar meanings)

- **Vertical Scan Results:** Some choices have the same words with different punctuation.
- **Vertical Scan Notes:** It looks like we need to decide whether commas should be placed after "Box," "geology," and/or "State."
- **Key Features in Surrounding Text:** The word "believes" is the verb being done by Jason Box. Box's title is listed after his name, with the word "an," instead of being listed before his name without any other wording; as trained test-takers, we know this means his title will need a comma sandwich around it.

Concepts in the question:

- **Comma Sandwich:** Choice(s) would create phrases improperly "sandwiched" between similar types of punctuation. When removed from the sentence, a properly formed sandwich leaves behind a grammatically acceptable sentence. (See page 448.)
- **Commas:** Choices include one or more commas. On the Writing and Language section, commas can be used to separate things in a list of three or more, to form a comma sandwich, or to introduce an independent clause after a dependent clause. (See pages 448-450.)
- **Dependent and Independent Clauses:** Answer choice(s) would incorrectly use a dependent or independent clause. An independent clause can stand alone as a sentence: it has a main subject/verb pair. A dependent clause is introduced by a conjunction or relative pronoun. (See page 445.)

ANSWER CHOICE ANALYSIS

A   **Incorrect:** This choice only has the first comma in the comma sandwich that needs to be around the phrase describing "Jason Box." (If we try to imagine that the sole comma in (A) is part of a sandwich for the phrase "but Jason Box," which extends back to the beginning of the sentence, then we have another problem, because removing that "sandwich" would also remove the word "but," which would change the relationship of this sentence to the one before it.)

B   **Incorrect:** This choice only has the second comma in the comma sandwich that needs to be around the phrase describing "Jason Box." The sole comma in this choice isn't used in any way that the College Board allows (it's not part of a comma sandwich, list, dependent clause, or quotation).

C ✓   **Correct:** The entire phrase "an associate professor of geology at Ohio State" is an appositive (in other words, a specific kind of comma sandwich) describing Jason Box, so that entire phrase should be sandwiched between two commas, as it is here.

D   **Incorrect:** This choice leaves out the phrase "at Ohio State" from the comma sandwich that needs to be around the phrase describing "Jason Box."

Answer choice patterns (see page 455): Wrong answers incorporate elements of the right answer.

Test 1, Question 16   TYPE: GRAMMAR/STYLE/PUNCTUATION (often no prompt; choices have similar meanings)

- **Vertical Scan Results:** Similar phrases with different short words and/or punctuation.
- **Vertical Scan Notes:** Should there be a semi-colon or a colon after "thaw?" Also, should "thaw" be followed by "and it was," "being," or no phrase?

- **Key Features in Surrounding Text:** The part of the sentence up to and including the word "thaw" could stand on its own as a sentence. The phrase "the 'dark snow' problem" can't stand on its own as a sentence, and that phrase explains what's described in the rest of the sentence.

Concepts in the question:

- **Colons:** Choices include one or more colons. A colon can be placed after a set of words that could be a sentence on their own, and before a demonstration or example of the idea before the colon. (See page 447.)
- **Semi-colons:** Choices include one or more semicolons. Semi-colons can be used to separate two sets of words that could each stand on their own as a full sentence. (See page 447.)

ANSWER CHOICE ANALYSIS

A	**Incorrect:** As we noted above, the phrase "the 'dark snow' problem" can't stand on its own as a sentence, so we can't use a semicolon to join it to the rest of the sentence, since semicolons can only be used on the SAT to join independent clauses.
B	**Incorrect:** This choice has essentially the same problem as (A): "and it was the 'dark snow' problem" is a dependent clause, and we can't use a semi-colon to separate a dependent clause from an independent clause.
C ✓	**Correct:** There should be a colon after "thaw" because everything leading up to the colon can stand alone as a sentence, and what comes after the colon is an explanation or demonstration of what comes before the colon: the text before the colon mentions "another factor," and the phrase after the colon explains that the other factor is "the 'dark snow' problem."
D	**Incorrect:** The easiest way to tell that this choice is wrong is to notice that (C) is shorter and grammatically acceptable.

Answer choice patterns (see page 455): Wrong answers incorporate elements of the right answer.

Test 1, Question 17   **TYPE: GRAMMAR/STYLE/PUNCTUATION (often no prompt; choices have similar meanings)**

- **Vertical Scan Results:** some choices are short phrases with no obvious similarity.
- **Vertical Scan Notes:** We need to find the acceptable way to refer back to "soot" (whether with "it," "soot," or "which"), or decide whether the whole phrase should be deleted.
- **Key Features in Surrounding Text:** The phrase "according to Box...soot" can stand on its own as a sentence, and that phrase is separated from the rest of the sentence by a comma, which we don't have the option to change.

Concepts in the question:

- **Comma Splice:** Answer choice(s) and/or surrounding text use commas to separate two groups of words that could each be sentences on their own. A comma can't be used in this way on the SAT Writing and Language section. (See page 447.)
- **Commas:** Choices include one or more commas. On the Writing and Language section, commas can be used to separate things in a list of three or more, to form a comma sandwich, or to introduce an independent clause after a dependent clause. (See pages 448-450.)
- **Dependent and Independent Clauses:** Answer choice(s) would incorrectly use a dependent or independent clause. An independent clause can stand alone as a sentence: it has a main subject/verb pair. A dependent clause is introduced by a conjunction or relative pronoun. (See page 445.)

ANSWER CHOICE ANALYSIS

A	**Incorrect:** This choice would result in two sets of words that could each stand alone as sentences being joined by a comma, which isn't allowed on the SAT. Those two sentences would be "According to Box...fires...produced...amounts of soot," and "some of it drifted... onto the ice sheet."
B	**Incorrect:** This choice can't be correct for the same basic reason (A) can't be correct. The only difference is that the second sentence in this case would be "some soot drifted...onto the ice sheet."
C ✓	**Correct:** This choice is correct because it's grammatically acceptable to the SAT, and it solves the problem from choices (A), (B), and (D). Notice that the word "which" makes the second phrase a dependent clause, so it's okay to join that clause to the rest of the sentence with a comma, according to the SAT's rules.
D	**Incorrect:** This choice can't be correct for the same basic reason (A) and (B) are wrong. (Deleting the underlined phrase causes the second independent clause in the original "sentence" to be "some drifted over Greenland in giant plumes of smoke and then fell as particles onto the ice sheet.").

Test 1, Question 18   **TYPE: GRAMMAR/STYLE/PUNCTUATION (often no prompt; choices have similar meanings)**

- **Vertical Scan Results:** Some choices have different forms of the same base word.
- **Vertical Scan Notes:** We need to find the correct form of the verb "to fall."
- **Key Features in Surrounding Text:** As trained test-takers, we notice that the thing doing the falling in the underlined phrase is the "soot" from earlier in the sentence. The other two verbs related to the soot are "produced" and "drifted," and the word "then" indicates that the falling happened right after the drifting.

Concepts in the question:

- **Parallelism:** Choices include options that would ignore a parallel structure in the surrounding text. The correct answer choice should match phrasing in the surrounding text when possible. (See page 458.)

- **Verb Tense/Conjugation:** Choices include different forms of the same verb. Look at the surrounding text to find each verb's subject. Also, look for other verbs that could indicate the proper tense for the verbs in the answer choices. (See page 437.)

ANSWER CHOICE ANALYSIS

A ✓   **Correct:** As trained test-takers, we know that issues of verb tense on the SAT are often resolved by looking at the surrounding text for other verb forms that must be paralleled by the form in a question. In this case, this choice makes the text say that soot "drifted...and then fell...." The word "then" tells us that one verb happens immediately after the other, so they should both be in the same form, according to the SAT's unwritten rules. (Of course, "*falled" is a form that doesn't exist in English, because "fall" is an irregular verb; "fell" is the form that parallels "produced" and "drifted" in the sentence.)

B   **Incorrect:** As we saw in the explanation for (A), we shouldn't change "fell" to "falls," because that would mean the falling would happen in the present, and not in the past, like the other verbs related to soot in this sentence.

C   **Incorrect:** This choice has a similar issue to (B). We shouldn't change "fell" to "will fall," because the falling needs to happen in the past, not the future, in order to parallel "produced" and "drifted."

D   **Incorrect:** We shouldn't change "fell" to "had fallen," because the verb needs to parallel "produced" and "drifted." Since all these verbs are happening in the same time frame, they should either all have a helping verb like "had," or none of them should. Since the other verbs don't have helping verbs, the right form of "fall" shouldn't have a helping verb in this case.

Test 1, Question 19 — TYPE: GRAMMAR/STYLE/PUNCTUATION (often no prompt; choices have similar meanings)

- **Vertical Scan Results:** Some choices include homophone pairs or triples.

- **Vertical Scan Notes:** We need to decide whether the pronoun should be singular or plural, and how to form the appropriate version of that pronoun.

- **Key Features in Surrounding Text:** The underlined phrase refers to the plural phrase "snow and ice," so that phrase needs to be plural. Also, the "ability" belongs to the snow and ice, so the underlined phrase needs to express the idea of possession.

Concepts in the question:

- **Confused Homophones:** Choices include different homophone pairs (such as "their" and "they're" or "too" and "to"). Read carefully—also, remember the correct formation of possessive pronouns, and remember to read contractions as their uncontracted forms (e.g. "it's" = "it is"). (See page 452.)

- **Plural/Possessive/Contraction:** Choices include the same noun ending in "-s" with or without an apostrophe before or after the "-s." Remember the three rules for forming possessives. Think of contractions in their uncontracted forms ("you're" = "you are"). (See page 441.)

- **Singular versus Plural:** Choices include singular and plural versions of the same base words that don't agree with other words in the surrounding text. Singular nouns must go with singular verb forms and singular pronouns. Plural nouns must go with plural verbs and pronouns. Think carefully about which words should match or agree with each other! (See page 443.)

ANSWER CHOICE ANALYSIS

A   **Incorrect:** The underlined phrase refers to "snow and ice," which are two things, so the phrase needs to be plural. Further, the word "it's" isn't possessive; that word is the contracted form of "it is," which makes no sense in the original sentence.

B   **Incorrect:** The underlined phrase refers to "snow and ice," so the phrase needs to be plural.

C   **Incorrect:** The underlined phrase refers to "snow and ice," so the phrase needs to be plural—but this is actually the word "there," which indicates a physical location, like the words "where" and "here," as opposed to the plural possessive pronoun "their."

D ✓   **Correct:** The underlined phrase refers to "snow and ice," so the phrase needs to be plural, and this is the correct possessive plural form of the pronoun "they."

Test 1, Question 20 — TYPE: READING COMPREHENSION (usually has a prompt; choices have different meanings)

- **RC Question sub-type:** Best Accomplishes X. (The prompt describes a goal of the author, and asks us which choice achieves that goal. The correct answer choice will plainly and directly demonstrate the task described in the prompt. See page 431.)

- **Subjective phrases to be ignored:** "best"

ANSWER CHOICE ANALYSIS

A   **Pattern:** Largely irrelevant. **Incorrect:** A "cycle" describes something circular that ends back at its own beginning. The text says, "the result is a self-reinforcing cycle. As the ice melts...," so the beginning of the cycle is the ice melting. That means the end of the cycle must return to the idea of ice melting. (A) is wrong because it doesn't say anything about ice melting.

B   **Pattern:** Largely irrelevant. **Incorrect:** This choice has the same basic problem as (A), and it's wrong for the same reasons.

C **Pattern: Direct contradiction. Incorrect:** As we noted in our discussion of (A), the correct answer needs to refer back to the idea of "melt[ing]" from the original sentence in order to describe a complete cycle. But this choice talks about "cool[ing]," which is kind of the opposite of melting.

D ✓ **Pattern: Correct.** The question asks us to complete "the description of a self-reinforcing cycle." As we saw in the discussion for (A), a "cycle" is a process that ends back at its own beginning. The beginning of the cycle in the text is the "ice melt[ing]," so the end of the cycle must return to the idea of "melting," as this choice does. This is the only choice that causes the text to demonstrate the idea of describing a cycle, as mentioned in the prompt, so it's correct.

Note Some untrained test-takers will see this question in practice and then make the mistake of thinking that the key idea in the question is that a cycle must start somewhere, follow a certain path, and then end up back where it started. But it's highly unlikely that you'll actually be tested on the idea of a "cycle" on test day! Instead, the lesson to learn from this question is that we always need to read and think carefully on the SAT, and remember the rules of the test. If we only think in vague, general terms about what a cycle is, we might think that (A), (B), or (D) could all be correct. But if we read and think carefully about the specific concepts in the question—which happen to involve cycles in this case—then it becomes clear that only (D) can possibly be right. On test day, you'll definitely see questions that require you to think precisely about the definitions of key terms, but it's unlikely that "cycle" will be one of those terms.

| **Test 1, Question 21** | **TYPE: GRAMMAR/STYLE/PUNCTUATION (often no prompt; choices have similar meanings)** |

- **Vertical Scan Results:** Similar phrases with different short words and/or punctuation.
- **Vertical Scan Notes:** We need to choose whether to include a comma after the word "itself." We also need to choose whether "with damage and," "possibly," or no phrase should appear after "itself."
- **Key Features in Surrounding Text:** The word before the underlined phrase is "repeat," which expresses the idea of something happening "again." The text includes the phrase "harmful effects," which expresses the idea of "damage." The text also includes the word "may," which expresses the idea that something will "possibly" happen.

Concepts in the question:

- **Redundancy:** Answer choices and/or surrounding text could combine to repeat the same concept unnecessarily. We should avoid words or phrases that directly repeat ideas in the immediate context. (See page 452.)

ANSWER CHOICE ANALYSIS

A **Incorrect:** The word "again" is redundant: "repeat" already conveys that the pattern is happening again. "Repeat" isn't underlined, so we can't change it, which means "again" is inappropriate, according to the SAT's rules.

B ✓ **Correct:** This is the shortest choice and it's grammatically acceptable, which makes it correct, according to the SAT's unwritten rules for Writing and Language questions that feature style, grammar, and/or punctuation. Also, every other choice is redundant in some way.

C **Incorrect:** The word "damage" is redundant: "harmful effects" already conveys that the pattern will cause damage. "Harmful effects" isn't underlined, so we can't change it, which means "damage" must be inappropriate, according to the SAT's rules.

D **Incorrect:** The word "possibly" is redundant: "may" already conveys that the repetition of the pattern is a possibility, not a certainty. "May" isn't underlined, so we can't change it, which means "possibly" is redundant, according to the SAT's rules.

Answer choice patterns (see page 454): Shortest grammatically acceptable choice is correct.

| **Test 1, Question 22** | **TYPE: READING COMPREHENSION (usually has a prompt; choices have different meanings)** |

- **RC Question sub-type:** Sentence or paragraph placement. (The prompt asks us where a sentence should go in a paragraph, or where a paragraph should go in the passage. The correct order will reflect a logical chronology, and/or will allow for pronouns in the sentences to refer to nouns in a logical way, and/or will place related concepts near one another. See page 432.)
- **Subjective phrases to be ignored:** "most"

ANSWER CHOICE ANALYSIS

A **Pattern: Causes text to refer to an idea that hasn't been mentioned yet. Incorrect:** In this sentence's current position, it refers to "this crucial information," but up to this point in the paragraph there's nothing for the phrase "this crucial information" to refer back to.

B **Pattern: Causes text to refer to an idea that hasn't been mentioned yet. Incorrect:** This choice has the same issue as (A): if sentence 4 were placed after sentence 1, it would refer to "this crucial information," but up to that point in the paragraph there isn't anything for the phrase "this crucial information" to refer back to.

C **Pattern: Causes text to refer to an idea that hasn't been mentioned yet. Incorrect:** This choice has the same issue as (A) and (B): the phrase "this crucial information" can't be referring to anything that's been mentioned by sentence 2.

D ✓ **Pattern: Correct.** Sentence 4 mentions Box gathering "this crucial information," so sentence 4 needs to come after another sentence that tells us what the word "this" in that phrase is referring to. Sentence 5 explains that the information is "just how much the soot is contributing to the melting of the ice sheet," so sentence 4 should appear after sentence 5 in order to satisfy the SAT's rules.

Test 1, Question 23 — TYPE: GRAMMAR/STYLE/PUNCTUATION (often no prompt; choices have similar meanings)

- **Vertical Scan Results:** Similar phrases with different short words and/or punctuation.
- **Vertical Scan Notes:** We need to choose from "soon got," "was promptly," "promptly," or no phrase in the first part of the underlined text, and we need to choose whether "worn" or "wore" is appropriate in the second part of the underlined text.
- **Key Features in Surrounding Text:** The sentence says the action in the underlined phrase happened "quickly." The surrounding sentences also use verb phrases in the past ("traded," "found," "read," etc.)

Concepts in the question:

- **Parallelism:** Choices include options that would ignore a parallel structure in the surrounding text. The correct answer choice should match phrasing in the surrounding text when possible. (See page 458.)
- **Redundancy:** Answer choices and/or surrounding text could combine to repeat the same concept unnecessarily. We should avoid words or phrases that directly repeat ideas in the immediate context. (See page 452.)
- **Verb Tense/Conjugation:** Choices include different forms of the same verb. Look at the surrounding text to find each verb's subject. Also, look for other verbs that could indicate the proper tense for the verbs in the answer choices. (See page 437.)

ANSWER CHOICE ANALYSIS

A   Incorrect: The word "soon" is redundant, because the word "quickly" already expresses the idea that "the novelty" wore off in a short period of time. Further, as we'll see below, (D) is shorter and grammatically acceptable, so (A) can't be right according to the SAT's unwritten rules.

B   Incorrect: The word "promptly" is redundant, because the word "quickly" already expresses the idea that "the novelty" wore off in a short period of time.

C   Incorrect: The word "promptly" is redundant in this choice, just as it was in (B).

D ✓ Correct: This is the shortest answer and it's grammatically acceptable. It also avoids the redundancy in all the other choices.

Answer choice patterns (see pages 454 and 455): Shortest grammatically acceptable choice is correct. Wrong answers incorporate elements of the right answer.

Note   Many test-takers will struggle with the verb conjugation aspect of this question, because "wear" is an irregular verb in English. But, as trained test-takers, we can notice that (A), (B), and (C) all involve redundant words that the College Board won't allow in the correct answer, which means we can tell (D) must be correct without even having to worry about the form of the verb "wear."

Test 1, Question 24 — TYPE: GRAMMAR/STYLE/PUNCTUATION (often no prompt; choices have similar meanings)

- **Vertical Scan Results:** Choices are long phrases/sentences.
- **Vertical Scan Notes:** Only (D) begins with "I," which is the thing being described by the participial phrase "having become frustrated trying to solve difficult problems."
- **Key Features in Surrounding Text:** The underlined phrase comes immediately after the phrase "having become frustrated trying to solve difficult problems," which is a participial phrase attached to an independent clause by a comma. As trained test-takers, we know that the first noun phrase after the comma should be the thing described by "having become frustrated trying to solve difficult problems."

Concepts in the question:

- **Dangling Participle:** The question involves descriptive phrases beginning with an "-ing" word that would describe the wrong word in context. Descriptive phrases starting with a word ending in "-ing" describe the first noun phrase in that sentence's independent clause. (See page 450.)

ANSWER CHOICE ANALYSIS

A   Incorrect: This choice would mean that "having become frustrated trying to solve difficult problems" describes "no colleagues," which doesn't make sense in context.

B   Incorrect: This choice would mean that "having become frustrated trying to solve difficult problems" describes "colleagues," which doesn't make sense in context.

C   Incorrect: This choice would mean that "having become frustrated trying to solve difficult problems" describes "ideas," which doesn't make sense—"ideas" can't get "frustrated."

D ✓ Correct: The phrase "having become frustrated trying to solve difficult problems" describes the speaker, so the next phrase that comes after the comma needs to mean the same thing as "the speaker." This option places "I" directly after that phrase, and "I" refers to the speaker, so this choice appropriately indicates that the speaker is the person who has become frustrated.

Note   The rule about words ending in "-ing" having to describe the first noun in an independent clause is a good example of the kind of rules that are followed by the SAT even though they aren't universally followed in the everyday speech of educated speakers of American English. Remember that your job on test day is always to pick the answer choice that satisfies the College Board's rules, not the rules that might be acceptable to your teachers or yourself!

Test 1, Question 25   TYPE: GRAMMAR/STYLE/PUNCTUATION (often no prompt; choices have similar meanings)

- **Vertical Scan Results:** Some choices are short phrases with no obvious similarity.
- **Vertical Scan Notes:** It looks like we need to pick the right word to go between "article" and "coworking."
- **Key Features in Surrounding Text:** The underlined phrase connects the word "article" and the phrase "coworking spaces."

Concepts in the question:

- **Prepositional Idioms:** Choices typically include prepositional phrases with no other recognizable grammatical similarities. On this type of question, if you can't determine which answer choice contains an acceptable prepositional idiom in American English, then you should guess at an answer and invest your time in questions that don't involve prepositional idioms. (See page 443.)

ANSWER CHOICE ANALYSIS
A   Incorrect: If an article covers a topic, it's unacceptable in American English to say the article is "into" that topic. (See note!)
B ✓   Correct: If an article covers a topic, it's acceptable in American English to say the article is "about" that topic. (See note!)
C   Incorrect: If an article covers a topic, it's unacceptable in American English to say the article is "upon" that topic. (See note!)
D   Incorrect: If an article covers a topic, it's unacceptable in American English to say the article is "for" that topic. (See note!)

Note   Remember that the College Board will include a few questions about prepositional idioms on the Writing and Language section; by definition, these questions don't follow any general rules that can be used to predict the correct answers to other prepositional idiom questions that you'll see on test day. When you see a question like this, you should mark the answer that seems best to you as quickly as possible, based on your gut feelings of the appropriate preposition in American English, and then move on to other questions where you can apply your knowledge of the test's rules and patterns to mark answers with certainty. See the training on prepositional idioms in the Grammar/Style/Punctuation Toolbox earlier in this Black Book (starting on page 443) for further explanation.

Test 1, Question 26   TYPE: GRAMMAR/STYLE/PUNCTUATION (often no prompt; choices have similar meanings)

- **Vertical Scan Results:** Some choices have the same words with different punctuation.
- **Vertical Scan Notes:** Should there be a comma after "equipment?" Should there be a comma, colon, or no punctuation after "as?"
- **Key Features in Surrounding Text:** The sentence uses the phrase "such as" to introduce a list of examples of "equipment."

Concepts in the question:

- **Colons:** Choices include one or more colons. A colon can be placed after a set of words that could be a sentence on their own, and before a demonstration or example of the idea before the colon. (See page 447.)
- **Commas:** Choices include one or more commas. On the Writing and Language section, commas can be used to separate things in a list of three or more, to form a comma sandwich, or to introduce an independent clause after a dependent clause. (See pages 448-450.)

ANSWER CHOICE ANALYSIS
A ✓   Correct: This choice appropriately uses a comma to separate the independent clause "the spaces…equipment" from the phrase "such as…machines." (We know from our training that the phrase "such as" doesn't require a comma after it.)
B   Incorrect: There shouldn't be a colon after "as," because the words in the sentence before the colon wouldn't be able to stand on their own as a sentence, which is something the SAT requires when we use a colon.
C   Incorrect: This choice has the same problem as (B), and is wrong for the same reason.
D   Incorrect: The College Board's unwritten rules don't allow us to use a comma after the phrase "such as," as we discussed in our training on comma usage.

Test 1, Question 27   TYPE: READING COMPREHENSION (usually has a prompt; choices have different meanings)

- **RC Question sub-type:** Transition phrase. (The choices include words or phrases showing a transition from the previous sentence, like "however," "instead of," "for example," etc. The transition phrase must reflect the relationship between the previous sentence and the sentence where the transition phrase appears. See page 431.)

ANSWER CHOICE ANALYSIS

A   **Pattern:** Direct contradiction. **Incorrect:** The word "however" would be appropriate if this sentence contained information that was somehow in opposition to the information in the previous sentence, but that's not the case. The fact that coworking spaces usually have standard office equipment doesn't contrast with the fact that those spaces also often include "small meeting areas" and "larger rooms." Further, the phrase "in these locations" is redundant because the sentence already says we're talking about what "the spaces often include."

B ✓   **Pattern:** Correct. The previous sentence mentions some "standard office equipment" that the coworking spaces usually have. This sentence lists additional resources that the spaces "often include," so it makes sense to introduce this sentence with the phrase "in addition to equipment" before mentioning other resources.

C   **Pattern:** Largely irrelevant. **Incorrect:** This choice would be appropriate if the previous sentence mentioned some reasons that lead to the ideas in this sentence, but no reasons are mentioned in the previous sentence.

D   **Pattern:** Same ballpark. **Incorrect:** This choice would be appropriate if this sentence mentioned more of the same kind of information found in the previous sentence, but that's not the case—the previous sentence discusses equipment in the coworking space, but this sentence describes some of the rooms included in the space.

❙ Test 1, Question 28   **TYPE: READING COMPREHENSION (usually has a prompt; choices have different meanings)**

- **RC Question sub-type:** Including/excluding a phrase/sentence. (The question asks whether a sentence should be included in the passage. The correct choice will include a comment that plainly describes the role of the phrase or sentence in the passage. Sentences that should be included will follow broad College Board standards for ideal sentences and paragraphs—including consistency with any figures in the passage—while sentences that shouldn't be included will not follow those standards. See page 433.)

ANSWER CHOICE ANALYSIS

A   **Pattern:** Direct contradiction. **Incorrect:** The underlined sentence *doesn't* provide a detail that supports the main topic of the paragraph, as this choice would require. The main topic of this paragraph is an explanation of what coworking spaces are, which we know because each sentence (other than this one) provides basic information about what a coworking space is, and what can be found in a coworking space. But the paragraph doesn't discuss the cost associated with running your own coworking business, so this sentence doesn't provide a relevant detail according to the SAT.

B   **Pattern:** Direct contradiction. **Incorrect:** The underlined sentence *doesn't* set up the main topic of the paragraph that follows, as this choice would require, because "setting up" a topic on the SAT means introducing that topic, and the cost of launching a coworking business doesn't get discussed in the next paragraph.

C ✓   **Pattern:** Correct. The underlined sentence provides a detail that isn't discussed elsewhere in this paragraph—this paragraph doesn't discuss the costs of running or starting a coworking business, or launching businesses in the United States, or anything like that. This is what the SAT means when it uses the phrase "blurs the focus," so (C) is correct.

D   **Pattern:** Direct contradiction. **Incorrect:** The underlined sentence doesn't repeat information from an earlier paragraph—no other paragraph discusses the cost of launching a coworking business.

❙ Test 1, Question 29   **TYPE: READING COMPREHENSION (usually has a prompt; choices have different meanings)**

- **RC Question sub-type:** Figure. (The prompt requires us to read a figure in order to find an answer that reflects the data in the figure. The correct answer will be directly supported by the information in the figure. Remember to read carefully and check for details such as column headings, axis-labels, legends, and so on. See pages 44-51.)

- **Subjective phrases to be ignored:** "most"

ANSWER CHOICE ANALYSIS

A   **Pattern:** Direct contradiction. **Incorrect:** The chart indicates that the dark gray bars represent the percentage of people surveyed who believe that the "Perceived Effect of Coworking" on a particular "Business Skill" was *positive*. With that in mind, we can see that the graph shows 64% of respondents said coworking spaces had a *positive* impact on "completing tasks in a given time," which is the opposite of what this choice says.

B ✓   **Pattern:** Correct. We can see that the graph shows 71% of respondents said coworking spaces had a *positive* impact on their creativity, since the dark-gray bar next to "creativity" on the graph has the number 71% next to it. Choice (B) accurately describes this data, so (B) is correct.

C   **Pattern:** Confused concepts. **Incorrect:** The topmost bar in the graph shows that 74% of respondents thought they experienced a positive effect on their business-related ideas, which isn't the same thing as saying that 74% of new business ideas originated in coworking spaces, as this choice would require.

D   **Pattern:** Confused concepts. **Incorrect:** The graph shows which percentage of respondents felt coworking spaces had a positive or negative impact on certain skills; it doesn't represent a percentage increase in their abilities. (Even if it did, the graph would show a *negative* impact of 12%, not a positive impact as (D) requires, since the light-gray bars indicate a negative impact.)

❙ Test 1, Question 30   **TYPE: GRAMMAR/STYLE/PUNCTUATION (often no prompt; choices have similar meanings)**

- **Vertical Scan Results:** Choices include most or all possible combinations of two options.

- **Vertical Scan Notes:** We need to choose between "who" and "whom," and we need to choose between "use" and "uses."
- **Key Features in Surrounding Text:** "People" is the thing that "who/whom" refers to, and "people" is also the thing doing the action "to use."

Concepts in the question:

- **Who versus Whom:** At least one answer choice involves "who" or "whom." "Who" is a subject pronoun (that does an action), and "whom" is an object pronoun (that receives an action). In other words, we can use "who" where "he" would be appropriate, and "whom" where "him" would be appropriate. (See page 439.)
- **Singular versus Plural:** Choices include singular and plural versions of the same base words that don't agree with other words in the surrounding text. Singular nouns must go with singular verb forms and singular pronouns. Plural nouns must go with plural verbs and pronouns. Think carefully about which words should match or agree with each other! (See page 443.)

ANSWER CHOICE ANALYSIS

A	**Incorrect:** "Whom" is inappropriate here because the underlined word is doing the action of the verb "use," not acting as the object of another verb or preposition. (A quick way to check this is to apply the "he/him" test, as we described in the training portion of this Black Book: we wouldn't say "him uses," so we can't say "whom uses.").
B	**Incorrect:** This choices has the same "who/whom" problem that (A) has. Also, "who" refers to the plural noun "people," so the verb needs to be in its plural form, which is "use," not "uses."
C	**Incorrect:** "Who" refers to the plural noun "people," so the verb needs to be in its plural form, "use," not "uses."
D ✓	**Correct:** As we noted in our discussions of the other choices, "who" is appropriate because it's doing the action of "using" in this sentence, and the word "use" needs to be in its plural form because "who" refers back to the plural word "people." We can also try the they/them test here—if we turn the phrase into a question and ask "who uses them?" the answer would be "they use…," not "*them use…" We know that "they" corresponds to "who" in this test, which again confirms that "who" is right. (See "Who versus whom" on page 439 of this Black Book for a refresher on the they/them and he/him test.)

Answer choice patterns (see page 455): Wrong answers incorporate elements of the right answer.

Test 1, Question 31   **TYPE: READING COMPREHENSION (usually has a prompt; choices have different meanings)**

- **RC Question sub-type:** Sentence or paragraph placement. (The prompt asks us where a sentence should go in a paragraph, or where a paragraph should go in the passage. The correct order will reflect a logical chronology, and/or will allow for pronouns in the sentences to refer to nouns in a logical way, and/or will place related concepts near one another. See page 432.)
- **Subjective phrases to be ignored:** "best"

ANSWER CHOICE ANALYSIS

A	**Pattern:** Causes events to be discussed out of chronological order. **Incorrect:** Sentence 1 says the speaker "decided to try using a coworking space." The sentence in the prompt describes the speaker taking a tour of the facility and starting to work, so it doesn't make sense to place this sentence about the speaker actually using the facility before he even decides to use the facility. Further, the word "thus" in sentence 1 would make no sense with the prompt sentence at the beginning of the paragraph.
B	**Pattern:** Causes events to be discussed out of chronological order. **Incorrect:** Sentence 2 says the speaker "chose a facility." The sentence in the prompt describes the coworker taking a tour of the facility and starting to work, so it doesn't make sense to place this sentence about the speaker actually using the facility before he even chooses which facility to use.
C ✓	**Pattern:** Correct. Sentence 1 describes how the speaker decided to use a coworking space. Sentence 2 describes how the speaker chose the particular space he wanted to try. In sentences 3 and 4, the speaker describes people appearing, and people working. So it seems like the speaker has actually gone to the coworking space between sentence 2 and sentence 3, but that isn't in the original version of the text. The sentence in the prompt describes the speaker "filling out a form," "taking a quick tour," taking a seat, and getting to work. Because the sentence in the prompt describes the speaker actually getting to the coworking space and beginning to work, that sentence should go between sentences 2 and 3, as (C) indicates.
D	**Pattern:** Causes events to be discussed out of chronological order. **Incorrect:** Sentence 3 says "more people appeared" "throughout the morning." The sentence in the prompt describes the coworker filling out a form, taking a tour of the facility, and starting to work. It doesn't make sense to place this sentence about the speaker getting started on his work at the coworking space *after* a sentence that describes people showing up throughout the morning—the speaker must arrive at the facility and find a seat *before* he can observe other people showing up throughout the morning.

Test 1, Question 32   **TYPE: GRAMMAR/STYLE/PUNCTUATION (often no prompt; choices have similar meanings)**

- **Vertical Scan Results:** Same words, different punctuation.
- **Vertical Scan Notes:** We need to choose from a colon, semi-colon, comma, or no punctuation after "colleagues."

- **Key Features in Surrounding Text:** The phrase "over time, I've gotten to know several of my coworking colleagues" can stand on its own as a complete sentence, and "another website developer, a graphic designer, a freelance writer, and several mobile app coders" are examples of the "colleagues" mentioned in the first half of the sentence.

Concepts in the question:

- **Colons:** Choices include one or more colons. A colon can be placed after a set of words that could be a sentence on their own, and before a demonstration or example of the idea before the colon. (See page 447.)
- **Commas:** Choices include one or more commas. On the Writing and Language section, commas can be used to separate things in a list of three or more, to form a comma sandwich, or to introduce an independent clause after a dependent clause. (See pages 448-450.)
- **Semi-colons:** Choices include one or more semicolons. Semi-colons can be used to separate two sets of words that could each stand on their own as a full sentence. (See page 447.)

ANSWER CHOICE ANALYSIS

A ✓ **Correct:** We need a colon after "colleagues" because all the words in the sentence before the colon could stand on their own as a sentence, and what comes after the colon is an example or explanation of what comes before the colon. This situation fits exactly with the College Board's rules for colon usage.

B **Incorrect:** There shouldn't be a semi-colon after "colleagues" because the part of the sentence after the semi-colon couldn't stand on its own as a complete sentence, which violates the College Board's rules for semicolon usage.

C **Incorrect:** We can't put a comma after "colleagues" because it changes the meaning of the sentence significantly: it would make the list of the people the speaker now knows include "coworking colleagues," a "developer," "a graphic designer," a "writer," "and several mobile app coders," instead of making the developer, designer, writer, and coders be *examples* of the colleagues. When we look at the rest of the paragraph, it's clear that the speaker is confining her remarks to the people at the coworking space, so the College Board's rules for paragraph structuring would require this sentence to talk only about those people, instead of introducing other people. For that reason, a comma isn't acceptable after the word "colleagues," even if it would create a grammatically acceptable sentence outside the context of this paragraph.

D **Incorrect:** We can't leave out any punctuation after "colleagues" because, as described in the explanation for choice (A), we need a colon there in order to connect the list of different colleagues to the rest of the sentence.

Test 1, Question 33   **TYPE: READING COMPREHENSION (usually has a prompt; choices have different meanings)**

- **RC Question sub-type:** Vocabulary In Context. (Choices include words or short phrases that have vaguely similar but not identical meanings. Most or all of the choices will seem vaguely appropriate, but only one choice will be correct when we think very carefully and specifically about the word means and how it can be used. See page 432.)

ANSWER CHOICE ANALYSIS

A ✓ ("Even those of us who work in disparate fields are able to <u>share advice</u> and help each other brainstorm.") **Correct:** The text mentions how the workers "help each other brainstorm." It makes sense to say they "share advice," because the idea of sharing advice means the workers are all both giving and receiving advice, which goes along with the idea that they "help each other." Only (A) clearly restates the idea that the workers are mutually helping one another, so this choice is correct.

B ("Even those of us who work in disparate fields are able to <u>give some wisdom</u> and help each other brainstorm.") **Pattern:** Same ballpark. **Incorrect:** This idea isn't stated in the text—the text doesn't say that the workers "give some wisdom," it says they "help each other brainstorm." Helping each other brainstorm means that the advice and ideas can potentially flow in all directions, while giving wisdom would involve information flowing in one direction. Further, not all brainstorming ideas are good, by definition, but wisdom is valuable and accurate, so this choice fails to restate the text in that way as well.

C ("Even those of us who work in disparate fields are able to <u>proclaim our opinions</u> and help each other brainstorm.") **Pattern:** Same ballpark. **Incorrect:** This might sound like it generally goes along with the text, but "proclaiming our opinions" just means saying out loud what you think about different things. It doesn't even mean that you're saying your opinions to anyone in particular, or that more than one person is involved. This doesn't go along with the idea of "help[ing] each other brainstorm," which must involve one person interacting with at least one other person; further, brainstorming is usually a matter of generating new ideas and advice, rather than gathering opinions.

D ("Even those of us who work in disparate fields are able to <u>opine</u> and help each other brainstorm.") **Pattern:** Same ballpark. **Incorrect:** This choice means basically the same thing as (C), and is wrong for the same reason.

Test 1, Question 34   **TYPE: READING COMPREHENSION (usually has a prompt; choices have different meanings)**

- **RC Question sub-type:** Transition phrase. (The choices include words or phrases showing a transition from the previous sentence, like "however," "instead of," "for example," etc. The transition phrase must reflect the relationship between the previous sentence and the sentence where the transition phrase appears. See page 431.)

ANSWER CHOICE ANALYSIS

A ✓ **Pattern: Correct.** It makes sense to introduce the statement in this sentence with the phrase "in broad terms," because that statement describes philosophy in broad, non-specific terms.

B **Pattern: Largely irrelevant. Incorrect:** This choice would be appropriate if this sentence gave an example of something mentioned in the previous sentence, but that's not the case.

C **Pattern: Largely irrelevant. Incorrect:** This choice would be appropriate if this sentence offered some kind of information or viewpoint that was the opposite of what was discussed in the previous sentence, but that's not the case.

D **Pattern: Largely irrelevant. Incorrect:** This choice would be appropriate if this sentence told us something that was true in spite of what was mentioned in the previous sentence, but that's not the case.

❚ Test 1, Question 35 TYPE: GRAMMAR/STYLE/PUNCTUATION (often no prompt; choices have similar meanings)

- **Vertical Scan Results:** Choices are long phrases/sentences. Some choices have different forms of the same base word.
- **Vertical Scan Notes:** We need to pick the choice that can be an acceptable part of a phrase that's attached to the front of an independent clause with a comma.
- **Key Features in Surrounding Text:** The underlined phrase is followed by the phrase "…the discipline encourages…".

Concepts in the question:

- **Commas:** Choices include one or more commas. On the Writing and Language section, commas can be used to separate things in a list of three or more, to form a comma sandwich, or to introduce an independent clause after a dependent clause. (See pages 448-450.)
- **Dangling Participle:** The question involves descriptive phrases beginning with an "-ing" word that would describe the wrong word in context. Descriptive phrases starting with a word ending in "-ing" describe the first noun phrase in that sentence's independent clause. (See page 450.)
- **Dependent and Independent Clauses:** Answer choice(s) would incorrectly use a dependent or independent clause. An independent clause can stand alone as a sentence: it has a main subject/verb pair. A dependent clause is introduced by a conjunction or relative pronoun. (See page 445.)
- **Phrase Proximity:** Answer choice(s) would place descriptive phrases next to ideas they don't describe. Descriptive phrases that don't begin with a word ending in "-ing" describe the closest noun phrase. (See page 451.)
- **Shorter is Better:** Choices include words or phrases that can be removed without impacting the meaning of the sentence or creating grammatical problems. Remember to avoid redundancy, and that the shortest grammatically acceptable choice (according to the College Board) is correct. (See page 454.)

ANSWER CHOICE ANALYSIS

A ✓ **Correct:** This is the shortest choice and it's grammatically acceptable, so we know that it's correct on the SAT. Also, this phrase avoids the problem in (B) and (C) because it doesn't include a verb like "speaking" to modify "the discipline."

B **Incorrect:** According to the SAT's rules, the structure of this phrase would mean that "the discipline" is the thing that's "speaking," which doesn't make any sense.

C **Incorrect:** This choice has the same essential problem as (B): The structure of this phrase means that "the discipline" is the thing that's "speaking," which doesn't make any sense.

D **Incorrect:** This choice is longer than (A), and (A) is grammatically acceptable according to the SAT, so we know this choice can't be right according to the test's unwritten rules.

Answer choice patterns (see page 454): Shortest grammatically acceptable choice is correct.

❚ Test 1, Question 36 TYPE: GRAMMAR/STYLE/PUNCTUATION (often no prompt; choices have similar meanings)

- **Vertical Scan Results:** Some choices have different forms of the same base word.
- **Vertical Scan Notes:** It looks like we need to pick the right form of "teach."
- **Key Features in Surrounding Text:** "Philosophy" is the thing doing the action in the underlined phrase. The second half of the sentence calls philosophy "the age-old discipline" and pairs it with the verb "offers."

Concepts in the question:

- **Dependent and Independent Clauses:** Answer choice(s) would incorrectly use a dependent or independent clause. An independent clause can stand alone as a sentence: it has a main subject/verb pair. A dependent clause is introduced by a conjunction or relative pronoun. (See page 445.)
- **Parallelism:** Choices include options that would ignore a parallel structure in the surrounding text. The correct answer choice should match phrasing in the surrounding text when possible. (See page 458.)
- **Verb Tense/Conjugation:** Choices include different forms of the same verb. Look at the surrounding text to find each verb's subject. Also, look for other verbs that could indicate the proper tense for the verbs in the answer choices. (See page 437.)

A   **Incorrect:** This choice would leave the dependent clause without a verb to agree with the subject "philosophy."

B ✓   **Correct:** This is the only option that gives the dependent clause a verb that agrees with the singular noun "philosophy." The word "teaches" also parallels the form of the verb "offers" later in the sentence.

C   **Incorrect:** This choice leaves the dependent clause without a verb to agree with the subject "philosophy."

D   **Incorrect:** This choice leaves the dependent clause without a verb to agree with the subject "philosophy."

Answer choice patterns (see page 455): Wrong answers incorporate elements of the right answer.

Test 1, Question 37   TYPE: READING COMPREHENSION (usually has a prompt; choices have different meanings)

- **RC Question sub-type:** Best Accomplishes X. (The prompt describes a goal of the author, and asks us which choice achieves that goal. The correct answer choice will plainly and directly demonstrate the task described in the prompt. See page 431.)
- **Subjective phrases to be ignored:** "most"

ANSWER CHOICE ANALYSIS

A   **Pattern:** Confused concepts. **Incorrect:** This sentence expands on what's in the *previous sentence*—the idea that philosophy is useful for professional achievement—not what's in the *following* sentence, as this choice would require. This choice doesn't demonstrate the idea of "set[ing] up the information that follows" as required by the prompt, so it's wrong.

B   **Pattern:** Direct contradiction. **Incorrect:** This choice has multiple issues. For one thing, it refers to "evidence" that never appears in the paragraph; for another thing, it talks about *increased offerings* in philosophy courses, but the next two sentences talk about *requirements* that students take philosophy courses (as opposed to courses being offered) and the fact that philosophy departments were eliminated (as opposed to increased).

C   **Pattern:** Confused concepts. **Incorrect:** This choice might seem tempting for test-takers who don't read carefully, because it goes along with the idea of philosophy not being widely studied. But the following sentence says not many *colleges require* a philosophy course—it doesn't say whether students *wanted to major* in philosophy, as this choice would require.

D ✓   **Pattern:** Correct. This choice mentions the idea of colleges "not support[ing] the study of philosophy," which introduces (or "sets up") the idea that "only 18 percent of American colleges required at least one philosophy course" and that "philosophy departments were eliminated."

Test 1, Question 38   TYPE: READING COMPREHENSION (usually has a prompt; choices have different meanings)

- **RC Question sub-type:** Transition phrase. (The choices include words or phrases showing a transition from the previous sentence, like "however," "instead of," "for example," etc. The transition phrase must reflect the relationship between the previous sentence and the sentence where the transition phrase appears. See page 431.)

ANSWER CHOICE ANALYSIS

A   **Pattern:** Confused relationships. **Incorrect:** This choice would be appropriate if this sentence expressed a conclusion based on the information in the previous sentence, but that's not the case. The philosophy departments weren't eliminated *because* only 18 percent of American colleges required a philosophy course; these are just two pieces of related information.

B   **Pattern:** Confused relationships. **Incorrect:** This means essentially the same thing as (A), and is wrong for the same reasons.

C ✓   **Pattern:** Correct. The previous sentence mentions that in 1994 not many colleges required philosophy courses, and this sentences says that around the same time, many philosophy departments were eliminated. The word "moreover" appropriately reflects the idea that this sentence provides information that further expands on the information from the previous sentence.

D   **Pattern:** Confused concepts. **Incorrect:** This choice would be appropriate if what was discussed in this sentence were somehow in opposition to the information in the previous sentence, but that's not the case.

Test 1, Question 39   TYPE: GRAMMAR/STYLE/PUNCTUATION (often no prompt; choices have similar meanings)

- **Vertical Scan Results:** Similar phrases with different short words and/or punctuation.
- **Vertical Scan Notes:** Should there be a comma after "writing?" Which phrase should appear after "writing?"
- **Key Features in Surrounding Text:** The second sentence provides a detail about an idea from the first sentence.

Concepts in the question:

- **Commas:** Choices include one or more commas. On the Writing and Language section, commas can be used to separate things in a list of three or more, to form a comma sandwich, or to introduce an independent clause after a dependent clause. (See pages 448-450.)

- **Dependent and Independent Clauses:** Answer choice(s) would incorrectly use a dependent or independent clause. An independent clause can stand alone as a sentence: it has a main subject/verb pair. A dependent clause is introduced by a conjunction or relative pronoun. (See page 445.)

- **Shorter is Better:** Choices include words or phrases that can be removed without impacting the meaning of the sentence or creating grammatical problems. Remember to avoid redundancy, and that the shortest grammatically acceptable choice (according to the College Board) is correct. (See page 454.)

ANSWER CHOICE ANALYSIS

A ✓   **Correct:** This is the shortest choice and it's grammatically acceptable according to the SAT, so this choice must be correct, as we know from our training.

B   **Incorrect:** This choice is arguably grammatically acceptable in the real world, but choice (A) is shorter and also grammatically correct, so this choice can't be right according to the SAT's unwritten rules.

C   **Incorrect:** This choice has the same problem as (B) and is wrong for the same reasons.

D   **Incorrect:** This choice has the same problem as (B) and is wrong for the same reasons.

Answer choice patterns (see page 454): Shortest grammatically acceptable choice is correct.

Test 1, Question 40   TYPE: GRAMMAR/STYLE/PUNCTUATION (often no prompt; choices have similar meanings)

- **Vertical Scan Results:** Some choices have different forms of the same base word.
- **Vertical Scan Notes:** It looks like we need to pick the right form of the verb "score."
- **Key Features in Surrounding Text:** The rest of this paragraph describes actions completed in the past: "have recognized," "have markedly increased," "has grown," "have found." Nothing in context tells us that the action in the underlined phrase happened in some other time frame. Also, if we remove the intervening phrase "intending to study philosophy in graduate school," we can say that the thing doing the action in the underlined phrase is the plural noun "students."

Concepts in the question:

- **Parallelism:** Choices include options that would ignore a parallel structure in the surrounding text. The correct answer choice should match phrasing in the surrounding text when possible. (See page 458.)
- **Singular versus Plural:** Choices include singular and plural versions of the same base words that don't agree with other words in the surrounding text. Singular nouns must go with singular verb forms and singular pronouns. Plural nouns must go with plural verbs and pronouns. Think carefully about which words should match or agree with each other! (See page 443.)
- **Verb Tense/Conjugation:** Choices include different forms of the same verb. Look at the surrounding text to find each verb's subject. Also, look for other verbs that could indicate the proper tense for the verbs in the answer choices. (See page 437.)

ANSWER CHOICE ANALYSIS

A   **Incorrect:** As we discussed above, the verb in the underlined phrase should involve the helping verb "to have," and should agree in number with the plural noun "students." But "has" is a singular form, so this choice can't be correct.

B ✓   **Correct:** As we discussed above, the verb in the underlined phrase should indicate an action completed in the past, and should agree in number with the plural noun "students." This choice does both, so it's correct.

C   **Incorrect:** "Scores" is a present-tense singular form, so this choice can't be correct for the reasons noted above.

D   **Incorrect:** "Scoring" is the "-ing" form of the verb, not a form that can agree with a plural subject or show that an action was completed in the past, so this choice can't be correct for the reasons noted above.

Test 1, Question 41   TYPE: GRAMMAR/STYLE/PUNCTUATION (often no prompt; choices have similar meanings)

- **Vertical Scan Results:** Some choices have different forms of the same base word.
- **Vertical Scan Notes:** We need to choose "student's" or "students," and we need to choose among "majoring," "major," and "majors."
- **Key Features in Surrounding Text:** The word "many" indicates that the noun in the underlined phrase should be plural. The underlined phrase is part of an independent clause that already includes the main verb "have," so the verb form in the right answer shouldn't be a main verb.

Concepts in the question:

- **Plural/Possessive/Contraction:** Choices include the same noun ending in "-s" with or without an apostrophe before or after the "-s." Remember the three rules for forming possessives. Think of contractions in their uncontracted forms ("you're" = "you are"). (See page 441.)
- **Verb Tense/Conjugation:** Choices include different forms of the same verb. Look at the surrounding text to find each verb's subject. Also, look for other verbs that could indicate the proper tense for the verbs in the answer choices. (See page 437.)

ANSWER CHOICE ANALYSIS

A   **Incorrect:** There shouldn't be an apostrophe in "students," because it doesn't make sense to say that a student possesses "majoring," or that "many student is majoring in philosophy."

B ✓   Correct: "Students" is the correct plural form of "student," which makes sense after the word "many" in the sentence. Also, "majoring" is the correct form, because if the form were "major," then "students" would be doing two main verbs ("major" and "have") without a conjunction like "and" to connect those verbs appropriately.

C   Incorrect: "Majoring" is the correct form, not "major," because if the form were "major," then "students" would be doing two main verbs ("major" and "have") without a conjunction like "and" to connect those verbs appropriately.

D   Incorrect: This choice would create several problems, any of which would be enough to make the sentence unacceptable on the SAT. For one thing, it would make the word "many" apply to the plural word "majors," not the singular word "student," so that the majors would be the things "hav[ing] no intention" and "plan[ning] to apply," which makes no sense, since a student's major in this context isn't a person. In short, the sentence would be a grammatical wreck if we made this choice.

Test 1, Question 42   **TYPE: READING COMPREHENSION (usually has a prompt; choices have different meanings)**

- RC Question sub-type: Including/excluding a phrase/sentence. (The question asks whether a sentence should be included in the passage. The correct choice will include a comment that plainly describes the role of the phrase or sentence in the passage. Sentences that should be included will follow broad College Board standards for ideal sentences and paragraphs—including consistency with any figures in the passage—while sentences that shouldn't be included will not follow those standards. See page 433.)

ANSWER CHOICE ANALYSIS

A   Pattern: Largely irrelevant. Incorrect: This might be a tempting choice because the author of the passage does discuss the idea of philosophy majors being employed, as this choice mentions. But the sentence in the prompt doesn't "reinforce" that point, as this choice would require—it just tells us something Plato used to do.

B   Pattern: Largely irrelevant. Incorrect: The sentence in the prompt doesn't say anything about an argument or counterargument from the text; it just tells us something about the Greek philosopher Plato.

C ✓   Pattern: Correct. As trained test-takers, we know that the College Board will say a sentence "blurs" the "focus" if it mentions ideas that aren't discussed or explained elsewhere in the paragraph. This choice correctly notes that the rest of the paragraph doesn't talk about ancient Greek philosophers or Plato or dialogues, so this choice is correct.

D   Pattern: Largely irrelevant. Incorrect: The sentence in the prompt doesn't "undermine[]" a "claim about employability," as this choice would require. The prompt sentence about Plato doesn't relate to employability in any way, so it neither undermines nor supports that idea.

Test 1, Question 43   **TYPE: GRAMMAR/STYLE/PUNCTUATION (often no prompt; choices have similar meanings)**

- **Vertical Scan Results:** Some choices are short phrases with no obvious similarity.
- **Vertical Scan Notes:** Should the underlined portion be "which," "that," or "and," or should it be deleted entirely?
- **Key Features in Surrounding Text:** The surrounding "sentence" isn't a grammatically acceptable sentence on the SAT. It currently lacks a main verb, because everything that appears after the conjunction "which" is a dependent clause, and what appears before "which" is not an independent clause.

Concepts in the question:

- **Dependent and Independent Clauses:** Answer choice(s) would incorrectly use a dependent or independent clause. An independent clause can stand alone as a sentence: it has a main subject/verb pair. A dependent clause is introduced by a conjunction or relative pronoun. (See page 445.)

ANSWER CHOICE ANALYSIS

A   Incorrect: As we see in the explanation for choice (D), there's no need for any word in this part of the sentence.

B   Incorrect: As we see in the explanation for choice (D), there's no need for any word in this part of the sentence.

C   Incorrect: As we see in the explanation for choice (D), there's no need for any word in this part of the sentence.

D ✓   Correct: There is no need to have any word at this point in the sentence—when the word is removed, the sentence is grammatically acceptable, because the phrase "that these skills are transferable across professions" is the subject of the verb "makes." Further, (A), (B), and (C) make the underlined phrase and everything after the underlined phrase part of a dependent clause, which leaves the sentence without an independent clause.

Note   This question is a little strange to many test-takers because they're not familiar with the use of the word "that" at the beginning of the sentence. In addition to its many other uses in American English, "that" can be attached to the beginning of a verb phrase to turn it into a noun phrase, as we can see in sentences like "I didn't know that you were here" or "That the sun will rise tomorrow is a hypothesis." It's unlikely that you'll need to be aware of this usage of the word "that" on test day, because it doesn't often appear on the SAT in a way that would prevent you from answering a question correctly if you weren't aware of it.

Test 1, Question 44   **TYPE: GRAMMAR/STYLE/PUNCTUATION (often no prompt; choices have similar meanings)**

- Vertical Scan Results: Some choices are short phrases with no obvious similarity.

- **Vertical Scan Notes:** It looks like we need to pick the possessive pronoun that fits in the given context.
- **Key Features in Surrounding Text:** The only noun in the surrounding text that can have a "lifetime" is the plural noun "students."

Concepts in the question:

- **Singular versus Plural:** Choices include singular and plural versions of the same base words that don't agree with other words in the surrounding text. Singular nouns must go with singular verb forms and singular pronouns. Plural nouns must go with plural verbs and pronouns. Think carefully about which words should match or agree with each other! (See page 443.)

ANSWER CHOICE ANALYSIS

A	**Incorrect:** This would be correct if the speaker were referring to the lifetime of himself and one or more other people, but, instead, she's referring to the lifetime of "students." (The passage never indicates that the author is a member of the group indicated by the word "students.").
B	**Incorrect:** This would be correct if the speaker were referring to the lifetime of one unnamed person, instead of the plural noun "students."
C	**Incorrect:** This choice means the same thing as (B) in context, and is wrong for the same reason.
D ✓	**Correct:** The context tells us that the underlined word needs to refer to the idea of the plural noun "students" possessing the "lifetime," since the sentence is about the "jobs" the students "can expect to hold" during that period of time. Since "students" is plural and third person, the correct possessive pronoun is "their."

TEST 2

Test 2, Question 1 — TYPE: GRAMMAR/STYLE/PUNCTUATION (often no prompt; choices have similar meanings)

- **Vertical Scan Results:** some choices are words that could easily be confused with one another. Some choices have different forms of the same base word(s).
- **Vertical Scan Notes:** It looks like we need to decide whether a form of "reduce/reduction" or "deduct" is acceptable, and then we need to pick which form of the acceptable word is appropriate.
- **Key Features in Surrounding Text:** The text says "public libraries...have experienced" the underlined phrase "...due to cuts," so the correct answer must be something libraries can experience, and must be related to cuts.

Concepts in the question:

- **Parallelism:** Choices include options that would ignore a parallel structure in the surrounding text. The correct answer choice should match phrasing in the surrounding text when possible. (See page 458.)
- **Verb Tense/Conjugation:** Choices include different forms of the same verb. Look at the surrounding text to find each verb's subject. Also, look for other verbs that could indicate the proper tense for the verbs in the answer choices. (See page 437.)

ANSWER CHOICE ANALYSIS

A	**Incorrect:** Some untrained test-takers will be tempted by this choice, because the idea of "reducing" seems to fit generally with the context of the passage. But when we consider the surrounding text and the SAT's preference for parallelism on the Writing and Language section, we can see that (B) is the only choice that's a plural noun like the word "cuts" elsewhere in the sentence. So (A) is wrong and (B) is right.
B ✓	**Correct:** As we just saw in the explanation for (A), the SAT's unwritten rules call for a plural noun here to parallel the word "cuts." Since (B) is the only plural noun, we know it must be correct.
C	**Incorrect:** (C) has two problems. First, it's not a plural noun, as we discussed for (A). Second, no form of "deduct" is really appropriate here, because it refers to the idea of taking money away from something, rather than awarding less money in the first place, which is what the text describes.
D	**Incorrect:** This choice is a singular verb-form that basically has the same two problems we saw in (C).

Answer choice patterns (see page 455): Wrong answers incorporate elements of the right answer.

Test 2, Question 2 — TYPE: READING COMPREHENSION (usually has a prompt; choices have different meanings)

- **RC Question sub-type:** Transition phrase. (The choices include words or phrases showing a transition from the previous sentence, like "however," "instead of," "for example," etc. The transition phrase must reflect the relationship between the previous sentence and the sentence where the transition phrase appears. See page 431.)

ANSWER CHOICE ANALYSIS

A   **Pattern:** Direct contradiction. **Incorrect:** The word "however" would be appropriate if the sentence discussed something unexpected, given the information in the previous sentence. But that's not the case—we would expect a cost like "staffing" to be "cut" if the "funds" were reduced.

B ✓   **Pattern:** Correct. The word "consequently" appropriately reflects the idea that the information from this sentence is the logical result of the information in the previous sentence. If the "operating funds" of libraries are reduced, it makes sense that as a result, the "staffing" of those libraries would be "cut." "Operating funds" must mean money (funds) used to make the library operate. "Staffing" means employing people, which costs money, so reduced funds would logically lead to reduced staff.

C   **Pattern:** Direct contradiction. **Incorrect:** The word "nevertheless" would be appropriate if this sentence told us something that is true in spite of what was mentioned in the previous sentence, but that's not the case.

D   **Pattern:** Largely irrelevant. **Incorrect:** The word "previously" would be appropriate if this sentence told us something that happened before the events in the earlier sentence, but the context doesn't give us any reason to think that's the case.

Test 2, Question 3   TYPE: GRAMMAR/STYLE/PUNCTUATION (often no prompt; choices have similar meanings)

- **Comma Sandwich:** Choice(s) would create phrases improperly "sandwiched" between similar types of punctuation. When removed from the sentence, a properly formed sandwich leaves behind a grammatically acceptable sentence. (See page 448.)

- **Vertical Scan Results:** Some choices have different forms of the same base word. Choices include most or all possible combinations of two options.

- **Vertical Scan Notes:** Should "which" appear before the verb? Should the verb form be "have" or "has?"

- **Key Features in Surrounding Text:** Once we recognize the intervening phrase "combined with the increasing accessibility of information via the Internet" and mentally remove it, we can see that the thing that did the leading was the "trend," which is a singular noun. So we need to choose the form of the verb "to have" that agrees with "trend."

Concepts in the question:

- **Intervening Phrase:** A phrase appears between two words that need to agree with each other. Identify which words need to agree with each other, and ignore extra phrases that appear between them. (See page 456.)

- **Verb Tense/Conjugation:** Choices include different forms of the same verb. Look at the surrounding text to find each verb's subject. Also, look for other verbs that could indicate the proper tense for the verbs in the answer choices. (See page 437.)

ANSWER CHOICE ANALYSIS

A ✓   **Correct:** The verb "has" agrees with its subject "this trend." Further, the sentence would become a fragment if we included the word "which" from (C) or (D), because it would turn the clause with the main verb into a dependent clause.

B   **Incorrect:** The verb "have" doesn't agree with its subject "this trend." (See the note at the end of this explanation.)

C   **Incorrect:** The verb "have" does not agree with its subject "this trend." Also, we know to leave out the pronoun "which," as we saw in the discussion of choice (A).

D   **Incorrect:** The pronoun "which" is inappropriate here as discussed in choice (A).

Answer choice patterns (see page 455): Wrong answers incorporate elements of the right answer.

> **Note**   Some untrained test-takers will fall for (B) because they'll think the subject of the verb is something like "this trend and accessibility," which could be a compound subject requiring a plural verb. But the phrase "combined with the increasing accessibility of information via the Internet" is an intervening phrase in a comma sandwich, which means it can be removed from the sentence without altering the grammatical structure of what's left behind; in other words, the phrases relating to the Internet aren't on the same structural level in the sentence as the words "this trend," so the verb isn't agreeing with those phrases. The verb only needs to agree with the phrase "this trend," which is why (A) is correct. To put it another way, if the sentence began "this trend and the increasing accessibility of information via the Internet," then we would need the plural verb form "have," but since "accessibility" was inside of a punctuation sandwich, it's not part of the main subject of this sentence.

Test 2, Question 4   TYPE: READING COMPREHENSION (usually has a prompt; choices have different meanings)

- **RC Question sub-type:** Including/excluding a phrase/sentence. (The question asks whether a sentence should be included in the passage. The correct choice will include a comment that plainly describes the role of the phrase or sentence in the passage. Sentences that should be included will follow broad College Board standards for ideal sentences and paragraphs—including consistency with any figures in the passage—while sentences that shouldn't be included will not follow those standards. See page 433.)

ANSWER CHOICE ANALYSIS

A ✓   **Correct:** The phrase from the prompt plainly demonstrates the idea described in this answer choice—the "e-books, audio and video materials, and online journals" are all "specific examples of the materials discussed in the sentence," since the sentence mentions "library materials…in nonprint formats" and that's what these items are. As trained test-takers, we see that (A) is the only choice whose explanatory text is demonstrated by the prompt and the passage, so it must be right, and we don't have to consider the second rule for questions that ask about including a phrase, as described on page 433.

B   Pattern: Largely irrelevant. Incorrect: The list in the prompt doesn't give a *reason* for the increase mentioned later in the sentence, as (B) requires (in fact, the list doesn't explicitly demonstrate or restate a reason for anything at all).

C   Pattern: Direct contradiction. Incorrect: As we saw in the explanation for choice (A), this information provides *relevant* examples of an idea already mentioned in the sentence, so every part of (C) is the opposite of the correct answer.

D   Pattern: Confused concepts. Incorrect: The information in the prompt provides *relevant* background on an aspect of a skill in which "librarians must now be proficient," so it doesn't "weaken[] the focus of the passage" according to the SAT's rules, as (D) requires.

| Test 2, Question 5 | TYPE: GRAMMAR/STYLE/PUNCTUATION (often no prompt; choices have similar meanings) |

- **Vertical Scan Results:** Similar phrases with different short words and/or punctuation.
- **Vertical Scan Notes:** It looks like we need to pick the acceptable phrase that describes the idea of circulation.
- **Key Features in Surrounding Text:** This sentence contains the plural nouns "materials," "formats," and "e-books." An acceptable answer choice can't use a plural pronoun in a way that makes it unclear which noun the pronoun is referring to, according to the SAT's unwritten rules.

Concepts in the question:

- **Pronoun Ambiguity:** Choices include pronouns that could refer to more than one phrase in the surrounding text. We can't use a pronoun on the SAT when it isn't clear what that pronoun refers to. (See page 441.)
- **Verb Tense/Conjugation:** Choices include different forms of the same verb. Look at the surrounding text to find each verb's subject. Also, look for other verbs that could indicate the proper tense for the verbs in the answer choices. (See page 437.)

ANSWER CHOICE ANALYSIS

A   Incorrect: This choice includes the plural pronoun "them," but it's not clear which plural noun in the surrounding text is being referred to by the word "them."

B   Incorrect: This choice has the same issue as (A).

C   Incorrect: This choice has the plural pronoun "their," which creates the same problem we saw in (A) and (B).

D ✓ Correct: This choice doesn't use a pronoun, so it doesn't have the ambiguous pronoun issue that the other choices have. Further, it's the shortest answer choice, and it's grammatically acceptable, so it's correct.

Answer choice patterns (see page 454): Shortest grammatically acceptable choice is correct.

Note   Many teachers and untrained test-takers will mistakenly assume that (B) is wrong because it uses the passive voice, but, as trained test-takers, we know that the College Board doesn't care about the passive voice! (B) is wrong because it uses an ambiguous pronoun. You don't need to worry about the passive voice on test day, because the College Board never uses the passive voice as the difference between a right answer and a wrong answer, even though some wrong answer choices might coincidentally include the passive voice. (If you're not familiar with the passive voice, don't worry about it! It won't be tested on the SAT Writing and Language section.)

| Test 2, Question 6 | TYPE: GRAMMAR/STYLE/PUNCTUATION (often no prompt; choices have similar meanings) |

- **Vertical Scan Results:** Some choices have different forms of the same base word.
- **Vertical Scan Notes:** We need to decide whether "librarians" should appear first in the underlined phrase, and whether the appropriate verb form is "catalog," "cataloging," or "to catalog."
- **Key Features in Surrounding Text:** The text says that librarians must be "compiling, [BLANK], and updating these collections." The verb form we choose must be parallel to "compiling" and "updating."

Concepts in the question:

- **Parallelism:** Choices include options that would ignore a parallel structure in the surrounding text. The correct answer choice should match phrasing in the surrounding text when possible. (See page 458.)
- **Verb Tense/Conjugation:** Choices include different forms of the same verb. Look at the surrounding text to find each verb's subject. Also, look for other verbs that could indicate the proper tense for the verbs in the answer choices. (See page 437.)

ANSWER CHOICE ANALYSIS

A   Incorrect: The SAT won't accept "catalog" here because the underlined phrase is mentioned in parallel with "compiling" and "updating," so the test will require the correct answer to end in "-ing."

B   Incorrect: This choice might trap some test-takers who don't pay enough attention when they read, because it ends with the word "cataloging." But the word "librarians" isn't acceptable here because the parallel phrases in the rest of the sentence

---

("compiling" and "updating") don't include a word like "librarians" immediately before their "-ing" words, so the underlined phrase shouldn't do that either.

C   Incorrect: "To catalog" can't be correct for the same reason discussed in the explanation for choice (A).

D✓   Correct: The structure of the word "cataloging" parallels the words "compiling" and "updating" in the list from the rest of the sentence, so it's correct.

Answer choice patterns (see page 455): Wrong answers incorporate elements of the right answer.

Test 2, Question 7   TYPE: GRAMMAR/STYLE/PUNCTUATION (often no prompt; choices have similar meanings)

- **Vertical Scan Results:** Choices are long phrases/sentences.
- **Vertical Scan Notes:** The answer choices are fairly long and will need to be analyzed a bit more closely to determine what's going on in this question. A few differences that might jump out include the different phrases regarding "training" and "teaching classes" in each choice.
- **Key Features in Surrounding Text:** The entire underlined text.

Concepts in the question:

- **Commas:** Choices include one or more commas. On the Writing and Language section, commas can be used to separate things in a list of three or more, to form a comma sandwich, or to introduce an independent clause after a dependent clause. (See pages 448-450.)
- **Dependent and Independent Clauses:** Answer choice(s) would incorrectly use a dependent or independent clause. An independent clause can stand alone as a sentence: it has a main subject/verb pair. A dependent clause is introduced by a conjunction or relative pronoun. (See page 445.)
- **Joining Two Sentences:** Each choice is a sentence that combines the two sentences in the underlined portion of the text. The correct answer must follow all rules for other question types without changing the meaning of the original sentences. (See page 453.)
- **Redundancy:** Answer choices and/or surrounding text could combine to repeat the same concept unnecessarily. We should avoid words or phrases that directly repeat ideas in the immediate context. (See page 452.)
- **Semi-colons:** Choices include one or more semicolons. Semi-colons can be used to separate two sets of words that could each stand on their own as a full sentence. (See page 447.)

ANSWER CHOICE ANALYSIS

A   Incorrect: Among other possible issues, the phrase "taught by them" is redundant with the phrase "many librarians teach." This breaks up the information about the classes the librarians teach into two separate, consecutive phrases: "many librarians teach classes in Internet navigation, database and software use" and "digital information literacy is taught by them," instead of one list of three types of classes expressed in a parallel structure without redundancy. This choice violates the College Board's rules regarding parallelism and redundancy, so it's wrong.

B✓   Correct: This option avoids the issues in the other answer choices and doesn't introduce any new issues. It uses commas in a way that's consistent with the SAT's rules: the phrase "whose training…search methods" is a comma sandwich that can be removed from the sentence without creating any grammatical problems, and the sentence ends with a comma-separated three-item list that includes "navigation," "database and software use, and…literacy" as three things that librarians teach.

C   Incorrect: As trained test-takers, we have to remember that "join 2 sentences" questions involve elements of both reading comprehension and grammar/style/punctuation. This choice is arguably grammatically acceptable, but, from a reading comprehension standpoint, it doesn't make a distinction between the training that librarians *receive*, and the training that the librarians *provide*. That distinction is clearly made in the original text, and in choice (B), the correct answer.

D   Incorrect: Again, we have to remember that "join 2 sentences" questions incorporate reading comprehension as well as grammar/style/punctuation. This choice says that librarians teach the classes *because* their training involves "courses on research and Internet search methods." But the original text just says that librarians' training includes particular courses, and that librarians teach particular classes, not that one is the *cause* of the other, as this choice would require. Since this choice doesn't restate the ideas in the original sentences, it's wrong.

Test 2, Question 8   TYPE: GRAMMAR/STYLE/PUNCTUATION (often no prompt; choices have similar meanings)

- **Vertical Scan Results:** Similar phrases with different short words and/or punctuation.
- **Vertical Scan Notes:** The first three choices are different conjunctions. One choice omits any conjunction at all.
- **Key Features in Surrounding Text:** The sentence begins with the conjunction "while."

Concepts in the question:

- **Dependent and Independent Clauses:** Answer choice(s) would incorrectly use a dependent or independent clause. An independent clause can stand alone as a sentence: it has a main subject/verb pair. A dependent clause is introduced by a conjunction or relative pronoun. (See page 445.)

ANSWER CHOICE ANALYSIS

A   **Incorrect:** Since the sentence begins with the word "while," adding the word "but" here would cause the sentence to consist of two dependent clauses, which isn't acceptable on the SAT.

B   **Incorrect:** This choice has the same basic problem as (A).

C   **Incorrect:** This choice has the same basic problem as (A). Also, the word "for" indicates that the clause following the underlined phrase is the reason for, or cause of, the information in the first half of the sentence, but that isn't the case.

D ✓   **Correct:** The first half of the sentence, up until the comma, is a dependent clause beginning with the word "while," and we need the sentence to have an independent clause in order to satisfy the College Board's rules. Only (D) fulfills that requirement, by omitting the conjunction in the middle of the sentence.

Test 2, Question 9   TYPE: READING COMPREHENSION (usually has a prompt; choices have different meanings)

- **RC Question sub-type:** Best Accomplishes X. (The prompt describes a goal of the author, and asks us which choice achieves that goal. The correct answer choice will plainly and directly demonstrate the task described in the prompt. See page 431.)
- **Subjective phrases to be ignored:** "most"

ANSWER CHOICE ANALYSIS

A   **Pattern: Same ballpark. Incorrect:** We need a choice that restates the idea of the resources described in this sentence being "especially valuable," or that demonstrates why they would be valuable. (When the College Board says one phrase "sets up" another, it means that one phrase introduces or begins discussing the other phrase.) The original version of the underlined phrase doesn't introduce the example at the end of the sentence, so (A) is wrong.

B ✓   **Pattern: Correct.** This choice "sets up" the examples at the end of the sentence, because it demonstrates why "free resources" related to getting a job would be "especially valuable" "during periods of economic recession." Note that this is the only choice with a word like "during," which indicates a change or specific circumstance, going along with the idea of the library being "especially" useful—in other words, no other choice includes a phrase to show that it's talking about a condition that only applies at certain times, as the word "especially" in the text requires.

C   **Pattern: Same ballpark. Incorrect:** (C) has the same issue as (A), and is wrong for the same reason.

D   **Pattern: Same ballpark. Incorrect:** This choice has the same problem as (A), and is wrong for the same reason.

> **Note**   The "examples given at the end of the sentence" as mentioned in the prompt are "help with online job searches" and "résumé and job material development." See "The College Board's Unique Phrasing" on page 457 for more on "sets up" questions.

Test 2, Question 10   TYPE: READING COMPREHENSION (usually has a prompt; choices have different meanings)

- **RC Question sub-type:** Vocabulary In Context. (Choices include words or short phrases that have vaguely similar but not identical meanings. Most or all of the choices will seem vaguely appropriate, but only one choice will be correct when we think very carefully and specifically about the word means and how it can be used. See page 432.)

ANSWER CHOICE ANALYSIS

A   ("An overwhelming number of public libraries also report that they provide help with electronic government resources related to income taxes, <u>law troubles,</u> and retirement programs.") **Pattern: Same ballpark. Incorrect:** (A) might tempt some untrained test-takers, but, as we'll see in our discussion of (B), the subtle difference between the words "troubles" and "issues" makes (A) wrong.

B ✓   ("An overwhelming number of public libraries also report that they provide help with electronic government resources related to income taxes, <u>legal issues,</u> and retirement programs.") **Correct:** (B) is right because the word "issues" fits precisely with the idea of something that someone could "provide help" with in the text, and also matches the kind of everyday situation demonstrated by the phrases "income taxes" and "retirement programs" in the text. A "trouble" is an inherently negative concept and might, in this context, indicate something like an arrest, while "issue" is a broader term in this context that lacks the level of negativity indicated by the word "trouble." There isn't anything in the surrounding text to support the idea of a negative word like "troubles."

C   ("An overwhelming number of public libraries also report that they provide help with electronic government resources related to income taxes, <u>concerns related to law courts,</u> and retirement programs.") **Pattern: Same ballpark. Incorrect:** Among other issues, the phrase "related to" doesn't work here because a concern related to a law court could technically be something along the lines of a problem with the court itself (such as how the electricity is supplied to the court, or what time the court opens in the morning), rather than a problem that a person might need to handle with the help of the legal system.

D ("An overwhelming number of public libraries also report that they provide help with electronic government resources related to income taxes, <u>matters for the law courts</u>, and retirement programs.") **Pattern:** Same ballpark. **Incorrect:** This choice has an issue similar to the one in (C).

Test 2, Question 11 — TYPE: READING COMPREHENSION (usually has a prompt; choices have different meanings)

- **RC Question sub-type:** Best Accomplishes X. (The prompt describes a goal of the author, and asks us which choice achieves that goal. The correct answer choice will plainly and directly demonstrate the task described in the prompt. See page 431.)
- **Subjective phrases to be ignored:** "most" "primary"

ANSWER CHOICE ANALYSIS

A **Pattern:** Largely irrelevant. **Incorrect:** This answer makes broad statements loosely related to ideas that appear in the text, but doesn't restate a claim from the passage: the passage mentions librarians and e-books, but never says "books and librarians have been around for a long time" before this sentence, as this choice would require.

B **Pattern:** Direct contradiction. **Incorrect:** The text *does* say that "librarians are hardly obsolete," which goes along with the idea that "librarians will continue to be employed by public libraries for the foreseeable future." But the passage says that "librarians' roles are actually expanding," so this choice's statement that their "roles have diminished significantly" is a contradiction of the writer's claim, not a restatement of it, as the prompt would require.

C ✓ **Pattern:** Correct. This choice is correct because it restates several ideas from the passage, just as the prompt requires. "Growth of electronic information" restates the idea of "rapid technological advances in information distribution." "Diversification of librarian's skills and services" restates the idea that "librarians must now be proficient curators of electronic information, compiling, [cataloging], and updating" collections of e-books. Calling librarians "savvy resource specialists" restates the idea that "librarians are especially valuable, because they offer free resources that may be difficult to find elsewhere."

D **Pattern:** Confused concepts. **Incorrect:** The text does mention in the second paragraph that librarians have "extensive training," and it does mention in the first paragraph that "budget cuts" have caused librarians to be "displaced." But the text never discusses the idea of librarians looking for other jobs, which means that this choice's phrase about having "other possible avenues of employment" isn't restating anything in the passage.

Test 2, Question 12 — TYPE: READING COMPREHENSION (usually has a prompt; choices have different meanings)

- **RC Question sub-type:** Transition phrase. (The choices include words or phrases showing a transition from the previous sentence, like "however," "instead of," "for example," etc. The transition phrase must reflect the relationship between the previous sentence and the sentence where the transition phrase appears. See page 431.)

ANSWER CHOICE ANALYSIS

A **Pattern:** Largely irrelevant. **Incorrect:** The phrase "on one hand" is used along with the phrase "on the other hand" to express two opposing ideas. For example, someone might say, "On one hand I love to exercise, but on the other hand I recently twisted my ankle, so I should probably rest." But there isn't another phrase in the text that begins with "on the other hand," so this choice can't be correct.

B ✓ **Pattern:** Correct. The previous sentence tells us that the speaker "expected to be impressed" by the "famous large paintings" at the Art Institute. This sentence mentions seeing a "10-foot wide" painting "in its full size." The phrase "for instance" appropriately reflects the idea that this sentence gives us a specific instance of one of the large paintings that was mentioned in the previous sentence.

C **Pattern:** Direct contradiction. **Incorrect:** This choice would be appropriate if this sentence provided information that contradicted what was discussed in the previous sentence, but that's not the case.

D **Pattern:** Same ballpark. **Incorrect:** This choice would be appropriate if this sentence expressed an idea that was a lot like the idea in the previous sentence, but that's not the case. This sentence expresses *an example* of the idea in the previous sentence, not a separate, similar idea.

Note Notice that (A) and (C) might be tempting because they both express the idea that the text contains two opposing concepts, and this paragraph mentions that the speaker was excited to see some big paintings but ended up enjoying small artwork instead. But the discussion of miniature artwork comes after the sentence discussed in this question, so that discussion isn't relevant in the context of this question.

Test 2, Question 13 — TYPE: GRAMMAR/STYLE/PUNCTUATION (often no prompt; choices have similar meanings)

- **Vertical Scan Results:** Some choices have the same words with different punctuation. Choices include most or all possible combinations of two options.
- **Vertical Scan Notes:** We need to decide whether there should be a comma after "painter" and/or after "George Seurat's."
- **Key Features in Surrounding Text:** The key feature of the surrounding text is the whole sentence containing this underlined phrase, because we need to determine whether there should be commas on either side of "George Seurat's."

Concepts in the question:

- **Comma Sandwich:** Choice(s) would create phrases improperly "sandwiched" between similar types of punctuation. When removed from the sentence, a properly formed sandwich leaves behind a grammatically acceptable sentence. (See page 448.)
- **Commas:** Choices include one or more commas. On the Writing and Language section, commas can be used to separate things in a list of three or more, to form a comma sandwich, or to introduce an independent clause after a dependent clause. (See pages 448-450.)

ANSWER CHOICE ANALYSIS

A   Incorrect: This choice would create a comma sandwich around "George Seurat's," but that isn't grammatically acceptable in context. We know that we can remove a comma sandwich from a sentence and leave a grammatically acceptable sentence behind, but if the comma sandwich were removed from this version of the sentence, the following would be left behind: "*On one hand, I couldn't wait to view painter 10-foot-wide *A Sunday Afternoon on the Island of La Grande Jatte* in its full size." In this version of the sentence, "I couldn't wait to view painter 10-foot-wide" would be meaningless.

B   Incorrect: The word "painter" describes "George Seurat," and we can't insert a comma between these two phrases, as we discussed on page 449 when talking about the rules for comma usage on the SAT Writing and Language section.

C   Incorrect: The phrase "painter George Seurat's" tells us who made the "10-foot-wide" painting," and there's no reason to insert a comma between these two phrases: this isn't part of a comma sandwich or any other valid use of a comma on the SAT Writing and Language section.

D ✓   Correct: As we discussed on page 449, the test doesn't allow us to insert a comma between a profession and a person's name when the profession comes before the name, as is the case here.

Answer choice patterns (see pages 454 and 455): Shortest grammatically acceptable choice is correct. Wrong answers incorporate elements of the right answer.

Test 2, Question 14   **TYPE: GRAMMAR/STYLE/PUNCTUATION (often no prompt; choices have similar meanings)**

- **Vertical Scan Results:** Some choices have the same words with different punctuation. Choices include most or all possible combinations of two options.
- **Vertical Scan Notes:** We need to decide whether "its" or "it's" is acceptable, and whether there should be a colon, semi-colon, or comma after "tiniest."
- **Key Features in Surrounding Text:** The thing that possesses the "tiniest" exhibit is the "museum," so we need the possessive form of the word "it" to indicate this relationship. Also, the sentence can stand on its own as an independent clause without the phrase "the Thorne Miniature Rooms," and "the Thorne Miniature Rooms" is an explanation of what that sentence describes. So we need a colon after the word "tiniest."

Concepts in the question:

- **Colons:** Choices include one or more colons. A colon can be placed after a set of words that could be a sentence on their own, and before a demonstration or example of the idea before the colon. (See page 447.)
- **Plural/Possessive/Contraction:** Choices include the same noun ending in "-s" with or without an apostrophe before or after the "-s." Remember the three rules for forming possessives. Think of contractions in their uncontracted forms ("you're" = "you are"). (See page 441.)
- **Semi-colons:** Choices include one or more semicolons. Semi-colons can be used to separate two sets of words that could each stand on their own as a full sentence. (See page 447.)

ANSWER CHOICE ANALYSIS

A   Incorrect: "It's" is unacceptable here because that word is the contracted form of "it is," and "one of it is tiniest" doesn't make any sense in context. Also, there shouldn't be a semi-colon after "tiniest" because semicolons are used to join independent clauses, but the part of the sentence after the semi-colon isn't an independent clause.

B   Incorrect: As we discussed for choice (A), there shouldn't be a semi-colon after "tiniest" because the words after the semi-colon can't stand on their own as a complete sentence.

C ✓   Correct: The possessive form "its" accurately reflects the idea that the "museum" is the thing that possesses the "tiniest" exhibit. Further, the sentence can stand on its own without the phrase "the Thorne Miniature Rooms," and "the Thorne Miniature Rooms" is an example of what that sentence describes, so it's okay to use a colon to introduce the phrase "the Thorne Miniature Rooms."

D   Incorrect: As we discussed for choice (A), the word "it's" is unacceptable here because that word is the contracted form of "it is," not the possessive form of the pronoun "it."

Answer choice patterns (see page 455): Wrong answers incorporate elements of the right answer.

- RC Question sub-type: Including/excluding a phrase/sentence. (The question asks whether a sentence should be included in the passage. The correct choice will include a comment that plainly describes the role of the phrase or sentence in the passage. Sentences that should be included will follow broad College Board standards for ideal sentences and paragraphs—including consistency with any figures in the passage—while sentences that shouldn't be included will not follow those standards. See page 433.)

ANSWER CHOICE ANALYSIS

A **Pattern:** Confused concepts. **Incorrect:** The sentence in the prompt does *not* provide historical context for the Thorne Miniature Rooms exhibit, as (A) would require. Nothing in context suggests that the *exhibit itself* is connected to the time of "King Louis XV's reign." The text simply says that *one of the rooms* was a replica of a room from that time period.

B **Pattern:** Confused concepts. **Incorrect:** The sentence in the prompt does *not* explain why salons are ornately decorated, as (B) would require. The sentence in the prompt mentions the "excesses of King Louis XV's reign," but this sentence never says anything about *why* salons would be ornately decorated; it doesn't even mention salons or rooms at all.

C ✓ **Pattern:** Correct. The previous sentence mentions the "replica of a salon," and the following sentence describes that miniature replica of a salon, while the sentence in the prompt doesn't say anything about the miniature salon, so it's correct to say the sentence from the prompt "interrupts the paragraph's description of the miniature salon," just as (C) requires.

D **Pattern:** Largely irrelevant. **Incorrect:** The sentence doesn't say anything at all about the interior designer of the salon, so we can't say this sentence implies anything about that designer's "political motivations," as this choice would require.

- **Vertical Scan Results:** Similar phrases with different short words and/or punctuation.

- **Vertical Scan Notes:** Should there be a comma after "legs?" Which phrase connects the two halves of the sentence in the way the College Board would prefer?

- **Key Features in Surrounding Text:** When we notice the intervening phrase "in keeping with the style of the time," it becomes easier to notice that the underlined phrase connects the parallel phrases "are characterized by elegantly curved arms and legs" and "are covered in luxurious velvet."

Concepts in the question:

- **Comma Splice:** Answer choice(s) and/or surrounding text use commas to separate two groups of words that could each be sentences on their own. A comma can't be used in this way on the SAT Writing and Language section. (See page 447.)

- **Dependent and Independent Clauses:** Answer choice(s) would incorrectly use a dependent or independent clause. An independent clause can stand alone as a sentence: it has a main subject/verb pair. A dependent clause is introduced by a conjunction or relative pronoun. (See page 445.)

- **Intervening Phrase:** A phrase appears between two words that need to agree with each other. Identify which words need to agree with each other, and ignore extra phrases that appear between them. (See page 456.)

ANSWER CHOICE ANALYSIS

A **Incorrect:** This version of the underlined phrase would create a comma splice, because everything before the comma in the underlined phrase could stand on its own as a sentence, and everything after the comma could stand on its own as a separate sentence. Remember the College Board never allows us to use a comma to join two independent clauses.

B **Incorrect:** This version of the underlined phrase has the same problem as choice (A), and is wrong for the same reason.

C ✓ **Correct:** This version of the underlined phrase appropriately uses the word "and" to connect the phrase "are covered in luxurious velvet" to the rest of the sentence. This is the only choice that doesn't create a grammatically unacceptable sentence according to the College Board.

D **Incorrect:** This version of the sentence arguably creates a grammatically acceptable (though slightly poetic) sentence *in the real world*, but it breaks the College Board's rules for comma usage! The College Board doesn't allow us to use a comma in place of the word "and" in a list of two things; in this sentence, "are characterized by…" and "are covered in…" are two phrases that both apply to the couch and chairs, and the College Board won't allow us to join them with just a comma—we need to use a conjunction like "and."

Note   This question is a great example of the importance of understanding how the College Board's rules and patterns differ from what you might encounter in class or in the real world! Remember that your job is to mark the answer that you know the test will reward based on your training, not your instincts from school.

- RC Question sub-type: Best Accomplishes X. (The prompt describes a goal of the author, and asks us which choice achieves that goal. The correct answer choice will plainly and directly demonstrate the task described in the prompt. See page 431.)

- Subjective phrases to be ignored: "most"

ANSWER CHOICE ANALYSIS

A   Pattern: Largely irrelevant. **Incorrect:** This option doesn't give a second example at all, which is required by the prompt. Instead, it just provides a detail about the first supporting example.

B ✓ Pattern: Correct. The "example already in the sentence" referred to by the prompt gives us the measurement of an item in the room, and this choice gives us the measurement of another item in the room.

C   Pattern: Same ballpark. **Incorrect:** This option does give us a "second supporting example," but that example isn't similar to the "example already in the sentence," as the prompt requires. This choice just mentions "tiny cushions," but "tiny" isn't a measurement in the way that "seven inches long" from the text is.

D   Pattern: Confused concepts. **Incorrect:** This option isn't actually another *example*, as the prompt requires. An example would name some specific item in the room and tell us how big it is, but this choice doesn't mention any specific item or its size. Instead, (D) is a general statement telling us that the scale in the first example was constant throughout the room.

Note   The "example already in the sentence" is "a couch, for example, is seven inches long."

Test 2, Question 18   TYPE: GRAMMAR/STYLE/PUNCTUATION (often no prompt; choices have similar meanings)

- **Vertical Scan Results:** Similar phrases with different short words and/or punctuation.
- **Vertical Scan Notes:** We need to decide whether a comma, colon, or no punctuation should appear after "furnished," and whether the underlined phrase should end with "by their," "but their," "their," or "whereas."
- **Key Features in Surrounding Text:** The choices offer us four ways to combine two sentences, so we need to consider all the text of both sentences, especially the main verbs in each sentence (which are both "are"), and the phrase "more sparsely" and "just as true," which indicate a kind of contradiction, since one phrase indicates two things are different, and one indicates that two things are the same.

Concepts in the question:

- **Colons:** Choices include one or more colons. A colon can be placed after a set of words that could be a sentence on their own, and before a demonstration or example of the idea before the colon. (See page 447.)
- **Commas:** Choices include one or more commas. On the Writing and Language section, commas can be used to separate things in a list of three or more, to form a comma sandwich, or to introduce an independent clause after a dependent clause. (See pages 448-450.)
- **Dependent and Independent Clauses:** Answer choice(s) would incorrectly use a dependent or independent clause. An independent clause can stand alone as a sentence: it has a main subject/verb pair. A dependent clause is introduced by a conjunction or relative pronoun. (See page 445.)

ANSWER CHOICE ANALYSIS

A   **Incorrect:** (A) has multiple issues. One problem is that the phrase "by their" would indicate that the "architectural features, furnishings, and decorations" actually furnished the rooms themselves, which isn't reflected in the original versions of the two sentences, and doesn't make any sense in context—the passage doesn't say that features can furnish rooms somehow. Perhaps a larger issue is that (A) would make the sentence ungrammatical, since it would have two main verb phrases ("are...furnished" and "are...true") without any conjunction or punctuation to allow those independent clauses to be joined.

B ✓ **Correct:** The first of the two sentences says the plainer rooms are "more sparsely furnished," and the second says those rooms are "just as true to the periods they represent." In other words, the first sentence uses the word "more," which means that one set of rooms *exceeds* the other in some way, while the second sentence uses the phrase "just as," which means the rooms are *equal* in some way. The contrast between the ideas of being different and being equal is accurately reflected in the word "but." Further, this choice uses a comma and the conjunction "but" to join the two sentences, which turns the second sentence into a dependent clause being joined to the first with a comma. Since this choice is grammatically acceptable according to the SAT *and* accurately restates the relationships in the relevant original text, we know it's the correct answer.

C   **Incorrect:** This version of the underlined phrase uses a colon, which would indicate that the second sentence is an example or further explanation of the first sentence. But as we just discussed with (B), the second sentence is *not* in agreement with the first; instead, the second sentence expresses an idea that contrasts with the first sentence.

D   **Incorrect:** This choice might be tempting to some untrained test-takers, because it seems very similar to choice (B) at first: both choices use a comma and a negating conjunction to tie the two original sentences together. But there's an important difference between (B) and (D)! (B) includes the word "their," while (D) omits it. Without the word "their," it's not clear that the "architectural features, furnishings, and decorations" belong to the "plainer rooms," so the sentence that's produced by (D) doesn't restate the relationship between the first sentence and the second sentence. This makes (D) wrong, since the correct answer must follow the College Board's grammatical rules without changing the meaning of the original text.

Test 2, Question 19 — TYPE: GRAMMAR/STYLE/PUNCTUATION (often no prompt; choices have similar meanings)

- **Vertical Scan Results:** Choices are long phrases/sentences.
- **Vertical Scan Notes:** (A) includes no verb, (B) includes "is," and (C) and (D) include "has." Also, (A) and (B) both begin with "a small table," while (C) and (D) begin with "the third wall has a."
- **Key Features in Surrounding Text:** The "stylistic pattern established earlier in the sentence" mentioned in the prompt must refer to the way the earlier parts of the sentence are written. All the answer choices mention a detail about "the room," and the other details mentioned earlier in the sentence are "a small sink and counter along one wall," and "a cast-iron wood stove and some hanging pots and pans against another wall."

Concepts in the question:

- **Parallelism:** Choices include options that would ignore a parallel structure in the surrounding text. The correct answer choice should match phrasing in the surrounding text when possible. (See page 458.)

ANSWER CHOICE ANALYSIS

A ✓ **Correct:** The other two examples mention items in the room ("a small sink and counter" and "a cast-iron wood stove and some hanging pots") and say where they are ("along one wall" and "against another wall") without using any verbs. This is the only choice that "matches" that "stylistic pattern," so it's correct.

B **Incorrect:** See the explanation for choice (A). This choice involves the verb "is," so it doesn't follow the pattern established by the earlier part of the sentence, which means it's wrong.

C **Incorrect:** See the explanation for choice (A). This choice involves the verb "has," so it doesn't follow the pattern from the earlier part of the sentence.

D **Incorrect:** See the explanation for (A). This choice involves the verb "has," so it's not correct.

Test 2, Question 20 — TYPE: GRAMMAR/STYLE/PUNCTUATION (often no prompt; choices have similar meanings)

- **Vertical Scan Results:** Some choices have different forms of the same base word.
- **Vertical Scan Notes:** We need to decide whether "visitor," "visitors'," or "visitors" is acceptable, and also whether "remark," "remarking," or "remarked" is acceptable.
- **Key Features in Surrounding Text:** The entire sentence in the question.

Concepts in the question:

- **Plural/Possessive/Contraction:** Choices include the same noun ending in "-s" with or without an apostrophe before or after the "-s." Remember the three rules for forming possessives. Think of contractions in their uncontracted forms ("you're" = "you are"). (See page 441.)
- **Singular versus Plural:** Choices include singular and plural versions of the same base words that don't agree with other words in the surrounding text. Singular nouns must go with singular verb forms and singular pronouns. Plural nouns must go with plural verbs and pronouns. Think carefully about which words should match or agree with each other! (See page 443.)

ANSWER CHOICE ANALYSIS

A **Incorrect:** Since "visitors'" is the plural possessive form, this choice would attribute a single remark to multiple visitors, which is something we know the College Board won't allow, as trained test-takers. The College Board would have been okay with saying that multiple visitors had multiple remarks, or that one visitor had one remark, but not with a statement that multiple visitors had one remark.

B **Incorrect:** This choice creates a disagreement between the word "a," which must describe a singular noun, and the word "visitors," which is plural. This is exactly the kind of singular-plural mismatch that trained test-takers know to stay alert for on the Writing and Language section.

C **Incorrect:** This choice would result in a run-on sentence (that is, two independent clauses with no punctuation between them). The first independent clause would be "As I walked...I overheard" and the second would be "a visitor remarked, 'You know...actually runs.'" Two independent clauses must be separated by either a semi-colon or a period on the SAT, so this choice can't be correct.

D ✓ **Correct:** This choice avoids the problems from the other answer choices. It's also the shortest choice, and it's grammatically acceptable, so, as trained test-takers, we know it's right.

- **Vertical Scan Results:** Choices are long phrases/sentences.
- **Vertical Scan Notes:** The main difference among all the answer choices is the location of the phrase "dotted with pin-sized knobs," and the punctuation around that phrase.
- **Key Features in Surrounding Text:** the underlined sentence.

Concepts in the question:

- **Phrase Proximity:** Answer choice(s) would place descriptive phrases next to ideas they don't describe. Descriptive phrases that don't begin with a word ending in "-ing" describe the closest noun phrase. (See page 451.)

ANSWER CHOICE ANALYSIS

A	**Incorrect:** Placing the phrase "another visitor" after the comma that follows the phrase "dotted with pin-sized knobs" makes it sound like the *visitor* is the thing "dotted with pin-sized knobs" according to the College Board's grammar rules.
B	**Incorrect:** This choice has a similar problem to the one in choice (A), and it's wrong for the same reasons.
C	**Incorrect:** This choice has the same problem as (A) and (B), and it's wrong for the same reasons.
D ✓	**Correct:** This is the only choice that puts the phrase "dotted with pin-sized knobs" next to what that phrase must describe, the word "drawers."

- **RC Question sub-type:** Sentence or paragraph placement. (The prompt asks us where a sentence should go in a paragraph, or where a paragraph should go in the passage. The correct order will reflect a logical chronology, and/or will allow for pronouns in the sentences to refer to nouns in a logical way, and/or will place related concepts near one another. See page 432.)
- **Subjective phrases to be ignored:** "most"

ANSWER CHOICE ANALYSIS

A	**Pattern:** Causes text to refer to an idea that hasn't been mentioned yet. **Incorrect:** The end of paragraph 1 mentions "the Thorne Miniature Rooms" exhibit, and paragraph 3 explains what that exhibit is. Meanwhile, paragraph 2 describes the narrator's personal experience viewing the exhibit. So paragraph 2 shouldn't occur between paragraphs 1 and 3, because paragraph 2 talks about the narrator's experience viewing the Thorne Miniature Rooms exhibit before even explaining what the exhibit is in paragraph 3.
B ✓	**Pattern:** Correct. Paragraph 4 begins by saying that the "architectural features, furnishings, and decorations" of "the plainer rooms" are "just as true to the periods they represent," so it belongs after a discussion of something else that was "true to the periods [it] represent[s]." This will allow the phrase "just as" to signal a comparison between the rooms in paragraph 4 and the more decorated rooms in paragraph 2. Also, this addresses the problem described in (A) by allowing paragraph 3, which explains what the Thorne Miniature Rooms exhibit is, to come before paragraph 2, which begins the description of the narrator's experience viewing the exhibit. As trained test-takers, we know that all of this means the College Board will reward us for placing paragraph 2 just before paragraph 4, which is the same as saying it should appear after paragraph 3.
C	**Pattern:** Causes text to introduce an idea that has already been discussed. **Incorrect:** As we saw in the explanation for (B), paragraph 2 needs to appear right *before* paragraph 4 so that the comparison near the beginning of paragraph 4 involving the phrase "just as true" makes sense.
D	**Pattern:** Causes text to introduce an idea that has already been discussed. **Incorrect:** As we saw in the explanation for choice (B), paragraph 2 needs to appear right before paragraph 4.

- **Vertical Scan Results:** Choices are long phrases/sentences.
- **Vertical Scan Notes:** We need to decide whether the phrase should begin with "living along" or "that live along," which phrase should appear after "North America," and whether there should be a comma after "America."
- **Key Features in Surrounding Text:** The entire sentence in the question.

Concepts in the question:

- **Comma Sandwich:** Choice(s) would create phrases improperly "sandwiched" between similar types of punctuation. When removed from the sentence, a properly formed sandwich leaves behind a grammatically acceptable sentence. (See page 448.)
- **Commas:** Choices include one or more commas. On the Writing and Language section, commas can be used to separate things in a list of three or more, to form a comma sandwich, or to introduce an independent clause after a dependent clause. (See pages 448-450.)

- **Dependent and Independent Clauses:** Answer choice(s) would incorrectly use a dependent or independent clause. An independent clause can stand alone as a sentence: it has a main subject/verb pair. A dependent clause is introduced by a conjunction or relative pronoun. (See page 445.)
- **Intervening Phrase:** A phrase appears between two words that need to agree with each other. Identify which words need to agree with each other, and ignore extra phrases that appear between them. (See page 456.)
- **Phrase Proximity:** Answer choice(s) would place descriptive phrases next to ideas they don't describe. Descriptive phrases that don't begin with a word ending in "-ing" describe the closest noun phrase. (See page 451.)
- **Shorter is Better:** Choices include words or phrases that can be removed without impacting the meaning of the sentence or creating grammatical problems. Remember to avoid redundancy, and that the shortest grammatically acceptable choice (according to the College Board) is correct. (See page 454.)
- **Verb Tense/Conjugation:** Choices include different forms of the same verb. Look at the surrounding text to find each verb's subject. Also, look for other verbs that could indicate the proper tense for the verbs in the answer choices. (See page 437.)

ANSWER CHOICE ANALYSIS

A ✓ **Correct:** This is the shortest choice and it's grammatically acceptable, so it's right. The phrase "living along the West Coast of North America" is an intervening phrase that describes the otters, and the plural verb form "help" agrees with the plural noun "otters," which is its subject. In other words, if we remove the intervening phrase, we're left with this basic sentence: "It has long been known that…otters…help…"

B **Incorrect:** This choice has several issues that prevent it from being correct. One is that it introduces a comma, which can be viewed as a change that turns the rest of the sentence into a phrase that interrupts the description of the sea otters that live along the coast. Alternatively, we could try to view the part of the sentence that comes after the comma as an independent clause, but then the phrase "it has long been known that sea otters living along the West Coast of North America" isn't a dependent clause, or a sandwiched phrase describing the word "they," or any other kind of phrase that the College Board allows. Further, as trained test-takers, we should already have noted that (A) is both shorter than (B) and grammatically acceptable, which means (A) must be right.

C **Incorrect:** This choice would turn the original sentence into a sentence fragment that began by saying something was known about otters, and then described two things the otters did as an aside ("live along the West Coast of North America" and "help keep kelp forests in their habitat healthy and vital"), without ever saying what was known about the otters according to the beginning of the sentence.

D **Incorrect:** This choice creates a sentence fragment similar to the fragment created by (C), but with the difference that the part of the sentence after the comma would be a sandwiched phrase giving more information about the coast. In this situation, the sentence fragment would begin by saying that something has long been known about otters, and then it would interrupt itself to explain which otters were being talked about by telling us where the otters lived, and then it would interrupt itself again to tell us some further information about where the otters lived…but it would never actually get around to telling us what was known about the otters. And, as we noted for (B) and (C), this choice also has the problem that it's longer than (A), and (A) is grammatically acceptable, so we know as trained test-takers that (D) can't be right.

Answer choice patterns (see pages 454 and 455): Wrong answers incorporate elements of the right answer. Shortest grammatically acceptable choice is correct.

Test 2, Question 24 — TYPE: READING COMPREHENSION (usually has a prompt; choices have different meanings)

- **RC Question sub-type:** Figure. (The prompt requires us to read a figure in order to find an answer that reflects the data in the figure. The correct answer will be directly supported by the information in the figure. Remember to read carefully and check for details such as column headings, axis-labels, legends, and so on. See pages 44-51.)

ANSWER CHOICE ANALYSIS

A **Pattern:** Confused concepts. **Incorrect:** The label on the left side of the chart tells us that the vertical bars measure the "number per square meter" of different animals in coastal areas. The legend tells us that information about "sea urchins" is expressed in the dark gray bars. When we look at the bottom of the chart, we see the middle set of bars provides information about areas with "otters present for 2 years or less." There's a small dark gray bar there, which means that there are still some sea urchins present. So we can't say that "two years or less of sea otters can *completely* eliminate sea urchins in a coastal area" (emphasis mine), as this choice would require, because the graph shows a non-zero number of sea urchins present in the middle cluster of bars, instead of zero urchins present. (This choice may have been tempting if an untrained test-takers confused the bars for "2 years or less" with the bars for "10 years or more.")

B ✓ **Pattern:** Correct. We can see that the dark gray bar above "no otters present" indicates the presence of around 5 or 6 sea urchins per square meter. Then the central dark gray bar, above "otters present for 2 years or less," indicates the presence of 1 or 2 sea urchins per square meter, showing that when otters were present for two years or less, the number of sea urchins per square meter dropped from roughly 5 to roughly 1. So we can see that "two years or less of sea otter presence" did, in fact, "reduce" the population density of sea urchins, just as this choice requires. (Notice that we didn't even specifically need to figure out that the number dropped from 5-ish to 1-ish—we only needed to be able to see that the dark gray bar on the left was bigger than the dark gray bar in the middle.)

C   **Pattern:** Direct contradiction. **Incorrect:** If we compare the change in dark bars to the change in light bars as we move from left to right, we see that a *falling* density of urchins coincided with a *rising* density of kelp, contradicting this answer choice. (C) may have been tempting if we misread the word "increase" as "decrease" in one of the places where it appears.

D   **Pattern:** Direct contradiction. **Incorrect:** The information on the chart above "otters present for 10 years or more" shows that kelp density is around 50, while sea urchin density is zero. This means the kelp density was *higher* than the urchin density, not *lower*, as this choice would require. Untrained test-takers might pick this choice if they confused the colors of the bars for kelp and sea urchins.

Note   Notice that (C) and (D) directly contradicted the text, but they could still be tempting if we looked at the wrong part of the chart, or misread the chart. This is one more example of why it's so important to read carefully on test day and make sure you don't give points away with unnecessary mistakes!

Test 2, Question 25   **TYPE: READING COMPREHENSION (usually has a prompt; choices have different meanings)**

- RC Question sub-type: Transition phrase. (The choices include words or phrases showing a transition from the previous sentence, like "however," "instead of," "for example," etc. The transition phrase must reflect the relationship between the previous sentence and the sentence where the transition phrase appears. See page 431.)

ANSWER CHOICE ANALYSIS

A   **Pattern:** Confused concepts. **Incorrect:** This choice would be appropriate if this sentence told us something that's true in spite of what was mentioned in the previous sentence, but that's not the case. There's nothing in the previous sentence that would suggest that the information in this sentence isn't true.

B✓   **Pattern:** Correct. The previous sentences tell us what happens "*with* sea otters" (emphasis mine), but then this sentence tells us what happens "*without* sea otters" (emphasis mine). The word "however" appropriately reflects the idea that what's discussed in this sentence contrasts with what was discussed in the previous sentence.

C   **Pattern:** Largely irrelevant. **Incorrect:** This choice would be appropriate if this sentence provided some conclusion based on the information in the previous sentence, but that's not the case.

D   **Pattern:** Direct contradiction. **Incorrect:** This choice would be appropriate if this sentence expressed a relationship that was similar to one from the previous sentence, but that's not the case—as we saw in the explanation for (B), this sentence discusses a situation that contrasts with a situation in the previous sentence.

Test 2, Question 26   **TYPE: READING COMPREHENSION (usually has a prompt; choices have different meanings)**

- RC Question sub-type: Including/excluding a phrase/sentence. (The question asks whether a sentence should be included in the passage. The correct choice will include a comment that plainly describes the role of the phrase or sentence in the passage. Sentences that should be included will follow broad College Board standards for ideal sentences and paragraphs—including consistency with any figures in the passage—while sentences that shouldn't be included will not follow those standards. See page 433.)

ANSWER CHOICE ANALYSIS

A ✓   **Pattern:** Correct. The phrase does establish the relationship between the level of carbon dioxide and global warming, as this choice requires: the sentence already in the text says "the amount of carbon dioxide in the atmosphere has increased 40 percent," and the phrase from the prompt says this carbon dioxide "result[ed] in a rise in global temperatures." The phrase in question plainly demonstrates the idea described in (A) alone, so (A) is correct.

B   **Pattern:** Wrong part of the passage. **Incorrect:** The phrase in question doesn't explain anything about sea otters and sea urchins. Instead, those animals are discussed elsewhere in the passage—not in the phrase from the question, as this choice and the prompt would require.

C   **Pattern:** Confused concepts. **Incorrect:** The phrase doesn't contradict the claim from the previous paragraph, because the phrase doesn't say anything about sea otters or kelp forests.

D   **Pattern:** Direct contradiction. **Incorrect:** The phrase doesn't blur the focus of the paragraph, as this choice would require: the Industrial Revolution is only mentioned to give additional information about the time period over which "the amount of carbon dioxide in the atmosphere has increased 40 percent." The phrase still mentions "a rise in global temperatures," so it maintains the focus of the rest of the paragraph.

Test 2, Question 27   **TYPE: GRAMMAR/STYLE/PUNCTUATION (often no prompt; choices have similar meanings)**

- **Vertical Scan Results:** Some choices have the same words with different punctuation.
- **Vertical Scan Notes:** Should the words "suggests" and "that" be joined by a comma, a dash, a comma and a quotation mark, or no punctuation?

- **Key Features in Surrounding Text:** The comma-sandwiched intervening phrase "by two professors at the University of California, Santa Cruz, Chris Wilmers and James Estes" makes understanding this sentence more challenging. If we remove that phrase, the beginning of the sentence is "A recent study suggests …" This makes it easier to see that no punctuation is needed in the underlined phrase.

Concepts in the question:

- **Commas:** Choices include one or more commas. On the Writing and Language section, commas can be used to separate things in a list of three or more, to form a comma sandwich, or to introduce an independent clause after a dependent clause. (See pages 448-450.)

- **Intervening Phrase:** A phrase appears between two words that need to agree with each other. Identify which words need to agree with each other, and ignore extra phrases that appear between them. (See page 456.)

ANSWER CHOICE ANALYSIS

A   **Incorrect:** When we remove the intervening phrase, this choice would give us "A recent study suggests, that kelp forests protected by sea otters can absorb…" The College Board won't let us insert a comma here, because the comma wouldn't be part of a comma sandwich, a comma-separated list, an introduction to a dependent clause, or any other thing that the SAT allows us to do with commas (see pages 448-450 for the SAT's comma rules.) Remember that the College Board prefers to avoid punctuation whenever possible on the Writing and Language section, unless there's a specific need for it.

B   **Incorrect:** This choice has a similar problem to the one in (A): it introduces a piece of punctuation—a dash—where there's no need for one (see the discussion of (D) below, and see page 450 of this Black Book for a refresher on dashes).

C   **Incorrect:** The easiest way to tell that (C) is wrong is that it introduces an open quotation mark with no closing quotation mark anywhere in sight. We can't have an open quotation mark without a closing quotation mark, so (C) is wrong.

D ✓ **Correct:** As trained test-takers, we know the College Board won't allow us to insert any punctuation to separate the verb "suggests" from the thing being suggested, for reasons we discussed for the other choices. We also need to remember that the College Board's default preference is to omit punctuation unless it's specifically required by the College Board's rules—for more, see the discussion of commas on the Writing and Language section starting on page 448 of this Black Book.

Answer choice patterns (see page 454): Shortest grammatically acceptable choice is correct.

Test 2, Question 28   **TYPE: READING COMPREHENSION (usually has a prompt; choices have different meanings)**

- **RC Question sub-type:** Vocabulary In Context. (Choices include words or short phrases that have vaguely similar but not identical meanings. Most or all of the choices will seem vaguely appropriate, but only one choice will be correct when we think very carefully and specifically about the word means and how it can be used. See page 432.)

ANSWER CHOICE ANALYSIS

A ✓ ("…as those where sea urchins are allowed to <u>devour</u> the kelp.") **Correct:** The first paragraph mentions that sea urchins "graze voraciously on kelp." The word "devour" has the same extreme connotation as the word "voraciously," so (A) restates a relevant idea from the text, which makes it correct.

B   ("…as those where sea urchins are allowed to <u>dispatch</u> the kelp.") **Pattern:** Same ballpark. **Incorrect:** "Dispatch" means something like "get rid of" or "send off." But as we saw in the explanation for (A), we need a choice that means the same thing as "graze voraciously," so this choice can't be correct.

C   ("…as those where sea urchins are allowed to <u>overindulge on</u> the kelp.") **Pattern:** Plausible, but not in the text. **Incorrect:** "Overindulge on" means to consume so much of something as to cause yourself harm. But the text doesn't restate the idea that the sea urchins eat so much they harm themselves, so this choice can't be correct.

D   ("…as those where sea urchins are allowed to <u>dispose of</u> the kelp.") **Pattern:** Same ballpark. **Incorrect:** This phrase has basically the same meaning as choice (B), and is wrong for the same reasons.

Test 2, Question 29   **TYPE: GRAMMAR/STYLE/PUNCTUATION (often no prompt; choices have similar meanings)**

- **Vertical Scan Results:** Choices include most or all possible combinations of two options. Some choices include homophone pairs or triples.

- **Vertical Scan Notes:** We need to decide whether the underlined phrase should be plural or singular, whether it should be possessive or a contraction, and what its correct form is.

- **Key Features in Surrounding Text:** The thing that has "terrestrial plant cousins" is kelp, so the underlined phrase needs to agree with "kelp" in number, and also express the idea that the "terrestrial plant cousins" belong to kelp. So we need a singular possessive pronoun.

Concepts in the question:

- **Plural/Possessive/Contraction:** Choices include the same noun ending in "-s" with or without an apostrophe before or after the "-s." Remember the three rules for forming possessives. Think of contractions in their uncontracted forms ("you're" = "you are"). (See page 441.)
- **Singular versus Plural:** Choices include singular and plural versions of the same base words that don't agree with other words in the surrounding text. Singular nouns must go with singular verb forms and singular pronouns. Plural nouns must go with plural verbs and pronouns. Think carefully about which words should match or agree with each other! (See page 443.)

ANSWER CHOICE ANALYSIS

A **Incorrect:** The correct answer needs to refer to the singular noun "kelp," but this choice is plural, so it can't be right.

B **Incorrect:** The underlined phrase should refer to the singular noun "kelp," but this choice is plural. Also, this choice is the contracted form of "they are," but we need a possessive form that shows the "terrestrial plant cousins" belong to "kelp." Either issue would be enough by itself to make this choice wrong.

C ✓ **Correct:** This is the correctly formed singular possessive pronoun "its," so this choice is correct.

D **Incorrect:** This choice is the contracted form of "it is," but we need a possessive form to show that the "terrestrial plant cousins" belong to "kelp."

> **Note** Notice that if you weren't sure whether "kelp" might be an irregular plural form, you could see that the singular verb "removes" right after the word "kelp" indicates that "kelp" must be a singular form.

Test 2, Question 30 **TYPE: GRAMMAR/STYLE/PUNCTUATION (often no prompt; choices have similar meanings)**

- **Vertical Scan Results:** Choices are long phrases/sentences.
- **Vertical Scan Notes:** Only choice (C) actually mentions otters; the other choices include a pronoun like "it" or "they."
- **Key Features in Surrounding Text:** The rest of this sentence doesn't mention any specific thing that "help[s] kelp forests to significantly decrease the amount of carbon dioxide." So this underlined phrase must include a noun that could do that action, according to the SAT's rules.

Concepts in the question:

- **Pronoun Ambiguity:** Choices include pronouns that could refer to more than one phrase in the surrounding text. We can't use a pronoun on the SAT when it isn't clear what that pronoun refers to. (See page 441.)
- **Singular versus Plural:** Choices include singular and plural versions of the same base words that don't agree with other words in the surrounding text. Singular nouns must go with singular verb forms and singular pronouns. Plural nouns must go with plural verbs and pronouns. Think carefully about which words should match or agree with each other! (See page 443.)

ANSWER CHOICE ANALYSIS

A **Incorrect:** This choice would include the word "they" without clearly indicating what the word "they" refers to: the word "they" could refer to the plural noun "scientists" from earlier in this sentence, or to the words "forests" or "otters" from earlier in the paragraph. As trained test-takers, we know the College Board's unwritten rules only allow us to use a pronoun when it's clear what the pronoun is referring to, so this choice must be wrong.

B **Incorrect:** This choice would include the word "it" without clearly indicating what "it" was referring to. The word "it" could be referring to the singular nouns "kelp," "carbon dioxide," "atmosphere," "fuel," "photosynthesis," "oxygen," or "air" from the previous sentence, or to whatever the word "this" is referring to earlier in the same sentence. As trained test-takers, we know this breaks the College Board's rules for unambiguous pronoun usage, so this choice must be wrong.

C ✓ **Correct:** This choice makes it clear that "sea otters" are what play a role, because this is the only choice that avoids ambiguous pronouns completely.

D **Incorrect:** This choice has the same pronoun issue that we saw in (A), and is wrong for the same reason.

Answer choice patterns (see page 455): Wrong answers incorporate elements of the right answer.

Test 2, Question 31 **TYPE: READING COMPREHENSION (usually has a prompt; choices have different meanings)**

- **RC Question sub-type:** Sentence or paragraph placement. (The prompt asks us where a sentence should go in a paragraph, or where a paragraph should go in the passage. The correct order will reflect a logical chronology, and/or will allow for pronouns in the sentences to refer to nouns in a logical way, and/or will place related concepts near one another. See page 432.)
- **Subjective phrases to be ignored:** "most"

ANSWER CHOICE ANALYSIS

A **Pattern:** Causes text to refer to an idea that hasn't been mentioned yet. **Incorrect:** This choice would cause the paragraph to refer to Wilmers and Estes by their last names alone, two sentences before the paragraph introduces Wilmers and Estes in sentence 3.

B   **Pattern:** Causes text to refer to an idea that hasn't been mentioned yet. **Incorrect:** This choice would place the sentence from the prompt immediately after the sentence that introduces Wilmer and Estes, but the sentence with the introduction doesn't describe anything that would cause the researchers to be "surprised," so the word "therefore" in the prompt sentence wouldn't be referring to anything.

C   **Pattern:** Causes text to refer to an idea that hasn't been mentioned yet. **Incorrect:** Like (B), this choice would place the sentence in a position that doesn't explain what "surprised" the researchers, which would make the word "therefore" in the sentence unacceptable according to the College Board's rules.

D✓   **Pattern:** Correct. Sentence 5 explains that scientists previously didn't recognize something about the role of otters with respect to carbon dioxide. This explains why the researchers could be "surprised," as the prompt sentence requires, and allows the word "therefore" in the prompt sentence to refer back to a logical cause for the surprise in sentence 5.

Test 2, Question 32	TYPE: READING COMPREHENSION (usually has a prompt; choices have different meanings)

- **RC Question sub-type:** Vocabulary In Context. (Choices include words or short phrases that have vaguely similar but not identical meanings. Most or all of the choices will seem vaguely appropriate, but only one choice will be correct when we think very carefully and specifically about the word means and how it can be used. See page 432.)

ANSWER CHOICE ANALYSIS

A   ("…having more otters will not automatically solve the problem of higher levels of carbon dioxide in the air.") **Pattern:** Largely irrelevant. **Incorrect:** This might be tempting to test-takers who don't read carefully, but (A) is wrong for two reasons: the word "having" could indicate some kind of ownership or authority, which isn't restated or demonstrated in the text, and the idea of "more otters" doesn't specifically indicate the otters will be interacting with the environment, as we see in (B).

B✓   ("…increasing the otter population will not automatically solve the problem of higher levels of carbon dioxide in the air.") **Correct:** This passage discusses "the presence of otters" in an "ecosystem," which is restated by the phrase "otter population" in (B). Note the subtle but important difference here between the idea of "increasing" a "population," which objectively describes the idea of raising the number of otters in the ecosystem, and the idea of "having more otters" in (A) and (D), which doesn't specifically reflect those key elements of the passage.

C   ("…the otters multiplying will not automatically solve the problem of higher levels of carbon dioxide in the air.") **Pattern:** Same ballpark. **Incorrect:** This choice is wrong because the idea of otters multiplying doesn't necessarily indicate an overall increase in the otter population. A population of otters can reproduce (or "multiply") while still dying off for unrelated reasons, which could potentially result in a population that decreases or stays the same size, rather than increasing.

D   ("…having more otters than other locations will not automatically solve the problem of higher levels of carbon dioxide in the air.") **Pattern:** Largely irrelevant. **Incorrect:** This choice has the same problem as choice (A), with the added problem of mentioning otters in other locations. The text doesn't describe the idea that the relative number of otters in one location as opposed to another has anything to do with removing carbon dioxide.

Test 2, Question 33	TYPE: GRAMMAR/STYLE/PUNCTUATION (often no prompt; choices have similar meanings)

- **Vertical Scan Results:** Some choices have the same words with different punctuation.
- **Vertical Scan Notes:** Should there be a semi-colon after "removed?" If not, where should the comma appear?
- **Key Features in Surrounding Text:** It looks like the underlined phrase helps to explain what the word "sequestered" means. Also, if we decide the semi-colon isn't acceptable here, it looks like we're going to create a "comma sandwich" with the comma after "sequestered" and the comma from choice (B), (C), or (D).

Concepts in the question:

- **Comma Sandwich:** Choice(s) would create phrases improperly "sandwiched" between similar types of punctuation. When removed from the sentence, a properly formed sandwich leaves behind a grammatically acceptable sentence. (See page 448.)
- **Commas:** Choices include one or more commas. On the Writing and Language section, commas can be used to separate things in a list of three or more, to form a comma sandwich, or to introduce an independent clause after a dependent clause. (See pages 448-450.)
- **Prepositional Idioms:** Choices typically include prepositional phrases with no other recognizable grammatical similarities. On this type of question, if you can't determine which answer choice contains an acceptable prepositional idiom in American English, then you should guess at an answer and invest your time in questions that don't involve prepositional idioms. (See page 443.)

ANSWER CHOICE ANALYSIS

A   **Incorrect:** The College Board won't let us place a semi-colon after "removed" because semicolons can only be used to join two independent clauses on the SAT, and the part of the sentence after the semi-colon isn't an independent clause because it can't stand on its own as a complete sentence.

B   **Incorrect:** This choice would create a comma sandwich around "or removed from." If we remove that phrase from the sentence, we're left with the ungrammatical phrase "carbon can be sequestered the atmosphere," so (B) can't be correct.

C   Incorrect: This choice would create a comma sandwich around "removed from." If we remove that phrase from the sentence, we're left with the ungrammatical phrase "carbon can be sequestered or the atmosphere," so (C) can't be correct.

D ✓   Correct: This choice would create a comma sandwich around "or removed." If we remove that phrase from the sentence, we're left with the grammatically acceptable phrase "carbon can be sequestered from the atmosphere," so (D) is correct.

Note   In order to answer this question correctly, it helps to know that, in context, the verb "sequestered" needs to be followed by the preposition "from." But even if we're not familiar with that idiom, we can still tell that the phrase "carbon can be sequestered the atmosphere" is ungrammatical, because there's nothing tying the noun "the atmosphere" back to the rest of the sentence.

Test 2, Question 34   **TYPE: GRAMMAR/STYLE/PUNCTUATION (often no prompt; choices have similar meanings)**

- **Vertical Scan Results:** Some choices are short phrases with no obvious similarity.
- **Vertical Scan Notes:** We have a variety of prepositional phrases to choose from, which strongly suggests that this question is testing our knowledge of a prepositional idiom.
- **Key Features in Surrounding Text:** The underlined phrase connects the word "practice" and a phrase explaining that practice.

Concepts in the question:

- **Prepositional Idioms:** Choices typically include prepositional phrases with no other recognizable grammatical similarities. On this type of question, if you can't determine which answer choice contains an acceptable prepositional idiom in American English, then you should guess at an answer and invest your time in questions that don't involve prepositional idioms. (See page 443.)

ANSWER CHOICE ANALYSIS

A   Incorrect: In context, "at which" isn't acceptable—see the note below!

B   Incorrect: In context, "from which" isn't acceptable—see the note below!

C   Incorrect: In context, "so that" isn't acceptable—see the note below!

D ✓   Correct: In context, "whereby" is an acceptable way to connect the word "practice" and the explanation of that practice.

Note   Remember that questions involving prepositional idioms often have explanations that feel unsatisfactory because there isn't really any logic behind prepositional idioms—they just reflect the commonly accepted usage of a certain phrase in American English. If you had trouble with this question, don't get hung up on it, because the odds of you needing to know the phrase "a practice whereby X happens" on test day are very low. Remember that the vast majority of questions on the Writing and Language section are based on rules and patterns that allow you to know with certainty if you've found the right answer; focus your energy on those questions, rather than on idiom questions like this. If you do that, then you can get an excellent score. See the training on prepositional idioms on page 443.

Test 2, Question 35   **TYPE: GRAMMAR/STYLE/PUNCTUATION (often no prompt; choices have similar meanings)**

- **Vertical Scan Results:** Some choices have the same words with different punctuation.
- **Vertical Scan Notes:** Should there be a comma, dash, semicolon, or nothing after "usefulness?"
- **Key Features in Surrounding Text:** The entire sentence in the question.

Concepts in the question:

- **Comma Sandwich:** Choice(s) would create phrases improperly "sandwiched" between similar types of punctuation. When removed from the sentence, a properly formed sandwich leaves behind a grammatically acceptable sentence. (See page 448.)
- **Commas:** Choices include one or more commas. On the Writing and Language section, commas can be used to separate things in a list of three or more, to form a comma sandwich, or to introduce an independent clause after a dependent clause. (See pages 448-450.)
- **Semi-colons:** Choices include one or more semicolons. Semi-colons can be used to separate two sets of words that could each stand on their own as a full sentence. (See page 447.)

ANSWER CHOICE ANALYSIS

A ✓   Correct: This choice would create a comma sandwich around the phrase "a practice whereby products are designed to have a limited period of usefulness." If we remove that phrase from the sentence, we're left with the grammatically acceptable phrase "Planned obsolescence has been a cornerstone..." So this choice is correct.

B   Incorrect: This choice would attempt to create the same punctuation sandwich described in choice (A), but that sandwich would involve two different types of punctuation—a comma and a dash. According to the rules of the SAT, punctuation sandwiches must have the same punctuation mark on either end (or a comma and a period if the sandwich appears at the end of a sentence), so this choice is incorrect.

C   Incorrect: There shouldn't be a semi-colon after "usefulness" because the part of the sentence before the semi-colon and the part of the sentence after the semi-colon wouldn't each stand on their own as complete sentences, and the College Board only lets us use semi-colons to separate independent clauses.

D   Incorrect: With no punctuation here, the entire sentence after the word "obsolescence" becomes an ungrammatical phrase describing "planned obsolescence." That would also mean there was no main verb for "planned obsolescence" to do, and the sentence would become a fragment.

Test 2, Question 36   **TYPE: READING COMPREHENSION (usually has a prompt; choices have different meanings)**

- **RC Question sub-type:** Vocabulary In Context. (Choices include words or short phrases that have vaguely similar but not identical meanings. Most or all of the choices will seem vaguely appropriate, but only one choice will be correct when we think very carefully and specifically about what the word means and how it can be used. See page 432.)

ANSWER CHOICE ANALYSIS

A   ("This approach increases sales, but it also stands in <u>austere</u> contrast to a time when goods were produced to be durable.") **Pattern:** Largely irrelevant. **Incorrect:** "Austere" means something like "strict" or "plain," so this choice doesn't restate or demonstrate anything from the passage, which means it's incorrect.

B   ("This approach increases sales, but it also stands in <u>egregious</u> contrast to a time when goods were produced to be durable.") **Pattern:** Confused concepts. **Incorrect:** "Egregious" means something like "really bad," so this choice isn't correct, because it doesn't restate or demonstrate anything from the passage.

C   ("This approach increases sales, but it also stands in <u>unmitigated</u> contrast to a time when goods were produced to be durable.") **Pattern:** Confused concepts. **Incorrect:** "Unmitigated" means something like "without anything to limit its impact," so this choice doesn't restate or demonstrate anything from the passage and isn't correct.

D✓   ("This approach increases sales, but it also stands in <u>stark</u> contrast to a time when goods were produced to be durable.") **Correct:** The correct answer should describe the "contrast" between products that are "designed to have a limited period of usefulness" and products that are "durable." "Stark" means something like "very striking" or "very obvious," which makes sense in this context— the "contrast" between something that isn't durable and something that is durable would be very obvious. The text demonstrates the idea of a "stark" contrast, so (D) is right.

Test 2, Question 37   **TYPE: READING COMPREHENSION (usually has a prompt; choices have different meanings)**

- **RC Question sub-type:** Best Accomplishes X. (The prompt describes a goal of the author, and asks us which choice achieves that goal. The correct answer choice will plainly and directly demonstrate the task described in the prompt. See page 431.)
- **Subjective phrases to be ignored:** "best"

ANSWER CHOICE ANALYSIS

A✓   **Pattern:** Correct. (A) supports the claim made in the sentence, because the idea that "repair methods are often specialized" supports the idea that mending goods would be difficult, which means it's "easier to replace" them, as the text says.

B   **Pattern:** Largely irrelevant. **Incorrect:** This choice doesn't support the claim made by the sentence, because the idea of obsolete goods becoming collectible items isn't related to whether or not it's "easier to replace goods than to mend them."

C   **Pattern:** Largely irrelevant. **Incorrect:** This choice doesn't support the claim made by the sentence, because the idea of goods "fall[ing] into disrepair again" isn't related to whether or not it's "easier to replace goods than to mend them."

D   **Pattern:** plausible, but not in the text. **Incorrect:** This choice doesn't support the claim made by the sentence, because the idea of new designs having bugs isn't related to whether or not it's "easier to replace goods than to mend them."

> **Note**   The "claim made by this sentence" as mentioned in the prompt is that "[planned obsolescence] also reinforces the belief that it is easier to replace goods than to mend them."

Test 2, Question 38   **TYPE: GRAMMAR/STYLE/PUNCTUATION (often no prompt; choices have similar meanings)**

- **Vertical Scan Results:** Choices include most or all possible combinations of two options. Some choices have the same words with different punctuation.
- **Vertical Scan Notes:** Is "fair" or "fare" appropriate? Is "then" or "than" appropriate? Should there be a comma between "fair" and "then?"
- **Key Features in Surrounding Text:** The text compares "the first Repair Café" to "an actual café," so the underlined phrase needs to include a word used to make comparisons—in this case, the word "than." The thing that "the first Repair Café" was "more like" must be something you could logically compare "an actual café" to. We can choose between "fare," an amount of money paid for a service, and "fair," a word describing a gathering of people and stalls. The paragraph describes people coming together to do something, which means "fair" is the appropriate choice.

Concepts in the question:

- **Commas:** Choices include one or more commas. On the Writing and Language section, commas can be used to separate things in a list of three or more, to form a comma sandwich, or to introduce an independent clause after a dependent clause. (See pages 448-450.)
- **Confused Homophones:** Choices include different homophone pairs (such as "their" and "they're" or "too" and "to"). Read carefully—also, remember the correct formation of possessive pronouns, and remember to read contractions as their uncontracted forms (e.g. "it's" = "it is"). (See page 452.)

ANSWER CHOICE ANALYSIS

A **Incorrect:** "Then" is an adverb that tells us when something happened, but in context we need the word "than" to allow the comparison between "the Repair Café" and "an actual café."

B ✓ **Correct:** This is the only choice the combines the words "fair" and "than," so it's correct. (A "fair" is an event where a lot of people gather, and "than" is a word used in comparisons; both of these usages are appropriate in this context.)

C **Incorrect:** As we discussed above, the appropriate word in context is "fair," not "fare."

D **Incorrect:** This choice has the same problem with the word "then" that we saw in (A), so it must be wrong. It also adds a comma between the two words that doesn't follow the SAT's rules for comma usage. Either issue would be enough by itself to make this choice wrong.

Answer choice patterns (see page 455): Wrong answers incorporate elements of the right answer.

Test 2, Question 39   **TYPE: GRAMMAR/STYLE/PUNCTUATION (often no prompt; choices have similar meanings)**

- **Vertical Scan Results:** Some choices have different forms of the same base word.
- **Vertical Scan Notes:** We need to pick the correct form of the verb "to want," and we need to decide whether "who," "whom," "she," or nothing should appear before the verb in the underlined phrase.
- **Key Features in Surrounding Text:** The underlined phrase needs to indicate that "Martine Postma" is the one doing the action described after the comma.

Concepts in the question:

- **Dangling Participle:** The question involves descriptive phrases beginning with an "-ing" word that would describe the wrong word in context. Descriptive phrases starting with a word ending in "-ing" describe the first noun phrase in that sentence's independent clause. (See page 450.)
- **Dependent and Independent Clauses:** Answer choice(s) would incorrectly use a dependent or independent clause. An independent clause can stand alone as a sentence: it has a main subject/verb pair. A dependent clause is introduced by a conjunction or relative pronoun. (See page 445.)
- **Verb Tense/Conjugation:** Choices include different forms of the same verb. Look at the surrounding text to find each verb's subject. Also, look for other verbs that could indicate the proper tense for the verbs in the answer choices. (See page 437.)
- **Who versus Whom:** At least one answer choice involves "who" or "whom." "Who" is a subject pronoun (that does an action), and "whom" is an object pronoun (that receives an action). In other words, we can use "who" where "he" would be appropriate, and "whom" where "him" would be appropriate. (See page 439.)

ANSWER CHOICE ANALYSIS

A **Incorrect:** According to the SAT's rules, this choice would indicate that the word "it" at the beginning of the sentence was the thing doing the "wanting." This is because the phrase "wanting to take a practical stand in a throwaway culture" starts with a word ending in "-ing," and the SAT's grammar rules say that the word ending in "-ing" in that situation (which is "wanting") modifies the first noun in the independent clause (which is "it").

B **Incorrect:** We know that "whom" functions like "him," and it wouldn't be acceptable to say "him wants to take a practical stand…," so this choice can't be correct. Another issue is that the verb "wants" is in the present tense, but past-tense verbs appear in other places in the paragraph ("was," "took place," "were," etc.).

C ✓ **Correct:** This choice would cause the verb "wanted" to refer clearly to Martine Postma, because it creates a comma sandwiched phrase beginning with "who" that is positioned immediately after the phrase "Martine Postma." Further, the verb "wanted" is in the past tense, which fits with other verbs in the paragraph related to the creation of the fair, as we discussed with choice (B).

D **Incorrect:** This choice would create an independent clause after the comma, resulting in a comma splice, which isn't allowed on the SAT. (See page 447 for more on comma splices.)

Answer choice patterns (see page 455): Wrong answers incorporate elements of the right answer.

- **RC Question sub-type:** Transition phrase. (The choices include words or phrases showing a transition from the previous sentence, like "however," "instead of," "for example," etc. The transition phrase must reflect the relationship between the previous sentence and the sentence where the transition phrase appears. See page 431.)

ANSWER CHOICE ANALYSIS

A   **Pattern:** Largely irrelevant. **Incorrect:** This choice would be appropriate if what was discussed in this sentence was not what one would expect based on the previous sentence, but that's not the case, because the straightforward nature of the goals is neither surprising nor unsurprising based on the information in the previous sentence.

B   **Pattern:** Largely irrelevant. **Incorrect:** This choice would be appropriate if this sentence provided some conclusion based on the information in the previous sentence, but that's not the case, because the straightforward nature of the goals doesn't follow as a consequence of the information in the previous sentence.

C   **Pattern:** Largely irrelevant. **Incorrect:** This choice would be appropriate if this sentence told us something that's true in spite of what was mentioned in the previous sentence, but that's not the case; as we explained in (A) and (B), there's no real connection or contrast of any kind between this sentence and the one before it.

D ✓   **Pattern:** Correct. No transition word is appropriate before the colon here, because there's no real relationship between the ideas in this sentence and those in the previous one, as we've seen in our discussions of the other choices.

> **Note**   This might look like a question about style or grammar at first glance, but in reality we're just picking which transition word, if any, should appear between the word "straightforward" and the colon.

- **Vertical Scan Results:** Some choices have different forms of the same base word.
- **Vertical Scan Notes:** We need to decide whether "they" should be part of the phrase, whether some form of "await" or "wait" is appropriate, and which form of the appropriate verb is acceptable.
- **Key Features in Surrounding Text:** The phrase immediately after the underlined phrase is "for service," so the correct answer choice must be one that can be followed by "for service."

Concepts in the question:

- **Phrase Proximity:** Answer choice(s) would place descriptive phrases next to ideas they don't describe. Descriptive phrases that don't begin with a word ending in "-ing" describe the closest noun phrase. (See page 451.)
- **Prepositional Idioms:** Choices typically include prepositional phrases with no other recognizable grammatical similarities. On this type of question, if you can't determine which answer choice contains an acceptable prepositional idiom in American English, then you should guess at an answer and invest your time in questions that don't involve prepositional idioms. (See page 443.)
- **Verb Tense/Conjugation:** Choices include different forms of the same verb. Look at the surrounding text to find each verb's subject. Also, look for other verbs that could indicate the proper tense for the verbs in the answer choices. (See page 437.)

ANSWER CHOICE ANALYSIS

A   **Incorrect:** The verb "to await" takes a direct object, which means it can't be followed by the preposition "for." For example, we could say "I await an answer," not "*I await *for* an answer." This choice can't be correct because the next word after the underlined phrase is "for."

B   **Incorrect:** This choice has the same problem as (A), and is wrong for the same reason.

C   **Incorrect:** This choice is incorrect because the sentence says patrons "can enjoy coffee and snacks and mingle with their neighbors" "while" the action in the underlined phrase takes place—but this choice uses a past-tense verb, which can't happen at the same time as the present-tense verbs in the rest of the sentence.

D ✓   **Correct:** This choice doesn't have the problems described in the explanations for the other answer choices. "Waiting for service" is an acceptable prepositional idiom in American English, and the form of the verb "wait" fits with the other verbs in the sentence that happen while the waiting is going on, such as "can enjoy."

Answer choice patterns (see page 455): Wrong answers incorporate elements of the right answer.

> **Note**   This question involves a prepositional idiom like the ones we discussed in the training for the Writing and Language section. There's no general rule for the words "wait," "await," or "for" that we can take from this question and apply to a future question using those words in a different way, so there's no point focusing too much on this question if you missed it. Instead, let the idiom in this question remind you of why it's so important to make sure you answer all the non-idiom questions correctly. See the training on prepositional idioms on page 443 for more on this.

- **RC Question sub-type:** Sentence or paragraph placement. (The prompt asks us where a sentence should go in a paragraph, or where a paragraph should go in the passage. The correct order will reflect a logical chronology, and/or will allow for pronouns in the sentences to refer to nouns in a logical way, and/or will place related concepts near one another. See page 432.)
- **Subjective phrases to be ignored:** "most"

ANSWER CHOICE ANALYSIS

A	**Pattern:** Causes text to introduce an idea that has already been discussed. **Incorrect:** In its current position, sentence 5 refers back to "the inaugural Repair Cafe" that was mentioned in sentences 1 and 2. It also tells us that other repair cafes have been held, which seems to be referred to in sentence 4, which has present-tense verbs that indicate repair cafes are still going on. For these reasons, the College Board will want us to move sentence 5 earlier in the paragraph so it's near the concepts it's referring to. The current location of sentence 5 also interrupts the description of the participants expressed in sentences 4 and 6, and doesn't solve the verb tense problem described in the explanation for choice (C).
B	**Pattern:** Causes text to refer to an idea that hasn't been mentioned yet. **Incorrect:** Sentence 5 can't go at the beginning of the paragraph because it says what has happened "since the inaugural Repair Café," and this placement would be before sentence 1 even tells us what a "Repair Café" is.
C ✓	**Pattern:** Correct. Sentences 1, 2, and 3 all describe "the first Repair Café" in the past tense. Then sentence 4 uses the present tense to describe how "participants bring all manner of damaged articles." This means we need something to go between sentence 3 and sentence 4 to account for the shift in tense. Moving sentence 5 after sentence 3 makes sense because sentence 5 describes how other events have been happening since the first Repair Cafe.
D	**Pattern:** Causes text to introduce an idea that has already been discussed. **Incorrect:** In this placement, sentence 5 has essentially the same problems we talked about for (A).

- **RC Question sub-type:** Including/excluding a phrase/sentence. (The question asks whether a sentence should be included in the passage. The correct choice will include a comment that plainly describes the role of the phrase or sentence in the passage. Sentences that should be included will follow broad College Board standards for ideal sentences and paragraphs—including consistency with any figures in the passage—while sentences that shouldn't be included will not follow those standards. See page 433.)

ANSWER CHOICE ANALYSIS

A	**Pattern:** Largely irrelevant. **Incorrect:** The sentence in the prompt doesn't provide examples of repair skills being lost, or examples of any skills at all, as this choice would require. The prompt sentence just says that as some jobs become more plentiful, other jobs are less needed; no mention is made of "specific repair skills."
B	**Pattern:** Confused concepts. **Incorrect:** The sentence in the prompt doesn't say anything about the statistic related to "the Netherlands' municipal waste," as this choice would require.
C ✓	**Pattern:** Correct. This choice accurately and plainly describes the relationship between the passage and the sentence in the prompt: the idea of "corporate and service-based jobs" increasing and "the need for people who work with their hands" diminishing isn't "further explained." Only (C) accurately describes the sentence in question, so it's correct.
D	**Pattern:** Largely irrelevant. **Incorrect:** The prompt sentence doesn't contradict any claims made in the rest of the paragraph, as this choice would require; what's discussed in this sentence doesn't even relate to rest of the paragraph.

- **Vertical Scan Results:** Some choices are short phrases with no obvious similarity; deleting a phrase is an option.
- **Vertical Scan Notes:** (A), (B), and (C) all seem to mean basically the same thing, which suggests they're all wrong.
- **Key Features in Surrounding Text:** The phrase immediately before the underlined phrase is "and other countries." The word "other" already expresses the idea of countries beyond those listed in this sentence.

Concepts in the question:

- **Redundancy:** Answer choices and/or surrounding text could combine to repeat the same concept unnecessarily. We should avoid words or phrases that directly repeat ideas in the immediate context. (See page 452.)

ANSWER CHOICE ANALYSIS

A	**Incorrect:** The phrase "on top of that" is redundant, because "other" already expresses the idea of countries beyond those listed in this sentence.
B	**Incorrect:** The phrase "in addition" is redundant, because "other" already expresses the idea of countries beyond those listed in this sentence.
C	**Incorrect:** The word "likewise" is redundant, because "other" already expresses the idea of countries beyond those listed.

D ✓   Correct: This is the shortest choice and it's grammatically acceptable, so it's right, according to the SAT's rules for Writing and Language questions that deal primarily with style and grammar. Further, all the other answer choices add a redundant phrase, which the College Board doesn't reward.

TEST 3

- **Vertical Scan Results:** Some choices have different forms of the same base word, similar phrases with different short words.
- **Vertical Scan Notes:** We need to decide whether "healthy" or "healthier" is acceptable, and whether "and more," "and they are," or "being more" is acceptable.
- **Key Features in Surrounding Text:** The underlined phrase appears in a list of phrases describing "employees." The first word in the list is the comparative form "happier," so the other adjectives in the list should be comparatives as well.

Concepts in the question:

- **Dangling Participle:** The question involves descriptive phrases beginning with an "-ing" word that would describe the wrong word in context. Descriptive phrases starting with a word ending in "-ing" describe the first noun phrase in that sentence's independent clause. (See page 450.)
- **Parallelism:** Choices include options that would ignore a parallel structure in the surrounding text. The correct answer choice should match phrasing in the surrounding text when possible. (See page 458.)

ANSWER CHOICE ANALYSIS

A ✓   Correct: This option makes the second and third adjectives in the list describing "employees" into their comparative forms, so their structure parallels the word "happier" earlier in the sentence. This satisfies the College Board's preference for answer choices that parallel the structure of the surrounding text when possible.

B   Incorrect: This choice is grammatically acceptable in real life, but it doesn't use the comparative form of "healthy," so it can't be correct on the SAT because it fails to parallel the structure of the word "happier" earlier in the sentence.

C   Incorrect: This choice has at least two issues. One issue is that it doesn't make the adjective "productive" parallel the comparative structures in the words "happier" and "healthier," as we discussed with (A). Another issue is that the insertion of "and they are" causes the structure of the sentence to change so that everything beginning with "and they are...controlled" is a dependent clause, with "studies have shown...healthier" left as the independent clause. This causes the independent clause to end in a list of two things without the word "and" between them, which is something the College Board doesn't allow us to do, as we discussed in the training for the Writing and Language section. Either of these issues by itself would be enough to make this choice wrong.

D   Incorrect: This choice turn the lists of three words describing "employees" into a list of two things, which would require the word "and" to appear between "happier" and "healthier," instead of the comma that appears there, as we mentioned in our discussion of (C). Further, according to the SAT's rules for participial phrases, it would cause the phrase "being more...controlled" to modify the noun "studies" instead of the noun "employees." Either issue would make (D) wrong.

Answer choice patterns (see page 455): Wrong answers incorporate elements of the right answer.

     Note   Notice that "happier" isn't underlined, so we can't change it, which means the other adjectives in the list must be changed to parallel the comparative form "happier."

- **RC Question sub-type:** Best Accomplishes X. (The prompt describes a goal of the author, and asks us which choice achieves that goal. The correct answer choice will plainly and directly demonstrate the task described in the prompt. See page 431.)
- **Subjective phrases to be ignored:** "most"

ANSWER CHOICE ANALYSIS

A   Pattern: Largely irrelevant. Incorrect: This choice talks about "temperature" in the "environment" of "employees," but the rest of the passage talks about natural light instead of artificial light in the workplace. This paragraph mentions "artificial lighting" and "increas[ing] the amount of natural light," the next paragraph talks about "lack of exposure to natural light," and so on. Since this phrase introduces an idea that doesn't get discussed again in the passage, it can't be an appropriate introduction to the passage, which means it's wrong.

B ✓   Pattern: Correct. As we saw in the explanation for choice (A), the passage discusses the impact of natural light in the workplace. This is the only choice that includes the idea of natural light—or even mentions light at all—so it's correct.

C   Pattern: Largely irrelevant. Incorrect: As we saw in the explanation for (A), the passage discusses natural light, so this choice that mentions "energy loss" isn't relevant to the passage, and can't be an "appropriate introduction" to the passage.

D   **Pattern:** Largely irrelevant. **Incorrect:** As we saw in for (A), the passage doesn't restate anything about employees asking for accommodations, so this choice can't be an "appropriate introduction" to the passage, which makes it incorrect.

Test 3, Question 3   TYPE: READING COMPREHENSION (usually has a prompt; choices have different meanings)

- **RC Question sub-type:** Including/excluding a phrase/sentence. (The question asks whether a sentence should be included in the passage. The correct choice will include a comment that plainly describes the role of the phrase or sentence in the passage. Sentences that should be included will follow broad College Board standards for ideal sentences and paragraphs—including consistency with any figures in the passage—while sentences that shouldn't be included will not follow those standards. See page 433.)

ANSWER CHOICE ANALYSIS

A   **Pattern:** Largely irrelevant. **Incorrect:** The "quantitative data" from the prompt sentence isn't "examined in the rest of the paragraph," as this choice would require—the idea of one group of workers sleeping 46 minutes more per night than another group of workers is never mentioned again. This choice incorrectly describes the prompt sentence, so it's wrong.

B   **Pattern:** Confused concepts. **Incorrect:** The sentence from the prompt doesn't "explain" anything about multiple "bodily functions" from the next sentence, as this choice would require; instead, it just provides a statistic about a single function: sleep. Like (A), this choice incorrectly describes the prompt sentence, so it's wrong.

C ✓   **Pattern:** Correct. The previous sentence ends by introducing the term "Circadian rhythms," and the following sentence immediately explains that term; in other words, the prompt sentence "interrupts the discussion of circadian rhythms," just as this choice requires—so this choice is correct.

D   **Pattern:** Largely irrelevant. **Incorrect:** As we saw for (C), the sentence should not be added to the paragraph. But the issue isn't sunlight exposure outside the office—even if the sentence accounted for that idea, the problem mentioned in our discussion of (C) wouldn't be solved. (D) accurately describes the sentence in question, but that sentence still doesn't follow the broader rules of ideal sentences and paragraphs on this section of the SAT, as we saw for (C), so (D) is wrong.

Test 3, Question 4   TYPE: GRAMMAR/STYLE/PUNCTUATION (often no prompt; choices have similar meanings)

- **Vertical Scan Results:** Some choices have the same words with different punctuation.
- **Vertical Scan Notes:** We need to decide whether "bodies," "bodies'," or "body's" is acceptable, and also whether "clocks," "clocks'," or "clock's" is acceptable.
- **Key Features in Surrounding Text:** The context makes it clear that the "biological clock" belongs to the body, so we need a possessive form of "body." Also, nothing in the text belongs to the "clock[s]," so we shouldn't have a possessive form of "clock[s]."

Concepts in the question:

- **Plural/Possessive/Contraction:** Choices include the same noun ending in "-s" with or without an apostrophe before or after the "-s." Remember the three rules for forming possessives. Think of contractions in their uncontracted forms ("you're" = "you are"). (See page 441.)
- **Singular versus Plural:** Choices include singular and plural versions of the same base words that don't agree with other words in the surrounding text. Singular nouns must go with singular verb forms and singular pronouns. Plural nouns must go with plural verbs and pronouns. Think carefully about which words should match or agree with each other! (See page 443.)

ANSWER CHOICE ANALYSIS

A   **Incorrect:** The "biological clocks" in this choice belong to the "body," so we need a possessive form of the word "body," instead of the plural form ("bodies") that appears in this choice.

B   **Incorrect:** Nothing in the text is possessed by the "clock[s]," so the possessive form "clocks'," with an apostrophe, is inappropriate here.

C ✓   **Correct:** This choice includes the possessive form of the word "body" ("body's") and the non-possessive plural form "clocks," so it's the only grammatically acceptable option.

D   **Incorrect:** Nothing in context belongs to a clock, so we shouldn't have the possessive form "clock's" that appears in this choice. Also, it wouldn't make sense if the phrase said "which are controlled by the body's biological clock is," so "clock's" as a contracted form of "clock is" wouldn't make sense here either.

Answer choice patterns (see page 455): Wrong answers incorporate elements of the right answer.

Note   Some test-takers might spend time trying to figure out if the proper form of the word "clock" should be singular or plural, rather than trying to figure out if it should be possessive. If we focus on whether it should be singular or plural without considering the answer choices first, we'll never reach a conclusion, since the sentence could make sense with either a singular or plural form of "clock," if we were going to re-write the sentence ourselves from scratch. But when we consider the choices, we see that some of them use a possessive form of "clock," which can't be appropriate here; of the choices that don't use a possessive form of "clock," only one is paired with a possessive form of "body," so that choice must be correct, and we never need to decide on our own whether "clock" should be singular or plural. Keep this in mind on test day, across the whole SAT: we can save a lot of time and frustration by focusing on the options the test is presenting us with, instead of just trying to imagine a perfect answer beforehand.

Test 3, Question 5 — TYPE: GRAMMAR/STYLE/PUNCTUATION (often no prompt; choices have similar meanings)

- **Vertical Scan Results:** Some choices have different forms of the same base word.
- **Vertical Scan Notes:** We need to choose the appropriate form of the verb "to be" from "is," "are," "is being," and "have been."
- **Key Features in Surrounding Text:** The underlined phrase needs to agree with the pronoun "which," which refers to the single noun "employee absenteeism."

Concepts in the question:

- **Verb Tense/Conjugation:** Choices include different forms of the same verb. Look at the surrounding text to find each verb's subject. Also, look for other verbs that could indicate the proper tense for the verbs in the answer choices. (See page 437.)

ANSWER CHOICE ANALYSIS

A ✓   **Correct:** The singular verb form "is" agrees with the singular noun "employee absenteeism." Also, this is the shortest choice and it's grammatically acceptable, so it's right.

B   **Incorrect:** The verb form needs to be singular so it can agree with the singular noun "employee absenteeism," so this choice can't be correct.

C   **Incorrect:** This choice is arguably grammatically acceptable in real life, but, as trained test-takers, we know that the College Board prefers the shortest grammatically acceptable choice on questions that test style and grammar, like this one. Choice (A) is both shorter and grammatically correct, so (C) can't be right.

D   **Incorrect:** The verb form needs to be singular to agree with the singular noun "employee absenteeism," so this choice can't be correct, much as we saw with (B).

Answer choice patterns (see page 455): Wrong answers incorporate elements of the right answer.

Test 3, Question 6 — TYPE: READING COMPREHENSION (usually has a prompt; choices have different meanings)

- **RC Question sub-type:** Best Accomplishes X. (The prompt describes a goal of the author, and asks us which choice achieves that goal. The correct answer choice will plainly and directly demonstrate the task described in the prompt. See page 431.)
- **Subjective phrases to be ignored:** "best"

ANSWER CHOICE ANALYSIS

A   **Pattern:** Plausible, but not in the text. **Incorrect:** The prompt refers to the "statement made in the previous sentence," which is that "employees who feel less than 100 percent…are also less prone to work at their maximal productivity." That statement is about employee *productivity*, but this choice talks about "employees' *morale*" (emphasis added), so it's not correct. Some test-takers may assume that morale and productivity would tend to improve at the same time, but the text doesn't say that, and we know we can't assume it, as trained test-takers.

B ✓   **Pattern:** Correct. As we saw in the explanation for choice (A), the statement in the previous sentence is related to employee productivity, and this choice that gives an example of "increase[d]...productivity" is the only one that "supports the statement made in the previous sentence." So this choice is correct.

C   **Pattern:** Largely irrelevant. **Incorrect:** As we saw for (A), the statement in the previous sentence is related to employee productivity, so this choice discussing "operational costs" doesn't support that statement, and must be wrong.

D   **Pattern:** Largely irrelevant. **Incorrect:** As we saw in the explanation for choice (A), the statement in the previous sentence is related to employee productivity, so this choice that discusses investments of "time and capital" is incorrect because it doesn't support that statement.

Test 3, Question 7 — TYPE: GRAMMAR/STYLE/PUNCTUATION (often no prompt; choices have similar meanings)

- **Vertical Scan Results:** Choices are long phrases/sentences.
- **Vertical Scan Notes:** The answer choices are fairly long and will need to be analyzed a bit more closely to determine what's going on in this question. A few differences that might jump out include the different forms of "constitute" in each choice, and the use of "aside from" in (A) and (B) but not in (C) and (D).
- **Key Features in Surrounding Text:** These two sentences combined will be the first sentence of this paragraph. The end of the previous paragraph described how worker productivity increased with the introduction of natural light. The rest of the current paragraph talks about how a building in Seattle saved a lot of money by using more natural light. So the sentence in this question needs to transition from the idea of artificial light increasing productivity to the idea of artificial light costing less money, according to the SAT's unwritten rules.

Concepts in the question:

- **Commas:** Choices include one or more commas. On the Writing and Language section, commas can be used to separate things in a list of three or more, to form a comma sandwich, or to introduce an independent clause after a dependent clause. (See pages 448-450.)
- **Dangling Participle:** The question involves descriptive phrases beginning with an "-ing" word that would describe the wrong word in context. Descriptive phrases starting with a word ending in "-ing" describe the first noun phrase in that sentence's independent clause. (See page 450.)
- **Dependent and Independent Clauses:** Answer choice(s) would incorrectly use a dependent or independent clause. An independent clause can stand alone as a sentence: it has a main subject/verb pair. A dependent clause is introduced by a conjunction or relative pronoun. (See page 445.)
- **Joining Two Sentences:** Each choice is a sentence that combines the two sentences in the underlined portion of the text. The right answer must follow all rules for other question types without changing the meaning of the original two sentences. (See page 453.)
- **Phrase Proximity:** Answer choice(s) would place descriptive phrases next to ideas they don't describe. Descriptive phrases that don't begin with a word ending in "-ing" describe the closest noun phrase. (See page 451.)

ANSWER CHOICE ANALYSIS

A ✓   **Correct:** As we discussed above, in order to follow the SAT's unwritten rules, the sentence should start out by talking about worker productivity (the idea discussed in the previous paragraph) and then transition into talking about energy consumption and the cost of artificial light (the idea discussed in this paragraph). The phrase "aside from" at the beginning of the sentence indicates clearly that the idea of lowered productivity has already been mentioned, and the word "also" then indicates that the sentence is moving on to a new idea. This is the only choice that meets those requirements, so it's the only acceptable option.

B   **Incorrect:** This version isn't acceptable on the SAT because, in a purely grammatical sense, the phrase "aside from lowering worker productivity" actually applies to the *cost* of the lights. In other words, this choice makes it sound like the cost itself is what lowers productivity, instead of the lights being the things that lower productivity. This differs from the meaning of the original text, so it's wrong on the SAT.

C   **Incorrect:** This choice would arguably be the most concise expression of the ideas from the text if we didn't have to consider the sentence in the context of the whole paragraph. But, as trained test-takers, we know that the answer to a "join 2 sentences" question must satisfy the College Board's requirements for both grammar/style/punctuation *and* sentence/paragraph structure; the problem with this choice is that it mentions "lower[ing] worker productivity" in the middle of the sentence, instead of using that phrase at the beginning of the sentence as a transition from the previous paragraph, like (A) does. Remember that the College Board expects us to group related ideas as near each other as possible on these kinds of questions.

D   **Incorrect:** As we noted in explaining (A) and (C), the College Board will want the correct answer to be a transition from the idea of lowered productivity to the idea of energy costs. This choice does mention both of those concepts, but it lacks a transitional phrase to show that the lowered productivity was mentioned in the previous paragraph, so the College Board will prefer (A), which includes the phrase "aside from."

Answer choice patterns (see page 455): Wrong answers incorporate elements of the right answer.

Note   This question is a great example of the importance of reading carefully and keeping the College Board's unwritten rules in mind—in other words, a great example of the importance of proper training. Many untrained test-takers would be confused by any or all of the wrong answers to this question, especially (C) and (D), because those sentences would probably be acceptable in most classroom settings.

Test 3, Question 8 — TYPE: GRAMMAR/STYLE/PUNCTUATION (often no prompt; choices have similar meanings)

- **Vertical Scan Results:** Similar phrases with different short words and/or punctuation; deleting a phrase is an option.
- **Vertical Scan Notes:** The question seems to ask us to choose the best way to say "yearly," but we also have the option of deleting the underlined phrase.
- **Key Features in Surrounding Text:** When we check the surrounding text, we see that "annual" describes "electricity cost reductions." Since the text already contains the idea of "annual," we don't need the phrases from (A), (B), or (C).

Concepts in the question:

- **Redundancy:** Answer choices and/or surrounding text could combine to repeat the same concept unnecessarily. We should avoid words or phrases that directly repeat ideas in the immediate context. (See page 452.)

ANSWER CHOICE ANALYSIS

A   **Incorrect:** As we discussed above, the text already says "annual," so the phrase in this option is redundant.
B   **Incorrect:** This choice has the same problem as (A).
C   **Incorrect:** This choice has the same problem as (A).

D ✓ **Correct:** As we discussed above, the text already says "annual," so the underlined phrase is redundant and should be deleted according to the SAT.

Note Notice that at first this question seems to ask us to choose the best way to express the idea of "yearly." That might seem challenging at first, because most of the choices are pretty similar. But when we notice that we have the option to delete the underlined phrase, and we remember to read the context, we can see that "annual" already appears in the text, and the underlined phrase is redundant.

Test 3, Question 9 — TYPE: READING COMPREHENSION (usually has a prompt; choices have different meanings)

- **RC Question sub-type:** Transition phrase. (The choices include words or phrases showing a transition from the previous sentence, like "however," "instead of," "for example," etc. The transition phrase must reflect the relationship between the previous sentence and the sentence where the transition phrase appears. See page 431.)

ANSWER CHOICE ANALYSIS

A **Pattern:** Confused concepts. **Incorrect:** This choice would be appropriate if this sentence expressed a conclusion based on the information in the previous sentence, but that's not the case here: the previous sentence mentions installing windows, but this choice refers to light tubes.

B **Pattern:** Confused concepts. **Incorrect:** This choice would be appropriate if this sentence told us something was true in spite of what was mentioned in the previous sentence, but that's not the case: nothing about installing windows would make it seem like installing light tubes was impossible.

C ✓ **Pattern:** Correct. This sentence introduces another option—or alternative—apart from what's mentioned in the previous sentence. The previous sentence mentions installing windows, and this sentence mentions installing light tubes instead. The paragraph tells us that these are two options for reconfiguring a building's lighting, so the word "alternatively" accurately restates the relationship between the two ideas in the two sentences.

D **Pattern:** Confused concepts. **Incorrect:** This choice would be appropriate if this sentence expressed an idea that was the last idea in a series of ideas, but that's not the case—the next sentence expresses another way to reconfigure a building's lighting.

Test 3, Question 10 — TYPE: GRAMMAR/STYLE/PUNCTUATION (often no prompt; choices have similar meanings)

- **Vertical Scan Results:** Similar phrases with different short words.
- **Vertical Scan Notes:** We need to decide whether "these," "they," "which," or "those" is acceptable, and also whether "are" or "being" is acceptable.
- **Key Features in Surrounding Text:** The underlined phrase needs to refer to "light tubes," since those are the "pipes...to capture...sunlight."

Concepts in the question:

- **Comma Splice:** Answer choices and/or surrounding text could be combined in ways that would use commas to separate two groups of words that could each be sentences on their own. A comma can't be used to join two groups of words that could each be sentences on their own. (See page 447.)

- **Dependent and Independent Clauses:** Answer choice(s) would incorrectly use a dependent or independent clause. An independent clause can stand alone as a sentence: it has a main subject/verb pair. A dependent clause is introduced by a conjunction or relative pronoun. (See page 445.)

- **Pronoun Ambiguity:** Choices include pronouns that could refer to more than one phrase in the surrounding text. We can't use a pronoun on the SAT when it isn't clear what that pronoun refers to. (See page 441.)

- **Verb Tense/Conjugation:** Choices include different forms of the same verb. Look at the surrounding text to find each verb's subject. Also, look for other verbs that could indicate the proper tense for the verbs in the answer choices. (See page 437.)

ANSWER CHOICE ANALYSIS

A **Incorrect:** This choice has two issues according to the SAT's rules. One issue is that the word "these" could grammatically refer to either of the plural nouns earlier in the sentence: "businesses" or "tubes." The other issue is that there's a comma after the word "tubes," but (A) would create an independent clause after that comma, so the comma would be joining two independent clauses, which isn't allowed on the SAT. Either issue would be enough by itself to make (A) wrong.

B **Incorrect:** This choice has the same two problems that we saw in (A).

C ✓ **Correct:** This phrase begins a dependent clause that explains what "light tubes" are, so it needs to begin with the relative pronoun "which," and it needs to be placed immediately after the phrase "light tubes."

D **Incorrect:** Like (A) and (B), this choice uses a plural pronoun ("those") that could grammatically be referring to either "businesses" or "tubes."

Answer choice patterns (see page 455): Wrong answers incorporate elements of the right answer.

- **Vertical Scan Results:** Some choices are short phrases with no obvious similarity; deleting a phrase is an option.
- **Vertical Scan Notes:** We need to decide whether the underlined phrase should be "through," "of," or "from," or whether it should be removed altogether.
- **Key Features in Surrounding Text:** The underlined phrase needs to connect "means" and the idea of "distributing natural light more freely."

Concepts in the question:

- **Prepositional Idioms:** Choices typically include prepositional phrases with no other recognizable grammatical similarities. On this type of question, if you can't determine which answer choice contains an acceptable prepositional idiom in American English, then you should guess at an answer and invest your time in questions that don't involve prepositional idioms. (See page 443.)

ANSWER CHOICE ANALYSIS

A   Incorrect: The phrase "means through distributing" isn't an acceptable prepositional idiom in American English. (See the explanation for (B) and the note for more!)

B ✓   Correct: The phrase "means of [X-ing]" is a common prepositional idiom in American English, where "[X-ing]" indicates an "-ing" form of a verb. So "means of distributing" is the only acceptable choice here.

C   Incorrect: As we saw in the discussion of (B), the acceptable phrase in context is "means of," not "means from." (See note!)

D   Incorrect: As we saw in the discussion of (B), the acceptable phrase in context is "means of," not just "means." (See note!)

      Note   As we noted in the Writing and Language training, the College Board occasionally tests your knowledge of idioms, which are phrases that you just have to know in order to answer a few questions correctly, because truly idiomatic phrases don't follow any general rule. In other words, there's nothing you can learn from this question about the words "means," "of," or "distributing" that would help you answer a future question about the proper use of any of those words, beyond just knowing that "means of distributing" is acceptable in American English. When the SAT tests an idiom, your best move is to mark the answer that sounds correct to your ear as quickly as you can, and then invest your time in non-idiom questions, since they follow generalized rules you've learned in your training. See the training on prepositional idioms on page 443 for more on this.

- **Vertical Scan Results:** Some choices have different forms of the same base word.
- **Vertical Scan Notes:** Should the underlined phrase be singular or plural, should it be one word or two, and should it express grammatical gender?
- **Key Features in Surrounding Text:** If we ignore the intervening phrase "traversing the American West by train in the mid-1800s," we see that the context before the underlined phrase reads "settlers often found [blank] in need of refreshment." So the word in the underlined phrase refers to "settlers," and should agree with that word in number.

Concepts in the question:

- **Pronoun Ambiguity:** Choices include pronouns that could refer to more than one phrase in the surrounding text. We can't use a pronoun on the SAT when it isn't clear what that pronoun refers to. (See page 441.)
- **Singular versus Plural:** Choices include singular and plural versions of the same base words that don't agree with other words in the surrounding text. Singular nouns must go with singular verb forms and singular pronouns. Plural nouns must go with plural verbs and pronouns. Think carefully about which words should match or agree with each other! (See page 443.)

ANSWER CHOICE ANALYSIS

A ✓   Correct: As we discussed above, the underlined phrase should agree with the plural noun "settlers." This choice is the correctly formed plural pronoun "themselves," so it's correct.

B   Incorrect: As we discussed above, the underlined phrase should agree with the plural noun "settlers," so these singular forms are wrong. Multiple "settlers" can't have a single "self," regardless of grammatical gender.

C   Incorrect: As we discussed above, the underlined phrase should agree with the plural noun "settlers." This option seems to be plural, but it's not the correct form of the plural pronoun "themselves," so this choice can't be right. (Even if we accidentally thought this choice was grammatically acceptable, we should still recognize that choice (A) is shorter and also grammatically acceptable, which means the College Board will credit (A) as the correct answer.)

D   Incorrect: This choice has the same problem as (B)—multiple "settlers" can't have a single "self."

Answer choice patterns (see page 455): Wrong answers incorporate elements of the right answer.

- **RC Question sub-type:** Best Accomplishes X. (The prompt describes a goal of the author, and asks us which choice achieves that goal. The correct answer choice will plainly and directly demonstrate the task described in the prompt. See page 431.)
- **Subjective phrases to be ignored:** "most"

ANSWER CHOICE ANALYSIS

A   **Pattern:** Direct contradiction. **Incorrect:** The word "despite" would indicate that Harvey's experience working for rail companies makes it less likely or expected that he'd open a restaurant for rail customers—but, if anything, that experience would make it *more* reasonable and expected for Harvey to open a business serving rail customers. So this choice is wrong.

B   **Pattern:** Largely irrelevant. **Incorrect:** The text doesn't give us any reason to think that living in New York and New Orleans has anything to do with restaurants or railroads, so this choice is incorrect.

C✓   **Pattern:** Correct. The previous sentences mention that people on trains needed "refreshment," and that "food available on rail lines was...terrible." The following sentence mentions that Fred Harvey "decided to open his own restaurant business to serve rail customers." If people want food and no good food is available, then it makes sentence to say that Fred Harvey would open a restaurant "to capitalize on the demand for good food." Notice that the phrase "demand for good food" restates the idea of a "need of refreshment" in spite of the "terrible quality" of food mentioned earlier in the paragraph.

D   **Pattern:** Confused concepts. **Incorrect:** If we delete the underlined portion, that means this choice provides no introduction at all to the sentence, so it can't be "the most logical introduction to the sentence," as the prompt requires.

- **Vertical Scan Results:** Similar phrases with different short words and/or punctuation.
- **Vertical Scan Notes:** Should there be a period, colon, comma, or semi-colon after "entrepreneur," and should "he" be included afterward?
- **Key Features in Surrounding Text:** As it's currently written, the first "sentence" that this underlined phrase overlaps is basically the fragment "Fred Harvey, an English-born entrepreneur." (Regardless of what happens with question 13, that "sentence" is still a fragment.) That fragment can't be an independent clause, so we know we'll need to join it somehow with the following sentence.

Concepts in the question:

- **Colons:** Choices include one or more colons. A colon can be placed after a set of words that could be a sentence on their own, and before a demonstration or example of the idea before the colon. (See page 447.)
- **Comma Sandwich:** Choice(s) would create phrases improperly "sandwiched" between similar types of punctuation. When removed from the sentence, a properly formed sandwich leaves behind a grammatically acceptable sentence. (See page 448.)
- **Commas:** Choices include one or more commas. On the Writing and Language section, commas can be used to separate things in a list of three or more, to form a comma sandwich, or to introduce an independent clause after a dependent clause. (See pages 448-450.)
- **Dependent and Independent Clauses:** Answer choice(s) would incorrectly use a dependent or independent clause. An independent clause can stand alone as a sentence: it has a main subject/verb pair. A dependent clause is introduced by a conjunction or relative pronoun. (See page 445.)
- **Intervening Phrase:** A phrase appears between two words that need to agree with each other. Identify which words need to agree with each other, and ignore extra phrases that appear between them. (See page 456.)
- **Semi-colons:** Choices include one or more semicolons. Semi-colons can be used to separate two sets of words that could each stand on their own as a full sentence. (See page 447.)

ANSWER CHOICE ANALYSIS

A   **Incorrect:** As we discussed above, there can't be a period after "entrepreneur" because that would basically result in the fragment "Fred Harvey, an English-born entrepreneur." (This issue would exist no matter which choice we make for question 13, because all of the choices for 13 would result in (A) creating a fragment for this question.)

B   **Incorrect:** There can't be a colon after "entrepreneur," because what appears before a colon must be able to stand alone as a complete sentence on the SAT. As we discussed for (A), there's no choice we can make for 13 that would cause the words leading up to "entrepreneur" in this sentence to be an independent clause.

C   **Incorrect:** There can't be a semi-colon after "entrepreneur," because what appears before a semi-colon must be able to stand alone as a complete sentence on the SAT. As we discussed above, no choice for question 13 would make it acceptable for a semicolon to appear after "entrepreneur."

D✓   **Correct:** This option creates a "comma sandwich" around the phrase "an English-born entrepreneur." We know this is grammatically acceptable because we can remove the phrase "an English-born entrepreneur" from the resulting sentence without creating any grammatical problems. The remaining sentence without that comma sandwich would basically read "...Fred Harvey decided to open his own restaurant business to serve rail customers." Any choice we make for question 13 would preserve this basic structure.

- **Vertical Scan Results:** Choices include most or all possible combinations of two options.
- **Vertical Scan Notes:** Is "was" or "were" acceptable? Is "its" or "their" acceptable?
- **Key Features in Surrounding Text:** When we ignore the intervening phrase "which constituted the first restaurant chain in the United States," we see that the "unique" thing with "high standards" is "these Harvey Houses." So the form of "to be" and the possessive pronoun in the underlined phrase should both agree in number with "Harvey Houses."

Concepts in the question:

- **Intervening Phrase:** A phrase appears between two words that need to agree with each other. Identify which words need to agree with each other, and ignore extra phrases that appear between them. (See page 456.)
- **Pronoun Ambiguity:** Choices include pronouns that could refer to more than one phrase in the surrounding text. We can't use a pronoun on the SAT when it isn't clear what that pronoun refers to. (See page 441.)
- **Singular versus Plural:** Choices include singular and plural versions of the same base words that don't agree with other words in the surrounding text. Singular nouns must go with singular verb forms and singular pronouns. Plural nouns must go with plural verbs and pronouns. Think carefully about which words should match or agree with each other! (See page 443.)

ANSWER CHOICE ANALYSIS

A	Incorrect: As we discussed above, both the form of "to be" and the possessive pronoun should agree in number with "Harvey Houses," so both "was" and "its" should be in the plural form.
B ✓	Correct: This choice is the only one that uses the two plural forms "were" and "their," as required to match the plural phrase "Harvey Houses."
C	Incorrect: This choice uses the singular form "was," which is inappropriate for reasons we noted in (A).
D	Incorrect: This choice uses "its," which is wrong for the reasons noted in (A).

- **RC Question sub-type:** Best Accomplishes X, Vocabulary-In-Context. (The prompt describes a goal of the author, and asks us which choice achieves that goal. The correct answer choice will plainly and directly demonstrate the task described in the prompt. Choices include words or short phrases that have vaguely similar but not identical meanings. Most or all of the choices will seem vaguely appropriate, but only one choice will be correct when we think very carefully and specifically about the word means and how it can be used. See page 432 for more.)
- **Subjective phrases to be ignored:** "best"

ANSWER CHOICE ANALYSIS

A	Pattern: Same ballpark. Incorrect: The underlined phrase describes the food that customers get when they travel by train, because "fare" is a synonym for "food" in this context (we may be able to realize this from the context of the sentence if we didn't already know it). Earlier in the text, that food was described as "generally of terrible quality," so we need a word that means "generally of terrible quality." But "sinister" means something like "evil" or "foreboding," which doesn't restate anything from the text. This choice *does* express a broadly negative idea, but it doesn't mean the same thing as "generally of terrible quality," so it's wrong.
B	Pattern: Same ballpark. Incorrect: As we saw in the explanation for (A), we need a word that means "generally of terrible quality." The word "surly" means something like "unpleasant" or "moody," and can only be applied to a person's attitude or behavior, so it can't be appropriate here.
C ✓	Pattern: Correct. As we saw in the explanation for choice (A), we need a word that means "generally of terrible quality." "Abysmal" can mean that, so (C) is right.
D	Pattern: Same ballpark. Incorrect: As we saw in the explanation for choice (A), we need a word that means "generally of terrible quality." "Icky" means something like "disgusting." This choice expresses a broadly negative idea, but being "icky" isn't really the same thing as being of terrible quality. For example, if you don't like bleu cheese, you could think that very high quality bleu cheese is disgusting or icky, because you just don't like it—in other words, something of great quality can still be disgusting to someone, depending on the situation.
Note	Several aspects of this question should interest us, as trained test-takers. For one thing, we should note that the correct answer is really the only choice that makes sense in the context of the passage if we read each word carefully—in other words, we didn't have to think about the "tone" of the passage to find the answer, even though the prompt told us we would need to. This is one more example of how the College Board often tries to mislead untrained test-takers by phrasing questions in ways that hide what the SAT really rewards. It's also interesting that we can tell (A),

(B), and (D) must all be wrong for the reasons noted above, even if we didn't know the meaning of the word in (C). This means it's possible to answer this question correctly, with total confidence, even if we don't know the word "abysmal," which is the right answer—of course, this kind of approach requires us to read carefully and keep the unwritten rules of the test in mind, which is why it's so important to train properly for test day.

Test 3, Question 17 — TYPE: READING COMPREHENSION (usually has a prompt; choices have different meanings)

- **RC Question sub-type:** Including/excluding a phrase/sentence. (The question asks whether a sentence should be included in the passage. The correct choice will include a comment that plainly describes the role of the phrase or sentence in the passage. Sentences that should be included will follow broad College Board standards for ideal sentences and paragraphs—including consistency with any figures in the passage—while sentences that shouldn't be included will not follow those standards. See page 433.)

ANSWER CHOICE ANALYSIS

A   **Pattern:** Direct contradiction. **Incorrect:** The sentence in question *is* relevant at this point in the passage, because it introduces the idea that "Harvey was not content to follow conventional business practices," and the rest of the paragraph talks about Harvey employing women, who "did not traditionally work in restaurants" at that time. This choice inaccurately describes the sentence in question, so it's wrong.

B   **Pattern:** Direct contradiction. **Incorrect:** This sentence does "logically follow" the previous paragraph according to the SAT's unwritten rules, because the second half of the previous paragraph discusses Harvey opening his restaurants, and the previous sentence tells us what happened when those restaurants opened.

C ✓   **Pattern:** Correct. As we saw in our discussion of (A), this sentence *does* provide a "logical introduction to the paragraph," because it says Harvey didn't "follow conventional business practices," and the next two sentence explain how Harvey did something that was "not traditionally" done at the time. This is the only choice that's accurately demonstrated by the relationship between the prompt sentence and the text, so it's correct.

D   **Pattern:** Confused concepts. **Incorrect:** The sentence doesn't provide any example that supports an argument from elsewhere in the passage, as this choice would require, so this choice is wrong.

Test 3, Question 18 — TYPE: GRAMMAR/STYLE/PUNCTUATION (often no prompt; choices have similar meanings)

- **Vertical Scan Results:** Choices are long phrases/sentences.
- **Vertical Scan Notes:** (B) is the only option that calls the "response" "overwhelming," but doesn't also call the response "tremendous."
- **Key Features in Surrounding Text:** the underlined phrase.

Concepts in the question:

- **Redundancy:** Answer choices and/or surrounding text could combine to repeat the same concept unnecessarily. We should avoid words or phrases that directly repeat ideas in the immediate context. (See page 452.)

ANSWER CHOICE ANALYSIS

A   **Incorrect:** "Tremendous" and "overwhelming" both express the idea that there was a lot of response to the advertisement—using both words isn't necessary, so the SAT will want us to delete one if we have the option, which is what (B) does.

B ✓   **Correct:** This is the only choice that doesn't unnecessarily use both "tremendous" and "overwhelming" to describe the response to the advertisement, so this is the only acceptable answer according to the College Board. Also, as trained test-takers, we should notice that (B) is both grammatically acceptable and the shortest option, which means it will be correct according to the SAT's unwritten rules for style/grammar/punctuation questions on the Writing and Language section.

C   **Incorrect:** This choice has the same problem as (A).

D   **Incorrect:** This choice has the same problem as (A).

Test 3, Question 19 — TYPE: GRAMMAR/STYLE/PUNCTUATION (often no prompt; choices have similar meanings)

- **Vertical Scan Results:** Similar phrases with different short words and/or punctuation.
- **Vertical Scan Notes:** Is "but" and/or "also" acceptable? Should "they" appear before the verb form? Also, is "helping" or "helped" acceptable?
- **Key Features in Surrounding Text:** The current version of the sentence includes a dependent clause ("but also….restaurant industry") without a main subject. We need an answer choice with an acceptable dependent clause, which will include both a main subject and a main verb.

Concepts in the question:

- **Pronoun Ambiguity:** Choices include pronouns that could refer to more than one phrase in the surrounding text. We can't use a pronoun on the SAT when it isn't clear what that pronoun refers to. (See page 441.)

- **Verb Tense/Conjugation:** Choices include different forms of the same verb. Look at the surrounding text to find each verb's subject. Also, look for other verbs that could indicate the proper tense for the verbs in the answer choices. (See page 437.)

ANSWER CHOICE ANALYSIS

A Incorrect: As we discussed above, without a main subject like "they," this phrase doesn't clearly convey which noun "helped."

B Incorrect: This choice has the same problem as (A).

C Incorrect: This choice has the same problem as (A).

D ✓ Correct: As we discussed above, this phrase needs to include the word "they," to convey clearly which noun "helped," and also to provide this dependent clause with a subject. Only (D) includes "they," so it's the only acceptable answer.

Answer choice patterns (see page 455): Wrong answers incorporate elements of the right answer.

Test 3, Question 20   TYPE: READING COMPREHENSION (usually has a prompt; choices have different meanings)

- **RC Question sub-type:** Best Accomplishes X. (The prompt describes a goal of the author, and asks us which choice achieves that goal. The correct answer choice will plainly and directly demonstrate the task described in the prompt. See page 431.)
- **Subjective phrases to be ignored:** "most"

ANSWER CHOICE ANALYSIS

A **Pattern:** Largely irrelevant. **Incorrect:** The previous sentence tells us the servers were "paid quite well for the time," and then gives details about the pay and benefits given to the workers. But (A) talks about "the growth of Harvey's business" and the "Santa Fe Railway." The concepts in (A) don't have any connection to the previous sentence, so it's wrong.

B **Pattern:** Largely irrelevant. **Incorrect:** This has essentially the same issue as (A). The idea of opening a lot of businesses doesn't involve any of the same concepts as the previous sentence, so (B) can't "logically follow the previous sentence" according to the SAT's unwritten rules.

C ✓ **Pattern:** Correct. The previous sentence tells us the servers received "tips, meals, room and board, laundry service, and travel expenses." (C) refers to those "benefits" and explains their impact on the Harvey Girls, which is demonstrated in the following paragraph. So this choice "logically follows" the previous sentence according to the SAT's unwritten rules.

D **Pattern:** Largely Irrelevant. **Incorrect:** This choice introduces the idea of "today's standards," which isn't restated or demonstrated in the relevant text. Instead, the previous sentence and the following sentences only make statements related to the time of the Harvey Houses, so a sentence that logically belongs with them (according to the SAT) can't introduce the unrelated idea of "today's standards."

Test 3, Question 21   TYPE: GRAMMAR/STYLE/PUNCTUATION (often no prompt; choices have similar meanings)

- **Vertical Scan Results:** Similar phrases with different short words and/or punctuation.
- **Vertical Scan Notes:** We need to decide whether a semi-colon, colon, or comma should appear after "ethic," and whether "and" should appear at the end of the underlined phrase.
- **Key Features in Surrounding Text:** The beginning of the sentence through the word "ethic" is a phrase that describes "the Harvey Girls," and the rest of the sentence is an independent clause.

Concepts in the question:

- **Colons:** Choices include one or more colons. A colon can be placed after a set of words that could be a sentence on their own, and before a demonstration or example of the idea before the colon. (See page 447.)
- **Commas:** Choices include one or more commas. On the Writing and Language section, commas can be used to separate things in a list of three or more, to form a comma sandwich, or to introduce an independent clause after a dependent clause. (See pages 448-450.)
- **Dependent and Independent Clauses:** Answer choice(s) would incorrectly use a dependent or independent clause. An independent clause can stand alone as a sentence: it has a main subject/verb pair. A dependent clause is introduced by a conjunction or relative pronoun. (See page 445.)
- **Semi-colons:** Choices include one or more semicolons. Semi-colons can be used to separate two sets of words that could each stand on their own as a full sentence. (See page 447.)

ANSWER CHOICE ANALYSIS

A Incorrect: On the SAT, a semi-colon can only appear between two groups of words that could each stand on their own as complete sentences. The part of this sentence leading up to the semi-colon can't stand on its own as a complete sentence, so this choice is wrong.

B Incorrect: On the SAT, a colon can only appear after a group of words that could stand on its own as a complete sentence. The part of the sentence leading up to the colon can't stand on its own as a complete sentence, so this choice is wrong.

C   Incorrect: Adding the word "and" to the clause after the comma makes it a dependent clause—but the phrase leading up to the comma isn't an independent clause. Since every acceptable sentence on the SAT must include an independent clause, the word "and" makes this choice wrong.

D✓   Correct: This is the only choice that correctly uses a comma to separate the phrase "living independently and demonstrating an intense work ethic" from the phrase it describes ("the Harvey Girls"); this choice also doesn't create any problem with the independent clause after the comma, as (C) did.

Answer choice patterns (see page 455): Wrong answers incorporate elements of the right answer.

| Test 3, Question 22 | TYPE: READING COMPREHENSION (usually has a prompt; choices have different meanings) |

- **RC Question sub-type:** Including/excluding a phrase/sentence. (The question asks whether a sentence should be included in the passage. The correct choice will include a comment that plainly describes the role of the phrase or sentence in the passage. Sentences that should be included will follow broad College Board standards for ideal sentences and paragraphs—including consistency with any figures in the passage—while sentences that shouldn't be included will not follow those standards. See page 433.)

ANSWER CHOICE ANALYSIS

A✓   **Pattern:** Correct. This phrase does "provide examples of the Harvey Girls' influence," because it says the Harvey Girls "inspir[ed] books, documentaries, and even a musical." Since this is the only choice that accurately describes the phrase in the prompt, it's correct.

B   **Pattern:** Largely irrelevant. **Incorrect:** The phrase doesn't "serve[] as a transitional point in the paragraph," as (B) requires. In other words, this point in the paragraph doesn't mark a shift from discussing one topic to discussing another topic.

C   **Pattern:** Largely irrelevant. **Incorrect:** This phrase shouldn't appear earlier in the passage, because it provides examples of how Harvey Girls were "a transformative force in the American West," so it needs to appear after that statement.

D   **Pattern:** Largely irrelevant. **Incorrect:** Nothing in this phrase "contradicts the main claim of the passage," as (D) requires.

| Test 3, Question 23 | TYPE: GRAMMAR/STYLE/PUNCTUATION (often no prompt; choices have similar meanings) |

- **Vertical Scan Results:** Choices are long phrases/sentences.
- **Vertical Scan Notes:** The answer choices are fairly long and will need to be analyzed a bit more closely to determine what's going on in this question. Some issues that might jump out at first glance include the placement of the phrase "when applied to apples" and whether the word "because" should be in the right answer.
- **Key Features in Surrounding Text:** The two entire underlined sentences.

Concepts in the question:

- **Comma Sandwich:** Choice(s) would create phrases improperly "sandwiched" between similar types of punctuation. When removed from the sentence, a properly formed sandwich leaves behind a grammatically acceptable sentence. (See page 448.)

- **Commas:** Choices include one or more commas. On the Writing and Language section, commas can be used to separate things in a list of three or more, to form a comma sandwich, or to introduce an independent clause after a dependent clause. (See pages 448-450.)

- **Intervening Phrase:** A phrase appears between two words that need to agree with each other. Identify which words need to agree with each other, and ignore extra phrases that appear between them. (See page 456.)

- **Joining Two Sentences:** Each choice is a sentence that combines the two sentences in the underlined portion of the text. The right answer must follow all rules for other question types without changing the meaning of the original two sentences. (See page 453.)

- **Phrase Proximity:** Answer choice(s) would place descriptive phrases next to ideas they don't describe. Descriptive phrases that don't begin with a word ending in "-ing" describe the closest noun phrase. (See page 451.)

ANSWER CHOICE ANALYSIS

A✓   **Correct:** This is the only choice that expresses the ideas from the two sentences in a logical order. The sentence starts by saying "when applied to apples," which specifies the situation being described in the sentence, since the previous sentence says MCP can also be applied to "other fruit." The sentence continues by saying "1-MCP lengthens storage life by three to four times," which tells us the effect of applying 1-MCP to apples. Next, the sentence says, "allowing producers to sell their apples in the off-season," which tells us the benefit of the idea that was just mentioned—lengthening the storage life. Finally, the sentence says, "months after the apples have been harvested," which provides additional information about the "off-season." So each component of the sentence provides more information about the previous component, which means similar concepts in the sentence are grouped as closely together as possible; as trained test-takers, we know this is one of the College Board's unwritten requirements for questions about ideal sentences or paragraphs. Further, we can see that this sentence restates the same concepts and relationships found in the original two sentences. Compare this choice to the wrong answers to see some arrangements of these concepts that wouldn't satisfy the College Board.

B   Incorrect: Unlike (A), this sentence presents ideas out of logical order by the SAT's standards, because it fails to arrange modifying phrases next to the ideas they modify. The sandwiched phrase "in the off-season" comes after the word "harvested," indicating that the harvest happens in the off-season— but that contradicts the original text, which says the *selling* is what happens in the off-season.

C   Incorrect: In this sentence, the phrase "when applied to apples" comes after the phrase "storage life," indicating the storage life is the thing being applied to apples—but this differs from the text, which says 1-MCP is the thing that's applied to the apples.

D   Incorrect: Like (C), this choice inserts the phrase "when applied to apples" immediately after the phrase "storage life," which differs in meaning from the original text.

Answer choice patterns (see page 455): Wrong answers incorporate elements of the right answer.

Test 3, Question 24   **TYPE: GRAMMAR/STYLE/PUNCTUATION (often no prompt; choices have similar meanings)**

- **Vertical Scan Results:** Similar phrases with different short words and/or punctuation.
- **Vertical Scan Notes:** The question seems to ask us to choose the best way to explain what something is, but we also have the option of deleting the underlined phrase.
- **Key Features in Surrounding Text:** When we check the surrounding text, we see that the underlined phrase is the beginning of a punctuation sandwich that describes the word before the punctuation sandwich. It's clear that the phrase in the punctuation sandwich describes "ethylene."

Concepts in the question:

- **Comma Sandwich:** Choice(s) would create phrases improperly "sandwiched" between similar types of punctuation. When removed from the sentence, a properly formed sandwich leaves behind a grammatically acceptable sentence. (See page 448.)
- **Comma Splice:** Answer choice(s) and/or surrounding text use commas to separate two groups of words that could each be sentences on their own. A comma can't be used in this way on the SAT Writing and Language section. (See page 447.)
- **Dangling Participle:** The question involves descriptive phrases beginning with an "-ing" word that would describe the wrong word in context. Descriptive phrases starting with a word ending in "-ing" describe the first noun phrase in that sentence's independent clause. (See page 450.)
- **Dependent and Independent Clauses:** Answer choice(s) would incorrectly use a dependent or independent clause. An independent clause can stand alone as a sentence: it has a main subject/verb pair. A dependent clause is introduced by a conjunction or relative pronoun. (See page 445.)

ANSWER CHOICE ANALYSIS

A   Incorrect: This choice would create a comma splice, because it uses a comma to separate two independent clauses.

B   Incorrect: According to the SAT's grammar rules, if we begin this phrase with an "-ing" word, as this choice would do, then we'd be saying that 1-MCP is the chemical that "causes fruit to ripen," instead of ethylene. This is because 1-MCP is the first noun in the independent clause that our phrase starting with the "-ing" word would be attached to.

C   Incorrect: This choice has the same problem as (A).

D ✓ Correct: This choice creates a comma sandwich that comes after the word "ethylene" and describes what ethylene does. Notice that this comma sandwich actually involves a comma and a period (rather than two commas), because the comma sandwich is the last phrase in the sentence, and we can't put a comma directly before a period.

Test 3, Question 25   **TYPE: READING COMPREHENSION (usually has a prompt; choices have different meanings)**

- **RC Question sub-type:** Vocabulary In Context. (Choices include words or short phrases that have vaguely similar but not identical meanings. Most or all of the choices will seem vaguely appropriate, but only one choice will be correct when we think very carefully and specifically about the word means and how it can be used. See page 432.)

ANSWER CHOICE ANALYSIS

A   ("While 1-MCP keeps apples <u>tight</u> and crisp for months, it also..." **Pattern:** Same ballpark. **Incorrect:** The underlined phrase must be a word we can logically use to describe "apples." It doesn't make sense to say that apples are "tight;" we could say that an article of clothing is tight if the clothing is very snug, and we could say a lid on a jar is closed tight if the jar is difficult to open— but we can't use "tight" to describe an apple in any normal context.

B ✓ ("While 1-MCP keeps apples <u>firm</u> and crisp for months, it also...") **Correct:** The underlined phrase must be a word we can use to describe "apples." We can say that apples are firm—when something is "firm," it gives a lot of resistance when you try to press your finger into it.

C   ("While 1-MCP keeps apples <u>stiff</u> and crisp for months, it also...") **Pattern:** Same ballpark. **Incorrect:** It doesn't make sense to say that apples are "stiff." We can say that uncooked spaghetti is stiff, and we can say our joints are stiff if they're hard to move in cold weather—but we can't use "stiff" to describe an apple in any normal context.

D   ("While 1-MCP keeps apples <u>taut</u> and crisp for months, it also...") **Pattern:** Same ballpark. **Incorrect:** Apples can't be "taut:" the word "taut" can only be used in situations where something is stretched, and apples can't be stretched. We can say a rope or a piece of fabric is taut, if it's pulled tight and nearly straight, but we can't say apples are "taut" on the SAT.

Test 3, Question 26   TYPE: GRAMMAR/STYLE/PUNCTUATION (often no prompt; choices have similar meanings)

- **Vertical Scan Results:** Some choices have different forms of the same base word.
- **Vertical Scan Notes:** It looks like we need to decide whether the underlined phrase should be singular or plural, and then decide what the correct form of the underlined phrase should be.
- **Key Features in Surrounding Text:** The sentence says "While 1-MCP keeps apples firm and crisp...it also limits [blank] scent production." So the word "it" refers to 1-MCP, and the underlined word refers to the plural noun "apples." Also, the "scent production" belongs to the "apples," so the underlined phrase needs to be possessive.

Concepts in the question:

- **Confused Homophones:** Choices include different homophone pairs (such as "their" and "they're" or "too" and "to"). Read carefully—also, remember the correct formation of possessive pronouns, and remember to read contractions as their uncontracted forms (e.g. "it's" = "it is"). (See page 452.)
- **Plural/Possessive/Contraction:** Choices include the same noun ending in "-s" with or without an apostrophe before or after the "-s." Remember the three rules for forming possessives. Think of contractions in their uncontracted forms ("you're" = "you are"). (See page 441.)
- **Pronoun Ambiguity:** Choices include pronouns that could refer to more than one phrase in the surrounding text. We can't use a pronoun on the SAT when it isn't clear what that pronoun refers to. (See page 441.)

ANSWER CHOICE ANALYSIS

A ✓   **Correct:** As we discussed above, the underlined phrase should be plural and possessive. This is the only correctly formed plural possessive pronoun in the answer choices, so it's correct.

B   **Incorrect:** As we discussed above, the answer should be plural and possessive. This choice may sound like the plural possessive form "their" in (A), but this word actually refers to a location, like the words "where" and "here."

C   **Incorrect:** As we discussed above, the answer should be plural and possessive—but this choice is *singular* and possessive.

D   **Incorrect:** As we discussed above, the answer should be plural and possessive—but this choice is neither. This option is the contracted form of the phrase "it is."

Test 3, Question 27   TYPE: GRAMMAR/STYLE/PUNCTUATION (often no prompt; choices have similar meanings)

- **Vertical Scan Results:** Some choices are short phrases with no obvious similarity.
- **Vertical Scan Notes:** The choices are all different pronouns, so we have to pick the one that works in the given sentence.
- **Key Features in Surrounding Text:** It looks like we need to pick a word to connect "consumers" with the action that the consumers perform, as reflected in the phrase, "will reject apples lacking the expected aroma."

Concepts in the question:

- **Comma Splice:** Answer choice(s) and/or surrounding text use commas to separate two groups of words that could each be sentences on their own. A comma can't be used in this way on the SAT Writing and Language section. (See page 447.)
- **Commas:** Choices include one or more commas. On the Writing and Language section, commas can be used to separate things in a list of three or more, to form a comma sandwich, or to introduce an independent clause after a dependent clause. (See pages 448-450.)
- **Dependent and Independent Clauses:** Answer choice(s) would incorrectly use a dependent or independent clause. An independent clause can stand alone as a sentence: it has a main subject/verb pair. A dependent clause is introduced by a conjunction or relative pronoun. (See page 445.)

ANSWER CHOICE ANALYSIS

A   **Incorrect:** The underlined phrase needs to be a pronoun that can represent "consumers," because the next phrase describes an action the "consumers" do. This choice isn't a personal pronoun, so it can't be a correct way to refer to consumers, since consumers are people.

B   **Incorrect:** This choice would create a comma splice, because everything before the underlined phrase can stand on its own as a sentence, and everything from the underlined phrase to the end of the sentence can stand on its own as a sentence.

C   **Incorrect:** This choice has the same problem as (A): it can't be used to refer to people.

D ✓   **Correct:** Only (D) provides a personal pronoun to represent "consumers," and doesn't create a comma splice.

Test 3, Question 28   TYPE: GRAMMAR/STYLE/PUNCTUATION (often no prompt; choices have similar meanings)

- **Vertical Scan Results:** Some choices are short phrases with no obvious similarity.

- **Vertical Scan Notes:** It looks like we need to pick a verb form that matches the context.
- **Key Features in Surrounding Text:** The underlined phrase is being used to compare the idea that "some fruits do not respond as well" to what "others [blank]." Since we're comparing these two actions, the verbs should be in the same form.

Concepts in the question:

- **Parallelism:** Choices include options that would ignore a parallel structure in the surrounding text. The correct answer choice should match phrasing in the surrounding text when possible. (See page 458.)
- **Verb Tense/Conjugation:** Choices include different forms of the same verb. Look at the surrounding text to find each verb's subject. Also, look for other verbs that could indicate the proper tense for the verbs in the answer choices. (See page 437.)

ANSWER CHOICE ANALYSIS

A	**Incorrect:** This choice is in the past tense, but the underlined phrase needs to correspond to the verb in the phrase "some fruits do not respond as well." (See the explanation for (B).)
B ✓	**Correct:** As trained test-takers, we know that the underlined phrase needs to parallel the verb phrase "some fruits do not respond as well," from earlier in the sentence, to satisfy the SAT's unwritten rules about parallelism. So the present-tense verb "do" is acceptable here, since it matches the present-tense helping verb "do" in the phrase "do not respond."
C	**Incorrect:** This choice gives us the present-tense form of a different helping verb from the one in the phrase "some fruits do not respond as well." As we saw in (B), the helping verb "do" is the one that needs to be paralleled in the correct answer.
D	**Incorrect:** This choice represents an action in the future, but the underlined phrase needs to correspond to the present-tense verb phrase from earlier in the sentence, as we described for (B).

Note	Don't worry if you're not familiar with the term "helping verb" as we used it in the explanations for these answer choices, because you don't need to know that term on test day—all you really need to notice is that the question offers us the chance to use parallelism, which means we need to make sure the things being compared are similar, according to the SAT's unwritten rules. Since the first part of the comparison involves a verb in the present tense, the second part also needs to involve a verb in the present tense.

Test 3, Question 29 **TYPE: GRAMMAR/STYLE/PUNCTUATION (often no prompt; choices have similar meanings)**

- **Vertical Scan Results:** Some choices have the same words with different punctuation.
- **Vertical Scan Notes:** We need to decide whether a comma, period, or no punctuation should appear after "pears," and whether a comma or colon should appear after "instance."
- **Key Features in Surrounding Text:** The "Bartlett pears" are an example of something "not respond[ing] well to 1-MCP treatment" from the previous sentence.

Concepts in the question:

- **Colons:** Choices include one or more colons. A colon can be placed after a set of words that could be a sentence on their own, and before a demonstration or example of the idea before the colon. (See page 447.)
- **Comma Sandwich:** Choice(s) would create phrases improperly "sandwiched" between similar types of punctuation. When removed from the sentence, a properly formed sandwich leaves behind a grammatically acceptable sentence. (See page 448.)
- **Comma Splice:** Answer choice(s) and/or surrounding text use commas to separate two groups of words that could each be sentences on their own. A comma can't be used in this way on the SAT Writing and Language section. (See page 447.)
- **Commas:** Choices include one or more commas. On the Writing and Language section, commas can be used to separate things in a list of three or more, to form a comma sandwich, or to introduce an independent clause after a dependent clause. (See pages 448-450.)
- **Dependent and Independent Clauses:** Answer choice(s) would incorrectly use a dependent or independent clause. An independent clause can stand alone as a sentence: it has a main subject/verb pair. A dependent clause is introduced by a conjunction or relative pronoun. (See page 445.)

ANSWER CHOICE ANALYSIS

A	**Incorrect:** This choice might be tempting to untrained test-takers who don't read the entire original sentence, because the phrase "for instance" is often found in a comma sandwich, as it would be in this choice. The problem with a comma sandwich here is that both of the clauses on either side of the commas are independent clauses, which means they could stand as full sentences by themselves. If we remove the comma sandwich completely, we're left with a run-on sentence, since we'd have two independent clauses next to each other with no period or semicolon. (Compare this choice to (C) for a similar situation.)
B ✓	**Correct:** This sentence is consistent with the rules for colons on the Writing and Language section. The text before the colon could stand on its own as a sentence, and the text after the colon is an example or explanation of the idea before the colon: the attributes of Bartlett pears that make them an example of "fruits...[that] do not respond well to 1-MCP" are explained.

C   Incorrect: This choice would create a comma splice because it would use a comma to join two sets of words that could each be full sentences on their own, which is against the College Board's rules.

D   Incorrect: On the SAT, a transition phrase like "for instance" needs to refer to an idea from the previous sentence, but this choice would make "for instance" refer to "take Bartlett pears," which makes the rest of the sentence sound like an example of Bartlett pears, or of taking Bartlett pears, which makes no sense in context.

Test 3, Question 30   TYPE: READING COMPREHENSION (usually has a prompt; choices have different meanings)

- **RC Question sub-type:** Sentence or paragraph placement. (The prompt asks us where a sentence should go in a paragraph, or where a paragraph should go in the passage. The correct order will reflect a logical chronology, and/or will allow for pronouns in the sentences to refer to nouns in a logical way, and/or will place related concepts near one another. See page 432.)
- **Subjective phrases to be ignored:** "most"

ANSWER CHOICE ANALYSIS

A   **Pattern:** Causes text to introduce an idea that has already been discussed. **Incorrect:** This placement would cause the text to mention that "some [fruits] even respond adversely" to 1-MCP after examples of fruits responding adversely have already been discussed: sentences 2 and 3 already explain that 1-MCP can limit the "scent production" of certain apples, which can cause consumers to "reject" apples. This placement makes even less sense because sentence 4 begins with the word "but," which should indicate that the sentence doesn't go along with the ideas in the sentence that comes before it.

B ✓   **Pattern:** Correct. This choice solves the problem in (A) by positioning sentence 4 to introduce the idea that some fruits respond adversely before any examples of responding adversely have been given. Note that the word "but" at the beginning of sentence 4 makes sense in this position, because the idea in sentence 4 doesn't go along with the idea in sentence 1.

C   **Pattern:** Causes text to introduce an idea that has already been discussed. **Incorrect:** This choice has the same problem as (A), and is wrong for the same reason.

D   **Pattern:** Causes text to introduce an idea that has already been discussed. **Incorrect:** This choice has the same problem as (A), and is wrong for the same reason.

Test 3, Question 31   TYPE: READING COMPREHENSION (usually has a prompt; choices have different meanings)

- **RC Question sub-type:** Figure. (The prompt requires us to read a figure in order to find an answer that reflects the data in the figure. The correct answer will be directly supported by the information in the figure. Remember to read carefully and check for details such as column headings, axis-labels, legends, and so on. See pages 44-51.)

ANSWER CHOICE ANALYSIS

A   **Pattern:** Confused concepts. **Incorrect:** When we read the passage carefully, we see that the underlined text must describe "the flesh of untreated Empire apples that are first stored in the open air" as compared to "untreated Empire apples that are immediately put into storage in a controlled environment." We can see on the graph that "untreated" apples are represented by the light gray bars. The data for apples first stored "in open air" is shown on the right-hand side of the graph, and the data for apples "placed immediately in controlled atmosphere" is shown to the left. When we compare the light gray bar on the right to the light gray bar on the left, we can see the apples that spent time in open air experienced much less browning than the apples that went immediately into the controlled atmosphere. So this choice is incorrect, but it may have been tempting for test-takers who accidentally compared the dark gray bar on the left to the light gray bar on the left.

B   **Pattern:** Direct contradiction. **Incorrect:** As we saw for (A), untreated Empire apples that spent time in open air had significantly less browning than untreated Empire apples that went right to the controlled atmosphere, so (B) is wrong.

C   **Pattern:** Direct contradiction. **Incorrect:** Again, as we saw with (A), untreated Empire apples that spent time in open air had significantly less browning than untreated Empire apples that went right to the controlled atmosphere, so (C) is wrong.

D ✓   **Pattern:** Correct. As we saw with (A), untreated Empire apples that spent time in open air experienced significantly less browning than untreated Empire apples that went right to the controlled atmosphere, so this choice is right.

Test 3, Question 32   TYPE: READING COMPREHENSION (usually has a prompt; choices have different meanings)

- **RC Question sub-type:** Figure. (The prompt requires us to read a figure in order to find an answer that reflects the data in the figure. The correct answer will be directly supported by the information in the figure. Remember to read carefully and check for details such as column headings, axis-labels, legends, and so on. See pages 44-51.)

ANSWER CHOICE ANALYSIS

A   **Pattern:** Direct contradiction. **Incorrect:** We can see on the graph that at least some of the flesh of Empire apples turns brown in all four situations represented on the graph, so we can't say there are any conditions under which the flesh doesn't turn brown, as this choice would require.

B ✓   **Pattern:** Correct. The dark gray bars on the graph represent apples treated with 1-MCP, and both dark gray bars show about 50 percent of the flesh browning, just as this choice describes.

C   **Pattern:** Direct contradiction. **Incorrect:** This choice has the same problem as (A) and is wrong for the same reasons: no part of the graph shows that any group of apples manages to have zero browning, as this choice would require.

D   **Pattern:** Largely irrelevant. **Incorrect:** This choice can't be right because the graph doesn't provide any information about how quickly the flesh turns brown; it only tells us *how much* of the flesh turns brown.

| Test 3, Question 33 | TYPE: READING COMPREHENSION (usually has a prompt; choices have different meanings) |

- RC Question sub-type: Best Accomplishes X. (The prompt describes a goal of the author, and asks us which choice achieves that goal. The correct answer choice will plainly and directly demonstrate the task described in the prompt. See page 431.)
- Subjective phrases to be ignored: "best"

ANSWER CHOICE ANALYSIS

A   **Pattern:** Plausible, but not in the text. **Incorrect:** We might imagine that the statement in (A) is true in real life, but the prompt asks for a conclusion that shows how the "shortcomings of 1-MCP...affect the actions of people in the fruit industry." (A) doesn't say anything about "the actions of people in the fruit industry," as the prompt requires, so it's wrong.

B   **Pattern:** Plausible, but not in the text. **Incorrect:** This choice has the same basic problem as (A): it doesn't mention the actions of people in the fruit industry, as the prompt requires.

C✓   **Pattern:** Correct. The prompt asks for a conclusion that shows how the "shortcomings of 1-MCP...affect the actions of people in the fruit industry." (C) does that, because it tells us what "fruit sellers" must do. Further, the phrase "must weigh the relative values of aroma, color, and freshness" tells us that 1-MCP doesn't allow fruit sellers to optimize all of these characteristics—they must choose from among them. This demonstrates the "shortcomings" of 1-MCP, as required in the prompt.

D   **Pattern:** Confused concepts. **Incorrect:** The question asks for a conclusion that shows how the "shortcomings of 1-MCP...affect the actions of people in the fruit industry." Instead, this choice tells us what "the fruit industry" can do because of the *benefits* of 1-MCP, like shipping and storing fruit "in ways that were impossible before." The choice doesn't tell us anything about what happens because of 1-MCP's *shortcomings*, as the prompt requires, so it's wrong.

| Test 3, Question 34 | TYPE: GRAMMAR/STYLE/PUNCTUATION (often no prompt; choices have similar meanings) |

- **Vertical Scan Results:** Similar phrases with different short words and/or punctuation.
- **Vertical Scan Notes:** We need to decide whether a period, semi-colon, or comma should appear after "Gothic," and whether "these" should appear before "works."
- **Key Features in Surrounding Text:** The first "sentence" that this underlined phrase overlaps is actually a fragment, because it doesn't contain any main verb: "from Michelangelo's David to Vincent van Gogh's series of self-portraits to Grant Wood's iconic image of a farming couple in American Gothic." Since that "sentence" has no independent clause, it can't be separated from the following sentence by a period or a semi-colon.

Concepts in the question:

- **Commas:** Choices include one or more commas. On the Writing and Language section, commas can be used to separate things in a list of three or more, to form a comma sandwich, or to introduce an independent clause after a dependent clause. (See pages 448-450.)
- **Dependent and Independent Clauses:** Answer choice(s) would incorrectly use a dependent or independent clause. An independent clause can stand alone as a sentence: it has a main subject/verb pair. A dependent clause is introduced by a conjunction or relative pronoun. (See page 445.)
- **Semi-colons:** Choices include one or more semicolons. Semi-colons can be used to separate two sets of words that could each stand on their own as a full sentence. (See page 447.)

ANSWER CHOICE ANALYSIS

A   **Incorrect:** As discussed above, the first "sentence" has no independent clause, so it can't be separated from the following sentence by a period.

B   **Incorrect:** This choice has the same problem as (A), since it also uses a period after a group of words that can't stand on its own as a sentence.

C   **Incorrect:** This choice has the same problem as (A) and (B), since the College Board's rules say that periods and semicolons can only be used to separate two groups of words that could each be sentences on their own.

D✓   **Correct:** This is the only choice that doesn't use a period or semi-colon after "Gothic," so it's the only acceptable answer according to the SAT.

Answer choice patterns (see page 455): Wrong answers incorporate elements of the right answer.

Note   Notice that once we realize the first "sentence" has no independent clause, and that (A), (B), and (C) must be wrong, we don't need to wonder whether the word "these" should be part of the correct answer, because only (D) features the necessary punctuation.

- **Vertical Scan Results:** Some choices have the same words with different punctuation.
- **Vertical Scan Notes:** We need to decide whether a comma, dash, semi-colon, or no punctuation should appear after "Coolidge".
- **Key Features in Surrounding Text:** This underlined phrase is the last word in a phrase that begins with "—popularized in" that describes the image of dogs playing poker.

Concepts in the question:

- **Punctuation Sandwich:** Choice(s) would create phrases improperly "sandwiched" between similar types of punctuation. When removed from the sentence, a properly formed sandwich leaves behind a grammatically acceptable sentence. (See page 450.)

ANSWER CHOICE ANALYSIS

A   **Incorrect:** The phrase "popularized in a series of paintings by American artist C. M. Coolidge" must be intended as a punctuation sandwich, because we can remove the phrase and leave behind a sentence with no grammatical problems. A punctuation sandwich needs the same punctuation on either end, and the other end of this punctuation sandwich uses a dash, not a comma, so (A) is wrong.

B ✓   **Correct:** As we saw in the explanation for (A), the underlined phrase is the end of a punctuation sandwich that begins with a dash, so the punctuation sandwich must end with a dash as well.

C   **Incorrect:** As we saw for (A), the underlined phrase is the end of a punctuation sandwich that begins with a dash, so that punctuation sandwich must end with a dash, not a semi-colon.

D   **Incorrect:** As we saw in the explanation for choice (A), the underlined phrase is the end of a punctuation sandwich that begins with a dash. That punctuation sandwich must also end with a dash, so this choice is incorrect.

- **Vertical Scan Results:** Some choices have different forms of the same base word.
- **Vertical Scan Notes:** We need to pick the appropriate form of the verb "to portray."
- **Key Features in Surrounding Text:** This sentence has the comma-sandwiched intervening phrase "including paintings and drawings tens of thousands of years old found on cave walls in Spain and France." When we remove that phrase, we're left with a much simpler sentence: "Yet some of the earliest known works of art [blank] animals." We can simplify further by removing the intervening phrase "of art," which leaves us with "Yet some of the earliest known works [blank] animals."

Concepts in the question:

- **Intervening Phrase:** A phrase appears between two words that need to agree with each other. Identify which words need to agree with each other, and ignore extra phrases that appear between them. (See page 456.)
- **Singular versus Plural:** Choices include singular and plural versions of the same base words that don't agree with other words in the surrounding text. Singular nouns must go with singular verb forms and singular pronouns. Plural nouns must go with plural verbs and pronouns. Think carefully about which words should match or agree with each other! (See page 443.)
- **Verb Tense/Conjugation:** Choices include different forms of the same verb. Look at the surrounding text to find each verb's subject. Also, look for other verbs that could indicate the proper tense for the verbs in the answer choices. (See page 437.)

ANSWER CHOICE ANALYSIS

A   **Incorrect:** As we discussed above, we need the form of "to portray" that would go with the plural noun "works." But this choice gives us the singular form "portrays," so it's wrong.

B   **Incorrect:** This choice would leave the sentence without a main verb, since no verb would be conjugated to pair with the plural noun "works," which is the subject of the sentence. When we remove the intervening phrases mentioned above and insert the verb form from this choice, we would be left with the fragment "*Yet some of the earliest known works portraying animals."

C ✓   **Correct:** When we remove the intervening phrases mentioned above, we're left with "Yet some of the earliest known works [blank] animals." This makes it clear that the verb in the underlined phrase should agree with "works," and we need the plural verb form "portray": "...earliest known works portray animals."

D   **Incorrect:** As we discussed above, we need the plural form "portray," but (D) gives us the singular form "has portrayed."

- **RC Question sub-type:** Best Accomplishes X. (The prompt describes a goal of the author, and asks us which choice achieves that goal. The correct answer choice will plainly and directly demonstrate the task described in the prompt. See page 431.)
- **Subjective phrases to be ignored:** "best"

ANSWER CHOICE ANALYSIS

A   **Pattern:** Largely irrelevant. **Incorrect:** The question asks for a choice that links the first paragraph "with the ideas that follow." The next paragraph talks about cats that hunt rodents at "one of Russia's great art museums." This option isn't related to those concepts in any way, so it's wrong.

B   **Pattern:** Same ballpark. **Incorrect:** The question asks for a choice that links the first paragraph "with the ideas that follow." The next paragraph talks about cats that hunt rodents at "one of Russia's great art museums." This choice might be tempting because it also mentions cats, but it mentions the idea of "special attention being paid to domestic animals such as cats," and the following paragraph doesn't say anything about "domestic animals such as cats" getting "special attention." In order for cats to get "special attention," other animals must get a lesser amount of attention. But the text doesn't compare cats in art to other animals in art, and it doesn't compare domestic animals in art to non-domestic animals in art. Since this option introduces an idea that doesn't appear later in the passage, it's not correct.

C   **Pattern:** Largely irrelevant. **Incorrect:** The question asks for a choice that links the first paragraph "with the ideas that follow." The next paragraph talks about cats that hunt rodents at "one of Russia's great art museums." This option says that most paintings are of people, which isn't discussed anywhere in the rest of the passage. That makes this choice incorrect.

D ✓   **Pattern:** Correct. The question asks for a choice that links the first paragraph "with the ideas that follow." The next paragraph talks about cats that hunt rodents at "one of Russia's great art museums," and this option mentions that "one museum in Russia" is an example of what's discussed in the first paragraph. So this choice restates an idea discussed in the rest of the passage, which makes it correct.

| **Test 3, Question 38** | **TYPE: GRAMMAR/STYLE/PUNCTUATION (often no prompt; choices have similar meanings)** |

- **Vertical Scan Results:** Some choices are short phrases with no obvious similarity.
- **Vertical Scan Notes:** It looks like we need to pick the proper form of the verb "scare."
- **Key Features in Surrounding Text:** As trained test-takers, we know that questions about the correct form of a verb often require us to find another verb in the original text whose form should be paralleled by the form of the correct answer. In this case, the underlined phrase describes something that "rodents" could do in addition to the phrase "damage the art." Since we're describing something else the rodents could do in a parallel phrase, this verb should appear in the same form as "damage" from earlier in the sentence.

Concepts in the question:

- **Parallelism:** Choices include options that would ignore a parallel structure in the surrounding text. The correct answer choice should match phrasing in the surrounding text when possible. (See page 458.)
- **Verb Tense/Conjugation:** Choices include different forms of the same verb. Look at the surrounding text to find each verb's subject. Also, look for other verbs that could indicate the proper tense for the verbs in the answer choices. (See page 437.)

ANSWER CHOICE ANALYSIS

A   **Incorrect:** As discussed above, the verb form should correspond to the verb "damage," so this past-tense form is wrong.

B   **Incorrect:** As discussed above, the verb form should correspond to the verb "damage," so this form isn't acceptable. (B) might have tempted someone who thought the verb in the underlined phrase should parallel the verb "ridding," but that's an action done by the cats, not the mice; when we read the whole sentence, we see that "scare off visitors" is something the rodents might do, not something the cats are trying to do, so the right answer shouldn't have the same structure as "ridding."

C ✓   **Correct:** As we discussed above, the verb form should correspond to the verb "damage" in the parallel phrase "damage the art," so this verb form "scare" is correct.

D   **Incorrect:** As we discussed above, the verb should correspond to the verb "damage," so this past-tense form isn't acceptable. (D) might have tempted someone who thought the verb in the underlined phrase should parallel the verb phrase "have guarded," but that's an action done by the cats, not the mice. (Compare this to (B), which tried to play a similar trick.)

| **Test 3, Question 39** | **TYPE: READING COMPREHENSION (usually has a prompt; choices have different meanings)** |

- **RC Question sub-type:** Sentence or paragraph placement. (The prompt asks us where a sentence should go in a paragraph, or where a paragraph should go in the passage. The correct order will reflect a logical chronology, and/or will allow for pronouns in the sentences to refer to nouns in a logical way, and/or will place related concepts near one another. See page 432.)
- **Subjective phrases to be ignored:** "most"

ANSWER CHOICE ANALYSIS

A   **Pattern:** Causes events to be discussed out of chronological order. **Incorrect:** Sentence 5 says Elizaveta "introduced...cats" as a way to "continu[e] the tradition." But with 5 in its current position, it's preceded by sentence 4, which doesn't mention anything that could be "the tradition" referred to in 5. Since sentences 3 and 5 both refer to the idea of "introduc[ing]" cats, they should be grouped together, according to the SAT's principle of locating similar ideas together when possible.

B   **Pattern:** Causes text to refer to an idea that hasn't been mentioned yet. **Incorrect:** This sentence refers to "continuing the tradition," but if we place it after sentence 1, we'll refer to "the tradition" before sentence 3 tells us what that tradition was.

C ✓ **Pattern:** Correct. As we saw in the explanation for (A), sentence 5 includes the idea of a tradition of introducing cats that's begun in sentence 3 (and not mentioned in any other sentence), so it needs to appear directly after sentence 3, according to the SAT's unwritten rules for ordering sentences in a paragraph.

D **Pattern:** Causes events to be discussed out of chronological order. **Incorrect:** This choice has the same basic issue as (A), except that it would result in two sentences appearing between sentence 3 and sentence 5, not just one sentence.

Test 3, Question 40 — TYPE: READING COMPREHENSION (usually has a prompt; choices have different meanings)

- **RC Question sub-type:** Vocabulary In Context. (Choices include words or short phrases that have vaguely similar but not identical meanings. Most or all of the choices will seem vaguely appropriate, but only one choice will be correct when we think very carefully and specifically about the word means and how it can be used. See page 432.)

ANSWER CHOICE ANALYSIS

A ("…officials recently <u>decreed</u> original paintings to be made…") **Pattern:** Same ballpark. **Incorrect:** To "decree" something means to make an official command or order. Further, the word "decree" isn't usually used in the context of physical objects like paintings; it's more frequently used to refer to rules, as in "the King decreed that polka dots could never appear on the royal stationery." Since the text doesn't support the idea that the "digital artist" was commanded to make the painting, and since "decree" doesn't fit well for the other reasons we mentioned, we know (A) can't be right.

B ✓ ("…officials recently <u>commissioned</u> original paintings to be made…") **Correct:** To "commission" something means to get someone to make something for you, usually a work of art. The context describes how "officials" got "digital artist Eldar Zakirov" to make six "original paintings," which is directly restated by the word "commissioned," so (B) is correct.

C ("…officials recently <u>forced</u> original paintings to be made…") **Pattern:** Same ballpark. **Incorrect:** The word "force" would be somewhat similar to the word "decree" in this context, so (C) is wrong for the same reasons (A) is wrong.

D ("…officials recently <u>licensed</u> original paintings to be made…") **Pattern:** Same ballpark. **Incorrect:** To "license" something means to allow someone to use that thing in return for a payment. For example, if an artist licenses a cartoon character to a car company, then the car company might have the right to use the character in a commercial. So the word "licensed" doesn't work here, for several reasons—for one thing, the text doesn't indicate that the artist paid the officials for the right to make the paintings.

Test 3, Question 41 — TYPE: GRAMMAR/STYLE/PUNCTUATION (often no prompt; choices have similar meanings)

- **Vertical Scan Results:** Some choices have the same words with different punctuation.
- **Vertical Scan Notes:** Should there be commas after "task," "artist," and/or "Zakirov?"
- **Key Features in Surrounding Text:** This sentence describes the person painting the cats, and we can see that the underlined phrase tells us that this person is a digital artist named Eldar Zakirov. Since all the answer choices involve comma placement, it looks like we'll need to rely on our awareness of the SAT's rules for things like comma sandwiches, especially as they apply to professions.

Concepts in the question:

- **Comma Sandwich:** Choice(s) would create phrases improperly "sandwiched" between similar types of punctuation. When removed from the sentence, a properly formed sandwich leaves behind a grammatically acceptable sentence. (See page 448.)
- **Commas:** Choices include one or more commas. On the Writing and Language section, commas can be used to separate things in a list of three or more, to form a comma sandwich, or to introduce an independent clause after a dependent clause. (See pages 448-450.)

ANSWER CHOICE ANALYSIS

A **Incorrect:** This choice would create a comma sandwich around the name of a profession that appears immediately before a person's name. We know the SAT doesn't allow us to use comma sandwiches in that scenario, so (A) must be wrong.

B **Incorrect:** This choice has the same fundamental problem as (A): it creates a comma sandwich around the name of a profession that appears immediately before a person's name, which the SAT doesn't allow.

C **Incorrect:** This choice avoids the comma sandwich around the phrase "digital artist," but it also includes a comma after "Zakirov" that isn't acceptable by itself on the SAT: if we pick (C), then that comma isn't part of an existing comma sandwich, list, quotation, or dependent clause. Since (C) doesn't follow the SAT's rules for comma usage, it must be wrong.

D ✓ **Correct:** This choice creates a comma sandwich around the phrase "digital artist Eldar Zakirov," which is appropriate because the phrase can be removed without causing any grammatical problems in the sentence. (D) also avoids creating a comma sandwich around the phrase "digital artist," which is important for the reasons we discussed in (A) and (B).

Answer choice patterns (see page 455): Wrong answers incorporate elements of the right answer.

Test 3, Question 42 — TYPE: READING COMPREHENSION (usually has a prompt; choices have different meanings)

- **RC Question sub-type:** Best Accomplishes X. (The prompt describes a goal of the author, and asks us which choice achieves that goal. The correct answer choice will plainly and directly demonstrate the task described in the prompt. See page 431.)

- Subjective phrases to be ignored: "most"

A ✓ **Pattern:** Correct. The question asks which choice "sets up the examples that follow." The following examples describe the cats with words like "aristocratic" and "stately," which match the word "noble" in this choice. The paragraph also uses the words "wise" and "thoughtful," and compares the eyes of one cat to "those of a trusted royal advisor;" these phrases demonstrate the idea of the cats being "worthy of respect," as this choice also requires. So we know (A) is correct.

B **Pattern:** Off by one or two words. **Incorrect:** This choice might be tempting to a lot of test-takers, but the word "unique" specifically means that the attributes of each cat are only possessed by that individual cat—in other words, if one cat has green eyes, for example, then the other cats don't also have that characteristic. That idea isn't present in the "examples that follow," so this choice can't be correct on the SAT.

C **Pattern:** Plausible, but not in the text. **Incorrect:** We might think that dressing a cat up in royal robes is "absurd" to us, but that idea isn't present in the "examples that follow." (C) doesn't demonstrate the idea from the prompt, so it's wrong.

D **Pattern:** Wrong part of the passage. **Incorrect:** The *previous* paragraph discusses how the cats hunt mice, but the prompt told us to find an answer choice that introduces ("sets up") ideas from "the examples that follow" the underlined phrase. The examples that follow the underlined phrase are descriptions of cat paintings; they don't discuss the idea of cats catching mice, so this choice is wrong.

Test 3, Question 43	TYPE: READING COMPREHENSION (usually has a prompt; choices have different meanings)

- **RC Question sub-type:** Including/excluding a phrase/sentence. (The question asks whether a sentence should be included in the passage. The correct choice will include a comment that plainly describes the role of the phrase or sentence in the passage. Sentences that should be included will follow broad College Board standards for ideal sentences and paragraphs—including consistency with any figures in the passage—while sentences that shouldn't be included will not follow those standards. See page 433.)

A **Pattern:** Largely irrelevant. **Incorrect:** The sentence in the prompt doesn't say anything about Peter the Great or cat paintings, so this choice doesn't describe the sentence accurately.

B **Pattern:** Confused concepts. **Incorrect:** This choice might seem tempting to some untrained test-takers because the passage discusses animals and Russian art, which are mentioned in this answer choice. But we can still see that the sentence in the prompt doesn't say anything about animals or Russian art, so this choice doesn't describe the sentence accurately.

C **Pattern:** Confused concepts. **Incorrect:** This choice might be tempting because it makes a true statement: the sentence in the prompt *does* fail to indicate "why the Winter Palace became an art museum." But as we see in the explanation for choice (D), the sentence in the question is irrelevant to the paragraph, and it would still be irrelevant even if the concern raised in this answer choice were addressed. Explaining why the palace became an art museum still wouldn't make this sentence relevant. Remember on this question type that when more than one answer choice describes the phrase or sentence accurately—like (C) and (D) in this question—the correct answer will be the one that excludes or includes a sentence for reasons that fit the College Board's broader rules about ideal sentences and paragraphs.

D ✓ **Pattern:** Correct. This passage does mention the State Hermitage Museum in Russia, but only as it relates to the connection between that museum and cats. The passage doesn't discuss how many buildings comprise the museum, or the history of those buildings, so the information in the prompt sentence is irrelevant on the SAT, just as this choice describes.

Test 3, Question 44	TYPE: READING COMPREHENSION (usually has a prompt; choices have different meanings)

- **RC Question sub-type:** Vocabulary In Context. (Choices include words or short phrases that have vaguely similar but not identical meanings. Most or all of the choices will seem vaguely appropriate, but only one choice will be correct when we think very carefully and specifically about the word means and how it can be used. See page 432.)

A ("...but these felines, by <u>mastering the art of killing mice and rats,</u> are benefactors of the museum...") **Pattern:** Same ballpark. **Incorrect:** This choice is incorrect because the fact that these "felines" were *mastering* the art of killing mice" (emphasis added) isn't specifically why they're important to the museum; in other words, from what the text says, they can be important to the museum and just be pretty good at killing mice and rats, without specifically dedicating themselves to becoming masters of it. Further, the rest of the sentence indicates that what appears in the underlined phrase makes the cats "benefactors of the museum." What benefits the museum isn't actually the killing of the mice and rats—it's the protection of the artwork, which this choice doesn't mention.

B ("...but these felines, by <u>acting as the lead predator in the museum's ecosystem,</u> are benefactors of the museum...") **Pattern:** Largely irrelevant. **Incorrect:** This choice is incorrect because the cats' possible status as "lead predator in the museum's ecosystem" wasn't specifically mentioned in the passage; even if it had been mentioned, their status isn't why they're important to the museum, according to the text. Whether the cat is the lead predator or some other animal is the lead predator isn't what helps the museum—what helps the museum is the fact that the cats kill mice and rats in the museum, and that doing so protects the artwork. This is the case regardless of who or what is the "lead predator." (B) also has the problem from (A) of not explaining that the protection of the artwork is what benefits the museum.

C   ("…but these felines, by <u>hunting down and killing all the mice and rats one by one,</u> are benefactors of the museum…") **Pattern:** Same ballpark. **Incorrect:** This choice has the same problem we saw in (A) and (B)—what makes the cats "benefactors of the museum" is the fact that they protect the artwork, which this choice doesn't mention.

D ✓   ("…but these felines, by <u>protecting the museum's priceless artworks from destructive rodents,</u> are benefactors of the museum…") **Correct:** The text says that "cats have guarded this famous museum, ridding it of mice, rats, and other rodents that could damage the art." This is directly related to the idea of "protecting the museum's priceless artworks from destructive rodents," just as this choice requires. This is the only choice that actually states why the cats are "benefactors of the museum," so we know it's right.

Note   Some test-takers might assume at first that this question is based on grammar, style, and/or punctuation, since it has no prompt. But when we scan through the answer choices, we see that they're all grammatically acceptable on the SAT, and that they discuss different concepts that are related to the concepts from the passage in different degrees. This means we'll need to use our reading-related testing skills to pick the answer choice that reflects concepts from the surrounding text appropriately.

TEST 4

Test 4, Question 1   TYPE: GRAMMAR/STYLE/PUNCTUATION (often no prompt; choices have similar meanings)

- **Vertical Scan Results:** Similar phrases with different short words and/or punctuation.
- **Vertical Scan Notes:** (B) is the only choice to include the pronoun "which."
- **Key Features in Surrounding Text:** An independent clause appears before the comma in the sentence: "Siqueiros was asked to celebrate tropical America in his work." So there can't be another independent clause after the comma, or the result will be a comma splice.

Concepts in the question:

- **Comma Splice:** Answer choices and/or surrounding text could be combined in ways that would use commas to separate two groups of words that could each be sentences on their own. A comma can't be used to join two groups of words that could each be sentences on their own. (See page 447.)
- **Dependent and Independent Clauses:** Answer choice(s) would incorrectly use a dependent or independent clause. An independent clause can stand alone as a sentence: it has a main subject/verb pair. A dependent clause is introduced by a conjunction or relative pronoun. (See page 445.)

ANSWER CHOICE ANALYSIS

A   **Incorrect:** This choice would make both sets of words on either side of the comma independent clauses, which would make this sentence a comma splice.

B ✓   **Correct:** The relative pronoun "which" makes the words after the comma a dependent clause, which avoids the comma splices that are created by the other answer choices.

C   **Incorrect:** This choice has the same problem as (A).

D   **Incorrect:** This choice has the same problem as (A).

Note   We don't need to know what "accordingly" means, or worry over whether it sounds strange, because every answer choice includes it.

Test 4, Question 2   TYPE: READING COMPREHENSION (usually has a prompt; choices have different meanings)

- **RC Question sub-type:** Transition phrase. (The choices include words or phrases showing a transition from the previous sentence, like "however," "instead of," "for example," etc. The transition phrase must reflect the relationship between the previous sentence and the sentence where the transition phrase appears. See page 431.)

ANSWER CHOICE ANALYSIS

A   **Pattern:** Direct contradiction. **Incorrect:** This choice would be appropriate if this sentence provided additional information that was similar to the information in the previous sentence, but that's not the case—the previous sentence describes Siqueiros painting during the day, and this sentence describes Siqueiros painting at night.

B ✓   **Pattern:** Correct. The previous sentence says Siqueiros painted "the mural's first two sections…during the day." But this sentence says he "painted the final section of the mural…at night." The word "however" appropriately reflects the contrast between the idea of painting during the day in the previous sentence, and the idea of painting at night in this sentence.

C   **Pattern:** Creates a grammatical issue. **Incorrect:** The word "although" can only be used to introduce a dependent clause, so this choice would make the entire sentence into a dependent clause, which is unacceptable on the SAT, because every acceptable sentence on the SAT must include an independent clause.

D   **Pattern:** Confused concepts. **Incorrect:** This choice would be appropriate if this sentence made a further statement that was a continuation of the ideas in the previous sentence, but that's not the case.

Test 4, Question 3   TYPE: GRAMMAR/STYLE/PUNCTUATION (often no prompt; choices have similar meanings)

- **Vertical Scan Results:** Some choices have the same words with different punctuation.
- **Vertical Scan Notes:** The choices let us follow the word "centerpiece" with a comma, semi-colon, dash, or no punctuation.
- **Key Features in Surrounding Text:** "The centerpiece" is a phrase that describes "the final section of the mural."

Concepts in the question:

- **Comma Sandwich:** Choice(s) would create phrases improperly "sandwiched" between similar types of punctuation. When removed from the sentence, a properly formed sandwich leaves behind a grammatically acceptable sentence. (See page 448.)
- **Semi-colons:** Choices include one or more semicolons. Semi-colons can be used to separate two sets of words that could each stand on their own as a full sentence. (See page 447.)

ANSWER CHOICE ANALYSIS

A   **Incorrect:** There should be a comma sandwich around "the centerpiece," but (A) omits the comma after "centerpiece."

B ✓   **Correct:** This choice completes the comma sandwich that equates "the final section" with "the centerpiece." We know this comma sandwich is appropriate because we can remove the sandwich without creating any grammatical issues or changing the meaning of the rest of the sentence.

C   **Incorrect:** There shouldn't be a semi-colon after "centerpiece" because the phrase "at night" isn't an independent clause (in other words, "at night" can't stand on its own as a complete sentence). Semicolons can only be used to join independent clauses on the SAT Writing and Language section.

D   **Incorrect:** A dash might have been appropriate if the entire phrase "the centerpiece" were sandwiched in dashes. But since the phrase "the centerpiece" is preceded by a comma, we need a comma to complete the punctuation sandwich correctly.

Test 4, Question 4   TYPE: READING COMPREHENSION (usually has a prompt; choices have different meanings)

- **RC Question sub-type:** Best Accomplishes X. (The prompt describes a goal of the author, and asks us which choice achieves that goal. The correct answer choice will plainly and directly demonstrate the task described in the prompt. See page 431.)
- **Subjective phrases to be ignored:** "best"

ANSWER CHOICE ANALYSIS

A ✓   **Pattern:** Correct. "Secrecy" restates the idea of "avoid[ing] scrutiny" mentioned in the last sentence of the previous paragraph, which establishes a connection between this sentence and that paragraph, as the prompt requires.

B   **Pattern:** Plausible, but not in the text. **Incorrect:** The idea of the sections being "on display" isn't connected to anything from the previous paragraph, so this choice can't be correct.

C   **Pattern:** Plausible, but not in the text. **Incorrect:** The idea of the community turning out "in large numbers" isn't connected to anything from the previous paragraph, so this choice can't be correct.

D   **Pattern:** Plausible, but not in the text. **Incorrect:** The idea of Siqueiros being "informed of people's reactions" isn't connected anything from the previous paragraph, so this choice can't be correct.

Note   Any of these choices could create a grammatically acceptable sentence; remember that the College Board wants you to "connect the sentence with the previous paragraph," which means finding a choice that restates an idea that appeared in the previous paragraph.

Test 4, Question 5   TYPE: READING COMPREHENSION (usually has a prompt; choices have different meanings)

- **RC Question sub-type:** Vocabulary In Context. (Choices include words or short phrases that have vaguely similar but not identical meanings. Most or all of the choices will seem vaguely appropriate, but only one choice will be correct when we think very carefully and specifically about the word means and how it can be used. See page 432.)

ANSWER CHOICE ANALYSIS

A   ("...when the mural was <u>confided</u>.") **Pattern:** Same ballpark. **Incorrect:** To "confide" means to tell someone a secret or an idea, but it doesn't make sense to say a physical object like a mural was "confided."

B   ("...when the mural was <u>promulgated</u>.") **Pattern:** Same ballpark. **Incorrect:** To "promulgate" means to make something known, or to spread an idea, but it doesn't make sense to say a physical object like a mural was "promulgated."

C   ("...when the mural was <u>imparted</u>.") **Pattern:** Same ballpark. **Incorrect:** In context, this choice means something similar to (A), and is wrong for the same reasons.

D ✓   ("...when the mural was <u>unveiled</u>.") **Correct:** the word "unveil" can describe the physical process of presenting a work of art to the public for the first time.

Note   (A) and (C) are essentially interchangeable in this context, and both are wrong. Some test-takers would be able to realize that the word "unveiled" refers to the idea of removing a covering from something, and would be able to tell that "unveil" must be correct even if they didn't know the meanings of the other words. If you didn't know any of the words for this question, remember not to worry too much about those words specifically, because you'll probably never see them on test day; instead, focus on improving your performance on other, more predictable question types.

Test 4, Question 6   **TYPE: GRAMMAR/STYLE/PUNCTUATION (often no prompt; choices have similar meanings)**

- **Vertical Scan Results:** Some choices have different forms of the same base word.
- **Vertical Scan Notes:** It looks like we need to pick the appropriate form of the verb "to include."
- **Key Features in Surrounding Text:** The verb in the underlined phrase is parallel to the verb "dominated" from earlier in the sentence.

Concepts in the question:

- **Parallelism:** Choices include options that would ignore a parallel structure in the surrounding text. The correct answer choice should match phrasing in the surrounding text when possible. (See page 458.)

ANSWER CHOICE ANALYSIS

A   **Incorrect:** This version of the verb doesn't follow the pattern established by "dominated" earlier in the sentence.

B ✓   **Correct:** This choice follows the pattern established by "dominated" earlier in the sentence: "The centerpiece...was dominated...and included..."

C   **Incorrect:** This choice has the same problem as (A).

D   **Incorrect:** This choice has the same problem as (A).

Answer choice patterns (see page 455): Wrong answers incorporate elements of the right answer.

Note   (D) incorporates a kind of past-tense form, just like the correct answer does, and forms a sentence that could be grammatically acceptable if it weren't on the SAT Writing and Language test...but (D) is still wrong because it doesn't follow the College Board's pattern of parallel structures being used when possible. Also note that some test-takers will misread this sentence and think it's possible to make it say, "images of native people being oppressed, including an eagle," but the actual text uses the word "and" instead of a comma, making (A) grammatically unacceptable. Issues like these are examples of why we need to make sure we read carefully at all times, and remember out training!

Test 4 Question 7   **TYPE: GRAMMAR/STYLE/PUNCTUATION (often no prompt; choices have similar meanings)**

- **Vertical Scan Results:** Some choices are short phrases with no obvious similarity.
- **Vertical Scan Notes:** We need to decide whether the underlined phrase should be "this," "it," "them," or "this movement."
- **Key Features in Surrounding Text:** There are a number of different nouns that the underlined phrase could refer to, such as "movement," "awareness," "identity," "Mexican Americans," and "artists." The correct answer must make it clear what the underlined phrase refers to.

Concepts in the question:

- **Pronoun Ambiguity:** Choices include pronouns that could refer to more than one phrase in the surrounding text. We can't use a pronoun on the SAT when it isn't clear what that pronoun refers to. (See page 441.)

ANSWER CHOICE ANALYSIS

A   **Incorrect:** It's not clear what the word "this" refers to in the sentence ("identity," "awareness," "movement,"...?).

B   **Incorrect:** This choice has the same problem as (A).

C   **Incorrect:** This choice has the same problem as (A).

D ✓   **Correct:** The phrase "this movement" makes it clear what the artists were associated with, avoiding the pronoun ambiguity that's forbidden by the College Board on the Writing and Language section.

Test 4 Question 8   **TYPE: GRAMMAR/STYLE/PUNCTUATION (often no prompt; choices have similar meanings)**

- **Vertical Scan Results:** Choices are long phrases/sentences.
- **Vertical Scan Notes:** The choices are long and will need to be analyzed a bit more closely to determine what's going on in this question. A few differences that might jump out include the different phrases with "result" and "explosion" in each choice, the placement of commas in (A) and (B), the lack of punctuation in (C), and the semi-colon in (D).
- **Key Features in Surrounding Text:** Both underlined sentences.

Concepts in the question:

- **Commas:** Choices include one or more commas. On the Writing and Language section, commas can be used to separate things in a list of three or more, to form a comma sandwich, or to introduce an independent clause after a dependent clause. (See pages 448-450.)
- **Dependent and Independent Clauses:** Answer choice(s) would incorrectly use a dependent or independent clause. An independent clause can stand alone as a sentence: it has a main subject/verb pair. A dependent clause is introduced by a conjunction or relative pronoun. (See page 445.)
- **Joining Two Sentences:** Each choice is a sentence that combines the two sentences in the underlined portion of the text. The right answer must follow all rules for other question types without changing the meaning of the original two sentences. (See page 453.)
- **Phrase Proximity:** Answer choice(s) would place descriptive phrases next to ideas they don't describe. Descriptive phrases that don't begin with a word ending in "-ing" describe the closest noun phrase. (See page 451.)
- **Pronoun Ambiguity:** Choices include pronouns that could refer to more than one phrase in the surrounding text. We can't use a pronoun on the SAT when it isn't clear what that pronoun refers to. (See page 441.)
- **Semi-colons:** Choices include one or more semicolons. Semi-colons can be used to separate two sets of words that could each stand on their own as a full sentence. (See page 447.)

ANSWER CHOICE ANALYSIS

A   Incorrect: Remember that the College Board wants us to group related ideas together as much as possible. This choice interrupts the phrase "an explosion of mural painting" with the phrase "the Chicano mural movement." Also, the phrase "an explosion, the Chicano mural movement," would mean "the Chicano mural movement" was a literal "explosion," which doesn't make any sense in context, as opposed to an "explosion of mural paintings."

B ✓   Correct: This choice avoids the problems from the other choices and doesn't create any new problems. The phrase "an explosion…in the 1970s" is a comma sandwich that describes the "movement" mentioned before the comma.

C   Incorrect: The word "resulting" should show that the explosion of painting happened because of the ideas mentioned at the end of the previous paragraph. That relationship is more clear if the phrase including some version of the word "result" appears at or near the beginning of this sentence, as it does in the other choices. Remember that the SAT wants us to group related ideas together.

D   Incorrect: In this choice, both uses of the pronoun "it" could refer grammatically to the singular noun "explosion" or to the singular noun "painting." The College Board doesn't allow us to use pronouns that could refer to more than one noun in the surrounding text, so (D) is unacceptable according to the College Board's unwritten rules.

Answer choice patterns (see page 455): Wrong answers incorporate elements of the right answer.

Test 4, Question 9   **TYPE: GRAMMAR/STYLE/PUNCTUATION (often no prompt; choices have similar meanings)**

- **Vertical Scan Results:** Similar phrases with different short words and/or punctuation; deleting a phrase is an option.
- **Vertical Scan Notes:** We need to find the acceptable way to convey the idea that that the murals were painted on infrastructure.
- **Key Features in Surrounding Text:** The underlined phrase is parallel to "in abandoned lots" and "on unused buildings," and therefore needs to match those phrases.

Concepts in the question:

- **Parallelism:** Choices include options that would ignore a parallel structure in the surrounding text. The correct answer choice should match phrasing in the surrounding text when possible. (See page 458.)

ANSWER CHOICE ANALYSIS

A   Incorrect: This choice includes the word "painted," which doesn't match the structure of the parallel phrases "in abandoned lots" and "on unused buildings" from earlier in the sentence, so it can't be correct, according to the rules and patterns of the SAT Writing and Language section.

B   Incorrect: This choice has the same problem as (A).

C ✓   Correct: This choice is just the preposition "on," which matches the structure of the parallel phrases "in abandoned lots" and "on unused buildings" earlier in the sentence.

D   Incorrect: This choice is grammatically unacceptable to the College Board. The phrase "or infrastructure" wouldn't fit with the rest of the sentence, because it lacks a preposition like "on." Note that prepositions are found in the parallel phrases "in abandoned lots" and "on unused buildings."

Test 4, Question 10   **TYPE: READING COMPREHENSION (usually has a prompt; choices have different meanings)**

- **RC Question sub-type:** Best Accomplishes X. (The prompt describes a goal of the author, and asks us which choice achieves that goal. The correct answer choice will plainly and directly demonstrate the task described in the prompt. See page 431.)

- Subjective phrases to be ignored: "most"

ANSWER CHOICE ANALYSIS

A ✓   **Pattern: Correct.** The first sentence in the paragraph says that other murals are being cleaned, restored, and repainted. Then the text describes Siqueiros's "América Tropical…after a lengthy and complex restoration process." If "América Tropical" has already been restored, then it demonstrates the idea of "leading the way" for other murals to be "clean[ed], restore[d], and repaint[ed]," because "América Tropical" went through a certain process before the other murals went through that process. Further, the phrase "once again" is appropriate with choice (A) because the rest of the passage describes "América Tropical" "leading the way" in another scenario: as the beginning of the Chicano mural movement. This choice does exactly what the prompt requires, so it's correct.

B   **Pattern: Confused concepts. Incorrect:** The text never indicates that the work has already been restored before the restoration described in the paragraph, so we can't pick a choice that says the piece is being restored "once again."

C   **Pattern: Confused concepts. Incorrect:** The text mentions that some murals "have not been well maintained," but it never says anything about any mural being "at risk of destruction," let alone América Tropical, so this choice can't be correct.

D   **Pattern: Direct contradiction. Incorrect:** The text doesn't say anything about the mural "awaiting" appreciation—in fact, the text calls the mural "a tourist attraction," demonstrating that it's already being appreciated. So (D) contradicts the text, rather than "set[ting] up" any information that follows, as the prompt requires.

Test 4, Question 11   TYPE: READING COMPREHENSION (usually has a prompt; choices have different meanings)

- **RC Question sub-type:** Including/excluding a phrase/sentence. (The question asks whether a sentence should be included in the passage. The correct choice will include a comment that plainly describes the role of the phrase or sentence in the passage. Sentences that should be included will follow broad College Board standards for ideal sentences and paragraphs—including consistency with any figures in the passage—while sentences that shouldn't be included will not follow those standards. See page 433.)

ANSWER CHOICE ANALYSIS

A   **Pattern: Largely irrelevant. Incorrect:** The sentence doesn't provide "historical context," as (A) would require. Historical context would mean information about what was going on in the world in the time period discussed in the passage outside of the topic that the passage focuses on, or what has happened in the world since then, or something along those lines.

B   **Pattern: Largely irrelevant. Incorrect:** As we'll see in the discussion for (C), the information in this sentence isn't "useful" because it just repeats information from earlier in the passage for no reason.

C ✓   **Pattern: Correct.** As this choice describes, the sentence in question just repeats information from a different paragraph. This is the only choice that is demonstrated by that sentence, so it's right.

D   **Pattern: Direct contradiction. Incorrect:** The claim in the sentence in the prompt is directly supported by other parts of the passage—the second paragraph tells us that Siqueiros's mural "did not please" the people who commissioned it, and this paragraph describes the mural today as a "tourist attraction" and an "inspiration." So we can see this choice doesn't accurately describe the sentence, which means it's wrong.

Test 4, Question 12   TYPE: GRAMMAR/STYLE/PUNCTUATION (often no prompt; choices have similar meanings)

- **Vertical Scan Results:** Similar phrases with different short words and/or punctuation; deleting a phrase is an option.
- **Vertical Scan Notes:** We need to pick the right version of the phrase with the verb "to purchase," or delete that phrase.
- **Key Features in Surrounding Text:** The underlined phrase is in the middle of the comparison between "organically grown crops" and "their conventionally grown counterparts."

Concepts in the question:

- **Parallelism:** Choices include options that would ignore a parallel structure in the surrounding text. The correct answer choice should match phrasing in the surrounding text when possible. (See page 458.)

ANSWER CHOICE ANALYSIS

A   **Incorrect:** When this phrase appears immediately after "than," it causes the comparison in the sentence to be between "crops" and "people," instead of between "crops" and "counterparts."

B   **Incorrect:** When this phrase appears immediately after "than," it causes the comparison in the sentence to be between "crops" and "purchase," instead of between "crops" and "counterparts."

C   **Incorrect:** When this phrase appears immediately after "than," it causes the comparison in the sentence to be between "crops" and "purchasing," instead of between "crops" and "counterparts."

D ✓   **Correct:** When this phrase is removed, it allows the phrase "their conventionally grown counterparts" to appear immediately after "than," which makes it clear that the comparison is between "organically grown crops" and "their conventionally grown counterparts."

Test 4, Question 13   TYPE: GRAMMAR/STYLE/PUNCTUATION (often no prompt; choices have similar meanings)

- **Vertical Scan Results:** Similar phrases with different short words and/or punctuation.
- **Vertical Scan Notes:** We need to decide whether the underlined phrase should include "these consumers," and whether the verb form should be "spending," "spend," "having spent," or "to spend."
- **Key Features in Surrounding Text:** In its current state, the sentence doesn't contain an independent clause, so we know we need to find an answer choice that fixes this problem.

Concepts in the question:

- **Dependent and Independent Clauses:** Answer choice(s) would incorrectly use a dependent or independent clause. An independent clause can stand alone as a sentence: it has a main subject/verb pair. A dependent clause is introduced by a conjunction or relative pronoun. (See page 445.)

ANSWER CHOICE ANALYSIS

A   **Incorrect:** This choice doesn't create a complete sentence with a subject and a main verb, so it's grammatically unacceptable to the College Board.

B ✓ **Correct:** This choice assigns the subject "these consumers" to the verb "spend," creating a complete sentence—that is, a sentence with an independent clause.

C   **Incorrect:** This choice has the same problem as (A).

D   **Incorrect:** This choice has the same problem as (A).

Test 4, Question 14   TYPE: GRAMMAR/STYLE/PUNCTUATION (often no prompt; choices have similar meanings)

- **Vertical Scan Results:** Choices are long phrases/sentences.
- **Vertical Scan Notes:** Every choice refers to the idea of growing food conventionally, but the choices use different wording and vary considerably in length.
- **Key Features in Surrounding Text:** The underlined phrase.

Concepts in the question:

- **Redundancy:** Answer choices and/or surrounding text could combine to repeat the same concept unnecessarily. We should avoid words or phrases that directly repeat ideas in the immediate context. (See page 452.)
- **Shorter is Better:** Choices include words or phrases that can be removed without impacting the meaning of the sentence or creating grammatical problems. Remember to avoid redundancy, and that the shortest grammatically acceptable choice (according to the College Board) is correct. (See page 454.)

ANSWER CHOICE ANALYSIS

A   **Incorrect:** (A) is grammatically acceptable, but (D) is shorter and also grammatically acceptable, so (A) can't be right.

B   **Incorrect:** This choice is redundant because the previous sentence already specifies that growing food conventionally means using pesticides and synthetic fertilizers.

C   **Incorrect:** This choice is redundant because the previous sentence already specifies that growing food conventionally is different from growing food organically.

D ✓ **Correct:** (D) is the shortest choice and it's grammatically acceptable, so it's right. It also avoids the redundancy of (B) and (C).

Note   The sentence doesn't need to specify that "conventionally grown" refers to the idea of not using pesticides and fertilizers, or that it's different from "organically grown," because those ideas are mentioned in other sentences in the paragraph.

Test 4, Question 15   TYPE: READING COMPREHENSION (usually has a prompt; choices have different meanings)

- **RC Question sub-type:** Transition phrase. (The choices include words or phrases showing a transition from the previous sentence, like "however," "instead of," "for example," etc. The transition phrase must reflect the relationship between the previous sentence and the sentence where the transition phrase appears. See page 431.)

ANSWER CHOICE ANALYSIS

A   **Pattern:** Confused concepts. **Incorrect:** This choice would be appropriate if this sentence provided some conclusion based on the information in the previous sentence, but that's not the case. In fact, this sentence contradicts the idea that people should spend money on organic food as described in the previous sentence.

B   **Pattern:** Confused concepts. **Incorrect:** This choice would be appropriate if this sentence made a further statement that was a continuation of the ideas in the previous sentence, but that's not the case.

C ✓   Pattern: Correct. The previous sentence tells us that some people spend more money to eat organic food than they would spend on conventionally grown food, and that they do this "in the name of health." But then this sentence says the evidence indicates there aren't "significant benefits" to choosing organic food. The word "however" appropriately reflects the idea that what's discussed in this sentence isn't what one would expect, given the information in the previous sentence.

D   Pattern: Confused concepts. **Incorrect:** This choice would be appropriate if this sentence expressed an idea that chronologically followed the previous idea, but that's not the case.

Test 4, Question 16   TYPE: READING COMPREHENSION (usually has a prompt; choices have different meanings)

- **RC Question sub-type:** Vocabulary In Context. (Choices include words or short phrases that have vaguely similar but not identical meanings. Most or all of the choices will seem vaguely appropriate, but only one choice will be correct when we think very carefully and specifically about the word means and how it can be used. See page 432.)

ANSWER CHOICE ANALYSIS

A   ("…advocates of organic food <u>preserve</u> that organic produce is healthier…") **Pattern:** Same ballpark. **Incorrect:** To "preserve" means to "keep" or "protect." It makes no sense to say that people "preserve that" something is true, so (A) must be wrong. It's probably included here because some untrained test-takers will accidentally associate the word "preserve" with the idea of "preservatives," which is vaguely relevant to the concepts in the rest of the passage, or to the type of food known as "preserves." It also looks like the word "persevere," which some test-takers might think is appropriate in context. Still, as trained test-takers, we can see that the word "preserve" is inappropriate the way it's being used in the passage.

B   ("…advocates of organic food <u>carry on</u> that organic produce is healthier…") **Pattern:** Largely irrelevant. **Incorrect:** To "carry on" means to "continue in spite of adversity" or "to keep going." It makes no sense to say that people "carry on that" something is true.

C ✓   ("…advocates of organic food <u>maintain</u> that organic produce is healthier…") **Correct:** To "maintain" means to "state a belief" or "to continue to believe something." It makes sense to say that people "maintain that" an "assertion" is true, as we see in this sentence.

D   ("…advocates of organic food <u>sustain</u> that organic produce is healthier…") **Pattern:** Same ballpark. **Incorrect:** To "sustain" means to "provide nourishment or support," or "to help survive." It makes no sense to say that people "sustain that" something is true. Note that this choice has a syllable in common with the correct answer ("-tain"), which might reflect an effort to confuse an untrained test-taker.

Test 4, Question 17   TYPE: READING COMPREHENSION (usually has a prompt; choices have different meanings)

- **RC Question sub-type:** Transition phrase. (The choices include words or phrases showing a transition from the previous sentence, like "however," "instead of," "for example," etc. The transition phrase must reflect the relationship between the previous sentence and the sentence where the transition phrase appears. See page 431.)

ANSWER CHOICE ANALYSIS

A ✓   Pattern: Correct. The phrase "for instance" appropriately reflects the idea that the previous sentence mentions research, and this sentence provides an example of that research.

B   Pattern: Direct contradiction. **Incorrect:** This choice would be appropriate if what was discussed in this sentence was surprising based on the previous sentence, but that's not the case.

C   Pattern: Confused concepts. **Incorrect:** This choice would be appropriate if the current sentence provided additional information that was of the same type as information from the previous sentence, such as adding items to a list from the previous sentence—but that's not the case.

D   Pattern: Confused concepts. **Incorrect:** This choice would be appropriate if the current sentence expressed an idea reflecting similar relationships to those in the previous sentence, but that's not the case.

Test 4, Question 18   TYPE: READING COMPREHENSION (usually has a prompt; choices have different meanings)

- **RC Question sub-type:** Including/excluding a phrase/sentence. (The question asks whether a sentence should be included in the passage. The correct choice will include a comment that plainly describes the role of the phrase or sentence in the passage. Sentences that should be included will follow broad College Board standards for ideal sentences and paragraphs—including consistency with any figures in the passage—while sentences that shouldn't be included will not follow those standards. See page 433.)

ANSWER CHOICE ANALYSIS

A   Pattern: Largely irrelevant. **Incorrect:** This sentence doesn't add a "relevant research finding." The number of markets that carry organic foods isn't discussed or expanded on elsewhere, so we can't call this sentence "relevant."

B   Pattern: Largely irrelevant. **Incorrect:** (B) might be tempting because it mentions an idea discussed in the passage—but the sentence in the prompt doesn't say anything about comparing the healthiness of organic and conventional foods.

C ✓   **Pattern: Correct.** This answer choice accurately says that the prompt sentence isn't relevant to the scientific evidence discussed in this paragraph. This is a true statement because the number of markets that sell organic foods has no bearing on whether organic foods are more or less nutritious than conventionally grown foods.

D   **Pattern: Largely irrelevant. Incorrect:** The prompt sentence doesn't introduce any new terms, so this choice is wrong because it doesn't describe how the prompt sentence relates to the paragraph.

> **Note**   We always need to remember to read carefully! The sentence in the prompt may be about the USDA, but that doesn't automatically make the sentence relevant to a discussion of whether organic food is healthier than conventional food.

Test 4, Question 19   TYPE: GRAMMAR/STYLE/PUNCTUATION (often no prompt; choices have similar meanings)

- **Vertical Scan Results:** Some choices have different forms of the same base word.
- **Vertical Scan Notes:** We need to pick the appropriate form of the verb "to have."
- **Key Features in Surrounding Text:** After we recognize the intervening phrase "of residue falling within such limits," we can see that the subject of the verb "to have" is the plural noun "amounts."

Concepts in the question:

- **Intervening Phrase:** A phrase appears between two words that need to agree with each other. Identify which words need to agree with each other, and ignore extra phrases that appear between them. (See page 456.)
- **Singular versus Plural:** Choices include singular and plural versions of the same base words that don't agree with other words in the surrounding text. Singular nouns must go with singular verb forms and singular pronouns. Plural nouns must go with plural verbs and pronouns. Think carefully about which words should match or agree with each other! (See page 443.)
- **Verb Tense/Conjugation:** Choices include different forms of the same verb. Look at the surrounding text to find each verb's subject. Also, look for other verbs that could indicate the proper tense for the verbs in the answer choices. (See page 437.)

ANSWER CHOICE ANALYSIS

A ✓   **Correct:** This is a plural form of the verb "to have." It's the only choice that agrees with the plural subject "amounts," so it's right.

B   **Incorrect:** This is a singular form of the verb "to have," so it doesn't agree grammatically with the subject "amounts."

C   **Incorrect:** This choice has the same problem as (B).

D   **Incorrect:** This choice has the same problem as (B).

> **Note**   Some untrained test-takers will incorrectly assume that the verb "have" needs to agree with the noun "residue," which could cause those test-takers to have a difficult time choosing from among the tenses in (B), (C), and (D). But we never needed to consider the correct tense of the verb, because the correct answer must include a plural verb, and only (A) is plural.

Test 4, Question 20   TYPE: READING COMPREHENSION (usually has a prompt; choices have different meanings)

- **RC Question sub-type:** Best Accomplishes X. (The prompt describes a goal of the author, and asks us which choice achieves that goal. The correct answer choice will plainly and directly demonstrate the task described in the prompt. See page 431.)
- **Subjective phrases to be ignored:** "most"

ANSWER CHOICE ANALYSIS

A   **Pattern: Largely irrelevant. Incorrect:** This sentence provides information about what it takes "to be labeled organic," but that doesn't reinforce any "claim about the safety of *nonorganic* food," which is what the prompt requires.

B   **Pattern: Largely irrelevant. Incorrect:** The issue with this choice is similar to what we saw in (A): information about what's absent from organic food doesn't tell us anything about the safety of *nonorganic* food, as the prompt requires.

C ✓   **Pattern: Correct.** The first two sentences of this paragraph specifically discuss the connection between food safety and the presence of pesticides, and this choice discusses the issue of reducing pesticides on produce—thereby making the produce safer. Since this choice contains a statement related to the "safety of nonorganic food" as required by the prompt, we know that (C) will be correct according to the SAT's rules and patterns.

D   **Pattern: Largely irrelevant. Incorrect:** Information about how much of the world's pesticides are used in the United States doesn't tell us anything about the safety of nonorganic food, which is what the prompt requires.

Test 4, Question 21   TYPE: GRAMMAR/STYLE/PUNCTUATION (often no prompt; choices have similar meanings)

- **Vertical Scan Results:** Choices include most or all possible combinations of two options.
- **Vertical Scan Notes:** We need to choose between "there" and "their," and between "is" and "are."

- **Key Features in Surrounding Text:** The plural noun "reasons" is the thing that the underlined phrase is introducing, so we need to use the plural verb form "are" to describe those reasons. Also, the context makes it clear that we need to use the preposition "there," not the possessive pronoun "their."

Concepts in the question:

- **Confused Homophones:** Choices include different homophone pairs (such as "their" and "they're" or "too" and "to"). Read carefully—also, remember the correct formation of possessive pronouns, and remember to read contractions as their uncontracted forms (e.g. "it's" = "it is"). (See page 452.)
- **Singular versus Plural:** Choices include singular and plural versions of the same base words that don't agree with other words in the surrounding text. Singular nouns must go with singular verb forms and singular pronouns. Plural nouns must go with plural verbs and pronouns. Think carefully about which words should match or agree with each other! (See page 443.)

ANSWER CHOICE ANALYSIS

A   **Incorrect:** "Their" is a possessive pronoun, but nothing in the sentence involves possession.

B ✓   **Correct:** As we discussed above, the context tells us we need the preposition "there" and the plural verb form "are" to introduce the plural noun "reasons."

C   **Incorrect:** The verb form "is" is singular, but the verb needs to agree with the plural noun "reasons."

D   **Incorrect:** "Their" is a possessive pronoun, but nothing in the sentence involves possession; the verb form "is" is singular, but the verb needs to agree with the plural noun "reasons."

Test 4, Question 22   TYPE: GRAMMAR/STYLE/PUNCTUATION (often no prompt; choices have similar meanings)

- **Vertical Scan Results:** Some choices have the same words with different punctuation.
- **Vertical Scan Notes:** Should a comma appear after "food?" Should a colon, comma, or no punctuation appear after "as?"
- **Key Features in Surrounding Text:** The part of the sentence after the word "as" is a list of examples of what is discussed in the first part of the sentence.

Concepts in the question:

- **Colons:** Choices include one or more colons. A colon can be placed after a set of words that could be a sentence on their own, and before a demonstration or example of the idea before the colon. (See page 447.)
- **Commas:** Choices include one or more commas. On the Writing and Language section, commas can be used to separate things in a list of three or more, to form a comma sandwich, or to introduce an independent clause after a dependent clause. (See pages 448-450.)
- **Dependent and Independent Clauses:** Answer choice(s) would incorrectly use a dependent or independent clause. An independent clause can stand alone as a sentence: it has a main subject/verb pair. A dependent clause is introduced by a conjunction or relative pronoun. (See page 445.)

ANSWER CHOICE ANALYSIS

A   **Incorrect:** The phrase "such as" shouldn't be followed by any punctuation when it's used to introduce an example of something. (See "No commas after conjunction expressions (unless a comma sandwich is involved)" on page 450 for more.)

B   **Incorrect:** The phrase "such as" shouldn't be followed by any punctuation when it's used to introduce an example of something. Further, a colon can only appear after a set of words that could stand on their own as a sentence.

C   **Incorrect:** This choice has the same problem as (A).

D ✓   **Correct:** The phrase "such as" can be preceded by a comma when the phrase is used to introduce an example, but it can't be sandwiched between commas, because a comma sandwich would indicate that the phrase "such as" could be removed and leave behind a grammatically acceptable sentence.

Test 4, Question 23   TYPE: READING COMPREHENSION (usually has a prompt; choices have different meanings)

- **RC Question sub-type:** Best Accomplishes X. (The prompt describes a goal of the author, and asks us which choice achieves that goal. The correct answer choice will plainly and directly demonstrate the task described in the prompt. See page 431.)
- **Subjective phrases to be ignored:** "best"

ANSWER CHOICE ANALYSIS

A   **Pattern:** Largely irrelevant. **Incorrect:** The idea of something changing someone's life doesn't express "genuine interest" as required by the prompt, so this choice can't be correct.

B   **Pattern:** Largely irrelevant. **Incorrect:** The prompt asks us to choose the word that expresses "genuine interest," but the word "galvanizing" has to do with motivating someone to take action—not expressing interest—so it isn't appropriate here according to the SAT's rules.

C ✓   **Pattern:** Correct. Describing something as "intriguing" does "convey an attitude of genuine interest," as the prompt requires, since "intriguing" means "interesting." So we know this choice is correct.

D   **Pattern:** Confused concepts. **Incorrect:** The word "weird" means "strange" or "unusual," which doesn't demonstrate the idea of "genuine interest" as the prompt requires, much as we saw with (A) and (B).

Note   Many test-takers may not know the word "galvanize," but it should probably still be possible to answer this question correctly by realizing that the word "intriguing" demonstrates the idea of "genuine interest" that the prompt asks for. If we don't know the word "intriguing," the best course of action would probably be to guess on this question as quickly as possible and move on. The bottom line here is that the prompt asks for a word that conveys interest, and only "intriguing" means "interesting." When we look at the question in this way, we don't need to worry about what the SAT considers to be "mockery," even though many untrained test-takers would waste their time trying to figure that out.

▌Test 4, Question 24   **TYPE: GRAMMAR/STYLE/PUNCTUATION (often no prompt; choices have similar meanings)**

- **Vertical Scan Results:** Similar phrases with different short words and/or punctuation.
- **Vertical Scan Notes:** We need to decide whether the phrase should begin with "it also," "and also," "but also," or none of those, and whether the verb form should be "illustrates" or "illustrating."
- **Key Features in Surrounding Text:** The phrase "not only" appears earlier in the same sentence, which means the sentence needs to include another phrase that begins with the word "but" in order to create a valid correlative conjunction.

Concepts in the question:

- **Correlative Conjunction:** Choices typically include variations on phrases that occur in common correlative conjunctions, such as "either…or," "not only…but also," or "both…and." Pick the choice that creates a standard correlative conjunction. (See page 444.)

ANSWER CHOICE ANALYSIS

A   **Incorrect:** This choice would cause the sentence not to include the word "but," which means the sentence wouldn't complete the correlative conjunction that began with "not only."

B   **Incorrect:** This choice has the same problem as (A).

C ✓   **Correct:** This is the only choice that correctly completes the correlative conjunction "<u>not only</u> yielded…<u>but also</u> illustrates."

D   **Incorrect:** This choice has the same problem as (A).

▌Test 4, Question 25   **TYPE: READING COMPREHENSION (usually has a prompt; choices have different meanings)**

- **RC Question sub-type:** Best Accomplishes X. (The prompt describes a goal of the author, and asks us which choice achieves that goal. The correct answer choice will plainly and directly demonstrate the task described in the prompt. See page 431.)
- **Subjective phrases to be ignored:** "most"

ANSWER CHOICE ANALYSIS

A   **Pattern:** Direct contradiction. **Incorrect:** The prompt asks for an answer that does two things: "sets up the contrast in the sentence" and "is consistent with the information in the rest of the passage." (A) isn't consistent with the rest of the passage. The third paragraph tells us "the veritable army of trained volunteers…can *sometimes* be replaced" (emphasis added). In other words, that "army" of volunteers can't *always* be replaced, so some people must still be doing "traditional, human-intensive data collection" as the paragraph describes, and we can't say that kind of collection "has all but disappeared."

B ✓   **Pattern:** Correct. This choice accomplishes both tasks mentioned in our discussion of choice (A): it says that traditional data collection "still has an important place," which contrasts with the end of the sentence that describes how "social media has opened new avenues for investigation." It's also consistent with the rest of the passage when it says that "human-intensive data collection" is still important. (As we saw in our discussion of (A), the third paragraph indicates that humans are still necessary to collect data.)

C   **Pattern:** Direct contradiction. **Incorrect:** This is inconsistent with the passage because the third paragraph discusses the use of social media, as opposed to "human-intensive data collection."

D   **Pattern:** Largely irrelevant. **Incorrect:** The text never mentions whether any results are questionable, so this choice can't be "consistent with the information in the rest of the passage" as the prompt would require.

▌Test 4, Question 26   **TYPE: GRAMMAR/STYLE/PUNCTUATION (often no prompt; choices have similar meanings)**

- **Vertical Scan Results:** Similar phrases with different short words and/or punctuation.
- **Vertical Scan Notes:** We need to decide whether a comma or period should appear after "scholars," and which phrase should appear at the end of the underlined text.
- **Key Features in Surrounding Text:** One sentence ends by mentioning "scholars," and the next sentence starts off by describing something that scholars do.

Concepts in the question:

- **Commas:** Choices include one or more commas. On the Writing and Language section, commas can be used to separate things in a list of three or more, to form a comma sandwich, or to introduce an independent clause after a dependent clause. (See pages 448-450.)
- **Redundancy:** Answer choices and/or surrounding text could combine to repeat the same concept unnecessarily. We should avoid words or phrases that directly repeat ideas in the immediate context. (See page 452.)
- **Who versus Whom:** At least one answer choice involves "who" or "whom." "Who" is a subject pronoun (that does an action), and "whom" is an object pronoun (that receives an action). In other words, we can use "who" where "he" would be appropriate, and "whom" where "him" would be appropriate. (See page 439.)

ANSWER CHOICE ANALYSIS

A   **Incorrect:** This option unnecessarily repeats the word "scholars;" as trained test-takers, we know that the College Board won't reward an answer choice on the Writing and Language section if it includes redundant phrasing.

B   **Incorrect:** This choice has the same problem as (A).

C   **Incorrect:** The word "but" indicates some kind of contradiction between the ideas that come before and after it, but there isn't any such contradiction in the text.

D ✓   **Correct:** This is the shortest grammatically acceptable option. It also avoids the possible redundancy of using the word "scholars" twice.

Answer choice patterns (see page 454455): Shortest grammatically acceptable choice is correct.

Test 4, Question 27   TYPE: READING COMPREHENSION (usually has a prompt; choices have different meanings)

- **RC Question sub-type:** Sentence or paragraph placement. (The prompt asks us where a sentence should go in a paragraph, or where a paragraph should go in the passage. The correct order will reflect a logical chronology, and/or will allow for pronouns in the sentences to refer to nouns in a logical way, and/or will place related concepts near one another. See page 432.)
- **Subjective phrases to be ignored:** "most"

ANSWER CHOICE ANALYSIS

A   **Pattern:** Causes text to refer to an idea that hasn't been mentioned yet. **Incorrect:** To satisfy the SAT's rules about sentence placement, the sentence we're adding needs to appear as close as possible to sentences that mention data gathering and the amount of time something takes, since those are the ideas in the sentence we're adding. But sentence 2 doesn't say anything about data gathering specifically, as opposed to any other phase of the "arduous work" that was needed to produce the dictionary, and sentence 3 doesn't say anything about data gathering being quicker than any other part of the process.

B   **Pattern:** Causes text to refer to an idea that hasn't been mentioned yet. **Incorrect:** This choice interrupts the initial description of the project with information about the finished project. In other words, the previous sentence and the following sentences are still describing what the project is, and this sentence tells us which part of the project ended up being quicker. Also, this placement would make it unclear what "their" from sentence 4 refers to.

C ✓   **Pattern:** Correct. Sentences 3 and 4 describe how the "data gathering" was done, how long it took, and what it was. Sentence 5 describes how "the work" that remained was expected to be done in 1976, but actually wasn't completed before the founder's death. (We know from sentence 2 that the work wasn't completed until 2012.) According to the SAT's rules for ordering sentences, it makes sense to describe "data gathering" as "the quick part" *after* explaining what the data gathering was and how long it took, but *before* explaining that the other part of the work took much longer than expected.

D   **Pattern:** Causes text to introduce an idea that has already been discussed. **Incorrect:** As we said for (C), this sentence needs to come *before* sentence 5, which talks about the part of the work that took more time than the data-gathering.

Test 4, Question 28   TYPE: GRAMMAR/STYLE/PUNCTUATION (often no prompt; choices have similar meanings)

- **Vertical Scan Results:** Some choices have different forms of the same base word.
- **Vertical Scan Notes:** We need to pick the right form of the verb "to require."
- **Key Features in Surrounding Text:** Once we recognize the intervening phrase "into regional English varieties," we can see that the subject of the underlined verb phrase is "research." So we need a singular verb form that agrees with the singular noun "research."

Concepts in the question:

- **Intervening Phrase:** A phrase appears between two words that need to agree with each other. Identify which words need to agree with each other, and ignore extra phrases that appear between them. (See page 456.)
- **Singular versus Plural:** Choices include singular and plural versions of the same base words that don't agree with other words in the surrounding text. Singular nouns must go with singular verb forms and singular pronouns. Plural nouns must go with plural verbs and pronouns. Think carefully about which words should match or agree with each other! (See page 443.)
- **Verb Tense/Conjugation:** Choices include different forms of the same verb. Look at the surrounding text to find each verb's subject. Also, look for other verbs that could indicate the proper tense for the verbs in the answer choices. (See page 437.)

A ✓   Correct: As we discussed above, the subject "research" requires a singular verb form, and this is the only choice with a singular verb form.

B   Incorrect: As we discussed above, the subject "research" requires a singular verb form, but "are requiring" is a plural form.

C   Incorrect: "have required" is a plural verb form, but the subject of the verb is the singular noun "research."

D   Incorrect: "require" is a plural verb form, but the subject of the verb is the singular noun "research."

Note   Many untrained test-takers will incorrectly assume that the correct answer has to agree with the plural noun "varieties," which will cause them to waste a lot of time trying to figure out whether (B), (C), or (D) uses the correct tense. There's no way to tell which tense should be correct, but we can notice that the correct answer must use a singular verb to agree with the word "research," and (A) is the only choice with a singular verb, so it must be correct, no matter what tense it is.

❙ Test 4, Question 29   TYPE: GRAMMAR/STYLE/PUNCTUATION (often no prompt; choices have similar meanings)

- **Vertical Scan Results:** Some choices have the same words with different punctuation.
- **Vertical Scan Notes:** Should there be a dash after "replaced?" Should there be a comma, semi-colon, colon, or no punctuation after "army?"
- **Key Features in Surrounding Text:** The words in the sentence up to and including the word "army" can stand on their own as a complete sentence, and everything that appears after the word "army" is an explanation of what "another army" is; that explanation can't stand on its own as a complete sentence.

Concepts in the question:

- **Colons:** Choices include one or more colons. A colon can be placed after a set of words that could be a sentence on their own, and before a demonstration or example of the idea before the colon. (See page 447.)
- **Commas:** Choices include one or more commas. On the Writing and Language section, commas can be used to separate things in a list of three or more, to form a comma sandwich, or to introduce an independent clause after a dependent clause. (See pages 448-450.)
- **Dependent and Independent Clauses:** Answer choice(s) would incorrectly use a dependent or independent clause. An independent clause can stand alone as a sentence: it has a main subject/verb pair. A dependent clause is introduced by a conjunction or relative pronoun. (See page 445.)
- **Punctuation Sandwich:** Choice(s) would create phrases improperly "sandwiched" between similar types of punctuation. When removed from the sentence, a properly formed sandwich leaves behind a grammatically acceptable sentence. (See page 450.)
- **Semi-colons:** Choices include one or more semicolons. Semi-colons can be used to separate two sets of words that could each stand on their own as a full sentence. (See page 447.)

A   Incorrect: This option doesn't include any punctuation to relate the phrase "another army" to the following explanation of what "another army" is, so it's wrong.

B   Incorrect: It's true that (B) would create a comma sandwich making all the words after the comma into an appositive describing the word "army," which would be grammatically acceptable on the SAT if it were the only change being made to the original sentence. But this sentence also introduces a dash after the word "replace," and there's no reason for that dash. As trained test-takers, we know that a dash can only be used on the Writing and Language section when it's part of a punctuation sandwich, or when it could be replaced by a colon, as we discussed on page 450.

C   Incorrect: There shouldn't be a semi-colon after "army" because the part of the sentence after the semi-colon wouldn't form an independent clause; in other words, it couldn't stand on its own as a complete sentence. Remember that the SAT Writing and Language section only allows us to use semicolons to join two complete sentences.

D ✓   Correct: A colon is appropriate here because everything in the sentence before the colon can stand on its own as a complete sentence, and what comes after the colon explains what is meant by "another army." This is consistent with the SAT's rules for colon usage, as discussed on page 447.

❙ Test 4, Question 30   TYPE: GRAMMAR/STYLE/PUNCTUATION (often no prompt; choices have similar meanings)

- **Vertical Scan Results:** Some choices include homophone pairs. Similar phrases with different short words and/or punctuation.
- **Vertical Scan Notes:** Is "sight," "cite," or "site" acceptable? Is "of" or "for" acceptable?
- **Key Features in Surrounding Text:** The term "social media" and the phrase "users are posting" make it clear that what's being discussed is a website, commonly called a "site."

Concepts in the question:

- **Confused Homophones:** Choices include different homophone pairs (such as "their" and "they're" or "too" and "to"). Read carefully—also, remember the correct formation of possessive pronouns, and remember to read contractions as their uncontracted forms (e.g. "it's" = "it is"). (See page 452.)
- **Prepositional Idioms:** Choices typically include prepositional phrases with no other recognizable grammatical similarities. On this type of question, if you can't determine which answer choice contains an acceptable prepositional idiom in American English, then you should guess at an answer and invest your time in questions that don't involve prepositional idioms. (See page 443.)

ANSWER CHOICE ANALYSIS

A   **Incorrect:** As we discussed above, the context makes it clear the first word in the underlined phrase should be "site," not "cite." (See the note below!)

B ✓   **Correct:** As we discussed above, the context makes it clear that the first word in the underlined phrase should be "site." Also, the prepositional idiom phrase "in search of" is acceptable in American English. (See the note below!)

C   **Incorrect:** As we discussed above, the context makes it clear that the first word in the underlined phrase should be "site," not "sight." Also, it's unacceptable in American English to say that someone is "in search for" something. (See the explanation for (B), and the note below!)

D   **Incorrect:** As we discussed above, the context makes it clear that the first word in the underlined phrase should be "site," not "cite." This choice also uses the preposition "for" inappropriately, just like (C) does. (See the explanation for (B), and the note below!)

Note   The phrase "in search of" is an example of the kind of prepositional idiom we discussed in the Grammar/Style/Punctuation Toolbox. But notice that we didn't actually need to know the correct form of that idiom to answer this question! As it turned out, only one choice correctly used the word "site" instead of "cite" or "sight," so we know (B) is correct even if we don't know which preposition should be used in this context. Keep this kind of thing in mind on test day, and don't waste energy on aspects of a question that may not be relevant!

Test 4, Question 31   **TYPE: READING COMPREHENSION (usually has a prompt; choices have different meanings)**

- **RC Question sub-type:** Figure. (The prompt requires us to read a figure in order to find an answer that reflects the data in the figure. The correct answer will be directly supported by the information in the figure. Remember to read carefully and check for details such as column headings, axis-labels, legends, and so on. See pages 44-51.)
- **Subjective phrases to be ignored:** "as closely as possible"

ANSWER CHOICE ANALYSIS

A   **Pattern:** Confused concepts. **Incorrect:** The text tells us that the first term for a soft drink "is commonly heard in the middle and western portions of the United States." If we look in the middle and western portions of the United States on the map, we see the color that's common to several states in the middle of the map and several states in the western portion of the map is dark gray. The key in the bottom left of the map tells us that the dark gray portion of the map is where the word "pop" is commonly used to describe soft drinks. So the first word in the correct answer choice should be "pop," not "soda." The text then tells us that the second term for a soft drink "is frequently used in many southern states." The coloring that appears in the south (and not anywhere else on the map) is the diagonal stripe pattern, and the key in the bottom left of the map tells us that the portion of the map with that pattern is where the word "coke" is commonly used. So the second word in the correct answer should be "coke," not "pop." Finally, the text tells us the third term in the correct answer "is predominant in the northeastern and southwest regions but used elsewhere as well." When we look at the map, we see that the light gray color appears in those areas, and the key tells us the light gray color corresponds to the word "soda." So the third word should be "soda," not "coke."

B   **Pattern:** Confused concepts. **Incorrect:** As we saw in the discussion for (A), the order should be "pop," "coke," "soda."

C ✓   **Pattern:** Correct. As we saw in the discussion for (A), the order should be "pop," "coke," "soda," so (C) is correct.

D   **Pattern:** Confused concepts. **Incorrect:** As we saw in the discussion for (A), the order should be "pop," "coke," "soda."

Note   This question is a great example of the way that the College Board likes to write questions that test relatively basic skills in a way that will frustrate and misdirect many untrained test-takers. Most test-takers can easily use the map to identify which terms are popular in which states, but the question is constructed in a way that will confuse a lot of people and cause them to misread small details in the text, prompt, or choices. Keep this kind of thing in mind on test day and remember to stay focused on details!

Test 4, Question 32   **TYPE: GRAMMAR/STYLE/PUNCTUATION (often no prompt; choices have similar meanings)**

- **Vertical Scan Results:** Some choices include homophone pairs or triples.
- **Vertical Scan Notes:** Should the underlined phrase begin with "they're," "their," or "there?" Should the underlined phrase end with "they're," "their," or "there?"

- **Key Features in Surrounding Text:** The first word in the underlined phrase expresses the idea that "findings" possess "true value." So we need a plural possessive pronoun form to be the first word in the underlined phrase. The last word in the underlined phrase expresses the idea that "findings" possess a "reminder." So, again, we need a plural possessive pronoun form to be the last word in the underlined phrase.

Concepts in the question:

- **Confused Homophones:** Choices include different homophone pairs (such as "their" and "they're" or "too" and "to"). Read carefully—also, remember the correct formation of possessive pronouns, and remember to read contractions as their uncontracted forms (e.g. "it's" = "it is"). (See page 452.)
- **Plural/Possessive/Contraction:** Choices include the same noun ending in "-s" with or without an apostrophe before or after the "-s." Remember the three rules for forming possessives. Think of contractions in their uncontracted forms ("you're" = "you are"). (See page 441.)

ANSWER CHOICE ANALYSIS

A		**Incorrect:** The first word in the underlined phrase should be a plural possessive pronoun to show that "findings" possess value. But "they're" is the contracted version of the phrase "they are," so (A) must be wrong.
B	✓	**Correct:** As we discussed above, the first and last words in the underlined phrase should both be plural possessive pronouns, and "their" is a plural possessive pronoun form.
C		**Incorrect:** As we discussed above, "they're" is the contracted version of the phrase "they are," but the last word in the correct answer choice needs to reflect the idea that the "findings" possess a "reminder."
D		**Incorrect:** The word "there" reflects a physical location, not a possessive relationship; as we discussed above, the last word in the correct answer needs to reflect possession.

Answer choice patterns (see page 455): Wrong answers incorporate elements of the right answer.

Test 4, Question 33   TYPE: READING COMPREHENSION (usually has a prompt; choices have different meanings)

- **RC Question sub-type:** Best Accomplishes X. (The prompt describes a goal of the author, and asks us which choice achieves that goal. The correct answer choice will plainly and directly demonstrate the task described in the prompt. See page 431.)
- **Subjective phrases to be ignored:** "most"

ANSWER CHOICE ANALYSIS

A	✓	**Pattern:** Correct. When we look back at the sentence in question, we see the phrase "not only...but...also," which indicates that the idea appearing after "but also" should be something of a surprise compared to the earlier half of the sentence, or that it should build on the earlier half of the sentence. (A) does that by pointing out that the Internet is a "source of data," not just a tool for gathering data. Since (A) is the only choice that fits this "not only...but...also" structure, it's correct.
B		**Pattern:** Confused concepts. **Incorrect:** As we saw in the discussion for (A), this paragraph isn't just about using the Internet to learn how people refer to soft drinks; the phrase beginning with "as interesting as Russ's findings are, though" indicates that the soft drink research isn't truly what makes the Internet valuable. The example of collecting information about terms used to refer to soft drinks is just one of the ways that information can be collected from the internet.
C		**Pattern:** Plausible, but not in the text. **Incorrect:** This statement may be true in general, but it isn't discussed anywhere in the passage, so it's not relevant to this question.
D		**Pattern:** Confused concepts. **Incorrect:** As we saw for (A), the idea appearing after "but also" should be slightly different from the earlier half of the sentence. But the first half of the sentence already indicates that that Internet is "helpful to researchers," since Russ is a researcher and the Internet has helped him. So this choice doesn't fit with the "not only...but...also" structure of the sentence.

Test 4, Question 34   TYPE: GRAMMAR/STYLE/PUNCTUATION (often no prompt; choices have similar meanings)

- **Vertical Scan Results:** Some choices have different forms of the same basic word.
- **Vertical Scan Notes:** We need to pick the right form of the verb "to be."
- **Key Features in Surrounding Text:** Every other verb in this sentence is in the present tense ("can take," "is," "is") and the context gives us no reason to think that the action described by the verb in this underlined phrase takes place at another time. So we need a verb form in the present tense.

Concepts in the question:

- **Parallelism:** Choices include options that would ignore a parallel structure in the surrounding text. The correct answer choice should match phrasing in the surrounding text when possible. (See page 458.)
- **Verb Tense/Conjugation:** Choices include different forms of the same verb. Look at the surrounding text to find each verb's subject. Also, look for other verbs that could indicate the proper tense for the verbs in the answer choices. (See page 437.)

A   **Incorrect:** As we discussed above, the context requires a present tense verb form, and this choice is a past tense form.

B   **Incorrect:** This choice has the same problem as (A).

C ✓   **Correct:** As we discussed above, the context requires a present tense verb form, and (C) is the only present tense form.

D   **Incorrect:** This choice has the same problem as (A).

Note   Many test-takers will be confused by the issue of whether the correct answer should agree with "number" or "steps" in the original sentence, but, as trained test-takers, we can avoid considering that issue when we realize that the rest of the sentence uses verbs in the present tense ("is" is used twice), which means "are" must be correct, since it's the only verb in the answer choices in the present tense.

Test 4, Question 35   TYPE: GRAMMAR/STYLE/PUNCTUATION (often no prompt; choices have similar meanings)

- **Vertical Scan Results:** Some choices have the same words with different punctuation.
- **Vertical Scan Notes:** We need to decide which punctuation should go on either end of the phrase "the settings, characters, and plots that make each game unique."
- **Key Features in Surrounding Text:** The phrase "The designer envisions the game's fundamental elements" can stand on its own as a sentence, but the other phrases in the sentence can't.

Concepts in the question:

- **Colons:** Choices include one or more colons. A colon can be placed after a set of words that could be a sentence on their own, and before a demonstration or example of the idea before the colon. (See page 447.)
- **Commas:** Choices include one or more commas. On the Writing and Language section, commas can be used to separate things in a list of three or more, to form a comma sandwich, or to introduce an independent clause after a dependent clause. (See pages 448-450.)
- **Punctuation Sandwich:** Choice(s) would create phrases improperly "sandwiched" between similar types of punctuation. When removed from the sentence, a properly formed sandwich leaves behind a grammatically acceptable sentence. (See page 450.)
- **Semi-colons:** Choices include one or more semicolons. Semi-colons can be used to separate two sets of words that could each stand on their own as a full sentence. (See page 447.)

ANSWER CHOICE ANALYSIS

A   **Incorrect:** On the SAT, *everything* that comes after the colon in a sentence must be an example of or elaboration on what comes before the colon. The phrase "and is thus a primary creative force behind a video game" doesn't satisfy this requirement, so this choice can't be correct.

B   **Incorrect:** This choice has the same problem as (A).

C ✓   **Correct:** This choice uses dashes to create an acceptable punctuation sandwich around the phrase "the settings, characters, and plots that make each game unique," because the entire sandwich can be removed without creating any grammatical issues in the sentence.

D   **Incorrect:** There can't be a semi-colon after "elements" or "unique" on the SAT because all the parts of the sentence separated by semi-colons couldn't stand on their own as complete sentences.

Note   Many untrained test-takers will assume that the original version of the sentence is okay because they'll misread the text and assume the sentence ends where the underlining ends, with the word "unique." Once more we see the critical importance of reading the answer choices very carefully!

Test 4, Question 36   TYPE: GRAMMAR/STYLE/PUNCTUATION (often no prompt; choices have similar meanings)

- **Vertical Scan Results:** Some choices have the same words with different punctuation.
- **Vertical Scan Notes:** We need to decide whether a comma, dash, or no punctuation should appear after "job," and whether a period, comma, or no punctuation should appear after "however."
- **Key Features in Surrounding Text:** The previous paragraph says "every video game…starts with a concept" from "the mind of a designer." This paragraph discusses what happens after the designer conceptualizes the game. So the idea expressed in the first sentence of this paragraph up through the word "however" is a reaction to the previous paragraph. That means we need this phrase to be punctuated in such a way that "however" refers only to the idea that appears in this sentence before the word "however," and not to the following sentence.

Concepts in the question:

- **Commas:** Choices include one or more commas. On the Writing and Language section, commas can be used to separate things in a list of three or more, to form a comma sandwich, or to introduce an independent clause after a dependent clause. (See pages 448-450.)
- **Comma Splice:** Answer choice(s) and/or surrounding text use commas to separate two groups of words that could each be sentences on their own. A comma can't be used in this way on the SAT Writing and Language section. (See page 447.)
- **Dependent and Independent Clauses:** Answer choice(s) would incorrectly use a dependent or independent clause. An independent clause can stand alone as a sentence: it has a main subject/verb pair. A dependent clause is introduced by a conjunction or relative pronoun. (See page 445.)

ANSWER CHOICE ANALYSIS

A	**Incorrect:** When we read the entire sentence carefully, we see that (A) would ultimately create a comma splice. In other words, it would cause a comma to be the punctuation between two groups of words that could each stand on their own as independent sentences. Since commas can't be used this way on the SAT, we know (A) must be wrong.
B ✓	**Correct:** This choice is the only one that follow the SAT's rules and patterns, because it results in two independent clauses being separated by a period.
C	**Incorrect:** This choice uses a dash in a way that the SAT forbids. On the SAT, a dash can be used in a punctuation sandwich or to replace a colon (see page 450 for more on dashes).
D	**Incorrect:** This choice would create a run-on sentence because it would join two independent clauses to each other without any punctuation (such as a semicolon or period) to divide them.

Note	This question is a great example of the importance of knowing the SAT's specific rules and patterns, rather than focusing on general grammar concepts that we might learn from a teacher or textbook! Many sources would accept (C) as a grammatical construction, but trained test-takers know that the College Board only allows us to use dashes in punctuation sandwiches or in a position where it would be okay to use a colon instead, and those situations don't apply in this question.

| Test 4, Question 37   TYPE: READING COMPREHENSION (usually has a prompt; choices have different meanings)

- **RC Question sub-type:** Including/excluding a phrase/sentence. (The question asks whether a sentence should be included in the passage. The correct choice will include a comment that plainly describes the role of the phrase or sentence in the passage. Sentences that should be included will follow broad College Board standards for ideal sentences and paragraphs—including consistency with any figures in the passage—while sentences that shouldn't be included will not follow those standards. See page 433.)

ANSWER CHOICE ANALYSIS

A	**Pattern:** Confused concepts. **Incorrect:** The sentence in the prompt doesn't "support a conclusion" in the next sentence, as this choice would require. The following sentence doesn't include a "conclusion" for the sentence in the question to support—it simply makes a statement about what designers need to do.
B	**Pattern:** Confused concepts. **Incorrect:** This sentence doesn't "illustrate" anything; it's just a general statement without any illustrative example or anecdote.
C	**Pattern:** Confused concepts. **Incorrect:** This isn't irrelevant; instead, it's redundant, as we'll see in the discussion for (D).
D ✓	**Pattern:** Correct. This sentence shouldn't be added because it's redundant—it simply rephrases the idea from the previous sentence that a concept for a game will never actually become a game "unless it is communicated effectively." Since (D) is the only choice that directly reflects the relationship between the sentence in the prompt and the text, (D) is right.

| Test 4, Question 38   TYPE: READING COMPREHENSION (usually has a prompt; choices have different meanings)

- **RC Question sub-type:** Best Accomplishes X. (The prompt describes a goal of the author, and asks us which choice achieves that goal. The correct answer choice will plainly and directly demonstrate the task described in the prompt. See page 431.)
- **Subjective phrases to be ignored:** "best"

ANSWER CHOICE ANALYSIS

A ✓	**Pattern:** Correct. This choice demonstrates the idea from the previous sentence, which says that a concept for a game must be "communicated effectively" to the other people working on the game.
B	**Pattern:** Wrong part of the passage. **Incorrect:** The question asks for an answer that "supports the point developed in this paragraph." This paragraph doesn't talk about imagination; imagination is only discussed in the previous paragraph.
C	**Pattern:** Largely irrelevant. **Incorrect:** Nothing in this paragraph (or in the entire text) discusses the idea of game designers carefully assessing their motivations, as this choice would require.
D	**Pattern:** Plausible, but not in the text. **Incorrect:** We might imagine that this would be a good skill for a video game designer to have, but that idea isn't stated "in this paragraph," as the prompt requires.

- RC Question sub-type: Transition phrase. (The choices include words or phrases showing a transition from the previous sentence, like "however," "instead of," "for example," etc. The transition phrase must reflect the relationship between the previous sentence and the sentence where the transition phrase appears. See page 431.)

ANSWER CHOICE ANALYSIS

A **Pattern:** Confused concepts. **Incorrect:** This choice would be appropriate if this sentence expressed a relationship that was the mirror image of one in the previous sentence, but that's not the case.

B **Pattern:** Direct contradiction. **Incorrect:** This choice would be appropriate if the current sentence told us something that was true in spite of what was mentioned in the previous sentence, but that's not the case.

C ✓ **Pattern:** Correct. The previous sentence says game designers must "generate extensive documentation" and "explain…ideas clearly." Then this sentence says anyone who wants to be a game designer has to be good at writing and speaking. The word "consequently" appropriately reflects the fact that this sentence expresses a conclusion based on the previous sentence.

D **Pattern:** Direct contradiction. **Incorrect:** This choice would be appropriate if what was discussed in this sentence was not what we'd expect based on the previous sentence, but that's not the case.

- **Vertical Scan Results:** Similar phrases with different short words and/or punctuation.
- **Vertical Scan Notes:** Should "both" be present in the correct answer? Should "writer" and "speaker" be plural, or singular? What should the word order be?
- **Key Features in Surrounding Text:** The thing in the sentence that "must be" what's described in the underlined phrase is "anyone," so the underlined phrase must describe something that "anyone" could be.

Concepts in the question:

- **Singular versus Plural:** Choices include singular and plural versions of the same base words that don't agree with other words in the surrounding text. Singular nouns must go with singular verb forms and singular pronouns. Plural nouns must go with plural verbs and pronouns. Think carefully about which words should match or agree with each other! (See page 443.)

ANSWER CHOICE ANALYSIS

A **Incorrect:** As we discussed above, the underlined phrase must describe something that "anyone" could be. According to the rules of the SAT, the word "anyone" can't refer to "writers and speakers," because "anyone" is singular, while "writers and speakers" is plural. In other words, any *one* person can't be *multiple* writers and speakers.

B ✓ **Correct:** As we saw for (A), the underlined phrase must describe something that the singular word "anyone" could grammatically agree with. "Anyone" can be a "writer and speaker," because the word "anyone" is grammatically singular, and "writer" and "speaker" are singular things that agree grammatically with the word "anyone."

C **Incorrect:** This choice has the same problem as (A).

D **Incorrect:** This choice has the same problem as (A).

Note Many untrained test-takers will focus incorrectly on trying to determine the proper word order, but trained test-takers are always on the lookout for singular/plural issues on the test; once we realize that the correct answer must be singular, we see that only (B) is possible. Let this be one more reminder of the importance of reading exactly what's on the page and remembering the SAT's rules and patterns!

- **Vertical Scan Results:** Choices are long phrases/sentences.
- **Vertical Scan Notes:** It looks like we need to find the acceptable way to express the idea of starting a career.
- **Key Features in Surrounding Text:** The underlined text itself.

Concepts in the question:

- **Redundancy:** Answer choices and/or surrounding text could combine to repeat the same concept unnecessarily. We should avoid words or phrases that directly repeat ideas in the immediate context. (See page 452.)
- **Singular versus Plural:** Choices include singular and plural versions of the same base words that don't agree with other words in the surrounding text. Singular nouns must go with singular verb forms and singular pronouns. Plural nouns must go with plural verbs and pronouns. Think carefully about which words should match or agree with each other! (See page 443.)

ANSWER CHOICE ANALYSIS

A **Incorrect:** The word "begin" already describes something that happens "initially," so "initially" is redundant.

B **Incorrect:** The words "start" and "begin" mean the same thing, so using both here is redundant according to the SAT.

C   Incorrect: Many untrained test-takers will have a vague sense that (C) is wrong, even if they can't pinpoint why. As trained test-takers, we can see that (D) is shorter and grammatically acceptable, which means (C) can't be the right answer to a grammar/style/punctuation question on the Writing and Language section of the SAT.

D ✓   Correct: This is the shortest choice and it's grammatically acceptable, so it's right, according to the SAT's unwritten rules.

Answer choice patterns (see page 454): Shortest grammatically acceptable choice is correct.

Test 4, Question 42	**TYPE: READING COMPREHENSION (usually has a prompt; choices have different meanings)**

- **RC Question sub-type:** Vocabulary In Context. (Choices include words or short phrases that have vaguely similar but not identical meanings. Most or all of the choices will seem vaguely appropriate, but only one choice will be correct when we think very carefully and specifically about the word means and how it can be used. See page 432.)

ANSWER CHOICE ANALYSIS

A   ("Courses in psychology and human behavior may help you develop emphatic collaboration skills.") **Pattern:** Same ballpark. **Incorrect:** The underlined phrase describes "collaboration skills," and the last sentence of the previous paragraph mentions that making video games is a "collaborative effort" and a video game designer must be a "team player." So the correct answer must be something that indicates that "collaboration skills" are necessary for a person who wants to be a video game designer. But "emphatic" means putting emphasis on something, or being very clear or direct about something, which isn't the same thing as saying "collaboration skills" are necessary in this context.

B   ("Courses in psychology and human behavior may help you develop paramount collaboration skills...") **Pattern:** Same ballpark. **Incorrect:** As we saw in the discussion of (A), the correct answer must be something that indicates that "collaboration skills" are necessary for a person who wants to be a video game designer. But "paramount" means that these skills are the most important part of making video games. The text never says collaboration skills are the *most* important part of being a game designer, as this choice would require, so it can't be correct.

C   ("Courses in psychology and human behavior may help you develop eminent collaboration skills.") **Pattern:** Same ballpark. **Incorrect:** As we saw for (A), the correct answer must be something that indicates that "collaboration skills" are necessary for a person who wants to be a video game designer. But "eminent" specifically describes a *person* who is famous or respected, and that doesn't make any sense in this context.

D ✓   ("Courses in psychology and human behavior may help you develop important collaboration skills...") **Correct:** As we saw in the discussion of choice (A), the correct answer must be something that indicates that "collaboration skills" are necessary for a person who wants to be a video game designer. The word "important" clearly reflects the idea that "collaboration skills" are necessary for game designers—if you must have collaboration skills to be a video game designer, then it makes sense to say collaboration skills are important in this context.

Note   Many trained test-takers will be able to tell (D) must be right even if they don't know the words "paramount" and "eminent." Remember that it's often possible to work around unknown words in this way!

Test 4, Question 43	**TYPE: GRAMMAR/STYLE/PUNCTUATION (often no prompt; choices have similar meanings)**

- **Vertical Scan Results:** Similar phrases with different short words and/or punctuation.
- **Vertical Scan Notes:** It looks like we need to determine whether the phrase "video game design" should appear at the beginning, middle, or end of the correct version of the underlined phrase.
- **Key Features in Surrounding Text:** The phrase "demanding and deadline driven" must describe the first thing that appears after the comma in the sentence.

Concepts in the question:

- **Dangling Participle:** The question involves descriptive phrases beginning with an "-ing" word that would describe the wrong word in context. Descriptive phrases starting with a word ending in "-ing" describe the first noun phrase in that sentence's independent clause. (See page 450.)

ANSWER CHOICE ANALYSIS

A ✓   **Correct:** Only (A) makes it clear that the phrase "demanding and deadline driven" appropriately describes the phrase "video game design," according to the SAT's rules for phrases with a word that ends in "-ing" joined to a sentence with a comma.

B   **Incorrect:** According to the SAT's rules, this choice would make the phrase "demanding and deadline driven" describe the word "choice," which doesn't make sense in the context of the paragraph.

C   **Incorrect:** This choice has a similar problem to (B): it would make the word "you" be the thing that's "demanding and deadline driven" according to the SAT's rules.

D   **Incorrect:** This choice has the same basic problem that (B) and (C) do: it would make "demanding and deadline driven" describe the word "choosing" according to the rules of the SAT.

- RC Question sub-type: Sentence or paragraph placement. (The prompt asks us where a sentence should go in a paragraph, or where a paragraph should go in the passage. The correct order will reflect a logical chronology, and/or will allow for pronouns in the sentences to refer to nouns in a logical way, and/or will place related concepts near one another. See page 432.)
- Subjective phrases to be ignored: "most"

ANSWER CHOICE ANALYSIS

A   **Pattern:** Causes text to introduce an idea that has already been discussed. **Incorrect:** This placement doesn't make sense, because sentences 3 and 4 already specifically describe the value of taking certain courses. There's no reason to say that "careful educational preparation" is necessary after we've already discussed the various educational preparations that should be made, so this sentence should appear earlier in the paragraph than it does.

B ✓   **Pattern:** Correct. This entire paragraph is about the educational preparation that aspiring game designers should undergo, so it makes sense to introduce the paragraph with a sentence like this, which makes a broad statement about the importance of "careful educational preparation."

C   **Pattern:** Causes text to introduce an idea that has already been discussed. **Incorrect:** (C) has the same problem as (A): it would make the paragraph introduce educational preparation in general after a sentence that mentions some specific courses.

D   **Pattern:** Direct contradiction. **Incorrect:** The sentence shouldn't be deleted because it makes a broad statement that introduces the topic discussed in this paragraph. For this reason—as we saw in our discussion of (B)—the sentence should appear before sentence 1.

Part 10: Essay Training

Before you begin training for the SAT Essay, you should make sure that your target schools actually want you to take it—many schools, including some of the most competitive, have decided that the SAT Essay doesn't reflect the type of educated, reflective writing that they want to see from their students. If your target schools do want you to submit an SAT Essay score, you'll find that the current version of the essay rewards a formulaic, shallow approach that's relatively easy to learn, and to implement on test day.

In this part, you'll learn the following:

- why the current version of the SAT Essay came into existence
- how the College Board has designed the SAT Essay
- the unwritten rules of the SAT Essay
- how to identify the author's thesis quickly, to make sure that you're writing on the correct subjects
- why you should choose to say that the author made a strong argument
- how little time the graders will spend on your essay, and the implications of those time restrictions for your writing
- the true impact of spelling and grammar errors on your score
- whether the length of your essay is important
- why the 5-paragraph format is probably best (even if your essay doesn't end up with exactly 5 paragraphs)
- why quotes matter, and how much of your essay should consist of them
- how to distinguish evidence from reasoning—and whether the distinction is actually all that important in practice
- how to identify stylistic elements and appeals to emotion
- how these ideas can be applied to sample SAT Essay prompts from the official practice tests
- a formula for generating a high-scoring SAT Essay efficiently
- why note-taking and essay-planning are generally bad ideas on test day, and how to avoid them
- how all the training concepts I teach you are directly reflected in the College Board's perfect-scoring sample essays
- and more . . .

SAT Essay Training

An excellent precept for writers: have a clear idea of all the phrases and expressions you need, and you will find them.
Ximénès Doudan

Overview and Important Reminders for the SAT Essay

Before we even start talking about how to do well on the SAT Essay, let's get something very clear: There's a good chance you don't even have to take the Essay part of the test, which means there's a good chance you don't even need to read this section.

The best way to find out if your target schools require you to submit the SAT Essay is to contact their admissions departments directly, or to visit their websites and look for the details of what they require as far as standardized testing is concerned. If your target schools don't require you to submit the optional SAT Essay score, then you can focus your training on the multiple-choice portions of the SAT.

Now, you may be wondering why the College Board made the SAT Essay optional in the current version of the test (the Essay was mandatory when it was first introduced in the 2005 version of the SAT, which preceded the current version of the SAT). The answer is telling: the overwhelming feedback—from educators, administrators, and test-takers—was that the original Essay was a horribly designed waste of everyone's time. As I pointed out in the earlier version of this Black Book, the previous version of the SAT Essay allowed test-takers to make up facts, and the main factor in determining the overall Essay score was the length of the essay, with almost no regard for content. The University of Pennsylvania summed up the situation well when it called the SAT Essay the "least predictive element of the overall Writing section of the SAT." Dr. Les Perelman, who was then a director of undergraduate writing at MIT, went even further when he said the old SAT Essay rewarded "exactly what we don't want to teach our kids."

So the College Board knew that educational professionals weren't enthusiastic about the idea of an SAT Essay, but it still didn't want to scrap the Essay completely. (One major economic motivation for not getting rid of the Essay is that the College Board wants some states to use the SAT as part of their common core testing programs, which require an essay.) The College Board's "solution" to the problems with the SAT Essay includes three major components:

1. Making the SAT Essay optional, so colleges and universities can choose whether they think it's worth their applicants' time. (At the time of this writing, fewer than 10% of colleges and universities require the SAT Essay.)

2. Changing the structure of the SAT Essay, so it doesn't seem to reward made-up facts in the same way that the previous version did. (As we'll see in a few pages, the current version of the Essay still rewards weak analysis and made-up reasoning, though.)

3. Changing the scoring of the SAT Essay, so it's harder for test-takers, colleges, and universities to attempt direct comparisons among scores. (As one example, how can we reliably compare the writing ability of a person who scores a 4/2/3 to a person who scores a 3/4/2, or even a 3/3/3? Each writer amassed 9 total points on the task, but their skills appear to be allocated differently according to the graders.)

The end result of all of this is that the SAT Essay is still bad at measuring writing ability, and there's still a way to game the current essay, just as there was a way to game the previous essay. We'll talk about how to do exactly that in this section.

SAT Essay Scoring

Before we go any farther, let's take a minute to discuss the SAT Essay's weird scoring process. We mentioned earlier that it seems like the College Board intentionally picked a scoring system that makes comparisons difficult among different test-takers, and especially between scores from the old version of the SAT Essay and scores from the new version of the SAT Essay.

First of all, the SAT Essay is now scored in three different areas: reading, writing, and analysis. Each grader awards a score of 1, 2, 3, or 4 in each area. The College Board *always* discusses those three scores separately. So if you score a 2 in reading, a 3 in writing, and a 2 in analysis, the College Board says your score is a 2/3/2, not a 7.

To make it more confusing, the Blue Book and the College Board's web site present sample essays with each section scored on the 1-4 scale . . . but, in real life, there will be *two* graders, and *each grader* will assign a score of 1-4 for each section. Those scores will be added together to result in an actual score *on each of the three sections* of 2, 3, 4, 5, 6, 7, or 8. So on your actual SAT score report, your SAT Essay score will be reported on a scale from 2-8 in three different areas. For example, you might get a 6 on reading, a 5 on writing, and a 7 on analysis, for a score of 6/5/7.

For the purposes of the training in this Black Book, we'll discuss the three SAT Essay scores on the 1-4 scale, mostly because that's how they're discussed in the official College Board materials that contain sample essays. That way, when you look at those sample essays and the scores they receive, and you read our discussion of those essays here, the scoring scale will be the same.

One more thing: even though the College Board doesn't talk about the combined total score, we'll sometimes talk about the combined total score as a way to understand the trends in the provided sample essays (for example, the correlation between the word count of the sample essays from the College Board and the total combined scores those sample essays received). Discussing the essay in these terms makes it much easier to draw meaningful comparisons.

Now that we're on the same page about SAT Essay scoring, let's get into our discussion of writing the essay itself.

Test Design Rules of the SAT Essay

As with the other parts of the SAT, you have to learn the rules of the essay if you want to do well on it. But be careful! The College Board's SAT Essay Scoring Rubric isn't very useful if you're trying to figure out exactly what to do on test day.

It might sound strange to say this, but most of the College Board's advice on how to write the SAT Essay is very, very bad, in the sense that many people who make an effort to follow it still end up with lower scores on the SAT Essay than they would like. Instead of following the rules that the College Board states explicitly, we'll do something much smarter—we'll figure out the rules that are implicitly revealed in the high- and low-scoring sample responses provided by the College Board in the Blue Book, and on the College Board's web site. We'll find that the rules revealed by actual high- and low-scoring sample essays released by the College Board are often very different from what the SAT claims to reward.

SAT Essay Rule 1: The Prompt is Always (Basically) the Same.

This rule is one that the College Board is upfront about: every single SAT Essay prompt follows the same format. There will be a passage of approximately 700 words, and then there will be a prompt asking you to analyze how the author made her argument.

The predictable prompt is good news for pretty much everybody, because it means test-takers will know ahead of time what kind of essay they'll need to write. (Remember—you won't know what the passage is about ahead of time, but you will know that the passage presents an argument on a subject, and that you'll need to write about that argument according to the standards we'll discuss in this section of the Black Book.)

There's one potential difficulty with this prompt, which we'll discuss in the next rule.

SAT Essay Rule 2: DON'T Offer Your Own Opinion on the Topic! Remember that Your Job is to Analyze the Argument in the Passage, Not Make Your Own Argument.

This is another rule that the College Board itself acknowledges. On many standardized tests, test-takers are expected to state a position on a topic and then defend that position. But on the SAT Essay, your response to the provided passage doesn't offer YOUR opinion on the topic in the passage—instead, your response is a discussion of how the author presented HER argument.

For example, if the passage is about rescuing beached whales, and the author makes an argument against rescuing beached whales, you can't write an essay about how you, personally, think beached whales should be rescued. Instead, you must write an essay about how the author made her argument—which facts and statistics she cited, what her reasoning was, what kind of wording she used, etc.

SAT Essay Rule 3: Use the College Board's Idea of the Author's Thesis.

As with most persuasive essays, the passage that you'll see on test day will usually be structured so that the author's opinion is stated in one or two sentences near the beginning or the end of the passage, in what many teachers would call a "thesis statement."

But you shouldn't try to hunt through the passage for the author's thesis on your own! The College Board will always provide its own statement of the author's thesis, in the box of text that appears after the passage on test day. Looking in that box of text is the best way to find the author's opinion, for two reasons:

- It's pretty fast, so you don't have to search through the passage itself.
- If you get the author's opinion from that box of text, you avoid any risk that you might misunderstand what the author was trying to say, because you're working directly from the College Board's own statement of the author's opinion.

The author's opinion will appear after the phrase "an argument to persuade [his/her/their] audience that . . ." For example, after the passage for the essay at the end of SAT Practice Test #1, we can see that the box says

> Write an essay in which you explain how Jimmy Carter builds an argument to persuade his audience that the Arctic National Wildlife Refuge should not be developed for industry.

So the author's opinion is the following:

> . . . the Arctic National Wildlife Refuge should not be developed for industry.

SAT Essay Rule 4: Say the Author did a Good Job.

Even though you won't be writing an essay about your position on the topic of the provided passage, your essay will still take a position, and that position will still be clearly stated in a thesis in your first paragraph (more on that later).

Your position will be that the author did a good job making her argument.

You might not actually agree with the author's argument, but, as we discussed previously, the point of the SAT Essay isn't for you to state your opinion on the topic in the passage. When we look at all the sample SAT Essay passages provided by the College Board, we can see that the College Board always provides a passage that includes plenty of evidence, reasoning, and persuasive language in support of a thesis—so it would be pretty hard for you to argue that the author *didn't* do a good job supporting her argument. Plus, more importantly, every single high-scoring sample essay available from the College Board at the time of this writing says that the author made an effective argument. So that's what we'll say, too.

So your introductory paragraph should include a sentence that clearly states in one way or another that the author makes an effective argument. (We'll discuss this introductory paragraph later in more detail.)

SAT Essay Rule 5: Graders Don't Spend Much Time or Thought on Grading Your Essay.

On the previous version of the SAT Essay, the College Board's graders generally spent less than 3 minutes on each essay they graded, and the evidence suggests that similar time constraints probably exist for graders of the current version of the essay. (For one thing, the number of grammatical and diction errors that exist even in "perfect" essays would tend to suggest that they aren't being read very closely. On top of that, making sure the graders consistently spend only a few minutes on each essay is actually a decent way to help standardize the grading process, because it helps ensure that each essay gets treated with the same degree of thoroughness—or lack of thoroughness. Finally, the College Board has tried hard to make the new SAT Essay seem like a better instrument than the previous Essay was, and one of the main criticisms of the previous Essay was the superficial way in which it was graded; in spite of these two facts, the College Board has never claimed that the new Essay is being graded in a way that allows graders to invest more time and thought, which further suggests that the timing situation hasn't changed much.)

Not only is each grader spending only a few minutes on your essay, but they also generally grade dozens of essays in a row. This makes it even less likely that your essay will stand out in a grader's mind.

It's important for you to appreciate the assembly-line nature of the grading process! Once you're aware of how little time and energy gets spent on grading your writing, you'll understand why some of the other rules in this section work the way they do: graders simply aren't able to spend the necessary time and energy to engage each essay on a deep level, so a lot of stuff ends up in "perfect" essays that doesn't really fit the official rubric.

So don't worry if the approach we discuss in this part of the Black Book feels different from the approach you normally take when you write an essay for school. It SHOULD feel different! The grading process for the SAT Essay is very different from the grading process for your school essays, so it only makes sense that the process of writing the SAT Essay will be different as well.

SAT Essay Rule 6: It's Okay to Have Some Spelling Mistakes and Imperfect Grammar.

The College Board's rubric for scoring the SAT Essay says that an essay that scores a 4 (the highest score possible) in Writing will be "free or virtually free of errors." But both of the perfect-scoring sample essays in the Blue Book contain multiple errors. In fact, those two essays and the perfect sample essay available on the College Board's website have dozens of errors among them. For example, the perfect-scoring sample essay called "Student Sample 6"—about the plastic bag ban—includes an error in the very first sentence (forming the possessive of the singular noun "Adam B. Summers" by adding an apostrophe instead of an apostrophe and an "s"), and another error in the first sentence of the third paragraph (a misspelling of the word "ethical"). The perfect-scoring sample essay called "Student Sample 7"—also about the plastic bag ban—contains errors such as using the object pronoun "us" instead of the subject pronoun "we" in the phrase "us consumers are confident," and using the word "that" in place of the word "than" in the comparative phrase "lower that [sic] we all assume."

Let me be clear about something: I'm not trying to pick on the authors of these essays for making grammatical mistakes on a timed essay during a standardized test! That's a totally normal thing for any writer under those circumstances. I'm just trying to demonstrate that your essay doesn't need to be free from grammatical errors to get a top score, because the perfect-scoring sample essays provided by the College Board aren't even close to being error-free.

Of course, you want to write clearly and well, and you want to avoid grammatical errors within reason, if you can help it—but don't waste time trying to proofread your essay and catch every single grammatical error. Instead, focus your time and energy on making sure your essay matches the standards we discuss in this section.

SAT Essay Rule 7: The Longer, the Better

As we previously discussed, the old SAT Essay came under a lot of fire for making the length of a test-taker's essay essentially the most important factor in determining that test-taker's score. The College Board seems to be presenting sample essays in a way that might have been an effort to make this connection less obvious—but the connection is still there, as we can see in the graph below.

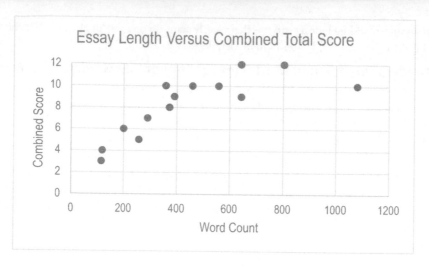

Essay Length Versus Combined Total Score

(Note that in the graph above, a 12 represents a perfect score, because we've combined the three scoring categories, and because the sample essays show a maximum score of 4 in each category, as discussed in the section called "SAT Essay Scoring" on page 545.)

All the high-scoring sample essays are fairly long and well-developed, while the low-scoring sample essays are much shorter. But be careful—an essay's score seems to correlate with its length to some extent, but that doesn't mean it's a good idea to write garbage just to fill up space on the page. What it means is that if you've written a short essay—around 300 words or less—your chances of scoring high seem to be just about zero. You'll want to shoot for roughly 600 – 700 words on your essay (about 2.5 to 3 handwritten pages for most people) if you're looking for a perfect score, which means you'll need to write roughly one to two lines per minute, assuming you finish reading the passage in 5 minutes, since you'll have a total of 50 minutes for all your reading and writing. This pace won't allow much time for revision, as we'll see when we discuss my step-by-step approach to the SAT Essay starting on page 556.

SAT Essay Rule 8: A Few Vocabulary Mistakes Aren't a Big Deal.

In the original SAT Essay, using big words incorrectly could hurt your score, so I always used to advise students to stick to words whose meanings they were sure of. But the perfect-scoring sample essays provided by the College Board for the current version of the SAT Essay frequently include big or exotic words that are used inaccurately, so it seems that the College Board's graders are no longer that concerned with perfect diction. (See the analysis of perfect-scoring SAT sample Essays starting on page 561 for specific examples of vocabulary mistakes in those essays.)

Still, I definitely would NOT advise throwing in big words you don't know just to try to impress the College Board's readers! It's unlikely that doing so would help. But if you end up accidentally misusing a couple of big words, it shouldn't hurt your score.

SAT Essay Rule 9: There's No Set Format (But Use a Version of the "5-Paragraph" Format).

The College Board doesn't specify a mandatory format for the SAT Essay—so, in theory, many formats could be acceptable on test day.

But as it turns out, all of the top-scoring essays I've seen have generally followed something similar to the standard 5-paragraph format commonly taught in American high schools. This format generally consists of an intro paragraph, three supporting "body" paragraphs with evidence to support the statements in the intro paragraph, and then a concluding paragraph that restates the ideas from the previous paragraphs.

If you end up altering the number of body paragraphs, so that you have two, four, or even five body paragraphs instead of the standard three, that's fine. For our purposes, you've still followed the "five-paragraph" format as long as you have an intro paragraph, a certain number of body paragraphs in support of the intro, and then a concluding paragraph.

There are four main reasons I advise you to use this general format:

1. The 5-paragraph format is the format that we find in all of the top-scoring essays provided by the College Board as examples, so we know the College Board graders are okay with it.

2. The 5-paragraph format lends itself well to a timed writing process, as we'll see in a few pages, because it doesn't require us to keep a lot of concepts in our mind at once. When we write the introduction paragraph, we need to think generally about the kinds of things we'll want to mention later in the essay, but not in a way that requires us to plan everything out in strict detail. After that, we just focus on each body paragraph by itself: when we're writing one body paragraph, we don't need to think about what the other paragraphs say. Finally, we write a conclusion that refers back to the ideas we just discussed in the previous paragraphs.

3. The 5-paragraph format makes it relatively easy for the grader to understand your position. The grader who reads your work will need to work quickly to identify key elements of your essay. When you use a standardized format with a clear distinction between different types of paragraphs, you make it easy for the grader to figure out what you're trying to say . . . which, in turn, makes it easier for the grader to award you high scores.

4. Most test-takers have used a similar (or identical) format in school, so it's relatively easy to apply the 5-paragraph format to the SAT Essay.

(Remember that we're not saying the 5-paragraph format is the *only* way to score high on the SAT Essay! We're just discussing the most teachable, predictable, user-friendly way to score high on the SAT Essay, in my experience with my students.)

SAT Essay Rule 10: Make Sure You Use Quotes—But Not Just to Pad Your Essay.

When you write your essay, you'll need to quote the provided passage, and you'll need to write at least 600-700 words (typically 2.5 to 3 handwritten pages) in less than an hour. A lot of test-takers in this situation will be tempted to use long quotes from the passage to fill up space on the page and hit their target word count—but don't give in to that temptation!

Even though a top-scoring essay will includes quotations from the passage, we can tell from the sample essays provided by the College Board that it matters what you say about those quotations. You can't just fill your essay with long quotes and expect a good score—you need to provide some analysis, as well. (We'll talk about how to provide this analysis in a few pages.)

As it turns out, the samples from the College Board show us that perfect-scoring essays are about 10% - 15% quotations by word count, which means the original words of the test-taker account for about 85% - 90% of those essays.

Of course, this doesn't mean that the College Board's graders will actually calculate the percentage of the words in your essay that are quoted from the passage, or that you should try to! But it does suggest that roughly one-tenth of your essay should consist of the author's words, and nine-tenths should consist of your analysis of those words, as a general rule of thumb. This ratio seems to offer you the best chance to make sure your analysis is grounded in what the passage has to say, without seeming like you're going overboard with quotes just to increase the length of your essay.

If you take a look at the top-scoring sample essays from the College Board and follow the guidelines in this section of the Black Book, you should be good to go.

Understanding the Parts of the SAT Essay Prompt

Every SAT Essay prompt will tell you to consider three main aspects of the argument in a passage:

1. evidence
2. reasoning
3. stylistic or persuasive elements

The prompt does provide a brief explanation of what the College Board means when it uses these three terms, but many untrained test-takers still have a hard time feeling confident when they apply these concepts on test day. For that reason, I'd like to take a few moments and lay out some of the concrete differences between evidence, reasoning, and stylistic/persuasive elements.

As we discussed in SAT Essay Rule 3 on page 546, the College Board will state the author's thesis in the box of text that appears after the passage. Remember that the thesis is the statement of the author's opinion—but the author doesn't expect to convince his audience that his opinion is right just by stating it!

He has to provide an argument to support his position, which is why he writes an entire passage instead of a single sentence. For purposes of the SAT Essay, the argument will include two main kinds of elements:

1. Logic, which involves the use of facts and rational thinking. In the context of our SAT Essay training, the logical side of the argument is the "evidence" and "reasoning" mentioned in the prompt.
2. Emotion, which involves affecting the reader's feelings so the reader will sympathize with the author. In the context of our SAT Essay training, the emotional side of the argument corresponds to the "stylistic and persuasive elements" mentioned in the prompt.

So evidence and reasoning are inherently related to the logical form of the author's argument, while style and persuasion reflect the emotional content of the author's message. With that fundamental division in mind, let's go into some details that will help you understand how to use these concepts on test day.

What is Evidence?

For our purposes, a piece of *evidence* is almost any statement an author makes in an attempt to support his position. For example, in the passage that appears in the SAT Essay section of SAT Practice Test #1, Jimmy Carter says that the Arctic National Wildlife Refuge has been protected "by both Democratic and Republican presidents." Carter presents this personal anecdote as evidence that people with different political philosophies can agree that the Arctic National Wildlife Refuge is worth saving.

Most of the statements in the SAT Essay passage you see on test day could be thought of as statements of evidence. Since these statements play such a large role in the process of writing your SAT Essay, I'll explain briefly how to recognize common kinds of evidence.

Bear in mind that most passages you'll see on the SAT Essay section will only use a handful of these kinds of evidence at most. Some passages might even cite other kinds of evidence, and of course you should feel free to analyze those other kinds of evidence if you see them on test day. But being familiar with the types of evidence below will give you a significant advantage over untrained test-takers, because there's a good chance you'll see at least a couple of the following on test day:

- **Numbers and statistics**
  Many readers and authors believe that numbers give an air of authority and official weight to an argument. Quantifying a claim can also make it seem more precise and believable. We can often identify numbers and statistics at a glance in a body of text. Our eyes might also be drawn to characters like percentage signs or decimals.

- **Historical or political events**
  Writers often refer to history (or to current politics) to show what the impact of a choice is likely to be, based on what the author claims to have been the historical precedent of similar choices. We can sometimes identify historical examples at a glance in a body of text because they involve numbers for years or centuries, or because they involve the proper names of historical figures.

- **Anecdotes and personal accounts**
  Some writers like to tell stories in support of their arguments. These stories are often personal narratives of things that happened to the author herself, but they can also focus on the experiences of other people. These kinds of stories can help a writer put a human face on a situation. They can also identify the writer with the argument in such a way that the reader is hesitant to disagree with the argument, because disagreeing with the argument would feel like personally insulting the writer. We can sometimes recognize these elements of arguments because they'll incorporate the word "I," or the name of another person involved in an anecdote.

Bear in mind that these aren't the only kinds of evidence that could appear in the passage, and you don't have to classify the evidence you find into one of these groups. There's no need to memorize these types of evidence and the ways that we can recognize them. We're only discussing these different types of evidence here to give you an idea of what kinds of statements in the text could be examples of evidence that you'll use in your essay.

What is Reasoning?

For the purposes of the SAT Essay section, *reasoning* consists of the underlying logic or assumption that connects an evidence statement back to the thesis. To continue the example we just talked about from Carter's passage, we could say that the reasoning that connects the comment about support from Democratic and Republican presidents back to Jimmy Carter's thesis would be an unstated idea like "if Democratic and Republican presidents can agree that the Arctic National Wildlife Refuge should be protected, then protecting that refuge must be a pretty reasonable idea that appeals to people with different political philosophies."

(Sometimes the reasoning that connects an evidence statement to the thesis will be stated directly in the passage, but it will often be unstated, too — in other words, there will often be situations where the author assumes that the reader will understand why evidence supports the author's thesis, even though the author doesn't spell out the connection. We'll see examples of this idea in a moment.)

Connecting evidence and reasoning: what, why, and how

If you're having trouble thinking of the way reasoning and evidence relate to each other, you can try to think of them in terms of questions that start with "what," "why," and "how." The answer to the "what" question tells us what the evidence is; the answer to the "why" and/or "how" questions lets us identify the reasoning that connects the evidence to the thesis.

- The **evidence** in an argument consists of the facts cited by the author: *What* does the author say?
- Part of the **reasoning** in an argument is the author's underlying purpose for mentioning a piece of evidence: *Why* does the author cite this piece of evidence in support of his thesis?
- Another aspect of the **reasoning** in an argument is a consideration of the impact on the reader: *How* does this evidence convince the reader to agree with the author?

The answers to these what-why-how questions will help us identify the evidence and reasoning that support the author's thesis.

Real-life examples of evidence and reasoning

Let's take a more in-depth look at evidence and reasoning at work in a real SAT Essay passage. We'll continue to look at the passage from the SAT Essay section from SAT Practice Test #1.

In the table below, the "Evidence" column contains examples of evidence statements from the passage. The "Reasoning" column shows the reasoning that connects the evidence back to the thesis of the passage. Remember that the reasoning may be directly stated in the passage, or it may be implied.

Thesis: The Arctic National Wildlife Refuge should not be developed for industry.	
Evidence *What does the author say in support of his thesis?*	Reasoning *Why does the author choose this evidence?* *How does the statement convince the reader?*
Carter says, "The Arctic National Wildlife Refuge stands alone as America's last truly great wilderness."	This statement creates a sense of urgency about preserving the refuge, because if the refuge is developed for industry, then there will be no "truly great wilderness" left in America.
Carter cites the "windswept coastal plain where polar bears and caribou give birth," as well as the "Brooks Range where Dall sheep cling to the cliffs and wolves howl in the midnight sun."	The description of the different animals in their separate environments gives the reader a sense of how many different kinds of wildlife would be impacted by the industrial development of the refuge, which drives home the point that this harmful industrial development should not happen.
Carter and his wife saw "ancient caribou trails" and "the brilliant mosaic of wildflowers, mosses, and lichens that hugged the tundra."	This description of the natural beauty of the refuge provides the reader with a vivid mental image of this faraway place, which helps to create a connection between the reader and the Arctic wilderness, so that the reader will agree that the wilderness should not be developed. The personal nature of the anecdote also gives the weight of Carter's reputation and image to his position that the refuge should not be developed for industry.
The land had a "timeless quality," and the Carters "watched muskox, those shaggy survivors of the Ice Age, lumber along braided rivers."	When Carter mentions the "timelessness" of the land, and the muskox who have lived there since the Ice Age, he drives home the point that the Alaskan National Wildlife Refuge has been

	the same for centuries. This insight makes it easy for the reader to take his side in thinking that the refuge must not be developed, because development would change the landscape.
"One of the most unforgettable and humbling experiences" the Carters ever had was when they "witnessed the migration of tens of thousands of caribou." He called this procession a "once-in-a-lifetime wildlife spectacle."	This description of such an incredible experience in the Arctic National Wildlife Refuge reminds the reader that if the land is developed, such an experience will no longer be possible, because the "proposed developments would forever destroy the wilderness character of America's only Arctic refuge." Carter thinks it would be bad if that "wilderness character" were destroyed, which is why he doesn't want those developments to happen.
The Arctic Refuge has been consistently protected "by both Republican and Democratic presidents."	The fact that a variety of people with different political alignments still support the refuge makes the reader feel like protecting the refuge must be a reasonable thing to do. It also lends the weight and credibility of the presidency to the statement that the refuge should not be developed for industry.
The original refuge was established in 1960, and Carter significantly expanded the refuge twenty years later.	Now the reader knows that Jimmy Carter himself has already taken action to defend the refuge, which gives his argument credibility.
Since Carter left office, "there have been repeated proposals to open the Arctic Refuge coastal plain to oil drilling," and those proposals haven't succeeded because of "tremendous opposition by the American people."	This statement establishes the popularity of the refuge by noting that many other people want to protect the refuge from drilling. This is likely to convince the reader because most readers will assume a popular position must be valid.
The Gwich'in Athabascan Indians are "indigenous people whose culture has depended on the Porcupine caribou herd for thousands of years."	This fact plays on the reader's sympathies, compelling the reader to agree with Carter in support of the rights of this native population and their ancient way of life, which will apparently be destroyed if the refuge is developed.
The oil in the Arctic Refuge might, at best, provide "1 to 2 percent of the oil our country consumes each day;" we can save more fuel by just "driving more fuel-efficient vehicles."	This statement shows that the benefits of drilling in the refuge would be minimal, which is another reason not to develop the refuge for industry.
There are "few places on earth as wild and free as the Arctic Refuge," and it will be a "grand triumph" to preserve this land.	This repetition of the idea that the Arctic Refuge is rare and endangered helps to underscore the importance of preserving the refuge for generations to come, strengthening the idea that the Refuge should not be developed for industry.

The table above gets pretty repetitive, but that's because I tried to include more or less every bit of evidence from the passage. As we'll see in this training section, you won't need to include nearly so many pieces of evidence in your actual essay. I included them here in an effort to help you see the way an essay's evidence and reasoning support its thesis.

What if we don't feel confident figuring out what the reasoning is?

You may notice that some of the text in the "Reasoning" column came from the passage, but a lot of it didn't. Remember that the reasoning is the underlying idea that connects the evidence to the thesis. Authors often assume that the reasoning will be understood by the reader without needing to be stated.

This might seem like a problem on a standardized test like the SAT. How can the College Board expect that readers will just "understand" what the reasoning is when it isn't always stated directly in the passage?

The College Board "solves" this problem by accepting just about any sort of reasoning that makes any kind of sense in context. This is good news for us as test-takers, because it means we don't have to worry about analyzing the passage in exactly the way the grader would analyze it. Instead, we just need to come up with some sort of reasoning—some kind of answer to the "how" and/or "why" questions—that could plausibly connect the evidence with the thesis. (Remember, too, that the grader is going to read your essay in only a few minutes, so there likely won't be time to dissect the details of the reasoning you find in the passage anyway, even if the grader wanted to do that.)

For example, the perfect-scoring sample essay called "Student Sample 6," about the plastic bag ban, refers to the following sentence from Adam B. Summers's essay about banning plastic bags:

> Believe me, I love sea turtles as much as the next guy.

The perfect-scoring test-taker says this sentence

> adds acceptance to those who don't care to act with regard for the environment

which is a statement of the author's reasoning in the passage. But notice that the passage doesn't actually mention people acting without regard for the environment! There's no strict textual basis in the passage for the reasoning provided by the test-taker. But the test-taker's statement kind of vaguely makes sense when discussing a passage arguing against a ban on plastic bags, so this kind of reasoning statement can appear in a perfect-scoring essay.

Similarly, a perfect-scoring sample essay available on the College Board's website at the time of this writing refers to the following sentence from the passage from the SAT Essay section of SAT Practice Test #4:

> At my family's cabin on a Minnesota lake, I knew woods so dark that my hands disappeared before my eyes.

The test-taker says this sentence

> challenges the audience to remember a time [when they were] in natural darkness.

But the passage never actually asks the reader to remember anything! Again, this kind of "analysis" of the passage's reasoning can appear in a perfect-scoring essay because it sounds vaguely plausible.

So don't worry too much that you might misidentify the reasoning in the passage. As long as the reasoning you identify is at least loosely connected to what the passage actually says, you should be in good shape.

Understanding Stylistic and Persuasive Elements

We just discussed the ideas of evidence and reasoning as they appear in the SAT Essay prompt. Those ideas were related to the passage's logical structure: the author cites evidence in support of the thesis, and his reasoning is the (often unstated) thought process that connects the evidence to the thesis.

Now, we'll discuss the "stylistic and persuasive elements" that are also referred to in the prompt for the SAT Essay. These elements are fundamentally different from what we've already talked about: instead of a logical analysis of *what* the author talks about in the passage, stylistic and persuasive elements relate to the author's use of specific words and short phrases to get an emotional response from the reader.

Let's look again at the passage from the SAT Essay section of SAT Practice Test #1. Here are some comments we might make about the stylistic and persuasive elements in that essay:

> When Carter describes the Arctic Refuge with words like "magnificent" and "truly great," he creates an emotional response in his audience, who will feel proud of such an exceptional place and unwilling to risk losing it.
>
> The author describes the caribou migration at the Arctic National Wildlife Refuge as "unforgettable" and "humbling." These powerful words evoke a sense of duty to protect such an awe-inspiring place.
>
> When Carter discusses the possibility of the refuge being developed for industry, he uses words like "saddened" and "tragedy," and says that such development would "destroy" and "disturb" the refuge. This repeated use of negative words creates a sense of fear and concern in the reader for the future of the refuge.

As we can see, words like "magnificent," "truly great," "unforgettable," "humbling," "saddened," "tragedy," "destroy," and "disturb" can all evoke an emotional response in the reader that's similar to the emotion felt by the author, which in turn makes it more likely that the reader will agree with the author.

How can we recognize stylistic and persuasive wording on test day?

One reliable way to recognize words and phrases that you can cite as examples of stylistic and persuasive elements on test day is to look out for extreme words that could be defined using the word "very." As we'll see, words that evoke an emotional response from the reader could mean something like very good, very bad, very happy, very sad, very big, very small, very exciting, very frightening, very important, very urgent, etc.

Here are some other words and phrases that evoke an emotional response, found in the passage from the SAT Essay section of SAT Practice Test #1:

- "vast" (very big)
- "towering" (very tall)
- "fortunate" (very lucky)
- "brilliant" (very bright)

- "great" (very good)
- "dramatic" (very substantial or noticeable)
- "once-in-a-lifetime" (very rare)
- "monumental" (very important)

- "grand triumph" (very big accomplishment)
- "extraordinary land" (very special place)
- . . . and so on

Conclusion

Now that we've seen several examples of the different elements mentioned in the SAT Essay prompt, you should have a better idea of how passages are structured on this part of the test:

- The author of the passage cites evidence to give logical support to the thesis; the reasoning that connects the evidence to the thesis is often unstated.

- The stylistic and persuasive elements of the passage are the emotionally charged words and phrases that induce the reader to feel what the author wants her to feel, and to support the argument on a personal level.

Recommended Structure for Your SAT Essay

As I mentioned earlier, there are probably many possible approaches that you could take to structuring a perfect-scoring SAT Essay. But here's the structure I recommend using, based on extensive analysis of the graded sample essays that have been released by the College Board, combined with decades of experience in helping lots and lots of people write top-scoring essays for a variety of standardized tests:

First, 1 Introductory Paragraph

Every high-scoring sample essay provided by the College Board starts with an introductory paragraph that states that the author of the provided passage did a good job making her argument, so your SAT Essay should start that way, too.

Next, 1 - 3 Body Paragraphs Discussing Evidence and Reasoning

In these paragraphs, you'll discuss the evidence and reasoning that you found in the passage. If you want, you can break up the evidence and reasoning into 2 or 3 categories, like "historical references," "statistics," and "economic impact" (or whatever else makes sense in the context of the passage), and then discuss each category of evidence (and the reasoning connected to that evidence) in its own paragraph. So you might have a body paragraph where you discuss historical references in the passage and the reasoning that connects those references to the thesis, and then you might have a second body paragraph that discusses statistics in the passage and the reasoning that connects those statistics back to the thesis. If you have time, you might have a third body paragraph that discusses economic considerations in the passage and the reasoning that connects those statistics back to the thesis.

You can also just discuss all your evidence and reasoning in one or two big body paragraphs about evidence and reasoning, if you prefer—you don't have to break the evidence and reasoning up into different categories and discuss them separately if you don't want to, but some students like to break it up that way.

(By the way, there's nothing magical about the idea of devoting 1 - 3 body paragraphs to evidence and reasoning. It's just that you'll need at least 1 body paragraph about evidence and reasoning, and it's unlikely that you'll have the time to write more than 3 body paragraphs on evidence and reasoning.)

Then, 1 Body Paragraph Discussing Stylistic and Persuasive Elements

Every perfect-scoring sample SAT Essay provided by the College Board at the time of this writing has a body paragraph about stylistic and persuasive elements that appears right before the conclusion paragraph, so you should plan to do the same thing. You may notice that some of the high-scoring sample essays from the College Board refer to this as the author's "appeal to emotion," or just "persuasive elements," or something else along those lines, but you can also just call it a paragraph about "stylistic and persuasive elements" if you want to keep it simple.

Finally, 1 Concluding Paragraph

Every high-scoring sample essay provided by the College Board ends with a concluding paragraph that basically sums up everything the test-taker has said in the earlier paragraphs, so—again—your essay should too.

In the next section, we'll discuss in more detail the step-by-step process you can follow to generate an SAT essay using this structure.

Recommended Step-By-Step Approach to the SAT Essay

This process is an effective way to organize your thoughts and write a response that closely imitates known high-scoring essays. Feel free to use it or adapt it to fit the situation—but make sure any adaptations you make are still in line with the rules for the SAT Essay in this Black Book.

In the example below, we'll write a response to sample practice essay #1 from the College Board's SAT Practice Test #1.

1. Identify the College Board's Statement of the Passage's Thesis by Looking in the Box of Text after the Passage.

As we discussed in Rule 3 a few pages ago, it's faster and smarter to use the College Board's statement of the passage's thesis, rather than spending the time to try to determine the thesis on our own and risking a misinterpretation of the passage.

In the case of the passage from SAT Practice Test #1, the College Board's statement of Carter's thesis is the following:

> the Arctic National Wildlife Refuge should not be developed for industry.

2. With the Thesis from Step 1 in Mind, Read the Provided Passage. Note the Author's Use of Evidence, Reasoning, Stylistic Elements, and Persuasive Elements. Consider Underlining These Elements for Later Reference as You Read the Passage.

We'll need to read most or all of the passage in order to know which parts of it we want to talk about. This reading should be a little different from the way we'd read a passage on the SAT Reading section, or on the Writing and Language section: on those sections, we know the test will ask us multiple-choice questions that guide us to specific portions of the passage and allow us to evaluate provided options to determine which choice follows the SAT's rules. But for the essay, it will be largely up to us to decide which aspects of the passage to talk about. This doesn't require us to read every single word of the passage with strict attention, but it does require us to pay attention in a way that isn't always necessary on other parts of the test.

The goal is to read the passage only once at the beginning of our writing process, and then just refer back to it in bits and pieces when we need quotes to analyze in our body paragraphs. This minimizes the overall time spent reading the passage, allowing us to spend more time on our actual writing, which gives us a better chance of approaching the length of 600 – 700 words (or typically 2.5 to 3 handwritten pages) that often correlates with perfect scores on the SAT Essay.

We also want to note (and possibly underline, if you so choose) some specific examples of evidence, reasoning, persuasive elements, and stylistic elements that jump out at us as we go through the passage.

3. Decide which Topics to Cover in Your Body Paragraphs. Remember that You'll Write 1 - 3 Body Paragraphs about Evidence and Reasoning, and 1 Body Paragraph about Stylistic/Persuasive Elements!

For the passage from SAT Practice Test #1, we might note the following elements being used:

- Personal anecdotes
- Historical events
- Statistics
- Appeals to emotions like pride, sorrow, and empathy

We probably won't have time to cover all four of those topics in our essay, but we can probably cover three of them.

As trained test-takers, we know that we'll need to have a body paragraph about stylistic and persuasive elements, so we'll want to make sure we cover the appeals to emotion. That means we need to choose two of the other topics to write about. I'll choose personal anecdotes and statistics, just because I feel like it—it would also be perfectly fine to write about historical events or some other topic entirely if you felt like there was enough evidence in the passage to discuss that topic in its own paragraph.

So I've decided my body paragraphs will focus on these elements:

- Personal anecdotes
- Statistics
- Appeals to emotions (in this case, pride, sorrow, and empathy)

(Remember that you can choose to just have one or two big body paragraphs that discuss all the different kinds of evidence together, along with the reasoning that connects that evidence to the thesis, if you prefer not to classify the different kinds of evidence you'll discuss into groups like "personal anecdotes" and "statistics." But you'll still need a separate paragraph to discuss stylistic and persuasive elements.)

4. Write your Introductory Paragraph.

When you set out to write your intro paragraph, it's important to remember that you probably won't be able to do much editing later on, since you'll need to write 600 – 700 words (probably around 2.5 to 3 handwritten pages) in order to have a good chance at making a perfect score. So your goal in this first paragraph is just to sketch out the main points of your essay in advance, without committing too heavily to any particular statements, because you don't want to say something that ends up needing to be changed when you're done with the rest of the essay.

I recommend you start by restating the information written in bold at the beginning of the passage (including the author and other basic information), and then accurately quote the author's position on the given topic, and say that the author successfully makes his argument. (Remember that we identified Carter's statement of his argument in the first step of this process.)

> In Jimmy Carter's foreword for Subhankar Banerjee's book "Arctic National Wildlife Refuge: Seasons of Life and Land, A Photographic Journey," Carter argues successfully that the "greatest gift we could pass on to future generations" would be to "preserve the Arctic Refuge in its pure, untrammeled state."

Next, you could restate the author's position with a quote or detail from the passage. (Note that I use the verb "maintains" instead of "argues" in this next sentence to try to keep it from being too obvious that I'm just repeating myself.)

> He maintains that "proposed developments" like "pipelines" and "drilling rigs" would "forever destroy the wilderness character of America's only Arctic refuge."

Finally, I'll say that the author uses the elements we selected in the previous step, and I'll mention again that the author does a good job with his argument. I'll also mention what that argument is one more time, using another quote I found. (If you can't easily incorporate another quote here, don't worry about it.)

> Carter effectively combines anecdotes and compelling statistics with appeals to emotions like pride and empathy in order to reinforce his position that the American people should "look beyond the alleged benefits of a short-term economic gain" to protect the "precious wilderness" of the Arctic.

5. Write Your First Body Paragraph, Focusing on the First Element of the Argument that You Want to Talk About.

In our case, personal anecdotes were one of the things I first noticed in Carter's argument, so I'll make them the focus of my first body paragraph. I'll start the paragraph by mentioning which type of evidence I'm going to explore here.

> Carter's personal experiences in the Arctic Refuge play a key role in his argument.

Now that we've got our topic sentence for this paragraph written, we'll begin giving supporting examples, keeping in mind that we need to analyze each piece of evidence we cite. We'll do this by discussing the author's reasoning, which means we explain *why* this piece of evidence supports the author's thesis, and *how* that evidence helps convince the reader.

Here's my first example sentence on the topic of Carter's personal anecdotes, which will cite the evidence portion of this example:

> He begins his story by telling the reader of his "fortunate opportunity" to go hiking in the Arctic Refuge years ago, when he saw "wildflowers, mosses, and lichens" sharing the "timeless" landscape with muskox.

With this sentence, I've asserted that Carter's evidence is his anecdote, which mentions things he saw while hiking. Now I'll explain "why" he does this, in the context of his argument:

> This reference to Carter's personal experiences in the rugged natural beauty of the Arctic Refuge establishes a sense of the area's importance. It also establishes that Carter knows firsthand what he's talking about.

Now that we've said what he did in the argument and why he did it, I'll explain how his choice convinces the reader to agree with his thesis. In other words, I'll explain the connection between this piece of evidence and Carter's thesis.

> After finishing the second paragraph of Carter's argument, the reader believes that Carter has a genuine appreciation for the Arctic Refuge, and that his appreciation is valid. The reader is now ready to consider anything that Carter has to say about the Refuge, and Carter will proceed to use this to his advantage.

Okay! Now we've finished our first analysis on the topic of Carter's personal anecdotes for our first body paragraph. All we need to do now is analyze another anecdote or two, depending on how much raw material we find in the passage and how much time we have left—remember that we still need to address at least a couple of other concepts in other body paragraphs, such as the use of statistics and the author's appeals to emotions.

I'll create the next analysis of evidence and reasoning all at once, to show you how that can work:

> Carter's personal tale of his time in the Refuge ends with him remembering how he was "saddened to think of the tragedy" that could occur if "developments" were allowed to "destroy the wilderness character of America's only Arctic Refuge." At this point, the reader sees that Carter has been building up to a plea for support of the preservation of the Refuge. Because the reader has already been won over by Carter's moving personal description of his time in the Refuge, it's easy to agree with his position.

At this point, we've provided two strong examples of evidence and reasoning for our first body paragraph. We should always include at least one example from the text in each body paragraph about evidence and reasoning, but two or more is better if we have time and we can find those examples in the text.

For now, I need to close out my first body paragraph before moving on to the next one. So I'll pad out this paragraph with a sentence that sets up the next paragraph:

> Thanks to Carter's personal narrative, the reader is now ready to learn more about the Refuge and why it should be saved.

6. Repeat Step 5 to Create Your Second Body Paragraph, Focusing on the Second Kind of Evidence and Reasoning that You Want to Talk About:

As we did for the first body paragraph, we'll construct the second body paragraph by combining an intro sentence, some examples of evidence from the text and the reasoning that connects those examples to the author's thesis, and a concluding sentence. Here's what that might look like (remember that we came up with "statistics" as the second element we wanted to talk about):

> After discussing his personal experiences, Carter turns his attention to the economic dimension of preserving the Refuge, citing a key statistic that seals his case. He says that oil from the Arctic Refuge "might provide 1 to 2 percent of the oil our country consumes each day." This shows the reader that the potential gain from drilling for oil in the Refuge is relatively small, which further reinforces Carter's argument that we shouldn't drill there. Carter puts this oil savings into perspective when he says, "we can easily conserve" more oil than we would get from the Refuge if people would just "driv[e] more fuel-efficient vehicles," which finally convinces the reader that it would be foolish to develop the refuge, since other measures would be preferable to damaging a pristine place like the refuge. The reader now realizes that Carter's argument has merit in objective terms, beyond the personal views he expressed earlier.

This second body paragraph is shorter than the first, but still adequately covers what it needs to, and gives a good analysis of the reasoning that connects the cited evidence to the thesis. Now I'll go ahead and add the third body paragraph—remember that all perfect-scoring sample essays include a body paragraph discussing stylistic and persuasive elements right before the concluding paragraph, so we'll discuss those elements here in a paragraph about appeals to emotion.

7. After You've Written Your Body Paragraphs about Evidence and Reasoning, Write a Body Paragraph about Stylistic and Persuasive Elements in the Passage.

As we mentioned on page 555, we'll need to discuss examples of the passage's appeals to emotion, and then include an explanation of how those particular examples convince the reader to agree with the author of the passage.

> But Carter doesn't just build his argument on solid evidence—he also makes subtle appeals to his readers' emotions. He uses many powerful phrases to describe the Refuge, calling it "America's last truly great wilderness;" near the end of his argument, he even says it's a "precious" symbol of our "national heritage." This wording deliberately evokes a sense of pride and personal involvement on the part of the reader. Carter also appeals to the reader's empathy when he mentions the Gwich'in Athabascan Indians by name and tells us that he personally feels moved by their "struggle to safeguard one of their precious human rights." Carter's descriptions of his own emotions effectively create an emotional response in the reader, who can't help but share the view that this wilderness must be preserved.

At this point, we've written three body paragraphs to support our introductory paragraph, and we're approaching both the time limit and the goal of 600 – 700 words (or about 2.5 to 3 handwritten pages) that we set for ourselves. Under the circumstances, it's time to wrap things up with a concluding paragraph.

8. Write Your Concluding Paragraph:

Make a broad statement about how the author uses the elements you noted in your body paragraphs to make his argument:

> Carter's mix of personal experience, statistical reasoning, and appeals to emotion makes it clear that the Arctic National Wildlife Refuge should not be developed for industry.

Restate the author's position with a quote or detail from the passage.

> As he says, "it will be a grand triumph for America if we can preserve the Arctic Refuge."

Say one more time that the author does a good job convincing us that his position is correct.

> Anyone who reads Carter's argument can be counted on to agree with him.

Complete Sample Essay

Here's the 694-word sample essay we just wrote, all in one place, in case you'd like to read it. Quotations from the passage account for roughly 15% of the essay's length.

> In Jimmy Carter's foreword for Subhankar Banerjee's book "Arctic National Wildlife Refuge: Seasons of Life and Land, A Photographic Journey," Carter argues successfully that the "greatest gift we could pass on to future generations" would be to "preserve the Arctic Refuge in its pure, untrammeled state." He maintains that "proposed developments" like "pipelines" and "drilling rigs" would "forever destroy the wilderness character of America's only Arctic refuge." Carter effectively combines anecdotes and compelling statistics with appeals to emotions like pride and empathy in order to reinforce his position that the American people should "look beyond the alleged benefits of a short-term economic gain" to protect the "precious wilderness" of the Arctic.

> Carter's personal experiences in the Arctic Refuge play a key role in his argument. He begins his story by telling the reader of his "fortunate opportunity" to go hiking in the Arctic Refuge years ago, when he saw "wildflowers, mosses, and lichens" sharing the "timeless" landscape with muskox. This reference to Carter's personal experiences in the rugged natural beauty of the Arctic Refuge establishes a sense of the area's importance. It also establishes that Carter knows firsthand what he's talking about. After finishing the second paragraph of Carter's argument, the reader believes that Carter has a genuine appreciation for the Arctic Refuge, and that his appreciation is valid. The reader is now ready to consider anything that Carter has to say about the Refuge, and Carter will proceed to use this to his advantage. Carter's personal tale of his time in the Refuge ends with him remembering how he was "saddened to think of the tragedy" that could occur if "developments" were allowed to "destroy the wilderness character of America's only Arctic Refuge." At this point, the reader sees that Carter has been building up to a plea for support of the preservation of the Refuge. Because the reader has already been won over by Carter's moving personal description of his time in the Refuge, it's easy to agree with his position. Thanks to Carter's personal narrative, the reader is now ready to learn more about the Refuge and why it should be saved.

> After discussing his personal experiences, Carter turns his attention to the economic dimension of preserving the Refuge, citing a key statistic that seals his case. He says that oil from the Arctic Refuge "might provide 1 to 2 percent of the oil our country consumes each day." This shows the reader that the potential gain from drilling for oil in the Refuge is relatively small, which further reinforces Carter's argument that we shouldn't drill there.

Carter puts this oil savings into perspective when he says, "we can easily conserve" more oil than we would get from the Refuge if people would just "driv[e] more fuel-efficient vehicles," which finally convinces the reader that it would be foolish to develop the refuge, since other measures would be preferable to damaging a pristine place like the refuge. The reader now realizes that Carter's argument has merit in objective terms, beyond the personal views he expressed earlier.

But Carter doesn't just build his argument on solid evidence—he also makes subtle appeals to his readers' emotions. He uses many powerful phrases to describe the Refuge, calling it "America's last truly great wilderness;" near the end of his argument, he even says it's a "precious" symbol of our "national heritage." This wording deliberately evokes a sense of pride and personal involvement on the part of the reader. Carter also appeals to the reader's empathy when he mentions the Gwich'in Athabascan Indians by name and tells us that he personally feels moved by their "struggle to safeguard one of their precious human rights." Carter's descriptions of his own emotions effectively create an emotional response in the reader, who can't help but share the view that this wilderness must be preserved.

Carter's mix of personal experience, statistical reasoning, and emotion makes it clear that the Arctic National Wildlife Refuge should not be developed for industry. As he says, "it will be a grand triumph for America if we can preserve the Arctic Refuge." Anyone who reads Carter's argument can be counted on to agree with him.

Notes on this Process

You've probably noticed that this formula is fairly repetitive—it restates ideas from the passage often, and uses roughly the same structure in each body paragraph, based on the same pattern of citing part of the passage and then explaining why and/or how that part of the passage convinces the reader to agree with the author's thesis. Don't let that bother you. As the high-scoring sample essays from the College Board demonstrate, this is the way the SAT rewards you for writing.

There are a few other aspects of this process that might seem strange to people who expect to treat the SAT Essay like a regular high school essay, and I'd like to address some of them now.

I don't recommend taking notes on the passage (beyond potentially underlining pieces of evidence that you want to refer to later), for these reasons:

- Note-taking generally makes test-takers nervous about time limits, and nervous about whether they're taking notes on the right aspects of the passage. In my experience, most test-takers perform worse when they're nervous.

- We don't really have to remember much in order to use the approach I recommend for the SAT Essay. When we read the passage through the first time, we just make a quick mental note of the general types of elements of the argument that we encounter (for example, we might just remember the author cites scientific studies, recounts a personal experience, and appeals to our emotions). We only need to remember these broad types of elements once, when we incorporate them in our opening paragraph. Then, for each body paragraph, we just glance up at the intro paragraph to remind ourselves which element we should be working on next, and then we glance back at the passage to find the quotes that are relevant to the element we're discussing in the current paragraph. At the end of the process, we create the conclusion paragraph by glancing back through the essay (especially the intro paragraph) to note the points we made, so we can restate them. We never need to keep a separate record of our analysis in any notes, because we're just writing our analysis straight into our essay as we think of it.

I don't recommend doing any separate planning, for reasons similar to the ones I have against note-taking, other than planning to follow the format discussed here. Further planning just eats up time that would be better spent trying to reach the 600 — 700-word goal, and we don't really need to plan anything anyway, since we already know we'll use a modified 5-paragraph format with an intro, some body paragraphs, and a conclusion. Each part of the essay can be generated more or less automatically according to the process we just discussed, so there's not really any need to write down anything separately beforehand.

An Analysis of Perfect-Scoring SAT Sample Essays from the Blue Book and from the College Board's Web Site

Since there are many ways to write the SAT Essay while still respecting the unwritten rules and patterns of the test, I think one of the best ways to see what a top-scoring SAT Essay really does is to analyze the two SAT Essays in the Blue Book that are provided as examples of the "perfect" SAT Essay, along with the only perfect-scoring essay sample that currently appears on the College Board's website, which you can find by navigating to https://collegereadiness.collegeboard.org/sample-questions/essay/1 .

Student Sample 6 (about the Plastic Bag Ban) from the Blue Book

Length

This essay is 642 words long, which would probably exceed two and a half pages if written out by hand on test day. This length is typical for an SAT Essay that receives a perfect score. Roughly 12% of the essay's length is made up of quotes from the passage.

Thesis

The introductory paragraph includes the following two sentences:

> By the end of this piece the reader will likely find themselves nodding in agreement with what Summers has to say, and this isn't just because he's right. Summers, like any good writer, employs tactical reasoning and persuasive devices to plead with the audience to take his side.

This direct statement that the author has made a convincing argument using certain literary devices or strategies is what we expect from a high-scoring SAT essay.

Structure

This essay is 4 paragraphs long, but still uses the basic "5-paragraph" structure we discussed in this section: it begins with an introductory paragraph, then has some supporting body paragraphs, and finally closes with a concluding paragraph.

The first paragraph is a normal intro paragraph, providing basic information about the passage, and stating that the author has done well presenting his argument.

The second paragraph focuses on the author's use of numbers to make his argument. Recall that citing statistics and numbers was one of the common elements of arguments that we talked about on page 550. You'll also see that the test-taker uses the analytical structure we talked about to mention evidence from the text and explain how it convinces the reader to agree with the author's thesis.

The third paragraph describes the passage's appeal to emotions, listing a number of examples of the wording used by the author, and explains how those examples support the author's position. The test-taker again uses analysis to show how the cited text causes the reader to agree with the author, as we can see in this quote:

> Appealing to environmentalists, too, Summers qualifies that they "have every right to try to convince people to adopt certain beliefs or lifestyles, but they do not have the right to use government force ..." A statement such as this is an attempt to get readers of either persuasion on his side, and his ingenius [sic] qualification only adds to the strength of his argument.

The first sentence in this quote cites the passage, and the second sentence tells us how that part of the passage convinces the reader to agree with the author's thesis.

The fourth paragraph is a normal concluding paragraph. It reiterates the various ways that the passage conveys and supports his position, and also reiterates that the passage does a good job convincing the reader.

This is basically the 5-paragraph format we discussed, except the second body paragraph is extra long and there's no third body paragraph.

Selected errors

In the first sentence, the author forms the possessive of the singular noun "Adam B. Summers" by adding an apostrophe instead of an apostrophe and an "s." In the third paragraph, the author uses the non-word "ethnical" in place of the word "ethical." In the same paragraph, the author also forgets the apostrophe in the possessive form "legislation's" and uses the subject pronoun "he" instead of the object pronoun "him" after the preposition "between." (Bear in mind that we're not criticizing the author of this essay when we point out these errors, especially since the author wasn't really given any time to proofread! I just want to show you evidence that essays can include several grammatical errors and score high.)

Student Sample 7 (about the Plastic Bag Ban) from the Blue Book

Length

This essay is 802 words long, which would probably exceed three pages if written out by hand on test day. This length is typical for an SAT Essay that receives a perfect score. Roughly 16% of the essay's length comes from quoting the passage.

Thesis

The introductory paragraph includes the following two sentences:

> Adam B. Summers has created a highly plausible argument that may change your answer next time you go grocery shopping. He has developed valid claims that are backed up with crucial evidence and has been able to properly persuade the reader by appealing to logos and other rhetorical strategies.

This direct statement that the author has made a convincing argument using certain literary devices or strategies is what we expect from a high-scoring SAT essay.

Structure

This essay uses a 5-paragraph format, just as we recommended in "Recommended Structure for Your SAT Essay" on page 555. The first paragraph provides basic information about the passage, and states that the author has made a good argument.

The second paragraph quotes or restates various parts of the passage, focusing primarily on the passage's use of numbers and discussion of the economic impact of eliminating plastic bags. We see a slightly less clear example of the author citing evidence and then explaining how the evidence convinces the reader to agree with the author's thesis, but that structure is still evident if we pay attention; each example from the text is followed by some discussion from the test-taker, but she waits until the end of the paragraph to explain how *all* the examples convince the reader to agree with the author by saying this:

> These four ideas are successfully connected and convince the reader to use plastic bags over paper bags and other types of reusable bags.

The third paragraph lists some sources and authorities that are used in the passage, and explains how those sources give weight to the author's position. Here, again, we see that the author waits until the end of the paragraph to explain (this time in two sentences) how the evidence cited in the paragraph causes the reader to agree with the author.

The fourth paragraph is a shorter one, focusing primarily on the author's appeal to emotion. (The test-taker uses the word "pathos" instead of the word "emotion," because a common trend in American high schools now is to analyze works in terms of the classical Greek constructs of logos, pathos, and ethos. If you're not familiar with those Greek terms, don't worry; you don't have to use them on test day.) The intro part of this paragraph is relatively long and reiterates the test-taker's earlier statements about the passage. The test-taker says the passage evokes an emotional response by reminding people to make the Earth a nice place to live, and reminding them that they might get sick if they ban plastic bags. Again, the final sentence explains how the material discussed in the paragraph convinces the reader of the author's thesis.

The fifth paragraph is a standard conclusion paragraph for an SAT Essay. It makes a couple of general statements about how the passage supported its position, and then reiterates that the passage does a good job convincing the reader to agree with the author.

This is pretty much exactly the same as the 5-paragraph format we discussed, except the supporting paragraphs in this example are a little less consistent as far as their structures.

Selected errors

In the second paragraph, the author unintentionally states that Summers himself misleads the readers, when in fact the readers are already being misled and Summers is the one showing them the truth. In the next sentence, the author uses the word "that" instead of "than." The phrase "Another claim by Summers . . ." later in the same paragraph is the beginning of a sentence fragment. A few sentences later, another fragment appears, this time starting with the phrase "A final claim by Summers."

The third paragraph includes the phrase "credible and believable," which is redundant because both words mean the same thing. The same sentence uses the object pronoun "us" instead of the subject pronoun "we," and inappropriately uses the preposition "of" after the word "confident." The fourth paragraph includes "evince" as a misspelling of "evidence," and uses the plural verb form "are" with the singular noun "use." Finally, the second-to-last sentence uses the object pronoun "us" instead of the subject pronoun "we" in the phrase "us readers can trust."

(Again—we're not pointing out all of these errors as a way of criticizing the authors! We're only doing it so you can see concrete evidence that essays with a number of errors can still score high. You should try to avoid errors as you write your essay, and you should look back over your essay if you end up having time to do that. But you shouldn't stress out about not having a lot of time—or any time—to proofread your work, because several grammatical errors won't stop you from getting a great score.)

The Perfect-Scoring Essay from the College Board's Web Site[3]

Length

This essay is 592 words long, which would probably be close to two and a half pages if written out by hand on test day; as we've seen repeatedly by now, this length of 2.5 or more pages is typical for an SAT Essay that receives a perfect score. Roughly 8% of the essay's word count comes from quotations of the original passage.

Thesis

The intro paragraph says the writer

> effectively builds his argument by using a personal anecdote, allusions to art and history, and rhetorical questions.

This is a straightforward statement that the passage has made a convincing argument using some of the common elements of arguments that we discussed, just as we'd expect to find in a high-scoring SAT essay.

Structure

This essay uses the standard 5-paragraph format, which, as you know by now, is typical of high-scoring SAT essays.

The first paragraph provides basic information about the passage, and says the passage makes an effective argument.

The second paragraph, which is the first body paragraph, focuses on the personal anecdote in the passage and includes the same kind of evidence-and-reasoning analysis we've seen in the other high-scoring essays.

The third paragraph (which is the second body paragraph) mentions points from the original passage that could be loosely classified as cultural examples, since they include references to art and to the perception of Paris in popular culture. We see reasoning provided in the analysis of each example of evidence, but no real conclusion statement for the paragraph.

The fourth paragraph (which is the last body paragraph) discusses the passage's appeal to the reader's emotions, also using the word "pathos" that we saw in an essay from the Blue Book (as we mentioned in our analysis of that essay, you don't need to use the word "pathos" in your essay if you don't want to—it's just a technical term that roughly describes the idea of playing on your readers' emotions to win someone over to your side in an argument). Here, again, we see the same kind of analysis from the other paragraphs in this essay, and the other essays discussed in this section.

Finally, the fifth paragraph is a standard conclusion paragraph for an SAT Essay. It uses only two sentences, just like the intro paragraph; in fact, it's almost a phrase-by-phrase restatement of the intro paragraph.

Selected errors

The second paragraph includes the ungrammatical phrase "there was 'woods . . . ','" instead of "there were 'woods . . . .'" It also uses "amass" reflexively in a way that makes no sense in the context of the essay, and the verb "reminiscing" as a transitive verb.

The fourth paragraph says the passage "draws out . . . ponderance," which makes no sense in American English. It also includes the non-word "gutthral," which may have been an attempt to write "guttural," and uses the word "multifaceted" in a way that suggests the test-taker doesn't know what "multifaceted" means.

(I want to stress once more that the purpose of listing these errors is not to attack the test-taker, but to provide solid proof that your writing doesn't have to be free of errors—or even particularly solid from a technical standpoint—in order to get a perfect score.)

Conclusion

These examples make it clear that the SAT Essay is predictable and standardized, and that writing the SAT Essay is very different from writing essays in the classroom. The basic 5-paragraph format, or some variation of it, will be found in most top-scoring SAT Essays, but isn't strictly necessary. Also, top-scoring essays typically don't demonstrate exceptionally advanced vocabularies or flawless grammar.

---

[3] At the time of this writing, the College Board has sample responses from two SAT Essays available on its web site that aren't in the Blue Book. Only one of these sample responses was given a perfect score. It can be found at the bottom of the page at the following URL: https://collegereadiness.collegeboard.org/sample-questions/essay/1

SAT Essay Quick Summary

This is a one-page summary of the major relevant concepts. Use it to evaluate your comprehension or jog your memory. For a more in-depth explanation, see the rest of this section.

The Big Secret: The SAT Essay isn't graded like a school essay, and shouldn't be written like one.

Your essay will analyze the argument made in the passage. Don't try to make your own argument on the topic from the passage.

The prompt is always basically the same.

Say the author did a good job presenting the argument in the passage.

Some imperfect grammar is okay. Showing off your vocabulary won't help. Just say what you mean using words you know.

Longer essays tend to score higher. Plan on 2 pages at a bare minimum. 2.5 or more is best.

There's no set format you must follow to get a good score, but I find it's best to stick with this one:

- 1 introductory paragraph
- 1-3 body paragraphs discussing evidence and reasoning
- 1 body paragraph discussing stylistic and persuasive elements
- 1 concluding paragraph

This structure is basically the 5-paragraph structure many students use in school. Since it's familiar, structured, and repetitive, it will be easy to write in the time allotted, and it will be easy for the grader to read and understand quickly.

Remember that you're not trying to stand out and write a "special" essay. You want to write one that's just like all the other high-scoring essays, so the grader can quickly read it, recognize that it's a good essay, give you a good score, and then move on.

Here's the process:

1. Identify the College Board's statement of the thesis in the box of text after the passage.
2. Read the passage with the thesis in mind. If you want, underline examples of evidence and/or stylistic and persuasive elements that you'll use in your essay.
3. Decide which topics you want to include in your essay. Remember that you can group your evidence and reasoning into different categories, or you can just write about all the evidence and reasoning in 1 or 2 body paragraphs.
4. Intro paragraph: Start your essay with a sentence that includes the name of the author, basic information about the passage, and a restatement of the author's thesis. Restate the author's position with a quote or detail from the passage. Mention the topics you'll discuss in your body paragraph(s).
5. Write 1-3 body paragraphs discussing the evidence that the author uses in the passage. In each of those paragraphs, discuss the reasoning that connect that evidence to the author's thesis, and explain how this convinces the reader to agree with that thesis.
6. Write 1 body paragraph discussing the author's use of stylistic and persuasive elements in the passage. Mention each example, and explain the impact that the example has on the reader and how this convinces the reader to agree with the author.
7. Conclusion: Say again that the author used the topics you discussed in your body paragraphs to defend whatever the author's thesis was. Use a quote or detail from the passage to restate that thesis. Finally, say one more time that the author's argument was convincing.

This is not the only way to get a high score on your essay, but in my experience it's the easiest and most reliable. Just make sure that it's long, that you quote or restate the passage accurately, and that you explain how everything you bring up from the text convinces the reader to agree with the author.

Refer to the example essays in the Blue Book and on the College Board's website to see what high-scoring essays look like.

Part 11: Closing Thoughts

By now, we've covered everything you need to know for test day. You've seen how the SAT is designed, you know how to exploit that design to maximize your score, and you've seen these ideas applied to four official SAT Practice Tests from the College Board. Now we'll close out this Black Book with some thoughts and observations that may be helpful for some readers . . . including guidance on how you can follow us for more advice on test-taking, admissions, lifestyle design, and other challenges facing high school and college students.

In this part of the Black Book, you'll learn the following:

- answers to frequently asked questions relating to the SAT and the process of training for it
- what it means to be an "SAT Machine," and how to become one
- how to shoot for an elite score, or even a perfect score
- what to do if American English isn't your first language
- why every question I've ever been asked about the SAT has basically the same answer
- how to connect with us online

Frequently Asked Questions

General Questions

How Long Will I Need to Practice?

There is no set amount of time that every student should plan to spend practicing. It varies heavily from person to person. Your goal should be to develop a deep understanding of the way the SAT works, not to log an arbitrary number of practice hours. For more on this, see "Things to Think about for Scheduling" on page 30 of this Black Book.

Where Did You Learn these Strategies?

I didn't "learn" these strategies in the sense of having some book or tutor explain them to me. I developed them on my own based on my own reasoning and analysis of the SAT and other tests. Over the years, I've refined both the strategies themselves and the way that I teach them to students, and adapted them to the College Board's occasional format changes, like the one that happened in 2016. For more on my background and the way it has informed my test-prep training, please see the relevant articles on my blog at www.TestingIsEasy.com.

What's the Best Way to Start Implementing Your Strategies?

The best way to get started is generally to learn the strategies in an abstract way first, and then to see several sample solutions that implement the strategies against real College Board SAT questions. Finally, it's important to try to implement the strategies yourself, and to try to figure things out on your own as much as you can when you get stuck. For more ideas on specific drills and exercises, please see "Drills and Exercises" on page 28. For a selection of videos that demonstrate the ideas in this book, please visit www.SATprepVideos.com (those sample videos are free to readers of this book).

Do these Strategies Work on the ACT? What about on the SAT Subject Tests?

All well-designed standardized tests must follow certain rules and patterns when they create their test questions—otherwise the tests wouldn't be standardized. But those particular rules and patterns don't have to be the same for every standardized test. ACT questions have their own standardized design elements that are different from those of SAT questions but still fairly similar to them. The SAT Subject Tests have the added wrinkle of involving a bit more subject-matter knowledge in most cases.

So the short answer is that the *specific* strategies in this Black Book are aimed at the SAT in particular. Some will work fairly well on other tests, and some won't. But the general idea of analyzing a standardized test in terms of rules and patterns can still be applied successfully against the ACT and the SAT Subject Tests.

If you like the material in this book, and you're also preparing for the ACT, you may be interested in my *ACT Prep Black Book*. I also have Black Books for the some SAT Subject Tests available.

What if I Want to Score a 1600? What if I Only Need to Score a 1000 (or 1200, or 1400, or Whatever)?

Contrary to popular belief, you don't need to use different strategies to reach different score levels, because the design of the SAT is constant. It would be more accurate to say that in order to score a 1600 you need to be roughly 99% accurate in your execution of the SAT strategies in this Black Book, while in order to score a 1400 you must be roughly 85% accurate, and in order to score a 1000 you must be a little less than 50% accurate, and so on.

So scoring higher isn't a question of learning separate strategies; it's a question of becoming more accurate and consistent when applying a fixed set of strategies. For more on how to do these things, see "Being an SAT Machine" on page 569 of this Black Book, and "The Nature of Elite Scores" on page 570.

What if I Can't Get the Strategies to Work?

Most students experience difficulty with some of these strategies at some point in their preparation, even if the difficulty is only limited to a single practice question.

This can be frustrating, of course—but it's actually a great opportunity to improve your understanding of the test, because the experience of figuring out how to overcome these temporary setbacks can be very instructive if we let it.

(Bear in mind that this discussion of how to handle difficult questions applies to a *practice situation*. As we discussed in "Part 4: Guessing and Time-Management on Test Day" starting on page 32 of this Black Book, if you're stumped by a question on test day, then you should skip that question and answer easier questions before coming back to the challenging question on a later pass.)

When a strategy doesn't seem to work against a particular question, the first thing to do is to make sure that the practice question is a real SAT question from the College Board. The next thing is to verify that you haven't misread the answer key—I can't tell you how many times a student has reported struggling with a question for a long time, only to realize that he had misread the answer key, and that the correct answer would have made sense the whole time.

Assuming that you're looking at a real College Board question, and assuming that you haven't misread the answer key, the next thing to consider is whether the strategy you're trying to apply is really relevant to the question. Sometimes people mistakenly try to apply a strategy for the Reading Test to a grammar/style/punctuation question on the Writing and Language Test, for instance.

If you're pretty sure the strategy you're trying to apply really should work on a particular question, then the issue is probably that you've overlooked some key detail of the question, or that you've misunderstood a word or two somewhere in the question. At this point, it can be a very useful exercise to start over from square one and go back through the question word-by-word, taking nothing for granted and making a sincere effort to see the question with new eyes.

If you do this well, you'll probably be able to figure out where you went wrong and why the question works the way it does. If you make an effort to incorporate the lessons from this experience into your future preparation, then it can be tremendously beneficial to your performance on test day.

On the other hand, if you keep staring at the question and you still can't figure out what the issue is, then I would recommend that you move on to something else for a while—but do make sure you come back to the troubling question at some point and try to work it out, because the standardized nature of the SAT makes it very likely that any troubling strategic issues you run into during practice will reappear on test day, in one form or another.

Of course, you can refer to its walkthrough in this Black Book for extra help in understanding the troublesome question.

Which Practice Books Should I Buy?

I designed this book so the only additional resources you would need are copies of SAT Practice Tests #1-4. Those tests are available in the "Blue Book," which is the College Board's *Official SAT Study Guide* (either the 2016 or 2018 Edition), and they're also available for free in PDF form on the College Board's website. For more on why this is so important, see "Only Work with Questions from the College Board!" on page 18 of this Black Book.

I'm Having a Hard Time Visualizing Some of Your Techniques. What Can I Do?

Visit www.SATprepVideos.com, where I've made some sample video solutions available for free to readers of this book, to help you visualize some of the techniques from this book more clearly.

Reading Questions

I Know You Say that the Answer to Each Question is Always Spelled Out on the Page, but I Found a Question Where that's not the Case. Now What?

I completely understand that there are some questions where the answer doesn't seem to be on the page somewhere, but I promise you that the issue is always—*always*—some error on the part of the test-taker, not on the part of the test. (This assumes that you're working with a real SAT question published by the College Board, of course. Fake questions from other companies don't have to follow any rules, and the strategies in this Black Book—the strategies for the real SAT—don't always apply to fake questions written by companies like Kaplan, McGraw-Hill, and so on. That's why it's so important to have access to SAT Practice Tests #1-4.)

So if you think you've found a real SAT question that doesn't follow the rules, you need to try to figure out where you've gone wrong. It may be that you haven't read some critical part of the text, or that you misread it, or that you misread an answer choice. It may be that some of the words on the page don't actually mean what you think they mean. It may be a combination of all of the above, or even something else. But, somewhere in there, you've made a mistake.

I know it can be frustrating to hunt back through the question and the text to find your mistake, but I strongly advise you to do so, especially if your goal is to score really high. The process of figuring out your mistake will help you understand the test much better, and greatly improve your future performance. (For more on these ideas, see "The Importance of Details: Avoiding "Careless Errors" on page 16, "How to Train for the SAT—Mastering the Ideas in this Black Book" on page 27, and "The Nature of Elite Scores" on page 570)

I Like My Answer to a Question Better than the College Board's Answer. Now What?

It's normal to feel like the College Board has done a bad job of deciding the correct answer to one of its own questions. But we have to work very hard to overcome that feeling. We need to understand that the SAT is a standardized test with questions and answers that can be reliably predicted because they follow certain rules and patterns. So your job isn't to find the answer choice that seems most satisfactory to you. Your job is to ask yourself, "Which choice will the SAT reward, based on the rules it follows for this type of question?"

What do I do for Questions about the Author's Attitude?

Questions about the author's attitude should be treated just like any other Reading question, even though they might seem like they require us to interpret the text. For more on these questions, please see "
What about "Attitude" Questions?" on page 73 of this Black Book.

Math Questions

Which Math Formulas are Most Important for the SAT?

If I had to pick, I would say that the formulas related to circles and triangles seem to me like they come up most often.
But that answer is kind of misleading, for three reasons:

1. Almost all the geometry formulas you could use on the SAT Math sections are included in the beginning of each SAT Math section, so it's not like you'll need to memorize how to find the area of a circle or anything.
2. In general, the best approach to the SAT Math sections doesn't rely primarily on formulas.

3. Many SAT Math questions couldn't be answered with formulas even if we wanted them to be.

For more on the right way to approach SAT Math, please see the part of this Black Book on SAT Math training, which starts on page 165.

Which Type of Calculator should I Use?

It's best to have a graphing calculator you're familiar with when you take the SAT. A graphing calculator isn't absolutely necessary, but it can be useful on some questions. You'll also want to make sure your calculator can find values of trigonometric functions in both radians and degrees.

Beyond that, I'd recommend that you use the brand and model of calculator that makes you feel the most confident on test day. It's also important to remember that a calculator can only do so much for you on the SAT, because the challenge with most SAT Math questions comes down to figuring out which basic math concepts are involved in a question, not doing some kind of complicated calculation. For more, see the part of this Black Book that deals with SAT Math, which starts on page 165.

Writing and Language Questions

I Found a Question Where the Right Answer Doesn't Follow the Rules of Grammar. How can that Be?

Remember that the College Board isn't necessarily following the grammar rules that you learned in school, or even the rules that native speakers of American English follow when they speak or write. Instead, the College Board has its own set of grammar rules. While those rules largely overlap with the current grammar of American English, there are some points where they differ sharply. Remember that your goal on the Writing and Language test isn't to make the sentences sound good to *you*, but to figure out which answer choice the College Board will reward based on the rules and patterns it follows. For more on this, see the part of this Black Book that deals with the SAT Writing and Language Test, which starts on page 428.

Being an SAT Machine

Trifles make perfection, and perfection is no trifle.

Michelangelo

In this book, I talk a lot about how to answer individual questions. Obviously, that's an important part of beating the SAT.

But you may have noticed that the processes and sample solutions get pretty repetitive pretty quickly. My students often complain, "After a while, doing these questions is just the same thing over and over . . ."

Some teachers might be insulted by that, but when I hear those magic words I just smile and say, "Exactly!" On a standardized test, when answering questions begins to feel repetitive and automatic, you know you've made a huge improvement.

Standardized Tests Have Standardized Questions

In writing the Black Book, my goal has been to teach you the unwritten rules of the test, so that you know how to attack every real SAT question you'll ever see. Never forget that the SAT is a test with rules and patterns that it has to follow, and once you start to unlock them you almost can't go wrong. It's almost like you turn into an SAT machine.

An SAT Machine at Work

One of the things I often do for students is show them how I would take a section of the test. I don't just show them the processes and strategies I use, although those are definitely important. I also show them the speed and the attitude I use on the test.

When I'm taking the SAT, I have an inner dialogue going on in my head. It's very simple and straightforward. I'm reading each question, thinking briefly about what kind of question it is, then walking myself through the various steps described in these pages. It's all second nature to me, and the layouts of my walkthroughs in this Black Book reflect this style of attack: there's a preliminary set of details I always notice before I start really solving each question, and then I go through my solution, and then I check everything over and make sure I haven't made any mistakes before I move on to the next question. When I think about answer choices, I'm ruthless about cutting them out—as soon as I see something wrong with an answer, it's gone.

Unless I get confused or lose my concentration, I usually finish each section in well under half the allotted time. And it's not because I'm rushing or anything. I just don't waste time thinking about any unnecessary aspects of the questions.

When I take a test, there's no dilly-dallying or second-guessing. I'm prepared, and I know what to expect, because I know the SAT is ALWAYS THE SAME in all the important ways. You'll see this kind of direct, efficient approach reflected in the way I've presented the walkthroughs in this book.

Becoming an SAT Machine

When most untrained test-takers take the SAT, they let their minds wander. They don't realize that every question has one clear answer, so they often waste their time trying to justify every answer choice to themselves. They don't have set processes to rely on. They don't know the recurring rules and patterns to look for in every question. In other words, they don't take advantage of any of the gaping holes in the SAT's armor. They're inefficient and unfocused, and their scores suffer for it.

So what do you do if you want to turn into a machine? The key thing is to remember that every question has one clear answer, and that you can find it. Stick to a game plan—know how to start in on any SAT question and keep going until you either arrive at the answer, decide to skip it for the moment, or use your chosen guessing approach on it. Then just keep working your system all the way through the test. That's it. Don't get distracted. Rely on the SAT to give you the same sorts of questions you've seen before—because it definitely will. It has to.

In a way, taking the SAT is similar to taking a driving test. You know in advance which skills you'll be asked to demonstrate and what rules you'll have to follow during the test; what you don't know is the specific situation you'll be in when you demonstrate each skill. Keep this in mind—stay flexible about applying what you know, but never forget that the range of things you can be asked to do on the SAT is very limited.

Also, as weird as it might sound, you should strive for the SAT to be boring and repetitive. Some people look at the SAT as a way to be creative— but what's the point of that? Find each answer, and practice finding it as efficiently as possible. You'll be attacking the test in a systematic, methodical way before you know it—and that's the secret to real SAT success. Save the creativity for other areas of your life.

The Nature of Elite Scores

It is not because things are difficult that we do not dare. It is because we do not dare that they are difficult.
Seneca the Younger

Imagine a hypothetical test with 100 questions of varying difficulty on various subjects. If you needed to answer any one question correctly, you could probably find one that seemed to be the easiest for you, and get it right.

Now imagine that you're working on the same imaginary test, and you've answered 90 questions correctly, and you want to get one more of the remaining ten. The odds are good that you've already answered all of the questions that were easiest for you. All that are left are the ones you skipped, and now you're more likely to be stuck than you were when you just started out.

Now imagine that you wanted to get nine of the ten remaining question, or even all ten. It would only get harder and harder, right?

My point is this: The more you improve on any test, the harder it is to keep improving. The more you succeed with the SAT, the rarer your opportunities for future success become. The more questions you master, the closer you come to having to deal with the questions you dislike most if you want to make any progress.

So making an elite score on the SAT (say, a combined score of 1500 or more) will require most people to prepare diligently and intelligently. Let's talk about how to do that.

Having the Right Attitude.

Your attitude is an important factor in preparing for the SAT.

Accountability

If you want a good score, *you* have to do it. That sentence is probably the most obvious one in this book, but it's also the most important. Every other strategy or attitude will fail you unless you take full accountability for your performance.

Many people feel that they have performance anxiety that makes them bad test-takers. Others think the test is biased against them. These people may be absolutely correct, but that will not help them improve their scores. The only thing that will help you improve is diligent, intelligent practice.

Thinking about nonspecific problems that you cannot fix will only distract you from other weaknesses that you *can* fix. When you conquer all the problems you can pinpoint, you may be surprised to find that there are no others left to deal with.

Persistence

You will fail in some way, however small or large, over the course of your SAT preparation. Everyone does. However, failure is as impermanent as you want it to be. If you are willing to work for it, every failure is literally another opportunity to succeed in the future.

Remember to keep working until you achieve the score you want. As your progress becomes more and more difficult, remind yourself that it's only because you've already come so far, and that you can go even further.

Practicing for the SAT

Performing on the SAT, like any other skill, becomes easier if you practice it.

Choosing Your Pace

You will need some amount of some kind of practice; the kind and amount depend on how well you've done so far, in which areas, and how well you want to do in the future. Refer to "How to Train for the SAT—Mastering the Ideas in this Black Book" on page 27 of this Black Book for more on how to approach your training for the SAT.

You also have to be responsible in your training. If you don't feel like you're practicing enough, or if you're not improving, then you need to put in more time, or go back to basics with the different sections of this book. Just keep working away at it. You get results depending on the quality of the work you put in, so if you want an elite score, remember: Work smarter *and* harder.

Assessing Weakness

As you practice you will notice certain areas of the test that seem to give you particular trouble. Take note, and work harder on those sections. There is no "I can't do it"—the information you need is there in every question, just learn to see it and use it. Don't be tempted to convince yourself that one question type is just too hard or flawed or has some other problem. You can do them all if you will only work on it.

When you do start to notice problem areas, see them as places where you have not yet succeeded, not places where you won't or can't succeed. Learn the difference between recognizing weakness and expecting failure.

Making it Count

You can spend all the time in the world practicing, but if it's mindless practice, then you won't improve. Practice actively and intelligently. Don't try to look up every word in the Reading section and memorize its meaning, but if you feel like you keep seeing a word with which you are unfamiliar (especially in the question prompts), go ahead and look it up and be sure you understand what it means; you might see it again somewhere.

However, if there is a word in the Math section that you don't understand, look it up every time. This isn't as extreme, since there are fewer of them in Math than in Reading or Writing, but you can't answer an SAT Math question without knowing the vocabulary involved.

Also, feel free to come up with your own tricks while practicing, but if your tricks don't work every time, then don't rely on them. When you've mastered all the techniques, you shouldn't just be right all the time; you should know that you're right, know why you're right, and know why the wrong answers are wrong—every time. Remember: if you're not getting 800s (or whatever your goal is) in practice, you probably won't get them on the real test.

Parting Advice

If you're putting in all this extra effort to reach an elite score, then you must have some larger goal in mind (improving your chances at a particular school, qualifying for a scholarship, or whatever). Keep that goal in mind. Let it motivate you to continue to work even when you don't want to. If you get your score report and you're not satisfied, think of it as a progress report and let your goal keep you working. Repeat this entire process thoroughly in order to optimize your improvement.

At the same time, treat each test as the real thing, because it is. Don't take a test thinking only that it will help you know what to do better later. It will, but always shoot for your goal or else you might not do as well as you can. Strive to do your best, *always*.

Advice for Non-Native Speakers of American English

Knowledge, then, is a system of transformations that become progressively adequate.
Jean Piaget

The SAT involves a lot of reading, so it poses special challenges for students who aren't native speakers of American English. There are things we can do to overcome these challenges to some extent.

First, Focus on Questions in Which Language is Not a Problem.

Before we start worrying about building up your vocabulary or grammar knowledge, the most important thing—and the easiest—is to focus on eliminating mistakes in the questions that you can understand well enough to answer with confidence. It doesn't make sense to try to learn a lot of big words if you haven't reached a point where knowing the words actually helps you to answer a question. So master the strategies in this book as much as you can before you start trying to memorize stuff.

Next, Focus on "Testing" Vocabulary.

Most non-native speakers waste time memorizing the same lists of words that native speakers used to memorize for earlier versions of the SAT. Instead, focus on the terms we discussed in "Critical Technical Terms for the SAT Reading Section" on page 69, as well as the terms in the SAT Math Toolbox (starting on page 168)—the kinds of words that actually frame the questions themselves, rather than the words that might show up as answer choices on Reading questions.

These are the kinds of words that native speakers would normally have no problems with, but that non-native speakers may never have studied specifically. They are absolutely critical if we want to understand what the test is actually asking us—and, most importantly, they are words that you will definitely encounter over and over again as you practice and take the real test.

The best way to discover which parts of "testing" vocabulary need your attention is to mark particular words and phrases that you encounter in real practice questions—again, pay particular attention to the prompts of the question rather than the answer choices, although "testing" vocabulary words can also appear in the answer choices. If you run into a word like "undermine" in 3 or 4 different questions and don't know what it means, then it's a good idea to go online and find the translation in your language.

Then Focus on SAT Grammar and SAT Style.

Notice that I'm specifically advising you to focus on learning *SAT grammar* and *SAT style*, which will be different from the grammar and style you learned when you studied English in school. You'll have to make small tweaks to your understanding of "textbook" English to answer every Writing and Language question on the SAT, but, again, those should be easy enough to take care of if you've been studying English for a while.

Finally, Consider the Essay.

If the schools that you're applying to are interested in the Essay portion of the SAT, then you need to try to write the best essay you can. As we discussed in the SAT Essay portion of this book, above-average length is an important indicator of a good score—but it's also important to try to avoid too much awkward phrasing. A little bit of awkwardness doesn't seem to hurt in most cases, but if you have a lot of it you increase the chance that an essay-grader will notice it and feel like he has to penalize you for it.

Also try to avoid using large words for their own sake. Remember that the graders don't care if your vocabulary is advanced. But if you use a lot of large words in a way that sounds forced and unnatural, you run the very real risk of making the grader think that your writing is awkward, which could make your essay hard to understand and result in a lower score. So stick with the grammatical structures and the vocabulary that you're sure of, and focus on getting the length and the organization of the essay right.

Conclusion

I hope you've found these tips useful. Remember that the SAT is a unique test, but it's also a very repetitive test, and even a very basic one in a lot of ways. By focusing on the issues I've pointed out above, you should hopefully be able to maximize your score without wasting your time on things that won't really help you.

Check Us Out Online

All you need to prepare for the SAT is this Black Book, and SAT Practice Tests #1-4 (which are available for free on the College Board's website, as well as in the College Board publication *The Official SAT Study Guide*, also called the Blue Book).

But if you'd like more from me—including sample videos and updates related to test preparation, admissions, and the college experience—please connect with me on the following channels:

SATprepVideos.com

This is where you can sign up for my e-mail newsletter and check out sample videos of question walkthroughs to see how I think through real SAT practice questions in real time.

YouTube.com/TestingIsEasy

This is my YouTube channel, where you can find sample videos from my online video courses, as well as videos about other aspects of test prep and admissions.

Facebook.com/TestingIsEasy

This is my Facebook page, the primary place where I keep in touch with my students, and also a place to share updates, interesting articles, commentary, and the occasional gif of a goat riding a dirt bike through a mall. This feed is also posted on Instagram.com/TestingIsEasy and Twitter.com/TestingIsEasy, if you prefer to follow it there.

TestingIsEasy.com

This is my main website and blog where you can find videos and articles about many different aspects of test preparation and college admissions.

And look for more soon—including a podcast where I answer your questions . . .

One Final Piece of Advice
(Or: Every Question I've Ever Been Asked about the SAT Has Basically the Same Answer)

The "paradox" is only a conflict between reality and your feeling of what reality "ought to be."
- Richard Feynman

I've helped a lot of people with a lot of standardized tests, and in a lot of formats. This means I've also gotten a lot of questions from a very wide variety of test-takers. Most of the time those questions are very polite and sincere, but sometimes they're downright accusatory—something along the lines of

> You said I could use a certain strategy on this kind of question, but it didn't work and my score went down. What are you, some kind of idiot?

So I wanted to close this book with some words of advice and encouragement for students who are still struggling.

First, the advice: In literally every single instance that I can recall in which a student has become frustrated with an idea in this Black Book, the underlying issue has always—ALWAYS—been that the student overlooked or misunderstood at least one key detail.

Let me say that again.

When you try to apply the ideas in this book to real SAT questions from the College Board and get frustrated by your inability to find correct answers reliably, the reason is nearly always that you've misread or misunderstood some important detail somewhere.

So when a question is giving you trouble, whether during practice or on test day, you must always, always, always assume you've made a mistake somewhere, and then set out to find and correct it. You need to develop an instinctive faith in the SAT's rules.

Let me also say, very clearly, that all of us—myself included—will run into situations in which we are completely certain that the College Board has finally made a mistake. No matter how convinced we may be that this is the case, we must remember that we're actually the ones who've made the mistake, and go back and re-evaluate our decisions until we figure out where we went wrong.

The most common type of mistake that I see students make is the general mistake of misreading something. Sometimes a question asks us to compare Passage 1 to Passage 2, but we choose the answer that compares Passage 2 to Passage 1 instead. Sometimes the question asks for the area and we find the perimeter. Sometimes we think a minus sign is a plus sign. And so on.

At other times, we may think we know something that actually turns out to be wrong. Yesterday I was talking to a student who incorrectly thought that "taciturn" meant "peaceful" (this is the kind of misunderstanding that often comes from memorizing lists of vocabulary words, by the way). Until a couple of months ago, I though "pied" meant something like "famous" or "skillful," because of the story *The Pied Piper*. But it turns out that "pied" just refers to something with patches of two or more colors, and I was completely wrong. These kinds of mistakes are harder to figure out during the actual moment of taking the test, because it's usually not possible to realize that something you believe isn't actually correct until after you've chosen the wrong answer and found out it's wrong.

No matter what the mistake, though, it ultimately comes down to some specific detail (or details) of the question that you've misunderstood in some way. When you can't figure out the answer to a question with certainty, your first instinct must be to take nothing for granted, and expect that you've overlooked or misunderstood something.

Now that I've finished with the advice, let me offer some encouragement. I know how hard it is to stare at a question and feel defeated. I know the frustration of being sure you've answered a question correctly and then finding out later you were wrong. And I know that it's tempting, in those moments, to reject what you've learned and assume the SAT really is unbeatable, like everybody says.

But I'm here to tell you that those moments of frustration are also the moments that offer the most opportunity for progress. When you've wrestled with a question for a while and then you finally figure out how it works and where you went wrong, you learn a tremendous lesson about the test, and about how you've been approaching it. And your score improves.

When you truly figure out a challenging question, you learn something that you'll be able to apply on future questions, because the SAT is standardized. You also develop a stronger trust in the design of the test, which will help you in the future. More importantly, though, you can learn something about your own problem-solving process, because you can start to figure out which parts of the question kept you from understanding it correctly in the first place, and you can start to reflect on the process you used to uncover and correct that mistake, so you can make that process much smoother in the future.

With the SAT, as with most areas of life, we make the most progress when we're confronted with a difficult situation that we eventually overcome. Good luck!

Thanks for Reading!

I've enjoyed sharing my SAT strategies with you, and I hope you've enjoyed learning how to beat the test, and that you're seeing good results with your practice sessions. It means a lot to me that so many students over the years have trusted me to help them at such an important time in their lives.

If this book has helped you, I would really appreciate it if you could tell your friends about it, or even go on Amazon and leave an honest review, if you'd like to do that.

Thanks again for reading, and I wish you the best of luck—with your preparation, and with everything else in your life.

Made in the USA
Middletown, DE
22 February 2019